www.wileyplus.com

ALL THE HELP, RESOURCES, AND PERSONAL SUPPORT YOU AND YOUR STUDENTS NEED!

www.wileyplus.com/resources

2-Minute Tutorials and all of the resources you & your students need to get started.

Student support from an experienced student user.

Collaborate with your colleagues, find a mentor, attend virtual and live events, and view resources.
www.WhereFacultyConnect.com

Pre-loaded, ready-to-use assignments and presentations. Created by subject matter experts.

Technical Support 24/7 FAQs, online chat, and phone support.
www.wileyplus.com/support

Your *WileyPLUS* Account Manager. Personal training and implementation support.

Financial Accounting
a user perspective
SIXTH CANADIAN EDITION

Robert E. Hoskin
UNIVERSITY OF CONNECTICUT

Maureen R. Fizzell
SIMON FRASER UNIVERSITY

Donald C. Cherry
DALHOUSIE UNIVERSITY

With Contributions by
Julia A. Scott
McGILL UNIVERSITY

JOHN WILEY & SONS CANADA, LTD.

Library and Archives Canada Cataloguing in Publication

Hoskin, Robert E., 1949-
    Financial accounting : a user perspective / Robert E. Hoskin, Maureen R. Fizzell, Don C. Cherry. -- 6th Canadian ed.

ISBN 978-0-470-67660-8

    1. Accounting--Textbooks.   I. Fizzell, Maureen   II. Cherry, Donald C.   III. Title.

HF5636.H68 2010   657'.044   C2010-905811-9

Production Credits
Acquisitions Editor: Zoë Craig
Vice President & Publisher: Veronica Visentin
Vice President, Publishing Services: Karen Bryan
Creative Director, Publishing Services: Ian Koo
Senior Marketing Manager: Aida Krneta
Editorial Manager: Karen Staudinger
Developmental Editor: Theresa Fitzgerald
Production Manager: Tegan Wallace
Editorial Assistant: Laura Hwee
Permissions Coordinator: Jessie Coffey
Typesetting: Lakeside Group
Cover Design: Interrobang Graphic Design Inc.
Cover Images: © Photo ephemera/Flickr/Getty Images
Printing and binding: Quad/Graphics

Printed and bound in the United States.
1 2 3 4 5 QG 15 14 13 12 11

John Wiley & Sons Canada, Ltd.
6045 Freemont Blvd.
Mississauga, Ontario L5R 4J3
Visit our website at: www.wiley.ca

WILEY

About the Authors

Maureen R. Fizzell

Maureen R. Fizzell, B.Ed, B.Comm., M.Sc., CMA, FCMA has been teaching at the university level for 26 years, nine years at the University of Saskatchewan and 17 years at Simon Fraser University, where she is now the Director of the Undergraduate Program in the Faculty of Business Administration. In 2003 she was named a CMA/SFU Business Academic Fellow, and in 2004 she was awarded the FCMA designation. Over her university career, she has taught financial accounting from the introductory to the advanced level.

Maureen is an active CMA member who has served on the B.C. Board of Directors on two occasions. She served on the CMA Canada National Board of Examiners from 2000 to 2004, and on the B.C. Board of Directors from 1997 to 1999 and again from 2003 to 2005. As well, she has been a member of the Saskatchewan Provincial Council, critiqued exams and acted as a liaison between university students and the Society. During her 26 years of teaching, Maureen has received numerous teaching awards, including: Most Effective Professor in the Classroom Award at the University of Saskatchewan in 1990, TD Canada Trust Distinguished Teaching Award in 1996, and membership on the Teaching Honour Roll in 1997 and 2010 at Simon Fraser University.

Donald C. Cherry

Donald C. (Don) Cherry, B.Comm., MBA, CMA, FCMA, has taught accounting for over 35 years. He began his teaching career at Seneca College in Toronto in 1974, and moved to Dalhousie University in Halifax in 1978. Don has taught a wide range of courses, from the introductory undergraduate level to advanced graduate and executive programs, and has won numerous teaching awards from both Commerce and MBA students.

In addition to teaching, at various times during his career Don served as Director of Dalhousie's Commerce Program, Associate Director of the School of Business, Associate Director of the Lester Pearson International Institute, Director of the Centre for Development Projects, and Director of the Centre for International Business Studies. As a result of a strong interest in economic development and social justice issues, he has worked in management education programs in over a dozen developing countries and been involved in numerous international development efforts.

Aside from his work on textbooks, Don has published articles in several accounting magazines and the proceedings of numerous conferences, and authored a number of case studies dealing with financial management issues. He has also been an active member of the Society of Management Accountants, including serving on the Provincial Council for Nova Scotia and the National Board of Examiners, and chairing the CMA Syllabus Committee.

About the Contributor

Julia A. Scott CA, CFA, MBA teaches accounting and financial statement analysis courses in the B Com program, the MBA program, and the Graduate Program in Accounting for students pursuing their CA designation at the Desautels Faculty of Management, McGill University. She has been teaching for more than 20 years at the university level both at McGill and previously at Bishop's University. Julia is a graduate of the Richard Ivey School of Business at The University of Western Ontario and the Schulich School of Business at York University. An active member of the Chartered Financial Analyst Institute, Julia consults and develops materials for CFA candidate preparation programs. Julia has authored numerous supplements to accounting textbooks and has been involved in grading professional exams for both the Ontario Institute of Chartered Accountants and the CFA Institute.

Dedications

To my family.
— MRF

To my dear wife and soul mate, Shirley — the lovely lady
who lights up my life.
— DCC

Preface

Background

Financial Accounting: A User Perspective strives to teach students about accounting information and how it affects decision-making, by complementing the fundamental procedural aspects of accounting with discussions about who uses accounting information and how they make decisions from it. This unique balance has been widely appreciated through previous editions of the text, and is just as relevant today as when it was first published in Canada in 1997. What has changed are the means available to instructors and students, to enhance the learning experience. With successive editions we have introduced a wealth of online resources and made the text the centre of an interactive learning environment with a unique set of technology tools. With the sixth edition we continue to provide extensive online support materials for both students and instructors through WileyPLUS.

The Evolution of This Textbook

While *Financial Accounting: A User Perspective* has been used successfully for many years, improvements and refinements continue to take place. Throughout the book, changes have been made to make the text even more "reader friendly" than the fifth edition. However, the main change to this edition is the integration of the new accounting standards.

- The text is written using the **International Financial Reporting Standards (IFRS)** required in Canada as of January 2011.

- Two international companies, H&M and HMV, are used throughout the book to fully demonstrate the use of the new standards. Numerous Canadian companies are also used, where appropriate, to illustrate accounting examples.

- Using IFRS involves a new "language"; this new terminology is emphasized using the *Summary of Equivalent Terms* in Chapter 1.

- Some of the key changes introduced with IFRS are summarized in *IFRS Insights* boxes throughout the text.

- Some of the differences between IFRS and Canada's **Accounting Standards for Private Entities (ASPE)** are also covered using comparative *IFRS versus ASPE* boxes.

Following is an outline of some of the other key pedagogical and content changes in this edition:

Pedagogical Changes

- There has been a significant restructuring of content in chapters 2-4 to provide clearer coverage of the preparer topics, such as the basic transactions in chapter 2, with a new set of transactions introduced in chapter 3 for more complete coverage. Also, detailed discussion of the Income Statement (Statement of Earnings) has been moved from chapter 3 to chapter 4.

- To enhance the conceptual focus of the book, further emphasis has been placed on *Earnings Management* boxes, included where appropriate in most chapters.

- **Seven varieties of assignment material:** Assessing Your Recall, Applying Your Knowledge, User Perspective Problems, Reading and Interpreting Published Financial Statements, Beyond the Book, Cases, and Critical Thinking Questions satisfy a wide variety of learning and teaching objectives. Over one-third of the assignment material is new with this edition.

- There is a set of **integrative questions** on reading and interpreting financial statements mid-way through the book, and an **integrative course project**, illustrating the impact of accounting estimates and policy choices, at the end of the book. Alternate versions of the integrative course project (with solutions) will be available on the companion website for instructors.

- *IFRS Insights* boxes have been added to further students' understanding of the new reporting standards and how they differ from past practice.

- To further clarify the new standards and how to apply them, there is a new box feature entitled *IFRS versus ASPE*, which provides a distinction for reporting for private enterprises.

- To illustrate the IFRS standards that are now required in Canada, examples from the financial statements of companies from outside of Canada have been used in greater numbers in this edition, because very few Canadian companies adopted the new IFRS standards prior to 2011.

- The number of different companies used to illustrate standards has been reduced in this edition and more excerpts from the same companies have been used to enable students to follow the selected companies through several different topics. The financial statements of these companies are also used in the assignment materials at the end of each chapter.

Content Changes

- Throughout the text, references to Canadian GAAP have been changed to references to IFRS.

- Additional descriptive labels and headings have been added, for easier reference by students and instructors.

- To enhance the clarity of the transaction analysis in Chapter 2, each of the 16 transactions analyzed is followed by a table that shows the accounts involved and the effects on the basic accounting equation. These tables are cumulative, so that by transaction 16 all of the previous transactions can be viewed on the table.

- The discussion of the transactions has been divided into 5 sub-sections — Analysis, Balance Sheet Effects, Cashflow Effect, Earnings Effect, and (in most cases) Related Concepts — to make the discussion easier for students to follow, retain, and refer to later.

- The more complex transactions and adjustments have been reserved for Chapter 3, rather than being partially introduced in Chapter 2.

- Chapter 3 now deals exclusively with the accounting cycle. The other material that was previously in this chapter has been moved to other chapters.

- The detailed discussion of the statement of earnings has been moved from Chapter 3 to Chapter 4, where it complements the discussion of revenue recognition.

- In Chapter 5, there is much more emphasis on understanding the statement of cash flows and interpreting the information contained in it.

- The T-account method of preparing cash flow statements has been replaced by a less technical, more intuitive method that focuses on underlying relationships rather than mechanical procedures. However, the T-account method is presented on the companion website, for those who want to use it.

- All of the examples and problems prior to Chapter 7 now use the perpetual inventory method for calculating the cost of goods sold, so that students will no longer be confused by a mix of periodic and perpetual methods in the early chapters.

- There is now more extensive coverage of bank loans and notes payable in Chapter 9, as well discussion of extended warranty sales, customer loyalty programs, and constructive liabilities.

- The discussion of deferred income tax and income tax disclosures has been revised and moved to chapter 10.

- New sections have been added to Chapter 10 to cover long-term notes and mortgages, and the treatment of both bonds and leases has been simplified.

- Amortization tables are now used for notes, mortgages, bonds and leases, to illustrate the similarities between these different forms of liabilities.

- Tables for the *Time Value of Money* have been moved from Chapter 10 to the inside back cover, for easy reference.

- In Chapter 12, more emphasis is now placed on the interpretation of ratio results from a user's perspective.

- The inside front cover now provides a list of *Key Ratios* discussed within the text.

- Efforts were made to alert students to potential areas of accounting where earnings management could take place. *Earnings Management* boxes are included in most chapters, to describe how the items under discussion could be affected by it.

Text Organization

In order to focus on the understanding and use of financial statements, and to emphasize the importance of topics such as decision-making, cash flows, and ratio analysis, this text is organized in a unique manner.

Chapter 1 lays the conceptual groundwork for the mechanics of the accounting system, and guides students through the annual report of fashion retailer H&M. The section on the users of financial statements ensures that students have a good understanding of who the people are that use the information in financial statements, what kind of decisions they make, and how the financial statements can provide information for them. Students learn basic accounting terminology and are introduced to the three major financial statements: statement of earnings, statement of financial position, and statement of cash flows. This chapter also presents background material on the IFRS standard-setting process and the conceptual framework underlying accounting. Financial ratios associated with specific topics under discussion are introduced in chapter 1 and in each chapter

Chapters 2 and 3 build on the basics from Chapter 1, providing the traditional presentation of the accounting system using the basic accounting equation, followed by a full explanation of the double entry accounting system and the accounting cycle. Both the earnings and cashflow effects of transactions are identified, to enable students to appreciate the differences between the statement of earnings and statement of cash flows that are crucial to understanding accrual basis financial statements.

Chapter 4 caps the coverage of the statement of earnings with a discussion of revenue recognition criteria and methods. This topic is often not emphasized in introductory texts. However, the revenue recognition policies established by a company have a major impact on its reported operating results. It is, therefore, important for students to have a good understanding of accounting policy choices early in the course. A detailed illustration of the format of the statement of earnings is also included in this chapter.

Chapter 5 reflects the importance of the statement of cash flows in at least two ways: it covers the interpretation as well as the construction of the statement, and the coverage occurs earlier than in most other introductory texts. Because this topic is a difficult one for many students, the chapter explains the linkage of the statement of cash flows to the operating policies of the company (accounts receivable, inventory, and accounts payable policies), which helps students to interpret the information in the operating activities section of the statement of cash flows. By the end of Chapter 5, students will have a basic understanding of the three major financial statements. However, because of the complexity of the statement of cash flows, the authors realize that some instructors may prefer to teach this topic later in the course. The chapter has therefore been designed so that it can be taught after Chapter 11 rather than after Chapter 4.

Chapters 6 through 11 discuss the major asset, liability, and equity accounts that students will see in published financial statements. In each of these chapters, students are alerted to the important aspects of these items so that they can better interpret financial accounting information. The chapter material and the assignment materials provide numerous examples of disclosures from the financial statements of real companies.

Financial statement analysis issues are discussed throughout the book and are summarized and extended in Chapter 12. Financial ratios associated with specific topics under discussion are introduced in each chapter. Thus, from their first exposure to accounting, students are given tools that can be used to analyze financial statements. By the time they reach Chapter 12, where financial statement analysis is dealt with in detail, they have already worked with most of the ratios. Chapter 12 gives them an opportunity to pull the analysis together and work with the total corporate entity. In some cases, this takes the coverage slightly beyond what is usual in introductory texts.

Because real corporations are complex and generally prepare consolidated financial statements, an appendix is included that covers long-term investments in other corporations and the consolidation process. Recognizing that consolidation procedures are complicated and beyond the usual scope of an introductory text, this discussion is kept as simple as possible. In keeping with the user orientation, the financial statement impacts of the consolidation policies are considered.

HALLMARK FEATURES OF THIS BOOK

The text's user orientation aims to prepare students for their future in business, no matter what their area of concentration, and has been successfully adopted at universities across Canada. In addition to the content and organizational features described above, some of the proven pedagogical features that support this approach are presented below.

The Use of Financial Statements

A unique balance between covering preparer material and presenting a user perspective runs throughout the book, and recognizes the fact that introductory courses are taken by both accounting and non-accounting students. Since virtually all introductory accounting students, both graduate and undergraduate, will become users of accounting information, while only relatively few will become preparers, this text focuses on the understanding and use of corporate financial statements as a primary source of accounting information. Over the years, instructors across the country have found the balanced perspective featured in this text to be a very effective way of preparing students for further work as users of accounting information, as well as providing a solid foundation for students who do further studies in accounting.

Integral to this approach is the extensive use of real financial statement data. Throughout the text, you will find excerpts from the annual reports of actual corporations, reprinted (whenever possible) exactly as they originally appeared. In this edition, many of the excerpts are from internationally-based corporations where IFRS has been in use for some time.

The annual report of a Swedish company, H&M, is presented in its entirety, along with a variety of excerpts from over 50 other international and Canadian corporations. Examples and problems using the H&M Annual Report are highlighted by means of the H&M logo in the margin. An Annual Report icon in the margin identifies material that has been extracted from actual annual reports and brief notes provide basic background information on the companies involved, in case students are not familiar with them. In addition, the annual reports of HMV plc, a British company, and other international Canadian and companies are available online.

The assignment materials for each chapter also include a set of problems focused on *Reading and Interpreting Published Financial Statements*, which require students to analyze and interpret actual corporate financial statements and related disclosures.

User Relevance

Another key feature that complements the use of real financial statements is the User Relevance section, found at the beginning of each chapter from Chapter 2 onward. This describes why the content of the chapter is important to users of accounting information as they make business decisions, and prepares students to view the material from a user perspective as they read. Also, throughout the chapter, there are frequent references to what users will see on financial statements and how that information is related to decision-making. To reinforce this, at the end of each chapter there is a set of assignment items called *User Perspective Problems*, which require students to consider issues and concepts from the perspectives of various users of financial statements.

International Perspectives

In this edition of the text, International Financial Reporting Standards (IFRS) were adopted as the main accounting standards described in the text. In some cases, both the standards and the terminology are different from the previous Canadian GAAP (e.g., the titles of financial statements). Despite the fact that some of the standards are more detailed than the previous Canadian GAAP, efforts were made to portray the information as clearly and simply as possible. Additional international material is set off from the main body in boxes that summarize how some countries' standards are different from IFRS.

IFRS vs. ASPE

Where there are important differences between the IFRS and the standards in place in Canada for private enterprises, the details are included in boxes titled *IFRS vs. ASPE*.

Ethics in Accounting

Ethical issues are raised in most chapters by special boxed-in sections. These exhibits are designed to raise students' consciousness regarding ethical issues, and to provide a source of in-class discussion topics. The focus of these boxes is on what students need to think about in order to act responsibly. This feature is complemented by additional material on ethical issues in accounting provided on the Companion Website.

Earnings Management

To provide students with some understanding of the impact that the management of earnings can have on the information on financial statements, boxes entitled *Earnings Management* were added to most chapters. Information about how earnings can be managed with respect to the topic under discussion in the chapter alerts students to the potential for manipulation of the information. This additional knowledge should make them more knowledgeable end users of the financial statements.

Crictical Thinking and Communication Skills

While many of the questions in the *Reading and Interpreting Published Financial Statements* sections present challenging problems, special critical thinking questions and cases have been included at the end of most chapters. These require students to critically analyze issues, and can be used as the basis for student papers, class discussions, or debates, and to provide opportunities for students to develop their written and oral communication skills. Additional help with their writing skills is available on the Companion Website.

In-Text Student Aids

Each chapter includes the following sections:

HELPFUL HINTS   These boxes provide students with tips to help avoid common difficulties.

PRACTICE PROBLEMS   The practice problems at the end of each chapter are designed to reinforce the main points in the text and provide examples to assist students when tackling the assignment materials. Students are provided with "Strategies for

Success" before they attempt the problems, and explanations of key points are included in the solutions provided. Additional practice problems are available on the Companion Website.

SYNONYMS & ABBREVIATIONS   This section presents a summary of common synonyms for key terms used in the chapter, as well as any common abbreviations that are used.

GLOSSARY   There is a glossary at the end of each chapter that defines the key terms introduced in the chapter. Key terms are boldfaced in purple the first time they are used. A searchable glossary is also available on the Companion Website.

ASSIGNMENT MATERIALS   There are nine types of assignment materials, to satisfy a variety of learning and teaching objectives.

1. The *Assessing Your Recall* questions are designed to assess students' understanding of the basic concepts and terms introduced in the chapter.

2. The *Applying Your Knowledge* problems ask students to apply the concepts and procedures discussed in the chapter in hypothetical situations. These problems are similar to those found in traditional texts, and will often reinforce the technical and procedural aspects of accounting. Also, alternate versions of these problems will be available on the Companion Website for instructors. This enables them to assign a different version to another group of students or a new version of the problems in another term.

3. The *User Perspective* questions have the students assume the role of a particular user and consider and discuss chapter topics from that perspective.

4. The *Reading and Interpreting Published Financial Statements* section is a hallmark feature of this book, and contains problems that make use of actual corporate financial statement disclosures. The problems typically involve some type of analysis and interpretation of financial statement data.

5. The *Beyond the Book* section provides an opportunity for instructors to have students do individual or group research. Students are asked to find financial information about a company of their choice and to answer questions about topics introduced in each chapter. The Beyond the Book section in Chapter 1 gives several library and Internet sources of corporate financial statements, which students can use throughout the course.

6. The *Cases* are hypothetical scenarios in which students are asked to identify problems, evaluate situations, and make recommendations. The required part of the Cases often asks for a written report. Additional Cases can be found on the Companion Website.

7. The *Critical Thinking Questions* often take students beyond the structured data in the chapter by asking them to consider controversial areas associated with one or more of the chapter's topics.

8. The *Integrative Questions* (mid-way through the book) provide an opportunity for students to take a comprehensive look at reading and interpreting financial statements and applying a user perspective to accounting data.

9. The *Integrative Course Project* (following Chapter 11) enables students to examine the impact that accounting estimates and policy choices can have on corporate financial statements and ratio analysis.

Instructor's Resources

All instructor resources are provided on the Instructor Resource site. Included in this convenient format are:

- Instructor's Manual
- Test Bank
- Solutions Manual
- PowerPoint Presentation Slides
- Clicker Questions

Learning Leveraged with Technology

We have created a complete suite of online tools to introduce students to the world of financial accounting. Cognizant of the fact that every school has different needs, Wiley provides you with a variety of technology resources, giving you flexibility to incorporate some or all of these tools into your classes and create the balance that is right for you and your students.

WILEY PLUS

WileyPLUS is an innovative online environment for effective teaching and learning.

It builds students' confidence and increases their likelihood of success, because it takes the guesswork out of studying by providing them with a clear roadmap: what to do, how to do it, and whether they did it right. This interactive approach focuses on:

DESIGN: The research-based design of *WileyPLUS* is based on proven instructional methods. Content is organized into small, manageable amounts of information, helping students build better time management skills.

ENGAGEMENT: Students can visually track their progress as they move through the material at a pace that is right for them, while individualized self-quizzes followed by immediate feedback helps to sustain their motivation to learn.

OUTCOMES: Self-assessment lets students know the exact outcome of their effort at any time. Advanced reporting features allows instructors to easily spot trends in the performance their classes in order to make more informed decisions. With *WileyPLUS*, students take more initiative so you'll have greater impact on their achievement in the classroom and beyond.

What do students receive with *WileyPLUS*?

- Confidence-boosting feedback and proof of progress, 24/7

- Context-sensitive feedback as they work on problems that are linked to relevant sections in the online digital textbook

- An easy-to-navigate framework, calendars, visual progress tracking, and self-evaluation tools that help students study more effectively

What do instructors receive with *WileyPLUS*?

- Reliable resources that reinforce course goals inside and outside of the classroom

- Media-rich course materials and assessment content—Instructor's Manual, Test Bank, PowerPoint® Slides, Learning Objectives, Interactive Tutorials, Videos, Solutions Manual, Study Guide, Computerized Test Bank, Pre- and Post- Lecture Quizzes, and much more

www.wileyplus.com

ACKNOWLEDGEMENTS

We would like to thank Robert Hoskin, who developed the original concept for this book and who put so much thought and energy into its construction many years ago.

We give great thanks to our contributor and collaborator, Julia Scott, for all of her work on this edition.

We would also like to acknowledge the many reviewers who provided very valuable comments on our plans for the sixth edition and on our writing as we progressed through the chapters. We have tried to incorporate as many of your suggestions as possible.

Reviewers:

Greg Berberich, *Wilfrid Laurier University*
Rob Ducharme, *University of Waterloo*
Catherine Fortin, *McGill University*
Steve Gibson, *Simon Fraser University*
Else Grech, *Ryerson University*
Scott Laing, *Dalhousie University*
Philippe Levy, *McGill University*
Anne MacDonald, *Simon Fraser University*
Michelle O'Gay, *Georgian College*
Patti Proulx, *Carleton University*
Traven Reed, *Canadore College*
Julia Scott, *McGill University*
Sara Stonehouse, *Wilfrid Laurier University*
Greg Streich, *SAIT Polytechnic*
Larry Tenenbaum, *McGill University*
Peggy Wallace, *Trent University*

We are very grateful to everyone at John Wiley & Sons Canada, Limited. Zoë Craig got us going on the sixth edition, and Theresa Fitzgerald structured all of the text material and ensured that the book was published with as few errors as possible. We also want to thank the many people who worked behind the scenes producing materials that make this book unique: David Schwinghamer, who copyedited the text; Alison Arnot, who researched and summarized many of the numerous news articles that bring the real business world into this book; Merrie-Ellen Wilcox, who proofread all of the pages; and Alan Yoshioka, who produced the index. We also want to thank Aida Krneta, who has developed creative ways of marketing this edition of the text. Last, but by no means least, sincere thanks go to all of the university/college representatives for all their energy and enthusiasm in promoting the merits of the book to instructors. There are several people who worked on supplemental material for the text that also deserve a special thank you:

Margo Burtch, *Seneca College*
Lynn de Grace, *McGill University*
Robert G. Ducharme, *University of Waterloo*
Rosalie Harms, *University of Winnipeg*
Steven Konvalinka-Plateo, *George Brown College*
Scott Laing, *Dalhousie University*
Gerlando La Rocca, *Vanier College*
Camillo Lento, *Lakehead University*
Helen Vallee, *Kwantlen Polytechnic University*

We would also like to thank the companies who granted us permission to reproduce their financial statements, especially H&M and HMV.

CONCLUDING REMARKS

We hope that both students and instructors will find the material in this book and its supplements interesting and helpful as they attempt to understand the complex and fascinating world of corporate financial reporting.

We have tried to be very careful in the editing of this book and the associated support materials, to minimize errors. Any remaining errors are, of course, our responsibility and we would appreciate hearing from you concerning any that you find. We also look forward to receiving any comments and suggestions that you would like to make, so that we can continue to improve this teaching and learning package.

Maureen Fizzell   Don Cherry
Simon Fraser University   Dalhousie University

November 2010

Brief Table of Contents

Table of Contents

OVERVIEW OF CORPORATE FINANCIAL REPORTING

LEARNING OBJECTIVES

After studying this chapter, you should be able to:

1. Define accounting and understand its relationship to economic decision-making.

2. Understand what an annual report is and what it contains.

3. Describe the major forms of business organization in which accounting is used.

4. Identify several users of financial statements and begin to understand how they use accounting information.

5. Know what the terms "generally accepted accounting principles" (GAAP) and "international financial reporting standards" (IFRS) mean.

6. Identify the qualitative characteristics and constraints of accounting information.

7. Describe the three fundamental business activities.

8. Identify the major financial statements and describe their main components.

9. Begin to understand the role of ethics in financial accounting.

Principle of Caution Fuels Growth

Fashion retailer H&M was established in Västerås, Sweden, in 1947 by Erling Persson. Its philosophy—to bring fashion and quality at the best price—has struck a chord internationally. By the end of 2009, the company was selling clothes and cosmetics in approximately 2,000 stores in 35 countries. H&M offers fashion for women, men, teenagers, and children, as well as its own brand of cosmetics, accessories, and footwear. The first H&M store in Canada opened in Toronto in March 2004, and by the end of 2009 the company had 51 stores in Ontario, Quebec, New Brunswick, Nova Scotia, Alberta, and British Columbia.

The successful growth and expansion of this fashion retailer can be traced to sound financial decision-making. "We have a principle that we call 'the principle of caution,' " says Nils Vinge, H&M's Head of Investor Relations. "One way of practising that is to always pay for the expansion with our own funds." In fact, the company has never used financing for an expansion, relying instead on the available funds from its strong cash flow and sound profitability.

The retailer also keeps its accounting information up to date. "If we deem a product to need a price markdown, we do it immediately in our books," explains Mr. Vinge.

"Cost consciousness is vital to the success story," he continues. "Historically, when our own success had continued for many consecutive years, the focus on costs might have fallen behind." Indeed, when the pace of increasing sales slowed down but costs continued to increase, profitability suffered and cost-cutting programs became necessary. "But we have learned from this," says Mr. Vinge. "The trick is to focus on costs when sales are good! If you

succeed with that, you will not have a problem when sales are weaker." He provides the example of 2009, when sales in the first nine months had been weaker than the company had hoped for, but profitability remained very high and there was no cost-cutting program.

This success comes down to benchmarking, says Mr. Vinge. "With 2,000 stores in 35 markets, everything is continuously benchmarked." H&M learned that using its accounting information to monitor the company's financial health can lead to future success and growth.

The opening story describes how a large international company grows and evolves and how accounting assists in that development. Whether you are performing day-to-day operations, borrowing money for a start-up or expansion, restructuring your organization, planning a new avenue of operations, or deciding to purchase or lease, you need to have information that will help you make the best decisions. One of the most important sources of that information is the accounting system. Mr. Vinge described how the close monitoring of accounting information has enabled **H&M** to use its own funds to grow and to remain profitable even in challenging economic times. H&M's "principle of caution" represents a tempered approach to managing the company. Other companies might choose to use a riskier philosophy by using borrowed funds to fuel expansion. As a user of accounting information, you will find that knowing a company's underlying management philosophy will help you assess the company's financial health. For Mr. Vinge and other business owners, accounting systems represent the backbone of their businesses.

WHAT IS A BUSINESS?

This book describes the role of accounting within a business setting. It is, therefore, important to start with an understanding of what a business **entity** is. Businesses usually plan to earn a profit for their owners. They usually sell products or services and/or invest in other businesses. The owners can be a single individual or thousands of people. A local business in your area may be owned by a few individuals, whereas a large company such as **Canadian Tire** likely has thousands of investors (owners). Accounting is present in all these entities.

WHAT IS ACCOUNTING?

Define accounting and understand its relationship to economic decision-making.

Accounting is an information system in which the underlying economic conditions of organizations—and, indeed, of individuals—are recorded, summarized, reported, and understood. Accounting can be as simple as balancing your personal cheque book or as complex as recording and reporting on the economic condition of a multinational corporation such as **Microsoft** or of a federal government such as the Government of Canada. All these entities need to know economic information in order to continue to operate efficiently and effectively. Accounting is the system that provides vital financial information. It provides the very framework around which people and organizations make decisions. It is therefore important that you, as a future user, have at least a basic understanding of what accounting is (and is not), what it is trying to accomplish, and how it does so.

The focus of this book is the accounting information produced by profit-oriented organizations, although we will occasionally refer to not-for-profit organizations or governments. We will concentrate mainly on the **financial statements**, which are management's reports to the companies' owners that summarize how the company performed during a particular period. They also tell users what the company owns, to whom it has obligations (debts), and what is left over after the obligations are satisfied (paid). There is also a statement that describes how cash flowed in and out of the company. The financial statements are the final set of documents produced at the end of an accounting period. They are included in a larger **annual report** that is the main method that management uses to report the results of the company's activities during the year. The annual report is sent to all owners, but many other parties that have an interest in the company (for example, lenders, analysts, and credit-rating agencies) also use it. Many companies include their most recent financial statements on their websites so that visitors can access them.

The primary goal of this book is to help you become an intelligent user of accounting information by enhancing your ability to read and understand corporate financial statements. You may become a manager, accountant, banker, or financial analyst, and even if you do not end up working directly in the finance industry, you will probably invest in the shares or bonds of a company at some point in your career. If you work in a company, whether in sales, human resources, or other areas, your decisions will probably have an impact on what is reported to owners. Whatever your business role, you will make decisions about companies, such as whether to invest in their shares, lend them money, or sell them goods or services on credit. In making these decisions, it will be important for you to understand the information that is presented in corporate financial statements. You must know not only what each piece of information tells you about the company, but also what it does not tell you. You should also become aware that some important information is not contained in the financial statements, yet could be useful in making certain decisions.

We have written this book for a broad readership, understanding that many of you will play multiple roles as owners (shareholders), creditors, and managers of companies. We have assumed that you know little or nothing about accounting. We have not assumed that you are training to be an accountant, although that may be your objective. Therefore, this book does not emphasize accounting procedures. Instead, it emphasizes the underlying concepts of accounting and the analysis of financial statements. However, it is not really possible to have a knowledgeable understanding of the end result of the accounting process without first having an overall view of how the accounting system works. For this reason, the first chapters present the mechanics of the accounting system. The remaining chapters are then devoted to more detailed accounting issues and concepts, and to a more in-depth analysis of financial statements.

Throughout the book, information from real companies is used to illustrate topics. Many of the companies that we have used for illustrations are non-Canadian companies because as of January 1, 2011, Canada changed the underlying standards that are used to collect, record, and report accounting information. The change was from Canadian standards to international financial reporting standards (IFRS). When we were writing this edition of the book, however, very few Canadian companies had changed to IFRS. We therefore chose companies from other parts of the world where IFRS was being used.

In addition to the many examples throughout the book of financial statement information from a variety of companies, we have also included Part II of the annual report of **H&M Hennes & Mauritz AB** (H&M) for 2009 in Appendix A at the end of the book. As you learned in the opening story, H&M is a Swedish company that sells clothing to women, men, and children in retail outlets in 35 countries, including Canada. It also sells merchandise via the Internet and by catalogue. Its annual report for 2009 was produced in two parts: Part I includes a description of its operations, including a discussion of the past year and its future plans. Part II includes the financial statements and the notes to the financial statements. You will find Part I on the book companion website, which is located at www.wiley.com/canada/hoskin. A second complete annual report, that of **HMV Group plc** (HMV) for 2010, has also been

LEARNING OBJECTIVE 2

Understand what an annual report is and what it contains.

www.wileyplus.com

H&M Part I,
HMV Group plc

included on the companion website. HMV, a United Kingdom company, is one of the world's leading retailers of music, videos, and games. Its merchandise is sold in HMV stores throughout Canada and other countries. The inclusion of two complete annual reports will provide you with more reference material to help your analysis of accounting information.

Many references will be made to the H&M and HMV reports throughout the book. Page numbers from these annual reports will be preceded by H&M- or HMV-. For example, page 10 from an annual report will be referred to as H&M-10 or HMV-10. At the end of each chapter, additional problems, labelled Beyond the Book, require you to find an annual report for a company of your own choosing or one suggested by your instructor. At most colleges and universities, students can access annual reports of other companies electronically. Reports for Canadian companies are also currently available on the Internet through the SEDAR filings. Your instructor may provide you with information about how to access this information on your campus, or you can contact your librarian.

Because different companies use slightly different terminology to refer to items in their financial statements, it is sometimes confusing to read them. To help you interpret these financial statements, at the end of most of this book's chapters you will find lists of abbreviations and synonyms. A glossary that briefly defines or explains the terms that are used is also provided at the end of each chapter.

accounting in the news

Print Is Still Important

While investor relations websites are great for storing reams of information or disseminating news quickly, most companies still rely on the traditional annual report, according to a survey of 2008 annual reports done by Toronto-based Craib Design & Communications and investor relations consulting firm Blunn & Company, which researched 680 annual reports from companies worldwide.

They found most of the leading companies in North America and Europe continue to devote substantial time and resources to the printed annual report, because only the printed report offers the required control over structure, pacing, and context.

The best printed annual reports, the surveyors say, contain highlights of the company's financial history, corporate governance, sustainability performance, and so on, with referrals to the investor relations website. The best investor relations websites offer a full annual report for downloading, as well as an on-line version that incorporates video and/or animation. The on-line annual report is easier to read and navigate, with features such as variable text size, related links, and key word search functions.

Source: http://www.craib.com/craib_public/pdf/ARTrends/AR-Trends08_LR.pdf

INTERNATIONAL PERSPECTIVES

With its recent adoption of IFRS, Canada has joined many other countries and moved the world one step closer to the establishment of a single set of accounting reporting standards. The United States has not yet adopted IFRS. It is working with the international accounting standard-setters on issues of mutual concern and planning to adopt IFRS before 2020.

The **Canadian Accounting Standards Board (AcSB)** has simplified the previous Canadian accounting reporting guidelines for private companies. Occasionally in the book, there are examples of how accounting standards in private companies might differ from those in public companies in Canada. These sections are in boxes like this so that you can easily identify discussions of private company standards, and not confuse them with IFRS.

FORMS OF ORGANIZATION

The financial information that is captured by the accounting system is used in many different types of organization: profit-seeking entities such as corporations; governing organizations such as federal, provincial, and municipal governments; service entities such as hospitals and academic institutions; and not-for-profit entities such as charities and clubs. Although these entities have different objectives, they all need information that tells their users whether they are financially sound, meeting their goals, and likely to remain viable in the future. Within the accounting system, as mentioned earlier, reports called financial statements attempt to capture financial information about an entity and present it to users so that they can make informed decisions. Because these entities have different structures and objectives, the accounting approaches that are associated with the statements may be different. To try to describe all the variations adequately would make this book too complicated. We are therefore *concentrating on the profit-seeking entities*, although we will occasionally add information about the other types of organization.

Although the accounting issues in this book also apply to some degree to the other forms of organization, our focus is the accounting issues that *corporations* face. Almost every large business in Canada is a corporation. Other forms of business include sole proprietorships, partnerships, limited partnerships, and Crown corporations. These forms of organization are discussed in more detail in Chapter 11.

In all business organizations, the owners make an initial investment in the business entity by contributing either cash or property, or both. In sole proprietorships and partnerships, this ownership interest is called the owner's or partners' capital. In a corporation, owners make similar investments in the company, but their ownership interest is called **shareholders' equity** and it is represented by documents known as **shares**. A share is simply a document that represents a small part of ownership in the corporation. The **owners** therefore are referred to as **shareholders** (or stockholders). One advantage of the corporate form of business is that shares are easily transferred between investors; one investor can sell his or her shares (i.e., ownership) in a company and another can buy them, usually without significantly affecting the company itself. Corporations whose shares are held by a large number of individuals or entities and that are traded on a public stock exchange (such as the Toronto Stock Exchange) are called **publicly traded corporations**. Some portion of their ownership will usually change hands every day. It is not as easy to transfer ownership in a sole proprietorship or a partnership. Corporations whose shares are held by a small number of individuals are sometimes called **privately held corporations**. The shares in these corporations do not trade on public stock exchanges, which makes the transfer of ownership more difficult. Except in some small corporations, shareholders typically are not involved in the day-to-day operation of the business. Because of the large number of shareholders and their lack of involvement in

LEARNING OBJECTIVE 3

Describe the major forms of business organization in which accounting is used.

day-to-day activities, the shareholders typically elect a **board of directors** to represent them. The board of directors then hires (and fires) individuals in senior executive positions to manage the day-to-day operations. Together, these senior executives, along with the managers they hire, are known as **management**. To keep shareholders informed of the performance of their investment in the company, management reports periodically to the shareholders. This information is sent to shareholders on a quarterly basis (every three months) in a quarterly report. The fourth-quarter report is combined with the reports from the previous three quarters to produce financial statements that cover the entire fiscal year. These annual financial statements are included in the company's annual report. It is these annual financial statements that we will be studying.

USERS OF FINANCIAL STATEMENTS

LEARNING OBJECTIVE 4

Identify several users of financial statements and begin to understand how they use accounting information.

Accounting is primarily concerned with the communication of financial information to users. Accountants must first identify what information they should communicate to users, then ensure that the company's accounting system will accurately collect and record this information so that it can be communicated. Because businesses are involved in many thousands of transactions each year, accountants must summarize this information in a format that is understandable, and therefore useful, to users. Accountants are very concerned that the information they provide is both relevant to users and reliable.

Although managers prepare annual reports and corporate financial statements primarily for shareholders, other users of financial data also analyze them. These include people who are internal to the company and others who are external to it. The various users do not have the same goals in their search for information. As mentioned previously, in the future you will probably be a user of financial information. What kind of user is still unclear. It is important, therefore, at this stage, to understand who the typical users of financial information are and what they want to know. At the end of each chapter, we have therefore included a series of questions entitled User Perspective Problems that describe situations to consider from different user perspectives. Exhibit 1-1 lists some of these users.

EXHIBIT 1-1

USERS OF FINANCIAL STATEMENT INFORMATION

Internal users:

Management

Board of directors

External users:

Shareholders

Potential investors

Creditors (for example, bankers and suppliers)

Regulators (for example, a stock exchange)

Taxing authorities

Other corporations, including competitors

Security analysts

Credit-rating agencies

Labour unions

Journalists

Internal Users

Management and the Board of Directors

Management and the board of directors, as primary internal users, use accounting data to make many decisions, such as pricing products, expanding operations, deciding whether to buy or lease equipment, and controlling costs. Because of their position inside the company, managers have access to many sources of financial information beyond what is included in the financial statements that external users see. Their use of these additional accounting data is important, but it is generally covered in books devoted to **managerial accounting** or **cost accounting** and will not be discussed in this book. Our focus will be on the value of accounting data to external users. **Financial accounting** courses are primarily aimed at the study of the accounting data provided to outside users through financial statements. In most business programs, students are required to take financial as well as managerial accounting courses in order to expose them to both types of accounting information.

Professional Profiles

External Users

The information that is disclosed in financial statements is sensitive to external users' needs because management, who prepares the statements, wants to communicate information to shareholders, creditors, and others about the company's financial status. Management can therefore disclose almost any information it considers important, although there are limitations set by various regulatory bodies. There may also be times when management does not want to disclose some information to certain users. The financial accounting reporting standards describe what must be disclosed, but they often allow latitude in the way the information is recorded and reported.

Shareholders and Potential Investors

Shareholders and potential investors need information that makes it possible to assess how well management has been running the company. They want to make decisions about buying more shares or selling some or all of the shares they already own. They will analyze the current share price (as reflected on the stock exchange) and compare it with the original price that they paid for the shares. Are the shares now worth more or less? They will also be comparing the share price with the company's underlying value, which is reflected in the financial statements and other sources of information they have about the company. They will also consider whether the people currently sitting on the board of directors are doing an adequate job of overseeing the management team they have selected. Is the company heading in the right direction? Is it making decisions that result in increased value to the shareholders? Information in the financial statements will help answer these questions. Other sources of information for these users include press releases, websites, business newspapers and magazines, and experts such as stockbrokers and financial advisors. Because shareholders are concerned with the company as a whole, they are probably the external users who have the broadest need for information.

Creditors

Creditors usually come from three major groups. The first group includes those who sell goods or services to the company and are willing to wait a short period of time for payment. Examples of these users are suppliers, employees, and government (with respect to payroll deductions). These users focus on the short-term cash level in the company because they want to be paid.

The second group consists of financial institutions, such as banks, that have loaned money to the company. The loans can either be short-term or extend over several years. Like the people in the first group, they are also interested in the company's cash level, but they often need to assess the cash flow further into the future, so their need for information is broader. They want not only repayment of the principal of the debt (the original amount that was loaned), but also payment of interest.

The third group comprises investors who have purchased long-term debt instruments such as corporate bonds from the company. Similar to banks, these users have both a long-term and a short-term interest in the company's cash level. These creditor groups use the financial statements as a source of information that enables them to assess the company's future cash flows. They will make their lending or investing decisions and set interest levels based on their assessment of how much risk there is of non-collection (i.e., of not being able to collect the amounts they loaned).

Regulators

The regulators who are interested in financial statements are numerous. For example, the government has regulations for how a business becomes incorporated and for its conduct after incorporation. It is interested in ensuring that the company follows these regulations. The stock exchanges on which shares are traded have regulations about the timing and format of information that companies must convey to them and to investors. If companies do not comply with those regulations, they could be delisted (their shares can no longer trade on the stock exchange), which greatly affects their ability to raise capital. Environmental groups also monitor the activities of companies, as they want to ensure that environmental standards are respected.

Taxing Authorities

Parliament, the federal **taxing authority** in Canada, has established the Canada Revenue Agency (CRA) as its collection agency. Parliament creates the rules for how taxable income (the earnings on which the tax amount is calculated) should be measured. The tax rules rely extensively on a company's financial statements in assessing the amount of tax that businesses have to pay, and there are several areas where these rules vary. Later in this book, we will describe some of these variations and explain their impact on the financial statements.

Other Users

Additional users of financial statement information include other companies, security analysts, credit-rating agencies, labour unions, and journalists. Other companies may want information about the performance of a company if they enter into co-operative agreements or contracts with that company. If it is a direct competitor, the company may want information that will help assess the competitor's strength and future plans. Security analysts and credit-rating agencies use the financial statements to provide information about the strengths and weaknesses of companies to people who want to invest. Labour unions need to understand the company's financial health in order to negotiate labour contracts with management. Companies often give journalists press releases that disclose financial information such as expected earnings. The journalists may refer to the actual financial statements to validate the information they were given and to supplement the original information.

All these users, with their various needs, use the same set of financial statements. It is therefore important that the financial statements provide information for the widest possible group of users. As you would guess, however, many pieces of information that particular users want cannot be found in the financial statements. Users must therefore find other sources of information as well.

DEVELOPMENT OF ACCOUNTING STANDARDS

When management begins the task of measuring, collecting, recording, and reporting financial information for users, it needs some guidelines to follow so that all users can read and understand the financial statements. If there were no guidelines, each company would develop its own information reporting system, and it would be difficult for users to evaluate the statements and compare them with those of other companies in order to make knowledgeable decisions. Each country has developed guidelines for this purpose.

LEARNING OBJECTIVE 5

Know what the terms "generally accepted accounting principles" (GAAP) and "international financial reporting standards" (IFRS) mean.

For Canada, the **International Accounting Standards Board (IASB)**, based in London, England, sets accounting recommendations and standards. These accounting recommendations and standards are in the *CICA Handbook* and have the force of law in Canada, as they are recognized in both federal and provincial statutes that regulate business corporations. To promote the development of international accounting standards, the IASB has developed relationships with the primary standard-setting bodies in many countries, including the Canadian Institute of Chartered Accountants (CICA) in Canada. Up until the adoption of IFRS, the CICA was responsible for setting standards in Canada. The IASB encourages countries to change their accounting standards so that they more closely resemble the international standards. Canada has now adopted those standards. Although the CICA is no longer setting the financial accounting reporting standards in Canada for publicly traded companies, it is involved in the work of the IASB, as it comments regularly on proposed standards and sometimes has a Canadian representative on the board.

In the United States, the **Financial Accounting Standards Board (FASB)** sets accounting standards for American corporations. In its deliberations about new standards and revision of old standards, the FASB is currently working closely with the IASB to develop a single set of financial reporting standards.

The set of accounting recommendations and standards that corporations use is referred to as generally accepted accounting principles, or **GAAP** (usually pronounced as "gap"). These principles have been developed using many different methods over time. For example, deductive methods start with some generally accepted definitions (of assets, liabilities, and income, for instance) and concepts, and then logically derive specific accounting methods and other accounting principles from them. This approach is similar to the process that mathematicians use in the development of mathematical theory. The problem with this approach has been the difficulty in achieving agreement about the underlying definitions and concepts. Inductive approaches generally consider the methods that are currently being used and then try to develop (induce) general principles from these methods. Current standard setting under the IASB combines both an inductive and a deductive approach. On the deductive side, the IASB has developed a set of underlying objectives and concepts called the Framework, or the **conceptual framework**. This framework has then been used deductively to justify new accounting standards and to revise old ones. On the inductive side, the conceptual framework and the new accounting standards have all been established by a political process of reaching consensus among the various users of financial information.

INTERNATIONAL PERSPECTIVES

The development of accounting standards has, in general, been specific to each country. Each country has developed its own standards, which reflect its political, social, and economic environment. However, with the development of world markets for both products and financial capital, there has been an increasing need for better understanding among countries regarding financial reporting. Over the years, many organizations have tried to set international accounting standards. The International Accounting Standards Board (IASB) has been the most successful. The IASB is an independent, private-sector body that is funded by donations from accounting organizations around the world and from the **International Federation of Accountants (IFAC)**. By the end of January 2009, the IASB had issued 41 **International Accounting Standards (IASs)** and 9 **International Financial Reporting Standards (IFRSs)**. The IASs were issued by the IASB's predecessor, the Board of the International Accounting Standards Committee (IASC).

As a future user of accounting information, it is important that you understand the concepts that underlie financial accounting. The conceptual framework that these concepts form is used to develop accounting guidelines for companies to follow when preparing their financial statements. The financial statements should describe what the entity owns, to whom it has obligations, and what is left over after the obligations are satisfied. They should also show how cash flowed in and out of the entity. The final purpose of financial statements should be to describe the results of the entity's operations.

Qualitative Characteristics and Constraints of Accounting Information

LEARNING OBJECTIVE 6

Identify the qualitative characteristics and constraints of accounting information.

Accounting data should possess four essential qualitative characteristics, which are limited by three possible constraints. Exhibit 1-2 provides a hierarchy of these qualitative characteristics and the constraints.

Understandability, the first qualitative characteristic, simply means that the information must be understandable to the user. For example, if you see an item called "Current portion of long-term debt" listed on a financial statement, you should understand that this means that the amount listed for this item will be paid in cash over the next 12 months to the entity that loaned the money to the company. If preparers of the financial statements were not interested in understandability, they would show the amount of long-term debt in total without pulling out the amount that has to be paid back in the next year. Then, users would not be able to assess the company's probable cash outflow in the coming year. The underlying assumptions behind this qualitative characteristic are that the users are reasonably well informed about accounting terminology and procedures and that they have a reasonable understanding of the business environment. As you probably do not yet have such a background, you are likely to find the financial statements more difficult to understand at first. As your knowledge of accounting grows, you will find statements easier to read.

CHARACTERISTICS AND CONSTRAINTS OF ACCOUNTING INFORMATION

EXHIBIT 1-2

Qualitative Characteristics

Understandability

Relevance

    Predictive value

    Confirmatory value

Reliability

    Faithful representation

    Substance over form

    Neutrality

    Prudence

    Completeness

Comparability

Constraints

Timeliness

Balance between benefits and cost

Balance between qualitative characteristics

Relevance refers to whether the information would make a difference in a decision. For example, if you were told that you had an exam next week, that fact would be relevant to you. It would affect what you planned to do with your time during the next week. However, if you were told that it was snowing at the North Pole, you would probably not find that relevant. In some cases, there are accounting reporting standards that direct management to record and/or disclose certain information that is considered relevant. For example, companies must report the market value (current selling price) of their short-term investments, which is likely a relevant piece of information to a user. If an investment is short-term, the company probably intends to sell it in the near future. Knowing the investment's market value allows the user to estimate potential cash inflow from the sale. In other cases, there is no clear standard and management must judge whether certain information would be relevant to users.

Relevant information may have two kinds of value: predictive value and confirmatory value. These two roles are interrelated. **Predictive value** means that the information is useful in predicting future results, such as income or cash flow, and therefore should be helpful to users who make decisions that depend on predictions of future events. Predictive value is based on an underlying assumption that the past is a good predictor of the future. The example in the previous paragraph has potential predictive value in that the market value of the investment may be a good predictor of future cash inflows.

Confirmatory value is information that allows users to evaluate the outcomes of previous decisions, giving them feedback on their past decisions. This can be helpful as users learn from their past successes and failures. Following the short-term investment example mentioned earlier, a user who later saw financial statements from after the sale of the investment could then determine whether the investment sold for the market value that was previously disclosed. If it did, the user would be confident that relying on the market value was a reasonable decision. If the investment sold for less or more, the user might decide that the market value was one piece of information, but that other sources of information are needed to better predict future cash inflows.

The relevance of economic information is also affected by its nature and **materiality**. If a company decides to begin selling its products outside of Canada, the nature of this decision affects the risks and probable future profit of the company. By its nature, this decision is relevant. Information is material if the exclusion or misstatement of the information would affect the decision-making of users. It is often difficult for accountants to determine the point at which something becomes material, and it may vary depending on the information.

accounting in the news

More Annual Reports Online

Since 2005, the majority of the FTSE 100 companies (the 100 most highly capitalized companies on the London Stock Exchange) have prepared online annual reports in HTML, PDF or JPG formats. HTML is the most common format enabling users to access only the portions of the reports with the information that they want. Most companies today will include their annual and quarterly reports on their websites so that users have easy access to their financial results.

The growth of the online reports enables users to access the financial information from multiple access points and devices. In the recent past, users had to request print copies of reports if they wanted information. The expansion of online materials makes it easier for users to get timely information.

The challenge for companies now is how to make their reports different from those of other companies. Technology is helping them do that.

Source: Corporate Eye, "Online Annual Reports: What's Next?" Blog by Lucy, August 18, 2009, http://www.corporate-eye.com/blog/2009/08/annual-reports-stretch-target/

Reliability of information rests on five fundamental characteristics: faithful representation, substance over form, neutrality, prudence, and completeness. Information is reliable if it is free from error and bias.

Faithful representation means that the information faithfully represents the attribute, characteristic, or economic event that it claims to represent. It is necessary to look for the underlying substance of the transactions when deciding how to account for them. For example, suppose the accounting system produces a dollar total for sales that is supposed to represent all sales made during a single year. This amount should include all sales made in that year and exclude all sales made in any other year. If it does, the information has representational faithfulness. Because the task of identifying, measuring, recording, and reporting financial transactions is complex, it is sometimes difficult to ensure that a representation is faithful.

Substance over form means that accountants need to convey the underlying substance of transactions rather than just record and report transactions according to required standards. Accountants must look beyond the accounting standards and ensure that the information that is conveyed captures the economic reality. For example, if a company sells inventory to a customer and promises to provide warranty service for a period of time, it is important that the sale be recorded and, at the same time, that the potential cost of the warranty service also be determined and reported. Presenting potential warranty costs gives the user a more complete picture of the total agreement with the customer.

Neutrality means that the information is not calculated or presented in a way that would bias users toward making certain desired decisions and not making other decisions that the company might find less desirable. For example, an inflated estimate of the value of inventory on hand is biased and not neutral. On the other hand, recording inventory at the value you paid for it is neutral.

Prudence refers to using caution when making judgements. Accounting transactions and measurements are not always exact. They often include uncertainties. For instance, in the example about disclosing possible warranty costs, accountants must use judgement in measuring the probability and the amount of the future costs. Prudence requires that accountants make estimates that do not overstate revenues and assets or understate expenses and liabilities. Accountants need to be careful because prudence does not give the freedom to understate or overstate items on purpose. Such information would no longer be neutral.

Completeness refers to the need to ensure that the financial statements contain all of the information that users need in order to make informed decisions. It is recognized that materiality and the cost of providing the information could put some restraints on the gathering and reporting of some information. Accountants must carefully weigh whether the usefulness of the information outweighs the cost of providing it.

INTERNATIONAL PERSPECTIVES—IFRS REQUIREMENTS

In May 2008, the IASB and FASB worked together on a complete review of the conceptual framework. Their first exposure draft (a discussion paper that contained proposed changes that the IASB was suggesting) considered the objectives and the qualitative characteristics and constraints of financial reporting information. The exposure draft suggested only two qualitative characteristics: relevance and faithful representation; and it suggested only two constraints on financial reporting: materiality and cost. The relevance characteristic is similar to the current definition of relevance, which includes predictive and confirmatory values. Faithful representation is much broader than the current definition. Rather than being part of reliability, it replaces reliability as the overall characteristic and includes items like neutrality, completeness, and freedom from material error that before were part of reliability. The other change described in the exposure draft is the ordering of the two characteristics. The exposure draft identifies the connection between economic events and relevance. It requires that relevance be applied first before faithful representation. The recommendation includes the additional characteristics of comparability, verifiability, timeliness, and understandability that it defines as enhancing characteristics. These proposed changes had not been finalized by the time this book was published.

Comparability, the fourth qualitative characteristic, generally refers to the ability to compare information produced by different companies, especially if they are in the same industry. A high degree of comparability allows for better comparisons across companies and potentially better decisions. Within GAAP, however, there are no guidelines that require all companies in an industry to use the same accounting methods. Because different methods will produce different financial statement amounts, it is important for users to understand what methods are available to companies and how the various methods will affect the accounting numbers. Comparability also refers to the ability to compare the financial statements of the same company over more than one time period. The information that is gained by comparing a company's results from one period to its results from another period is enhanced when a company applies the same accounting methods in both periods. Much of the predictive value of accounting information depends on the long-term data trends. If a company uses different methods to produce that information over time, the information has less predictive value.

There are three overriding **constraints** that can affect the information provided by management: timeliness, the balance between benefit and cost, and the balance between qualitative characteristics.

Timeliness is important because old information quickly loses its relevance to users. If the information is not timely, it may lose its ability to make a difference in a decision. For example, if you were interested in investing in a company, you would want to see its financial statements. Public companies produce financial statements for the public every three months (quarterly) and annually. It normally takes a company three weeks to produce quarterly results after the end of the quarter and two to three months to produce the annual report after the company's year end. If it is June and the most recent financial statements you can find are dated March 31, is this timely information? With the rapid changes in the business environment, timeliness will become even more important in decision-making. In the future, companies may need to publish monthly financial statements in order to satisfy users' demand for timely information. At the same time, however, as companies rush to produce timely information, management must be aware that producing information before all aspects of an economic event are known may compromise the reliability of that information.

The **balance between benefit and cost** states simply that the value of the benefits that are expected to be had from information should exceed the cost of producing it. The value of the benefits provided by information, however, is very difficult to measure. This can lead to problems because the company pays the costs of producing the information, yet the benefits are mainly for outside users. For example, a company could consider publishing financial statements every week instead of every three months. This would make the information more timely for outside users, but publishing the financial statements every week would be very costly in hours to produce them and ensure their accuracy. If it perceived that the benefit of providing weekly financial statements to external users was not great enough, the company would not produce them, because the cost would exceed the benefit.

Because the economic events that accounting is conveying in the financial statements are complex, it is often difficult to determine the appropriate **balance between qualitative characteristics**. It is sometimes necessary to reduce the emphasis on one characteristic in order to favour another one. Professional judgement is often required to meet the underlying objective of financial statements, which is to provide information that is useful for decision-making. For example, assume a company has a piece of equipment that it purchased a few years earlier to use in its manufacturing business. It has the original invoice from when it purchased the equipment, and therefore has a reliable amount to use when reporting. The company later makes changes to its product line and decides to sell the piece of equipment as it no longer needs it. However, it does not have a buyer and does not have a reliable potential selling price. Because it plans to sell the equipment, reporting it at its potential selling price would be relevant to users. The question that arises is this: should it use an estimate of the selling price in order to provide relevant information or should it continue to report the equipment at its original cost because it is a reliable amount? It is for decisions like this that we have the constraint of achieving a balance between qualitative characteristics.

These qualitative characteristics and constraints help form the underlying basis on which accounting standards are established. As we discuss them in the book, referring back to these characteristics and constraints should help you understand and remember the standards that are being used.

accounting in the news

Responsibilities of Corporate Directors

In a recent court case, the directors of Feltex Carpets Limited, a New Zealand company, were charged under the New Zealand Financial Reporting Act (FRA) for failing to comply with the applicable reporting standards. One of Feltex's loan agreements had a covenant (special agreement) that the company had not met. This meant that the company could be required to repay the total amount of the debt. In the financial statements, the company had not reported the breach of this covenant nor had the loan been reported as due within one year. The financial statements had it listed as a long-term liability.

The directors are responsible for the content of the financial statements and they are required to ensure that they are prepared according to the required standards. Because New Zealand was switching from it New Zealand standards to IFRS, the directors had hired an accounting firm to review the financial statements to ensure that all of the standards had been met. Both the accounting firm and the company's CFO and CEO assured the directors that there were no significant issues with respect to compliance with the standards. The directors' defense was that they had relied on the expert advice of the accounting firm and the CFO and CEO.

In the FRA, it stipulates that directors can rely on expert advice in performing their responsibilities. The court agreed that the directors had taken all "reasonable and proper steps" to comply with the reporting standards. There can be significant consequences for directors when accounting standards are not followed because the ultimate responsibility for the content of the financial statements rests with them.

Source: Martin Wiseman and Pavanie Edirisuriya, "Directors' ability to rely on employees and advisors – what does the Feltex case tell us?" DLA PHILLIPS FOX, August 13, 2010, http://www.dlaphillipsfox.com/article/868/Directors-ability-to-rely-on-employees-and-advisors—what-does-the-Feltex-case-tell-us

BUSINESS ACTIVITIES

To understand the information in financial statements, it is useful to think about the fundamental types of activities that all businesses engage in and report on. The basic activities of businesses are **financing, investing**, and **operating**.

LEARNING OBJECTIVE 7

Describe the three fundamental business activities.

Financing Activities

Financing refers to the activity of obtaining **funds** (cash) in order to buy major assets, such as the buildings and equipment that almost every business uses. This activity is necessary, of course, to start the business, but it also continues as the business grows, expands its operations, and replaces old buildings and equipment. Funds are obtained from two primary sources outside the company: **creditors** and **investors**. Creditors expect to be repaid on a timely basis and often charge the business, in the form of interest, for the use of their money, goods, or services. The amount to be repaid is generally a fixed (pre-determined) amount. Examples of creditors are banks that offer both short-term and long-term loans, and suppliers who are willing to provide goods and services today with the expectation of being paid for those products later. Investors, on the other hand, invest in the company in the hope that their investment will generate a profit. They earn profits either by receiving **dividends** (payments of funds from the company to the shareholders) or by selling their shares to another investor. Of course, investors may experience either a gain (receive more than the initial amount paid for the shares) or a loss (receive less than the initial amount paid for the shares) when the sale occurs.

A primary internal source of new funds for any company is the profit it makes that is not paid out to shareholders in dividends. These profits are called **retained earnings**. Remember how H&M finances its growth into new markets? It does not expand unless it has sufficient internally generated funds to fund the expansion. If a company is not profitable, or if all profits are distributed to shareholders as dividends, the only way it can expand is to get more funds from investors (existing shareholders or new investors) or borrow from creditors. How much to borrow from creditors and how much to obtain from investors are important decisions that the company's management must make. Those decisions can determine whether a company grows, goes bankrupt, or is bought by another company. Examples of financing activities follow:

TYPICAL FINANCING ACTIVITIES

Borrowing money
Repaying loans
Issuing shares
Repurchasing shares
Paying dividends on shares

Investing Activities

Once a company obtains funds, it must invest them to accomplish its goals. Most companies make both long-term and short-term investments in order to carry out the activities that help them achieve their goals. Most short-term investments (such as the purchase of raw materials and inventories) are related to the day-to-day operations of the business and are therefore considered operating activities. Many long-term investments are related to the purchase of property, plant, and equipment that can be used to produce goods and services for sale. Companies can also consider investing in the shares of other companies either long-term or short-term. Examples of investing activities follow:

TYPICAL INVESTING ACTIVITIES

Purchase of property, plant, and equipment
Sale of property, plant, and equipment
Purchase of the shares of other companies
Sale of the shares of other companies

Operating Activities

Operating activities are all activities associated with developing, producing, marketing, and selling the company's products and/or services. While financing and investing activities are necessary to conduct operations, they tend to occur on a more sporadic basis than operating activities. Day-to-day ongoing activities are generally classified as operations. Examples of operating activities follow:

TYPICAL OPERATING ACTIVITIES

Sales to customers
Collections of amounts owed by customers
Purchases of inventory
Payments of amounts owed to suppliers
Payments of expenses such as wages, rent, and interest
Payments of taxes owed to the government

The financial statements provide information about a company's operating, financing, and investing activities. By the end of this book, you should be able to interpret financial statements as they relate to these activities. As mentioned previously, to help you become a successful user of financial statement information, in Appendix A at the back of the book we present Part II of the annual report of the Swedish company H&M Hennes & Mauritz AB. A survey of the various types of information contained in this annual report follows.

H&M ANNUAL REPORT

Part II of the 2009 annual report for H&M contains the information that will be discussed in detail in this book. H&M's **fiscal year** runs from December 1 to November 30 of the following year. The company has labelled the report as its 2009 annual report, with its financial statements showing the financial information for the fiscal year December 1, 2008, to November 30, 2009. As mentioned earlier, references to its page numbers are prefixed by H&M-. H&M's annual report may appear very complex even though H&M is a fairly uncomplicated company. We decided to use H&M's annual report because it is a good example of annual reporting, illustrates almost all the reporting issues discussed in this book, and offers you the challenge of understanding a modern company. The pain you may first experience in trying to understand H&M's financial information will be rewarded by the gains you make in understanding a real business organization.

A survey of typical types of information contained in H&M's annual report follows.

**Annual Report
Walk Through**

Corporate Profile

Part I of the annual report (on the companion website) has extensive sections describing the company's business activities during the year. H&M sells mainly clothing and accessories for women, men, and children. It sells through store outlets, as well as internet and catalogue sales.

When you evaluate a company for the first time, it is extremely important to know what kind of business it is in so that you can assess its risk level. You may be deciding whether to invest in the company or lend it money. The decision will be heavily influenced by the risk being taken. An investment in an oil exploration company, for instance, would have a much greater risk than an investment in a grocery store chain. An oil exploration company may not find any oil or it might find oil when the price of oil on the market is low. Both of these scenarios mean that your investment faces some high risks of not generating a profit or perhaps not even returning the money you invested. In contrast, people need to buy many of the products that a grocery store sells, so as long as it can purchase fresh products and sell them at a profit, it will probably continue to operate. When you read a company's financial statements, you must always weigh the financial results against the investment's level of risk. Turning to H&M, we see that it sells mainly clothing and, therefore, must ensure that the products it sells are the products that people want to buy. The clothing industry is constantly changing and companies like H&M need to stay on the leading edge of fashion in order to be successful. On H&M-4 of Part II of the report, H&M states that it has 1,988 stores (some of which are **franchises**) located in 35 markets. The business description on H&M-4 tells us more about how extensive its operations are. While its business is concentrated mainly in Europe, it has recently expanded into North America. By having its stores in highly populated areas, it is increasing the probability that it will be profitable (assuming, of course, that it is selling merchandise that people want to buy). All of this information is useful in your risk assessment of the company.

Message to Shareholders

The message to shareholders from a senior executive is an important part of an annual report. On H&M-14 and H&M-15 in Part I of H&M's annual report, CEO Karl-Johan Persson provides a brief overview of past events that have affeced the company and provides some insights into H&M's future plans. He discusses the effect of the economic downturn on the company, the company's substantial expansion in 2009, the value of designer collections, the keys to the company's success, its commitment to social and environmental responsibility, and the challenges that the company faces.

Management Discussion and Analysis

The Management Discussion and Analysis section of the annual report is required of all publicly traded companies in Canada and the United States. It provides an overview of the previous year, a discussion of the risks facing the company, and some information about future plans. Many companies use this part of the report to make more extensive, detailed comments on the company and its operating results. As a Swedish company, H&M includes this information in a section called "Administration Report" (H&M-4 to H&M-9 in Part II). This section provides an opportunity for senior management to discuss the company's performance with shareholders. Often the information is presented from the perspective of the company's various divisions. It includes information about significant events and about sales, profits, and cash flow during the year. The discussion focuses on the financial aspects of the business, including pricing strategies, expenses, earnings, liquidity, environmental and corporate social responsibility, expansion and future development, taxes, events after the end of the current year, and executive compensation policies.

On page H&M-8, there is a discussion of the risks and uncertainties facing the company. It focuses on the external threats of operating in the fashion industry, the weather, changes in the purchasing behaviour of customers, textile quotas, launching new concepts, and foreign currency. Earlier we mentioned that because H&M was in the clothing business, it needed to stay on the leading edge of the fashion world. It must anticipate what clothing and accessories people will want, then make or purchase those items, and finally sell them at competitive prices so that it can make a profit. The Administration Report section tells you how it expects to do that. As a user of financial information, you should read this section carefully to understand the level of risk associated with the company.

Page H&M-33 of Part II includes a five-year summary that highlights the changes that have occurred in H&M over this extended period. Such a summary allows a user to identify possible trends that may continue into the future. While this summary is often included in the Management's Discussion and Analysis section of an annual report, H&M includes it in the notes to its financial statements.

Board of Directors and Management

Somewhere in every annual report there is a list of the company's board of directors. The directors often hold positions in other companies as well. These directors are elected by shareholders to act as their representatives. They provide advice and counsel to company management, have broad powers to vote on issues that are relevant to shareholders (e.g., the declaration of dividends), and can hire and fire management. The annual report also often includes a listing of the company's senior management. For H&M, the list of the board of directors and senior officers, along with their pictures, can be found on pages H&M-40 and H&M-41. The pictures are followed by brief biographies of each of the directors. All of this information is included in an extensive report called the "Corporate Governance Report 2009" (H&M-35 to H&M-45).

Over the last several years, there has been an increased interest in the responsibilities of corporate boards. In 2002, the United States Congress passed the **Sarbanes-Oxley Act** in response to several accounting scandals in the previous years. This act established new standards regarding the qualifications of board members and their responsibilities. The effects of this act have spilled over into Canada because many companies in Canada are also operating in the United States, and because most companies recognize the value of having stronger boards. For more information on the duties and responsibilities of boards, go to the following website: http://www.managementhelp.org/boards/brdrspon.htm.

Financial Section

The remainder of Part II of H&M's annual report contains all the financial information about the company's performance and status (H&M-10 to H&M-47). In general, this section contains the following major components:

COMPONENTS OF THE FINANCIAL SECTION

Statement of management's responsibility
Auditors' report
Financial statements:
  Statement of comprehensive income
  Statement of financial position
  Statement of changes in equity
  Statement of cash flows
  Notes to the financial statements
  Statement on corporate governance

Each of these components is discussed at some length in the sections that follow. Virtually all the disclosure contained in this section of the annual report is in compliance with either the IFRS or those of the securities commission in the country where the company has its head office.

In this chapter, we will describe three of the four major statements that appear in all sets of financial statements: the **statement of comprehensive income**, the **statement of financial position**, and the **statement of cash flows**. In addition to these, a company will often include a statement of changes in equity, which will be discussed later in this book.

LEARNING OBJECTIVE 8

Identify the major financial statements and describe their main components.

STATEMENT OF COMPREHENSIVE INCOME This statement is also known as the **income statement**, the **statement of earnings**, or the **statement of profit or loss**. It describes the results of the operating activities from the beginning to the end of the current period. The results of those activities add up to the net earnings (**net income** or net profit, or net loss if the amount is negative) amount or "bottom line." In companies, **net earnings** is defined as income less expenses. **Income** is money or resources that flow into the company as a result of such ordinary activities as sales (also known as **revenues**) and from gains (selling items for more than their original cost). **Expenses** are money or resources that flow out of the company to enable the inflow of income, such as the cost of the goods that are sold in sale transactions. Losses (selling items at less than their carrying value) are part of expenses.

There may be a delay in recognizing some expenditures as expenses. Because items such as machinery help generate revenues over several years, over the course of the machine's life we normally recognize in each period only a portion of the original cost as an expense. This expense treatment is called **depreciation**. Eventually, over the life of the machine, the entire cost will be expensed in determining net earnings.

Refer to the Group Income Statement of H&M in Exhibit 1-3. It is called a group income statement because it includes the financial information for the main or parent company plus the financial information of all the other companies that it controls. In Canada we use the term "consolidated" for this. The time period of the statement is indicated at the top, where it reads, "1 December–November 30" followed by two columns labelled 2009 and 2008. The 2009 year amounts are included in the inside column. The outside column, the 2008 year amounts, is included for comparison so that users can see changes from the previous year. The revenues and expenses are the amounts recognized during each of the fiscal years that ended on November 30, 2009, and November 30, 2008. The statement is a report of the company's operating performance during the year; it measures the inflow of revenues and the outflow of expenses from the shareholders' perspective. For this reason, it is sometimes called a **flow**

statement. Another way of putting it is that the earnings statement captures the net change in the shareholders' wealth, as measured in the accounting records, across a designated time period. In this case, that time period is one year.

Note: H&M is a Swedish company and, therefore, reports its amounts in Swedish currency, kronor, rather than in dollars. The abbreviation or code for kronor is SEK. At the time of the writing of the book, SEK 6.6 equalled 1 Canadian dollar (CAD).

Revenue In the statement, there are revenues called "Sales including VAT" and "Sales excluding VAT." VAT refers to value added tax, which is similar to GST in Canada. The VAT is remitted to the government at regular intervals. Because it does not belong to the company, H&M has shown the sales value without the VAT. This is the amount that is used for subsequent calculations. The sales excluding VAT represents the inflow of resources from the sale of inventory in H&M's various stores. Depending on a company's operating activities, you might also find revenue from performing services or earning interest. Below its operating profit, H&M indicates an amount for interest income. How much detail a company gives in its income statement depends on the usefulness of the disclosure. Since H&M is involved only in the sale of apparel and accessories, the statement can be quite simple.

Revenues are also classified into different types so that shareholders (and other users of financial statements) can forecast the company's future performance. Because of the differences in the nature of various aspects of a company, the growth rates of the different types of revenues and expenses may differ greatly. If the revenues and expenses were not broken down into different types, it would be very difficult for the reader of the financial statements to forecast them accurately.

H&M 2009 ANNUAL REPORT

EXHIBIT 1-3

annual report

GROUP INCOME STATEMENT
SEK M

1 DECEMBER – 30 NOVEMBER	2009	2008
Sales including VAT	118,697	104,041
Sales excluding VAT, Note 3, 4	101,393	88,532
Cost of goods sold, Note 6, 8	-38,919	-34,064
GROSS PROFIT	**62,474**	**54,468**
Selling expenses, Note 6, 8	-38,224	-32,185
Administrative expenses, Note 6, 8, 9	-2,606	-2,145
OPERATING PROFIT	**21,644**	**20,138**
Interest income	467	1,060
Interest expense	-8	-8
PROFIT AFTER FINANCIAL ITEMS	**22,103**	**21,190**
Tax, Note 10	-5,719	-5,896
PROFIT FOR THE YEAR	**16,384**	**15,294**

All profit is assignable to the parent company H & M Hennes & Mauritz AB's shareholders.

	2009	2008
Earnings per share, SEK*	19.80	18.48
Number of shares	827,536,000	827,536,000

* Before and after dilution.

Expenses Costs and expenses are also listed under various categories, including cost of goods sold (or cost of sales, or cost of merchandise sold), selling expenses (or operating expenses), and administrative expenses. These cost and expense categories explain the company's performance in more detail. You will notice on H&M's income statement that there are references to Notes 6, 8, and 9. These notes, on H&M-23 to H&M-25, include more details about these expenses. Note 8 refers to depreciation, which, as we saw earlier, is the allocation of a portion of the original cost of a long-lived asset to a period. H&M owns buildings, equipment, and vehicles that it uses to sell its inventory and thereby generate revenue. The cost of using these items (their depreciation) is included every year as an expense. The last expense, "Tax," is listed as a separate expense because its amount depends on both the revenues and expenses that are reported. Taxes are calculated on the amount of revenue that is greater than expenses. On H&M's income statement, the tax amount is SEK 5,719 million for the current year.

At the bottom of the income statement is an **earnings per share** disclosure. Basic earnings per share is the company's net income divided by the average number of **common shares** that are outstanding (owned by shareholders of the company) during the year. Shareholders find this calculation useful since it puts the performance of their investment into perspective. In other words, a shareholder who holds 10,000 shares of H&M can determine his or her share of the earnings during the period. In the fiscal year ending November 30, 2009, H&M earned SEK 19.80 per share. Therefore, that investor's share of the earnings for 2009 would be SEK 198,000. The board of directors decides how much of the earnings, if any, will be paid to shareholders as dividends.

On some income statements, there will also be a fully *diluted* earnings per share amount, which is normally lower than the basic earnings per share. H&M has indicated that its earnings per share before and after dilution is the same. Advanced financial accounting courses discuss fully diluted earnings per share in more detail.

When businesses expand, they often establish other companies or buy shares in other companies. Because these other companies are separate legal entities, the parent companies can expand operations and diversify their risk. As previously mentioned, H&M is a straightforward company, with most of its operations concentrated in retail sales in Europe and other parts of the world. However, unlike other retail clothing stores, H&M has its own design and buying department that creates the collections it sells. In 2007, H&M (the **parent company**) transferred its central design, buying, and inventory functions to a separate company that it owns called H&M Hennes & Mauritz GBC AB. This **subsidiary company** is a separate business entity that owns the inventory until it is delivered to the stores. When H&M prepares its annual financial statements, it prepares group financial statements. These **group financial statements** combine all the elements of the subsidiary's financial statements with the parent company's financial statements. There is more detail about **consolidated financial statements** in Appendix B at the end of the book.

By reviewing the income statement for H&M, you can see that the net profit (net income or net earnings) for 2009 were SEK 16,384 million. You will notice that the net profit increased from the SEK 15,294 million of the previous year. Companies often round amounts to the nearest hundred, thousand or, in the case of very large companies, million. The currency units in which the numbers are expressed must be stated somewhere on the statement. Usually, they can be found in parentheses at the top of the statement. H&M tells you that its numbers are in millions of kronor (SEK M).

This brings up an issue that was discussed earlier in the section on the development of accounting standards: materiality. If an auditor were to find a $2,000 mistake when trying to verify how fairly the statements presented the earnings of a company, how much difference would it make, assuming the company rounded its amounts to the nearest thousand? The answer is it would not make much difference in the overall analysis of the company's financial status. On the other hand, a $2,000 mistake in the tax reporting of an individual's earnings would certainly get the attention of the Canada Revenue Agency. How material an item is often depends, in part, on the size of the entity.

Below is a list of some of the more common items you can expect to see on statement of earnings.

COMMON STATEMENT OF EARNINGS ITEMS

Sales Revenues	The total amount of sales of goods and/or services for the period.
Other Income	Various types of revenues or income to the company other than sales, including interest income.
Cost of Goods Sold	The cost of the units of inventory that were sold during the period.
Selling, General, and Administrative Expense	The total amount of other expenses (e.g., salaries, rent) during the period that do not fit into any other category.
Depreciation Expense	The allocation of part of the cost of long-lived items such as equipment.
Interest Expense	The amount of interest incurred on the company's debt during the period.
Income Tax Expense (Provision for Taxes)	The taxes levied on the company's profits during the period.

STATEMENT OF FINANCIAL POSITION This statement is also known as a **balance sheet**. The group balance sheet for H&M is shown in Exhibit 1-4. The term "financial position" indicates that this statement presents the company's financial status at a particular point in time. In fact, at the top of the statement, the words "30 November, 2009, 2008," appear, indicating that the amounts in the statement are those that existed on November 30, 2009, and November 30, 2008, respectively. These dates may also be considered the beginning and end points of the current accounting period. In the transition from one accounting period to the next, the ending balances of one accounting period become the beginning balances of the next accounting period. The balance sheet has often been described as a snapshot of a company's financial position at a particular point in time.

The format of this balance sheet is typical of European balance sheets and is different from most Canadian ones. The H&M balance sheet lists the long-term assets first (labelled fixed assets), followed by the current assets. Most Canadian balance sheets will list the current assets first. On the liability and equity part of the balance sheet, H&M begins with the equity and follows with the long-term liabilities and then the current liabilities. Most Canadian balance sheets will begin with current liabilities, followed by long-term liabilities and then equity. Other than stating that assets and liabilities must be identified as current and long-term, there is no standard that requires either the European or Canadian format. The differences in the way the balance sheets are presented reflects the different ways that accounting standards and traditions have developed in different parts of the world.

So what makes up the company's financial position? Individuals, if asked about their own financial position, would probably start by listing what they own, such as a car, a computer, or a house, and then list what they owe to others, such as bank loans and credit card balances. What is owned less what is owed would be a measure of their net worth (wealth or equity) at a particular point in time. A company lists exactly the same types of things in its balance sheet. In H&M's statement, there are two major categories: **assets**, and **liabilities** and equity (often called shareholders' equity in Canada).

EXHIBIT 1-4

H&M 2009 ANNUAL REPORT

annual report

GROUP BALANCE SHEET
SEK M

30 NOVEMBER	2009	2008
ASSETS		
FIXED ASSETS		
Intangible fixed assets		
Brands, Note 11	396	443
Customer relations, Note 11	110	123
Leasehold rights, Note 11	744	659
Goodwill, Note 11	424	431
	1,674	1,656
Tangible fixed assets		
Buildings and land, Note 12	492	480
Equipment, tools, fixtures and fittings, Note 12	14,319	11,961
	14,811	12,441
Long-term receivables	551	476
Deferred tax receivables, Note 10	1,246	1,299
TOTAL FIXED ASSETS	18,282	15,872
CURRENT ASSETS		
Stock-in-trade	10,240	8,500
Current receivables		
Accounts receivable	1,990	1,991
Other receivables	889	1,206
Prepaid expenses, Note 13	937	948
	3,816	4,145
Short-term investments, Note 14	3,001	–
Liquid funds, Note 15	19,024	22,726
TOTAL CURRENT ASSETS	36,081	35,371
TOTAL ASSETS	54,363	51,243

30 NOVEMBER	2009	2008
EQUITY AND LIABILITIES		
EQUITY		
Share capital, Note 17	207	207
Reserves	1,514	1,410
Retained earnings	22,508	20,039
Profit for the year	16,384	15,294
TOTAL EQUITY	40,613	36,950
Long-term liabilities*		
Provisions for pensions, Note 18	254	228
Deferred tax liabilities, Note 10	2,038	1,818
Other provisions, Note 19	368	368
	2,660	2,414
Current liabilities**		
Accounts payable	3,667	3,658
Tax liabilities	439	1,279
Other liabilities	2,531	3,255
Accrued expenses and prepaid income, Note 21	4,453	3,687
	11,090	11,879
TOTAL LIABILITIES	13,750	14,293
TOTAL EQUITY AND LIABILITIES	54,363	51,243
Pledged assets and contingent liabilities	–	–

* Only provisions for pensions are interest-bearing.
** No current liabilities are interest-bearing.

Assets When asked for a simple definition of an asset, many people reply that it is something of value that the company either owns or has the right to use. In fact, the accounting definition of an asset is very similar. In this book, assets are things that meet the following criteria: (1) they are a resource controlled by an entity; (2) the entity expects future economic benefits from the use or sale of the resource; and (3) the event that gave the entity control of the resource has already happened. The word "future" has been added to "economic benefits," since the company would not want to list things that had value in the past but do not have value in the future. Because of concerns expressed about the interpretation of future economic benefits, the IASB is considering shortening the definition to "a present economic resource to which the entity has a right or other access that others do not have."[1] For this edition of the book, the current IASB Framework definition will be used.

CHARACTERISTICS OF AN ASSET

1. A resource controlled by an entity.
2. The company expects future economic benefits from the use or sale of the resource.
3. The event that gave the company control of the resource has already happened.

The assets that H&M lists in its balance sheet include:

- liquid funds (in Canada often called cash and cash equivalents), short-term investments, accounts receivable, other receivables, prepaid expenses, and stock-in-trade (often called inventories)
- deferred tax receivables, long-term receivables
- buildings and land, equipment, tools, fixtures and fittings (often called fixed assets)
- brands, customer relationships, leasehold rights, and goodwill (often called intangible assets because they do not have any physical form)

While later chapters discuss in more detail how each of these assets meets the criteria of control and future economic benefits, we can look at H&M's inventory as an example for now. Control of the inventory (the stock-in-trade) is proven either by possession of the inventory or by legal documentation. The inventory has future economic benefits because the company can later sell it and receive cash in the amount of the selling price. The presence of the inventory or the underlying documents of the purchase indicates that the event that gave the company control has already happened.

The total assets of H&M as at November 30, 2009, were SEK 54,363 million. A list of assets normally found in a balance sheet follows:

COMMON BALANCE SHEET ASSETS

Cash	The amount of currency that the company has, including amounts in bank accounts.
Short-Term (Temporary) Investments	Short-term investments in securities of other companies, such as treasury bills, shares, and bonds.
Accounts Receivable	Amounts owed to the company that result from credit sales to customers.

---

1. FASB Technical Plan and Project Updates, 2009, p. 2.

COMMON BALANCE SHEET ASSETS (cont'd)	
Inventory	Goods held for resale to customers.
Prepaid Expenses	Expenses related to items that have been paid for but have not yet been used. An example is insurance that is paid in advance.
Capital Assets	Land, buildings, equipment, vehicles, and intangibles that the company uses over the long term. Fixed assets are investments in physical assets such as land, buildings, and equipment. Intangibles are investments in assets without physical substance such as patents, trademarks, and goodwill.

H&M prepares a **classified balance sheet**, in which the assets and liabilities are classified as **current** and **non-current** (H&M uses the term "fixed assets"). For assets, "current" means that the asset will be turned into cash or be consumed (used up) in the next year or operating cycle, whichever is longer. The **operating cycle** of a company refers to the time period between the initial investment of cash in products or services and the return of cash from the sale of the product or service. Most companies have several operating cycles in a year.

Assets such as cash, accounts receivable, and inventories are classified as current, and assets such as long-term assets (fixed assets in the case of H&M) are classified as non-current. In Canada, assets and liabilities are frequently listed on the balance sheet in liquidity order. **Liquidity** refers to how quickly the company can turn the asset into cash or will use the cash to settle (pay) an outstanding liability. Non-current assets are the least liquid because they will be used over a long time period and will not be quickly turned into cash. Accounts receivable, on the other hand, are amounts owed to the company by customers who bought goods or services on credit. Normally, these will be collected quickly. Therefore, accounts receivable are fairly liquid. In the case of H&M, its accounts receivable are likely from credit card sales. It will collect the credit card amounts from companies such as VISA or MasterCard within a few days. Inventories are less liquid than accounts receivable since they must be sold first, which often results in an account receivable. Cash is then received when the account receivable is collected. H&M's balance sheet is in order of how permanent the asset is rather than how liquid.

An **unclassified balance sheet** is a balance sheet in which there are no labels to indicate whether an asset or liability is current or non-current. Even in an unclassified balance sheet, however, assets and liabilities are still listed primarily in the order of their liquidity or permanency. For instance, stock-in-trade, accounts receivable, other receivables, prepaid expenses, short-term investments, liquid funds, and the various fixed assets will have the same order as in the H&M report even if they are not specifically identified as current or non-current.

Liabilities A simple definition of liabilities might be amounts that the company owes to others. The accounting definition of liabilities encompasses this concept and, consistent with the earlier definition of assets, refers to items that require a future event, which in this case is the sacrifice of resources. In most cases, the resource is cash, but a company could satisfy a liability with services or goods. For example, a warranty liability could be satisfied with a new part or with the services of a repairperson. Like assets, liabilities also arise from past events.

In Exhibit 1-4, the liabilities in H&M's classified balance sheet include accounts payable, tax liabilities, other liabilities, accrued expenses and prepaid income, provisions for pensions, deferred tax liabilities, and other provisions. Note that H&M labels the current (short-term) liabilities and long-term liabilities as such. Many companies will label the current liabilities and then list the long-term liabilities without putting a label on them. Current liabilities are those that will require the use of current assets or will be replaced by another current liability in the next year or operating cycle, whichever is longer. The following list includes some of the more common liabilities found in financial statements:

COMMON BALANCE SHEET LIABILITIES

Bank Indebtedness   Amounts owed to the bank on short-term credit.

Accounts Payable   Amounts owed to suppliers from the purchase of goods on credit.

Notes Payable   Amounts owed to a creditor (bank or supplier) that are represented by a formal agreement called a note (sometimes called a promissory note). Notes payable often have an interest component, whereas accounts payable usually do not.

Dividends Payable   Amounts owed to shareholders for dividends that are declared by the board of directors.

Accrued Liabilities   Amounts owed to others based on expenses that have been incurred by the company but are not yet due, such as interest expense and warranty expense.

Income Taxes Payable Amounts owed to taxing authorities.

Long-Term Debt   Amounts owed to creditors over periods longer than one year.

Deferred Tax Liabilities Amounts representing probable future taxes the company will have to pay.

Shareholders' Equity The last major category in the balance sheet is the section called **equity**. It is frequently referred to as shareholders' equity. In H&M's section on equity, note the listings for share capital, reserves, retained earnings, and profit for the year. Most companies will include profit for the year in the retained earnings amount and not list it as a separate item.

This section captures the value of the shareholders' interest in the company, as measured by the accounting recommendations and guidelines. Note that the total assets equal the total liabilities plus the equity. H&M lists both as SEK 54,363 million on November 30, 2009. This relationship is described by the **basic accounting equation**.

BASIC ACCOUNTING EQUATION

Assets = Liabilities + Shareholders' Equity

This equation gives meaning to the term "balance sheet." If the equation is rearranged, you can see that shareholders' equity is equal to assets minus liabilities.

BASIC ACCOUNTING EQUATION (REARRANGED)

Shareholders' Equity = Assets − Liabilities
(Net Assets)

To state this relationship another way, shareholders' equity is the difference between what the investors own and what the company owes to others, as measured in the **accounting records**. Because of this relationship, shareholders' equity is sometimes called the company's **net assets** ("net" refers to the assets' value less the liabilities) or the net book value of the company. It is the equivalent of an individual's personal net worth. The shareholders' wealth as measured by the accounting statements is a residual concept. The shareholders can claim the assets that are left over after paying all the liabilities.

Note that the shares' market value is another measure of the shareholders' wealth in the company. By **market value**, we mean the price at which the shares trade in the stock market. This value could be very different from the book value of share-holders' equity because accounting records are not necessarily based on market values or expectations.

We can look at the proportion of liabilities and shareholders' equity on the balance sheet to better understand a company's financing strategy. For H&M, total liabilities are SEK 13,750 million and total shareholders' equity is SEK 40,613 million, for a total of SEK 54,363 million. The proportion of liabilities is 25.3% (SEK 13,750 ÷ SEK 54,363 × 100), which is one-quarter of the total financing. This means that H&M uses more shareholders' equity than debt to finance its activities. Specifically, it gets 74.7% of its financing from shareholders' equity. This low percentage of debt to equity reflects the company's philosophy of not expanding unless there is enough internal financing. The higher the proportion of debt to equity, the greater the financial risk facing the company.

Shareholders' equity is usually composed of at least two accounts: **share capital** and retained earnings. The first account, share capital (some companies use the term **capital stock**), records the amount that the investors originally paid (invested) for the shares that the company issued. The second account, retained earnings, keeps track of the company's earnings less any amounts that the company pays to the share-holders in dividends. Dividends are only paid to shareholders when the payment is approved by a vote of the board of directors. The change in a company's retained earnings during a given period can be explained by the net income less the dividends declared, as follows:

CHANGE IN RETAINED EARNINGS

Change in Retained Earnings = Net Income − Dividends

Other accounts can appear in this section (H&M has an account called reserves). The early part of this book will ignore these other accounts in order to concentrate on share capital and retained earnings. The other accounts will be discussed in later sections of the book. A list of some of the more common account titles that appear in the shareholders' equity section follows:

COMMON BALANCE SHEET
"SHAREHOLDERS' EQUITY ACCOUNTS"

Share Capital   Represents the shares that the company has issued, usually stated at an amount equal to what investors originally paid for the shares. This can be referred to as capital stock. Shares can be of different types, with different rights and privileges attached to each type.

Retained Earnings   The company's earnings (as measured on the Income Statement) that have been kept (retained) and not paid out in the form of dividends.

STATEMENT OF CASH FLOWS The statement of cash flows, sometimes called the **cash flow statement**, is a flow statement that is, in some ways, similar to the income statement.

H&M's consolidated statement of cash flows is in Exhibit 1-5. It measures inflows and outflows of cash during a specific time period. Note how the words at the top of the statement indicate that the statement is for 1 December to 30 November 2008 and 2009, which is the same terminology used on the income statement. The difference is that instead of measuring the increase and decrease in shareholders' wealth, this statement measures the increase and decrease in cash and highly liquid assets and liabilities called "cash equivalents." Remember that a liquid item is one that can be converted quickly to cash. Since cash is very important to the company's operations, this statement is vital to any user's evaluation of a business.

The cash flow statement has three sections that report the sources and uses of cash and cash equivalents for the three business activities described earlier: operating, financing, and investing.

SUBSECTIONS OF THE CASH FLOW STATEMENT

Cash flow from operating activities
Cash flow from financing activities
Cash flow from investing activities

In order to evaluate a company's liquidity position, users need to evaluate where cash is coming from and where it is being spent. H&M generated a positive cash flow of SEK 17,973 million from its operating activities in the fiscal year ending November 30, 2009.

Operating activities include all inflows and outflows of cash related to the company's sale of goods and services. The starting point in this section is frequently net earnings (or net income or profit) from the income statement. There are adjustments to this number because the recognition (recording) of revenues and expenses (as will be seen in future chapters) does not necessarily coincide with the receipt and payment of cash. For instance, sales could be either cash sales or sales on account (i.e., customers can pay at a later date, resulting in an accounts receivable rather than cash). Expenses may also be paid later if the company is given credit by its suppliers (this would result in an account payable). Because operating activities are the backbone of the company,

EXHIBIT 1-5   **H&M 2009 ANNUAL REPORT**

annual report

GROUP CASH FLOW STATEMENT
SEK M

1 DECEMBER – 30 NOVEMBER	2009	2008
Profit after financial items*	22,103	21,190
Provision for pensions	26	72
Depreciation	2,830	2,202
Tax paid	–6,468	–5,940
Cash flow from current operations before changes in working capital	18,491	17,524
Cash flow from changes in working capital		
Current receivables	–71	–1,343
Stock-in-trade	–1,740	–183
Current liabilities	1,293	1,968
CASH FLOW FROM CURRENT OPERATIONS	17,973	17,966
Investment activities		
Investments in leasehold rights	–180	–446
Investments in/sale of buildings and land	–25	–23
Investments in fixed assets	–5,481	–4,724
Adjustment of consideration/acquisition of subsidiaries	7	–555
Change in short-term investments, 4–12 months	–3,001	4,900
Other investments	–75	–242
CASH FLOW FROM INVESTMENT ACTIVITIES	–8,755	–1,090
Financing activities		
Dividend	–12,825	–11,584
CASH FLOW FROM FINANCING ACTIVITIES	–12,825	–11,584
CASH FLOW FOR THE YEAR	–3,607	5,292
Liquid funds at beginning of financial year	22,726	16,064
Cash flow for the year	–3,607	5,292
Exchange rate effect	–95	1,370
Liquid funds at end of financial year**	19,024	22,726

* Interest paid for the Group amounts to SEK 8 m (8). Received interest for the Group amounts to SEK 466 m (1,070).

** Liquid funds and short-term investments at the end of the financial year amounted to SEK 22,025 m (22,726).

a positive cash flow from operations is essential to the company's health. H&M's liquidity position improved slightly from the previous year, when its cash flow from operations was SEK 17,966 million.

The negative cash flow of SEK −12,825 million from **financing activities** indicates that H&M brought in less cash from outside sources than it used; the company paid dividends (SEK 12,825 million). Financing activities, as you will recall, are transactions that either generate new funds from investors or return funds to investors. Investors can be either shareholders or lenders, and the typical activities in this category are the issuance and repurchase of shares and the issuance and repayment of debt. H&M did not seek external funding from either shareholders or loan facilities (banks and other lending institutions).

Investing activities generally involve the purchase and sale of long-term assets such as property, plant, and equipment, and investments in other companies. All of these activities can be seen from the disclosure by H&M. The negative cash flow of SEK −8,755 million from investing activities results from the investment in leasehold rights (SEK −180 million), investments in and sale of buildings and land (SEK −25 million), investments in fixed assets (SEK −5,481 million), the acquisition of subsidiaries (SEK 7 million), the change in short-term investments (SEK −3,001 million), and the purchase of other investments (SEK −75 million). The company will use these assets for its future operating activities.

It is important to note that H&M did not need to go to outside sources to pay for its investment in fixed assets. It generated sufficient cash from its operating activities (SEK 17,973 million) to pay for them. If the current year is an indicator of future results, the future operating activities will generate a positive cash flow and the company's investment in new fixed assets will have been worthwhile. These amounts in 2009 indicate that H&M is doing quite well with respect to cash flow.

Chapter 5 discusses the preparation and interpretation of the cash flow statement in greater detail. For now, confine your study of this statement to understanding what its three sections are measuring.

SUMMARY OF FINANCIAL STATEMENTS

Statement of Earnings	Measures the operating performance of a company over a period of time.
Statement of Financial Position	Measures the resources controlled by a company (assets) and the claims on those resources (liability and equity holders) at a given point in time.
Statement of Cash Flows	Measures the change in cash flow through operating, financing, and investing activities over a period of time.

NOTES TO THE FINANCIAL STATEMENTS You may have noticed that some items in the financial statements direct the reader to specific notes. In such notes to the financial statements (H&M-18 to H&M-30), management gives more detail about the items. For example, on H&M's income statement, the tax item includes a reference to Note 10. Note 10 (H&M-25) goes into greater detail about taxes owed, deferred taxes, and tax rates. By including additional explanations in notes rather than on the financial statements, management keeps the company's statements simple and uncluttered. The note disclosures help achieve the qualitative characteristics of understandability, faithful representation, and completeness. They also increase the probability that the information will be useful for decision-making.

A full discussion of notes will be left to succeeding chapters, but some attention should be paid to the note that discusses the company's Accounting Principles. It is usually the first note, as it is in H&M's financial statements (H&M-18). Within IFRS, there are choices and judgements to be made by management. This note describes the choices this particular company made. The auditors, of course, review these choices for how well they conform with IFRS.

As you progress through the book, you will learn that the choices that management makes have important implications for how to interpret the statements. As an example, note how on page H&M-21, H&M's stock-in-trade (inventories) are valued at the lower of acquisition cost and net realizable value. The note further describes how the acquisition cost and net realizable value are measured. These are acceptable methods under IFRS for valuing inventory, but other alternative methods are also acceptable. Valuing the inventory under these methods will produce a different amount in the inventory account on the balance sheet, and a different net income on the income statement, from what a similar company would produce under an alternative method. Comparing two companies that use two different methods would pose difficulties. To help users compare various companies, management must therefore disclose in this note the major accounting principles that it uses.

SEGMENTED INFORMATION Information about various **segments** of the company is provided in the notes to the financial statements. This is a requirement for any company that has more than one significant segment. A segment represents a business activity. H&M has only one operating segment: the retail sale of apparel and accessories. However, it made sales outside of Sweden, which means that it has to report the amount of those sales (see page H&M-23). H&M provides information on the Nordic region, the Euro zone excluding Finland, and the rest of the world. Only 16.1% of H&M's sales were in the Nordic region, where it has its head office. A further 56.4% of its sales are in the other parts of Europe and 27.5% are in the rest of the world. This information is important to users because it helps explain the kinds of risks an investor takes when buying H&M's shares. Segments can differ significantly with regard to risk and are affected in different ways by such economic factors as commodity prices, inflation, exchange rates, and interest rates. An overall assessment of the company's risk must take into consideration the relative amounts that are invested in each of these segments. Because companies produce consolidated (group) financial statements that provide aggregate information, it would be difficult to assess segment risks without this additional information.

STATEMENT OF MANAGEMENT'S RESPONSIBILITY In this section, management states that it is responsible for the contents of the annual report. It also discusses the steps it has taken to ensure the safekeeping of the company's assets and it assures shareholders that it is operating in an ethical and responsible way. This statement is a Canadian requirement. Because it is not required in Sweden, H&M does not have the equivalent of this statement.

INDEPENDENT AUDITORS' REPORT It is important to remember that the financial statements are prepared by the company's management. They are reporting on the results of their management of activities. Because shareholders do not participate in the day-to-day activities of the company, it is impossible for them to evaluate the validity of the financial statements. To have an external evaluation of the financial statements, the shareholders hire independent auditors to express an opinion about the fairness of the presentation of the company's results and the conformity to accounting standards. In Sweden and some other European countries, the auditors use the phrase "true and fair view" to express their evaluation of the statements, which is more specific than the phrase "present fairly," which is normally used in Canada.

ethics in accounting

The management of a company, through the direction given to it by the board of directors, has both a moral and a legal obligation to safeguard the investment that shareholders have made in the company and entrusted to the care of management. To ensure that management fulfills this stewardship function over the company's resources, shareholders typically provide some incentives for and controls over management. You have probably heard about stock option plans and bonuses given to top management. These additional compensation arrangements are often tied to the company's financial performance and provide incentives for management to make decisions that are in the best interests of the shareholders. H&M has provided extensive information about its remuneration for senior executives (H&M-6 to 8). This information is intended to show shareholders and others that it is open and accountable for its decisions.

Sometimes bonus compensation is given in years when the financial performance is down. When this occurs, shareholders and others often question the ethics of the decision. For example, in March 2009, AIG (a major financial institution in the United States) announced a payment of $165 million to its executives. Taxpayers and politicians were outraged because a few months earlier, AIG was in severe financial trouble. It accepted $170 billion from the U.S. government to help it weather the sub-prime mortgage crisis that was affecting the banking sector and causing several banks to declare bankruptcy. Taxpayers and politicians believed that the executives should not be rewarded when past management decisions had led to the current financial crisis.

Source: Trish Turner, "Tax AIG Executive Bonuses, Dodd Says," FOXNews.com, March 16, 2009, http:// www.foxnews.com/politics/2009/03/16/tax-aig-executive-bonuses-dodd-says.

LEARNING OBJECTIVE 9

Begin to understand the role of ethics in financial accounting.

Auditors are professionally trained accountants who add credibility to the financial statements by expressing their professional opinion about their fairness. The auditors review the financial statements, visit the company to verify various procedures, check supporting documentation, confirm the reasonableness of financial numbers, and investigate any discrepancies they find. Because they are independent from the company and are knowledgeable about IFRS requirements, they can provide assurance to the shareholders that IFRS has been followed in the preparation of the statements. Exhibit 1-6 contains the auditors' report for H&M for 2009.

Companies such as H&M are not audited by one person alone, but by a firm of auditors. Auditors apply a set of procedures to test the financial statements to determine if they comply with IFRS and to assess the fairness of the presentation. Audit reports are often expressed in a standard format of three major sections. The first major section states which financial statements have been audited and that the financial statements are the responsibility of management. The second section states that the auditors' responsibility is to express an opinion about the financial statements. This section explains how the auditors conducted the audit using generally accepted auditing standards. To be able to express their opinion, the auditors need to examine enough audit evidence. The third section is the auditors' opinion about the financial statements.

EXHIBIT 1-6   H&M 2009 ANNUAL REPORT

annual report

AUDITORS' REPORT

To the Annual General Meeting of H & M Hennes & Mauritz AB (publ) Corporate identity number 556042-7220

We have audited the annual accounts, consolidated accounts, accounting records and the administration of the Board of Directors and the Managing Director of H & M Hennes & Mauritz AB for the financial year 1 December 2008 to 30 November 2009. The company's annual accounts and consolidated accounts are included in this document on pages 4–31. These accounts, the administration of the company and compliance with the Annual Accounts Act in the preparation of the annual report and the application of IFRS international accounting standards, as adopted by the EU, and of the Annual Accounts Act to the consolidated accounts are the responsibility of the Board of Directors and the Managing Director. Our responsibility is to express an opinion on the annual accounts, the consolidated accounts and the administration based on our audit.

Our audit was conducted in accordance with generally accepted auditing standards in Sweden. This means that we planned and performed the audit in order to obtain a high, but not absolute, degree of assurance that the annual accounts and consolidated accounts are free from material misstatement. An audit includes examining, on a test basis, evidence supporting the amounts and disclosures in the accounts. An audit also includes assessing the accounting principles used and their application by the Board and the Managing Director and evaluating the significant assessments made by the Board and the Managing Director in preparing

the annual accounts and consolidated accounts, as well as assessing the overall presentation of information in the annual accounts and the consolidated accounts. As a basis for our opinion concerning discharge from liability, we examined significant decisions, actions taken and circumstances in the company to be able to determine the liability, if any, to the company of any Board member or the Managing Director. We also examined whether any Board member or the Managing Director has, in any other way, acted in contravention of the Companies Act, the Annual Accounts Act or the Articles of Association. We believe that our audit provides a reasonable basis for our opinion set out below.

The annual report has been prepared in accordance with the Annual Accounts Act and gives a true and fair view of the company's and the Group's earnings and financial position in accordance with generally accepted accounting principles in Sweden.

The consolidated accounts have been compiled in accordance with IFRS international accounting standards, as adopted by the EU, and the Annual Accounts Act and give a true and fair view of the Group's earnings and financial position. The administration report is consistent with the other section of the annual accounts and the consolidated accounts.

We recommend to the Annual General Meeting that the income statement and balance sheet of the parent company and the Group be adopted, that the profit for the parent company be dealt with in accordance with the proposal in the administration report and that the members of the Board of Directors and the Managing Director be discharged from liability for the financial year.

Stockholm, 28 January 2010

Ernst & Young AB

Erik Åström
Authorised Public Accountant

The audit report of H&M (Exhibit 1-6) follows this format. Its format is the standard format for an **unqualified opinion**. This means that the financial statements present fairly or, in the case of H&M, are a true and fair view, in all material respects of the financial position, results of operations, and cash flows of the entity in conformity with generally accepted accounting principles.

In Canada, the unqualified or **clean opinion** is the most common audit opinion. Companies prefer to have a clean opinion attached to their financial statements. If the auditors are considering an opinion other than an unqualified one, they inform management about the reason(s) for the opinion before the financial statements are issued. Management then has an opportunity to change the financial statements to resolve the problem(s) the auditors have detected. If the issue is controversial, there may be some negotiation between management and the auditors as to how best to resolve the problem. If no resolution is reached and management decides to issue the statements as originally prepared, a **qualified** or **adverse opinion** will be included

accounting in the news

Auditor Says Golf Resort's Financial Not Up to Par

A report by the former auditor of Bear Mountain Resort—a golf, hotel, and commercial and residential project near Victoria, BC—has accused head, Len Barrie, co-owner of the Tampa Bay Lightning, and other senior members of the complex's management team of misappropriating funds. The Victoria accounting firm of Norgaard Neale Camden Ltd. made the report to Bear Mountain's executive committee in January 2009. It then resigned as the auditor on April 15 because it felt some financial transactions were illegal and because Bear Mountain's directors did not take action.

The auditor's report listed more than 20 transactions going back to 2007 that it found questionable. Among the transactions, the auditor said it discovered that almost $2.5 million in construction costs on Mr. Barrie's personal residence were charged to the partnership. The report also said $2.5 million was funnelled from Bear Mountain to pay for Mr. Barrie's share of the Lightning through Scansa Construction Ltd., a company owned by Mr. Barrie's brother-in-law. Mr. Barrie said all monies from those transactions were repaid to the Bear Mountain partnership. He said the $2.5 million was part of a $5 million shareholder distribution he received, which was approved by Bear Mountain's shareholders.

Source: David Shoalts, "Scathing audit of golf empire accuses Canadian NHL owner of misusing funds," *The Globe and Mail*, September 1, 2009

with the statements. This rarely happens in practice because the problems are usually resolved before issuing the statements. In extreme cases, as the article above indicates, sometimes the auditors withdraw from an audit if they do not think they can find enough information to verify the amounts on the financial statements.

In any set of financial statements, users should read the auditors' report because it can alert them to major problems the company may be experiencing. In other words, it can provide a red flag. Readers must then investigate further to make their own assessments of the extent of the problems. Also, it is important to recognize that there may be significant problems that the auditors did not identify with their tests or that are beyond the responsibility of the auditors. An unqualified opinion means that the financial statements are a fair representation of the company's financial position. It does not mean that the company is necessarily in good financial health. It is up to the user to determine what the financial position is by reading the statements carefully.

Throughout this discussion of the parts of an annual report, we have used many terms that are equivalent to other terms. The following is a summary of these terms:

SUMMARY OF EQUIVALENT TERMS	
Statement of earnings	Income statement; Statement of income; Earnings statement; Statement of profit and loss; Statement of operations
Statement of financial position	Balance sheet
Statement of cash flows	Cash flow statement
Net earnings	Net income; Net profit

The Changing Face of the Large Public Accounting Firms

Most large companies are audited by large accounting firms because of the required size and expertise of the audit team. Until the late 1980s, the eight largest accounting firms were known as the Big Eight. The Big Eight audited virtually all the large companies in Canada and, as international firms themselves, many companies in other parts of the world. In the late 1980s, two mergers among the Big Eight resulted in what became known as the Big Six. In 1998, a merger between two of the Big Six, **Price Waterhouse** and **Coopers & Lybrand**, was finalized to form **PricewaterhouseCoopers**, the largest public accounting firm in Canada. This created the Big Five. In 2001, however, in the United States, **Enron**, which was audited by one of the Big Five, **Arthur Andersen**, went bankrupt. In the subsequent investigation, it was determined that the auditors had shredded Enron documents; Andersen was thus charged with obstruction of justice and found guilty. Andersen no longer carries an accounting practitioner licence in the United States. The remaining Big Four firms are, in alphabetical order, **Deloitte & Touche**, **Ernst & Young**, **KPMG**, and PricewaterhouseCoopers. There are also several large and medium-sized national accounting firms that perform audits in Canada.

In Canada, there are three professional accounting organizations that establish the professional standards followed by accountants. The members of the Canadian Institute of Chartered Accountants are called Chartered Accountants (CAs); CMA Canada is the organization of the Certified Management Accountants (CMAs); and the Certified General Accountants Association of Canada represents the Certified General Accountants (CGAs). These professional accountants perform audits, supervise and perform accounting functions inside organizations, and provide decision-making functions inside and outside organizations. Canada is one of the few countries in the world that has more than one professional accounting body. In the past, there have been attempts to combine the three bodies into one, but so far these attempts have been unsuccessful.

ethics in accounting

WILEY PLUS
www.wileyplus.com

Ethics in Accounting

Shareholders hire auditors to review the financial statements presented to them by the company's management. The auditors, as they conduct their review, must maintain their independence from the company's management team. In order to ensure their independence and encourage ethical behaviour, the professional accounting organizations have developed codes of professional conduct. The codes state the responsibilities of professional accountants to the public, clients, and colleagues. For example, accountants normally cannot audit companies in which they own shares. In addition, the codes describe the scope and nature of the services provided by auditors. Each professional accounting organization has also developed a peer review process to monitor its members in the performance of audit work.

What do professional accountants do? Accountants, whether they are in public practice (i.e., work in an accounting firm) or in industry, government, or education, provide their clients and employers with information and advice so that they can make effective, informed decisions. They are often strategic advisors who are part of a company's management team. Accountants do not perform much of the day-to-day recording of transactions and events, although some of them may have some supervisory role over those who do perform this function. Today, most financial information is collected in computer systems that allow the data to be rapidly summarized into financial statements and other reports. Computerized accounting systems present a special challenge for auditors but enable managers to access financial information as often as they want. With up-to-the-minute data, financial statements can be updated in real time.

INTERNATIONAL PERSPECTIVES—IFRS REQUIREMENTS

The International Federation of Accountants (IFAC) defines independence as independence of mind and independence in appearance. Independence of mind means that the auditors do not have any external factors that could compromise their ability to exercise objectivity and professional scepticism. Independence in appearance means that there should be no circumstances associated with the auditors that, if they came to light, could lead an external person to reasonably conclude that the auditors' judgement could be compromised. The auditors' value to the shareholders and other users of financial statements lies in their knowledge of accounting and in their arms-length relationship with the company's management team.

EARNINGS MANAGEMENT

Because many accounting standards allow companies to choose among different measurement methods that can impact the information on financial statements, management can select methods that can raise or lower income and report revenues and/or expenses at different times. When management selects accounting methods to achieve a specific reporting objective, it is called **earnings management**. As a user of the financial statement information, it is important that you recognize the circumstances that make it possible for earnings to be managed. Throughout the book we will be including information about earnings management in boxes like this one.

SUMMARY

In this chapter, we discussed what a business is, what accounting is, and what financial statements are. We looked at the activities in which companies engage. We discussed the various users of financial reporting information and provided an overview of the types of information that they would need. We included a brief introduction to the development of accounting standards that underlie practice so that you can begin to understand the basic concepts that govern how we collect and report financial information.

Most of the chapter provided a detailed explanation of the various components of an annual report, using H&M as an example. In the annual report, you discovered the information components of three major financial statements: the statement of income, the statement of financial position (balance sheet), and the statement of cash flow. Subsequent chapters will build on this framework. Chapters 2 through 5 discuss the mechanics of preparing these statements and provide more information about their decision-making value. Chapters 6 through 11 discuss details of individual asset, liability, and shareholders' equity accounts. Chapter 12 considers financial statement analysis to provide some tools to interpret and link the major financial statements. Throughout the book, we will be introducing ratios that relate to the chapter topic. In Chapter 1, we introduced the ratio of liabilities to the total of liabilities plus shareholders' equity. This ratio tells you to what extent the company is using debt and equity to finance its activities. Appendix B provides some understanding of complex business organizations and the major accounting issues related to mergers, acquisitions, and consolidated financial statements.

PRACTICE PROBLEM

www.wileyplus.com

Additional Practice Problems

The Practice Problems reinforce your understanding of major sections in the chapter. One or more questions have been created to illustrate the topics and demonstrate how you can use the information. Answers are provided so that you can check your knowledge. You can use these questions as examples when working on other questions assigned by your instructor.

The major financial statements of **The Forzani Group Ltd.** from its 2009 annual report are included in Exhibit 1-7. The Forzani Group Ltd. is Canada's largest retailer of sports products. It operates stores like SportChek and Coast Mountain Sports. Note that its fiscal year end is February 1, 2009. As with H&M, we are going to refer to these as the 2009 financial statements and use them to answer a series of questions. Note that the format of Forzani's consolidated balance sheet is different from that of H&M. It first lists the current assets, then the long-term assets, next the current liabilities, and finally the long-term liabilities and shareholders' equity. This format is typical of balance sheets in Canada.

1. Find the following amounts in the statements:

   a. Total revenues for fiscal year 2009

   b. Total cost of sales for fiscal year 2009

   c. Total operating and administrative expenses for fiscal year 2009

   d. Interest expense for fiscal year 2009

   e. Income tax expense (current and future) for fiscal year 2009

   f. Net income (earnings) for fiscal year 2009

   g. Inventory at the end of fiscal year 2009

   h. Accounts payable and accrued liabilities at the beginning of fiscal year 2009

   i. Shareholders' equity at the end of fiscal year 2009

   j. Retained earnings at the beginning of fiscal year 2009

   k. Cash provided from operating activities in fiscal year 2009

   l. Cash payments, net of disposals (sales), to acquire capital assets in fiscal year 2009

   m. Cash used in the repayment of debt in fiscal year 2009

   n. Cash proceeds from issuing new shares in fiscal year 2009

   o. Cash provided from (used for) investing activities in fiscal year 2009

2. Does Forzani finance its business primarily with debt or with shareholders' equity? Support your answer with appropriate data.

3. List the two largest sources of cash and the two largest uses of cash in fiscal year 2009. (Consider operating activities to be a single source or use of cash.)

4. Does Forzani use a classified balance sheet? Explain.

THE FORZANI GROUP LTD. 2009 ANNUAL REPORT

EXHIBIT 1-7A

annual report

Consolidated Balance Sheets
(in thousands)

As at	February 1, 2009	February 3, 2008
ASSETS		
Current		
Cash	$ 3,474	$ 47,484
Accounts receivable	84,455	75,506
Inventory (Note 3)	291,497	319,445
Prepaid expenses (Note 4)	2,827	14,501
	382,253	456,936
Capital assets (Note 5)	196,765	188,621
Goodwill and other intangibles (Note 6)	91,481	89,335
Other assets (Note 7)	9,280	3,863
Future income tax asset (Note 12)	9,681	16,209
	$ 689,460	$ 754,964
LIABILITIES		
Current		
Indebtedness under revolving credit facility (Note 8)	$ 17,130	$ -
Accounts payable and accrued liabilities	277,820	279,910
Current portion of long-term debt (Note 8)	7,501	51,863
	302,451	331,773
Long-term debt (Note 8)	126	6,586
Deferred lease inducements	47,811	55,089
Deferred rent liability	5,893	6,033
	356,281	399,481
SHAREHOLDERS' EQUITY		
Share capital (Note 11)	147,161	157,105
Contributed surplus	6,401	7,210
Accumulated other comprehensive earnings (loss)	863	(8)
Retained earnings	178,754	191,176
	333,179	355,483
	$ 689,460	$ 754,964

See accompanying notes to the consolidated financial statements

practice problems

THE FORZANI GROUP LTD. 2009 ANNUAL REPORT

annual report

Consolidated Statements of Operations
(in thousands, except per share data)

	For the 52 weeks ended February 1, 2009	For the 53 weeks ended February 3, 2008
Revenue		
Retail	$ 994,043	$ 969,256
Wholesale	352,715	361,753
	1,346,758	1,331,009
Cost of sales	863,239	852,608
Gross margin	483,519	478,401
Operating and administrative expenses		
Store operating	277,089	251,630
General and administrative	109,328	103,801
	386,417	355,431
Operating earnings before undernoted items	97,102	122,970
Amortization of capital assets	47,613	44,468
Interest	5,175	5,797
Loss on sale of investment (Note 21)	–	864
	52,788	51,129
Earnings before income taxes	44,314	71,841
Income tax expense (recovery) (Note 12)		
Current	6,273	27,439
Future	8,716	(3,049)
	14,989	24,390
Net earnings	$ 29,325	$ 47,451
Earnings per share (Note 11(c))	$ 0.94	$ 1.40
Diluted earnings per share (Note 11(c))	$ 0.93	$ 1.39

See accompanying notes to the consolidated financial statements

THE FORZANI GROUP LTD. 2009 ANNUAL REPORT

EXHIBIT 1-7C

annual report

Consolidated Statements of Cash Flows
(in thousands)

	For the 52 weeks ended February 1, 2009	For the 53 weeks ended February 3, 2008
Cash provided by (used in) operating activities		
Net earnings	$ 29,325	$ 47,451
Items not involving cash:		
Amortization of capital assets	47,613	44,468
Amortization of deferred finance charges	377	738
Amortization of deferred lease inducements	(11,500)	(11,109)
Rent expense (Note 9)	152	524
Stock-based compensation (Note 11(d))	(174)	2,756
Future income tax expense (recovery)	8,716	(3,049)
Loss on sale of investment (Note 21)	–	864
Unrealized loss on ineffective hedges	321	44
	74,830	82,687
Changes in non-cash elements of working capital related to operating activities (Note 9)	20,913	23,737
	95,743	106,424
Cash provided by (used in) financing activities		
Net proceeds from issuance of share capital (Note 11(b))	2,384	13,273
Share repurchase via normal course issuer bid (Note 11(e))	(44,027)	(33,331)
Long-term debt	(51,199)	(19,198)
Revolving credit facility	17,130	–
Lease inducements received	4,221	7,648
Dividends paid (Note 11(f))	(9,327)	(2,472)
	(80,818)	(34,080)
Changes in non-cash elements of financing activities (Note 9)	(1,121)	(1,698)
	(81,939)	(35,778)
Cash provided by (used in) investing activities		
Capital assets	(52,139)	(40,660)
Other assets	(2,998)	2,151
Acquisition of wholly-owned subsidiaries (Note 17)	–	(8,774)
	(55,137)	(47,283)
Changes in non-cash elements of investing activities (Note 9)	(2,677)	1,363
	(57,814)	(45,920)
Increase (decrease) in cash	(44,010)	24,726
Net cash position, opening	47,484	22,758
Net cash position, closing	$ 3,474	$ 47,484

See accompanying notes to the consolidated financial statements

STRATEGIES FOR SUCCESS:

▶ Start by reviewing Forzani's three financial statements. Refresh your understanding of the kinds of information found in each statement.

▶ As you work through the list of items in question 1, try to remember which financial statement to look at by linking in your mind the name of the item identified and the financial statement on which it is included. As you work through more problems like this, you will become more familiar with what is on each statement.

▶ To answer question 2, first reread the section in the balance sheet discussion that explains shareholders' equity. The discussion of H&M's use of liabilities and share-holders' equity to finance its operations should be helpful.

SUGGESTED SOLUTION TO THE PRACTICE PROBLEM

To find the answers to the above questions, you will need to examine closely the three financial statements that have been provided.

1. The following answers are found on the financial statements included in Exhibits 1-7A, B, and C:

   a. Total revenues in 2009: $1,346,758 thousand. Revenues are reported on the income statement, which Forzani calls a statement of operations.

   b. Total cost of sales in 2009: $863,239 thousand. The cost of sales is a type of expense. Expenses are reported on the income statement.

   c. Total operating and administrative expenses in 2009: $386,417 thousand. Expenses are reported on the income statement.

   d. Interest expense in 2009: $5,175 thousand. Expenses are reported on the income statement.

   e. Income tax expense (current and future) in 2009: $14,989 thousand ($6,273 + $8,716). Expenses are reported on the income statement.

   f. Net income (earnings) in 2009: $29,325 thousand. The earnings are reported on the income statement.

   g. Inventories at the end of 2009: $291,497 thousand. Inventories are assets, which are reported on the balance sheet.

   h. Accounts payable and accrued liabilities at the beginning of 2009: $279,910 thousand (the end of 2008 is the same as the beginning of 2009). Liabilities are reported on the balance sheet.

   i. Shareholders' equity at the end of 2009: $333,179 thousand. Shareholders' equity is reported on the balance sheet.

   j. Retained earnings at the beginning of 2009: $191,176 thousand (again, you need to look to the end of 2008 to find the beginning of 2009). The retained earnings are a part of shareholders' equity that is reported on the balance sheet.

k. Cash provided from operating activities in 2009: $95,743 thousand. The cash provided by various business activities is reported on the statement of cash flows. Operating activities are shown in the first section of this statement.

l. Cash payments, net of disposals (sales), to acquire capital assets in 2009: ($52,139 thousand) (The net addition of capital assets is reported under the investing section on the statement of cash flows). Putting the amount in parentheses indicates that it is a negative number. In other words, cash was used.

m. Cash used in the repayment of debt in fiscal year 2009: ($51,199 thousand). The cash used for various business activities is reported on the statement of cash flows. The repayment of debt is a financing activity.

n. Cash proceeds from issuing new shares in 2009: $2,384 thousand. The cash proceeds for various business activities is reported on the statement of cash flows. Issuing shares is a financing activity.

o. Cash provided from (used for) investing activities in 2009: ($57,814 thousand). The cash provided by various business activities is reported on the statement of cash flows. Investing activities are one of the three main sections on this statement.

On the statement of cash flows you will notice that Forzani has adjusted both the financing activities and the investing activities by amounts labelled as "non-cash elements." Some of the amounts that it included in these two sections were amounts for which cash was neither received nor paid. Most companies include only the cash segments of transactions. To provide more information to users, Forzani has chosen to show the amounts of the transactions in total and then separate out the noncash parts.

2. Forzani uses marginally more liabilities than shareholders' equity to finance its business. You can see this when you compare the total liabilities with the total liabilities plus shareholders' equity (on the balance sheet) as follows:

Total liabilities (02/01/09): $356,281 thousand

Total shareholders' equity (02/01/09): $333,179 thousand

Total liabilities and shareholders' equity: $689,460 thousand

Total liabilities are, therefore, 52% ($356,281 ÷ $689,460 × 100) of Forzani's total sources of financing. Because debt must be repaid, it is important for users to understand how much of the company's activities are being financed by debt. The greater the percentage of debt to total liabilities and shareholders' equity, the more risk there is that the company may not be able to repay its debt when it comes due. Forzani is fairly conservative in carrying only 52% of its financing as debt.

3. The two largest sources of cash are proceeds from the operating activities, $95,743 thousand, and proceeds from the revolving credit facility, $17,130 thousand. The two largest uses are the acquisition of new capital assets ($52,139 thousand), and the repayment of long-term debt ($51,199 thousand).

4. Forzani does use a classified balance sheet. It has labelled a section for current assets and current liabilities but not for the non-current assets and liabilities. It has included the non-current assets and liabilities in a separate section after the total of the current assets and liabilities. It has not, however, given you a total for the non-current assets or liabilities. It has, instead, given you total assets and total liabilities.

practice problems

ABBREVIATIONS USED

AcSB	Accounting Standards Board	GAAP	Generally accepted accounting principles
CA	Chartered Accountant		
CGA	Certified General Accountant	IAS	International Accounting Standards
CICA	Canadian Institute of Chartered Accountants	IASB	International Accounting Standards Board
CMA	Certified Management Accountant	IFAC	International Federation of Accountants
CRA	Canada Revenue Agency		
FASB	Financial Accounting Standards Board	IFRS	International Financial Reporting Standards

SYNONYMS

Balance sheet **❙** Statement of financial position
Balance sheet equation **❙** Accounting equation
Books **❙** Accounting records **❙** Accounting information system
Capital assets **❙** Property, plant, and equipment **❙** Plant assets **❙** Fixed assets
Cash flow statement **❙** Statement of cash flows
Depreciation **❙** Amortization
Earnings statement **❙** Statement of earnings **❙** Income statement **❙**
    Statement of income **❙** Statement of comprehensive income **❙**
    Profit and loss statement **❙** Statement of operations
Equity **❙** Owner's equity **❙** Partners' equity **❙** Shareholders' equity
Group financial statements **❙** Consolidated financial statements
Inventory **❙** Stock-in-trade
Liabilities **❙** Debt **❙** Obligations
Managerial accounting **❙** Cost accounting
Net earnings **❙** Net income **❙** Net profit
Retained earnings **❙** Earnings retained in the business **❙**
    Earnings reinvested in the business
Share capital **❙** Common shares **❙** Capital stock

GLOSSARY

Accounting records   The accounting system (usually computerized) in which financial transactions are recorded and stored.

Accounting Standards Board (AcSB)   The CICA committee that sets accounting standards in Canada.

Adverse opinion   Synonym for qualified opinion.

Amortization   Synonym for depreciation.

Annual report   An annual document prepared and published by a corporation in which it reports on its business activities during the year. The report includes the corporation's annual financial statements.

Assets   Elements of the balance sheet that have probable future benefits that can be measured, are owned or controlled by the company, and are the result of a past transaction.

Auditor   A professionally trained accountant who examines a company's accounting records and financial statements to determine whether they fairly present the company's financial position and operating results in accordance with GAAP.

Balance between benefit and cost   A constraint that states that the cost of implementing a new accounting standard should be less than the benefits it brings.

Balance between qualitative characteristics   A constraint that results in decisions that will sometimes favour one qualitative characteristic over another.

Balance sheet A financial statement showing a company's asset, liability, and shareholders' equity account balances at a specific point in time.

Basic accounting equation The equation that describes the relationship between assets, liabilities, and shareholders' equity: Assets = Liabilities + Shareholders' Equity.

Board of directors The governing body of a company elected by the shareholders to represent their ownership interests.

Books Synonym for a company's accounting records.

Capital stock Synonym for share capital.

Cash flow statement A financial statement that shows the cash flows of a company during the accounting period, categorized into operating, investing, and financing activities.

Classified balance sheet A balance sheet in which the assets and liabilities are listed in liquidity order and are categorized into current and non-current sections.

Clean opinion Synonym for unqualified opinion.

Common shares The shares a company issues to its owners. Shares represent the ownership interest in a company.

Comparability A required quality that accounting information has when financial statement readers are able to compare different sets of financial statements over time.

Completeness A required quality that accounting information has when it provides enough information for users to be able to make informed decisions.

Conceptual framework Also known as the Framework. The framework that, together with the IFRS, guides the IASB as it sets new accounting standards.

Confirmatory value A required quality that accounting information has when it is relevant to decision-makers because it provides feedback on their previous decisions.

Consolidated financial statements Financial statements that represent the combined financial results of a parent company and its subsidiaries.

Constraints Aspects of accounting information that limit the use of some of the qualitative characteristics.

Cost accounting A branch of accounting that studies how cost information is used within the company.

Creditors Individuals or entities that are owed something by the company.

Current asset/liability For assets, current means that the asset will be turned into cash or consumed in the next year or operating cycle of a company. For liabilities, current means that the liability will require the use of cash or the rendering of a service, or will be replaced by another current liability, within the next year or operating cycle of the company.

Depreciation The expense taken each period that is based on the usage of a long-lived asset, such as equipment. Depreciation is the process that uses a systematic and rational method to allocate a portion of the cost of a long-lived asset to each of the years of its useful life.

Dividends Payments made to shareholders that represent a return on their investment in a company. Dividends are paid only after they are declared by the board of directors.

Earnings management Management decisions to deliberately record and report accounting information in a way that will achieve a specific reporting objective.

Earnings per share A ratio calculated by dividing the earnings for the period by the average number of shares outstanding during the period.

Entity The business about which the financial statements report, usually a company.

Equity A term sometimes used to describe the sum of liabilities and shareholders' equity. It is also sometimes used to refer simply to the shareholders' equity section, which can lead to some confusion in its use.

Expenses The resources used in the production of revenues by a company, representing decreases in the shareholders' wealth.

Faithful representation A required quality that accounting information has when the information accurately represents the attribute or characteristic that it claims to represent.

Financial accounting The study of the accounting concepts and principles that are used to prepare financial statements for external users.

Financial Accounting Standards Board (FASB) The regulatory body that sets accounting standards in the United States.

Financial statements Reports from the management of a company to its owners summarizing how the company performed during a particular period. Specific financial statements are the balance sheet, the income statement, and the statement of cash flows.

Financing activities The company's activities that raise funds to support the other activities of the company. The two major ways to raise funds are to issue new shares or borrow money.

Fiscal year The one-year period that represents a company's operating year.

Flow statement A statement that describes certain types of company inflows and outflows. The cash flow statement and the income statement are both examples of this type of statement.

Franchise A business structure in which a business with products or services contracts other business owners to sell the products or services in a structured manner so that customers are offered the same products or services regardless of the business owners.

Funds Resources, usually money, that the company obtains and uses to purchase assets or conduct operations.

GAAP Generally accepted accounting principles. The set of accounting recommendations and guidelines that corporations use in measuring, recording, and reporting financial accounting information.

Group financial statements Term used in Europe for consolidated financial statements.

Income Term used to describe the inflow of resources that increase shareholders' equity but are not the result of shareholder activities. Income includes revenues and gains.

Income statement A financial statement that measures the results of a company's operating activities over a period of time, in terms of profitability.

International Accounting Standards (IAS) The early international financial accounting standards that were developed before the IFRS.

International Accounting Standards Board (IASB) The committee that develops the international financial accounting standards.

International Federation of Accountants (IFAC) The international association of professional accountants who work together to develop and promote international financial reporting standards.

International Financial Reporting Standards (IFRS) The international financial reporting standards that are currently being developed by the IASB.

Investing activities Company activities involving long-term investments. Primarily investments in property, plant, and equipment, and in the shares of other companies.

Investors Individuals or entities that acquire shares of a company as an investment.

Liability An element of the balance sheet that leads to a probable future sacrifice of a company's resources.

Liquidity The length of time required to turn an asset into cash.

Management The individuals responsible for running (managing) the company.

Managerial accounting The study of the preparation and uses of accounting information by a company's management.

Market value The amount that an item would generate if it were sold.

Materiality A concept used to indicate items that will affect decision-making. In auditing, it means those items that are large enough to have a significant effect on the evaluation of a company's financial results.

Net assets Assets minus liabilities. Net assets are equal to shareholders' equity.

Net earnings The profits generated by a company during a specified time period. Net earnings are determined by subtracting expenses from a company's revenues.

Net income Synonym for net earnings.

Neutrality A required quality that accounting information has when the methods or principles that have been applied are unbiased regarding the potential outcomes for the company, rather than chosen for the company's self-interest.

Non-current asset/liability Assets or liabilities whose lives extend beyond one year or the operating cycle.

Operating activities A company's activities that involve the sale of goods and services to customers.

Operating cycle The time period between the initial investment of cash in products or services and the return of cash from the sale of the products or services.

Owners Synonym for shareholders.

Parent company A company that owns and controls other companies.

Predictive value A required quality that accounting information has when the information is relevant to decision-makers because it helps predict the future.

Privately held corporation A company whose shares are held by a few individuals; they do not trade in a public stock market.

Prudence A required quality that accounting information has when professional judgements and estimates that have been made in the financial statements ensure that assets and income are not overstated.

Publicly traded corporation A company whose shares are traded in a public stock market.

Qualified opinion An audit opinion that expresses some exception to the fair presentation of the financial results.

Relevance A required quality that accounting information has when the information has an impact on the user's decisions.

Reliability A required quality that accounting information has when the information can be depended on with respect to verifiability, representational faithfulness, neutrality, and conservatism.

Retained earnings Earnings that are kept within the company and not paid out to shareholders in the form of dividends.

Revenues Inflows of resources to the company that result from the sale of goods and/or services.

Sarbanes-Oxley Act An act passed by the United States Congress in 2002 that established new standards for corporate boards, management, and accounting firms.

Segments Divisions or units within a company that report revenues and expenses as a unit and about which management decisions are made as a unit.

Share A document representing a unit of investment in a corporation.

Share capital The shares issued by a company to its owners. Shares represent the ownership interest in the company.

Shareholders The individuals or entities that own shares in a company.

Shareholders' equity The section of the balance sheet that represents the shareholders' wealth; it is equivalent to the assets less the liabilities.

Statement of cash flows Synonym for cash flow statement.

Statement of comprehensive income An additional financial statement that is either attached to a statement of earnings or produced as a separate financial statement and which reports on activities that affect equity but are not ordinary operating activities.

Statement of earnings Synonym for income statement.

Statement of financial position Synonym for balance sheet.

Statement of profit and loss Synonym for income statement.

Subsidiary company A company that is owned and controlled by a parent company.

Substance over form The quality of accounting information that requires that the accounting information reflect the substance of the transaction rather than just its legal form.

Taxing authority An agency that assesses and collects taxes from a company.

Timeliness A required quality that accounting information has when the information is current enough to be relevant to decision-makers.

Unclassified balance sheet A balance sheet that does not classify assets and liabilities into current and non-current categories.

Understandability A required quality that accounting information has when it is prepared with enough information and in a clear enough format for users to comprehend it.

Unqualified opinion An audit opinion that states that the financial statements present fairly the company's financial position and operating results in conformity with GAAP.

ASSIGNMENT MATERIAL

Assessing Your Recall

1-1 Describe the role that accounting plays in the management of a business.

1-2 Explain the difference between a public corporation and a private corporation.

1-3 Identify at least three major users of corporate financial statements, and briefly state how these users might use the information from the statements.

1-4 Discuss the meaning of generally accepted accounting principles, and describe the organizations that establish these principles.

1-5 What role does the International Accounting Standards Board have in the setting of standards in Canada?

1-6 List and briefly describe the major qualitative characteristics that accounting information should possess, according to the Framework developed by the IASB.

1-7 Describe and illustrate the three major types of activities in which all companies engage.

WILEY **PLUS**
www.wileyplus.com

Self-Assessment Quiz

1-8 Describe and illustrate the three major categories of items that appear in a typical balance sheet.

1-9 How is the statement of earnings related to the three major types of business activities?

1-10 Describe the purpose of the three main financial statements that are contained in all annual reports.

1-11 Explain the purpose behind the notes to the financial statements.

1-12 What role does the management discussion and analysis section of an annual report play in informing users about a company?

1-13 What is the purpose of the auditors' opinion, and what types of opinion can auditors render?

1-14 Describe the impact of the use of computers on the collection and reporting of financial information.

Applying Your Knowledge

1-15 (Importance of accounting)
In the opening story to this chapter, Nils Vinge credited H&M's long-term success to "the principle of caution."

> ### Required:
> a. Describe what he meant by "the principle of caution" and how this philosophy impacted business decisions.
> b. According to Mr. Vinge, what role does accounting play in H&M's success?

1-16 (Apply qualitative characteristics)
The BMAC Company purchased land many years ago for $100,000 as a potential site for a new building. No building was ever constructed. A comparable lot near the site was recently sold for $350,000.

> ### Required:
> a. At what value should BMAC carry the land on its balance sheet? Support your answer with consideration for the prudence, faithful representation, and relevance of the information that would result.
> b. If BMAC wanted to borrow money from a bank, what information about the land would the bank want to know? Explain your answer.
> c. What information about the land would potential investors in BMAC want to know? Explain your answer.

1-17 (Apply qualitative characteristics)
Provide an example of how the characteristics of relevance and reliability may be in conflict when valuing an asset on the balance sheet. Which characteristic do you think is more important? Why?

1-18 (Apply qualitative characteristics)
Matrix Technologies designs and installs computer software for businesses. Recently, it learned that one of its major customers, representing 20% of annual sales, is in financial difficulty and is unlikely to be ordering for some time. Matrix is about to issue its quarterly report to shareholders.

> ### Required:
> Do you think the information about the customer should be disclosed in the quarterly report? Support your answer by referring to the qualitative characteristics described in this chapter.

1-19 (Apply qualitative characteristics)

Many users of the information in financial statements have difficulty understanding and evaluating that information. Suggest two reasons for this difficulty. How have the accounting standard-setters tried to help users in this regard?

1-20 (Identify financing, investing, and operating transactions)

For a company like **Canadian Tire**, provide two examples of transactions that you would classify as financing, investing, and operating activities.

1-21 (Identify financing, investing, and operating transactions)

For a company like **Hudson Bay Company** (a retailer), provide two examples of transactions that you would classify as financing, investing, and operating activities.

1-22 (Identify financing, investing, and operating transactions)

For a company like **Scotiabank**, provide two examples of transactions that you would classify as financing, investing, and operating activities.

1-23 (Compare statement of earnings and cash flow statement)

Compare and contrast the purpose of the income statement and the purpose of the cash flow statement. Outline how they are similar.

1-24 (Compare statement of earnings and balance sheet accounts)

On what financial statement would you expect to find sales revenue, and what does it represent? On what financial statement would you expect to find accounts receivable, and what does it represent? What is the connection between these two accounts?

1-25 (Compare statement of earnings and balance sheet accounts)

On what financial statement would you expect to find wages payable, and what does it represent? On what financial statement would you expect to find wages expense, and what does it represent? What is the connection between these two accounts?

1-26 (Classify items on financial statements)

Use the following abbreviations to answer this question:

CA	Current assets
NCA	Non-current assets
CL	Current liabilities
NCL	Non-current liabilities
SC	Share capital
RE	Retained earnings
IS	Statement of earnings item
SCF	Statement of cash flows item

Required:

Classify the following items according to where they would appear in the financial statements:

a. Accounts payable
b. Rent revenue
c. Interest expense
d. Property, plant, and equipment
e. Short-term investment in the shares of another company
f. Sales to customers
g. Repayment of a loan owed to a financial institution
h. Common shares
i. Cash
j. Mortgage payable (debt due in 10 years)

1-27 (Classify items on financial statements)

Use the same abbreviations as in 1-26 to answer the following question.

Required:

Classify the following items according to where they would appear in the financial statements:

a. Rent payable
b. Amounts owed by customers of the company
c. Administrative expense
d. Acquisition of a long-term bank loan
e. Purchase of office supplies with cash
f. Net earnings for the year
g. Cash proceeds from the sale of old equipment
h. Increase in the cash balance for the year
i. Income taxes expense
j. Cost to the company of inventory sold to customers this year

1-28 (Classify items on financial statements)

Use the same abbreviations as in 1-26 to answer the following question.

Required:

Classify the following items according to where they would appear in the financial statements:

a. Intangible assets
b. Interest revenue
c. Cash collections from amounts owed by customers on account
d. Cost of developing a new advertising campaign
e. Earnings over the years that have not been paid to shareholders as dividends
f. Revenue from the provision of services to customers
g. Dividends paid
h. Increase in a bank loan (additional borrowings)
i. Office supplies used this year
j. An investment in the shares of another corporation (the intent is to not sell the investment in the near future)

1-29 (Classify items on statement of cash flows)

Use the following abbreviations to answer this question:

OA   Operating activities item
FA   Financing activities item
IA   Investing activities item

Required:

Classify each of the following transactions according to whether they are operating, financing, or investing activities:

a. Payment of employee wages
b. Cash collected from customers for sales
c. Payment of dividends
d. Purchase of land for an office building
e. Repayment of debt owed to a financial institution
f. Purchase of shares of another company
g. Cash received as rent payment from a tenant in a building owned by the company
h. Issuance of shares

1-30 (Classify items on statement of cash flows)

Use the same abbreviations as in 1-29 to classify each of the following transactions according to whether they are operating, financing, or investing activities:

   a. Sale of an investment in another company's shares
   b. Net earnings
   c. Cash paid to suppliers of inventory
   d. Acquisition of a long-term bank loan
   e. Depreciation of the factory building
   f. Purchase of a truck used for deliveries
   g. Payment of dividends

1-31 (Identify items on balance sheet and statement of earnings)

Indicate whether each of the following items will be reported in the balance sheet (BS), statement of earnings (SE), both the balance sheet and statement of earnings (B), or neither statement (N)—for example, it might appear only on the cash flow statement.

   a. Cash
   b. Land acquired four years ago
   c. Prepaid rent
   d. Interest revenue
   e. Sales of goods and services
   f. Dividends paid to shareholders
   g. Rent expense
   h. Sales anticipated next period
   i. Payment made to reduce the principal amount of a bank loan
   j. Common shares issued when the company was organized five years ago

1-32 (Identify items on balance sheet and statement of earnings)

Indicate whether each of the following items will be reported in the balance sheet (BS), statement of earnings (SE), both the balance sheet and statement of earnings (B), or neither statement (N)—for example, it might appear only on the cash flow statement.

   a. Notes receivable
   b. Interest revenue from a short-term investment
   c. Common shares
   d. Accounts payable
   e. Depreciation expense on a building
   f. Interest expense
   g. Cash from the issuance of shares
   h. Wages payable
   i. Interest expense owed and paid on a bank loan
   j. Retained earnings

1-33 (Relationship of balance sheet and income statement)

In question 1-31 or 1-32, did you identify any items that appeared on both the balance sheet and statement of earnings? Would you expect to? Explain by describing the nature of each financial statement.

1-34 (Determine missing balance sheet amounts)

Calculate the missing balance sheet amounts in each of the following independent situations:

	A	B	C	D
Current assets	$?	$ 600,000	$180,000	$ 990,000
Non-current assets	780,000	?	390,000	?
Total assets	?	1,335,000	?	1,650,000
Current liabilities	375,000	345,000	135,000	390,000
Non-current liabilities	?	330,000	?	225,000
Shareholders' equity	638,000	?	330,000	?
Total liabilities and shareholders' equity	1,350,000	?	?	?

1-35 (Determine missing balance sheet amounts)

Calculate the missing balance sheet amounts in each of the following independent situations:

	A	B	C	D
Current assets	$ 650,000	$?	$150,000	$320,000
Non-current assets	?	380,000	?	760,000
Total assets	1,800,000	?	360,000	?
Current liabilities	750,000	170,000	50,000	410,000
Non-current liabilities	500,000	?	120,000	?
Shareholders' equity	?	425,000	?	400,000
Total liabilities and shareholders' equity	?	800,000	?	?

1-36 (Determine missing retained earnings amounts)

The change in retained earnings from the beginning of the year to the end of the year is the result of net earnings minus dividends for the year. Calculate the missing amounts in the reconciliation of retained earnings in each of the following independent situations:

	A	B	C	D
Retained earnings, Dec. 31, 2011	$100,000	$420,000	$?	$ 930,000
Net earnings	40,000	?	550,000	290,000
Dividends declared and paid	10,000	50,000	225,000	?
Retained earnings, Dec. 31, 2012	?	530,000	1,800,000	1,080,000

1-37 (Prepare simple statement of earnings)

Jason Chan operates a takeout pizza business called A Slice of Life. During the month of November, the following things occurred: he paid $7,692 for pizza ingredients, $1,200 for rent, $220 for the telephone system, $670 for electricity, and $420 for water. He took in $23,870 from selling pizzas, and he used up $7,130 worth of ingredients to make the pizzas. He paid his employees $5,120 for the month.

> **Required:**
> a. Prepare a statement of earnings to determine how much A Slice of Life earned in November.
> b. Are there any other costs that might have been incurred in November but are not listed?

1-38 (Prepare simple statement of earnings)

Lydia Cravette operates a florist shop called Scents Unlimited. During the month of May, the following things occurred: she spent $160 on the telephone system and $370 on electricity and water; the rent on the premises was $1,500; she took in $24,730 from selling flowers and plants; the cost of the flowers from a local grower was $10,733; she paid $329 for gas and repairs to the delivery vehicle; and she paid her employees $7,000 in wages.

> **Required:**
> a. Prepare a statement of earnings to determine how much Scents Unlimited earned in May.
> b. Are there any other costs that might have been incurred in May but are not listed?

1-39 (Prepare simple statement of earnings)

Michelle Fontaine runs an outdoor adventure company called Call of the Wild Ltd. Her busiest months are June through September, although, if the weather holds, she extends her excursions into October and November. For the month of July, she recorded the following items: she paid $49,860 for employee wages; she spent $14,610 on advertising; people paid her $171,430 for excursions that took place in July; the supplies used in July cost $25,629; the telephone and electricity in the office came to $1,532; and it cost $3,460 for gas and repairs on the vehicles.

Required:

a. Prepare a statement of earnings to determine how much Call of the Wild earned in July.

b. Are there any other costs that might have been incurred in July but were not listed?

1-40 (Prepare simple balance sheet)

Problem 1-37 introduced Jason Chan and his pizza business. At the end of November, the following items were in his records:

Supply of ingredients	$ 670
Wages owed to employees	1,460
Loan owed to the bank	11,000
Cash held in a chequing account	3,490
Cost of ovens and refrigerators	14,300
Prepaid rent for December	1,200
Common shares	5,000
Retained earnings	2,200

Required:

a. Identify each of the items in his records as an asset, liability, or shareholders' equity item.

b. Prepare a balance sheet for the end of November.

c. Jason Chan does not have accounts receivable in his records. Explain why it is unlikely that he will have an account called accounts receivable. Under what business circumstances would it be necessary for him to have such an account?

1-41 (Prepare simple balance sheet)

Problem 1-38 introduced Lydia Cravette and her florist shop. At the end of May, the following items were in her records:

Inventory	$ 1,100
Wages owed to employees	950
Loan owed to the bank	8,000
Cash held in a chequing account	8,361
Cost of refrigerator used to store the flowers	18,695
Prepaid rent for June	1,500
Common shares	18,000
Retained earnings	2,706

Required:

a. Identify each of the items in her records as an asset, liability, or shareholders' equity item.

b. Prepare a balance sheet for the end of May.

c. Lydia Cravette does not have accounts receivable in her records. Explain why it is unlikely that she will have an account called accounts receivable. Under what business circumstances would it be necessary for her to have such an account?

1-42 (Prepare simple balance sheet)

Problem 1-39 introduced Michelle Fontaine and her outdoor adventure company. At the end of July, the following items were in her records:

Loan owed to the bank	$24,000
Supplies on hand to be used in August	13,420
Cash in bank accounts	33,670
Common shares	20,000
Cost of tents and rafts	34,100
Retained earnings	56,450
Amounts prepaid by customers for trips to be taken in August	19,140
Vehicles	38,400

Required:

a. Identify each of the items in her records as an asset, liability, or shareholders' equity item.
b. Prepare a balance sheet for the end of July.
c. Does Michelle Fontaine have any inventory? Explain.
d. Michelle Fontaine does not have accounts receivable in her records. Explain why it is unlikely that she will have an account called accounts receivable. Under what business circumstances would it be necessary for her to have such an account?

1-43 (Identify assets and liabilities)

For each of the following companies, list at least two types of assets and one type of liability that you would expect to find on its balance sheet (try to include at least one item for each company that is unique to its type of business):

a. **Bombardier Inc.** This Quebec-based company manufactures transportation equipment and other industrial products.
b. **Sobeys Inc.** This company operates grocery stores across Canada.
c. **McCain Foods Limited.** This New Brunswick company prepares frozen vegetables, including Super fries.
d. **Royal Bank.** This is a major commercial bank.
e. **Suncor Energy Inc.** This company develops oil from the tar sands in Northern Alberta.
f. **Westjet Airlines.** This is an airline company.
g. **Danier Leather Inc.** This company designs and sells leather clothing.

1-44 (Identify statement of earnings items)

For each of the companies listed in Problem 1-43, list at least two line items that you would expect to find on its statement of earnings (try to include at least one item for each company that is unique to its type of business).

1-45 (Identify statement of cash flow items)

For each of the companies listed in Problem 1-43, list at least two line items that you would expect to find on its statement of cash flows (try to include at least one item for each company that is unique to its type of business).

User Perspective Problems

1-46 (Use of accounting information)

You are a junior accountant for a grocery store chain. Your company operates in Ontario and Quebec but wants to expand into Western Canada. The controller is sending you to Calgary to find a location for the store.

Required:

Make a list of information that you want to collect while you are in Calgary.

1-47 (Use of accounting information)

Continuing with Problem 1-46, it turns out that while in Calgary you find two locations. One is for sale and the other for rent.

a. What information do you want to collect about the property that is for sale so that the controller can evaluate this option?
b. What information do you want to collect about the property that is for rent so that the controller can compare this option to the purchase alternative?

1-48 (Information for decision-making)

Suppose that the IASB proposed that inventory is to be accounted for at its current market price (what you could sell it for) rather than its historical cost. Provide an argument that supports or opposes this change on the basis of relevance and reliability.

1-49 (Information for decision-making)

One of the alternatives under IFRS is that equipment used in manufacturing a company's product can be accounted for at its current market price (what the equipment could be sold for) rather than its depreciated historical cost (original cost minus accumulated depreciation). Provide an argument that supports or opposes this method on the basis of relevance and reliability.

1-50 (Information for decision-making)
How does the preparation of a classified balance sheet help the statement user predict a company's future cash flows? What qualitative characteristic(s) is/are illustrated?

1-51 (Information for decision-making)
Suppose that you started your own company that assembles and sells laptop computers. You do not manufacture any of the parts yourself. The computers are sold through orders received over the Internet and through mail orders.

> *Required:*
> Make a list of the information that would be relevant to running this business. Then discuss how you would reliably measure this information so that you can make effective decisions.

1-52 (Information for decision-making)
Suppose that you own and operate a company. You need to raise money to expand your operation, so you approach a bank for a loan. The loan officer has asked you for financial statements prepared according to IFRS.

> *Required:*
> a. Why would the loan officer make such a request?
> b. Assuming that your statements were prepared according to IFRS, how could you convince the loan officer that this was so?
> c. What items on your financial statements would be of the most interest to the loan officer?

1-53 (Value of auditors)
In order for a company's shares to be listed (traded) on a Canadian stock exchange, the company's annual financial statements must be audited by an independent auditor. Why is an audit important to shareholders? Why does the auditor have to be independent?

1-54 (Raising new capital)
Suppose that your best friend wants to start a new business that provides website development services to customers. Your friend has some savings to start the business but not enough to buy all the equipment that she thinks she needs. She has asked you for some advice about how to raise additional funds.

> *Required:*
> Give her at least two alternatives and provide the pros and cons for each alternative.

1-55 (Value of future-oriented information)
From time to time there have been calls from the user community for management to disclose its own forecasts of future expectations, such as net earnings.

> *Required:*
> a. As an external user of the financial statements, discuss the relevance and reliability of this type of information.
> b. Why might management be reluctant to disclose future-oriented information?

1-56 (Distribution of dividend to shareholders)
The board of directors of a public company is having its monthly meeting. One of the items on the agenda is the possible distribution of a cash dividend to shareholders. If the board decides to issue a cash dividend, the decision obliges the company to issue cash to shareholders based on the number of shares each shareholder owns.

> *Required:*
> Before making its decision, what information about the company should the board consider? Think of the items on the financial statements that you saw in this chapter.

Reading and Interpreting Published Financial Statements

Financial Analysis Assignments

1-57 (Financial statements of H&M)

Base your answers to the following questions on the financial statements for H&M in Appendix A at the end of the book. In the questions below, the year 2009 refers to H&M's fiscal year that ends November 30, 2009, and the year 2008 refers to the prior fiscal year ending November 31, 2008.

a. Determine the amount of dividends that H&M declared in 2009. On which financial statement(s) did you find this information?

b. Find the following amounts in the statements:
   i. Revenues from the sale of merchandise in 2009
   ii. Cost of sales and selling, general and administrative expenses, in 2009
   iii. Interest expense in 2009
   iv. Income tax expense in 2009
   v. Net earnings in 2008
   vi. Inventories at the end of 2008
   vii. Accounts payable and accrued liabilities at the beginning of 2009
   viii. Retained earnings at the end of 2009
   ix. Long-term debt at the beginning of 2009 (include the current portion of long-term debt)
   x. Cash flows generated from operating activities in 2009
   xi. Cash payments to acquire fixed assets in 2009
   xii. Cash proceeds from the issuance of capital stock in 2009
   xiii. Cash flows generated from (used for) financing activities in 2008
   xiv. Cash payments to reduce long-term debt in 2009

c. List the two largest sources of cash and the two largest uses of cash in 2009. (Consider operations to be a single source or use of cash.)

d. Suggest two reasons why net earnings were SEK 16,384 million in 2009, yet cash flows generated from operations were SEK 17,973 million.

e. During 2009, total sales revenue was approximately SEK 12.861 million higher than in 2008. However, net earnings in 2009 was only SEK 1,090 million higher than in 2008. By examining the statement of earnings, try to explain where the additional sales revenue went.

1-58 (Financial statements of Michelin Group)

Base your answers to the following questions on the 2009 financial statements for **Michelin Group** in Exhibit 1-8. This international French company manufactures and sells tires.

a. Michelin has issued consolidated financial statements. What does the word "consolidated" at the top of a financial statement tell you about the company's structure?

b. Michelin prepared a classified balance sheet. Calculate the difference between the current assets and current liabilities at the end of 2009, and at the end of 2008. This amount is referred to as working capital. Did the company's working capital improve in 2009? Explain. (Note that Michelin has followed the European balance sheet structure of putting the most permanent assets first and shareholders' equity first on the other side of the balance sheet.)

c. Find the following amounts in Michelin's statements (note that the amounts are in millions of Euros):
   i. Sales revenues in 2009
   ii. Cost of sales in 2009
   iii. Interest expense (cost of debt) in 2008
   iv. Income tax expense in 2009
   v. Net income (earnings) in 2008

MICHELIN GROUP 2009 ANNUAL REPORT

EXHIBIT 1-8A

annual report

CONSOLIDATED INCOME STATEMENT

(in EUR million, except per share data)	Dec. 31 2009	Dec. 31 2008	Dec. 31 2007	Dec. 31 2006	Dec. 31 2005
Net sales	**14,807**	**16,408**	**16,867**	**16,384**	**15,590**
Cost of sales	(10,527)	(12,024)	(11,760)	(11,653)	(10,835)
Gross income	**4,280**	**4,384**	**5,107**	**4,731**	**4,755**
Sales and marketing expenses	(1,650)	(1,730)	(1,738)	(1,799)	(1,775)
Research and development expenses	(506)	(499)	(561)	(591)	(565)
General and administrative expenses	(1,113)	(1,161)	(1,069)	(965)	(999)
Other operating income and expenses	(149)	(74)	(94)	(38)	(48)
Operating income before non-recurring income and expenses	**862**	**920**	**1,645**	**1,338**	**1,368**
Non-recurring profits	-	-	-	-	256
Non-recurring expenses	(412)	(77)	(326)	(220)	(50)
Operating income	**450**	**843**	**1,319**	**1,118**	**1,574**
Cost of net debt	(292)	(330)	(294)	(315)	(310)
Other financial income and expenses	40	(3)	29	135	30
Share of profit/(loss) from associates	9	10	17	4	6
Income before taxes	**207**	**520**	**1,071**	**942**	**1,300**
Income tax	(103)	(163)	(299)	(369)	(411)
Net income	**104**	**357**	**772**	**573**	**889**
• Attributable to Shareholders of the Company	106	360	774	572	889
• Attributable to non-controlling interests	(2)	(3)	(2)	1	-
Earnings per share (in euros)					
• Basic	0.71	2.46	5.32	3.95	6.13
• Diluted	0.71	2.46	5.22	3.94	6.12

     vi.   Intangible assets at the end of 2009 (note that goodwill is an intangible asset)

     vii. Trade receivables (accounts receivable) at the beginning of 2009

     viii. Share capital at the end of 2009

     ix.   Property, plant, and equipment at the end of 2009

     x.   Cash produced from operating activities in 2009

     xi.   Cash payments to acquire intangibles and property, plant, and equipment in 2008

     xii. Cash used for the payment of dividends in 2009

     xiii. Cash produced or used for financing activities in 2009

  d. Did Michelin finance the company's assets mainly from creditors (total liabilities) or from shareholders (shareholders' equity) in 2009? Support your answer with appropriate calculations.

  e. List the two largest sources of cash and the two largest uses of cash in 2009. (Consider cash generated from operating activities to be a single source or use of cash.)

  f. Suggest some reasons why net income was €104 million in 2009, yet cash generated from operating activities was €2,123 million.

  g. Because Michelin manufactures the tires it sells, it must devote resources to the development of new materials and designs for tires. This activity is called research and development. How much did Michelin spend in 2009 on research and development? Where did you find this amount? In terms of size, what percentage is research and development expense relative to gross income?

EXHIBIT 1-8B **MICHELIN GROUP 2009 ANNUAL REPORT**

annual report

CONSOLIDATED BALANCE SHEET

(in EUR million)	2009	2008	2007	2006	2005
Goodwill	403	401	401	438	444
Other intangible assets	321	310	200	181	192
Property, plant and equipment (PP&E)	6,782	7,046	7,124	6,848	6,577
Non-current financial assets and other assets	712	382	452	449	435
Investments in associates and joint ventures	71	65	62	71	50
Deferred tax assets	942	896	926	1,005	1,227
Non-current assets	**9,231**	**9,100**	**9,165**	**8,992**	**8,925**
Inventories	2,994	3,677	3,353	3,342	3,225
Trade receivables	2,314	2,456	2,993	3,237	3,273
Current financial assets	165	173	35	79	229
Other current assets	583	732	573	544	618
Cash and cash equivalents	1,231	456	330	680	611
Current assets	**7,287**	**7,494**	**7,284**	**7,882**	**7,956**
TOTAL ASSETS	**16,518**	**16,594**	**16,449**	**16,874**	**16,881**
Share capital	295	290	288	287	287
Share premiums	1,987	1,944	1,885	1,863	1,845
Reserves	3,210	2,874	3,109	2,527	2,379
Non-controlling interests	3	5	8	11	16
Total equity	**5,495**	**5,113**	**5,290**	**4,688**	**4,527**
Non-current financial liabilities	3,568	3,446	2,925	2,736	3,092
Employee benefit obligations	2,374	2,448	2,567	2,730	3,049
Provisions and other non-current liabilities	1,105	760	895	818	801
Deferred tax liabilities	40	39	61	58	71
Non-current liabilities	**7,087**	**6,693**	**6,448**	**6,342**	**7,013**
Current financial liabilities	760	1,440	1,145	2,157	1,647
Trade payables	1,249	1,504	1,642	1,776	1,792
Other current liabilities	1,927	1,844	1,924	1,911	1,902
Current liabilities	**3,936**	**4,788**	**4,711**	**5,844**	**5,341**
TOTAL EQUITY AND LIABILITIES	**16,518**	**16,594**	**16,449**	**16,874**	**16,881**

1-59   (Financial statements of Mosaid Technologies Incorporated)
Base your answers to the following problems on the 2009 financial statements of Mosaid Technologies Incorporated in Exhibit 1-9. Mosaid Technologies is an Ontario corporation that licenses and develops semiconductor and communication technologies. It designs memory technology and supplies semiconductor technologies around the world. In the questions below, the year 2009 refers to Mosaid Technologies' fiscal year that ends April 30, 2009, and the year 2008 refers to the prior fiscal year ending April 30, 2008.

a. Determine the amount of dividends that Mosaid Technologies declared in 2009. On which financial statement did you find this information? Determine the amount of dividends that Mosaid Technologies paid in 2009. On which financial statement did you find this information?

b. Find the following amounts in the statements of Mosaid Technologies:
   i.   Revenues in 2009
   ii. Research and development expense in 2009

MICHELIN GROUP 2009 ANNUAL REPORT

EXHIBIT 1-8C

annual report

CONSOLIDATED CASH FLOW STATEMENT

(in EUR million)	2009	2008	2007	2006	2005
Net income	**104**	**357**	**772**	**573**	**889**
Adjustments					
• Cost of net debt	292	330	294	315	310
• Other financial income and expenses	(40)	3	(29)	(135)	(30)
• Income tax	103	163	299	369	411
• Amortization, depreciation and impairment of intangible assets and PP&E	940	928	823	871	803
• Non-recurring income and expenses	412	77	326	220	(206)
• Share of loss/(profit) from associates	(9)	(10)	(17)	(4)	(6)
EBITDA adjusted (before non-recurring income and expenses)	**1,802**	**1,848**	**2,468**	**2,209**	**2,171**
Other non-cash income and expenses	(28)	10	(26)	(75)	(22)
Change in provisions, including employee benefit obligations	(372)	(268)	(175)	(229)	(147)
Cost of net debt and other financial income and expenses paid	(207)	(266)	(277)	(311)	(284)
Income tax paid	(19)	(275)	(294)	(182)	(261)
Change in working capital, net of impairments	947	(134)	166	(221)	(426)
Cash flows from operating activities	**2,123**	**915**	**1,862**	**1,191**	**1,031**
Purchases of intangible assets and PP&E	(707)	(1,289)	(1,484)	(1,379)	(1,292)
Proceeds from sale of intangible assets and PP&E	47	52	106	102	84
Equity investments in consolidated companies, net of cash acquired	(1)	(1)	(106)	(41)	(41)
Disposals of equity investments in consolidated companies, net of cash sold	10	5	-	(3)	(3)
Purchases of available-for-sale investments	(5)	(62)	(5)	(60)	(17)
Proceeds from sale of available-for-sale investments	29	6	19	146	2
Cash flows from other financial assets	(109)	15	41	5	112
Cash flows from investing activities	**(736)**	**(1,274)**	**(1,429)**	**(1,230)**	**(1,155)**
Proceeds from issuance of shares	2	36	14	11	-
Proceeds from increase of non-controlling interests in the share capital of subsidiaries	-	-	-	-	14
Dividends paid to Shareholders of the Company	(65)	(230)	(208)	(193)	(179)
Proceeds of the issuance of convertible bonds	-	-	694	-	-
Cash flows from financial liabilities	(667)	768	(1,262)	311	(739)
Other cash flows from financing activities	(20)	(93)	(12)	(7)	(50)
Cash flows from financing activities	**(750)**	**481**	**(774)**	**122**	**(954)**
Effect of changes in exchange rates	**2**	**4**	**(9)**	**(14)**	**34**
Increase/(decrease) of cash and cash equivalents	639	126	(350)	69	(1,044)
Cash and cash equivalents as at 1 January (as adjusted, without bank overdrafts of EUR 136 million in 2009)	592	330	680	611	1,655
Cash and cash equivalents as at 31 December	**1,231**	**456**	**330**	**680**	**611**

The complete consolidated financial statements may be found in the 2009 Registration Document.

    iii.   Foreign exchange gain in 2008
    iv.   Income tax expense in 2009
    v.   Net income (loss) in 2009
    vi.   Accounts receivable at the end of 2009
    vii.   Accounts payable and accrued liabilities at the beginning of 2009
    viii. Retained earnings at the end of 2009
    ix.   Other long-term liabilities at the end of 2009 (current and long-term)
    x.   Cash produced from operating activities in 2009
    xi.   Cash payments to acquire short-term marketable securities in 2009
    xii.   Cash used to repay the mortgage in 2008
    xiii. Cash proceeds from new share issuances in 2009
    xiv. Cash produced or used for investing activities in 2009

EXHIBIT 1-9A

MOSAID TECHNOLOGIES INC. 2009 ANNUAL REPORT

Consolidated Balance Sheets
(In thousands of Canadian Dollars)

Year Ended	April 30, 2009	April 30, 2008
Current Assets		
Cash and cash equivalents	$ 32,899	$ 22,133
Marketable securities (Note 15)	18,888	36,246
Accounts receivable	10,434	12,304
Prepaid expenses	759	486
Other asset (Note 15)	446	-
Future income taxes recoverable (Note 11)	11,519	11,015
	74,945	82,184
Capital assets (Note 3)	563	957
Acquired intangible assets (Note 3)	79,402	70,130
Future income taxes recoverable (Note 11)	17,549	16,988
	$172,459	$170,259
Current Liabilities		
Accounts payable and accrued liabilities	$ 6,341	$ 7,723
Income tax payable	1,432	356
Deferred revenue	3,432	1,146
Other liability (Note 15)	-	318
Current portion of other long-term liabilities (Note 5)	20,869	5,345
	32,074	14,888
Deferred gain on sale-leaseback (Note 4)	1,039	1,797
Other long-term liabilities (Note 5)	28,799	31,195
	61,912	47,880
Shareholders' Equity (Note 6)		
Share capital (Note 7)	94,741	100,403
Contributed surplus (Note 6)	3,753	2,997
Retained earnings	11,607	19,297
Accumulated other comprehensive income (Note 6)	446	(318)
	110,547	122,379
	$172,459	$170,259

See accompanying Notes to the Consolidated Financial Statements

Carl Schlacte
Chairman of the Board

Normand Paquette
Director and Chairman of the Audit Committee

MOSAID TECHNOLOGIES INC. 2009 ANNUAL REPORT

EXHIBIT 1-9B

annual report

Consolidated Statements Of Income And Retained Earnings

(In thousands of Canadian Dollars, except per share amounts)

Year Ended	April 30, 2009	April 30, 2008
Revenues	**$ 62,538**	$ 55,072
Operating expenses		
Patent portfolio management	**5,048**	4,834
Patent licensing and litigation	**21,230**	13,643
Research and development (Note 9)	**2,274**	2,351
General and administration	**4,406**	4,312
Foreign exchange loss (gain)	**6,791**	(3,393)
Stock-based compensation (Note 8)	**790**	550
Patent amortization and imputed interest	**13,881**	13,223
	54,420	35,520
Income from operations	**8,118**	19,552
Net interest income (Note 10)	**1,621**	2,130
Income before income tax expense and discontinued operations	**9,739**	21,682
Income tax expense (Note 11)	**4,923**	10,827
Income before discontinued operations	**4,816**	10,855
Discontinued operations income (net of tax) (Note 12)	**1,029**	7,619
Net income	**5,845**	18,474
Dividends	**10,320**	10,958
Normal course issuer bid (Note 7)	**3,215**	5,120
Retained earnings, beginning of year	**19,297**	16,901
Retained earnings, end of year	**$ 11,607**	$ 19,297
Earnings per share (Note 13)		
Basic – before discontinued operations	**$0.47**	$0.99
Diluted – before discontinued operations	**$0.47**	$0.98
Basic – net earnings	**$ 0.57**	$ 1.69
Diluted – net earnings	**$ 0.57**	$ 1.67
Weighted average number of shares		
Basic	**10,324,043**	10,962,648
Diluted	**10,337,827**	11,057,861

See accompanying Notes to the Consolidated Financial Statements

EXHIBIT 1-9C

annual report

MOSAID TECHNOLOGIES INC. 2009 ANNUAL REPORT

Consolidated Statements Of Cash Flows

(In thousands of Canadian Dollars)

Year Ended	April 30, 2009	April 30, 2008
Operating		
Income before discontinued operations	$ 4,816	$10,855
Items not affecting cash		
Amortization of capital assets and acquired intangible assets	10,320	9,653
Stock-based compensation	790	550
Loss on disposal of capital assets	76	95
Unrealized foreign exchange loss (gain) on other long-term liabilities	6,536	(3,999)
Future income tax	(1,065)	6,743
	21,473	23,897
Change in non-cash working capital items from continuing operations (Note 14)	(745)	(9,341)
	20,728	14,556
Investing		
Acquisition of capital assets and acquired intangible assets	(9,152)	(1,708)
Acquisition of short-term marketable securities	(60,135)	(119,460)
Proceeds on disposal and maturity of short-term marketable securities	77,493	110,090
	8,206	(11,078)
Financing		
Repayment of mortgage	-	(4,346)
Increase in long-term liabilities	(3,633)	(4,081)
Repurchase of common shares	(8,415)	(10,324)
Dividends	(10,320)	(10,958)
Funding of Restricted Share Unit Plan	(825)	-
Issue of common shares	268	2,702
	(22,925)	(27,007)
Net cash inflow (outflow) from continuing operations	6,009	(23,529)
Net cash inflow from discontinued operations (Note 12)	4,757	22,266
Net cash inflow (outflow)	10,766	(1,263)
Cash and cash equivalents, beginning of year	22,133	23,396
Cash and cash equivalents, end of year	$32,899	$22,133
Supplementary Information:		
Cash on hand and bank balances		
Short-term investments	$ 6,438	$ 8,126
	26,461	14,007
Total cash and cash equivalents	$32,899	$22,133

See accompanying Notes to the Consolidated Financial Statements

c. Did Mosaid Technologies finance its business primarily from creditors (total liabilities) or from shareholders (shareholders' equity) in 2009? Support your answer with the appropriate calculations.

d. List the two largest sources of cash and the two largest uses of cash in 2009. (Consider operations to be a single source or use of cash.)

e. The short-term marketable securities decreased on the balance sheet from $36,246 thousand in 2008 to $18,888 thousand in 2009. Using information from the cash flow statement, explain the net change in this account.

f. Total assets of Mosaid Technologies at April 30, 2009, and April 30, 2008, were $172,459 thousand and $170,259 thousand, respectively. Total shareholders' equity at these dates was $110,547 thousand and $122,379 thousand, respectively. Calculate the ratio of total liabilities to total assets for each of the 2009 and 2008 fiscal years. Explain the change from 2008 to 2009.

1-60 (Financial statements of Carnival Corporation & PLC)

Base your answers to the following problems on the 2009 financial statements of **Carnival Corporation & PLC** in Exhibit 1-10. Carnival Corporation is a global cruise company combining Carnival Corporation, which is incorporated in Panama, and Carnival PLC, which is incorporated in England and Wales. It operates several cruise lines, including Carnival Cruises, Holland America, and Princess Cruises, that offer cruises in Europe, North America, and Australia.

a. Find the following amounts in the statements:
   i. Total revenues in 2009
   ii. Total operating expenses in 2009
   iii. Depreciation and amortization in 2008
   iv. Income tax expense in 2008
   v. Net income in 2009
   vi. Inventories at the beginning of 2009
   vii. Accounts receivable at the end of 2008
   viii. Retained earnings at the end of 2009
   ix. Total long-term debt at the end of 2009
   x. Cash flows from operating activities in 2009
   xi. Cash payments to acquire property and equipment in 2008
   xii. Dividends paid in 2009
   xiii. Cash produced or used for investing activities in 2009

b. Did Carnival Corporation finance its business primarily from creditors (total liabilities) or from shareholders (shareholders' equity) in 2009? Support your answer with appropriate calculations.

c. List the two largest sources of cash and the two largest uses of cash in 2009. (Consider operating activities to be a single source or use of cash.)

d. Carnival Corporation prepared a classified balance sheet. Calculate the difference between the current assets and current liabilities at the end of 2009, and at the end of 2008. This amount is referred to as working capital. Did the company's working capital improve in 2009? Explain.

e. Carnival Corporation operates several cruise lines. When customers book cruises, they usually pay for the cruise several weeks or months before the cruise occurs. Because the cruise has not yet happened, Carnival does not record the payment as revenue. Instead it recognizes its obligation by recording the payment as a liability. Find this liability on the company's balance sheet. What is it called? What are the amounts for 2009 and 2008?

EXHIBIT 1-10A   **CARNIVAL CORPORATION & PLC 2009 ANNUAL REPORT**

CONSOLIDATED STATEMENTS OF OPERATIONS
(in millions, except per share data)

	Years Ended November 30,		
	2009	**2008**	**2007**
Revenues			
Cruise			
Passenger tickets	$ 9,985	$11,210	$ 9,792
Onboard and other	2,885	3,044	2,846
Other	287	392	395
	13,157	14,646	13,033
Costs and Expenses			
Operating			
Cruise			
Commissions, transportation and other	1,917	2,232	1,941
Onboard and other	461	501	495
Payroll and related	1,498	1,470	1,336
Fuel	1,156	1,774	1,096
Food	839	856	747
Other ship operating	1,997	1,913	1,717
Other	236	293	296
Total	8,104	9,039	7,628
Selling and administrative	1,590	1,629	1,579
Depreciation and amortization	1,309	1,249	1,101
	11,003	11,917	10,308
Operating Income	2,154	2,729	2,725
Nonoperating (Expense) Income			
Interest income	14	35	67
Interest expense, net of capitalized interest	(380)	(414)	(367)
Other income (expense), net	18	27	(1)
	(348)	(352)	(301)
Income Before Income Taxes	1,806	2,377	2,424
Income Tax Expense, Net	(16)	(47)	(16)
Net Income	$ 1,790	$ 2,330	$ 2,408
Earnings Per Share			
Basic	$ 2.27	$ 2.96	$ 3.04
Diluted	$ 2.24	$ 2.90	$ 2.95
Dividends Declared Per Share		$ 1.60	$ 1.375

The accompanying notes are an integral part of these consolidated financial statements

CARNIVAL CORPORATION & PLC 2009 ANNUAL REPORT

EXHIBIT 1-10B

annual report

CONSOLIDATED BALANCE SHEETS

(in millions, except par values)

	November 30, 2009	November 30, 2008
ASSETS		
Current Assets		
Cash and cash equivalents	$ 538	$ 650
Trade and other receivables, net	362	418
Inventories	320	315
Prepaid expenses and other	298	267
Total current assets	1,518	1,650
Property and Equipment, Net	29,870	26,457
Goodwill	3,451	3,266
Trademarks	1,346	1,294
Other Assets	650	733
	$36,835	$33,400
LIABILITIES AND SHAREHOLDERS' EQUITY		
Current Liabilities		
Short-term borrowings	$ 135	$ 256
Current portion of long-term debt	815	1,081
Convertible debt subject to current put option		271
Accounts payable	568	512
Accrued liabilities and other	874	1,142
Customer deposits	2,575	2,519
Total current liabilities	4,967	5,781
Long-Term Debt	9,097	7,735
Other Long-Term Liabilities and Deferred Income	736	786
Commitments and Contingencies (Notes 6 and 7)		
Shareholders' Equity		
Common stock of Carnival Corporation; $.01 par value; 1,960 shares authorized; 644 shares at 2009 and 643 shares at 2008 issued	6	6
Ordinary shares of Carnival plc; $1.66 par value; 226 shares authorized; 213 shares at 2009 and 2008 issued	354	354
Additional paid-in capital	7,707	7,677
Retained earnings	15,770	13,980
Accumulated other comprehensive income (loss)	462	(623)
Treasury stock; 24 shares at 2009 and 19 shares at 2008 of Carnival Corporation and 46 shares at 2009 and 52 shares at 2008 of Carnival plc, at cost	(2,264)	(2,296)
Total shareholders' equity	22,035	19,098
	$36,835	$33,400

The accompanying notes are an integral part of these consolidated financial statements.

CARNIVAL CORPORATION & PLC 2009 ANNUAL REPORT

CONSOLIDATED STATEMENTS OF CASH FLOWS
(in millions)

	Years Ended November 30,		
	2009	2008	2007
OPERATING ACTIVITIES			
Net income	$ 1,790	$ 2,330	$ 2,408
Adjustments to reconcile net income to net cash provided by operating activities			
Depreciation and amortization	1,309	1,249	1,101
Share-based compensation	50	50	64
Other	37	(37)	26
Changes in operating assets and liabilities, excluding businesses acquired and sold			
Receivables	81	(70)	(119)
Inventories	10	(8)	(57)
Prepaid expenses and other	7	(18)	(56)
Accounts payable	74	(66)	109
Accrued and other liabilities	29	37	163
Customer deposits	(45)	(76)	430
Net cash provided by operating activities	3,342	3,391	4,069
INVESTING ACTIVITIES			
Additions to property and equipment	(3,380)	(3,353)	(3,312)
Purchases of short-term investments	(4)	(4)	(2,098)
Sales of short-term investments	2	11	2,078
Acquisition of business, net of cash acquired and sales of businesses	(33)		(339)
Other, net	31	91	(75)
Net cash used in investing activities	(3,384)	(3,255)	(3,746)
FINANCING ACTIVITIES			
Principal repayments of revolver	(1,749)	(3,314)	(135)
Proceeds from revolver	1,166	3,186	1,086
Proceeds from issuance of other long-term debt	2,299	2,243	2,654
Principal repayments of other long-term debt	(1,273)	(1,211)	(1,656)
(Repayments of) proceeds from short-term borrowings, net	(288)	138	(1,281)
Dividends paid	(314)	(1,261)	(990)
Purchases of treasury stock	(188)	(98)	(326)
Sales of treasury stock	196	15	
Proceeds from settlement of foreign currency swaps	113		
Other, net	(55)	(13)	44
Net cash used in financing activities	(93)	(315)	(604)
Effect of exchange rate changes on cash and cash equivalents	23	(114)	61
Net decrease in cash and cash equivalents	(112)	(293)	(220)
Cash and cash equivalents at beginning of year	650	943	1,163
Cash and cash equivalents at end of year	$ 538	$ 650	$ 943

The accompanying notes are an integral part of these consolidated financial statements.

BEYOND THE BOOK

The Beyond the Book problems give you the opportunity to find and use company information from outside this book.

1-61   (Use the library and other sources to find company information)
Familiarize yourself with the resources that are available at your university to acquire information about corporations. Most universities have some type of electronic database that contains financial statement information. The following is a short list of resources that may be available:

LEXIS/NEXIS Database   This is an incredibly large database that contains all sorts of news and financial information about companies. It contains information about Canadian, U.S., and international companies. The financial information is in full text form.

Compact/Disclosure Canada   This database contains descriptive and financial data for more than 8,500 public, private, and Canadian government–owned (Crown) corporations. It provides more than 60 financial items, including assets, liabilities, sales, profits, number of employees, and selected ratios.

EDGAR Filings   The EDGAR Filings are electronic forms of the SEC filings in the U.S. that are included in the LEXIS/NEXIS database but are also accessible through the Internet at www.sec.gov/edgar.shtml.

ABI Inform (UMI, Inc.)   This database contains full-text information from numerous business periodicals.

SEDAR website (www.sedar.com)   This site contains most securities-related information required by the Canadian securities regulatory authorities and is probably your best source for financial statements of Canadian companies on the Internet.

You can also search the Internet for sites that list information about companies. Most companies that have a website have a section on investor information. In this section, they often include their most recent financial reports and news releases.

1-62   (Find information about a new company)
Choose a company and answer the following questions:
   a. What are the products (or product lines) and/or services that it sells? Please be as specific as possible.
   b. Who are the company's customers?
   c. In what markets, domestic and global, does the company sell its products and/or services?
   d. Who are the company's major competitors?
   e. What are the major inputs that the company needs in order to produce its product? Who are the suppliers of these inputs?
   f. Are any of the items listed in the questions above changing substantially? Use a two-year time span to answer this question.

To help you answer the questions above, first collect several articles about the company that cover the most recent two-year period. Try to find at least three longer articles. Use these as references to write a two- to three-page background paper about the company. If the company has a website (most companies do), it will probably have useful news releases there.

1-63   (Find information about a new company)

Go to the Student website and find the annual report of **HMV Group plc.** for 2009. Answer the following questions:

    a.   What are the major sections of the annual report?
    b.   What are the three most important points in the letter to the shareholders?
    c.   What are the titles of the major financial statements in the report?
    d.   What are the company's total assets, total liabilities, and total shareholders' equity? What percentage of the company's total assets is financed through liabilities?
    e.   Is the balance sheet classified or unclassified? If it is classified, what are the major categories?
    f.   What are the net sales in the most recent year? Are they up or down from the previous year? (Answer in both dollar and percentage amounts.)
    g.   What is the net income and earnings per share in the most recent year? Are these amounts up or down from the previous year? (Answer in both dollar and percentage amounts.)
    h.   What is the net cash provided (used) by operating, financing, and investing activities for the most recent year?
    i.   What is the last day of the company's fiscal year?
    j.   Who are the independent auditors and what type of opinion did they give on the company's statements?

1-64   (Find information about a new company)

Choose a company, find its most recent annual report, and answer the following questions:

    a.   What are the major sections in its annual report?
    b.   What are the three most important points in the letter to the shareholders?
    c.   What are the titles of the major financial statements in the report?
    d.   What are the company's total assets, total liabilities, and total shareholders' equity? What percentage of the company's total assets is financed through liabilities?
    e.   Is the balance sheet classified or unclassified? If it is classified, what are the major categories?
    f.   What are the net sales in the most recent year? Are they up or down from the previous year? (Answer in both dollar and percentage amounts.)
    g.   What is the net income and earnings per share in the most recent year? Are these amounts up or down from the previous year? (Answer in both dollar and percentage amounts.)
    h.   What is the net cash provided (used) by operating, financing, and investing activities for the most recent year?
    i.   What is the last day of the company's fiscal year?
    j.   Who are the independent auditors and what type of opinion did they give on the company's statements?

Cases

1-65   Born to be Wiled

WILEY PLUS
www.wileyplus.com

Case Primer

Born to be Wiled is owned by Fraser Grant, a designer of upscale women's clothing. He started by selling his early creations to small boutiques in Toronto. Customers liked the colours and fabrics he used and enjoyed the unique styling of the garments. Demand for his clothing rose to the point where he opened his own store on a fashionable street in Montreal. As the sole owner of his business, he has used up most of his personal resources in getting his store operational. He has visited his local bank seeking additional financing so that he can hire more people to assist in the various aspects of his business. The bank wants to see his financial statements. The financial statements do not need to be audited, but the bank wants them to follow IFRS.

You are an accountant employed by a local accounting firm and Fraser Grant has been your client for several years. In the past, you have prepared his annual financial statements and completed his business tax return. He has approached you because he wants to know what IFRS are and whether you can prepare his financial statements using them.

Required:

Prepare a memo to Fraser Grant addressing his concerns.

1-66   Rust Consulting

Heather Rust is the owner-operator of a small consulting business. She has recently taken a brief accounting seminar and was introduced to the idea of the qualitative characteristics of accounting information. She is having some difficulty understanding the concept of faithful representation. She thinks that this is an odd label for a qualitative characteristic. She does not understand what it means or why it is important for financial information.

Required:

Using the concepts discussed in the text, explain to Heather Rust what faithful representation is and why it is important.

Critical Thinking Question

1-67   (The cost of the 2010 Olympics)

In the article "Costing the 2010 Winter Olympic Games" (*CGA Magazine*, January– February 2010), Andrew Allentuck discusses the various ways of determining the total cost of hosting the games in Vancouver.

a. Find this article in your library and identify the issues that he raises in discussing how to arrive at a total cost for the 2010 Olympic Games.
b. We often think that accounting is black and white and that it is just a matter of measuring events and putting the numbers in a report. Why is the measurement issue so challenging for the Olympics?
c. Do businesses have some of the same measurement issues that affect the costing of the 2010 Olympics? If so, identify what some of the business issues could be.

ANALYZING TRANSACTIONS AND THEIR EFFECTS ON FINANCIAL STATEMENTS

LEARNING OBJECTIVES

After studying this chapter, you should be able to:

1. Describe the basic accounting equation and each of its components.

2. Analyze simple transactions to determine their effects on the basic accounting equation and the financial statements.

3. Describe the difference between accrual-basis accounting and cash-basis accounting.

4. Explain how inventory is accounted for when it is purchased and when it is sold.

5. Identify operating activities and describe their effects on the financial statements.

6. Explain the basic concepts of revenue recognition and expense matching.

7. Prepare a simple set of financial statements, reflecting a series of business transactions.

8. Explain the basic classification of items on a statement of financial position.

9. Calculate three ratios for assessing a company's profitability.

10. Begin to analyze the information provided by a statement of cash flows.

A Recipe for Success—The Evolution of a Business

Ever since high school, Chris Emery and Larry Finnson had known they wanted to go into business together. Sure enough, one day Mr. Emery's grandmother came up with an irresistible recipe for a vanilla fudge treat, and Krave's Candy Company was born. In 1996, with $20,000 scraped together from family and friends, the two Winnipeg entrepreneurs set up some old kettle cookers in a tiny industrial space and started churning out 80-pound batches of the sweets, which they called Clodhoppers.

In its first year of operation, Krave's sold its product mostly through local retailers and craft fairs. Ten years later, in 2006, they sold the Clodhoppers trademark to Brookside Foods Ltd., a manufacturer of chocolate-covered fruit and nuts based in Abbotsford, B.C. Today, Chris and Larry's Clodhoppers are sold in stores across Canada, including Wal-Mart, Zellers, Safeway, and The Bay, as well as in Blockbuster video outlets across North America.

While their company enjoyed remarkable success, Mr. Emery and Mr. Finnson, neither of whom had any prior business experience, learned a lot along the way. "At the beginning, we just thought we'd fire up a manufacturing plant and start making millions of pounds of candy and be rich within two years," says Mr. Finnson. "It didn't work out that way. It was step by step for everything from manufacturing to money."

During Krave's start-up period, the pair ran into unanticipated expenses. "First, we needed a computer; then there was the development of the packaging and artwork; plus we had to hire people to help us make the candy," Mr. Emery recalls. "Before we knew it, the money was pretty much spent." Meanwhile, as their sales continued to climb, the two had to find more cash to finance their expansion, including much needed upgrades to their production equipment: the

large mixers, cooling tunnels, and other devices used in the manufacturing process.

When Krave's purchased two form-and-fill machines to weigh and package the candy, the company ensured adequate cash flow by financing the purchase with a term loan from its bank, which it got on the basis of its strong financial statements. During that first decade, as the company continued to grow, Mr. Emery and Mr. Finnson kept their financing balanced among several sources, including a venture capitalist, a traditional bank, and the Business Development Bank of Canada.

Clodhoppers' financial information is now included in the more complicated accounting structure of Brookside Foods, which is a large corporation. Information on production planning, warehouse management, product tracing, shipment scheduling, budgeting, and sales commissions for the Clodhoppers product line is added to similar information for other Brookside products to provide an overall picture of the company's operations. Still, whether running a large company like Brookside or the two-person start-up that Krave's once was, "The most important thing is to know your numbers," Mr. Finnson says, "and how your business works from A to Z."

Chris Emery and Larry Finnson started **Krave's Candy** as a small company and grew the business through hard work and effective marketing. They started with a product that they thought customers would want, and have proven that they were right. Now that their company has been taken over by **Brookside Foods**, several variations of their original Clodhoppers product are sold throughout North America.

It is well known that many new businesses do not survive, so what did Mr. Emery and Mr. Finnson do that made Krave's such a success? First, they had a product that people liked and would buy. Second, they worked hard at producing and distributing it. They had to ensure that the quality of the product remained consistent as they moved to producing it in larger batches. They also had to get the product to consumers. They chose to go to craft fairs first, and to convince local retailers to carry their product. As the name "Clodhoppers" became known, they were able to convince multi-outlet retailers such as The Bay, Zellers, and Shoppers Drug Mart to carry their product. This was the start of their real growth.

However, along with growth comes a need for additional funding. It is financing that often causes young companies their greatest problems, and Krave's was no exception. Within a very short time, the founders had exhausted their original investment of $20,000. Fortunately, however, by that time they were able to convince a bank that they were an acceptable credit risk. As the business evolved, they used multiple sources of funds (including a venture capitalist, as discussed in the *Accounting in the News* item on the following page). Investors were convinced that they had a good product, that the company was well managed, and that there was growth potential.

Behind all of its success and through all of its decisions, Krave's had to use its accounting information to manage the business. As young companies grow, the owners sometimes lose track of the numbers, especially if the growth is rapid. However, Mr. Emery and Mr. Finnson did not make that mistake. They knew that they had to keep track of all aspects of their business, and that the accounting numbers and financial statements were the tools that would enable them to do this. Therefore, as the company expanded its manufacturing and marketing operations, it also increased its accounting staff. In addition, it used computer technology to analyze its financial data efficiently and effectively.

The way Mr. Emery and Mr. Finnson started their business is typical of how many small businesses begin, with their funding obtained from personal savings, families, and friends. Financial institutions are often reluctant to take chances on new companies until they see some indicators of success, so alternative sources of financing are often required. One such source is called "venture capital," which refers to financing provided to relatively new, potentially high-risk companies to enable them to get established.

accounting in the news

Canadian Venture Capital Financing

In the aftermath of the 2008 crisis in financial markets and the onset of a global recession, deal activity in the Canadian venture capital (VC) market in 2009 reached its lowest level since the mid-1990s. A total of $1.0 billion was invested across the country, a 27% decrease from the $1.4 billion invested in 2008, according to a report by Canada's Venture Capital & Private Equity Association (CVCA) and Thomson Reuters.

The number of VC-backed entrepreneurial firms in Canada also dropped in 2009, though not as much as the dollars invested. A total of 331 companies were financed, 15% fewer than the 388 companies financed in 2008. Amounts invested per company averaged $3.1 million in 2009, compared with $3.5 million in 2008 and $5.1 million in 2007.

The overall decline in domestic VC activity was partly offset by an increase in Quebec. A total of $431 million was invested in Quebec, up 10% from the $392 million invested in 2008, giving it a leading 43% share of the Canadian total last year. In contrast, $288 million was invested in Ontario in 2009, 50% below the $575 million invested in 2008. As a result, Ontario accounted for only 28% of the Canadian total, its lowest market share since the early 1990s.

CVCA news release, February 17, 2010,
http://www.cvca.ca/files/News/CVCA_Q4_2009_VC_Press_Release_Final.pdf

USER RELEVANCE

If accounting information is to be useful, it must be (among other things) understandable and relevant. In order for users like Mr. Emery and Mr. Finnson to understand the information that is provided on financial statements, they must have at least some basic knowledge of the accounting system: what items are identified, measured, and recorded; how those items are recorded; and how financial statements are generated from the recorded data. Without that knowledge, they will have difficulty understanding the importance and relevance of accounting reports, and may not be able to use them effectively to make the best decisions.

The accounting system measures, records, and compiles information on the effects that economic events have on a company. To interpret the information in financial statements, you need to understand how accounting information is obtained and the guidelines for how it is presented in the financial statements. Only then can you use accounting information sensibly to make decisions. Chapter 1 provided an overview of the types of information that are presented in financial statements. This chapter and the next explain how accountants collect and classify that information.

THE BASIC ACCOUNTING EQUATION

In this chapter, we will demonstrate how a typical set of **transactions** affects a company's **accounts**, and how the three major financial statements are prepared using the transaction information. We will start with the basic accounting equation discussed in Chapter 1, which is the basis of all accounting systems.

LEARNING OBJECTIVE 1

Understand the basic accounting equation and each of its components.

BASIC ACCOUNTING EQUATION

Assets = Liabilities + Shareholders' Equity

A company's assets, liabilities, and shareholders' equity are reported on its statement of financial position, which is commonly referred to as the balance sheet. For this reason, the basic accounting equation is often called the *balance sheet equation*.

As transactions are recorded in the accounting system, the two sides of this equation must always remain equal. The statement of financial position provides readers with information about this equality at the beginning and end of the current accounting period—usually by showing the beginning amounts (from the previous period) in the outside column, and the ending amounts (from the current period) in the inside column. A statement with the amounts for two or more periods is called a comparative statement. Refer to H&M's balance sheet (statement of financial position) in Exhibit 1-4 for an example of this.

Users of financial information typically want to know more than just the statement of financial position amounts. They usually want to know how and why the company's financial position changed from the beginning of the period to the end. A statement of earnings and a statement of cash flows are both useful for this. In the remainder of this chapter, a set of accounts illustrating the basic accounting equation will be used to record typical transactions for a small company, and a statement of earnings and a statement of cash flows will be constructed from this information.

Companies are generally required to prepare financial statements at least once a year. However, because the financial statements provide information that is useful to management, owners, and other users, most companies prepare them more often (for example, semi-annually, quarterly, monthly, weekly, or even daily). The period of time that the financial statements cover is referred to as *the accounting period*. In the example we will use, the company prepares financial statements at the end of each month, so the accounting period is one month.

In Chapter 1, we explained that one of the components of shareholders' equity, share capital, increases when the owners invest money in the company and are issued shares. We also showed you that the other main component of shareholders' equity, retained earnings, increases when the company generates earnings or net income (which consists of revenues minus expenses), and decreases when the company declares dividends (distributions of earnings to the owners). In short, *revenues increase retained earnings; expenses and dividends decrease retained earnings.*

To help you understand the links between the financial statements and how various items are affected by transactions, each of the amounts in the retained earnings column will be labelled R for revenues, E for expenses, or D for dividends. Similarly, to help us prepare the statement of cash flows, we will label each of the amounts in the cash column as O for operating activities, F for financing activities, or I for investing activities, to indicate in which section of the statement they will be presented.

TRANSACTION ANALYSIS AND THE BASIC ACCOUNTING EQUATION

LEARNING OBJECTIVE 2

Analyze simple transactions and describe their effects on the basic accounting equation and the financial statements.

The basic accounting equation can now be used to illustrate the fundamentals of the accounting system and the preparation of financial statements. We will use typical transactions for a retail sales company to demonstrate the analysis of transactions and how they affect the financial statements.

Assume that a business called Demo Company Limited is formed as a corporation on January 1, 2011. During the month of January it engages in a number of basic transactions, as described in the sections that follow. We will discuss each of the transactions to analyze its effects on the company's accounts and financial statements.

Sample Transactions

At the beginning of January:

1. The owners invested $17,500 cash and Demo Company issued shares to them.

2. The company used $4,500 of the cash received from the investors to buy equipment.

3. Demo paid $360 cash for an insurance policy.

4. To raise additional financing, the company borrowed $10,000 from its bank.

During the rest of January:

5. Demo purchased some land for $15,000.

6. The company bought $23,000 of inventory from suppliers, on account (i.e., Demo will pay for the goods at a later date).

7. The company sold some goods to customers for $13,000, on account (i.e., Demo will receive payment for the goods at a later date).

8. The cost of the goods that were sold and removed from the company's inventory in Transaction 7 was $9,000.

9. Demo received $11,000 from its customers as payments on their accounts (which originated in Transaction 7.)

10. The company made payments of $13,500 to its suppliers on account (which originated in Transaction 6.)

11. Demo paid the following costs for the month of January: $2,000 for salaries; $500 for rent; $300 for utilities.

12. Dividends in the amount of $250 were declared and paid.

At the end of January, Demo's accountant noted that the following adjustments were required:

13. Depreciation expense must be recorded for the equipment. The accountant determined that the equipment should be depreciated by $150 for the month.

14. Insurance expense must be recognized for January. The insurance policy (which was purchased in Transaction 3) covers the six-month period from January 1 to June 30, 2011.

15. Interest expense must be recognized for the month. The interest rate charged on the bank loan (which originated in Transaction 4) is 6% per year. Although the loan itself does not have to be repaid for five years, the interest on it has to be paid quarterly.

16. Income tax expense must be recognized for the month, even though the company does not have to pay the tax until later. Demo's income tax rate is 25%.

Transaction Analysis

For each event or transaction that affects an organization, accountants must analyze its economic substance to decide what accounts are affected and by how much. We call this **transaction analysis**. It is at this stage of the accounting process that accounting knowledge is most needed. In addition to determining the economic substance of each transaction, accountants must know the accounting principles and guidelines that apply to the various situations that arise.

In the following subsections, we will analyze the economic substance of each of the transactions listed above, and discuss the related accounting principles underlying them. In addition, for each transaction we will show the accounts involved and the effects on the basic accounting equation, by entering the amounts in a table with columns for each of the asset, liability, and shareholders' equity accounts. Since the specific assets and liabilities that Demo Company will need are not known in advance, we will start with a basic table and add columns to it as we proceed through the analysis. Whenever we encounter a new account, we will add a new column to the table.

Transaction 1: Issuance of Shares for Cash

Demo Company issued shares in exchange for $17,500 received in cash from investors.

ANALYSIS   The company's shareholders invested $17,500 in the company, in exchange for ownership rights represented by share certificates. The money the company received is recorded as an asset (cash), and the ownership rights are recorded as shareholders' equity (share capital).

The analysis of this transaction and its effects on the basic accounting equation are summarized below:

ANALYSIS OF TRANSACTION 1

Assets (specifically, Cash) **increased** by $17,500
Shareholders' Equity (specifically, Share Capital) **increased** by $17,500

EFFECTS ON THE BASIC ACCOUNTING EQUATION

	Assets	=	Liabilities	+	Shareholders' Equity	
	Cash	=		+	Share capital	+ Retained earnings
Tr. 1	+17,500 F				+17,500	

Note that these entries keep the two sides of the basic accounting equation equal (in balance).

CASHFLOW EFFECT   Since this transaction provides financing for the company, the cash inflow of $17,500 is classified as a financing activity and therefore has been designated with an F.

EARNINGS EFFECT   Since this transaction does not involve revenues or expenses, there is no effect on the company's earnings.

RELATED CONCEPTS—The nature of revenue   It is important to note that, although the issuance of shares results in an inflow of resources into the business, *revenue* cannot be recorded when a company sells shares to investors. Revenue has to be *earned from operations* of the business, and therefore only arises when the company sells goods or services to customers. The issuance of shares—even if the transaction is described as a "sale of shares"—does not involve customers, and consequently does not constitute sales revenue and will not be reported on the statement of earnings.

Transaction 2: Purchase of Equipment for Cash

Demo Company used $4,500 of its cash to buy equipment.

ANALYSIS Because the purchase required an outflow of cash, this asset decreased. At the same time, another asset—equipment—increased. The equipment is an asset, rather than an expense, because it will be used in the operations of the business and provide future benefits.

The analysis of this transaction and its effects on the basic accounting equation are summarized below:

ANALYSIS OF TRANSACTION 2

Assets (specifically, Cash) **decreased** by $4,500
Assets (specifically, Equipment) **increased** by $4,500

EFFECTS ON THE BASIC ACCOUNTING EQUATION

	Assets		=	Liabilities	+	Shareholders' Equity	
	Cash	+ Equip.	=		+	Share capital	+ Retained earnings
Tr. 1	+17,500 F					+17,500	
Tr. 2	−4,500 I	+4,500					

Again, notice that the equilibrium of the basic accounting equation has been maintained.

The equipment purchased is regarded as a *long-term* asset because the company will use it over several future accounting periods. The value of this asset will be used up over those future periods, and the amount that is consumed each period will be shown as *depreciation expense*. The expensing of part of the cost of the equipment is shown later, as one of the adjustments that is made at the end of the accounting period.

CASHFLOW EFFECT Transactions involving long-term assets are classified as investing activities. Accordingly, the cash outflow of $4,500 has been designated with an I.

EARNINGS EFFECT Since no revenue or expense is involved in this transaction, there is no effect on the company's earnings. The equipment is an asset; the expense (depreciation) related to it will be recorded later, as the asset is used.

RELATED CONCEPTS—Accrual-basis versus cash-basis accounting The treatment of this transaction is based on an assumption of **accrual-basis** accounting. Under accrual accounting, costs (such as the cost of the equipment) are only classified as expenses if and when the item is consumed; until that time, the cost is recorded as an asset. In this transaction, therefore, the purchase of the equipment is not recorded as an expense. The equipment is recorded as an asset, because it will be used in the future. One asset (cash) has simply been exchanged for another asset (equipment) and there is no effect on the company's income, or change in its shareholders' equity.

LEARNING OBJECTIVE 3

Describe the difference between accrual-basis accounting and cash-basis accounting.

Accrual-basis accounting is very different from **cash-basis** accounting, which classifies costs as expenses whenever cash is spent. In a cash-basis system, the purchase of equipment would be recorded as an expense and reported on the statement of earnings. However, as will be discussed in detail in Chapter 4, cash-basis accounting violates generally accepted accounting principles (GAAP). The accrual basis is consistent with GAAP, is used by most businesses, and will be used throughout this book.

Transaction 3: Purchase of Insurance

Demo Company paid $360 in cash for an insurance policy.

ANALYSIS   This transaction is an example of a **prepaid expense**. The cost of insurance coverage is paid in advance of the coverage period. Therefore, at the date of the payment the cost of the policy should be shown as an asset, since it has not been used up yet. Only as time passes will the asset (the insurance coverage) be consumed.

Because the purchase required an outflow of cash, this asset decreased. However, another asset—prepaid insurance—increased.

The analysis of this transaction and its effects on the basic accounting equation are summarized below:

HELPFUL HINT

Note that this is an example of the concept that a cost can be classified as either an asset or an expense, depending on whether or not it has expired (i.e., been consumed). *Unexpired* costs are assets, while *expired costs* are expenses.

ANALYSIS OF TRANSACTION 3

Assets (specifically, Prepaid Insurance) **increased** by $360
Assets (specifically, Cash) **decreased** by $360

EFFECTS ON THE BASIC ACCOUNTING EQUATION

	Assets			=	Liabilities		+	Shareholders' Equity	
	Cash	+ Equip.	+ Prepaid insur.	=			+	Share capital	+ Retained earnings
Tr. 1	+17,500 F							+17,500	
Tr. 2	−4,500 I	+4,500							
Tr. 3	**−360 O**		**+360**						

CASHFLOW EFFECT   This transaction decreases cash by the $360 payment, which represents an operating cash flow and has therefore been designated with an O.

EARNINGS EFFECT   Since this transaction does not involve revenue or expenses, there is no effect on the company's earnings. The insurance is not an expense until it is used up.

Transaction 4: Loan from Bank

Demo Company borrowed $10,000 from the bank.

ANALYSIS   In addition to issuing shares to investors, a company can also raise money by taking out a loan. In this case, Demo borrowed $10,000 from the bank. The effect of this transaction is to increase cash and create an obligation (liability) that shows the amount owed to the bank.

The amount that was borrowed is called the **principal** of the loan. The principal does not include **interest**. As time passes, interest will be added to the amount owed to the bank. For example, if the interest rate on this loan is 6% per year (interest rates are generally stated on an annual basis), the interest added during the first year of the loan will be 6% of the $10,000 principal, $600. Using accounting terminology, interest accrues on the loan as time passes. At the point of acquiring the loan, however, only the principal is recorded; since no time has passed since the loan was taken out, no interest has accrued.

The analysis of this transaction and its effects on the basic accounting equation are summarized below:

ANALYSIS OF TRANSACTION 4

Assets (specifically, Cash) **increased** by $10,000

Liabilities (specifically, Bank Loan) **increased** by $10,000

EFFECTS ON THE BASIC ACCOUNTING EQUATION

	Assets			=	Liabilities	+	Shareholders' Equity	
	Cash	+ Equip.	+ Prepaid insur.	=	Bank loan	+	Share capital	+ Retained earnings
Tr. 1	+17,500 F						+17,500	
Tr. 2	−4,500 I	+4,500						
Tr. 3	−360 O		+360					
Tr. 4	+10,000 F				+10,000			

CASHFLOW EFFECT   Since taking out a loan from the bank is a financing activity, the resulting cash inflow is designated with an F.

EARNINGS EFFECT   Since no revenue or expense is involved in this transaction, there is no effect on the company's earnings.

RELATED CONCEPTS—The nature of revenue   As with the issuance of shares (discussed in Transaction 1), taking out a loan creates an inflow of resources into the business; however, no revenue is recorded when a company borrows money. Revenue has to be earned from the operations of the business. Getting financing from creditors does not involve selling goods or services to customers, and consequently does not involve revenue. (In fact, as we will see in Transaction 15, the opposite occurs: when interest is charged on the debt, interest *expense* must be recorded.)

Transaction 5: Purchase of Land for Cash

Demo Company purchased land for $15,000.

ANALYSIS   The purchase of land for cash means that cash decreases by the amount of the purchase price and another asset, land, increases by the same amount.

The analysis of this transaction and its effects on the basic accounting equation are summarized below:

ANALYSIS OF TRANSACTION 5

Assets (specifically, Cash) **decreased** by $15,000

Assets (specifically, Land) **increased** by $15,000

EFFECTS ON THE BASIC ACCOUNTING EQUATION

	Assets				=	Liabilities		+	Shareholders' Equity	
	Cash	+ Equip.	+ Prepaid insur.	+ Land	=	Bank loan		+	Share capital	+ Retained earnings
Tr. 1	+17,500 F								+17,500	
Tr. 2	−4,500 I	+4,500								
Tr. 3	−360 O		+360							
Tr. 4	+10,000 F					+10,000				
Tr. 5	−15,000 I			+15,000						

CASHFLOW EFFECT   Since purchasing a long-term capital asset such as land is classified as an investing activity, the resulting cash outflow is designated with an I.

EARNINGS EFFECT   Since this transaction does not involve revenues or expenses, there is no effect on the company's earnings.

RELATED CONCEPTS   Land is an asset because it has probable future value and the company holds title to it. The probable future value can be viewed as either its future sale price or the value to be derived from its future use. As with other assets, land should be recorded at its acquisition cost. Unlike other long-term capital assets, however, land is not depreciated. This is because it is not consumed the way other capital assets are. Capital assets such as buildings and equipment can be used for only a limited period of time beforc they wear out from use, but land can typically be used for an unlimited period.

Transaction 6: Purchase of Inventory on Account

Demo Company purchased $23,000 of inventory, on account.

ANALYSIS   "On account" means that Demo has been extended credit by its suppliers and will be required to pay for the inventory at a later date.

The substance of this transaction is that the company has received an asset (inventory) from a supplier and, in exchange, has given the supplier a promise to pay for the inventory at a later date. The promise to pay represents an obligation of the company and is therefore recorded as a liability. These types of liabilities are usually referred to as **accounts payable**.

The term "account payable" means an account that Demo will have to pay in the future. It must be recorded as a liability on the day the inventory is purchased, even though the payment is not due until later.

The analysis of this transaction and its effects on the basic accounting equation are summarized below:

ANALYSIS OF TRANSACTION 6

Assets (specifically, Inventory) **increased** by $23,000

Liabilities (specifically, Accounts Payable) **increased** by $23,000

EFFECTS ON THE BASIC ACCOUNTING EQUATION

	Assets					=	Liabilities		+	Shareholders' Equity	
	Cash	+ Equip.	+ Prepaid insur.	+ Land	+ Inven- tory +	=	Bank loan	+ Accts. payable	+	Share capital	+ Retained earnings
Tr. 1	+17,500 F									+17,500	
Tr. 2	−4,500 I	+4,500									
Tr. 3	−360 O		+360								
Tr. 4	+10,000 F						+10,000				
Tr. 5	−15,000 I			+15,000							
Tr. 6					**+23,000**			**+23,000**			

CASHFLOW EFFECT   This transaction has no immediate impact on cash, since no cash has changed hands yet. Cash will be affected later, when the company pays the amount owed to the supplier.

EARNINGS EFFECT   Since no revenue or expense is involved in this transaction, there is no effect on the company's earnings. Net earnings (and therefore retained earnings) will be affected only when the inventory is sold.

RELATED CONCEPTS   As with Transactions 2, 3, and 5, this transaction involves the purchase of an asset. The inventory will be held until it is sold, and should be shown as an asset on the statement of financial position until that time. The cost of goods purchased for inventory is, therefore, classified as an asset until the company sells the inventory. There is no immediate impact on the statement of earnings from this transaction. It will only affect the statement of earnings later, when the inventory is sold.

As with most other assets, the valuation principle for inventory is that it should be recorded at its acquisition cost (i.e., the price paid to obtain it). Accordingly, the inventory is recorded at the amount that the company has to pay for it (its cost), not the amount it will be sold for (its resale value).

Accounts payable are generally settled in a short time period (typically 30 days), and there is generally no interest charged on accounts payable, even though they are equivalent to loans from the supplier.

Occasionally, inventory or other assets are purchased on longer-term credit and a formal loan document called a **note payable** is prepared, as evidence of the liability. In the case of a note payable, interest is usually charged. The interest would be recorded as an expense and as either an outflow of cash, if it is paid, or as an additional liability (interest payable) if it is going to be paid later. Accounting for interest is explained further in Transaction 15.

Transaction 7: Sales on Account

Demo Company sold some of its inventory to customers, on account, for $13,000.

ANALYSIS   The substance of a sale transaction is that a company exchanges an asset that it has for an asset that a customer has. The sale may involve goods (items of inventory), if the company is a retailer, wholesaler, or manufacturer; or it may involve services, if the company is a service provider. In this case, Demo sells goods and the asset it provides is inventory. The asset it receives in exchange from its customers is generally cash, but other possibilities exist. For example, companies often agree to make

LEARNING OBJECTIVE 4

Explain how inventory is accounted for when it is purchased and when it is sold.

sales based on customers' promises to pay later. These are called **sales on account**, or **credit sales**, and they result in the company getting the right to receive payment, usually called **accounts receivable**, in exchange for its goods. An account receivable is an amount that the seller is entitled to receive in the future, when the payment is due from the customer. It is recorded as an account receivable on the day the sale occurs, even though the amount is not due to be received until later.

Because this is an exchange, there are two parts of the transaction to consider: the inflow of the asset that is received, and the outflow of the asset that is given up. The inflow results in an increase in an asset (accounts receivable) and is also recorded as a revenue, which causes an increase in the shareholders' equity (retained earnings). The outflow results in a decrease in an asset (inventory) and is also recorded as an expense, which causes a decrease in the shareholders' equity (retained earnings). If the inflow or revenue is *more* than the outflow or expense, the company has generated income or a **profit** from the transaction. If the inflow (revenue) is less than the outflow (expense), the company has experienced a **loss** on the exchange.

LEARNING OBJECTIVE 5

Identify operating activities and describe their effects on the financial statements.

The increases and decreases in shareholders' equity from sales transactions such as this are typically called **sales revenue** and **cost of goods sold** (a type of expense), respectively.

Because the analysis which follows focuses on the basic accounting equation, the effects of both the sales revenue and the cost of goods sold (expense) will be shown as affecting the retained earnings portion of shareholders' equity. Remember from our earlier discussion that *net income (revenues minus expenses) increases retained earnings*. Therefore, it should be logical that *revenues increase retained earnings and expenses decrease retained earnings*. Showing revenues and expenses as increases or decreases in retained earnings is a temporary shortcut that we use in this chapter, to introduce you to the analysis of transactions. In future chapters, revenues and expenses will be recorded in their own accounts.

The remaining question in the analysis is how to value the inflow and the outflow. The inflow (revenue) should be recorded using the *selling price* of the goods being sold, while the outflow (expense) should be recorded using Demo's cost of the goods sold. Based on the information in Transaction 7, the selling price of the goods sold was $13,000. Therefore, retained earnings (sales revenue) and assets (accounts receivable) will both be increased by $13,000.

Transaction 7 gives no information about the cost of the goods that were sold; this is covered in Transaction 8. Although it may seem odd to analyze and record these two simultaneous events separately, it is necessary because they involve two different values: the retail price at which Demo sells the goods to its customers, and the cost price at which Demo bought the goods from its suppliers. For the same reason, when a clerk in a store rings up a sale, a record is made of the sales revenue and the increase in cash (or accounts receivable, in the case of a sale on account), but the salesperson usually does not know the cost of the item that is being sold. The cost is determined and recorded separately, as it will be for Demo in Transaction 8.

The analysis of Transaction 7 and its effects on the basic accounting equation are summarized below:

ANALYSIS OF TRANSACTION 7

Assets (specifically, Accounts Receivable) **increased** by $13,000
Shareholders' Equity (specifically, Retained Earnings) **increased** by $13,000

EFFECTS ON THE BASIC ACCOUNTING EQUATION

	Cash	+ Equip.	+ Prepaid insur.	+ Land	+ Inven- tory	+ Accts. receiv.	= Bank loan	+ Accts. payable	+	Share capital	+ Retained earnings
	Assets						= **Liabilities**			+ **Shareholders' Equity**	
Tr. 1	+17,500 F									+17,500	
Tr. 2	−4,500 I	+4,500									
Tr. 3	−360 O		+360								
Tr. 4	+10,000 F						+10,000				
Tr. 5	−15,000 I			+15,000							
Tr. 6					+23,000			+23,000			
Tr. 7						**+13,000**					**+13,000 R**

Notice that the basic accounting equation is still in balance after these entries are made.

CASHFLOW EFFECT   This transaction has no immediate effect on cash. Because this sale is on account, the effect on cash will not occur until Demo collects the account receivable.

EARNINGS EFFECT   Since sales are revenues that will be reported on the statement of earnings, the amount in the retained earnings column has been designated with an R.

RELATED CONCEPTS—Revenue recognition   The timing of the recognition of revenues and expenses is an important decision that management must make in record-ing transactions and preparing financial statements. There is an underlying conflict between reporting income information in a *timely* manner and being assured that the information is *reliable*.

Consider three possible points in time for when a sale could be recorded:

1. At one extreme, it might be argued that a company should record a sale as soon as a customer signs a contract for the future delivery of inventory, even though the goods have not yet been delivered and the customer has not yet paid for them.

2. At the other extreme, it might be argued that the sale should not be recorded until the entire process has been completed (i.e., when the company has made the delivery and the customer has paid for the goods).

3. As an intermediate position, it might be argued that the sale should be recorded when the company delivers the goods, even though the customer has not yet paid for them.

- In the first case, the company would be assuming that it will eventually deliver the goods to the customer and collect the cash from the sale. However, these are both uncertain events that may not materialize. A statement of earnings prepared on this basis would be very timely but not totally reliable, and shareholders might be misled into thinking that the company is doing better than it really is.

- In the second case, by delaying recognition of the sale until the goods have been delivered and the cash has been collected, all the uncertainty will have been resolved; however, a significant amount of time may have passed. A statement of earnings prepared on this basis would be totally reliable but not very timely, and would not provide a good measure of the company's business activity during the period(s) before the cash is collected.

- In the third case, by delaying recognition of the sale until the goods have been delivered the uncertainty about the delivery will be resolved, but not the uncertainty about the collection of the cash. A statement of earnings prepared on this basis would be less timely but more reliable than the first case, and more timely but less reliable than the second case.

LEARNING OBJECTIVE 6

Explain the basic concepts of revenue recognition and expense matching.

The accrual basis of accounting attempts to balance the trade-off between timeliness and reliability, and measures performance (by recording revenues and expenses) in the period in which the performance takes place. Under the accrual basis of accounting, **revenue recognition criteria** are used to determine when revenue should be recorded (i.e., when the earning process has been substantially completed). Chapter 4 discusses these criteria in detail, so the following discussion will deal only with general principles.

Generally, revenue should not be recorded when a customer places an order or signs a contract (as described in the first case above), because the company has not completed the major things it must do to earn the revenue. The company must still deliver the goods, which is a major part of the earning process. On the other hand, it would not usually be necessary for the company to wait until the cash is collected and the entire process is finished (as described in the second case above) before the revenue could be recognized. In most situations, the revenue can be recorded when the company delivers the goods (as described in the third case above), as long as it is *reasonably* sure that it will be able to collect the cash.

The revenue recognition criteria used under the accrual basis of accounting provide shareholders with assurance that the amounts reported as revenues and expenses on the statement of earnings are reasonable, and that it is very likely that the revenues and expenses that have been recorded will ultimately result in similar cash flows.

As mentioned earlier, the alternative to the accrual basis is the cash basis of accounting. If the cash basis were used, events would be recorded whenever their cash effects occur. For example, sales revenue would be recorded when cash is received from customers, and the cost of goods sold expense would be recorded when the cash is paid for purchases of inventory. As a result, on this basis you could record revenues from selling inventory in a later accounting period than the expenses for purchasing it. Or, if the company purchased its inventory on account (to be paid for later), you could record revenues from selling the inventory in an earlier period than you record the expenses for purchasing it. In either case, you would have the revenue recorded in one accounting period and its associated expense in another, and the statement of earnings would not show the company's performance in a meaningful way. This is the main reason why the cash basis of accounting is not used very often. (In the past, most not-for-profit organizations used the cash basis, but today most of them have switched to the accrual basis of accounting. However, the cash basis is still used by some not-for-profit organizations, farmers, fishers, and professional service companies.)

For a retail business such as Demo Company, the revenue recognition criteria are generally met when the inventory is transferred to the customer. Therefore, in the preceding analysis, the result of Transaction 7 is to recognize revenues (which increases the retained earnings). We assume that once the goods have been delivered, Demo knows how much it has earned and is reasonably sure that it will be able to collect its accounts receivable. Therefore, it should recognize revenues when the goods are transferred to customers, and not wait until the cash is collected.

Another equally important aspect of accrual-basis accounting is the **matching concept**. This principle of accounting requires that all the costs that are associated with generating sales should be matched on the statement of earnings with the revenue that has been earned. That is, the cost of goods sold (and any other expenses) related to this revenue should be recognized in the same period and reported on the same statement of earnings as the sales revenue. Transaction 8 deals with the cost of goods sold related to this transaction.

Transaction 8: Cost of Goods Sold

The cost of the items that were sold and removed from inventory during January was $9,000.

ANALYSIS As explained in the analysis of Transaction 7, there are two parts to sales transactions. Transaction 7 dealt with the revenue side of the January sales. In this transaction, the costs or expenses that are to be matched with the revenues are analyzed.

The effect of the outflow of the items that were sold is to decrease both the assets (inventory) and the shareholders' equity (retained earnings) by the cost of the goods that have been sold to customers. The cost of goods sold is an expense, which decreases the net income and retained earnings. It is one of the many expenses that the company will show on its statement of earnings.

The analysis of this transaction and its effects on the basic accounting equation are summarized below:

ANALYSIS OF TRANSACTION 8

Assets (specifically, Inventory) **decreased** by $9,000

Shareholders' Equity (specifically, Retained Earnings) **decreased** by $9,000

EFFECTS ON THE BASIC ACCOUNTING EQUATION

	Cash	+ Equip.	+ Prepaid insur.	+ Land	+ Inven-tory	+ Accts. receiv.	=	Bank loan	+ Accts. payable	+	Share capital	+ Retained earnings
Tr. 1	+17,500 F										+17,500	
Tr. 2	−4,500 I	+4,500										
Tr. 3	−360 O		+360									
Tr. 4	+10,000 F							+10,000				
Tr. 5	−15,000 I			+15,000								
Tr. 6				+23,000					+23,000			
Tr. 7						+13,000						+13,000 R
Tr. 8					−9,000							−9,000 E

CASHFLOW EFFECT This transaction has no effect on cash. The cash flow effects of inventory transactions occur when payments are made for the goods that were purchased.

EARNINGS EFFECT The cost of goods that have been sold is an expense that will be reported on the statement of earnings. Accordingly, the amount in the retained earnings column has been designated with an E.

RELATED CONCEPTS—The matching principle As explained earlier, in the analysis of Transaction 7, when revenues are recognized the matching concept requires that the expenses associated with those revenues be recognized as well. Under accrual-basis accounting, the cost of inventory is held in an asset account until it is sold; when it is sold, it is transferred to an expense account. This illustrates a very important concept, so further elaboration is warranted: Under accrual-basis accounting, *a cost can be classified as either an asset or an expense, depending on its nature.*

- If the cost represents something that still has value to the company and will be of economic benefit to it in the future, it is classified as an asset and reported on the statement of financial position.

- If the cost represents something that has already given up its value to the company and will not be of further benefit to it in the future, it is classified as an *expense* and reported on the statement of earnings.

Many costs are initially classified as assets but eventually reclassified as expenses. For example, while Demo holds the inventory, its cost is recorded as an asset (inventory); but when the inventory is sold, its cost ceases to be an asset and must be transferred to an expense account (cost of goods sold). For a retailer such as Demo, the inventory's cost is the wholesale price that Demo paid to acquire it.

Transaction 9: Collections from Customers on Account

During the month, Demo Company received $11,000 from customers as payments on their accounts.

ANALYSIS The receipt of cash from customers increases Demo's cash. Because the company received this money from its customers as payments on their accounts, the value of the accounts receivable decreases by the amount of the payments received.

The analysis of this transaction and its effects on the basic accounting equation are summarized below:

ANALYSIS OF TRANSACTION 9

Assets (specifically, Cash) **increased** by $11,000
Assets (specifically, Accounts Receivable) **decreased** by $11,000

EFFECTS ON THE BASIC ACCOUNTING EQUATION

	Cash	+ Equip.	+ Prepaid insur.	+ Land	+ Inven- tory	+ Accts. receiv.	=	Bank loan	+ Accts. payable	+		Share capital	+ Retained earnings
Tr. 1	+17,500 F											+17,500	
Tr. 2	−4,500 I	+4,500											
Tr. 3	−360 O		+360										
Tr. 4	+10,000 F							+10,000					
Tr. 5	−15,000 I			+15,000									
Tr. 6					+23,000				+23,000				
Tr. 7					+13,000								+13,000 R
Tr. 8					−9,000								−9,000 E
Tr. 9	+11,000 O					−11,000							

CASHFLOW EFFECT Since collecting cash from customers is a basic operating activity for a business, the amount in the cash column has been designated with an O to indicate that it will be reported under operating activities on the statement of cash flows.

EARNINGS EFFECT It is extremely important to note that this transaction does not involve revenues, and therefore does not affect the company's earnings.

RELATED CONCEPTS The effect on the company's earnings was recorded earlier, in Transaction 7, when the original sale occurred and the revenue was earned. Since the revenue was already recognized when the sale was made, there is no revenue recorded when the account is collected; one asset (accounts receivable) is simply replaced by another asset (cash).

Accounts receivable are generally short-term credit arrangements (typically for a period of 30 days), and do not usually involve interest charges. If this were a **note receivable** (indicating that a formal document had been prepared and signed, as evidence of the obligation), interest charges would probably be specified. When the customer's payment includes interest, the amount of cash received is more than the selling price and the extra amount is recorded as interest revenue.

Transaction 10: Payments to Suppliers on Account

Demo Company made payments of $13,500 on its accounts payable.

ANALYSIS Cash payments made by the company result in a decrease in an asset— cash. In this case, because the payment is being made for goods that were purchased earlier, on account, there is a corresponding decrease in a liability—accounts payable.

The analysis of this transaction and its effects on the basic accounting equation are summarized below:

ANALYSIS OF TRANSACTION 10

Assets (specifically, Cash) **decreased** by $13,500
Liabilities (specifically, Accounts Payable) **decreased** by $13,500

EFFECTS ON THE BASIC ACCOUNTING EQUATION

	Assets						=	Liabilities		+	Shareholders' Equity	
	Cash	+ Equip.	+ Prepaid insur.	+ Land	+ Inven- tory	+ Accts. receiv.	=	Bank loan	+ Accts. + payable	+	Share capital	+ Retained earnings
Tr. 1	+17,500 F										+17,500	
Tr. 2	−4,500 I	+4,500										
Tr. 3	−360 O		+360									
Tr. 4	+10,000 F							+10,000				
Tr. 5	−15,000 I			+15,000								
Tr. 6					+23,000				+23,000			
Tr. 7						+13,000						+13,000 R
Tr. 8					−9,000							−9,000 E
Tr. 9	+11,000 O					−11,000						
Tr. 10	**−13,500 O**								**−13,500**			

CASHFLOW EFFECT Because paying cash to its suppliers is a basic operating activity for a business, the amount in the cash column has an O beside it to indicate that the cash outflow will be reported under operating activities on the statement of cash flows.

EARNINGS EFFECT   Note that paying this debt does not result in an expense being recorded; there is simply a decrease in an asset and a corresponding decrease in a liability. Therefore, there is no effect on the company's earnings.

RELATED CONCEPTS   Accounts payable are, of course, the opposite of accounts receivable. Whenever a purchase or sale is made on account, the party making the purchase records an account payable, and the party making the sale records an account receivable.

With *accounts payable*, there are typically no interest charges (unless the accounts are overdue). However, longer-term financing arrangements (usually represented by *notes payable*) almost always involve interest charges. When interest is involved, the total amount paid to settle the obligation has to be divided between the amount that is repayment of the original liability (i.e., the principal amount of the debt) and the amount that is payment of the interest expense.

Note again that shareholders' equity (retained earnings) is not affected by Transaction 10. The income effects related to inventory are recorded in the period when the inventory is *sold*, because that is when the cost of the inventory is transferred to an expense account (cost of goods sold). This could occur either before or after the payment of cash to the supplier.

Transaction 11: Cash Expenses

Demo Company paid the following costs for the month of January: $2,000 for salaries; $500 for rent; $300 for utilities (telephone, electricity, water, etc.).

ANALYSIS   Because they were incurred to operate the business for the month of January, rather than to acquire something that will be used up in the future, the costs in this transaction should be recorded as expenses for January. (Remember that *unexpired costs* are assets, and *expired costs* are expenses.) Expenses reduce net earnings for the period, which will reduce retained earnings.

Because the payments of these costs required outflows of cash, the asset cash is decreased. This is counter-balanced (i.e., the accounting equation is kept in balance) by a decrease in the retained earnings portion of shareholders' equity, representing the effect of the expenses. Note that, in order to provide as much information as possible about the operation of the business, each of these expenses is listed separately. This ensures that when the statement of earnings is prepared the details of the company's expenses can be shown.

The analysis of this transaction and its effects on the basic accounting equation are summarized below:

ANALYSIS OF TRANSACTION 11

Assets (specifically, Cash) **decreased** by $2,000, $500, and $300
Shareholders' Equity (specifically, Retained Earnings) **decreased** by $2,000, $500, and $300

CASHFLOW EFFECT   Since these payments are related to the operation of the business, they are classified as operating cash flows. Accordingly, the amounts entered in the cash column have an O beside them.

EARNINGS EFFECT   Since these costs are expenses, the amounts listed in the retained earnings column have an E beside them and will be reported on the statement of earnings.

EFFECTS ON THE BASIC ACCOUNTING EQUATION

	Cash	+ Equip.	+ Prepaid insur.	+ Land	+ Inven-tory	+ Accts. receiv.	= Bank loan	+ Accts. payable	+	Share capital	+ Retained earnings
Tr. 1	+17,500 F									+17,500	
Tr. 2	−4,500 I	+4,500									
Tr. 3	−360 O		+360								
Tr. 4	+10,000 F						+10,000				
Tr. 5	−15,000 I			+15,000							
Tr. 6					+23,000			+23,000			
Tr. 7						+13,000					+13,000 R
Tr. 8					−9,000						−9,000 E
Tr. 9	+11,000 O					−11,000					
Tr. 10	−13,500 O							−13,500			
Tr. 11	**−2,000 O**										**−2,000 E**
	−500 O										−500 E
	−300 O										−300 E

Transaction 12: Declaration and Payment of Dividends

Demo Company declared and paid dividends of $250.

ANALYSIS   Dividends are payments to the shareholders of the company, as authorized by the company's board of directors. They distribute part of the company's earnings to its owners. They are not expenses, because they are not incurred to operate the business and generate revenues.

When dividends are declared (i.e., announced by the directors of the company), the effect is to reduce the shareholders' equity (retained earnings) and either to decrease the assets (cash), if the dividends are paid immediately, or to increase the liabilities (dividends payable), if they are to be paid later. In this case, the dividends were declared and paid, so cash is reduced.

The analysis of this transaction and its effects on the basic accounting equation are summarized below:

ANALYSIS OF TRANSACTION 12

Assets (specifically, Cash) **decreased** by $250

Shareholders' Equity (specifically, Retained Earnings) **decreased** by $250

CASHFLOW EFFECT   Because dividends are related to the company's shares (which are a primary source of financing for a business), the payment of dividends is generally classified as a financing activity. Accordingly, the outflow in the cash column has an F beside it.

EFFECTS ON THE BASIC ACCOUNTING EQUATION

	Cash	+ Equip.	+ Prepaid insur.	+ Land	+ Inven- tory	+ Accts. receiv.	=	Bank loan	+ Accts. payable	+	+ Share capital	+ Retained earnings
Tr. 1	+17,500 F										+17,500	
Tr. 2	−4,500 I	+4,500										
Tr. 3	−360 O		+360									
Tr. 4	+10,000 F							+10,000				
Tr. 5	−15,000 I			+15,000								
Tr. 6					+23,000				+23,000			
Tr. 7						+13,000						+13,000 R
Tr. 8					−9,000							−9,000 E
Tr. 9	+11,000 O					−11,000						
Tr. 10	−13,500 O							−13,500				
Tr. 11	−2,000 O											−2,000 E
	−500 O											−500 E
	−300 O											−300 E
Tr. 12	−250 F											−250 D

EARNINGS EFFECT   Notice that, in the shareholders' equity section of the equation, the decrease in the retained earnings column has a D beside it to indicate that this amount represents dividends, not expenses. This is an important distinction because, although dividends and expenses both reduce a company's retained earnings, dividends are not part of the calculation of net income and do not appear on the statement of earnings.

RELATED CONCEPTS   Dividends are determined and announced (declared) by a vote of a company's board of directors. On the date of declaration, they become a legal obligation of the company. If there is a delay between the date the dividends are declared and the date they are paid, a liability (dividends payable) exists between these dates. In the case of Demo Company, however, the dividends are declared and paid in the same accounting period, so the dividends payable account is ignored.

Dividends explain part of the change in retained earnings from the beginning of the period to the end of the period. As discussed previously, net earnings (consisting of revenues minus expenses) increase a company's retained earnings, and dividends declared decrease the retained earnings.

Finally, note once again that dividends are not expenses and do not appear on the statement of earnings.

Transaction 13: Depreciation Expense

Demo Company's accountant determined that the equipment should be depreciated by $150 for the month of January.

ANALYSIS   Whenever an expenditure is made to acquire an asset, there are three general questions to ask about the nature of the transaction:

1. Has an asset been created?

2. If so, what is the value of the asset?

3. When is the value of the asset consumed, or when does the asset cease to exist?

To answer the first question, the criteria for recognizing an asset must be considered. Does the item have probable future value, and does the company own it or have the exclusive right to use it? If the answers to both of these questions are yes, an asset exists and should be recorded.

When Demo originally purchased its equipment, the answer to both of these asset recognition questions was yes. Demo owned the equipment and it had future value, because the equipment was to be used to help operate the business and thus generate revenues. The equipment, therefore, was recorded as an asset when it was purchased (in Transaction 2).

The answer to the second question, regarding the value of the asset, is simply that, according to GAAP, the equipment is valued at its acquisition cost (sometimes called **historical cost**). In this example, the $4,500 that was paid for the equipment when it was purchased represents its historical cost.

The third question (When is the value of the asset consumed, or when does the asset cease to exist?) is a little more difficult to answer. For an asset such as inventory, the answer is relatively simple: the value of the asset is consumed and the asset ceases to exist when it is sold. As a result, inventory simply stays on the statement of financial position as an asset until it is sold; when it is sold, its cost is transferred to an expense (cost of goods sold) on the statement of earnings. For an asset such as equipment, the answer is more complicated. In the case of a long-term asset such as equipment, the asset's value is consumed as time passes and the equipment is used. Consequently, the asset's **useful life** (the time until it will cease to have value) must be estimated. For example, the equipment may be expected to last for five years, at which time it will either be sold, traded in for a new piece of equipment, or discarded.

Because an asset such as equipment is used up over time, its value does not simply stay unchanged on the statement of financial position from one period to another. Instead, to fairly measure the company's net income and satisfy the matching principle, some of its cost should be shown as an expense for each of the periods in which it is used. In other words, we should transfer some of the cost of the asset to an expense account each period, so that the cost of using the equipment will appear on the statement of earnings at the same time as the revenues that are generated from using it. The portion of the asset's cost that is transferred to expense each period is called **depreciation** or **amortization**.

The amount of depreciation (or amortization) expense in any particular period should reflect the portion of the asset's value that was used up during that time. There are many factors to consider in determining the appropriate amount, and therefore many methods for calculating how much the depreciation expense should be each period. Chapter 8 discusses these methods in detail.

The simplest and most common method is **straight-line depreciation**. It assumes that an asset's value is consumed evenly throughout its life and therefore charges the same amount of depreciation expense in each accounting period. The formula for calculating straight-line depreciation is:

$$\text{Straight-Line Depreciation} = \frac{\text{Original Cost} - \text{Estimated Residual Value}}{\text{Estimated Useful Life}}$$

Note that two estimates are required in this calculation. First, the useful life of the asset must be estimated. This could be expressed in years or months, depending on the length of the accounting period. In the Demo Company example, we will be preparing financial statements at the end of each month, so the depreciation expense should be calculated as an amount per month. The second estimate is the **residual value** of the asset. This is how much the asset is expected to be worth at the end of its useful life. For example, if Demo's equipment is expected to have a useful life of two years (24 months) and a residual value of $900 at the end of its life, the monthly depreciation would be calculated as follows:

$$\text{Straight-Line Depreciation} = \frac{\$4{,}500 - \$900}{24 \text{ months}}$$

$$= \$150 \text{ per month}$$

At the end of each month, Demo would reduce the value of the asset (the equipment) on the statement of financial position by $150, and show a $150 expense (depreciation) on the statement of earnings.

The analysis of this transaction and its effects on the basic accounting equation are summarized below:

ANALYSIS OF TRANSACTION 13

Assets (specifically, Equipment) **decreased** by $150
Shareholders' Equity (specifically, Retained Earnings) **decreased** by $150

EFFECTS ON THE BASIC ACCOUNTING EQUATION

	Assets						=	Liabilities		+	Shareholders' Equity	
	Cash	+ Equip.	+ Prepaid insur.	+ Land	+ Inven- tory	+ Accts. receiv.	=	Bank loan	+ Accts. + payable	+	Share capital	+ Retained earnings
Tr. 1	+17,500 F										+17,500	
Tr. 2	−4,500 I	+4,500										
Tr. 3	−360 O		+360									
Tr. 4	+10,000 F							+10,000				
Tr. 5	−15,000 I			+15,000								
Tr. 6					+23,000				+23,000			
Tr. 7						+13,000						+13,000 R
Tr. 8					−9,000							−9,000 E
Tr. 9	+11,000 O					−11,000						
Tr. 10	−13,500 O								−13,500			
Tr. 11	−2,000 O											−2,000 E
	−500 O											−500 E
	−300 O											−300 E
Tr. 12	−250 F											−250 D
Tr. 13		−150										−150 E

CASHFLOW EFFECT   This transaction has no effect on cash. The cash outflow for the equipment occurred in the period when it was purchased. There might be a cash *inflow* in the future, when the equipment is sold at the end of its useful life. However, during the asset's life, depreciation simply transfers a portion of the equipment's cost from the asset account to an expense account; it does not involve cash.

EARNINGS EFFECT   Notice that the amount deducted in the retained earnings column has an E beside it, indicating that it is an expense and will therefore be reported on the statement of earnings.

RELATED CONCEPTS—Depreciation   As will be discussed further in Chapter 8, the choice of which depreciation method should be used is influenced by several factors, including the nature of the asset and how the company will use it. To achieve a good matching of revenues and expenses, a company should choose the depreciation method that best reflects the pattern of the economic benefits that will be received from using the asset.

HELPFUL HINT

The process of depreciating a capital asset is just one example of how a cost can be initially recorded as an asset but eventually transferred to an expense as time passes and the cost expires (i.e., the benefits provided by the asset are consumed). Conceptually, it is similar to how a prepaid expense is handled, as illustrated in Transaction 14.

Note that, in the table above, the $150 reduction of the asset's value has been taken directly out of the equipment account. In actual practice, however, the reduction in the value of a capital asset due to depreciation is kept in a separate account, called **accumulated depreciation**. Over time, this account collects (i.e., accumulates) all the reductions in the asset's value. When a statement of financial position is prepared, the balance in the accumulated depreciation account is deducted from the balance in the capital asset account, and the net amount (i.e., the *remaining* cost of the asset) is shown. You will see this in Demo Company's statement of financial position, on page 105. An account such as accumulated depreciation is called a **contra-asset**, because it is offset against, or deducted from, the related asset.

By using a separate account for the accumulated depreciation, both the original cost of the asset and the amount that has been written off through depreciation can be reported. This is desirable, because users of financial statements often find it helpful to know both the original cost of an asset and its remaining cost.

Transaction 14: Insurance Expense

Insurance expense has to be recorded for January. The insurance policy (which was purchased in Transaction 3) covers the six-month period from January 1 to June 30, 2011.

ANALYSIS   As discussed in the analysis of Transaction 3, insurance is an example of a prepaid expense because the cost of the insurance coverage was paid in advance of the coverage period. Therefore, at the beginning of January when the insurance policy was purchased, it was recorded as an asset since it had not been used up yet. Only as time passes is the asset (the insurance coverage) consumed.

In this example, the portion of the coverage that is consumed as each month passes is one month out of six, or one-sixth of the total cost. Therefore, we should charge $1/6 \times \$360 = \$60$ to expense each month, to spread the cost of the insurance evenly over the coverage period. Accordingly, for the month of January, $60 of the insurance cost should be treated as an expense. The remaining $300 of the insurance cost at the end of January should be treated as an asset, representing the value of the remaining coverage that will be consumed in the future (i.e., between February 1 and June 30).

The analysis of this transaction and its effects on the basic accounting equation are summarized below:

HELPFUL HINT

Remember that costs can be classified as either expenses or assets, depending on whether or not they have expired (i.e., been consumed). *Expired costs* relate to the past and are reported on the statement of earnings as expenses; *unexpired costs* relate to the future and are reported on the statement of financial position as assets.

ANALYSIS OF TRANSACTION 14

Shareholders' Equity (specifically, Retained Earnings) **decreased** by $60

Assets (specifically, Prepaid Insurance) **decreased** by $60

EFFECTS ON THE BASIC ACCOUNTING EQUATION

	Cash	+ Equip.	+ Prepaid insur.	+ Land	+ Inventory	+ Accts. receiv.	= Bank loan	+ Accts. payable	+	+ Share capital	+ Retained earnings
Tr. 1	+17,500 F									+17,500	
Tr. 2	−4,500 I	+4,500									
Tr. 3	−360 O		+360								
Tr. 4	+10,000 F						+10,000				
Tr. 5	−15,000 I			+15,000							
Tr. 6					+23,000			+23,000			
Tr. 7						+13,000					+13,000 R
Tr. 8					−9,000						−9,000 E
Tr. 9	+11,000 O					−11,000					
Tr. 10	−13,500 O							−13,500			
Tr. 11	−2,000 O										−2,000 E
	−500 O										−500 E
	−300 O										−300 E
Tr. 12	−250 F										−250 D
Tr. 13		−150									−150 E
Tr. 14			**−60**								**−60 E**

CASHFLOW EFFECT   This transaction is similar to the preceding one, and has no effect on cash. The cash outflow for the insurance was shown when the asset was purchased. During each period of the asset's life, adjustments such as this are made to transfer a portion of the cost of the insurance from the asset account to an expense account; these adjustments do not involve cash.

EARNINGS EFFECT   Notice that the deduction under retained earnings has an E beside it, indicating that this is an expense which will be reported on the statement of earnings for January.

You should also note that the balance in the prepaid insurance account will now be the correct amount as of the end of January ($300, representing five remaining months of insurance coverage), because when we recorded Transaction 3 we added $360 to the prepaid insurance column and in this transaction we deducted $60 from it.

RELATED CONCEPTS—The matching principle   The initial handling of prepaid expenses as assets is dictated by the accrual basis of accounting and the principle of matching expenses with revenues in the proper accounting periods. In this case, although the cash payment for the insurance is made in January, we cannot classify the entire $360 as an expense of that month. Rather, the cost must be spread over the six-month period of the insurance coverage. As each month goes by, one-sixth of the insurance cost must be transferred to an expense account.

Exhibit 2-1 shows a timeline illustrating the effects of a prepaid expense and the timing issue involved. Part of the cost will be an expense on the statement of earnings in the current period, and the remaining portion will be an asset carried forward on the statement of financial position into the following period.

PREPAID EXPENSES: General Model

EXHIBIT 2-1

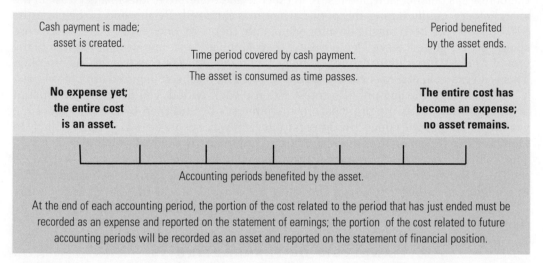

Exhibit 2-2 illustrates how the general concepts related to prepaid expenses are applied to the specific case of Demo's insurance policy.

PREPAID EXPENSES: Insurance Example

EXHIBIT 2-2

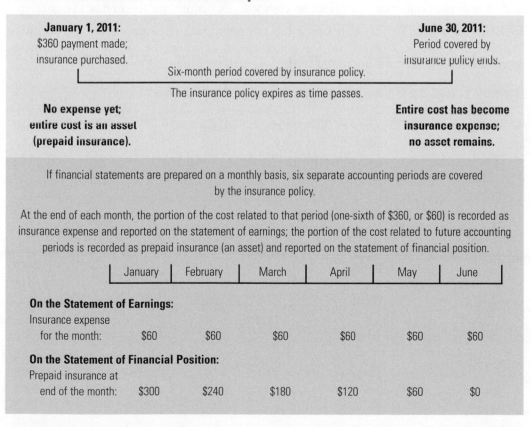

	January	February	March	April	May	June
On the Statement of Earnings: Insurance expense for the month:	$60	$60	$60	$60	$60	$60
On the Statement of Financial Position: Prepaid insurance at end of the month:	$300	$240	$180	$120	$60	$0

Transaction 15: Interest Expense

Interest expense has to be recognized for the month of January. The interest rate on the bank loan (which originated in Transaction 4) is 6% per year, and interest payments are to be made quarterly (i.e., at the end of every three months).

ANALYSIS   Interest is the amount charged by lenders for the use of their money. From the borrower's point of view, interest is an expense and therefore results in a decrease in the shareholders' equity during the period when it is incurred. By the end of January, the $10,000 loan has been outstanding for one month; therefore, one month's interest expense should be recognized. Since Demo has not yet paid the interest (and will not pay it until the end of March), it has to recognize a liability now for its obligation to pay the interest later. This is an example of an **accrued expense**: a cost that has been incurred but not yet paid.

To calculate the amount of interest expense each period, you multiply the amount of the loan (known as the principal) by the interest rate and then by the fraction of the year that has passed (since the interest rate is always expressed as a yearly rate). In Demo's case, the amount of interest incurred in January is $10,000 \times 6\% \times 1/12 = \$50$. The shareholders' equity (retained earnings) will therefore be decreased by $50, to recognize the interest expense, and a liability (interest payable) will be increased by $50, to recognize the obligation to pay the interest when it is due at the end of the quarter.

The analysis of this transaction and its effects on the basic accounting equation are summarized below:

ANALYSIS OF TRANSACTION 15

Shareholders' Equity (specifically, Retained Earnings) **decreased** by $50

Liabilities (specifically, Interest Payable) **increased** by $50

CASHFLOW EFFECT   This transaction does not affect cash. Because the interest on this loan is only paid quarterly, the effect on cash will not occur until the end of the quarter.

EARNINGS EFFECT   Even though it has not been paid, the interest on the loan is an expense and will be reported on the statement of earnings for the month of January. Accordingly, the amount deducted in the retained earnings column has an E beside it.

EFFECTS ON THE BASIC ACCOUNTING EQUATION

	Cash	+ Equip.	+ Prepaid insur.	+ Land	+ Inven- tory	+ Accts. receiv.	= Bank loan	+ Accts. payable	+ Interest payable	+ Share capital	+ Retained earnings
Tr. 1	+17,500 F									+17,500	
Tr. 2	−4,500 I	+4,500									
Tr. 3	−360 O		+360								
Tr. 4	+10,000 F						+10,000				
Tr. 5	−15,000 I			+15,000							
Tr. 6					+23,000		+23,000				
Tr. 7						+13,000					+13,000 R
Tr. 8					−9,000						−9,000 E
Tr. 9	+11,000 O					−11,000					
Tr. 10	−13,500 O							−13,500			
Tr. 11	−2,000 O										−2,000 E
	−500 O										−500 E
	−300 O										−300 E
Tr. 12	−250 F										−250 D
Tr. 13		−150									−150 E
Tr. 14			−60								−60 E
Tr. 15									+50		−50 E

RELATED CONCEPTS—Accrued expenses Accrual-basis accounting requires that expenses be recognized in the period when they are incurred, rather than when they are paid. This is so they appear on the statement of earnings in the appropriate period and are matched against the revenues that they help to generate. Accrued expenses therefore result in liabilities that appear on the statement of financial position at the end of the period, representing the expenses that have been incurred by that date and will be paid at a future date.

Exhibit 2-3 illustrates how accrued expenses are recognized on the statement of earnings in the period when they are incurred, and result in a related liability on the statement of financial position until they are paid in a future period.

ACCRUED EXPENSES: General Model

EXHIBIT 2-3

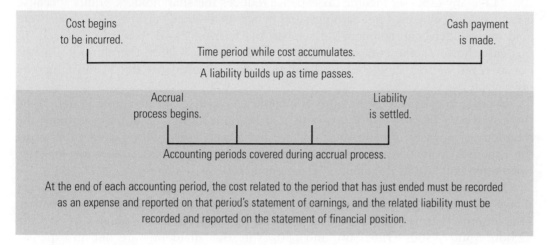

Cost begins to be incurred.		Cash payment is made.
	Time period while cost accumulates.	
	A liability builds up as time passes.	

Accrual process begins.		Liability is settled.
	Accounting periods covered during accrual process.	

At the end of each accounting period, the cost related to the period that has just ended must be recorded as an expense and reported on that period's statement of earnings, and the related liability must be recorded and reported on the statement of financial position.

Exhibit 2-4 illustrates how the general concepts related to accrued expenses are applied to the specific example of the interest on Demo Company's loan.

ACCRUED EXPENSES: Interest Example

EXHIBIT 2-4

January 1, 2011:		**March 31, 2011:**
$10,000 borrowed; interest begins to be incurred.		Quarterly interest payment is made
	Three-month period covered by quarterly interest payment.	
	Interest expense and interest payable accrue as time passes.	

If financial statements are prepared on a monthly basis, three separate accounting periods are covered by each quarterly interest payment.

At the end of each month, the cost related to that period ($10,000 × 6% × 1/12, or $50) is recorded as interest expense and reported on the statement of earnings. At the same time, a liability for the amount to be paid in the future is recorded and reported on the statement of financial position.

	January	February	March	
On the Statement of Earnings:				
Interest expense for the month:	$50	50	$50	
On the Statement of Financial Position:				
Interest payable at the end of the month:	$50	$100	$150	before the payment is made;
			$0	after the payment is made.

Transaction 16: Income Tax Expense

Income tax expense must be recognized each accounting period, even though the company does not have to pay the tax until later. Demo's income tax rate is 25%.

ANALYSIS Businesses that are incorporated, such as Demo Company Limited, must pay taxes on the income they earn. This income tax is an expense of doing business in Canada, and therefore must be recognized on the company's statement of earnings. In addition, if the tax has not yet been paid, the amount owed must be reported on the statement of financial position as a liability. This is another example of an accrued expense (i.e., a cost of operating the business that has been incurred but not yet paid).

Like any expense, income tax expense reduces the shareholders' equity (because it reduces the company's net earnings, and hence its retained earnings). If the tax were paid immediately, the company's assets (in the form of cash) would be reduced. In this case, however, the company will not pay the tax until later; therefore, its cash is not affected at this time, but its liabilities are increased (in the form of income tax payable).

In order to calculate the amount of income tax expense, we need to first determine the company's *income before tax*. This can be done quite easily by examining the retained earnings column in the table we have been constructing, and subtracting the expenses from the revenue. Since revenue minus expenses equals income, this calculation will give us the amount of income before tax.

To illustrate this process for Demo Company, refer to the table on page 98 that shows the effects of all the preceding transactions on the basic accounting equation. The retained earnings column lists revenue of $13,000 and expenses of $9,000, $2,000, $500, $300, $150, $60, and $50. Note that dividends are not an expense, and are therefore not included in this calculation. By subtracting the expenses from the revenue, Demo's income before tax is found to be $940 (i.e., 13,000 − 9,000 − 2,000 − 500 − 300 − 150 − 60 − 50 = 940). Applying the income tax rate of 25% to this amount, Demo's income tax expense is found to be $235 (i.e., 0.25 × 940 = 235).

The analysis of this transaction and its effects on the basic accounting equation are summarized below:

ANALYSIS OF TRANSACTION 16

Shareholders' Equity (specifically, Retained Earnings) **decreased** by $235

Liabilities (specifically, Income Tax Payable) **increased** by $235

CASHFLOW EFFECT This transaction does not affect cash. The effect on cash will occur later, when the income tax liability is paid.

EARNINGS EFFECT The income tax that will have to be paid for January is an expense and will be reported on the statement of earnings for the month. Accordingly, the amount deducted in the retained earnings column has an E beside it.

EFFECTS ON THE BASIC ACCOUNTING EQUATION

	Cash	+ Equip.	+ Prepaid insur.	+ Land	+ Inven-tory	+ Accts. receiv.	=	Bank loan	+ Accts. payable	+ Interest payable	+ Inc. tax payable	+	Share capital	+ Retained earnings
							Assets =	Liabilities					Shareholders' Equity	
Tr. 1	+17,500 F												+17,500	
Tr. 2	−4,500 I	+4,500												
Tr. 3	−360 O		+360											
Tr. 4	+10,000 F							+10,000						
Tr. 5	−15,000 I			+15,000										
Tr. 6					+23,000				+23,000					
Tr. 7						+13,000								+13,000 R
Tr. 8					−9,000									−9,000 E
Tr. 9	+11,000 O					−11,000								
Tr. 10	−13,500 O								−13,500					
Tr. 11	−2,000 O													−2,000 E
	−500 O													−500 E
	−300 O													−300 E
Tr. 12	−250 F													−250 D
Tr. 13		−150												−150 E
Tr. 14			−60											−60 E
Tr. 15										+50				−50 E
Tr. 16											+235			**−235 E**

RELATED CONCEPTS—The accrual basis of accounting As stated earlier, the accrual basis of accounting requires that expenses be recognized in the period when they are incurred so they appear on the statement of earnings in the appropriate period. This means that even if a company does not have to pay its income tax until later, it must still record the income tax expense that has been incurred during the current accounting period. At the same time, cash will be reduced for any portion of the tax that is paid, and a liability will be recorded for any portion of it that will be paid later. This accrual process ensures that the tax expense appears on the statement of earnings in the period that it relates to, and that a tax liability for the amount owing appears on the statement of financial position at the end of that period. Doing this enables the financial statements to present a true picture of the company's economic performance and financial position.

Although profit-oriented companies have long adhered to these requirements, governments have been slower to move to the accrual basis of accounting, as the following report illustrates.

This completes the analysis of the transactions of Demo Company Limited, for the month of January. Exhibit 2-5 shows the combined effects of these transactions on the basic accounting equation, and the resulting account balances at the end of January.

accounting in the news

Accrual-based Accounting in the Federal Government

Since 2003, the Canadian government has presented its financial statements using the full accrual basis of accounting. The move to full accrual accounting from the previous standard of "modified accrual accounting" shifted the focus of financial reporting from expenditures (recorded when funds are spent) to expenses (recorded when resources are used). This change resulted in the recording of tens of billions of dollars in additional assets and liabilities in the country's financial statements, including:

- inventories and prepaid expenses
- capital assets such as land, buildings, ships, and aircraft
- taxes receivable and taxes payable
- liabilities for pension plans for employees and veterans, as well as for health, dental, disability, and worker's compensation benefits
- liabilities related to such items as the cleanup of contaminated military sites, obligations under capital lease arrangements, and additional liabilities for Aboriginal claims

Prior to 2003, these items did not appear on Canada's statement of financial position, or balance sheet. Instead, they were charged against the annual surplus or deficit in the year the assets were acquired, the cash was received, or the liabilities were paid.

The Finance Department reports that the adoption of full accrual accounting provides a more complete measure of the government's financial position. It also reduces the distortions that arise through the timing of cash receipts and payments, and it properly allocates the costs of expensive capital items over the periods of their use, rather than simply the period when they were acquired. The result is a better estimation of the costs of government programs from year to year.

Source: Finance Canada

Note that, because this is a new company, the beginning balances in all the accounts are zero. However, if a company has account balances from previous periods it is essential to include them, because the statement of financial position totals must be cumulative.

Exhibit 2-5 provides all the information required to prepare Demo's financial statements: the statement of earnings, the statement of financial position, and the statement of cash flows. We will now look at each of these.

**EFFECTS OF DEMO COMPANY'S TRANSACTIONS IN JANUARY 2011
ON THE BASIC ACCOUNTING EQUATION**

EXHIBIT 2-5

	Cash	+ Equip.	+ Prepaid insur.	+ Land	+ Inven- tory	+ Accts. receiv.	=	Bank loan	+ Accts. payable	+ Interest payable	+ Inc. tax payable	+	Share capital	+ Retained earnings
				Assets			=			Liabilities		+	Shareholders' Equity	
Beginning balances	0	+ 0	+ 0	+ 0	+ 0	+ 0	=	0	+ 0	+ 0	+ 0	+	0	+ 0
Tr. 1	+17,500 F												+17,500	
Tr. 2	−4,500 I	+4,500												
Tr. 3	−360 O		+360											
Tr. 4	−10,000 F							+10,000						
Tr. 5	−15,000 I			+15,000										
Tr. 6					+23,000				+23,000					
Tr. 7						+13,000								+13,000 R
Tr. 8					−9,000									−9,000 E
Tr. 9	+11,000 O					−11,000								
Tr. 10	−13,500 O								−13,500					
Tr. 11	−2,000 O													−2,000 E
	−500 O													−500 E
	−300 O													−300 E
Tr. 12	−250 F													−250 D
Tr. 13		−150												−150 E
Tr. 14			−60											−60 E
Tr. 15										+50				−50 E
Tr. 16											+235			−235 E
Ending balances	2,090	+ 4,350	+ 300	+ 15,000	+ 14,000	+ 2,000	=	10,000	+ 9,500	+ 50	+ 235	+	17,500	+ 455

Total Assets $37,740 = Total Liabilities and Shareholders' Equity $37,740

Legend: F Financing Activity   I Investing Activity   O Operating Activity   R Revenue   E Expense   D Dividend

FINANCIAL STATEMENTS

Statement of Earnings

If necessary, you should refer to Chapter 1 for a description of the statement of earnings.

The statement of earnings can be constructed from the information recorded in the retained earnings column in Exhibit 2-5. Since we labelled each of the amounts that affected retained earnings with an R to indicate a revenue, an E to indicate an expense, or a D to indicate dividends, this will be an easy task. Each of the revenue and expense items in the retained earnings column of Exhibit 2-5 has to be reported on the statement of earnings.

LEARNING OBJECTIVE 7

Prepare a simple set of financial statements, reflecting a series of business transactions.

In its simplest form, the statement of earnings would be presented as follows. While it would normally be prepared on a comparative basis, because this is Demo's first month of operations there are no figures from previous periods for comparison.

DEMO COMPANY LIMITED
STATEMENT OF EARNINGS
FOR THE MONTH ENDED JANUARY 31, 2011

Revenue:	
Sales	$13,000
Expenses:	
Cost of goods sold	(9,000)
Salaries	(2,000)
Rent	(500)
Utilities	(300)
Depreciation	(150)
Insurance	(60)
Interest	(50)
Income tax	(235)
Net earnings	$ 705

There are many other ways to organize and present the information on the statement of earnings; however, the net result would be the same. There is a detailed discussion of the statement of earnings and its alternative formats in Chapter 4.

Note that, because they are not an expense, dividends do not appear on the statement of earnings. Rather, they are a distribution of a portion of the earnings to the shareholders, and therefore affect retained earnings. The combination of the income earned and the dividends declared during the period explains the change in retained earnings, as follows:

Beginning balance of retained earnings (January 1, 2011)	$ 0
Add: Net earnings in January	705
Deduct: Dividends declared in January	(250)
Ending balance of retained earnings (January 31, 2011)	$455

Statement of Financial Position

At the bottom of Exhibit 2-5, you can see the net result of Demo's January transactions. These figures represent the amounts that should appear on the company's statement of financial position at the end of the month. However, **the table presented in Exhibit 2-5 is not a statement of financial position**. Although the same ending balances from Exhibit 2-5 will be shown on the statement of financial position, we have to reorganize the data and present it in a more formal manner.

The statement of financial position could be presented as shown below. Like all the financial statements, the statement of financial position would normally be prepared on a comparative basis; however, this being Demo's first month, there are no comparative figures.

Notice that the equipment is first shown at its original cost of $4,500; then the portion that has been written off (i.e., the $150 of depreciation that has been charged to date) is deducted, leaving the remaining amount of $4,350. This net amount is usually referred to as the asset's **book value** or **carrying value**.

You should also note that Demo's statement of financial position is indeed balanced; that is, the company's total assets are equal to the sum of its liabilities and shareholders' equity (as they must be, to satisfy the basic accounting equation).

DEMO COMPANY LIMITED
STATEMENT OF FINANCIAL POSITION
JANUARY 31, 2011

Current assets:			
Cash		$ 2,090	
Accounts receivable		2,000	
Inventory		14,000	
Prepaid insurance		300	
			$18,390
Non-current assets:			
Land		15,000	
Equipment, at its original cost	$4,500		
Less: Accumulated depreciation	(150)		
		4,350	
			19,350
Total assets			**$37,740**
Current liabilities:			
Accounts payable		$ 9,500	
Interest payable		50	
Income tax payable		235	
			$ 9,785
Non-current liabilities:			
Bank loan			10,000
Total liabilities			**19,785**
Shareholders' equity:			
Share capital		$17,500	
Retained earnings		455	
Total shareholders' equity			**17,955**
Total liabilities and shareholders' equity			**$37,740**

This is a **classified statement of financial position**, which means that the assets and liabilities have been categorized as current and non-current.

As you may recall from Chapter 1, **current assets** include short-term items such as cash, accounts receivable (that will be converted to cash within a year), and inventory and prepaid expenses (that will be sold or consumed within a year). Within the current assets section, the individual items are generally listed in the order of their **liquidity**—i.e., how quickly they can be converted into cash. Thus, the most liquid

LEARNING OBJECTIVE 8

Explain the basic classification of items on a statement of financial position.

current assets, cash and accounts receivable, are listed first, followed by inventory and then items such as prepaid expenses (the least liquid).

Assets that will last more than one year, such as land and equipment, are classified as **non-current assets**. Within the non-current assets section, the items are typically listed in order of permanency, starting with the assets with the longest lives. Thus, land will usually be listed first, followed by buildings, and then equipment, vehicles, and so on—based on the length of time these assets will be useful to the company.

Current liabilities are short-term obligations that will be paid within one year, such as accounts payable and accrued liabilities. Since Demo's bank loan is not due to be repaid for five years, it is classified as a **non-current liability**. Within the liabilities, the individual items are generally listed according to how quickly they will require the use of cash. Those that will become due soonest are usually listed first; those with the longest durations are typically listed last. However, there is no firm requirement; the items can be listed in whatever order the company thinks is most informative.

Variations in Statement of Financial Position

Although the statement of financial position always has separate sections for assets, liabilities, and shareholders' equity, there are many variations in how these can be presented. For example, in the sequence of the items on the statement of financial position typical European practice is the opposite of that in North American practice. This was first discussed in Chapter 1, when we looked at H&M's balance sheet. For another example, look at the consolidated balance sheet or statement of financial position for the Lindt & Sprüngli Group, which is reproduced in Part A of Exhibit 2-6. (You might be familiar with some of this company's chocolate products, marketed under the Lindt brand.)

Notice that, on Lindt & Sprüngli's balance sheet, the assets section begins with the non-current assets, followed by the current assets. On the other side of its balance sheet, the liabilities and shareholders' equity sections are reversed; shareholders' equity is shown *before* the liabilities. Within the liabilities section, the non-current liabilities are listed first, then the current liabilities.

HMV Group uses another variation in format for its balance sheet. Notice in Part B of Exhibit 2-6 that, after HMV lists its assets and liabilities (with, in both cases, the non-current items before the current items), it subtracts the total liabilities from the total assets to get the **net assets**. It then lists the shareholders' equity and shows that the total equity is equal to the net assets. (From the basic accounting equation, Assets = Liabilities + Shareholders' Equity, we know that Assets − Liabilities = Shareholders' Equity. Since, by definition, Net Assets = Assets − Liabilities, the shareholders' equity must be equal to the net assets.)

In conclusion, it is the content of the financial statements that is important, not the order of the items within them. Any format that is meaningful to the users is acceptable.

USING RATIOS TO ANALYZE FINANCIAL STATEMENTS

The statement of earnings shows that Demo Company operated profitably during the month of January, with net earnings of $705. By itself, however, knowing that the income was $705 tells users very little. To understand a company's profitability more fully, users will often use **ratio analysis**, which you will see frequently throughout this text.

EXAMPLES OF DIFFERENCES IN STATEMENT OF FINANCIAL POSITION PRESENTATION: Lindt & Sprüngli Group 2009 ANNUAL REPORT

EXHIBIT 2-6A

annual report

CONSOLIDATED BALANCE SHEET

	Notes	December 31, 2009 CHF million	%	December 31, 2008 CHF million	%
ASSETS					
Property, plant and equipment	7	834.2		839.4	
Intangible assets	8	17.9		13.4	
Financial assets	9	84.0		80.0	
Deferred tax assets	10	4.1		2.9	
Total non-current assets		**940.2**	**38.0%**	**935.7**	**38.8%**
Inventories	11	424.6		437.9	
Accounts receivable	12	656.0		709.5	
Other receivables		62.9		70.3	
Accrued income		9.0		19.3	
Derivative assets	13	8.2		33.9	
Marketable securities	14	7.9		11.3	
Cash and cash equivalents	15	367.2		192.0	
Total current assets		**1,535.8**	**62.0%**	**1,474.2**	**61.2%**
Total assets		**2,476.0**	**100.0%**	**2,409.9**	**100.0%**
LIABILITIES					
Share and participation capital	16	22.8		22.7	
Treasury stock		−29.5		− 0.8	
Retained earnings and other reserves		1,624.4		1,457.1	
Total shareholders' equity		**1,617.7**	**65.3%**	**1,479.0**	**61.4%**
Loan	17	1.1		0.8	
Deferred tax liabilities	10	25.6		29.0	
Pension liabilities	18	135.6		132.0	
Other non-current liabilities		10.7		9.8	
Provisions	19	47.9		34.1	
Total non-current liabilities		**220.9**	**8.9%**	**205.7**	**8.5%**
Accounts payable to suppliers	20	172.7		168.5	
Other accounts payable		37.9		32.4	
Current tax liabilities		30.3		30.2	
Accrued liabilities	21	364.3		332.7	
Derivative liabilities	13	13.4		67.5	
Bank and other borrowings	17	18.8		93.9	
Total current liabilities		**637.4**	**25.8%**	**725.2**	**30.1%**
Total liabilities		**858.3**	**34.7%**	**930.9**	**38.6%**
Total liabilities and shareholders' equity		**2,476.0**	**100.0%**	**2,409.9**	**100.0%**

The accompanying notes form an intregal part of the consolidated statements.

EXHIBIT 2-6B

annual report

EXAMPLES OF DIFFERENCES IN STATEMENT OF FINANCIAL POSITION PRESENTATION: HMV Group 2009 ANNUAL REPORT

Balance sheets

	Notes	Group as at 24 April 2010 £M	Group as at 25 April 2009 £M	Group as at 24 April 2010 £M	Company as at 25 April 2009 £M
Assets					
Non-current assets					
Property, plant and equipment	14	**167.3**	161.9	**0.1**	0.2
Intangible assets	16	**122.2**	73.0	–	–
Investments in subsidiaries and joint venture	17	–	–	**695.6**	673.6
Investments accounted for using the equity method	17	**13.0**	14.7	–	–
Deferrred income tax asset	11	**30.1**	26.1	**12.6**	9.8
Trade and other receivables	18	**12.7**	1.2	–	–
		345.3	276.9	**708.3**	683.6
Current assets					
Inventories	19	**247.8**	213.9	–	–
Trade and other receivables	18	**80.7**	71.6	**28.3**	75.4
Derivative financial instruments	24	**0.1**	0.1	**0.1**	–
Current income tax recoverable		**1.8**	1.3	–	–
Cash and short-term deposits	20	**29.7**	52.7	**48.9**	15.8
		360.1	339.6	**77.3**	91.2
Total assets		**705.4**	616.5	**785.6**	774.8
Liabilities					
Non-current liabilities					
Deferred income tax liabilities	11	**(1.6)**	(0.1)	–	–
Retirement benefit liabilities	32	**(39.0)**	(21.0)	**(39.0)**	(20.7)
Interest-bearing loans and borrowings	22	**(11.8)**	(5.0)	–	–
Provisions	23	**(1.1)**	(0.2)	–	–
		(53.5)	(26.3)	**(39.0)**	(20.7)
Current liabilities					
Trade and other payables	21	**(442.4)**	(415.5)	**(7.8)**	(201.0)
Current income tax payable		**(20.8)**	(17.2)	**(0.9)**	(2.3)
Interest-bearing loans and borrowings	22	**(84.5)**	(53.3)	**(227.5)**	(75.1)
Derivative financial instruments	24	**(0.8)**	–	–	–
Provisions	23	**(3.0)**	(4.6)	–	–
		(551.5)	(490.6)	**(236.2)**	(278.4)
Total liabilities		**(605.0)**	(516.9)	**(275.2)**	(299.1)
Net assets		**100.4**	99.6	**510.4**	475.7
Equity					
Equity share capital	29	**347.1**	347.1	**347.1**	347.1
Other reserve – own shares	29, 30	**(0.6)**	(2.7)	**(0.6)**	(2.7)
Hedging reserve	29	**0.1**	0.1	–	–
Foreign currency translation reserve	29	**12.9**	14.0	–	–
Capital reserve	29	**0.3**	0.3	**0.3**	0.3
Retained earnings		**(260.4)**	(259.2)	**163.6**	131.0
Equity attributable to shareholders of the Parent Company		**99.4**	99.6	**510.4**	475.7
Minority interests		**1.0**	–	–	–
Total equity		**100.4**	99.6	**510.4**	475.7

A ratio divides one financial statement amount by another, so that users can compare related amounts. As seen in the financial statements illustrated so far, meaningful relationships can be derived from many numbers. Ratios allow users to compare companies of different sizes, or to compare the same company's situation at various times. Ratio analysis can be used to assess things such as profitability, the effectiveness of management, and the company's ability to meet debt obligations. In Chapter 1, we discussed how the ratio of a company's total liabilities to its total liabilities plus shareholders' equity could be used to indicate how much a company relies on debt financing. As we introduce new topics, we will show additional ratios that can help users understand and evaluate a set of financial statements. In addition to this, Chapter 12 presents a complete discussion of these ratios.

We will now use Demo Company's financial statements to examine *profitability ratios*. Profitability ratios are usually constructed by comparing some measure of the company's profit (net income or earnings) to the amount invested, or by comparing the profit to the company's revenues. We will calculate three such measures.

Profitability Ratios

The **profit margin ratio** is calculated by dividing the company's profit (or income) by the revenues that produced the profit. For Demo Company, this ratio is calculated by dividing its $705 of net earnings by its $13,000 of sales revenue, giving a result of 0.0542. This indicates that Demo earned, as profit, 5.42% of the amount of its revenue. Stated another way, after the related expenses were deducted from the sales revenues that were generated by the company in January, 5.42% of the revenues remained with the company as income.

LEARNING OBJECTIVE 9

Calculate three ratios for assessing a company's profitability.

The **return on assets** is another measure of profitability. It is calculated by dividing the company's profit (or income) by its average total assets.

Like all the amounts on the statement of financial position, the amount for total assets is determined at particular points in time. For Demo, the relevant points in time are January 1 and January 31, 2011 (i.e., the beginning and end of the current accounting period). To get a measure of the total assets during the period *between* these two dates, we would normally calculate the *average*. However, since Demo had no beginning balances for January, the average amount would not be very meaningful in this situation. Therefore, we will simply use the amount for total assets at the end of the period.

In January 2011, Demo's return on assets was its $705 of net earnings divided by its $37,740 of total assets, giving a result of 0.0187 or 1.87%. Remember that a company's reason for having assets is to use them to generate profits. Demo's return on assets of 1.87% means that during its first month of operations it earned profit at the rate of $1.87 for each $100 that was invested in its assets.

The third measure of performance is the **return on equity**. This ratio compares the return (or income) earned to the amount invested by the shareholders, represented by the total shareholders' equity. (Again, we would normally calculate the *average* shareholders' equity. However, an average amount would not be very meaningful for the month of January, because it was the company's first period of operations and the beginning balances were zero. Therefore, we will simply use the amount for total shareholders' equity at the end of January.)

The return on equity for Demo during January is then calculated by dividing its $705 of net earnings by its $17,955 of shareholders' equity, giving a result of 0.0393, or 3.93%. This measure shows that in the month of January Demo's shareholders earned a 3.93% return on their investment in the company. It also means that during its first month of operations the company earned profit at the rate of $3.93 for each $100 that was invested by the owners.

Ratios are most useful when they are compared to the company's past performance, or with other companies in the same industry. Chapter 12 provides an extensive discussion of these and other ratios and how to interpret them.

Statement of Cash Flows

A statement of cash flows will now be constructed, using the information in the cash column in Exhibit 2-5. The statement of cash flows explains the changes in the amount of cash, by detailing the company's operating, financing, and investing activities (as described in Chapter 1).

Remember that, to make it easier to prepare this statement, we marked all the cash transactions in the exhibit with an O to indicate an operating activity, an F to indicate a financing activity, or an I to indicate an investing activity. All that we need to do now is arrange the items under these three headings and present the data in a more formal manner, as follows.

DEMO COMPANY LIMITED
STATEMENT OF CASH FLOWS
FOR THE MONTH ENDED JANUARY 31, 2011

Cash from operating activities:		
Cash received from customers	$11,000	
Cash paid for insurance	(360)	
Cash paid to suppliers	(13,500)	
Cash paid for salaries	(2,000)	
Cash paid for rent	(500)	
Cash paid for utilities	(300)	
Total cash flow from operating activities		$ (5,660)
Cash from investing activities:		
Cash paid for purchase of equipment	(4,500)	
Cash paid for purchase of land	(15,000)	
Total cash flow from investing activities		(19,500)
Cash from financing activities:		
Cash received from issuance of shares	17,500	
Cash received from bank loan	10,000	
Cash paid for dividends	(250)	
Total cash flow from financing activities		27,250
Net change in cash during the period		2,090
Cash balance on January 1, 2011		0
Cash balance on January 31, 2011		$ 2,090

Note that the final amount shown above is what is shown for cash on the statement of financial position.

You might have noticed that the operating activities section of Demo's statement of cash flows is somewhat different from H&M's, which was shown in Exhibit 1-5. The reason is that GAAP allows this section to be presented using either a *direct* or an *indirect* method. The direct method has been used here, whereas the indirect method is used by H&M. Chapter 5 will explain this difference and provide a detailed discussion of the statement of cash flows.

Generally speaking, with regard to interpreting a statement of cash flows, when you look at its three main sections you should bear in mind that

LEARNING OBJECTIVE 10

Begin to analyze the information provided by a statement of cash flows.

- *operating activities* are normally expected to generate a net *inflow* of cash

- *investing activities* are normally expected to result in a net *outflow* of cash

- *financing activities* are normally expected to result in a net *inflow* of cash

In Demo Company's case, notice that the statement of cash flows shows that there was a net cash *outflow* from its operating activities, even though its operations in January were profitable (as indicated by the statement of earnings). The other two sections of Demo's statement of cash flows conform to what would normally be expected: its investing activities resulted in a net cash outflow, and its financing activities resulted in a net cash inflow.

As the only really obvious cause for concern is the negative cash flow from operating activities, we would want to examine why Demo Company is experiencing this cash drain even though it is profitable. Although it is not unusual for a new business to have a negative cash flow from operations during its early stages, it should be clear that a company cannot continue to operate indefinitely with its day-to-day operations consuming cash, rather than generating it. In fact, cash flow problems are why many new businesses fail in their first year.

Analyzing why a company is having difficulty generating cash from its operating activities is beyond the scope of this chapter, but Demo's situation represents an important issue that will be addressed in various sections of this book, particularly in Chapter 5. For now, it is important to understand that, while the statement of earnings provides important information about a company's performance, it does not reveal everything that should be known about the period's activities. The statement of cash flows provides additional useful information about the company's operations that is not provided by the statement of earnings.

SUMMARY

This chapter introduced the process for recording transactions in an accounting system, using the basic accounting equation to analyze the effects of various events. A set of business transactions was examined in detail, and the effects of these transactions on the basic accounting equation were illustrated. Related concepts and underlying accounting principles were also discussed. Based on an analysis of how a series of transactions affected the basic accounting equation, the three main financial statements were developed.

The explanations that accompanied the transactions and financial statements in this chapter built on the information provided in Chapter 1. In the next chapter, we will continue the Demo Company example and use it to illustrate, in a more formal manner, how the accounting system works.

PRACTICE PROBLEM

You should carefully work through the following problem, and then check your work against the suggested solution. Doing this problem will reinforce and extend what you have learned in this chapter.

Exhibit 2-7 shows the statement of financial position of Sample Company Ltd.

EXHIBIT 2-7

SAMPLE COMPANY LTD.
Statement of Financial Position
December 31, 2010

Cash		$ 4,500
Accounts receivable		2,500
Inventory		7,500
Prepaid rent		1,000
Total current assets		15,500
Equipment, at its original cost	$11,000	
Less: Accumulated depreciation	(1,500)	
		9,500
Total assets		$25,000
Accounts payable		$ 3,100
Accrued salaries payable		1,000
Income tax payable		300
Total current liabilities		4,400
Bank loan		3,500
Total liabilities		7,900
Share capital		10,600
Retained earnings		6,500
Total shareholders' equity		17,100
Total liabilities and shareholders' equity		$25,000

The following transactions occurred during 2011:

Additional Practice Problems

1. Additional inventory was purchased for $39,700 on account.

2. Goods with selling prices totalling $80,000 were sold, all on account.

3. The company received $78,400 from customers as payments on accounts receivable.

4. The company paid $37,300 to suppliers on its accounts payable.

5. The cost of the goods that were sold during the year totalled $38,200.

6. Additional shares were sold to investors for $4,000 cash.

7. New equipment was purchased for $5,000 cash during the year.

8. Dividends of $1,500 were declared and paid during the year.

9. Employees earned salaries for the year totalling $20,500. (Hint: The next transaction deals with the *payment* of salaries. Therefore, at this point the salaries should be recorded as *payable*.)

10. Cash payments for salaries during the year totalled $20,800.

11. The rent for each month was always prepaid on the last day of the previous month. Accordingly, a payment of $1,000 had been made on December 31, 2010, for the rent for the month of January 2011. The rent payments during 2011 were $1,000 per month from January 31 through November 30, and $1,200 on December 31 (because the rent was increased for 2012). (Hint: Record the payments as *prepaid* rent, initially; then, as a separate transaction, transfer the cost for the year 2011 to rent *expense*.)

12. Interest on the bank loan, at 8%, was paid on December 31, 2011. At the same time, $400 of the loan principal was repaid.

13. Depreciation expense on the company's equipment totalled $2,000 for the year.

14. The income tax rate is 30%. Tax payments of $1,900 were made during the year.

Required

a. Analyze the effects of each of the transactions on the company's accounts, using the basic accounting equation (as illustrated in this chapter).

b. Use your answer for part "a" of this problem to prepare a statement of earnings, statement of financial position, and statement of cash flows.

c. Calculate the following ratios for the year 2011:
   i.   Profit margin ratio
   ii. Return on assets
   iii. Return on equity

STRATEGIES FOR SUCCESS:

▶ Start by setting up a table, such as the one that was constructed in this chapter. Use the account titles from the statement of financial position (given in Exhibit 2-7) as the column headings. Enter the beginning balances as the first line of data in the table.

▶ Begin your analysis of each transaction by thinking about what items are affected by it, bearing in mind that there must be at least two. Then determine whether each of those items is increasing or decreasing, and enter the effects in the table.

▶ As you enter the effects of each transaction, ensure that the basic accounting equation remains balanced (i.e., Assets = Liabilities + Shareholders' Equity).

▶ Watch for key words such as "collected," "received," or "paid," indicating that cash has increased or decreased. On the other hand, "on account" means that the collection, receipt, or payment will occur later; in the meantime, an account receivable or account payable will exist.

▶ Remember that revenues have to be *earned* by selling goods or services. Issuing shares in the company does not generate revenue, because the money that comes in has not been earned by operating the business; it has simply been invested by the owners. Similarly, collecting accounts receivable from customers does not generate revenue; the revenue is earned and recorded when the goods are sold, not when the accounts are collected.

▶ Be careful to distinguish between expenses and assets. Expenses are costs that have been used up or consumed in the process of operating the business and generating revenues; assets are costs that have not yet been consumed and can be used to operate the business and generate revenues in the future.

SUGGESTED SOLUTION TO PRACTICE PROBLEM

The basic accounting equation analysis (part "a" of the problem) is shown in Exhibit 2-8. The entries are numbered to match the transaction numbers in the problem. The financial statements (required for part "b") are shown in Exhibits 2-9, 2-10, and 2-11. Following these, the ratios (required for part "c") are presented.

EXHIBIT 2-8 **ANALYSIS OF TRANSACTIONS: Sample Company Ltd.**

	Cash	+ Accts. receiv.	+ Inven- tory	+ Prepaid rent	+ Equip.	= Accts. payable	+ Salaries payable	+ Bank loan	+ Inc. tax payable	+ Share capital	+ Retained earnings
Ending balances	4,500	+ 2,500	+ 7,500	+ 1,000	+ 9,500	= 3,100	+ 1,000	+ 3,500	+ 300	+ 10,600	+ 6,500
Tr. 1		+39,700				+39,700					
Tr. 2		+80,000									+80,000 R
Tr. 3	+78,400 O	−78,400									
Tr. 4	−37,300 O					−37,300					
Tr. 5			−38,200								−38,200 E
Tr. 6	+4,000 F									+4,000	
Tr. 7	−5,000 I			+5,000							
Tr. 8	−1,500 F										−1,500 D
Tr. 9							+20,500				−20,500 E
Tr. 10	−20,800 O						−20,800				
Tr. 11	−12,200 O			+12,200							
				−12,000							−12,000 E
Tr. 12	−280 F										−280 E
	−400 F							−400			
Tr. 13				−2,000							−2,000 E
Tr. 14									+2,106		−2,106 E
	−1,900 O								−1,900		
Ending balances	7,520	+ 4,100	+ 9,000	+ 1,200	+ 12,500	= 5,500	+ 700	+ 3,100	+ 506	+ 14,600	+ 9,914

Total Assets $34,320 = Total Liabilities and Shareholders' Equity $34,320

Legend: O Operating Activity   F Financing Activity   I Investing Activity   R Revenue   E Expense   D Dividend

Explanations follow for selected transactions:

Transactions 9 and 10: Salaries

The amount of salaries earned by employees during the period should be shown as an expense for the company. The amount of salaries *paid* during the period reflects the payment of salaries from the previous period (i.e., the beginning balance in the accrued salaries payable account), as well as partial payment of salaries for the current period. The ending balance in the salaries payable account reflects salaries that have been earned by employees during the current period but have not yet been paid.

Transaction 11: Rent

There were 12 rent *payments* during 2011: the first 11 were for $1,000 each, and the last was for $1,200. (11 × $1,000) + (1 × $1,200) = $12,200

The rent *expense* for 2011 is calculated differently, however. The beginning balance in prepaid rent reflects the payment that was made on December 31, 2010, for January 2011. This plus the amounts paid for the other 11 months of 2011 constitute the rent expense for the year. In other words, the rent expense is the expired cost for January through December 2011: 12 months × $1,000 per month = $12,000.

The final payment of $1,200 on December 31, 2011, applies to the first month of 2012 and is, therefore, an *asset* at the end of 2011. This appears as the ending balance in the prepaid rent account.

Transaction 12: Interest

Because the interest expense was paid during the year, there is no accrued liability at the end of the period. The cash payments for interest, in this case, are the same as the expense. The expense is calculated by multiplying the principal ($3,500) by the interest rate (8%) for one year.

Note that repaying the principal of a loan does not create an expense; it simply reduces the loan liability. The *expense* related to the loan is the *interest* charged on it.

Although it would seem logical to view an interest payment as a *financing* cash flow, most companies treat the payment of interest as an *operating* cash flow. Accordingly, in this book we will classify interest payments as operating activities. You should be aware, however, that some companies classify interest payments as financing activities.

Transaction 14: Income tax

To determine the tax expense for the period, the amount of *income before tax* must first be determined. This is found by subtracting the expenses from the revenues, all of which are listed in the retained earnings column in Exhibit 2-8. Thus, the income before tax is $7,020 (i.e., 80,000 − 38,200 − 20,500 − 12,000 − 280 − 2,000 = 7,020). Since Sample Company's tax rate is 30%, its income tax expense is then calculated by taking 30% of its income before tax, resulting in $2,106 (i.e., 0.30 × 7,020 = 2,106).

The beginning balance in the income tax payable account was tax owing from 2010 that was paid in 2011. The ending balance in the tax payable account will be paid in 2012.

The amounts on the statement of earnings are the ones designated with either an R or an E (indicating Revenue or Expense) in the retained earnings column of Exhibit 2-8.

EXHIBIT 2-9

SAMPLE COMPANY LTD.
Statement of Earnings
For the year ended December 31, 2011

Revenues:	
Sales	$ 80,000
Expenses:	
Cost of goods sold	$(38,200)
Salary expense	(20,500)
Rent expense	(12,000)
Depreciation expense	(2,000)
Interest expense	(280)
Income tax expense	(2,106)
Net earnings	$ 4,914

EXHIBIT 2-10

SAMPLE COMPANY LTD.
Statement of Financial Position
As at December 31, 2011

		2011		2010
Assets				
Current Assets				
Cash		$ 7,520		$ 4,500
Accounts receivable		4,100		2,500
Inventory		9,000		7,500
Prepaid rent		1,200		1,000
Total current assets		21,820		15,500
Equipment, at its original cost	$16,000		$11,000	
Less: Accumulated depreciation	(3,500)		(1,500)	
		12,500		9,500
Total assets		**$34,320**		**$25,000**
Liabilities				
Current liabilities				
Accounts payable		$ 5,500		$ 3,100
Accrued salaries		700		1,000
Income tax payable		506		300
Total current liabilities		6,706		4,400
Bank loan		3,100		3,500
Total liabilities		9,806		7,900
Shareholders' equity				
Share capital		14,600		10,600
Retained earnings		9,914		6,500
Total shareholders' equity		24,514		17,100
Total liabilities and shareholders' equity		**$34,320**		**$25,000**

The amounts reported on the statement of financial position for 2011 are simply the ending balances from Exhibit 2-8.

Note that the ending balance for retained earnings equals the beginning balance plus the net earnings minus the dividends declared (i.e., $6,500 + 4,914 − 1,500 = $9,914).

EXHIBIT 2-11

SAMPLE COMPANY LTD.
Statement of Cash Flows
For the year ended December 31, 2011

Cash from operating activities:		
Cash received from customers	$78,400	
Cash paid to suppliers	(37,300)	
Cash paid for salaries	(20,800)	
Cash paid for rent	(12,200)	
Cash paid for interest	(280)	
Cash paid for income tax	(1,900)	
Total cash flow from operating activities		$5,920
Cash from investing activities:		
Cash paid for purchase of new equipment		(5,000)
Cash from financing activities:		
Cash received from investors for shares	4,000	
Cash paid for dividends	(1,500)	
Cash paid for repayment of bank loan	(400)	
Total cash flow from financing activities		2,100
Overall increase in cash during the year		3,020
Beginning balance of cash		4,500
Ending balance of cash		$7,520

The amounts reported on the statement of cash flows are those in the cash column of Exhibit 2-8, each of which was designated O, I, or F (indicating an Operating activity, Investing activity, or Financing activity).

Note that the ending balance reported on the statement of cash flows agrees with the cash balance reported on the statement of financial position at the end of 2011.

$$\text{Profit margin ratio} = \frac{\text{Net earnings}}{\text{Sales revenue}} = \frac{\$4,914}{\$80,000} = 0.061 = 6.1\%$$

$$\text{Return on assets} = \frac{\text{Net earnings}}{\text{Average total assets}} = \frac{\$4,914}{(\$25,000 + \$34,320) \div 2} = 0.166 = 16.6\%$$

$$\text{Return on equity} = \frac{\text{Net earnings}}{\text{Average total equity}} = \frac{\$4,914}{(17,100 + \$24,514) \div 2} = 0.236 = 23.6\%$$

Note that we have calculated the *average* total assets and the *average* total shareholders' equity, to get amounts that are representative of the entire year.

practice problems

SYNONYMS

Amortization ▎ Depreciation
Book value ▎ Carrying value
Credit purchase ▎ Purchase on account
Credit sale ▎ Sale on account
Earnings ▎ Income/Profit

WILEY
PLUS
www.wileyplus.com

GLOSSARY

Accounts payable   Liabilities that result when inventory or supplies are purchased on credit. They represent an obligation to pay cash to suppliers in the future.

Accounts receivable   Assets that result when goods or services are sold on credit. They represent the right to receive cash from customers in the future.

Accrual basis   The accounting basis, used by almost all companies, that recognizes revenues and expenses in the period when they are earned or incurred, and not necessarily in the period when the related cash inflows and outflows occur.

Accrued expense   An expense that has been incurred and reported on the statement of earnings, but not yet been paid for; consequently, a related liability is reported on the statement of financial position.

Amortization   A synonym for depreciation.

Book value   The value carried in the accounting system (or "on the company's books") for an item. A synonym for carrying value.

Carrying value   A synonym for book value.

Cash basis   The accounting basis, used by some entities, that recognizes revenues and expenses when the cash inflows or outflows occur.

Classified statement of financial position   A statement of financial position in which the assets and liabilities sections are subdivided into current (or short-term) and non-current (or long-term) items.

Contra-asset   An account whose balance is offset against, or deducted from, a related asset.

Cost of goods sold   The expense that records the acquisition value of the inventory that was sold during the period.

Credit purchase   A business transaction in which a buyer acquires goods or services from a seller in exchange for the buyer's promise to pay cash at a later date. This is also referred to as a purchase on account, because it creates an account payable on the buyer's books.

Credit sale   A business transaction in which a seller provides goods or services to a buyer in exchange for the buyer's promise to pay cash at a later date. This is also referred to as a sale on account, because it creates an account receivable on the seller's books.

Current assets   Short-term assets that will generally be converted into cash or consumed within one year.

Current liabilities   Short-term debts or obligations that will be settled within one year.

Depreciation   The expense that records the usage of a non-current asset, such as equipment, for the period. Depreciation is a process that allocates the cost of a non-current asset to each of the periods in the asset's useful life. Depreciation is sometimes referred to as amortization.

Dividends declared   A distribution of assets (usually cash) to the shareholders of a company. The board of directors votes to declare the distribution, at which point it becomes a legal obligation of the company. The distribution of cash occurs at a date specified at the time of declaration.

Historical cost   A valuation method that values assets at the amounts that were paid to obtain them.

Liquidity   A quality of an asset that describes how quickly it can be converted into cash. Assets that can be converted into cash quickly have high liquidity.

Loss   A reduction in shareholders' equity that results when the value of the resources that flowed into the company (i.e., revenues) are less than the value of the resources that flowed out (i.e., expenses). A net loss is the opposite of net earnings, income, or profit.

Matching concept   A concept in accounting that requires all expenses related to the production of revenues to be recorded during the same time period as the revenues. The expenses are said to be matched with the revenues on the statement of earnings.

Net assets   Total assets minus total liabilities. Mathematically, the net assets must equal the shareholders' equity.

Non-current assets   Assets that will last and provide future benefits for more than one year.

Non-current liabilities   Debts or obligations that will not be settled within one year.

Note payable   A liability represented by a formal document that states the amount owed to a creditor. It is similar to an account payable, except that the note constitutes legal documentation that the buyer has promised to make payment in the future. The note usually specifies the amount, due date, and interest rate.

Note receivable   An asset represented by a formal document that states the amount due from a customer. It is similar to an account receivable, except that the note constitutes legal documentation that the seller has the right to receive payment in the future. The note usually specifies the amount, due date, and interest rate.

Prepaid expense   An asset representing a past expenditure whose benefits are expected to be consumed in a future accounting period. A prepaid expense represents a past cash outflow for which the company will receive future economic benefits. It is sometimes called a deferred expense.

Principal   The amount of a debt, excluding interest.

Profit   A synonym for earnings or income.

Profit margin ratio   A ratio that compares the net earnings (or profit or income) during an accounting period to the related revenues.

Purchase on account   A purchase in which the buyer gives a promise to the seller to pay at a later date. A synonym for credit purchase.

Residual value   The estimated value of an asset at the end of its useful life. The estimate is made when the asset is purchased, in order to calculate the amount to be depreciated each period.

Return on assets   A ratio that compares the net earnings (or income or profit) for the period to the company's assets.

Return on equity   A ratio that compares the net earnings (or income or profit) for the period to the shareholders' equity in the company.

Revenue recognition criteria   Conditions that must be satisfied for revenues to be recognized in the accounting system.

Sale on account   A sale in which the seller receives a promise from the buyer to pay at a later date. A synonym for credit sale.

Sales revenue   The amount of sales recognized and reported on the statement of earnings during the accounting period, based on the revenue recognition criteria.

Straight-line depreciation   A method of calculating depreciation in which the amount of expense for each period is found by dividing an asset's cost (less any residual value) by its estimated useful life.

Transaction   An exchange of resources with an outside entity, or an internal event that affects the balances in individual asset, liability, or shareholders' equity accounts.

Transaction analysis   The process by which an accountant decides what accounts are affected, and by how much, when an economic transaction or event occurs.

Useful life   The estimated period of time over which a capital asset (such as equipment) is expected to be used.

ASSIGNMENT MATERIAL

Assessing Your Recall

2-1   Explain the difference between an asset and a liability.

2-2   Describe how the basic accounting equation (or *balance sheet equation*) is used to analyze how transactions are recorded in the accounting system.

2-3   Discuss why dividends do not appear on the statement of earnings but do appear on the statement of cash flows.

2-4   What are the advantages and disadvantages of using the accrual basis of accounting rather than the cash basis?

2-5   Identify the three major sections in the statement of cash flows, and briefly describe the nature of the items that appear in each section.

WILEY **PLUS**
www.wileyplus.com

Self-Assessment Quiz

2-6 Indicate whether each of the following statements is true or false:

a. The cash basis of accounting recognizes revenues when they are received.
b. In the cash basis of accounting, there is no such thing as a prepaid rent account.
c. In the accrual basis of accounting, paying an account payable creates an expense.
d. In the accrual basis of accounting, interest should be recognized only when it is paid.
e. Cash receipts from customers increase accounts receivable.
f. Expenses increase shareholders' equity.
g. Dividends are an expense of doing business and should appear on the statement of earnings.
h. Interest paid on bank loans is reported in the investing activities section of the statement of cash flows.

2-7 What are revenue recognition criteria, and how does the matching concept relate to these criteria?

2-8 Explain how a prepaid expense (such as rent) is handled under accrual-basis accounting.

2-9 Explain how an accrued expense (such as interest) is handled under accrual-basis accounting.

2-10 Explain what depreciation is, and how it is calculated using the straight-line method.

Applying Your Knowledge

2-11 (Determine missing amounts using financial statement relationships)

For the two independent cases that follow, determine the missing amount for each letter. (Hint: You might not be able to calculate them in the order in which they appear.)

	Case 1	Case 2
Revenues	A	29,000
Expenses	17,000	25,000
Net earnings	2,000	F
Dividends declared	500	G
Retained earnings:		
Beginning of year	6,000	10,000
End of year	B	11,000
Total assets:		
Beginning of year	C	H
End of year	28,000	I
Total liabilities:		
Beginning of year	9,000	10,500
End of year	D	9,500
Share capital:		
Beginning of year	1,000	J
End of year	E	8,500
Additional investments made by shareholders		
during the year	$4,000	$ 3,500

2-12 (Determine net earnings or loss from statement of financial position changes)

The following are from a company's statements of financial position:

	Dec. 31, 2010	Dec. 31, 2011
Total assets	$110,000	$125,000
Total liabilities	$80,000	$85,000

During 2011, the company issued additional shares for $7,000 and declared dividends of $4,000.

Required:

Calculate what the company's net income or loss must have been for the year 2011. Be sure to indicate whether your answer represents net earnings or a net loss.

2-13 (Determine revenues, expenses, and dividends)

The following information for the current year was obtained from the accounting records of Safari Supplies Corporation:

Retained earnings, beginning	$ 96,000
Retained earnings, ending	105,600
Sales	448,800
Cost of goods sold	272,000
Selling expenses	63,300
General and administrative expenses	38,800
Dividend revenue	4,800
Interest revenue	2,200
Interest expense	1,200
Income taxes expense	26,400

Required:

Calculate the following items:

a. Total revenues
b. Total expenses
c. Net earnings
d. Dividends declared

2-14 (Determine statement of earnings and statement of financial position amounts)

Rhaman Company had the following transactions in its first month of operations:

1. The owner invested $10,000 cash in the business, plus some office furniture and equipment that had originally cost her $3,000 but was currently worth only $1,000.

2. Additional equipment costing $4,000 was purchased for cash.

3. Supplies costing $500 were purchased for cash.

4. Inventory costing $5,000 was acquired on account. Later in the month, the company paid half of the amount owed. It will pay the remainder next month.

5. The entire inventory was sold to customers for $8,000. The company received half of this amount in cash and will receive the remainder next month.

6. By the end of the month, $400 of the supplies were used up.

7. The equipment was amortized $100 for the month.

8. Operating expenses paid in cash during the month were $1,900.

9. Dividends of $200 were declared and paid during the month.

Required:

a. Calculate the following amounts for the month:
   i. Sales revenue
   ii. Cost of goods sold
   iii. Total expenses other than cost of goods sold
   iv. Net earnings or loss
b. Calculate the following amounts as of the end of the month:
   i. Cash on hand
   ii. Total assets other than cash
   iii. Total liabilities
   iv. Share capital
   v. Retained earnings

2-15   (Cash basis versus accrual basis)

Based on the following transactions, calculate the revenues and expenses that would be reported (a) on the cash basis and (b) on the accrual basis:

    i.   Credit sales to customers totalled $35,000.

    ii.   Cash sales totalled $115,000.

    iii. Cash collections on account from customers totalled $30,000.

    iv. Cost of goods sold during the period was $85,000.

    v.   Payments made to suppliers of inventory totalled $75,000.

    vi. Wages of $32,500 were paid during the year. In addition, wages of $2,500 remained unpaid at year end; there were no wages unpaid at the beginning of the year.

    vii. Halfway through the year, a one-year insurance policy was purchased at a cost of $1,000.

2-16   (Cash basis versus accrual basis)

Based on the following transactions, calculate the revenues and expenses that would be reported (a) on the cash basis and (b) on the accrual basis:

    i.   Inventory costing $70,000 was purchased on account.

    ii.   Inventory costing $60,000 was sold for $100,000. Eighty percent of the sales were for cash.

    iii. Cash collected from credit customers (i.e., who bought on account) totalled $20,000.

    iv. A lease was signed at the beginning of the year, requiring monthly payments of $1,000. The rent for the first month was paid when the lease was signed. After that, the $1,000 rent was paid on the last day of each month, to cover the following month.

    v.   Office supplies costing $5,500 were purchased for cash. At the end of the year, $500 of the office supplies were still unused.

    vi. Wages of $37,500 were paid during the year. Also, wages of $500 remained unpaid at year end.

2-17   (Nature of retained earnings)

Explain why you agree or disagree with the following statement: "Retained earnings are like money in the bank. If you are running out of cash, you can always use some of your retained earnings to pay your bills."

2-18   (Statement of earnings and statement of cash flows)

Compare and contrast the purpose of the statement of earnings and the statement of cash flows. Outline how they differ, and briefly describe their relationship to the statement of financial position.

2-19   (Transaction analysis and the basic accounting equation)

For each of the following transactions, indicate the effect on the basic accounting equation (assets = liabilities + shareholder's equity):

    a. Issuance of shares for cash

    b. Purchase of land for cash

    c. Sale of services to a customer on credit

    d. Receipt of cash from customers as payments on their accounts

    e. Payment of cash to shareholders as a distribution of earnings

    f. Receipt of a loan from a bank

    g. Payment of interest on the bank loan

    h. Purchase of inventory on credit

    i.   Payment of an account payable

    j.   Payment to a courier company for delivering goods to a customer

    k. Payment of an insurance premium to cover the following year

    l.   Depreciation of equipment

2-20   (Transaction analysis)

For each of the transactions below, indicate which accounts are affected and whether they are increased or decreased:

a. Sold shares for cash.
b. Borrowed money from a bank.
c. Bought equipment from a supplier on credit.
d. Bought inventory from a supplier, partly for cash and partly on account.
e. Sold inventory to a customer on account. (Hint: Your answer should deal with both the revenue and the related expense.)
f. Made a payment to a supplier on account.
g. Received a payment from a customer on account.
h. Bought office supplies for cash.
i. Declared and paid a dividend.
j. Accrued the interest on the money that was borrowed in transaction "b" (i.e., recognized the interest but did not pay it).
k. Paid for the equipment that was purchased on credit in transaction "c."
l. Used some of the office supplies that were purchased in transaction "h."

2-21   (Transaction analysis)

For each of the following transactions, indicate how (a) net earnings and (b) cash flows are affected. For each, state whether there will be an increase, a decrease, or no effect, and the amount (if any):

i.   Issued shares to investors for $60,000.
ii.   Purchased inventory from suppliers for $2,500, on account.
iii.   Sold a unit of inventory for $500, on account. The unit had cost $300 and was already in inventory prior to its sale.
iv.   Purchased equipment for $10,000 cash.
v.   Made a payment of $1,000 on accounts payable.
vi.   Used $300 of office supplies. The supplies were purchased for cash in an earlier period.
vii.   Received a payment of $700 from a customer for inventory previously sold on account.
viii. Declared (but did not yet pay) a dividend of $2,000.
ix.   Paid the $2,000 dividend that was declared above.
x.   Depreciated equipment by $500.

2-22   (Transaction analysis and the basic accounting equation)

Analyze the following transactions and show their effects on the basic accounting equation, by preparing a table like the one in Exhibit 2-8:

a. Received $150,000 from investors buying shares in the company.
b. Bought land for $50,000. Paid half in cash, with the remainder to be paid in six months.
c. Bought inventory costing $45,000, on account.
d. Sold inventory costing $35,000 to customers, on account, for $52,000.
e. Paid $1,000 of taxes that were owed from the previous period.
f. Borrowed $25,000 from a bank. The interest on the loan is 6% per year.
g. Depreciated equipment by $1,200.
h. Paid $750 for supplies to be used in the future.
i. Paid $250 to the power company for electricity used during the period.
j. Declared and paid dividends of $8,000.

2-23   (Transaction analysis and the basic accounting equation)

Dr. Walter Wong completed the following business transactions during the month of November:

i.   Incorporated a veterinary practice by investing (a) $30,000 in cash and (b) equipment worth $20,000.
ii.   Rented a furnished office and clinic, and paid $1,500 in rent for the month of November.
iii.   Purchased medical supplies on account, $850.
iv.   Performed veterinary services and immediately collected $2,400 for the work.
v.   Paid for the medical supplies that were purchased in transaction c.
vi.   Provided $700 of additional veterinary services, on account.

vii. Used $350 of the medical supplies that were purchased in transaction c.

viii. Received $500 in partial payment for the services that were provided in transaction f.

ix. Paid the November telephone bill for the office, $75.

x. Received a bill of $250 for advertising, but decided not to pay it until next month.

xi. Paid rent on the office for the months of December and January, totalling $3,200.

xii. Dr. Wong paid $1,000 from the clinic's bank account for repairs to his vacation villa in Cuba. (Hint: Before recording it, think about the nature of this transaction and the definition of an expense.)

Required:

Analyze these transactions and show their effects on the basic accounting equation for November, by preparing a table like the one in Exhibit 2-8.

2-24 (Transaction analysis and the basic accounting equation)

Show how each of the following transactions affects the basic accounting equation (assets = liabilities + shareholders' equity), and identify the ones that have an immediate impact on the statement of earnings and/or the statement of cash flows:

a. Bought parts and supplies inventory for $15,000, on account. (The company repairs and services vehicles, and will use these parts and supplies for repairs.)

b. Paid $12,000 to suppliers for the purchases that were made in transaction "a."

c. Received $20,000 in cash for repairing and servicing vehicles; another $5,000 of work was done on account.

d. Collected $3,000 from customers for the work that was done on account in transaction "c."

e. In the repair work done in transaction "c," $10,000 of the parts and supplies inventory was used.

f. The owners invested a further $25,000 in the business, and shares were issued to them.

g. Received utility (electricity, water, and telephone) bills for the month that totalled $600. Paid all these bills except for $100 that will be paid next month.

h. Borrowed $50,000 from the bank.

i. Bought a vehicle hoist for $45,000.

j. Paid the employees their wages for the month, $9,000.

k. Recorded accrued interest of $200 on the bank loan. The interest will be paid when the loan is due, in one year.

l. Some of the parts that were used in the repair of the vehicles have warranties. The company estimates that $500 in free replacements will be necessary in the future, under the terms of the warranties. (Hint: This is an expected future cost to the company. Remember that if revenue is recognized in the current period, the matching principle requires that all the associated expenses be recognized in the same accounting period.)

2-25 (Transaction analysis and the basic accounting equation)

For each of the following transactions, indicate (a) what the immediate effect will be on the basic accounting equation, and (b) what other effects, if any, there will be in the future as a result of the transaction:

i. Sold inventory to customers for cash.

ii. Sold inventory to customers on account.

iii. Collected cash from customers as payments on their accounts.

iv. Purchased inventory on account.

v. Paid suppliers for goods purchased on account.

vi. Purchased production equipment for cash.

vii. Paid for an insurance policy on an office building.

viii. Borrowed money from the bank.

ix. Bought a patent, which gives the company the exclusive right to use an improved production process.

x. Provided warranties to customers for free repair or replacement of any defective products that were sold to them. (See transaction "l" in Problem 2-24 for more information about this type of transaction.)

2-26 (Transaction analysis and the basic accounting equation)

Show the effect of each of the following transactions on the basic accounting equation, by preparing a table like the one in Exhibit 2-8. The company's fiscal year end is December 31.

a. On January 1, 2011, the company borrowed $15,000 from the bank.

b. On December 31, 2011, the company paid the interest on the bank loan in transaction "a." The interest rate is 6%.

c. On January 1, 2011, the company bought equipment for $10,000 cash.

d. On December 31, 2011, the company recorded depreciation on the equipment, using the straight-line method. The equipment has an estimated useful life of six years and an estimated residual value of $1,000.

e. Purchases of inventory on account during the year totalled $87,500.

f. Sales for the year totalled $147,500, of which $17,500 was for cash and the remainder was on account.

g. The cost of the products sold from inventory during the year was $85,000.

h. Payments to suppliers for inventory purchases totalled $73,000 during the year.

i. Collections on account from customers totalled $116,000 for the year.

j. Employees earned wages of $48,400 during the year, which were recorded as Wages Payable.

k. All employee wages were paid by the end of the year except the wages for the last week in December, which totalled $1,200.

l. Dividends were declared and paid in the amount of $1,000.

2-27 (Transaction analysis and the basic accounting equation)

Show the effect of each of the following transactions on the basic accounting equation, by preparing a table like the one in Exhibit 2-8. The fiscal year end of the company (which has been operating for several years) is December 31.

a. Consumed $1,000 of office supplies during the year. The supplies were purchased for cash the previous year.

b. Purchased $32,000 of inventory on account during the year.

c. Made sales of $60,000 during the year, of which $24,000 were cash sales.

d. Paid $36,000 owed to suppliers on accounts payable. (This included some amounts owed from the previous year.)

e. Collected $34,000 due from customers on accounts receivable. (This included some amounts due from the previous year.)

f. Paid an insurance premium of $800 on March 31 that provides coverage for the 12-month period starting April 1. The company had no insurance prior to this.

g. Determined that the cost of the inventory sold during the year was $39,000. (This included some inventory purchased the previous year.)

h. Paid $7,000 for operating expenses during the year.

i. On December 31, the company recognized the amount of insurance expense incurred during the period. (Refer to transaction "f.")

j. Recorded $3,600 of depreciation for the year on the company's equipment.

k. Declared (but did not immediately pay) dividends of $400 each quarter, for a total of $1,600.

l. By the end of the year, $1,200 of the dividends were paid.

2-28 (Determine amounts using the basic accounting equation)

Ballentine Company Ltd. has assets of $100,000, liabilities of $40,000, and shareholders' equity of $60,000. Refer to the basic accounting equation (assets = liabilities + shareholders' equity) to answer each of the following independent questions:

   a. At what amount will assets be stated, if total liabilities decrease by $5,000 and shareholders' equity remains constant?
   b. Go back to the original data. At what amount will assets be stated, if total liabilities increase by $3,000 and shareholders' equity increases by $4,000?
   c. Go back to the original data. At what amount will shareholders' equity be stated, if the company pays $7,000 of its liabilities?
   d. Go back to the original data. At what amount will liabilities be stated, if total assets decrease by $7,000 and shareholders' equity increases by $2,000?
   e. Go back to the original data. At what amount will shareholders' equity be stated, if the company declares a $1,000 dividend but does not pay it?

2-29 (Prepare a statement of earnings)

Sara's Bakery had the following account balances at the end of 2011:

Supplies on hand	$ 4,000
Wages expense	42,000
Sales	178,000
Cash	24,000
Supplies used	14,000
Accounts payable	8,000
Rent expense	12,000
Share capital	90,000
Accounts receivable	10,000
Cost of goods sold	101,000
Equipment	95,000
Accumulated depreciation	7,500
Depreciation expense	2,500
Retained earnings	22,500
Dividends declared	2,000
Prepaid rent	1,000
Wages payable	1,500

Required:
   a. Prepare a statement of earnings for the year ended December 31, 2011.
   b. In answering part "a," you did not need to use all the accounts provided. For each item that you did not use, explain why you did not include it on the statement of earnings.

2-30 (Prepare a statement of earnings)

The Garment Tree Ltd. sells clothing. At the end of 2011, it had the following account balances:

Accounts receivable	$ 9,000
Rent expense	12,000
Inventory	18,000
Retained earnings	11,000
Advertising expense	5,000
Cash	6,000
Wages expense	32,000
Dividends declared	1,000
Miscellaneous expense	3,000
Wages payable	2,000
Share capital	15,000
Prepaid rent	1,000

Cost of goods sold	57,000
Accounts payable	6,000
Sales	110,000

Required:

a. Prepare a statement of earnings for the year ended December 31, 2011.

b. In answering part "a," you did not need to use all the accounts provided. For each item that you did not use, explain why you did not include it on the statement of earnings.

2-31 (Prepare a statement of financial position)

Tree Top Restaurants Ltd., a chain that has several restaurants in cities across Canada, had the following account balances at December 31, 2011:

Retained earnings	$ 60,000
Wages payable	10,000
Accounts receivable	90,000
Bank loan (due in five years)	250,000
Buildings	260,000
Accumulated depreciation on buildings	30,000
Accounts payable	82,000
Prepaid insurance	8,000
Share capital	200,000
Cash	53,000
Land	100,000
Taxes payable	5,000
Inventory	46,000
Furniture and equipment	90,000
Accumulated depreciation on furniture and equipment	10,000

Required:

Prepare a classified statement of financial position for Tree Top Restaurants Ltd. for December 31, 2011.

2-32 (Calculate net income and retained earnings; prepare statement of financial position)

Little Tots Ltd. sells children's clothing. At the end of December 2011 (its first year of operations), it had the following account balances:

Accounts receivable	$ 2,500
Rent expense	3,600
Cash	3,500
Wages payable	400
Display counters and other store fixtures	5,500
Accumulated depreciation	500
Depreciation expense	500
Wages expense	26,000
Prepaid rent	300
Cost of goods sold	34,900
Sales revenue	69,900
Bank loan (due in two years)	4,800
Advertising expense	800
Accounts payable	2,000
Electricity expense	300
Dividends declared	1,200
Share capital	10,000
Interest paid on bank loan	100
Inventory	8,000
Other expenses	400
Retained earnings	?

Required:

a. Calculate the net earnings for the year, by adding the revenue and deducting all the expenses.

b. Calculate the retained earnings, by following the process outlined below:

Balance in retained earnings at the beginning of the year	$ 0*
Add: Net earnings for the year	?
Deduct: Dividends declared during the year	
Balance in retained earnings at the end of the year	?

*The beginning balance is zero because this was the company's first year of operations.

c. Prepare a classified statement of financial position.

2-33 (Calculate income and retained earnings; prepare statement of financial position)
On December 31, 2011 (the end of its first year of operations), Minute Print Company had the following account balances:

Bank loan (due in three years)	$ 40,000
Wages expense	93,000
Materials and supplies on hand	68,000
Dividends payable	1,500
Sales	486,000
Cash	24,000
Materials and supplies used	214,500
Wages payable	4,500
Prepaid rent	2,000
Interest paid on loan	2,500
Rent expense—equipment	100,000
Dividends declared	3,000
Accounts payable	8,000
Share capital	30,000
Rent expense—premises	24,000
Accounts receivable	30,000
Other expenses	9,000
Retained earnings	?

Required:

a. Identify the accounts that would appear on the statement of earnings, and use them to calculate the net earnings for the year.

b. Find the amount of retained earnings at December 31, 2011, by subtracting the dividends declared from the net earnings you calculated in part "a."

c. Prepare a classified statement of financial position for December 31, 2011. Use the retained earnings amount calculated in part "b."

2-34 (Prepare statement of earnings and statement of financial position)
The Wizard's Corner, a company that sells video games and related items, had the following account balances at the end of June 2011:

Cost of goods sold	$103,000
Share capital	33,000
Advertising expense	6,000
Equipment	20,000
Accumulated depreciation	9,000
Depreciation expense	2,000
Dividends declared	3,000
Accounts payable	11,000
Inventory	28,000

Wages expense	36,000
Sales	160,000
Accounts receivable	15,000
Rent expense	12,000
Cash	10,000
Prepaid rent	1,000
Wages payable	2,000
Retained earnings (as at July 1, 2010)	21,000

Required:
a. Prepare a statement of earnings for the year ended June 30, 2011.
b. Calculate the amount of retained earnings as at June 30, 2011.
c. Prepare a statement of financial position as at June 30, 2011.

2-35 (Transaction analysis and financial statement preparation)
Singh Company started business on January 1, 2011. The following transactions occurred in 2011:

1. On January 1, the company issued 10,000 shares for $250,000.

2. On January 2, the company borrowed $50,000 from the bank.

3. On January 3, the company purchased land and a building for a total of $200,000 cash. The land was recently appraised at a fair market value of $60,000. (Note: Because the building will be depreciated in the future and the land will not, these two assets should be recorded in separate accounts.)

4. Inventory costing $130,000 was purchased on account.

5. Sales to customers totalled $205,000. Of these, $175,000 were sales on account.

6. The cost of the inventory that was sold to customers in transaction 5 was $120,000.

7. Payments to suppliers on account totalled $115,000.

8. Collections from customers on account totalled $155,000.

9. Payments to employees for salaries were $55,000. In addition, there was $2,000 of unpaid salaries at year end.

10. The interest on the bank loan was recognized and paid each month. The interest rate on the loan was 6%.

11. The building was estimated to have a useful life of 30 years and a residual value of $20,000. The company uses the straight-line method of depreciation.

12. The company declared dividends of $7,000 on December 15, 2011, to be paid on January 15, 2012.

Required:
a. Analyze the effects of each of the transactions on the basic accounting equation, using a table like the one in Exhibit 2-8.
b. Prepare a statement of financial position, a statement of earnings, and a statement of cash flows for 2011.

2-36 (Transaction analysis and financial statement presentation)
The Hughes Tools Company started business on October 1, 2011. Its fiscal year runs through to September 30 the following year. The following transactions occurred in the fiscal year that started on October 1, 2011, and ended on September 30, 2012.

1. On October 1, 2011, Jill Hughes invested $175,000 to start the business. Hughes is the only owner. She was issued 10,000 shares.

2. On October 1, Hughes Tools borrowed $225,000 from a venture capitalist (a lender who specializes in start-up companies).

3. On October 1, the company rented a building. The rental agreement was a two-year contract requiring quarterly rental payments (every three months) of $15,000, payable in advance. The first payment was made on October 1, 2011 (covering the period from October 1 to December 31). Thereafter, payments were due on December 31, March 31, June 30, and September 30 for each three-month period that followed. All the rental payments were made as specified in the agreement.

4. On October 1, the company purchased equipment costing $220,000 for cash.

5. Initial inventory was purchased for $90,000 cash.

6. Additional purchases of inventory during the year totalled $570,000, all on account.

7. Sales during the year totalled $800,000, of which $720,000 were on account.

8. Collections from customers on account totalled $650,000.

9. Payments to suppliers on account totalled $510,000.

10. The cost of the inventory that was sold during the year was $560,000.

11. Selling and administrative expenses totalled $86,500 for the year. Of this amount, $4,000 was unpaid at year end.

12. Interest on the loan from the venture capitalist was paid at year end (September 30, 2012). The interest rate on the loan is 10%. In addition, $25,000 of the loan principal was repaid at that time.

13. The equipment was depreciated based on an estimated useful life of 10 years and a residual value of $20,000.

14. The company's income tax rate was 30%. Before the end of the year, $12,000 in income taxes was paid; the remainder was still owing at year end.

15. The company declared and paid a dividend of $7,000.

Required:
a. Show the effects of the transactions on the basic accounting equation, by preparing a table like the one in Exhibit 2-8.
b. Prepare a statement of earnings, statement of financial position, and statement of cash flows for the year.
c. Comment on the results of the company's first year of operations.

2-37 (Transaction analysis and financial statement preparation)

A.J. Smith Company started business on January 1, 2011, and the following transactions occurred in its first year:

1. On January 1, the company issued 12,000 shares at $25 per share.

2. On January 1, the company purchased land and a building from another company in exchange for $80,000 cash and 6,000 shares. The land's value is approximately one-quarter of the total value of the transaction. (Hint: You need to determine a value for the shares using the information given in transaction 1, and the land and building should be recorded in separate accounts.)

3. On March 31, the company rented out a portion of its building to Frantek Company. Frantek is required to make quarterly payments of $7,500 on March 31, June 30, September 30, and December 31 of each year. The first payment, covering the period from April 1 to June 30, was received on March 31, and the other payments were all received as scheduled.

4. Equipment worth $120,000 was purchased on July 1, in exchange for $60,000 cash and a one-year note with a principal amount of $60,000 and an interest rate of 10%. No principal or interest payments were made during the year.

5. Inventory costing $250,000 was purchased on account.

6. Sales were $300,000, of which credit sales were $250,000.

7. The inventory sold had a cost of $190,000.

8. Payments to suppliers totalled $205,000.

9. Accounts receivable totalling $200,000 were collected.

10. Operating expenses amounted to $50,000, all of which were paid in cash.

11. The building purchased in transaction 2 is depreciated using the straight-line method, with an estimated useful life of 20 years and an estimated residual value of $30,000.

12. The equipment purchased in transaction 4 is depreciated using the straight-line method, with an estimated useful life of 10 years and an estimated residual value of $5,000. Because the equipment was purchased on July 1, only a half year of depreciation is recognized in 2011.

13. The company's income tax rate is 30%. It paid $10,000 of its income tax to the Canada Revenue Agency before the end of the year; the remainder will be paid in the first quarter of 2012.

14. Dividends of $20,000 were declared during the year, of which $5,000 remained unpaid at year end.

Required:
a. Show the effects of the transactions on the basic accounting equation, by preparing a table like the one in Exhibit 2-8.
b. Prepare a statement of financial position, statement of earnings, and statement of cash flows for 2011.
c. Comment on the company's results for its first year of operations.

2-38 **(Correct a statement of earnings and statement of financial position)**
Kim Moore owns a small auto repair shop, which has been in operation for a few years. The following statements attempt to summarize the shop's operations for the month of January and its financial position at that time:

MOORE REPAIRS
Statement of Earnings
For the month ending January 31, 2012

Revenues:		
Repair fees earned	$18,000	
Accounts receivable	15,500	
Bank loan	5,500	
		$39,000
Expenses:		
Rent expense	$ 6,000	
Miscellaneous expenses	600	
Parts and supplies on hand	8,800	
Accounts payable	3,800	
Dividends declared	2,000	
Net earnings		21,200
		$17,800

MOORE REPAIRS
Statement of Financial Position
January 31, 2012

Assets		Shareholders' Equity	
Cash	$ 7,000		
Parts and supplies used	2,600	Share capital	$13,600
Salaries and wages expense	5,000	Retained earnings, January 1	6,600
Total assets	$14,600	Total shareholders' equity	$20,200

Kim realizes that something is wrong with these statements, because she knows that the statement of financial position is supposed to balance. She is sure that the amounts are correct, but not so sure that she has put everything in its proper place.

Required:

Prepare a corrected statement of earnings for the month of January, and statement of financial position as of January 31. (Hint: You will have to calculate the ending balance of retained earnings.)

2-39 (Prepare a statement of cash flows)

The following items should appear on a statement of cash flows for Gordon Company for its fiscal year ending on March 31, 2012. Organize these items into a formal statement of cash flows, and then comment briefly on the company's health.

Proceeds from the issuance of shares	$25,000
Dividends paid	3,000
Cash balance on March 31, 2012	4,000
Payments to employees for salaries	10,000
Cash payments for other expenses	2,000
Cash receipts from customers	14,000
Repayment of bank loan	3,000
Proceeds from the sale of old equipment	1,000
Cash balance on April 1, 2011	8,000
Cash invested in shares of Tim Hortons Inc.	2,000
Cash disbursements to suppliers	9,000
Payment for purchase of equipment	15,000

2-40 (Transaction analysis from both parties' perspectives)

Most transactions take place between two independent entities. How you record a particular transaction depends on whose perspective you take. For each of the following transactions, explain how it would affect the basic accounting equation of each entity.

a. Loan from a bank: from the borrower's and the bank's perspectives
b. Cash sales: from the seller's and the customer's perspectives
c. Investment made by Company A in shares of Company B, with the shares being obtained directly from Company B: from Company A's and Company B's perspectives
d. Investment made by Company A in shares of Company B, with the shares being purchased through the Toronto Stock Exchange; that is, the shares had previously been issued by Company B and now trade in the stock market: from Company A's and Company B's perspectives
e. Purchase of inventory on account: from the buyer's and the seller's perspectives
f. Deposit paid by a customer on the purchase of inventory to be delivered at a later time: from the supplier's and the customer's perspectives

User Perspective Problems

2-41 (Areas of risk in a new company)

Assume that you are a commercial loan officer for a bank. The two owners of **Krave's Candy Company** (see the opening story) come to the bank for a loan shortly before the last of their initial $20,000 of financing has been spent. Prepare a list of things that you would want to know about the company's operations before you decide whether to loan them any money.

2-42 (Accrual-basis versus cash-basis accounting, and manipulation of earnings)

Under the accrual basis of accounting, revenues are recognized when the revenue recognition criteria are met and expenses are then matched with the revenues, according to the matching concept. Discuss the opportunities that management has to manipulate the amount of earnings reported to shareholders under the accrual basis compared with the cash basis.

2-43 (Cash basis of accounting)

Under the cash basis of accounting, the purchase of a new piece of equipment for cash would be treated as an expense of the accounting period when the purchase occurred.

    a. If you were a shareholder, how would this treatment affect your assessment of the company's earnings and financial position?

    b. If you were a prospective buyer of the company (someone who wanted to purchase all the company's shares), how would this treatment affect your assessment of the company as a potential acquisition?

2-44 (Warranty expense and tax implications)

Under accrual-basis accounting, warranty expenses are typically estimated and accrued in the period when the sales are made. If you were in a position to set income tax regulations, would you allow companies to deduct warranty expenses at the time of the sale, or would you make the companies wait until they have actually provided the warranty services? Why?

Reading and Interpreting Published Financial Statements

2-45 (Determination of items from an international company's financial statements)

Base your answers to the following questions on the financial statements of **H&M AB.** in Appendix A (near the end of the book).

    a. Calculate the growth in the following accounts from 2008 to 2009.
       i. Sales (excluding VAT)
       ii. Profit for the year
       iii. Total assets
       iv. Total equity
    Would you expect each of these accounts to grow at the same rate? Why or why not? Comment on the growth rates you calculated.

    b. Based on your analysis from part "a", do the equity investors finance more of the company in 2009 than they did in 2008?

    c. Calculate the following ratios for each of the two years presented. (Note that, in order to be able to calculate these ratios for each of the years, you will have to use the total assets for each year and the total shareholders' equity for each year in your ratios, rather than average total assets and average shareholders' equity.)
       i. profit margin ratio
       ii. return on assets
       iii. return on equity
    Comment on your results. Do the results from part "a" help you interpret the changes in these ratios?

Financial Analysis Assignments

2-46 **(Determination of items from a Canadian company's financial statements)**
Base your answers to the following questions on the 2010 balance sheet and statement of operations of **Research in Motion Limited (RIM)** in Exhibit 2-12. RIM is the manufacturer of the Blackberry. Although it is a Canadian company based in Waterloo, Ontario, RIM prepares its financial statements in U.S. dollars and under U.S. GAAP. However, the general format and accounting policies are similar to the financial statements you have seen so far.

a. In the Shareholders' Equity section, what does the $2,207,609 in common shares represent?
b. In the Shareholders' Equity section, what does the $5,274,365 in retained earnings represent?
c. Does RIM use more liabilities or shareholders' equity to finance its total assets?
d. How much did total assets grow in 2010 over 2009? What were the major areas (or accounts) that accounted for the growth?
e. If RIM were to pay the income taxes payable, in the current liabilities section, what would be the effect on the basic accounting equation?
f. On the Statement of Operations, RIM discloses separately the revenues and cost of sales for its two lines of business: devices and other, and service and software. Calculate the gross margin (the sales revenue less the cost of sales) of each line of business, in dollars and as a percentage of revenues. Are the lines more or less profitable in 2010 than in 2009? Which line is more profitable?

 **EXHIBIT 2-12A** **RESEARCH IN MOTION LIMITED 2010 ANNUAL REPORT**

annual report

Consolidated Statements of Operations

(United States dollars, in thousands, except per share data)

	For the Year Ended		
	February 27, 2010	February 28, 2009	March 1, 2008
Revenue			
Devices and other	$ 12,535,998	$ 9,410,755	$ 4,914,366
Service and software	2,417,226	1,654,431	1,095,029
	14,953,224	11,065,186	6,009,395
Cost of sales			
Devices and other	7,979,163	5,718,041	2,758,250
Service and software	389,795	249,847	170,564
	8,368,958	5,967,888	2,928,814
Gross margin	6,584,266	5,097,298	3,080,581
Operating expenses			
Research and development	964,841	684,702	359,828
Selling, marketing and administration	1,907,398	1,495,697	881,482
Amortization	310,357	194,803	108,112
Litigation	163,800	–	–
	3,346,396	2,375,202	1,349,422
Income from operations	3,237,870	2,722,096	1,731,159
Investment income	28,640	78,267	79,361
Income before income taxes	3,266,510	2,800,363	1,810,520
Provision for income taxes	809,366	907,747	516,653
Net income	$ 2,457,144	$ 1,892,616	$ 1,293,867
Earnings per share			
Basic	$ 4.35	$ 3.35	$ 2.31
Diluted	$ 4.31	$ 3.30	$ 2.26

See notes to consolidated financial statements

RESEARCH IN MOTION LIMITED 2010 ANNUAL REPORT

Consolidated Balance Sheets

(United States dollars, in thousands)

EXHIBIT 2-12B

annual report

	As at	
	February 27, 2010	February 28, 2009
Assets		
Current		
Cash and cash equivalents	$ 1,550,861	$ 835,546
Short-term investments	360,614	682,666
Accounts receivable, net	2,593,742	2,112,117
Other receivables	206,373	157,728
Inventories	621,611	682,400
Other current assets	285,539	187,257
Deferred income tax asset	193,916	183,872
	5,812,656	4,841,586
Long-term investments	958,248	720,635
Property, plant and equipment, net	1,956,581	1,334,648
Intangible assets, net	1,326,363	1,066,527
Goodwill	150,561	137,572
Deferred income tax asset	–	404
	$ 10,204,409	$ 8,101,372
Liabilities		
Current		
Accounts payable	$ 615,620	$ 448,339
Accrued liabilities	1,638,260	1,238,602
Income taxes payable	95,650	361,460
Deferred revenue	67,573	53,834
Deferred income tax liability	14,674	13,116
	2,431,777	2,115,351
Deferred income tax liability	141,382	87,917
Income taxes payable	28,587	23,976
	2,601,746	2,227,244
Commitments and contingencies		
Shareholders' Equity		
Capital Stock		
Preferred shares, authorized unlimited number of non-voting, cumulative, redeemable and retractable	–	–
Common shares, authorized unlimited number of non-voting, redeemable, retractable Class A common shares and unlimited number of voting common shares.		
Issued – 557,328,394 voting common shares (February 28, 2009 – 566,218,819)	2,207,609	2,208,235
Treasury stock (note 11)		
February 27, 2010 – 1,458,950 (February 28, 2009 – nil)	(94,463)	–
Retained earnings	5,274,365	3,545,710
Additional paid-in capital	164,060	119,726
Accumulated other comprehensive income	51,092	457
	7,602,663	5,874,128
	$ 10,204,409	$ 8,101,372

See notes to consolidated financial statements

On behalf of the Board:

John Richardson
Director

Mike Lazaridis
Director

2-47 **(Determination of items from a Canadian company's financial statements)**
Base your answers to the following questions on the 2010 financial statements of **Magnotta Winery Corporation** in Exhibit 2-13. (Magnotta Winery has vineyards in Ontario and Chile, and produces, imports, exports, and retails beer and spirits, as well as wine and ingredients for making wine.)

    a. Assuming that all the sales were on account, determine the amount of cash that was collected from customers in fiscal 2010.

    b. Assuming that all the transactions that flow through the *accounts payable and accrued liabilities* account are related to purchases of inventory, determine the amount of cash that was paid to suppliers in fiscal 2010.

    c. How miuch cash did Magnotta have at the end of fiscal 2010?

    d. What amount of retained earnings did the company have at the end of fiscal 2010?

EXHIBIT 2-13A

annual report

MAGNOTTA WINERY CORPORATION 2010 ANNUAL REPORT

Consolidated Statement of Earnings, Comprehensive Income and Retained Earnings

Years ended January 31, 2010 and 2009

	2010	2009
Net sales	$ 24,172,809	$ 24,046,671
Cost of goods sold, excluding amortization of property plant and equipment	13,935,458	14,172,992
Amortization of property, plant and equipment (production)	524,864	511,764
Total cost of goods sold	14,460,322	14,684,756
Gross profit	9,712,487	9,361,915
Expenses:		
Selling, administration and other	4,717,334	4,400,094
Retirement allowance (note 10)	1,600,000	–
Amortization of property, plant and equipment (non-production)	595,471	698,676
Interest:		
Long-term debt	372,567	449,700
Bank indebtedness	128,232	184,714
	7,413,604	5,733,184
Earnings before income taxes	2,298,883	3,628,731
Income taxes (recovery) (note 8):		
Current	1,131,422	1,043,261
Future	(422,653)	(58,459)
	708,769	984,802
Net earnings and comprehensive income	1,590,114	2,643,929
Retained earnings, beginning of year	27,984,313	25,340,384
Retained earnings, end of year	$ 29,574,427	$ 27,984,313
Earnings per common share (note 7):		
Basic	$ 0.12	$ 0.19
Diluted	0.11	0.19

See accompanying notes to consolidated financial statements.

e. Did the company declare dividends during fiscal 2010? How did you determine this?

f. Why do you think Magnotta reports amortization of property, plant, and equipment in two different places on the statement of earnings?

g. Calculate the following ratios for fiscal 2010. (Note that, in order to be able to calculate these ratios for each of the years, you will have to use the total assets for each year and the total shareholders' equity for each year in your ratios, rather than average total assets and average shareholders' equity.)

    i. profit margin ratio

    ii. return on assets

    iii. return on equity

h. Comment on your results in part "g".

MAGNOTTA WINERY CORPORATION 2010 ANNUAL REPORT

EXHIBIT 2-13B

annual report

Consolidated Statements of Cash Flows
Years ended January 31, 2010 and 2009

	2010	2009
Cash provided by (used in):		
Operations:		
Net earnings	$ 1,590,114	$ 2,643,929
Items not involving cash:		
Amortization of property, plant and equipment	1,120,335	1,210,440
Retirement allowance (note 10)	1,040,000	–
Future income taxes	(422,653)	(58,459)
Unrealized foreign exchange loss (gain)	(6,001)	76,032
Change in non-cash operating working capital:		
Accounts receivable	(29,522)	95,195
Inventories	(2,031,155)	(2,738,908)
Income taxes receivable/payable	328,109	(463,702)
Prepaid expenses and deposits	(21,268)	(6,512)
Accounts payable and accrued liabilities	131,462	362,519
	1,699,421	1,120,534
Financing:		
Decrease in long-term debt	(687,574)	(763,453)
Repayment of notes receivable for share capital	116,250	116,250
Increase (decrease) in bank indebtedness	(631,927)	344,539
	(1,203,251)	(302,664)
Investments:		
Purchase of property, plant and equipment	(496,170)	(1,162,101)
Decrease in cash and cash equivalents	–	(344,231)
Cash and cash equivalents, beginning of year	–	344,231
Cash and cash equivalents, end of year	$ –	$ –
Supplemental cash flow information:		
Interest paid	$ 529,030	$ 730,822
Income taxes paid (net of income tax recovery)	875,125	1,506,963

See accompanying notes to consolidated financial statements.

EXHIBIT 2-13C

annual report

MAGNOTTA WINERY CORPORATION 2010 ANNUAL REPORT

Consolidated Balance Sheets
January 31, 2010 and 2009

	2010	2009
Assets		
Current assets:		
Accounts receivable	$ 590,322	$ 560,800
Inventories (note 2)	29,878,758	27,847,603
Income taxes receivable	137,511	465,620
Future income taxes (note 8)	83,130	4,453
Prepaid expenses and deposits	268,306	247,038
	30,958,027	29,125,514
Property, plant and equipment (note 3)	20,468,725	21,092,890
Winery licenses	251,516	251,516
	$ 51,678,268	$ 50,469,920
Liabilities and Shareholders' Equity		
Current liabilities:		
Bank indebtedness (note 4)	$ 5,249,398	$ 5,881,325
Accounts payable and accrued liabilities	1,568,495	1,437,033
Current portion of long-term debt (note 5)	1,041,811	784,920
Current portion of retirement allowance (note 10)	300,000	–
	8,159,704	8,103,278
Long-term debt (note 5)	5,665,914	6,616,380
Long-term retirement allowance (note 10)	740,000	–
Future income taxes (note 8)	482,856	826,832
Shareholders' equity:		
Share capital (note 6)	6,961,617	6,961,617
Notes receivable for share capital (note 9(b))	(116,250)	(232,500)
Other paid-in capital	210,000	210,000
Retained earnings	29,574,427	27,984,313
	36,629,794	34,923,430
Commitments (note 13)		
	$ 51,678,268	$ 50,469,920

See accompanying notes to consolidated financial statements.

On behalf of the Board:

Rossana Di Zio Magnotta
Director

Owen McManamon
Director

2-48 **(Determination of items from a Canadian company's financial statements)**
Base your answers to the following questions on the 2009 financial statements of **WestJet Airlines Ltd.** provided in Exhibit 2-14. (Calgary-based WestJet, known for its corporate culture and providing customers with a user-friendly travel experience, has grown from a small regional airline to one that provides services throughout Canada and to some international destinations.)

  a. Assuming that all the sales were on account, determine the amount of cash that was collected from customers in 2009.
  b. Why do you think WestJet does not report a cost of goods sold account on their statement of earnings?
  c. Explain what the account *advance ticket sales* in the current liabilities section of the balance sheet represents. What type of transaction gave rise to this liability? What will cause this liability to decrease?
  d. How much money did WestJet raise in 2009 by issuing shares? Assuming the shares were all issued for cash, what was the effect on the accounting equation of the share issuance?
  e. How much did WestJet spend on acquiring new aircraft in 2009? If they financed the acquisitions with long-term debt, what was the effect on the accounting equation?

2-49 **(Determination of items from a Canadian company's financial statements)**
Base your answers to the following questions on the financial statements of **WestJet Airlines Ltd.** in Exhibit 2-14. (Calgary-based WestJet, known for its corporate culture and providing customers with a user-friendly travel experience, has grown from a small regional airline to one that provides services throughout Canada and to some international destinations.)

  a. Calculate the following ratios for each of the two years presented. (Note that, in order to be able to calculate these ratios for each of the years, you will have to use the total assets for each year and the total shareholders' equity for each year in your ratios, rather than average total assets and average shareholders' equity.)
     i.   profit margin ratio (use total revenues)
     ii. return on assets
     iii. return on equity
  b. Comment on WestJet's profitability during 2008 and 2009.

2-50 **(Determination of items from an international company's financial statements)**
Base your answers to the following questions on the consolidated financial statements and Note 25 of **Domino's Pizza Enterprises Limited** in Exhibit 2-15. (Domino's Pizza Enterprises is an Australian-based company that operates 776 outlets selling pizza and other fast foods in Australia, New Zealand, and Europe.)

  a. Determine the amount of dividends *declared* during fiscal 2009. Where did you find this information?
  b. How does the declaration of dividends affect the accounting equation?
  c. Determine the amount of dividends *paid* during fiscal 2009. Where did you find this information?
  d. How does the payment of dividends affect the accounting equation?
  e. What percentage of total assets is invested in inventories? Would you expect Domino's to have a relatively large or small level of inventory, as a portion of total assets, compared to a company like H&M? Why?
  f. Why does the account "Borrowings" appear in two places on the balance sheet? What is the difference between the two accounts?
  g. What are the largest two expenses on Domino's income statement?

EXHIBIT 2-14A

annual report

WESTJET AIRLINES LTD. 2009 ANNUAL REPORT

CONSOLIDATED STATEMENT OF EARNINGS

For the years ended December 31
(Stated in thousands of Canadian dollars, except per share amounts)

	2009	2008
		Restated – see note 2
Revenues:		
Guest revenues	$ 2,067,860	$ 2,301,301
Charter and other revenues	213,260	248,205
	2,281,120	2,549,506
Expenses:		
Aircraft fuel	570,569	803,293
Airport operations	352,333	342,922
Flight operations and navigational charges	298,762	280,920
Marketing, general and administration	208,316	211,979
Sales and distribution	172,326	170,693
Depreciation and amortization	141,303	136,485
Inflight	112,054	105,849
Aircraft leasing	103,954	86,050
Maintenance	96,272	85,093
Employee profit share	14,675	33,435
	2,070,564	2,256,719
Earnings from operations	210,556	292,787
Non-operating income (expense):		
Interest income	5,601	25,485
Interest expense	(67,706)	(76,078)
Gain (loss) on foreign exchange	(12,306)	30,587
Loss on disposal of property and equipment	(1,177)	(701)
Gain (loss) on derivatives (note 13(b))	1,828	(17,331)
	(73,760)	(38,038)
Earnings before income taxes	136,796	254,749
Income tax expense: (note 9)		
Current	2,690	2,549
Future	35,928	73,694
	38,618	76,243
Net earnings	$ 98,178	$ 178,506
Earnings per share: (note 10(c))		
Basic	$ 0.74	$ 1.39
Diluted	$ 0.74	$ 1.37

The accompanying notes are an integral part of the consolidated financial statements.

WESTJET AIRLINES LTD. 2009 ANNUAL REPORT

EXHIBIT 2-14B

annual report

CONSOLIDATED BALANCE SHEET

As at December 31
(Stated in thousands of Canadian dollars)

	2009	2008
		Restated – see note 2
Assets		
Current assets:		
Cash and cash equivalents (note 4)	$ 1,005,181	$ 820,214
Accounts receivable	27,654	16,837
Future income tax (note 9)	2,560	8,459
Prepaid expenses, deposits and other (note 14(a))	56,239	53,283
Inventory	26,048	17,054
	1,117,682	915,847
Property and equipment (note 5)	2,307,566	2,269,790
Intangible assets (note 6)	14,087	12,060
Other assets (note 14(a))	54,367	71,005
	$ 3,493,702	$ 3,268,702
Liabilities and shareholders' equity		
Current liabilities:		
Accounts payable and accrued liabilities	$ 231,401	$ 249,354
Advance ticket sales	286,361	251,354
Non-refundable guest credits	64,506	73,020
Current portion of long-term debt (note 7)	171,223	165,721
Current portion of obligations under capital leases (note 8)	744	395
	754,235	739,844
Long-term debt (note 7)	1,048,554	1,186,182
Obligations under capital leases (note 8)	3,358	713
Other liabilities (note 14(a))	19,628	24,233
Future income taxes (note 9)	278,999	241,740
	2,104,774	2,192,712
Shareholders' equity:		
Share capital (note 10(b))	633,075	452,885
Contributed surplus	71,503	60,193
Accumulated other comprehensive loss (note 14(c))	(14,852)	(38,112)
Retained earnings	699,202	601,024
	1,388,928	1,075,990
Commitments and contingencies (note 12)		
	$ 3,493,702	$ 3,268,702

The accompanying notes are an integral part of the consolidated financial statements.

On behalf of the Board:

Sean Durfy, Director   Hugh Bolton, Director

EXHIBIT 2-14C

annual report

WESTJET AIRLINES LTD. 2009 ANNUAL REPORT

CONSOLIDATED STATEMENT OF CASH FLOWS

For the years ended December 31
(Stated in thousands of Canadian dollars)

	2009	2008
		Restated – see note 2
Operating activities:		
Net earnings	$ 98,178	$ 178,506
Items not involving cash:		
Depreciation and amortization	141,303	136,485
Amortization of other liabilities	(7,595)	(937)
Amortization of hedge settlements	1,400	1,400
Unrealized (gain) loss on derivative instruments	(2,406)	6,725
Issuance of shares pursuant to employee share purchase plan	11,071	–
Loss on disposal of property and equipment	1,504	1,809
Stock-based compensation expense	13,440	13,485
Income tax credit receivable	(1,952)	–
Future income tax expense	35,928	73,694
Unrealized foreign exchange loss (gain)	8,440	(34,823)
Change in non-cash working capital (note 14(b))	19,350	84,242
	318,661	460,586
Financing activities:		
Increase in long-term debt	33,855	101,782
Repayment of long-term debt	(165,757)	(179,397)
Decrease in obligations under capital leases	(406)	(375)
Issuance of shares	172,463	227
Share issue costs	(7,468)	–
Shares repurchased	–	(29,420)
Decrease (increase) in other assets	3,427	(4,135)
Change in non-cash working capital	(1,463)	(4,111)
	34,651	(115,429)
Investing activities:		
Aircraft additions	(118,686)	(114,470)
Aircraft disposals	27	84
Other property and equipment and intangible additions	(48,155)	(90,663)
Other property and equipment and intangible disposals	134	172
Change in non-cash working capital	–	5,147
	(166,680)	(199,730)
Cash flow from operating, financing and investing activities	186,632	145,427
Effect of foreign exchange on cash and cash equivalents	(1,665)	21,229
Net change in cash and cash equivalents	184,967	166,656
Cash and cash equivalents, beginning of year	820,214	653,558
Cash and cash equivalents, end of year	$ 1,005,181	820,214
Cash interest paid	$ 67,973	$ 76,604
Cash taxes paid	$ 3,369	$ 2,305

The accompanying notes are an integral part of the consolidated financial statements.

DOMINO'S PIZZA ENTERPRISES LIMITED 2009 ANNUAL REPORT

EXHIBIT 2-15A

annual report

BALANCE SHEET
AS AT 28 JUNE 2009

	NOTE	CONSOLIDATED 2009 $'000	CONSOLIDATED 2008 $'000	COMPANY 2009 $'000	COMPANY 2008 $'000
CURRENT ASSETS					
Cash and cash equivalents	33(A)	17,426	12,645	6,987	6,750
Trade and other receivables	9	23,248	24,728	7,147	5,624
Other financial assets	10	279	554	5,200	554
Inventories	11	3,598	3,525	1,443	1,848
Current tax assets	8	13	-	-	110
Other	16	2,691	6,083	1,489	3,034
		47,255	47,535	22,266	17,920
Non-current assets classified as held for sale	12	-	2,369	-	-
TOTAL CURRENT ASSETS		**47,255**	**49,904**	**22,266**	**17,920**
NON-CURRENT ASSETS					
Other financial assets	10	21,179	16,402	48,241	54,652
Property, plant & equipment	13	30,505	30,412	22,224	21,787
Deferred tax assets	8	2,107	2,393	559	147
Goodwill	14	43,803	41,118	29,024	26,789
Other intangible assets	15	4,241	1,726	1,884	1,107
Other	16	170	202	105	132
TOTAL NON-CURRENT ASSETS		**102,005**	**92,253**	**102,037**	**104,614**
TOTAL ASSETS		**149,260**	**142,157**	**124,303**	**122,534**
CURRENT LIABILITIES					
Trade and other payables	18	25,977	27,901	11,806	13,620
Borrowings	19	74	118	48	58
Other financial liabilities	20	889	177	889	80
Current tax liabilities	8	1,561	477	1,511	-
Provisions	21	1,981	2,113	1,954	2,090
Other	22	7	-	-	-
TOTAL CURRENT LIABILITIES		**30,489**	**30,786**	**16,208**	**15,848**
NON-CURRENT LIABILITIES					
Borrowings	19	20,977	28,448	20,789	28,279
Other financial liabilities	20	1,686	2,011	1,686	2,011
Provisions	21	310	409	310	409
Other	22	893	1,249	-	-
TOTAL NON-CURRENT LIABILITIES		**23,866**	**32,117**	**22,785**	**30,699**
TOTAL LIABILITIES		**54,355**	**62,903**	**38,993**	**46,547**
NET ASSETS		**94,905**	**79,254**	**85,310**	**75,987**
EQUITY					
Issued capital	23	63,411	55,649	63,411	55,649
Reserves	24	182	176	311	1,163
Retained earnings	25	31,312	23,429	21,588	19,175
TOTAL EQUITY		**94,905**	**79,254**	**85,310**	**75,987**

Notes to the financial statements are included on pages 66 to 123.

EXHIBIT 2-15B

annual report

DOMINO'S PIZZA ENTERPRISES LIMITED 2009 ANNUAL REPORT

CASH FLOW STATEMENT
FOR THE FINANCIAL YEAR ENDED 28 JUNE 2009

	NOTE	CONSOLIDATED		COMPANY	
		2009 $'000	2008 $'000	2009 $'000	2008 $'000
CASH FLOWS FROM OPERATING ACTIVITIES					
Receipts from customers		265,497	257,902	162,136	175,450
Payments to suppliers and employees		(238,326)	(235,681)	(143,394)	(158,960)
Interest received		1,640	890	1,090	612
Interest and other costs of finance paid		(1,552)	(2,086)	(1,468)	(2,018)
Income taxes paid		(2,099)	(2,432)	(1,725)	(2,380)
Net cash provided by operating activities	33(F)	**25,160**	**18,593**	**16,639**	**12,704**
CASH FLOWS FROM INVESTING ACTIVITIES					
Payment for investment and business operations, net of cash acquired	33(B)	(8,466)	(9,639)	(6,669)	(8,304)
(Loans to)/repaid from related parties, third parties and franchisees		(3,708)	(7,129)	700	(9,129)
Payment for property, plant & equipment		(5,799)	(8,603)	(4,224)	(3,801)
Proceeds from sale of businesses and other non-current assets		9,675	17,978	3,441	14,971
Payments for intangible assets		(3,253)	(1,162)	(1,411)	(712)
Investment in subsidiaries		-	-	(53)	(65)
Net cash used in investing activities		**(11,551)**	**(8,555)**	**(8,216)**	**(7,040)**
CASH FLOWS FROM FINANCING ACTIVITIES					
Proceeds from borrowings		118	11,000	31	11,000
Repayment of borrowings		(8,631)	(16,633)	(8,512)	(15,181)
Dividends paid		(4,246)	(3,915)	(4,246)	(3,915)
Proceeds from issue of equity securities		4,541	3,915	4,541	3,915
Net cash (used in)/provided by financing activities		**(8,218)**	**(5,633)**	**(8,186)**	**(4,181)**
NET INCREASE IN CASH AND CASH EQUIVALENTS		**5,391**	**4,405**	**237**	**1,483**
CASH AND CASH EQUIVALENTS AT THE BEGINNING OF THE FINANCIAL YEAR		**12,645**	**7,862**	**6,750**	**5,267**
Effects of exchange rate changes on the balance of cash held in foreign currencies		(610)	378	-	-
CASH AND CASH EQUIVALENTS AT THE END OF THE FINANCIAL YEAR	33(A)	**17,426**	**12,645**	**6,987**	**6,750**

Notes to the financial statements are included on pages 66 to 123.

DOMINO'S PIZZA ENTERPRISES LIMITED 2009 ANNUAL REPORT

EXHIBIT 2-15C

annual report

INCOME STATEMENT
FOR THE FINANCIAL YEAR ENDED 28 JUNE 2009

	NOTE	CONSOLIDATED 2009 $'000	CONSOLIDATED 2008 $'000	COMPANY 2009 $'000	COMPANY 2008 $'000
Revenue	5	239,015	229,587	149,151	156,955
Other income	7(A)	1,631	1,582	1,031	573
Food and paper expenses		(81,885)	(83,389)	(33,464)	(43,979)
Employee benefits expense		(59,938)	(55,879)	(43,522)	(43,495)
Plant and equipment costs		(4,490)	(5,237)	(4,959)	(5,227)
Depreciation and amortisation expense	7	(6,449)	(6,198)	(4,685)	(4,670)
Occupancy expenses		(7,970)	(7,688)	(5,199)	(5,476)
Finance costs	6	(1,552)	(2,086)	(1,468)	(2,018)
Marketing expenses		(11,514)	(12,811)	(10,982)	(11,970)
Store related expenses		(6,820)	(8,507)	(5,338)	(6,238)
Communication expenses		(4,347)	(4,288)	(3,882)	(3,710)
Other expenses		(35,418)	(28,068)	(22,876)	(23,575)
PROFIT BEFORE TAX	7	**20,263**	**17,018**	**13,807**	**7,170**
Income tax expense	8	(4,910)	(5,184)	(3,924)	(2,354)
PROFIT FOR THE YEAR FROM CONTINUING OPERATIONS		**15,353**	**11,834**	**9,883**	**4,816**
DISCONTINUED OPERATIONS					
Profit for the year from discontinued operations		-	-	-	-
PROFIT FOR THE YEAR		**15,353**	**11,834**	**9,883**	**4,816**

EARNINGS PER SHARE

From continuing operations:

	NOTE	CONSOLIDATED 2009	CONSOLIDATED 2008		
Basic (cents per share)	26	22.6	18.4		
Diluted (cents per share)	26	22.5	18.3		

Notes to the financial statements are included on pages 66 to 123.

EXHIBIT 2-15D **DOMINO'S PIZZA ENTERPRISES LIMITED 2009 ANNUAL REPORT**

NOTES TO THE
FINANCIAL STATEMENTS
25. RETAINED EARNINGS

	CONSOLIDATED		COMPANY	
	2009	**2008**	**2009**	**2008**
	$'000	**$'000**	**$'000**	**$'000**
Balance at beginning of financial year	23,429	18,522	19,175	21,286
Net profit for the year	15,353	11,834	9,883	4,816
Dividends provided for or paid (note 27)	(7,470)	(6,927)	(7,470)	(6,927)
Balance at end of financial year	**31,312**	**23,429**	**21,588**	**19,175**

BEYOND THE BOOK

2-51 (Examine a Canadian company's annual report)

Find the annual report of a Canadian company in the retailing business, and answer the following questions:

    a. Who are the independent auditors for this company? Did they give the company an unqualified opinion?

    b. How important is inventory relative to the other assets on the company's statement of financial position (or balance sheet)?

    c. Does the company finance its business primarily with debt (funds borrowed from creditors) or with equity (funds invested by owners)?

    d. Read through the *management discussion and analysis* and determine whether there is any information there that is not included in the financial statements. If you were a shareholder, would you think the extra information is important? Why or why not?

    e. How many directors does the company have? What positions do they hold? Are any of them directors of other companies?

2-52 (Research a Canadian company)

Find at least three articles in the financial press about the company you chose for Problem 2-53. Write a one-page summary that discusses the nature of the company's markets and the forecast for this sector of the economy. (Hint: You might find recent articles about the company on its website.)

Cases

2-53   Wroad Wrunner Courier Service

At the end of her first year of university, Nola Lam decided that she wanted a summer job that would keep her outside enjoying the nice weather, so she set up her own courier service. She invested savings of $800 in the company, which she incorporated and called *Wroad Wrunner*. In addition, her parents loaned the company $2,200 to help it get started. Since this was a business venture, Nola insisted on paying interest on this loan and her parents agreed to charge a rate of 6% per year.

Nola then negotiated the purchase of a used car for the business for $4,000. The company made a down payment of $750 on the car, and financed the remainder of the purchase price at an interest rate of 12% per year. Nola estimated that the car could be sold at the end of the summer for $3,500.

Wroad Wrunner began operations on May 1, and continued until August 31. Although she did not keep any formal accounting records, at the end of the summer Nola put together the following additional information related to the business:

1. During the summer, the company made payments of $623 on the car, which included interest of $123 and principal of $500.

2. No payments (of either interest or principal) were made on the loan from her parents.

3. Nola paid herself a salary of $1,500 per month for the four months that the business operated.

4. Payments for other operating costs (including advertising, insurance, gas, etc.) totalled $1,100. In addition, there were unpaid bills totalling $100 at the end of August.

5. Courier charges collected from customers totalled $9,300. In addition, customers still owed $300 for services performed in the last two weeks of August.

6. After the close of business on August 31, there was a balance of $3,777 in the company's bank account, plus a "float" of $50 in the car.

Required:

a. Analyze the transactions that affected the business during the summer. Prepare a statement of earnings for *Wroad Wrunner* for the four-month period ending on August 31, and a statement of financial position on that date.

b. Comment on the profitability of the business during its four-month period of operations. How much did Nola make from her venture during the summer?

c. Comment on the financial position of the company on August 31. If Nola dissolves the business before she returns to university, will there be enough cash to pay off the liabilities?

2-54   Daisy-Fresh Dry Cleaning

Daisy-Fresh Dry Cleaning is in the process of preparing its annual financial statements. The owner of the business is not an accountant, but likes to prepare the financial statements himself. Most of the business transactions are straightforward and can be easily recorded; however, the owner is having trouble determining how to account for the following events that occurred in during the year:

1. On January 1, the company purchased a three-year insurance policy for $3,000. Because the entire amount had to be paid when the policy took effect, the owner charged $3,000 to expense in the current year.

2. On July 1, the company bought a new dry-cleaning machine for $10,000. Although it is expected to have a five-year life, the owner thinks he would only get $2,000 for it if he sold it now, so he recorded an asset of $2,000 and an expense of $8,000.

3. On October 31, the company borrowed $10,000 from a bank. Since the loan does not have to be repaid until four years later, the owner does not think it should be reported as a payable on this year's statement of financial position.

4. No interest has to be paid on the loan until October 31 of next year, so the owner did not record any interest this year.

5. On December 31, the company declared and paid a dividend of $10,000. Because it is not an expenditure that will produce future benefits and is therefore not an asset, the owner recorded this payment as an expense.

Required:

Advise the owner as to how the above transactions should be recorded and reported in the financial statements for the current year.

2-55 Mega Manufacturing

Mega Manufacturing has calculated the following financial ratios, based on the company's comparative financial statements for 2011 and 2010:

	2011	2010	INDUSTRY AVERAGE
Profit Margin Ratio	18%	20%	16%
Return on Assets	10%	8%	12%
Return on Equity	12%	10%	14%

Briefly explain what each of the ratios indicates, and comment on the company's performance during this two-year period.

Critical Thinking Question

2-56 (Consider the value of an ownership interest in a company)

One of the shareholders of The Canadian Cookies and Cakes Company is considering selling her one-third ownership and therefore wants to determine her equity in the cookie shop, using the correct accounting principles. The following transactions have occurred since the shop started operations at the beginning of this year:

1. The company borrowed $30,000 from the bank to help get the business started, and repaid $10,000 of this before year end. Shareholders also contributed $30,000 to get the business started.

2. Ingredients costing $42,000 were purchased on account, and 80% of these ingredients were used in goods that were baked and sold during the year. Before the end of the year, payments of $37,000 were made for these ingredients.

3. Baking ovens were rented for $12,000 cash, paid at the rate of $1,000 per month. At the end of the year, the company purchased its own ovens for $46,000 cash.

4. Employees earned wages of $30,000 during the year; the company withheld income taxes of $3,000 from their paycheques, which it will forward to the Canada Revenue Agency early next year. In other words, although the employees' wages were $30,000, the company deducted income taxes and paid only the remaining $27,000 net amount to the employees; it will pay the $3,000 of income taxes directly to the CRA. (Note that these income taxes relate to the *employees'* earnings, not the company's earnings. Consequently, they are recorded as part of the company's wages expense, not as income taxes expense.)

5. Interest on the bank loan for the year totalled $1,600, but has not yet been paid.

6. Various other expenses totalled $15,000 for the year, but only $13,500 of this amount was paid before the end of the year.

7. After $98,000 was collected from the sale of goods (which was the full sales amount), the cash balance at the end of the year was $12,500, and net income of $5,800 was reported.

Required:

a. Show calculations to prove that the ending cash balance was $12,500 and the net income for the year was $5,800.

b. Prepare a statement of financial position for the bakery as of the end of the year.

c. If the shareholder sells her one-third ownership interest in the bakery, what does the foregoing tell you regarding how much she should expect to get for her shares?

chapter 3

PROCESSING DATA THROUGH THE ACCOUNTING SYSTEM

LEARNING OBJECTIVES

After studying this chapter, you should be able to:

1. Explain the role of debits and credits in the accounting system.

2. Explain the difference between permanent and temporary accounts.

3. Identify and explain the steps in the accounting cycle.

4. Build a chart of accounts based on transactions that affect the company's assets, liabilities, and/or shareholder equity.

5. Analyze transactions and record them in journal entry format.

6. Post transactions from the journal to the ledger.

7. Prepare a trial balance and use it to identify errors.

8. Make adjusting entries to prepare an adjusted trial balance.

9. Prepare financial statements.

10. Explain closing entries and why they are necessary.

Learning to Handle the Dough

For generations, grandmothers in Grant Hooker's family would make a pastry of flattened, whole-wheat dough as a special treat, called a BeaverTail®, which became a Sunday staple with Mr. Hooker's own kids during the 1970s.

Mr. Hooker sold the family secret to the public for the first time in 1978, at a music festival near Killaloe, Ontario. The crowd loved it. The delectable dough was then served up at several Ottawa Valley agricultural fairs throughout that fall. Encouraged by the enthusiasm for his treats, Mr. Hooker, a builder by trade, trademarked the name "BeaverTails" and built his own booth in Ottawa's Byward Market in 1980 to sell them full-time. However, sales weren't as swift as at the fairs.

Undaunted, Mr. Hooker secured permission to sell BeaverTails on the Rideau Canal during Ottawa's Winterlude festival. "We had lineups down the lake," he says. The whole family—Mr. Hooker's wife Pamela, and teenage son Nicholas and daughter Lisa—pitched in, giving out free samples and letting people know the treats were for sale year-round in the Market.

Within three years, BeaverTails Canada Inc. had the contract to sell all the food on the Rideau Canal and employed 450 people. The business continued to grow; BeaverTails began franchising in 1990 and now includes 97 locations across Canada, 2 in the United States, and 2 in the Kingdom of Saudi Arabia.

At first, keeping track of the money was straightforward and didn't require a formal accounting system. It meant little more than staying on top of how much was owed to suppliers and staff, and in rent and utilities. Mr. Hooker, who has no formal business training, got along fine simply managing the chequebook.

But this changed with franchising. "We weren't just selling products to people for cash, putting the cash in the bank, and then writing

cheques for what we owed," says Mr. Hooker. "We were into receivables; people owed us money." The company also had liabilities—in the form of an operating loan from a bank.

Mr. Hooker hired an accountant to build the accounting system, working closely with him to learn how it worked. The breakthrough point for him, he says, was understanding that "cash is a debit on the balance sheet." Assets (from the balance sheet) and expenses (from the statement of earnings) have normal debit balances. Liabilities and shareholders' equity (from the balance sheet) and revenues (from the statement of earnings) have normal credit balances. To increase the amount in an account, an entry has to be the same type as the balance, he adds. That is, debits increase debit accounts and credits increase credit accounts.

Now that he understands the basics of the accounting system, Mr. Hooker monitors it very closely. He insists that his accountant provide him with "TAMFS"—timely, accurate, monthly financial statements. "That is an absolute necessity any time a business grows to where the owner puts his trust in somebody else to handle the money," he says. A lesson this entrepreneur learned as his business grew.

Now that you understand the basic accounting equation and can work through the analysis of some transactions, we are going to take you further into the practical side of accounting. We are going to show you how data is recorded in an accounting system so that organizations can easily extract information and summarize it into financial statements and other reports.

When you were working through Chapter 2, you used columns in tables to record the effects of transactions on the basic accounting equation. You could probably see that if you had to handle large volumes of accounts and transactions, this type of framework would become awkward to manage. Since real companies typically have hundreds of accounts and thousands of transactions, the accounting system for recording, summarizing, and reporting information about their economic activities requires something more elaborate than columnar tables.

USER RELEVANCE

Why is it important for users to have a good understanding of how accounting data are collected, stored, and reported? All business owners, such as Grant Hooker of BeaverTails, must understand how the financial statements reflect the company's business activities, especially if the owner intends to use the financial results to make decisions.

Investment analysts, who advise others on buying or selling shares, should also have in-depth knowledge of how an accounting system works. In order to understand what the numbers on financial statements mean, financial analysts need to know how the numbers are determined, and how relevant they are in understanding a company's overall profitability and financial position. Creditors, such as loan officers, need an in-depth understanding of the accounting process so that they can assess whether future cash flows will be adequate to meet the existing obligations, plus any future ones being contemplated. To do so, they need to understand what types of transactions affect which financial statement amounts.

Users should also be aware that decisions should not be made on single amounts or ratios. Rather, decision-makers should review the full set of results, because changes in one area of the financial statements will often have implications for other areas, which could affect the conclusions that are drawn.

DOUBLE-ENTRY ACCOUNTING SYSTEMS

The recording of transactions in a table or spreadsheet that has columns reflecting the basic accounting equation is sufficient if the entity has only a few transactions to record. This type of system is usually called a **synoptic journal**, and is used, for example, by community clubs that only need to maintain information about the dues they collect and the limited number of activities they undertake. However, using columnar tables or spreadsheets is cumbersome when large numbers of accounts and transactions are involved. To overcome this problem, accountants have developed a special system to record transactions, which utilizes debits and credits and is known as the **double-entry accounting system**.

Before we introduce the role of debits and credits in an accounting system, we should point out that the method that we used to record transactions in Chapter 2 was a type of double-entry system, because each transaction affected two columns. In this way, we were able to keep the basic accounting equation in balance as each transaction was recorded. This principle also applies to double-entry accounting systems that use debits and credits rather than pluses and minuses, and that record the effects of transactions in accounts rather than columns.

Debits and Credits

We will demonstrate the debit-credit system by using a simplified form of accounts, called **T accounts**. In the illustration below, notice that when this method is used to depict accounts the basic shape is a large letter T. Note also that the left side of a T account is known as the **debit** side, and the right side as the **credit** side.

LEARNING OBJECTIVE 1

Explain the role of debits and credits in the accounting system.

GENERAL FORM OF A "T ACCOUNT"

Name of account

Debit side	Credit side

Thus, at the most basic level, the words "debit" and "credit" in accounting simply refer to the left and right sides of an account. As you will soon see, whether an entry on the debit (left) or credit (right) side of an account indicates an increase or a decrease depends on the type of account involved.

The T account concept can be used for each specific asset, liability, and shareholders' equity account. Therefore, instead of the columns that we used for recording transactions in Chapter 2, from this point onward each asset, liability, and shareholders' equity item will have its own T account.

Regardless of the type of account (asset, liability, or shareholders' equity), items recorded on the left side are called debits and items recorded on the right side are called credits. However, note this key distinction: *for asset accounts, the balances are debits* (i.e., recorded on the left side of the account), *while for liability and shareholders' equity accounts, the balances are credits* (i.e., recorded on the right side of the account). This is the basic "rule" regarding debits and credits in accounting.

This allows us to express the balancing nature of the accounting system in terms of debits and credits, rather than in terms of the basic accounting equation. By recording asset balances on the left side of their accounts and liability and shareholders' equity balances on the right side of their accounts, we can maintain the basic accounting equation (i.e., Assets = Liabilities + Shareholders' Equity) by ensuring that the sum of all the debits in the accounts equals the sum of all the credits (i.e., Debits = Credits). If transactions are recorded correctly, in terms of debit entries and credit entries, the total debits will always equal the total credits and the accounting system will be "balanced."

For example, Exhibit 3-1 shows how the balances for Demo Company at the end of January 2011 would be presented in T accounts. (As you probably recall, Demo Company was used to illustrate transactions in Chapter 2.) The accounts and balances are the same as those shown on Demo's statement of financial position for January 31, 2011, which was presented on page 105.

HELPFUL HINT

To remember which side of an account is the debit side and which is the credit side, think of the equation Debits = Credits. The word "Debits" is on the left side of this equation, and debit entries are always recorded on the left side of an account. Similarly, the word "Credits" is on the right side of the equation, and credit entries are always recorded on the right side of an account.

EXHIBIT 3-1

ACCOUNTS SHOWING THE BALANCES FOR DEMO COMPANY AS OF JANUARY 31, 2011

Cash (A)			Accounts Payable (L)	
Bal. Jan. 31/11	2,090		Bal. Jan. 31/11	9,500

Accounts Receivable (A)			Interest Payable (L)	
Bal. Jan. 31/11	2,000		Bal. Jan. 31/11	50

Inventory (A)			Income Tax Payable (L)	
Bal. Jan. 31/11	14,000		Bal. Jan. 31/11	235

Prepaid Insurance (A)			Bank Loan (L)	
Bal. Jan. 31/11	300		Bal. Jan. 31/11	10,000

Land (A)			Share Capital (SE)	
Bal. Jan. 31/11	15,000		Bal. Jan. 31/11	17,500

Equipment (A)			Retained Earnings (SE)	
Bal. Jan. 31/11	4,500		Bal. Jan. 31/11	455

Accumulated Depreciation—Equipment (XA)	
	Bal. Jan. 31/11	150

HELPFUL HINT

To remember the sides on which different types of account balances should appear, think of the basic accounting equation (Assets = Liabilities + Shareholders' Equity). Assets are on the left side of this equation; hence, balances for assets are recorded on the left side of their T accounts. Similarly, liabilities and shareholders' equity are on the right side of the equation; hence, balances for liabilities and permanent shareholders' equity accounts are recorded on the right side of their T accounts.

Notice the letters in the illustration, beside each of the account names. These letters will be used throughout this book to designate the type of account: (A) indicates an asset account, (L) a liability account, and (SE) a shareholders' equity account. These letters are intended to remind you of the type of account involved, and help you deal with it correctly.

In addition to these basic account categories, we will use (XA) to represent a contra-asset. At this point, we have only encountered one contra-asset, **Accumulated Depreciation**. However, other contra accounts will be introduced later. Remember that, when a statement of financial position is prepared, contra-assets are reported as deductions from their related assets. That is why the balance in Demo's **contra-asset account**, Accumulated Depreciation, is a *credit* while the balance in its related asset account, Equipment, is a *debit*. The fact that they are opposites indicates that one partially offsets the other.

Note that all of Demo's assets have debit balances, recorded on the left side of their T accounts, while all of its liabilities and shareholders' equity accounts have credit balances, recorded on the right side of their T accounts. Also remember that the accounting system ensures that Assets = Liabilities + Shareholders' Equity by keeping the total of the debit amounts equal to the total of the credit amounts.

We can now extend the basic rule regarding debits and credits, as follows:

- Because *asset accounts* have *debit balances*, *increases* in asset accounts are recorded as *debits*. It logically follows that *decreases* in assets are recorded as *credits*.

- Because *liability and shareholders' equity accounts* have *credit balances*, *increases* in liability and shareholders' equity accounts are recorded as *credits*. It logically follows that *decreases* in liabilities and shareholders' equity are recorded as *debits*.

Notice that asset accounts are treated in the opposite manner to liability and shareholders' equity accounts, in terms of debits and credits: debits increase assets, but decrease liabilities and shareholders' equity; credits increase liabilities and shareholders' equity, but decrease assets. Thus, whether the term "debit" or "credit" indicates an increase or decrease depends on the type of account.

Exhibit 3-2 illustrates the appropriate entries for asset, liability, and shareholders' equity accounts. This summarizes what are often referred to as "**the rules of debit and credit**."

ENTRIES TO T ACCOUNTS:
A Summary of the Rules of Debit and Credit

EXHIBIT 3-2

An Asset Account		A Liability Account	
Beginning balance **Increases**	Decreases	Decreases	Beginning balance **Increases**
Ending balance			Ending balance

A Shareholders' Equity Account	
Decreases	Beginning balance **Increases**
	Ending balance

Increases and balances go on the **debit** side.

Increases and balances go on the **credit** side.

HELPFUL HINT

Remember that increases in accounts *are recorded in the same way as the account balances:*

- Asset account balances are debits; increases in assets are also recorded as debits.

- Liability and Shareholders' Equity account balances are credits; increases in liabilities and shareholders' equity are also recorded as credits.

The easiest way to remember these rules is to focus on how *increases* are recorded for each type of account. Logically, decreases are recorded on the opposite side of the account. Also, since there will be more increases than decreases (because you cannot take more out of an account than you put into it), *account balances will be on the same side as the increases.*

As you would expect, since *contra-assets* are deductions from their related assets, they are recorded in the same way as *decreases in asset accounts* (i.e., as *credits*). In terms of balances, since asset accounts have debit balances, it is logical that contra-asset accounts have the opposite (i.e., credit balances).

Statement of Financial Position

One way to think about the accounts and debits and credits is to imagine that the accounting system is a warehouse that is balanced on a central point (like the equal sign between the two parts of the basic accounting equation). In the warehouse, the company has boxes on both sides, which maintain the balance. The boxes themselves are weightless, which means you do not need to have the same number of boxes on each side. Weight is added when something is put in a box. Each box represents an account. When the company needs to keep track of information about a specific financial item, it creates a new box, and labels it so that everyone knows what is in that box. For example, there would be a box (or account) labelled Cash on one side of the warehouse and another labelled Share Capital on the other side.

As financial activities are recorded, things are added to or removed from the appropriate boxes. In order to preserve the balance, if you add something to an asset box on one side of the warehouse, you have to either take something out of another asset box, on the same side of the warehouse, or go to the other side of the warehouse and add something to one of the boxes there (a liability or a shareholders' equity box).

Debiting and crediting accounts is like putting things into boxes and taking things out. All the asset boxes are kept on the left side of the warehouse, and each time you add something to an asset box, you debit it; each time you take something out of an asset box, you credit it. All the liability and shareholders' equity boxes are on the right side of the warehouse, where the opposite is true. Each time you put something into a liability or shareholders' equity box, you credit it; each time you take something out, you debit it. If you are careful to ensure that every debit to a box is counterbalanced with a credit to another box, the warehouse will remain balanced. Periodically, you can check all the boxes to see what is in each one, and use this information to prepare a statement of financial position.

LEARNING OBJECTIVE 2

Explain the difference between permanent and temporary accounts.

The accounts shown in Exhibits 3-1 and 3-2 are all statement of financial position accounts. Therefore, they have balances that carry over from one period to the next. (Recall that a statement of financial position shows what the entity has at that point in time, to be carried forward to future periods.) Therefore, statement of financial position accounts are sometimes called **permanent accounts**.

One of the permanent accounts is retained earnings. You learned in Chapter 1 that the change in retained earnings during a given period is the increase or decrease due to the net income or loss (the difference between the revenues and expenses for the period) and the decrease due to the dividends declared. In order to keep track of the individual revenue and expense amounts, as well as the dividends declared during the period, the retained earnings account can be subdivided into several separate accounts. These separate accounts are called **temporary accounts** because they are used temporarily, during the accounting period, to keep track of the revenues, expenses, and dividends. At the end of the accounting period, the balances in the temporary accounts are transferred into the retained earnings account.

While revenues, expenses, and dividends declared are all shareholders' equity accounts, increases and decreases in them are handled differently. For revenues, credits represent increases (and debits represent decreases). For expenses and dividends declared, the opposite is true: debits represent increases (and credits represent decreases). The logic of this is directly connected to their effect on shareholders' equity: revenues increase shareholders' equity and thus are recorded as credits, while expenses decrease shareholders' equity and so are recorded as debits. Therefore, revenue accounts have credit balances, expense accounts have debit balances, and the dividends declared account has a debit balance (until these balances are eliminated when they are transferred to the retained earnings account at the end of the period).

Exhibit 3-3 shows the subdivision of the retained earnings account into the temporary revenue, expense, and dividends declared accounts.

RETAINED EARNINGS:
Revenues, Expenses, and Dividends Accounts

EXHIBIT 3-3

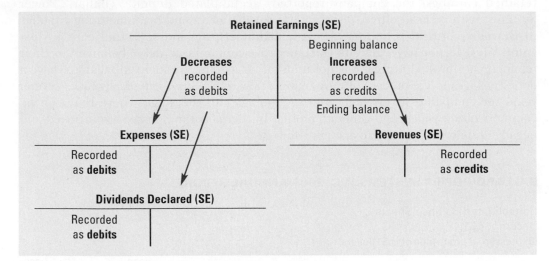

Notice that the rules of debit and credit for these accounts follow the overall rule for shareholders' equity: increases in shareholders' equity are recorded as credits, and decreases in shareholders' equity are recorded as debits. Therefore,

- since revenues increase the shareholders' equity, they are recorded as credits
- since expenses and dividends decrease shareholders' equity, they are recorded as debits.

Several other things should be noted about the revenue, expense, and dividends declared accounts.

First, at the beginning of each new accounting period, the balance in each of these accounts is always zero. Because these accounts are used to keep track of the revenues, expenses, and dividends declared during the current period, their beginning balances must be zero so that amounts from previous periods will not be combined with those of the current period.

At the end of each accounting period, the balance in each of the temporary revenue and expense accounts is used to prepare the statement of earnings, and is then transferred into the permanent retained earnings account, along with the dividends, to produce the ending balance in the retained earnings account.

In this way, the retained earnings account keeps track of the *cumulative* amounts of revenues and expenses less dividends, and the temporary accounts keep track of only the amounts for the *current period*. In other words, using our warehouse example, the contents of the revenue, expense, and dividends declared boxes are all dumped into the retained earnings box at the end of each period. A revenue box, with a credit balance, will increase the retained earnings (which also has a credit balance). An expense or dividends declared box, with a debit balance, will decrease the retained earnings.

The debit balances in the expense and dividends declared accounts are probably best understood by remembering that they both represent decreases in the shareholders' equity. Because shareholders' equity is represented by a credit balance, decreases in it must be represented by debit balances. At the end of the period, when the balances in the temporary accounts are transferred to retained earnings, the debit balances in the expense and dividends accounts will normally be offset by the credit balances in the revenue accounts, leaving the retained earnings account with an overall credit balance.

However, if expenses have exceeded revenues (i.e., the company has suffered losses), it is possible to have a debit balance in the retained earnings account. A debit balance in the retained earnings account indicates negative retained earnings, and is

HELPFUL HINT

- Increases in revenues are recorded as credits, and revenue accounts have credit balances.

- Increases in expenses are recorded as debits, and expense accounts have debit balances.

- Dividends declared are recorded as debits, and the dividends declared account has a debit balance.

called a deficit. For example, if you look at the balance sheet (statement of financial position) of **Ballard Power Systems Inc.** in Exhibit 3-4, you will see that, rather than retained earnings, the company reported "accumulated deficit." (Ballard Power Systems, with its head office, research and development, and manufacturing facilities in Burnaby, British Columbia, designs, manufactures, and sells fuel cells.) Most companies do not have deficits (i.e., negative amounts or debit balances in their retained earnings). However, it is not unusual for a company such as Ballard to have a deficit, as it is in the process of developing a new technology. It typically takes several years for companies to perfect such technologies to the stage where they can be commercialized widely and generate profits. In the meantime, losses are incurred and negative retained earnings are accumulated.

EXHIBIT 3-4

annual report

BALLARD POWER SYSTEMS INC. 2009 ANNUAL REPORT

Consolidated Balance Sheets
December 31,
(Expressed in thousands of U.S. dollars)

	2009	2008 (revised = note 1(c)(ii))
Assets		
Current assets:		
Cash and cash equivalents	$ 43,299	$ 54,086
Short-term investments	38,932	31,313
Accounts receivable (notes 4 & 17)	12,903	18,856
Inventories (note 5)	9,168	10,402
Prepaid expenses and other current assets	2,114	1,434
	106,416	116,091
Property, plant and equipment (note 6)	39,320	38,755
Intangible assets (note 7)	824	3,726
Goodwill	48,106	48,106
Investments (note 8)	632	1,765
Other long-term assets	50	–
	$ 195,348	$ 208,443
Liabilities and Shareholders' Equity		
Current liabilities:		
Accounts payable and accrued liabilities (notes 9 & 17)	$ 20,321	$ 21,819
Deferred revenue	1,607	947
Accrued warranty liabilities	7,813	3,841
Current portion of obligation under capital lease (note 10)	316	–
	30,057	26,607
Long-term liabilities (notes 11 & 12)	4,632	23,349
Obligation under capital lease (note 10)	1,739	–
	36,428	49,956
Shareholders' equity:		
Share capital (note 13)	835,358	832,711
Contributed surplus (notes 2 & 13)	284,510	283,466
Accumulated deficit	(960,712)	(957,454)
Accumulated other comprehensive loss	(236)	(236)
	158,920	158,487
	$ 195,348	$ 208,443

UNDERSTANDING THE ACCOUNTING CYCLE

We are now ready to look at the whole system by which transactions are first measured, recorded, and summarized, and then communicated to users through financial statements. This system is called the **accounting cycle** because it is repeated each accounting period.

Exhibit 3-5 illustrates the complete cycle. Each of the steps will be discussed in the subsections that follow.

As we proceed through a discussion of the accounting cycle, we will demonstrate each stage by continuing the Demo Company example that we began in Chapter 2. In that chapter, we analyzed Demo's January transactions, recorded their effects in a columnar table, and used the table to prepare the company's financial statements for the month of January. In this chapter, we will use Demo's February transactions to explain how these would be handled in a formal accounting system and illustrate each of the steps in the accounting cycle.

A system for maintaining accounting records can be as simple as a notebook, in which everything is processed by hand, or as sophisticated as an on-line system in which most of the processing is done by computers. We will use a simple manual system to illustrate the accounting cycle. However, the same underlying processes apply to any accounting system, no matter how simple or sophisticated it is.

LEARNING OBJECTIVE 3

Identify and explain the steps in the accounting cycle.

www.wileyplus.com

Animated Tutorials & Videos: Accounting Cycle Tutorial

The Chart of Accounts

Imagine a company that has just been formed and whose managers need to set up an accounting system. One of the first things they must determine is what information they need to run the business. What information is important for them to make well-

THE ACCOUNTING CYCLE

EXHIBIT 3-5

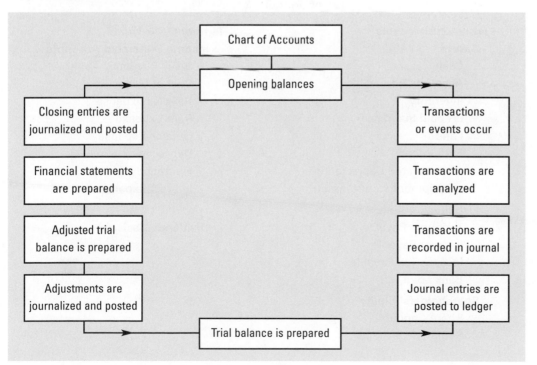

informed decisions? What information is needed by outside users? What is required to satisfy financial reporting standards? Accounting systems are information systems, so managers should decide at the outset what information they need in order to operate the business and satisfy the requirements of other users. These needs vary, so even companies in the same type of business will develop their own unique information systems and use different accounts.

Once a company has decided what accounts it needs to have, in order to get the information that it requires, the types of accounting information to be recorded in the accounting system (represented by the accounts to be used) are generally summarized in a **chart of accounts**. The chart of accounts is the starting point for the company's accounting cycle. However, the chart of accounts is dynamic, rather than something that cannot be changed. As the business changes, it may need to have different types of accounts. For example, suppose that the company did not originally provide credit to its customers; all of its sales were for cash. In that case, there would have been no need for an accounts receivable account. Later, if the company decided to allow customers to buy on credit, it would need to add an accounts receivable account to its chart of accounts.

Although there are certain account titles that are commonly used, an account can be given any name that makes sense to the company and describes the account's purpose. In an actual accounting system, each of the accounts in the chart of accounts would also be identified by a number that indicates the sequence of the accounts and makes it easier to record transactions in a computerized system. In this book, accounts will be designated by their names and not by account numbers.

LEARNING OBJECTIVE 4

Build a chart of accounts based on transactions that affect the company's assets, liabilities, and/or shareholder equity.

EXHIBIT 3-6

DEMO COMPANY'S CHART OF ACCOUNTS

Demo Company's Chart of Accounts
(as of January 31, 2011)

Permanent Accounts	Temporary Accounts
Assets	**Income Statement Accounts**
Cash	Sales Revenue
Accounts Receivable	Cost of Goods Sold
Inventory	Salaries Expense
Prepaid Insurance	Rent Expense
Land	Utilities Expense
Equipment	Depreciation Expense
Accumulated Depreciation—	Insurance Expense
Equipment (contra-asset)	Interest Expense
Liabilities	Income Tax Expense
Accounts Payable	**Dividends Declared**
Interest Payable	
Income Tax Payable	
Bank Loan	
Shareholders' Equity	
Share Capital	
Retained Earnings	

Exhibit 3-6 shows the chart of accounts for Demo Company, as of the end of January 2011. It consists of all the accounts that were used to record Demo's transactions in Chapter 2.

Later in this chapter, as we record Demo's February transactions, we will need to create some new accounts; as new accounts are created, they are added to the company's chart of accounts.

Notice that the accounts are listed in the chart of accounts in the order in which they will appear on the financial statements. Accounts are kept in this order so that it is easy to locate them in the ledger, and to facilitate the preparation of the financial statements. If account numbers are assigned to the accounts, a different set of account numbers will usually be assigned to each section of the financial statements. For example, many companies using four-digit account numbers will assign numbers between 1000 and 1999 to current assets only, so that all the accounts given those numbers will be easily identifiable as current assets. When the computer system prepares a statement of financial position, in the current assets section it will list these accounts in numerical order, according to the account numbers they were assigned.

The Opening Balances

As indicated in the chart of accounts, the permanent accounts are the statement of financial position accounts: assets, liabilities, and the main shareholders' equity accounts (at this stage, the share capital and retained earnings). The balances of the permanent accounts at the beginning of each accounting period are the amounts carried forward from the end of the previous accounting period. Exhibit 3-1 shows the opening balances in Demo's *permanent* accounts at the beginning of February 2011 (i.e., the amounts brought forward from its statement of financial position at the end of January, as determined in Chapter 2). Demo's *temporary* accounts at the beginning of February will all have zero balances, since every company starts each new accounting period with zero balances in its temporary accounts.

Exhibit 3-7 presents the complete set of Demo Company's accounts at the beginning of February 2011. Note that the balances in the permanent accounts are the same as those in Exhibit 3-1, and that the balances in all the temporary accounts are zero.

Note that there is a T account for each account listed in the chart of accounts (Exhibit 3-6). Also note that the temporary accounts for revenues, expenses, and dividends declared have been segregated from the permanent accounts, since only the permanent accounts have balances brought forward from the end of the previous accounting period.

TRANSACTIONS

The next step in the accounting cycle is to identify whether an event or transaction has occurred that affects the company's assets, liabilities, and/or shareholders' equity. If so, its effects on the company's accounts will have to be analyzed and recorded.

Evidence of a transaction or event is usually some sort of "source document"—a document that is received or created by the company indicating that something that needs to be recorded has happened. Examples of source documents include invoices, cheques, cash register tapes, bank deposit slips, and shipping documents.

EXHIBIT 3-7

DEMO COMPANY'S T ACCOUNTS, WITH BEGINNING BALANCES AS AT FEBRUARY 1, 2011

Permanent Accounts:

Cash (A)				Accounts Payable (L)	
Bal. Jan. 31/11	2,090			Bal. Jan. 31/11	9,500

Accounts Receivable (A)				Interest Payable (L)	
Bal. Jan. 31/11	2,000			Bal. Jan. 31/11	50

Inventory (A)				Income Tax Payable (L)	
Bal. Jan. 31/11	14,000			Bal. Jan. 31/11	235

Prepaid Insurance (A)				Bank Loan (L)	
Bal. Jan. 31/11	300			Bal. Jan. 31/11	10,000

Land (A)				Share Capital (SE)	
Bal. Jan. 31/11	15,000			Bal. Jan. 31/11	17,500

Equipment (A)				Retained Earnings (SE)	
Bal. Jan. 31/11	4,500			Bal. Jan. 31/11	455

Accumulated Depreciation—Equipment (XA)	
Bal. Jan. 31/11	150

Temporary Accounts:

Sales Revenue (SE)				Depreciation Expense (SE)	
		Bal. Jan. 31/11	0	Bal. Jan. 31/11	0

Cost of Goods Sold Expense (SE)				Insurance Expense (SE)	
Bal. Jan. 31/11	0			Bal. Jan. 31/11	0

Salaries Expense (SE)				Interest Expense (SE)	
Bal. Jan. 31/11	0			Bal. Jan. 31/11	0

Rent Expense (SE)				Income Tax Expense (SE)	
Bal. Jan. 31/11	0			Bal. Jan. 31/11	0

Utilities Expense (SE)				Dividends Declared (SE)	
Bal. Jan. 31/11	0			Bal. Jan. 31/11	0

Analyzing Transactions

LEARNING OBJECTIVE 5

Analyze transactions and record them in journal entry format.

When a transaction or event has occurred, the accountant must analyze it to determine what accounts have been affected and how the transaction should be recorded in the accounting system. We introduced this phase of the process in Chapter 2, where we analyzed the effects of various transactions on the basic accounting equation and recorded the results by entering positive and negative amounts in a columnar table. In this chapter— and throughout the remainder of this book—we will analyze the effects of transactions to see how they should be recorded as debits and credits in a company's accounts.

Routine transactions, such as the purchase or sale of goods, need to be analyzed only once. After that, each subsequent purchase or sale transaction is handled in the same way and can be entered into the accounting system without further analysis. Unique and unusual transactions require special analysis, however, and sometimes require the services of a professional accountant who understands the use of appropriate accounting methods, according to generally accepted accounting principles, practices, and standards.

Recording Transactions in a Journal

After an accountant has decided how to record transactions, appropriate entries must be made in the accounting system. The initial entries are usually made in what is known as a **journal**. A journal is a chronological listing of all the events that are recorded in the accounting system. A journal could be as simple as a piece of paper on which a chronological list of the transactions that have occurred is recorded, but most organization's journals are now kept in computerized form. Each complete entry made in the journal shows the effects of a transaction or business event on the company's accounts, and is called a **journal entry**.

When entries are made to record transactions in a journal, they are always dated and often each of them is given a sequential entry number. Then, the names of the accounts affected by the transaction, and the amounts involved, are listed. The accounts being debited are listed first, followed by the accounts being credited, and the credit portions are indented. Finally, an explanation of the transaction is often included with the journal entry, for future reference.

To summarize the preceding paragraph, complete journal entries typically consist of the date and entry number, a listing of the names of the accounts affected (with their account numbers, if applicable), and the amounts being debited and credited, followed by a brief explanation. In this book, we will use the following format for presenting journal entries:

	BASIC FORMAT FOR A JOURNAL ENTRY		
Date and/or entry number	**Name of account debited**	**Amount debited**	
	Name of account credited		**Amount credited**
	A brief explanation of the transaction.		

As illustrated above, when journal entries are made the customary practice is to list the accounts that are being debited before the accounts that are being credited, and to indent the accounts that are being credited. Of course, each complete journal entry must keep the accounting system balanced; that is, the amount debited must equal the amount credited. (Accounting software generally contains internal subroutines that automatically check journal entries to ensure that they are balanced, and alert the user to any problems that must be fixed before proceeding.)

We will now illustrate the process of analyzing transactions and recording them as journal entries by working through Demo's February transactions. Each transaction will be presented and analyzed, to determine what accounts are affected and whether they should be debited or credited. Then the journal entry to record the transaction will be presented. You should study this material carefully to ensure that you understand how the rules of debit and credit are applied and how journal entries are used to record transactions in an accounting system.

HELPFUL HINT

Accountants frequently use the abbreviation Dr. and Cr. for debit and credit, respectively (even though there is no "r" in "debit").

Transaction 1: Repayment of Loan

On February 1, 2011, Demo Company pays off $1,000 of the principal of its bank loan.

ANALYSIS   Since Demo is paying off part of its bank loan, this liability account should be reduced. At the same time, the company is making a cash payment, so this asset account should be reduced.

Note that repaying the *principal* of a loan does not involve an expense. The expense associated with a loan is the *interest* charged on it, which is recorded separately.

ANALYSIS OF TRANSACTION 1

Liabilities (Bank Loan) **decreased** by $1,000

Assets (Cash) **decreased** by $1,000

These changes in the accounts are now translated into debits and credits. The rules of debit and credit specify that liability accounts have credit balances. Therefore, they are reduced by making debit entries. Accordingly, the liability account Bank Loan must be debited. Conversely, asset accounts have debit balances and therefore are reduced by making credit entries. Accordingly, the asset account Cash must be credited. Thus, this transaction is recorded in the journal as follows:

JOURNAL ENTRY FOR TRANSACTION 1

Date	Entry number	Names of accounts debited and credited	Amount debited	Amount credited
Feb. 1	1	Bank Loan (L)	1,000	
		Cash (A)		1,000
		Repayment of bank loan.		

Transaction 2: Prepayment of Rent

On February 1, Demo Company signs a one-year lease agreement for office and storage space. The rent is to be $450 per month, and Demo pays the first and last months' rent (a total of $900) immediately. Thereafter, the monthly rent is to be paid on the first day of each month.

ANALYSIS Since the company is paying rent in advance, an asset is created (which would usually be called Prepaid Rent). At the same time, the company is making a cash payment, so this asset account should be reduced.

Like insurance, which is also paid in advance (discussed in Chapter 2), rent should not be recorded as an expense until the cost has *expired* (been used up). This is why rent expense is not recorded at this time.

ANALYSIS OF TRANSACTION 2

Assets (Prepaid Rent) increased by $900

Assets (Cash) decreased by $900

We now translate these changes into debits and credits for the journal entry. The rules of debit and credit specify that asset accounts have debit balances. Therefore, they are increased by making debit entries, and decreased by making credit entries. Accordingly, the asset account Prepaid Rent must be debited, and the asset account Cash must be credited. Thus, this transaction is recorded in the journal as follows:

JOURNAL ENTRY FOR TRANSACTION 2

Date	Entry number	Names of accounts debited and credited	Amount debited	Amount credited
Feb. 1	2	Prepaid Rent (A)	900	
		Cash (A)		900
		Payment of rent in advance.		

Transaction 3: Purchase of Inventory on Account

On February 5, the company buys $30,000 of additional inventory on account.

ANALYSIS As we saw in Chapter 2, when goods are purchased to be sold in the future, the asset Inventory is increased. At the same time, since the purchase is on account and payment will not be made until later, the liability Accounts Payable is increased.

ANALYSIS OF TRANSACTION 3

Assets (Inventory) increased by $30,000

Liabilities (Accounts Payable) increased by $30,000

We now translate these changes in the accounts into debits and credits. The rules of debit and credit specify that asset accounts have debit balances, and are therefore increased by making debit entries. Conversely, liability accounts have credit balances, and are increased by making credit entries. Accordingly, the asset Inventory must be debited, and the liability Accounts Payable must be credited. Thus, this transaction is recorded in the journal as follows:

JOURNAL ENTRY FOR TRANSACTION 3

Date	Entry number	Names of accounts debited and credited	Amount debited	Amount credited
Feb. 5	3	Inventory (A)	30,000	
		Accounts Payable (L)		30,000
		Purchase of inventory on account.		

Transaction 4: Sales for Cash and on Account

On February 8, the company sells goods to customers for $40,000. Of these sales, $4,000 are for cash; the remaining $36,000 are on account.

ANALYSIS   When goods are sold to customers, the company's assets are increased and *revenue* is earned, equal to the *selling price* of the goods that have been sold—i.e., the amount that is received, or will be received, from the sale. In this case, the assets Cash and Accounts Receivable are increased by $4,000 and $36,000, respectively, and revenue of $40,000 is recognized. (Remember that, under the accrual basis of accounting, revenue is generally recognized when the sale is made, not when the cash is collected.) Because it affects the net earnings and, ultimately, the retained earnings, revenue is a shareholders' equity account.

ANALYSIS OF TRANSACTION 4

Assets increased by $40,000 (Cash of $4,000 and Accounts Receivable of $36,000)
Shareholders' Equity increased by $40,000 (recorded as Sales Revenue)

These changes in the accounts are now translated into debits and credits. Assets are increased by making debit entries. Accordingly, the asset accounts Cash and Accounts Receivable must both be debited. Conversely, the rules of debit and credit specify that shareholders' equity is increased by making credit entries. Therefore, the Sales Revenue account must be credited. Thus, this transaction is recorded in the journal as follows:

JOURNAL ENTRY FOR TRANSACTION 4

Date	Entry number	Names of accounts debited and credited	Amount debited	Amount credited
Feb. 8	4	Cash (A)	4,000	
		Accounts Receivable (A)	36,000	
		Sales Revenue (SE)		40,000
		Sale of goods for cash and on account.		

Notice that the above journal entry has three parts. However, the sum of the two debit parts (4,000 and 36,000) is equal to the credit part (40,000), so the entry as a whole is in balance. This illustrates the fact that, although every journal entry must have at least one debit and one credit, a journal entry can have any number of debit and credit parts, as long as the sum of the amounts debited is equal to the sum of the amounts credited. The term **compound journal entry** is used for a journal entry that has more than two parts.

Transaction 5: Cost of Goods Sold

The company determines that the cost of the goods that were sold on February 8 is $27,000.

ANALYSIS   As you should recall from Chapter 2, when goods are sold their cost must be removed from the asset account Inventory and transferred to the expense account Cost of Goods Sold. In other words, in addition to the revenue that is earned when a sale is made, the company's assets are decreased and an *expense* is incurred, equal to the *cost* of the goods that have been sold. In this case, the asset Inventory is decreased by $27,000 and an expense of the same amount is recognized. Because they affect the net earnings and, ultimately, the retained earnings, expenses are shareholders' equity accounts.

ANALYSIS OF TRANSACTION 5

Shareholders' Equity decreased by $27,000 (recorded as Cost of Goods Sold)

Assets (Inventory) **decreased** by $27,000

We now translate these changes into debits and credits for the journal entry. Shareholders' equity is decreased by making debit entries. Therefore, the Cost of Goods Sold account must be debited. At the same time, since assets are decreased by making credit entries, the Inventory account must be credited. Thus, this transaction is recorded in the journal as follows:

JOURNAL ENTRY FOR TRANSACTION 5

Date	Entry number	Names of accounts debited and credited	Amount debited	Amount credited
Feb. 8	5	Cost of Goods Sold (SE)	27,000	
		Inventory (A)		27,000
		Removal of goods sold from inventory.		

Transactions 4 and 5 are logically linked, because when goods are sold the company's assets are increased and *revenue* is earned (equal to the *selling price* of the goods that have been sold), and at the same time the company's assets are decreased and an expense is incurred (equal to the *cost* of the goods that have been sold). Subtracting the expense from the revenue reveals the amount of profit made on the sale. In this case, goods costing $27,000 were sold for $40,000, resulting in a **gross profit** of $13,000. This is referred to as gross profit because there are many other expenses—salaries, rent, utilities, etc.—that have to be deducted to determine the company's *net* profit or earnings for the period. (In accounting, the term "gross" is generally used to refer to the initial amount of an item, before certain deductions from it have been made; and the term "net" is used to refer to the final amount of an item, after the deductions from it have been made.)

Transaction 6: Purchase of Supplies for Cash

On February 10, Demo Company buys office supplies for $500 cash.

ANALYSIS Whenever something is purchased to be used in the future, it should be recorded as an asset. We will refer to this asset account as Office Supplies on Hand. Since cash is paid for the purchase, the asset account Cash is decreased.

Note that, since these office supplies will be used in the future operations of the business, there is no expense recorded at this point. Eventually, when the supplies are consumed, their cost will be transferred to an expense account; however, as long as they are on hand they are an asset. This is similar to the treatment of merchandise inventory, prepaid insurance, and prepaid rent.

ANALYSIS OF TRANSACTION 6

Assets (Office Supplies on Hand) **increased** by $500

Assets (Cash) **decreased** by $500

We now translate these changes in the accounts into debits and credits. The rules of debit and credit specify that asset accounts have debit balances, and are therefore increased by making debit entries and decreased by making credit entries. Accordingly, the asset Office Supplies on Hand must be debited, and the asset Cash must be credited. Thus, this transaction is recorded in the journal as follows:

JOURNAL ENTRY FOR TRANSACTION 6

Date	Entry number	Names of accounts debited and credited	Amount debited	Amount credited
Feb. 10	6	Office Supplies on Hand (A)	500	
		Cash (A)		500
		Purchase of supplies for cash.		

Transaction 7: Purchase of Equipment for Cash

On February 12, the company buys additional equipment for $3,000 cash.

ANALYSIS This is similar to Transaction 6. Equipment is purchased to be used in the future, so the asset Equipment is increased. At the same time, since it is a cash purchase, the asset Cash is decreased.

As with the office supplies in Transaction 6, the equipment will be used in the future operations of the business. Therefore, at this point it is an asset. Eventually, however, as the value of the equipment is consumed, its cost will have to be transferred to an expense account. For long-term assets like equipment, whose benefits are used up gradually over many accounting periods, this is done through the process of depreciation (discussed in Chapter 2).

ANALYSIS OF TRANSACTION 7

Assets (Equipment) increased by $3,000

Assets (Cash) decreased by $3,000

Asset accounts have debit balances, and are therefore increased by making debit entries and decreased by making credit entries. Accordingly, the asset Equipment must be debited, and the asset Cash must be credited. Therefore, this transaction is recorded in the journal as follows:

JOURNAL ENTRY FOR TRANSACTION 7

Date	Entry number	Names of accounts debited and credited	Amount debited	Amount credited
Feb. 12	7	Equipment (A)	3,000	
		Cash (A)		3,000
		Purchase of equipment for cash.		

Transaction 8: Issuance of Shares for Cash

On February 15, shareholders invest an additional $5,000 cash in the business.

ANALYSIS   As we saw in Chapter 2, when people invest cash in a business they are issued shares in the company, as evidence of their investment. Consequently, the company has an increase in its assets, in the form of Cash, and an increase in its shareholders' equity, in the form of Share Capital.

ANALYSIS OF TRANSACTION 8

Assets (Cash) increased by $5,000

Shareholders' Equity (Share Capital) increased by $5,000

Assets are increased by making debit entries. Accordingly, the asset account Cash must be debited. Conversely, the rules of debit and credit specify that shareholders' equity is increased by making credit entries. Therefore, the Share Capital account must be credited. Thus, this transaction is recorded in the journal as follows:

JOURNAL ENTRY FOR TRANSACTION 8

Date	Entry number	Names of accounts debited and credited	Amount debited	Amount credited
Feb. 15	8	Cash (A)	5,000	
		Share Capital (SE)		5,000
		Issuance of shares for cash.		

Transaction 9: Collections from Customers on Account

On February 18, Demo collects all but $5,000 of the amounts due from its customers.

ANALYSIS Notice that the amount given in the description of this transaction is not the amount of cash that was collected. Rather, it is the amount that was not collected; in other words, it is the ending balance of accounts receivable.

This illustrates an important difference in the type of information you may be given regarding a transaction, which you will encounter in some cases. Rather than simply being given the amount of the transaction, you may be given the remaining *balance* in a related account. In such cases, you will have to use the given information to logically determine the amount to be recorded in the journal entry.

In this case, in order to prepare the journal entry for this transaction we need to determine the amount of cash that was collected. This can be done by using the following relationships:

The beginning balance in Accounts Receivable (from Exhibit 3-7)	$ 2,000
+ The sales on account during the period (from Transaction 4)	36,000
= The total amount of accounts receivable to be collected	38,000
− The ending balance in Accounts Receivable (given in this transaction)	(5,000)
= The amount of accounts receivable collected during the period	$33,000

As discussed in Chapter 2, when a company receives payments from its customers on account, one asset (Cash) increases and another asset (Accounts Receivable) decreases. No revenue is recognized when cash is collected on account, because under the accrual basis of accounting the revenue is recognized when the sale is made, not when the cash is collected.

ANALYSIS OF TRANSACTION 9

Assets (Cash) **increased** by $33,000
Assets (Accounts Receivable) **decreased** by $33,000

Asset accounts have debit balances, and are therefore increased by making debit entries and decreased by making credit entries. Accordingly, the asset Cash must be debited, and the asset Accounts Receivable must be credited. Thus, this transaction is recorded in the journal as follows:

JOURNAL ENTRY FOR TRANSACTION 9

Date	Entry number	Names of accounts debited and credited	Amount debited	Amount credited
Feb. 18	9	Cash (A)	33,000	
		Accounts Receivable (A)		33,000
		Collection of customers' accounts.		

Note again that the $5,000 given in the description of this transaction does not appear in the journal entry. Rather, since it was a balance, it was used to calculate the $33,000 recorded in the above entry. From this point onward, you will have to watch for situations like this, in which you are given information about the balance in an account, rather than the amount of a particular transaction. In these cases, you will need to bear in mind that a balance is not recorded with a journal entry; a balance is the net amount remaining in an account, as a result of all the preceding transactions affecting that account. Therefore, if you are trying to record a transaction but are given information regarding the balance in an account, you will need to use it—together with your knowledge of the logical relationships affecting that account—to calculate the amount to be recorded in the journal entry, as we did for this transaction. We will see more examples of this process in later transactions.

Transaction 10: Payments to Suppliers on Account

On February 20, Demo Company makes payments of $34,000 on its accounts payable.

ANALYSIS   As we discussed in Chapter 2, when a company pays for previous purchases on account, both its liabilities (Accounts Payable) and its assets (Cash) are reduced.

ANALYSIS OF TRANSACTION 10

Liabilities (Accounts Payable) **decreased** by $34,000

Assets (Cash) decreased by $34,000

Liabilities have credit balances, and are therefore decreased by making debit entries. Accordingly, the liability Accounts Payable must be debited. Conversely, assets have debit balances, and are therefore decreased by making credit entries, so the Cash account must be credited. Thus, this transaction is recorded in the journal as follows:

JOURNAL ENTRY FOR TRANSACTION 10

Date	Entry number	Names of accounts debited and credited	Amount debited	Amount credited
Feb. 20	10	Accounts Payable (L)	34,000	
		Cash (A)		34,000
		Payment of accounts due to suppliers.		

Transaction 11: Salaries Expense

On February 25, the company pays $2,500 for salaries. In addition, it still owes $300 to employees for time worked during February, which will be paid in March.

ANALYSIS   According to the accrual basis of accounting, the amount of salaries expense that should be recorded each period is the amount that is *incurred* that period, rather than simply the amount that is *paid* during the period. Therefore, the amount of salaries expense to be recorded for the month of February is $2,500 + $300 = $2,800.

It should be noted that Demo did not have any salaries payable at the end of January. (This can be confirmed by checking the balances in Exhibit 3-7.) If there had been salaries payable at the beginning of February (i.e., brought forward from January), this amount would have been deducted in the calculation above. This is because, if you are calculating the amount of salaries expense to be recorded for the month of *February*, any salaries paid during February for the month of *January* should be excluded from the February expense.

Since expenses reduce net income and, ultimately, retained earnings, the salaries expense causes a decrease in shareholder's equity. At the same time, assets (in the form of Cash) are decreased by the amount paid, and liabilities (in the form of Salaries Payable) are increased by the amount owing.

ANALYSIS OF TRANSACTION 11

Shareholders' Equity decreased by $2,800 (recorded as Salaries Expense)

Assets (Cash) **decreased** by $2,500

Liabilities (Salaries Payable) **increased** by $300

Shareholders' Equity is decreased by making debit entries. Therefore, since expenses are temporary shareholders' equity accounts, the Salaries Expense account must be debited. Because assets are decreased by making credit entries, the Cash account must be credited. Since liabilities are increased by making credit entries, the Salaries Payable account must also be credited. Thus, this transaction is recorded in the journal as follows:

JOURNAL ENTRY FOR TRANSACTION 11

Date	Entry number	Names of accounts debited and credited	Amount debited	Amount credited
Feb. 25	11	Salaries Expense (SE)	2,800	
		Cash (A)		2,500
		Salaries Payable (L)		300
		Recognition of salaries for February.		

This is another example of a compound journal entry. Note that although it has two credits and only one debit, the amount debited equals the total amount credited.

Transaction 12: Declaration of Dividends to Be Paid Later

On February 28, dividends of $400 are declared. However, they will not be paid to the shareholders until March.

ANALYSIS   Dividends have to be recorded as soon as they are declared. If they are not paid immediately, the declaration creates a legal obligation for the company to make the payment later, which means that a liability has to be recorded.

Dividends reduce shareholder's equity, by reducing the amount of retained earnings. They are usually recorded in a temporary account called Dividends Declared.

At the same time, if they are not paid they increase liabilities (in the form of Dividends Payable) by the amount owing.

ANALYSIS OF TRANSACTION 12

Shareholders' Equity decreased by $400 (recorded as Dividends Declared)
Liabilities (Dividends Payable) **increased** by $400

Shareholders' Equity is decreased by making debit entries. Therefore, the temporary shareholders' equity account called Dividends Declared is debited. At the same time, since liabilities are increased by making credit entries, the Dividends Payable account must be credited. Accordingly, this transaction is recorded in the journal as follows:

JOURNAL ENTRY FOR TRANSACTION 12

Date	Entry number	Names of accounts debited and credited	Amount debited	Amount credited
Feb. 28	12	Dividends Declared (SE)	400	
		Dividends Payable (L)		400
		Declaration of dividends to be paid in March.		

This completes Demo Company's transactions for February. Exhibit 3-8 shows the company's journal at this stage, with all the transactions recorded in it. The first four journal entries have been colour-coded for easy reference in the following section, which illustrates the posting process.

RECORDING IN JOURNAL, LEDGER, AND TRIAL BALANCE

Posting to the Ledger

Although the journal provides an important chronological record of the effects of each transaction on the accounts, the information in the journal is not organized in a way that is very useful for most purposes. For example, if a manager wanted to know the balance in the cash account, the accountant would have to take the beginning balance of cash and add or subtract all the journal entries that affected cash. To prepare financial statements, the accountant would have to go through this process for all of the accounts, in order to determine their ending balances. If the company had hundreds of journal entries, this would be extremely time-consuming and inefficient. Therefore, to provide more efficient access to information about the cumulative effects of transactions on individual accounts, the next step in the accounting cycle transfers the data in the journal to the accounts in the ledger. This process is called posting.

The **ledger** is the collection of all the accounts used by a company. **Posting** is the process of transferring the information from the journal entries to the ledger accounts.

Each account in the ledger represents a separate, specific T account, and includes the name of the account (and its number, if applicable), its beginning balance, and then

LEARNING OBJECTIVE 6

Post transactions from the journal to the ledger.

EXHIBIT 3-8

DEMO COMPANY'S JOURNAL SHOWING ITS TRANSACTION ENTRIES FOR THE MONTH OF FEBRUARY

Date	Entry number	Names of accounts debited and credited	Amount debited	Amount credited
Feb. 1	1	Bank Loan (L)	1,000	
		Cash (A)		1,000
		Repayment of bank loan.		
Feb. 1	2	Prepaid Rent (A)	900	
		Cash (A)		900
		Payment of rent in advance.		
Feb. 5	3	Inventory (A)	30,000	
		Accounts Payable (L)		30,000
		Purchase of inventory on account.		
Feb. 8	4	Cash (A)	4,000	
		Accounts Receivable (A)	36,000	
		Sales Revenue (SE)		40,000
		Sale of goods for cash and on account.		
Feb. 8	5	Cost of Goods Sold (SE)	27,000	
		Inventory (A)		27,000
		Removal of goods sold from inventory.		
Feb. 10	6	Office Supplies on Hand (A)	500	
		Cash (A)		500
		Purchase of supplies for cash.		
Feb. 12	7	Equipment (A)	3,000	
		Cash (A)		3,000
		Purchase of equipment for cash.		
Feb. 15	8	Cash (A)	5,000	
		Share Capital (SE)		5,000
		Issuance of shares for cash.		
Feb. 18	9	Cash (A)	33,000	
		Accounts Receivable (A)		33,000
		Collection of customers' accounts.		
Feb. 20	10	Accounts Payable (L)	34,000	
		Cash (A)		34,000
		Payment of accounts due to suppliers.		
Feb. 25	11	Salaries Expense (SE)	2,800	
		Cash (A)		2,500
		Salaries Payable (L)		300
		Recognition of salaries for February.		
Feb. 28	12	Dividends Declared (SE)	400	
		Dividends Payable (L)		400
		Declaration of dividends to be paid in March.		

a listing of all the postings that affected the account during the period. Each posting includes the date of the transaction and the transaction number, as well as the amount debited or credited. The date and transaction number enable users to cross-reference the amounts in the ledger with the related entries in the journal, and thus determine the source of each of the amounts that has been posted to the accounts.

Exhibit 3-7 presented Demo Company's ledger accounts *before* the February transactions were posted, while Exhibit 3-9 shows its ledger *after* the February transactions have been posted. Four new accounts have been added (Prepaid Rent, Office Supplies On Hand, Salaries Payable and Dividends Payable), because we needed them to record new types of transactions that occurred in February. These new accounts would also be added to the company's chart of accounts, which was presented in Exhibit 3-6.

To make it easier to see how the posting process transfers the information from the journal (Exhibit 3-8) to the accounts in the ledger (Exhibit 3-9), the first four entries in the journal have been colour-coded to match the related postings in the ledger. For example, in Exhibit 3-8 the journal entry on February 1 for Transaction 1 indicates that the Bank Loan account is to be debited $1,000 and the Cash account is to be credited $1,000. In Exhibit 3-9, you will see that $1,000 has been posted as a debit to the Bank Loan account, by entering it on the left side of that T account; $1,000 has also been posted as a credit to the Cash account, by entering it on the right side of that T account; and both have been cross-referenced to the journal by the notation "Trans. #1, Feb. 01/11."

Similarly, in Exhibit 3-8 the journal entry on February 1 for Transaction 2 indicates that the Prepaid Rent account is to be debited and the Cash account is to be credited, in the amount of $900. In Exhibit 3-9, you will see that $900 has been posted as a debit to the Prepaid Rent account (by entering it on the left side of that T account) and as a credit to the Cash account (by entering it on the right side of that T account), and both have been cross-referenced to the journal by the notation "Trans. #2, Feb. 01/11."

You should follow this same process to see how the journal entries for Transactions 3 and 4, shown in Exhibit 3-8, have been transferred to the T accounts in the ledger in Exhibit 3-9. Once you have traced these amounts from their origins in the journal to their individual accounts in the ledger, you should have a good understanding of what "posting" means. It is a mechanical process, and all of the entries in the journal are transferred to the accounts in the ledger in the same way.

Posting to the ledger can be done monthly, weekly, daily, or at any frequency desired. The timing of the postings is determined to some extent by management's (or the shareholders') need for up-to-date information. If managers need to know the balance in a particular account, say Cash, on a daily basis, then the postings have to be done at least daily. If management needs to know the amount of cash available on an hourly basis, then the postings have to be done at least hourly.

Many computer systems account for transactions in "real time," meaning that accounts are updated instantaneously, as each transaction occurs. Once a journal entry has been completed, such systems automatically post the information to the ledger accounts. Other computer systems collect journal entries in batches and post them all at one time (for example, at the end of each day). In general, since managers like to have information sooner rather than later, the number of real-time accounting systems continues to increase as the cost of computer technology continues to decrease.

At this point, it is important to note that a system consisting only of journal entries would make it difficult for managers to know the balances in the accounts. On the other hand, a system of only ledger accounts, without the original journal entries, would make it difficult to understand the sources of the amounts in the accounts. Accounting systems need both journal entries and ledger accounts in order to collect information in a way that makes it readily accessible and as useful as possible.

EXHIBIT 3-9

DEMO COMPANY'S LEDGER AFTER THE FEBRUARY TRANSACTIONS HAVE BEEN POSTED TO IT

Permanent Accounts:

Cash (A)

Balance	Jan. 31/11	2,090				
			Entry #1	Feb. 01/11	1,000	
			Entry #2	Feb. 01/11	900	
Entry #4	Feb. 08/11	4,000				
			Entry #6	Feb. 10/11	500	
			Entry #7	Feb. 12/11	3,000	
Entry #8	Feb. 15/11	5,000				
Entry #9	Feb. 18/11	33,000				
			Entry #10	Feb. 20/11	34,000	
			Entry #11	Feb. 25/11	2,500	
Balance	Feb. 28/11	2,190				

Accounts Receivable (A)

Balance	Jan. 31/11	2,000				
Entry #4	Feb. 08/11	36,000				
			Entry #9	Feb. 18/11	33,000	
Balance	Feb. 28/11	5,000				

Inventory (A)

Balance	Jan. 31/11	14,000				
Entry #3	Feb. 05/11	30,000				
			Entry #5	Feb. 08/11	27,000	
Balance	Feb. 28/11	17,000				

Prepaid Insurance (A)

Balance	Jan. 31/11	300

Prepaid Rent (A)

Balance	Jan. 31/11	0
Entry #2	Feb. 01/11	900
Balance	Feb. 28/11	900

Office Supplies on Hand (A)

Balance	Jan. 31/11	0
Entry #6	Feb. 10/11	500
Balance	Feb. 28/11	500

Land (A)

Balance	Jan. 31/11	15,000

Equipment (A)

Balance	Jan. 31/11	4,500
Entry #7	Feb. 12/11	3,000
Balance	Feb. 28/11	7,500

Accumulated Depreciation—Equipment (XA)

Balance	Jan. 31/11	150

Accounts Payable (L)

			Balance	Jan. 31/11	9,500	
Entry #10	Feb. 20/11	34,000	Entry #3	Feb. 05/11	30,000	
			Balance	Feb. 28/11	5,500	

Interest Payable (L)

		Balance	Jan. 31/11	50

Income Tax Payable (L)

		Balance	Jan. 31/11	235

Salaries Payable (L)

		Balance	Jan. 31/11	0
		Entry #11	Feb. 25/11	300
		Balance	Feb. 28/11	300

Dividends Payable (L)

		Balance	Jan. 31/11	0
		Entry #12	Feb. 28/11	400
		Balance	Feb. 28/11	400

Bank Loan (L)

			Balance	Jan. 31/11	10,000
Entry #1	Feb. 01/11	1,000			
			Balance	Feb. 28/11	9,000

Share Capital (SE)

		Balance	Jan. 31/11	17,500
		Entry #8	Feb. 15/11	5,000
		Balance	Feb. 28/11	22,500

Retained Earnings (SE)

		Balance	Jan. 31/11	455

DEMO COMPANY'S LEDGER AFTER THE FEBRUARY TRANSACTIONS HAVE BEEN POSTED TO IT (cont'd)

EXHIBIT 3-9

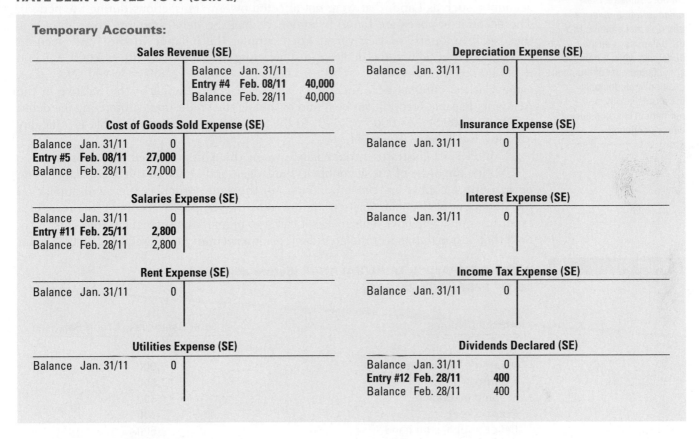

Temporary Accounts:

Sales Revenue (SE)

Balance	Jan. 31/11	0
Entry #4	**Feb. 08/11**	**40,000**
Balance	Feb. 28/11	40,000

Cost of Goods Sold Expense (SE)

Balance	Jan. 31/11	0
Entry #5	**Feb. 08/11**	**27,000**
Balance	Feb. 28/11	27,000

Salaries Expense (SE)

Balance	Jan. 31/11	0
Entry #11	**Feb. 25/11**	**2,800**
Balance	Feb. 28/11	2,800

Rent Expense (SE)

Balance	Jan. 31/11	0

Utilities Expense (SE)

Balance	Jan. 31/11	0

Depreciation Expense (SE)

Balance	Jan. 31/11	0

Insurance Expense (SE)

Balance	Jan. 31/11	0

Interest Expense (SE)

Balance	Jan. 31/11	0

Income Tax Expense (SE)

Balance	Jan. 31/11	0

Dividends Declared (SE)

Balance	Jan. 31/11	0
Entry #12	**Feb. 28/11**	**400**
Balance	Feb. 28/11	400

Finally, it should be noted that, since each journal entry must have equal debits and credits, if the journal entries are posted properly, the ledger should always be in balance (i.e., the total of the debit amounts in the accounts should be equal to the total of the credit amounts).

Preparing a Trial Balance

LEARNING OBJECTIVE 7

Prepare a trial balance and use it to identify errors.

While most errors should be detected at the journal entry and posting phases of the accounting cycle, some errors may persist. As stated earlier, most computerized systems will not post a journal entry unless the debits equal the credits. These systems catch most errors at the input stage. In manual systems, however, errors may not be detected when journal entries are being made. Moreover, even if the debits equal the credits at the journal entry stage, it is possible for the amounts to be posted incorrectly to the accounts. A useful tool for detecting errors in the ledger is to produce a **trial balance**.

The trial balance is a listing of all the account balances in the ledger at a specific point in time. To use our warehouse example, we would look into each of the boxes and make a list of the final amount in each of them. A check can then be done to ensure that the total of all the balances on the debit side equals the total of all the balances on the credit side. If these amounts are not equal, a mistake has been made at some point during the process and it must be found and corrected before proceeding.

Notice in Exhibit 3-9 that, in addition to the February transactions having been posted, the ending balance in each account has been calculated (except for those accounts, such as Land, that were not affected by any transactions during the period). The account balances are found by simply adding the debit amounts and subtracting the credit amounts, or vice versa. For example, the balance in the Cash account can be found by adding the debits and subtracting the credits: 2,090 + 4,000 + 5,000 + 33,000 − 1,000 − 900 − 500 − 3,000 − 34,000 − 2,500 = 2,190. Note that, since Cash is an asset account, the balance is a debit. Similarly, the balance in the Accounts Payable account can be found by adding the credits and subtracting the debit: 9,500 + 30,000 − 34,000 = 5,500. In this case, since Accounts Payable is a liability account, the balance is a credit.

Exhibit 3-10 illustrates a trial balance, using the data presented in Exhibit 3-9.

Notice the order of the accounts in the ledger, and hence in the trial balance. The permanent accounts are presented first (in the same order as they will appear on the statement of financial position), followed by the temporary accounts (the revenues, expenses, and dividends). This makes it easier to prepare the financial statements. Also, note that although the accumulated depreciation account has a credit balance, it is not

EXHIBIT 3-10

DEMO COMPANY'S TRIAL BALANCE (before adjustments)
AS OF FEBRUARY 28, 2011

Account Names	Debit Balances	Credit Balances
Cash	$ 2,190	
Accounts receivable	5,000	
Inventory	17,000	
Prepaid insurance	300	
Prepaid rent	900	
Office supplies on hand	500	
Land	15,000	
Equipment	7,500	
Accumulated depreciation—equipment		$ 150
Accounts payable		5,500
Interest payable		50
Income tax payable		235
Salaries payable		300
Dividends payable		400
Bank loan		9,000
Share capital		22,500
Retained earnings		455
Sales revenue		40,000
Cost of goods sold expense	27,000	
Salaries expense	2,800	
Rent expense	0	
Utilities expense	0	
Depreciation expense	0	
Insurance expense	0	
Interest expense	0	
Income tax expense	0	
Dividends declared	400	
Totals	$78,590	$78,590

a liability; it is a *contra-asset* account, representing the portion of the equipment's cost that has been used up and written off, through depreciation, thus far.

The purpose of a trial balance is to assist in detecting errors that may have been made in the recording process. If the ledger does not balance (i.e., if the total of all the debit balances in the accounts does not equal the total of all the credit balances), this indicates that something is wrong. In such cases, there is no point in proceeding until the errors have been found and corrected. This makes the preparation of a trial balance a very useful step in the accounting cycle. However, it is important to realize that, because a trial balance only checks whether the total of the debit balances in the ledger accounts equals the total of the credit balances, it cannot detect all types of errors. For example:

- The trial balance will still balance if the correct amount was debited or credited, but to the wrong account (for example, if a purchase of office supplies was debited to the Inventory account, rather than to the Office Supplies account).

- If an incorrect amount was recorded (for example, if a $450 transaction was recorded as a $540 transaction, for both the debit and credit portions of the entry), the trial balance will still balance.

- The trial balance will also not detect the complete omission of an entire journal entry. If neither the debit nor the credit portions of a journal entry were posted, the totals on the trial balance will still be equal.

Despite these limitations, the preparation of a trial balance is very helpful in detecting many other types of common errors in the recording process, and is an important step in the accounting cycle.

Recording Adjusting Entries

If an error is detected in the trial balance phase, it must be corrected. A journal entry to correct an error is one type of **adjusting entry** that is made at the end of the accounting period. A second, routine type of adjusting entry is made for accounting events that were not recognized and recorded during the period. These reflect the objective of the adjusting entry phase of the accounting cycle: to ensure that all the appropriate revenues and expenses have been recorded and reported for the period. Common examples of adjustments that must be made at the end of an accounting period are recording the depreciation of capital assets, recognizing the portions of prepaid expenses that have expired, recording interest and other accrued liabilities, recognizing the cost of supplies that were used up during the period, and recording income taxes. We introduced some basic adjustments in Chapter 2; in this chapter, we will continue our discussion of adjustments and demonstrate how the appropriate journal entries are made.

Notice that the types of items that need to be adjusted generally relate to the passage of time: the depreciation of capital assets, the expiration of prepaid expenses, the accrual of interest, and the consumption of supplies all occur on a daily basis. However, because recording them every day would be impractical, they are typically updated only at the end of the accounting period, through adjusting entries. In most situations there is no external transaction at the end of a period to signal that an adjustment needs to be made—only the passage of time. As a result, the ending balances in the accounts have to be carefully reviewed to determine those that need to be adjusted.

HELPFUL HINT

If you prepare a trial balance that does not balance, here are some tips for finding your error:

- First, calculate the difference between the total debits and the total credits, and look for this amount in either the question or your answer.
- Divide the difference from the first step by 2, and check to see whether a debit for this amount has been recorded as a credit, or vice versa.
- Divide the difference from the first step by 9. If it divides evenly—with no decimals—check for a *transposition error:* two digits that have been reversed (for example, 765 written as 756, or 432 written as 234).

LEARNING OBJECTIVE 8

Make adjusting entries to prepare an adjusted trial balance.

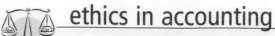

ethics in accounting

Ethics in Accounting

Many adjusting entries require management to make estimates and exercise judgement, providing opportunities for managers to manipulate earnings and statement of financial position values.

For example, suppose that you, as an accountant for a company, are asked to postpone the write-off of some old equipment. The equipment has not been used for some time, and it is clear to you that it will never be used again. You therefore think that it should be written off immediately. However, the write-off would need to be recognized as a loss (like an expense on the statement of earnings) and, since the amount involved is large, it would have a significant negative impact on the company's income for the period. Management has asked you to postpone the write-off because the company has applied for a large loan from the bank, and the loss from the write-off would have a negative impact on the bank's assessment of the company. What should you do?

As you consider your response to this, or any, ethical question, it is sometimes helpful to think about who will be affected by your decision (including yourself), and how it will help or hurt them. Particularly, think of who the users or potential users of the financial statements are, and how they might be affected by your action (or inaction). This should help you structure a fuller understanding of the situation and make an ethical decision.

It is essential that financial statements not be presented in a way that could mislead, or potentially harm, a user—such as the bank, in this case.

Under the accrual basis of accounting, companies must apply the *revenue recognition* principles (introduced in Chapter 2 and discussed in detail in Chapter 4) to ensure that all the revenues earned in an accounting period are identified, recorded, and reported in that period. They must also apply the *matching* principle to ensure that all the expenses incurred to generate those revenues are identified, recorded, and reported in that period. Therefore, in order to properly measure a company's net income and financial position, end-of-period adjustments to the revenues and expenses, and to the related assets and liabilities, are an essential step in the accounting cycle.

As stated earlier, end-of-period adjustments are very important. They ensure that all events and transactions related to the period have been accounted for, and thus make the financial statements as accurate as possible. We will illustrate the adjusting process by working through Demo Company's adjustments as of February 28, 2011.

At the end of February, Demo's accountant reviews the accounts in the trial balance and notes that adjustments need to be made for interest, rent expense, office supplies, utilities, depreciation, insurance, and income tax. This is a fairly typical set of adjustments, so we will now analyze each of these items and prepare the appropriate adjusting journal entries.

Entry 13: Interest Adjustment

Interest on the company's bank loan must be recognized for the month of February. (As noted in Chapter 2, the loan originated on January 1 and has an interest rate of 6% per year. However, the interest does not have to be paid until the end of March.)

ANALYSIS   From the borrower's point of view, interest is an expense and therefore causes a decrease in shareholders' equity in the period when it is incurred. Since Demo is preparing financial statements each month, the interest for January was recognized at the end of January (in Chapter 2); the interest to be recognized now is only for the month of February. Since the company has not yet paid the interest (because it is not due to be paid until the end of March), it has to recognize a liability for its obligation to pay the interest later.

Recall that Demo Company paid off $1,000 of its bank loan on February 1 (see Transaction 1), which reduced the principal amount from $10,000 to $9,000. This can be confirmed by looking at the amount shown for the Bank Loan on the trial balance in Exhibit 3-10. To calculate the amount of interest expense for February, the principal amount of the loan is multiplied by the interest rate and the fraction of the year that has passed. In this case, the amount of interest incurred in February is $9,000 \times 6\% \times 1/12 = $45. Shareholders' equity (retained earnings) will therefore be decreased by $45, as a result of the interest expense, and a liability (interest payable) will be increased by the same amount, to recognize the obligation to pay this interest when it is due at the end of March.

ANALYSIS OF INTEREST ADJUSTMENT

Shareholders' Equity decreased by $45 (recorded as Interest Expense)

Liabilities (Interest Payable) **increased** by $45

The rules of debit and credit specify that shareholders' equity is decreased by making debit entries. Accordingly, the Interest Expense account must be debited. Conversely, liabilities are increased by making credit entries, so the Interest Payable account must be credited. Thus, this adjustment is recorded in the journal as follows:

JOURNAL ENTRY FOR INTEREST ADJUSTMENT

Date	Entry number	Names of accounts debited and credited	Amount debited	Amount credited
Feb. 28	13	Interest Expense (SE)	45	
		Interest Payable (L)		45
		Recognition of February interest on loan.		

Entry 14: Rent Adjustment

Rent expense must be recognized for the month of February.

ANALYSIS From the tenant's point of view, rent is an expense and therefore causes shareholders' equity to decrease in the period when it is incurred. Since Demo Company is operating on a monthly accounting cycle, the rent expense to be recognized at this point is only for February.

Recall that Demo signed a lease agreement on February 1 and paid $900 to cover the first and last months' rent, which was recorded as an asset called Prepaid Rent (see Transaction 2). This can also be seen by looking at the amount shown for Prepaid Rent on the trial balance in Exhibit 3-10. One month's worth of this asset, $450, was used up during the first month of the lease, February, and therefore now has to be removed from the Prepaid Rent account and put into the Rent Expense account. Shareholders' equity (retained earnings) will therefore be decreased by $450, as a result of the rent expense, and the asset (prepaid rent) will be decreased by the same amount.

This transfer—out of an asset account and into an expense account—is necessary because, as of the end of February, this $450 cost no longer relates to the future and therefore should no longer appear on the statement of financial position; it was incurred to operate the business during the past month, and therefore belongs on this period's statement of earnings.

ANALYSIS OF RENT ADJUSTMENT

Shareholders' Equity decreased by $450 (recorded as Rent Expense)

Assets (Prepaid Rent) decreased by $450

The rules of debit and credit specify that shareholders' equity is decreased by making debit entries, so the Rent Expense account must be debited. Conversely, assets are decreased by making credit entries, so the Prepaid Rent account must be credited. Thus, this adjustment is recorded in the journal as follows:

JOURNAL ENTRY FOR RENT ADJUSTMENT

Date	Entry number	Names of accounts debited and credited	Amount debited	Amount credited
Feb. 28	14	Rent Expense (SE)	450	
		Prepaid Rent (A)		450
		Recognition of rent expired in February.		

Entry 15: Office Supplies Adjustment

Demo Company checks its office supplies at the end of the month and determines that the cost of the items that are still on hand is $300.

ANALYSIS Recall that the company bought $500 of office supplies on February 10 and recorded them as an asset (Transaction 6). This can also be seen by looking at the amount shown for Office Supplies on Hand in the trial balance (Exhibit 3-10). However, a portion of these supplies was consumed during February and should now be recorded as an expense. Hence, an adjustment is required.

In cases such as this, accountants usually determine how much of the asset has been used up during the period indirectly, by checking how much is still on hand. The difference between the amount that was on hand previously and the amount that is on hand now represents the amount that was used up during the period. In this case, Demo originally had $500 of office supplies on hand but now has only $300 worth of supplies, which indicates that supplies costing $200 have been consumed.

The general formula to be used in such situations is as follows:

Cost of supplies on hand at the beginning of the period	$ 0
+ Cost of supplies purchased during the period (Transaction 6)	500
= Total cost of supplies available to be consumed	500
− Cost of supplies on hand at the end of the period (given in this transaction)	(300)
= Cost of supplies consumed during the period	$200

Shareholders' equity (retained earnings) will therefore be decreased by $200, as a result of the office supplies expense, and the asset (office supplies on hand) will be decreased by the same amount. As with the preceding adjustment, this transfer—out of an asset account and into an expense account—is necessary because, as of the end of February, this $200 of cost will not benefit the future and therefore should not appear on the statement of financial position; it was consumed in operating the business during the past month, and therefore belongs on this period's statement of earnings.

ANALYSIS OF OFFICE SUPPLIES ADJUSTMENT

Shareholders' Equity decreased by $200 (recorded as Office Supplies Expense)

Assets (Office Supplies on Hand) decreased by $200

Since shareholders' equity is decreased by making debit entries, the Office Supplies Expense account must be debited. Conversely, because assets are decreased by making credit entries, the Prepaid Rent account must be credited. Thus, this adjustment is recorded in the journal as follows:

JOURNAL ENTRY FOR OFFICE SUPPLIES ADJUSTMENT

Date	Entry number	Names of accounts debited and credited	Amount debited	Amount credited
Feb. 28	15	Office Supplies Expense (SE)	200	
		Office Supplies on Hand (A)		200
		Recognition of supplies consumed in February.		

Note that the $300 given in the original description of this adjustment does not appear in the journal entry. Rather, since that amount was a remaining balance, it was used to calculate the $200 recorded in the entry. Bear in mind that a balance is the net amount remaining in an account as a result of all the preceding transactions that affected the account. Therefore, if you need to make a journal entry but are only given the ending balance in an account, you have to use that information—together with your knowledge of the logical relationships affecting that account—to calculate the amount to be recorded in the journal entry, as we did here and in Transaction 9.

Entry 16: Utilities Adjustment

Demo's accountant noted that the company received a bill for $315 for utilities used in February. However, the company does not plan to pay the bill until March.

ANALYSIS   According to the accrual basis of accounting, the amount of expense that should be recorded each period is the amount that is *incurred* that period, rather than simply the amount that is *paid* during the period. Therefore, utilities expense of $315 must be recorded for the month of February, even though it will not be paid until March.

Since expenses reduce net income and, ultimately, retained earnings, the utilities expense causes a decrease in shareholder's equity. At the same time, liabilities are increased by the amount owing.

ANALYSIS OF UTILITIES ADJUSTMENT

Shareholders' Equity decreased by $315 (recorded as Utilities Expense)

Liabilities (Utilities Payable) **increased** by $315

Since shareholders' equity is decreased by making debit entries, and expenses are temporary shareholders' equity accounts, the Utilities Expense account must be debited. Since liabilities are increased by making credit entries, the Utilities Payable account must be credited. Thus, this transaction is recorded in the journal as follows:

JOURNAL ENTRY FOR UTILITIES ADJUSTMENT

Date	Entry number	Names of accounts debited and credited	Amount debited	Amount credited
Feb. 28	16	Utilities Expense (SE)	315	
		Utilities Payable (L)		315
		Recognition of utilities for February.		

Entry 17: Depreciation Adjustment

Demo Company's accountant determined that the depreciation on the equipment for the month of February should be $250.

ANALYSIS As discussed in Chapter 2, because the value of the equipment is used up over time, some of its cost should be shown as an expense in each of the periods when it is used. The matching principle requires that we transfer some of the cost of the asset to an expense account each period, so that the cost of using the equipment will appear on the statement of earnings in the same time periods as the revenues generated from using the equipment. This process is called depreciation (or amortization).

In the preceding chapter, we illustrated how the depreciation for January could be calculated. The amount of depreciation for February will be different, because the company purchased additional equipment this month (Transaction 7). However, since depreciation calculations will be covered in detail in Chapter 8, at this point we will simply accept the amount determined by Demo's accountant, $250, as the correct amount for February.

Consequently, the company should report a $250 expense (depreciation) on the statement of earnings and reduce the value of the asset (equipment) on the statement of financial position by a further $250. However, as discussed in Chapter 2, we do not reduce the equipment account directly; instead, we record the reduction in the value of the equipment in its contra-account, accumulated depreciation, and show this as a deduction from the equipment when we prepare the statement of financial position.

ANALYSIS OF DEPRECIATION ADJUSTMENT

Shareholders' Equity decreased by $250 (recorded as Depreciation Expense)

Assets decreased by $250 (recorded as Accumulated Depreciation)

Since all expenses are debits (because shareholders' equity is decreased by making debit entries), the Depreciation Expense account must be debited. Conversely, because assets are decreased by making credit entries, the contra-asset account Accumulated Depreciation must be credited. Therefore, this adjustment is recorded in the journal as follows:

JOURNAL ENTRY FOR DEPRECIATION

Date	Entry number	Names of accounts debited and credited	Amount debited	Amount credited
Feb. 28	17	Depreciation Expense (SE)	250	
		Accumulated Depreciation (XA)		250
		Recognition of depreciation for February.		

When the statement of financial position is prepared, the credit balance in the contra-asset, Accumulated Depreciation, will be deducted from the debit balance in the related asset, Equipment, to show users the net remaining cost of the equipment. This approach enables financial statement users to see both the original cost of the equipment and the portion that remains to be used in future periods.

EARNINGS MANAGEMENT

As mentioned in Chapter 1, many accounting standards allow choices between alternatives, and this sometimes enables management to select methods that raise or lower the revenues and/or expenses that are reported in the financial statements. Adjustments illustrate this potential problem well, because they often not only involve choices between alternative methods but also require the use of significant estimates. For example, there are many different methods for calculating depreciation, and they require estimates of useful lives and residual values.

Accountants have an ethical duty to try to ensure that financial statements are prepared in an unbiased manner, so that they present a fair picture of the company's earnings and financial position. Nevertheless, adjusting entries presents many opportunities for managers to engage in *earnings management*, and users of financial statements have to be aware that biased presentations are a possibility.

Entry 18: Insurance Adjustment

The cost of insurance coverage for the month of February must be recognized.

ANALYSIS   Since Demo is operating on a monthly accounting cycle, insurance expense must be recognized each month. As discussed in Chapter 2, the company paid $360 for a six-month policy, so the monthly cost is one-sixth of the total. Since the initial cost was recorded as an asset, Prepaid Insurance, each month we must make an entry to transfer the portion that has expired, $60, out of this account and into the Insurance Expense account.

ANALYSIS OF INSURANCE ADJUSTMENT

Shareholders' Equity decreased by $60 (recorded as Insurance Expense)

Assets (Prepaid Insurance) decreased by $60

Since the rules of debit and credit specify that shareholders' equity is decreased by making debit entries, the Insurance Expense account must be debited. Conversely, since assets are decreased by making credit entries, the Prepaid Insurance account must be credited. Thus, this adjustment is recorded in the journal as follows:

JOURNAL ENTRY FOR INSURANCE ADJUSTMENT

Date	Entry number	Names of accounts debited and credited	Amount debited	Amount credited
Feb. 28	18	Insurance Expense (SE)	60	
		Prepaid Insurance (A)		60
		Recognition of insurance expired in February.		

Entry 19: Income Tax Adjustment

Income tax expense must be recognized for each accounting period. As you may recall from Chapter 2, Demo's income tax rate is 25%.

ANALYSIS Since Demo operates on a monthly accounting cycle, income tax expense must be recognized each month—even though the company does not have to pay the tax until later. Income tax is an expense of doing business, and therefore must be reported on the statement of earnings. In addition, if the tax has not been paid, the amount owed must be reported as a liability on the company's statement of financial position.

Like any expense, income tax expense reduces the company's net earnings, and hence its retained earnings and shareholders' equity. If the tax is paid, the company's assets (in the form of cash) are reduced. In Demo's case, however, the tax does not have to be paid until later, so cash is not affected at this time. Instead, liabilities are increased (in the form of income tax payable).

Before we can calculate the amount of income tax expense, we need to first determine the company's *income before tax*. To facilitate this, we will now post the adjusting journal entries to the accounts in the ledger.

Exhibit 3-11 shows the portion of Demo Company's journal with the preceding adjustments for February, and Exhibit 3-12 shows Demo's accounts after these adjusting entries have been posted from the journal to the ledger. For easy reference, the postings for the adjusting entries are in blue.

Notice that, compared to the previous view of Demo's ledger (presented in Exhibit 3-9), the company's ledger now contains two new accounts: Office Supplies Expense and Utilities Payable. These have been added because we needed them to record some of the adjustments (entries 15 and 16). These new accounts would also be added to the company's chart of accounts.

DEMO COMPANY'S JOURNAL SHOWING ITS ADJUSTING ENTRIES FOR FEBRUARY (except the adjustment for income tax)

EXHIBIT 3-11.

Date	Entry number	Names of accounts debited and credited	Amount debited	Amount credited
Feb. 28	13	Interest Expense (SE)	45	
		Interest Payable (L)		45
		Recognition of February interest on loan.		
Feb. 28	14	Rent Expense (SE)	450	
		Prepaid Rent (A)		450
		Recognition of rent expired in February.		
Feb. 28	15	Office Supplies Expense (SE)	200	
		Office Supplies on Hand (A)		200
		Recognition of supplies consumed in February.		
Feb. 28	16	Utilities Expense (SE)	315	
		Utilities Payable (L)		315
		Recognition of utilities for February.		
Feb. 28	17	Depreciation Expense (SE)	250	
		Accumulated Depreciation (XA)		250
		Recognition of depreciation for February.		
Feb. 28	18	Insurance Expense (SE)	60	
		Prepaid Insurance (A)		60
		Recognition of insurance expired in February.		

HELPFUL HINT

Notice that each of these adjusting entries involves both a balance sheet account and an income statement account. That is, one half of each adjusting entry (either the debit or the credit) is an asset or liability account, while the other half of the entry is a revenue or expense account.

DEMO COMPANY'S LEDGER AFTER THE ADJUSTING ENTRIES HAVE BEEN POSTED (except the adjustment for income tax)

EXHIBIT 3-12

Permanent Accounts:

Cash (A)

Balance Jan. 31/11	2,090	
		Entry #1 Feb. 01/11 1,000
		Entry #2 Feb. 01/11 900
Entry #4 Feb. 08/11	4,000	
		Entry #6 Feb. 10/11 500
		Entry #7 Feb. 12/11 3,000
Entry #8 Feb. 15/11	5,000	
Entry #9 Feb. 18/11	33,000	
		Entry #10 Feb. 20/11 34,000
		Entry #11 Feb. 25/11 2,500

Accounts Payable (L)

Entry #10 Feb. 20/11 34,000	Balance Jan. 31/11	9,500
	Entry #3 Feb. 05/11	30,000

Accounts Receivable (A)

Balance Jan. 31/11	2,000	
Entry #4 Feb. 08/11	36,000	
		Entry #9 Feb. 18/11 33,000

Interest Payable (L)

	Balance Jan. 31/11	50
	Entry #13 Feb. 28/11	45

EXHIBIT 3-12

DEMO COMPANY'S LEDGER AFTER THE ADJUSTING ENTRIES HAVE BEEN POSTED (cont'd) (except the adjustment for income tax)

Permanent Accounts (cont'd):

Inventory (A)					
Balance	Jan. 31/11	14,000			
Entry #3	Feb. 05/11	30,000			
			Entry #5	Feb. 08/11	27,000

Prepaid Insurance (A)					
Balance	Jan. 31/11	300			
			Entry #18	Feb. 28/11	60

Prepaid Rent (A)					
Balance	Jan. 31/11	0			
Entry #2	Feb. 01/11	900			
			Entry #14	Feb. 28/11	450

Office Supplies on Hand (A)					
Balance	Jan. 31/11	0			
Entry #6	Feb. 10/11	500			
			Entry #15	Feb. 28/11	200

Land (A)			
Balance	Jan. 31/11	15,000	

Equipment (A)			
Balance	Jan. 31/11	4,500	
Entry #7	Feb. 12/11	3,000	

Accumulated Depreciation—Equipment (XA)					
			Balance	Jan. 31/11	150
			Entry #17	Feb. 28/11	250

Income Tax Payable (L)					
			Balance	Jan. 31/11	235

Salaries Payable (L)					
			Balance	Jan. 31/11	0
			Entry #11	Feb. 25/11	300

Dividends Payable (L)					
			Balance	Jan. 31/11	0
			Entry #12	Feb. 28/11	400

Utilities Payable (L)					
			Balance	Jan. 31/11	0
			Entry #16	Feb. 28/11	315

Bank Loan (L)					
			Balance	Jan. 31/11	10,000
Entry #1	Feb. 01/11	1,000			

Share Capital (SE)					
			Balance	Jan. 31/11	17,500
			Entry #8	Feb. 15/11	5,000

Retained Earnings (SE)					
			Balance	Jan. 31/11	455

Temporary Accounts:

Sales Revenue (SE)					
			Balance	Jan. 31/11	0
			Entry #4	Feb. 08/11	40,000

Cost of Goods Sold Expense (SE)			
Balance	Jan. 31/11	0	
Entry #5	Feb. 08/11	27,000	

Salaries Expense (SE)			
Balance	Jan. 31/11	0	
Entry #11	Feb. 25/11	2,800	

Depreciation Expense (SE)			
Balance	Jan. 31/11	0	
Entry #17	Feb. 28/11	250	

Insurance Expense (SE)			
Balance	Jan. 31/11	0	
Entry #18	Feb. 28/11	60	

Interest Expense (SE)			
Balance	Jan. 31/11	0	
Entry #13	Feb. 28/11	45	

DEMO COMPANY'S LEDGER AFTER THE ADJUSTING ENTRIES HAVE BEEN POSTED (cont'd) (except the adjustment for income tax)

EXHIBIT 3-12

Temporary Accounts (cont'd):

Rent Expense (SE)			Income Tax Expense (SE)		
Balance Jan. 31/11	0		Balance Jan. 31/11	0	
Entry #14 Feb. 28/11	450				

Utilities Expense (SE)		
Balance Jan. 31/11	0	
Entry #16 Feb. 28/11	315	

Office Supplies Expense (SE)			Dividends Declared (SE)		
Balance Jan. 31/11	0		Balance Jan. 31/11	0	
Entry #15 Feb. 28/11	200		Entry #12 Feb. 28/11	400	

To determine the company's income before tax, we can now examine its ledger accounts and calculate the revenues minus the expenses. As you should recall, these are all listed in the *temporary accounts* section of the ledger in Exhibit 3-12. In Demo's case, the result is $40,000 - 27,000 - 2,800 - 450 - 315 - 200 - 250 - 60 - 45 = $8,880. (Remember that dividends are not an expense, and therefore are not involved in the calculation of income.) Applying Demo's tax rate of 25% to this yields the income tax expense for the period: $0.25 \times \$8,880 = \$2,220$.

ANALYSIS OF INCOME TAX ADJUSTMENT

Shareholders' Equity decreased by $2,220 (recorded as Income Tax Expense)
Liabilities (Income Tax Payable) **decreased** by $2,220

The rules of debit and credit specify that shareholders' equity is decreased by making debit entries, so the Income Tax Expense account must be debited. Since liabilities are increased by making credit entries, the Income Tax Payable account must be credited. Thus, this transaction is recorded in the journal as follows:

JOURNAL ENTRY FOR INCOME TAX ADJUSTMENT

Date	Entry number	Names of accounts debited and credited	Amount debited	Amount credited
Feb. 28	19	Income Tax Expense (SE)	2,220	
		Income Tax Payable (L)		2,220
		Recognition of income tax in February.		

Exhibit 3-13 presents Demo's ledger after the final adjusting entry, for income tax, has been posted. In addition, the balances in the accounts as of the end of February have been calculated and recorded.

EXHIBIT 3-13

DEMO COMPANY'S LEDGER AFTER ALL THE ADJUSTING ENTRIES HAVE BEEN POSTED AND THE ENDING BALANCES RECORDED

Permanent Accounts:

Cash (A)

Balance	Jan. 31/11	2,090				
			Entry #1	Feb. 01/11	1,000	
			Entry #2	Feb. 01/11	900	
Entry #4	Feb. 08/11	4,000				
			Entry #6	Feb. 10/11	500	
			Entry #7	Feb. 12/11	3,000	
Entry #8	Feb. 15/11	5,000				
Entry #9	Feb. 18/11	33,000				
			Entry #10	Feb. 20/11	34,000	
			Entry #11	Feb. 25/11	2,500	
Balance	Feb. 28/11	2,190				

Accounts Receivable (A)

Balance	Jan. 31/11	2,000			
Entry #4	Feb. 08/11	36,000			
			Entry #9	Feb. 18/11	33,000
Balance	Feb. 28/11	5,000			

Inventory (A)

Balance	Jan. 31/11	14,000			
Entry #3	Feb. 05/11	30,000			
			Entry #5	Feb. 08/11	27,000
Balance	Feb. 28/11	17,000			

Prepaid Insurance (A)

Balance	Jan. 31/11	300			
			Entry #18	Feb. 28/11	60
Balance	Feb. 28/11	240			

Prepaid Rent (A)

Balance	Jan. 31/11	0			
Entry #2	Feb. 01/11	900			
			Entry #14	Feb. 28/11	450
Balance	Feb. 28/11	450			

Office Supplies on Hand (A)

Balance	Jan. 31/11	0			
Entry #6	Feb. 10/11	500			
			Entry #15	Feb. 28/11	200
Balance	Feb. 28/11	300			

Land (A)

Balance	Jan. 31/11	15,000

Equipment (A)

Balance	Jan. 31/11	4,500
Entry #7	Feb. 12/11	3,000
Balance	Feb. 28/11	7,500

Accumulated Depreciation—Equipment (XA)

	Balance	Jan. 31/11	150
	Entry #17	Feb. 28/11	250
	Balance	Feb. 28/11	400

Accounts Payable (L)

			Balance	Jan. 31/11	9,500
			Entry #3	Feb. 05/11	30,000
Entry #10 Feb. 20/11		34,000			
			Balance	Feb. 28/11	5,500

Interest Payable (L)

Balance	Jan. 31/11	50
Entry #13	Feb. 28/11	45
Balance	Feb. 28/11	95

Income Tax Payable (L)

Balance	Jan. 31/11	235
Entry #19	Feb. 28/11	2,220
Balance	Feb. 28/11	2,455

Salaries Payable (L)

Balance	Jan. 31/11	0
Entry #11	Feb. 25/11	300
Balance	Feb. 28/11	300

Dividends Payable (L)

Balance	Jan. 31/11	0
Entry #12	Feb. 28/11	400
Balance	Feb. 28/11	400

Utilities Payable (L)

Balance	Jan. 31/11	0
Entry #16	Feb. 28/11	315
Balance	Feb. 28/11	315

Bank Loan (L)

			Balance	Jan. 31/11	10,000
Entry #1 Feb. 01/11		1,000			
			Balance	Feb. 28/11	9,000

Share Capital (SE)

Balance	Jan. 31/11	17,500
Entry #8	Feb. 15/11	5,000
Balance	Feb. 28/11	22,500

Retained Earnings (SE)

Balance	Jan. 31/11	455

DEMO COMPANY'S LEDGER AFTER ALL THE ADJUSTING ENTRIES HAVE BEEN POSTED AND THE ENDING BALANCES RECORDED (cont'd)

EXHIBIT 3-13

Temporary Accounts:

Sales Revenue (SE)

	Balance	Jan. 31/11	0
	Entry #4	Feb. 08/11	40,000
	Balance	Feb. 28/11	40,000

Depreciation Expense (SE)

Balance	Jan. 31/11	0	
Entry #17	Feb. 28/11	250	
Balance	Feb. 28/11	250	

Cost of Goods Sold Expense (SE)

Balance	Jan. 31/11	0	
Entry #5	Feb. 08/11	27,000	
Balance	Feb. 28/11	27,000	

Insurance Expense (SE)

Balance	Jan. 31/11	0	
Entry #18	Feb. 28/11	60	
Balance	Feb. 28/11	60	

Salaries Expense (SE)

Balance	Jan. 31/11	0	
Entry #11	Feb. 25/11	2,800	
Balance	Feb. 28/11	2,800	

Interest Expense (SE)

Balance	Jan. 31/11	0	
Entry #13	Feb. 28/11	45	
Balance	Feb. 28/11	45	

Rent Expense (SE)

Balance	Jan. 31/11	0	
Entry #14	Feb. 28/11	450	
Balance	Feb. 28/11	450	

Income Tax Expense (SE)

Balance	Jan. 31/11	0	
Entry #19	Feb. 28/11	2,220	
Balance	Feb. 28/11	2,220	

Utilities Expense (SE)

Balance	Jan. 31/11	0	
Entry #16	Feb. 28/11	315	
Balance	Feb. 28/11	315	

Office Supplies Expense (SE)

Balance	Jan. 31/11	0	
Entry #15	Feb. 28/11	200	
Balance	Feb. 28/11	200	

Dividends Declared (SE)

Balance	Jan. 31/11	0	
Entry #12	Feb. 28/11	400	
Balance	Feb. 28/11	400	

Preparing an Adjusted Trial Balance

After all the adjusting entries have been recorded and posted, an **adjusted trial balance** is prepared. This is done to ensure that the total debits in the accounts still equal the total credits; any imbalance must be corrected before the financial statements are prepared.

Exhibit 3-14 shows the adjusted trial balance for Demo Company as of the end of February. It is simply a listing of all the accounts and their balances; all the information has been taken directly from the ledger in Exhibit 3-13.

Note that, although the adjusted trial balance is dated February 28, 2011, the amount shown for retained earnings is the balance as of January 31 (the end of the preceding period). This is because all the changes affecting retained earnings in the current period are recorded in the temporary accounts (for revenues, expenses, and dividends declared). When the *closing entries* are made, the balances in the temporary accounts will be transferred into the retained earnings account and its balance will be brought up to date.

EXHIBIT 3-14

**DEMO COMPANY'S ADJUSTED TRIAL BALANCE
AS OF FEBRUARY 28, 2011**

Account Names	Debit Balances	Credit Balances
Cash	$ 2,190	
Accounts receivable	5,000	
Inventory	17,000	
Prepaid insurance	240	
Prepaid rent	450	
Office supplies on hand	300	
Land	15,000	
Equipment	7,500	
Accumulated depreciation—equipment		$ 400
Accounts payable		5,500
Interest payable		95
Income tax payable		2,455
Salaries payable		300
Dividends payable		400
Utilities payable		315
Bank loan		9,000
Share capital		22,500
Retained earnings		455
Sales revenue		40,000
Cost of goods sold	27,000	
Salaries expense	2,800	
Rent expense	450	
Utilities expense	315	
Office supplies expense	200	
Depreciation expense	250	
Insurance expense	60	
Interest expense	45	
Income tax expense	2,220	
Dividends declared	400	
Totals	$81,420	$81,420

LEARNING OBJECTIVE 9

Prepare financial statements.

PREPARING FINANCIAL STATEMENTS AND CLOSING ENTRIES

Preparing the Financial Statements

After the adjusted trial balance has been prepared and any necessary corrections have been made, the financial statements for the period can be prepared. The statement of earnings is the first statement to be prepared, using the information for the revenue and expense accounts listed in the adjusted trial balance.

Exhibit 3-15 shows Demo Company's statement of earnings for the month of February, with comparative amounts for the preceding period.

DEMO COMPANY'S STATEMENT OF EARNINGS FOR THE MONTH OF FEBRUARY
(with comparative figures for the month of January)

EXHIBIT 3-15

	February 28, 2011	January 31, 2011
Revenue:		
Sales	$ 40,000	$ 13,000
Expenses:		
Cost of goods sold	(27,000)	(9,000)
Salaries	(2,800)	(2,000)
Rent	(450)	(500)
Utilities	(315)	(300)
Office supplies	(200)	–
Depreciation	(250)	(150)
Insurance	(60)	(60)
Interest	(45)	(50)
Income tax	(2,220)	(235)
Net income	$ 6,660	$ 705

At this point, we are illustrating the simplest format for the statement of earnings. There many other ways to organize and present the information in a statement of earnings. These will be discussed in Chapter 4.

The revenue and expenses on the statement of earnings for February have been taken directly from the information presented for these accounts in the lower portion of Exhibit 3-14, the adjusted trial balance. Remember, however, that the last account listed in Exhibit 3-14, dividends declared, is not an expense account; consequently, it is not included on the statement of earnings. The amounts for January have simply been brought forward from the statement of earnings presented in Chapter 2 (page 104).

The statement of financial position is prepared next, but to do so we need to first determine the new balance in retained earnings, as of the end of February. As you may recall from Chapter 2, the following formula is used each accounting period to calculate the updated amount of retained earnings:

> Retained Earnings at the end of the preceding period
> + Net Earnings (or − Net Loss) for the current period
> − Dividends Declared in the current period
> = Retained Earnings at the end of the current period

Applying this to Demo Company, its retained earnings on February 28 would be determined as follows:

Retained Earnings at the end of January (from Chapter 2, page 104; or from the adjusted trial balance, Exhibit 3-14)	$ 455
+ Net Income for February (from the statement of earnings, Exhibit 3-15)	6,660
− Dividends Declared in February (from the adjusted trial balance, Exhibit 3-14)	(400)
= Retained Earnings at the end of February	$ 6,715

The remaining statement of financial position data can be taken directly from the balances for the permanent accounts, shown in the upper portion of the adjusted trial balance (Exhibit 3-14).

Exhibit 3-16 shows Demo Company's statement of financial position as of the end of February, with comparative amounts for the preceding period.

As we discussed in Chapter 2, other formats can be used to present the statement of financial position. However, for examples in this book we will generally use a format similar to what is shown in Exhibit 3-16.

EXHIBIT 3-16

DEMO COMPANY'S STATEMENT OF FINANCIAL POSITION AT THE END OF FEBRUARY

(with comparative figures for the end of January)

	February 28, 2011		January 31, 2011	
Current assets:				
Cash		$ 2,190		$ 2,090
Accounts receivable		5,000		2,000
Inventory		17,000		14,000
Prepaid insurance		240		300
Prepaid rent		450		–
Office supplies		300		–
		25,180		18,390
Non-current assets:				
Land		15,000		15,000
Equipment, at its original cost	$ 7,500		$ 4,500	
Less: Accumulated depreciation	(400)		(150)	
		7,100		4,350
		22,100		19,350
Total assets		**$47,280**		**$37,740**
Current liabilities:				
Accounts payable		$ 5,500		$ 9,500
Interest payable		95		50
Income tax payable		2,455		235
Salaries payable		300		–
Dividends payable		400		–
Utilities payable		315		–
		9,065		9,785
Non-current liabilities:				
Bank loan		9,000		10,000
Total liabilities		18,065		19,785
Shareholders' equity:				
Share capital	$22,500		$17,500	
Retained earnings	6,715		455	
Total shareholders' equity		29,215		17,955
Total liabilities and shareholders' equity		**$47,280**		**$37,740**

As you can see, Demo's statement of financial position at the end of February reflects the data listed in the adjusted trial balance for the permanent accounts, with the exception of retained earnings. That is, the amounts for the assets, liabilities, and share capital have been taken directly from Exhibit 3-14; only the amount for retained earnings had to be calculated (as we did, by adding the net income for February and deducting the dividends declared).

Notice how the contra-asset account Accumulated Depreciation is shown on the statement of financial position as a deduction from (or contra to) the associated asset account, Equipment. You should also notice how the balance in the accumulated depreciation account has grown from $150 at the end of January to $150 + $250 = $400 at the end of February. Over the life of the equipment, the balance in the accumulated depreciation account will continue to grow, by the amount of depreciation that is recorded each period. In other words, the *depreciation expense* amounts that are reported on the statement of earnings each period are added up (or accumulated) in the *accumulated depreciation* account that is reported on the statement of financial position. As each accounting period goes by, the accumulated depreciation balance will increase and the net remaining value of the asset will decrease, reflecting the fact that the equipment's value is used up as time passes.

The final major financial statement to be prepared is the statement of cash flows. However, since Chapter 5 is devoted entirely to this topic, we will defer any further discussion of the statement of cash flows until it is covered in detail in Chapter 5.

Preparing the Closing Entries

To complete the accounting cycle, the balances in the temporary accounts must be reset to zero, so that they will be ready to record data for the next accounting cycle. We do this by transferring the balances in the temporary accounts to retained earnings (which is a permanent account). The entries that accomplish this are called **closing entries**.

The first step in the closing process is to eliminate all the balances in the revenue and expense accounts, and transfer the net amount to the retained earnings account. To do this, we *debit the revenues* (to eliminate their credit balances), *credit the expenses* (to eliminate their debit balances), and *credit retained earnings* (to increase retained earnings by the difference between the revenues and the expenses, which equals the net earnings for the period).*

The second step in the closing process is to eliminate the balance in the dividends declared account and transfer it to the retained earnings account. To do this, we credit Dividends Declared (to eliminate its debit balance) and debit Retained Earnings (to reduce the retained earnings by the amount of dividends declared during the period).

Exhibit 3-17 shows the closing entries for Demo Company at the end of February.

LEARNING OBJECTIVE 10

Explain closing entries and why they are necessary.

*In some cases, the expenses will be larger than the revenues, resulting in a net loss for the period. If so, the retained earnings account would have to be debited (to decrease it).

EXHIBIT 3-17

DEMO COMPANY'S JOURNAL SHOWING ITS CLOSING ENTRIES FOR THE MONTH OF FEBRUARY

Date	Entry number	Names of accounts debited and credited	Amount debited	Amount credited
Feb. 28	20	Sales Revenue (SE)	40,000	
		Cost of Goods Sold (SE)		27,000
		Salaries Expense (SE)		2,800
		Rent Expense (SE)		450
		Utilities Expense (SE)		315
		Office Supplies Expense (SE)		200
		Depreciation Expense (SE)		250
		Insurance Expense (SE)		60
		Interest Expense (SE)		45
		Income Tax Expense (SE)		2,220
		Retained Earnings (SE)		6,660
		Closing the revenue and expense accounts, and increasing the retained earnings by the amount of income earned this period.		
Feb. 28	21	Retained Earnings (SE)	400	
		Dividends Declared (SE)		400
		Closing the dividends declared account, and decreasing the retained earnings by the amount for this period.		

HELPFUL HINT

Points to remember about closing entries:
- The revenues are debited and the expenses credited, to eliminate their balances; the difference between these is the net earnings, which goes into retained earnings.
- The dividends declared account is credited, to eliminate its balance; since dividends reduce retained earnings, the retained earnings account is debited.

Exhibit 3-18 shows Demo's ledger after the above closing entries have been posted to the accounts. For easy reference, the postings for the closing entries are in red.

It is important for you to realize that the closing entries have achieved two key objectives:

- The balance in the retained earnings account has been brought up to date, by adding the income earned and deducting the dividends declared during the period that has just ended.

- The balances in all of the temporary accounts have been reset to zero, so that they are ready to start the next accounting period.

HELPFUL HINT

Be sure to note that, although it is involved in the closing process, the retained earnings account is not closed. It is a permanent (statement of financial position) account, which is updated by the closing process.

Rather than the simplified two-entry closing process that has been illustrated above, some companies use a four-entry closing process in which (1) the revenues are closed into another temporary account, called the **Income Summary**; (2) the expenses are also closed into the Income Summary account; (3) the Income Summary account is then closed into the Retained Earnings account; (4) the Dividends Declared account is closed into the Retained Earnings account. The combined effect of entries (1), (2), and (3) under this approach is equivalent to the first closing entry that we made for Demo Company, and entry (4) under this approach is identical to the second closing entry that we made for Demo. Either of these approaches is acceptable, as they both produce the same results.

In a computerized accounting system, the software package will perform the closing process automatically, when it is instructed to do so. Since the closing entries are

DEMO COMPANY'S LEDGER AFTER THE CLOSING ENTRIES HAVE BEEN POSTED `EXHIBIT 3-18`

Permanent Accounts:

Cash (A)

Balance	Jan. 31/11	2,090				
			Entry #1	Feb. 01/11	1,000	
			Entry #2	Feb. 01/11	900	
Entry #4	Feb. 08/11	4,000				
			Entry #6	Feb. 10/11	500	
			Entry #7	Feb. 12/11	3,000	
Entry #8	Feb. 15/11	5,000				
Entry #9	Feb. 18/11	33,000				
			Entry #10	Feb. 20/11	34,000	
			Entry #11	Feb. 25/11	2,500	
Balance	Feb. 28/11	2,190				

Accounts Payable (L)

			Balance	Jan. 31/11	9,500
			Entry #3	Feb. 05/11	30,000
Entry #10 Feb. 20/11	34,000				
			Balance	Feb. 28/11	5,500

Accounts Receivable (A)

Balance	Jan. 31/11	2,000			
Entry #4	Feb. 08/11	36,000			
			Entry #9	Feb. 18/11	33,000
Balance	Feb. 28/11	5,000			

Interest Payable (L)

			Balance	Jan. 31/11	50
			Entry #13	Feb. 28/11	45
			Balance	Feb. 28/11	95

Inventory (A)

Balance	Jan. 31/11	14,000			
Entry #3	Feb. 05/11	30,000			
			Entry #5	Feb. 08/11	27,000
Balance	Feb. 28/11	17,000			

Income Tax Payable (L)

			Balance	Jan. 31/11	235
			Entry #19	Feb. 28/11	2,220
			Balance	Feb. 28/11	2,455

Prepaid Insurance (A)

Balance	Jan. 31/11	300			
			Entry #18	Feb. 28/11	60
Balance	Feb. 28/11	240			

Salaries Payable (L)

			Balance	Jan. 31/11	0
			Entry #11	Feb. 25/11	300
			Balance	Feb. 28/11	300

Prepaid Rent (A)

Balance	Jan. 31/11	0			
Entry #2	Feb. 01/11	900			
			Entry #14	Feb. 28/11	450
Balance	Feb. 28/11	450			

Dividends Payable (L)

			Balance	Jan. 31/11	0
			Entry #12	Feb. 28/11	400
			Balance	Feb. 28/11	400

Office Supplies on Hand (A)

Balance	Jan. 31/11	0			
Entry #6	Feb. 10/11	500			
			Entry #15	Feb. 28/11	200
Balance	Feb. 28/11	300			

Utilities Payable (L)

			Balance	Jan. 31/11	0
			Entry #16	Feb. 28/11	315
			Balance	Feb. 28/11	315

Land (A)

Balance	Jan. 31/11	15,000

Bank Loan (L)

			Balance	Jan. 31/11	10,000
Entry #1	Feb. 01/11	1,000			
			Balance	Feb. 28/11	9,000

Equipment (A)

Balance	Jan. 31/11	4,500
Entry #7	Feb. 12/11	3,000
Balance	Feb. 28/11	7,500

Share Capital (SE)

			Balance	Jan. 31/11	17,500
			Entry #8	Feb. 15/11	5,000
			Balance	Feb. 28/11	22,500

Accumulated Depreciation—Equipment (XA)

			Balance	Jan. 31/11	150
			Entry #17	Feb. 28/11	250
			Balance	Feb. 28/11	400

Retained Earnings (SE)

			Balance	Jan. 31/11	455
			Entry #20	Feb. 28/11	6,660
Entry #21 Feb. 28/11	400				
			Balance	Feb. 28/11	6,715

EXHIBIT 3-18

DEMO COMPANY'S LEDGER AFTER THE CLOSING ENTRIES HAVE BEEN POSTED (cont'd)

Temporary Accounts:

Sales Revenue (SE)

				Balance	Jan. 31/11	0		
				Entry #4	Feb. 08/11	40,000		
				Balance	Feb. 28/11	40,000		
Entry #20 Feb. 28/11		40,000						
				Balance	Feb. 28/11	0		

Depreciation Expense (SE)

Balance	Jan. 31/11	0				
Entry #17	Feb. 28/11	250				
Balance	Feb. 28/11	250				
			Entry #20 Feb. 28/11		250	
Balance	Feb. 28/11	0				

Cost of Goods Sold Expense (SE)

Balance	Jan. 31/11	0		
Entry #5	Feb. 08/11	27,000		
Balance	Feb. 28/11	27,000		
			Entry #20 Feb. 28/11	27,000
Balance	Feb. 28/11	0		

Insurance Expense (SE)

Balance	Jan. 31/11	0		
Entry #18	Feb. 28/11	60		
Balance	Feb. 28/11	60		
			Entry #20 Feb. 28/11	60
Balance	Feb. 28/11	0		

Salaries Expense (SE)

Balance	Jan. 31/11	0		
Entry #11	Feb. 25/11	2,800		
Balance	Feb. 28/11	2,800		
			Entry #20 Feb. 28/11	2,800
Balance	Feb. 28/11	0		

Interest Expense (SE)

Balance	Jan. 31/11	0		
Entry #13	Feb. 28/11	45		
Balance	Feb. 28/11	45		
			Entry #20 Feb. 28/11	45
Balance	Feb. 28/11	0		

Rent Expense (SE)

Balance	Jan. 31/11	0		
Entry #14	Feb. 28/11	450		
Balance	Feb. 28/11	450		
			Entry #20 Feb. 28/11	450
Balance	Feb. 28/11	0		

Income Tax Expense (SE)

Balance	Jan. 31/11	0		
Entry #19	Feb. 28/11	2,220		
Balance	Feb. 28/11	2,220		
			Entry #20 Feb. 28/11	2,220
Balance	Feb. 28/11	0		

Utilities Expense (SE)

Balance	Jan. 31/11	0		
Entry #16	Feb. 28/11	315		
Balance	Feb. 28/11	315		
			Entry #20 Feb. 28/11	315
Balance	Feb. 28/11	0		

Office Supplies Expense (SE)

Balance	Jan. 31/11	0		
Entry #15	Feb. 28/11	200		
Balance	Feb. 28/11	200		
			Entry #20 Feb. 28/11	200
Balance	Feb. 28/11	0		

Dividends Declared (SE)

Balance	Jan. 31/11	0		
Entry #12	Feb. 28/11	400		
Balance	Feb. 28/11	400		
			Entry #20 Feb. 28/11	400
Balance	Feb. 28/11	0		

the final step in the accounting cycle, you should make sure you have made all the appropriate adjustments, and prepared and reviewed the financial statements, before you instruct the program to close the books for the period.

At this stage, some companies would prepare a **post-closing trial balance**. This would include only the permanent (statement of financial position) accounts, because all the temporary accounts now have zero balances. A post-closing trial balance serves as a final check on the accounting system, to ensure that it is in balance, before any transactions for the next period are recorded. This is an optional final step in the accounting cycle, and we are not illustrating it here.

Accounting Cycle Frequency

One final issue to look at is the question of how often the accounting cycle should be completed. In other words, how long should an accounting period be? Or, put differently, how often should financial statements be prepared? The answer is that financial statements should be prepared as often as necessary to provide timely information to management, shareholders, and other users. Since this preparation can be costly, especially in a manual accounting system, there is a trade-off between the benefits of having up-to-date information and the cost of preparing the financial statements. In some businesses it is essential to have up-to-date information on a regular basis, so daily or weekly financial statements may be needed. In other businesses, monthly statements are probably sufficient. For companies whose shares are traded on a public stock exchange, there is a requirement to file financial statements quarterly, as well as annually. Regardless of the time period, however, the accounting cycle steps and procedures described above are the same.

The frequency with which financial statements are prepared is sometimes expressed in terms of how often a company **closes the books**. If, as in our Demo example, the company closes its books every month, the company's accounting cycle is one month long. In such cases, adjusting entries are made on a monthly basis, so that the financial statements are as accurate as possible, and the temporary accounts are reset each month.

With a computerized accounting system, financial statements can very easily be generated weekly, monthly, quarterly, semi-annually, on a year-to-date basis, or for any specified time period. The accounting software can isolate all the transactions that were recorded for a particular period, and then prepare financial statements that include only the appropriate transactions. Because financial statements can be generated very quickly and easily in a computerized accounting system, it is feasible to produce them more frequently.

SUMMARY

This chapter built on the concepts introduced in Chapter 2 and explained the procedures underlying how financial information is collected, recorded, summarized, and reported in an actual accounting system. You should now understand debits and credits, journal entries, ledger accounts, trial balances, adjusting entries, and closing entries.

Whether in a manual accounting system or a computerized one, the underlying structures and processes are the same. In a computerized accounting system, the software takes care of the mechanical tasks, such as posting journal entries to the ledger accounts, preparing trial balances and financial statements, and closing the accounts. However, people with knowledge of accounting are still required to formulate transaction entries, make appropriate adjustments, and so on.

After the in-depth discussion of the accounting cycle presented in this chapter, you should be starting to feel more familiar and comfortable with accounting concepts, terms, and procedures. As you work through the problems at the end of this chapter, remember that the more effort you put in at this point, the easier the course will become later.

PRACTICE PROBLEM

Exhibit 3-19 presents the statement of financial position of Template Company as of December 31, 2010.

a. Prepare a set of T accounts for Template Company, and enter the opening balances from the December 31, 2010, statement of financial position (in Exhibit 3-19).

b. Using the transaction data that follows, prepare journal entries for the company's 2011 transactions and adjustments, and post the journal entries to the T accounts. Open new accounts as you need them.

c. Prepare a statement of earnings for 2011, and a classified, comparative statement of financial position (showing amounts at the beginning and end of the year).

d. Prepare the journal entries to close the accounts at the end of the year, and post the closing entries to the T accounts.

EXHIBIT 3-19

TEMPLATE COMPANY STATEMENT OF FINANCIAL POSITION, DECEMBER 31, 2010

**Template Company
Statement of Financial Position
December 31, 2010**

Assets			
Current Assets			
Cash	$ 37,000		
Accounts receivable	39,500		
Inventory	43,000		
Prepaid rent	15,000		
Total current assets			$134,500
Capital Assets			
Building and equipment, at cost	$350,000		
Less: Accumulated depreciation	100,000		
		$250,000	
Office furniture, at cost	76,000		
Less: Accumulated depreciation	16,000		
		60,000	
Total capital assets			310,000
Total Assets			$444,500
Liabilities			
Current Liabilities			
Accounts payable	$ 33,000		
Wages payable	9,000		
Taxes payable	6,000		
Total current liabilities		$ 48,000	
Non-Current Liabilities			
Long-term debt		75,000	
Total Liabilities			$123,000
Shareholders' Equity			
Share capital	$185,000		
Retained earnings	136,500		
Total Shareholders' Equity			321,500
Total Liabilities and Shareholders' Equity			$444,500

Transactions for 2011:

1. Sales for the year totalled $760,000, all on account.

2. A review of accounts receivable at the end of 2011 showed a balance of $35,000 remaining at that time.

3. Purchases of new equipment totalled $40,700, all paid in cash.

4. Depreciation for 2011 totalled $19,600. Eighty percent of this amount was related to the building and equipment, and the remainder to the office furniture.

5. Rent was paid quarterly, in advance, on March 31, June 30, September 30, and December 31. Payments of $15,000 each were made on March 31 and June 30. Starting with the September 30 payment, the rent increased to $16,500 per quarter.

6. The wages that were shown as payable as of December 31, 2010, were paid in 2011. In addition, the employees earned wages of $150,000 during the year. As of December 31, 2011, $11,000 of this amount had not yet been paid to the employees.

7. Purchases of inventory, all on account, amounted to $431,000. (This is the only item that affects accounts payable.)

8. On December 31, 2011, the company owed inventory suppliers a total of $36,000.

9. The cost of the goods sold during the year was $417,000.

10. The interest rate on the long-term debt is 8%, and the interest is paid on December 31 each year. On September 30, 2011, the company borrowed $15,000 in additional long-term debt, with the same interest terms.

11. Other selling and administrative expenses of $45,000 were paid in cash.

12. The company's net income is taxed at 30%. Some tax payments were made during the year, but $4,180 was still owed to the Canada Revenue Agency as of December 31, 2011.

13. The company declared $5,000 in dividends in each quarter of 2011. These dividends were payable on April 15, 2011; July 15, 2011; October 15, 2011; and January 15, 2012.

STRATEGIES FOR SUCCESS:

▶ Rather than using pluses and minuses to show the effects of the transactions in a table (as we did in Chapter 2), you will now use debits and credits to record them as journal entries in T accounts. As you record the effects of the transactions, ensure that the total amount of debits equals the total amount of credits.

▶ Remember that debits are used to record increases in assets, while credits are used to record increases in liabilities and shareholders' equity accounts. Decreases are recorded in the opposite manner.

▶ Within the shareholders' equity group of accounts, bear in mind that investments made by the owners and revenues earned by the business both represent increases in shareholders' equity, and are therefore recorded as credits. On the other hand, dividends distributed to the owners and expenses incurred by the business both represent decreases in shareholders' equity, and are therefore recorded as debits.

▶ Bear in mind that *expenses* are costs that have been used up in the process of operating the business and generating revenues, while *assets* are costs that have not yet been consumed and will therefore be used to operate the business and generate revenues in the future.

▶ Analyze each transaction by thinking about what items are affected, and whether each of those items is increased or decreased. Then, based on the types of accounts involved and the rules of debit and credit (as summarized in Exhibits 3-2 and 3-3), determine what should be debited and what should be credited.

▶ When you encounter items that describe how much *remains*, remember that a remaining amount represents a balance in an account, rather than a transaction. Therefore, if you are told how much remains at the end of the period, you have to work backwards to determine what transaction must have occurred to create that ending amount. Then you can record the transaction in the manner described above.

SUGGESTED SOLUTION TO PRACTICE PROBLEM

The journal entries for Template Company are shown in Exhibit 3-20. Extended explanations for the more complex transactions are also provided.

EXHIBIT 3-20

TEMPLATE COMPANY'S JOURNAL ENTRIES FOR 2011

1.	Accounts Receivable (A)	760,000	
	Sales Revenue (SE)		760,000
	Made sales on account.		
2.	Cash (A)	764,500	
	Accounts Receivable (A)		764,500
	Collected accounts receivable.		
3.	Building and Equipment (A)	40,700	
	Cash (A)		40,700
	Purchased new equipment.		
4.	Depreciation Expense (SE)	19,600	
	Accumulated Depreciation—Building and Equipment (XA)		15,680
	Accumulated Depreciation—Office Furniture (XA)		3,920
	Depreciated the capital assets.		
5a.	Prepaid Rent (A)	63,000	
	Cash (A)		63,000
	Paid rent (in quarterly instalments).		
5b.	Rent Expense (SE)	61,500	
	Prepaid Rent (A)		61,500
	Recorded rent expired in 2011.		
6a.	Wages Payable (L)	9,000	
	Cash (A)		9,000
	Paid wages owed from 2010.		
6b.	Wage Expense (SE)	150,000	
	Wages Payable (L)		150,000
	Recorded wages due for 2011.		

TEMPLATE COMPANY'S JOURNAL ENTRIES FOR 2011 (cont'd)

EXHIBIT 3-20

6c. Wages Payable (L)	139,000	
Cash (A)		139,000
Recorded wages paid for 2011 ($150,000 − $11,000).		
7. Inventory (A)	431,000	
Accounts Payable (L)		431,000
Bought inventory on account.		
8. Accounts Payable (L)	428,000	
Cash (A)		428,000
Made partial payment to suppliers.		
9. Cost of Goods Sold (SE)	417,000	
Inventory (A)		417,000
Recorded cost of inventory sold.		
10a. Cash (A)	15,000	
Long-Term Debt (L)		15,000
On September 30, borrowed additional funds.		
10b. Interest Expense (SE)	6,300	
Cash (A)		6,300
On December 31, paid interest on long-term debt.		
11. Selling and Administrative Expenses (SE)	45,000	
Cash (A)		45,000
Paid selling and administrative expenses.		
12a. Income Tax Expense (SE)	18,180	
Taxes Payable (L)		18,180
Recorded income taxes owed for the year.		
12b. Taxes Payable (L)	20,000	
Cash (A)		20,000
Recorded partial payment of income taxes.		
13a. Dividends Declared (SE)	20,000	
Dividends Payable (L)		20,000
Recorded dividends declared (4 × $5,000).		
13b. Dividends Payable (L)	15,000	
Cash (A)		15,000
Paid first three dividends (3 × $5,000).		

Transaction 2: Accounts Receivable

The information provided is the ending balance in the account. The cash collections are calculated based on the beginning and ending balances in Accounts Receivable combined with the amount of sales on account during the year, as follows:

Beginning balance of Accounts Receivable	$ 39,500
Add: Sales on account (new accounts receivable)	760,000
Total accounts receivable to be collected	799,500
Deduct: Ending balance of Accounts Receivable	35,000
Payments received on account	$764,500

Note that, after the journal entries for Transactions 1 and 2 are posted to the T accounts, the ending balance in the Accounts Receivable account will be the specified $35,000.

Transaction 4: Depreciation

The depreciation for the period is split between the building and equipment, and the office furniture. Both of these can use the same depreciation expense account (or they could be recorded in separate expense accounts); however, the accumulated depreciation must be recorded in separate contra-asset accounts, to be reported on the statement of financial position.

An accumulated depreciation account is referred to as a contra-asset, because it represents the portion of the asset that has been written off. Accordingly, it has a balance opposite to the related asset account (i.e., an asset has a debit balance, while a contra-asset has a credit balance). On the statement of financial position, the accumulated depreciation balance is deducted from the cost of the related asset.

Transaction 5: Rent

a. The total cash *payments* during the period are $(2 \times \$15,000) + (2 \times \$16,500) = \$63,000$. At the time these payments are made, they constitute an asset—prepaid rent.

b. The beginning balance in the Prepaid Rent account on December 31, 2010, of $15,000 represents the payment made on December 31, 2010, covering the rent for the first quarter of 2011. The first two payments in 2011 (of $15,000 each, on March 31 and June 30) cover quarters two and three. The third payment of $16,500 on September 30 covers the fourth quarter. Therefore, the rent expense for 2011 should be the sum of these amounts, or $[3 \times \$15,000] + \$16,500 = \$61,500$. The last payment made (of $16,500 on December 31, 2011) applies to the first quarter of 2012 and therefore should be the ending balance in the Prepaid Rent account. After the two journal entries for Transaction 5 have been posted to the T accounts, the ending balance in the Prepaid Rent account will be the specified $16,500.

Also note that various other combinations of entries could be made to record these events. Any journal entries that result in the correct balances in the accounts are acceptable.

Transaction 6: Wages

We have assumed that the company first paid the wages owed from 2010 (in entry 6a). We have also assumed that the wages earned by the employees are first recorded as an expense and a liability (in entry 6b); then the liability is reduced when the wages are paid (in entry 6c). This is typically how companies account for wages. However, other combinations of entries could be made to record these events, and any journal entries that result in the correct balances in the accounts are acceptable.

Note that, as a result of these entries, there is a balance of $11,000 in wages payable at the end of the year, which is the amount that had not yet been paid to the employees.

Transaction 8: Accounts Payable

The beginning and ending balances in Accounts Payable, together with the amount of new purchases made on account during the year, are used to calculate the amount that was paid on account during 2011, as follows:

Beginning balance of Accounts Payable	$ 33,000
Add: Purchases on account (new accounts payable)	431,000
Total accounts payable to be paid	464,000
Deduct: Ending balance of Accounts Payable	36,000
Payments made during the period	$428,000

Note that, after the journal entries for Transaction 8 have been posted to the T accounts, the ending balance in Accounts Payable will be the specified $36,000.

Transaction 10: Interest

For the first nine months of the year, the interest is calculated on the initial balance of $75,000; for the last three months of the year, it is calculated on the new amount of debt, $90,000. The total interest for the year is therefore calculated as follows:

$75,000 \times 8\% \times 9/12 =$	$4,500
$90,000 \times 8\% \times 3/12 =$	1,800
Interest expense	$6,300

Transaction 12: Income Taxes

Taxes are calculated on the income before taxes. This can be calculated by going through the transactions and adjustments recorded in either the journal entries or the T accounts, and adding the revenues and subtracting the expenses. You should find that the income before taxes is $760,000 − 417,000 − 150,000 − 19,600 − 61,500 − 6,300 − 45,000 = $60,600. The tax expense is then calculated as 30% of this amount: $0.30 \times \$60,600 = \$18,180$.

The ending balance in the Taxes Payable account is then used to calculate how much Template Company must have paid in taxes in 2011, as follows:

Beginning balance of Taxes Payable	$ 6,000
Add: Tax expense for the period (new taxes payable)	18,180
Total taxes to be paid	24,180
Deduct: Ending balance of Taxes Payable	4,180
Tax payments made during the period	$20,000

Transaction 13: Dividends

The first three dividends declared in 2011 were paid in cash. Because the last dividend is still payable as at December 31, a new account, Dividends Payable, will appear on the statement of financial position.

The T accounts are shown in Exhibit 3-21. The opening balances (from December 31, 2010) have been shown in bold, and the posted transactions for 2011 are numbered. Exhibit 3-22 (page 207) shows the 2011 financial statements for Template Company. Exhibit 3-23 (page 208) presents Template Company's closing journal entries.

TEMPLATE COMPANY'S T ACCOUNTS FOR 2011

EXHIBIT 3-21

The opening balances in the accounts have been brought forward from December 31, 2010. The amounts shown in red are the closing entries (required for part d of the problem).

Cash (A)

	37,000		
2	764,500	40,700	3
10a	15,000	63,000	5a
		9,000	6a
		139,000	6c
		428,000	8
		6,300	10b
		45,000	11
		20,000	12b
		15,000	13b
	50,500		

Accounts Receivable (A)

	39,500		
1	760,000	764,500	2
	35,000		

Accounts Payable (L)

		33,000	
8	428,000	431,000	7
		36,000	

Wages Payable (L)

		9,000	
6a	9,000	150,000	6b
6c	139,000		
		11,000	

Taxes Payable (L)

		6,000	
12b	20,000	18,180	12a
		4,180	

EXHIBIT 3-21

TEMPLATE COMPANY'S T ACCOUNTS FOR 2011 (cont'd)

Inventory (A)

7	43,000 431,000	417,000	9
	57,000		

Prepaid Rent (A)

5a	15,000 63,000	61,500	5b
	16,500		

Building and Equipment (A)

3	350,000 40,700		
	390,700		

Accumulated Dep.—B & E (XA)

		100,000 15,680	4
		115,680	

Office Furniture (A)

	76,000	
	76,000	

Accumulated Dep.—O.F. (XA)

		16,000 3,920	4
		19,920	

Dividends Payable (L)

13b	15,000	0 20,000	13a
		5,000	

Long-Term Debt (L)

		75,000 15,000	10a
		90,000	

Common Shares (SE)

		185,000
		185,000

Retained Earnings (SE)

15	20,000	136,500 42,420	14
		158,920	

Temporary Accounts:

Sales Revenue (SE)

		0 760,000	1
14	760,000		
		0	

Wage Expense (SE)

6b	0 150,000		
		150,000	14
	0		

Rent Expense (SE)

5b	0 61,500		
		61,500	14
	0		

Selling & Admin. Expense (SE)

11	0 45,000		
		45,000	14
	0		

Cost of Goods Sold (SE)

9	0 417,000		
		417,000	14
	0		

Depreciation Expense (SE)

4	0 19,600		
		19,600	14
	0		

Interest Expense (SE)

10b	0 6,300		
		6,300	14
	0		

Income Tax Expense (SE)

12a	0 18,180		
		18,180	14
	0		

Dividends Declared (SE)

13a	0 20,000		
		20,000	15
	0		

TEMPLATE COMPANY'S 2011 FINANCIAL STATEMENTS

EXHIBIT 3-22

Template Company
Statement of Earnings
For the year ended December 31, 2011

Sales revenue	$760,000
Less expenses:	
Cost of goods sold	(417,000)
Wage expense	(150,000)
Depreciation expense	(19,600)
Rent expense	(61,500)
Interest expense	(6,300)
Selling and administrative expense	(45,000)
Income tax expense	(18,180)
Net income	$ 42,420

Template Company
Statement of Financial Position
December 31, 2011 and 2010

	2011		2010
Assets			
Current Assets			
Cash		$ 50,500	$ 37,000
Accounts receivable		35,000	39,500
Inventory		57,000	43,000
Prepaid rent		16,500	15,000
Total current assets		159,000	134,500
Capital Assets			
Building and equipment	$390,700		$350,000
Less: Accumulated depreciation	115,680		100,000
	275,020		250,000
Office furniture	76,000		76,000
Less: Accumulated depreciation	19,920		16,000
	56,080		60,000
Total capital assets		331,100	310,000
Total Assets		$490,100	$444,500
Liabilities			
Current Liabilities			
Accounts payable		$ 36,000	$ 33,000
Wages payable		11,000	9,000
Taxes payable		4,180	6,000
Dividends payable		5,000	—
Total current liabilities		56,180	48,000
Non-Current Liabilities			
Long-term debt		90,000	75,000
Total Liabilities		146,180	123,000
Shareholders' Equity			
Share capital	$185,000		$185,000
Retained earnings	158,920		136,500
Total Shareholders' Equity		343,920	321,500
Total Liabilities and Shareholders' Equity		$490,100	$444,500

EXHIBIT 3-23

TEMPLATE COMPANY'S CLOSING ENTRIES

14. Sales revenue (SE)	760,000	
Cost of goods sold (SE)		417,000
Wage expense (SE)		150,000
Depreciation expense (SE)		19,600
Rent expense (SE)		61,500
Interest expense (SE)		6,300
Selling and administrative expense (SE)		45,000
Income tax expense (SE)		18,180
Retained earnings (SE)		42,420
To close the revenue and expense accounts		
and add the net income to retained earnings.		
15. Retained earnings (SE)	20,000	
Dividends declared (SE)		20,000
To close the revenue and expense accounts		
and add the net income to retained earnings.		

These entries have also been posted to the ledger (T accounts) in Exhibit 3-21. For easy reference, the closing entries are in red.

Note that, after posting the closing entries, all the revenue and expense accounts and the dividends declared account have zero balances. They are now ready to start the new accounting cycle for 2012. Also, the retained earnings account has been updated to reflect the cumulative amount as at the end of 2011.

ABBREVIATIONS USED

A   Asset account
L   Liability account
SE   Shareholders' equity account
XA   Contra-asset account

SYNONYMS

Posting the accounts **|** Posting to the ledger

GLOSSARY

Accounting cycle   The sequence of steps that occurs in the recording, summarizing, and reporting of events in the accounting system.

Accumulated depreciation   The total amount of depreciation that has been taken on an asset, up to a particular point in time.

Adjusted trial balance   A listing of the accounts and their balances after the adjusting entries have been made, but before the closing entries have been made.

Adjusting entries   Journal entries made at the end of the accounting period to record an event or transaction that was not recorded during the period. Events or transactions that are not signalled in any other way are recorded through adjusting entries.

Chart of accounts   A listing of the names of the accounts used in a particular accounting system.

Closing the books   The process by which a company makes closing entries to complete one accounting period and set the balances in the temporary accounts to zero, in preparation for the next period. The temporary accounts are closed into the retained earnings account.

Closing entries   Entries made at the end of the accounting period to transfer the balances from the temporary revenue, expense, and dividend accounts into the retained earnings account.

Compound entry   A journal entry with more than two parts (i.e., multiple debits and/or multiple credits). Of course, as with any journal entry, the total amount debited must equal the total amount credited.

Contra-asset account   An account used to record reductions in a related asset account. An example is accumulated depreciation.

Credit   A reference to the right side of an account, or an entry made to the right side of an account.

Debit   A reference to the left side of an account, or an entry made to the left side of an account.

Double-entry accounting system   An accounting system that maintains the equality of the basic accounting equation by requiring that each entry have equal amounts of debits and credits.

Gross profit   The difference between the revenue from the sales and the cost of the goods that were sold.

Income summary account   An optional account that is often used when closing the books, to summarize all the temporary income statement accounts (revenues and expenses) before transferring the net income to retained earnings.

Journal   The portion of the accounting system in which transactions and events are originally recorded, in chronological order.

Journal entry   An entry made in a journal to record a transaction or event.

Ledger   The portion of the accounting system in which transactions and events are summarized in accounts. Amounts are posted from the journal to the ledger.

Permanent accounts   Accounts whose balances carry over from one period to the next. All statement of financial position accounts are permanent accounts.

Post-closing trial balance   A trial balance prepared after the closing entries have been journalized and posted to the accounts. Since all the temporary accounts have zero balances at this point, it usually lists only the permanent accounts (i.e., statement of financial position accounts, whose balances are carried forward into the next period). This is an optional final step in the accounting cycle.

Posting the accounts   The process of transferring the information recorded in journal entries to the ledger accounts. A synonym for posting to the ledger.

Posting to the ledger   The process of transferring the information recorded in journal entries to the ledger accounts. A synonym for posting the accounts.

Rules of debit and credit   For assets, increases are recorded with debits, and decreases with credits; for liabilities and shareholders' equity, increases are recorded with credits, and decreases with debits.

Synoptic journal   A journal in which transactions are recorded in a spreadsheet format. Each account is assigned its own column, and amounts are added or subtracted inside the columns.

T account   A simplified format for representing a ledger account, resembling the letter T.

Temporary accounts   Accounts used to keep track of information temporarily during each accounting period. The balances in these accounts are eventually transferred to a permanent account (retained earnings) at the end of the period by making closing entries.

Trial balance   A listing of all the ledger accounts and their balances. Used to check whether the total of the debit balances is equal to the total of the credit balances.

ASSIGNMENT MATERIAL

Assessing Your Recall

3-1   In general terms, explain the role of each of the two main financial statements for a business enterprise: the statement of earnings and the statement of financial position. Outline the type of information that each statement presents, and the basic difference between the types of items that appear on the statement of earnings versus those that appear on the statement of financial position.

www.wileyplus.com

Self-Assessment Quiz

3-2 Indicate whether each of the following statements is true or false:

    a. Under the accrual basis of accounting, when cash is collected on accounts receivable revenue is recorded.

    b. Cash receipts from customers are debited to accounts receivable.

    c. The cash basis of accounting recognizes expenses when they are incurred.

    d. Under the cash basis of accounting, there is no such thing as a prepaid rent account.

    e. Asset accounts and expense accounts have debit balances.

    f. Credits increase asset accounts.

    g. Revenues are recorded with credit entries.

    h. Dividends are an expense of doing business and should appear on the statement of earnings.

3-3 Indicate whether each of the following accounts normally has a debit balance or a credit balance:

    a. Sales Revenue
    b. Rent Expense
    c. Prepaid Rent
    d. Bank Loan
    e. Investment in Shares of X Company
    f. Accounts Receivable
    g. Accounts Payable
    h. Retained Earnings
    i. Dividends Declared
    j. Dividends Payable
    k. Depreciation Expense

3-4 Indicate whether each of the following accounts normally has a debit balance or a credit balance:

    a. Inventory
    b. Cost of Goods Sold
    c. Prepaid Insurance
    d. Wages Expense
    e. Wages Payable
    f. Interest Revenue
    g. Equipment
    h. Accumulated Depreciation—Equipment
    i. Long-Term Debt
    j. Share Capital
    k. Cash

3-5 The retained earnings account has a credit balance, and credit entries are used to record increases in this account. Explain why expense accounts (which are transferred to retained earnings when they are closed) have debit balances, and debit entries are used to record increases in these accounts.

3-6 List the steps in the accounting cycle, and briefly explain each step.

3-7 Why is it important for users of financial statements to have an understanding of how transactions are recorded, summarized, and reported?

3-8 In the adjusted trial balance part of the accounting cycle, the retained earnings account has its beginning-of-period balance, whereas the rest of the permanent accounts have their end-of-period balances. Explain why this is so.

3-9 Explain what is meant by the term "prepaid expense," including how a prepaid expense arises and where it is reported in the financial statements.

3-10 Explain what is meant by the term "accrued expense," including how an accrued expense arises and where it is reported in the financial statements.

3-11 Explain how a prepaid expense differs from an accrued expense.

3-12 If a company fails to record an accrued expense at the end of an accounting period, what effect will this omission have on the current period's financial statements, and on the next period's financial statements?

3-13 Explain the meaning of "depreciation expense" and "accumulated depreciation," including how they differ and where each of these items appears in the financial statements.

3-14 Explain why closing entries are made, by stating the two objectives that are accomplished by making closing entries.

3-15 Discuss why one company might close its books monthly and another might close them weekly.

3-16 Describe the standard format of the statement of financial position.

3-17 Explain the meaning of the terms "current" and "non-current" as they apply to the statement of financial position.

3-18 Explain the meaning of the term "liquidity."

Applying Your Knowledge

3-19 **(Determine effects of transactions on statement of financial position accounts)**
Ann and Greg Fenway run a small art gallery and custom framing business. Explain how the basic statement of financial position accounts of assets, liabilities, and shareholders' equity would be affected by each of the following transactions and activities:

    a. Framing materials are purchased on credit.
    b. Payment is made for the framing materials that were purchased previously.
    c. Wages are paid to their assistant in the shop.
    d. Pictures are purchased by the gallery for cash.
    e. A picture is sold for cash, at a profit.
    f. A receivable is collected on a framing project that was completed for a customer last month.
    g. A loan from the bank is repaid, with interest.
    h. Depreciation on the equipment is recognized.
    i. Framing glue is spilled on some materials and they have to be discarded.

3-20 **(Determine effects of transactions on statement of financial position accounts)**
Gagnon's Autobody Ltd. repairs and paints automobiles after accidents. Explain how the basic statement of financial position accounts of assets, liabilities, and shareholders' equity would be affected by each of the following transactions and activities:

    a. Gagnon's Autobody purchases new spray-painting equipment. The supplier gives the company 60 days to pay.
    b. The company pays for the spray-painting equipment that was purchased above.
    c. Supplies such as paint and putty are purchased for cash.
    d. The company pays for a one-year liability insurance policy.
    e. The company pays its employees for work done.

f. A car is repaired and repainted. The customer pays the deductible required by her insurance policy, and the remainder of the bill is sent to her insurance company.

g. Cash is collected from the customer's insurance company.

3-21 (Construct journal entries)

For each of the following transactions, construct journal entries:

a. Inventory costing $3,100 is purchased on account.

b. A payment of $3,000 was made on accounts payable.

c. Inventory costing $1,800 is sold on account for $2,700. (Hint: Two journal entries are required.)

d. Accounts receivable of $2,000 are collected.

e. Office supplies costing $1,400 were purchased on account.

f. Office supplies costing $500 were consumed during the period.

g. New equipment costing $7,500 is purchased for cash.

h. The company borrows $12,000 from a bank.

i. The company issues common shares for $20,000.

j. Wages totalling $6,300 were earned by employees and paid to them.

k. The company paid $2,000 on its bank loan, which included $150 of interest.

l. The company paid $2,500 for the monthly rent on its leased premises.

m. Land costing $23,000 was purchased. The company paid $3,000 in cash and the remainder was financed with a mortgage (a long-term loan).

3-22 (Construct journal entries)

Chapati Company started business on January 1, 2011. Some of the events that occurred in its first year of operations follow:

1. An insurance policy was purchased on February 28 for $1,800.

2. During the year, inventory costing $140,000 was purchased, all on account.

3. Sales to customers totalled $200,000. Of these, $40,000 were cash sales.

4. Payments to suppliers (for inventory that had been purchased earlier) totalled $110,000.

5. Collections from customers on account during the year totalled $140,000.

6. Customers paid $25,000 in advance payments for goods that will be delivered later.

7. Equipment worth $140,000 was purchased on October 1 for $40,000 cash and a two-year, 10% note with a principal amount of $100,000.

8. Salaries totalling $44,000 were paid to employees during the year.

9. The board declared dividends of $12,000 in December 2011, to be paid in January 2012.

10. A year-end review revealed that the insurance policy (in item 1) was for one year of coverage that began on March 1, 2011.

11. The equipment that was purchased on October 1, 2011, is to be amortized using the straight-line method, with an estimated useful life of 10 years and an estimated residual value of $20,000.

12. No interest was paid on the note during the year.

13. A physical count at year end revealed $20,000 of unsold inventory still on hand.

14. It was determined that 80% of the goods that were paid for in advance (in item 6) had been delivered to the customers by the end of the year.

15. In addition to the salaries that were paid during the year, salaries of $4,000 remained unpaid at the end of the year.

Required:
Prepare journal entries for each of the above transactions and adjustments.

3-23 (Journalize, post, and prepare trial balance)
Sweet Dreams Chocolatiers Ltd. began operations on January 1, 2011. During its first year, the following transactions occurred:

1. Issued common shares for $200,000 cash.

2. Purchased $475,000 of inventory on account.

3. Sold inventory on account for $640,000. The original cost of the inventory that was sold was $380,000.

4. Collected $580,000 from customers on account.

5. Paid $430,000 to suppliers for the inventory previously purchased on account.

6. Bought a delivery vehicle for $36,000 cash.

7. Paid $26,000 for rent, including $2,000 related to the next year.

8. Incurred $20,000 of other expenses, of which $18,000 was paid.

9. Recorded $2,000 of depreciation on the vehicle.

10. Declared and paid dividends of $6,000.

Required:
a. Prepare journal entries to record each of the above transactions.
b. Create T accounts and post the journal entries to the T accounts.
c. Prepare a December 31, 2011, trial balance.

3-24 (Journalize, post, and prepare trial balance)
Sparkling Clean Dry Cleaners Inc. began operations on January 1, 2011. In its first year, the following transactions occurred:

1. Issued common shares for $150,000 cash.

2. Purchased dry cleaning equipment for $75,000 cash.

3. Purchased cleaning supplies, on account, for $9,600.

4. Used $8,400 of the supplies in cleaning operations.

5. Collected $124,000 from customers for dry cleaning.

6. Borrowed $15,000 from the bank on July 1, 2011, at an interest rate of 8% per year.

7. Paid wages of $49,000 to employees. In addition to this, $1,000 of wages were owed to employees at the end of the year.

8. Amortized the equipment by $3,000 for the year.

9. Paid $22,000 for utilities (telephone, electricity, and water).

10. Paid interest on the bank loan described in transaction 6.

Required:
a. Prepare journal entries to record each of the above transactions.
b. Create T accounts and post the journal entries to the T accounts.
c. Prepare a December 31, 2011, trial balance.

3-25 (Journalize, post, and prepare trial balance and closing entries)
Refer to Problem 2-35 in Chapter 2 for Singh Company.

  a. Prepare journal entries for each of the transactions and adjustments listed in the problem.
  b. Prepare the necessary T accounts and post the journal entries to them.
  c. Prepare an adjusted trial balance.
  d. Prepare the closing entries and post them to the T accounts.

3-26 (Journalize, post, and prepare trial balance and closing entries)
Refer to Problem 2-36 in Chapter 2 for The Hughes Tools Company.

  a. Prepare journal entries for each of the transactions and adjustments listed in the problem.
  b. Prepare the necessary T accounts and post the journal entries to them.
  c. Prepare an adjusted trial balance.
  d. Prepare the closing entries and post them to the T accounts.

3-27 (Journalize, post, and prepare trial balance and closing entries)
Refer to Problem 2-37 in Chapter 2 for A.J. Smith Company.

  a. Prepare journal entries for each of the transactions and adjustments listed in the problem.
  b. Prepare the necessary T accounts and post the journal entries to them.
  c. Prepare an adjusted trial balance.
  d. Prepare the closing entries and post them to the T accounts.

3-28 (Determine statement of earnings amounts)
Jake Redding owns and operates a tire and auto repair shop named Jake's Jack'em and Fix'em Shop. During the current month, the following activities occurred:

  1. The shop charged $8,500 for repair work done during the month. All but one of his customers paid in full. The one customer who had not yet paid owed Jake $500. Jake still has the car in the shop's parking lot and he intends to keep it until the customer pays the bill. The $500 is included in the $8,500.

  2. The total cost of parts and oil purchased during the month was $2,900. Jake pays for the parts with cash, but the oil is purchased in bulk from a supplier on 30 days' credit. At the end of the month, he still owes $400 to this supplier.

  3. The cost of the parts that were used in repair work during the month was $2,600.

  4. Jake paid $750 monthly rent on the repair shop on the first day of the month, and since he had extra cash on hand at the end of the month he paid another $750 to cover the next month's rent.

  5. On the 10th of the month, Jake paid the previous month's utility bills of $250. At the end of the month, he received this month's utility bills, totalling $230, which he intends to pay on the 10th of next month.

  6. Jake paid a friend $500 for helping him in the repair shop, and also gave him a new set of tires from the shop's stockroom. These tires had cost Jake $300, and could have been sold to customers for $400.

  7. Other expenses related to operating the repair shop for the month totalled $875. All of these were paid during the month, as well as $125 that was owed from the previous month.

  8. During the last week of the month, a customer dropped off her vehicle for repair work. Jake set aside $600 of parts to be used in these repairs, but he has not yet had time to do any work on this job.

Required:
With reference to the concepts discussed so far in the book, determine the amounts that would properly be reported in the statement of earnings for Jake's shop this month, and calculate the net earnings for the month. If an item is excluded, explain why.

3-29 **(Determine statement of earnings amounts)**
Jan Wei owns a cycle store that sells equipment, clothing, and other accessories. During the month of June, the following activities occurred:

1. The business earned $30,000 from the sale of bicycles, clothing, and accessories. Half the sales were for cash and the other half was paid for with credit cards. The money for the credit card sales, less a 3% charge, was collected from the credit card company.

2. The merchandise that was sold originally cost $17,400.

3. Jan purchased additional merchandise on credit for $20,800.

4. Jan paid $18,000 to the suppliers of the merchandise purchased above.

5. The telephone, electricity, and water bills for the month came to $430. All but one of these bills, for $130, was paid by the end of the month.

6. Other expenses for the month totalled $2,100. They were all paid in cash, except the depreciation expense, which was $600.

7. At the end of May, Jan had an 8% loan for $5,000 outstanding with the bank. On the last day of June, Jan paid the monthly interest that was owed on the loan, and also paid $500 on the loan principal.

8. On the last day of June, a customer ordered a $1,300 bicycle. Jan did not have it in stock, so it was ordered and will be delivered in July. Since it was a special order, the customer paid a $300 deposit on it.

Required:
With reference to the concepts discussed so far in the book, determine the amounts that would properly be reported in the June statement of earnings for Jan's shop, and calculate the net earnings for the month. If an item is excluded, explain why.

3-30 **(Determine expenses using matching principle)**
For each of the following independent cases, apply the matching concept to determine how much of the cost should be recognized as expense in each of the months of September, October, and November:

1. A new lease for the business premises goes into effect on October 1 and increases the rent from $1,000 to $1,150 per month. The rent for the next month is always prepaid on the last day of the current month. Accordingly, rent of $1,000 was paid on September 30, and $1,150 was paid on October 31 and November 30.

2. The company borrowed $12,000 on September 1. The loan is to be repaid on December 1, along with $300 of interest.

3. The company purchased a large supply of lubricant for $2,000 on September 1. The lubricant is to be used in the company's operations and is expected to last for four months.

4. Employees work Monday through Friday and are paid each Monday for the previous week's work. The payroll for the week of Monday, September 29 to Friday, October 3 (paid on October 6) is $10,000. The payroll for the week of Monday, October 27 to Friday, October 31 (paid on November 3) is $10,500.

3-31 (Determine previous account balances)

Selected items from the adjusted trial balance for Puzzle-Solver Consulting Services as of January 31, 2012, follow:

Partial Adjusted Trial Balance as of January 31, 2012

	Debit balances	Credit balances
Supplies on Hand	$ 800	
Prepaid Insurance	2,400	
Salaries Payable		$ 900
Unearned Fees		1,000
Fees Earned		7,000
Salaries Expense	4,100	
Insurance Expense	400	
Supplies Used	300	

Required:

a. If supplies costing $1,000 were purchased in January, determine what the balance in the Supplies on Hand account must have been at the beginning of the month.

b. If the insurance amounts relate to a policy with an original term of one year, determine the total premium that was paid and the date on which the policy was purchased.

c. If the amount paid for salaries during the month was $3,000, determine what the balance in the Salaries Payable account must have been at the beginning of the month.

d. If there are no accounts receivable, and the amount of fee payments received during the month was $3,000, determine what the balance in the Unearned Fees account must have been at the beginning of the month.

3-32 (Journalize, post, prepare statement of earnings and statement of financial position, and prepare closing entries)

On December 31, 2010, Clean and White Linen Supplies Ltd. had the following account balances:

Cash	$90,000
Accounts receivable	96,000
Uniforms for sale	60,000
Supplies on hand	2,000
Investment in Golden Company	80,000
Equipment	330,000
Accumulated depreciation	90,000
Accounts payable	60,000
Wages payable	8,000
Long-term bank loan, 7%	150,000
Share capital	250,000
Retained earnings	100,000

In 2011, the following transactions occurred:

1. On January 1, paid $3,900 for a three-year fire insurance policy.

2. Purchased additional uniforms on credit for $120,000.

3. Sold uniforms for $180,000 on account. The inventory that was sold had been purchased for $100,000.

4. Performed cleaning services for customers for $520,000. One-quarter of this amount was paid in cash and the remainder was on account.

5. Paid $130,000 to suppliers to settle some of the accounts payable.

6. Received $246,000 from customers in settlement of amounts owed to the company.

7. Paid $12,000 for advertising.

8. At the end of 2011, paid the interest on the bank loan for the year, as well as $30,000 on the principal.

9. Received a $3,000 dividend from the investment in Golden Company.

10. Paid $15,000 for utilities for the year.

11. Paid dividends of $12,000 at the end of the year.

12. Paid $102,000 for wages during the year. At year end, the company still owed $2,000 to the employees for the last week of work in December.

13. Amortized the equipment for the year. The company had bought its equipment at the beginning of 2008, and it was expected to last 10 years and have a residual value of $30,000.

14. Made an adjustment for the cost of the insurance that expired in 2011.

Required:
a. Prepare journal entries to record each of the above transactions and adjustments.
b. Create T accounts. Enter the beginning balances from 2010, post the 2011 journal entries, and determine the ending balances for 2011.
c. Prepare an adjusted trial balance, and ensure that the total of the debit balances is equal to the total of the credit balances. (If your totals are not equal, you should use the procedures outlined in the Helpful Hint on page 179 to try to locate the error.)
d. Prepare a statement of earnings and a statement of financial position for 2011.
e. Prepare the closing entries and post them to the T accounts.

3-33 **(Prepare journal entries, trial balances, and closing entries)**
Evergreen Retail Company, whose fiscal year end is December 31, had the following transactions in its first year of operations:

1. Issued common shares for $65,000 cash on January 1, 2011.

2. Borrowed $15,000 of additional financing from the bank on January 1, 2011.

3. Bought equipment for $25,000 cash, also on January 1, 2011.

4. Made $60,000 of inventory purchases on account.

5. Had total sales of $92,000, of which $28,000 were on account. The cost of the products sold was $44,000.

6. Bought office supplies for $800 cash.

7. Collected payments of $24,000 from customers on their accounts.

8. Paid suppliers $25,000 for the inventory that had been purchased on account.

9. Paid employees $36,200.

10. Paid the interest on the bank loan on December 31, 2011. The interest rate was 8%.

11. Declared dividends of $2,000, which will be paid in 2012.

Information for adjusting entries:

12. The equipment purchased on January 1 has an estimated useful life of eight years and an estimated residual value of $1,000 at the end of its life.

13. Office supplies costing $200 were still on hand at the end of the year.

14. Wages in the amount of $800 were owed to employees at the end of the year. These will be paid early in 2012.

Required:

a. Prepare journal entries for transactions 1 through 11.

b. Set up T accounts, post the 2011 transactions, and calculate the unadjusted balance in each account.

c. Prepare a trial balance, and ensure that the total of the debit balances is equal to the total of the credit balances. (If your totals are not equal, you should use the procedures outlined in the Helpful Hint on page 179 to try to locate the error.)

d. Prepare journal entries for adjustments 12 to 14.

e. Post the adjusting entries, and recalculate the balances in the accounts involved.

f. Prepare the closing entries, post them to the T accounts, and calculate the final balance in each account.

3-34 **(Journalize, post, prepare statement of earnings and statement of financial position, and prepare closing entries)**
Perfect Pizza had the following account balances at December 31, 2010:

Cash	$ 33,000
Accounts receivable	15,000
Ingredients and supplies inventory	10,000
Prepaid rent	3,000
Equipment	60,000
Accumulated depreciation—equipment	30,000
Delivery vehicles	80,000
Accumulated depreciation—delivery vehicles	36,000
Accounts payable	7,000
Wages payable	2,000
Share capital	110,000
Retained earnings	16,000

During 2011, the following transactions occurred:

1. Purchases of ingredients and supplies (ingredients and supplies inventory) were $230,000, all on account.

2. Sales of pizzas for cash were $510,000, and sales of pizzas on account were $40,000.

3. The company paid $88,000 for wages and $42,000 for other expenses.

4. Payments for ingredients and supplies purchased on account totalled $220,000.

5. Collections from customers for sales on account totalled $50,000.

6. Ingredients and supplies valued at $225,000 were used in making pizzas.

7. A dividend of $15,000 was declared and paid at the end of the year.

Information for adjusting entries:

8. At the end of 2011, the amount of rent paid in advance was $1,500.

9. Wages owed to employees at the end of 2011 were $2,500.

10. The equipment had an estimated useful life of eight years, with no residual value.

11. The delivery vehicles had an estimated useful life of six years with a residual value of $8,000.

Required:
a. Prepare journal entries for transactions 1 through 7. Create new accounts as necessary.
b. Set up T accounts. Enter the beginning balances from 2010, post the 2011 journal entries, and determine the unadjusted balance in each account.
c. Prepare a trial balance.
d. Prepare journal entries for adjustments 8 through 11. Post these journal entries to the T accounts, and determine the adjusted balance in each account.
e. Prepare an adjusted trial balance.
f. Prepare a statement of earnings and statement of financial position for 2011.
g. Prepare the closing entries, post them to the T accounts, and determine the final balance in each account.

3-35 (Prepare journal entries, trial balances, and closing entries)
Genesis Sportswear Ltd. is a wholesale company that buys sports clothing from manufacturers and sells it to retail stores. It had the following transactions in its first year of operations. The company's fiscal year end is December 31.

1. Common shares were issued for $60,000.

2. An insurance premium that provides coverage for the 12-month period starting March 1 was bought for $1,200 on February 15.

3. Clothing was purchased for $75,000 on account.

4. Employees were paid $46,900 in wages.

5. Other operating expenses totalled $10,000. Of this amount, $9,000 was paid during the year; the remainder was due to be paid early in the next year.

6. Sales recorded for the period totalled $105,000, all on credit.

7. The cost of the inventory sold during the year was $62,000.

8. Cash collections on customer accounts totalled $96,000.

9. Payments to suppliers for clothing purchased totalled $54,000.

10. New equipment was purchased for $15,000 cash.

11. Dividends of $6,000 were declared but not yet paid.

Adjusting entries (Hint: You may need to use information recorded in the first 11 transactions.):

12. Recognized the amount of insurance expense that was incurred during the period.

13. Recorded depreciation of $2,000 on the equipment.

Required:
a. Prepare journal entries to record transactions 1 through 11.
b. Create T accounts, post the journal entries to them, and determine the unadjusted balance in each account.
c. Prepare a trial balance.
d. Prepare journal entries for items 12 and 13, post these adjustments, and calculate the adjusted balances in the affected accounts.
e. Prepare the closing entries, post them to the T accounts, and determine the final balance in each account.

3-36 (Determine amounts to appear in financial statements)

The following is the final trial balance (after the adjusting and closing entries had been made) for Hartman Company as at August 31, 2011. Hartman adjusts and closes its books at the end of each month.

	Debit balances	Credit balances
Cash	$ 6,000	
Accounts receivable	40,000	
Merchandise inventory	90,000	
Prepaid rent	8,000	
Equipment	18,000	
Accumulated depreciation		$ 3,000
Accounts payable		32,000
Note payable		30,000
Accrued interest payable		1,500
Share capital		50,000
Retained earnings		45,500
	$162,000	$162,000

Hartman's transactions in September 2011 and all relevant data for month-end adjustments follow:

1. Sales on account were $41,000.

2. Payments of $37,000 were collected from customers on their accounts.

3. Cash sales were $50,000.

4. Merchandise was purchased for $39,000 on account.

5. The cost of merchandise sold in September was $59,000.

6. Payments of $33,000 were made to suppliers for accounts owing.

7. Advertising costs of $3,000 were paid.

8. Employees were paid $15,000 in wages.

9. Wages of $1,000 were earned by employees but not yet paid.

10. Miscellaneous expenses of $9,000 were paid in cash.

11. The rent was paid in advance to December 31, 2011. The payment was made earlier in the year.

12. The equipment was purchased on September 1, 2010 (one year before the start of the current month), and is expected to have a total useful life of six years.

13. The note payable was dated March 1, 2011, and the principal is due to be repaid in two equal instalments on March 1, 2012 and 2013. Interest on the note, at a rate of 10% per year, is also to be paid on March 1, 2012 and 2013.

Required:

Based on the above information, answer the following questions:

a. What amount should Hartman report as revenue for September?
b. What amount should Hartman report as wages expense for September?
c. What amount should Hartman report as rent expense for September?
d. What amount should Hartman report as interest expense for September?
e. As of the end of September, what should the balance in Hartman's cash account be?
f. As of the end of September, what is the amount of Hartman's accounts receivable?
g. As of the end of September, what should the balance in Hartman's merchandise inventory account be?

h. As of the end of September, what is the amount of Hartman's accounts payable?
i. Is the equipment expected to have any value at the end of its useful life?
j. As of September 30, 2011, what is the net book value of Hartman's equipment?
k. What amount should be shown under Long-Term Liabilities, on Hartman's statement of financial position as of September 30, 2011?

3-37 (Prepare adjusting entries)

The trial balance for Cozy Fireplaces Inc. for December 31, 2011, follows:

	Debit balances	Credit balances
Cash	$ 89,000	
Accounts receivable	38,000	
Inventory	95,000	
Office supplies	5,000	
Prepaid rent	46,000	
Land	80,000	
Building	150,000	
Accumulated depreciation		$ 19,500
Accounts payable		21,400
Salaries and wages payable		0
Interest payable		0
Income tax payable		0
Deposits from customers (revenue received in advance)		12,400
Bank loan, 9%, long-term		40,000
Share capital		150,000
Retained earnings		16,700
Sales		840,000
Cost of goods sold	482,000	
Salaries and wages	95,000	
Rent expense	0	
Office supplies used	0	
Depreciation expense	0	
Interest expense	0	
Miscellaneous expenses	14,000	
Income tax expense	0	
Dividends declared	6,000	
Totals	$1,100,000	$1,100,000

Additional information for adjusting entries:

1. The deposits from customers were for future deliveries. As of December 31, three-quarters of these goods had been delivered.

2. There is $2,000 in salaries and wages owed at year end.

3. Rent is paid in advance on the last day of each month. There was a balance of $3,000 in the prepaid rent account on January 1, 2011. At the end of January, $3,000 was paid for the February rent and was debited to the prepaid rent account. All the rent payments during the year were treated the same way. The rent for July to December increased to $4,000 per month. (Hint: Determine the amount of rent expense for 2011, as well as the correct amount that has been prepaid for 2012, and make an adjustment that will bring both these accounts to the correct balances.)

4. A count of the office supplies at year end revealed that $500 of supplies were still on hand.

5. The building is being depreciated over 20 years with a residual value of $20,000.

6. The bank loan was taken out on April 1, 2011. The first interest payment is due on April 1, 2012.

7. Income tax for the year should be calculated using a tax rate of 30%. (Hint: After you finish the other adjusting entries, you will have to determine the *income before income tax* and then calculate the tax as 30% of this amount.)

Required:
Prepare the adjusting entries for the year 2011.

3-38 **(Prepare adjusting entries)**
The following trial balance before adjustments is for Snowcrest Ltd on December 31, 2011:

	Debit balances	Credit balances
Cash	$ 10,000	
Inventory	24,000	
Advances to salespeople (prepaid sales commissions)	2,000	
Office supplies	3,000	
Equipment	56,000	
Accumulated depreciation—equipment		$ 4,000
Deposits from customers (revenue received in advance)		6,000
Bank loan		20,000
Share capital		40,000
Retained earnings		9,000
Sales revenue		230,000
Cost of goods sold	130,000	
Sales commissions	34,000	
Office salaries	25,000	
Rent expense	6,600	
Miscellaneous expenses	15,000	
Dividends declared	3,400	
Totals	$309,000	$309,000

Data for adjusting entries:

1. As of December 31, 2011, 80% of the commissions that had been paid in advance to the salespeople had been earned.

2. A count of the office supplies at the end of the year revealed that $600 of supplies were still on hand.

3. Depreciation on the equipment for 2011 was $1,000.

4. The deposits from customers were advance payments for future deliveries of goods. By December 31, 2011, two-thirds of these deliveries had been made.

5. The bank loan was a six-month loan taken out on October 1, 2011. The interest rate on the loan is 9%, but the interest is not due to be paid until the note is repaid on March 1, 2012.

6. Office salaries owed at year end and not yet recorded were $500.

7. The rent expense figure includes $600 paid in advance for January 2012.

8. Income tax for the year should be calculated using a tax rate of 25%. (Hint: After you finish the other adjusting entries, determine the *income before income tax* and then calculate the tax as 25% of this amount.)

Required:
Prepare the adjusting entries for the year 2011.

3-39 (Determine statement of earnings and statement of financial position values)
The following information was available for Brilliant Consulting Company at its year end, December 31, 2011:

1. During the year, the company agreed to provide certain consulting services to a client for a fee of $10,000, which was received in advance. At the end of the year, it was estimated that 85% of the services had been provided.

2. The Office Supplies account had a balance of $350 at the beginning of the year and additional supplies costing $950 were purchased during the year. At the end of the year, a count of the office supplies indicated that supplies costing $250 remained on hand.

3. A new "business occupancy" tax was introduced by the municipal government in 2011, and the company was required to pay $1,800 to cover the period from April 1, 2011, to March 31, 2012.

4. The company rents some surplus space in its building to a tenant for $1,500 per quarter, payable in advance. The agreement began on September 1, 2011, and the tenant paid $1,500 on that date and an additional $1,500 on December 1.

5. Another tenant rents space in the company's building for $750 per month, due on the first day of each month. The agreement began several years ago and the tenant has paid the rent as scheduled every month, except for the most recent one. At year end, the rent for December 2011 was still outstanding.

6. During the year, the company engaged an advertising agency and paid $3,000 for its services. In addition to this, there were unpaid advertising bills at year end totalling $450; these are due in January 2012.

Required:
For each of the items above, indicate what should appear on the statement of earnings for the year ended December 31, 2011, and on the statement of financial position as of that date.

3-40 (Determine statement of earnings and statement of financial position values)
The Great Graphics Group began operations on January 1, 2010. At the end of its second year of operations, and before any adjustments had been made, the trial balance was as follows:

	Debit balances	Credit balances
Cash	$ 8,600	
Accounts Receivable	13,500	
Prepaid Insurance	1,800	
Equipment	48,000	
Accumulated Depreciation		$ 3,300
Accounts Payable		11,000
Unearned Consulting Fees		7,500
Notes Payable		18,000
Share Capital		22,000

Retained Earnings		7,200
Graphic Design Fees Revenue		45,500
Salaries Expense	33,000	
Supplies Expense	3,300	
Advertising Expense	1,700	
Rent Expense	2,700	
Utilities Expense	1,900	
	$114,500	$114,500

Analysis reveals the following additional data for adjustments to be made:

1. There were $2,000 of supplies on hand at year end.

2. The note payable was issued on October 1, 2011. It is a nine-month note, with an interest rate of 9% per year. The interest does not have to be paid until July 1, 2012, when the note is due to be repaid.

3. The balance in the Prepaid Insurance account is the premium paid for a one-year policy that began March 1, 2011.

4. By year end, $4,500 of the amount recorded in the Unearned Consulting Fees account had been earned.

5. At year end, $3,000 of additional graphic design fees had been earned, but not yet billed or recorded. The work was completed in December 2011, and the clients will pay for it in January 2012.

6. The equipment was acquired on April 1, 2010, and is being amortized at a rate of $4,400 per year.

Required:
Calculate the amount that should appear (after adjustments) on the December 31, 2011, financial statements for each of the following items:

a. On the statement of earnings, related to supplies
b. On the statement of financial position, related to interest
c. On the statement of financial position, related to insurance
d. On the statement of earnings, related to consulting fees
e. On the statement of earnings, related to graphic design fees
f. On the statement of financial position, as the net book value of the equipment

3-41 (Determine effects of omitted adjustment)
When it was preparing its financial statements for the year ended December 31, 2011, a company failed to record $3,000 of accrued salaries. These salaries were paid, and recorded as an expense, in 2012.

Required:
State the effect (if any) that this error will have on each of the following financial statement items:

a. Net earnings for 2011
b. Total assets on December 31, 2011
c. Total liabilities on December 31, 2011
d. Total shareholders' equity on December 31, 2011
e. Net earnings for 2012
f. Total assets on December 31, 2012
g. Total liabilities on December 31, 2012
h. Total shareholders' equity on December 31, 2012

3-42 (Determine adjusted balances; prepare statement of earnings and statement of financial position)

On December 31, 2011, Information Inc. completed its third year of operations. The following list of account balances (which are not arranged in any particular order) was assembled by a student working in the company's business office on a part-time basis while taking his first accounting course:

Accounts receivable	$150,000	Advertising expense	$ 76,000
Interest expense	2,000	Cash	20,000
Note receivable	26,000	Merchandise inventory	140,000
Cost of goods sold	590,000	Dividends declared	12,000
Share capital	570,000	Unearned rent revenue	6,000
Building	360,000	Insurance expense	6,300
Accumulated depreciation,		Retained earnings	
equipment	20,000	(January 1, 2011)	177,000
Land	160,000	Equipment	200,000
Accumulated depreciation,		Miscellaneous expense	5,200
building	40,000		
Sales	963,000	Accounts payable	72,700
Telecommunications expense	2,500	Salaries expense	125,000
Note payable	30,000	Office supplies inventory	3,700

The foregoing items are correct, but the following information was not taken into consideration:

1. The amount shown as insurance expense includes $900 for coverage during the first two months of 2012.

2. The note receivable is a six-month note that has been outstanding for four months. The interest rate is 10% per year. The interest will be received by the company when the note becomes due at the end of February 2012.

3. As of December 31, 2011, the office supplies still on hand are worth $600.

4. On November 1, 2011, the company rented surplus space in its building to a tenant for $1,000 per month, payable in advance for six months.

5. Depreciation for 2011 is $10,000 on the building and $20,000 on the equipment.

6. Employees earned $3,000 of salaries in December 2011 that will not be paid until the first scheduled pay day in 2012.

7. Additional dividends of $50,000 were declared in December 2011, but will not be paid until January 2012.

Required:

a. Determine the amounts that would appear in an adjusted trial balance for Information Inc. as of December 31, 2011.

b. Prepare a statement of earnings for the year ended December 31, 2011.

c. Calculate the amount of retained earnings as of December 31, 2011.

d. Prepare a classified statement of financial position as of December 31, 2011.

3-43 (Calculate income and retained earnings; prepare statement of financial position)

Little Lads and Ladies Ltd. sells children's clothing. At the end of December 2011, it had the following adjusted account balances, which are listed in random order:

Cash	$ 3,000
Wages payable	500
Supplies used	4,200
Equipment	23,000
Wages expense	25,000

Prepaid rent	400
Cost of goods sold	32,000
Sales	66,450
Accounts receivable	10,000
Rent expense	4,800
Bank loan (due in two years)	3,800
Advertising expense	750
Accounts payable	5,000
Electricity	600
Dividends declared	1,200
Depreciation	500
Share capital	20,000
Telephone expense	200
Interest charged on bank loan	300
Accumulated depreciation	1,500
Retained earnings	17,600
Inventory	8,000
Other expenses	400
Supplies on hand	800
Interest payable	300

Required:
a. Identify the statement of earnings accounts and calculate the net earnings (or loss) for the year.
b. Determine the amount of retained earnings at the end of 2011.
c. Prepare a classified statement of financial position as of December 31, 2011.

3-44 (Calculate income and retained earnings; prepare statement of financial position)
Your assistant prepared the following adjusted trial balance data for Commerce Company on December 31, 2011. The accounts are arranged in alphabetical order.

Accounts payable	$36,000	Land	$70,000
Accounts receivable	67,000	Mortgage payable	48,000
Accumulated depreciation	20,000	Note payable (short-term)	15,000
Building	72,000	Other expenses	13,000
Cash	24,000	Prepaid insurance	500
Cost of goods sold	110,000	Retained earnings	31,500
Depreciation expense	4,500	Salaries and wages	60,000
Dividends declared	12,400	Salaries and wages owed	3,000
Dividends payable	4,000	Sales	179,800
Expired insurance	1,400	Selling expenses	27,000
Income tax payable	2,000	Service fees earned	93,100
Income tax provision	8,000	Share capital	85,000
Interest on mortgage and note	1,700	Supplies on hand	800
Interest payable	300	Supplies used	2,200
Inventory	30,000	Unearned revenue	1,200
Long-term investment in Key		Utilities expense	2,400
Company shares	12,000		

Required:
a. Calculate the net income for the year ended December 31, 2011.
b. Determine the retained earnings balance as at the end of the year.
c. Prepare a classified statement of financial position as of December 31, 2011.

3-45 (Prepare statement of financial position—manufacturing company)

The following adjusted trial balance data are for Novasco Manufacturing Corporation as at December 31, 2011. (Note: The accounts are listed in alphabetical order, first for debit balances, then for credit balances.)

	Debit balances	Credit balances
Accounts receivable	$ 77,000	
Administration and general expenses	75,000	
Cash	30,000	
Cost of goods sold	430,000	
Dividends declared	35,000	
Finished goods inventory	140,000	
Interest expense	25,000	
Loss on sale of equipment	2,100	
Prepaid insurance	3,000	
Property, plant, and equipment	280,000	
Provision for income taxes	19,600	
Raw materials inventory	55,000	
Selling expenses	95,300	
Short-term investments	65,000	
Work-in-process inventory	95,000	
Accounts payable		$ 65,000
Accrued expenses payable		18,000
Accumulated depreciation		65,000
Dividends payable		7,000
Due to the Canada Revenue Agency		13,000
Interest revenue		10,000
Long-term debt		250,000
Retained earnings		114,000
Sales		650,000
Share capital		150,000
Short-term borrowings		85,000
	$1,427,000	$1,427,000

Required:
Prepare a classified statement of financial position for Novasco Manufacturing Corporation as at December 31, 2011.

3-46 (Determine missing amounts in financial statements)

Lee's Enterprises Ltd. suffered serious flood damage that destroyed most of its accounting records. The following statements were reconstructed from the records that were recovered, but many of the amounts are missing:

	2010	2011
Statement of Earnings		
Revenues	A	200,000
Expenses	B	K
Net Income	15,000	L
Retained Earnings		
Opening Balance	C	M
Net Income	D	20,000
Dividends	5,000	N
Ending Balance	E	O

Statement of Financial Position

Current Assets	F	30,000
Other Assets	54,000	P
Total Assets	G	80,000
Current Liabilities	10,000	Q
Long-Term Liabilities	H	10,000
Total Liabilities	40,000	R
Common Stock	I	20,000
Retained Earnings	20,000	S
Total Shareholders' Equity	34,000	55,000
Total Equity and Liabilities	J	T

The following information is also available, to help you determine the missing amounts:

1. The company's retained earnings balance at the end of 2009 was $10,000.

2. The company's profit margin ratio was 15% in 2010 and 10% in 2011.

3. In both 2010 and 2011, the company's current assets were twice the amount of the current liabilities.

Required:

For each of the letters above, determine the missing dollar amount that will complete the financial statements. (Hint: It might not be possible to find all the missing amounts in the order they are presented in. You may have to skip over some, initially, and come back to them after you have determined other items.)

3-47   (Determine missing amounts in financial statements)

Rao's Recycling Centre suffered a serious fire that destroyed most of the firm's accounting records. The following statements were reconstructed from the records that were recovered, but many of the amounts are missing:

	2010	2011
Statement of earnings		
Revenues	A	180,000
Expenses	B	K
Net Income	14,000	L
Retained earnings		
Opening Balance	C	M
Net Income	D	18,000
Dividends	5,000	N
Ending Balance	20,000	O
Statement of financial position		
Current Assets	E	30,000
Other Assets	54,000	P
Total Assets	F	90,000
Current Liabilities	10,000	Q
Long-Term Liabilities	G	20,000
Total Liabilities	40,000	R
Common Stock	H	25,000
Retained Earnings	I	S
Total Shareholders' Equity	J	55,000
Total Equity and Liabilities	74,000	T

The following information is also available, to help you determine the missing amounts:

1. The company's profit margin ratio was 10% in both 2010 and 2011.

2. In both 2010 and 2011, the company's current assets were twice the amount of the current liabilities.

Required:
For each of the letters above, determine the missing dollar amount that will complete the financial statements. (Hint: It might not be possible to find all the missing amounts in the order they are presented in.)

User Perspective Problems

3-48 (Establish chart of accounts)

Saskco Chicken Products is a new company established by four entrepreneurs from Moose Jaw, Saskatchewan. They intend to purchase live chickens, process them, and sell them as frozen pieces. They anticipate hiring 17 workers to process the chickens. The four owners will work in the business and have the following titles: President (overseeing the whole operation, including finance and accounting), VP Procurement (in charge of purchasing chickens from farmers), VP Operations (in charge of the processing operations), and VP Marketing.

The president has hired you to help the company set up a computerized accounting system. First she wants you to create a list of account titles that you think the company will need for its operations. Second, for each account title, she wants you to provide a brief explanation of its nature and your reason for including it in the chart of accounts.

3-49 (Discuss end-of-period accounting process)

Accounting system procedures require some time at the end of each accounting period to check for errors, make adjusting entries, prepare the financial statements, etc. In recent years, most companies have been under pressure to speed up this end-of-period process. Discuss the incentives that companies might have to make this a faster process.

3-50 (Discuss necessity of month-end adjustments)

In order to monitor and control its operations, your company prepares monthly financial statements. An executive meeting is held in the latter part of each month to review the previous month's statements and discuss the company's progress.

A new member of the executive team asks why these meetings are not held at the beginning of each month. The chief financial officer (CFO) replies that, because of the adjustments that have to be made, the financial statements are not ready until near the middle of the month. This prompts someone to ask, "Is it really necessary to make adjustments every month? Couldn't the process be simplified and sped up by only making adjustments for the year-end statements? After all, the monthly financial statements are only used internally, for management control purposes; only the year-end statements are used externally and therefore have to conform with financial reporting standards."

The CFO asks you to prepare a response to these questions with a brief discussion of the shortcomings of unadjusted financial statements, including the reliability of the results and the possibility of manipulation.

3-51 (Assess performance and set goals)

Northland Enterprises sells and services snowmobiles and other recreational vehicles, and has reported the following revenues and expenses for the year ended December 31, 2011:

Sales of recreational vehicles	$6,000,000
Sales of replacement parts	800,000
Revenue from repair work (parts and labour)	1,100,000
Interest earned on investments	40,000
Cost of recreational vehicles sold	3,400,000
Cost of replacement parts sold	490,000
Cost of labour and parts used for repair work	400,000
Shipping and delivery costs	280,000
Selling and administrative salaries	450,000
Other operating expenses	500,000
Interest expense on mortgage	70,000
Loss on sale of old equipment	10,000
Income tax expense	740,000

Required:

a. Prepare a 2011 statement of earnings for Northland Enterprises in a format that you think will be useful for management analysis.

b. Which aspect of the company's operations (sales of recreational vehicles, sales of replacement parts, or repair work) seems to be the most profitable?

c. In 2010, Northland had total revenues of $7,200,000 and a profit margin rate (net income divided by revenues) of 18%. The company's goals for 2011 were to achieve total revenues of at least $8,000,000 and a profit margin rate of at least 20%. Did Northland attain its goals in 2011?

d. In setting its goals for revenues and return on revenues for future periods, what types of factors do you think Northland should take into consideration?

Reading and Interpreting Published Financial Statements

Financial Analysis Assignments

3-52 **(Transactions from financial statements)**

Use the financial statements for **H&M AB** in Appendix A at the end of the book to answer the following questions.

a. Assume that H&M made all of their purchases of inventory (stock-in-trade) on account and in one single purchase, and also assume they recorded all of the cost of goods sales in a single entry. Prepare the journal entries H&M would have used to record the purchases and the cost of goods sold.

b. Assume the tax liabilities in current liabilities on the balance sheet arise only from the tax expense on the income statement. Using only the information on the income statement, prepare the journal entry that H&M would have used to record income tax expense for fiscal 2009 (assuming it was not paid at that time). Prepare the journal entry to record the amount that H&M paid for income taxes during the 2009 fiscal year, based on the information in the balance sheet.

c. Identify one account in each of the following sections of the balance sheet that would have required an adjusting entry. Briefly explain what the entry would have been (you do not need to prepare it or attempt to quantify it) and why the adjustment is necessary.

    i. Fixed assets

    ii. Current assets

    iii. Current liabilities

d. Prepare the closing entries that H&M would have used at the end of the year.

3-53 **(Financial statement items and transactions)**

Lindt & Sprüngli AG (Lindt) is a maker of fine chocolates based in Switzerland. Use their consolidated balance sheet, income statement, and cash flow statement, presented in Exhibit 2-6A and Exhibit 3-24, to answer the following questions.

a. There is a large difference between Lindt's net income and its cash from operating activities in 2009. The largest item contributing to the difference is Depreciation, amortization, and impairments. (For simplicity at this point you can ignore impairments and assume the entire expense consists of depreciation and amortization charges.)

    1. What were the Net income, Cash from operations, and Depreciation and amortization for 2009? Where did you find those amounts?

    2. What would have been the journal entry to record the depreciation and amortization?

    3. Explain why depreciation is added back to net income in determining cash from operating activities.

b. What amount of dividends did Lindt pay during 2009? Where did you find that information? What would have been the journal entries to record the declaration of the dividends and the subsequent payment of the dividends?

c. Compare the profitability of Lindt in 2009 to 2008 using the profit margin ratio (Refer to Chapter 2 if you need to review the profit margin ratio.) Using the additional information Lindt provides on the income statement, discuss the main factors that have led to the change in the profit margin ratio from 2008 to 2009.

LINDT & SPRÜNGLI GROUP 2009 ANNUAL REPORT

EXHIBIT 3-24A

annual report

CONSOLIDATED FINANCIAL STATEMENTS
OF THE LINDT & SPRÜNGLI GROUP

CONSOLIDATED INCOME STATEMENT

	Note	2009 CHF million	2009 %	2008[1] CHF million	2008[1] %
INCOME					
Sales		2,524.8	100.0%	2,573.2	100.0%
Other income	22	13.9		11.7	
Total income		**2,538.7**	**100.6%**	**2,584.9**	**100.4%**
EXPENSES					
Material expenses		−905.6	−36.0%	−957.6	−37.1%
Changes in inventories		−7.2	−0.3%	36.4	1.4%
Personnel expenses	23	−571.8	−22.6%	−544.6	−21.2%
Operating expenses		−672.0	−26.6%	−658.6	−25.6%
Depreciation, amortization and impairment	7, 8	−117.3	−4.6%	−99.3	−3.9%
Total expenses		**−2,273.9**	**−90.1%**	**−2,223.7**	**−86.4%**
Operating profit		264.8	10.5%	361.2	14.0%
Income from financial assets	24	5.4		10.1	
Expense from financial assets	24	−7.2		−20.6	
Income before taxes		263.0	10.4%	350.7	13.6%
Taxes	25	−69.9		−89.2	
Net income		**193.1**	**7.6%**	**261.5**	**10.2%**
Attributable to shareholders		193.1		261.5	
Non-diluted earnings per share/10 PC (in CHF)	26	850.9		1,157.5	
Diluted earnings per share/10 PC (in CHF)	26	850.9		1,140.4	

1) 2008 comparatives have been adjusted. See note 2.

EXHIBIT 3-24B

annual report

LINDT & SPRÜNGLI GROUP 2009 ANNUAL REPORT

CONSOLIDATED FINANCIAL STATEMENTS
OF THE LINDT & SPRÜNGLI GROUP

CONSOLIDATED CASH FLOW STATEMENT

CHF million	Note	2009		2008
Net income		193.1		261.5
Depreciation, amortization and impairment	7, 8, 14	117.3		104.6
Changes in provisions and value adjustments		7.5		−9.4
Decrease (+) / increase (−) of accounts receivable		71.3		21.9
Decrease (+) / increase (−) of inventories		15.3		−52.5
Decrease (+) / increase (−) of prepayments and other receivables		6.0		−6.6
Decrease (+) / increase (−) of accrued income		20.2		−10.3
Decrease (−) / increase (+) of accounts payable		2.6		−46.2
Decrease (−) / increase (+) of other payables and accrued liabilities		34.9		−11.0
Non-cash effective items		1.9		42.7
Cash flow from operating activities (operating cash flow)		**470.1**		**294.7**
Investments in property, plant and equipment	7	−115.2		−193.7
Disposals of property, plant and equipment		0.9		0.4
Investments in intangible assets	8	−8.3		−4.9
Disposals (+) / investments (−) in financial assets		−1.0		−0.8
Marketable securities				
Investments		−9.3		−9.7
Disposals		14.0		28.7
Cash flow from investment activities		**−118.9**		**−180.0**
Proceeds from borrowings		–		56.6
Repayments of bonds / borrowings	17	−77.5		−105.1
Repayments of loans		−0.1		−2.5
Capital increase (including premium)	16	13.4		24.3
Purchase of treasury stock		−29.9		−0.8
Sale of treasury stock		1.3		–
Dividends paid to shareholders		−82.4		−74.9
Cash flow from financing activities		**−175.2**		**−102.4**
Net increase (+) / decrease (−) in cash and cash equivalents		**176.0**		**12.3**
Cash and cash equivalents as at January 1	15	**192.0**		**189.1**
Exchange gains / (losses) on cash and cash equivalents		**−0.8**	191.2	**−9.4**	179.7
Cash and cash equivalents as at December 31	15	**367.2**		**192.0**
Interest received from 3rd parties[1]		4.1		10.6
Interest paid to 3rd parties[1]		7.0		12.9
Income tax paid[1]		81.0		75.0

1) Included in cash flow from operating activities.

The accompanying notes form an intregal part of the consolidated statements.

3-54 (Financial statement items with a deficit)

Groupe Bikini Village Inc. (Bikini Village) operates 63 retail stores selling beach and travel clothing throughout Eastern Canada. Use their consolidated financial statements, presented in Exhibit 3-25, to answer the following questions.

  a. As at January 30, 2010 what is the cumulative amount of losses the company has incurred since incorporation?

  b. Explain why it was not possible for the company to pay any dividends in the year ending January 30, 2010.

  c. If the company continues to lose money at the same rate as in the most recent year, how long would it take for the shareholders' equity to be totally eliminated? Which users of the financial statements would be concerned with the decreasing shareholders' equity? Why?

GROUPE BIKINI VILLAGE INC. 2009 ANNUAL REPORT

EXHIBIT 3-25A

annual report

Statements of Cash Flows

(in thousands of dollars)

	Year ended	
	January 30, 2010	January 31, 2009 Restated Note 3
	$	$
Operating activities		
Net Loss	(1,477)	(440)
Adjustments (Note 16)	1,592	1,718
	115	1,278
Net changes in non-cash working capital items (Note 16)	1,669	(1,784)
Operating activities	1,784	(506)
Financing activities		
Purchase of share capital	–	(230)
Issuance of convertible debentures	–	2,000
Repayment of convertible debentures	(525)	–
Rental inducement	227	208
Reimbursement of long-term debt	(231)	(42)
Financing activities	(529)	1,936
Investing activities		
Acquisition of capital assets	(1,518)	(2,766)
Acquisition of intangible assets	(154)	(488)
Investing activities	(1,672)	(3,254)
Net changes in cash	(417)	(1,824)
Cash at beginning	4,346	6,170
Cash at end	3,929	4,346

See accompanying notes

d. Compare the net loss for the most recent year with the cash from operating activities. Explain how it is possible for the net income to be negative but the cash from operations to be positive. What kind of accounts or transactions would typically be included in the "Adjustments"?

EXHIBIT 3-25B

annual report

GROUPE BIKINI VILLAGE INC. 2009 ANNUAL REPORT

Statements of Operations and Comprehensive Loss

(in thousands of dollars, except per share amounts)

	Year ended	
	January 30, 2010	January 31, 2009 Restated Note 3
	$	$
Operating revenue	**41,022**	40,844
Cost of goods sold, operating and administrative expenses (Note 5)	**40,535**	39,559
Interest (Note 6)	**766**	446
Amortization	**1,590**	1,385
	42,891	41,390
Loss before income taxes	**(1,869)**	(546)
Income taxes recovery (Note 7)	**(392)**	(106)
Net loss and comprehensive loss	**(1,477)**	(440)
Loss per share, basic and diluted (Note 8)	**(0.01)**	–
Weighted average number of shares outstanding	**167,678,115**	171,996,196

Statements of Deficit

(in thousands of dollars)

	Year ended	
	January 30, 2010	January 31, 2009 Restated Note 3
	$	$
Deficit, beginning of period as previously reported	**(19,617)**	(19,339)
Adjustment to opening deficit resulting from adoption of new accounting standard Section 3031 - Inventories net of income taxes of $103,000	**–**	207
Adjustment to opening deficit resulting from adoption of new accounting standard Section 3064 - Intangible assets, net of income taxes of $15,000 ($36,000 in 2008)	**(28)**	(73)
Deficit, beginning of period as restated	**(19,645)**	(19,205)
Net loss	**(1,477)**	(440)
Deficit, end of period	**(21,122)**	(19,645)

See accompanying notes

e. During the year, the company purchased capital assets and intangible assets. Prepare the journal entries the company would have used to record each of those purchases, assuming they paid cash. (Hint: The amounts purchased are not equal to the increases in these accounts on the balance sheet.)

f. Assuming the amortization taken during the year was only related to the capital assets and not to the intangible assets; prepare the adjusting journal entry the company would have made to record the amortization expense for the year. (Hint: Amortization can be recorded the same way as depreciation.)

GROUPE BIKINI VILLAGE INC. 2009 ANNUAL REPORT

EXHIBIT 3-25C

annual report

Balance Sheets

(in thousands of dollars)

As at	January 30, 2010	January 31, 2009 Restated Note 3
	$	$
Assets		
Current assets		
Cash	3,929	4,346
Accounts receivable	167	149
Income taxes	4	270
Inventories	6,223	7,922
Prepaid charges	580	441
Future income taxes (Note 7)	266	450
	11,169	13,578
Capital assets (Note 9)	7,903	7,599
Intangible assets (Note 10)	497	487
Future income taxes (Note 7)	443	–
	20,012	21,664
Liabilities and shareholders' equity		
Liabilities		
Current liabilities		
Accounts payable and accrued liabilities	5,268	5,235
Current portion of long-term debt and convertible debentures (Note 11 and 12)	1,159	756
	6,427	5,991
Deferred lease credits	629	404
Long-term debt (Note 11)	528	727
Liability component of convertible debentures (Note 12)	2,360	2,972
Future income taxes (Note 7)	–	129
	9,944	10,223
Shareholders' equity		
Share capital (Note 13)	27,702	27,702
Equity component of convertible debentures (Note 12)	1,137	1,137
Contributed surplus	2,351	2,247
Deficit	(21,122)	(19,645)
	10,068	11,441
	20,012	21,664

3-55 (Determining items on a Canadian financial statement)

Base your answers to the following questions on the balance sheet and statement of income of **Dorel Industries Inc.** in Exhibit 3-26. Based in Canada, Dorel manufactures juvenile products (strollers, car seats, etc.), bicycles, and home furniture at facilities throughout the world.

a. Assuming that all the sales were on account, prepare a single journal entry to record the sales for 2009 and another entry to record the amount that was collected from customers in 2009.

b. Prepare a single journal entry to record the cost of goods sold for 2009.

c. As a manufacturer of products such as baby strollers, car seats, bicycles, and home furniture, what types of costs do you think Dorel incurs in producing the inventory?

d. Compare the profitability of Dorel in 2009 to 2008, using the profit margin ratio and the return on assets. (Refer to Chapter 2 if you need to review the two ratios. Note that, in order to be able to calculate the return on assets for both years, you will have to use the total assets for each year, rather than average total assets.)

e. During 2009 Dorel acquired four companies that produce or distribute bicycles or juvenile products in Belgium and Australia. Acquisitions normally result in an increase in assets for the acquiring company (Dorel). What was the change in Dorel's total assets from 2008 to 2009? Which asset had the largest change? Comment on your findings.

EXHIBIT 3-26A

annual report

DOREL INDUSTRIES INC. 2009 ANNUAL REPORT

Consolidated Balance Sheets

As at December 30, 2009 and 2008
(All figures in thousands of U.S. dollars)

	AS AT DECEMBER 30, 2009	AS AT DECEMBER 30, 2008
	$	$
	Reclassified (Note 12)	
ASSETS		
CURRENT ASSETS		
Cash and cash equivalents (Notes 24)	19,847	16,966
Accounts receivable (Notes 5 and 14)	349,990	316,267
Income taxes receivable	16,264	19,798
Inventories (Note 6)	399,866	509,467
Prepaid expenses	17,358	16,236
Future income taxes (Note 22)	38,042	37,342
	841,367	916,076
PROPERTY, PLANT AND EQUIPMENT (Note 7)	153,279	158,895
INTANGIBLE ASSETS (Notes 2 and 8)	401,831	395,742
GOODWILL (Note 25)	569,824	540,187
OTHER ASSETS (Notes 2, 9 and 14)	35,879	19,573
	2,002,180	2,030,473

DOREL INDUSTRIES INC. 2009 ANNUAL REPORT

EXHIBIT 3-26B

annual report

Consolidated Balance Sheets

As at December 30, 2009 and 2008

(All figures in thousands of U.S. dollars)

	AS AT DECEMBER 30, 2009	AS AT DECEMBER 30, 2008
	$	$
	Reclassified (Note 12)	
LIABILITIES		
CURRENT LIABILITIES		
Bank indebtedness (Notes 10 and 14)	1,987	4,398
Accounts payable and accrued liabilities (Notes 11 and 14)	339,294	380,915
Income taxes payable	26,970	30,164
Future income taxes (Note 22)	85	2,713
Current portion of long-term debt (Notes 12 and 14)	122,508	8,879
	490,844	427,069
LONG-TERM DEBT (Notes 12 and 14)	227,075	450,704
PENSION & POST-RETIREMENT BENEFIT		
OBLIGATIONS (Note 15)	20,939	20,072
FUTURE INCOME TAXES (Note 22)	128,984	111,874
OTHER LONG-TERM LIABILITIES (Notes 13 and 14)	25,139	6,010
SHAREHOLDERS' EQUITY		
CAPITAL STOCK (Note 16)	174,816	177,422
CONTRIBUTED SURPLUS	20,311	16,070
RETAINED EARNINGS	818,707	738,113
ACCUMULATED OTHER COMPREHENSIVE INCOME	95,365	83,139
	914,072	821,252
	1,109,199	1,014,744
	2,002,180	2,030,473

EXHIBIT 3-26C

DOREL INDUSTRIES INC. 2009 ANNUAL REPORT

Consolidated Statements of Income

For the years ended December 30, 2009 and 2008
(All figures in thousands of U.S. dollars, except per share amounts)

	2009	2008
	$	$
Sales	2,125,459	2,164,767
Licensing and commission income	14,655	17,113
TOTAL REVENUE	2,140,114	2,181,880
EXPENSES		
Cost of sales (Notes 2 and 3)	1,634,570	1,670,481
Selling, general and administrative expenses	316,168	316,782
Depreciation and amortization (Note 2)	27,366	26,510
Research and development costs (Note 8)	17,184	13,245
Restructuring costs (Note 3)	104	726
Interest on long-term debt	14,969	21,162
Other interest	1,406	961
	2,011,767	2,049,867
Income before income taxes	128,347	132,013
Income taxes (Note 22)		
Current	24,952	17,002
Future	(3,839)	2,156
	21,113	19,158
NET INCOME	107,234	112,855
EARNINGS PER SHARE (Note 23)		
Basic	3.23	3.38
Diluted	3.21	3.38

BEYOND THE BOOK

3-56   (Examine financial statement disclosures)
Find the annual report of a Canadian company that is listed on a Canadian stock exchange, and answer the following questions about it:

   a. Has the company prepared a classified balance sheet (statement of financial position)? If not, look for an explanation and state it briefly.

   b. Referring to items in the balance sheet, explain what liquidity is and how it is reflected in the preparation of the balance sheet.

   c. Discuss how important inventory is, compared to the other assets on the company's balance sheet. Also address how important capital assets (property, plant, and equipment) are to the company.

   d. Does the company rely more heavily on debt financing or equity financing?

   e. How many directors does the company have? What is their average age? What percentage of the board is female?

3-57   (Find additional information about a company)
For the company you selected in Problem 3-56, find at least three articles in the financial press that discuss the nature of this company's markets, and that forecast what the future may be for this sector of the economy. Write a one-page summary of your findings.

Cases

3-58   Al's Gourmet Fish

Leadfoot Al decided to retire from a successful career in stock car racing and invest all his winnings in a fish farm. He had majored in genetics in college, and he experimented with many different species of fish before coming up with a catfish that had the texture and taste of ocean trout. After incorporating Al's Gourmet Fish Company and operating for two years, he decided to explore expansion possibilities. He talked with his banker about getting a loan and presented a statement of earnings for the current year, based strictly on cash flows, as follows:

Cash collected from sale of fish		$520,000
Less: Feed purchases	$460,000	
Purchase of new fish tank	40,000	
Wages paid	80,000	
Other operating expenses paid	20,000	600,000
Operating loss		(80,000)
Plus: Proceeds from sale of land		130,000
Net earnings		$ 50,000

From discussions with Al, the banker learned the following:

   1. Of the cash collected in the current period from sales of fish, $120,000 was for shipments delivered to customers last year. All the sales made this year were collected before the end of the year.

   2. The fish feed can be stored indefinitely, and about 40% of this year's purchases were still on hand at year end.

   3. Two fish tanks were purchased last year at a total cost of $80,000. These tanks, along with the one purchased at the beginning of this year, were used all year. Each tank is expected to last five years.

4. The amount for wages includes $60,000 paid to Al, as compensation for his time devoted to the business.

5. There was a total of $1,000 in bills for other operating expenses for the current year that had not been recorded or paid by year end.

6. The land that was sold for $130,000 had been purchased two years ago for $90,000.

Required:
Provide Al and his banker with answers to the following questions:

a. What amount of revenue from the sale of merchandise should be reported in this period?
b. What amount of expense for fish food should be reported in this period? How should the remainder of the food be reported?
c. Should some amount for the fish tanks be included in calculating the earnings for the current period? If so, how much?
d. Is it alright for Al's company to pay him wages?
e. What amount for "other operating expenses" should be included in calculating the earnings for the current period?
f. The land was sold for more than its original purchase price. The difference between the selling price and the purchase price of a capital asset is called a gain, and is included on the statement of earnings in the period of the sale. What amount should be included in the company's earnings as the gain on the sale of the land?
g. How much did Al earn from his business this year?
h. Comment on whether you think Al should stay in the fish business or go back to auto racing. In addition to financial factors, briefly describe several non-financial considerations that would be relevant to this decision.

3-59 Sentry Security Services

Samir Sarkov incorporated Sentry Security Services and began operations on January 1, 2011. After a busy year, Samir thinks his business has done well, at least in terms of the volume of work done. However, he has asked for your help in determining the financial results.

The company's accounting records, such as they are, have been kept by Mr. Sarkov's son. Although he kept good records of all the cash received and spent by the business during the year, he has no formal training in accounting. At the end of the year he prepared the following statement:

Sentry Security Services
Statement of Cash Receipts and Disbursements
For the Year Ended December 31, 2011

Cash Receipts:		
Invested in the business by the Sarkov family	$ 25,000	
Received from customers for services provided	75,000	
Borrowed from the Provincial Bank	15,000	
		$115,000
Cash Disbursements:		
Paid to the Provincial Bank	6,500	
Rent paid	6,500	
Security equipment purchased	18,000	
Wages paid	37,000	
Security services truck payments	25,000	
Insurance premiums paid	2,000	
Security system parts and supplies purchased	15,000	110,000
Cash remaining (equals the bank balance)		$ 5,000

After reviewing the records, you confirm that the amounts are correct, and you also discover these additional facts:

1. The business does most of its work for cash, but at the end of the year customers owe $5,000 for security services that were provided on account.

2. The amount borrowed from the Provincial Bank is a three-year loan, with an interest rate of 10% per year.

3. The amount paid to the bank during the year includes $1,500 of interest on the loan and $5,000 of principal.

4. The rental contract for the company's space covers a two-year period and requires payments of $500 per month, paid at the beginning of each month. In addition, the last month's rent had to be paid in advance. All the required payments have been made as scheduled.

5. The security equipment was purchased at the beginning of the year and has an estimated five-year lifespan, after which it will be worthless.

6. In addition to the wages that were paid during 2011, $250 is owed to employees for overtime that was worked during the last few days of the year. This will be paid early in 2012.

7. The security services truck payments consist of $21,000 paid to purchase the truck at the beginning of the year plus $4,000 paid for gas, oil, and repairs during the year. Mr. Sarkov expects to use the truck for four years, after which he thinks he should be able to get about $1,000 for it as a trade-in on a new truck.

8. The $2,000 for insurance resulted from paying premiums on two policies at the beginning of the year. One policy cost $700 for one year of insurance coverage; the other policy cost $1,300 for two years of coverage.

9. In addition to the $15,000 of parts and supplies that were purchased and paid for during the year, creditors have billed the business $500 for parts and supplies that were purchased and delivered but not paid for.

10. An inventory count at the end of the year shows that $1,750 of unused parts and supplies are still on hand.

Required:
a. Prepare an accrual-basis statement of earnings for the year ended December 31, 2011, and a classified statement of financial position for Sentry Security Services at the end of the year. (Hint: You may find it helpful to use T accounts for recording the transactions and adjustments, and then determining the ending balances.)
b. Comment on the company's performance during its first year of operations, and its financial position at the end of the year.

3-60 Shirley's Snack Shop

Shirley Sze incorporated Shirley's Snack Shop on April 30, 2011, by investing $5,000 in cash. The following is a summary of the other events affecting the business during its first eight months of operations:

1. On May 1, Shirley acquired a licence from the municipality at a cost of $150. The licence allows her to operate the snack shop for a period of one year.

2. On May 2, she borrowed $10,000 from the bank and used most of it to buy equipment costing $9,600. The interest rate on the loan is 10%, and the interest is to be paid annually (i.e., each May). The entire principal amount is repayable at the end of three years. Shirley estimates that the equipment will last 10 years, after which it will be scrapped. On December 31, 2011, she estimated that the equipment could have been sold for $9,200.

3. At the beginning of September, Shirley realized that she should have liability insurance and purchased a one-year policy effective immediately. The premium paid was $750.

4. Her business is located in a small shop near the university campus. The rental cost is $900 per month and she has paid nine months of rent thus far.

5. Shirley paid herself a salary of $1,000 a month, and a part-time assistant earned wages of $350 each month. However, she has not yet paid her assistant his wages for December.

6. Shirley's purchases of food supplies, on account, cost a total of $22,500. All but $4,500 of this has been used, and she still owes the supplier $4,000. Of the food supplies that have been used, most went into snacks that were sold to customers; however, Shirley ate some of them herself, as on-the-job meals. She estimates that the snacks she consumed were purchased from the supplier at a cost of approximately $200, and would have been priced to sell to her customers for approximately $400.

7. According to her bank records, Shirley received $42,300 from her customers and deposited this in the bank during the period. However, a customer still owes her $500 for snacks provided for a company party held shortly before the end of the year. The balance in her bank account on December 31 is $9,750.

8. Shirley thinks that she has had fairly successful operations since opening the business. However, she has no idea how to calculate its net earnings or determine its financial position.

Required:
a. Provide Shirley with a statement of earnings for the eight-month period ended December 31, 2011, and a statement of financial position as of that date.
b. Comment on the snack shop's performance during its first eight months of operations, and its financial standing as at December 31, 2011.

3-61 Mbeke's Hardware Store
In the middle of January, 2012, Mark Mbeke, the owner of Mbeke's Hardware Store, decided to expand the business by buying out a local lumberyard. To finance the purchase, Mark had to obtain financing from a local bank. The bank asked Mark to provide financial statements for the year ended December 31, 2011, as support for the loan application.

Over the last year, Mark was so busy managing the store that he had no time to review the financial aspects of its operations. However, when the company's bookkeeper provided him with a set of hastily prepared financial statements for 2011, Mark was pleasantly surprised to see that the hardware store's net earnings had increased from $60,000 in 2010 to $90,000 in 2011. He commented, "With financial results like these—a 50 percent increase in earnings during the past year—we should have no trouble getting the loan." However, further investigation revealed the following:

1. On January 2, 2012, the company repaid a $140,000 loan in full, including interest. The loan was a one-year, 10% term loan. No interest expense was recorded in 2011.

2. On January 3, 2012, wages of $10,000 were paid. A review of the time cards shows that these wages relate to work done in the last week of 2011.

3. Goods that originally cost $11,000 and were sold in December 2011 for $15,000 were returned by the customer on January 4, 2012. Accompanying the goods was a letter that stated, "As we agreed on December 30, 2011, these goods are not what we had ordered and are therefore being returned for full credit."

4. Mbeke's Hardware received bills totalling $2,000 in the first week of January, 2012, for utilities and other operating costs incurred in 2011. They were immediately recorded as accounts payable when they were received.

Mark is concerned that some of these transactions may affect the company's financial statements for the year 2011, and therefore its ability to obtain the necessary bank financing.

Required:
a. Calculate the effect of each of these items on the store's net earnings for 2011.
b. By what percentage did the store's earnings increase (or decrease) over the last year?
c. In light of this information, how should Mark proceed?
d. What should the bank do to ensure that it is being provided with accurate financial information?

3-62   Downunder Company

You have been retained by Downunder Company to straighten out its accounting records. The company's trusted accountant for the past 25 years suddenly retired to a tropical island in the South Pacific and, in his rush to get away, he seems to have misplaced the company's accounting records. Now the bank has asked for the latest financial statements, so it can determine whether to renew the company's loan. Luckily, you managed to find the following listing of accounts and their balances, in alphabetical order, written on the back of one of the accountant's travel brochures.

Amount invested by owners (for shares)	$20,000
Amounts due to suppliers	13,000
Amounts due from customers	20,200
Cash in bank account	1,000
Cash on hand (in cash box)	100
Cost of inventory sold to customers	41,000
Cost of inventory still on shelves	7,900
Depreciation accumulated on equipment	4,000
Depreciation expense	2,000
Equipment (original cost)	51,500
Interest expense	500
Loan balance owed to Rational Bank	15,000
Miscellaneous expenses	8,000
Sales to customers	93,600
Wages expense	27,500
Wages owed to employees (not yet paid)	1,200

Required:
a. Based on the information available, prepare a statement of earnings for the year 2011 and a statement of financial position as at December 31, 2011. Note that there is no amount available for retained earnings, so you will have to enter whatever amount is required to make the statement of financial position balance.
b. Identify several additional pieces of information that would be needed for preparing more complete and accurate financial statements. (Hint: Think in terms of the types of adjustments that would normally be made.)

chapter 4

REVENUE RECOGNITION AND STATEMENT OF EARNINGS

LEARNING OBJECTIVES

After studying this chapter, you should be able to:

1. Describe the cash-to-cash cycle of a retail company.

2. List and explain the basic criteria for revenue recognition.

3. Define earnings management as it relates to revenue recognition and explain why and how it can occur.

4. Describe the specific revenue recognition criteria and how they apply to the sale of goods, the provision of services, and the use by others of a company's assets.

5. Explain the impact that various revenue recognition methods have on earnings recognition.

6. Calculate amounts to be recognized under the percentage of completion method.

7. Understand the difference between a multi-step statement of earnings and a single-step one.

8. Describe the criteria for unusual or infrequent items and discontinued operations.

9. Describe how the return on investment can give you one measure of performance.

10. Calculate the return on investment under some basic scenarios.

Charting a Course—
When to Recognize Revenue

"**A** more adventurous and realistic look at the world and how people travel through it" is what *Outpost* magazine offers readers through real-life stories of journeys off the beaten track. Since its March 1996 launch, the Toronto-based publication has grown from a quarterly to six issues per year and seen its circulation climb to approximately 28,000.

What does it take to keep a magazine running smoothly? Publisher Matt Robinson says it pays to have a revenue recognition policy that makes sense.

"Advertising is our principal source of revenue," explains Mr. Robinson. "We bill on a per-issue basis. Payment is against service rendered, so billing has to take place when the issue is published." Since *Outpost* publishes every other month, the company sends out a new set of invoices every eight weeks or so.

Outpost's advertisers can then take anywhere from 30 to 90 days to pay. "We follow the standard 30–60 90 days to collect on invoices that all companies follow," says Mr. Robinson. "We begin to place pressure on clients after 30 days, first with a phone call, then a letter, and then through other collection resources, if necessary. We also offer a two percent early payment discount to encourage clients to pay their invoices within 10 days." Meanwhile, the magazine has to pay all its principal suppliers—the printer, landlord, and contributors.

"Circulation revenue does help mitigate cash flow issues between invoicing and payments," says Mr. Robinson. When *Outpost* sells a subscription, it recognizes the entire sale as revenue right away. "Magazines are atypical in that we get people to pay up front before the service is rendered," he points out. Subscriptions can begin and end with any issue, with each individual subscriber having his or her renewal dates. To recognize the revenue on a per-issue basis for every subscriber would be too complicated and cumbersome for a small operation like *Outpost*. The liability created by recognizing revenue on issues not yet published is understood.

As for newsstand sales, the company typically receives payment from distributors six months after an issue has gone out, based on the number of copies left over. The magazine is unable to plan for revenue from distributors with any kind of accuracy, despite the fact that it has already paid production and shipping costs for those magazines, says Mr. Robinson.

Outpost's own spending is focused on boosting circulation figures, and thus increasing revenues. Its website and participation in consumer shows are two areas where it markets itself. The magazine has also sponsored several speaking tours for Ian Wright, host of the travel show *Pilot Guides*, which airs on OLN (formerly Outdoor Life Network). "Because we're a small business, we like to keep focused on the core product," says Mr. Robinson. "Increasing the number of subscribers is a priority."

The opening story describes a company that publishes an adventure magazine called *Outpost*. The magazine publishing industry is very competitive. Among other things, it is difficult to find a focus that will attract readers year after year. *Outpost* has managed to do this despite the downturn in the travel market since the recent rise in fuel costs and the slowdown in the economy.

From an accounting perspective, the company provides an opportunity to look at a variety of revenue models, as it has three distinct sources of revenue, including the most important one, its advertising revenue. As *Outpost* has contracts with advertisers for ads in future issues of its magazine, the main question that arises is when it should recognize this revenue. When it signs the agreement with the advertiser? When it puts the advertisement in the magazine? When it gets paid for the advertisement? *Outpost*'s practice is to recognize revenue when it sends an invoice to the advertiser, which is done as each issue is published. This delays the recognition of revenue until the invoice is sent, and it also means that the receipt of cash from the advertiser happens after the revenue has been recognized.

The second form of revenue is from individual subscribers. These people pay in advance. Subscriptions are of varying lengths and start at different times during the year. *Outpost* first recognizes this revenue when it receives the subscription request and the money. However, the company is also aware that some of this revenue should not be included in an accounting period if the company must provide additional issues to the subscriber in the following periods. As a result, while *Outpost* initially recognizes the total amount paid by the subscriber as revenue, it later backs out some of this revenue and records it as a liability. This liability is then reduced as the remaining issues are sent to the subscriber, which has the effect of then recognizing the revenue.

The third form of revenue is from sales of magazines to distributors who supply retailers with individual copies to sell. In this case, the company does not even know how much revenue it has earned until about six months after it sends the magazines to the distributors. It receives revenue from the number of issues sold and gets the unsold issues back from the distributors. This means that the revenue recognition is delayed until the cash is received, which is much later than when the magazines were issued. *Outpost* has little choice here as to when to recognize this revenue. It must wait until it knows how much has been earned.

Outpost's three sources of revenue thus provide an introduction to some guidelines that companies can use when making decisions about when to recognize revenue.

In Chapters 1 through 3, three basic financial statements were described, and we saw that two of these, the statement of earnings and the statement of cash flows, measure the company's performance across a time period. In this chapter, the accounting concepts and guidelines for the recognition of earnings are discussed, more detail is provided about the statement of earnings, and some of the problems that are inherent in performance measurement are considered. Chapter 5 is a more detailed discussion of the statement of cash flows and the measurement of performance using cash flows.

USER RELEVANCE

Why is it important for users to know about the **recognition** of revenue? First, the revenue amount is often the largest single amount on the financial statements. Total revenues need to be large enough to cover all the expenses. When users see that total revenues are greater than total expenses (when the company has a positive net earnings), they take this as a sign that the company is viable, that it has the ability to take advantage of opportunities, and that it is growing. On the other hand, companies can and do sometimes experience losses—a signal that all is not well with the company. When losses occur, it is important for users to evaluate both the size and cause of the loss. They need to observe the company over time to see how serious the problems are.

When evaluating revenue information, users also want to assess the quality of the earnings: how well management's decisions are reflected in predictable earnings. All earnings must, at some time, translate into cash. Cash is essential to a company's ultimate survival. One way to measure the quality of earnings is to compare the cash flow from operations (statement of cash flows) with the net earnings. If these two amounts are moving together (both up or both down) and if the cash flow is greater than the net earnings, we consider the earnings to be of high quality. If the two amounts do not move together and if the cash flow is less than the net earnings, we consider the earnings to be of low quality.

The second reason users need to be aware of a company's revenue recognition policies is that the revenues that are earned by companies are not all the same, as our opening story showed. Sometimes cash is received when the revenue is recognized; sometimes it precedes it or comes after it. A company can have different revenue recognition policies associated with different types of revenue. Users need to be aware of the

accounting in the news

Rolling Stone Goes Digital

Rolling Stone magazine has sought—and likely found—a new revenue stream with the revamping of its website. The magazine has put complete digital replicas of its 43-year archive on-line, along with its current issue, and is charging readers for access to them. In doing so, *Rolling Stone* has become one of the most prominent magazines to add a "pay wall" to make money on the Web. The magazine's home page will remain mostly free, offering news updates and slide shows of bands on tour; however, reminders will be placed throughout that full access to *Rolling Stone*'s latest issue as well as its archive going back to 1967 is available once credit card information is provided. A one-month pass costs $3.95; annual access is $29.99 and includes a print subscription, which usually costs $19.95 a year. Print subscribers do not get Web access.

Rolling Stone, like the rest of the publishing industry, had a painful 2009—it sold nearly 20% fewer ads than the year before. However, it still has a devoted print readership—average paid circulation in 2009 was about 1.5 million, up from 1.3 million in 2000. With the average age of its readership at 30, the magazine continues to be profitable.

Source: Andrew Vanacore, "*Rolling Stone*'s Archive Going Online, for a Price," *The Globe and Mail*, April 16, 2010.

company's revenue recognition policies so that they can make judgements about the validity of the revenue amount that is reported. As the article on the previous page shows, sometimes investors are surprised by the revenue source.

Rolling Stone magazine has found a new source of revenue. While other magazine and newspaper companies are making more of their products available on the internet usually for no cost, *Rolling Stone* has decided to charge people who want to see back issues of their magazine. Many newspapers allow access to their feature stories for free but charge for their other features. If you buy a paper subscription to a newspaper, you often get access to the total on-line version. *Rolling Stone* has gone the opposite way. If you pay for the on-line subscription, you will receive the paper version but if you pay for the paper version, you do not get access to the on-line version. *Rolling Stone* has repackaged an old product in a creative way and is earning revenue on it again.

As you will see later in this chapter, there are standards under IFRS for revenue recognition. Those standards can, however, be applied in various ways. Even within the same industry, companies may choose to recognize the same type of revenue in a different manner. In evaluating a company's performance, it is therefore very important to understand the impact of various revenue recognition policies on the financial statements, and therefore essential to read the disclosures about revenue recognition that accompany the financial statements.

Before we look at the revenue recognition policies in detail, it is important to first understand how cash typically flows through a company. As you saw in the opening story, cash and revenue sometimes coincide and sometimes do not.

CASH-TO-CASH CYCLE

LEARNING OBJECTIVE 1

Describe the cash-to-cash cycle of a retail company.

As we have seen, corporate managers engage in three general types of activities: financing, investing, and operating. Let's focus for a moment on operating activities (the ones that generate most of the revenue).

Operating activities include all the normal, day-to-day activities of every business that almost always involve cash. These activities include the normal buying and selling of goods and/or services for the purpose of earning profits. The typical business operation involves an outflow of cash that is followed by an inflow of cash, a process commonly called the **cash-to-cash** cycle. Exhibit 4-1 shows the cash-to-cash cycle of a typical retail company. Each phase in the cycle is discussed in the following subsections.

Cash

The initial amount of cash in a company comes from the original investment by shareholders and from any loans that the company may have received as start-up financing. To simplify matters, let us assume that the company is being totally financed by shareholders—i.e., without any loans.

Acquisition of Inventory

Before the company acquires the inventory that it will sell to customers or will use to provide its services, it must first undertake the investing activities of acquiring property, plant, and equipment. It then hires labour and purchases the first shipments of

CASH-TO-CASH CYCLE OF A RETAIL COMPANY

EXHIBIT 4-1

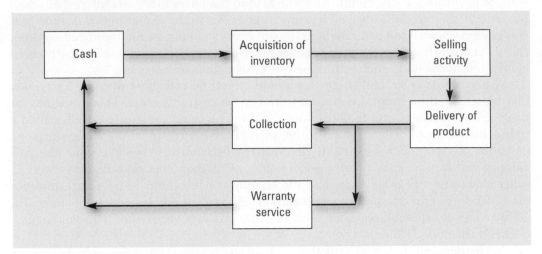

inventory (or signs contracts to acquire them). Note that in a retail company, the costs in this initial phase may be larger than those of a service-oriented company. If you visualize even a small retail store, the amount of inventory that must be purchased to initially fill the shelves can be substantial.

Selling Activity

The selling phase includes all activities that are designed to promote and sell the product. These may include pricing the product, advertising the product, hiring and managing a sales force, establishing retail sales outlets, contracting with agencies, signing supply agreements, and attending trade shows, among other activities. The end results of this phase are sales contracts between buyers and the seller. These may be verbal agreements, where a customer selects and pays for a product, or formal written documents. For most retail companies selling to customers, the agreement occurs when the goods are paid for in the sales outlet (the store). Some companies, however, sell to other businesses or to large enterprises such as hospitals or schools. For these sales, it is more likely that a formal contract is drawn up, specifying prices, times of delivery, and methods of payment.

Delivery of Product

Once a sales contract has been agreed upon, the product must be delivered to the customer. Depending on the type of product, this may be instantaneous (as in a grocery store), or it may take time (as with a car dealership). Some sales contracts require periodic deliveries of inventory (as with fresh produce to a restaurant).

Collection

Upon delivery of the product, collection of the sales price in cash may be immediate, as in a shoe store, or it could take place at some later date, resulting in an amount owing at the time of delivery, which is called an **account receivable**. Payment at a later date is the same as the seller making a loan to the buyer and accepting the risk that the buyer will not pay (this is called credit risk). The loan to the buyer may carry interest charges, but usually no interest is charged if payment is made within a short period of time that is specified (typically 30 to 60 days). If the buyer does not pay within the specified time, the seller may try to get the product back (repossession) or may try other methods to collect on the account, such as turning it over to a collection agency.

Other events could also occur that would affect the collection of cash. The goods may be returned for various reasons, resulting in no cash collection. The goods may be damaged in shipment, and the buyer may ask for a price adjustment (generally called a **price allowance**). There may also be an incentive built in to encourage prompt payment of cash, such as a **cash discount**, which means that less than the full amount will be accepted as full payment. Just as *Outpost* does with its advertisers, a seller may offer a 2% price discount if the account is paid within 10 days instead of the usual 30 days. These terms are sometimes stated as 2/10 net 30, which means that a 2% discount is offered if payment is made within 10 days; otherwise, the total amount is due at the end of 30 days.

In the opening story, you read about customers paying for a magazine subscription in advance. In this instance, the company has the cash before using cash to generate magazines. Collecting cash is not a concern for the company, but creating the magazine issues to satisfy the obligation to the customers is. In accepting the cash, the company is agreeing to produce future issues of the magazine and must plan its future activities to satisfy that obligation.

Warranty Service

Some goods carry a written or implied guarantee of quality. Automobiles, for example, are warranted for a certain number of years or for a certain number of kilometres. During this period, the seller is responsible, to some extent, for product replacement or repair. Because the provision of warranty work often involves additional outlays of cash for employees' time and for the purchase of repair parts, warranty service affects the ultimate amount of cash that is available at the end of the cycle. Many retail outlets today that sell products with warranties will cover the warranty for a period of time— perhaps three to six months—and will then sell additional warranty coverage to the customer. If the product needs to be repaired within the extended warranty time, the company has additional funds to offset the cost of that repair. If no repair is needed, the company earns an additional revenue amount.

Summary of the Cash-to-Cash Cycle

The net amount left in cash after this cycle is completed is then available to purchase more goods and services in the next cycle. If the cash inflows are less than the cash outflows, the amount of cash available is reduced, and the company may be unable to begin a new cycle without getting additional cash from outside the company in the form of equity or debt. If cash inflows exceed cash outflows, the company can expand its volume of activity, add another type of productive activity, or return some of the extra cash to shareholders in the form of dividends.

Note that the order of the phases in the cash-to-cash cycle may be different from one company to the next. For example, a transportation contractor such as **Bombardier** may do most of its selling activity early in the cycle to obtain contracts to deliver products at a future date, with much of the acquisition of raw materials and production taking place after the contract is signed. Also, in some companies, the separate phases may take place simultaneously. At **Safeway**, for example, the delivery of groceries to the customer and the collection of cash happen at the same time.

REVENUE RECOGNITION

Managers do not want to wait until the end of the cash-to-cash cycle to assess the performance of their company, because they must make day-to-day decisions that will ultimately affect the final cash outcome. If they wait until the end, they may not be able to make appropriate adjustments. For example, if the first few items sold result in significant uncollected accounts or require significant warranty service, they might want to rethink their policies on granting credit and providing warranties. If the cost of warranty service is too high, they might also want to purchase better quality inventory so the products last longer. Furthermore, the cash-to-cash cycle is a continuous process that is constantly beginning and ending for different transactions. There is no specific point in time at which all the cash-to-cash transactions reach an end.

To measure operating performance as accurately as possible, accountants divide normal operating activities into two groups, called revenues and expenses. **Revenues** are the inflows of cash or other benefits from the business's normal operating activities when these inflows result in an increase in equity that did not come from contributions from equity holders. It is important to note that revenues result from normal operating activities. There are other activities that result in increases in equity that are not from ordinary operating activities. These are not called revenues. Revenues usually involve the sale of goods, the provision of services or allowing others to use the company's assets in exchange for interest, dividends, or royalties. **Expenses** are the costs incurred to earn revenues. The difference between revenues and expenses, called **net earnings** (or **net income**), is one of the key measurements of performance. The expression "in the red" is related to net earnings. In the past, if a company had a negative net earnings (expenses > revenues), the net loss figure was actually written in red ink. The expression came to mean that a company had experienced a loss. Similarly, but less commonly used, the expression "in the black" meant that you had a positive net earnings.

Some companies make profits by charging higher prices, others by controlling costs. New companies in industries where there are already established players face difficult challenges. Note the article on the following page.

The need for timely information in decision-making is an argument for recognizing revenue as early as possible in the cash-to-cash cycle. The earlier in the cycle that revenue is recognized, however, the greater the number of estimates that are needed to measure the net performance. For example, if the company chooses to recognize revenue when the product is delivered to customers (a common practice for many businesses), it will have to make estimates regarding the collectibility of the receivables, the possibility of the customer returning the goods, and the costs of warranty service. To measure the return (profitability) on the sale of a product accurately, these items should be considered; otherwise, the company may be overestimating the profit on the sales of its products. To produce the most accurate measurement of net operating performance, all costs related to the earning of revenues are matched to the revenues they helped earn. In accrual accounting, this is called **matching** (see Chapter 2). Matching

accounting in the news

Discount Fares Not Enough to Cover Costs

Blaming the downturn in the economy and high fuel costs, Zoom Airlines, an Ottawa- based company, suspended operations and filed for bankruptcy protection on August 28, 2008, when one of its planes was seized in Scotland and another in Calgary. The airport authorities in the two locations were owed substantial amounts and held the airplanes to force the airline to pay the amounts owed. Zoom Airlines, a low-fare transatlantic airline, began operating in 2002 hoping to tap into the casual traveller market. It was a small airline operating a small number of airplanes with flights to 15 locations, mainly in Canada and Europe. It offered both scheduled and chartered services. When the seizures occurred, passengers were left stranded, often far from home, and had to scramble to find alternative flights. Those who had purchased tickets for future flights had little hope of recovering their ticket costs.

Source: "Zoom Stops Operations, Strands Passengers," CTV News, August 28, 2008, http://www.ctv.ca/servlet/ArticleNews/story/CTVNews/20080828/zoom_airline_080828/20080828?hub=TopStories

requires the simultaneous recognition of all costs that are or will be incurred (in the past, present, or future) to produce the revenue.

The question of when to recognize revenue is quite straightforward for some industries (e.g., clothing retailers like H&M). Revenue is recognized when the customer buys the goods in the store. Normally customers pay cash or use a debit or credit card, which means that the collection of cash for the sale is not an issue. While there are no warranty costs for a clothing retailer to consider, items are sometimes returned. Returns are often handled by giving the customer another article of clothing, if one is available, or the value of the returned clothing as a credit to buy a different article. Some retailers return the original cash paid. Clothing stores also usually put a time frame on returns (typically, customers have two weeks to return merchandise), which means the issue of returns is a known quantity very quickly. For other industries, the decision is not as clearly defined. For a manufacturing company such as Bombardier (a maker of trains and airplanes), contracts are signed, merchandise such as a rail car is manufactured, the merchandise is delivered, money is collected from the customer (usually some time after delivery), and warranty services are provided on the merchandise sold. When should such a company recognize revenue: when the contract is signed, when the goods are delivered, when the cash is collected, or when the warranty period expires and all obligations related to the sale have been satisfied?

The earlier in the cash-to-cash cycle the company chooses to recognize revenues, the less reliable the company's estimate of the effects of future events. On the other hand, however, the company receives more timely information. To reduce the uncertainty that is inherent in estimating future events, the company would need to recognize revenues later in the cash-to-cash cycle, when those estimates are more reliable, but the information would be less useful for making management decisions. The decision about when to recognize revenue is a very important one for managers, because it has a major impact on net earnings. Knowing about the revenue recognition policy is also important for users, so that they can assess the reliability of the information and the quality of the earnings.

There is obviously a conflict between the desire to measure performance on a timely basis (early in the cycle) and the ability to measure performance reliably (late in the cycle). **Revenue recognition criteria** have been developed within IFRS (IAS 18) to resolve this conflict and to produce a measure of performance that is intended to balance the need for timely information with the need for reliable information. The issue is further complicated when the company is involved in two or more lines of business that have different cash-to-cash cycles. A revenue recognition policy must be developed for each line and it is possible that they may not be the same.

Two basic criteria must be met before a revenue item can be recognized. The first is that it is probable that economic benefits will flow to the company. This condition is normally met when the activity that generated the revenue (sometimes referred to as the **performance**) is substantially completed—in other words, when the earnings process is substantially complete. In general, this would mean that the company has completed most of what it agreed to do and there are very few costs still to be incurred in the cash-to-cash cycle, or the remaining costs can be reasonably estimated, or both. Another way to consider this factor is to determine whether all the risks and rewards of the goods or services have been transferred to the buyer. If they have, there is very little left for the seller to do.

The second criterion is the requirement that the revenue can be reliably measured. This is often straightforward. When goods or services are sold for cash or an agreed selling price (an account receivable), the **measurement** is easy to determine. Sometimes, however, goods or services are sold in exchange for other products, services, or assets (other than accounts receivable). Now the measurement is more difficult. The accountant must examine the value of the goods or services sold and compare it with the value of the products, services, or assets received. In deciding which of these values to use, the accountant will look for the most reliable amount—the amount that can be most objectively determined. If the amount of revenue cannot be measured, it cannot be recognized. Within the measurement issue, there must be reasonable assurance that the amounts earned can be realized, or collected, from the buyer. If cash is given at the time of sale, this assurance is automatically satisfied. If, however, the goods or services are sold on credit, the seller must be reasonably assured that the amount owing will be collected. Companies rarely sell goods or services on credit without a credit check on the buyer. This is to provide assurance of the probable future collection of the accounts receivable. Even with this assurance, it is possible that some customers will not pay the amounts owed. Because of this possibility, companies that recognize credit sales as revenue must, in the same period, recognize an expense that measures the probable uncollectibility of the accounts receivable. This is to keep the revenues from being overstated. We call this expense "bad debt expense." More will be said about this expense in Chapter 6.

LEARNING OBJECTIVE 2

List and explain the basic criteria for revenue recognition.

BASIC REVENUE RECOGNITION CRITERIA

1. The probable inflow of economic benefits to the company.
   a. The performance has been achieved.
   b. The risks and rewards are transferred and/or the earnings process is substantially complete with respect to the sale.
2. The amount earned can be measured.

In conclusion, if it is probable that future economic benefits will flow to the company and if the amounts earned can be reliably measured, revenues should be recognized in the financial statements. These conditions are usually met at the time of delivery of the product to the customer, so this is the point at which many companies recognize their revenues. The following sections discuss various applications of revenue recognition, including at the sale of goods to the customer and the sale of services.

Earnings Management

LEARNING OBJECTIVE 3

Define earnings management as it relates to revenue recognition and explain why and how it can occur.

The criteria for revenue recognition, and the matching of expenses with revenues, make it possible for management to evaluate the company's revenue stream and establish a revenue recognition policy that best reflects the company's operating results. Sometimes management deliberately chooses how and when to recognize revenues and costs so that net earnings are higher or lower in particular accounting periods, or smoother over time. This practice is called **earnings management**.

It is not easy for external users of financial statements to determine if earnings management is taking place, because companies are often very complex. They are engaged in many diversified activities, and it is not possible for users to have a thorough knowledge of all their activities. Sometimes external bodies like the Ontario Securities Commission, or the Securities and Exchange Commission (SEC) in the United States, question a company's revenue recognition policy. As the following story shows, sometimes people within the organization itself identify accounting issues.

accounting in the news

School Board Does Homework in Financial Management

Many news stories in recent years have featured corporations restating their financials due to accounting errors. But sound accounting is necessary in all sectors. Teachers in the Langley School District in British Columbia called for financial reform after noting significant accounting errors. Langley School District, which comprises almost 50 schools and has an annual budget of about $150 million, had amassed a $14 million deficit, even though school districts are not allowed to run deficits under the B.C. *School Act*. The Langley Teachers' Association called on the Education Minister to appoint a special advisor, as had been done for the Vancouver School Board, which had been deemed "unable or unwilling to manage its resources to protect the interests of the students."

When the Langley School District's financial problems were first identified in 2009, it arranged a review by an outside accounting firm and asked the provincial auditor general to review its financial management. The Deloitte & Touche review found a series of accounting errors, including schools getting authorization to spend money without approval or funding. Some parents and teachers in Langley have called for a forensic audit to determine how a modest projected surplus in 2009 turned into a multi-million-dollar deficit in 2010. Provincial staff have been working with the school board staff to come up with a plan to eliminate the deficit.

Source: Wendy Stueck, "Teachers to Take Calls for Financial Reform to B.C. Minister's Doorstep," *The Globe and Mail*, April 22, 2010.

The teachers in the Langley School District called for an investigation into the accounting issues facing the school district. School districts are not-for-profit organizations. As such, they do not have the same access to funds as a profit organization does. It is therefore vital that they have well-formulated processes for managing expenditures. When those processes are not in place, the money spent can exceed the money available, and a deficit results.

Earnings management can be related to the early or late recognition of revenues and/or to the recognition of expenses before or after their related revenues have been recognized. Because it is difficult to detect, users of financial statements rely on auditors to determine whether accounting standards have been applied appropriately or not. Companies that deliberately manage their earnings may be able to affect the market's valuation of their shares, but when earnings management is discovered such companies usually pay a heavy price through shareholder lawsuits and the lowering of their share values.

In the next section, as you read through the different ways that revenue can be recognized, keep earnings management in mind. For each revenue stream, consider whether earnings management could occur. If it could, would it still meet the revenue recognition criteria?

Applications of Revenue Recognition

The revenue recognition criteria can be met at different points in the cash-to-cash cycle. The point at which different companies recognize revenues varies accordingly, as you observed in the opening story about *Outpost* magazine. IAS 18 provides revenue recognition criteria for specific types of transactions: the sale of goods, provision of services, and use of the company's assets by others. This section will provide more detail on each of these transactions.

LEARNING OBJECTIVE 4

Describe the specific revenue recognition criteria and how they apply to the sale of goods, the provision of services, and the use by others of a company's assets.

Revenue Recognition for the Sale of Goods

For the sale of goods, there are five specific revenue recognition criteria[1] that must be met before revenue can be recognized:

- There has been a transfer of the risks and rewards to the buyer.
- The company no longer has managerial involvement or control over the goods sold.
- The revenue can be measured reliably.
- It is probable that economic benefits from the transaction will flow to the seller.
- The costs incurred or to be incurred with respect to the transaction can be measured reliably.

Recognition at the time of sale The most common point at which sales revenues are recognized is the time of sale and/or shipment of the goods to the customer. Once the goods have been taken by or shipped to the customer, the company has usually completed everything it has to do for the transaction. The title to the goods has been transferred, which transfers the risks and rewards to the buyer, and the company no longer has control over the goods. This meets the first two criteria listed above. At the time of sale, the amount that is earned is known and measureable. Often the customer will pay cash, which provides immediate economic benefits to the seller. If the company sells the goods

1. IAS 18.14.

on credit, the amount owed is also measurable. However, the company will have to be reasonably assured of collection of the account receivable before revenue can be recognized. Most companies will not sell on credit if they have doubts about the future collectibility of the amount. An estimate of potential uncollectibility must be made and an allowance for uncollectible accounts established. At the time of sale, the seller usually knows the costs that are related to the transaction. Thus, the last three criteria are also met.

Outpost magazine recognizes two of its revenues at the time of sale. The time of sale occurs when an issue has been printed and sent to subscribers and distributors. At this point, it has completed the earning process on that issue. It recognizes the revenue from individual subscribers and the revenue from advertisers on a per-issue basis. Prior to releasing an issue, the company can measure how much it has earned because subscribers have paid in advance and advertisers have signed a contract that specifies how much they will pay for advertisements in each issue. The only unknown at the point of sale is whether the advertisers will pay when they receive the bill from the magazine. The company would need to estimate the likelihood of uncollectibility of its advertising revenue. The issues sent to distributors pose more of a problem for *Outpost*. It has completed the printing of the issues but it will have to wait six months before it knows how much has been earned. It needs to wait until distributors provide information about how many issues were sold and how many issues are being returned before it can measure its earnings. Therefore, because revenue must be measureable to be recognized, *Outpost* cannot recognize this revenue at the time of delivery.

In annual reports, most companies state their revenue recognition policy as part of the first note, which includes a summary of the company's significant accounting policies. For example, in its 2009 financial statements, **Brickworks Limited** states its revenue recognition policy in Note 1 (c) to the financial statements. Brickworks Limited is an Australian company that manufactures and sells bricks, tiles, and building supplies. It also sells land and handles waste management. Part of its revenue recognition statement follows:

BRICKWORKS LIMITED (2009)

Revenue

Sales revenue is recognized when the significant risks and rewards of ownership of the items sold have passed to the buyer, and the revenue is also able to be measured reliably.

For revenue from the sale of goods, this occurs upon the delivery of goods to customers.

For revenue from the sale of land held for resale, this is recognized at the point at which any contract of sale in relation to industrial land has become unconditional, and at which settlement has occurred for residential land.

Profits on disposal of investments and property, plant and equipment are recognized at the point where title to the asset has passed.

This is a fairly detailed statement from Brickworks. Note that it frequently refers to the transfer of the risks and rewards of ownership. Note as well the timing of the recognition—when the product is delivered to its customers. Brickworks also has revenue from interest and dividends that will be discussed later in this section. Like *Outpost*, Brickworks has different types of revenue and must establish different revenue recognition policies.

If a company's revenue is very homogeneous, it will need only a simple statement about revenue recognition. **Maple Leaf Foods Inc.**, in Note 2 (d) to its 2009 financial statements, states: "The Company recognizes revenues from product sales upon transfer of title to customers. Revenue is recorded at the invoice price for each product. An estimate of sales incentives provided to customers is also recognized at the time of sale and is classified as a reduction in reported sales. Sales incentives include various rebate and promotional programs provided to the Company's customers. " Maple Leaf Foods is a Canadian-based food processing company that sells to retail, wholesale, food service, industrial, and agricultural customers. It sells meat and bakery products, as well as feed for animals. Although it has several different customers, it has a single type of revenue (sale of a product) that does not require lengthy disclosure.

Sometimes when you read the description of a company's revenue recognition policy, you will see reference to the term "F.O.B." F.O.B. means "free on board" and is a legal term to describe the point at which title to the goods passes from the seller to the buyer. It is used by companies like Maple Leaf Foods that deliver goods in large volumes to customers. If the goods are shipped F.O.B. shipping point, the title (ownership) passes after the goods leave the seller's loading dock (the shipping point). If they were shipped F.O.B. destination, the goods would remain the property of the seller until they reached their destination: the buyer's receiving dock. The way the goods are shipped will affect the point at which revenue can be recognized. The point at which title to the goods passes is a clear indication that the seller has earned the revenue. Prior to that point, the seller is still responsible for the goods.

To illustrate revenue recognition at the time of sale, assume that Hawke Company sells 1,000 units of its product during 2011 at $30 per unit. Also assume that the costs of these units totalled $22,000 and that, at the time of sale, Hawke estimated they would cost the company an additional $500 in warranty expenses in the future. Ignoring all other operating expenses, the statement of earnings for Hawke for 2011 would appear as in Exhibit 4-2.

REVENUE RECOGNITION AT TIME OF SALE

EXHIBIT 4-2

HAWKE COMPANY
Statement of Earnings
For the period ended December 31, 2011

Revenues	$30,000
Cost of goods sold	22,000
Gross profit	8,000
Warranty expense	500
Net income	$ 7,500

Note that although Hawke Company may not have incurred any actual warranty expenses yet, it recognizes an expense for its estimate of what the future warranty costs might be. Recognizing the warranty expense is appropriate because the future warranty costs are directly related to the revenue. Therefore, if the company wants to recognize the revenue before it knows the actual warranty cost, it must estimate what those costs might be so that the income is not overstated. At the same time as it recognizes the warranty expense, it recognizes a liability for these future costs. When actual costs are incurred, the liability is then reduced and no further expense is recognized. In its revenue recognition note, Maple Leaf Foods said that it estimated the cost of the sales incentives and recognized them at the same time as a reduction to the revenue. This treatment is similar to Hawke's treatment of warranty costs.

In some cases, a company might receive a deposit for a product to be delivered in the future. Because it is unlikely that the revenue recognition criteria would be met by this transaction (until the product is delivered, the title has not passed and the risks and rewards of ownership have not been transferred to the buyer), the revenue from this order would not be recorded until the goods are delivered. The deposit is therefore recorded as unearned revenue, deferred revenue, or revenue received in advance (a liability account that represents an obligation either to deliver the goods or to return the deposit). For example, if Hawke Company received a $500 deposit on an order, it would make the following entry:

Cash (A)	500	
Unearned revenue (L)		500

When the goods are delivered, the liability to provide the product is satisfied (the company has completed what it had to do in the sale and the title to the goods has passed to the buyer), and the deposit can then be recognized as a revenue item with the following entry:

Unearned revenue (L)	500	
Sales revenue (SE)		500

Companies that require deposits or advance payments on products or services may disclose this in their footnote on revenue recognition. Note that liabilities are created for the obligation to provide the service or product in the future. Typical disclosures for this type of situation are shown here for **WestJet Airlines Ltd.** (2009).

WESTJET AIRLINES LTD. (2009)

1. Summary of Significant Accounting Policies

  d) Revenue recognition

    (i) Guest revenues

      Guest revenues, including the air component of vacation packages, are recognized when air transportation is provided. Tickets sold but not yet used are reported in the consolidated balance sheet as advance ticket sales.

    (ii) Charter and other revenues

      Charter and other revenues include charter revenue, cargo revenue, net revenues from the sale of the land component of vacation packages, ancillary revenues and other.

      Charter and cargo revenue is recognized when air transportation is provided. Revenue from the land component of vacation packages is generated from providing agency services equal to the amount paid by the guest for products and services less payment to the travel supplier, and are reported at the net amounts received. Revenue from the land component is deferred as advanced ticket sales and recognized in earnings on completion of the vacation.

      Ancillary revenues are recognized as the services and products are provided to the guests. Included in ancillary revenues are fees associated with guest itinerary changes or cancellations, excess baggage fees, buy-on-board sales and pre-reserved seating fees.

      Included in other revenue is revenue from expired non-refundable guest credits recognized at the time of expiry.

Users should be aware of one other aspect of revenue recognition: sales returns. In many retail stores, customers are allowed to return merchandise. Usually a time is specified, such as 10 days or one month. When goods are returned, the company either returns the amount paid or gives a credit that allows the customer to buy new merchandise. Technically, the company should take into consideration the cost of possible returns when it recognizes revenue; otherwise, its income may be overstated. In reality, the time period in which returns are allowed is usually short, which means that the income is not materially misstated if the returns are recorded when they happen. For companies that sell to other companies (business-to-business sales), the returns can be substantial. For example, in the bookselling business, publishers often accept back from booksellers the books that have not been sold. This can result in a substantial amount of returns, depending on how well a book sells. If such companies want to recognize revenue when they ship books to a bookseller, they must estimate the amount of returns and recognize that amount when the revenue is recognized. The issue of returns has been particularly problematic for companies that sell through the Internet. Note the following example:

accounting in the news
Growth of On-line Shopping

On-line shopping has been growing steadily in Western Europe. The most popular items bought are books, followed by travel and clothing. Among the big drawbacks that discourage customers from buying on-line are shipping costs and the difficulty to return goods. Buying clothing on-line is difficult because many customers like to feel items and try them on before buying them. This is not possible with on-line shopping, so on-line sellers of clothing have a much higher return rate than a physical retail outlet would have.

Source: Katie Deatsch, "Online Shopping is Growing Steadily in Western Europe, Forrester Says," *Internet Retailer*, March 27, 2009. http://www.internetretailer.com/2009/03/27/online-shopping-is-growing-steadily-in-western-europe-forrester

Recognition at the time of contract signing Even though the point of sale—or more correctly, the point at which title to the product is transferred to the buyer from the seller—is the most common method used to recognize revenues, several situations exist that require exceptions to this application of revenue recognition. Over the years, certain types of transactions have caused concern among investors and accountants because of how the companies chose to recognize revenues. One of those was in the area of retail land sales. This industry initially recognized revenues at the date of contract signing. In the case of retail land sale companies, it was the land sale agreement. The problem was that a considerable amount of uncertainty existed regarding future costs on the seller's part subsequent to contract signing, and to the collectibility of the receivables from buyers. Questions were raised as to whether any of the revenue recognition criteria were being met.

The uncertainty stemmed from industry practices. Retail land sale companies often sell land before it is developed and therefore have yet to incur the development costs. This means that the seller has not completed all the things that must be done; the seller still has continuing management involvement in the development of the property. There is also the problem of matching the future development costs to the revenues. Remember that if you want to recognize revenue before all the costs associated with the sale are incurred (note the warranty example), you must be able to estimate those future costs so that they can be recognized simultaneously with the revenue (according to the matching principle). Sales contracts typically require low down payments and sometimes include below-market interest rates to entice buyers to sign contracts. These conditions make it relatively easy for a buyer to back out of the transaction before all the cash is collected, thereby negating the sale and raising the possibility that future economic benefits may not flow to the seller.

Given that the earning process was rarely complete, and there were uncertainties with regard to future costs and the collectibility of the receivables, revenue for retail land sale companies is now only recognized at the time of contract signing if certain minimum criteria are met. These criteria require, first, that there be only minimal costs yet to be incurred (this means that the seller has completed substantially all the things that have to be done to conclude the sale), and second, that the receivables created in the transaction have a reasonable chance of being collected.

Recognition at the time of production Revenue recognition at the time of production was common in two industries: mining and long-term construction. If the product's market value and sale are both fairly certain at the time of production, as it was in certain mining operations, then the inventories produced can be valued at their net realizable value (selling price) and the resulting revenues can be recognized immediately. The reason for this practice was that the critical event in the revenue earning process for the mine was not the ore's sale, but its production. If the market for the ore was well established with fairly stable prices and there were buyers for the ore, the sale was assured as soon as the ore was produced. By recording the revenues as soon as possible, these companies had more timely information for making decisions. Although this was an acceptable practice at the time, it no longer is. The current mining market is unstable, as prices for various ores fluctuate daily. Therefore, resource companies now delay the recognition of the revenue until the ore is actually delivered. Many companies manage the risk of changing prices by purchasing forward contracts to sell their ore at a fixed price. A forward contract is an agreement between a buyer and a seller that establishes a fixed selling price.

The following example presents the revenue recognition method of the international mining company **Barrick Gold Corporation**, which operates gold and copper mines:

BARRICK GOLD CORPORATION (2009)

5. Revenues
Revenue Recognition
We record revenue when the following conditions are met: persuasive evidence of an arrangement exists; delivery and transfer of title (gold revenue only) have occurred under the terms of the arrangement; the price is fixed or determinable; and collectability is reasonably assured.

Note that for Barrick Gold Corporation, the earning process is complete when title to the gold has passed. At this point, the sale's final amount is certain. Because it uses forward or option contracts, the amount earned is known for certain. A forward or option contract stipulates the amount that will be received for the gold in the future.

The other industry that recognizes revenue at the time of production is the long-term construction industry, which has a long production period. In this industry, revenue is recognized using the **percentage of completion method**, which recognizes a portion of a project's revenues and expenses during the construction period based on the percentage of completion. The basis for determining the percentage completed is usually the costs incurred relative to the estimated total costs.

As an example, suppose that Solid Construction Company agrees to construct a building for $300 million. It will take three years to build, and the company expects to incur costs of $75 million, $105 million, and $30 million in 2011, 2012, and 2013, respectively. The total expected cost is $210 million and, therefore, the profit on the project is expected to be $90 million. Assuming that all goes according to plan, Exhibit 4-3 shows how Solid Construction would recognize the revenues and expenses (and related profits) during the three years with the percentage of completion method.

LEARNING OBJECTIVE 5

Explain the impact that various revenue recognition methods have on earnings recognition.

REVENUE RECOGNITION WITH THE PERCENTAGE OF COMPLETION METHOD
(amounts in millions)

EXHIBIT 4-3

Year	Degree of Completion		Revenue Recognized	Expenses Recognized	Profit
1	$ 75 ÷ $210 =	36%	36% × 300 = $108	$ 75	$33
2	$105 ÷ $210 =	50%	50% × 300 = $150	105	45
3	$ 30 ÷ $210 =	14%	14% × 300 = $ 42	30	12
		100%	$300	$210	$90

The formulae to arrive at these amounts are as follows:

$$\frac{\text{Expenses for this period}}{\text{Total cost of project}} = \text{Percentage completed}$$

$$\text{Percentage completed} \times \text{Total revenue} = \text{Revenue to be recognized this period}$$

How well does the percentage of completion method meet the revenue recognition criteria? The total revenue can be measured reliably and, because of the construction contract, it is probable that the economic benefits will flow to the builder. For many long-term construction contracts, the buyer is often billed periodically during the construction process. The periodic billing and collection provide the seller with the ability to estimate collectability. The costs incurred to date are known and can be recognized when the revenue is recognized. It is also possible to reliably measure the cost to complete the contract and the stage of the contract. Has the builder transferred the risks and rewards of ownership to the buyer? It is assumed that the transfer of the risks and rewards of ownership are transferred as the contract proceeds through the building phases. This is not the same as the title but is accepted as a sufficient basis for recognizing revenue.

Instead of waiting until all the contract work has been completed (which can take several years), this method allows the company to measure how much work has been completed so far and then recognize as revenue the same percentage of the total contract price. The expenses for the period and the percentage of revenue earned are recognized each period, which provides timely information to users. The total revenue

LEARNING OBJECTIVE 6

Calculate amounts to be recognized under the percentage of completion method.

from the contract is known before the work begins. The company also has an estimate of the total costs that it expects to incur. As actual costs are incurred and some of the work is completed, we can calculate how much of the contract is finished and, therefore, how much revenue has been earned. We do that using the formulae in Exhibit 4-3.

The disclosure below for **Bombardier Inc.** (used as an example earlier in this chapter) for the fiscal year ending January 31, 2010, illustrates the percentage of completion method of revenue recognition.

BOMBARDIER INC. (2010)

Revenue recognition

Aerospace programs Revenues from the sale of commercial aircraft and light business aircraft (*Learjet* Series) are recognized upon final delivery of products and presented in manufacturing revenues.

Medium and large business aircraft (*Challenger* and *Global* Series) contracts are segmented between green aircraft (i.e., before external painting and installation of customer-selected interiors and optional avionics) and completion. Revenues are recognized based on green aircraft deliveries (when certain conditions are met), and upon final acceptance of interiors and optional avionics by customers. Revenues for green aircraft delivery and completion are presented in manufacturing revenues.

Long-term contracts Revenues from long-term contracts related to designing, engineering, or manufacturing of products, including vehicle and component overhaul, are recognized using the percentage-of-completion method of accounting. The percentage of completion is generally determined by comparing the actual costs incurred to the total costs anticipated for the entire contract, excluding costs that are not representative of the measure of performance. Vehicle and component overhaul revenues are presented in services revenues. System and signaling revenues are presented in other revenues. All other long-term manufacturing contract revenues are presented in manufacturing revenues.

Revenues from maintenance service contracts entered into on or after December 17, 2003, are recognized in proportion to the total costs originally anticipated to be incurred at the beginning of the contract and are presented in services revenues. Maintenance service contracts entered into before this date are recognized using the percentage-of-completion method of accounting.

Revenues from other long-term service contracts are generally recognized as services are rendered and are presented in services revenues.

Estimated revenues from long-term contracts include revenues from change orders and claims when it is probable that they will result in additional revenues in an amount that can be reliably estimated.

If a contract review indicates a negative gross margin, the entire expected loss on the contract is recognized in cost of sales in the period in which the negative gross margin is identified.

In some cases, it may not be possible to measure how much of the project is completed, which would make it difficult to measure the revenue earned. There could also be a question about the future collectability on the contract, although it is doubtful that a company would continue work on a project if it was concerned about the future payment for its work. If it is not possible to reliably estimate future costs and revenues, revenue can only be recognized at an amount equal to the construction costs already incurred, and assuming also that the recognized revenue will be collectible.

With the percentage of completion method, if an overall loss is projected on the project, IFRS requires that the loss be recognized as soon as it is identified. For example, if, at the end of 2012, the total estimated costs to complete the Solid Construction contract were $315 million (instead of the original $210 million), an overall loss of $15 million would be indicated for the contract. At the end of 2012, Solid Construction would have to recognize a loss of $48 million (the overall loss of $15 million plus the $33 million in profit recognized in 2011). This loss would offset the $33 million profit reported in 2011 and would result in a net loss at this point of $15 million on the contract. If the actual costs equalled the new estimated costs in 2013, no additional profit or loss would be recorded in 2013, as the overall loss on the contract would already have been recognized. The details for an expected loss on a long-term contract do not need to be learned until you take an intermediate accounting course. For now, however, it is important that you understand that contract losses can occur and that the total potential loss is recognized in the year that the loss is determined. Note that Bombardier has a statement about how it recognizes expected contract losses.

Recognition at the time of collection Except for cash sales, revenue recognition criteria are almost always met before cash is collected. Therefore, for reporting purposes, the collectibility of cash rarely delays the recognition of revenue. Magazines such as *Outpost* have one of those rare circumstances. When *Outpost* sends magazines to a distributor for sale on newsstands, it does not know how much it has earned until it receives the money from the distributor six months later. It has no choice but to delay the recognition of revenue.

There are other circumstances under which the collection of receivables is so uncertain that accounting standards would require that revenue recognition be postponed until cash is actually collected. Some companies allow their customers to pay for their merchandise through instalments over an extended period of time. Many companies that sell merchandise this way have learned about the probability of collecting all the amounts owed by their customers. These companies will recognize revenue at the time of the original sale and recognize the probability of uncollectibility at the same time. However, there are rare situations where it is not possible to estimate the probability of collection. In these rare cases, the company would need to delay the recognition of revenue until the actual cash is received.

Revenue Recognition for Delivery of Services

Companies that earn revenue from the delivery of services are a growing sector of the economy. The revenue recognized by WestJet for passenger flights is service revenue. Bombardier, as well, described how it accounts for maintenance and long-term service contracts. The criteria for the recognition of service revenue are very similar to the criteria for the sale of goods[2]:

- The amount of revenue can be measured reliably.

- It is probable that economic benefits from the service will flow to the provider.

2. IAS 18.20.

- The stage of completion of the service can be measured reliably.

- The costs incurred or to be incurred with respect to the transaction can be measured reliably.

Revenue from the provision of services is normally recognized in the period when the service is completed. If the service takes a long time to complete, the percentage of completion method is used when the costs and the probable revenue can be measured reliably. Financial institutions are one of the largest providers of services. **The Toronto-Dominion Bank**, one of Canada's major banks, describes its revenue recognition policy as follows:

TORONTO-DOMINION BANK (2009)

Note 1 Summary of Significant Accounting Policies
Revenue Recognition
Investment and securities services include asset management, administration and commission fees, and investment banking fees. Asset management administration and commissions fees from investment management and related services, custody and institutional trust services and brokerage services are all recognized over the period in which the related service is rendered. Investment banking fees include advisory fees, which are recognized as income when earned, and underwriting fees, net of syndicate expenses, which are recognized as income when the Bank has rendered all services to the issuer and is entitled to collect the fee.

Card services include interchange income from credit and debit cards and annual fees. Fee income, including service charges, is recognized as earned, except for annual fees, which are recognized over a 12-month period.

Revenue from the Use by Others of a Company's Assets

Companies can also earn revenue by allowing others to use their assets. The revenue is in the form of interest, dividends, or royalties. The recognition of the revenue from these sources follows the basic revenue recognition criteria plus additional specifications depending on the type of revenue.

Interest revenue is recognized after the issuance of the interest-bearing asset and is proportional to the time that has passed. For example, if a company accepts a $5,000, 3-month, 5% interest-bearing note receivable from a customer on February 1, 2011, interest will be earned on March 1, April 1, and May1, and would be calculated as follows for each month: $5,000 \times 0.05 \times 1/12 = \$20.83$.

The journal entries for this note receivable would be as follows:

Feb. 1 (acceptance of note receivable)		
Note receivable (A)	5,000.00	
Sales (SE)		5,000.00
Mar. 1 (recognition of first month's interest)		
Interest receivable (A)	20.83	
Interest revenue (SE)		20.83

Apr. 1 (recognition of second month's interest)

Interest receivable (A)	20.83	
Interest revenue (SE)		20.83

May 1 (recognition of third month's interest)

Interest receivable (A)	20.83	
Interest revenue (SE)		20.83

May 1 (collection of note and interest owed)

Cash (A)	5,062.49	
Note receivable (A)		5,000.00
Interest receivable (A)		62.49

When a company owns shares (has an investment) in another company, it may receive dividends from the other company. When dividends are declared by the board of directors of the other company, the company is legally obligated to distribute the dividends to shareholders in proportion to the number of shares owned. For example, assume that Hawke Company buys 500 shares in Axle Corporation. On June 1, 2011, the board of directors of Axle Corporation declared a dividend of $0.07 per share payable to shareholders on June 21, 2011. Hawke Company would record the following:

June 1 (date dividend declared)

Dividends receivable (A)	35	
Dividend revenue (SE)		35

June 21 (date dividend payment received)

Cash (A)	35	
Dividends receivable (A)		35

If a company owns a licence, copyright, patent, or other intangible asset, it could allow other companies to use the rights associated with the asset in return for a royalty. Royalty revenue is recognized on the accrual basis according to the contractual agreement that outlines the amount and timing of the payments. For example, assume that on September 24, 2011, Hawke Company purchased 10 airport taxi licences from the city for $5,000 each. Hawke does not own taxis but intends to resell the rights to individual taxi owners for $300 a month, payable monthly. On October 1, Hawke Company drew up a contract with Jonathan Wittly for the use of one taxi licence for six months. Hawke would record the following transactions:

Sept. 24 (purchase of taxi licences)

Taxi licences (A)	50,000	
Cash (A)		50,000

Oct. 1 (no journal entry because Jonathan Wittly has not used the licence yet)

Oct. 31 (one month of royalties earned by Hawke)

Licence royalty receivable (A)	300	
Licence royalty revenue (SE)		300

Companies often earn these types of revenue in addition to selling goods or performing services. As the following note shows, Brickworks Limited, the company you met earlier in the chapter and that sells bricks, tiles, and other building products, also has the kind of revenue described above:

BRICKWORKS LIMITED (2009)

Revenue

Interest revenue is recognized on a time proportionate basis that takes into account the effective interest rate applicable to the net carrying amount of the financial asset.

Dividend revenue is recognised when the right to receive a dividend has been established. Dividends received from associates and joint venture entities are accounted for in accordance with the equity method of accounting.

Rental revenue is recognized on an accrual basis

Revenue Recognized from Multiple Lines of Business

In businesses that have multiple lines of business or that sell products in either standard or customized models, the revenue recognition criteria may be met at different points for different products. The disclosures that follow for **Finning International Inc.** illustrate this point. Finning International is the largest Caterpillar equipment dealer in the world. Caterpillar equipment includes large construction and mining equipment like large earth movers used in highway construction.

FINNING INTERNATIONAL INC. (2009)

1. **Significant accounting policies**
   (o) **Revenue Recognition**
   Revenue recognition, with the exception of cash sales, occurs when there is a written arrangement in the form of a contract or purchase order with the customer, a fixed or determinable sales price is established with the customer, performance requirements are achieved, and ultimate collection of the revenue is reasonably assured. Revenue is recognized as performance requirements are achieved in accordance with the following:

   • Revenue from sales of equipment is recognized at the time title to the equipment and significant risks of ownership passes to the customer, which is generally at the time of shipment of the product to the customer;

   • Revenue from sales of equipment includes construction contracts with customers that involve the design, installation, and assembly of power and energy equipment systems. Revenue is recognized on a percentage of completion basis proportionate to the work that has been completed which is based on associated costs incurred;

   • Revenue from equipment rentals and operating leases is recognized in accordance with the terms of the relevant agreement with the customer, either evenly over the term of that agreement or on a usage basis such as the number of hours that the equipment is used; and

   • Revenue from product support services includes sales of parts and servicing of equipment. For sales of parts, revenue is recognized when the part is shipped to the customer or when the part is installed in the customer's equipment. For servicing of equipment, revenue is recognized as the service work is performed. Product support is also offered to customers in the form of long-term maintenance and repair contracts. For these contracts, revenue is recognized on a basis proportionate to the service work that has been performed based on the parts and labour service provided. Parts revenue is recognized based on parts list price and service revenue is recognized based on standard billing labour rates. Any losses estimated during the term of the contract are recognized when identified.

ethics in accounting

Pressures to show profit or growth in revenues, or both, can create ethical dilemmas for managers and accountants. Some of these pressures are self-imposed, particularly if the manager's compensation is tied to reported profits or revenues. Other pressures may be externally imposed by someone more senior in the organization or by the shareholders. Suppose, for example, that you are the accountant of a company division and the division manager has asked you to make an adjusting entry for the period to recognize a large order. Revenue in your company is usually recorded when the goods are shipped, not when the order is placed. The manager has indicated that this order will bump the division over its sales target for the year and that the bonuses of several managers in the division will be significantly affected. She has also said that the company is about to issue more common shares and that the company would like to show improved results from last year to get the most favourable price for the shares that will be issued. What should you do? Identify the individuals who will be helped and hurt by your decision, in order to help you determine what to do.

Ethics in Accounting

The choice of a revenue recognition policy is one of the critical policy decisions for a company. Current and future profitability measures will be affected by when revenue is recognized. Companies must choose a revenue recognition policy that is appropriate for their revenue streams and must disclose what that policy is so that users can make informed decisions.

STATEMENT OF EARNINGS FORMAT

One of the most fundamental objectives of financial reporting is to ensure that financial statements provide information that is useful to the users. To be useful, the information should enable investors, creditors, and other users to understand the enterprise's performance and financial position, and help them assess the amount, timing, and certainty of future net cash flows to the enterprise.

As you learned in Chapter 1, the purpose of the statement of earnings is to provide information about the company's performance. The statement summarizes all the revenues and expenses to show the net earnings or net income. The information is primarily historical. The revenues are the historical amounts received or receivable from the sale of goods and services, and the expenses are based on the amounts actually paid or payable for the goods and services that were used to produce the revenues. Some of the expenses may represent very old costs—for example, the depreciation of very old assets such as buildings.

For the statement of earnings to provide information about future cash flows, the connection between the amounts presented in the statement and those future cash flows must be understood. As you learned in this chapter, accrual-basis accounting requires that revenues and expenses be recorded at amounts that are ultimately expected to be received or paid in cash. For example, to estimate the actual amount of cash that will be collected from sales, the company estimates the amount of sales that will not be collected (bad debts) and deducts that amount from the sales. On the expense side, estimates are made for some expenses where amounts are not yet paid, such as for warranties or taxes. In both cases, the figures reflect management's estimates about future cash flows. Thus, the statement of earnings provides information to readers about management's assessment of the ultimate cash flows that will result from the period's operations. This means that the statement of earnings, prepared according to IFRS on an accrual basis, actually provides more information about future cash flows than a statement of earnings prepared on a cash basis, which only reflects the cash flows that have already occurred.

A second aspect of providing information about future cash flows is the statement's forecasting ability. If trends in the revenues and expenses over several time periods are examined, the revenues and expenses that will occur in the future may be predicted (assuming that trends in the past continue into the future). An understanding of how revenues and expenses are related to cash flows will allow a reasonable prediction of the amount of cash flows that will result in future periods.

The ability to predict future revenues and expenses depends on the type of item being considered, the industry in which the company operates, and the company's history. If the business is in a fairly stable product line, the sales revenues and cost of goods sold figures may be reasonably predictable. However, this type of forecasting is much more difficult for new businesses and new products.

Some other types of items on the statement of earnings are not very predictable. Sales of capital assets, for example, tend to be more sporadic than normal sales of goods or services. Some items may occur only once and cannot, therefore, be projected into the future. For example, the closing of a plant or the sale of a business unit is an event that has implications for the statement of earnings in the current period, but will likely not be repeated in the future.

To enable readers of the statement of earnings to make the best estimates or projections of future results, the continuing items should be separated from any non-continuing items. For this reason, the format of the statement is designed to highlight these differences.

Understand the difference between a multi-step statement of earnings and a single-step one.

In general terms, there are two approaches to presenting information on a statement of earnings: the multi-step format and the single-step format. We will illustrate and discuss the multi-step format first.

Exhibit 4-4 provides an overview of the major sections of a typical statement of earnings presented in the **multi-step format**.

MULTI-STEP STATEMENT OF EARNINGS FORMAT

EXHIBIT 4-4

Earnings from operations:		
Sales or service revenues	$XXX	
Cost of goods or services sold	(XXX)	
Gross profit (or *gross margin*)	XXX	
Other operating revenues	XXX	
Other operating expenses (e.g., selling, general, and administrative expenses)	(XXX)	
Earnings from operations		$XXX
Earnings from non-operating sources:		
Interest revenue and expense	$XXX	
Other non-operating revenues and expenses	XXX	
Gains (losses) on sales of capital assets or investments	XXX	
Earnings from non-operating sources		XXX
Gains (losses) from unusual or infrequent events		XXX
Earnings from continuing items, before tax		$XXX
Income tax expense (or *provision for income taxes*)		(XXX)
Earnings from continuing items (or *income before discontinued operations*)		$XXX
Gains (losses) from discontinued operations (net of tax)		XXX
Net earnings (income)		$XXX

The sections that follow discuss each of the major components.

Earnings from Operations

This section provides information about the revenues and expenses that result from selling goods and services. The operations that are reported are the company's normal operating activities that are expected to continue in the future. Later in the statement, there are sections for items that are not part of regular activities, including the results of any operations that management has decided to discontinue.

A distinguishing feature of many multi-step statements of earnings is that the statement starts with sales less the cost of the goods sold (or cost of sales), to arrive at a **gross profit** or **gross margin** amount. If a company's major source of revenue is selling goods, it must make enough profit or margin from the sales of its goods to cover all the other costs of operating the business. By examining the gross margin, users can assess the profitability of the company's products. You can also calculate a gross margin percentage, which is the gross margin divided by the sales. You can then use this percentage to evaluate a company's performance over time (by noting whether this percentage has been increasing, decreasing, or remaining stable) and to compare it with other companies in the same industry. The gross margin can therefore be a very informative and useful figure.

Following this, other normal operating revenues (if any) will be added, and all the usual operating expenses will be deducted, to show the amount of income that was generated from regular business operations that will continue in the future. For predictive purposes, this is usually a key figure on the statement of earnings.

Earnings from Non-Operating Sources

This section of the statement of earnings reports the results of transactions that are not part of the company's core operations. The typical types of items found here are interest income and expense, gains or losses on disposals of capital assets (such as property, plant, and equipment), and other events or transactions that are not considered part of the company's core business operations. IFRS guidelines do not strictly specify what should be included in each section of a multi-step statement.

Earnings from Unusual or Infrequent Events

Sometimes unusual or infrequent events occur that the company wants to segregate from the rest of its results so that statement readers can better understand the nature of the events and assess their continuing or noncontinuing status. For example, losses associated with a labour dispute or costs related to restructuring the organization might be reported here. Rather than being reported in a section by themselves, however, these types of items are often reported with the other non-operating items, discussed above.

Corporate Income Taxes

After the statement sections that have been discussed so far, there is a line item for corporate **income tax expense**, which is calculated on the net of all the items listed above. Sometimes the term **provision for income taxes** is used instead of income tax expense. Taxes are calculated based on the aggregate (total) income to this point.

The tax expense listed on a company's statement of earnings may not be the actual taxes that will be paid to the Canada Revenue Agency. The rules to calculate the taxes owed to the government are specified in the *Income Tax Act* and regulations. Although many of these rules parallel the accounting guidelines, there are some tax regulations that differ significantly from IFRS. When the amount of income tax expense for the period differs from the amount of tax that must be paid in the current period, the difference is shown as **deferred income tax**. This means that additional taxes will likely be paid in future years, as some of the income that was recognized currently, under accounting principles, becomes taxable in the future, based on the rules in the *Income Tax Act*. More will be said about these dual income tax calculations in future chapters.

Discontinued Operations

An additional item may appear after the calculation of income tax expense: **discontinued operations**. When a company has decided to discontinue a significant segment of its operations, it is important to segregate the results of the discontinuance from the ongoing operations. This item, therefore, appears below all the other items on the statement of earnings, including the income tax. This enables readers to focus on the earnings before the discontinued operations (frequently called *earnings from continuing operations*) as a key figure for predicting future income.

Because it appears after the calculation of income taxes, the tax effects of discontinued operations must be reported along with the items themselves. The company must pay taxes on these items, just as it does on the items in the upper part of the statement of earnings; so discontinued operations are reported on what is known as a **net-of-tax basis**. This means that the tax effect of each such item is subtracted from the original amount to produce a net, after-tax amount. If, for example, discontinued operations result in a gain of $1,000 before taxes and the tax on this is $400, the net-of-tax amount would be a $600 gain (i.e., the $1,000 gain minus the $400 tax expense related to it). Losses from discontinued operations are handled in the same way. For example, if discontinued operations result in a loss of $1,000 before taxes, which saves the company $400 in taxes (due to the deductibility of the loss), the net-of-tax amount would be a $600 loss (i.e., the $1,000 loss minus the $400 tax saving arising from it).

Discontinued operations are significant segments of the company that management has decided to eliminate. There are specific criteria for deciding what constitutes a discontinued operation; however, the basic idea is that this category involves dispositions where the business unit or segment can be clearly distinguished, both operationally and for financial reporting purposes, from the rest of the enterprise.

Once management has discontinued a segment of the company or a separately identifiable portion of its business, there are two types of results that must be reported in the discontinued operations section of the statement of earnings:

- The income earned by operating the business segment since the decision to discontinue it must be reported separately from other (continuing) income. Since the company has exited from this portion of its operations, it is important to show users what effect the discontinued business segment had on income.

- The gain or loss on the closure and disposal of the discontinued business segment must also be reported in the discontinued operations section of the statement of earnings.

Variations in Statement of Earnings Formats

An alternative to the multi-step format of the statement of earnings illustrated thus far is the **single-step format**. Exhibit 4-5 shows this approach.

Note that this method of presenting the statement of earnings contains the same data as the multi-step format shown earlier; the differences relate to how the data are organized in the statement. Although there are many variations in practice, the general idea of the single-step format is that all the revenues and gains (other than any related to discontinued operations) are listed together. Then, all the expenses and losses (other than any related to discontinued operations) are listed. As a result, there are fewer subsections and subtotals in a single-step statement, than in a multi-step statement.

To ensure that you grasp the difference between the multi-step and single-step approaches to the statement of earnings, take a few minutes to compare Exhibits 4-4 and 4-5. Notice that although they are organized quite differently, the same line items appear in each statement of earnings format. You should also note that, regardless of whether you use the multi-step or single-step format, discontinued operations have to be segregated in the bottom portion of the statement and shown on a net-of-tax basis.

EXHIBIT 4-5

SINGLE-STEP STATEMENT OF EARNINGS FORMAT

Revenues and gains:		
Sales or service revenues	$XXX	
Other operating revenues	XXX	
Interest revenue	XXX	
Other non-operating revenues	XXX	
Gains on sales of capital assets or investments	XXX	
Gains from unusual or infrequent events	XXX	
Total revenues and gains		$XXX
Expenses and losses:		
Operating expenses (e.g., cost of goods or services sold, selling expenses, general andadministrative expenses)	$XXX	
Interest expense	XXX	
Other non-operating expenses	XXX	
Losses on sales of capital assets or investments	XXX	
Losses from unusual or infrequent events	XXX	
Income tax expense (or *provision for income taxes*)	XXX	
Total expenses and losses		XXX
Earnings from continuing items (or *income before discontinued operations*)		$ XXX
Gains (losses) from discontinued operations (net of tax)		**XXX**
Net earnings (income)		$ XXX

Remember that the discontinued operations will not form part of the earnings in the future, so it is important to allow users to see what will continue into the future and what will not.

It should be noted that Exhibits 4-4 and 4-5 illustrate "pure" forms of multi-step and single-step statements of earnings. In actual practice, companies often use hybrid forms of these approaches, combining elements of both the multi-step and single-step formats in their statement of earnings. The statement of earnings for **WestJet Airlines** for 2009, which is shown in Exhibit 4-6, provides a good example of a hybrid form of presentation that includes elements of both the multi-step and single-step formats. It has revenues and expenses segregated (single-step characteristic) and then it has a segment that includes non-operating items (multi-step characteristic).

It should also be noted that published financial statements are often very condensed, with several items combined and presented as one line item. A consequence of this practice is that information on individual revenues and expenses is often unavailable. In particular, many companies do not disclose their cost of goods sold. Instead, they combine the cost of goods sold amount with other operating expenses and report the combined figure as a single amount. (An example of this can be seen in the income statement for H&M, in Appendix A. **H&M** combines its cost of goods sold with some of its salaries and depreciation, and reports these items as a single amount with reference to Notes 6 and 8.) The usual reason for doing this is that, for competitive reasons, companies do not wish to reveal their cost of goods sold. Unfortunately, when the cost of goods sold is not disclosed, it is not possible to calculate a gross profit figure; as a result, the statement of earnings is less informative and useful to readers.

WESTJET AIRLINES LTD. 2009 ANNUAL REPORT

EXHIBIT 4-6

Consolidated Statement of Earnings

For the years ended December 31
(Stated in thousands of Canadian dollars, except per share amounts)

	2009	2008
		Restated – see note 2
Revenues:		
Guest revenues	$ 2,067,860	$ 2,301,301
Charter and other revenues	213,260	248,205
	2,281,120	2,549,506
Expenses:		
Aircraft fuel	570,569	803,293
Airport operations	352,333	342,922
Flight operations and navigational charges	298,762	280,920
Marketing, general and administration	208,316	211,979
Sales and distribution	172,326	170,693
Depreciation and amortization	141,303	136,485
Inflight	112,054	105,849
Aircraft leasing	103,954	86,050
Maintenance	96,272	85,093
Employee profit share	14,675	33,435
	2,070,564	2,256,719
Earnings from operations	210,556	292,787
Non-operating income (expense):		
Interest income	5,601	25,485
Interest expense	(67,706)	(76,078)
Gain (loss) on foreign exchange	(12,306)	30,587
Loss on disposal of property and equipment	(1,177)	(701)
Gain (loss) on derivatives (note 13(b))	1,828	(17,331)
	(73,760)	(38,038)
Earnings before income taxes	136,796	254,749
Income tax expense: (note 9):		
Current	2,690	2,549
Future	35,928	73,694
	38,618	76,243
Net earnings	$ 98,178	$ 178,506
Earnings per share: (note 10(c)):		
Basic	$ 0.74	$ 1.39
Diluted	$ 0.74	$ 1.37

The accompanying notes are an integral part of the consolidated financial statements.

Examples of Actual Statements of Earnings

Exhibit 4-7, which shows the consolidated income statement for **Michelin Group**, provides an example of the multi-step income statement format. Michelin is an international company with its headquarters in France. Its main product line is the manufacture and sale of tires. Notice that its income statement begins with sales minus cost of sales, to give a subtotal called gross income. This represents the profit that was earned on the company's sales. Then, the company's operating expenses (i.e., its sales and marketing, research and development, general and administrative, and other expenses) and non-recurring profits and expenses related to its operations are shown, resulting in a subtotal for operating income. The statement then includes non-operating items, including cost of debt (interest expense), other financial income and expenses, and its share of profit/losses from associates (companies in which it is holding a block of shares), which are added or deducted to give a subtotal for *income before taxes*. Finally, the income taxes are deducted, giving the net income for the year.

EXHIBIT 4-7

annual report

EXAMPLE OF A MULTI-STEP INCOME STATEMENT; MICHELIN GROUP 2009 ANNUAL REPORT

CONSOLIDATED INCOME STATEMENT

(in EUR million, except per share data)	2009	2008	2007	2006	2005
Net sales	14,807	16,408	16,867	16,384	15,590
Cost of sales	(10,527)	(12,024)	(11,760)	(11,653)	(10,835)
Gross income	4,280	4,384	5,107	4,731	4,755
Sales and marketing expenses	(1,650)	(1,730)	(1,738)	(1,799)	(1,775)
Research and development expenses	(506)	(499)	(561)	(591)	(565)
General and administrative expenses	(1,113)	(1,161)	(1,069)	(965)	(999)
Other operating income and expenses	(149)	(74)	(94)	(38)	(48)
Operating income before non-recurring income and expenses	862	920	1,645	1,338	1,368
Non-recurring profits	-	-	-	-	256
Non-recurring expenses	(412)	(77)	(326)	(220)	(50)
Operating income	450	843	1,319	1,118	1,574
Cost of net debt	(292)	(330)	(294)	(315)	(310)
Other financial income and expenses	40	(3)	29	135	30
Share of profit/(loss) from associates	9	10	17	4	6
Income before taxes	207	520	1,071	942	1,300
Income tax	(103)	(163)	(299)	(369)	(411)
Net income	104	357	772	573	889
• Attributable to Shareholders of the Company	106	360	774	572	889
• Attributable to non-controlling interests	(2)	(3)	(2)	1	-
Earnings per share (in euros)					
• Basic	0.71	2.46	5.32	3.95	6.13
• Diluted	0.71	2.46	5.22	3.94	6.12

In Exhibit 4-8, the consolidated statements of earnings and statements of comprehensive income for **Suncor Energy Inc.** provide an example of a statement of earnings prepared using the single-step format. Suncor is a major North American energy producer focused on the oil sands of northern Alberta. Notice that all the company's revenues are listed together, totalling $25,480 million for the year ended December 31, 2009. Then all its expenses (except income taxes) are listed, totalling $24,191 million, resulting in earnings before taxes of $1,289 million for 2009. After corporate taxes totalling $143 million (of which $725 million will likely result in tax savings in the future), Suncor Energy shows net earnings for the year of $1,146 million.

Earnings Per Share

IFRS stipulates that **earnings per share** figures must be reported, either in the statement of earnings itself or in a note accompanying the financial statements. The earnings per share figures express the amount of income earned during the period in relation to

**EXAMPLE OF A SINGLE-STEP STATEMENT OF EARNINGS;
SUNCOR ENERGY INC. 2009 ANNUAL REPORT**

EXHIBIT 4-8

annual report

CONSOLIDATED STATEMENTS OF EARNINGS

For the years ended December 31 ($ millions)	2009	2008 (restated)	2007 (restated)
Revenues			
Operating revenues (notes 4 and 22)	**18 658**	18 179	15 193
Less: Royalties	**(1 199)**	(890)	(691)
Operating revenues (net of royalties)	**17 459**	17 289	14 502
Energy supply and trading activities (notes 4 and 5)	**7 577**	11 320	2 782
Interest and other income (note 2e)	**444**	28	30
	25 480	28 637	17 314
Expenses			
Purchases of crude oil and products	**7 383**	7 582	6 414
Operating, selling and general (note 15)	**6 641**	4 186	3 450
Energy supply and trading activities (notes 4 and 5)	**7 381**	11 323	2 870
Transportation	**427**	246	160
Depreciation, depletion and amortization	**2 306**	1 049	864
Accretion of asset retirement obligations	**155**	64	48
Exploration (note 21)	**268**	90	95
Loss on disposal of assets	**66**	13	7
Project start-up costs	**51**	35	68
Financing expenses (income) (note 6)	**(487)**	917	(211)
	24 191	25 505	13 765
Earnings Before Income Taxes	**1 289**	3 132	3 549
Provisions for (Recovery of) Income Taxes (note 7)			
Current	**868**	514	382
Future	**(725)**	481	184
	143	995	566
Net Earnings	**1 146**	2 137	2 983
Net Earnings Per Common Share (dollars) (note 8)			
Basic	**0.96**	2.29	3.23
Diluted	**0.95**	2.26	3.17
Cash dividends	**0.30**	0.20	0.19

CONSOLIDATED STATEMENT OF COMPREHENSIVE INCOME

Years ended December 31 ($ millions)	2009	2008	2007
Net earnings	**1 146**	2 137	2 983
Other comprehensive income (loss), net of tax (notes 4 and 20)			
Change in foreign currency translation adjustment	**(332)**	350	(195)
Gain on derivative contracts designated as cash flow hedges	**2**	—	5
Comprehensive Income	**816**	2 487	2 793

See accompanying Summary of Significant Accounting Policies and Notes.

the number of common shares held by the owners. Although this can be a complex calculation in some situations, in essence it is a simple one that consists of dividing the earnings by the number of common shares outstanding during the period. If the number of common shares outstanding changed during the year, a weighted average number of shares must be used. Calculating a weighted average means determining each increase or decrease in the number of shares outstanding during the year and calculating an average based on the length of time each level of shares remained outstanding. For example, if a company started the year with 100,000 shares and on July 1, issued an additional 20,000 shares, the weighted average number of shares would be:

$$100,000 \times 6/12 = 50,000$$
$$120,000 \times 6/12 = \underline{60,000}$$
$$110,000 \text{ weighted average number of shares outstanding}$$

Look at the disclosure of earnings per share in Exhibit 4-8 for Suncor Energy. The basic earnings per share figure was $0.96 for 2009 (versus $2.29 for 2008 and $3.23 for 2007). Note that another earnings per share amount is also reported, called diluted earnings per share. The **diluted earnings per share** figure is usually lower than the basic earnings per share; for Suncor, it was $0.95 for 2009 (versus $2.26 for 2008 and $3.17 for 2007). The inclusion of the diluted earnings per share figure is a signal to users that the company has some financial instruments such as convertible debt (the company will allow the debt holder to turn it in and receive shares in exchange), or some obligations such as stock options given to its employees, that could result in more common shares being issued. Since the earnings per share amount is calculated by dividing the earnings by the number of shares outstanding, if more shares are issued, then the amount earned per share could decline. The diluted earnings per share amount shows how much the earnings per share would have declined if new shares had been issued as a result of existing financial instruments and obligations.

In addition, when companies have discontinued operations, they must report earnings per share amounts based on the income both before and after such items. This means that, in an extreme case in which a company had financial instruments or obligations that could result in more common shares being issued, as well as discontinued operations, the company would have to report four earnings per share amounts: both basic and diluted earnings per share, and calculated for both on the earnings before discontinuing operations and on the net earnings. Chapter 12 discusses earnings per share calculations in more detail.

Comprehensive Income

The Accounting Standards Board and the IFRS require companies to report comprehensive income, as well as net earnings, in their financial statements. **Comprehensive income** is defined as the total change in the shareholders' equity (or net assets) of the enterprise from non-owner sources. It includes all the changes in shareholders' equity during a period, not including investments by owners or distributions to owners. Net earnings is, therefore, part of comprehensive income because it causes a change in retained earnings, which is part of shareholders' equity.

Besides net earnings, there are other items that cause changes in shareholders' equity. For example, some gains and losses (such as certain gains or losses arising from the translation of foreign currencies, unrealized gains or losses arising from changes in the fair values of certain types of financial investments, and unrealized gains and losses from revaluations of long-term assets to market value) are not included in the determination of net earnings but are included in comprehensive income. Comprehensive income is therefore broader than net earnings. It includes net earnings plus a few other specified items.

Some of the concepts and procedures related to this issue are very complex. At this introductory level, you should focus on the basic concept that companies are required to present certain gains and losses outside net income, in a category referred to as **other comprehensive income**, which will then be combined with the net earnings to give the comprehensive income or loss. These other elements of the comprehensive income may be presented on the statement of earnings, immediately below the net income, or in a separate statement that begins with the net earnings. In either case, the final total is the comprehensive income for the period. In Exhibit 4-8, Suncor presents a statement entitled statement of comprehensive income just below its statement of earnings.

The concept of comprehensive income is based on an all-inclusive approach to earnings measurement. This means that all transactions affecting the net change in shareholders' equity during a period are to be included when determining income, except contributions (or investments) by the owners and distributions (or dividends) to them. To illustrate the reason for introducing the concept of comprehensive income, we will now see a simplified example of the distinction between net income and other comprehensive income.

Assume that a company buys shares in another company as a long-term investment. If the market value of this investment increases during the period, but the investment is still held, the increase in value can be reported in the net earnings, or the company could elect to include the gain in other comprehensive income. Because the gain is not considered realized until the investment is sold, the company may decide that it is better to include the gain in other comprehensive income so that there are no fluctuations in net earnings when the investment is revalued to market every year. (Bear in mind that, until the investment is sold, an unrealized gain is not "locked in." If the market value decreases before the investment is sold, the unrealized gain could be reduced or eliminated, or become a loss.) Later, when the investment is sold and the gains/losses are realized, the total change in value will be recognized as a gain/loss and transferred to net earnings.

Companies have to present comprehensive income and its components in a financial statement displayed with the same prominence as the rest of the financial statements. This statement must show net earnings, each component of other comprehensive income (on a net-of-tax basis), and the total comprehensive income. Note again that net earnings, as traditionally defined, is a component of comprehensive income (i.e., net earnings + other comprehensive income = total comprehensive income). Companies can decide to include other comprehensive income at the bottom of the statement of earnings (it is often called the statement of earnings and other comprehensive income) or they can prepare a separate statement of comprehensive income as Suncor does.

Exhibit 4-9 presents Finning International Inc.'s **statement of comprehensive income** from its 2009 annual financial statements.

As stated earlier, Finning International is a company that sells and services large construction equipment that carry the CAT brand. Note that the statement starts with net income. The first line under the net income states that all items are listed net of income tax. The items included are currency translation adjustments, unrealized gains on net investment hedges, tax recovery (expense) on net investment hedges, unrealized gains (losses) on cash flow hedges, realized losses on cash flow hedges, reclassified to earnings, and tax recovery (expense) on cash flow hedges. It is not important that you understand what all of these items mean. You should know, however, that there are some items that are not included in net earnings and retained earnings but are included in shareholders' equity and that might in the future be transferred to net earnings.

On the balance sheet, **accumulated other comprehensive income** would be shown, along with (but separate from) retained earnings. The shareholders' equity

EXHIBIT 4-9

annual report

FINNING INTERNATIONAL INC. 2009 ANNUAL REPORT

CONSOLIDATED STATEMENT OF COMPREHENSIVE INCOME

For years ended December 31 ($ thousands)	2009	2008
Net income	$ 130,823	$ 95,996
Other comprehensive income (loss), net of income tax		
Currency translation adjustments	(165,606)	60,536
Unrealized gains on net investment hedges	55,594	496
Tax recovery (expense) on net investment hedges	(18,040)	1,658
Foreign currency translation and gain (losses) on net investment hedges	(128,052)	62,690
Unrealized gains (losses) on cash flow hedges	10,318	(11,851)
Realized losses on cash flow hedges, reclassified to earnings	2,657	1,565
Tax recovery (expense) on cash flow hedges	(2,348)	3,375
Gains (losses) on cash flow hedges	10,627	(6,911)
Comprehensive income	$ 13,398	$ 151,775

section of Finning International is presented in Exhibit 4-10 to illustrate where it appears on the balance sheet.

Rather than presenting the details on the balance sheet itself, most companies will summarize the changes in their shareholders' equity accounts in a separate statement, and then present only the final amounts on the balance sheet. The statement of changes in equity will be discussed in more detail in Chapter 11.

PERFORMANCE MEASUREMENT

LEARNING OBJECTIVE 9

Describe how the return on investment can give you one measure of performance.

Now that you have a good idea about the various ways that revenue can be recognized and a better understanding of the components of the statement of earnings, let's use that information to have a closer look at how we can measure performance. After making an investment, investors want to know how well their investment is performing. To put this in a simple context, suppose an investment is made in a savings account at a bank. The money is put in the bank so that it can earn something and it is safe. Periodically, the bank provides information that details any new deposits or withdrawals and any interest earned on the savings. The interest earned can then be compared with the balance in the account to indicate the investment's performance. The comparison of the interest earned to the balance in the account is called a ratio. Ratios can help us assess performance.

The Return on Investment (ROI) Ratio as a Measure of Performance

A common measure of business performance is a ratio called the **return on investment (ROI)**, which is generally calculated as follows (in Chapter 12 we will discuss several other ratios that also calculate returns):

SHAREHOLDERS' EQUITY SECTION OF A BALANCE SHEET— FINNING INTERNATIONAL INC. 2009 ANNUAL REPORT

EXHIBIT 4-10

annual report

CONSOLIDATED BALANCE SHEETS

December 31 ($ thousands)	2009	2008
SHAREHOLDERS' EQUITY		
Share capital (Note 7)	$ 557,052	$ 554,966
Contributed surplus	33,509	25,441
Accumulated other comprehensive loss	(293,869)	(176,444)
Retained earnings	1,218,994	1,163,141
Total shareholders' equity	1,515,686	1,567,104
	$3,671,435	$4,720,375

SIGNED

The accompanying Notes to the Consolidated Financial Statements are an integral part of these statements.

$$ROI = \frac{Return}{Average\ investment}$$

LEARNING OBJECTIVE 10

Calculate the return on investment under some basic scenarios.

In the case of the bank account, the numerator is the interest earned during the period, and the denominator is the average amount invested over the period. By averaging the denominator, additional deposits or withdrawals made during the period are taken into account. A simple average of the beginning balance and the ending balance in the investment is often used; however, more sophisticated averaging methods may be more appropriate. Suppose the average investment in a bank account was $1,000, and the return was $50. The ROI from the investment would be calculated as follows:

$$ROI = \frac{\$50}{\$1,000} = 5\%$$

Based on this return, two questions might be asked: (1) Is this a good return on investment? And (2) how confident is the investor that this really is the return? To answer the first question, the return on this investment should be compared with the returns that could have been earned on alternative investments, or with the returns that similar investors are earning. If the next best alternative of similar risk would have returned only 4%, the bank account was a good investment. If, however, investors are earning 6.5% for similar investments, it would seem that this was not the best investment.

To answer the second question, the investors must assure themselves that their $1,000 investment plus their $50 return is really worth $1,050 today. Ultimately, the only way to be sure that the investment is worth $1,050 is to sell the investment—that is, to withdraw the $1,050 from the bank. If the investors do not sell the investment, there is still some chance that the bank will not have the money to repay them; the bank might, for example, file for bankruptcy. In the late 1980s and early 1990s, this was not an inconceivable event, as several small Canadian banks went out of business. More recently, several banks in the United States have gone out of business. In Canadian banks that are insured by the Canada Deposit Insurance Corporation (CDIC), small accounts (those up to $100,000) are insured so that, even in the event of a bank

HELPFUL HINT

Risk is the potential that you will not earn the interest that you are expecting and/or that you will not be able to get your initial investment back when you want it. Both of these aspects of risk depend on the investment's financial health and viability.

collapse, the investor would still be repaid by the CDIC. A bank account of this type is about the safest investment you can make. An uninsured account would not give you the same comfort level regarding the possible failure of the banking institution.

Now suppose that instead of investing in a savings account, an investment is made in a house. Assume that the house is bought for investment purposes for $250,000. The buyer is hoping the property value will rise. Assume also that there are no further cash outlays or inflows during the year from this investment. To assess the return on the investment, the investment's value at the end of the period must be determined. This value could be estimated by getting the house appraised by a real estate agent, or by comparing the house with the selling prices of similar houses in the area that have recently sold. In either case, the value will be an estimate. Confidence in these estimates will surely be lower than the confidence in the return earned from the investment in the savings account at the bank. In fact, the only certain way to determine the return on the house would be to sell it. If the investor does not want to sell the property, however, the only alternative would be to use an estimate of the selling price to measure performance. If the investor estimates the selling price to be $270,000, the ROI will be calculated as follows:

$$\text{ROI} = \frac{\$270,000 - \$250,000}{\$250,000} = 8\%$$

Measuring the performance of a business is much like estimating the return on the investment in a house. The business makes investments in capital assets (property, plant, and equipment), inventory, accounts receivable, and other assets, and it periodically measures the performance of these investments. However, it does not want to sell its investment in these assets at the end of every accounting period simply to determine the proper ROI. It must, therefore, estimate any changes in the value of its assets and liabilities that may have occurred during the accounting period, and report these as net earnings. We then use that net earnings amount to calculate two more specific kinds of ROI that you will see in greater detail later in the book. The first is a return on assets (ROA). This ratio measures the amount of income earned per $1 of assets. It attempts to provide the user with information about how effectively the assets are being used to generate earnings. The second ratio is the return on equity (ROE). This ratio measures the amount of income earned per $1 invested in the company's shares. It provides users with information about the amount of return being earned by shareholders. They can compare this ROE with investments of other types and risks to determine whether investing in this company is still a good idea.

Some of the changes in value (returns) are easy to measure, such as the interest earned on a savings account. Other changes, such as the change in the value of property, plant, and equipment, are not as easily measured, as the example concerning the investment in a house demonstrates. Because accounting data should be reliable as well as relevant (as we discussed in Chapter 1), accountants have established concepts and guidelines for recognizing the changes in value of assets and liabilities. This ensures that the measurement of performance that is most commonly used (net earnings) reliably measures the effects of the transactions that took place during the period.

Net Earnings as a Measure of Performance

The statement of earnings attempts to measure the return to the shareholders on their investment in the company; that is, it measures changes in shareholders' wealth in the company. The accounting value of this shareholders' wealth is measured by the value of shareholders' equity accounts. Remember that these accounts include common shares, retained earnings, and accumulated other comprehensive income.

Shareholders' equity accounts are typically affected by three general types of transactions: shareholder investment activities, the declaration of dividends, and transactions that result in profits or losses. Shareholders may invest more money in the company by buying, for example, new shares when they are issued. This does not directly affect their return on the investment, but does affect the amount of investment they have in the company. Second, shareholders may receive a dividend (via a declaration by the board of directors) that reduces their wealth in the company by reducing the company's total assets. This also does not directly affect the return on investment, but again affects the amount of the investment. Finally, transactions that result in profits or losses will affect shareholders' wealth through their effects on retained earnings. It is this last set of transactions and their impact on value that are measured by the statement of earnings.

Because the company does not want to sell its investments at the end of each period to determine its performance, the net earnings amount is used as part of several ratios that inform users about how their investment is doing. Now that you have a better idea of the various ways that revenue can be determined, you can better assess the underlying strength of the net earnings amount. You also understand the value of reading the notes to the financial statements to learn about the company's revenue recognition policy.

SUMMARY

In this chapter, we first discussed the importance of revenue to a company's overall health, which led to an explanation of why we have established revenue recognition criteria. We then explained the cash-to-cash cycle and its importance in understanding a company's performance. Tied to the cash-to-cash cycle are the concepts underlying the recognition of revenue. We introduced the concept of earnings management to increase your awareness of how the management of a company can set revenue and expense recognition policies to make its net earnings higher or lower in particular accounting periods, or smoother over time. We looked at revenue recognition for the sale of goods, the rendering of services, and the receipt of revenues from allowing others to use the company's assets in return for interest, royalties, and dividends. In the sale of goods discussion, we illustrated revenue recognition at the time of sale, at contract signing, at the time of production, and at the time of collection. We explored these concepts to improve your understanding of net earnings as a measure of business performance. Companies use different revenue recognition criteria according to the type of revenue they are generating. When assessing a company's performance, it is important to understand the type of revenue the company is generating and the revenue recognition policy it has established. If you know these two things, you will be better able to understand its cash-to-cash cycle. We then built on your previous understanding of the statement of earnings. We showed you some of the complexities of the statement of earnings, such as earnings from operations, non-operating earnings, unusual or infrequent items, income taxes, discontinued operations, and earnings per share. We introduced a new statement, the statement of comprehensive income. As we progress through the text, you will have some of these items explained more fully. We then concluded the chapter with a brief look at some measures of performance, or returns on investment. These measures enable users to better assess how their investments are doing.

While net earnings is a useful measure of performance, it is not the only measure in which users of financial statements should be interested. In the next chapter, the cash flow statement is considered. We had a brief look at this statement in Chapters 1 and 2. Chapter 5 will explore it in more detail by showing how the statement is created and how to interpret its information. We will also discuss the implications for a company's health of some matters that are not shown on the statement of earnings.

PRACTICE PROBLEM 1

Additional Practice Problems

Jonathan, Anthony, and Kendra operate a bicycle shop, The Silver Spoke. They sell assembled bicycles and bicycle accessories. They have a shop in the back where Kendra repairs bicycles. Occasionally they are given a contract to assemble 20 to 50 bicycles for a major retailer. Customers use either cash or credit cards when buying bicycles or bicycle accessories. For minor repairs, the customer pays when the repairs are done. For major repairs, The Silver Spoke asks for a down payment equal to 25% of the repair's estimated cost. The remaining 75% is paid when the work is complete. When the company assembles bicycles for another retailer, it bills the retailer when the work is done. The company normally receives payment within 30 days of submitting the bill.

Required:
Based on the revenue recognition criteria, recommend when The Silver Spoke should recognize revenue for each of its various revenue-generating activities. Provide a rationale for each of your recommendations.

STRATEGIES FOR SUCCESS:

▶ Start by identifying the various ways that The Silver Spoke generates revenue. Then look at the flow of cash from each type of revenue. Next, identify when the company has completed the performance required for each type of revenue—when the customer takes possession of the goods, when the work that was agreed to is finished, when the amount earned is known, or when the total of the costs associated with the revenue is known.

▶ Remember to look for things that take a long time to do versus those that are completed in a short time. If the time is short, probably the time of sale/delivery of the goods is appropriate. If the time is long, you may need to look at percentage of completion or collection of cash.

▶ Keeping these items in mind, go back through your notes on the various applications of revenue recognition and select the most appropriate method of revenue recognition.

PRACTICE PROBLEM 2

Suppose that Guenther Construction Ltd. is in the construction business. In 2011, it enters into a contract with a customer to construct a building. The contract price is $10 million, and the building's estimated cost is $6 million. The construction is estimated take three years to complete.

Required:
Prepare a schedule of the revenues and expenses that would be recognized in income in each of the three years with each of the following methods:

a. Recognition of income at contract signing.

b. Percentage of completion method, assuming the following schedule of estimated costs:

Year	Amount
2011	$3,000,000
2012	$1,800,000
2013	$1,200,000

STRATEGIES FOR SUCCESS:

▶ Part "a" asks for the recognition of revenue at contract signing. Remember that recognizing the income at contract signing will result in the immediate recognition of all the revenue and an estimate of all the expenses. Because of the length of time to complete the contract, it is unlikely that this would satisfy the performance criteria for revenue recognition.

▶ Create a table similar to the one in this chapter that shows the year, degree of completion, recognized revenue, recognized expenses, and profit. This will create a framework for your answer to part "b."

SUGGESTED SOLUTION TO PRACTICE PROBLEM 1

Sales of bicycles and bicycle accessories: The company should recognize revenue at the time of sale. Since the customer leaves with the merchandise, there is a transfer of title and the company's involvement with the goods therefore stops. The amount earned is also measurable and has been collected either in cash or through a credit card. The costs associated with the sale are known as well.

Minor repairs: The company should recognize revenue when the work is completed. Similar to the situation with the sale of bicycles, the company's work is complete, the customer has paid, so the amount of revenue can be measured reliably, and the costs associated with the repairs are also known.

Major repairs: The company should recognize revenue when the work is completed. When the customer makes the 25% down payment, the work has not yet been started. As well, the total amount owed is still unknown, although it has been estimated to determine the 25% down payment. Therefore, the revenue cannot be measured reliably. The costs associated with the work may also not be known yet. The company should record the down payment as unearned revenue. When the repairs are done, the company will have completed the work (therefore earned the revenue) and the total amount owed is known. The customer pays for the work with cash or a credit card so the collectibility is assured. All of the costs associated with the work are also known. At this time, revenue recognition criteria have been met. Although it is a major repair, the work will likely be completed in a reasonably short time, which means the delay in revenue recognition will not be very long.

Assembly contract: The company should recognize revenue when the assembly work is complete. At the time of the contract signing, although the company knows how much it will receive and is confident that it will receive that amount, it has not yet assembled any bicycles. Because a substantial amount of work remains to be done, the company has not earned the revenue. When the work is complete, the amount earned is known and it is reasonable to assume that the company will collect the amount owed. As well, the costs associated with the assembly of the bicycles are also known. At this time, the revenue recognition criteria have been met and revenue should be recognized.

SUGGESTED SOLUTION TO PRACTICE PROBLEM 2

a. Recognizing revenue at the time of contract signing would probably not be appropriate because of the contract's extended construction period. If it were appropriate, all the profit, $4 million ($10 million – $6 million), would be recognized in the first year and none in later years. As well, all of the estimated costs would also have to be recognized.

practice problems

b. Percentage of completion method (answers in thousands)

Year	Degree of Completion			Revenue Recognized		Expenses Recognized	Profit
2011	$3,000 ÷ $6,000 =	50%		50% × $10,000 =	$ 5,000	$3,000	$2,000
2012	$1,800 ÷ $6,000 =	30%		30% × $10,000 =	$ 3,000	1,800	1,200
2013	$1,200 ÷ $6,000 =	20%		20% × $10,000 =	$ 2,000	1,200	800
		100%			$10,000	$6,000	$4,000

ABBREVIATIONS USED

F.O.B.   Free on board
ROA   Return on assets
ROE   Return on equity
ROI   Return on investment

SYNONYMS

Gross margin ▌ Gross profit
Net earnings ▌ Net income
Statement of earnings ▌ Income statement
Tax expense ▌ Provision for taxes ▌ Tax provision

GLOSSARY

Account receivable   An amount owing as a result of the sale of a product or service.

Accumulated other comprehensive income   A component of shareholders' equity representing the cumulative amount of unrealized increases and decreases in the values of the net assets of the entity. Once realized, these gains/losses are transferred to retained earnings.

Cash discount   A reduction in the amount that has to be paid on an account payable or receivable if payment is made within a specified time limit.

Cash-to-cash cycle   A company's operating cycle: its operating activities beginning with the initial outlays of cash to buy a product or to provide a service and ending with the replacement of cash through collections from customers.

Comprehensive income   The total change in the shareholders' equity (net assets) of the entity from non-owner sources. Includes net income as well as other components, which generally represent unrealized gains and losses.

Deferred income tax   An asset or liability representing tax on the difference between the accounting balance of assets/liabilities at a given point in time and the tax balance of the same assets/liabilities. These differences arise when the company uses one method for accounting purposes and a different method for tax purposes. This concept is discussed in more detail in Chapter 8.

Diluted earnings per share   An earnings per share calculation that shows what the company's basic earnings per share would have been reduced to if financial instruments such as convertible debt or obligations such as employee stock options had caused more common shares to be issued.

Discontinued operations   Business operations that have been (or are being) phased out or sold and will, therefore, not continue in the future. They are reported separately on the statement of earnings.

Earnings management   The deliberate choice of revenue and expense recognition methods that will increase or decrease net income in particular accounting periods or smooth them over time.

Earnings per share A calculation in which income or earnings are divided by the average number of common shares outstanding during the period.

Expenses The costs incurred to earn revenues.

Gross margin Sales minus cost of goods sold. Synonym for gross profit.

Gross profit Synonym for gross margin.

Income tax expense The expense for income taxes. A synonym for provision of taxes.

Matching principle The concept that requires all expenses related to the production of revenues to be recorded during the same time period as the related revenues. The expenses are said to be matched with the revenues.

Measurement The process of determining an appropriate amount or value for some attribute of the item being measured.

Multi-step statement of earnings A statement of earnings in which revenues and expenses from different sources are shown in separate sections.

Net earnings The difference between revenues and expenses. Synonym for net income.

Net income Synonym for net earnings.

Net-of-tax basis The presentation of a gain or loss with the related income tax deducted from it, to show the remaining amount after tax.

Operating activities Activities involving the cash effects of the normal operations of a business, such as the buying and selling of goods and services.

Other comprehensive income Changes in net asset values representing unrealized gains and losses, which are not included in net earnings but are included in comprehensive income.

Percentage of completion method A method of revenue recognition used in the construction industry in which a percentage of the profits that are expected to be realized from a given project is recognized in a given period, based on the percentage of the project's completion. The percentage completed is typically measured as the fraction of costs incurred to date relative to the total estimated costs to complete the project.

Performance The work associated with the generation of revenue. Used in a similar way to the term "earned."

Price allowance An adjustment made to the selling price of a good or service to satisfy a customer, typically for some defect in the good or service provided.

Provision for income taxes The expense for income tax. A synonym for income tax expense.

Recognition Recording an event in the accounting system and/or reporting an item in a financial statement, including both the description and the amount.

Return on investment (ROI) A measure of an investment's performance, calculated as the ratio of the return from the investment to the average amount invested.

Revenue recognition criteria Criteria developed that specify the conditions under which revenue should be recognized.

Revenues The inflows of cash or other assets from the normal operating activities of a business, which mainly involve the sale of goods, provision of services, or allowing others to use the company's assets.

Single-step statement of earnings A statement of earnings in which all revenues are listed in one section and all expenses (except income tax, perhaps) are listed in a second section.

Statement of comprehensive income A statement showing net income plus other components of other comprehensive income, combined to produce the total comprehensive income.

ASSIGNMENT MATERIAL

Assessing Your Recall

4-1 Draw a diagram of a typical cash-to-cash cycle of a retail company and briefly explain the cycle's various components.

4-2 List the two basic revenue recognition criteria that exist under IFRS.

4-3 What are the three types of revenue that are typical of many companies?

4-4 Describe the five criteria for revenue recognition from the sale of goods.

WILEY PLUS
www.wileyplus.com

Self-Assessment Quiz

4-5 Explain the meaning of "performance has been achieved."

4-6 What is the most common point at which revenue is recognized for the sale of goods? How does this point meet the five criteria for revenue recognition?

4-7 Describe the revenue recognition method that is recommended for long-term construction contracts. What information do you need to know in order to apply this method?

4-8 Describe how revenue is recognized for mining companies that extract ore.

4-9 Explain the meaning of the matching principle.

4-10 Describe the accounting treatment for a deposit made by a customer for the future delivery of inventory. Using the revenue recognition criteria, explain the rationale for this treatment.

4-11 Identify and briefly describe the major sections of a multi-step statement of earnings.

4-12 How does the single-step statement of earnings differ from the multi-step statement of earnings? Do they produce different net income? Explain.

4-13 What two types of disclosures are made in the statement of earnings with regard to discontinued operations? Why are these items segregated to the bottom of the statement of earnings?

4-14 What kind of items are included on the statement of comprehensive income? Explain where these items are included in shareholders' equity.

4-15 Explain how ROI measures performance.

Applying Your Knowledge

4-16 (Revenue recognition criteria)

In the opening story to this chapter, the owner of *Outpost* magazine explained how the company recognizes revenue. Using the revenue recognition criteria described in this chapter, explain the appropriateness of *Outpost*'s revenue recognition policies for revenue from advertisers and revenue from subscribers.

4-17 (Revenue recognition and statement of earnings)

Vanessa Simon and Juan Cassetto started a landscaping company as a way of earning money for the summer. They purchased two lawn mowers for $250 each, a leaf blower for $59, and various smaller items, such as rakes, a shovel, canvas, clippers, and pails, which cost them $63. Vanessa rented her father's van for $100 per month. They began work in May and worked through to the middle of September. They had several regular customers who paid them for managing their yards either once or twice a week. These customers paid them at the end of each week. They did the landscaping for three malls, watering and planting flowers and trimming hedges. They left an invoice with the mall manager every two weeks and received a cheque for the work the following week. They set up a separate bank account for their company and deposited money when they were paid. On September 15, they tallied up what they had earned over the summer. They had deposited $14,350 in the bank account, which represented the amount received from customers. One customer still owed them $150 for work and has promised to pay them on September 20. The final cheque from the mall manager for $136 had not arrived yet. In addition to the original amount spent at the beginning of summer, they paid for the following items: $100 per month for their two cell phones, $450 for gas and $39 for an oil change for the van, $20 for sunscreen, $250 for gas and oil for the lawn mowers, and $600 to rent a trailer to carry their equipment. Vanessa still owes her father for renting the van for the half month in September.

> **Required:**
> Prepare as much of the income statement for Simon and Cassetto as you can, showing the proper amount of revenue and any expenses that should be included. Show all calculations. Using the revenue recognition criteria, justify the revenue recognition method you

selected. Do you have a cost of goods sold? Why or why not? What other expenses do you think they would probably have?

4-18 (Revenue recognition and statement of earnings)

Dimitri Chekhov owns a medium-sized Russian restaurant called The Steppes. Most of his business is from customers who enjoy in-restaurant lunches and dinners and pay before they leave. He also provides catered food for functions outside of the restaurant. Because he needs to prepare the food in large quantities and transport it to the venue, he requires these customers to make a 40% deposit at the time of booking the event. The remaining 60% is due on the day of the function.

During 2011, the restaurant took in $736,432 from restaurant and catered sales. At year end, December 31, 2011, the catered sales amount included $12,678 for a convention scheduled for January 12, 2012. Dimitri paid $198,108 for food supplies during the year and $248,572 for wages for the chefs and other restaurant staff. The restaurant owed $6,161 in wages to its staff at year end, which will be paid on January 4, 2012, as part of the normal bi-weekly pay schedule.

> **Required:**
> Prepare as much of the income statement for The Steppes as you can, showing the amount of sales and any other amounts that should be included. Show all calculations. Using the revenue recognition criteria, justify the revenue recognition method you selected. Do you have a cost of goods sold? Why or why not? What other expenses do you think the restaurant probably has?

4-19 (Revenue recognition and statement of earnings)

The Warm as Toast Company installs furnaces and fireplaces in homes and businesses. Each furnace and fireplace carries a four-year warranty. During 2011, the company had sales of $835,000. Customers paid half of the sales price when they arranged for an installation and the other half when the furnace or fireplace was installed. At year end, $76,000 of the sales amount represented amounts paid for furnaces or fireplaces that were not yet installed and for which the second half of the payment had not yet been received. The cost associated with the sales was $407,000 for the furnaces and fireplaces that had been installed that year. An additional cost of $198,000 was incurred for the labour associated with the installation. The accountant estimated that total future warranty costs associated with the installed items would likely be $46,000 over the next five years.

> **Required:**
> Prepare as much of the income statement for The Warm as Toast Company for 2011 as you can, showing the proper amount of sales, cost of goods sold, gross profit, and any other amounts that can be included. Show all calculations. What other expenses do you think the company would probably have?

4-20 (Revenue recognition on long-term contract)

Allied Construction Company has signed a three-year contract to construct an apartment complex for $64 million. The expected costs for each year follow (in millions):

2011	$ 7.2
2012	20.1
2013	18.7
Total	$46.0

The apartment complex will be completed in 2013.

> **Required:**
> Calculate the total revenue, expense, and profit for each year using the percentage of completion method.

4-21 (Revenue recognition on long-term contract)

Atlantic Ferries arranged for Columbus Shipbuilders to build three new ferries for its Nova Scotia to Prince Edward Island run. Atlantic agreed to pay $22.5 million for the ferries ($7.5 million each). The contract was signed on June 30, 2011, with a delivery date of September 30, 2013. Atlantic agreed to pay the $22.5 million as follows:

$4 million at the signing of the contract
$9.5 million on December 31, 2012
$9 million on September 30, 2012 (at completion)

The following costs were incurred by Columbus Shipbuilders (in millions):

2011	$ 3.2
2012	7.1
2013	6.9
Total	$17.2

Required:

a. Calculate the revenue, expense, and profit (ignoring interest) that Columbus Shipbuilders should report for each of the three years, using the percentage of completion method.
b. What should Columbus Shipbuilders do if, in 2010, it determines that it will cost more than $22.5 million to complete the three ferries?

4-22   (Revenue recognition on a layaway sale)

Enchanted Brides sells complete bridal ensembles. The most expensive part of the ensemble is the wedding gown. Recognizing that some of its customers may not have enough immediate funds to purchase one of its gowns, the store provides a layaway plan. The customer selects a gown and the store agrees to hold the gown until it is paid for. The store sets up a monthly payment schedule for the customer, extending the payment time over six months to a year. The store charges an additional $35 for storage fees and $100 in possible default charges. If all payments are made on schedule, the default charge reduces the final payment. If the customer defaults, the $100 is not refunded.

Required:

Using the revenue recognition criteria, explain how the store should account for the monthly payments from the customer. Should the $35 storage fee be treated as revenue? Why or why not? Should the $100 default charge be treated as revenue? Why or why not? When should the store recognize the original cost of the wedding gown?

4-23   (Revenue recognition on gift cards)

The Carrot Top is a trendy clothing store that is very popular with young teens. Because it is difficult to select clothes that young people might wear, the store offers gift cards to parents, friends, and relatives. The cards are very popular, particularly for birthdays. When a card is purchased, the cashier identifies the purchase as a gift card and activates the card so that it can be used within 24 hours. There is no time limit on when the card must be used.

Required:

Using the revenue recognition criteria, explain how the store should account for the purchase of a gift card. Discuss how the store could account for gift cards that are not used. Is there a time when the store could assume that the card will not be used?

4-24   (Revenue recognition on long-term contract)

Concord Construction Inc. agreed to build a new science building on the Northern University campus. Both parties signed the contract on October 31, 2011, for $60 million, which is to be paid as follows:

$5 million at the signing of the contract
$15 million on December 31, 2011
$30 million on December 31, 2012
$10 million at completion, on August 15, 2013

The following costs were incurred by Concord Construction (in millions):

2011	$ 9.2
2012	20.4
2013	16.4
Total	$46.0

Required:
a. Calculate the revenue, expenses, and profit (ignoring interest) that Concord Construction should report for each of the three years, using the percentage of completion method.
b. Explain how this method appropriately allows Concord Construction to show the company's performance under the contract.

4-25 (Revenue recognition on long-term contract)

Cougar Builders Ltd. takes on both short- and long-term contracts. For short-term contracts (nine months or less), it recognizes expenses as they are incurred and revenue when the contract is complete, unless the contract is not complete by year end. When the contract spans two accounting periods, it uses the percentage of completion method for that contract. For long-term contracts (over nine months), it uses the percentage of completion method. It recently agreed to do two contracts. On June 30, 2011, the company agreed to a six-month contract to replace the bricks on the outside of an apartment building. The contract was for $650,000 and the company expected to incur costs of $480,000. The contract was completed by December 20, 2011, and had actual costs of $510,000.

The second contract was for the construction of a new apartment complex for $5,620,000. The contract was signed on August 1, 2011, and was expected to be finished by September 30, 2012. The expected costs for the contract are as follows:

Year	Cost
2011	$1,408,075
2012	2,676,985
Total	$4,085,060

Cougar Builders closes its books every December 31.

Required:
a. For each of the two contracts, determine the revenue, expense, and profit (loss) as at December 31, 2011.
b. Explain why the accounting method chosen for the two types of contracts is appropriate for Cougar Builders.

4-26 (Revenue recognition on long-term contract)

On June 21, 2011, Three Rivers Concrete Company signed a contract with Premier Power Incorporated to construct a dam over a river in northern British Columbia. The contract price was $42 million, and it was estimated that the project would cost Three Rivers Concrete $27 million to complete over a three-year period. On June 21, 2011, Premier Power paid Three Rivers Concrete $1.2 million as a default deposit. In the event that Premier Power backed out of the contract, Three Rivers Concrete could keep this deposit. Otherwise, the default deposit would apply as the final payment on the contract (assume, for accounting purposes, that this is treated as a deposit until contract completion). The other contractual payments are as follows:

Date	Amount
Oct. 15, 2011	$14,280,000
Apr. 15, 2012	6,120,000
Dec. 15, 2012	8,160,000
Mar. 15, 2013	7,956,000
Aug. 10, 2013	4,284,000
Total	$40,800,000

Estimated construction costs were as follows:

Year	Amount
2011	$12,150,000
2012	9,450,000
2013	5,400,000
Total	$27,000,000

The contract was completed on September 30, 2013. Solid Concrete closes its books on December 31 each year.

Required:

Calculate the revenue, expense, and profit to be recognized in each year, using the percentage of completion method.

4-27 (Revenue recognition decision)

After graduating with a degree in computer systems and design, Terry Park set up a business to design and produce computer games for arcades. Terry hired two other designers because of the anticipated volume of business. One designer, Kim, is paid an hourly wage. The second, Sandy, is paid 50% of the revenue received by Terry on the games designed or redesigned by Sandy. Terry rents an office where they all work and provides all the necessary equipment, supplies, and other items. Terry is not paid a wage but keeps all of the profits earned.

Terry realized there were two kinds of business: speculative design and custom design. For the speculative designs, Terry or one of the designers would think of a new game and design, program, and test it. Terry would then try to sell it to a distribution company, for either a fixed price or a percentage (which ranges from 10% to 25%) of the total revenues earned by the game. To date, Terry has sold three of the four games produced. He is currently negotiating the sale of the fourth game.

For the custom design business, Terry would receive an order from a distribution company for either the design of a new game or the redesign of an existing game (which occurs frequently because games have a useful life of only six months as players quickly get bored with them). Terry negotiates either a fixed fee payable upon completion, or an hourly rate based on the estimated length of time it should take to redesign the game. Terry sets the hourly rate based on the perceived difficulty of the project, but the rate is always at least triple the amount paid to Kim. For the hourly rate contracts, Terry submits monthly invoices showing the number of hours worked on the project.

Required:

a. Describe Terry's cash-to-cash cycle.
b. What revenue recognition options are open to Terry? Which one(s) would you recommend and why?
c. Using your recommended revenue recognition policy, how would you account for all of the costs incurred by Terry?

4-28 (Revenue recognition decision)

Juan Hernadez had seen many signs advertising house painters during the previous summers. Between his third and fourth year of university, he decided that he would start a painting business so that he could earn enough money to pay his tuition in the fall. He talked with a fellow student who ran a business like this the previous summer and knew the rates that he could charge. He made the following decisions: When he had a customer sign a contract for the inside or outside painting of a house, he would ask for a 20% down payment. The remainder of the contract price would be required when the job was completed. He made a deal with a local paint supplier for a discount on paint and other supplies. He assumed that most of the brushes and other painting supplies would be worth very little by summer's end, but he would sell off other supplies, such as ladders, when summer ended. If he needed a piece of equipment to do a job that he would likely not need again, he would rent it. His parents provided him with $500 in start-up money that needed to be repaid when he closed his business.

Required:

a. Describe Juan's cash-to-cash cycle.

b. What revenue recognition options are open to him? Which one would you recommend and why?

c. Using your recommended revenue recognition policy, how would Juan account for all the costs for his various contracts?

d. How should he account for the original loan that he received from his parents?

4-29 (Revenue recognition decision)

Sonya's Christmas Tree Company began operations on April 1, 2011, when she bought a parcel of land on which she intended to grow Christmas trees. The normal growth time for a Christmas tree is approximately six years, so she divided her land into seven plots. In 2011, she planted the first plot with trees and watered, cultivated, and fertilized her trees all summer. In 2012, she planted her second plot with trees and watered, cultivated, and fertilized both planted plots. She continued with her plantings and cultivation every year through 2017, when she planted the last plot. On November 1, 2017, she harvested the first plot of trees that she had planted in 2011. In 2018, she replanted the first plot.

Required:

a. Describe Sonya's cash-to-cash cycle.

b. What revenue recognition options are open to her? Which one would you recommend and why?

c. Using your recommended revenue recognition policy, how would Sonya account for all her costs for growing the trees?

4-30 (Revenue recognition decision)

Sparkling Cleaners operated six outlets in the city. At each outlet, customers could drop off clothes to be either dry cleaned or laundered. Clothes were normally ready for pickup within one to three days, and customers paid with cash, debit, or credit when they picked them up. Sparkling Cleaners had a central facility at which the clothing was cleaned. The company also had large contracts with hospitals and hotels. Under these contracts, laundry was picked up daily, cleaned, and returned the following day, and the customer was sent a weekly invoice for the laundry cleaned that week. Payment was due before the next invoice was sent out. Whenever a payment had not yet been received by the time that the next invoice needed to be sent, the unpaid amount was added to the new invoice.

Required:

a. Describe Sparkling Cleaners' cash-to-cash cycle. To do this, you will need to determine the types of expenditures that the company will likely incur in the operation of its business, as well as outline when the company receives cash in return for its services.

b. What revenue recognition options are open to the company with respect to its two types of customers? Which one would you recommend for each type of customer and why?

4-31 (Revenue recognition decision)

Carolina Dubasov enjoyed working with wood. She had a workshop set up in her backyard where she built articles of furniture, including tables, chairs, chests of drawers, end tables, and desks. She called her workshop C's Den of Wood. Every Saturday, she opened her workshop to the public and sold items of furniture that she had completed. Customers paid with cash or credit card. Sometimes customers asked her to make specific articles such as a table and six chairs or a bedroom suite. For these customers, she would draw up the plans. When the customer agreed to the design and the wood, she drew up a contract and asked for a 30% down payment. When the furniture was 60% completed, she showed it to the customer and collected another 30%. She collected the final 40% of the contract price when the furniture was completed.

Required:

a. Describe Carolina's cash-to-cash cycle.

b. What revenue recognition options are open to Carolina? Which one(s) would you recommend and why?

c. Using your recommended revenue recognition policy, how would you account for all the costs incurred by Carolina?

d. If a customer had signed a contract for a roll-top desk, paid the 30% down payment, and then decided he did not want the desk, should Carolina return the 30% down payment? Why or why not? How can she protect her business from this possibility?

4-32 (Statement of earnings presentation)

The following information is for Rooftop Ltd. for the year ended December 31, 2011:

Cost of goods sold	$175,000
Dividends declared	4,900
Dividend revenue	2,100
Gain on expropriation of land	5,600
Gain on sale of land	5,880
Interest expense	7,000
Loss from earthquake damage	13,300
Loss from flood damage	11,620
Income from operations of the company's Wholesale Division, which was closed (discontinued) during the year	2,800
Loss on sale of the Wholesale Division	44,800
Operating expenses	63,000
Sales revenue	287,000

The income tax rate is 40%. The company had 10,000 common shares outstanding throughout the entire year, and is located in a part of Ontario where earthquakes have rarely occurred before but floods have been known to happen in the past.

Required:

Prepare a statement of earnings, in single-step format, based on the information. (Note: Expropriation is a process by which governments can take over private property for public purposes. When property is expropriated, the owner has no choice but to sell it to the government.)

4-33 (Calculate ROI)

Calculate the ROI for the following independent investments:

a. Maria Chevas bought a GIC (guaranteed investment certificate) on June 1 for $3,000. The certificate reached maturity on December 1 (it was a six-month certificate). On December 1, she cashed in the certificate and received her original $3,000 back plus $37 in interest.

b. On January 2, Jim Wilson bought 10 shares of a pharmaceutical company for $12.00 a share. At year end, he received a dividend of $0.30 per share. At that time, the shares were trading for $12.50 per share.

c. Susan Blanchard bought a 25% interest in an outdoor adventure partnership for $15,000. During the year, the partnership earned net income of $50,000.

d. The Free-flow Plumbing Company had $250,000 in net assets (shareholders' equity) at the beginning of the year, and $280,000 at the end. During the year, it earned net income of $60,000.

e. Anastasia Kostovia bought a condo in Ottawa for $125,000. One year later, a real estate agent suggested that she could sell the condo for $130,000.

4-34 (Calculate ROI)

Calculate the ROI for the following independent investments:

a. The Cordova family bought a home in Calgary for $320,000. Two years later, a real estate agent told them that they could probably sell their home for $390,000.

b. Melrose Motor Company bought an investment in a supply company for $110,000. During the year, it received $4,000 in dividends.

c. Jack Valaas bought 5,000 shares in his sister's retail company for $20,000. The company earned net income of $72,000, which resulted in earnings per share of $3.75.

d. Margot Chan bought 10 shares in Transit Airlines for $6.60 per share. One year later, she had not received a dividend but the shares were selling at $8.10 per share.

e. Downing Disposal Company had $1,340,000 in assets at the beginning of the year and $1,150,000 at the end of the year. During the year, it earned net income of $120,000. (Assume that no new shares were issued during the year and no dividends were declared.)

User Perspective Problems

4-35 (Revenue recognition and earnings)

Financial analysts frequently refer to the quality of a company's earnings. By quality, they mean that the earnings are showing growth and are good predictors of future earnings. If you were looking for evidence of a company's quality of earnings, what would you look for on the financial statements?

4-36 (Changing revenue recognition policy to affect earnings)

Suppose that a company is currently private (its shares do not trade on a public stock exchange) but it is considering going public (issuing shares on a public stock exchange). Discuss the incentives that the company might have to misstate its income statement via its revenue recognition policies. If a company decided to change its revenue recognition policy to enhance its earnings, would the investors realize what it was doing? Where would a new investor look for information about the changes?

4-37 (Revenue recognition)

Suppose that a company has short- and long-term construction contracts. Explain how using the percentage of completion method for revenue recognition could meet the accounting requirements for both types of contracts.

4-38 (Revenue recognition)

Suppose that your company sells appliances to customers under sales contracts that require them to pay for the appliance in monthly payments over one year. Describe a revenue recognition policy that would be appropriate for this type of sale. How should the company account for the fact that some customers might not make the payments as required?

4-39 (Short-term borrowing)

Suppose that a company would like to increase a short-term loan outstanding that it has with a local financial institution. The institution currently requires monthly payments on the loan. Would the financial institution be interested in receiving periodic financial statements from the company? Why? If it did receive financial statements, what items would it find of most interest?

4-40 (Revenue recognition policy and management performance measurement)

Suppose that you are the sales manager of a company with an incentive plan that provides bonuses based on meeting sales targets. Explain how meeting your sales target is affected by the company's revenue recognition policies.

4-41 (Revenue recognition policy and sales targets)

Suppose that you are the vice-president in charge of marketing and sales in a large company. You want to boost sales, so you have developed an incentive plan that will provide a bonus to the salespeople based on the revenue they generate. At what point would you recommend that the company count a sale: when the salesperson generates a purchase order, when the company ships the goods, or when the company receives payment for the goods? Explain.

4-42 (Revenue recognition policy for accounting and tax purposes)
The guidelines for revenue recognition for accounting are not always the same as the rules for revenue recognition for tax purposes. Describe some incentives a company might have for setting its revenue recognition policy for accounting. Describe some incentives that the government might have for setting the rules for revenue recognition for tax purposes.

4-43 (Revenue recognition policy and return policies)
In the toy manufacturing industry, it is common to allow customers (retail stores) to return unsold toys within a specified period of time. Suppose that a toy manufacturer's year end is December 31 and that the majority of its products are shipped to customers during the last quarter of the year (October to December) in anticipation of the holiday season. Is it appropriate for the company to recognize revenue upon shipment of the product? Refer to revenue recognition criteria to support your answer.

4-44 (Revenue recognition policy and modes of shipping goods)
Suppose that an exporter in Vancouver sells goods to a customer in Australia. The goods are shipped by cargo vessel. For goods that are in transit at year end, what recognition should the Vancouver exporter make in its financial statements? Support your answer based on revenue recognition criteria.

4-45 (Revenue recognition for car leases)
Suppose that you are the owner of a car dealership that sells and leases cars. When customers lease a vehicle, they are required to sign a three- or five-year lease. A lease is a contract whereby the customer agrees to make monthly payments for the duration of the lease period. There are penalties if the customer decides to return the vehicle before the end of the lease. During the lease, the customer is required to keep the vehicle in good condition with respect to mechanical operations and appearance. When the customer returns the vehicle at the end of the lease, it is inspected for damage. The customer is often expected to pay for mechanical work or repainting that is required. Using revenue recognition criteria, explain when you would recognize the revenue from the monthly lease payments. How is your decision affected by your awareness that the customers pay a penalty if they return the vehicle early and that they pay for any damages at the end of the lease term?

4-46 (Advertising revenue recognition)
Suppose the sports channel on television sells $10 million in advertising slots to be aired during the games that it broadcasts during the World Cup. Suppose also that these slots are contracted out during the month of October with a down payment of $2 million. The ads will be aired in June and July of the following year. If the sports channel's fiscal year end is December 31, how should it recognize this revenue in its financial statements?

4-47 (Revenue recognition for gift certificates)
Suppose that **The GAP** (a clothing retailer) sells gift certificates for merchandise. During the Christmas holiday period, it issues $500,000 in gift certificates. If the company's fiscal year end is December 31, how should it recognize the issuance of these gift certificates in its financial statements at year end? Explain your answer in relation to the revenue recognition criteria.

4-48 (Revenue recognition on software sales)
Suppose that Solution Software Company produces inventory tracking software that it sells to retail companies such as **Canadian Tire**. The software keeps track of what inventory is on hand and where it is located. It automatically adjusts the information when items are sold and alerts the company when new inventory needs to be ordered. The software package sells for $100,000 and the company agrees to customize it to the buyer's operations, which can take several months. If the fiscal year end is September 30 and the company sells 10 software units in August, how should it recognize these sales in the financial statements at year end? Use the revenue recognition criteria to support your answer.

4-49   (Revenue and expenses associated with obsolete inventory)
Suppose that you are the auditor of Nichol's Department Store and, during your audit of the company's inventory, you observe a significant amount of inventory that appears to be extremely old. How would you recommend that the company deal with this inventory, and how will it affect the revenues and expenses recognized during the period? Explain the incentives that management might have for keeping the inventory in its warehouse.

Reading and Interpreting Published Financial Statements

4-50   (Revenue recognition for multiple products)
Brickworks Limited is an Australian company whose main activity is to manufacture clay and concrete bricks, tiles, and terracotta shingles that it sells for residential and industrial construction. Its other operations include timber products sales, land sales, and waste management services.

Financial Analysis Assignments

> *Required:*
> Using the revenue recognition criteria, describe how Brickworks should recognize revenue for its brick sales, its land sales, and its waste management services. You might find it useful to find out more about the company by going to its website at www.brickworks.com.au

4-51   (Catalogue production, revenue recognition, and matching)
Marks and Spencer (M&S) is a British company that sells clothing, home and furniture items, home electronics, food, and other items from retail stores and over the Internet. The cost of Internet shopping site development and maintenance is fairly substantial for a company such as M&S. Considering that these costs occur before any revenue can be generated from the sale of items through the Internet site, discuss how they could be recorded in the accounting system so that they can be matched with the revenue that is eventually generated.

4-52   (Apply revenue recognition criteria)
Qantas Airways Limited is the major airline company in Australia. The company's statement of financial position (balance sheet) as at June 30, 2009, is presented below in Exhibit 4-11. In Note 1(G) to the financial statements, Qantas describes its passenger, freight, and tours and travel revenue policy:

> Passenger and freight revenue is included in the Income Statement at the fair value of the consideration received net of sales discount, passenger and freight interline/IATA commission and GST. Tours and travel revenue is included in the Income Statement as the net amount of commission retained by Qantas. Passenger recoveries (including fuel surcharge on passenger tickets) are disclosed as part of net passenger revenue. Freight fuel surcharge is disclosed as part of net freight revenue. Other sales commissions paid by Qantas are included in expenditure.
>
> Passenger, freight and tours and travel sales are credited to revenue received in advance and subsequently transferred to revenue when passengers or freight are uplifted or when tours and travel air tickets and land content are utilized. Unused tickets are recognized as revenue using estimates regarding the timing of recognition based on the terms and conditions of the ticket. Changes in these estimation methods could have a material impact on the financial statements of Qantas.

> *Required:*
> a. Referring to the balance sheet, what was the value of the transportation that Qantas was committed to provide at year end in 2009 and 2008?
> b. Referring to the revenue recognition criteria, explain why Qantas's revenue recognition policy is appropriate.
> c. Qantas passengers can earn frequent flyer miles each time they fly with Qantas. When passengers have earned enough frequent flyer miles, they can travel free on Qantas. How should Qantas account for these free trips?

EXHIBIT 4-11

annual report

QANTAS AIRWAYS LIMITED 2009 ANNUAL REPORT

Balance Sheets

as at 30 June 2009

		Qantas Group		Qantas	
		2009	2008	2009	2008
CURRENT ASSETS	Notes	$M	$M	$M	$M
Cash and cash equivalents	10	3,617	2,599	3,404	2,461
Receivables	11	1,054	1,435	2,296	2,705
Other financial assets		561	1,076	561	1,078
Inventories	12	250	216	199	163
Current tax receivable		128	–	137	–
Assets classified as held for sale	13	26	41	23	28
Other		330	249	295	228
Total current assets		5,966	5,616	6,915	6,663
NON-CURRENT ASSETS					
Receivables	11	522	532	2,258	785
Other financial assets		344	347	344	347
Investments accounted for using the equity method	14	387	404	–	–
Other investments	15	3	3	766	553
Property, plant and equipment	16	12,155	12,341	10,763	10,834
Intangible assets	17	664	448	317	299
Other		8	9	6	8
Total non-current assets		14,083	14,084	14,454	12,826
Total assets	3	20,049	19,700	21,369	19,489
CURRENT LIABILITIES					
Payables	19	1,833	2,174	2,156	2,599
Revenue received in advance	20	3,109	3,267	2,688	2,895
Interest-bearing liabilities	21	608	587	726	664
Other financial liabilities		641	960	641	960
Provisions	22	507	484	436	417
Current tax liabilities		–	113	–	111
Deferred lease benefits/income		16	19	11	15
Total current liabilities		6,714	7,604	6,658	7,661
NON-CURRENT LIABILITIES					
Revenue received in advance	20	1,232	1,083	1,232	1,083
Interest-bearing liabilities	21	4,895	3,573	6,626	3,964
Other financial liabilities		268	475	268	475
Provisions	22	533	423	458	377
Deferred tax liabilities	18	607	757	606	767
Deferred lease benefits/income		35	50	34	45
Total non-current liabilities		7,570	6,361	9,224	6,711
Total liabilities	3	14,284	13,965	15,882	14,372
Net assets		5,765	5,735	5,487	5,117
EQUITY					
Issued capital	23	4,729	3,976	4,729	3,976
Treasury shares		(58)	(61)	(58)	(61)
Reserves	23	7	450	44	474
Retained earnings		1,043	1,366	772	728
Equity attributable to members of Qantas		5,721	5,731	5,487	5,117
Minority interest		44	4	–	–
Total equity		5,765	5,735	5,487	5,117

4-53 **(Apply revenue recognition criteria)**

According to Note 2(e) to its 2009 financial statements, the revenue policy of **Catalyst Paper Corporation**, a leading North American newsprint and specialty paper products manufacturer, is as follows:

> **Revenue Recognition**
>
> The Company recognizes revenues upon shipment when persuasive evidence of an arrangement exists, prices are fixed or determinable, title of ownership has transferred to the customer and collection is reasonably assured. Sales are reported net of discounts, allowances and rebates.

> *Required:*
> a. Describe Catalyst Paper's revenue recognition policy and explain how it satisfies the revenue recognition criteria.
> b. Explain what the term "F.O.B. shipping point" means. After reading the revenue recognition criteria stated by Catalyst Paper, do you think that it ships its products F.O.B. shipping point? Explain your reasoning.

4-54 **(Apply revenue recognition criteria)**

The revenue recognition policy of **Imperial Metals Corporation**, a Canadian gold and copper mining company, is as follows, from Note 1 to its 2009 financial statements:

> Estimated mineral revenue, based upon prevailing metal prices, is recorded in the financial statements when title to the concentrate transfers to the customer which generally occurs on date of shipment. Revenue is recorded in the statement of income net of treatment and refining costs paid to counterparties under terms of the off take arrangements. The estimated revenue is recorded based on metal prices and exchange rates on the date of shipment and is adjusted at each balance sheet date to the date of settlement metal prices. The actual amounts will be reflected in revenue upon final settlement, which is usually four to five months after the date of shipment. These adjustments reflect changes in metal prices and changes in quantities arising from final weight and assay calculations.

> *Required:*
> a. Describe Imperial Metals' revenue recognition method. Explain why this method conforms with the IFRS criteria for revenue recognition. Include consideration of the treatment of estimated revenues and settlement adjustments (adjustments caused by changes in metal prices and changes in quantities arising from final weight and assay calculations).
> b. What alternative revenue recognition policies and recording could Imperial Metals use that would also conform with IFRS?

4-55 **(Statement of earnings items)**

High Liner Foods Inc. processes and markets seafood products throughout Canada, the United States, and Mexico under the High Liner and Fisher Boy brands. It also produces private label products and supplies restaurants and institutions. Using High Liner Foods' consolidated statements of income for 2009, which appear in Exhibit 4-12, answer the following questions:

> a. Has High Liner Foods used a single-step or a multi-step income statement? What aspects of the statement influenced your answer?
> b. Calculate High Liner Foods' gross profit rate (gross profit divided by net sales) for 2009 and 2008. Did the company's gross profit, as a percentage of its revenue, increase or decrease?
> c. Calculate High Liner Foods' net profit rate (net earnings divided by net sales) for 2009 and 2008. Did the company's net profit, as a percentage of its revenue, increase or decrease?
> d. High Liner Foods reports both "basic" and "diluted" earnings per share (EPS). Briefly explain the difference between these two terms and why the figures for diluted EPS are lower than those for basic EPS.

Financial Analysis Assignments

EXHIBIT 4-12

annual report

HIGH LINER FOODS INCORPORATED 2009 ANNUAL REPORT

For the fifty-two weeks ended January 2, 2010
(with comparative figures for the fifty-three weeks ended January 3, 2009)

CONSOLIDATED STATEMENTS OF INCOME
(in thousands of Canadian dollars, except per share information)

	For the fifty-two weeks ended, January 2, 2010	For the fifty-three weeks ended, January 3, 2009
Sales	$ 627,186	$ 615,993
Cost of sales *(notes 2b and 16)*	492,564	482,454
Distribution expenses *(note 2b)*	32,352	36,997
Gross profit	102,270	96,542
Foreign exchange gain (loss)	264	(1,234)
Selling, general and administrative expenses *(note 2b)*	(65,571)	(63,860)
Business acquisition integration costs	(460)	(4,879)
Amortization of intangible assets *(note 4)*	(1,499)	(1,383)
Interest expense:		
Short-term	(1,680)	(2,695)
Long-term	(3,765)	(3,768)
Loss on asset disposals	(492)	(402)
Non-operating transactions	(922)	(84)
Income before income taxes	28,145	18,237
Income taxes *(note 9)*		
Current	(2,548)	(3,002)
Future	(5,850)	(1,043)
Total income taxes	(8,398)	(4,045)
Net income	$ 19,747	$ 14,192

PER SHARE EARNINGS
Earnings per common share *(note 10)*

Basic	$ 1.07	$ 0.88
Diluted	$ 1.07	$ 0.77
Weighted average common shares outstanding *(note 10)*		
Basic	18,384,940	15,059,296
Diluted	18,396,067	18,203,100

See accompanying notes to the financial statements

4-56 (Income statement items)

Gildan Activewear Inc. is a marketer and manufacturer of quality T-shirts, sport shirts, and fleeces. It sells the apparel to wholesale distributors as undecorated shirts, which are subsequently decorated with designs and logos.

Using Gildan Activewear's consolidated statements of earnings and comprehensive income, which appear in Exhibit 4-13, answer the questions below:

- a. Has Gildan Activewear used a single-step or a multi-step income statement? What aspects of the statement influenced your answer?
- b. Calculate Gildan Activewear's gross profit rate (gross profit divided by net sales) for 2009, 2008, and 2007. Did the company's gross profit, as a percentage of its revenue, increase or decrease?
- c. Calculate Gildan Activewear's net profit rate (net earnings divided by net sales) for 2009, 2008, and 2007. Did the company's net profit, as a percentage of its revenue, increase or decrease?
- d. Gildan Activewear reported both "basic" and "diluted" earnings per share (EPS). Briefly explain the difference between these two terms and why each of these amounts may be important to users.

GILDAN ACTIVEWEAR INC. 2009 ANNUAL REPORT

EXHIBIT 4-13

annual report

CONSOLIDATED STATEMENTS OF EARNINGS AND COMPREHENSIVE INCOME
Years ended October 4, 2009, October 5, 2008 and September 30, 2007
(in thousands of U.S. dollars, except per share data)

	2009	2008	2007
		(recast–note 1)	*(recast–note 1)*
Net sales	$ 1,038,319	$ 1,249,711	$ 964,429
Cost of sales	807,986	911,242	705,546
Gross profit	230,333	338,469	258,883
Selling, general and administrative expenses	134,785	142,760	99,926
Restructuring and other charges (note 16)	6,199	5,489	28,012
Operating income	89,349	190,220	130,945
Financial (income) expense, net (note 19(b))	(304)	9,240	5,420
Non-controlling interest in consolidated joint venture	110	230	1,278
Earnings before income taxes	89,543	180,750	124,247
Income taxes (note 14)	(5,786)	34,400	(4,815)
Net earnings and comprehensive income	$ 95,329	$ 146,350	$ 129,062
Earnings per share (note 15):			
Basic EPS	$ 0.79	$ 1.21	$ 1.07
Diluted EPS	0.79	1.20	1.06

See accompanying notes to consolidated financial statements.

4-57 (Income statement items)

As its name suggests, **West Fraser Timber Co. Ltd.** is a Canadian forest products company that produces lumber, wood chips, fibreboard, plywood, pulp, linerboard, kraft paper, and newsprint. Using West Fraser Timber's consolidated statements of earnings and comprehensive income, which appear in Exhibit 4-14, answer the questions below:

   a. Has West Fraser Timber presented a single-step or a multi-step income statement? What aspects of the statement influenced your answer?
   b. Calculate West Fraser Timber's gross profit rate (gross margin divided by revenue) for 2009 and 2008. Did the company's gross margin, as a percentage of its revenue, increase or decrease?

EXHIBIT 4-14

annual report

WEST FRASER TIMBER CO. LTD. 2009 ANNUAL REPORT

Consolidated Statements of Earnings and Comprehensive Earnings
For the years ended December 31, 2009 and 2008

(in millions of Canadian dollars, except earnings per share)

	2009	2008
Sales	$ 2,611.8	$ 3,188.5
Costs and expenses		
Cost of products sold	1,930.9	2,363.3
Freight and other distribution costs	449.1	534.4
Export taxes	47.3	54.3
Amortization	265.2	281.2
Selling, general and administration	107.8	108.5
Asset impairments (note 9)	156.9	–
Restructuring charges (note 10)	46.9	–
	3,004.1	3,341.7
Operating earnings	(392.3)	(153.2)
Other		
Interest expense – net (note 12)	(28.9)	(36.1)
Exchange gain (loss) on long-term debt	50.1	(68.0)
Other income (expense) (note 13)	(1.4)	36.9
Earnings before income taxes	(372.5)	(220.4)
Recovery of (provision for) income taxes (note 14)		
Current	57.7	18.8
Future	(26.0)	64.5
	31.7	83.3
Earnings	$ (340.8)	$ (137.1)
Earnings per share (note 15)		
Basic and diluted	$ (7.96)	$ (3.20)
Comprehensive earnings		
Earnings	$ (340.8)	$ (137.1)
Other comprehensive earnings		
Foreign exchange translation gain (loss) on investment in self-sustaining foreign operations	(61.5)	94.9
Comprehensive earnings	$ (402.3)	$ (42.2)

c. Calculate the company's net profit rate (net earnings divided by revenue) for 2009 and 2008. Did the company's net profit, as a percentage of its revenue, increase or decrease?

d. West Fraser Timber has included other comprehensive income at the bottom of its statement of earnings. What is other comprehensive income? What item is included by West Fraser Timber under other comprehensive income?

BEYOND THE BOOK

4-58 (Revenue recognition policies used)

Using an electronic database, select a company in the oil and gas industry. Then use the information on its financial statements and in the notes to the financial statements to answer the following questions:

a. Describe the types of revenue that the company generates.

b. Describe the policies that the company uses for revenue recognition for its various revenues. Using the revenue recognition criteria, explain why the company's policies are suitable for the revenues it generates.

4-59 (Financial statement disclosures)

Find the annual report of a Canadian company that is listed on a Canadian stock exchange, and answer the following questions:

a. Does the company prepare a single-step or multi-step income statement (statement of earnings)? Briefly explain your answer.

b. Does the company have any discontinued operations? If so, search through the information provided with the financial statements and explain why this item was classified in this way.

c. Has the company reported diluted earnings per share? If so, how do the amounts reported for diluted EPS compare to the amounts reported for basic EPS?

Cases

4-60 Quebec Supercheese Company (QSC)

Quebec Supercheese Company (QSC) produces many varieties of cheese that are sold in every province in Canada, mainly through large grocery stores and specialty cheese shops. The cheese is produced at its factory in Montreal and shipped across Canada using commercial refrigerated trucks that pick up the cheese at the factory loading dock. All cheese is shipped F.O.B. shipping point, meaning that the purchasers pay for the trucking and assume responsibility for the cheese as soon as the trucks pick it up at the factory. In accordance with IFRS, QSC recognizes the sale as soon as the trucks load the cheese, as the purchasers have title and responsibility for the cheese at this point.

QSC is not happy with these arrangements because it has received many complaints from purchasers about spoilage. Even though the purchasers and their truckers have full responsibility for this spoilage, many disputes have occurred because the truckers insist the cheese is spoiled when they pick it up. QSC is considering setting up its own fleet of trucks to deliver its cheese across Canada. It estimates that the additional freight costs can be regained through the higher prices it would charge for including shipping in the price (F.O.B. destination).

WILEY
PLUS
www.wileyplus.com

Case Primer

If the company makes the deliveries, the title to the cheese will not transfer until the cheese is delivered. QSC's president was not happy when she learned that sales would be recognized and recorded only upon delivery to the customer, since she knew that an average of five days' sales are in transit at all times because of the distances involved. One day's sales total approximately $100,000 on average. The effect of this change would be an apparent drop in sales of $500,000 and a $50,000 decrease in net income in the year of the change.

Required:
a. Advise the president about revenue recognition guidelines.
b. Do you see a solution that could change the shipping method while avoiding the resulting effect on the income statement?

4-61   Windsor Contracting Ltd.

Windsor Contracting Ltd. has been delaying the recognition of revenue until its contracts are complete. In the past, the company has focused on performing small renovation and home improvement jobs that typically lasted from two weeks to three months. The company has a very good reputation for quality work and fair pricing. Due in large part to its strong reputation, the company has begun to expand its operations to include larger contracts that may take up to two years to complete. Dan Fielding, the president, is thrilled with the company's success but is a little concerned about accepting these larger contracts. He contacts you, John Philpot, a local accountant, to obtain some advice on the accounting for these larger long-term contracts.

"John," Dan says to you, "I'm concerned about accepting these long-term contracts. If I can't recognize any of the revenue associated with these jobs until they're completed, my income statement is going to look very poor for the years when the contracts are in progress but not completed. I'll need financing to undertake these large jobs and the bank needs a yearly income statement to support my line of credit. What do you suggest?"

Required:
As John Philpot, write a memo to Dan Fielding, addressing his concerns. Your memo should focus on a discussion of the percentage of completion method of accounting for revenue recognition and how this method would meet the needs of Windsor Contracting. The memo should also include a discussion of any estimates that Windsor will have to make to apply this method of revenue recognition.

4-62   Mountainside Appliances

Danielle Madison owns a store called Mountainside Appliances that sells several different brands of refrigerators, stoves, dish washers, washers, and dryers. Each of the appliances comes with a factory warranty on parts and labour that is usually one to three years. For an additional charge, Danielle offers customers more extended warranties. These extended warranties come into effect after the manufacturers' warranties end.

Required:
Using IFRS guidelines for revenue recognition, discuss how Danielle should account for the revenue from the extended warranties.

4-63   Furniture Land Inc.

Furniture Land Inc. is a producer and retailer of high-end custom-designed furniture. The company produces only to special order and requires a one-third down payment before any work begins. The customer is then required to pay one-third at the time of delivery and the balance within 30 days after delivery.

It is now February 1, 2011, and Furniture Land has just accepted $3,000 as a down payment from H. Gooding, a wealthy stockbroker. As per the contract, Furniture Land is to deliver the custom furniture to Gooding's residence by June 15, 2011. Gooding is an excellent customer and has always abided by the contract terms in the past. If Furniture Land cannot make the delivery by June 15, the contract terms state that Gooding has the option of cancelling the sale and receiving a full reimbursement of any down payment.

Required:

As Furniture Land's accountant, describe what revenue recognition policy the company should be using. Prepare all journal entries related to the sale in a manner that supports the revenue recognition policy you chose.

Critical Thinking Questions

4-64 (Revenue recognition decision-making)

Alliance Atlantis Communications Inc. is a fully integrated supplier of entertainment products to the television and motion picture production industries. One of its products is television series that it sells to TV networks. Often these series involve the development of an idea and production of a pilot show. This is followed by attempts to market the show to television stations. If the series is sold, weekly shows are produced for later airing by participating stations.

Required:

Discuss the revenue generation process of this kind of television series, emphasizing the critical points in the revenue recognition process and pointing out the similarities and differences between the revenue process for Alliance Atlantis and for a company that manufactures television sets.

THE STATEMENT OF CASH FLOWS

LEARNING OBJECTIVES

After studying this chapter, you should be able to:

1. Understand the importance of cash, and cash flow management, to a company's financial health.

2. Explain the relationship between the statement of cash flows and the statement of earnings, and how both are used in assessing management performance.

3. Explain lead/lag relationships, in terms of the cash-to-cash cycle for a retail company.

4. Describe some solutions to common cash flow problems.

5. Identify the three major types of activities that are disclosed in a statement of cash flows, and describe the components of each activity.

6. Prepare a statement of cash flows, using a comparative statement of financial position and a statement of earnings.

7. Interpret a statement of cash flows and use the information from it and other financial statements to analyze a company's financial health.

Maintaining Your Cash Flow Doesn't Have to Be Frantic

Having been the creative force behind advertisements and promotional material for a variety of companies, the producer of several award-winning television shows and documentaries, and the company behind the Academy-award–nominated visual effects in *Superman Returns* and *Poseidon*, Winnipeg-based Frantic Films has experienced nothing less than a meteoric rise from small 1997 start-up to internationally recognized producer of world-class content.

After 10 years of astounding success, in 2007 Frantic Films sold its visual effects division to Prime Focus Group, India's largest film and television post-production company. "Our VFX Division needed to become significantly larger to compete with the giants in the industry," says Frantic's CEO Jamie Brown. "Prime Focus allowed it to do so, while Frantic focused on its core film and television production businesses."

The company now has three divisions. Its Film and Television division has produced hundreds of hours of award winning programs that have sold to well over 100 countries worldwide. The Branded Content and Commercial division creates targeted entertainment programming, such as television commercials and corporate promotional videos, as well as animation, short films, and documentaries. Its third division, Red Apple Entertainment, was acquired in 2008 and produces lifestyle and factual programs in Toronto.

The company's success is due in large part to maintaining a healthy cash flow. "Cash flow is critical to any company's success," says Mr. Brown. "We carefully forecast at least 12 months ahead and do all our due diligence to consider all variables in revenue and expense, always erring on the side of being cautious in our approach."

Frantic Film's television productions begin with some preliminary work on the concept. Then,

once the company has buy-in for a show from a network, it secures a licensing fee and a contract, which includes the show's budget and financial plan. Frantic then gets a line of credit from a bank. "The budget is fixed regardless of any contingencies faced, and payments can be delayed if deliverables take longer than anticipated, so careful project management, on-time deliveries, and prompt invoice issuance and follow-up are critical to managing cash flow," Mr. Brown explains.

While contracts may last for only a set time period and television show production work is cyclical, Frantic still has to pay its full-time staff salaries and administrative expenses, so ideally the contracts overlap to some degree. Lately, avoiding too much down time is not a problem. Frantic has more than 10 television shows in various stages of production and averages 15 to 20 commercial and branded content productions in the works at any given time.

Whether a profit-oriented business like **Frantic Films** in the opening story or a not-for-profit entity such as a cultural group or charity, every organization needs to manage its cash flows. Management's ability to predict when cash will be coming in and going out, and to plan in advance for how any cash shortfalls will be covered, is essential to the health of any organization. For most organizations, cash prediction and management is a fine balancing act. At any point in time, a business such as Frantic Films is engaged in many different projects and contracts of varying lengths, and most require the company to make up-front investments and then wait for the cash to be received later, often over extended periods of time. This makes effective cash management essential to its survival.

If a company does not manage its cash flows well and therefore has difficulty paying its debts on time, its credit rating will suffer. Suppliers and lenders will be reluctant to continue to sell goods on credit or loan money to the company. At best, this will affect the company's ability to grow. At worst, it could contribute to an eventual slide into bankruptcy.

In Chapter 4, the basic concepts underlying the recognition of revenue and the measurement of earnings were discussed. Although this is a very important perspective on a company's performance, other aspects that affect the company's overall health are not adequately captured by the statement of earnings. For example, creditors want to be able to assess a company's ability to pay the interest on its debt and eventually repay the debt in full when it comes due. However, because they are based on accrual accounting, the revenues and expenses on the statement of earnings do not necessarily correspond to the company's cash inflows and outflows, and therefore do not provide the information that creditors need. Creditors and other outside users of financial information need some way to assess an organization's cash flows and predict its future cash position. The **statement of cash flows** provides this perspective on an organization's performance, by summarizing its cash inflows and outflows and highlighting the activities that resulted in the net change in its cash position during the period.

USER RELEVANCE

Some users consider the statement of cash flows to be the most important financial statement in determining a company's future prospects. Remember the three basic activities of a business that were described in Chapters 1 and 2: operating activities, investing activities, and financing activities. Users look at these activities on the statement of cash flows to assess a company's financial health.

In particular, users will examine the statement to see whether the **operating activities**—the lifeblood of any company—are generating a positive **cash flow**. After all, the operating activities are the reasons for having established the company, and what its growth or decline will be based on. A positive cash flow from operating activities indicates that, as a result of its basic business operations, more cash flowed into the company than out. That cash may then be used for other activities, such as purchasing new assets, repaying debts, or paying dividends to shareholders. A negative cash flow from operations indicates that, as a result of its regular operating activities, more cash flowed out of the company than in. This may mean that investments have to be curtailed and/or external sources of financing have to be found to provide the required cash.

Under **investing activities**, users can examine the company's decisions to buy and sell long-term assets, as well as any long-term investments in other companies. This information enables users to assess the company's investment strategy when it comes to replacing assets that are needed to continue, and perhaps expand, its operations.

Users also need to examine a company's **financing activities**, to determine what decisions it made during the period about debt and equity. Did it incur more debt or pay some off, issue new shares, and/or pay dividends? This information enables users to evaluate the company's financial strength and strategy, and to estimate its reliance on debt versus equity financing in the future.

Many users still consider the statement of earnings to be the most important statement, but they will examine it together with the statement of cash flows and statement of financial position to try to fully understand and analyze a company. As a future user of financial information, it is important that you know what to look for on the statement of cash flows and understand what the amounts in its various categories mean. For this reason, we are going to show you both how the statement is developed and how you should analyze it.

WHY ANOTHER FLOW STATEMENT?

The statement of earnings was the first flow statement we examined. To demonstrate why another flow statement is needed, we will use the hypothetical example of Ajax Company, whose essential information follows.

LEARNING OBJECTIVE 1

Understand the importance of cash, and cash flow management, to a company's financial health.

Ajax Company Example—Overview of Operations

BACKGROUND

The company was established in December 2010 with an investment of $150,000. Its only activities in December were to spend $132,000 on capital assets and $4,000 on inventory, so as to be ready to commence sales in January 2011. The capital assets will be depreciated at a rate of $2,000 per month, starting in January 2011.

PRODUCT LINE

Ajax Company sells circuit-board components to cell phone manufacturers.

SUPPLIER CREDIT

The components cost Ajax $4 each. Ajax's suppliers do not allow it to purchase the components on credit, so payment for all inventory must be made in cash when it is ordered.

SALES AND CUSTOMER CREDIT

Ajax has set a selling price of $7 per component. Ajax allows its customers up to 30 days to pay for the components they buy. For simplicity, it is assumed that all customers pay Ajax one month after a sale.

Ajax is a new company and is expecting rapid growth in sales. Exhibit 5-1 shows this growth during the first three months of 2011. The company expects its sales to continue to grow at the rate of 1,000 units per month for at least the next year.

INVENTORY POLICY

Ajax's suppliers are located overseas, so it cannot get components from them instantly. Therefore, it must maintain sufficient inventory to ensure that units are available when customers need them. Since the components take about four weeks to arrive, they have to be purchased at the beginning of each month in order to be on hand by the end of the month and ready for the next month's sales. This means that each month Ajax has to purchase the number of components that it expects to sell the next month. This relationship can be seen in the data in Exhibit 5-1. Notice that there is sufficient inventory on hand at the beginning of each month to cover what is sold that month, and that the units purchased each month are equal to the units sold in the following month.

EXHIBIT 5-1

AJAX COMPANY—INVENTORY PURCHASES AND SALES DATA

	January	February	March
Units in beginning inventory	1,000	2,000	3,000
Units purchased during the month	2,000	3,000	4,000
Units available for sale	3,000	5,000	7,000
Units sold	1,000	2,000	3,000
Units in ending inventory	2,000	3,000	4,000

Performance Evaluation Using the Statement of Earnings and Statement of Cash Flows

LEARNING OBJECTIVE 2

Explain the relationship between the statement of cash flows and the statement of earnings, and how both are used in assessing management performance.

As previous chapters have shown, a company's economic performance can be measured by constructing a statement of earnings. Assuming that the revenues are recognized at the time of sale and that no other expenses are incurred, Exhibit 5-2 shows the statement of earnings for each of Ajax's first three months of 2011.

As Exhibit 5-2 shows, the amount of net earnings is growing very quickly, which is good news to shareholders and managers. If sales continue to increase, this growth in earnings should continue and the investment in Ajax should be very profitable.

AJAX COMPANY—STATEMENT OF EARNINGS

EXHIBIT 5-2

	January	February	March
Sales revenues (number of units sold × $7)	$ 7,000	$14,000	$ 21,000
Cost of goods sold (number of units sold × $4)	(4,000)	(8,000)	(12,000)
Depreciation expense	(2,000)	(2,000)	(2,000)
Net earnings	$ 1,000	$ 4,000	$ 7,000

Exhibit 5-3 shows Ajax's statement of financial position at the end of each month. (Since Ajax is not able to purchase on credit, there are no liabilities in this simplified example.) The trends in cash, accounts receivable, and inventory shown in Exhibit 5-3 reflect the rapid growth of the business. Accounts receivable reflects the increasing level of sales, as does inventory, because the ending inventory is also a function of sales.

AJAX COMPANY—STATEMENT OF FINANCIAL POSITION

EXHIBIT 5-3

	Dec. 31	Jan. 31	Feb. 28	Mar. 31
Cash	$ 14,000	$ 6,000	$ 1,000	$ (1,000)
Accounts receivable (from the sales in Exhibit 5-2)	0	7,000	14,000	21,000
Inventory (number of units in Exhibit 5-1 × $4)	4,000	8,000	12,000	16,000
Capital assets	132,000	132,000	132,000	132,000
Accumulated depreciation	0	(2,000)	(4,000)	(6,000)
	$150,000	$151,000	$155,000	$162,000
Share capital	$150,000	$150,000	$150,000	$150,000
Retained earnings	0	1,000	5,000	12,000
	$150,000	$151,000	$155,000	$162,000

The disturbing trend in Exhibit 5-3 is, of course, the decline in the amount of cash on hand: by the end of February, the company will have a very small cash balance and by the end of March it will have a negative cash balance. This is a very serious problem because, unless it can make arrangements for some form of financing to cover its cash shortfall, Ajax will not be able to make its required purchases during March—even though the business is very profitable!

Operating with a negative cash balance is only possible if the company's bank permits it to overdraw its account—that is, if the bank allows more cash to be withdrawn than was deposited. A negative cash balance is really a loan from the bank. This type of loan arrangement is called a **line of credit**, and companies often have one with their bank to cover circumstances like this. The bank sets a limit on how much can be borrowed in this way, and also establishes a repayment schedule if the line of credit is used.

To understand why the company's cash declined during the first quarter of the year, its **cash-to-cash cycle** must be considered. (As you should recall, the cash-to-cash cycle was introduced in Chapter 4.) Exhibit 5-4 illustrates the basic elements of Ajax Company's cash-to-cash cycle.

EXHIBIT 5-4

AJAX COMPANY—CASH-TO-CASH CYCLE

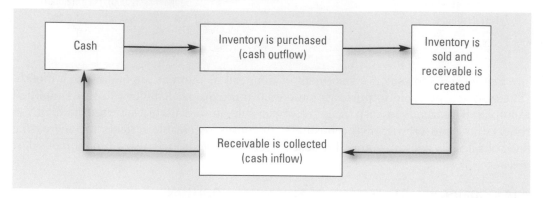

LEARNING OBJECTIVE 3

Explain lead/lag relationships, in terms of the cash-to-cash cycle for a retail company.

The cash-to-cash (or **cash conversion**) cycle illustrates the **lead/lag relationship** between the cash going out to buy inventory and the cash coming in from collections of accounts receivable.[1] In this simplified example, units are always bought for cash and are sold on credit in the following month. Thus, there is a one-month lag between the outflow of cash for inventory purchases and the sale of those units; and once the units are sold there is another one-month lag between the sale and the collection of the accounts receivable, because the company's policy is to allow customers 30 days to pay. Consequently, the total lag between cash outflow and cash inflow is two months.

Since the statement of earnings is prepared on an accrual basis and measures performance in terms of the revenues earned and the expenses incurred during a particular time period, regardless of whether the revenues are collected in cash or the expenses are paid in cash during that period, it is not very useful in tracking cash flows. Because a company cannot operate without enough cash, it makes sense to prepare a separate statement to measure the company's performance on a cash basis. Hence the need for a statement of cash flows.

The decline in the cash balance during the first three months of 2011 (shown in Exhibit 5-3) occurs because the growth in sales forces Ajax to buy more and more units each month. As a result, the cash payments for inventory purchases in a given month exceed the cash collections from the previous month's sales. As a result, even though the amount of net earnings is positive from the outset and is increasing each month, the company's cash position is declining.

The statement of cash flows cannot replace the statement of earnings—both provide very useful information. The statement of earnings summarizes the profitability of

---

1. If the company purchased goods on account, this would also affect its cash-to-cash cycle. More specifically, the use of suppliers' credit would reduce the length of the cash conversion cycle (the gap between when cash is paid out for the purchase of goods and when cash is collected from their sale), because it delays the time when the purchaser pays out cash. However, since Ajax Company does not purchase on account, this does not apply in this example.

the company's operations, while the statement of cash flows summarizes the cash flows. To analyze the operations of any company properly, you must consider both the profits and the cash flows. In the long run, the total profits and the net cash flows will be very similar; but they may be very different for any single month or year, or even over a period of several months or years.

To understand the usefulness of the information provided by the statement of cash flows, think of managing cash as one of the basic tasks of managing a company. Management must always ensure that sufficient cash is on hand both to operate the business and generate profits now and to invest in assets that will produce profits in the future. Simply producing profits now is not sufficient to ensure the company's long-term survival. Without enough cash to make investments in revenue-producing assets, the company's long-term viability is in jeopardy.

Exhibit 5-5 shows Ajax's statement of cash flows for the first three months of 2011. As can be seen from this exhibit, the company's cash flows are negative during that period. The receipts in the statement of cash flows are the collections from the previous month's sales, and the payments are the inventory purchase costs for the current month. (The inventory costs can be calculated by taking the units purchased in Exhibit 5-1 and multiplying them by the cost of $4 per unit.)

AJAX COMPANY—STATEMENT OF CASH FLOWS

EXHIBIT 5-5

	December	January	February	March
Operating activities:				
Cash received from collections of A/R	$ 0	$ 0	$ 7,000	$ 14,000
Cash paid for purchases of inventory	(4,000)	(8,000)	(12,000)	(16,000)
	(4,000)	(8,000)	(5,000)	(2,000)
Financing activities:				
Cash received from owners	150,000	0	0	0
Investing activities:				
Cash paid for purchases of capital assets	(132,000)	0	0	0
Net cash flow	**14,000**	**(8,000)**	**(5,000)**	**(2,000)**
Cash balance at beginning of month	0	14,000	6,000	1,000
Cash balance at end of month	$ 14,000	$ 6,000	$ 1,000	$ (1,000)

The statement of cash flows paints a very different picture of Ajax's performance during the first quarter of 2011 than does the statement of earnings. Cash flow is obviously a serious problem, and the company must consider how it will be able to buy inventory during March so that it can continue doing business in April.

In order to determine whether the problem will persist, Ajax should prepare a forecast for the next several months. In practice, companies usually prepare these forecasts for 12-month, 24-month, and even 36-month periods. This provides them with the information they need to manage their cash flows and plan in advance for any shortfalls.

Assuming continued growth in sales of 1,000 units a month for Ajax Company, and no changes in its collection terms or inventory purchase and payment policies, Exhibit 5-6 presents the forecast for the months of April through June.

EXHIBIT 5-6

AJAX COMPANY: APRIL–JUNE FORECAST

STATEMENT OF EARNINGS	April	May	June
Sales revenues	$ 28,000	$ 35,000	$ 42,000
Cost of goods sold	(16,000)	(20,000)	(24,000)
Depreciation expense	(2,000)	(2,000)	(2,000)
Net earnings for month	**$ 10,000**	**$ 13,000**	**$ 16,000**

STATEMENT OF CASH FLOWS	April	May	June
Operating activities:			
Cash received from collections of A/R	$ 21,000	$ 28,000	$ 35,000
Cash paid for purchases of inventory	(20,000)	(24,000)	(28,000)
	1,000	4,000	7,000
Financing activities:			
Cash received from owners	0	0	0
Investing activities:			
Cash paid for purchases of capital assets	0	0	0
Net cash flow for month	**1,000**	**4,000**	**7,000**
Cash balance at beginning of month	(1,000)	0	4,000
Cash balance at end of month	$ 0	$ 4,000	$ 11,000

As can be seen from Exhibit 5-6, earnings will continue to grow by $3,000 each month, and the net cash flow will be positive and continually improving during the second quarter of the year. There will be a small positive cash balance in May and a large one by the end of June. Thus, the "cash crunch" that Ajax experiences during March and April will be a temporary phenomenon related to the lead/lag relationship between the cash going out to buy inventory and the cash coming in from collections of accounts receivable, as discussed earlier. The key things to note from the Ajax example are that the company cannot have a negative cash balance without making special arrangements with its bank, and something must be done to ensure that the underlying problem will not continue for too long. However, with proper planning and advance discussions with bankers or investors, management can make appropriate arrangements to deal with this type of situation.

Solutions to the Cash Flow Problem

LEARNING OBJECTIVE 4

Describe some solutions to common cash flow problems.

The cash flow difficulties that Ajax is experiencing are typical of many new companies. These problems have three fundamental causes: **high growth rates** in sales, significant **lead/lag relationships** in cash inflows and outflows, and **inadequate financing** or undercapitalization. The term "**capitalization**" in this situation refers to how much cash the company begins with.

Start-up companies generally experience rapid growth of sales. This increase in sales requires them to buy or produce more and more inventory, as well as to expand their storage and operating capacity. Buying more inventory and expanding capacity both require cash.

accounting in the news

No Special Funds for Special Effects Firm

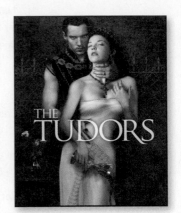

C.O.R.E. Digital, Ontario's largest animation and special-effects studio, was forced into bankruptcy after the provincial government backed out of financing negotiations with the 16-year-old Toronto company and the Royal Bank of Canada. By mid-March 2010, C.O.R.E. was in default on loans, lines of credit, and rent to the tune of $7.3 million, and had to lay off 120 staff and shut down production on several projects, including work on the TV miniseries *The Tudors*. C.O.R.E.'s experience underlines the difficulty of its line of business, which has tight margins, a small labour pool, and high capital costs. While the Ontario government decided not to help C.O.R.E., it did commit $263-million over 10 years to Ubisoft, a French-owned video and computer games maker, which promised to create 800 jobs in Ontario over the next decade. One reason Ubisoft was a better investment for the province, an industry observer noted, is that Ubisoft owns intellectual property and earns trailing royalties after the games are released—that is, Ubisoft has ongoing cash flow. Once C.O.R.E. finished a project it didn't receive any more revenue, making it a riskier business investment.

Source: Michael Posner, "Death of C.O.R.E. still a mystery," *The Globe and Mail*, April 9, 2010.

Compounding the growth problem is the presence of significant lead/lag relationships between the company's cash inflows and outflows. As long as the product can be sold for more than the cost to produce or buy it, if there is no lead/lag relationship, there is no cash flow problem. Most companies, however, do have some significant lead/lag relationships in their cash flows, and these are magnified in periods of high growth.

Finally, start-up companies tend to be undercapitalized—that is, they do not have a large enough pool of cash to start with. When large cash needs appear, caused by rapid growth and the lead/lag relationships, these companies do not have enough cash reserves to get them through prolonged periods of net cash outflows.

Most start-up companies (as well as other companies in rapid growth phases) will experience cash flow problems at some point. In Ajax's case, these problems lead to a crisis during the months of March and April, which could be resolved by addressing one or more of the underlying causes. Specifically, Ajax could reduce its rate of growth, increase its capitalization by getting more initial cash in the company, and/or reduce the lead/lag relationship between cash payments and collections. Solutions to Ajax's cash flow problems are discussed in the following subsections, where we address each of the three causes of its cash flow difficulties.

Alleviating cash flow problems by reducing the rate of growth One way to solve Ajax's problem is to slow down the sales growth rate. Exhibit 5-7 shows what happens to the cash flows when the rate of growth in sales is reduced to 750 units per month rather than 1,000 (with all other facts and assumptions unchanged). You can see from the exhibit that this solves the cash flow problem, because the lowest cash balance is $3,750. The net cash flows are still negative in January, February, and March, but the cash balance is sufficient to absorb these initial cash outflows. By April, the net cash flow has become positive and the company's cash balance has started to increase.

Reducing the growth rate may not be the best response, however, because (a) it will reduce the net earnings and (b) it may hurt the company in the long run, as it attempts to develop a strong customer base. Limiting the growth in sales may divert customers to

EXHIBIT 5-7

CASH FLOWS UNDER A STRATEGY OF REDUCING THE GROWTH RATE

Statement of Cash Flows for Ajax Company if the growth in sales is reduced from 1,000 to 750 additional units per month

	December	January	February	March	April
Operating activities:					
Cash received from A/R	$ 0	$ 0	$ 5,250	$ 10,500	$ 15,750
Cash paid for purchases	(3,000)	(6,000)	(9,000)	(12,000)	(15,000)
	(3,000)	(6,000)	(3,750)	(1,500)	750
Financing activities:					
Cash received from owners	150,000	0	0	0	0
Investing activities:					
Cash paid for capital assets	(132,000)	0	0	0	0
Net cash flow	**15,000**	**(6,000)**	**(3,750)**	**(1,500)**	**750**
Cash balance at beg. of month	0	15,000	9,000	5,250	3,750
Cash balance at end of month	$ 15,000	$ 9,000	$ 5,250	$ 3,750	$ 4,500

competing companies and, if these customers develop loyalties to the competitors, Ajax's long-term potential may be reduced.

Alleviating cash flow problems by increasing the amount of capitalization
A second way to solve the cash problem is to address the undercapitalization problem—that is, to start with more cash. This larger amount of cash may be obtained in numerous ways. Two typical ways are to issue additional shares in the company (equity financing) and to borrow the cash (debt financing).

If Ajax issues new shares, the cash flow projections will have to be adjusted to incorporate the additional cash inflow from the investors and any subsequent outflows for dividends. If money is borrowed, the cash flow projections will have to be adjusted for the initial inflow from the borrowing, and for the payments of principal and interest that will have to be made in the future.

Exhibit 5-8 shows what will happen if an additional $5,000 is obtained in December from the issuance of shares. Note that this approach also solves the cash flow problem, as the lowest cash balance is $4,000.

Although this strategy of increasing the company's capitalization may seem like an easy way to eliminate its cash flow problems, it is not without its own problems. Although the net earnings would not be affected under this strategy, the rate of return that the owners earn on their investment in the company would be slightly lower, because $155,000 (rather than $150,000) is invested to yield the same amount of earnings. In addition, if more shares are issued, the current Ajax shareholders may have to give up some of their control of the company, and they may not want to do this. It may also be difficult to find additional investors who are willing to take the risk of buying shares in a new company.

As an alternative, Ajax might want to use debt financing, by borrowing money. A potential problem with this strategy, however, is that Ajax may not be able to convince a lender that it is worthy of a loan, or, if it does find one, it may have to pay a very high interest rate. Lenders are typically very skeptical of new ventures.

Alleviating cash flow problems by reducing the lead/lag relationships   The third way to solve Ajax's cash flow problem is to change the lead/lag relationships

CASH FLOWS UNDER A STRATEGY OF INCREASING THE COMPANY'S CAPITALIZATION

EXHIBIT 5-8

Statement of Cash Flows for Ajax Company if the initial investment by owners is increased from $150,000 to $155,000

	December	January	February	March	April
Operating activities:					
Cash received from A/R	$ 0	$ 0	$ 7,000	$ 14,000	$ 21,000
Cash paid for purchases	(4,000)	(8,000)	(12,000)	(16,000)	(20,000)
	(4,000)	(8,000)	(5,000)	(2,000)	1,000
Financing activities:					
Cash received from owners	155,000	0	0	0	0
Investing activities:					
Cash paid for capital assets	(132,000)	0	0	0	0
Net cash flow	**19,000**	**(8,000)**	**(5,000)**	**(2,000)**	**1,000**
Cash balance at beg. of month	0	19,000	11,000	6,000	4,000
Cash balance at end of month	$ 19,000	$ 11,000	$ 6,000	$ 4,000	$ 5,000

between the cash inflows and outflows, and thereby reduce the length of the company's cash conversion cycle. There are many ways to do this. For example, if Ajax made some of its sales on a cash basis or by credit card, or reduced the credit period for customers who buy on account, the time difference between the cash outflows and inflows each month would be reduced. As an illustration of this, Exhibit 5-9 shows what will happen if Ajax makes one-quarter of its sales for cash and three-quarters on credit (with the sales on account still being collected in 30 days).

CASH FLOWS UNDER A STRATEGY OF CHANGING THE LEAD/LAG RELATIONSHIPS

EXHIBIT 5-9

Statement of Cash Flows for Ajax Company if 25% of its sales are made for cash and 75% are made on account

	December	January	February	March	April
Operating activities:					
Cash sales	$ 0	$ 1,750	$ 3,500	$ 5,250	$ 7,000
Cash received from A/R	0	0	5,250	10,500	15,750
Cash paid for purchases	(4,000)	(8,000)	(12,000)	(16,000)	(20,000)
	(4,000)	(6,250)	(3,250)	(250)	2,750
Financing activities:					
Cash received from owners	150,000	0	0	0	0
Investing activities:					
Cash paid for capital assets	(132,000)	0	0	0	0
Net cash flow	**14,000**	**(6,250)**	**(3,250)**	**(250)**	**2,750**
Cash balance at beg. of month	0	14,000	7,750	4,500	4,250
Cash balance at end of month	$ 14,000	$ 7,750	$ 4,500	$ 4,250	$ 7,000

As you can see, this would also solve Ajax's cash flow problem, as the cash balance never gets lower than $4,250. The big advantage of this strategy is that, if successfully implemented, it would maintain the original earnings with no additional investment. This strategy may be risky, however, because customers may not be happy with having to pay cash and may be able to get better terms from competitors. Consequently, the company might lose some of its customer base and jeopardize its long-term prospects.

Another strategy would be for Ajax to make its purchases on account, rather than on a cash basis. Currently, Ajax is required to pay cash for the inventory that it buys from its suppliers. This may be understandable, because suppliers are often reluctant to sell inventory to a new company on credit, since it has no track record for assessing its creditworthiness. Once Ajax gets established, they may be willing to let it buy on credit. But establishing creditworthiness takes time, so one of the other strategies that we described will probably have to be used to solve Ajax's initial cash flow problem.

As the article below indicates, despite being profitable, companies involved in real estate development often have cash flow challenges. This is because they have significant lead/lag relationships affecting their cash flows, since it often takes a considerable length of time to complete a project and, although units in the development may be sold early in the process, most of the cash does not begin to flow back to the developer until the project is complete and customers take possession.

accounting in the news

Revelstoke Receives Revitalization

The Vancouver-based Gaglardi family, owner of Sandman Inn hotels and Denny's restaurants, stepped in to revitalize the debt-ridden Revelstoke Mountain Resort in 2010.

The Revelstoke ski hill had opened three years earlier and the resort's first two condo projects reportedly sold out within three hours. But the timing for such a huge development couldn't have been worse. By the fall of 2008, the global recession hit and real estate sales dropped off. About 20% of first-phase sales at Revelstoke Mountain were to Americans who couldn't complete the transactions. Those purchasers lost their 20% deposits and their units were resold.

Northland Properties Corp., run by the Gaglardi family, has invested $200,000,000 to develop the resort, including $100,000,000 in inherited debt that it has paid off. A billion-dollar, 15-year plan is now in place for an international luxury getaway that will consist of the highest vertical runs in North America; more than 100 runs; 20 lifts; cat, heli, and back-country skiing from one base; and an 18-hole golf course. By the time the project is complete, there will be about 5,000 new housing units and 500,000 sq. ft. of commercial and retail space.

Northland says it has made about $140,000,000 in condo presales, with three-quarters of all condos sold or close to sold. But the recreational property market is still far behind the residential property market in terms of recovery, and progress is slow. Ski hills, with their snowmaking and maintenance costs, often don't make money. It's the real estate around them that generates earnings. And when a recession hits, consumers usually don't think about purchasing vacation properties.

Source: Kerry Gold, "Rx for a resort going down hill," *The Globe and Mail*, April 8, 2010, http://www.theglobeandmail.com/real-estate/rx-for-a-resort-going-down-hill/article1528420/

It should now be clear to you that (1) cash flow considerations are extremely important, and (2) a statement of cash flows provides additional information that is not captured by the statement of earnings and statement of financial position. For managers or other financial statement users, it is important to understand the relationship between the company's earnings, its cash-to-cash cycle, and its statement of cash flows. It is also extremely important when evaluating a company's performance and cash position to understand how its receivables, payables, and inventory policies affect its cash flows.

We will now turn to the components of cash flow analysis. Then we will illustrate the preparation of a statement of cash flows. Finally, we will discuss how users interpret the statement of cash flows to assess a company's financial health.

UNDERSTANDING THE STATEMENT OF CASH FLOWS

Definition of Cash and Cash Equivalents

As we saw above, proper management of cash is one of the critical tasks for managers in any organization. Having too little cash on hand results in not being able to pay liabilities and expenses, which may make it necessary to engage in short-term borrowing. Having too much cash on hand is also inefficient. Cash held in chequing accounts typically earns little or no interest. It is much better to invest excess cash in a temporary investment that will earn interest. The proper management of cash therefore involves not only managing cash itself, but also short-term borrowings and temporary investments. Thus, in considering what cash flows are to be summarized in the statement of cash flows, we must consider not only cash itself but the broader concept of *cash and cash equivalents*, sometimes called the **cash position**.

We use the term **cash equivalents** to include short-term, highly liquid investments that can readily be converted into known amounts of cash. They must be close enough to maturity that there is little risk of changes in their value, due to changes in interest rates or other economic factors. The time frame suggested is three months or less. Items that commonly meet these criteria are Government of Canada treasury bills and demand notes receivable from other companies. A demand note must be paid on demand, which means that it is very liquid.

Cash equivalents also include temporary borrowings that companies use to cover their cash shortages for short periods of time, such as bank overdrafts, lines of credit, or demand loans. However, a normal short-term bank loan would not be considered a cash equivalent, because it has a fixed duration and is therefore not equivalent to "negative cash." Rather, a normal bank loan (even a short-term one) would be considered a financing activity.

Components of Cash Flows

LEARNING OBJECTIVE 5

In discussing the components of cash flows, we are revisiting concepts that were introduced in Chapter 1, where we discussed the three components of managing any business. First, you must engage in financing activities: getting funding from shareholders or lenders to provide sufficient capitalization for the business. Next, you must engage in investing activities: acquiring long-term assets that will be used in the business to produce revenues

Identify the three major types of activities that are disclosed in a statement of cash flows, and describe the components of each activity.

and profits. Finally, you must engage in operating activities: carrying on the revenue-generating activities for which the company was established. The statement of cash flows summarizes all of the company's cash flows into these three types of activities.

Exhibit 5-10 presents the consolidated cash flow statement for **Lindt & Sprüngli Group** (a Swiss chocolate company) for the years ended December 31, 2009 and 2008. Lindt's financial statements are presented in millions of Swiss francs (CHF).

Note that Lindt's statement of cash flows is divided into the three primary business activities: operating activities, with a net cash *inflow* of 470.1 million Swiss francs for 2009; investment activities, with a net cash *outflow* of 118.9 million francs for 2009; and financing activities, with a net cash *outflow* of 175.2 million francs for 2009. Combining these three sections, the overall net increase in cash and cash equivalents for 2009 is 176 million francs. The final portion of the statement of cash flows shows that—when this is combined with the 192 million Swiss francs of cash and cash equivalents that Lindt had at the beginning of the year (together with an adjustment for the negative effect of changes in foreign exchange rates of 0.8 million francs)—the company has cash and cash equivalents of 367.2 million francs at the end of the year. Thus, the statement of cash flows summarizes all the cash flows that led to the change in the company's cash position during the year.

At the bottom of the statement of cash flows, Lindt includes supplementary information about the amount of interest that was received and paid in cash (4.1 and 7 million francs, respectively, during 2009), and the amount of income tax that was paid in cash (81 million Swiss francs, in 2009). Since interest and taxes are major factors for most companies, and are used in many financial ratios, these additional disclosures are provided to enable users to see the impact of interest and taxes on cash flows and to facilitate certain types of financial analysis.

Financing Activities

Financing activities are the activities involved in obtaining resources from lenders and shareholders, and making payments to those lenders and shareholders. Transactions that are classified as financing activities usually involve balance sheet accounts that are associated with short- and long-term debt, and with equity capital. Typical cash inflows come from issuing bonds, mortgages, notes, and other borrowings, or shares. Outflows include the repayment of the principal of debt obligations, the payment of interest on debt, the repurchase of shares, and the payment of dividends to shareholders.

HELPFUL HINT

Interest and dividend payments can be classified as either operating or financing activities. However, *interest payments* are usually treated as *operating activities*, and *dividend payments* are usually treated as *financing activities*.

A special word is needed about interest and dividends. Companies pay interest to lenders in exchange for the use of their money, and they pay dividends to shareholders for much the same reason. Even though interest is associated with debt, which is a financing activity, interest payments are usually included in the *operating* section of the statement of cash flows. Dividend payments, on the other hand, are usually treated as financing activities—as you would probably expect them to be, because they are associated with the issuance of shares, which is a financing activity. International Financial Reporting Standards allow companies to report interest and dividend payments as either operating activities or financing activities. In this book, we do what most Canadian companies do, which is to treat interest payments as operating activities and dividend payments as financing activities.

LINDT & SPRÜNGLI 2009 ANNUAL REPORT

EXHIBIT 5-10

annual report

CONSOLIDATED CASH FLOW STATEMENT
For the years ended December 31, 2009 and 2008

(in millions of Swiss francs)	Note	2009	2008
Net income		193.1	261.5
Depreciation, amortization and impairment	7, 8, 14	117.3	104.6
Changes in provisions and value adjustments		7.5	−9.4
Decrease (+) / increase (−) of accounts receivable		71.3	21.9
Decrease (+) / increase (−) of inventories		15.3	−52.5
Decrease (+) / increase (−) of prepayments and other receivables		6.0	−6.6
Decrease (+) / increase (−) of accrued income		20.2	−10.3
Decrease (−) / increase (+) of accounts payable		2.6	−46.2
Decrease (−) / increase (+) of other payables and accrued liabilities		34.9	−11.0
Non-cash effective items		1.9	42.7
Cash flow from operating activities (operating cash flow)		**470.1**	**294.7**
Investments in property, plant and equipment	7	−115.2	−193.7
Disposals of property, plant and equipment		0.9	0.4
Investments in intangible assets	8	−8.3	−4.9
Disposals (+) / investments (−) in financial assets		−1.0	−0.8
Marketable securities			
Investments		−9.3	−9.7
Disposals		14.0	28.7
Cash flow from investment activities		**−118.9**	**−180.0**
Proceeds from borrowings		–	56.6
Repayments of bonds / borrowings	17	−77.5	−105.1
Repayments of loans		−0.1	−2.5
Capital increase (including premium)	16	13.4	24.3
Purchase of treasury stock		−29.9	−0.8
Sale of treasury stock		1.3	–
Dividends paid to shareholders		−82.4	−74.9
Cash flow from financing activities		**−175.2**	**−102.4**
Net increase (+) / decrease (−) in cash and cash equivalents		**176.0**	**12.3**
Cash and cash equivalents as at January 1	15	**192.0**	**189.1**
Exchange gains / (losses) on cash and cash equivalents		**−0.8** **191.2**	**−9.4** **179.7**
Cash and cash equivalents as at December 31	15	**367.2**	**192.0**
Interest received from 3rd parties[1]		4.1	10.6
Interest paid to 3rd parties[1]		7.0	12.9
Income tax paid[1]		81.0	75.0

1) Included in cash flow from operating activities.

The accompanying notes form an intregal part of the consolidated statements.

In Lindt's cash flow statement, we can see that the company engaged in the following financing activities during 2009:

- It had no proceeds from new borrowings, but repaid 77.5 + 0.1 = 77.6 million Swiss francs that had been borrowed earlier.

- The company increased its equity capital by 13.4 million francs, by issuing additional shares. However, this was offset by the fact that it spent a net amount of 29.9 − 1.3 = 28.6 million francs buying back some of its shares (which is referred to as treasury stock). Overall, its share capital decreased during the year by 28.6 − 13.4 = 15.2 million francs.

- Lindt spent 82.4 million francs to pay dividends to its shareholders during the year.

Investing Activities

Transactions that are classified as investing activities usually involve balance sheet accounts that are classified as long-term assets. Typical transactions in this section are acquisitions and disposals of capital assets (such as property, plant, and equipment) and other long-term investments (such as shares in other companies). Purchases or sales of short-term investments that are not classified as cash equivalents are also included in the investing section.

In Lindt's statement of cash flows, we see that the company engaged in the following investing activities in 2009:

- It spent cash of 115.2 million Swiss francs on investments in new property, plant, and equipment, and received cash of 0.9 million francs from disposals of old property, plant, and equipment, for a net cash outflow related to capital assets of 114.3 million francs.

- It spent cash of 8.3 million francs on investments in intangible assets.

- It spent cash of 1 million francs on investments in financial assets.

- It received 14 million francs from disposals of marketable securities and spent 9.3 million on investments in marketable securities, for a net cash inflow of 4.7 million Swiss francs.

Note that Lindt had large outflows of cash for investing activities in both 2009 and 2008. This is typical of most companies. Usually, as companies go through the normal process of replacing long-lived assets, they spend much more for the new assets they require than they get from selling the old ones they no longer need. This usually results in a substantial net cash outflow related to investing activities.

Before moving on to operating activities, it is important to note that the amounts that are reported on the statement of cash flows for the acquisition of capital assets are the amounts of *cash* used by the company in making the acquisitions. For example, consider a company that purchased a building for $800,000, paid $200,000 down, and assumed a long-term mortgage liability for the balance of $600,000. The statement of cash flows would show only the cash outflow of $200,000, under investing activities. Neither the remaining $600,000 of the acquisition cost of the asset nor the $600,000 representing the new mortgage liability would appear on the statement of cash flows, because the only cash flow involved in this transaction was $200,000. Consequently, when this company reports an outflow of $200,000 on its statement of cash flows for the purchase of a building, this does not mean that the cost of the building was $200,000. Rather, it indicates that the cash paid for the purchase was $200,000.

Operating Activities

Operating activities include all other cash transactions not covered by financing or investing activities. The operating activities section typically includes the cash flows that result directly from the sale of goods and services to customers. Transactions that are classified as operating activities typically involve balance sheet accounts that are classified as current assets and current liabilities. The major cash inflow is from the collection of revenues from customers, and the major cash outflow is from payments to suppliers (for inventory, materials, labour, and so on). As mentioned earlier, interest payments are usually also included as operating activities on the statement of cash flows, even though they are related to debt financing. One other cash flow worth noting in the operating section is payments for taxes. Even though taxes are affected by all three types of activities, taxes are reported in the operating section of the statement of cash flows.

A complete record of the cash generated by a company's operating activities would show the amounts of cash received from revenues and collections from customers as inflows, and the amounts of cash paid for expenses and payments to suppliers as outflows. This method of presentation, called the **direct approach**, is theoretically very informative, and its use is encouraged by both the Canadian Institute of Chartered Accountants and the International Accounting Standards Board. When we prepared the statement of cash flows for Demo Company in Chapter 2, we used the direct approach. However, it is rarely used in practice. The method normally used in published cash flow statements is the **indirect approach**, which is the approach used by Lindt & Sprüngli Group. Note that these two approaches differ only in the format and content of the operating activities section. The investing and financing activities sections are the same under both approaches.

Using the indirect approach, the operating section starts with reported net earnings and then shows adjustments to convert the net earnings to a cash basis and arrive at the net cash flows from operations. The adjustments are in two groups. The first group consists of adjustments to eliminate items that are included in net earnings but do not involve cash flows. The second group consists of adjustments for the changes in various current assets and current liabilities, to convert the revenue and expense amounts that are included in net earnings from the accrual basis to their cash values.

In Lindt's statement of cash flows shown in Exhibit 5-10, note that the amount of net earnings is the starting point, but it is first adjusted by the items listed directly below it: depreciation, amortization, and impairment, and changes in provisions and value adjustments. This group of adjustments eliminates items that are included in the calculation of net earnings but do not involve cash flows. Unlike other expenses, depreciation, amortization, and impairment expenses do not involve cash payments. They merely involve recognizing the decline in value of long-term assets. The cash outflows related to these assets occurred when the assets were purchased, which may have happened several years ago and would have been reported as an outflow of cash at that time, in the investing activities section of the statement of cash flows. To illustrate this point, note the journal entries in the following example:

When the asset was purchased:
Dr. Equipment (A)	10,000	
Cr. Cash (A)		10,000

When the asset is depreciated:
Dr. Depreciation expense (SE)	1,000	
Cr. Accumulated depreciation (XA)		1,000

There was a cash outflow when the asset was purchased, but when it is depreciated there is no effect on cash. Like all expenses, depreciation, amortization, and impairment are subtracted when the net earnings amount is being calculated; but since these particular expenses do not represent cash outflows, they are added back to the net earnings on the statement of cash flows. This is part of the process of converting the amount of net earnings to the amount of net cash flow from operating activities. You can think of this as an elimination adjustment: on the statement of earnings, these expenses are deducted; on the statement of cash flows, they are added. The net result is that these items are eliminated (because, from a cash flow perspective, they have no effect).

The logic behind the adjustment for the changes in provisions and value adjustments is similar. As an example, let's examine the case of a value adjustment to record a $2,000 increase in the value of some investments that the company owns. The journal entry to record this increase in value would be as follows:

Dr. Investments	2,000	
Cr. Gain from increase in value of investments		2,000

The gain (or income) recorded above would be added when calculating net earnings. However, as you can see from the above journal entry, there was no cash flow related to it. Therefore, since it was added on the earnings statement, it has to be deducted—to eliminate it—on the statement of cash flows (because, from a cash flow perspective, it has no effect).

Gains or losses on disposals of fixed assets require similar adjustments, which will be illustrated later in this chapter.

As mentioned above, the second group of adjustments includes the changes in various current assets and current liabilities, in order to convert the related revenue and expense amounts (included in the net earnings) to their cash values. These adjustments in the second group are needed because not all revenues and expenses result in cash flows in the current period. For example, if the balance in accounts receivable has increased during the period, this means that not all the revenues were collected in cash; some will be collected later. Similarly, if the amount of accrued expenses payable has increased during the period, this means that not all the expenses were paid in cash; some will be paid later. Adjusting the net earnings amount by the changes in these current asset and current liability accounts during the period is the final part of the process of converting the net earnings amount from its accrual basis to a cash basis.

To illustrate and explain these adjustments, we will look at three examples.

Example 1: Accounts receivable   Look at the line related to accounts receivable on Lindt's cash flow statement. The description "Decrease (+) / Increase (−) of accounts receivable" indicates that if there was a *decrease* in accounts receivable during the year, it will be shown as a *positive* amount; if there was an *increase* in accounts receivable, it will be shown as a *negative* amount. Why would a decrease be positive and an increase be negative? The reason is that, *since this is a statement of cash flows, we need to show the effect on the cash* that flowed into or out of the company as a result of the change in its accounts receivable.

The easiest way to think of this is as follows: If the accounts receivable decrease, this has a positive effect on the amount of cash coming into the company (because the decrease in accounts receivable indicates that the accounts have been collected, resulting in a larger amount of cash). On the other hand, if the accounts receivable increase this has a negative effect on the amount of cash coming into the company (because the increase in accounts receivable indicates that they have not yet been collected, resulting in a smaller amount of cash).

Example 2: Inventories Look at the line related to inventories on Lindt's cash flow statement. The description "Decrease (+) / Increase (−) of inventories" indicates that if there was a decrease in inventories during the year, it will be shown as a positive amount; alternatively, if there was an increase in inventories, it will be shown as a negative amount. Again, the logic behind this apparent contradiction is that, since this is a statement of cash flows, we need to show the effect on the *cash* that flowed into or out of the company as a result of the change in its inventories. If the inventories *decrease*, this has a *positive* effect on the amount of cash in the company (because the decrease in inventories indicates that there have been more goods sold than purchased, resulting in a larger amount of cash). On the other hand, if the inventories *increase*, this has a *negative* effect on the amount of cash in the company (because the increase in inventories indicates that there have been more goods purchased than sold, resulting in a smaller amount of cash).

Examples 1 and 2 both deal with changes in a **current asset**, and both followed the same pattern. Based on these we can state the following rule, which can be applied to the change in any current asset: When making adjustments to convert the net earnings to the cash flow from operating activities, *a decrease in a current asset* has a positive effect on cash, and therefore *is added on the statement of cash flows*; conversely, *an increase in a current asset* has a negative effect on cash, and therefore *is deducted on the statement of cash flows*.

Example 3: Accounts payable Look at the line related to accounts payable on Lindt's cash flow statement. The description "Decrease (−) / Increase (+) of accounts payable" indicates that if there was a decrease in accounts payable during the year, it will be shown as a negative amount; if there was an increase in accounts payable, it will be shown as a positive amount. The reason a decrease in accounts payable has a negative effect on the amount of cash is that the decrease indicates that the accounts payable have been paid, which means that a smaller amount of cash is left in the company. On the other hand, an increase in accounts payable has a positive effect on the amount of cash because the increase indicates that the accounts payable have not been paid, which means that a larger amount of cash is left in the company.

Example 3 dealt with the change in a **current liability**. Based on this, we can state the following rule, which can be applied to the change in any current liability: When making adjustments to convert the net earnings to the cash flow from operating activities, *a decrease in a current liability* has a negative effect on cash, and therefore *is deducted on the statement of cash flows*; conversely, an increase in a *current liability* has a positive effect on cash, and therefore *is added on the statement of cash flows*.

Note that, as you might have expected, changes in current assets affect cash flows in the opposite direction from changes in current liabilities. Only the changes in current assets are handled in a counter-intuitive manner on the statement of cash flows, with decreases being added and increases being deducted. Changes in current liabilities are handled as one would expect, with decreases being deducted and increases being added.

EASTERN ENTERPRISES LTD.—STATEMENT OF EARNINGS

EXHIBIT 5-11

For the year ended December 31, 2011

Sales revenue		$136,000
Cost of goods sold		(80,000)
Gross profit margin		56,000
Salaries expense	$ 9,600	
Rent expense	7,100	
Miscellaneous cash expenses	1,100	
Depreciation expense	20,000	
Total operating expenses		$ (37,800)
Earnings from operations		18,200
Gain on sale of property, plant, and equipment		300
Interest expense		(2,500)
Earnings before income tax		16,000
Income tax expense		(3,500)
Net earnings		$ 12,500

EASTERN ENTERPRISES LTD.—STATEMENT OF FINANCIAL POSITION

EXHIBIT 5-12

	Dec. 31, 2011	Dec. 31, 2010
Cash	$ 6,050	$ 19,500
Accounts receivable	10,000	13,000
Inventory	40,000	30,000
Prepaid rent	600	500
Total current assets	56,650	63,000
Property, plant, and equipment	159,000	107,000
Accumulated depreciation	(69,200)	(50,000)
Net fixed assets	89,800	57,000
Total assets	$146,450	$120,000
Accounts payable	$ 9,000	$ 5,100
Notes payable	2,500	1,000
Accrued salaries payable	100	350
Dividends payable	450	250
Total current liabilities	12,050	6,700
Bonds payable	46,000	40,000
Total liabilities	58,050	46,700
Share capital	29,000	25,000
Retained earnings	59,400	48,300
Total shareholders' equity	88,400	73,300
Total liabilities and shareholders' equity	$146,450	$120,000

An Intuitive Approach to Preparing a Statement of Cash Flows

Statement of Cash Flows: Direct Approach

Our objective is to construct a statement of cash flows from the information given above. The information provided is fairly typical, although somewhat simplified for illustrative purposes. Using this information, we have to determine all the cash flows that occurred during the year to produce the balances shown above.

Several methods can be used to determine the underlying cash flows. Two common techniques used to derive the data for the statement of cash flows are the *T-account method*[2] and *the worksheet method*. However, we will not use either of these methods, as they tend to focus on mechanical procedures rather than the underlying concepts. Instead, we will simply examine the information provided in the statement of earnings and the statement of financial position, and use this information to logically determine the related cash flows. This less technical approach will allow us to focus on how the information that is provided, combined with your knowledge of accounting and financial statements, can be used to determine the underlying transactions and their effects on the company's cash flows.

We will show the preparation of a statement of cash flows using only the *indirect* approach, because virtually all published statements of cash flows are presented in this format. However, since International Financial Reporting Standards encourage the use of the direct method—and in the future they may require it—we have included the T-account preparation of the statement of cash flows using the *direct* approach on the companion website.

Exhibit 5-13 shows the skeleton of a statement of cash flows for Eastern Enterprises. This will be our starting point for analyzing the company's cash flows. Before we proceed, you should note the following points:

- The title of the statement indicates that it covers a period of time (in this case, the year 2011)—in the same way that the statement of earnings does.

- The skeleton allows for the items to be categorized into the three basic types of business activities discussed previously: operating, investing, and financing. The operating section is usually larger than the others, so more space has been provided for it.

- Eastern's net earnings (from Exhibit 5-11) have been entered as the first item in the operating activities section, because the amount of net earnings is always the starting point for determining the cash flows from operating activities.

- Eastern's beginning and ending cash balances have been entered, from Exhibit 5-12. When the remainder of the statement has been completed, it will explain how the company's activities during the year caused its cash balance to decline from $19,500 at the end of 2010 to $6,050 at the end of 2011.

  Before we even start the analysis of Eastern's cash flows during 2011, we can observe that the change in its cash balance was significant. The company's cash on hand at the end of the year was less than one third of the amount that it had on hand at the beginning of the year ($6,050 ÷ $19,500 = 0.31 or 31%).

---

2. The preparation of the statement of cash flows using the T-account method is explained and illustrated on the companion website for this book (www.wiley.com/canada/hoskin).

EASTERN ENTERPRISES LTD.—STATEMENT OF CASH FLOWS

EXHIBIT 5-13

For the year ended December 31, 2011

Operating activities

Net earnings	$ 12,500
Adjustments to convert the net earnings to the cash flow from operating activities:	
	———

Investing activities

	———

Financing activities

	———
Cash balance at beginning of year	19,500
Cash balance at end of year	$ 6,050

Determining the Cash Flows from Operating Activities

In the indirect approach to the statement of cash flows, the operating activities section is constructed by starting with the net earnings amount and then adjusting it to its net cash flow equivalent. Under this approach, the net earnings are initially assumed to increase cash by the same amount. (If there is a net *loss*, it is initially assumed to *decrease* cash by the same amount). As we have already discussed, however, this is not accurate because some of the items included in earnings do not represent cash flows. For example, as discussed earlier, depreciation has no effect on cash. Also, some of the revenues and expenses that are included in net earnings do not involve cash flows in the current period (such as sales that have been made on account but not yet collected, or salaries that have been incurred but not yet paid). Therefore, adjustments have to be made for changes in the related statement of financial position accounts (such as accounts receivable and salaries payable).

Applying this general logic to the specific case of Eastern Enterprises Ltd., the operating activities section of the statement of cash flows can be completed as follows. Each of the steps has been colour-coded, so that you can easily refer to the related items in Exhibit 5-14.

Step 1: Examine the statement of earnings for items that do not involve cash flows and/or do not involve operating activities. Once these items have been identified, they need to be eliminated.

The first thing you should always look for is *depreciation expense*. In Eastern's case, the depreciation for 2011 was $20,000 (from Exhibit 5-11). Since this amount was subtracted in the calculation of earnings but did not involve cash, it has to be added in the calculation of cash flows, to eliminate it. Refer to Exhibit 5-14 to see how this has been entered on the statement of cash flows.

Amortization, depletion, impairments, and other write-downs in asset valuations are treated the same way.

The next thing you should look for is any *gains or losses on disposals of assets*. In Eastern's case, there was a $300 gain on the sale of property, plant, and equipment (from Exhibit 5-11). Since this transaction involves long-term assets, it is an investing activity and therefore does not belong in the operating activities section. Since the gain was *added* in the calculation of net earnings, it has to be *subtracted* here, to eliminate it from the calculation of cash flows from operations. Look at Exhibit 5-14 to see how this has been entered on the statement of cash flows. If there had been a loss on the sale of property, plant, and equipment, the opposite would have to be done: losses are *subtracted* in the calculation of net earnings, so they are *added* on the statement of cash flows (to eliminate them).

Gains or losses on revaluations of assets are treated in the same way.

Step 2: Make adjustments for the changes in each of the current assets (other than cash) and current liabilities that are related to operating activities.

Eastern's statement of financial position lists the following current assets (other than cash): accounts receivable, inventory, and prepaid rent. Each of these accounts is related to the company's operating activities, so we will now make an adjustment for the change in each of them.

As you should recall from our earlier discussion, in order to get the cash flow from operations, *increases* in current assets have to be *subtracted* on the statement of cash flows, and decreases in current assets have to be *added* (if you have trouble understanding this, you should re-read the examples and explanations on pages 322–323 before continuing). For Eastern Enterprises, the accounts receivable decreased by $3,000; the inventory increased by $10,000; and the prepaid rent increased by $100 (from Exhibit 5-12). Refer to Exhibit 5-14 to see how these adjustments have been entered on the statement of cash flows.

For current liabilities, Eastern's statement of financial position lists the following: accounts payable, notes payable, accrued salaries payable, and dividends payable.

We have to make an adjustment for the change in each of these accounts. However, only two of them—accounts payable and accrued salaries payable—relate to the company's *operating* activities; the other two—notes payable and dividends payable—relate to the company's *financing* activities. Accordingly, we will make the adjustments for accounts payable and accrued salaries payable now, in the operating section, and make the adjustments for notes payable and dividends payable later, in the financing section.

As you should recall from our earlier discussion, increases in current liabilities have to be added on the statement of cash flows, and decreases in current liabilities have to be subtracted. For Eastern Enterprises, the accounts payable increased by $3,900, and the accrued salaries payable decreased by $250 (from Exhibit 5-12). Look at Exhibit 5-14 to see how these have been entered on the statement of cash flows.

Determining the Cash Flows from Financing and Investing Activities

Step 3: Use the additional information provided about the company to determine the cash flows related to these transactions.

As you may recall, in addition to the statements of earnings and financial position, the following information was provided for Eastern's transactions in 2011:

1. The company sold equipment that had a net book value of $200 for $500 cash, thus recording a gain of $300. The equipment had an original cost of $1,000.

2. The company borrowed an additional $8,000 by issuing bonds.

Item 1 of the additional information gives details of a transaction involving the sale of some equipment. Notice that the equipment had a net book value of $200 and an original cost of $1,000. Since the term *net book value* means the original cost minus the accumulated depreciation, this is an indirect way of telling us that the accumulated depreciation on the equipment was $800. (Net book value of $200 = Original cost of $1,000 − Accumulated depreciation; therefore, Accumulated depreciation = $1,000 − $200, or $800.)

Considerable detail is often provided about disposals of fixed assets such as this. However, you should bear in mind that, for purposes of the statement of cash flows, what really matters is the amount of cash that was received from the sale. In this case, the amount of cash is given: $500; so it can be entered directly into the statement of cash flows. Since transactions involving the purchase and sale of long-term assets are classified as investing activities, this is recorded in the investing activities section. Refer to Exhibit 5-14 to see how this has been entered on the statement of cash flows.

Sometimes you will not be told how much cash was received. In these cases, you will have to analyze the available data to determine what the amount of cash must have been. For example, suppose you were only told that the company sold equipment that had a book value of $200. You could use the following process to determine the amount of cash received: Logically, a *gain* on a sale indicates that the item was sold for *more* than its book value, and a *loss* on a sale indicates that the item was sold for *less* than its book value. Since gains and losses are reported on the statement of earnings, looking at that statement will reveal whether there was a gain or a loss on the sale, as well as the amount of the gain or loss. In Eastern's case, the statement of earnings (in Exhibit 5-11) shows a gain on the sale of property, plant, and equipment of $300. Thus, we can determine that the equipment was sold for $300 more than its book value of $200, which means that it was sold for $500.

Item 2 of the additional information tells us that Eastern Enterprises borrowed an additional $8,000 by issuing bonds in 2011. This means that cash of $8,000 was received as a result of this financing activity and therefore has to be reported on the statement of cash flows. Look at Exhibit 5-14 to see how this has been entered on the statement.

Step 4: **To finish the investing activities section, check each of the non-current asset accounts to ensure that all the changes in their balances have been accounted for. If you find any changes that have not yet been dealt with, determine their cash effects and report them on the statement of cash flows.**

Investing activities involve the acquisition and disposal of non-current assets. Accordingly, the changes in each of the non-current asset accounts have to be examined, to determine if they affected cash and should be included in the investing activities section.

Eastern's only non-current asset is property, plant, and equipment, which had a balance of $107,000 at the beginning of the period (from Exhibit 5-12). Remember that, since this is an asset account, the balance reflects the original *cost* of these assets. We also know, from the preceding step, that equipment with a cost of $1,000 was sold during the year. When the disposal was recorded, this cost would have been removed from the fixed asset account, bringing its balance down to $106,000. Since the balance at the end of the period was $159,000 (from Exhibit 5-12), we can deduce that additional property, plant, and equipment costing $53,000 must have been purchased during the period.

As no information was provided about this acquisition, we have to assume that it was a simple cash purchase. Since purchases and sales of long-term assets are classified

---

HELPFUL HINT

When an account such as property, plant, and equipment is affected by more than one transaction during the period, you may find it helpful to use a T account to organize the known data and determine any missing amount. For example, here is how a T account could be used to determine how much additional property, plant, and equipment Eastern Enterprises purchased in 2011:

Property, Plant, and Equipment

Beginning bal. (from Exhibit 5-12)	107,000		
		1,000	Cost of equip. sold (given)
Balance after sale of equip.	106,000		
Cost of P, P, & E purchased	**53,000**	←	**This is the missing amount, which will produce the ending balance.**
Ending bal. (from Exhibit 5-12)	159,000		

as investing activities, an outflow of $53,000 has to be reported in the investing activities section. Refer to Exhibit 5-14 to see how this has been entered on the statement of cash flows.

Step 5: To finish the financing activities section, check each financing liability and shareholders' equity account to ensure that all the changes in their balances have been accounted for. If you find any changes that have not yet been dealt with, determine and report their cash effects on the statement of cash flows.

Financing activities generally involve non-current liabilities and shareholders' equity. However, they also involve some *current* liabilities. Recall that earlier (in Step 2 of this analysis), we found that Eastern Enterprises has two current liabilities that are related to its financing activities: notes payable and dividends payable. Accordingly, the changes in these two current liability accounts, as well as the changes in each of the non-current liability and shareholders' equity accounts, have to be considered at this point. Any effects they had on cash have to be determined and included in the financing activities section of the statement of cash flows.

Eastern's notes payable increased by $1,500 during the year (from Exhibit 5-12). Since an increase in notes payable can only result from borrowing more money and issuing additional notes, we can conclude that the company borrowed an additional $1,500 in cash during 2011. Accordingly, this cash receipt has to be reported in the financing activities section of the statement of cash flows. Look at Exhibit 5-14 to see how it has been entered on the statement.

Eastern's only non-current liability is bonds payable, which had a balance of $40,000 at the beginning of the period (from Exhibit 5-12). We know from Step 3 that $8,000 of additional bonds were issued during the year. When this issuance was recorded, the balance in the bonds payable account would have been increased to $48,000. Since the balance in the account at the end of the period was only $46,000 (from Exhibit 5-12), we can deduce that $2,000 of bonds payable must have been repaid/retired during the period. Because this would have involved a cash payment, it has to be reported on the statement of cash flows. Look at Exhibit 5-14 to see how this has been entered in the financing section.

HELPFUL HINT

Remember that, although most current liabilities relate to *operating* activities, some relate to *financing* activities. Examples are short-term bank loans or notes payable that have been used to obtain financing through borrowing, and dividends payable.

HELPFUL HINT

Here is another example of how a T account can help you organize the known data and determine a missing amount. It shows how the Bonds Payable account can be used to determine the amount of bonds that Eastern Enterprises retired during 2011:

		Bonds Payable	
		40,000	Beginning bal. (from Exhibit 5-12)
		8,000	Bonds issued in 2011 (given)
		48,000	Balance after bonds issued
Bonds retired during 2011	2,000	◄— **This is the missing amount, which will produce the ending balance.**	
		46,000	Ending bal. (from Exibit 5-12)

In the shareholders' equity section of its statement of financial position, Eastern lists the usual two accounts: share capital and retained earnings. The share capital account had a balance of $25,000 at the beginning of the period and $29,000 at the end (from Exhibit 5-12). Since no other information is provided, we have to assume that $4,000 of additional shares were issued during the period. Because this would have involved a cash receipt, it has to be reported on the statement of cash flows. Refer to Exhibit 5-14 to see how this has been entered in the financing activities section.

Eastern's retained earnings account had a balance of $48,300 at the beginning of the period (from Exhibit 5-12). The key to analyzing retained earnings is to remember what affects this account: Each period, it is increased by the net earnings (or decreased by a net loss), and decreased by the dividends declared. Since Eastern had net earnings of $12,500 in 2011, this would have increased the retained earnings balance to $60,800. Since the ending balance in the retained earnings account was only $59,400 (from Exhibit 5-12), we can deduce that dividends of $1,400 must have been *declared* during the year. However, this does not necessarily mean that dividends of $1,400 were *paid* in 2011. Recall that Eastern has a dividends payable account, which increased by $200 during the year (from Exhibit 5-12). Combining these two pieces of information, we can conclude that although dividends of $1,400 were *declared* during the period, dividends of $1,200 must have been *paid* in 2011. Look at Exhibit 5-14 to see how this has been reported in the financing section of the statement of cash flows.

EXHIBIT 5-14

EASTERN ENTERPRISES LTD.—STATEMENT OF CASH FLOWS

For the year ended December 31, 2011

Operating activities

Net earnings	$ 12,500
Adjustments to convert the net earnings to the cash flow from operating activities:	
Depreciation expense	20,000
Gain on sale of property, plant, and equipment	(300)
Decrease in accounts receivable	3,000
Increase in inventory	(10,000)
Increase in prepaid rent	(100)
Increase in accounts payable	3,900
Decrease in accrued salaries payable	(250)

Investing activities

Cash received from sale of property, plant, and equipment	$ 500
Cash paid for purchase of property, plant, and equipment	(53,000)

Financing activities

Cash received from issuance of bonds payable	$ 8,000
Cash received from issuance of notes payable	1,500
Cash paid for retirement of bonds payable	(2,000)
Cash received from issuance of shares	4,000
Cash paid for dividends	(1,200)

Cash balance at beginning of year	19,500
Cash balance at end of year	$ 6,050

We can now complete Eastern's statement of cash flows by simply entering a subtotal for each of the three sections, and then combining these into an overall net change in cash for the period. This has been done in Exhibit 5-15. We can ensure that the overall change in cash for the period is the correct amount by combining it with the beginning cash balance to see if it produces the ending cash balance. In Eastern's case, $19,500 − $13,450 = $6,050, which confirms that all the cash flows for the period have been identified.

Finally, as you may recall from earlier in the chapter, the amount of cash received or paid for interest and income tax should be disclosed as supplementary information, at the bottom of the statement of cash flows. Eastern's statement of earnings (Exhibit 5-11) shows interest expense of $2,500 and income tax expense of $3,500. Since there were no related accounts—for items such as interest payable, income tax payable, or deferred income tax—on its statement of financial position (Exhibit 5-12), the amounts that were recorded as expenses must have been paid in cash. We have noted these cash payments at the bottom of Exhibit 5-15, for the benefit of users who want this information.

As an alternative to presenting the supplementary disclosures (about the amount of cash used for interest and income tax) on the statement of cash flows, this information may be provided in the notes accompanying the financial statements.

As a final point, we should note that Eastern Enterprises did not have any *cash equivalents*. Many companies have cash equivalents in the form of short-term investments that are extremely liquid and fixed in value. These have to be added to the cash balance, to determine the amount of *cash* and *cash equivalents*. On the other hand, some companies have negative cash equivalents, in the form of bank overdrafts or debts that are payable on demand. These have to be subtracted from the cash balance, to determine the amount of cash and cash equivalents. If a company has cash equivalents, the statement of cash flows has to show the net change in cash and cash equivalents, rather than just cash itself, during the accounting period.

HELPFUL HINT

Here is a final example of how a T account can help you organize the known data and determine a missing amount. It shows how the Retained Earnings account can be used to determine the amount of dividends that Eastern Enterprises declared in 2011:

Retained Earnings

		48,300	Beginning bal. (from Exhibit 5-12)
		12,500	Net earnings for 2011 (given)
		60,800	Balance after earnings added
Dividends declared in 2011	1,400	←	This is the missing amount, which will produce the ending balance.
		59,400	Ending bal. (from Exhibit 5-12)

As a final point to ensure that you have understood the foregoing, look at the amounts for 2009 shown in Lindt's cash flow statement (in Exhibit 5-10) for the three examples used above:

1. The amounts shown for the changes in accounts receivable are 71.3 for 2009 and 21.9 for 2008. Since this is a *current asset* account and the amounts are *positive*, this indicates that there was a *decrease* in the accounts receivable in both years.

2. The amounts shown for the changes in inventories are 15.3 and −52.5. Since this is a *current asset* account and the amount for 2009 is *positive*, this indicates that there was a *decrease* in Lindt's inventories during 2009; conversely, since the amount for 2008 is *negative*, this indicates that there was an *increase* in Lindt's inventories during 2008.

3. The amounts shown for the changes in accounts payable are 2.6 and −46.2. Since this is a *current liability* account and the amount for 2009 is *positive*, this indicates that there was an *increase* in the accounts payable during 2009; conversely, since the amount for 2008 is *negative*, this indicates that there was a *decrease* in the accounts payable during 2008.

INTERNATIONAL PERSPECTIVES

U.S. GAAP and IFRS Requirements

Although the accounting standards in the United States and International Financial Reporting Standards related to the statement of cash flows are generally very similar to current Canadian practice, here are a couple of differences that are worth noting:

- Under U.S. GAAP, interest payments must be classified as *operating* cash flows; under IFRS, they can be classified as either *operating* or *financing* cash flows.

- Under U.S. GAAP, dividends received on investments must be classified as *operating* cash flows; under IFRS, they can be classified as either *operating* or *investing* cash flows.

PREPARING THE STATEMENT OF CASH FLOWS

To illustrate the preparation of a statement of cash flows, we will use a new hypothetical example. Exhibit 5-11 shows the statement of earnings for Eastern Enterprises Ltd. for the year 2011, and Exhibit 5-12 shows Eastern's statement of financial position for the year ended December 31, 2011 (with comparative figures for 2010).

The following additional information is provided regarding Eastern's transactions in 2011:

1. The company sold equipment that had a net book value of $200 for $500 cash, thus recording a gain of $300. The equipment had an original cost of $1,000.

2. The company borrowed an additional $8,000 by issuing bonds.

EXHIBIT 5-15

EASTERN ENTERPRISES LTD.—STATEMENT OF CASH FLOWS

For the year ended December 31, 2011

Operating activities		
Net earnings	$ 12,500	
Adjustments to convert the net earnings to the cash flow from operating activities:		
Depreciation expense	20,000	
Gain on sale of property, plant, and equipment	(300)	
Decrease in accounts receivable	3,000	
Increase in inventory	(10,000)	
Increase in prepaid rent	(100)	
Increase in accounts payable	3,900	
Decrease in accrued salaries payable	(250)	
Cash flow from operating activities		$28,750
Investing activities		
Cash received from sale of property, plant, and equipment	$ 500	
Cash paid for purchase of property, plant, and equipment	(53,000)	
Cash flow from investing activities		(52,500)
Financing activities		
Cash received from issuance of bonds payable	$ 8,000	
Cash received from issuance of notes payable	1,500	
Cash paid for retirement of bonds payable	(2,000)	
Cash received from issuance of shares	4,000	
Cash paid for dividends	(1,200)	
Cash flow from financing activities		10,300
Net change in cash during the year		(13,450)
Cash balance at beginning of year		19,500
Cash balance at end of year		$ 6,050
Supplementary disclosures:		
Cash paid for interest	$2,500	
Cash paid for income tax	3,500	

INTERPRETING CASH FLOW INFORMATION

The most important part of cash flow analysis is interpreting what the statement of cash flows reveals about the company. Three basic questions can serve as a start for the analysis of this statement:

1. *Is the cash from operating activities sufficient to sustain the company over the long term?* A company can be healthy in the long run only when it produces a reasonable amount of cash from its operations. Although cash can be obtained from financing activities (issuance of new debt or shares) and from investment activities (the sale of investments or capital assets), these sources are limited and cannot sustain the company forever.

2. *Do any of the items on the statement of cash flows suggest that the business may be having problems?* For example, a large increase in accounts receivable may indicate that the company is having difficulties collecting its receivables; a large increase in inventories may indicate that it is having trouble selling its products; a large increase in accounts payable may indicate that the company is having difficulty paying its bills; large disposals of fixed assets may indicate that it is contracting, rather than expanding; and large increases in debt financing without counter-balancing increases in equity may indicate that the company is having trouble attracting investors.

3. *Of the sources and uses of cash, which ones are related to items or activities that will continue from period to period, and which are sporadic or non-continuing?* A large source or use of cash in one period may not have long-term implications if it will not continue in the future. To address this question, the historical trend in the cash flow data must be considered.

While some users will be interested in what has happened to cash in the current period, most are likely to be more interested in predicting the company's future cash flows. For example, a bank loan officer wants assurance that, if money is loaned to the company, the company will be able to pay it back. A stock analyst, on the other hand, will want to know what cash flows can be expected over a long period of time, to ensure an adequate return on an investment in the company's shares. Users interested in the company's future will analyze this statement to try to decide which cash flows will continue in the future and which will not.

In addition to deciding which cash flows are likely to continue, users will want to assess whether the cash inflow from operations will be sufficient to cover the company's investing and financing activities over the long term. There is a limit to the cash inflows that can be achieved from investing and financing activities. Investing inflows are limited by the kinds of returns that can be earned from investments in long-term assets and the level of investment made by the company. Financing inflows are limited by the willingness of lenders and shareholders to invest their money in the company. As the level of debt rises, so does the risk; consequently, the interest rate that must be paid will also increase. At some level of debt, the company becomes so risky that lenders will simply not lend more. Because the inflows from investing and financing are limited, the company, if it is to remain in business, must generate sufficient cash inflows from operating activities to make the principal, interest, and dividend payments associated with the financing activities, and to continue investing at appropriate levels in property, plant, and equipment and other long-term assets.

LEARNING OBJECTIVE 7

Interpret a statement of cash flows and use the information from it and other financial statements to analyze a company's financial health.

Eastern Enterprises, as an example, generated $28,750 from operations. Assuming that these are continuing operations (as opposed to discontinued operations) and that Eastern is in a fairly stable industry, you would expect operating cash flow of approximately this amount to continue into the future. One way to evaluate this would be to look at the trend in cash flow from operations over the last several years, to see how stable this figure has been. The next question to address is whether this flow is sufficient to cover Eastern's continuing cash needs.

If you look at the uses of cash in the investing and financing activities sections, you will see that Eastern spent $53,000 to buy new property, plant, and equipment; $2,000 to pay off debt; and $1,200 to pay dividends. It is likely that purchasing new capital assets will be a continuing need, because plant and equipment wear out over time. But does the company spend about $53,000 to purchase fixed assets every year, or was the amount of this year's spending significantly larger (or smaller) than usual? If Eastern buys approximately $53,000 of fixed assets every year, you could quickly conclude that the cash from operations will not be sufficient in the long run to pay for this one need, not to mention the company's other needs. However, the fact that Eastern has a total of only $159,000 of property, plant, and equipment suggests that $53,000 purchased in a single year is an unusually large amount. A reasonable estimate of the average amount spent on capital assets might be, say, one-tenth of the total amount, or $15,900 per year. This year's cash flow from operations would have been sufficient to pay for this need, with almost $13,000 left over to pay for other needs. The reasonableness of this estimate could be checked by looking at the trend in spending for property, plant, and equipment over the last several years, to determine the average amount of spending.

The repayment of debt is another item that generally continues from year to year, but (as discussed below) it is not so dependent on cash flows from operations. Almost all companies carry a certain amount of debt. The level of debt financing is often measured by comparing the amount of debt with the amount of equity financing. This measure is called a **debt to equity ratio**.

$$\text{Debt to equity ratio} = \frac{\text{Total liabilities}}{\text{Total shareholders' equity}}$$

For Eastern Enterprises, this ratio at year end was $58,050 ÷ $88,400 = 0.657. This indicates that the amount of Eastern's debt financing is 65.7% of the amount of its equity financing. As will be discussed in Chapter 12, there is a theoretical optimal mix of debt and equity financing that will maximize the rate of return to shareholders. Most companies try to maintain this optimal mix in their financing. Therefore, if some debt must be paid off in a given year (which would lower the debt to equity ratio), it is generally replaced by new borrowing (which would bring the ratio back to its original level). This process of replacing old debt with new debt is sometimes called "refinancing" or "rollover of debt."

With regard to its debt financing, Eastern Enterprises paid off some long-term debt in the form of bonds payable, but at the same time took on additional long-term debt, increasing the long-term borrowings by a net amount of $6,000. (Perhaps the company saw an opportunity to take on long-term debt at attractive interest rates.)

Eastern also took on some additional short-term debt financing, in the form of notes payable. This short-term debt will probably require a cash payoff in a relatively short period of time, whereas the long-term borrowings will require cash payments over a longer period. If the company experiences short-term cash flow shortages, short-term debt can be a problem. As a reader of the financial statements, you should consider how soon a company's debt will become due, because this will affect its need for cash. In the notes to the financial statements, companies usually describe their borrowings quite extensively, including information about interest rates and due dates.

In addition to its operations and borrowings, Eastern also generated a significant amount of cash from the issuance of shares. As well as helping the company's cash flow situation, this also helps counterbalance the additional debt and keep the debt to equity ratio reasonably stable.

Once a company has started to pay dividends, the payment of dividends is generally considered a continuing need. Companies are usually very reluctant to reduce or stop the payment of dividends, because this would send a negative signal to investors about their future prospects. Since the amount of dividends paid is affected by the number of shares outstanding, some growth in the total dividend payments would be expected when additional shares are issued. Eastern Enterprises is, in fact, in this position. New shares were issued in 2011, and this will probably mean more dividends will be paid in future years. In Eastern's case, however, the dividend payments are a relatively small amount, so a slight increase in dividends will not have a significant impact on the company's cash flows.

The final source of cash for Eastern Enterprises was from the sale of equipment. However, this cannot be considered a continuing source of cash and, in any case, the cash inflow from the sale of the old equipment was a very small amount.

In summary, Eastern required $56,200 in cash to cover its investing and financing payments—for the purchase of property, plant, and equipment, the retirement of debt, and dividends. It generated a total of $42,750 from its operating activities, the sale of capital assets, and the issuance of debt and shares. This left a shortfall of $13,450 for the period, which was covered by the beginning cash balance. Consequently, cash declined by $13,450 during the period, from $19,500 to $6,050. If all the items in the statement of cash flows were continuing items, Eastern could continue to operate for only about half a year before it would run out of cash. However, nothing definitive can be said about Eastern's cash flow health, because not enough historical data are available. You could say that, if all the items are continuing, Eastern Enterprises will be in trouble next year. If, on the other hand, purchases of property, plant, and equipment are generally much lower than this year's level, then Eastern may be in reasonable shape.

Cash from operating activities can also be examined further, to determine whether there are any apparent problems in the company's operations. This analysis is easily done using the indirect format of the statement of cash flows, as we have illustrated. For Eastern Enterprises, the operating section shows that two major contributors to the cash flow from operations during this period were the decrease in accounts receivable and the increase in accounts payable. This gives some information about the company's management of receivables and payables, which are critical in determining the lead/lag relationship in the cash-to-cash cycle. In general, these two accounts would be expected to move in unison. When business increases, a company usually generates both more receivables and more payables. When business slows down, both these accounts generally decrease. For Eastern, though, they are moving in opposite directions (with accounts receivable decreasing and accounts payable increasing). This should lead you to question why these accounts are changing in opposite directions. It could mean that there have been changes in the management of the company's receivables or payables, or both.

Another concern in the cash flow from operating activities section is the significant increase in Eastern's inventory level during the period, which reduced the cash flow from operations. If a business is expanding, you would expect a larger inventory. But increased sales normally mean that a larger amount of accounts receivable should also be present, which was not the case. Again, this should raise a red flag and lead you to ask *why* the inventory has increased so much. Perhaps Eastern is stockpiling inventory in anticipation of, say, a strike affecting its suppliers; or it could be that the company's product is not selling very well and management has not reduced its purchases of inventory sufficiently. This situation may lead to excessive inventory costs and/or obsolete inventory that cannot be sold.

Note that, even though depreciation expense is the largest adjustment on Eastern's statement of cash flows, we have not commented on it. This is because depreciation does not affect a company's cash flows. It is important that you realize this. To illustrate this point, consider what would have happened if Eastern's depreciation for 2011 had been $25,000 rather than $20,000. The higher depreciation expense would have produced lower earnings, of $23,750 rather than $28,750. As a result, the operating activities section of the statement of cash flows would have started with net earnings of $23,750 plus an adjustment for depreciation of $25,000, rather than net earnings of $28,750 plus an adjustment for depreciation of $20,000. Clearly, the overall result would be the same, regardless of how large or small the depreciation amount might be. Therefore, you should never make a comment suggesting that if the depreciation had been higher the company's cash flow from operations would have been higher, or vice versa.

Finally, in terms of analyzing cash flows, it should be mentioned that many analysts use a shortcut to estimate the cash flow from operations, by simply taking the net earnings and adding back the depreciation. Although this approach ignores all the adjustments due to the other items that are shown in Exhibit 5-15, it gives a quick and often reasonably close approximation of the cash received from operating activities. In the case of Eastern Enterprises for 2011, this shortcut approach would produce a figure of $32,500 as an approximation of the cash flow from operations (i.e., $12,500 of net earnings + $20,000 of depreciation), whereas the precise amount (as shown on the statement of cash flows) is $28,750.

An Analysis of Le Château's Statement of Cash Flows

As another example of how the information provided by this statement can be interpreted, refer to the statement of cash flows for **Le Château Inc.** in Exhibit 5-16. Le Château is a major Canadian retailer of men's and women's clothing, footwear, and accessories, based in Montreal.

As most Canadian companies do, Le Château uses the indirect approach for the operating activities section of its statement of cash flows. Accordingly, it starts with its net earnings and then makes adjustments to convert the net earnings to the net cash flows related to its operating activities.

LE CHÂTEAU 2009 ANNUAL REPORT

EXHIBIT 5-16

annual report

CONSOLIDATED STATEMENTS OF CASH FLOWS Years ended January 30, 2010 and January 31, 2009
[In thousands of Canadian dollars]

	2010 $	2009 $
	[52 weeks]	[53 weeks]
OPERATING ACTIVITIES		
Net earnings	29,837	38,621
Adjustments to determine net cash from operating activities		
Depreciation and amortization	17,216	16,705
Write-off of fixed assets	538	585
Amortization of deferred lease inducements	(1,540)	(1,414)
Future income taxes	734	(642)
Stock-based compensation [note 8]	341	836
	47,126	54,691
Net change in non-cash working capital items related to operations [note 13]	(7,554)	(15,402)
Deferred lease inducements	2,071	2,532
Cash flows related to operating activities	41,643	41,821
FINANCING ACTIVITIES		
Repayment of capital lease obligations	(1,008)	(1,384)
Proceeds of long-term debt	15,000	18,000
Repayment of long-term debt	(9,512)	(10,074)
Issue of capital stock upon exercise of options	2,696	614
Purchase of Class A subordinate voting shares for cancellation	—	(10,537)
Dividends paid	(17,010)	(20,496)
Cash flows related to financing activities	(9,834)	(23,877)
INVESTING ACTIVITIES		
Decrease in short-term investments	11,643	9,711
Increase in long-term investments	(10,000)	—
Additions to fixed assets and intangible assets	(20,075)	(21,467)
Cash flows related to investing activities	(18,432)	(11,756)
Increase in cash and cash equivalents	13,377	6,188
Cash and cash equivalents, beginning of year	10,034	3,846
Cash and cash equivalents, end of year	23,411	10,034
Supplementary information:		
Interest paid during the year	1,503	1,798
Income taxes paid during the year	15,929	22,009

See accompanying notes

First, Le Château presents a group of adjustments for the non-cash items that are included in its net earnings (depreciation and amortization, write-off of fixed assets, amortization of deferred lease inducements, future income taxes, and stock-based compensation).

Next, there is an adjustment for the net change in non-cash working capital items that are related to the company's operations. **Working capital** refers to a company's current assets and current liabilities, or the excess of its current assets over its current liabilities. Rather than showing the changes in the individual current asset and current liability accounts that are related to its operations, Le Château has presented the overall change in all these accounts as a summary amount, described as *net change in non-cash working capital items related to operations*. Many companies do this, to avoid having a long list of cuurent asset and current liability account adjustments in their statements of cash flows. In order to get more information about the individual components, you would have to examine the statement of financial position and the notes to the financial statements.

You do not need to be concerned about the final item in the operating activities section of Le Château's statement of cash flows—deferred lease inducements—as it is beyond the scope of an introductory text.

Note that Le Château produced a substantial amount of cash from its operating activities ($41,643 thousand in fiscal 2010) and that the amount was virtually the same as the prior year (when it was $41,821 thousand), even though the net earnings differed greatly ($29,837 thousand in fiscal 2010 versus 38,621 thousand in 2009).

Within the financing activities section of the statement of cash flows, it is important to note whether the changes in the company's financing are in the form of debt (which involves legal obligations for making future payments) or equity (which does not). The major points that should be observed with respect to Le Château's financing activities follow:

- The company increased its debt financing by approximately $4.5 million during fiscal 2010. The proceeds from long-term debt were $15 million (representing additional borrowings during the year), while the company spent approximately $1 million to repay capital lease obligations and approximately $9.5 million to repay long-term debt.

- The company's equity financing also increased during fiscal 2010. In addition to the approximately $2.7 million of cash that was received from the issue of capital stock, the company's retained earnings increased by approximately $12.8 million (net earnings of approximately $29.8 million minus dividends of approximately $17 million).

- In total, the increase in Le Château's equity of approximately $15.5 million ($2.7 million in share capital plus $12.8 million in retained earnings) was much larger than the increase in its debt financing of approximately $4.5 million. Thus, the company is limiting its financial risk.

The investing activities section of Le Château's statement of cash flows reveals the following points:

- The company reduced its short-term financial investments in favour of long-term ones, receiving cash of approximately $11.6 million from the decrease in its short-term investments and paying cash of $10 million to increase its long-term investments. This suggests that the company does not expect to need access to this cash in the near future.

- By far the largest use of cash for Le Château (approximately $20.1 million in fiscal 2010) was for additions to its fixed assets and intangible assets. Since this is is greater than the amount of depreciation, amortization, and write-offs of fixed assets (which totalled approximately $17.8 million), the company is increasing its investment in long-term productive capacity.

- These latter amounts—related to Le Château's investment in long-term productive capacity—are very similar to the prior year, when approximately $21.5 million was spent on additions to fixed assets and intangible assets while depreciation, amortization and write-offs of fixed assets totalled approximately $17.3 million.

Returning to the overall analysis, it should be noted that Le Château's cash flow from operations in fiscal 2010 was sufficient to cover the company's needs for both its financing and investing activities, with an excess of approximately $13.4 million left to increase its cash and cash equivalents. This exceeded, by a wide margin, the company's performance on a cash basis in fiscal 2009, when the amount generated by the company's operations was sufficient to cover its financing and investing activities and leave an excess of approximately $6.2 million to increase its cash and cash equivalents. As a result, Le Château's balance of cash and cash equivalents increased from approximately $3.8 million at the beginning of fiscal 2009 to approximately $23.4 million at the end of fiscal 2010. In conclusion, the company seems to perform extremely well in terms of generating cash, and to be in a very strong liquidity position.

SUMMARY

This chapter opened with a discussion about the importance of effective cash management and stressed that, for a business to be successful in the long run, both cash flows and profits must be generated. We demonstrated how a company can be very profitable, yet at the same time, have serious cash flow problems.

We outlined the types of insights that users can obtain from the cash flow information that is summarized in the statement of cash flows, and how this is an important supplement to the information provided in the statement of earnings and the statement of financial position. We also went through the statement of cash flows, describing its three essential components and the kinds of activities that are included in each section.

We then described the procedures for preparing a statement of cash flows, illustrating that it is more complex than the statement of financial position and the statement of earnings. To prepare the statement of cash flows, you need to analyze both the comparative statement of financial position and the statement of earnings, as well as additional information.

For users of financial statements, the concepts in the last part of this chapter are more important than the actual preparation of the statement. It outlined how the statement of cash flows can be interpreted and used to assess a company's current and future cash flows. We stressed that it is particularly important to see a positive cash flow from operating activities. The cash flow from operations is the lifeblood of a company; in the long run, it is through operations that the company will live or die.

The next six chapters provide details of the main items that appear in the statement of financial position. They will give you a better understanding of the source and significance of the amounts that appear in the financial statements, and make you a more informed user of them.

www.wileyplus.com

Additional Practice Problems

PRACTICE PROBLEM 1

The 2011 statement of financial position and statement of earnings of Hayes Industries Inc. are presented in Exhibit 5-17. Hayes manufactures and distributes a broad range of clothing and provides related services to retailers.

EXHIBIT 5-17A

HAYES INDUSTRIES INC.—STATEMENT OF FINANCIAL POSITION

(in thousands)	May 31, 2011	May 31, 2010
Assets		
Current assets:		
Cash and cash equivalents	$ 2,224	$ 3,226
Accounts receivable	83,962	75,165
Inventories	169,978	114,465
Prepaid expenses	14,213	14,873
Total current assets	270,377	207,729
Property, plant, and equipment	110,343	101,870
Less: Accumulated depreciation	(71,693)	(69,653)
Total assets	$309,027	$239,946
Liabilities		
Current liabilities:		
Notes payable	$ 43,500	$ 19,500
Accounts payable	54,331	45,023
Accrued interest	1,463	3,521
Other accrued expenses	19,811	22,143
Income tax payable	4,732	4,352
Dividends payable	1,740	1,555
Total current liabilities	125,577	96,094
Long-term debt	50,000	15,000
Total liabilities	175,577	111,094
Shareholders' Equity		
Share capital	26,587	25,909
Retained earnings	106,863	102,943
Total shareholders' equity	133,450	128,852
Total liabilities and shareholders' equity	$309,027	$239,946

The following additional information is also provided (all amounts are in thousands):

Property, plant, and equipment that had an original cost of $9,657 and accumulated depreciation of $5,765 was sold in fiscal 2011.

Required:

Prepare the statement of cash flows for Hayes for the year ended May 31, 2011, using the indirect approach.

HAYES INDUSTRIES INC.—STATEMENT OF EARNINGS

EXHIBIT 5-17B

(in thousands, except per share amounts)
For the year ended

	May 31, 2011	May 31, 2010
Net sales	$656,985	$624,568
Costs and expenses:		
Cost of goods sold	541,284	498,790
Selling, general, and administrative	84,965	83,707
Depreciation	7,805	7,502
Interest	4,136	2,297
	638,190	592,296
Earnings from operations	18,795	32,272
Loss on sale of property, plant, and equipment	1,170	–
Earnings before income tax	17,625	32,272
Income tax	7,050	13,070
Net earnings	$ 10,575	$ 19,202
Net earnings per share	$ 1.22	$ 2.23

STRATEGIES FOR SUCCESS:

▶ Start by setting up the skeleton of a statement of cash flows, with three sections labelled Operating Activities, Investing Activities, and Financing Activities. Leave a lot of space for the Operating Activities, as this is usually the biggest section.

▶ Enter the net earnings as the first item under Operating Activities. Also enter the beginning and ending balances of cash and cash equivalents, at the bottom of the statement.

▶ Step 1: Check the statement of earnings for depreciation expense and any gains or losses on disposals of long-term assets. Once these items have been identified, they need to be eliminated.

▶ Step 2: Finish the operating activities section by making an adjustment for the change in each of the current assets (other than cash) and current liabilities that are related to operating activities.

▶ Step 3: Use the additional information provided in the problem to determine the related cash flows. For disposals of capital assets, remember that it is the cash proceeds received that should appear on the statement of cash flows, under investing activities.

▶ Step 4: Check each of the non-current asset accounts, to ensure that all the changes in their balances have been accounted for. If you find any changes that have not yet been dealt with, determine their cash effects and report them under investing activities.

▶ Step 5: Check each financing liability and shareholders' equity account, to ensure that all the changes in their balances have been accounted for. If you find any changes that have not yet been dealt with, determine and report their cash effects in the financing activities section.

practice problems

> ## STRATEGIES FOR SUCCESS (cont'd):
>
> ▶ When all of the accounts on the statement of financial position have been dealt with, enter sub-totals for each of the three sections and the overall total. This should equal the difference between the beginning and ending balances of cash and cash equivalents.

PRACTICE PROBLEM 2

Based on the statement of cash flows prepared for Practice Problem 1 and statements of cash flows for Hayes Industries Inc. for 2010 and 2009 (the previous two years) shown in Exhibit 5-18, answer the following questions:

EXHIBIT 5-18

HAYES INDUSTRIES INC.—STATEMENT OF CASH FLOWS

	(in thousands) For the year ended	
	May 31, 2010	May 31, 2009
Operating Activities:		
Net earnings	$ 19,202	$ 14,786
Adjustments to convert net earnings to net cash from operating activities:		
Depreciation	7,040	6,457
(Gain) loss on sale of property, plant, and equipment	488	(212)
(Increase) decrease in:		
Receivables	(7,072)	(935)
Inventories	(11,872)	(19,687)
Prepaid expenses	(652)	(2,363)
(Decrease) increase in:		
Accounts payable	10,120	(3,734)
Accrued interest	1,458	646
Other accrued expenses	970	432
Income tax payable	–	(402)
Net cash provided (used) by operating activities	19,682	(5,012)
Investing Activities:		
Paid for purchase of property, plant, and equipment	(9,395)	(8,550)
Proceeds from sale of property, plant, and equipment	415	2,324
Net cash used by investing activities	(8,980)	(6,226)
Financing Activities:		
Additions to short-term borrowings	1,000	18,500
Repayments of long-term debt	(4,913)	(14,734)
Additions to long-term debt	–	10,000
Paid to purchase and retire shares	(1,885)	(2,448)
Paid for dividends	(5,956)	(5,486)
Net cash provided (used) by financing activities	(11,754)	5,832
Net change in cash during period	(1,052)	(5,406)
Cash at beginning of period	4,278	9,684
Cash at end of period	$ 3,226	$ 4,278

a. Discuss the company's ability to meet its needs for cash over the last three years, and comment on the continuing nature of the major items that have appeared during these years.

b. Explain why so much cash was consumed by the company's operations in fiscal 2011.

SUGGESTED SOLUTION TO PRACTICE PROBLEM 1

Since we are determining the cash flows for fiscal 2011, only the data that relates to 2011 is relevant. The statement of earnings for 2010 is not relevant, and is therefore not used in this analysis. (Although the statement of financial position data for 2010 is used, this is because it represents the balances at the beginning of 2011.)

The completed statement of cash flows for Hayes Industries for fiscal 2011 is shown below. Explanations for certain items follow the statement.

HAYES INDUSTRIES INC.
Statement of Cash Flows
For the year ended May 31, 2011

Operating activities		
Net earnings	$ 10,575	
Adjustments to convert net earnings to net cash from operating activities:		
Depreciation	7,805	
Loss on sale of property, plant, and equipment	1,170[a]	
Increase in accounts receivable	(8,797)	
Increase in inventories	(55,513)	
Decrease in prepaid expenses	660	
Increase in accounts payable	9,308	
Decrease in accrued interest	(1,058)	
Decrease in other accrued expenses	(2,332)	
Decrease in income tax payable	(620)	
Cash used for operating activities		$(38,802)
Investing activities		
Received from sale of property, plant, and equipment	2,722[b]	
Paid for purchase of property, plant, and equipment	(18,130)[c]	
Cash used for investing activities		(15,408)
Financing activities		
Received from issuance of notes payable	24,000[d]	
Received from additional long-term borrowing	35,000[e]	
Received from issuance of shares	678[f]	
Paid for dividends	(6,470)[g]	
Cash provided by financing activities		53,208
Decrease in cash and cash equivalents during year		(1,002)
Beginning balance of cash and cash equivalents		3,226
Ending balance of cash and cash equivalents		$ 2,224
Supplementary information:		
Interest paid during year		$ 6,194[h]
Income tax paid during year		$ 6,670[i]

Explanations:

a. As with depreciation, since the loss was subtracted on the statement of earnings, it has to be added on the statement of cash flows (to eliminate it, because it is related to an investing activity, not an operating activity).

b. The additional information provided in the problem states that the property, plant, and equipment that was sold had an original cost of $9,657 and accumulated depreciation of $5,765; thus, its net book value was $9,657 − $5,765 = $3,892. The statement of earnings shows a loss on the sale of these assets, which indicates that the amount received was less than their book value. Specifically, the proceeds must have been $2,722 (i.e., $3,892 − $1,170).

c. The beginning balance of property, plant, and equipment was $101,870. Removing the $9,657 cost of the assets that were sold during the year reduces the balance in this account to $92,213. Since the ending balance of $110,343 is higher than this, we can conclude that additional assets must have been purchased. Specifically, the cost of the new assets must have been $18,130 (i.e., $110,343 − $92,213).

d. Since the beginning balance of notes payable was $19,500 and the ending balance was $43,500, we can conclude that additional notes must have been issued during the year, representing additional borrowing of $24,000.

e. Since the beginning balance of long-term debt was $15,000 and the ending balance was $50,000, we can conclude that there must have been additional long-term borrowing during the year, amounting to $35,000.

f. Since the beginning balance of share capital was $25,909 and the ending balance was $26,587, we can conclude that additional shares must have been issued during the year. Specifically, the value of the shares that were issued must have been $678, bringing in cash of the same amount.

g. The beginning balance of retained earnings was $102,943. Adding the $10,575 that was earned during the year increases the retained earnings to $113,518. Since the ending balance of $106,863 is lower than this, we can conclude that dividends must have been declared. The amount of the dividends *declared* must have been $6,655 (i.e., $113,518 − $106,863). However, not all the dividends were paid, because the amount of dividends payable increased by $185 during the year (from a balance of $1,555 at the beginning of the year to $1,740 at the end of the year). Therefore, the amount of dividends *paid* during the year must have been $6,470 (i.e., $6,655 − $185).

h. The interest *expense* for the year was $4,136. However, the amount of interest payable decreased by $2,058 during the year (from a balance of $3,521 in the accrued interest account at the beginning of the year to $1,463 at the end of the year). Therefore, the amount of interest *paid* during the year must have been $6,194 (i.e., $4,136 + $2,058).

i. The income tax *expense* for the year was $7,050. However, the amount of income tax payable increased by $380 during the year (from a balance of $4,352 at the beginning of the year to $4,732 at the end of the year). Therefore, the amount of income tax *paid* during the year must have been $6,670 (i.e., $7,050 − $380).

SUGGESTED SOLUTION TO PRACTICE PROBLEM 2

a. The two major continuing needs for cash over the last three years have been the purchase of property, plant, and equipment and the payment of dividends. These items have consumed an average of almost $12 million per year for the purchase of property, plant, and equipment, and an average of approximately $6 million per year for the payment of dividends. The dividend payments have been increasing steadily, by roughly 10% per year. The property, plant, and equipment purchases also increased by about 10% from 2009 to 2010, but then increased by over 90% from 2010 to 2011. In other words, the company's expenditures for new fixed assets almost doubled during the current year. It would be important to investigate why there were such large outlays for property, plant, and equipment acquisitions in 2011.

Only in 2010 did Hayes produce enough cash from its operating activities to cover these needs. In both 2009 and 2011, the company's operating activities consumed cash (i.e., there was a negative cash flow from operations). In particular, a very large amount of cash—almost $39 million—was consumed by the company's operations in 2011.

During 2009, since operations did not provide cash, additional borrowings—with a net amount of almost $14 million—were used to meet the company's cash needs. Hayes also drew down its cash balance quite significantly in 2009, to cover the rest of its needs. Its cash balance declined by more than 50% from the beginning of 2009 to the end of the year. Similarly, since operations again failed to provide cash, during 2011 the company again used additional borrowings—this time totalling $59 million, from the issuance of notes payable and additional long-term borrowing—to cover its requirements.

It should also be noted that there has been a shift in the company's debt structure during this three-year period, with the amount of short-term borrowings increasing by a total of roughly $44 million while the long-term debt increased by a net amount of about $25 million. Thus, a higher proportion of the company's overall debt is now in the form of short-term borrowings. This increases the financial risk associated with this company, since short-term debt is riskier than long-term financing.

As an alternative to debt financing, the company could have used more equity financing. However, in both 2009 and 2010, rather than bringing in cash by selling shares it used cash to purchase and retire shares. Hayes did bring in a small amount of cash by issuing some shares in 2011; however, over the three-year period there was a net decrease in its share capital. Offsetting this, because the net earnings were consistently higher than the dividends, its retained earnings increased each year—which provided additional equity financing.

To summarize the main points regarding 2011, the company's cash flow from operations was a very large negative amount, and the expenditures for property, plant, and equipment and dividend payments were the largest in the three-year period. Hayes primarily covered these items by taking on large amounts of additional debt, in the form of both short-term notes payable and long-term debt. (A look at the statement of financial position shows that the company's short-term notes payable more than doubled during 2011, while its long-term debt more than tripled.) This has significant implications for the future because this debt will involve additional interest expense that will affect net earnings, and these borrowings will require future cash outflows for both interest and principal payments.

b. In analyzing the operating section of the statement of cash flows, it is clear that the biggest negative adjustment over the last three years has been the change in inventories. These changes represent very significant increases in inventories. Over the three-year period, inventories have increased by about $87 million. During 2011 alone, inventories increased by roughly $56 million. Looking at the other financial statements (in Exhibit 5-17) confirms that there is clearly a problem here. From 2010 to 2011, the company's inventories increased by almost 50%, while its sales increased by only about 5%. It would be important to know why the levels of inventories have increased so much.

Accounts receivable have also been steadily increasing over the three-year period, and increased more than one would have expected during 2011. From 2010 to 2011, the company's receivables increased by almost 12% (from Exhibit 5-17A). Since this is more than twice the percentage increase in sales, one would want to determine whether the company has lengthened its credit terms; if not, the increase in receivables may indicate that Hayes is having trouble collecting from its customers.

Offsetting the increase in receivables, the company's accounts payable also increased during 2010 and 2011. From the statement of financial position (in Exhibit 5-17A), we can see that in 2011 the amount of accounts payable increased by more than 20% over the 2010 level. Since this is more than four times the percentage increase in sales, one would want to determine why this occurred. While it helps the company's cash flow situation, it may also indicate that the company is having trouble paying its bills and is therefore slowing down its payments to suppliers.

Of course, the fact that the company had very low net earnings in 2011 was a major cause of its very poor cash flow from operating activities in the current year. From 2009 to 2010, the company's net earnings increased by about 30%—which greatly improved its cash flow from operations in 2010. By contrast, from 2010 to 2011 its net earnings decreased by about 45%—which greatly worsened its cash flow from operations in 2011. Nevertheless, the biggest concern is definitely the increase in the level of inventory. The reason for the very large growth in inventories, particularly in 2011, should definitely be investigated.

GLOSSARY

Capitalization The amount of resources contributed to the company by its shareholders and debt holders. However, the term "capitalization" is used in several ways in accounting. In addition to the above, it can also mean the recording of an asset or the deferral of a cost.

Cash conversion cycle The period of time between when cash is disbursed for the purchase of inventory and when cash is received from selling the inventory and collecting the accounts receivable. Synonym for cash-to-cash cycle.

Cash equivalents Current assets that are very liquid and readily convertible into cash, or current liabilities that may require the immediate use of cash. Examples are short-term investments and bank overdrafts or lines of credit.

Cash flow The net change in cash that occurs from the beginning of an accounting period to the end of the period.

Cash position The cash balance, or the amount of cash and cash equivalents (if any) held by a company.

Cash-to-cash cycle The period of time between when cash is disbursed for the purchase of inventory and when cash is received from selling the inventory and collecting the accounts receivable. Synonym for cash conversion cycle.

Debt to equity ratio The ratio that is calculated by dividing the total liabilities by the total shareholders' equity. It indicates the extent to which the company relies on debt financing in comparison to equity financing.

Direct approach A method of presenting the cash flow from operations that shows the direct gross amounts of cash receipts from revenues and cash payments for expenses.

Financing activities The activities of a company that are related to obtaining resources from investors or debt holders. Repayments of resources to shareholders and debt holders are also considered part of these activities.

Indirect approach A method of presenting the cash flow from operations in which the amount of net earnings is adjusted for all the non-cash revenues or expenses, to convert the net earnings from an accrual-basis amount to its cash-basis equivalent.

Investing activities The activities of a company that are related to the acquisition or disposal of long-term assets.

Lead/lag relationships The relationships between the recognition of revenues and expenses, for statement of earnings purposes, and the related cash inflows and outflows.

Line of credit An arrangement with a financial institution that allows a company to overdraw its bank account. The overdrawn amounts become a loan that must be repaid.

Operating activities The activities of a company that are related to selling goods and services to customers, and other basic day-to-day activities related to operating the business.

Statement of cash flows A financial statement that summarizes the cash flows of the company during the accounting period, categorized into operating, investing, and financing activities.

Working capital The liquid funds available for use in the company. Calculated as current assets minus current liabilities.

ASSIGNMENT MATERIAL

Assessing Your Recall

5-1 Discuss why, in addition to preparing a statement of earnings, it is important for companies to also prepare a statement of cash flows.

5-2 Discuss how a company's policies regarding receivables, inventory, and payables affect its cash flows relative to the earnings generated in a given period.

5-3 In terms of cash flows, what is meant by a lead/lag relationship?

5-4 For a company with a cash flow problem, list at least three potential reasons for the problem and suggest a possible solution for each.

5-5 Describe the three major categories of activities that are shown on the statement of cash flows.

5-6 Discuss the major difference between the direct approach and the indirect approach for presenting the operating section of a statement of cash flows.

5-7 Explain why it is important to a company's financial health to have a positive cash flow from operations.

5-8 Explain why, under the indirect approach, depreciation is added to the net earnings to calculate the cash flow from operations. Is depreciation a source of cash, as this treatment seems to suggest?

5-9 Explain what the outcome will be if a company increases its depreciation charges in an attempt to increase its cash flow from operations.

5-10 In what section of the statement of cash flows (operating, financing, or investing) would each of the following items appear?

    a. Issuance of shares to investors
    b. Payment of dividends to shareholders
    c. Purchase of new property, plant, and equipment
    d. Proceeds from the sale of old property, plant, and equipment
    e. Gain or loss on the sale of property, plant, and equipment
    f. Net earnings

Self-Assessment Quiz

    g. Proceeds from a bank loan

    h. Retirement of debt

    i. Proceeds from the sale of long-term securities

    j. Net change in inventories

5-11   Indicate whether each of the following items should be classified as an operating, investing, or financing activity on the statement of cash flows. If an item does not belong on the statement, indicate why.

    a. Declaration of dividends on shares, to be paid later

    b. Payment of dividends on shares

    c. Purchase of operating equipment

    d. Receipt of cash from the sale of a warehouse

    e. Receipt of cash through a long-term bank loan

    f. Interest payments on a long-term bank loan

    g. Acquisition of land for cash

    h. Purchase of the company's own shares on the stock market

    i. Investment in another company by buying some of its shares

    j. Net decrease in accounts payable

5-12   Explain why the net cash flow from investing activities is usually a negative amount.

5-13   Explain how the net cash flow from financing activities could be a negative amount.

5-14   When analyzing the statement of cash flows, explain why it is important to compare the current year's amounts with those of prior years.

Applying Your Knowledge

5-15   **(Cash flow and sales growth)**

Explain why a high sales growth rate can create significant cash flow problems for a company.

5-16   **(Cash flow and capital assets)**

Explain how the timing of cash flows relates to the purchase, use, and ultimate disposal of property, plant, and equipment.

5-17   **(Cash flow and interest)**

Discuss how cash flows from interest are usually classified in the statement of cash flows, and whether you think this is appropriate.

5-18   **(Effect of transactions on cash flows)**

Classify each of the following transactions as increasing, decreasing, or having no effect on cash flows:

    a. Purchasing inventory from a supplier on account

    b. Purchasing office supplies and writing a cheque to cover the amount

    c. Selling inventory to a customer on account

    d. Buying a building by making a down payment and taking out a mortgage for the balance of the amount owed

    e. Depreciating capital assets

    f. Making a payment on a bank loan, where the amount paid includes interest and a portion of the principal

    g. Issuing new shares

    h. Declaring and paying dividends to shareholders

    i. Paying wages owed to employees

    j. Receiving interest owed from a customer

5-19   **(Effect of transactions on cash flows)**

Classify each of the following transactions as increasing, decreasing, or having no effect on cash flows:

   a. Prepaying rent for the month
   b. Accruing the wages owed to employees at the end of the month, to be paid on the first payday of the next month
   c. Selling bonds to investors
   d. Buying the company's own shares on the stock market
   e. Selling merchandise to a customer who uses a debit card to pay for the purchase
   f. Paying for inventory purchased earlier on account
   g. Buying new equipment for cash
   h. Selling surplus equipment at a loss
   i. Paying the interest owed on a bank loan
   j. Paying the income taxes owed for the year

5-20 (Effect of transactions on cash flows)

For each of the following items, (1) identify the accounts affected and give the amounts by which they would be increased or decreased; (2) state the amount of any cash flow and whether cash is increased or decreased; and (3) identify how each item would be reported in the statement of cash flows.

   a. Annual interest of 6% is paid on $500,000 of bonds payable that were issued last year.
   b. A licence was purchased for $50,000 at the beginning of this year. The licence is being amortized over five years at a rate of $10,000 per year.
   c. Old equipment is sold for $40,000. The asset originally cost $160,000 and has accumulated depreciation of $125,000.
   d. New equipment is purchased for $200,000. A cash payment of $50,000 is made and a long-term note for $150,000 is issued for the remainder.
   e. A down payment of $2,000 is received in advance from a customer.
   f. Income tax expense for the year is $85,000: $70,000 of this amount was paid during the year and the remainder will be paid next year.

5-21 (Effect of transactions on cash flows)

For each of the following items, (1) identify the accounts affected and give the amounts by which they would be increased or decreased; (2) state the amount of any cash flow and whether cash is increased or decreased; and (3) identify how each item would be reported in the statement of cash flows.

   a. Inventory costing $300,000 was purchased on account.
   b. A new vehicle costing $30,000 was purchased. The company paid $5,000 as a down payment and the remaining $25,000 was financed through a loan.
   c. Surplus land was sold for $80,000, which was $20,000 more than its original cost.
   d. During the year, the company made a payment of $20,000 on its debt; $2,500 of this amount was for the interest owed on the debt.
   e. Research and development expenditures of $45,000 were charged to expense as they were incurred.
   f. The company declared and paid dividends of $30,000.

5-22 (Effect of transactions on cash flows)

A company had the following transactions during its most recent fiscal period:

   1. Paid rent of $39,000 during the year, which included $3,000 for the first month of next year.

   2. Paid $11,700 of income taxes owed from the previous period.

   3. Borrowed $50,000 from the bank, to be repaid in two years.

   4. Bought inventory from suppliers on credit for $315,000.

   5. Paid $290,000 cash on accounts payable.

   6. Issued additional shares for $120,000 cash.

7. Paid wages of $27,000 to employees.

8. Recorded $500 of wages owed to employees at the end of the period.

9. Purchased a new machine for $18,000 cash.

10. Sold an old machine having a book value (cost minus accumulated depreciation) of $3,000 for $4,000 cash.

11. Recorded depreciation expense of $2,400 on machinery.

12. Sold inventory to customers on credit for $510,000. The inventory had a cost of $305,000.

13. Paid $2,000 for advertising.

14. Bought office supplies for $5,000 cash, $3,500 of the supplies were used during the period.

15. Paid $3,600 interest on the amount borrowed.

16. Collected $480,000 on accounts receivable.

17. Declared and paid dividends of $6,300.

Required:

a. For each of the transactions listed above, use the following format to indicate the transaction's effect on the statement of financial position categories:

Transaction Number	Cash	Other Current Assets	Non-Current Assets	Current Liabilities	Non-Current Liabilities	Shareholders' Equity

b. For each transaction that affects cash, state whether it relates to an operating, investing, or financing activity.

5-23   (Effect of transactions on cash flows)

A company had the following transactions during its most recent fiscal period:

1. A total of 5,000 shares were issued at $30 per share.

2. Equipment worth $120,000 was purchased for $80,000 cash and shares worth $40,000.

3. A bank loan for $100,000 was taken out and is due in five years.

4. Sales contracts totalling $150,000 were signed, and deposits totalling $30,000 were received in cash.

5. One of the sales contracts in transaction 4 was subsequently cancelled by the customer. The deposit on this contract was $10,000; $8,000 of the deposit was returned and the rest was forfeited as a cancellation penalty.

6. Merchandise inventory costing $210,000 was purchased on account.

7. Goods costing $10,000 were found defective and returned to the suppliers. These goods had been purchased on account, and no payment had yet been made for them.

8. Payments of $250,000 were made to suppliers on account.

9. Sales totalled $450,000, of which $90,000 was on account.

10. Equipment with a cost of $10,000 and $2,000 of accumulated depreciation was destroyed by fire. The insurance company paid $7,000 in compensation for the loss.

11. The company purchased 100 shares of Pradar Company at $50 per share as a short-term investment.

12. The company purchased 50,000 shares of Zider Company at $10 per share, in an effort to buy a controlling interest in Zider (a supplier).

13. Patents on a new manufacturing process were purchased for $15,000.

14. Interest expense of $2,500 for the year was paid in cash.

15. Equipment with a net book value of $35,000 was sold for $30,000. The buyer paid $20,000 cash and agreed to pay the remaining $10,000, plus interest, in the future.

16. Warranty services costing $5,000 were provided to customers during the year. A provision for warranty services had been recorded earlier, in a separate transaction.

17. Depreciation for the year totalled $20,000.

18. Dividends of $7,000 were declared, of which $5,000 remained unpaid at year end.

Required:

a. For each of the transactions listed above, use the following format to indicate the effect on the statement of financial position categories:

Transaction Number	Cash	Other Current Assets	Non-Current Assets	Current Liabilities	Non-Current Liabilities	Shareholders' Equity

b. For each transaction that affects cash, state whether it relates to an operating, investing, or financing activity.

5-24   (Cash flow from operations)

For each of the following independent cases, calculate the cash flow from operations:

	Case I	Case II	Case III
Sales revenues	$380,000	$575,000	$936,000
Cost of goods sold	210,000	330,000	620,000
Selling and admin. expenses	65,000	95,000	105,000
Depreciation expense	7,000	18,000	28,000
Interest expense	3,000	1,000	2,000
Income tax expense	18,000	35,000	45,000
Dividends paid	7,000	5,000	25,000
Increase/(Decrease) in			
Accounts receivable	(2,500)	5,000	(8,500)
Inventories	4,000	(8,000)	14,000
Property, plant, and equipment	50,000	(10,000)	60,000
Accounts payable	3,500	(6,500)	4,200
Interest payable	(1,500)	1,200	(500)
Income tax payable	2,500	(1,500)	6,500
Mortgage payable	20,000	(40,000)	10,000
Share capital	30,000	(5,000)	80,000

5-25 (Cash flow from operations)

For each of the following independent cases, calculate the cash flow from operations:

	Case I	Case II	Case III
Sales revenues	$453,000	$790,000	$960,000
Cost of goods sold	235,000	420,000	550,000
Depreciation expense	40,000	70,000	80,000
Other operating expenses	50,000	60,000	70,000
Interest expense	15,000	20,000	35,000
Gain (loss) on sale of equipment	9,000	(15,000)	(14,000)
Dividends paid	6,000	10,000	12,000
Increase/(Decrease) in			
Accounts receivable	14,000	(16,000)	15,000
Inventory	(20,000)	25,000	(30,000)
Prepaid expenses	1,000	(2,400)	(2,600)
Property, plant, and equipment	220,000	(70,000)	150,000
Accounts payable	(8,000)	12,000	(8,000)
Interest payable	3,000	(8,000)	5,000
Bonds payable	(20,000)	50,000	60,000
Share capital	70,000	(10,000)	120,000

5-26 (Prepare financial statements)

The statement of financial position for Cool Air Ltd. as at the end of 2010 and its trial balance as at the end of 2011 follow:

COOL AIR LTD.
Statement of Financial Position
December 31, 2010

Assets

Cash	$ 31,000	
Accounts receivable	20,000	
Notes receivable	10,000	
Inventories	41,000	
Total current assets		$102,000
Property, plant, and equipment	320,000	
Accumulated depreciation	(71,000)	
Total non-current assets		249,000
Total assets		$351,000

Liabilities and shareholders' equity

Accounts payable	$ 10,000	
Salaries payable	27,000	
Interest payable	6,000	
Total current liabilities		$ 43,000
Bonds payable		100,000
Total liabilities		143,000
Share capital	200,000	
Retained earnings	8,000	
Total shareholders' equity		208,000
Total liabilities and shareholders' equity		$351,000

COOL AIR LTD.
Trial Balance
December 31, 2011

	Debits	Credits
Cash	$ 8,500	
Accounts receivable	25,000	
Prepaid rent	12,000	
Inventories	37,500	
Property, plant, and equipment	350,000	
Accumulated depreciation		$ 91,000
Accounts payable		24,000
Interest payable		18,000
Salaries payable		12,000
Bonds payable		20,000
Share capital		230,000
Retained earnings		8,000
Dividends declared	4,000	
Sales		704,000
Cost of goods sold	551,000	
Depreciation expense	20,000	
Rent expense	24,000	
Interest expense	27,000	
Salaries expense	48,000	
Totals	$1,107,000	$1,107,000

Required:

a. Prepare a statement of earnings, and a calculation of retained earnings, for the year ended December 31, 2011.

b. Prepare a statement of financial position as of December 31, 2011.

c. Prepare a statement of cash flows for the year ended December 31, 2011.

5-27 (Prepare statement of cash flows)

The statement of financial position for Johnson Company at the beginning and end of 2011 follows:

JOHNSON COMPANY
Statement of Financial Position

	Dec. 31, 2011	Dec. 31, 2010
Assets		
Current assets:		
Cash	$ 50,000	$ 55,000
Accounts receivable	81,000	95,000
Inventories	92,000	75,000
Prepaid expenses	30,000	40,000
Total current assets	253,000	265,000
Property, plant, and equipment	795,000	750,000
Accumulated depreciation	(325,000)	(300,000)
Total non-current assets	470,000	450,000
Total assets	$723,000	$715,000

Liabilities and shareholders' equity

Current liabilities:

Accounts payable	$ 33,000	$110,000
Wages payable	20,000	40,000
Total current liabilities	53,000	150,000
Bonds payable	125,000	100,000
Total liabilities	178,000	250,000
Shareholders' equity:		
Share capital	320,000	275,000
Retained earnings	225,000	190,000
Total shareholders' equity	545,000	465,000
Total liabilities and shareholders' equity	$723,000	$715,000

Additional information:

1. No property, plant, or equipment was sold.

2. Depreciation expense was $25,000.

3. No long-term debt was repaid.

4. Net earnings were $35,000.

5. No dividends were declared or paid.

Required:

Prepare a statement of cash flows for the year ended December 31, 2011.

5-28 (Prepare statement of cash flows)

Athabasca Company reported the following abbreviated statement of financial position and statement of earnings for 2011:

ATHABASCA COMPANY
Comparative Statement of Financial Position

	Dec. 31, 2011	Dec. 31, 2010
Cash	$ 60,000	$ 70,000
Accounts receivable	120,000	140,000
Inventory	320,000	280,000
Property, plant, and equipment	700,000	650,000
Less: Accumulated depreciation	(260,000)	(230,000)
Total assets	$940,000	$910,000
Accounts payable	$ 82,000	$ 85,000
Wages and salaries payable	8,000	10,000
Bonds payable	350,000	400,000
Share capital	200,000	150,000
Retained earnings	300,000	265,000
Total liabilities and shareholders' equity	$940,000	$910,000

ATHABASCA COMPANY
Statement of Earnings
For the year ended December 31, 2011

Sales	$450,000
Cost of goods sold	240,000
Gross profit	210,000

Other expenses:

Supplies expense	$ 15,000	
Depreciation expense	30,000	
Wages and salaries	100,000	
Other operating expenses	5,000	
Interest expense	24,000	174,000
		36,000
Other income		8,000
Net earnings		$ 44,000

Required:

a. Prepare a statement of cash flows for Athabasca Company for the year ended December 31, 2011.

b. Was the cash flow generated by the company's operating activities during the year larger or smaller than the net earnings? Should these two amounts be the same? Explain.

c. Was the change in the amount of working capital during the year the same amount as the net earnings? Should these two amounts be the same? Explain. (Hint: Working capital = current assets − current liabilities.)

5-29 **(Prepare statement of cash flows)**

Statements of financial position for Janxen Jeans Company for 2011 and 2010 follow:

JANXEN JEANS COMPANY
Comparative Statement of Financial Position

	Dec. 31, 2011	Dec. 31, 2010
Assets		
Current assets		
Cash	$ 180,000	$ 178,000
Accounts receivable	120,000	133,000
Notes receivable	50,000	71,000
Inventories	439,000	326,000
Total current assets	789,000	708,000
Non-current assets		
Land	545,000	500,000
Machinery	483,000	238,000
Accumulated depreciation	(143,000)	(98,000)
Total non-current assets	885,000	640,000
Total assets	$1,674,000	$1,348,000
Liabilities		
Current liabilities		
Accounts payable	$ 125,000	$ 158,000
Interest payable	17,000	10,000
Total current liabilities	142,000	168,000
Long-term debt	350,000	200,000
Total liabilities	492,000	368,000
Shareholders' equity		
Share capital	650,000	550,000
Retained earnings	532,000	430,000
Total shareholders' equity	1,182,000	980,000
Total liabilities and shareholders' equity	$1,674,000	$1,348,000

Additional information:

1. Net earnings during 2011 were $145,000.

2. An old machine that cost $70,000 was sold for $4,000 less than its $20,000 book value (cost minus accumulated depreciation).

3. Depreciation expense was $95,000.

4. There were no repayments of long-term debt in 2011.

5. Dividends declared and paid during the year were $43,000.

Required:

Prepare a statement of cash flows for the year ended December 31, 2011.

5-30 (Prepare statement of cash flows)

Financial statement data for Metro Moving Company for 2011 follow:

METRO MOVING COMPANY
Comparative Statement of Financial Position

	Dec. 31, 2011	Dec. 31, 2010
Assets		
Cash	$ 68,600	$ 49,100
Accounts receivable	95,000	59,400
Prepaid insurance	30,000	20,000
Total current assets	193,600	128,500
Property, equipment, and vehicles	400,000	345,000
Accumulated depreciation	(110,400)	(105,900)
Total non-current assets	289,600	239,100
Total assets	$483,200	$367,600
Liabilities and shareholders' equity		
Accounts payable	$ 21,500	$ 18,600
Wages payable	3,000	4,000
Total current liabilities	24,500	22,600
Bank loan	50,000	60,000
Total liabilities	74,500	82,600
Share capital	200,000	200,000
Retained earnings	208,700	85,000
Total shareholders' equity	408,700	285,000
Total liabilities and shareholders' equity	$483,200	$367,600

METRO MOVING COMPANY
Statement of Earnings
For the year ended December 31, 2011

Moving revenue		$450,000
Gain on sale of vehicles		4,000
		454,000
Expenses		
Vehicle maintenance	$102,400	
Wages expense	134,000	
Depreciation expense	59,500	
Interest expense	5,400	
Total expenses		301,300
Net earnings		$152,700

Additional information:

1. Vehicles that cost $65,000 and had a net book value of $10,000 were sold for $14,000.

2. New vehicles were purchased for cash.

3. A cash payment was made to reduce the bank loan.

4. Dividends of $29,000 were declared and paid during the year.

Required:

Prepare a statement of cash flows for Metro Moving Company for the year ended December 31, 2011.

5-31 **(Prepare statement of cash flows)**

Financial statement data for Gibbons Electronics Company for 2011 follow:

GIBBONS ELECTRONICS COMPANY
Comparative Statement of Financial Position

	Dec. 31, 2011	Dec. 31, 2010
Assets		
Cash	$ 285,000	$ 295,000
Accounts receivable	334,000	384,000
Inventory	311,000	266,000
Prepaid insurance	50,000	35,000
Total current assets	980,000	980,000
Property, plant, and equipment	650,000	590,000
Accumulated depreciation	(165,000)	(130,000)
Net capital assets	485,000	460,000
Total assets	$1,465,000	$1,440,000
Liabilities and shareholders' equity		
Accounts payable	$ 60,000	$ 50,000
Wages payable	15,000	10,000
Unearned revenue	50,000	35,000
Income taxes payable	55,000	45,000
Total current liabilities	180,000	140,000
Bond payable	490,000	575,000
Total liabilities	670,000	715,000
Share capital	350,000	285,000
Retained earnings	445,000	440,000
Total shareholders' equity	795,000	725,000
Total liabilities and shareholders' equity	$1,465,000	$1,440,000

GIBBONS ELECTRONICS COMPANY
Statement of Earnings
For the year ended December 31, 2011

Sales revenue		$3,855,000
Gain on sale of equipment		10,000
		3,865,000
Expenses		
Cost of goods sold	$2,105,000	
Wages expense	353,000	
Depreciation expense	95,000	
Other operating expenses	555,000	
Interest expense	60,000	
Income taxes	345,000	
Total expenses		3,513,000
Net earnings		$ 352,000

Additional information:

1. Old equipment that cost $100,000 and had been depreciated a total of $60,000 was sold for $50,000.

2. New equipment was purchased for cash during the year.

3. Some of the bonds were repaid during the year.

4. New shares were issued for cash during the year.

5. Dividends were declared and paid during the year.

Required:

Prepare a statement of cash flows for Gibbons Electronic Company for the year ended December 31, 2011. Include supplementary information to disclose the amounts paid for interest and income taxes.

5-32　**(Prepare statement of cash flows)**

Financial statement data for Comfort Shoes Company for 2011 follow:

COMFORT SHOES COMPANY
Comparative Statement of Financial Position

	Dec. 31, 2011	Dec. 31, 2010
Assets		
Cash	$ 97,000	$ 94,000
Accounts receivable	32,000	26,000
Inventory	135,000	90,000
Prepaid expenses	40,000	42,000
Total current assets	304,000	252,000
Property, plant, and equipment	420,000	370,000
Accumulated depreciation	(168,000)	(129,000)
Total non-current assets	252,000	241,000
Total assets	$556,000	$493,000
Liabilities and shareholders' equity		
Accounts payable	$ 31,000	$ 35,000
Interest payable	3,000	2,000
Income tax payable	9,000	5,000
Total current liabilities	43,000	42,000
Mortgage payable	90,000	120,000
Total liabilities	133,000	162,000
Share capital	200,000	140,000
Retained earnings	223,000	191,000
Total shareholders' equity	423,000	331,000
Total liabilities and shareholders' equity	$556,000	$493,000

COMFORT SHOES COMPANY
Statement of Earnings
For the year ended December 31, 2011

Sales	$970,000	
Gain on sale of equipment	6,000	
		$976,000
Expenses		
Cost of goods sold	$550,000	
Wages expense	95,000	
Utilities expense	160,000	

Depreciation expense	69,000	
Interest expense	6,000	
Total expenses		880,000
Net earnings		$ 96,000

Additional information:

1. Old equipment with an original cost of $40,000 and a net book value of $10,000 was sold for cash. (Hint: You have to determine the cash proceeds from the sale of this equipment. To do so, remember that any difference between the net book value and the proceeds is a gain or loss on the sale, which is reported on the statement of earnings.)

2. New equipment was purchased for cash. (Hint: You have to determine the cost of this equipment, by analyzing the changes in the property, plant, and equipment account.)

3. The transactions that affected the mortgage payable and share capital accounts were cash transactions.

4. Dividends were declared and paid during the year. (Hint: You have to determine the amount of the dividends by analyzing the changes in the retained earnings account.)

Required:

a. Prepare a statement of cash flows for Comfort Shoes Company for the year ended December 31, 2011.

b. Briefly comment on the most significant information revealed by the statement of cash flows that you prepared for Comfort Shoes.

5-33 (Prepare statement of cash flows)

Data follows for SlowFood Restaurants Inc., which has a December 31 year end:

	2011	2010
Assets		
Cash	$ 90,000	$ 80,000
Accounts receivable	60,000	75,000
Inventory	70,000	60,000
Property, plant, and equipment	100,000	80,000
Accumulated depreciation	(25,000)	(20,000)
Land	200,000	100,000
	$ 495,000	$ 375,000
Liabilities and shareholders' equity		
Accounts payable	$ 120,000	$ 155,000
Wages payable	25,000	20,000
Bonds payable	100,000	20,000
Share capital	160,000	130,000
Retained earnings	90,000	50,000
	$ 495,000	$ 375,000

Additional information:

1. Net earnings for 2011 were $70,000.

2. In 2011, the company sold old equipment with a cost of $10,000 and a net book value of $3,000. The sale resulted in a loss of $1,000. (Hint: To determine the cash received from the sale of this equipment, remember that the loss on the sale is the difference between the net book value of the asset and the amount received from selling it.)

3. The company acquired new equipment costing $30,000 during the year and, to conserve cash, issued shares in exchange.

4. Depreciation expense for the year was $12,000.

5. No bonds were repaid during the year.

Required:

a. Use the information above to prepare a statement of cash flows for SlowFood Restaurants Inc.

b. Comment briefly on the most significant information revealed by SlowFood's statement of cash flows.

5-34 (Prepare statement of cash flows)
The following information is from the accounting records of Khalid Company:

Statement of Earnings Data
for the Year Ended December 31, 2011

Sales	$142,000
Cost of goods sold	(84,000)
Depreciation expense	(10,000)
Other operating expenses	(34,000)
Earnings from operations	14,000
Gain on sale of investments	6,000
Loss on sale of equipment	(2,000)
Net earnings	$ 18,000

Statement of Financial Position Data
as at December 31

	2011	2010
Cash	$ 80,000	$ 68,000
Accounts receivable	34,000	24,000
Inventory	28,000	32,000
Long-term investments	–	18,000
Property, plant, and equipment	196,000	154,000
Accumulated depreciation	(78,000)	(96,000)
Total assets	$260,000	$200,000
Accounts payable	$ 29,000	$ 38,000
Bonds payable	70,000	20,000
Share capital	110,000	100,000
Retained earnings	51,000	42,000
Total liabilities and shareholders' equity	$260,000	$200,000

Additional data regarding the acquisition and disposal of capital assets:

1. Equipment with a cost of $30,000 and accumulated depreciation of $28,000 was sold for cash in 2011. (Hint: You have to determine the cash proceeds from the sale. To do so, remember that any difference between the net book value and the proceeds from the sale is a gain or loss, which is reported on the statement of earnings.)

2. New equipment was acquired during the year, and $50,000 of bonds payable were issued in full payment for it.

3. Other additions to property, plant, and equipment were purchased for cash.

Required:

Prepare a statement of cash flows for Khalid Company for the year ended December 31, 2011.

5-35 (Prepare statement of cash flows)

Condensed financial data for NextWave Company follow:

NEXTWAVE COMPANY
Comparative Statement of Financial Position

	Dec. 31, 2011	Dec. 31, 2010
Assets		
Cash	$ 66,700	$ 47,250
Accounts receivable	76,800	57,000
Inventories	121,900	92,650
Long-term investments	84,500	97,000
Property, plant, and equipment	280,000	235,000
Accumulated depreciation	(79,500)	(70,000)
	$550,400	$458,900
Liabilities and shareholders' equity		
Accounts payable	$ 52,700	$ 49,200
Income taxes payable	12,000	18,000
Bonds payable	100,000	70,000
Share capital	230,000	200,000
Retained earnings	155,700	121,700
	$550,400	$458,900

NEXTWAVE COMPANY
Statement of Earnings Data
For the year ended December 31, 2011

Sales revenue		$437,500
Gain on sale of equipment		3,700
		441,200
Less		
Cost of goods sold	$200,500	
Operating expenses (excluding depreciation)	63,800	
Depreciation expense	49,700	
Income taxes	40,000	354,000
Net earnings		$ 87,200

Additional information:

1. Some of the long-term investments were sold at their book value (or carrying value). As a result, there was no gain or loss on this transaction.

2. Equipment costing $47,000 was sold for $10,500, which was $3,700 more than its book value at the time of disposal.

Required:

a. Prepare the company's statement of cash flows for 2011.

b. Calculate the amount of cash that was paid for income taxes during 2011.

5-36 (Prepare statement of cash flows)

A comparative statement of financial position and a statement of earnings for Standard Card Company follow:

STANDARD CARD COMPANY
Statement of Financial Position

	Dec. 31, 2011	Dec. 31, 2010
Assets		
Current assets		
Cash	$134,000	$111,000
Accounts receivable	83,000	78,000
Inventories	200,000	110,000
Prepaid insurance	10,000	20,000
Total current assets	427,000	319,000
Non-current assets		
Equipment	305,000	350,000
Accumulated depreciation	(67,000)	(75,000)
Total non-current assets	238,000	275,000
Total assets	$665,000	$594,000
Liabilities		
Current liabilities		
Accounts payable	$ 88,000	$ 83,000
Interest payable	3,000	4,000
Unearned revenue	13,000	18,000
Total current liabilities	104,000	105,000
Long-term debt	100,000	150,000
Total liabilities	204,000	255,000
Shareholders' equity		
Share capital	200,000	115,000
Retained earnings	261,000	224,000
Total shareholders' equity	461,000	339,000
Total liabilities and shareholders' equity	$665,000	$594,000

STANDARD CARD COMPANY
Statement of Earnings
For the year ended December 31, 2011

Sales		$207,000
Expenses		
Cost of goods sold	$ 97,000	
Depreciation expense	12,000	
Insurance expense	10,000	
Interest expense	8,000	
Loss on sale of equipment	13,000	
Income tax	23,000	
Total expenses		163,000
Net earnings		$ 44,000

Additional information:

The loss on the sale of equipment occurred when a relatively new machine with a cost of $100,000 and accumulated depreciation of $20,000 was sold because a technological change had made it obsolete.

Required:

Prepare a statement of cash flows for the year ended December 31, 2011.

5-37 (Prepare statement of cash flows)

Steele Company had a $54,000 cash balance at the beginning of 2011. The company reported net earnings of $120,000 for the year. Included in the company's statement of earnings were depreciation expense of $60,000, interest expense of $20,000, and income tax expense of $44,000. The following also occurred in 2011:

1. Accounts receivable increased by $34,000.

2. Inventory increased by $18,000.

3. Equipment costing $120,000 was purchased; $50,000 of this amount was paid in cash and a mortgage was signed for the remaining $70,000.

4. Accounts payable decreased by $20,000.

5. Wages payable decreased by $12,000.

6. Unearned revenue increased by $10,000.

7. Income tax payable decreased by $8,000.

8. Interest payable increased by $5,000.

9. Long-term notes payable of $10,000 were repaid.

10. Cash dividends of $30,000 were declared and paid.

Required:

To help Steele Company's management team better understand its cash flows, do the following:

a. Calculate the cash generated from operating activities.
b. Calculate the cash flow related to investing activities.
c. Calculate the cash flow related to financing activities.
d. Prepare a statement of cash flows for Steele Company for 2011.

5-38 (Prepare statement of cash flows)

Downsview Company had a $163,000 cash balance at the beginning of 2011. The company reported net earnings of $285,000 for the year. Included in the company's statement of earnings were depreciation expense of $66,000, interest expense of $32,000, and income tax expense of $102,000. The following also occurred in 2011:

1. Accounts receivable increased by $13,000.

2. Accounts payable increased by $5,500.

3. Inventory increased by $7,000.

4. Prepaid rent decreased by $1,200.

5. The plant and equipment account increased by $400,000. A piece of equipment that had a cost of $54,000 and a net book value of $18,000 was sold during the year for $22,000.

6. Interest payable decreased by $3,000.

7. Income taxes payable increased by $3,700.

8. The company issued $200,000 of bonds.

9. The company repurchased $40,000 of its shares.

10. Cash dividends of $50,000 were declared and paid.

Required:
To help Downsview Company's management team better understand its cash flows, do the following:

a. Calculate the cash generated from operating activities.
b. Calculate the cash flow related to investing activities.
c. Calculate the cash flow related to financing activities.
d. Prepare a statement of cash flows for Downsview Company for 2011.

5-39 (Determine cash collected from customers and paid to suppliers)

Southbend Company had sales of $734,000 for the year. The company reported accounts receivable of $54,000 at the end of last year and $60,000 at the end of this year. Southbend's cost of goods sold this year was $440,000. In last year's statement of financial position, the company reported inventory of $62,000 and accounts payable of $32,000. In this year's statement of financial position, Southbend reported inventory of $66,000 and accounts payable of $38,000.

Required:
a. Calculate the amount of cash that Southbend Company collected from its customers during the year.
b. Calculate the amount of cash that Southbend paid to its suppliers for inventory during the year.

5-40 (Determine cash collected from customers and paid to suppliers)

Practical Company had sales of $315,000 for the year. The company reported accounts receivable of $30,000 at the end of last year and $34,000 at the end of this year. Practical's cost of goods sold this year was $246,000. In last year's statement of financial position, the company reported inventory of $49,000 and accounts payable of $33,000. In this year's statement of financial position, Practical reported inventory of $43,000 and accounts payable of $37,000.

Required:
a. Calculate the amount of cash that Practical Company collected from customers during the year.
b. Calculate the amount of cash that Practical paid to suppliers for inventory during the year.

5-41 (Convert between cash and accrual amounts)

Balances in the current asset and current liability accounts of Keith's Crafts Company follow:

	Dec. 31, 2011	Dec. 31, 2010
Current assets		
Cash	$ 31,200	$ 24,500
Accounts receivable	135,600	139,900
Merchandise inventory	321,000	279,600
Prepaid insurance	9,000	6,000
Current liabilities		
Bank loan	5,000	15,000
Accounts payable (for purchases of merchandise)	231,400	210,300
Dividends payable	3,700	19,500
Unearned sales revenue	17,500	5,900

Required:
a. If the total amount of cash received from customers in 2011 was $2,000,000, calculate the amount of sales revenue that was earned during the year.
b. If the amount of cash paid to suppliers for merchandise inventory in 2011 was $1,500,000, calculate the cost of the goods that were sold during the year.
c. If the insurance expense for 2011 was $18,000, calculate the amount of cash that was paid for insurance during the year.

5-42 (Convert from cash to accrual basis)

The following is selected information for 2011 from the accounting records of Greg's Gear, Limited:

	January 1	December 31
Accounts receivable	$ 77,500	$ 84,200
Merchandise inventory	110,000	125,000
Prepaid operating expenses	4,200	1,800
Accumulated depreciation	76,000	90,000
Accounts payable (for purchases of merchandise)	49,000	38,500
Accrued operating expenses payable	3,500	5,200
Unearned rent revenue	1,200	1,600
Cash collected from customers during the year	$963,000	
Cash paid to suppliers for merchandise during the year	640,000	
Cash paid for operating expenses during the year	122,800	
Cash received from tenants during the year	14,500	

There were no disposals of property, plant, and equipment during the year.

Required:

Prepare a condensed statement of earnings for Greg's Gear, Limited, reporting the revenues and expenses for the year ended December 31, 2011, on an accrual basis.

5-43 (Interpret statement of cash flows)

The following are the comparative statements of cash flows for Yellow Spruce Incorporated:

YELLOW SPRUCE INCORPORATED
Statements of Cash Flows
(in millions)

	2011	2010	2009
Operating activities			
Net earnings	57	86	98
Add back:			
Depreciation	82	75	65
Loss (gain) on sale of investments	2	–	(11)
Effect of changes in working capital items:			
Receivables	(38)	30	(39)
Inventories	(21)	(17)	(21)
Prepaid expenses	4	13	(9)
Accounts payable	27	(12)	35
Net cash inflow from operations	113	175	118
Investing activities			
Acquisition of non-current assets	(154)	(161)	(152)
Acquisition of investments	(23)	(51)	(72)
Proceeds from sale of non-current assets	16	11	27
Net cash outflow for investing activities	(161)	(201)	(197)
Financing activities			
Issuance of long-term debt	213	156	332
Repayment of long-term debt	(131)	(72)	(93)
Issuance of shares	12	–	–
Repurchase of shares	–	(38)	(84)
Dividends paid	(16)	(14)	(15)
Net cash flow from financing activities	78	32	140

Overall increase (decrease) in cash	30	6	61
Cash position at beginning of year	100	94	33
Cash position at end of year	130	100	94

Required:

a. Discuss the company's ability to meet its needs for cash over these three years, and comment on the continuing nature of the major items that have appeared over this time period.

b. Comment on the changes in Yellow Spruce's accounts receivable, accounts payable, and inventory levels over these three years.

c. How did Yellow Spruce finance its repayment of long-term debt and its acquisition of non-current assets in 2011?

d. Describe how the company's long-term financing has changed during this three-year period, in terms of the proportion of debt versus equity. (Hint: Start by calculating the total amount of the increase or decrease in long-term debt, and comparing it to the total amount of the increase or decrease in shareholders' equity.)

User Perspective Problems

5-44 (Cash flows from operations)

In this chapter, we have emphasized the importance of carefully analyzing the operating section of the statement of cash flows. In fact, the operating activities section is always the first one listed on the statement. From a user perspective, explain why this section is so important for understanding a company's financial health.

5-45 (Cash flow and compensation plans)

If you were the owner of a company and wanted to establish a management compensation plan to motivate your top managers, would you want to base your performance targets on cash flows from operations or on earnings from operations? Discuss the pros and cons of using these two measures of performance.

5-46 (Format of the statement of cash flows from a lender's perspective)

As a lender, discuss whether you would be satisfied with the current method of classifying cash flows into only three categories. In addition, comment on the usual classification of interest cash flows, and whether you think classifying them under operating activities is appropriate.

5-47 (Statement of cash flows and lending decisions)

From the perspective of a bank loan officer, discuss why the statement of cash flows may or may not be more important than the statement of earnings when you are analyzing a company that is applying for a loan.

5-48 (Accrual accounting and cash flows)

Loan officer Han Blackford once commented that cash flow analysis has risen in importance due to a "trend over the past 20 years toward capitalizing costs and deferring more and more expenses. Although the practice may match expenses and revenues more closely, it has also made it harder to find the available cash in a company, and easier for lenders to wind up with a loss." He further noted that recessions draw attention to the need for better warning signals of the sort that cash flow analysis could provide.

Required:

a. Why would the process of capitalizing costs (i.e., recording them as assets to be amortized over future periods) match expenses and revenues more closely, yet make it harder to find the cash available in a company?

b. Discuss the difference between earning power and solvency, why both are essential for a successful business, and how current financial statements provide measures of each.

c. Explain why unexpected bankruptcies would draw attention to cash flow analysis. Your response should include a discussion of why the statements of earnings and financial position might not adequately alert users to impending bankruptcies.

5-49 (Statement of cash flows and investing decisions)

From the perspective of a stock analyst, discuss why the statement of cash flows may or may not be more important than the statement of earnings, when analyzing a company to make a recommendation about investing in its shares.

5-50 (Analyze investment decision)

Jacques Rousseau is considering investing in Health Life Ltd., a pharmaceutical company. He read in the paper that this company is doing cancer research and is close to a breakthrough in developing a new drug that will be effective against bone cancer. The author of the article said that this was a good time to buy because, once the breakthrough happens, the share price is going to rise very rapidly. Jacques therefore decided to look at the company's most recent financial statements.

On the statement of financial position, he saw that the company had a significant amount of cash and short-term investments. It had some assets listed as "buildings and equipment under capital leases," which he interpreted to mean that the company was leasing its buildings and equipment rather than owning them. When he looked at the statement of earnings, he saw that there was no revenue. By far the largest expense was for research and development. The company had a loss during the current year, and the total retained earnings on the statement of financial position was in a deficit position. He thought that this made sense, because the company had yet to make its first medical breakthrough. The company had little debt, and its shares were recorded at approximately $35 million. When he looked at the notes, he saw that there were about seven million shares issued. In fact, one million of those shares had been issued during the current year.

Required:

Help Jacques with his decision, by answering the following questions:

a. Do you think that investing in this company would be risky? Explain.
b. Does the fact that Health Life is holding a large amount of cash and short-term investments mean that management is doing a good job? Explain in detail.
c. Is it possible for Jacques to make a rough estimate of how much longer the cash and short-term investments will last, assuming that the company does not get its breakthrough? What information would help him make this estimate?
d. Based on the number of shares that have been issued and the amount that is recorded in the share capital account, it is obvious that many investors have concluded that this is a good investment. Think carefully about this, and then list three or four advantages and disadvantages of buying shares in Health Life at this time.

5-51 (Interpret statement of cash flows data)

The 2011 financial statements of Green Company include the following statement of cash flows:

GREEN COMPANY
Statement of Cash Flows
For the year ended December 31, 2011

Operating:		
Net earnings	$ 644,000	
Adjustments to convert to cash:		
Depreciation	230,000	
Gain on sale of operating assets	(14,000)	
Change in current assets other than cash	(120,000)	
Change in current liabilities	80,000	
Cash provided by operations		$ 820,000
Investing:		
Purchase of operating assets	(1,200,000)	
Sale of operating assets	400,000	
Cash used for investing		(800,000)

Financing:

Issuance of shares	1,000,000	
Retirement of bonds	(1,300,000)	
Dividends paid	(250,000)	
Cash used for financing		(550,000)
Decrease in cash		$ (530,000)

Required:

a. Did Green Company increase or decrease its current assets, other than cash, during 2011? Is this change consistent with an increase in sales, or a decrease in sales, during the period? Explain.

b. From an investor's point of view, has Green Company become more risky or less risky in 2011? Explain.

c. Does Green Company appear to be expanding or contracting its operations? How can you tell? What other financial statement information might you examine to determine whether the company is expanding or contracting its operations?

d. Does Green appear to be able to maintain its productive capacity without additional financing? Explain.

5-52 (Interpret operating section)

The operating activities section of Johann Manufacturing Company's statement of cash flows is shown below. In answering the questions after the statement, assume that the net cash flows from Johann's investing and financing activities were zero (i.e., that the cash inflows within the investing and financing sections were offset by the cash outflows).

JOHANN MANUFACTURING COMPANY
Statement of Cash Flows
For the year ended December 31, 2011

Cash flows from operations:		
Net earnings		$632,000
Adjustments to convert earnings to cash flows:		
Depreciation	$110,000	
Loss on sale of investments	50,000	160,000
Change in current items other than cash:		
Accounts receivable	$(80,000)	
Inventory	20,000	
Prepaid expenses	(45,000)	
Accounts payable	75,000	
Income tax payable	(14,000)	(44,000)
Cash provided by operations		748,000
Cash balance, January 1		566,000
Cash balance, December 31		$1,314,000

Required:

Use the preceding information to answer the following questions. If a question cannot be answered based on the information given, indicate why.

a. Has the depreciation expense increased or decreased in comparison to last year?

b. Have the accounts receivable increased or decreased this year? Explain briefly.

c. Has the inventory increased or decreased this year? Explain how this affects cash.

d. Does the company appear to be more inclined, or less inclined, to prepay expenses than in the past? Does this help or hurt its cash position? Explain briefly.

e. Compared with last year, does the company seem to be relying more heavily, or less heavily, on trade credit to finance its activities? Explain briefly.

f. If you were a potential creditor, would you see any warning signs in the statement of cash flows that you would want to investigate before lending money to Johann Manufacturing? Explain briefly.

g. Johann has $2 million of bonds maturing in January 2012. It does not have a bond sinking fund (i.e., a cash fund that can be used to repay the bond debt) set aside to pay off the bonds. Do you think Johann will be able to meet its obligation to pay off the bonds, without obtaining additional long-term financing? Explain briefly.

Reading and Interpreting Published Financial Statements

5-53 **(Analyze an international company's statement of cash flows)**
Use the consolidated cash flow statement for **H&M AB** in Appendix A at the end of the book to answer the following questions.

a. In total, how much did H&M's cash and cash equivalents change during 2008? Was this an increase or a decrease? How much did H&M's cash and cash equivalents change during 2009? Was this an increase or a decrease?

b. Did H&M increase or decrease the amount of inventory it holds (stock-in-trade) in 2009? By how much? Where did you find this information?

c. Did H&M repay any outstanding debt during 2009?

d. Comment on H&M's sources and uses of cash during 2008 and 2009. Which types of cash flow (operating, investing, or financing) provided the main sources of cash? How did H&M spend its cash?

e. If you were a user of H&M's financial statements—a banker or an investor—how would you interpret the pattern of cash flows you identified in part "d"? Do you think H&M is a risky company? Do you think it is growing rapidly?

5-54 **(Analyze a Canadian company's statement of cash flows)**
Exhibit 5-19 shows the consolidated statement of cash flows of **Loblaw Companies Limited** for the years ended January 2, 2010, and January 3, 2009. Despite the fact that the actual ending dates were in 2010 and 2009, the financial statements cover the fiscal period 2009 and 2008 and are therefore referred to as 2009 and 2008, respectively. Loblaw Companies distribute food, general merchandise, and financial products and services through stores across Canada, including Superstore, Extra Foods, Dominion, Fortinos, No Frills, Independent, Zehrs, Dominion and Provigo, as well as Loblaws. Their brands include President's Choice, no name, and Joe Fresh Style.

Required:

a. What was the percentage increase in Loblaw's net earnings before minority interest, and in its cash flows from operating activities, from 2008 to 2009? What is the main item that explains the different growth rates?

b. The change in non-cash working capital is a net figure for all the changes in the current asset and current liability accounts. As a large retailer, what do you think Loblaw's largest current asset and current liability would most likely be? Using those two accounts, explain what could have occurred to lead to the change in non-cash working capital amount in 2009.

c. Examine the investing activities section of the statement of cash flows and comment on the main differences between 2009 and 2008.

d. Examine the financing activities section of Loblaw's statement of cash flows and comment on the main differences between 2009 and 2008.

e. What was the company's balance of cash and cash equivalents at the end of 2007, at the end of 2008, and at the end of 2009?

f. Discuss Loblaw's ability to meet its need for cash during 2008 and 2009.

EXHIBIT 5-19

annual report

LOBLAW COMPANIES LIMITED 2009 ANNUAL REPORT

Consolidated Cash Flow Statements

For the years ended January 2, 2010 and January 3, 2009 ($ millions)	2009 (52 weeks)	2008 (53 weeks)
Operating Activities		
Net earnings before minority interest	$ 667	$ 560
Depreciation and amortization	589	550
Future income taxes	(29)	27
Settlement of equity forward contracts (note 24)	(55)	–
Change in non-cash working capital	707	(284)
Other	66	107
Cash Flows from Operating Activities	**1,945**	960
Investing Activities		
Fixed asset purchases	(971)	(750)
Short term investments	(216)	45
Proceeds from fixed asset sales	27	125
Credit card receivables, after securitization (note 8)	8	82
Business acquisitions – net of cash acquired (note 3)	(204)	–
Franchise investments and other receivables	6	(37)
Other	102	(43)
Cash Flows used in Investing Activities	**(1,248)**	(578)
Financing Activities		
Bank indebtedness	(50)	50
Short term debt	(190)	(228)
Long term debt (note 16)		
Issued	402	301
Retired	(167)	(424)
Capital securities issued (note 19)	–	218
Common shares retired (note 20)	(56)	–
Dividends	(112)	(288)
Cash Flows used in Financing Activities	**(173)**	(371)
Effect of foreign currency exchange rate changes on cash and cash equivalents (note 7)	(59)	87
Change in Cash and Cash Equivalents	465	98
Cash and Cash Equivalents, Beginning of Year	528	430
Cash and Cash Equivalents, End of Year	**$ 993**	$ 528

See accompanying notes to the consolidated financial statements.

5-55 (Analyze an international company's statement of cash flows)
Exhibit 1-10C on page 68 shows the consolidated statements of cash flows for **Carnival Corporation & PLC** for the years ended November 30, 2007, 2008, and 2009. Carnival Corporation is a global cruise company that operates several lines—including Carnival Cruises, Princess Cruises, and Holland America—offering cruises in Europe, North America, and Australia.

> ***Required:***
> a. Calculate the percentage change in net income and the change in cash provided by operating activities, from 2007 to 2009. Did the cash provided by operating activities change by more or less than the net income? Would this be a positive sign or a negative one?
> b. When customers book a cruise, they usually pay for it several weeks or months before the cruise occurs. Because the cruise has not happened yet, Carnival does not record the payment as revenue. Instead, it recognizes its obligation as a liability called customer deposits. Based on the changes in customer deposits in 2008 and 2009, do you think Carnival's revenues are increasing or decreasing? Are there any other changes in the operating activities section that would support your conclusion?
> c. How much did Carnival invest in property and equipment in 2009?
> d. In general, what activities are used by Carnival to finance its investing activities?
> e. Has Carnival issued any shares over the three year period? (Ignore the items related to treasury shares.)
> f. Companies like to maintain or increase dividends paid to shareholders, and try to avoid decreasing dividends per share. Comment on Carnival's pattern of dividend payments over the three years, using the information in the statement of cash flows and your conclusion in part "e."

5-56 (Analyze a Canadian company's statement of cash flows)
Exhibit 5-20 shows the consolidated statements of cash flows for **Maple Leaf Foods Inc.** for the years ended December 31, 2009 and 2008. With headquarters in Toronto, Maple Leaf is a food processing company with operations across Canada, the United States, Europe, and Asia. It produces meats and meat products, including fresh and frozen pork, chicken, and turkey products, and, in its agribusiness group, livestock nutrition products and pet foods.

> ***Required:***
> a. In 2008 Maple Leaf incurred a loss of $36,857 thousand yet had cash provided by operating activities of $195,483 thousand. Explain how it is possible for a company to lose money but have a strong cash inflow from operating activities.
> b. In 2009 the company earned $52,147 thousand but the cash provided by its operating activities decreased substantially. Given the increase in net earnings, explain the change in cash provided by operating activities from 2008 to 2009. If you were a shareholder of Maple Leaf Foods, what additional information would you like to have regarding these changes?
> c. In the operating activities section there is an adjustment for the change in non-cash operating working capital. Give an example of one of the account adjustments that could be included in that total adjustment.
> d. Examine the financing activities section of Maple Leaf's statement of cash flows and comment on the main differences between 2009 and 2008.
> e. Examine the investing activities section of Maple Leaf's statement of cash flows and comment on the main differences between 2009 and 2008.

EXHIBIT 5-20

annual report

MAPLE LEAF FOODS INC. 2009 ANNUAL REPORT

consolidated statements of cash flows

Years ended December 31

(In thousands of Canadian dollars)	2009	2008
CASH PROVIDED BY (USED IN)		
Operating activities		
Net earnings (loss)	$ 52,147	$ (36,857)
Add (deduct) items not affecting cash		
Depreciation and amortization	149,489	149,219
Stock-based compensation (Note 14)	18,400	17,160
Non-controlling interest	7,902	7,212
Future income taxes	(7,390)	(23,254)
Loss (gain) on sale of property and equipment	1,137	(4,724)
Gain on sale of investments	(501)	–
Amortization of terminated interest rate swaps	2,106	4,391
Change in fair value of derivative financial instruments	(13,373)	12,851
Change in other long-term receivables	90	893
Decrease (increase) in net pension asset	962	(27,489)
Change in provision for restructuring and other related costs	15,046	37,859
Other	(7,828)	6,066
Change in non-cash operating working capital	(128,981)	52,156
Cash provided by operating activities	$ 89,206	$ 195,483
Financing activities		
Dividends paid	(20,913)	(20,769)
Dividends paid to non-controlling interest	(672)	(755)
Increase in long-term debt	–	415,000
Decrease in long-term debt	(262,795)	(22,715)
Proceeds on issuance of share capital (Note 12)	1,480	5,143
Shares repurchased for cancellation (Note 12)	–	(11,814)
Issuance of equity units (Note 12)	–	69,106
Purchase of treasury stock (Note 12)	(3,190)	(11,341)
Other	3,110	1,994
Cash provided by (used in) financing activities	$(282,980)	$ 423,849
Investing activities		
Additions to property and equipment	(162,893)	(206,220)
Proceeds from disposal of property and equipment	23,717	19,727
Acquisition of businesses – net of cash acquired (Note 20)	–	(62,962)
Proceeds on sale of investments	1,540	1,053
Purchase of Canada Bread shares (Note 20)	–	(32,643)
Other	(145)	(40)
Cash used in investing activities	$(137,781)	$(281,085)
Increase (decrease) in cash and cash equivalents	(331,555)	338,247
Cash and cash equivalents, beginning of year	356,624	18,377
Cash and cash equivalents, end of year	$ 25,069	$ 356,624

See accompanying Notes to the Consolidated Financial Statements

5-57 (Consideration of financing strategy)

The statements of cash flows for **RONA Inc.** are presented in Exhibit 5-21. (RONA operates approximately 700 stores of various sizes and formats across Canada and is the largest Canadian distributor and retailer of hardware, renovation, and gardening products.)

Examine the company's financing activities during the period 2008–2009. What general trends do you observe? What effect would these financing activities have on the proportion of RONA's total financing that is provided by debt (funds borrowed from creditors) versus that provided by equity (funds invested by owners)? What does this tell you about how the company's level of financial risk changed over the two years? What are some of the possible future implications of this?

5-58 (Analyze a Canadian company's statement of cash flows, discontinued operations)

Exhibit 1-9C on page 64 shows the consolidated statements of cash flows for **Mosaid Technologies Incorporated** for the years ended April 30, 2009 and 2008. An Ontario corporation, Mosaid licenses and develops semiconductor and communication technologies. It designs memory technology and supplies semiconductor technologies around the world. In fiscal 2007, Mosaid decided to sell its Systems Division assets to outside parties, and to stop development of its Semiconductor Intellectual Property. Consequently, the results of operations related to these two areas are reported in the statement of cash flows as discontinued operations.

Required:

a. For the combined two-year period, calculate the net cash inflow (outflow) from continuing operations and the net cash inflow from discontinued operations. As a user of the financial statements, would these findings cause you to be concerned about Mosaid Technologies' ability to generate cash flows in the future?

b. For the net cash inflow (outflow) from continuing operations in 2008 and 2009, comment on which activity is the main source of cash and which is the main use of cash. As a user of the financial statements, would these findings change your opinion about Mosaid Technologies' ability to generate cash flows continuing into the future, compared to your conclusion in part "a"?

c. For both 2009 and 2008, compare the cash from operations to the net income and identify the main items that account for the differences between these two figures.

d. What changes have occurred with the share capital of Mosaid Technologies?

e. Did Mosaid Technologies' retained earnings increase or decrease in 2009? Explain your conclusion.

f. Using your conclusions from parts "d" and "e," do you think the portion of total assets financed by equity has increased or decreased in 2009? Explain your conclusion.

EXHIBIT 5-21

annual report

RONA INC. 2009 ANNUAL REPORT

CONSOLIDATED CASH FLOWS

Years ended December 27, 2009 and December 28, 2008
(In thousands of dollars)

2009

	2009	2008 (Restated–Note2)
Operating activities		
Net earnings	$ 138,252	$ 156,451
Non-cash items		
Depreciation and amortization	103,160	100,958
Derivative financial instruments	(1,116)	1,192
Future income taxes	9,225	(2,917)
Net gain on disposal of assets	(2,358)	(2,796)
Impairment charge on fixed assets held for sale	2,050	–
Compensation cost relating to stock option plans	946	1,518
Compensation cost relating to share unit plans	2,557	1,091
Non-controlling interest	5,331	5,152
Other items	1,975	3,465
	260,022	264,114
Changes in working capital items (Note 8)	22,752	83,373
Cash flows from operating activities	282,774	347,487
Investing activities		
Business acquisitions (Note 9)	(3,734)	(4,824)
Advances to joint ventures and other advances	5	8,139
Other investments	(3,995)	(3,155)
Fixed assets	(115,713)	(161,869)
Intangible assets	(46,186)	(34,276)
Other assets	(4,837)	(10,565)
Disposal of fixed assets	6,291	11,686
Disposal of investments	2,422	10,618
Cash flows from investing activities	(165,747)	(184,246)
Financing activities		
Bank loans and revolving credit	(43,046)	(131,518)
Other long-term debt	646	8,560
Repayment of other long-term debt and redemption of preferred shares	(15,819)	(33,946)
Issue of common shares	176,936	5,592
Cash dividends paid by a subsidiary to non-controlling interest	(1,470)	(2,450)
Expenses relating to the issue of common shares	(7,362)	–
Cash flows from financing activities	109,885	(153,762)
Net increase in cash	226,912	9,479
Cash, beginning of year	12,345	2,866
Cash, end of year	$ 239,257	$ 12,345
Supplementary information		
Interest paid	$ 25,493	$ 33,165
Income taxes paid	$ 49,450	$ 75,508

The accompanying notes are an integral part of the consolidated financial statements.

BEYOND THE BOOK

5-59 (Analyze a statement of cash flows)

For a company of your own choosing, answer the following questions based on its statement of cash flows:

a. Summarize the results for cash from operating, investing, and financing activities over the last two years.

b. Explain any significant changes in the items listed in part "a," from last year to this year.

c. Treating operations as a single source, what were the three most significant sources of cash in the most recent year?

d. Within the investing and financing sections, what were the four most significant uses of cash in the most recent year?

e. How has the company been financing its investing activities—through operating activities, financing activities, or both? Support your answer with numbers from the statement of cash flows.

Cases

5-60 Atlantic Service Company

Atlantic Service Company was established five years ago to provide services to the home construction industry. It has been very successful, with assets, sales, and profits increasing each year. However, Atlantic is experiencing serious cash shortages and is in danger of going into bankruptcy, because it cannot pay its suppliers and already has a very substantial overdraft at its bank. The president has asked you to analyze the statement of cash flows for the years 2011 and 2010, and then write a memo that (a) explains what appears to be causing the cash shortage and (b) recommends a plan to save the company from bankruptcy.

ATLANTIC SERVICE COMPANY
Statement of Cash Flows
As of December 31

	2011	2010
Operating activities:		
Net earnings	$200,000	$185,000
Adjustments to convert earnings to cash flows:		
Depreciation expense	25,000	20,000
Gain on sale of investments	3,000	2,000
Changes in non-cash working capital:		
Increase in accounts receivable	(35,000)	(25,000)
Increase in inventory	(30,000)	(20,000)
Increase in prepaid expenses	(5,000)	(4,000)
Increase in accounts payable	52,000	43,000
	210,000	201,000
Financing activities:		
Repayment of short-term bank loan	(100,000)	(60,000)
Renewal of short-term bank loan	180,000	100,000
Dividends paid	(15,000)	(10,000)
	65,000	30,000
Investing activities:		
Purchase of equipment	(300,000)	(250,000)
Net decrease in cash during year	(25,000)	(19,000)
Cash position (bank overdraft) at beginning of year	(29,000)	(10,000)
Cash position (bank overdraft) at end of year	$(54,000)	$(29,000)

5-61 Robertson Furniture Ltd.

Kayla Moss has just received a small inheritance from her grandparents' estate. She would like to invest the money and is currently reviewing several opportunities. A friend has given her the financial statements of Robertson Furniture Ltd., a company she found on the Internet. Kayla has reviewed the financial statements and is ready to invest in Robertson Furniture.

Before she invests, Kayla comes to you for some financial advice, because she knows you are taking an accounting course and may be able to give her some insights into the financial statements. She is convinced that this company will be a profitable investment because the statement of financial position indicates that the company's cash balances have been increasing very rapidly, from only $8,000 two years ago to $354,000 now.

Kayla has copied Robertson's statement of cash flows for you, so that you can see how much cash the company has been able to generate each year.

ROBERTSON FURNITURE LTD.
Statement of Cash Flows
As of December 31

	2011	2010
Operating activities:		
Net earnings (loss)	$ (4,000)	$ 12,000
Add back items not representing cash flows:		
Depreciation expense	20,000	40,000
Loss on disposal of property, plant, and equipment	12,000	10,000
Loss on sale of investments	4,000	3,000
Adjustment for working capital items:		
Increase in accounts receivable	(40,000)	(36,000)
Increase in inventories	(54,000)	(42,000)
Decrease in prepaid insurance	8,000	2,000
Increase in accounts payable	45,000	28,000
Cash flow from operating activities	(9,000)	17,000
Financing activities:		
Issuance of bonds payable	100,000	20,000
Issuance of shares	50,000	30,000
Payment of dividends	(2,000)	(20,000)
Cash flow from financing activities	148,000	30,000
Investing activities		
Sale of property, plant, and equipment	70,000	22,000
Sale of investments	50,000	20,000
Cash flow from investing activities	120,000	42,000
Overall increase in cash during year	257,000	89,000
Cash—beginning of year	97,000	8,000
Cash—end of year	$354,000	$ 97,000

Required:

a. Comment on Robertson Furniture's statement of cash flows and address Kayla's opinion that, in light of the amount of cash it has generated, the company must be a good investment.

b. Based on the results of your analysis of Robertson's statement of cash flows, outline several points that Kayla should investigate about this company before investing her inheritance in it.

5-62   Ridlow Shipping

Jim Shea is an accountant at King and Associates, which is an accounting firm based in Halifax, Nova Scotia. The firm specializes in dealing with small business clients who generally are very successful business people but have limited accounting knowledge.

Owen Ridlow is a client and the sole owner of Ridlow Shipping. He recently called Jim with some questions about the financial statements prepared for the year ended December 31, 2011. During the conversation, Owen made the following comment: "Jim, I am wondering why I have to pay you guys to prepare a statement of cash flows. I understand the importance of the statement of financial position and the statement of earnings; but since I always know how much cash I have in the bank and I reconcile my bank accounts regularly, why do I need a statement of cash flows? It seems to me that paying to have this statement prepared is an unnecessary expense."

Required:

Do you think Owen is at all justified in making this comment? Outline several points that Jim should raise in his discussion with Owen to explain the importance of the statement of cash flows and justify the need for it. Support your answer by referring to Ridlow Shipping's most recent statement of cash flows, which follows.

RIDLOW SHIPPING LTD.
Statement of Cash Flows
As of December 31

	2011	2010
Operating activities:		
Net earnings	$206,250	$254,500
Add back items not representing cash flows:		
Depreciation	40,000	50,000
Loss on sale of investments	6,000	2,000
Adjustment for working capital items:		
Decrease (increase) in accounts receivable	(40,000)	16,000
Increase in inventories	(5,000)	(2,000)
Decrease in prepaid rent	750	500
Increase (decrease) in accounts payable	45,000	(28,000)
Net cash provided by operating activities	253,000	293,000
Financing activities:		
Repayment of bonds	(100,000)	–
Issuance of shares	50,000	–
Payment of dividends	(75,000)	(75,000)
Net cash consumed by financing activities	(125,000)	(75,000)
Investing activities:		
Sale of investments	50,000	20,000
Purchase of capital assets	(215,000)	(197,000)
Net cash consumed by investing activities	(165,000)	(177,000)
Overall increase (decrease) in cash during year	(37,000)	41,000
Cash balance at beginning of year	50,000	9,000
Cash balance at end of year	$ 13,000	$ 50,000

5-63   Jones Printing

Ben Jones would like to expand his small printing business to include a new computerized colour printing system. To finance the purchase of this equipment, Ben has applied for a loan from a government venture capital agency. The agency requires a complete set of financial statements before it can approve any loan application, and assigns an employee to each applicant to help prepare the necessary financial statements.

You have been assigned to assist Ben with his application, and he has provided you with a statement of earnings and a statement of financial position for his business. You explain to Ben that a complete set of financial statements includes a statement of cash flows, and that one will have to be prepared for his company before the loan application can be processed. Ben does not understand the purpose of the statement of cash flows and what types of information he will have to gather in order to have one prepared for his business.

Required:

Prepare a brief memo to Ben explaining the purpose and structure of the statement of cash flows and outlining any additional information, beyond the statement of earnings and statement of financial position, that he will have to provide to enable you to prepare a statement of cash flows for his business.

Critical Thinking Question

5-64   Kralovec Company

As discussed in the chapter, there are two methods for presenting the information in the operating activities section of the statement of cash flows: the direct method and the indirect method. Accounting standards generally express a preference for the direct method but also allow the indirect method. The vast majority of companies prepare their statements of cash flows using the indirect method of presentation.

Presented below are two statements of cash flows for Kralovec Company. In the first one, the operating activities section is presented using the direct method; in the second statement, the indirect method is used.

KRALOVEC COMPANY
Statement of Cash Flows
For the year ended December 31, 2011

(1)   Direct Method

Cash flows from operating activities		
Cash collections from customers		$ 6,446,000
Cash payments for operating expenses		(4,883,000)
Cash payments for interest		(80,000)
Cash payments for income taxes		(313,000)
Net cash provided by operating activities		1,170,000
Cash flows from investing activities		
Sale of machinery	$ 140,000	
Purchase of machinery	(750,000)	
Net cash used by investing activities		(610,000)
Cash flows from financing activities		
Retirement of bonds	(100,000)	
Payment of dividends	(200,000)	
Net cash used by financing activities		(300,000)
Net increase in cash during year		260,000
Cash at beginning of year		130,000
Cash at end of year		$ 390,000

(2) Indirect Method

Cash flows from operating activities

Net earnings		$ 705,000
Adjustments to convert net earnings to net cash provided by operating activities:		
Depreciation expense	$ 470,000	
Loss on sale of machinery	34,000	
Increase in accounts receivable	(100,000)	
Decrease in inventories	35,000	
Increase in accounts payable	21,000	
Decrease in interest payable	(5,000)	
Increase in taxes payable	10,000	465,000
Net cash provided by operating activities		1,170,000
Cash flows from investing activities		
Sale of machinery	140,000	
Purchase of machinery	(750,000)	
Net cash used by investing activities		(610,000)
Cash flows from financing activities		
Retirement of bonds	(100,000)	
Payment of dividends	(200,000)	
Net cash used by financing activities		(300,000)
Net increase in cash during year		260,000
Cash at beginning of year		130,000
Cash at end of year		$ 390,000

Required:

a. As discussed in Chapter 1, understandability is an important qualitative characteristic of financial statements. With this in mind, compare the two statements above and comment on the understandability of the direct versus the indirect method of presentation in the operating activities section. Which approach do you think most users of financial statements would prefer?

b. Looking only at the first statement (presented using the direct method), analyze the cash flow data for Kralovec Company and note any significant points that can be observed from it, regarding the company's operations during the year. Then repeat this process, looking only at the second statement (presented using the indirect method).

c. Based on your experience in working through part "b," which method of presentation do you find more useful for analyzing the cash flow data, understanding the company's operations, and identifying points to be investigated further?

chapters 1–5

READING AND INTERPRETING PUBLISHED FINANCIAL STATEMENTS

INTEGRATIVE QUESTIONS ON CHAPTERS 1–5

The following questions deal with material covered in the first five chapters of the book. They are intended to review and reinforce students' knowledge of where various items can be found in the financial statements and how the information contained in the statements can be used, at a basic level, to assess a company's performance and financial position. These questions are based on the financial statements of **HMV Group plc** for 2010, with comparative figures for 2009, which are available on the companion website for the book (**www.wiley.com/canada/hoskin**). On the income statement, you should base your answers on the columns for the Total figures (including exceptional items) for each year.

1. Answer the following questions, using HMV's financial statements and the notes that accompany them:

   a. What was the amount of profit earned for 2010?

   b. How much net cash was produced from operating activities in 2010?

   c. What was the amount of accounts receivable (trade and other) at the beginning of 2010?

   d. What was the amount of intangible assets at the end of 2010?

   e. What was the amount of trade and other payables at the beginning of 2010?

   f. What was the total amount of non-current liabilities at the end of 2010?

   g. What was the balance in the retained earnings account at the beginning of 2010?

   h. What was the dollar value of the common shares (equity share capital) at the end of 2010?

   i. How much was the profit on disposal of property plant, and equipment in 2010?

   j. How much cash was paid to acquire property, plant, and equipment in 2010?

   k. What was the amount of depreciation expense for 2010?

2. a. At the end of each of the years presented, what percentage of HMV's total assets was in the form of inventories?

   b. What percentage of HMV's total assets was in the form of property, plant, and equipment?

   c. Explain why you think HMV has more money invested in inventory than in property plant, and equipment. (Hint: Think about how HMV operates. Do you think they are primarily retailers or manufacturers? Where do they sell their goods from?)

3. Suppose that an analyst reports that the market value of HMV's property, plant, and equipment at the end of 2010 was approximately £200 million. Assuming this is accurate, explain why HMV's balance sheet reports a value of £167.3 million.

4. Is HMV's financing mainly from creditors (debt) or from shareholders (equity)? You can answer this question by simple observation, without doing any calculations.

5. Calculate the ratio of total liabilities to total assets at the end of each of the years presented, and comment on how it changed during the year ended April 24, 2010.

6. In 2009, HMV's cash flow from operating activities was more than its net earnings—which is typical. In 2010, however, its cash flow from operating activities was less than its net earnings. Identify the primary reason for this change. If you were considering investing in HMV, would this change in cash flow from operating activities concern you? Explain.

7. In the operating activities section of HMV's cash flow statement, what do the amounts labelled "Movement in" represent? Explain why some of these amounts are negative and some are positive, and whether they represent increases or decreases in the related accounts.

8. a. The cash flow statement reveals that HMV purchased capital assets in 2010, and also paid dividends. Compare the total of these two amounts to the profit for the year and to the cash from operating activities. Comment on your findings.

   b. Compare the amount of dividends paid in 2010 to (1) the cash balance at the beginning of the year, and (2) the retained earnings at the beginning of the year. Comment on your findings.

9. Did HMV issue any new shares during 2010 or 2009? How did you determine this?

10. In total, how many common (ordinary) shares has HMV issued? Where did you find this information?

11. What were HMV's Basic EPS for 2009 and 2010? Compare the Basic EPS to the dividends paid per share.

12. Considering your responses to questions 8 and 11, comment on HMV's dividend policy.

13. HMV is a publicly traded company, listed on the London Stock Exchange, and the price of its common shares at April 23, 2010, was about £82.00 per share. Use this information to calculate the total market value of HMV's common shares at that date. Compare this with the value of shareholders' equity as at April 24, 2010, as represented in the balance sheet. If these two values are different, explain why.

14. In your own words, explain HMV's revenue recognition policy and how it conforms to IFRS.

15. Calculate the return on assets and return on equity for each of the two years presented. (Note: To calculate these ratios for both years, you will have to use the total assets for each year and the total shareholders' equity for each year, rather than average total assets and average shareholders' equity).

16. In percentage terms, how much did HMV's *revenue* increase from 2009 to 2010? How much did its *profit* increase (in percentage terms) during the same period?

17. Calculate HMV's *gross* profit rate (gross profit divided by revenues) for 2009 and 2010. Did the company's gross profit, as a percentage of its revenue, increase or decrease during 2010?

18. Calculate HMV's *net* profit rate (profits divided by net revenues) for 2009 and 2010. Did the company's net profit, as a percentage of its revenue, increase or decrease during 2010?

19. Considering your responses to questions 15–18, comment on HMV's profitability during 2009 and 2010.

chapter 6

CASH, SHORT-TERM INVESTMENTS, AND ACCOUNTS AND NOTES RECEIVABLE

LEARNING OBJECTIVES

After studying this chapter, you should be able to:

1. Discuss the main control issues related to cash.

2. Prepare a bank reconciliation and make the related adjustments.

3. Describe the general criteria for classifying and valuing investments.

4. Explain why certain types of investments are reported at their market value.

5. Prepare the journal entries for acquiring, holding, and selling short-term investments.

6. Explain why it is important to consider the potential uncollectibility of accounts receivable, or "bad debts."

7. Identify two methods for recognizing bad debts, and describe the proper circumstances for using each method.

8. Differentiate between two approaches for estimating the amount of future bad debts.

9. Describe the main types of notes receivable and the circumstances for using them.

10. Calculate the interest on notes receivable and prepare the necessary journal entries.

11. Calculate the current ratio, quick ratio, and accounts receivable turnover ratio.

12. Explain how the current ratio, quick ratio, and accounts receivable turnover ratio help users analyze a company's short-term liquidity.

What If They Won't Pay?

After more than 20 years in operation, sales are still brisk at Stiff Sentences Inc. Based in Ottawa and, lately, Shanghai, the 15-person company recorded receivables of about $2 million in 2009 and expected to reach $3 million in 2010. Its product? Words. Eloquent, powerful words, usually in full sentences, written for clients in such vehicles as websites, blogs, speeches, annual reports, advertising copy, and other communication tools. Occasionally, Stiff Sentences also sells its words in ones and twos, as it creates names for companies, products, and campaigns.

Most of the company's clients, which have included Microsoft, Alcatel-Lucent, Nokia, the United States Air Force, the Bank of Canada, the CBC, ACE Limited, and countless government departments and agencies, are satisfied customers who bring repeat business and keep the 11 seasoned writers busy. But because the company sells a creative process rather than a tangible item, judgements on the quality of its products are always subjective.

So, despite strict quality control procedures—the company has been ISO-9000 certified since 1999—"it can happen," says Deborah Johnson, co-owner and CFO, "that a client isn't happy with the final result. The biggest problems come when we don't find out about an issue until we're trying to determine why the bill hasn't been paid two months later." To avoid these situations, the company retains an outsourced receivables clerk who works from home and calls clients as soon as an invoice becomes overdue. As a result, overdue accounts are usually resolved before any invoices become uncollectible.

Still, when there are disagreements, "we try to work something out," Ms. Johnson explains. Sometimes the work is redone; often, however, Stiff Sentences ends up writing off all or part of the fee as a bad debt. The writers involved share in the responsibility in such cases. "They're not employees, but associated companies," Ms. Johnson says, explaining that the company's financial relationship with the writers is much like that of a real estate company with its agents. "They pay a fee to belong to the group, they work independently, and they keep a percentage of the revenue from the work they do."

Most of the writers make an excellent living (rare in the writing trade). But while they share in the profits at Stiff Sentences, they also share in the risk. Writers are paid twice a month for work completed to date; but if the fee for a job is written off and the writer has already been paid for working on it, he or she refunds the payment.

"It's critical, therefore, that we keep focused on who's responsible for what in each job," stresses Ms. Johnson. Of course, it's also important to keep these uncollectible amounts to a minimum. "The best way to do that is to stay on top of our receivables," she explains. "The other thing that helps is to make sure we're serving people well. We routinely conduct customer satisfaction surveys and the feedback has been extremely valuable."

Our opening story talks about a growing company's efforts to control its accounts receivable and limit the number of uncollectible accounts, or bad debts. Since sales on credit are a common form of business transaction (particularly business-to-business transactions), accounts receivable are a major asset for many companies. And, as discussed in Chapter 5, the collection of customers' accounts is also a major source of cash. It should not be surprising, therefore, that determining the value of the accounts receivable and estimating the amount that will be collected in cash is important for both external financial reporting and sound internal financial management.

In addition to keeping an eye on accounts receivable, good financial management also means investing excess cash on hand until it is needed. Short-term investments thus become another part of the cash-to-cash cycle for many companies and an essential element in any assessment of a company's liquidity. This chapter discusses accounting and management control issues related to an organization's most liquid assets—its cash, its short-term investments, and its receivables.

USER RELEVANCE

As mentioned above, the three major topics discussed in this chapter—cash, short-term investments, and accounts and notes receivable—are a company's most liquid assets. It is mainly from these items that the company will meet its immediate, short-term financial obligations. Users therefore need to have a good understanding of these items on financial statements. For example, while cash seems to be straightforward, in reality it constitutes a series of things, including physical money, amounts in bank accounts, cheques, and money orders, to name just some of them. For their part, short-term investments are an indication to users that a company is managing its cash. It is taking cash that it does not need immediately and investing it to generate income rather than lie idle. When the cash is later needed, the company will then sell these investments, so it needs to be able to determine their value. Accounts receivable, meanwhile, are typically due within 30 days. However, as a user you need to be aware of the potential uncollectibility of some accounts, and of any agreements that allow customers more than the usual time to pay.

Having these items on the financial statements enables users to evaluate a company's liquidity, or short-term ability to meet its obligations. A deeper understanding of these items will improve your ability to assess a company's short-term vulnerability.

The assets discussed in this chapter are unique since they are all either cash or soon will be. In accounting terms, we often refer to them as **monetary** assets because their value is fixed in current monetary terms. Obviously, they are very important to every business since, as we learned in Chapter 5, sufficient cash must be available at all times to pay for purchases and other obligations as they become due.

In this chapter, the accounting methods and principles that apply to cash, short-term investments, and accounts and notes receivable are considered. In each account category, we discuss the recognition criteria, valuation methods, statement of earnings and balance sheet implications, financial statement analysis considerations, and other issues that are important to understanding that account category. The complexities of financial statement analysis associated with this group of accounts are discussed in this chapter, and in each subsequent chapter, in a section entitled "Statement Analysis Considerations."

CASH

In Chapter 1, we discussed the criteria that are used to decide whether, for accounting purposes, something is an asset. Assets are identified as items that (1) are controlled by the company, (2) are expected to provide future economic benefits from their use or sale, and (3) arose from a past event. In this chapter, we will use these criteria to decide why and how we categorize cash, short-term investments, and accounts and notes receivable as assets.

Cash meets the criterion of being controlled by the company. Ownership of cash is generally evidenced by possession: currency, cheques, money orders, etc., on hand, and money deposited in banks. Currency (bills and coins) is difficult to differentiate, except by using serial numbers on bills. It is therefore a very difficult asset to control. To address this problem, companies use financial institutions extensively and conduct more and more cash transactions electronically with credit or debit cards and computer transfers, thus eliminating most of the physical handling of cash. This makes the control of cash much easier and the processing of transactions much more efficient.

All companies must establish effective internal control procedures to govern how they handle and control their cash. Auditors review the internal control systems established by companies and design special audit procedures to test whether these controls adequately safeguard the handling and recording of cash. More will be said about internal controls later in this chapter, especially as they relate to cash.

Cash meets the future economic benefit criterion. It derives its value from its ability to be exchanged for goods and services in the future, which is also called its **purchasing power**. Cash serves as the medium of exchange in every economy, but it relies on the individuals who use it to have faith in the economy. If there is a loss of confidence about its exchangeability in the future, the currency loses its value. For example, a few years ago, Argentina experienced difficulty making its international borrowing repayments. Until early 2002, the country's currency, the peso, was tied one-to-one with the American dollar. However, in an attempt to get greater control of its economy, Argentina unpegged its currency from the U.S. dollar. People in Argentina immediately became concerned that the peso would lose value, and attempted to withdraw their money from banks so that they could invest it in assets that would not lose value. It was feared that there would be a full "run on the banks," which could have precipitated a complete collapse of the Argentine economy. To prevent this from happening, the country on several occasions froze bank accounts and prevented depositors from withdrawing their money. By the middle of 2002, the Argentine peso had dropped to half its former value. By early 2010, it had declined further, to about 26 American cents.

The third criterion, the occurrence of a past event that transferred the cash to the company, is also met. Cash flowing in or out of a company is a clear signal that a transaction has taken place; if cash is present, a past event must have occurred.

Cash Valuation Methods

Knowing that cash meets the recognition criteria, the next issue is how to record cash in the accounting system. For the cash account, and for all other accounts discussed in this text, there are several possible valuation methods. Although some of these methods are not allowed under IFRS, they are allowed in other countries and we will discuss all these methods so that you are aware of the concepts on which current practices are based. A separate section of this chapter focuses on the current IFRS requirements. In some cases, the methods used under IFRS are a combination of the various possible valuation methods that are discussed here.

One possible method of valuing cash is to record it at its face value. This means that as long as cash is held, its value is assumed not to change. If we had $100 in cash, the cash would be valued at $100. If that same $100 were present several months later, it would still be valued at $100. Its face value does not change.

Even though the face value of the $100 does not change, its ability to be converted into goods and services—its purchasing power—may change. Purchasing power is affected by inflation and deflation. During periods of inflation, cash sustains a loss in value, or purchasing power, as it becomes exchangeable for fewer goods and services. In other words, if prices have risen the $100 will buy fewer goods and services than it could before. Although the face value attribute does not change, the purchasing power attribute does. If we were to use the attribute of purchasing power to value cash (instead of face value), then in this example a loss would have to be recognized for the decrease in the currency's purchasing power during the accounting period. This example shows that the choice of which attribute of cash to measure is critical to how cash is valued on the balance sheet and how it affects the statement of earnings.

accounting in the news

Burger Prices and Exchange Rates

The Economist magazine has been illustrating countries' purchasing power with its Big Mac index since 1986. The index is based on the theory of purchasing-power parity (PPP), which says that exchange rates should adjust to equalize the prices of goods and services around the world. The survey conducted by *The Economist* compares the price of a McDonald's Big Mac in various countries and determines what exchange rates would make the cost of buying a Big Mac in the United States the same as its cost in other countries. These rates are then compared with actual exchange rates, providing a measure of how under- or overvalued the currencies are.

According to the Big Mac index, the most overvalued currency in the world in 2009 was the Norwegian krone. According to the index, it is valued at 96% above its purchasing power. This made the price of a Big Mac in Oslo equivalent to approximately US$7.00, compared to an average price for a Big Mac in the U.S. of $3.58. The most undervalued currency in the survey was the Chinese yuan, which is undervalued by 49%. As a result, a Big Mac in China costs the equivalent of just US$1.83. As it did for the Norwegian krone, the survey also suggested that the Canadian dollar was overvalued: a Big Mac in Canada cost the equivalent of US$3.97, or 10% more than it did in its home country.

Source: "Taste and See," *Economist.com*, January 6, 2010.

What Is Canadian Practice?

In Canada, there is an underlying assumption, referred to as the **unit-of-measure assumption**, which specifies that the results of business activities should be measured in terms of a **monetary unit** (e.g., the Canadian dollar). This precludes valuing items in terms of purchasing power; cash is, therefore, measured at its face value rather than by any other method. Many companies in Canada that have the majority of their transactions with entities in the United States will produce their financial statements using the U.S. dollar as their monetary unit.

While the unit-of-measure assumption requires that Canadian currency be measured at face value, this is not the case for foreign currencies. Suppose, for example, that a company does business with a German customer and that the agreement with the customer is denominated in euros (the currency used by most European countries). This means that the customer is required to pay in euros, rather than Canadian dollars. The Canadian company will receive euros, and may hold a certain balance of euros at the beginning and the end of the accounting period. Because this asset is measured in a different monetary unit than the rest of the company's assets, a conversion will have to be made from euros to Canadian dollars.

In Canada, the conversion of euros into dollars is done using the exchange rate that exists on the date of the balance sheet. For example, suppose the exchange rate is 1 euro = 1.38 Canadian dollars at the beginning of the year and 1 euro = 1.43 Canadian dollars at the end of the year. Further, suppose that the company holds 10,000 euros at the beginning and the end of the year. Exhibit 6-1 shows how the euros would be valued on the balance sheet. You can see that, while there is no gain or loss during the year in terms of euros, there is a gain in terms of their value in Canadian dollars. This gain will appear on the statement of earnings and will be called a foreign currency translation gain.

FOREIGN CURRENCY VALUATION

EXHIBIT 6-1

Date	Amount of Foreign Currency	Exchange Rate	Value of Foreign Currency in Canadian Dollars
Jan. 1	10,000 euros	1 euro = $1.38	$13,800
Dec. 31	10,000 euros	1 euro = $1.43	$14,300
Gain	0 euros		$ 500

Exchange rates are determined in the foreign currency markets. Reasons for changes in the exchange rates of currencies are difficult to pinpoint precisely but, in theory, one major cause is the difference in inflation rates in the two countries. Individuals who hold currencies in countries with high inflation rates lose more purchasing power than those in countries with low inflation rates. Exchange rates adjust to compensate for these differences in purchasing power. In effect, accounting standards recognize the changes in purchasing power of foreign currencies by allowing the dollar value of the foreign currencies to rise and fall with the changes in exchange rates.

Internal Control and Cash Management

Despite the issues discussed so far, accounting for cash is relatively straightforward: you simply report how much cash the company owns. By cash, we mean currency, cheques, money orders, bank drafts, and amounts in bank accounts that can be used with very short notice.

LEARNING OBJECTIVE 1

Discuss the main control issues related to cash.

The main issues with cash are the control of cash to ensure that it is not lost or stolen, and the management of cash balances. Proper control of cash includes policies such as ensuring that all cash is deposited into bank accounts daily (or even more frequently), using secure safes and tills to hold cash until it is deposited, writing cheques or using debit or credit cards instead of using cash to pay expenses, and keeping as little cash on hand as possible. Control of cash is a key part of a company's **internal control system**.

Management is responsible for safeguarding the organization's assets and ensuring that they are used effectively and efficiently. To accomplish this, policies and procedures must be established to help protect and manage the organization's assets, especially vulnerable ones such as cash, inventory, supplies, and equipment. Collectively, these measures are referred to as a system of internal control. The accounting system is a very important component of this. In addition to generating financial statements for reporting to external stakeholders, an accounting system has to establish and maintain control over the organization's operations, resources, and records. An effective record-keeping system must—without being too burdensome or bureaucratic—help management monitor and control the organization's assets and thereby prevent the misappropriation of property and the inefficient use of resources. A comprehensive internal control system encompasses much more than accounting and related records, however; physical safeguards, insurance protection, appropriate operating policies, and good human resources management are also important elements of an internal control system.

The following are some of the key elements of an effective internal control system (a fuller discussion of internal control principles, procedures, and challenges is available on the companion website for the text):

Internal Control

1. **Physical measures** are designed to protect the assets from theft, diversion, damage, or destruction. Management needs to protect the assets by ensuring that premises and resources are secure through, for example, the use of locks and/or alarms. In the case of cash, this means depositing cash in the bank regularly and keeping cash that is on the premises securely stored in tills and safes.

2. **Clear assignment of responsibilities**   An essential characteristic of internal control is the assignment of responsibility to specific individuals. Control is most effective when only one person is responsible for each task. To illustrate, assume that at the end of the day the cash on hand in a store is less than the amount rung up on the cash register. If only one person has operated the register, responsibility for the shortage can be determined immediately. If more than one individual has worked the register, it may be impossible to determine who is responsible for the shortage, unless each person is assigned a separate cash drawer.

   In addition to the performance of routine tasks, responsibility must also be assigned for the establishment of general policies and the handling of exceptional situations.

3. **Separation of duties**   Employees will have opportunities to defraud a company if, for example, they are in charge of purchasing assets, inspecting them on arrival to ensure that what was ordered has been received, recording the receipt of the assets in the accounting system, authorizing payment for them, and making the payment. To reduce this opportunity for fraud, management should ensure that different people are responsible for each of these activities.

   For cash, separation of duties means that one person receives cash, another is authorized to write cheques, and a third records the receipts or payments of cash in the accounting records. Personnel who receive, disburse, or otherwise handle cash should not maintain, or even have access to, the cash records. In this regard, it is important to bear in mind that "cash" transactions can occur in many forms. In addition to currency and cheques, cash transactions include credit card and debit card transactions, and other direct payments such as EFT (electronic funds transfers) to and from the company.

4. **Independent verification**   When one person is responsible for verifying the work of another, behaving dishonestly without being detected requires collusion. Therefore, good systems of internal control provide for independent internal verification. This involves the review, comparison, and reconciliation of data prepared by employees. Ideally, for maximum efficiency combined with control, the work of one employee should, whenever possible, provide a reliable basis for cross-checking the work of another employee, without duplication of effort.

   In small companies, achieving the appropriate level of separation of duties and independent verification is more difficult because of the limited number of employees. In this case, the owners or top management must sometimes perform some of the key tasks and periodically verify the work of employees.

5. **Proper documentation procedures**   Documents provide evidence that transactions and events have occurred, as well as an "audit trail" by which things can be traced back, if necessary. For example, the cash register tape is documentation for the amount of revenue earned and cash received. Similarly, a shipping document indicates that the goods have been shipped, and the sales invoice indicates that the customer has been billed for the goods. By adding a signature (or initials) to the documents, the individual responsible for the transaction or event can be identified. Whenever possible, documents should be prenumbered and all the documents should be accounted for.

6. **An effective record-keeping and reporting system**   Management must establish an accounting system in which all transactions are processed on a timely basis, source documents related to the transactions are handled and stored in an appropriate manner, only authorized personnel record transactions and access data in the accounting system, and all personnel who record transactions and prepare reports have the appropriate training.

   Although our focus for internal control and security systems is primarily on safeguarding companies' assets, the same types of concerns extend to the protection of information about their clients and customers. If clients and customers are not confident that sensitive information about them (especially their financial information) will be safeguarded, they may not be comfortable doing business with the organization.

Bank Reconciliations

An important internal control procedure that is used by almost every company is the **bank reconciliation**, which ensures that any differences between the accounting records for cash and the bank records are identified and explained.

Every bank account has a corresponding general ledger account in the company's accounting system. The company's records and the bank's records ultimately reflect the same transactions, such as cash deposits and cheques written, but the transactions may be recorded at different times. For example, suppose that a company writes, records, and

LEARNING OBJECTIVE 2

Prepare a bank reconciliation and make the related adjustments.

accounting in the news

Keep Tabs on Employee Expense Claims

Effective internal control includes keeping tabs on employee expense claims. Fraudulent reimbursement of common expenses like meals, entertainment, and hotel rooms accounts for 20% of cash misappropriation workplace fraud in Canada. In its 2007 report, *Detecting Occupational Fraud in Canada*, the Association of Certified Fraud Examiners found that the typical Canadian organization loses 5% of its annual sales to fraud each year. Of these occupational frauds, 42% were committed by employees, 39% by managers, and 19% by owners/executives.

Expense fraud is defined as any scheme where employees claim reimbursement for fictitious or inflated business expenses. Employees may claim reimbursement for personal expenses by reporting them as business-related; they may inflate the amount of the actual expenses and pocket the difference; they may "double-dip" by claiming legitimate expenses more than once; or they may submit fake expenses claiming reimbursement for purchases that never took place.

Expense fraud can result in costly and time-consuming investigations and lawsuits, lost jobs, and even jail time. In April 2009, a former Newfoundland cabinet minister was found guilty of submitting falsified, forged, and duplicitous expense claims while in public office and was sentenced to two years less a day in jail. He allegedly overspent $467,653 from his constituency allowance account—more than five times the approved limit.

Source: "No Free Lunch — Employee Expense Fraud Is More Serious Than You May Think," *The Globe and Mail*, October 13, 2009.

mails a cheque to a supplier on October 27, and the supplier receives the cheque and deposits it in its bank account on November 1. The supplier's bank then forwards the cheque to the company's bank through the banking clearing system, which withdraws the money from the company's account on November 3. Because the transaction takes several days to complete, the cheque will be outstanding from the time the company records it on October 27 until the bank shows it as a withdrawal from the company's account on November 3. While the cheque is outstanding, the two records (the general ledger account and the bank's record) will be different. As illustrated below, there can also be other reasons for differences between the company's cash records and the bank's records. The bank reconciliation is the process that accounts for all these differences.

The bank reconciliation procedure consists of identifying the items that are causing the cash balance recorded by the company to differ from the balance recorded by the bank. This involves comparing the company's cash records with the bank's records so that an adjustment can be made for any item that has been recorded by the company or the bank, but not yet both.

The process of preparing a bank reconciliation is quite straightforward, if you bear in mind that the objective is to determine what the cash balance would be if the same items were recorded in both sets of records (i.e., the company's and the bank's). Accordingly, when an item is identified as being recorded in one set of records but not in the other, or recorded differently in one set of records than in the other, that item has to be included in the reconciliation. Whether it is added or deducted depends on whatever needs to be done with it, logically, to determine what the correct cash balance would be if each item were recorded correctly in both sets of records.

The following information about Gelardi Company will illustrate the process of preparing a bank reconciliation. As you consider each of the items that follow, refer to Exhibit 6-2 to see how the item is presented on the bank reconciliation:

- The balance in the company's cash account in the general ledger on October 31, 2011, was $9,770.44. This is the starting point for the company portion of the bank reconciliation, labelled "Balance per the ledger."

- The balance in Gelardi's bank account on October 31 was $8,916.39. This is the starting point for the bank portion of the reconciliation, labelled "Balance per the bank."

The accountant reviewed the bank statement, compared the transactions recorded on it to the transactions recorded in the ledger account, and discovered the following differences. Note that the description of each item is followed by an explanation of how it was handled on the bank reconciliation.

- One of Gelardi's customers paid its account by making an electronic transfer from its bank into the company's account. The amount appeared on the bank statement as an "EFT" (Electronic Funds Transfer) in the amount of $312.98. Until the bank statement was reviewed, the company was not aware that this payment had been received.

  Since this transaction has been recorded by the bank but not by Gelardi, an adjustment has to be made in the company portion of the reconciliation. As the item is a cash receipt of $312.98, this amount has to be added to the balance per the ledger.

- The bank statement showed that cheque number 885 (which Gelardi Company had issued to pay for an advertising expense) was recorded by the bank as $246.81, while the company recorded this cheque as $426.81. A review of the cancelled cheques accompanying the bank statement showed that the amount recorded by the bank was correct.

  Since this was an error made by the company, an adjustment has to be made to the balance per the ledger. The amount of the error was $426.81 − $246.81 = $180.00. Since the company reduced its cash balance by $180.00 too much when it recorded this cheque, this amount needs to be added back to get the correct balance.

- The bank subtracted a charge of $25.75 from the company's bank account for October, but Gelardi's accountant had not yet recorded it in the company's books. (Typically, the company only becomes aware of these charges when it reviews the bank statement.)

  Since this charge has been deducted from the bank account but not from Gelardi's cash account, it is listed as a deduction in the company portion of the reconciliation, to reduce the ledger account balance by the amount of the charge.

- The bank statement showed that $500.00 was deducted from Gelardi's account by the bank as payment on a loan. The company's accountant only remembered that the payment was due this month when he saw it on the bank statement.

  Since this payment has been deducted from the bank account but not from Gelardi's cash account, it is listed as a deduction in the company portion of the reconciliation, to reduce the ledger account balance by the amount of the payment.

- The bank returned a cheque from one of Gelardi's customers marked "NSF" (Not Sufficient Funds). This was a cheque for $186.80 that a customer had given the company in payment for merchandise purchased earlier. Gelardi had accepted the cheque, recorded it as an increase to the cash account, and deposited it in its bank account. The bank had increased the balance in Gelardi's account to reflect this deposit. However, when Gelardi's bank sent the cheque to the customer's bank for payment, it was informed that the customer did not have enough money in his account to cover the cheque. Consequently, Gelardi's bank removed the amount from Gelardi's account and returned the cheque to the company.

Since this "bounced cheque" has been deducted from Gelardi's bank account but not from its cash account, it is listed as a deduction in the company portion of the reconciliation, to reduce the ledger account balance by the amount of this charge. Gelardi will now need to contact the customer to collect the amount owed.

- The last deposit of the month, for $1,035.62, was made as a night deposit on October 31 and therefore was not recorded by the bank until the beginning of November. Consequently, it did not appear on the October bank statement.

  Since this deposit has been added to Gelardi's cash account but not to its bank account, it is listed as an addition in the bank portion of the bank reconciliation, to increase the bank balance to the amount that will be available when this deposit is processed by the bank. The bank probably recorded the addition to Gelardi's account on November 1 or 2 when it recorded the night deposits. As of October 31, however, the bank's and company's accounts are different.

- The bank deducted a cheque written by Gardeli Company from Gelardi Company's account. The amount of the cheque was $127.53.

  Since this was an error made by the bank, an adjustment has to be made to the balance per the bank. Since $127.53 was mistakenly taken out of Gelardi's bank account, this amount has to be added back to get the correct balance. Gelardi will need to inform the bank of the error.

- Cheque number 873 for $262.89, cheque number 891 for $200.00, and cheque number 892 for $65.78 were still outstanding. (They were mailed to suppliers, but had not yet been processed by the bank.)

  Since these cheques have been deducted from Gelardi's cash account but not from its bank account, they are listed as deductions in the bank portion of the reconciliation, to reduce the bank balance to the amount that will be available when these cheques are processed by the bank.

HELPFUL HINT

The main objective of a bank reconciliation is to determine the correct cash balance. Therefore, items that the bank has not yet recorded must be added to, or deducted from, the balance shown on the bank statement, while items that the company has not yet recorded must be added to, or deducted from, the balance shown in the company's cash account.

Using this information, the accountant would prepare a bank reconciliation as in Exhibit 6-2.

Notice that the two adjusted balances are equal, indicating that all the differences between the company's records and the bank's records with respect to cash have been identified and dealt with, and the correct amount of cash available at the end of October is $9,550.87.

After the bank reconciliation is complete, the accountant needs to make journal entries to adjust the cash account in the company's ledger so that it reflects the information shown in the reconciliation. The entries for Gelardi Company are presented in Exhibit 6-3, with an explanation for each one.

It is important to note that a journal entry is made for each of the items shown in the company portion of the bank reconciliation (but not for those in the bank portion). After posting the above entries to the ledger, the balance in the cash account would be the correct amount: $9,550.87.

Bank reconciliations are an important control procedure. They ensure that all transactions affecting the bank account have been properly recorded, so the company knows that no transactions have been missed or recorded incorrectly. They are normally made each month for every bank account, as soon as the bank statements are received.

GELARDI COMPANY BANK RECONCILIATION
October 31, 2011

EXHIBIT 6-2

Balance per the ledger		$ 9,770.44
Add:	EFT from customer on account	312.98
	Correction of error made by the company	
	(cheque number 885 recorded for wrong amount)	180.00
Deduct:	Bank charges	(25.75)
	Automatic deduction for loan payment	(500.00)
	NSF cheque	(186.80)
Adjusted cash balance		$ 9,550.87
Balance per the bank		$ 8,916.39
Add:	Outstanding deposit	1,035.62
	Correction of error made by the bank	127.53
Deduct:	Outstanding cheques	
	#873	(262.89)
	#891	(200.00)
	#892	(65.78)
Adjusted bank balance		$ 9,550.87

JOURNAL ENTRIES ARISING FROM THE BANK RECONCILIATION IN EXHIBIT 6-2

EXHIBIT 6-3

Cash (A)	312.98	
Accounts receivable (A)		312.98

To record the EFT payment received from a customer on account.
(Notice that this is recorded like any other collection on account.)

Cash (A)	180.00	
Advertising expense (SE)		180.00

To correct the error made in recording cheque number 885.
(Note that this entry increases the cash account and decreses the advertising expense,
which was originally recorded as a debt of $426.81 but should have been $246.81.)

Bank charges expense (SE)	25.75	
Cash (A)		25.75

To record the bank charges for the month of October.
(Note that this is recorded like any other payment of an expense.)

Bank loan payable (L)	500.00	
Cash (A)		500.00

To record the payment made to reduce the bank loan.
(Notice that this is recorded like any other payment of a liability.)

Accounts receivable (A)	186.80	
Cash (A)		186.80

To reinstate the account receivable from a customer who paid with an NSF cheque.
(This is the reverse of the entry that was made when the cheque was originally received.)

As previously stated, duties must be separated appropriately for effective internal control. In terms of the bank reconciliation, this means that the person who reconciles the bank account must not be the person who is responsible for either doing the banking or maintaining the accounting records. This will ensure that any errors or discrepancies will be found and properly corrected. This also ensures that no individual has an opportunity to misappropriate cash and then change the books to cover the fraud.

ethics in accounting

Internal control considerations raise ethical questions about management's attitude toward employees and how it treats them. Should management assume that all employees are basically dishonest and will steal if they think they can get away with it? Or should management simply establish controls to ensure that employees are not presented with temptations and opportunities to steal? In considering such questions and determining what internal control measures to establish, management must also consider the impact on the employees' motivation. The dilemma is that employees generally have a more positive attitude toward their jobs and, consequently, better motivation when they feel they are trusted.

If an organization expects its employees to be loyal and honest, it must be fair in how it deals with them. This means they must be motivated to do a good job and be adequately compensated for doing it. If employees do not feel that the organization treats them well or fairly, they may not care about serving the organization well or fairly; they may even be motivated to "get even" with the organization by circumventing the internal control system and/or engaging in theft. For example, the control that is normally provided by segregation of duties can be circumvented if employees engage in collusion (that is, if they agree to work together in order to cover up fraud). Although it may be impossible to prevent this entirely, collusion is much less likely to occur in organizations whose employees are well motivated and feel that they are being treated fairly.

It is certainly not our intention to suggest that all, most, or even many employees, customers, and suppliers are dishonest, but rather to highlight management's responsibilities. In particular, if management expects others to behave in an ethical manner, it must recognize that it too has ethical responsibilities. These responsibilities include

- ensuring that its employees are compensated fairly, so that they will not feel that they are justified in helping themselves to more of the organization's assets; and

- ensuring that its employees, customers, or suppliers are not put into situations in which they may be tempted to engage in dishonest activities, due to management's failure to maintain an effective system of internal controls.

The other issue associated with cash is cash management. Proper cash management involves maintaining sufficient cash in readily accessible bank accounts to be able to make payments when the need arises, while at the same time not keeping excessive amounts of cash. Cash is a non-earning asset; that is, it does not earn a return (except, perhaps, a small amount of interest). For this reason, companies usually try to keep as much of their cash invested in income-earning assets as they safely can. (Income-earning assets include short-term investments, which are discussed later in this chapter.) A company's cash management policies are critical for effectively managing its cash position and maximizing its total earnings. Advanced cash management techniques are not discussed in this book, but are a very important aspect of financial management for the company's shareholders and other stakeholders.

Statement Analysis Considerations

Sometimes a company's cash withdrawals from its bank are restricted because of a feature known as **compensating balances**. These are minimum balances that must be maintained in the bank account to avoid significant service charges or, in some cases, to satisfy restrictive loan covenants (clauses in loan agreements that are designed to reduce the risk for the lender). A company might also choose to restrict a portion of its cash for a specific use. In such cases, the restricted cash should be segregated on the statements from other amounts of cash. Other than these considerations, and those presented when discussing the cash flow statement in Chapter 5, there are no special considerations regarding cash for financial statement analysis purposes.

SHORT-TERM INVESTMENTS

As discussed in the last section, managing cash is an important part of managing a company. One of the major aspects of cash management is the company's need to minimize its cash balance, given that current or chequing accounts normally earn no returns. One way to convert cash into an earning asset is to invest it in short-term, or temporary, **marketable securities**. These are financial assets that are publicly traded or otherwise easily converted back to cash: they include debt securities (treasury bills, bonds, or guaranteed investment certificates) and equity securities (shares) in another entity or money market–type mutual funds. The investor's usual intention in acquiring them is simply to hold them as income-generating alternatives to cash; they will be sold when the cash is needed for other purposes or the selling price is right. The more actively the security is traded, the easier it is to convert it back into cash when the cash is needed. The ability to turn an investment back into cash quickly is known as **liquidity** and is a critically important consideration in managing the company's cash position.

> ### LEARNING OBJECTIVE 3
>
> *Describe the general criteria for classifying and valuing investments.*

Financial investments that are not marketable or otherwise easily liquidated generally do not qualify as current assets, because they might not be easily converted into cash within a year. Instead, they would probably be classified as non-current investments. The discussion in this section is restricted to short-term, marketable securities that are held as current assets.

The probable future value of investments comes from two sources. One source is the periodic payments that these investments produce while they are being held. In the case of debt instruments, these payments are interest. When debt instruments have maturity dates of three months or less, they are often classified as cash equivalents (as discussed in Chapter 5) because they will quickly become a known amount of cash. Periodic payments received from equity securities are dividends. Because equity securities do not have maturity dates and their values fluctuate, they are never classified as cash equivalents.

The second source of an investment's value is the value of the security when it is sold in the future. If the intention is to hold the security for a short period (less than one year), the current market value or resale price is very relevant and important. If the intention is to hold it for a long or indefinite period, the current market value is less relevant and important. The latter type of security may therefore be accounted for differently and reported in a separate section of the balance sheet, for long-term investments.

The uncertainty, or risk, associated with the future value of investments relates to both the periodic payments and the ultimate sales value. For example, there is a risk that the issuers of debt may default on the interest payments. This not only causes uncertainty about the periodic payments but also reduces the value of a security in terms of its final price. If a company cannot make interest payments, it is unlikely that it will be able to pay back the principal when the debt matures. With equity securities, there is no guarantee of the dividends (if any) that will be paid; nor is there any guarantee of the ultimate value of the shares. The company may prosper, increasing the future selling price of its shares; or it may fail, rendering the shares worthless.

The uncertainty regarding a security's future cash flows is sometimes seen in the volatility of its price in the securities markets. You are probably well aware of the volatility of the markets for equity securities (shares). For example, during the one-year period from February 2009 to February 2010, the shares of **Research In Motion** (the maker of the BlackBerry) varied from a low of around $40 to a high of $72. The variability in price is partially due to the highly competitive technology markets in which this company operates. However, share prices fluctuate for many reasons, some of which relate to general economic conditions rather than company-specific factors.

Volatility also exists in the markets for debt securities (bond markets). While macro-economic factors have an impact, the degree of volatility is also affected by the level of risk or uncertainty, which depends on the type of security and the financial health of the issuing entity. Debt securities, for example, may be viewed as quite safe if they are issued by the government. At the other extreme are corporate bonds issued by very highly leveraged companies where total liabilities greatly exceed the total shareholders' equity. These bonds are sometimes called "junk bonds." Junk bonds pay very high interest rates to compensate for their high level of risk.

The ownership criterion for these assets is relatively straightforward. For some securities, pieces of paper representing ownership (share certificates and bond certificates) can be held by the owner. In many cases, however, no certificates are issued and the evidence of ownership consists of records maintained by an outside party (such as an investment dealer or a trust company).

Valuation Methods

One method that could be used to value investments is to record them at their original acquisition costs, or **historical costs**. With this method, changes in an investment's market value have no effect on the balance sheet or statement of earnings until the investment is actually sold. When the investment is sold, the difference between its original cost and its final market value is recognized and is called a **realized gain or loss**. In addition, investment income is recognized as periodic payments are received in the form of dividends or interest revenue.

A second method would be to value investments at their **market values**. In its pure form, this method means that changes in the market values of the investments would cause changes in the carrying values reported on the balance sheet, and produce corresponding gains or losses on the statement of earnings. Changes in market values while investments are held are called **unrealized gains or losses**. When investments are sold, the change in value (from the original purchase price to the final selling price) is considered a realized gain or loss. In addition, any periodic receipts of dividends or interest revenue are recognized as income.

A third method for valuing investments is the **lower of cost and market (LCM)** method. This is a hybrid of the two methods discussed above, historical cost and market value. The lower of cost and market method uses historical cost (i.e., the amount paid for the securities when they were purchased) unless the market value is less than the cost, in which case the market value is used. Note that this combination of the above methods is intended to report a conservative figure. Under the LCM method, investments are shown at their original cost unless their market value has declined to below the cost, in which case the investments' value on the balance sheet is reduced to their market value and an unrealized loss is recognized on the statement of earnings. Under this method, no gains (resulting from market values being higher than cost) are recognized until the investment is sold.

What Is Canadian Practice?

LEARNING OBJECTIVE 4

Explain why certain types of investments are reported at their market value.

For the last several years in Canada, the method of accounting for temporary investments has been market value. With the adoption of IFRS in Canada, most short-term investments will continue to be reported at their **fair (market) value**.

Because short-term investments are generally held in place of cash, the intention of this standard is to value them at the amount of cash that could be received from selling them. This provides information that is more relevant to readers of the financial statements. The standard also recognizes that the market values of such investments are usually easily determinable, objective, and verifiable. Thus, the market value information will also be reliable.

INTERNATIONAL PERSPECTIVES

Although there are some differences in details, IFRS for dealing with *financial instruments* is generally consistent with U.S. GAAP. Most short-term marketable securities are carried and reported at their fair market values.

There is, however, one type of investment that is not carried at market value. Instruments that have fixed cash payments and a maturity date can be carried at cost if the company intends to hold the investment to maturity and if the company is financially capable of waiting that long to convert the investment to cash. Because of the requirement for fixed cash payments and a maturity date, these investments are usually guaranteed investment certificates or debt instruments such as bonds. Many bonds are five or more years to maturity. If a company purchased a long-term bond that it intended to hold to maturity, the bond would not be classified as a short-term investment. The company would, however, carry it at cost if it met the criteria described in this paragraph.

The requirement that all investments be carried at market value except those described in the previous paragraph is outlined in IFRS 9. This standard was approved in 2009 with an implementation date set for 2013. Companies were encouraged to adopt this standard earlier than 2013, so you could see financial statements using the new standard as well as some using the previous one. Because of this dichotomy, it is necessary to understand a little about the standards that are being replaced.

As the standards being replaced are quite complex—the details will be left to intermediate or advanced accounting courses—the following is a simplified overview of the approach to accounting for investments or **financial instruments**.

Four types of financial instruments are identified:

1. Held for trading

2. Available for sale

3. Held to maturity

4. Loans and receivables

Each of these four categories is accounted for differently:

1. *Held for trading investments* are a portfolio of investments that a company holds with the intent of trading to diversify the company's sources of revenue. They are valued at their fair (market) values, with any related gains and losses included in net earnings.

2. *Available for sale investments* are investments that the company intends to sell when the price is right. These are usually individual investments and can be short- or long-term. They are valued at their fair (market) values,[1] with related gains and losses included in other comprehensive income[2] until disposition, and then transferred to net income.

3. *Held to maturity investments* are valued at their amortized costs, using the effective interest method.[3] These investments are similar to the investments described in IFRS 9 that maintain the investment at cost rather than market value.

4. *Investments in loans and receivables* are valued using the effective-interest method.

Note that the first two categories above, *held for trading investments* and *available for sale investments*, will both report the investments at their market values on each balance sheet date. This practice, sometimes referred to as **marked to market**, represents a significant departure from the accounting principle of reporting assets at their historical costs.

This older standard was somewhat controversial because it specified four different accounting treatments for various types of investments, thereby increasing the number of ways in which various types of assets are valued on the balance sheet. Because of this complexity, the IASB developed IFRS 9 to simplify the accounting for investments. Therefore, for simplicity, we will treat all short-term investments that are not intended to be held to maturity as held for trading investments. This means we will report them on the balance sheet at their fair market values, and any resulting gains or losses will be reported on the statement of earnings as part of net earnings. The investments with fixed cash payments and maturity dates will be reported at cost if the company intends to hold them to maturity.

Proper accounting for financial instruments or investments presents several other issues that must be resolved. The first is one of classification. When a company invests in a security, or financial instrument, it must first decide whether to classify the investment as a current or non-current asset. The classification is generally based on the intention of management and on the marketability of the asset. If management intends to hold the security for less than one year, and if it is readily marketable, it will be classified as a current asset. Otherwise, it will be classified as non-current, in which case the account will generally be referred to as a long-term investment.

HELPFUL HINT

Here is a brief summary of what you should know about the valuation of short-term investments. Although there are different categories for investments and specific requirements in how to account for them, at the introductory level it is sufficient to know that short-term investments will generally be valued at their current market values on each balance sheet date. When gains or losses arise on these investments because of changes in their values, these gains or losses will generally be reported directly in net earnings.

---

1. If reliable market values are not available, the investments are valued at cost.
2. Comprehensive income is discussed in Chapter 4.
3. The effective interest method is discussed in Chapter 10.

Equity securities raise another important issue in accounting for investments. Most equity securities are shares that entitle the owner to vote for the board of directors, which has direct authority over management. Therefore, when a company invests in shares of another company, the buyer will usually have some voting power, based on the number of shares that it owns. The larger the proportion of shares owned by the buyer, the more influence or control it can exercise over the other company. For short-term investments, there is usually no intention on the part of the buying company to exercise influence or control. In fact, the number of shares usually purchased as a short-term investment (a relatively small number) does not allow a buying company to exercise much influence or control. With long-term investments in shares, however, there may be some intention to exercise influence or control over the other company. In some cases, for example, the acquiring company will buy all the outstanding shares of another company. In this case, the acquiring company exercises absolute control over the acquired company. The accounting for an investment in which a company exercises significant influence or control (a "strategic investment") is different from when the company has little or no influence (a "non-strategic investment"). The accounting for investments with significant influence or control is discussed in Appendix B at the end of this book. This chapter considers only non-strategic short-term investments in securities.

The data in Exhibit 6-4 for Clifford Company will be used to illustrate the application of the market value method to short-term investments, as well as other aspects of accounting for them. Assume that Clifford's year end is December 31 and that it prepares financial statements on a quarterly basis. You will notice that Clifford bought

CLIFFORD COMPANY

Data related to short-term investments

EXHIBIT 6-4

Security	Type	Quarter Acquired	Acquisition Cost	Quarter Sold	Selling Price
Company X	Bonds	1	$10,000	3	$11,000
Company Y	Shares	1	$20,000	4	$18,500
Company Z	Shares	1	$30,000		NA

Security	Cost	Fair (market) values at the end of			
		Quarter 1	Quarter 2	Quarter 3	Quarter 4
Company X	$10,000	$10,500	$12,000	NA	NA
Company Y	20,000	17,500	21,000	$18,000	NA
Company Z	30,000	29,000	28,000	29,000	$31,500
Total portfolio	$60,000	$57,000	$61,000	$47,000	$31,500

Dividends/Interest Received

Quarter	Amount
1	$1,200
2	$1,200
3	$ 700
4	$ 700

three securities during the first quarter (the first three months) of the year. The exhibit then tracks the performance of these investments during the year, determining the value of each security at the end of each quarter until it is sold. Dividend and interest payments received are also included.

Initial Acquisition

Prepare the journal entries for acquiring, holding, and selling short-term investments.

If Clifford Company makes many such investments, the details of each one would probably be recorded in its own **subsidiary account**. The short-term investments account would then be a **control account** that holds the sum of all the subsidiary accounts (see below).

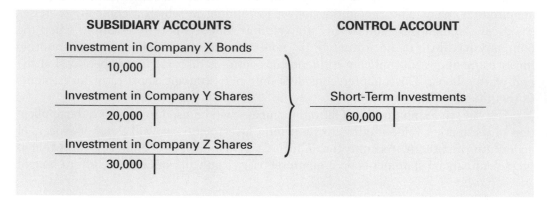

SUBSIDIARY ACCOUNTS	CONTROL ACCOUNT
Investment in Company X Bonds	
10,000	
Investment in Company Y Shares	Short-Term Investments
20,000	60,000
Investment in Company Z Shares	
30,000	

In such cases, only the control account is reported in the financial statements, and individual transactions are recorded in the subsidiary accounts. Thus, the following entry would record Clifford Company's acquisition of the short-term investments during the first quarter of the year:

Investment in Company X (A)	10,000	
Investment in Company Y (A)	20,000	
Investment in Company Z (A)	30,000	
Cash (A)		60,000

In order to simplify the illustration that follows, however, we will assume that Clifford Company makes few such purchases and therefore uses a single Short-Term Investments account, rather than separate accounts for the investments in Company X, Company Y, and Company Z. Under this approach, the entry to record the purchase of the investments is as follows:

Short-Term Investments (A)	60,000	
Cash (A)		60,000

Dividend and Interest Recognition

Dividend and interest income is recognized each period as it is earned. In the case of Clifford Company, we will assume that all dividend and interest income is received in cash. However, you should realize that the interest could be accrued and result in interest receivable rather than cash, and the dividends could have been declared but not paid, which would result in dividends receivable. In Exhibit 6-4, the dividends and interest from all three investments have been aggregated into one amount. The entry to record the dividend/interest in Quarter 1 is as follows:

Cash (A)	1,200	
Dividend/interest revenue (SE)		1,200

Recognition of Gains and Losses

At each financial statement date, the company will determine the aggregate market value of its portfolio of short-term investments. Note in Exhibit 6-4 that, on the balance sheet at the end of Quarter 1 (March 31), the portfolio should be carried at $57,000 because this is the market value. The write down from the cost of $60,000 would result in an unrealized loss of $3,000, which would appear on the statement of earnings.

The following entry is made on March 31, to record the reduction in the carrying value of the short-term investments and the unrealized loss:

Unrealized loss on short-term investments (SE)	3,000	
Short-term investments (A)		3,000

The preceding debit entry reduces the current period's net earnings, because these unrealized losses are shown on the statement of earnings. The balance in the short-term investments account is now $57,000. Within the portfolio, Company X would now be carried at $10,500, Company Y at $17,500, and Company Z at $29,000.

In Quarter 2, Clifford Company again recognizes dividend/interest revenue. This is recorded exactly as it was in Quarter 1. At the end of Quarter 2 (June 30), the company applies the market valuation rule again. Note from Exhibit 6-4 that the portfolio's market value has increased from $57,000 to $61,000. (In fact, it has gone up above the original cost of the securities; however, the original cost is no longer relevant.) This means that Clifford can record a $4,000 unrealized gain, to bring the portfolio up from the previous $57,000 to its current market value of $61,000.

The entry on June 30 to record the increase in the value of the securities is as follows:

Short-term investments (A)	4,000	
Unrealized gain on short-term investments (SE)		4,000

Within the portfolio, Company X will now be carried at $12,000, Company Y at $21,000, and Company Z at $28,000.

In Quarter 3, the company recognizes dividend/interest revenue of $700, recorded as follows:

Cash (A)	700	
Dividend/interest revenue (SE)		700

Clifford also sells the Company X bonds for $11,000 during Quarter 3. Since, as shown in Exhibit 6-4, these securities (at the end of Quarter 2) were valued at their market value of $12,000, the sale results in a realized loss of $1,000. The sale is recorded as follows:

Cash (A)	11,000	
Loss on sale of short-term investments (SE)	1,000	
Short-term investments (A)		12,000

At the end of Quarter 3 (September 30), the company applies the market valuation rule again. Note from Exhibit 6-4 that the combined market value of the two remaining securities in the portfolio has decreased from $49,000 (i.e., $21,000 + 28,000) at the end of Quarter 2 to $47,000 at the end of Quarter 3. This means that Clifford Company must record a $2,000 unrealized loss, to bring the portfolio's value down to its current market value. The entry on September 30 to record the decrease in the value of the Company Y and Company Z shares is as follows:

| Unrealized loss on short-term investments (SE) | 2,000 | |
| Short-term investments (A) | | 2,000 |

Within the portfolio, Company Y will now be carried at $18,000 and Company Z at $29,000.

Finally, in Quarter 4 the company again recognizes dividend/interest revenue of $700, which is recorded exactly as it was in Quarter 3.

Clifford also sells the Company Y shares during Quarter 4, for $18,500. Since, as shown in Exhibit 6-4, these securities (at the end of Quarter 3) were valued at their market value of $18,000, the sale results in a realized gain of $500. The sale is recorded as follows:

Cash (A)	18,500	
Gain on sale of short-term investments (SE)		500
Short-term investments (A)		18,000

At the end of Quarter 4 (December 31), the company applies the market valuation rule again. Note from Exhibit 6-4 that the market value of the one remaining security in the portfolio has increased from $29,000 at the end of Quarter 3 to $31,500 at the end of Quarter 4. This means that a $2,500 unrealized gain will be recorded, to bring the portfolio's value up to its current market value. The entry on December 31 to record the increase in the value of the Company Z shares is as follows:

| Short-term investments (A) | 2,500 | |
| Unrealized gain on short-term investments (SE) | | 2,500 |

Exhibit 6-5 summarizes the effects on the statement of earnings and balance sheet of applying the market valuation, as well as the other events that affected these short-term securities during the year.

In a typical set of financial statements, the disclosure of the effects of transactions involving short-term investments tends to be somewhat limited because of the small size of these transactions relative to the company's other operating revenues and expenses. Many companies will simply list a line item for short-term investments on the balance sheet, stating that the securities are carried at their market value. Similarly, on the statement of earnings, there may be few details about the amount of dividend or interest

PARTIAL FINANCIAL STATEMENTS FOR CLIFFORD COMPANY

EXHIBIT 6-5

Partial Statement of Earnings for the quarter ended	March 31	June 30	September 30	December 31
Unrealized gain (loss) on short-term investments	$(3,000)	$ 4,000	$(2,000)	$ 2,500
Realized gain (loss) on sale of short-term investments	–	–	(1,000)	500
Dividend/interest revenue	1,200	1,200	700	700
Partial Balance Sheet as at	**March 31**	**June 30**	**September 30**	**December 31**
Short-term investments (at fair market value)	$57,000	$61,000	$47,000	$31,500

revenue earned during the period, or the amount of realized and unrealized gains and losses that have been recognized. When the amounts are significant, however, a note to the financial statements generally provides the details.

Finally, refer to the third quarter, when Clifford sold the investment in Company X bonds for $11,000. Bonds have a face amount or maturity value (in this case $10,000) that the purchaser will receive when the bonds mature. The fact that Clifford sold the bonds for $11,000 indicates that they had not reached maturity yet. If they had, Clifford would have received only $10,000. Between the date of issue and the date of maturity, it is possible that the market value of the bonds (which is determined by the forces of supply and demand) will be either higher or lower than their face value, depending on competing interest rates and other economic factors.

ACCOUNTS RECEIVABLE

Accounts receivable are amounts owed by customers from normal business transactions of selling goods and services on credit. The control criterion for accounts receivable is evidenced either by a formal contractual agreement or by some other less formal documentation, such as a sales invoice. The sale itself represents the past event that gave rise to the account receivable. The probable future economic benefits would be satisfied by the fact that a receivable is the right to receive payment at some future date.

The value of the cash that is to be received in the future is affected by the same uncertainties that we described in the earlier section on cash. In addition to those uncertainties, there is also the uncertainty of whether customers will pay the cash as agreed. Defaults by customers are called **bad debts**.

Other uncertainties with accounts receivable are that the customer might return the goods for credit, the customer might request a price adjustment if the goods are damaged in shipment, or the customer might pay less than what is listed on the invoice if a discount is allowed for prompt payment. All these factors can affect the certainty of collecting accounts receivable and complicate the determination of the appropriate valuation amount.

Accounts Receivable Valuation Methods

An account receivable is a right to receive a certain amount at some point in the future. A simple way to value the receivable is to add up the gross payments called for in the agreement. This gross payments method ignores the effects of bad debts (customers who do not pay), returns, and so forth, as well as the effects of the time value of money.

A second method for valuing an account receivable is to take into consideration the time value of the gross payments to be received. The time value of money is the concept that a dollar received in the future is worth less than a dollar received today. The reasoning here is that a company can invest a dollar received today and have more than a dollar in the future. Therefore, if the company has a receivable for $100 to be received a month from now, this asset is worth less than $100 today. Using the terminology of the time value of money, we would want to calculate the **present value** of the receivable's future cash flows. We would discount the future payments, using an appropriate interest rate, to arrive at this present value. (Present value concepts and calculations are illustrated in Chapter 10. You can also see the companion website to the text for a full discussion of the calculation of present values.)

A third method is to consider the possibility that the receivable may not be paid. This could result from a default by the customer or from the return of the goods. Partial payment might also result if the customer pays early, taking advantage of a cash discount, or if the customer demands a price reduction (because, for example, the goods were not exactly as ordered or were received in damaged condition). Incorporating these events into the valuation process would mean reducing the value of the receivable. This alternative can be used in conjunction with either the first (gross payments) or the second (present value) method of valuing the accounts receivable.

Finally, a valuation method based on the market value of the accounts receivable might also be considered. Accounts receivable can be sold to other parties, who later collect the payments from the customers. The process of selling accounts receivable is called **factoring**. If a ready market is available in which to sell the receivables, the market price could be used to value them.

What Is Canadian Practice?

Most Canadian companies show receivables at their gross payment amount less appropriate allowances for bad debts, returns, and so forth. Ideally, using present values would be more appropriate, but only if the amounts are material. If there is little difference between the present values and the gross payments, as occurs with receivables that are expected to be paid in a relatively short time, the gross payments can be used. The use of present values adds some complications to the accounting for receivables and, unless using present values makes a significant difference, it is probably not worth the effort. For most companies, the time between a sale and its collection is relatively short (30 to 60 days). As a result, unless interest rates are extremely high, the differences between the present values and the gross payments would be relatively small. For this reason, most companies account for their receivables using the gross amount rather than present values.

Allowances for returns, bad debts, and so on are necessary because the company must be careful not to overstate the value of its assets or the amount of its income from sales to customers. For example, consider a company that sells $100,000 of goods during the accounting period, all on account. The entry to record this transaction is the following:

| Accounts receivable (A) | 100,000 | |
| Sales revenue (SE) | | 100,000 |

If the company anticipates that it will collect the entire $100,000, the preceding entry would appropriately state the effects of the transaction on the company's assets and income. However, if the company anticipates that some customers will not pay, this entry overstates the value of the accounts receivable, as well as the amount of shareholders' equity.

The likelihood that a customer will default on payments depends on the customer's creditworthiness. A company can improve its chances of receiving payments by performing credit checks on its customers before it grants them credit. However, the company must balance its desire to sell its products to the customer with the risk that the customer will not pay. Too strict a credit policy will mean that many customers will be denied credit and may therefore purchase their goods from other suppliers. Too loose a credit policy, and the company may lose more money from bad debts than it gains from additional sales. The company should do a cost-benefit analysis to decide what its credit policy should be.

The company must also stay aware of changes in the industry it operates in and changes in the economy in general. Changes in interest rates, inflation, or the global economy can quickly affect a customer's credit status.

In addition to a policy on bad debts, other policies can affect the amounts collected. One of these is the company's policy regarding returns. Can customers return goods, and under what circumstances? Again, the policy's strictness or looseness will have an effect on whether customers will buy goods from the company.

Several years ago, a large Canadian publishing and distribution company filed for bankruptcy protection while it attempted to restructure its organization. One main cause of its financial difficulty was the demands placed on it by one of its major customers, a large bookseller. The customer had extended its payment terms to 250 days from its former 90 days. To make matters worse, often, instead of making its payments in 250 days, the customer returned unsold books to settle its debts. The long delays in receiving payments, coupled with the fact that the company had to pay its own suppliers in 90 days, drained the company of cash and pushed it into financial difficulty. Here is a situation where customer returns affected not only the company's revenue picture but its cash flow as well. In the end, the company was unable to avoid bankruptcy.

A second policy that should be considered is whether to give discounts for early payment. If the company decides to offer a discount to customers who pay their accounts promptly, the amount of cash that will be collected from receivables will depend on the number of customers who pay early and therefore get the discount, which, in turn, will depend on the attractiveness of the discount. If the amounts involved are expected to be significant, adjustments will be necessary to the amounts recorded in accounts receivable, as well as in the sales revenue account.

The accounting methods for anticipated bad debts or doubtful (sometimes referred to as uncollectible) accounts are illustrated in the next section. Similar methods could be used to account for the other adjustments to accounts receivable, such as for returns or discounts; however, these will not be illustrated here. For a complete description of the accounting for returns and discounts, you should refer to an intermediate accounting text.

Accounting for doubtful accounts requires adjusting the value of the accounts receivable on the balance sheet, as well as recognizing the related bad debt expense on the statement of earnings. Some businesses use the **direct write-off method**, but most companies use what is called the **allowance method** to recognize doubtful accounts. We will therefore discuss the allowance method first.

LEARNING OBJECTIVE 7

Identify two methods for recognizing bad debts, and describe the proper circumstances for using each method.

The Allowance Method of Accounting for Bad Debts

Let's begin by noting two key points already discussed earlier in the text. First, the matching concept requires that when a company recognizes revenue from a sale, it must at the same time recognize all the expenses relating to that sale. Second, bad debts are technically not expenses; they are reductions in revenues. Nevertheless, they are usually recorded as expenses, and must be recognized at the same time as the related revenues. Because, at the point of sale, the company does not know which customers will end up as bad debts, it must estimate what portion of the amount due will ultimately be uncollectible. These estimates are usually based on the company's past experience with its customers. New businesses usually have little basis for initial estimates, and so must use some other method (such as data from Statistics Canada, or advice from an accounting firm) to make their estimates.

Returning to the example of our preceding journal entry for $100,000 in sales, assume that the company estimates that $2,500 of the $100,000 will ultimately prove to be uncollectible. As the company is not able to identify the specific customers who will not pay, the $2,500 cannot be reduced directly through specific accounts receivable in the subsidiary ledger (in which individual accounts are maintained for each customer). Therefore, the following entry instead records this amount in an account that is contra to the accounts receivable control account. This contra account, which is usually called the **allowance for doubtful accounts**, reduces the aggregate amount of the accounts receivable by the anticipated effects of the **uncollectible accounts**. The journal entry to recognize the bad debts expense and create an allowance for future write-offs (an adjusting entry, usually made at the end of the accounting period) is as follows:

Bad debts expense (SE)	2,500	
Allowance for doubtful accounts (XA)		2,500

The allowance for doubtful accounts has a credit balance because its purpose is to show that the debit balance amount in the accounts receivable will not be fully collected. In effect, it reduces the accounts receivable total to the net amount of cash that the company actually expects to receive. The allowance account is contra to accounts receivable and, therefore, shown as a deduction from that current asset on the balance sheet. If these were the only transactions affecting these accounts, the amounts would be presented as follows:

Accounts receivable (gross)	$100,000
Less: Allowance for doubtful accounts	2,500
Net accounts receivable	$ 97,500

Note that the entry above has the effect of reducing the net carrying value of the accounts receivable by $2,500, from $100,000 to $97,500. The accounts receivable are now stated at the amount that the company ultimately expects to collect in cash, which is often referred to as the **net realizable value**. At the same time, the bad debts expense reduces the net earnings by the same amount.

Notice that this is similar to the way in which accumulated depreciation reduces the value of the associated capital asset, while depreciation expense is recorded as a reduction of the net earnings.

HELPFUL HINT

Do not confuse **adjustments for bad debts** (which recognize the bad debts expense and increase the allowance for doubtful accounts) with the **write-offs of bad debts** (which decrease both the allowance for doubtful accounts and the accounts receivable).

The actual **write-off** of an account receivable, under the allowance method, usually occurs at a later date. The company's decision that a particular account is uncollectible and should be written off is usually based on a bad debts write-off policy. For example, the policy may state that accounts will be written off as uncollectible if they have been outstanding for more than 180 days. This policy is based on the company's experience with collecting from its customers, and usually means that the probability of collecting the account after 180 days is so small that it is not worth pursuing. Assume now that the company in our example writes off accounts that have not been collected within 180 days. Also assume that, in accordance with this policy, non-payments result in $2,800 of actual write-offs. With the allowance method, this means that we have now specifically identified the customer accounts that are bad, which we were unable to identify at the time we recognized the bad debts expense. Because we recognized the expense when the estimate was made, no further expense should be recognized when the accounts are written off. We simply remove the specific accounts from accounts receivable and remove an equivalent amount from the allowance account (because that portion of the allowance has been used). The entry to write off accounts receivable against the allowance that was provided for this purpose would be as follows:

Allowance for doubtful accounts (XA)	2,800	
Accounts receivable (A)		2,800

What happens if one of the accounts that we have written off is later paid by the customer? This is called a **recovery**. Under the allowance method, recoveries are accounted for by first reinstating the account receivable and then recording its collection. This is accomplished by reversing the write-off entry and then showing the normal cash collection entry. For example, the following two entries would be made if an account worth $400 was recovered after having been written off:

Accounts receivable (A)	400	
Allowance for doubtful accounts (XA)		400

To reinstate an account that was previously written off.

Cash (A)	400	
Accounts receivable (A)		400

To record the collection of the account referred to above.

Note that one net entry (debiting cash and crediting the allowance for doubtful accounts) could be made to accomplish the recording of this transaction. However, if no entry is made to the accounts receivable account, the customer's account will always be shown in the records as having been a bad debt. For this reason, it is preferable to make the two entries.

Assume next that the company began the year with an accounts receivable balance of $10,000 and a balance in its allowance for doubtful accounts of $1,000. In addition to the transactions recorded above, it had $95,200 of collections from its customers during the year. Exhibit 6-6 illustrates the entries and balances in the associated items on the balance sheet (i.e., the accounts receivable and the allowance for doubtful accounts) and on the statement of earnings (i.e., the sales revenue and the bad debts expense).

The ending balance in the accounts receivable account ($12,000) represents those accounts that remain to be collected, as at the end of the accounting period. In our example, the maximum amount of time that any of these accounts can have been outstanding is 180 days; any account beyond that time is written off. The ending

HELPFUL HINT

The allowance for doubtful accounts is a contra asset, and therefore a permanent account whose balance is cumulative and carried forward from one period to another. However, bad debts expense (like all expenses) is a temporary account and therefore begins each period with a zero balance.

EXHIBIT 6-6

ACCOUNTS UNDER THE ALLOWANCE METHOD OF ACCOUNTING FOR BAD DEBTS

BALANCE SHEET ACCOUNTS				STATEMENT OF EARNINGS ACCOUNTS	
Accounts Receivable				**Sales Revenue**	
Beginning Balance	10,000				
Credit Sales	100,000				100,000
		95,200	Cash collections		
		2,800	Write-offs		
Reinstatement	400				
		400	Cash collection		
Ending Balance	12,000				

Allowance for Doubtful Accounts				**Bad Debts Expense**	
		1,000	Beginning balance		
		2,500	Estimated bad debts	2,500	
Write-offs	2,800				
		400	Reinstatement		
		1,100	Ending balance		

balance in the allowance for doubtful accounts is the remaining allowance that applies to the ending balance in accounts receivable. In other words, the company has provided an allowance for $1,100 of the remaining $12,000 in accounts receivable to be written off in the future.

In most financial statements, the allowance account is netted against the accounts receivable account to produce a single line item on the balance sheet. In the example above, this would be $10,900 (i.e., the balance of $12,000 in accounts receivable minus the balance of $1,100 in the allowance for doubtful accounts). Few companies provide details of the amount of the allowance, either by showing the balance in the allowance for doubtful accounts or by including information about it in the notes to the financial statements.

The final, but vitally important, point to consider under the allowance method of accounting for bad debts is the method that is used to estimate the amounts that will not be collectible. The two methods that are commonly used are called the **percentage of credit sales method** and the **aging of accounts receivable method**. Each of these methods will be discussed in the following sections.

Estimating Bad Debts under the Allowance Method

LEARNING OBJECTIVE 8

Differentiate between two approaches for estimating the amount of future bad debts.

In order to use the allowance method of accounting for bad debts, companies must estimate the amount of the expected uncollectible accounts at the end of each period. Two bases can be used to determine this amount: (1) a percentage of the credit sales made during the period, and (2) an aging analysis of the accounts receivable outstanding at the end of the period. Both bases are generally accepted in accounting, so the choice for any particular company is management's decision. It depends on whether management wishes to focus on income measurement (i.e., matching expenses and revenues), or to focus on asset valuation (i.e., determining the net realizable value of the accounts receivable). The following table summarizes this difference:

PERCENTAGE OF CREDIT SALES METHOD	AGING OF ACCOUNTS RECEIVABLE METHOD
Focuses on earnings measurement by using the sales revenue as the basis for calculating the bad debts expense.	**Focuses on asset valuation** by using the accounts receivable as the basis for calculating the allowance for doubtful accounts.
Emphasizes earnings statement relationships by ensuring that the amount of expense is logically related to the amount of revenue.	**Emphasizes balance sheet relationships** by ensuring that the balance in the contra asset account is logically related to the balance in the asset account.

In short, the conceptual difference between these two approaches is that the percentage of credit sales method results in a better matching of expenses with revenues and therefore a better estimate of the net earnings, while the aging of accounts receivable method produces a better estimate of the net realizable value of the accounts receivable.

We will now look at the procedure to follow for each of these approaches.

The Percentage of Credit Sales Method of Estimating Bad Debts

The percentage of credit sales method of estimating bad debts is based on the assumption that the amount of bad debt expense is a function of the total sales made on credit. The bad debt expense for the period is estimated by multiplying the credit sales for the period by an appropriate percentage. The percentage is usually determined based on the company's collection history. In the previous example, assume that the $2,500 of bad debt expense resulted from using 2.5% of credit sales as an estimate of the bad debts (2.5% of the $100,000 in credit sales would have resulted in the estimated bad debt expense of $2,500).

In a new company, the percentage may be determined initially by considering the bad debts experience of other companies in the same industry. Subsequently, all companies must from time to time adjust their estimate of the percentage that will be uncollectible to reflect the company's recent credit experience and changes in general economic conditions. If the company is experiencing more write-offs than were estimated, the percentage should be increased. Companies typically do not go back to prior periods to adjust the percentage or recalculate the bad debts expense. Therefore, an overestimate or underestimate in one period will be corrected by an adjustment to the percentage used in a subsequent period. The appropriate percentage can be affected by the types of customers that the company has, changes in its credit policies, and general economic conditions. For example, during an economic downturn or recession, bad debts percentages often rise.

As mentioned at the beginning of this discussion, this basis of estimating bad debts emphasizes the matching of expenses with revenues. Accordingly, because the focus is on the amount of the expense rather than on the amount of the allowance, when the adjusting entry is made (to record the bad debts expense and increase the allowance for doubtful accounts) *the existing balance in the allowance account is not taken into consideration under this approach*. The ending balance in the allowance for doubtful accounts is therefore simply the net total of the various entries in that account, which is $1,100 in our example. There is thus no predetermined percentage relationship between the ending balance in the allowance account and the related accounts receivable account, and it has nothing directly to do with the percentage that is used to estimate the bad debts expense. In our example, the ratio of the ending balance in the allowance account to the ending balance in the accounts receivable account works out to be about 9.2% ($1,100 ÷ $12,000 = 0.0917). This is considerably higher than the 2.5% bad debts that the company estimated as its percentage of credit sales. This is not necessarily inconsistent, however, because a higher percentage of the accounts receivable that are still outstanding at the end of the period may be doubtful. For example, many of the remaining receivables may be older accounts, which means that the probability of not collecting them is greater.

The Aging of Accounts Receivable Method of Estimating Bad Debts

Under the aging of accounts receivable method, management estimates a percentage relationship between the amount of receivables and the expected write-offs of uncollectible accounts. This could be a single percentage assigned to the receivables as a whole; but the reliability of the estimate will be improved if it is based on different percentages for different age categories of receivables. The process of dividing the receivables into various age categories, reflecting the length of time the balances have been outstanding, is called aging the accounts receivable. An example of an aging schedule, based on the previous example, is shown in Exhibit 6-7. Note that the total amount of accounts receivable is $12,000—the same as it was in Exhibit 6-6.

After an aging schedule has been prepared, the expected bad debt losses are estimated by applying percentages, based on past experience, to the totals in each category. The longer a receivable has been outstanding, the higher the probability that it will be

EXHIBIT 6-7

EXAMPLE OF AN AGING SCHEDULE FOR ACCOUNTS RECEIVABLE

Customer's name	Total balance	Number of days the account receivable has been outstanding				
		1–30	31–60	61–90	91–120	121–180
T. E. Bansal	$ 2,700	$ 2,700				
R. C. Lortz	3,000	1,850	$ 1,150			
I. M. Owen	1,700		900	$ 800		
A. Rashad	1,100				$ 1,100	
O. L. Su	2,500	950	1,550			
T. Woznow	1,000					$ 1,000
	$12,000	$ 5,500	$ 3,600	$ 800	$ 1,100	$ 1,000

uncollectible. As a result, the estimated percentage of uncollectible accounts increases as the age of the receivables increases.

Exhibit 6-8 shows how the aging schedule can be used to calculate the estimated amount of uncollectible accounts. Note the increasing percentages by age category, from 1% to 65%.

The total estimated write-offs figure represents the amount of existing receivables that are expected to become uncollectible in the future. *Thus, the resulting amount ($1,390) represents the required balance in the allowance for doubtful accounts. Accordingly, the amount of the bad debts adjusting entry is the difference between the required balance and the existing balance in the allowance account.*

To determine the amount of the required adjustment for bad debts, we first have to calculate the existing balance in the allowance for doubtful accounts. In our example, this works out to a *debit* balance of $1,400 (indicating that a greater amount of accounts receivable were written off than was anticipated by the amount in the allowance account), as shown in Exhibit 6-9. We then compare this to the required ending balance—a *credit* of $1,390, as calculated in Exhibit 6-8—and determine that a credit adjustment of $2,790 ($1,400 + $1,390) is needed in order to change the balance in the allowance for doubtful accounts from the existing amount to the required amount.

Note that although the required ending balance is always a credit (since the allowance is a contra asset account), the existing balance may be either a debit or credit. In cases like our example, where the balance before adjustment is a debit, you have to add that amount to the required ending balance (a credit), in order to get the amount of the adjustment that has to be made. However, if the balance before adjustment is a credit, you have to subtract that amount from the required ending balance (also a credit), in order to determine the amount of the adjustment that is needed. In either case, the end result is the same: the final balance in the allowance for doubtful accounts is adjusted to the amount that the aging schedule indicates as the expected amount of accounts receivable that will be written off as bad debts in the future.

HELPFUL HINT

Under the percentage of sales method, you adjust the allowance account *by* the amount calculated when you multiply the given percentage by the credit sales figure; under the aging of receivables method, you adjust the balance in the allowance account *to* the amount indicated by the aging analysis.

EXHIBIT 6-8

USING AN AGING SCHEDULE TO ESTIMATE THE REQUIRED ALLOWANCE FOR DOUBTFUL ACCOUNTS

Customer's name	Total balance	Number of days the account receivable has been outstanding				
		1–30	31–60	61–90	91–120	121–180
T. E. Bansal	$ 2,700	$ 2,700				
R. C. Lortz	3,000	1,850	$ 1,150			
I. M. Owen	1,700		900	$ 800		
A. Rashad	1,100				$ 1,100	
O. L. Su	2,500	950	1,550			
T. Woznow	1,000					$ 1,000
	$12,000	$ 5,500	$ 3,600	$ 800	$ 1,100	$ 1,000
Estimated percentage uncollectible		1%	5%	15%	35%	65%
Total estimated write-offs	**$ 1,390**	$ 55	$ 180	$ 120	$ 385	$ 650

EXHIBIT 6-9

ACCOUNTS USING THE AGING OF ACCOUNTS RECEIVABLE METHOD

BALANCE SHEET ACCOUNTS				INCOME STATEMENT ACCOUNTS	
Accounts Receivable				**Sales Revenue**	
Beginning balance	10,000				
Credit sales	100,000				100,000
		95,200	Cash collections		
		2,800	Write-offs		
Reinstatement	**400**				
		400	Cash collection		
Ending balance	12,000				

Allowance for Doubtful Accounts					
		1,000	Beginning balance		
Write-offs	2,800				
		400	Reinstatement		
Balance before adj.	1,400			**Bad Debts Expense**	
		2,790	Estimated bad debts	2,790	
		1,390	Ending balance		

Before leaving our example, notice that these two methods produced different results. Under the percentage of credit sales method, we ended the year with bad debts expense of $2,500 and an allowance for doubtful accounts with a balance of $1,100 (as shown in Exhibit 6-6). Under the aging of accounts receivable method, we ended the year with bad debts expense of $2,790 and an allowance for doubtful accounts with a balance of $1,390 (as shown in Exhibit 6-9). The company's financial statements will therefore differ, depending on the method that it uses. Both methods are based on estimates, so neither can be said to be conclusively better than the other.

If it is based on a careful aging analysis, the aging of accounts receivable method will normally result in a better approximation of the net realizable value of the receivables than the percentage of credit sales method. However, the matching of expenses with revenues may not be as good, if significant amounts of customers' accounts have been outstanding for more than a year (because, under these circumstances, the bad debts expense for the current year will include amounts applicable to the sales of prior years).

INTERNATIONAL PERSPECTIVES

Reports from Other Countries

In some countries (for example, France and Germany), the estimate of uncollectible accounts is accomplished by considering the circumstances of individual accounts, rather than by estimating an overall percentage rate such as with the percentage of credit sales method. This method is similar to the aging of accounts receivable, which is used widely in Canada and by some companies in Japan.

The Direct Write-Off Method of Accounting for Bad Debts

The direct write-off method is often used by companies with an insignificant amount of bad debts. Rather than recognizing an estimated amount for bad debts expense in the period of the sale and providing an allowance for future write-offs, the direct write-off method recognizes the bad debts expense in the period in which the company decides that certain accounts are, in fact, uncollectible.

Assume that we are using the same policy as with the allowance method: accounts are written off after 180 days. In our example, $2,800 worth of accounts receivable were identified as being more than 180 days overdue and therefore should be written off. With the direct write-off method, the entry to record this is as follows:

Bad debts expense (SE)	2,800	
Accounts receivable (A)		2,800

Note that *no allowance for doubtful accounts is used with the direct write-off method*, and the debit to the bad debts expense account reduces net earnings in the period in which the uncollectible accounts receivable are written off.

As is the case whenever accounts are written off, the credit entries to accounts receivable refer to specific customer accounts; the company has reached the point where it is able to identify exactly who is not going to pay. For example, the $2,800 might be in two specific accounts, a $1,600 account from Joe Lee and a $1,200 account from Mary Smith. The overall accounts receivable balance (in the control account, in the general ledger) is supported by a subsidiary ledger (similar to the subsidiary ledger used with short-term investments) in which separate receivable accounts are maintained for each customer. This entry would cause reductions in the accounts of both Joe Lee and Mary Smith.

The direct write-off method is a simple way to account for bad debts. The company makes every reasonable effort to collect the account, and when it finally decides that an account is uncollectible, it records the entry to remove it from the accounting system. The problem with this method is that it violates the matching concept discussed in Chapter 4. As you will recall, the matching concept states that all the expenses related to the production of revenue should be recognized simultaneously with the revenue (i.e., recognized in the same period in which the revenue is recognized). The direct write-off method could often result in the revenue being recognized in one accounting period, and the associated bad debt expense being recorded in a later period. If bad debts are not significant, this mismatching will not be material and can be ignored. If bad debts are significant, however, this mismatching can distort the measurement of income enough for the direct write-off method to be unacceptable. The appropriate method to use when bad debts are significant is the allowance method.

Finally, note that bad debt expense is somewhat different from other expenses. It is more like a reduction in a revenue account, since it represents revenue the company will never receive. In recognition of this, a few companies report it as a direct reduction of the sales revenue amount on the statement of earnings. The majority of companies, however, show bad debts as an operating expense rather than as a reduction of revenues.

HELPFUL HINT

There are two main methods for dealing with bad debts: the direct write-off method and the allowance method. If the allowance method is used (as it should be whenever bad debts are significant), there are two alternative approaches to estimating the amount of bad debts: the aging of accounts receivable method and the percentage of credit sales method.

accounting in the news

Canadians and Their Debt

Through the struggle out of the recession in 2009, the average Canadian household debt rose to $96,100, which is higher than the average household's annual income. This was the highest average debt carried by Canadians in recent history. Close to 60 percent of Canadians admitted that they would be in trouble if a paycheque were delayed. More Canadians are now running behind in mortgage and credit card payments. Housing prices rose late in 2009, but there were also concerns that the higher prices may collapse in the near future, leaving homeowners with mortgage amounts that are greater than the value of their homes. The debt level will become an even greater concern if inflation takes hold and interest rates start to rise, making it even harder for Canadians to meet their debt payments. In February 2010, the federal finance minister brought in new regulations for mortgages that he hoped would slow down the rapid move by Canadians into debt levels that could become problematic.

Source: Canwest News Service, "Canadians Drowning in Debt," *Vancouver Sun*, February 16, 2010.

NOTES RECEIVABLE

Types of Notes Receivable

LEARNING OBJECTIVE 9

Describe the main types of notes receivable and the circumstances for using them.

Notes receivable are very similar to accounts receivable in their basic characteristics. The recognition criteria and valuation methods for notes receivable are the same as for accounts receivable. The difference between an account receivable and a note receivable is that the note receivable is a more formal agreement, referred to as a **promissory note**. A promissory note is a written contract between two parties, the maker and the payee. The maker promises to pay specific amounts, either upon demand by the payee or at a definite date in the future. Exhibit 6-10 is an example of a promissory note receivable.

EXHIBIT 6-10

PROMISSORY NOTE RECEIVABLE

$500	*Toronto, Ont. April 4, 2011*
(Principal amount)	(Location and date)

3 months after the date _____ *Josephine Lumbargi* _____ promises to pay

(Name of maker)

to the order of _____ *Cameo Sportswear* _____

(Name of payee)

for the value received with annual interest of _____ *10%* _____

(Interest rate)

_____

(Signature of maker)

Interest may be shown explicitly as a part of the note, or it may be implicit in the contractual payments. When interest is explicit, it is typically calculated by multiplying the interest rate by the face value of the note and the time factor. The presumption here is that the face value is the amount that has been borrowed via the note. A note in which the interest is implicit (not stated directly) specifies the amount to be paid at maturity; consequently, its face value will be larger than the initial amount borrowed. The interest is the difference between the amount borrowed and the face value. This type of note is sometimes called a **discounted note**.

The payment period for notes is generally longer than for accounts receivable, but if the maturity date is within a year, the notes are considered current assets. Long-term notes receivable are classified in the non-current assets section, along with long-term investments.

Notes are most commonly arranged with banks or other financial institutions. These financial institutions may require that the maker of the note put up some type of **collateral** for the note. Collateral is an asset that the lender (the note's *payee*) has the right to receive if the borrower (the note's *maker*) defaults on the note. As an example, if an individual purchases a car with a loan from a bank, the bank would use the car as collateral for the loan. If the person defaults on the loan, the bank could reclaim the car and sell it to satisfy the outstanding debt.

A note secured by collateral is called a **secured note**. If the borrower or maker is very creditworthy, the lender or payee may agree to issue an **unsecured note**, which means no collateral is specified.

Companies will sometimes agree to accept a note from a customer if the customer cannot pay an account receivable within the normal payment period. If the customer wants a longer time period in which to pay, the company may agree to this arrangement, provided that the customer signs a promissory note and pays interest on the outstanding debt covered by the note. Extending credit beyond the normal credit terms without demanding interest is not effective cash management.

Interest on Notes Receivable

As stated earlier, interest on notes receivable can be either implied or explicit. A note with implied interest might state that the maker of the note agrees to pay $1,100 at maturity, in exchange for $1,000 received today. The maker is borrowing $1,000 and, as the maturity payment is $1,100, the difference ($100) is interest. A note with explicit interest might state that the maker agrees to pay the principal amount of $1,000 at maturity plus interest at a rate of 10% (always stated as an annual rate, unless otherwise indicated) in exchange for $1,000 received today (see Exhibit 6-10). The dollar amount of interest in this case depends on how long the period is between now and maturity.

Short-term notes receivable generally require the interest payments to be calculated using **simple interest** calculations. Long-term notes, on the other hand, generally use **compound interest** calculations. Compound interest calculations are discussed in the "Time Value of Money" section on the companion website and also in Chapter 10. Simple interest calculations are demonstrated in the following equation. Interest charges are calculated based on the amount borrowed, the interest rate, and the amount of time that has passed.

LEARNING OBJECTIVE 10

Calculate the interest on notes receivable and prepare the necessary journal entries.

www.wileyplus.com

Time Value of Money

FORMULA FOR SIMPLE INTEREST:

Interest = Principal × Interest Rate × Time

The principal is the amount borrowed; the interest rate is specified in the note and is stated on a yearly basis; the time is the period that has elapsed, stated as a fraction of a year. The time that has elapsed is generally measured in days. While the actual number of days can be used, many companies simplify the calculation by treating each month as 30 days and, therefore, treating 360 days as being equivalent to one year. The example that follows illustrates the calculation of interest and the accounting for notes receivable, and uses the 360-day convention.

On August 31, Cellar Company agrees to accept a $2,000 note from Byer Company to satisfy an outstanding account receivable. (This could happen, for example, if Byer is having trouble meeting its payments or temporarily has some more pressing needs for its cash.) The note has a maturity of six months (180 days) and an interest rate of 12%. Cellar's fiscal year end is December 31.

When it receives the note on August 31, Cellar makes the following entry:

Notes receivable (A)	2,000	
Accounts receivable (A)		2,000

To record the receipt of a note in settlement of an account receivable.

The above entry records the elimination of the account receivable and its replacement by a note receivable.

On December 31, Cellar must make adjusting entries and close its books. This means that it must record the accrual of interest on the note from Byer. The interest through December 31 (four months after receiving the note) is calculated as follows:

$$\text{Interest} = \text{Principal} \times \text{Interest Rate} \times \text{Time}$$
$$= \$2,000 \times 12\% \times \frac{120}{360}$$
$$= \$80$$

The entry to record the accrued interest on December 31 is:

Interest receivable (A)	80	
Interest revenue (SE)		80

To accrue interest for the period August 31–December 31.

At the end of February, Cellar will receive payment of the principal and interest from Byer. Cellar will have to record the accrual of interest for the months of January and February, as well as the receipt of the cash. The calculation of interest is similar to the earlier one, but for only two months:

$$\text{Interest} = \text{Principal} \times \text{Interest Rate} \times \text{Time}$$
$$= \$2,000 \times 12\% \times \frac{60}{360}$$
$$= \$40$$

Two entries are shown on February 28. The first records the accrual of the interest, and the second records the receipt of the cash. (One combined entry could have been made.)

Interest receivable (A)	40	
Interest revenue (SE)		40

To accrue interest for the period December 31–February 28.

Cash (A)	2,120	
Notes receivable (A)		2,000
Interest receivable (A)		120

To record receipt of the principal of the note plus interest for six months.

In order to receive cash for a note without waiting until its maturity date, the payee may sell the note to another party. This is the same as factoring accounts receivable. The note may be sold with or without **recourse**, meaning that if the maker does not pay the note at maturity, the third party that bought the note will (if the arrangement is with recourse) or will not (if it is without recourse) have the right to collect the amount owed from the original payee. Further information about accounting for the factoring of notes receivable can be found in intermediate accounting courses.

Relatively few short-term notes receivable appear on balance sheets, because they are not very common and their amounts are usually relatively minor. Normally, in external financial statements, such notes receivable are grouped with accounts receivable.

EARNINGS MANAGEMENT

Management usually cannot use the accounting for cash as a way to manage earnings. They could, however, work with the calculation of the allowance for doubtful accounts. Because the calculation of the bad debt expense requires the use of estimates, some change in those estimates could be used to manage earnings. However, the bad debt expense is usually not a very significant amount, so any manipulations would not have a large effect. Similarly, estimates of warranty costs, returns, and discounts would provide avenues for some management of earnings, but again the effects would likely be small.

STATEMENT ANALYSIS CONSIDERATIONS

Short-Term Liquidity

As discussed in Chapter 1, and earlier in this chapter, liquidity refers to the company's ability to convert assets into cash so that liabilities can be paid. An important part of the analysis of short-term liquidity comes from considering the short-term monetary assets on the balance sheet. There are two very common ratios that provide quantitative measures of short-term liquidity: the current ratio and the quick ratio.

> **LEARNING OBJECTIVE 11**
>
> *Calculate the current ratio, quick ratio, and accounts receivable turnover ratio.*

CURRENT RATIO

The **current ratio** is measured by comparing the current assets to the current liabilities. It is calculated as follows:

$$\text{Current ratio} = \frac{\text{Current assets}}{\text{Current liabilities}}$$

Remember that current assets are those that are going to be converted into cash within the next year or operating cycle, and that current liabilities are going to require the use of cash within the next year or operating cycle. As such, this ratio should normally be greater than 1; otherwise, the company may have difficulty meeting its debt obligations in the coming year. The general guideline used for this ratio is that, in order to provide a reasonable margin of safety for most businesses, the current ratio should be 2 or greater. However, this can vary significantly, depending on the type of business and the types of assets and liabilities that are considered current.

> **LEARNING OBJECTIVE 12**
>
> *Explain how the current ratio, quick ratio, and accounts receivable turnover ratio help users analyze a company's short-term liquidity.*

Refer to the balance sheet of **Sony Corporation** in Exhibit 6-11A. The current ratio for Sony Corporation at the end of March 2009 was less than 1, calculated as follows:

CURRENT RATIO—SONY CORPORATION

$$\text{Current ratio} = \frac{¥3,620,635}{¥3,810,900} = 0.95$$

This represents a drop in Sony's current ratio during 2009. At the end of the preceding year it was higher, at 1.25 (5,009,663 ÷ 4,023,367).

One caveat: the current ratio is sometimes manipulated by a company at year end. This ratio may not, therefore, be a very reliable measure of liquidity. For example, consider a company that has $10,000 in current assets (consisting of $3,000 in cash and $7,000 in inventory) and $5,000 in current liabilities just before the end of the year. Its current ratio would be 2 ($10,000 ÷ $5,000). Suppose that the company uses all its $3,000 in cash to pay off $3,000 worth of current liabilities at year end. This greatly improves the current ratio, increasing it to 3.5 ($7,000 ÷ $2,000), and the company looks more liquid. Notice, however, that the company is actually less liquid. In fact, it is very illiquid in the short term because it has no cash, and must sell its inventory and wait until it collects on those sales before it will have any cash to pay its bills. In this case, the current ratio is deceptive. Therefore, a second short-term liquidity ratio, the "quick ratio," is used to provide more insight into the company's liquidity.

QUICK RATIO

As illustrated in the above example, one problem with the current ratio is that some assets in the current assets section may be much less liquid than others. For example, inventory is less liquid than accounts receivable, which are less liquid than cash. In some types of businesses, inventory is very illiquid because of the long period of time required for it to be sold and the cash collected. The current ratio in such cases will not adequately measure the company's short-term liquidity. Therefore, the **quick ratio** is also used to assess short-term liquidity. It differs from the current ratio as the numerator excludes inventories and any accounts listed after inventories, because they cannot (in most cases) be converted into cash quickly. It is calculated as follows:

$$\text{Quick ratio} = \frac{\text{Current assets} - \text{Inventory} - \text{Prepaid expenses}}{\text{Current liabilities}}$$

The general guideline used for this ratio is that it should be 1 or more. However, this also depends somewhat on the type of industry. For Sony Corporation (refer to the balance sheet in Exhibit 6-11A), the ratio at the end of March 2009 was as follows:

QUICK RATIO—SONY CORPORATION

$$\text{Quick ratio} = \frac{¥3,620,635 - ¥813,068 - ¥189,703 - ¥586,800}{¥3,810,900} = 0.53$$

SONY CORPORATION 2009 ANNUAL REPORT

EXHIBIT 6-11A

annual report

Consolidated Balance Sheets
Sony Corporation and Consolidated Subsidiaries—As of March 31

	Yen in millions	
	2008	2009
ASSETS		
Current assets:		
Cash and cash equivalents	1,086,431	660,789
Call loan in the banking business	352,569	49,909
Marketable securities	427,709	466,912
Notes and accounts receivable, trade	1,183,620	963,837
Allowance for doubtful accounts and sales returns	(93,335)	(110,383)
Inventories.	1,021,595	813,068
Deferred income taxes.	237,073	189,703
Prepaid expenses and other current assets.	794,001	586,800
Total current assets	5,009,663	3,620,635
Film costs	304,243	306,877
Investments and advances:		
Affiliated companies.	381,188	236,779
Securities investments and other	3,954,460	4,561,651
	4,335,648	4,798,430
Property, plant and equipment:		
Land	158,289	155,665
Buildings	903,116	911,269
Machinery and equipment.	2,483,016	2,343,839
Construction in progress	55,740	100,027
	3,600,161	3,510,800
Less—Accumulated depreciation	2,356,812	2,334,937
	1,243,349	1,175,863
Other assets:		
Intangibles, net	263,490	396,348
Goodwill	304,423	443,958
Deferred insurance acquisition costs	396,819	400,412
Deferred income taxes.	198,666	359,050
Other	496,438	511,938
	1,659,836	2,111,706
Total assets	12,552,739	12,013,511

(Continued on following page)

EXHIBIT 6-11A **SONY CORPORATION 2009 ANNUAL REPORT (cont'd)**

annual report

Consolidated Balance Sheets
Sony Corporation and Consolidated Subsidiaries—As of March 31

	Yen in millions	
	2008	2009
LIABILITIES AND STOCKHOLDERS' EQUITY		
Current liabilities:		
Short-term borrowings	63,224	303,615
Current portion of long-term debt	291,879	147,540
Notes and accounts payable, trade	920,920	560,795
Accounts payable, other and accrued expenses	896,598	1,036,830
Accrued income and other taxes	200,803	46,683
Deposits from customers in the banking business	1,144,399	1,326,360
Other	505,544	389,077
Total current liabilities	4,023,367	3,810,900
Long-term liabilities:		
Long-term debt	729,059	660,147
Accrued pension and severance costs	231,237	365,706
Deferred income taxes	268,600	188,359
Future insurance policy benefits and other	3,298,506	3,521,060
Other	260,032	250,737
Total long-term liabilities	4,787,434	4,986,009
Total liabilities	8,810,801	8,796,909
Minority interest in consolidated subsidiaries	276,849	251,949
Stockholders' equity:		
Common stock, no par value—		
2008—Shares authorized 3,600,000,000, shares issued 1,004,443,364	630,576	
2009—Shares authorized 3,600,000,000, shares issued 1,004,535,364		630,765
Additional paid-in capital	1,151,447	1,155,034
Retained earnings	2,059,361	1,916,951
Accumulated other comprehensive income—		
Unrealized gains on securities, net	70,929	30,070
Unrealized losses on derivative instruments, net	(3,371)	(1,584)
Pension liability adjustment	(97,562)	(172,709)
Foreign currency translation adjustments	(341,523)	(589,220)
	(371,527)	(733,443)
Treasury stock, at cost		
Common stock (2008—1,015,596 shares)	(4,768)	
(2009—1,013,287 shares)		443,958)
	3,465,089	2,964,653
Total liabilities and stockholders' equity	12,552,739	12,013,511

SONY CORPORATION 2009 ANNUAL REPORT

EXHIBIT 6-11B

annual report

Consolidated Statements of Income
Sony Corporation and Consolidated Subsidiaries—Years ended March 31

	Yen in millions		
	2007	2008	2009
Sales and operating revenue:			
Net sales..	7,567,359	8,201,839	7,110,053
Financial service revenue	624,282	553,216	523,307
Other operating revenue.................................	104,054	116,359	96,633
	8,295,695	8,871,414	7,729,993
Costs and expenses:			
Cost of sales..	5,889,601	6,290,022	5,660,504
Selling, general and administrative......................	1,788,427	1,714,445	1,686,030
Financial service expenses...............................	540,097	530,306	547,825
(Gain) loss on sale, disposal or impairment of assets, net.....	5,820	(37,841)	38,308
	8,223,945	8,496,932	7,932,667
Equity in net income (loss) of affiliated companies	78,654	100,817	(25,109)
Operating income (loss)	150,404	475,299	(227,783)
Other income:			
Interest and dividends.................................	28,240	34,272	22,317
Foreign exchange gain, net	—	5,571	48,568
Gain on sale of securities investments, net.................	14,695	5,504	1,281
Gain on change in interest in subsidiaries and equity investees..	31,509	82,055	1,882
Other...	20,738	22,045	24,777
	95,182	149,447	98,825
Other expenses:			
Interest	27,278	22,931	24,376
Loss on devaluation of securities investments...............	1,308	13,087	4,427
Foreign exchange loss, net..............................	18,835	—	—
Other...	17,474	21,594	17,194
	64,895	57,612	45,997
Income (loss) before income taxes and minority interest	180,691	567,134	(174,955)
Income taxes:			
Current	67,081	183,438	80,521
Deferred	(13,193)	20,040	(153,262)
	53,888	203,478	(72,741)
Income (loss) before minority interest	126,803	363,656	(102,214)
Minority interest in income (loss) of consolidated subsidiaries...	475	(5,779)	(3,276)
Net income (loss)......................................	126,328	369,435	(98,938)

Note that we have subtracted the amount for "Deferred income taxes" (along with the inventory and prepaid expenses) from the total current assets in the above calculation. We have done so because it was listed at the end of the current assets section on Sony's balance sheet, which implies that it is not very liquid. Remember that the current assets are listed in the order of their liquidity.

As shown in the above calculation, Sony's quick ratio for 2009 was less than 1. At the end of the preceding year it was somewhat higher, at 0.74 ([5,009,663 − 1,021,595 − 237,073 − 794,001] ÷ 4,023,367). Thus, Sony's quick ratio (like its current ratio) dropped during 2009.

Accounts Receivable Turnover Ratio

A company's cash flows are critical to its profitability and even to its survival. Because most companies receive a significant amount of operating cash from the collection of their accounts receivable, the analysis of a company's short-term liquidity should consider the company's success in collecting its accounts receivable. One common ratio to assess the management of accounts receivable is the **accounts receivable turnover ratio**. This is calculated by dividing the credit sales for the period by the average accounts receivable, as follows:

$$\text{Accounts receivable turnover ratio} = \frac{\text{Credit sales}}{\text{Average accounts receivable}}$$

Calculating this ratio from financial statement data usually requires you to assume that all the sales are credit sales. If the analyst has more detailed information about the composition of sales, then some adjustment can be made in the numerator to include only the sales on account. In addition, information in the financial statements may indicate that not all receivables are from customers. Therefore, a more sophisticated calculation would include only customer receivables in the denominator, as only these relate to the credit sales figure in the numerator.

As an example, consider the information provided in Exhibit 6-11 from the financial statements of Sony Corporation. A quick review of this information shows that Sony has included accounts receivable with notes receivable. Because notes receivable often have a longer collection time, the inclusion of both these items may distort this ratio. The company also includes the allowance for doubtful accounts, which needs to be deducted to arrive at the average receivable amount in the denominator. The accounts receivable were lower at the end of March 2009 compared to March 2008. This should not be a surprise, however, because Sony's sales were lower in 2009. The following calculation shows how this decline in sales affected Sony's collection rate for 2009:

ACCOUNTS RECEIVABLE TURNOVER—SONY CORPORATION

$$\text{Receivables turnover rate} = \frac{¥7,110,053}{(¥853,454 + ¥1,090,285) \div 2} = \frac{¥7,110,053}{¥971,870} = 7.3$$

In this context, turnover means how often the accounts receivable are "turned over," or how often they are collected in full and replaced by new accounts. Thus, the turnover analysis above shows that Sony's accounts were collected and replaced by new receivables approximately 7.3 times during the year.

Another way to analyze the performance of accounts receivable collection is to calculate the average number of days required to collect the accounts. This analysis assumes that the sales are spread evenly over a 365-day year. (In accounting we often use the convention of a 365-day year even if the accounting year has more or fewer days.) The calculation divides the number of days in the year (365) by the accounts receivable turnover rate. Using this calculation, Sony's average collection period for accounts receivable was 50 days (365 ÷ 7.3) in 2009.

It would be very useful to compare this with the company's normal credit terms. If its normal credit terms are 30 days, then you would expect that the number of days to collect receivables would be 30 days or fewer. Companies usually do not disclose their credit policy time frames or terms. Bear in mind, however, that Sony does not sell products directly to end customers; rather, it sells to retailers, which then sell to consumers. The credit terms for business-to-business sales are often longer than 30 days. Remember that the denominator also includes notes receivable, which often have a longer collection period. Sony's average collection period of 50 days in 2009 is probably very reasonable, and an indication of good receivables management. One way to check the reasonableness of the ratio would be to compare it with a competitor's.

It would also be very informative to compare the above ratios for Sony in 2009 with the results for the preceding year. Unfortunately, we do not know the amount of accounts receivable at the end of 2007, which is needed to calculate the average balance outstanding during 2008. (In order to get around this frequently encountered problem, analysts often base their calculations on end-of-year balances, although average balances are preferable.)

Finally, trends over time should be considered with respect to bad debts. For example, when analyzing a company, you may find that the amounts written off over the last several years have been increasing. Whether this is good or bad, though, depends on how the accounts receivable balance has changed over the same time period. To address this question, a ratio of the amount written off to the total amount of receivables could be calculated. If this ratio has been increasing over the last several years, it may represent some relative degradation in the quality of the receivables. If this were to continue, it would not be good news for the company.

Another way to address the same issue would be to compare the ratio of the ending balance in the allowance for doubtful accounts with the ending balance in the accounts receivable. An increase in this ratio over time would indicate that a higher percentage of the ending accounts receivable was considered uncollectible. This, too, would be a concern.

SUMMARY

In this chapter, we have discussed four major types of current assets that are either cash or about to become cash. We discussed how each could be valued and what the current Canadian practice is for valuation. For cash, we spent some time outlining the importance of internal controls. For short-term investments, we described how these will generally be reported at their fair market values at the end of each period. We discussed the measuring and recording of potential bad debts associated with accounts receivable. The discussion of notes receivable included a section on how to account for the interest that is earned on notes.

The discussion of these four types of current assets was completed with the introduction of three ratios: the current ratio, the quick ratio, and the accounts receivable turnover ratio, which can be used to assess a company's short-term liquidity.

The next chapter considers the last major component of current assets: inventory. Because of the complexities associated with accounting for inventory and the cost of goods sold, an entire chapter is devoted to this discussion.

www.wileyplus.com

Additional Practice Problems

PRACTICE PROBLEM 1

Exhibit 6-12 provides information about the short-term investments of Labbé Ltée.

Required:
Assuming that Labbé prepares financial statements on a quarterly basis, construct the journal entries that it would make each quarter to record the above events.

EXHIBIT 6-12

LABBÉ LTÉE.

Security	Quarter Acquired	Acquisition Cost	Quarter Sold	Selling Price
Alpha Co.	1	$20,000	–	–
Beta Co.	1	$30,000	4	$29,000
Gamma Co.	1	$15,000	2	$18,000

		Market Values at the End of			
Security	Cost	Quarter 1	Quarter 2	Quarter 3	Quarter 4
Alpha	$20,000	$21,000	$22,000	$17,000	$15,000
Beta	30,000	32,000	36,000	37,000	–
Gamma	15,000	14,000	–	–	–
	$65,000	$67,000	$58,000	$54,000	$15,000

Dividends/Interest Received

Quarter	Amount
1	$650
2	$525
3	$550
4	$150

All dividends are received in cash each quarter.

STRATEGIES FOR SUCCESS:

▶ Remember that short-term investments in marketable securities such as these are generally reported at their market value on each balance sheet date (rather than at their original cost or the lower of cost and market).

▶ Gains and losses arising from increases and decreases in market values while the securities are still held are referred to as *unrealized*. This differentiates them from realized gains and losses, which are recognized when the securities are sold.

▶ Do not confuse dividends received on a company's investments with dividends declared and paid by the company. Dividends received are a form of revenue, or income, from investments.

solution to practice problems

PRACTICE PROBLEM 2

During 2011, Kumar Company sold $150,000 of goods on credit and collected $135,000 from its customers on account. The company started the period with a balance of $15,000 in accounts receivable and a balance in the allowance for doubtful accounts of $450. During 2011, Kumar wrote off $2,725 of accounts receivable. Kumar estimates that 2% of its credit sales will ultimately be uncollectible.

Required:

a. Show the journal entries that would be made during the year that affect accounts receivable and the allowance for doubtful accounts. Then, calculate the amount of bad debts expense for 2011 and make the journal entry to record it.

b. What amount(s) would be reported on the balance sheet at the end of 2011 regarding accounts receivable?

c. Now assume that, instead of using the percentage of credit sales method to estimate its bad debts expense, Kumar Company performed an aging analysis of its accounts receivable at the end of 2011 and determined that it should have an allowance for doubtful accounts of $1,000. How would this affect your answers to parts "a" and "b" above?

STRATEGIES FOR SUCCESS:

▶ Bear in mind that the allowance method recognizes bad debts expense at the end of each period, when adjusting entries are made, and provides an allowance for accounts that will be written off. Therefore, when write-offs occur, they are debited to the allowance account rather than to the expense account.

▶ Remember that the percentage of credit sales approach applies the estimated percentage to the credit sales to determine the appropriate amount of bad debts expense. When the adjusting journal entry is made to record this, the existing balance in the allowance for doubtful accounts is ignored.

▶ In the aging of accounts receivable approach, the aging analysis indicates the appropriate amount of allowance for doubtful accounts. The existing balance in the allowance for doubtful accounts must be taken into consideration to determine the correct amount for the adjusting journal entry.

PRACTICE PROBLEM 3

Domino's Pizza Enterprises Limited is an Australian company that has pizza outlets in Australia, New Zealand, France, Belgium, and the Netherlands.

Required:

Using the balance sheets and income statement of Domino's Pizza Enterprises in Exhibit 2-15A and C on pages 143-145, calculate the current ratio, quick ratio, accounts receivable turnover rate, and average collection period for fiscal 2009. Write a brief interpretation of what these ratios tell you about Domino's Pizza.

STRATEGIES FOR SUCCESS:

▶ Remember that the quick ratio includes only the most liquid current assets. Inventories and other less liquid assets should be excluded.

▶ In any ratio that involves a comparison between amounts from the income statement and amounts from the balance sheet (such as the accounts receivable turnover ratio), the balance sheet amounts should, if possible, be averages.

practice problems

SUGGESTED SOLUTION TO PRACTICE PROBLEM 1

The journal entries that Labbé Ltée would make each quarter are as follows:

Quarter 1

Acquisition entry:

Short-term investments (A)	65,000	
Cash (A)		65,000

Dividend entry:

Cash (A)	650	
Dividend revenuc (SE)		650

Realized gain or loss on sale of investments:
None, because no investments were sold this quarter.

Unrealized gain or loss on securities held:

Short-term investments (A)	2,000	
Unrealized gain on short-term investments (SE)		2,000

To record increase in market value from $65,000 to $67,000. Alpha now has a value of $21,000, Beta of $32,000, and Gamma of $14,000.

Quarter 2

Dividend entry:

Cash (A)	525	
Dividend revenue (SE)		525

Realized gain or loss on sale of investments:

Cash (A)	18,000	
Gain on sale of short-term investment (SE)		4,000
Short-term investments (A)		14,000

Unrealized gain or loss on securities held:

Short-term investments (A)	5,000	
Unrealized gain on short-term investments (SE)		5,000

To record increase in market value from $53,000 ($21,000 + 32,000) to $58,000. Alpha now has a value of $22,000 and Beta of $36,000.

Quarter 3

Dividend entry:

Cash (A)	550	
Dividend revenue (SE)		550

Realized gain or loss on sale of investments:
None, because no investments were sold this quarter.

Unrealized gain or loss on securities held:

Unrealized loss on short-term investments (SE)	4,000	
Short-term investments (A)		4,000

To record decrease in market value from $58,000 to $54,000. Alpha now has a value of $17,000 and Beta of $37,000.

Quarter 4

Dividend entry:

Cash (A)	150	
Dividend revenue (SE)		150

Realized gain or loss on sale of investments:

Cash (A)	29,000	
Loss on sale of short-term investment (SE)	8,000	
Short-term investments (A)		37,000

Unrealized gain or loss on securities held:

Unrealized loss on short-term investments (SE)	2,000	
Short-term investments		2,000

To record decrease in market value from $17,000 to $15,000. Alpha now has a value of $15,000.

SUGGESTED SOLUTION TO PRACTICE PROBLEM 2

a. The following journal entries would be made during the year by Kumar Company:

To record the credit sales:

Accounts receivable (A)	150,000	
Sales revenue (SE)		150,000

To record the collections from customers:

Cash (A)	135,000	
Accounts receivable (A)		135,000

To record the write-off of bad debts:

Allowance for doubtful accounts (XA)	2,725	
Accounts receivable (A)		2,725

Calculation of bad debts expense equal to 2% of credit sales:
0.02 × $150,000 = $3,000

Year-end adjustment to record the bad debts expense:

Bad debts expense (SE)	3,000	
Allowance for doubtful accounts (XA)		3,000

b. The balance sheet at the end of 2011 would show the following:

Accounts receivable	$27,275 *	
Less: Allowance for doubtful accounts	725 **	
Net carrying value of accounts receivable		$26,550

or

Accounts receivable (net of allowance for doubtful accounts)$26,550

*Beginning balance $15,000 + Credit sales $150,000 − Cash collections $135,000 − Write-offs $2,725
**Beginning balance $450 − Write-offs $2,725 + Adjustment $3,000

c. The first three journal entries would not be affected; they would be exactly the same as shown above. The calculation of the bad debts expense would differ, though, and requires that you first determine the balance in the allowance for doubtful accounts before adjustment, as follows:

Beginning balance $450 (credit) − Write-offs $2,725 (debit) =
Balance before adjustment $2,275 (debit)

This must then be compared with the required allowance, as estimated by the aging analysis of the accounts receivable outstanding at year end. As stated in the problem, this indicated that an allowance of $1,000 was required. In order to adjust the existing balance in the allowance account (a debit of $2,275) to the required balance (a credit of $1,000), an adjustment must be made which credits the allowance account by

$3,275 and debits the bad debts expense by the same amount. The year-end adjustment would therefore be as follows:

Bad debts expense (SE)	3,275	
Allowance for doubtful accounts (XA)		3,275

The balance sheet at the end of 2008 would show the following:

Accounts receivable	$27,275	
Less: Allowance for doubtful accounts	1,000	
Net carrying value of accounts receivable		$26,275
or		
Accounts receivable (net of allowance for doubtful accounts)		$26,275

SUGGESTED SOLUTION TO PRACTICE PROBLEM 3

Current ratio:

$$\frac{\$47,255}{\$30,489} = 1.55$$

Quick ratio:

$$\frac{\$47,255 - 3,598 - 13 - 2,691 \ (\text{or} \ \$17,426 + 23,248 + 279)}{\$30,489} = 1.34$$

Note that we have assumed that all the current assets listed before inventories are highly liquid and therefore should be included in the numerator of the quick ratio calculation.

Accounts receivable turnover ratio:

$$\frac{\$239,015}{(\$23,248 + 24,728) \div 2} = 9.96$$

Average collection period for accounts receivable:

$$365 \text{ days} \div 9.96 = 36.6 \text{ days}$$

Interpretation:

The current ratio is below the "rule of thumb" level of 2 but above 1, which indicates that Domino's Pizza has one and a half times as many current assets as liabilities. In addition, the quick ratio is above the "rule of thumb" level of at least 1, which indicates that the company has enough highly liquid assets to cover its current liabilities. In general terms, then, both these ratios seem to be good.

If you were to also calculate the previous year's figures for these ratios, you should get a result of 1.62 for the current ratio and 1.23 for the quick ratio, thus showing that the current ratio has declined slightly but the quick ratio has improved.

The accounts receivable turnover rate, at 9.96 times per year, appears reasonable. It indicates that the receivables are collected, on average, every 36.6 days. If the normal collection policy is 30 to 60 days, collecting on average every 36.6 days is acceptable. If you were to read Note 5, which is referenced on the income statement for the revenue, you would see that Domino's Pizza has a variety of revenue types from the sale of goods and the rendering of services, to interest and royalty revenue. As well, the accounts receivable amount on the balance sheet is referred to as trade and other receivables. There may be amounts included that have collection times shorter or longer than an average of 30 to 60 days. Because of the mix of revenues and receivables, it is difficult to draw conclusions about the company's success at collecting its accounts receivable. The calculated numbers indicate, however, that it does not have a problem with its collections.

solution to practice problems

GLOSSARY

Accounts receivable   Assets of a seller that represent the promise made by a buyer to pay the seller at some date in the future.

Accounts receivable turnover ratio   A ratio that divides the total credit sales (if known) by the average accounts receivable. It indicates the number of times during the year that the accounts receivable balance is collected in total.

Aging of accounts receivable method   The process of analyzing customers' accounts and categorizing them by how long they have been outstanding. Usually done as a basis for estimating what amounts may be uncollectible.

Allowance for doubtful accounts   A contra account to the accounts receivable, reflecting the estimated amount of accounts receivable that will be uncollectible and eventually have to be written off.

Allowance method   A method used to value accounts receivable by estimating the amount of accounts receivable that will not be collected in the future. Makes it possible to recognize bad debts expense in the period of the sale.

Bad debt   An account receivable that cannot be collected.

Bank reconciliation   The procedure that is used to identify the differences between a company's cash balance and its bank balance. This enables the company to ensure that everything is correctly recorded and to determine the correct amount of cash available.

Collateral   An asset that is pledged as security for a debt. If the borrower defaults on the debt, the lender receives title to the asset, which can then be sold to cover the amount owed.

Compensating balances   Minimum balances that must be maintained in a bank account if one is to avoid significant service charges or, in some cases, to satisfy restrictive loan covenants.

Compound interest   Interest that is calculated by adding the interest earned in one period to the principal amount and multiplying the total by the interest rate to calculate the interest for the next period. The interest earned in one period then earns interest itself in subsequent periods. See Chapter 10 for a more complete discussion.

Control account   An account that contains the overall amounts related to a particular item in the financial statements, with the details recorded in subsidiary accounts. For example, the control account for Accounts Receivable would contain the total balance for all the company's receivables, while a set of subsidiary accounts

for Accounts Receivable would contain the balances for each of the individual customers. The balance in the control account should equal the sum of all the balances in the related subsidiary accounts.

Current ratio   A ratio that is calculated by dividing the total current assets by the total current liabilities and is a measure of short-term liquidity.

Direct write-off method   A method that only recognizes bad debts when the actual accounts receivable are written off. No estimates of future write-offs are made, and no allowance for doubtful accounts is used.

Discounted note   A note in which the interest is implicit (not stated directly). The note specifies the amount to be paid at maturity, which is larger than the initial amount borrowed. The interest is the difference between the amount borrowed and amount repaid.

Factoring   The process of selling accounts receivable to a third party to generate immediate cash.

Fair (market) value   The economic value of an item as determined in a transaction between independent parties. The amount that the item could be bought or sold for in an open marketplace. Often simply called "market value."

Financial instruments   Financial assets, financial liabilities, and certain equity items.

Historical cost   A valuation attribute or method that values assets at the amounts paid to obtain them.

Internal control system   The set of policies and procedures established by an enterprise to safeguard its assets and ensure the integrity of its accounting system.

Liquidity   An organization's short-term ability to convert its assets into cash to be able to meet its obligations and pay its liabilities.

Lower of cost and market (LCM)   A valuation method that reports an asset's value at the lower of its historical cost and its current market value.

Marked to market   The practice of reporting an investment at its current market value, rather than at its original cost or the lower of cost and market.

Marketable securities   Shares or debt securities that actively trade in a market.

Market value   The economic value of an item as determined in a transaction between independent parties. The amount for which the item could be bought or sold in an open marketplace. Often called "fair value."

Monetary   An attribute of an asset or liability that indicates that the item's value is a fixed number of monetary units (such as Canadian dollars).

Monetary unit   The nominal units that are used to measure assets and liabilities. The monetary unit used is usually the local currency unit (such as the Canadian dollar).

Net realizable value   The amount that a company normally expects to receive in cash from selling an item (less the normal costs associated with selling the item).

Note receivable   An asset that represents the right of the holder of the note to receive a fixed set of cash payments in the future.

Percentage of credit sales method   A method of estimating bad debts expense by using a percentage of the credit sales for the period.

Present value   The equivalent value, at the present time, of a future payment or series of payments. The present value is lower than the future value, because the latter implicitly includes interest.

Promissory note   A document in which the issuer (maker) of the note agrees to pay fixed amounts to the holder (payee) of the note at some point in the future.

Purchasing power   An attribute of an asset that measures its ability to be exchanged for goods and services.

Quick ratio   A ratio that is calculated by dividing the most liquid current assets (primarily cash, short-term investments, and accounts receivable) by the total current liabilities. Is another measure of short-term liquidity.

Realized gain or loss   A gain or loss that is the result of a completed transaction, such as the sale of an asset. (In general, it means that cash or an agreement to pay cash has been received in exchange.)

Recourse   A provision in agreements to sell receivables in which the buyer of the receivables has the right to return them to the seller if the buyer is unable to collect the receivables.

Recovery (of accounts receivable)   The reinstatement and collection of an account receivable that was previously written off.

Secured note   A promissory note in which the promise to pay is backed by collateral that can be seized if payment is not made.

Securities   Financial instruments, usually representing debt or equity (shares), which may be publicly traded.

Simple interest   Interest that is calculated by multiplying the interest rate in the agreement by the principal involved. Interest earned in one period does not earn interest in subsequent periods.

Subsidiary account   A specific account from a set of similar accounts whose total is presented in a control account that is shown as a single item in the financial statements. For example, a set of subsidiary accounts for Accounts Receivable would contain the balances due from each of the individual customers, while the control account for Accounts Receivable would contain the total balance for all the company's receivables. The sum of all the balances in the subsidiary accounts should equal the balance in the related control account.

Uncollectible accounts   Accounts receivable that are deemed to be bad debts. The point at which they are deemed uncollectible is generally established by company policy.

Unit-of-measure assumption   An assumption that all transactions should be measured using a common unit (in Canada, the Canadian dollar).

Unrealized gain or loss   A gain or loss recognized in the financial statements that has not resulted in the receipt of cash or the right to receive cash, but represents a change in value of an asset prior to its sale.

Unsecured note   A promissory note for which no asset or collateral has been pledged to guarantee repayment.

Write off   The process of removing an account receivable from a company's books when the account is deemed uncollectible.

ASSIGNMENT MATERIAL

Assessing Your Recall

6-1   Explain what the unit-of-measure assumption means in accounting.

6-2   Discuss why cash can be affected by purchasing-power risk, and why inventory may or may not be subject to this risk.

6-3   Explain why internal control is so important, especially for cash. Describe three types of internal control measures that organizations can put in place.

6-4   Identify the special challenge that small organizations face regarding the implementation of effective internal control systems.

6-5   Explain the purpose of a bank reconciliation and how it relates to internal control.

6-6   What are the guidelines that accountants use to decide whether an investment should be classified as a current asset?

6-7   What valuation method is used to report most short-term investments on the balance sheet?

6-8   Explain the difference between realized and unrealized gains and losses on short-term investments.

6-9   Investments in debt instruments are sometimes valued differently from investments in equity instruments. Explain what this different treatment is and what criteria must be met before this alternative valuation can be used.

6-10   What is an "allowance for doubtful accounts"? Your explanation should include what type of account it is, why it is created, and how it is used.

6-11   Identify two methods for estimating uncollectible accounts under the allowance method of accounting for bad debts, and outline how to implement each of these methods.

6-12   Describe and compare the allowance method and the direct write-off method for determining bad debts expense.

6-13   Why is the allowance method of accounting for bad debts more consistent with accounting standards than the direct write-off method? Under what circumstances is the direct write-off method acceptable?

6-14   How is a note receivable different from an account receivable?

6-15   Describe two ratios that measure current liquidity, and compare the information they provide.

6-16   Describe a ratio that can be used to assess the management of accounts receivable, and explain what information it provides.

Applying Your Knowledge

6-17   (Reconciliation of personal bank account)

Grace Ho notices that the balance recorded in her cheque book at the end of the month is $1,287, while the balance shown on her bank statement for the same date is $1,543. Examining the cheques listed on the bank statement, she sees that two cheques she wrote totalling $251 have not yet cleared the bank. Also, she notices that a cheque that she wrote for $86 that did clear was mistakenly recorded in her cheque book as $68. In addition, a $50 cheque given to her by a co-worker was returned for insufficient funds, and the bank charged her a $15 fee because of this cheque. The bank had also processed an electronic deposit of $100 to her account, which she had not yet recorded. Finally, the bank deducted a monthly service charge, but the bank statement is smeared and she cannot determine the amount of the charge.

> **Required:**
> Calculate the amount of the bank service charge.

6-18   (Preparation of bank reconciliation)

Infinity Emporium Company received the monthly statement for its bank account, showing a balance of $66,744 on August 31. The balance in the cash account in the company's accounting system at that date was $71,952. After comparing the cheques written by the company and those deducted from the bank account in August, the company's accountant determined that all six cheques (totalling $6,180) that had been outstanding at the end of July were processed by the bank in August; however, five cheques written in August, totalling $4,560, were outstanding on August 31. A review of the deposits showed that a deposit made by the company on July 31 for $11,532 was recorded by the bank on August 1, and an August 31 deposit of $12,240 was recorded in the company's accounting system but had not yet been recorded by the bank. The August bank statement also showed a service fee of $24, a customer's cheque in the amount of $204 that had been returned NSF, a bank loan payment of $900 that the bank had deducted automatically, and a customer's note for $3,600 that the bank had collected for Infinity Emporium and deposited in its account.

Required:

a. Prepare a bank reconciliation as at August 31. (Hint: Items that were outstanding last month but have been processed this month should no longer affect the bank reconciliation, since both the company and the bank now have them recorded.)

b. How much cash does Infinity Emporium actually have available as at August 31?

c. Explain how the adjusted (corrected) balance of cash, as determined by the bank reconciliation, could be higher than both the balance shown on the bank statement and the balance shown in the company's cash account.

d. Prepare adjusting journal entries to record all the necessary adjustments to bring the cash account to its correct balance.

6-19 (Placement of items on bank reconciliation)

Henri Heinz is preparing a bank reconciliation for his business, Heinz Company. Indicate whether each of the following items would be added to the bank balance, deducted from the bank balance, added to the cash account balance, or deducted from the cash account balance. If any of the items do not have to be included in the bank reconciliation, explain why.

a. A deposit of $2,310 at the end of the previous month was processed by the bank on the first day of this month.

b. A $683 cheque written by Heinz Company was erroneously processed through its account at $638.

c. The bank statement showed a service charge of $15 for the month. Heinz Company has not yet recorded this charge in its cash account.

d. A customer deposited an amount owed to Heinz Company directly into its bank account. Henri had not recorded it yet.

e. Three cheques written by Heinz Company totalling $6,842 have not yet been processed by the bank.

f. The bank lists a customer cheque that was received by Heinz and deposited in the company's bank account as "Not Sufficient Funds" (NSF).

g. A deposit of $1,280 made by Heinz Company was recorded by the bank as $1,290. Heinz Company had made an error in counting the money before making the deposit.

h. Three cheques that were outstanding at the end of the previous month are shown on the bank statement as having been processed by the bank this month.

i. Cash received by Heinz Company on the last day of the month and deposited that evening is not shown on the bank statement.

j. An automatic payment for the company's electricity bill was processed by the bank. Heinz Company had received notification from the electrical company, and recorded the amount as a payment earlier in the month.

k. A loan to Heinz Company from the bank became due on the 21st of the month and the bank deducted the payment from the company's account. Henri had forgotten about the loan coming due.

6-20 (Preparation of bank reconciliation)

Kinte Products Limited had a balance in its cash account of $38,755 on October 31, 2011. This included $2,650 of cash receipts from October 31, which had not yet been deposited in the bank. On the same date, its bank account had a balance of $42,301. Comparing the bank statement with the company's records indicated that the following cheques were outstanding on October 31:

#1224	$1,991
#1230	1,336
#1232	2,286
	$5,613

The following were shown on the bank statement and not yet recorded by the company:

- $376 deducted for a customer's cheque that was returned to Kinte Products marked NSF

- $420 added as a result of the direct deposit of a tax refund from the Canada Revenue Agency

- $1,200 added as a result of a note collected by the bank and deposited in the company's account, representing $1,000 of principal and $200 of interest

- $34 deducted for service charges for the month

In the process of preparing the data for its bank reconciliation, the company discovered that it had made an error in recording one of its deposits for cash sales during the month. The actual amount deposited was $2,282, but Kinte Products had recorded it as $2,882. The bank had also made an error in recording one of the company's cheques that was a payment to a supplier on account. The cheque had been issued in the amount of $336, but the bank processed it as $363.

Required:
a. Prepare a bank reconciliation for Kinte Products Limited as at October 31, 2011.
b. Prepare any journal entries required to adjust the cash account as at October 31.

6-21 (Preparation of bank reconciliation)

The April 30, 2011, bank statement for Comet Company showed a cash balance of $7,582. The cash account, according to the company's records on April 30, had a balance of $4,643. The following additional data were revealed during the reconciliation process:

1. A deposit of $652 that had been made by the company on March 31 was processed by the bank in April, and a deposit of $1,531 made on April 30 had not yet been processed by the bank.

2. The bank statement listed a deposit for $360 that was mistakenly put in Comet Company's bank account; it should have gone to Comment Company's account.

3. Comet Company determined that there were three cheques that had not yet been processed by the bank: #466 for $1,250; #467 for $520; and #470 for $1,350.

4. The bank had collected a note receivable for $1,000 from one of Comet Company's customers. An additional $15 in interest had been added to its account.

5. The bank service charge for the month was $25.

Required:
a. Prepare a bank reconciliation for Comet Company as at April 30, 2011.
b. What cash balance should Comet Company report on its April 30, 2011, balance sheet?
c. Prepare the journal entries that are required to bring Comet Company's cash account to its correct balance.

6-22 (Valuation of short-term investments)

On September 1, Duggan Company purchased 100 common shares of Green Company for $100 each and 200 common shares of White Company for $50 each. On December 31, the common shares of Green were selling at $95 and the common shares of White were selling at $55. Duggan considers the shares to be short-term, held-for-trading investments.

Required:
a. At what amount will these investments be reported on the December 31 balance sheet?
b. What other balance sheet or income statement account will be affected by the accounting treatment of these securities? What will the effect be?

6-23 (Dividends and rate of return earned on short-term investments)

During the period September 1 to December 31, Duggan Company received dividends from the two companies in Problem 6-22. Green Company paid dividends of $4 per share, and White paid dividends of $1.50 per share.

Required:
a. What amount of dividend revenue will Duggan report for the period?
b. One of Duggan Company's goals is to attain an annual return on investments of at least 10% (before tax). Has it met this goal during the period?

6-24 (Short-term investments: journal entries and earnings)

The following transactions relate to Waterway Investments for 2011 and 2012. Waterway closes its books on December 31 each year.

2011

July 20 — Waterway purchased 5,000 common shares of Meta-Solid Corporation at $20 per share, plus a brokerage commission of 1% of the purchase price. Waterway sent a cheque to its stockbroker for the total amount.

September 13 — Meta-Solid Corporation declared a dividend of $0.50 per share, to be paid on October 4.

October 9 — Waterway Investments received the dividend cheque from Meta-Solid Corporation.

December 31 — The market value of Meta-Solid Corporation's common shares was $25 per share.

2012

January 19 — Waterway sold the common shares of Meta-Solid Corporation at $24.50 per share. A brokerage commission of 1% of the total proceeds was deducted, and Waterway received a cheque from its stockbroker for the net amount.

Required:
a. Prepare journal entries to record the preceding transactions and events in the books of Waterway Investments, assuming that the shares are considered a short-term, held-for-trading investment. (Note: We have not discussed accounting for commissions to stockbrokers or brokerage fees. Therefore, in answering this question, try to use your knowledge of basic accounting principles to determine how they should be treated.)
b. What amount would be reported for this investment in Waterway's balance sheet on December 31, 2011?
c. What amount of gain or loss would be reported with respect to this investment in 2011? In 2012?
d. What was the overall rate of return earned on this investment?

6-25 (Valuations and journal entries for short-term investments)

Corona Company holds a portfolio of short-term investments. The portfolio's acquisition costs and aggregate market values were as follows. None of the securities were sold during this period.

Month Ended	Acquisition Cost of Securities Purchased During Month	Aggregate Market Value of Securities Held at End of Month
September 30	$450,000	$410,000
October 31	50,000	480,000
November 30	20,000	510,000
December 31	20,000	530,000
	$540,000	

Required:

a. Assuming that Corona adjusted its short-term investments monthly, what amount would appear on its balance sheets at the end of each month for these investments?

b. Give the journal entries to record the transactions and adjustments required for each month.

c. What is the amount of the total gain or loss on the portfolio during this four-month period?

6-26 (Valuation of short-term investments)

On July 1, Upper Company purchased 500 shares each of Jack, Queen, and King companies at a cost of $52, $28, and $40 per share, respectively. On December 31, the market values of the shares were $58, $16, and $38, respectively. Upper considers the shares to be short-term, held-for-trading investments.

Required:

a. At what amount will the investments be reported on the December 31 balance sheet?

b. What other balance sheet or income statement account will be affected by the accounting treatment of these securities? What will the effect be?

6-27 (Dividends and rate of return earned on short-term investments)

During the period from July 1 to December 31, Upper Company received dividends of $4, $2, and $3 per share, respectively, from the common shares of Jack, Queen, and King companies acquired in Problem 6-26.

Required:

a. What amount will Upper Company report for dividend revenue for the period?

b. During this period, has Upper Company accomplished its goal of earning a 12% annual return (before tax) on its short-term investments?

6-28 (Short-term investments: evaluating investment decision)

Birch Company invested in the following securities:

Date of Purchase	Name of Company	Amount Paid	Market Price Dec. 31 2011	Dec. 31 2012
February 2011	Silver	$80,000	$70,000	$72,000
March 2011	Platinum	45,000	40,000	56,000
June 2011	Copper	22,000	32,000	25,000

All of the securities are common shares and Birch considers them all to be held for trading. Birch received no dividends from its investments in 2011; however, dividends of $7,000, $1,000, and $1,400 were received from Silver, Platinum, and Copper, respectively, during 2012.

The chair of Birch's executive committee says she needs more information from you to determine whether or not the company should continue to invest excess cash in this manner.

Required:

a. Identify the accounts that would be used and the amounts that would be recorded by Birch Company during 2011 in accounting for its investments.

b. Provide the same information for 2012 for each of the investments.

c. Calculate the amount of net earnings reported each year, assuming Birch reported operating earnings (excluding earnings from investments) of $90,000 in 2011 and $110,000 in 2012.

d. Explain why taking into consideration both the dividends received and the change in the market value of the shares is important in evaluating the performance of short-term investments.

6-29 **(Accounts receivable and uncollectible accounts: percentage of credit sales method)**
Dundee Company started business on January 1 of the current year. The company made total sales of $900,000 during the year, of which $150,000 were cash sales. By the end of the year, Dundee had received payments of $675,000 from its customers on account. It also wrote off as uncollectible $10,000 of its receivables when it learned that the customer who owed this amount had filed for bankruptcy. That was Dundee Company's only entry related to bad debts for the period.

Dundee's management decides to adopt the allowance method of accounting for bad debts. Since Dundee is a new company and does not have past experience to base its own estimates on, it decides to use 3% of credit sales as an estimate for its bad debt expense, which is the average percentage for its industry.

Required:

a. What amount of bad debts expense would Dundee Company report on its statement of earnings for the year?

b. What allowance for doubtful accounts balance would be reported on the balance sheet at the end of the year?

c. What accounts receivable balance would be reported on the balance sheet at the end of the year?

d. Evaluate the reasonableness of the balance in the allowance for doubtful accounts at the end of the year.

6-30 **(Accounts receivable and uncollectible accounts: percentage of credit sales method)**
Majestic Equipment Sales Company, which sells only on account, had a $120,000 balance in its accounts receivable and a $4,200 balance in its allowance for doubtful accounts on December 31, 2011. During 2012, the company's sales of equipment were $820,000, and its total cash collections from customers were $780,000.

During the year, the company concluded that customers with accounts totalling $6,000 would be unable to pay, and wrote these receivables off. However, one of these customers subsequently made a payment of $850. At the end of 2012, management decided that it would use an estimate for bad debts of 1% of its credit sales.

Required:

a. Prepare the journal entries to record all the 2012 transactions, including the adjustment for bad debts expense at year end.

b. Show how the accounts receivable section of the balance sheet at December 31, 2012, would be presented.

c. What amount of bad debts expense would appear in the statement of earnings for the year ended December 31, 2012?

6-31 **(Accounts receivable and uncollectible accounts: percentage of credit sales method)**
The trial balance of M&D Inc. shows a $50,000 outstanding balance in accounts receivable at the
end of the first year of operations, December 31, 2011. During the fiscal year, 75% of the total
credit sales were collected and no accounts were written off as uncollectible. The company
estimated that 1.5% of the credit sales would be uncollectible. During the following year, 2012,
the account of J. Morgan, who owed $500, was judged uncollectible and was written off. At the
end of the year, on December 31, 2012, the amount previously written off was collected in full
from J. Morgan.

> **Required:**
> a. Prepare the necessary journal entries for recording all the preceding transactions in
>   the accounting system of M&D Inc.
> b. Show the accounts receivable section of the balance sheet at December 31, 2011.

6-32 **(Accounts receivable and uncollectible accounts: percentage of credit sales method)**
A large corporation recently reported the following amounts on its year-end balance sheets:

	2011	2012
Accounts receivable	$8,400,000	$8,800,000
Allowance for doubtful accounts	95,000	105,000

A footnote to these statements indicated that the company uses a percentage of its credit sales to
determine its bad debts expense, that $60,000 of uncollectible accounts were written off during
2011 and $80,000 of uncollectible accounts in 2012, and that there were no recoveries of
accounts written off.

> a. Determine the amount of bad debts expense that must have been recorded by the
>   company for 2012.
> b. How were the company's net receivables affected by the write-off of the $80,000 of
>   accounts in 2012?
> c. How was the company's net earnings affected by the $80,000 write-off of accounts in 2012?

6-33 **(Accounts receivable and uncollectible accounts: aging of receivables method)**
The following is an aging schedule for a company's accounts receivable as at December 31, 2011:

Customer's name	Total amount owed	Current (not yet due)	Number of days past due			
			1–30	31–60	61–90	Over 90
Aber	$ 20,000		$ 9,000	$11,000		
Bohr	30,000	$ 30,000				
Chow	35,000	15,000	5,000		$15,000	
Datz	18,000					$18,000
Others	158,000	95,000	15,000	13,000	15,000	20,000
	$261,000	$140,000	$29,000	$24,000	$30,000	$38,000
Estimated percentage that will be uncollectible		3%	6%	10%	25%	50%
Estimated value of uncollectibles	$ 34,840	$ 4,200	$ 1,740	$ 2,400	$ 7,500	$19,000

On December 31, 2011, the unadjusted balance in the allowance for doubtful accounts is a credit of $9,000.

Required:
a. Journalize the adjusting entry for bad debts on December 31, 2011.
b. Journalize the following selected events and transactions in 2012:
   - On March 1, an $800 customer account that originated in 2012 is judged uncollectible.
   - On September 1, an $800 cheque is received from the customer whose account was written off as uncollectible on March 1.
c. Journalize the adjusting entry for bad debts on December 31, 2012, assuming that the unadjusted balance in the allowance for doubtful accounts at that time is a *debit* of $1,000 and an aging schedule indicates that the estimated value of uncollectibles is $33,500.

6-34 **(Accounts receivable and uncollectible accounts: aging of receivables method)**
Xanadu Ltd. has accounts receivable totalling $142,800 and a $3,640 credit balance in its allowance for doubtful accounts prior to adjustment on December 31, 2011. The company uses an aging analysis of its receivables as the basis for estimating its uncollectible accounts.

The aging analysis shows the following:

Month of Sale	Accounts Receivable on Dec. 31
December	$ 91,000
November	26,040
September and October	16,800
July and August	8,960
	$142,800

The company's estimates of bad debts are as follows:

Age of Accounts	Estimated % Uncollectible
Current	2%
1–30 days past due	12%
31–90 days past due	25%
Over 90 days past due	40%

Required:
a. Determine the total estimated uncollectibles as at December 31.
b. Prepare the adjusting entry for the expected bad debts expense as at December 31, 2011.

6-35 **(Accounts receivable and uncollectible accounts: aging of receivables method)**
On December 31, 2011, Ajacks Company reported the following information in its financial statements:

Accounts receivable	$1,193,400
Allowance for doubtful accounts	81,648
Bad debts expense	80,448

During 2012, the company had the following transactions related to receivables:

1. Sales were $10,560,000, of which $8,448,000 were on account.

2. Collections of accounts receivable were $7,284,000.

3. Write-offs of accounts receivable were $78,000.

4. Recoveries of accounts previously written off as uncollectible were $8,100.

Required:

a. Prepare the journal entries to record each of the four items above.

b. Set up T accounts for the accounts receivable and the allowance for doubtful accounts and enter their January 1, 2012, balances. Then post the entries from part "a" and calculate the new balances in these accounts.

c. Prepare the journal entry to record the bad debts expense for 2012. Ajacks Company uses the aging of accounts receivable method and has prepared an aging schedule, which indicates that the estimated value of the uncollectible accounts as at the end of 2012 is $93,000.

d. Show what would be presented on the balance sheet as at December 31, 2012, related to accounts receivable.

6-36 (Accounts receivable and uncollectible accounts: aging of receivables method)
The following information relates to Bedford Company's accounts receivable:

Accounts receivable balance on December 31, 2011	$ 900,000
Allowance for doubtful accounts balance on December 31, 2011	55,000
Credit sales made in 2012	5,800,000
Collections from customers on account in 2012	4,900,000
Accounts receivable written off in 2012	70,000
Accounts previously written off that were recovered in 2012 (not included in the collections above)	6,000

An aging analysis estimates the uncollectible receivables on December 31, 2012, to be $80,000. The allowance account is to be adjusted accordingly.

Required:

a. Calculate the ending balance in accounts receivable, as at December 31, 2012.

b. Calculate the allowance for doubtful accounts balance, before adjustment, as at December 31, 2012

c. Calculate the bad debts expense for the year 2012.

6-37 (Percentage of credit sales and aging of accounts receivable methods)
Clean Sweep Ltd. manufactures several different brands of vacuum cleaners from hand-held models to built-in central vacuums. It sells its products to distributors on credit, giving customers 30 days to pay. During the year ending June 30, 2011, Clean Sweep recorded sales of $550,000. At June 30, the company prepared the following aging schedule:

Receivable Amount	Number of Days Outstanding	Estimated Percentage That Will Be Collected
$150,000	Less than 30	96%
50,000	31 to 45	93%
75,000	46 to 90	90%
100,000	More than 90	75%

The allowance for doubtful accounts had a balance of $19,000 before the year-end adjustment was made.

Required:

a. Prepare the adjusting entry to bring the allowance for doubtful accounts to the desired level.

b. Clean Sweep's sales manager thinks the company would increase sales if it extended its normal collection cycle to 60 days from its current 30 days. Should the president accept or reject this recommendation? Why? What factors should be considered in making this decision?

c. What suggestions would you make regarding Clean Sweep's management of its accounts receivable?

6-38 (Comparison of all methods of accounting for uncollectible accounts)
DejaVu Company has been in business for several years and has the following information for its operations in the current year:

Total credit sales	$3,000,000
Bad debts written off in the year	60,000
Accounts receivable balance on December 31 (after writing off the bad debts above)	500,000

Required:

a. Assume that DejaVu Company decides to estimate its bad debts expense at 2% of credit sales:
  i. What amount of bad debts expense will the company record if it has a *credit* balance (before adjustment) of $5,000 in its allowance for doubtful accounts on December 31?
  ii. What amount of bad debts expense will it record if there is a *debit* balance (before adjustment) of $5,000 in its allowance for doubtful accounts on December 31?

b. Assume that DejaVu Company estimates its bad debts based on an aging analysis of its year-end accounts receivable, which indicates that a provision for uncollectible accounts of $40,000 is required:
  i. What amount of bad debts expense will the company record if it has a *credit* balance (before adjustment) of $5,000 in its allowance for doubtful accounts on December 31?
  ii. What amount of bad debts expense will it record if there is a *debit* balance (before adjustment) of $5,000 in its allowance for doubtful accounts on December 31?

c. What amount of bad debts expense will DejaVu report if it uses the direct write-off method of accounting for bad debts?

d. State the two main reasons for using the allowance method to account for bad debts, rather than the direct write-off method.

6-39 (Comparison of all methods of accounting for uncollectible accounts)
Crystal Lights Company manufactures and sells light fixtures for homes, businesses, and institutions. All of its sales are made on credit to wholesale distributors. Information for Crystal Lights for the current year follows:

Total credit sales	$3,500,000
Uncollectible accounts written off in the year	17,500
Accounts receivable at December 31 (after writing off the uncollectible accounts above)	450,000

Required:

Assume that Crystal Lights estimates its bad debts based on an aging analysis of its year-end accounts receivable, which indicates that a provision for uncollectible accounts of $34,000 is required:

a. If there is a *debit* balance of $6,000 in its allowance for doubtful accounts on December 31, before adjustment,
  i. What amount will the company report on its income statement as bad debts expense?
  ii. What amount will it report on its balance sheet as the net value of its accounts receivable?

b. If there is a $6,000 *credit* balance in the allowance for doubtful accounts on December 31, before adjustment,
  i. What amount will the company report on its income statement as bad debts expense?
  ii. What amount will it report on its balance sheet as the net value of its accounts receivable?

Assume that Crystal Lights decides to estimate its bad debts expense at 1% of credit sales:

c. If there is a *debit* balance of $6,000 in its allowance for doubtful accounts on December 31, before adjustment,
   i. What amount will the company report on its income statement as bad debts expense?
   ii. What amount will it report on its balance sheet as the net value of its accounts receivable?
d. If there is a $6,000 *credit* balance in the allowance for doubtful accounts on December 31, before adjustment,
   i. What amount will the company report on its income statement as bad debts expense?
   ii. What amount will it report on its balance sheet as the net value of its accounts receivable?

Assume that Crystal Lights uses the direct write-off method of accounting for bad debts:

e. What amount will the company report on its income statement as bad debts expense?
f. What amount will it report on its balance sheet as the net value of its accounts receivable?
g. Briefly outline the main advantages of the allowance method of accounting for bad debts.

6-40   (Note receivable with interest calculations)

On August 31, 2011, a company accepted a note receivable from a customer whose $6,000 account was overdue. The note is due in eight months and has an interest rate of 8%.

Required:
a. How much interest will be earned on this note in total?
b. What journal entry should the company make to record the receipt of the note?
c. What adjusting entry should the company make regarding this note for its December 31, 2011, year end?
d. What journal entry should the company make when the note is collected on April 30, 2012?

6-41   (Note receivable with interest calculation)

On February 1, 2011, North Company sold equipment to South Company for $18,040. In payment for the equipment, North accepted a six-month, 9% note. The interest is payable when the note matures. North's year end is June 30.

Required:
a. Prepare all necessary journal entries associated with this note, including the end of year entries and the receipt of payment from South.
b. What items regarding this note would be included on North's balance sheet and statement of earnings on June 30, 2011?

6-42   (Note receivable with interest calculation)

On October 1, 2011, Sussex Bank loaned $2,800 to Sharrie Zhang to buy a computer. She was expecting to have $3,000 at the end of January 2012 when a guaranteed investment certificate she owned reached maturity. Sharrie signed a four-month note with interest at 8%. All interest is to be paid at the end of January when the note is due. Sussex Bank's year end is December 31.

Required:
a. Calculate how much interest has been earned by Sussex Bank by the end of December and by the time the note is due.
b. Prepare the journal entries that Sussex Bank would make at the end of December and when the note is collected in full.

6-43   (Note receivable with interest calculations)

On June 1, Moon Company determined that it would not be able to pay the account receivable that it was due to pay Gamma Company on that date. Moon was confident that it would have the necessary cash early in the next year. It therefore signed a nine-month, 9% note for the $14,000 that it owed. The interest on this note will be paid when the note matures. Gamma Company's fiscal year end is June 30.

Required:

a.   Prepare Gamma's journal entries in June for this note.

b.   Prepare Gamma's journal entry (or entries) to record the receipt of the full amount owed on March 1.

6-44   (Current and quick ratios)

The following amounts were reported by Liquid Company in its most recent balance sheet:

Cash	$ 40,000
Accounts receivable	130,000
Short-term investments	18,000
Inventory	390,000
Prepaid insurance	35,000
Capital assets (net)	960,000
Accounts payable	85,000
Wages payable	37,000
Income tax payable	45,000
Sales tax payable	10,000
Short-term notes payable	90,000
Five-year bank loan	50,000

Required:

a.   Calculate the current ratio and quick ratio for Liquid Company.

b.   Based on a review of other companies in its industry, the management of Liquid Company thinks it should maintain a current ratio of 2.2 or more, and a quick ratio of 0.9 or more. Its current and quick ratios at the end of the prior year were 2.1 and 0.8, respectively. How successful has the company been in achieving the desired results this year?

c.   How could the company improve its current position? What risks, if any, may be associated with the strategy you have suggested?

6-45   (Liquidity evaluation)

The following balance sheet accounts and amounts were for Classic Ltd. on October 31:

	2011	2010
Capital assets	$350,000	$343,000
Bank loan (long-term)	322,000	336,000
Prepaid expenses	2,800	4,200
Accumulated amortization	123,200	117,600
Taxes payable	19,600	16,800
Inventory	315,000	322,000
Wages payable	36,400	33,600
Accounts receivable	64,400	51,800
Unearned revenue	67,200	56,000
Retained earnings	84,000	72,800
Common shares	70,000	70,000
Cash	67,200	50,400
Accounts payable	77,000	68,600

Required:

a. Prepare a classified comparative balance sheet for Classic Ltd. as at October 31, 2011.

b. Calculate the amount of Classic's working capital (current assets minus current liabilities) at the end of its fiscal years 2011 and 2010. Has the company's working capital position improved or deteriorated during this period?

c. Calculate Classic's current ratios at the end of its fiscal years 2011 and 2010. Has its current ratio improved or deteriorated during this period?

d. Calculate Classic's quick ratios at the end of its fiscal years 2011 and 2010. Has the company's quick ratio improved or deteriorated during this period?

e. Based on the results from parts "b," "c," and "d," do you think Classic's overall liquidity position improved or deteriorated during this period?

f. How might Classic evaluate whether its overall liquidity is adequate?

User Perspective Problems

6-46 (Internal control and audit process)

You are the auditor of a medium-sized business with annual revenues of approximately $10 million. Before you begin the audit, you review the company's internal control system.

a. Why is this preliminary step necessary? What are you hoping to learn?

b. If you reviewed the company's internal control system before last year's audit, is it necessary to do it again this year? Explain why or why not.

6-47 (Bank reconciliation and cash management)

As a manager of a company, explain why a bank reconciliation would be important to your cash management.

6-48 (Impact of negative cash balance)

Assume that you are a shareholder of a large retail company. When you received the annual report, you noticed that the company did not have any cash recorded on the balance sheet. Instead, there was an item in the current liabilities section called "Bank overdraft." What does this represent? Should you be concerned? What ratio analysis could you do that might help you assess the seriousness of this situation?

6-49 (Market value of short-term investments and decision-making)

As a loan officer at a bank, why would you be interested in the market value of a company's short-term investments? Would you want them reported on the balance sheet at their market value, or would you be satisfied with just the disclosure of the market valuation in the notes accompanying the financial statements? Explain your reasoning.

6-50 (Market value of short-term investments and decision-making)

As a shareholder, why would you be interested in the market value of a company's short-term investments? Would you also want to know their cost? Explain your reasoning.

6-51 (Estimation of uncollectible accounts receivable)

Suppose there is a stock option plan at See Saw Company that rewards managers for achieving a certain level of reported net income. What incentives might this create for management to influence the estimate of the uncollectible portion of the accounts receivable?

6-52 (Accounts receivable and uncollectible accounts)

Ontario Company is involved in the manufacture and sale of high-quality racing and mountain bicycles. At the end of 2011, Ontario's balance sheet reported total accounts receivable of $250,000 and an allowance for doubtful accounts of $18,000. During 2012, the following events occurred:

1. Credit sales in the amount of $2,300,000 were made.

2. Collections of $2,250,000 were received on account.

3. Customers with total debts to Ontario Company of $38,000 were declared bankrupt, and those accounts receivable were written off.

4. Bad debts expense for 2012 was recorded as 2% of credit sales.

As the chief financial officer for Ontario Company, you have been asked by a member of the executive committee to do the following:

a. Explain the effects of each of the above transactions on the company's financial statements.
b. Show how the accounts receivable will be reported on Ontario's balance sheet as at December 31, 2012.
c. Evaluate the adequacy of the company's allowance for doubtful accounts as at December 31, 2012.

6-53 (Accounts receivable and uncollectible accounts)
Lowrate Communications is in the cellular telephone industry. The following selected information has been compiled for the company (in thousands of dollars):

	2011	2010	2009
Accounts receivable (net)	$ 1,469.8	$ 1,230.6	$ 1,044.8
Allowance for doubtful accounts	128.9	121.9	118.0
Accounts written off	305.4	267.6	296.8
Bad debt expense	312.4	271.5	267.0
Sales	12,661.8	11,367.8	10,420.0

Required:
a. In each of the three years presented, what percentage of the company's total accounts receivable is estimated to be uncollectible?
b. In each of the three years presented, what percentage of the sales revenue is the bad debts expense?
c. Did Lowrate's collection of accounts receivable improve or deteriorate over this three-year period?
d. The cloning of cellular telephones is a serious problem. (Cloning involves copying the access and billing codes from cellular phones belonging to others.) Cell phone companies typically absorb the charges for unauthorized calls, which amount to very large sums of money. If cloning and other types of signal theft continue to be problems as the cellular telephone and other wireless communication businesses grow, how will the financial statements of companies like Lowrate Communications be affected?

Reading and Interpreting Published Financial Statements

6-54 (Cash and short-term investments)
Qantas Airways Limited is Australia's largest domestic and international airline, and provides both passenger and cargo services.

On its balance sheet as at June 30, 2009, Qantas reported cash and cash equivalents of 3,617 million Australian dollars (AUD). The notes accompanying its financial statements revealed that this amount included investments of AUD3,002 million. The notes also stated that the investments are readily convertible into a known amount of cash and that their value is unlikely to change significantly.

Required:
a. Explain what Qantas means when it says that the investments are readily marketable. What can you infer from this about the company's cash management practices?
b. Explain why a company would choose to put cash into short-term investments rather than a savings account at a financial institution.

6-55 (Cash and short-term investments; current, quick, and accounts receivable turnover ratios)

Refer to the consolidated balance sheets and statements of income and retained earnings for **Leon's Furniture Limited**, which are presented in Exhibit 6-13. (Leon's sells furniture, appliances, and electronics through its approximately 64 home furnishing stores located across Canada.)

> *Required:*
> a. Notice that the first two current assets listed on the balance sheets are cash and cash equivalents and marketable securities. Why would these short-term investments in marketable securities not be treated as cash equivalents? Is it possible that there are other short-term investments included in cash and cash equivalents? If so, what can you infer about them?
> b. Calculate the following ratios for both 2009 and 2008:
>   i.   Current ratio
>   ii. Quick ratio
>   iii. Accounts receivable turnover ratio. Use the balance of accounts receivable at each year end, rather than average balances, for this calculation.
> c. Comment on the ratio results and any significant trends.

6-56 (Accounts receivable and credit risk)

Big Rock Brewery Income Trust produces, markets, and distributes craft beers from its brewery in Calgary, with several brands selling across Canada.

One of the reporting requirements for financial instruments is that a company must disclose if it has a high concentration of receivables from certain customers or categories of customers, because this may increase the company's level of credit risk as it depends greatly on the ability of those customers to pay their accounts. In accordance with this requirement, in its 2009 annual report, Big Rock Brewery disclosed that "substantially all of [its] accounts receivable are from provincial government liquor authorities."

How would this disclosure affect your assessment of Big Rock's level of credit risk?

6-57 (Analysis of accounts receivable)

The 2009 financial statements of **Winpak Ltd.** contained the following information, in thousands of US dollars. (Winpak sells high-quality packaging materials and packaging machines.)

	2009	2008
Sales	$505,991	$512,037
Receivables (net of allowances for doubtful accounts of $1,761 in 2009 and $1,663 in 2008)	$70,354	$64,570

> *Required:*
> a. What percentages of Winpak's accounts receivable were considered uncollectible in each of 2009 and 2008? Is the trend favourable or unfavourable?
> b. Calculate Winpak's accounts receivable turnover rates for 2009 and 2008 using the ending balances of the receivables for each year rather than the average receivables. Is the trend favourable or unfavourable?
> c. What was the average number of days taken by Winpak to collect its accounts receivable in 2009? In 2008? Do these figures provide insights beyond what the results in part "b" showed? Explain.

6-58 (Accounts receivable, uncollectible accounts, and average collection periods)

In its annual report for 2010, **HMV Group plc** showed total revenues of £2,016.6 million for 2010 versus £1,956.7 million for 2009, and net accounts receivable balances of £80.7 million at the end of 2010 versus £71.6 million at the end of 2009. The notes that accompanied the financial statements revealed that it provided for impairment of its accounts receivable of

EXHIBIT 6-13A

annual report

LEON'S FURNITURE LIMITED 2009 ANNUAL REPORT

CONSOLIDATED BALANCE SHEETS

As at December 31 (in thousands)	2009	2008
Assets		
Current		
Cash and cash equivalents	$ 58,301	$ 39,483
Marketable securities	94,337	83,194
Restricted marketable securities (NOTE 8(D))	18,088	16,598
Accounts receivable	31,501	30,291
Income taxes recoverable	–	2,037
Inventory	83,957	92,904
Future tax assets (NOTE 7)	1,133	270
Total current assets	$ 287,317	$ 264,777
Prepaid expenses	1,560	1,490
Goodwill (NOTE 13)	11,282	11,282
Intangible assets, net (NOTES 6 AND 13)	5,334	5,401
Other receivables	–	419
Future tax assets (NOTE 7)	11,465	10,752
Property, plant and equipment, net (NOTE 5)	212,198	219,287
	$ 529,156	$ 513,408
Liabilities and Shareholders' Equity		
Current		
Accounts payable and accrued liabilities	$ 83,880	$ 95,247
Income taxes payable	1,958	–
Customers' deposits	15,632	14,119
Dividends payable	4,938	4,952
Deferred warranty plan revenue	16,150	15,267
Total current liabilities	$ 122,558	$ 129,585
Deferred warranty plan revenue	22,248	21,712
Redeemable share liability (NOTE 10)	383	285
Future tax liabilities (NOTE 7)	8,829	8,468
Total liabilities	$ 154,018	$ 160,050
Shareholders' equity		
Common shares (NOTE 11)	17,704	16,493
Retained earnings	357,576	338,960
Accumulated other comprehensive loss (NOTE 12)	(142)	(2,095)
Total shareholders' equity	$ 375,138	$ 353,358
	$ 529,156	$ 513,408

SEE ACCOMPANYING NOTES

On behalf of the Board:

(Signed:)   (Signed:)

Director   Director

EXHIBIT 6-13B

annual report

CONSOLIDATED STATEMENTS OF INCOME AND RETAINED EARNINGS

Years ended December 31 (in thousands except shares outstanding and earnings per share)	2009	2008
Sales	$ **703,180**	$ 740,376
Cost of sales	**419,819**	440,360
Gross profit	$ **283,361**	$ 300,016
Operating expenses (income)		
Salaries and commissions	$ **103,977**	$ 112,270
Advertising	**34,732**	33,752
Rent and property taxes	**12,165**	11,268
Amortization	**16,562**	16,253
Employee profit-sharing plan	**4,177**	4,321
Other operating expenses	**42,359**	46,447
Interest income, net	**(3,165)**	(4,836)
Other income	**(9,980)**	(13,595)
	$ **200,827**	$ 205,880
Income before income taxes	**82,534**	94,136
Provision for income taxes (NOTE 7)	**25,670**	30,746
Net income for the year	$ **56,864**	$ 63,390
Retained earnings, beginning of year	**338,960**	307,068
Dividends declared	**(33,951)**	(26,873)
Excess of cost of share repurchase over carrying value of related shares (NOTE 11)	**(4,297)**	(4,625)
Retained earnings, end of year	$ **357,576**	$ 338,960
Weighted average number of common shares outstanding		
Basic	**70,714,089**	70,729,548
Diluted	**73,321,382**	72,817,871
Earnings per share		
Basic	$ **0.80**	$ 0.90
Diluted	$ **0.78**	$ 0.87
Dividends declared per share		
Common	$ **0.48**	$ 0.38
Convertible, non-voting	$ **0.14**	$ 0.14

SEE ACCOMPANYING NOTES

£0.6 million in 2009 (£1.2 million in 2008). It does not try to measure the uncollectibility of its accounts receivable, because it believes that it has minimal levels of credit risk because of the nature of its retail business. (HMV sells music and movies through HMV outlets in several countries, including Canada.)

Required:

a. What percentage of revenue is HMV's accounts receivable in each of these years?
b. Explain the difference between measuring and recording the impairment of accounts receivable and measuring and recording potential collectibility.
c. Do you think that using impairment instead of uncollectibility fits with the qualitative characteristics discussed in Chapter 1? Explain.

6-59 (Current ratio, quick ratio, and accounts receivable turnover ratio)

High Liner Foods Incorporated processes and markets prepared frozen seafood throughout Canada, the United States, and Mexico under the High Liner and Fisher Boy brands. It also produces private label products, and supplies restaurants and institutions. Exhibit 6-14 presents the company's consolidated balance sheets and statements of income (loss) from its 2009 annual report.

Required:

a. Calculate the following ratios for both 2009 and 2008:
   i.   Current ratio
   ii. Quick ratio
   iii. Accounts receivable turnover ratio (Use the balance of accounts receivable at each year end for this calculation, rather than average balances.)
b. Comment on the results of the above ratio calculations and any significant trends they reveal.

HIGH LINER FOODS INCORPORATED 2009 ANNUAL REPORT

Consolidated balance sheets

(in thousands of Canadian dollars)		January 2, 2010		January 3, 2009
ASSETS (notes 6 and 7)				
Current:				
Cash and cash equivalents	$	1,953	$	7,032
Accounts receivable (note 2a)		59,553		63,873
Income tax receivable		1,288		45
Inventories (note 2b)		119,586		146,863
Prepaid expenses		2,024		1,782
Future income taxes (note 9)		3,846		1,533
Total current assets		188,250		221,128
Property, plant and equipment (note 5)		59,528		59,016
Other:				
Future income taxes (note 9)		349		833
Other receivables and sundry investments		243		133
Employee future benefits (note 12)		7,391		3,477
Intangible assets (note 4)		19,785		24,065
Goodwill (note 4)		28,701		30,767
		56,469		59,275
	$	304,247	$	339,419
LIABILITIES AND SHAREHOLDERS' EQUITY				
Current:				
Bank loans (note 6a)	$	22,786	$	39,931
Accounts payable and accrued liabilities (note 6b)		54,876		73,611
Income taxes payable		29		2,443
Current portion of long-term debt (note 7)		4,582		–
Current portion of capital lease obligations (note 7)		864		458
Total current liabilities		83,137		116,443
Long-term debt (note 7)		50,848		63,939
Long-term capital lease obligations (note 7)		2,700		513
Other long-term liabilities		1,254		2,112
Future income taxes (note 9)		4,688		–
Employee future benefits (note 12)		4,540		563
Shareholders' Equity (see Statement of Changes in Shareholders' Equity):				
Common shares (note 8)		108,804		109,787
Contributed surplus		364		364
Retained earnings		64,690		49,897
Accumulated other comprehensive loss		(16,778)		(4,199)
		157,080		155,849
	$	304,247	$	339,419

Contingencies (note 21)

See accompanying notes to the financial statements.

On behalf of the Board:

(Signed:)

(Signed:)

Henry E. Demone, Director

David J. Hennigar, Director

Consolidated statements of income

(in thousands of Canadian dollars, except per share information)		For the 52 weeks ended, January 2, 2010		For the 53 weeks ended, January 3, 2009
Sales	$	627,186	$	615,993
Cost of sales (notes 2b and 16)		492,564		482,454
Distribution expenses (note 2b)		32,352		36,997
Gross profit		102,270		96,542
Foreign exchange gain (loss)		264		(1,234)
Selling, general and administrative expenses (note 2b)		(65,571)		(63,860)
Business acquisition integration costs		(460)		(4,879)
Amortization of intangible assets (note 4)		(1,499)		(1,383)
Interest expense:				
Short-term		(1,680)		(2,695)
Long-term		(3,765)		(3,768)
Loss on asset disposals		(492)		(402)
Non-operating transactions		(922)		(84)
Income before income taxes		28,145		18,237
Income taxes (note 9)				
Current		(2,548)		(3,002)
Future		(5,850)		(1,043)
Total income taxes		(8,398)		(4,045)
Net income	$	19,747	$	14,192
PER SHARE EARNINGS				
Earnings per common share (note 10)				
Basic	$	1.07	$	0.88
Diluted	$	1.07	$	0.77
Weighted average common shares outstanding (note 10)				
Basic		18,384,940		15,059,296
Diluted		18,396,067		18,203,100

See accompanying notes to the financial statements.

Beyond the Book

6-60 (Accounts receivable and related allowances)

Torstar Corporation publishes newspapers, most notably the *Toronto Star*, and digital properties, including thestar.com, Toronto.com, LiveDeal.ca, Workopolis, and Olive Canada Network. It also has a book publishing segment, Harlequin Enterprises. The following amounts, in millions of dollars, were taken from its 2009 annual report:

	2009	2008
Operating revenues	$1,451,259	$1,533,753
Receivables (net of allowances of $13,398 in 2009 and $18,939 in 2008)	$331,334	$363,381

Required:

a. For each year, express the allowances (i) as a percentage of the revenues and (ii) as a percentage of the receivables. Do these percentages seem rather high?

b. Notes 2 and 9 accompanying Torstar's 2009 financial statements provided additional information on the allowances for its receivables. (You can easily access Torstar's financial statements though either the company's website or the SEDAR website.) The accounts receivable balance given in this problem does not agree with the amounts given on Torstar's balance sheet. Read the two notes and explain the source of the difference in these balances. Should the book returns be included here?

6-61 (Examine and analyze company's financial statements)

Follow your instructor's guidelines for choosing a company and do the following:

a. Prepare an analysis of the company's cash (and cash equivalents, if applicable), short-term investments or marketable securities, gross accounts receivable, and allowance for doubtful accounts, by listing the beginning and ending balances in these accounts and calculating the net change, in both dollar and percentage terms, for the most recent year.

b. If any of the accounts in part "a" has changed more than 10%, suggest an explanation for this change.

c. If the company has any short-term investments or marketable securities, determine if there were any gains or losses recognized during the year, and describe where they were reported in the financial statements.

d. Calculate the following ratios for the most recent two years and then comment on both their reasonableness and any significant changes in them:
   i.   Bad debts expense divided by net sales
   ii. Allowance for doubtful accounts divided by gross accounts receivable
   iii. Accounts receivable turnover rate and average collection period (in days)

6-62 (Examine and compare different companies' financial statements)

Refer to the financial statements of a large retail company, a large resource company (such as one in the energy, forestry, or mining industries), and a large financial institution (such as a bank or insurance company). Prepare a short report outlining your findings on the following points:

a. Summarize the cash and other financial asset balances held by each company. Be sure to review the balance sheet accounts and all the related notes.

b. Make a list comparing the companies' operating characteristics that might affect the amount of financial assets they would have on hand. For example, which of the three businesses would likely have the most dependable and predictable cash inflows and outflows? Which of the companies would realize most of its profits from holding financial assets?

c. Look at the companies' cash flow statements and determine the major sources of cash inflows and outflows during the past year. Did the companies borrow significant amounts of money during the year? Did they have significant share issues? What types of major investments did they make?

Cases

6-63 Versa Tools Inc.

Versa Tools Inc. is a small tool and die manufacturing shop located in southwestern Ontario. The company's main shareholder, Arthur Henderson, is becoming increasingly concerned about the safety and security of the company assets and, in particular, its cash. In the past, Arthur handled all the cash transactions. However, with increasing production levels and plans to expand into a plastics division, he has been too busy to be able to continue with this hands-on approach.

Currently, there is only one person in the accounting department, a clerk who is responsible for recording all the cash receipts and disbursements and for depositing all the cash. Because she is so busy, cash is usually deposited in the bank only once a week. Until it is deposited, all cash collected is locked in a desk drawer in the main office.

The accounting clerk has no formal accounting education. In fact, she is a graduate of a local art school and is working at Versa only to earn enough money to move to Toronto and begin a career as a graphic artist. She often notes the cash receipts on slips of paper until she has time to enter them into the computer system several days later.

Finally, Arthur has not been preparing bank reconciliations. When asked about the bank reconciliations, he replied, "I'm so busy running the business that I don't have time to check every item on the bank statement each month. Besides, with the high fees that it charges us each month, shouldn't I be able to rely on the bank to keep an accurate record of the balance in our account?"

> ### Required:
> Prepare a memo to Arthur outlining the basic cash controls that should be put into place at Versa Tools Inc. to ensure the proper management and protection of its cash.

6-64 Slackur Company

Slackur Company is a very profitable small business. However, it has not given much consideration to internal controls. For example, in an attempt to keep its clerical and office expenses to a minimum, the company has combined the jobs of cashier and bookkeeper. As a result, Rob Rowe handles all the cash receipts, keeps the accounting records, and prepares the monthly bank reconciliations.

On November 30, 2011, the balance on the company's bank statement was $18,380.00. The outstanding cheques on that date were #143 for $241.75, #284 for $258.25, #862 for $190.71, #863 for $226.80, and #864 for $165.28. Included with the statement was a bank credit memorandum in the amount of $300, indicating the bank's collection of a note receivable for Slackur on November 25, and a debit memorandum in the amount of $50 for the bank's service charges for the month. Neither of these had been recorded by Slackur Company.

The company's cash account had a balance of $21,892.72 on November 30, 2011, which included a substantial amount of undeposited cash on hand. Because he needed cash for holiday shopping and knew that the company's internal controls were weak, Rob decided to take some of the undeposited cash for his personal use and report undeposited cash of only $3,845.51. In an effort to conceal his theft, he then prepared the following bank reconciliation:

Balance per bank statement, November 30		$18,380.00
Add: Undeposited receipts		3,845.51
Less: Outstanding cheques		
No. 862	$190.71	
No. 863	226.80	
No. 864	165.28	(582.79)
Add: Note collected by bank		300.00
Less: Bank service charges		(50.00)
Corrected bank balance, November 30		$21,892.72
Cash balance per books, November 30		$21,892.72

When he presented this to the general manager, she called the bank to determine whether the undeposited receipts on November 30 had since been deposited, and was happy to hear the bank confirm that Rob Rowe had made a cash deposit of $3,845.51 on the morning of December 1. She then reviewed the bank reconciliation to satisfy herself that the items on it seemed reasonable, and that it was balanced. Assuming that everything must be in order, she then thanked Rob for his good work and made a mental note to herself that he should be given a $500 year-end bonus.

Required:
a. Determine the amount of cash stolen by Rob Rowe. (Hint: Prepare a corrected bank reconciliation, treating the true amount of undeposited cash as an unknown. Then solve for this unknown, and compare the reported amount of undeposited cash to the true amount.)
b. Explain what Rowe did in the bank reconciliation that he prepared to try to conceal his theft. (Hint: You should be able to identify items whose combined effects match the amount of the discrepancy that you calculated in part "a.")
c. What should Slackur Company do differently to prevent this type of occurrence?

6-65 Sanjay Supplies Limited

Sanjay Supplies Limited is concerned about its ability to pay its debts. Analyze the information below and explain why Sanjay is experiencing problems with its cash balance. What could Sanjay do to reduce these problems?

Sanjay Supplies Limited
Selected Financial Information (in thousands)

Years ended October 31	2011	2012	2013
Sales on credit	$12,700	$14,100	$17,100
Cash	210	60	20
Short-term investments (cashable on demand)	40	—	—
Accounts receivable	1,180	1,510	1,980
Inventories	940	1,250	1,470
Short-term bank loans (payable on demand)	—	140	560
Accounts payable	610	490	340
Other short-term liabilities	80	80	80

6-66 Bestway International

Bestway International is an import-export company. Due to the nature of its business, the company often has significant amounts of cash on hand. Some of this cash has been invested in other companies as a means of achieving vertical integration. These investments are intended to be held for many years. At other times, Bestway's management invests extra cash in short-term investments. Management believes that it is better to have excess cash earning some return rather than just sitting in a bank account.

On December 31, 2011, Bestway's year end, the company had the following short-term equity investments in marketable securities:

Investment	Cost	Market Value on December 31, 2011
Royal Bank: 10,000 common shares	$48 per share	$54 per share
Petro-Canada: 10,000 common shares	$52 per share	$59 per share

Both these investments were purchased with the intention of selling them as soon as they rose significantly in value or Bestway needed the cash, whichever occurred first.

Bestway's CEO has recently approached you, the corporate controller, with some exciting news. The company plans to sell a significant bond issue in 2012 to provide funding for a large expansion into Eastern European markets. The CEO wants the statement of earnings for 2012 to be as strong as possible, and therefore tells you to record all the investments at their cost in the balance sheet on December 31, 2011, so that the increase in value will be reflected as a large gain when they are sold in 2012.

The CEO says he knows that assets are usually recorded at their cost, and that accountants tend to be conservative. Accordingly, he does not see any problem with showing the investments at their cost at the end of 2011, and waiting until they are sold in 2012 to report any gain on them.

Required:

Is the CEO correct? Refer to accounting principles in preparing your response to the CEO's position. Your response should include an outline of the proper accounting treatment for short-term investments such as these, and a brief explanation of the reasoning behind it.

6-67 Heritage Mill Works

Heritage Mill Works sells finished lumber and mouldings to a variety of housing contractors. Given the nature of the business, most of its sales are on credit, and careful management of credit and bad debts is a critical success factor for this business. The normal credit period is 60 days.

The company's owners place significant emphasis on the operating results as they appear on the statement of earnings. They believe that accurate net earnings are the best indicator of any business's success. The owners are currently looking at revising their credit-granting policies in light of a number of large write-offs that were made in the past year. They are also wondering whether notes receivable should be used in the future for certain types of customers and for very large sales.

Karen Starkly is the accounts receivable clerk for the business and has been asked by the controller to prepare an estimate of bad debts expense for the company, to be used in preparing the annual financial statements. The company had sales of $3,450,000 during the year, of which 90% were on credit. Historically, the percentage of bad debts has varied from 2% to 4% of credit sales. Bad debts are usually higher in times of economic downturns. Karen notes that business has been strong this year for the entire industry, since interest rate reductions have led to a boom in new housing starts.

The balance in the accounts receivable account on December 31 is $330,000. During the year, the company had written off $73,400 of accounts receivable as uncollectible.

Required:

a. Provide the controller with an estimate of the bad debts expense for the current period. Be prepared to justify your recommendation to the controller.
b. Comment on the magnitude of the accounts receivable that were written off as uncollectible during the year.
c. Discuss the trade-offs that must be considered when deciding credit-granting policies.
d. Explain why it might be appropriate to use notes receivable for certain types of customers or very large sales.
e. What other steps could this company take to reduce the risk of not collecting its receivables in the future?

Critical Thinking Questions

6-68 (Accounts receivable and doubtful accounts)

Sierra Wireless, Inc. produces and markets a range of products, such as wireless modems for mobile computers and vehicle-mounted modems, which allow users to access wireless data and voice communication networks using laptop computers or hand-held mobile computing devices. The company's consolidated financial statements reported the following in its 2009 annual report (in U.S. thousands):

	2009	2008
Revenues	$526,384	$567,308
Accounts receivable, net of allowance for doubtful accounts of $6,504 in 2009 and $1,989 in 2008	$ 86,466	$ 67,058

Required:

a. Is the balance in Sierra Wireless Inc.'s accounts receivable at the end of 2009 significantly higher or lower than it was at the end of 2008? Support your answer with a calculation of the percentage increase or decrease.

b. Is the balance in its allowance for doubtful accounts significantly higher or lower at the end of 2009, compared with the end of 2008? Support your answer with a calculation of the percentage increase or decrease.

c. What possible explanations can you suggest for such a big change in the relationship between the company's accounts receivable and its allowance for doubtful accounts in 2009?

6-69 (Assess internal control procedures)

The MegaMax Theatre is located in the MetroMall and employs six cashiers. Two of them work from 12:30 to 6:00 p.m., and the other four from 6:00 to 11:30 p.m. The cashiers receive payments from customers and operate machines that eject serially numbered tickets. Some customers use debit or credit cards, but most payments are cash. The rolls of admission tickets are inserted and locked into the machines by the theatre manager at the beginning of each cashier's shift.

The cashiers' booths are located just inside the entrance to the lobby of the theatre. After purchasing their tickets, customers take them to a doorperson stationed at the entrance to the theatre, about 10 metres from the cashiers' booths. The doorperson tears each ticket in half and drops the ticket stub into a locked box. The other half of the ticket is returned to the customer.

At the end of each cashier's shift, the theatre manager removes the ticket rolls from each cashier's machine, counts the cash and then totals it with the debit card and credit card transactions. Each cash count sheet is initialled by the cashier involved. The cash receipts from the first shift are stored in a safe located in the manager's office until the end of the day.

At the end of the day, the manager deposits the cash receipts from both shifts in a bank night deposit vault located in the mall. In addition, the theatre manager sends copies of the cash count sheets and the deposit slip to the company controller to be verified, and to the accounting department to be recorded.

Finally, the manager compares the total amount received by each of the cashiers to the number of tickets they issued, and notes any discrepancies, which are then discussed with the cashiers before their next shift.

Required:

a. Outline the main internal control considerations for cash receipts generally, and briefly discuss how they apply to MegaMax Theatre's cash receipts procedures.

b. Discuss any weaknesses in the current internal control system that could enable a cashier and/or doorperson to misappropriate cash.

chapter 7

INVENTORY

LEARNING OBJECTIVES

After studying this chapter, you should be able to:

1. Discuss the importance of inventory to a company's overall success.

2. Describe the valuation criteria for inventory in Canada.

3. Describe how the lower of cost and net realizable value rule is applied to inventory.

4. Explain the difference between the perpetual inventory system and the periodic inventory system.

5. Discuss some criteria that companies use when choosing an inventory system.

6. Describe the two cost flow assumptions and calculate cost of goods sold and ending inventory under each.

7. Describe management's responsibility for internal control measures related to inventory.

8. Estimate a value for ending inventory using the cost-to-sales ratio method.

9. Calculate the inventory turnover ratio and explain how it can be interpreted by users.

Selling Seeds from P.E.I.

In 1939, Veseys Seeds first began operations, filling orders using a spoon and kitchen scale, and tracking inventory on the back of little cards. Almost 70 years later, the York, Prince Edward Island, mail order company processes more than 100,000 customer orders each year, shipping to gardeners across Canada and the United States. Today, the company has state-of-the-art inventory and bookkeeping software that enables it to maintain a perpetual inventory system that automatically updates with each transaction.

Veseys' inventory has grown to include hundreds of different vegetable, flower, and herb seeds, as well as a wide range of bulbs, gardening accessories, and tools. Since seeds—which Veseys purchases in bulk and packages on site—are sold in five different packet sizes, the company has to keep track of thousands of individual items sold through its six printed catalogues, a retail outlet, and its website—which now brings in about 40 percent of total sales.

"Our entire inventory is stored in a database, so to create a purchase order, we simply type in a vendor name and item number, and the current price and ordering information pops up," explains John Barrett, Sales and Marketing Director at Veseys. "When the product arrives, our receiver verifies the shipment against the original purchase order. As a result, at any given time, our customer sales staff can tell whether an item is available or not, or if it's back-ordered."

Because Veseys uses a just-in-time system—it buys seeds in large quantities but packages them in increments—an item may occasionally show up as unavailable when in fact it is currently in packaging and will be on the shelf by the end of the day. "When that happens, our staff does an override and the sale goes through," says Mr. Barrett. "We control our own destiny when it comes to creating the inventory, unlike other companies that are dependent on outside suppliers. This way, basically, nothing is ever out of stock."

But the just-in-time system has posed a challenge for tracking Internet-based orders. Veseys' website is not fully integrated with the system. Although orders from the website are automatically entered, they are reviewed and processed by staff each day. "If we let the website run by itself, at 3 a.m. when somebody orders something from Manitoba and the computer tells them we're out of stock on an item, that person ends up not ordering it," explains Mr. Barrett. "With our system, we'll make sure they get that item."

In addition to tracking inventory, the system produces reports such as sales by week or by category. It can even show the number of items and dollar revenue per item on any page of Veseys' catalogues. "By comparing those figures with what we've bought so far, I can come up with a pretty good estimate of what we're going to need," Mr. Barrett says. "In the end, it will tell me whether I've bought too much or too little based on my projections. Due to the nature of our business, we can't have any surplus. Our product is alive, and it has to be sold and planted within a certain period of time or it's finished."

Purchasing, stocking, and selling inventory is a complicated process. Veseys Seeds is particularly vulnerable because its products have a short shelf life. Management must have enough seeds in stock to fill orders as they come in because customers want to get the seeds planted and growing. They are not willing to wait. There are also many other seed companies and if Veseys does not have the seeds that customers want, they may go elsewhere. At the same time, management must not overstock. Any seeds that are not sold will have to be discarded. Keeping the inventory at just the right level requires Veseys to generate up-to-date information about past sales, current demand, and current inventory levels. Veseys uses a perpetual inventory system (which keeps track of each sale and purchase of inventory as it happens) to give managers information about current inventory levels, enabling them to place orders with suppliers on a daily basis. Veseys' management of inventory is further complicated by its three modes of sales: store outlet, catalogues, and Internet. All customer personnel must have access to the same information and must update that information with each sale so that the next order is processed with the most current information possible. Management of inventory is a complicated process, but it is essential to the efficient sale of goods.

Inventory is any item purchased by a company for resale to customers or to be used in the manufacture of items to be sold to customers. For any retailer or manufacturer that sells goods to customers, inventory is generally its most important asset. The company's success or failure depends on buying or making inventory with a unit cost that is lower than its selling price. It also depends on buying or making the inventory that people want to buy. Management must be very careful to buy or make the right items, at the right cost, and in the right quantities so that sufficient profit can be made on sales to cover all the other necessary business expenditures.

Visualize, for a moment, a store like **HMV** that sells CDs, tapes, and movies. Imagine the complications that can arise with inventory. To begin, the store must select from its suppliers the music and movies that people want to buy, and do so in sufficient quantities to ensure that it does not run out of any particular item (called a **stockout**), which typically forces buyers to go to another store where they may buy more than just the item that was out of stock. At the same time, it must ensure that it does not have too many items in inventory, because that increases storage and handling costs and there is the risk of obsolescence. Next, it needs to make sure that it sets prices that are competitive but, at the same time, high enough to provide sufficient profit for the company. Then, with all items priced and in stock, the store must provide safeguards so that people cannot steal the inventory. And, finally, complicating all these activities even further are the variety and volume of items typically sold by any one store.

USER RELEVANCE

LEARNING OBJECTIVE 1

Discuss the importance of inventory to a company's overall success.

When you think about inventory, you probably think about items you have recently purchased in stores. Inventory includes not only those items, but much more. To a property developer, inventory is land and buildings; to a forest products company, it is logs, lumber, and pulp; to a recycler, it is old newspapers, plastic bottles, and aluminum cans. Exhibit 7-1 includes two other examples of inventory.

EXAMPLES OF INVENTORY

Suncor Energy Inc. is an integrated oil and gas company operating in the tar sands in Northern Alberta. Exhibit 7-1A shows Note 11 from its 2009 annual report, which describes its inventory.

SUNCOR ENERGY INC. 2009 ANNUAL REPORT

annual report

Excerpt from the Notes to the Statements

11. INVENTORIES

($ millions)	2009	2008
Crude oil	781	459
Refined products	1,303	247
Materials, supplies and merchandise	532	203
Energy trading commodity inventories[1]	355	–
Total	2,971	909

[1] As described in note 4, certain physical trading commodity contracts are no longer being used for the company's expected purchase, sale or usage requirements. Inventories related to these derivative contracts are now recorded at fair value less costs to sell with the associated gains and losses and the underlying settlement of inventory recorded on a net basis in Energy Supply and Trading Activities revenue.

During 2009, inventories of $14.9 billion (2008 – $15.7 billion) were expensed. There were no write-downs of inventories in 2009 (2008 – $40 million) and no reversals of write-downs were recorded in 2009 and 2008.

Brickworks Limited, an Australian company, manufactures and sells floor and wall tiles, bricks and terracotta tiles, and roofing materials. It also sells industrial land. Exhibit 7-1B shows Note 13 from its 2009 annual report, which lists its land held for resale.

BRICKWORKS LIMITED 2009 ANNUAL REPORT

annual report

Excerpt from the Notes to the Statements

13. Land held for resale

(Tabular amounts in thousands of Australian dollars)	2009	2008
(a) Current	50,461	95,108
(b) Non-Current	30,722	34,649

The investment in inventory can be substantial, so companies manage inventory levels carefully to maximize their return and minimize their costs. For example, to better track its inventory in transit and in its warehouses, several years ago Wal-Mart developed a sophisticated tracking method known as Radio Frequency ID (RFID), which uses computer chips with tiny antennas on inventory pallets to know where each pallet is. That technology is now being used for other purposes by other organizations.

accounting in the news

Medical Supply Company Tracks Its Inventory

Elite Medical Supply is a supplier of medical equipment for disorders of the spine as well as products for electrotherapy and bone growth stimulation. Many of its products are used by patients covered by the home health care industry in the U.S., and, in response to concerns about home care fraud, the home health care industry has begun to make unannounced visits to patients. Through Radio Frequency ID (RFID) tags supplied by Cybra Corporation, and which Elite Medical has attached to its equipment, Elite Medical can quickly retrieve its inventory records and match them to patients and home care providers to ensure that the right people are using the right equipment.

Source: "CYBRA's EdgeMagic To Help Medical Supply Company Comply with Medicare and Medicaid Initiatives," Cybra Corporation press release, March 23, 2009, http://www.cybra.com/press/202-em-article2.html

For companies whose major source of revenue is the sale of inventory, managing the inventory inflows and outflows can mean the difference between success and failure. As a user of financial information, you should therefore make yourself aware of the types of inventory that a company sells. You should also determine the gross profit (sales minus cost of goods sold) that the company earned in the current year and over the last several years. Has the company been earning enough gross profit to cover its other costs? Has that profit been increasing, decreasing, or staying constant?

A variety of accounting methods for estimating the total cost of inventory have been developed and are acceptable under IFRS. This makes the accounting for inventory a fairly complicated process. As a user, you need to be aware of what those methods are and how each one affects the gross profit and the net earnings amounts. Because companies are required to disclose their inventory costing method(s), once you know the method, you can make some assumptions about how it is affecting income. The basics of inventory accounting are covered in this chapter so that you will have a reasonable understanding of how inventory is measured, recorded, and reported. You can then use this information to make informed evaluations of companies.

INVENTORY RECOGNITION AND COST OF GOODS SOLD

Does inventory meet the criteria for being recognized as an asset? The future economic benefits criterion is met through a company's ability to sell its inventory in the future and use the proceeds to buy other goods and services. However, as long as inventory has not yet been sold, the collection of cash from its sale is even more uncertain than collecting accounts receivable. Inventory involves all the uncertainties associated with the collection of accounts receivable, as well as two others that are unique to this asset: finding buyers, and the obsolescence and spoilage of inventory. If a sufficient number of buyers cannot be found at the initial price set for the product or service, the price may have to change in order to attract buyers. A second uncertainty is obsolescence and spoilage. Computer hardware, for instance, is at considerable risk of becoming obsolete. Spoilage, on the other hand, is a major factor for food inventories.

With respect to the second criterion for recognizing an asset, control of inventories is evidenced by possession and by legal title. Usually ownership of low-priced inventories is evidenced by possession because it is impractical to keep track of their legal title. They are also very much like cash in terms of management, with adequate controls being necessary to protect them from loss or theft. Ownership of high-priced inventories may also be evidenced by possession, but there are generally legal documents that also prove ownership. The ownership of automobiles, for instance, is evidenced by the registration of serial numbers.

The fact that the company possesses inventory indicates that a past transaction occurred which meets the third criterion for recognizing an asset.

Inventory, therefore, meets the recognition criteria for an asset, and should be recorded as such in the company's accounting system. The next question is the amount to record, which depends on the valuation or measurement criteria that are applied. The final concern is the cost of goods sold amount, which represents the expense side of the inventory asset. Once inventory is sold, it is no longer an asset and its cost is reported on the statement of earnings as cost of goods sold and matched against the revenue that the sale generated. Determining what that cost is can, however, be problematic. Much of the discussion in this chapter will therefore centre on first establishing an appropriate cost for the inventory and then doing the same for the cost of goods sold.

VALUATION CRITERIA

The valuation method allowed under IFRS is a combination of several valuation approaches. The standards generally specify that cost should be used as long as this figure does not differ materially from more recent costs. If it does, the company can use one of a number of methods to recognize a decline in inventory value. Before this is discussed in detail, however, we need to examine the different approaches to valuation.

LEARNING OBJECTIVE 2

Describe the valuation criteria for inventory in Canada.

Historical Cost

One possible valuation method is to carry inventory at its historical cost. According to this method, inventory is recorded at its cost on the date it was acquired. In the purest application of this method, there is no recognition of changes in the inventory's market value while it is held. Earnings are recognized only when the inventory is sold. At that time, a profit or loss is recorded.

Market Value

A second possible valuation method is to carry inventory at its market value. To apply this method, the term "**market**" must first be more clearly defined. Inventory really has two markets. The first is the market in which the company buys its products. In the case of a retailer, this is called the **wholesale market**. If the market price can be found in the market where the inventory is bought (the wholesale market), the term "**replacement cost**" is used and refers to what it would cost the company to replace the inventory today. The market from which the inventory is bought is called the **input market** or the **entry market**, since the products enter the company from this market. Note that for a manufacturing company, because numerous costs are incurred when constructing a product, there may be several markets from which the company buys its inventory (raw materials) to create the finished product.

Another measure of market value might be obtained from the market in which the company sells its products. This is called the **retail market**. (The company, of course, hopes prices in the retail market are higher than those in the wholesale market so that it can earn a profit.) The markets in which companies sell their products are sometimes referred to as **output markets** or **exit markets**. In accounting terminology, the exit price is sometimes referred to as the **net realizable value (NRV)**, which is the net amount that can be realized from the sale of the product in question. Net realizable value is not the same as selling price. The "net" part of NRV refers to the company's need to net some costs against the selling prices. For example, there are generally some selling costs that must be incurred to sell a product. Net realizable value is then the selling price less the costs necessary to sell the item. In a manufacturing company, some inventory is not ready for sale (work-in-process). Net realizable value, in this case, is the selling price less the selling costs as well as the costs necessary to complete the item.

There is one final issue for the definition of market. The markets referred to in the preceding paragraphs are assumed to be the normal markets in which the company does normal business. There are also markets for goods that must be sold quickly (such as in a liquidation sale) or in abnormally large or small quantities. The prices in these markets do not reflect the value of inventory in its normal use and should not be used in valuing the inventory of a going concern (a company that will continue to operate in the foreseeable future). These markets may be important in valuing inventory, however, if the company is in bankruptcy or going out of business. Under these distress conditions, normal accounting procedures would not be appropriate, because the conditions violate the **going-concern assumption** that underlies financial accounting.

REPLACEMENT COST If a company uses a pure replacement cost valuation system, inventory is carried at its replacement cost. At acquisition, replacement cost is the same as historical cost. As the company holds the inventory, however, unrealized increases and decreases in value are recognized as the inventory's replacement cost changes. The statement of financial position reflects the inventory's replacement cost at the end of each period, and the statement of earnings shows the unrealized profits and losses. At the time of sale, the only additional profit or loss that is recognized is the difference between the replacement cost at the date of sale and the selling price. This difference is called a realized profit or loss.

NET REALIZABLE VALUE A pure net realizable value system records inventory at its net realizable value. At the date of acquisition, this means that a profit or loss is recorded equal to the difference between the historical cost and the net realizable value. While the inventory is held, this system requires that changes in net realizable value be recognized as unrealized profits or losses. At the time of ultimate sale, no profit is recognized, because the item has already been recorded at its net realizable value.

What Is Canadian Practice?

Historical cost is used extensively in Canada. However, when the use of historical cost results in a figure that is materially different from recent cost figures, companies should apply a lower of cost and net realizable value rule at the end of the period. If net realizable value is lower than historical cost, the inventory is recorded at the lower amount (the NRV). This impacts the inventory amount on the statement of financial position and a loss is recorded on the statement of earnings. In Canada, most companies describe their inventories as being valued at the lower of cost and net realizable value. In order to understand the implications for inventory, we will first discuss what should be included in the cost of inventory, and then consider how to apply the lower of cost and net realizable value rule.

ACQUISITION COSTS

The cost value that is originally assigned to inventory should contain all **laid-down costs**. For a retailer, laid-down costs include the invoice price, as well as any customs, tariff and excise duties, and freight and cartage costs (costs to transport the inventory, often simply called **transportation in** or **freight in**). As a practical matter, it is often difficult to assign a specific dollar amount of freight and cartage to a specific item of inventory. Imagine, for example, that a major grocery store received a new shipment of inventory that contained everything from cereal boxes to heads of lettuce. It would be totally impractical to assign freight costs to a single head of lettuce. Therefore, many companies do not assign these costs to inventory, but treat them instead as period costs in the period in which they are incurred and add them to the cost of goods sold.

The following equation is often used when valuing inventory:

> Beginning inventory (amount on hand at the beginning of the year)
> + Purchases of inventory made during the year
> _____
> = Total cost of goods available for sale during the year

Once you have the cost for the total goods available for sale during the year, you can deduct the cost of the goods that remain unsold at the end of the year (called ending inventory). The resulting amount is the cost of the goods that you have sold (called cost of goods sold).

If you include the transportation costs, the calculation of cost of goods sold becomes:

> Beginning inventory
> + Purchases
> + Transportation in
> _____
> = Cost of goods available for sale
> − Ending inventory
> _____
> = Cost of goods sold

For a manufacturing company, the inventory costs are more complicated. Typically, a manufacturing company buys materials that it intends to use to make new products. These materials are called raw materials and their cost is kept in a raw materials inventory account. The cost assigned to this account includes the cost of the materials plus any transportation costs. The company takes the raw materials and begins to make its new products. The process of manufacturing involves additional costs, such as workers' labour costs, the costs of the machines and buildings, and the cost of utilities to run the manufacturing facilities. The labour costs associated with manufacturing are referred to as direct labour, and all of the other more indirect costs are referred to as overhead. A typical product's cost therefore includes the cost of raw materials, direct labour, and overhead.

A company uses three inventory accounts in the manufacturing process: the raw materials inventory account, a work-in-process account, and a finished goods account. The work-in-process account collects all of the costs (raw materials, direct labour, and overhead) that are incurred as the product is being made. Once the product is complete, the full cost of making the product is transferred from the work-in-process account to the finished goods account. Products that are sold are then deducted from the finished goods account. Exhibit 7-2 illustrates how the costs flow through the three inventory accounts to cost of goods sold.

EXHIBIT 7-2

MANUFACTURING COST FLOWS

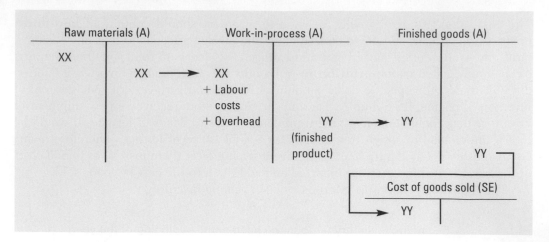

Exhibit 7-3 presents the 2009 inventory disclosure of the manufacturing company **Maple Leaf Foods Inc.** Maple Leaf Foods is a Canadian company that prepares and sells meats, meals, and bakery products.

EXHIBIT 7-3

annual report

MAPLE LEAF FOODS INC. 2009 ANNUAL REPORT

Excerpted from the Notes to the Statements

4. Inventories

(In thousands of Canadian dollars)	2009	2008
Raw materials	$ **49,644**	$ 62,014
Work in process	**54,164**	55,933
Finished goods	**182,687**	197,723
Packaging	**25,697**	27,208
Spare parts	**37,717**	34,536
	$ **349,909**	377,414

Lower of Cost and Net Realizable Value

Because inventory is crucial to the success of companies in the retail and manufacturing business, users are very interested in its value. When inventory is listed as a current asset on the balance sheet, users assume that it will be sold in the subsequent period for at least its stated value, but more optimistically, at a profit. During any given accounting period, however, economic circumstances may arise that negatively affect the inventory's value. At the end of every accounting period, most companies therefore compare the cost of the inventory with its market value and apply the lower of cost and net realizable value rule. To do so, companies can use either the direct method or the allowance method.

Under the direct method, the ending inventory is reduced to the lower NRV, which causes the cost of goods sold amount to rise in the statement of earnings. In the subsequent year, the lower value that has been assigned to the inventory becomes part of the cost of goods sold because the ending inventory of one year becomes the beginning inventory of the next year. Under the allowance method, the inventory account remains at the original cost and an allowance account is used to hold the decline in value. The allowance account, which is shown contra to the inventory on the balance sheet, is usually adjusted each year to reflect the inventory's changing value. The lower of cost and net realizable value is normally applied to individual items but can be applied to groups of similar items when it is impractical to apply it to individual items.

LEARNING OBJECTIVE 3

Describe how the lower of cost and net realizable value rule is applied to inventory.

Under the direct method, the unrealized losses that result from the application of the lower of cost and net realizable rule are often hidden in the cost of goods sold expense. Remember that the cost of goods sold calculation is:

> Cost of beginning inventory
> + Purchases
> + Transportation in
> ─────────────────────────
> = Goods available for sale
> − Ending inventory
> ─────────────────────────
> = Cost of goods sold

If the inventory's NRV is lower than the calculated cost amount, ending inventory is assigned the lower value. If the ending inventory value goes down, the cost of goods sold expense goes up, thereby incorporating the loss. Under this method, users will not know how large the loss was. In the following example, assume that the cost of the ending inventory was $14,000 and its NRV was $12,000.

	Before applying lower of cost and NRV	After applying lower of cost and NRV
Cost of beginning inventory	$ 10,000	$ 10,000
Purchases	370,000	370,000
Transportation in	5,000	5,000
Cost of goods available for sale	385,000	385,000
Ending inventory	14,000	12,000
Cost of goods sold	$371,000	$373,000

Note that when the ending inventory was reduced to the NRV of $12,000, the cost of goods sold increased to $373,000. In other words, the loss in the value of the inventory is now included in the cost of goods sold.

Under the allowance method, a separate loss account is created to hold the amount of the loss. It is usually called Loss Due to Market Decline of Inventory. This loss account could be listed separately on the statement of earnings but is more frequently summarized with other expenses, which are listed after Cost of Goods Sold. Similar to the direct method, the amount of the loss is frequently not disclosed as an individual item in the statement of earnings. Companies would probably disclose the loss in inventory value as a separate item if it were a material amount. They could also discuss it in a note to the financial statements.

Canada follows the IFRS standards that require the use of the net realizable value. This makes sense because if the selling price has dropped below the cost, the company may experience a loss in the next period, when the inventory is sold. Because the decline in value occurred in the current period, we reduce the value of the inventory in the current period. Then when it is sold in the next period, it will sell at no profit if the selling price does not change.

Exhibit 7-4 includes the inventory disclosure for **Finning International Inc.**, which distributes and services heavy equipment and related products, many under the CAT brand. Note that it uses net realizable value, as well as specific identification and weighted average cost, in its inventory disclosure. More will be said about these other cost bases later in the chapter.

EXHIBIT 7-4

FINNING INTERNATIONAL INC. 2009 ANNUAL REPORT
Excerpt from the Notes to the Statements

1. (e) *Inventories*

Inventories are assets held for sale in the ordinary course of business, in the process of production for sale, or in the form of materials or supplies to be consumed in the production process or in the rendering of services. Inventories are stated at the lower of cost and net realizable value. Cost is determined on a specific item basis for on-hand equipment, and on a weighted average cost basis for parts and supplies. The cost of inventories includes all costs of purchase, conversion costs, and other costs incurred in bringing inventories to their existing location and condition. In the case of internal service work in process on equipment, cost includes an appropriate share of overhead costs based on normal operating capacity.

INTERNATIONAL PERSPECTIVES

Reports from Other Countries

Most countries require the application of a lower of cost and market rule. Some countries, such as the United States, refer to it as the lower of cost or market rule. The application of this rule, however, can vary across countries. The market value used in the rule is interpreted to mean replacement cost in a few countries (Japan, for example), whereas in many more countries it is interpreted as net realizable value (France, Germany, and the United Kingdom, for example). The International Accounting Standards Board (IASB) defines market value as net realizable value. The United States uses three values for market (net realizable value, net realizable value less a normal profit margin, and replacement cost) when it requires that, regardless of how high the replacement costs are, the company cannot carry the inventory at a value higher than net realizable value (called a ceiling value). In addition, the carrying value cannot be lower than net realizable value less a profit margin (called a floor value). Another difference is that the United States is almost alone in viewing the write down of inventory as permanent. Most other countries, including Canada, either require or permit the recovery of value back to original cost if the market recovers.

INVENTORY SYSTEMS

Now that we have discussed the valuation of inventory in a general way, we need to look at various systems companies have developed to manage the volume and variety of inventory that they purchase and subsequently sell. Keeping track of inventory units and their associated costs is essential to managing the company profitably. Information on the units sold and those in inventory is necessary for intelligent decisions about pricing, production, and reordering. An inventory system is needed to keep track of this information. As you saw in our opening story, computerized inventory systems are making inventory management easier.

At least two types of information about inventory are needed. The first is the number of units sold during a period and the number that remain. This information is needed to establish a value for cost of goods sold, to trigger the reordering of inventory, or to set the level of production for the current period. It may also be necessary to fill sales orders. The second type of information is data about the cost of goods sold during the period and the cost of those that remain. This information is needed to prepare the financial statements, to evaluate performance, and to make pricing decisions.

Some inventory systems keep track of units of inventory but not their cost; others keep track of both units of inventory and cost. Systems that keep track of units but not costs are referred to as physical inventory systems. Major grocery chains, for example, have their cash registers connected to computers that record the sale of each item of inventory when the item is scanned for its bar code. The computerized inventory system is programmed to trigger new orders when the number of items remaining drops to a predetermined level. Unless the computer program is very sophisticated, it will not identify the purchase cost of the item sold.

Systems that keep track of the number of units and the costs associated with units of inventory are referred to as cost inventory systems. A cost inventory system can most easily be implemented when the inventory items are uniquely identifiable. For example, a car dealership records the unique characteristics of each vehicle that it buys for resale. When a vehicle is sold, it is relatively easy to record the sale of that specific vehicle and to record its original cost to the dealer. A grocery store, on the other hand, would have more difficulty determining the original cost of a can of peas because it would have to identify the case from which the can was sold. The bar code on the can tells the computer simply that it is a can of a particular brand of peas. With the increasing sophistication of computer technology, more businesses are now able to convert to cost inventory systems and manage their inventories with more precision.

It is important for you to understand how inventory flows through any inventory system. To illustrate these flows, consider the inventory T account in Exhibit 7-5. The company starts the period with a certain amount of beginning inventory that, in a physical inventory system, is the number of units and, in a cost inventory system, is the number of units multiplied by the cost of those units. These amounts are known from the end of the last period. The number of units purchased during the period and the cost of those purchases are known from the invoices for the period (in the case of a manufacturer, the debits are for direct materials, labour, and overhead, all of which are known during the period). The cost of goods sold (the number of units sold in a physical system) and the cost (number) of units left in ending inventory are unknown. The sum of the cost of the beginning inventory and that of purchases is called the cost of **goods available for sale**. The problem is deciding how to divide the total cost between the cost of goods sold and the cost of those that remain in ending inventory. Whatever inventory system is implemented, it must be able to allocate cost of the goods available for sale between the cost of goods sold and ending inventory.

EXHIBIT 7-5

INVENTORY INFORMATION

Inventory (A)			
Beginning balance	KNOWN		
Purchases	KNOWN	?????	Cost of goods sold
Ending balance	?????		

The type of inventory system used depends on the type and size of inventory involved and the cost of implementing the system. We will discuss two general types of inventory systems: perpetual and periodic systems.

Perpetual Inventory Systems

LEARNING OBJECTIVE 4

Explain the difference between the perpetual inventory system and the periodic inventory system.

Perpetual inventory systems may be either physical inventory systems or cost inventory systems. They keep track of units or their associated costs, or both, on a continuous basis. Veseys Seeds uses a perpetual system. This means that when a unit is sold, it (or its cost) is immediately removed from the inventory account. In terms of the T account in Exhibit 7-5, a credit is made to the account at the time of sale. The ending balance in the account can be calculated at any time to provide information about what is left in the account. In this type of system, the ending inventory balance and the cost of goods sold account are always up to date in terms of units and/or costs. Therefore, the information provided by this type of system is the most current for decision purposes.

Up-to-date information, which is useful in any business, is crucial to some businesses, such as car dealerships. In the automobile business, the sales personnel must know what stock is still available for sale so that a car is not sold twice. Because selling prices are negotiated and the costs of different cars may vary dramatically, the cost of a specific car must be known at the time of sale so that an appropriate price can be negotiated that will enable the company to earn a profit. The dealer's profitability depends on up-to-date information. Fortunately, the cost of keeping track of this information on a perpetual basis is not very high because the number of units of inventory is relatively small and each vehicle can be uniquely identified.

Contrast this with the decisions faced by the owner of a hardware store. Prices are not negotiated at the time of sale, but rather each item is pre-priced and customers pay the stated price. Therefore, knowing the cost of each unit on a per-sale basis is not as important. The amount of inventory must be known in order to reorder stock, but reordering is probably not done daily. The cost of keeping track of each inventory item on a perpetual basis would be fairly substantial because the hardware store deals with numerous items in relatively large quantities. Consider, for example, using the perpetual system to keep track of all the types of nuts and bolts the store sells. The cost of implementing a perpetual system in this case would probably outweigh the benefits of having up-to-date information. Therefore, the hardware store would no doubt develop a periodic inventory system.

Periodic Inventory Systems

In a **periodic inventory system**, there is no entry to record the reduction in inventory at the time of sale. Within the inventory system there may be no mechanism to determine the cost of the item at the time it is sold. In a retail store, for example, clerks know an item's retail price because it is written on the sales tag, but they probably do not know the cost of the item to the store. To determine the amount sold and the amount left in inventory, the company must periodically stop business and physically count the units that are left, and then assign costs to them. The cost of goods sold is then determined by subtracting the ending inventory value established by the count from the sum of the beginning inventory value and the purchases made during the period. This process assumes that all items included in the cost of goods sold were indeed sold, which may not always be the case. If items were stolen or misplaced, they would not be on the shelves or in the warehouse when the inventory was counted, and the company would assume they had been sold. With a periodic inventory system, the company does not have up-to-date information during the period regarding the level of inventory or the cost of goods sold. It therefore needs to develop other methods to determine reorder points.

The counting and costing of ending inventory can be an expensive process, particularly for companies with large amounts of inventory. The company must close during the counting process and perhaps even turn away business. It must also pay individuals to do the counting. Because of the cost, it generally makes sense to count inventory only once a year. For internal control purposes, some companies count key items of inventory more frequently than once a year and often prepare financial statements more frequently than once a year. Accountants have therefore developed estimation methods that are used to establish inventory values for these interim reports.

A company may use a perpetual system to keep track of the physical units (remember the use of bar codes in the grocery store) but, because of the difficulty of determining unit costs, it may use a periodic system to assign costs to units. This type of mixed system provides up-to-date information regarding the number of units available to aid in reordering or production decisions. It does not provide up-to-date cost information. This may be perfectly acceptable to management if up-to-date unit information is more important than cost information.

Costs and Benefits of System Choice

One of the key factors in the choice of inventory systems is the cost of maintaining the system. The perpetual system provides better, more current information than the periodic system, but does so at a higher cost. However, as inventory computer software becomes more sophisticated, the implementation of perpetual systems has become a real possibility for companies that formerly would not have considered it. For example, the introduction of the bar code scanner in the grocery business has allowed stores to keep track of units of inventory on a perpetual basis. As well, with the introduction of **electronic data interchange (EDI)**, some retailers use this information to automatically reorder inventory directly from the wholesaler or manufacturer. An EDI system links the seller's inventory system computers with the computers in the supplier's inventory system. When the seller's inventory drops to a pre-specified level, a new order is automatically generated that tells the supplier to send a new shipment of inventory.

With a perpetual system, managers can make better business decisions. From the system, they know what items are selling and how many items they still have. They can more accurately determine what items to reorder and when that new order should be placed. In a periodic system, managers must develop other techniques to determine the information that the perpetual system provides. For example, they might have a card placed near the bottom of a stack of merchandise. When the merchandise is sold and the card is visible, it is a signal that more must be ordered. This is a very crude system that depends on the card not being removed and on someone noticing it when it

LEARNING OBJECTIVE 5

Discuss some criteria that companies use when choosing an inventory system

becomes visible. Managers also use estimation methods in the periodic system to provide them with the information they need.

One advantage of the perpetual basis that we have not yet discussed is the identification of **inventory shrinkage**. Shrinkage refers to losses of inventory due to theft, damage, and spoilage. Periodic systems are incapable of identifying shrinkage because shrinkage appears as part of the cost of goods sold when the ending inventory value is subtracted from the beginning inventory plus purchases. A perpetual system can identify shrinkage because the system tells the company what the ending inventory should be. The company can then do a count to see what is actually left in its physical inventory. The difference is the shrinkage. Physically counting the inventory is necessary under both systems and the fact that shrinkage can be identified under the perpetual system is a bonus. Companies with perpetual systems may, however, stagger the counting of inventories so that not all inventories are counted at the same time. The closest that a periodic system can come to the perpetual system in identifying shrinkage is to use estimation methods. A company may be able to estimate how much inventory should be on hand. When it counts the inventory, it can then compare it with the estimated amount and get a crude measure of shrinkage.

accounting in the news

Inventory Losses Shrink Retail Profits

Each year the Global Retail Theft Barometer reports on statistics about retail theft and waste (called shrinkage) in 41 countries and regions. Prepared by the Centre for Retail Research in England, the report covers the year from July 1 to June 30. In 2009, theft and waste cost retailers $114.8 billion (1.43% of global retail sales). This is a 5.9% increase over the previous year. Shrinkage varied across different types of goods, with clothing and accessories having the highest and liquor, wine and beer having the lowest. Average shrinkage rose in 38 of the 41 countries. Companies are training staff in the detection of theft and are using more technology in an attempt to reduce this drain on their profits.

Source: Neto Baltic, *The Global Retail Theft Barometer 2009*, http://www.neto-baltic.com/en/2009-11-12

The cost of an inventory system must be balanced against the benefits of the information it provides. The main benefit of the perpetual system is its timely information. When inventory information is needed on a timely basis for pricing, reordering, or other important decisions, the benefits of the perpetual system must be carefully considered even though the system is likely to be more expensive.

COST FLOW ASSUMPTIONS

In order to determine the cost of goods sold and the cost of ending inventory, the cost of specific units must somehow be linked to the actual physical units that either were sold (cost of goods sold) or remain in ending inventory. For some businesses, this is not difficult because the physical units are unique and records are kept that specifically identify the unit and its cost. Under these circumstances, the company can match the physical units with their costs using the **specific identification method**. **Finning International Inc.** (Exhibit 7-4) would be able to identify the cost of its on-hand equipment in its inventory. Each piece of equipment would have its own invoice price and registration number and would therefore be unique.

In some businesses, specifically identifying costs of individual physical units is not feasible. Consider a shoe retailer that buys multiple styles, sizes, and colours of shoes in a single order. If the retailer never ordered the same shoe again, it would be possible to determine the cost of a specific pair of shoes. However, once a second order is placed and arrives at the store, it is no longer possible to identify whether a specific pair of shoes came from the first order or from the second unless the retailer took the time to mark the second purchase to distinguish it from the first. It is unlikely that retailers would incur the additional cost of specifically identifying each new order. Therefore, in businesses in which specific identification is not feasible, a logical assumption is generally made about how costs flow through the company.

Inventory Cost Flow Tutorial

POSSIBLE COST FLOW ASSUMPTIONS

1. The first item purchased is the first item sold (FIFO).
2. The cost of the items is determined using an average of the cost of the items purchased.

As we get into the various cost flow possibilities, we are going to describe the **cost flow assumptions** related to a perpetual inventory system only. The reason for restricting the choice to the perpetual system is that, with the advent of new inventory software, it is a common system used by businesses and we want to concentrate on showing you the methods and their financial statement implications, rather than working through four methods (two under each system). If you are interested in seeing the cost assumptions under the periodic system, we have included a description of them in the Appendix at the end of this chapter. Under the periodic system, the average method (which is called weighted average) will produce slightly different inventory cost amounts. FIFO will produce the same amounts under both the perpetual and periodic systems.

LEARNING OBJECTIVE 6

Describe the two cost flow assumptions and calculate cost of goods sold and ending inventory under each.

INTERNATIONAL PERSPECTIVES—IFRS REQUIREMENTS

International accounting standards (IFRS) allow both perpetual and periodic inventory systems but limit the cost flow choices to specific identification, FIFO, and weighted average. A fourth method, **last-in, first-out (LIFO)**, is no longer recognized as acceptable. Up until January 1, 2008, LIFO was acceptable in Canada as well.

ethics in accounting

Determining the ending balance in inventory is crucial not only for determining the statement of financial position value for inventory, but also for establishing the cost of goods sold for the statement of earnings. Any overstatement of ending inventory will result in an understatement of cost of goods sold and, therefore, an overstatement of earnings. There are many situations that put pressure on managers and employees to show higher net income, such as budget targets and bonus plans. There may also be incentives to overstate ending inventory if it is to serve as collateral for loans. Auditors are interested in validation of ending inventory values and are typically required under audit guidelines to be present at the physical count of ending inventory to make sure inventory counts are accurate and costs have been appropriately assigned.

Ethics in Accounting

Note that, as we go through the following assumptions, we are discussing cost flows, not physical flows. We will be suggesting logical assumptions for cost flows that may be entirely opposite to the way inventory physically flows through the company. To illustrate these assumptions, we will use the data in Exhibit 7-6 for Rhoda's Appliances, Inc.

Two cost flow assumptions—first-in, first-out (FIFO) and moving average (the name given to the average method under the perpetual system)—constitute two logical ways of assigning costs to units sold or remaining in inventory. FIFO assumes that the first unit purchased is also the first unit sold, hence first-in, first-out. Moving average assigns an average cost to both cost of goods sold and ending inventory each time there is a sale. Let's look at each of these approaches in more detail.

EXHIBIT 7-6

RHODA'S APPLIANCES, INC.
Inventory of Refrigerators

Date		Units	Unit cost	Total
January 1	Beginning inventory	6	$450	$ 2,700
January 10	Purchase #1	15	475	7,125
January 20	Purchase #2	12	480	5,760
Goods available for sale		33		$15,585
Sale record				
		Units	Unit price	Total
January 15	Sale #1	16	$725	$11,600
January 25	Sale #2	10	750	7,500
		26		$19,100

Rhoda's Appliances starts the period with six refrigerators in inventory. Note that the beginning inventory cost is $2,700 and that the unit cost is $450. Only in the very first period of operations are the beginning values in inventory the same under both assumptions. Because different cost flow assumptions assign costs to units in different ways, in subsequent periods each assumption will result in different per-unit amounts being assigned to ending inventory, which in turn becomes beginning inventory for the next period. Each of these cost flow assumptions is discussed in the following subsections. Refer to Exhibit 7-6 as each method is discussed.

First-In, First-Out (FIFO)

The **first-in**, **first-out**, or **FIFO**, method is the most commonly used method in Canada, although average cost is a very close second. FIFO assigns the first costs to the first units sold. This means that ending inventory units will be matched to costs for the most recent purchases. One way to visualize this method is to consider the flow through a pipeline, as shown in Exhibit 7-7. Purchases enter one end of the pipeline. As new purchases are made, they enter the same end of the pipeline, pushing the first purchases further into the pipe. Goods that get sold come out the other end of the pipeline.

Therefore, the ones that get sold first are also the ones that entered the pipeline first. The goods still left in the pipeline at the end of the period are the ending inventory. While the acronym FIFO is appropriate for this method, it refers to what happens to the cost of goods sold, not to the ending inventory. A more accurate acronym for ending inventory is **LISH**, for **last-in**, **still-here**.

FIFO VISUALIZATION

EXHIBIT 7-7

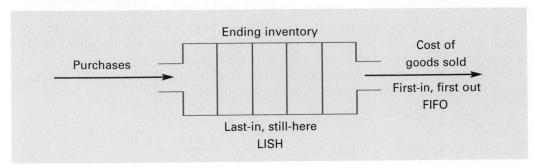

Each time inventory is sold, we need to determine the cost of the inventory sold and reduce the inventory account by that amount. Using the Rhoda's Appliances data (Exhibit 7-6) and the FIFO assumption, we can assign a cost to the cost of goods sold and ending inventory as follows:

First Sale, January 15
Cost of goods sold (16 units)

6	units @ $450 (beginning inventory)		$2,700
+10	units @ $475 (first purchase)		4,750
16	units		$7,450

Ending inventory (5 units)

5	units @ $475 (first purchase)		$2,375

Second Sale, January 25
Cost of goods sold (10 units)

5	units @ $475 (left over from first sale)		$2,375
+ 5	units @ $480 (second purchase)		2,400
10	units		$4,775

Ending inventory (7 units)

7	units @ $480 (second purchase)		$3,360

Total cost of goods sold for the period = $7,450 + $4,775 = $12,225
Ending inventory at the end of the period = $3,360

Note that the sum of the units in cost of goods sold (16 + 10) and ending inventory (7) equals the 33 units in goods available for sale. The sum of the dollar amounts ($12,225 + $3,360) equals the dollar amount of the goods available for sale, $15,585. As inventory is sold, the cost of goods sold is calculated using the earliest inventory purchases. As those items are used to determine a cost for the inventory sold, we move forward to the next inventory that has been purchased. The perpetual system provides management with a timely flow of information about what has been sold and what remains in inventory. An actual physical count of the inventory will still be required. If the physical count does not agree with the accounting records as to what should be in ending inventory, the records will need to be adjusted to reflect the actual number of units.

FIFO describes quite accurately the physical flow of goods in most businesses. For example, in grocery stores, new items are put behind old items on the shelf. Because customers usually select the item at the front of the shelf, the older items are sold first. If the grocery store did not rotate inventory in this way, some items would sit on the shelf for months, risking spoilage.

Under IFRS, the matching of costs to physical units does not depend on the physical flow of goods. IFRS attempts to provide the best measure of periodic net income, which is not necessarily achieved by choosing a cost flow assumption that matches the physical flow of the goods. Under FIFO, the costs assigned to the cost of goods sold are the costs from beginning inventory and from earlier purchases. The costs assigned to ending inventory are the most recent purchase costs.

Moving Average

The **moving average** method, the second most commonly used method in Canada, calculates an average cost each time there is a new purchase of inventory. When items are sold, the calculated average cost is used to assign a cost to both the units that are sold and those that remain in ending inventory. Exhibit 7-8 illustrates this method. Imagine inventory as a liquid stored in a tank, such as gasoline at a service station. Purchases of new gasoline are dumped into the tank and mixed with beginning inventory and previous purchases. Inventory that is sold is therefore a mixture of beginning inventory and recent purchases.

In the moving average method, the average cost is calculated by taking the total cost of the goods available for sale **after each purchase** and dividing it by the number of units available for sale at that time to produce an average cost per unit. This unit cost is then assigned to all the units sold until there is another purchase. Using Rhoda's Appliances (Exhibit 7-6) and the moving average assumption, let's work through the assignment of costs for each sale.

EXHIBIT 7-8

MOVING AVERAGE VISUALIZATION

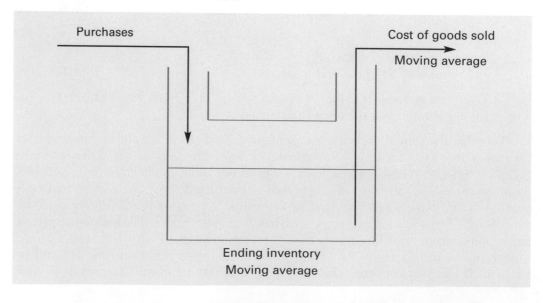

Calculation of first average cost after the first purchase:

Jan. 10	6	units @ $450 (beginning inventory)	$2,700
	+15	units @ $475 (first purchase)	7,125
	21	units	$9,825

First average cost = $9,825 ÷ 21 = $467.857

First Sale, January 15 (16 units)
    Cost of goods sold = 16 × $467.875 = $7,485.71
    Remaining inventory (5 units) = $9,825 − $7,485.71 = $2,339.29

Calculation of second average cost after the second purchase:

Jan. 20	5	units (left over from first purchase)	$2,339.29
	+12	units @ $480 (second purchase)	5,760.00
	17	units	$8,099.29

Second average cost = $8,099.29 ÷ 17 = $476.429

Second Sale, January 25 (10 units)
    Cost of goods sold = 10 × $476.429 = $4,764.29
    Remaining inventory (7 units) = $8,099.29 − $4,764.29 = $3,335.00

Total cost of goods sold for the period = $7,485.71 + $4,764.29 = $12,250.00
Ending inventory at the end of the period = $3,335.00

Note that the average method produces different results on the statement of earnings and statement of financial position than FIFO does. Because it produces a lower pre-tax income than FIFO when prices are rising, many companies in Canada choose it for tax purposes. They like the higher net income produced by FIFO for reporting to their shareholders and so will maintain two sets of inventory records. This is acceptable practice. The recent increase in the use of the average method for reporting purposes indicates that many companies are choosing to maintain only one set of inventory records.

Cost Flow Assumption Choice

The two cost flow assumptions we have discussed are in accordance with IFRS. Given free choice, which method should Rhoda's Appliances use to represent the operating results for the period? This depends on the fundamental objectives of management. Examine Exhibit 7-9 to see the different financial statement effects of each of the two assumptions.

The owner of Rhoda's Appliances would probably like to use moving average because it produces the smaller amount of profit and would therefore result in the smallest amount of tax liability.

Managers in Rhoda's Appliances may, however, be more interested in getting a bonus to increase their own compensation. If Rhoda's managers calculate their bonuses based on reported net earnings, they would be more likely to choose FIFO, which produces the highest amount of net earnings when prices are rising. Managers may also be tempted to use FIFO if the company has a loan agreement with a lender that requires it to maintain a specified current ratio (current assets/current liabilities) and the company is in danger of not meeting the required ratio test. When prices are rising, first-in, first-out produces the highest value of inventory that goes into the numerator of the current ratio.

EXHIBIT 7-9

FINANCIAL STATEMENT RESULTS

	Cost flow assumption	
Statement of earnings	FIFO	Moving average
Sales revenue	$19,100	$19,100
Cost of goods sold	12,225	12,250
Gross profit	$ 6,875	$ 6,850
Statement of financial position		
Inventory	$ 3,360	$ 3,335

HELPFUL HINT

Note that the difference between the higher gross profit, $6,875, and the lower gross profit, $6,850, is only $25. Remember that this is only on a few items within one specific inventory type. A company like Rhoda's Appliances would have many different kinds of refrigerators, as well as other appliances such as dishwashers, dryers, and stoves. The combination of these items probably would produce a much more dynamic difference in the gross profit.

Political sensitivity may also influence the cost flow assumption decision. Suppose the company is in the oil and gas industry, and recent disruptions in world oil markets have caused the price of oil to rise significantly. Consumer advocates have been accusing the industry of profiting from this situation by raising prices beyond what is required by the change in world prices. They advocate an excess profits tax on the industry. In this situation, the company may want to avoid reporting income at any higher level than is necessary. Moving average may be the best choice to minimize the income effects of these changing prices.

EARNINGS MANAGEMENT

Earlier in the book, we discussed the deliberate choice by management of accounting methods that will achieve specific reporting results — earnings management. The previous discussion about what methods companies should choose illustrates a situation where earnings management could be effectively used. However, the results of one method over another only achieve a desired amount if prices continue to rise or fall. If they do not move consistently in one direction, the financial statements will show the opposite impact to what may have been wanted. Because comparability is an important underlying characteristic of accounting, management cannot switch methods if prices start to move in the opposite direction. Earnings management, therefore, does not always produce the desired results.

INTERNATIONAL PERSPECTIVES

Reports from Other Countries

The predominant practice around the world with regard to cost flow assumptions is to assume either FIFO or moving average (also known as weighted average). Some countries, like the United States, use a third method, called last-in, first-out (LIFO). In this costing method, the cost of goods sold is assigned costs from the most recent purchases. As countries move to adopt IFRS, the use of LIFO will decrease.

The choice of cost flow assumption depends on the nature of the inventory, but the same assumption does not have to apply to all inventories held by a company. For example, note the multiple inventory methods used by **Suncor Energy Inc.** in Exhibit 7-10.

SUNCOR ENERGY INC. 2009 ANNUAL REPORT
Excerpted from the Notes to the Statements, Summary of significant accounting policies

EXHIBIT 7-10

(h) *Inventories*

Inventories of crude oil and refined products, other than inventories held for trading purposes, are valued at the lower of cost (using the first-in, first-out (FIFO) method) and net realizable value. Costs include direct and indirect expenditures incurred in bringing an item or product to its existing condition and location. Materials and supplies are valued at the lower of average cost and net realizable value.

Inventories held for trading purposes in the company's energy supply and trading operations are carried at fair value less costs to sell and any changes in fair value are recognized as gains or losses within Energy Supply and Trading Activities revenue in the Consolidated Statements of Earnings.

INVENTORY ISSUES FOR MANAGEMENT

In a company that sells inventory as part of its business, effective management of the inventory is critical to the company's success. One of the issues facing management is the safekeeping of the inventory. Like the management of cash, it is important to have internal control procedures to ensure that the inventory is not lost or stolen, that it is in the right place at the right time, that it does not spoil or get damaged prior to sale, and that it does not become obsolete. Some inventory is easily identifiable (for example, large equipment), but many kinds of inventory are like cash in that one item looks identical to another. Some companies put electronic markers on the inventory that must be removed when the item is purchased or an alarm will sound when the item leaves the premises. The RFID tags mentioned earlier not only identify the inventory but also tell you where it is.

Companies must also safeguard their inventory from theft by their employees. This involves some of the physical methods already mentioned and also accounting system safeguards. The person who orders the inventory is not the one who checks the inventory against the purchase order when it arrives. A third person enters the information about the arrival of the inventory in the accounting system. This division of duties prevents employees from ordering inventory, having it delivered somewhere else, and then recording it in the system as having been received.

Another issue facing management is the cost of inventory storage. As the cost of real estate rises, it becomes expensive to have large warehouses full of inventory. The longer an item is stored, the higher the costs will be and the greater the probability that it will become obsolete, damaged, or misplaced. Management needs to develop ordering and delivery strategies that will enable inventory to be sold as quickly as possible after it has been delivered. The shorter the storage time, the lower the cost. Some companies have moved to "just-in-time" (JIT) delivery strategies where the inventory is delivered as the customer is ready to buy it. In order to facilitate a "just-in-time" system, the company

Describe management's responsibility for internal control measures related to inventory.

needs to have contractual agreements with its suppliers to deliver on demand. Wal-Mart has one of the most efficient inventory delivery systems. It makes very high demands on its suppliers with respect to quality, supply, price, and delivery time. Suppliers who do not meet its demands are replaced with other suppliers.

Auditors also play an important role with respect to inventory management. The auditors review the company's internal control systems to ensure that safeguards are in place to physically protect and record and report inventory. During the annual audit, the auditors are present when the inventory is counted so that they can verify the amount and valuation of the inventory on hand for the financial statements. Over the years, there have been many stories about internal attempts to fool auditors. For example, one of the most famous inventory scandals involved salad oil and the Allied Crude Vegetable Oil company. The owner of the company had huge petroleum tanks that he claimed were full of salad oil. He borrowed money based on the value of the oil in the tanks. The claims were supported by warehouse delivery receipts. The tanks were in fact mostly full of salt water but had enough salad oil floating on top that inspectors assumed the whole tank was full of salad oil. Even when the tanks were checked by inserting poles into the tanks to measure the depth of the oil, the oil on the top of the water coated the poles as they passed through to the bottom of the tank, thus validating the amount of oil claimed. The fraud was eventually discovered and the owner went to prison for seven years. From experiences such as this, auditors have learned that what it says on the outside of boxes or tanks may not describe what is actually inside.

INVENTORY ESTIMATION

LEARNING OBJECTIVE 8

Estimate a value for ending inventory using the cost-to-sales ratio method.

There are several occasions when a company needs to know the cost of goods sold or inventory value but either chooses not to count inventory (since it would be too costly to close the business to do so) or, simply cannot count it (it has been stolen or destroyed). In these cases, the company may attempt to estimate the cost of goods sold amount in order to prepare monthly income statements. It may need to estimate the amount and value of inventory for insurance purposes if the inventory is destroyed or stolen. As mentioned earlier, under the periodic system it is difficult to determine inventory shrinkage. Companies will often estimate the inventory before they start the annual physical inventory count so that they can determine if shrinkage has occurred.

Using the Cost-to-Sales Ratio

One way to estimate the cost of goods sold is to multiply the sales revenue for the period (a figure that is readily available) by the normal cost-to-sales ratio. The normal cost-to-sales ratio reflects the normal markup that the company applies to its products. For example, a company that normally marks up its products by 50% would price an item that costs $60 at $90. The cost-to-sales ratio then is 67% ($60/$90). If the sales for a given month are $12,000, the estimated cost of goods sold is $8,040 (67% × $12,000).

This cost-to-sales ratio can be used to estimate ending inventory as well. The company would be able to determine the cost of the goods available for sale by referring to the accounting records and finding the beginning inventory and the purchases for the period. For example, if the beginning inventory is $2,000 and the purchases for the period were $9,000, the goods available for sale would be $11,000.

Beginning inventory	$ 2,000
Purchases	9,000
Goods available for sale	$11,000
Cost of goods sold (above calculation)	8,040
Ending inventory	$ 2,960

If we use the cost-to-sales ratio and the sales amount from the previous paragraph, we can determine that the cost of goods sold is $8,040 for the period. Because we know that goods available for sale must equal cost of goods sold plus ending inventory, all we need to do is subtract the calculated cost of goods sold ($8,040) from the goods available for sale ($11,000) to find the cost of ending inventory ($2,960). This method is often referred to as the **gross margin estimation method**.

STATEMENT ANALYSIS CONSIDERATIONS

Because of the diversity of cost flow assumptions that companies can make and the significant differences that these assumptions can cause in the financial statements, adjustments must be made when inventory ratios are compared across companies. Cross-industry analyses are most affected by cost flow assumptions. Analyses of the same company over time are not affected as much, as long as the inventory method has been consistently applied (the company used FIFO or moving average all the time). Changes in the cost flow assumption over time make time series analyses difficult. When using the inventory or cost of goods sold amounts in ratio analysis, keep these points in mind as you evaluate your results.

LEARNING OBJECTIVE 9

Calculate the inventory turnover ratio and explain how it can be interpreted by users.

Inventory Turnover

The one ratio that looks exclusively at inventory is the **inventory turnover** ratio. This ratio tells the user how fast inventory is sold or how long it is held before it is sold. It is calculated as follows:

$$\text{Inventory turnover} = \frac{\text{Cost of goods sold}}{\text{Average inventory}}$$

The numerator contains the cost of goods sold, which measures the costs assigned to all the items of inventory that were sold. The denominator contains the average inventory. Average inventory is used, where possible, rather than ending inventory because it represents a more appropriate measure of inventory levels if the inventory level has changed over the year. Average inventory is the beginning inventory plus the ending inventory in a year, divided by two. Inventory turnover for **H&M** for 2009 was:

$$\frac{\text{SEK 38,919}}{\dfrac{(\text{SEK 10,240} + \text{SEK 8,500})}{2}} = 4.15$$

H&M

If the turnover is 4.15, it takes H&M about 88 days to sell an average-sized batch of inventory. The 88 days is calculated by dividing the number of days in a year (365) by the inventory turnover. This will tell you approximately how many days inventory is held before it is sold. For H&M, the number of days that inventory was held in 2009 was

$$365 \text{ days} \div 4.15 = 88 \text{ days}$$

In order to determine whether a turnover of 4.15 is reasonable for H&M, you would need to calculate the ratio for previous years so that you could see if it was changing. You should also compare H&M's ratio with those of other companies in the same industry to see how it compares with its competitors. A look at the 2008 inventory turnover shows that turnover was virtually the same in 2008. Because H&M sells clothing, selling the inventory approximately every three months is reasonable because it will be bringing in new clothing each time the season changes.

$$\frac{\text{SEK } 34{,}064}{\dfrac{(\text{SEK } 8{,}500 + \text{SEK } 7{,}969)}{2}} = 4.14$$

$$365 \div 4.14 = 88 \text{ days}$$

Other Ratios

Other ratios are affected by the use of FIFO versus moving average if they contain inventory figures or the cost of goods sold. Because these two costing assumptions reflect costs in similar time frames, there will not be dramatic differences. If costs are rising, the choice of moving average can cause statement of financial position ratios to be lower than they would be with FIFO.

S U M M A R Y

This chapter discussed inventory—a current asset that is vital to a company's health—and its related expense—the cost of goods sold. Because of the many kinds of inventory, managing all aspects of inventory is a very complex task. Managers need to order the right kind and amount of inventory, price it competitively (but high enough to ensure that the company makes a profit), and safeguard it so that it cannot be stolen. Over time, accountants have developed two major systems for accounting for inventory: the perpetual system, which keeps a continuous record of the inventory on hand, and the periodic system, which records the purchase of inventory but does not cost the amount that has been sold until the end of an accounting period. Within these two systems, three methods are currently used under IFRS for assigning costs to inventory: specific identification, FIFO, and the average method. When unit costs are changing, each of these methods results in a different cost for ending inventory and cost of goods sold. Users need to be aware of how these methods are used so that they can factor their effect into any ratio analysis that they perform. Because counting inventory to determine the amount on hand is a costly endeavour, accountants have developed methods for estimating inventory. Estimates are used for interim reports, for determining inventory values when it has been stolen or destroyed, and for establishing a pre-count value against which management is able to compare the actual physical inventory count. In this chapter, we described the cost-to-sales ratio method for estimating inventory. We finished the chapter by discussing the inventory turnover ratio, a ratio that helps users evaluate the management of inventory.

At this point, all the major current asset accounts have been covered, and attention turns next to the non-current assets, which have longer lives than current assets. The benefits from these assets become evident over much longer time periods than those of current assets. The next chapter considers the most common non-current asset accounts, capital assets, with an emphasis on property, plant, and equipment.

PRACTICE PROBLEM 1

The following information relates to the merchandise inventory of Aspen Corporation for the month of October:

		Units	Cost
October 1	Beginning inventory	3,500	$70,000
October 3	Purchased	4,200	$88,200
October 7	Sold	2,600	
October 15	Sold	1,900	
October 23	Purchased	2,050	$45,100
October 29	Sold	3,300	
October 31	Purchased	1,750	$35,875

Required:

Calculate the cost of goods sold and ending inventory as at October 31 using a perpetual inventory system and the following cost flow assumptions:

a. FIFO

b. Moving average

WILEY PLUS
www.wileyplus.com

Additional Practice Problems

STRATEGIES FOR SUCCESS:

▶ The easiest way to start is to create a table with the dates, purchases, and sales listed chronologically. Once you have the table constructed, calculate the unit cost of the beginning inventory and the various purchases. To complete the requirements for FIFO, you will need the unit costs. Determine the following amounts: total units available for sale, total units sold, total units in ending inventory, and total cost of goods available for sale. These amounts will make solving of the problem easier and provide you with benchmarks that will tell you if you are on the right track.

▶ To calculate FIFO amounts, start at the top of your spreadsheet and work downward, using up the values for beginning inventory first and then moving on to the various purchases. For moving average, move to your first purchase and calculate an average cost of inventory using that purchase plus the amounts in beginning inventory. Use this cost to determine cost of goods sold for your first sale. When you have calculated the total cost of goods sold and determined ending inventory for each costing method, do a quick check by adding the cost of goods sold to the ending inventory amount. It should equal the goods available for sale.

practice problems

PRACTICE PROBLEM 2

The balance sheets and income statements from the 2009 annual report of **High Liner Foods Incorporated** are shown in Exhibit 6-14. Further inventory data is provided in Note 2b shown in Exhibit 7-11. High Liner Foods is a Canadian company that processes and sells seafood products to major grocery store outlets, restaurants, and institutions in North America.

a. In 2009, High Liner Food's net income increased from $14,192 thousand in 2008 to $19,747 thousand. Based solely on the sale of inventory, can you suggest reasons why the net income increased in 2009?

b. Calculate the inventory turnover for High Liner Foods for 2009. Provide a brief discussion of what this ratio means.

c. Calculate the current ratio for High Liner Foods for 2009 and 2008. How important is the inventory value in this ratio?

STRATEGIES FOR SUCCESS:

▶ Think about the relationship between inventory valuation and net income. For a company that sells goods, inventory is vital to its health. As you work through what is required, note how large the inventory is on the balance sheet relative to other assets and how large the sales and cost of goods sold are on the statement of income. Managing inventory efficiently and effectively is critical to a company's success.

▶ Note as well the limited amount of information that a user can get about an important item like inventory.

SUGGESTED SOLUTION TO PRACTICE PROBLEM 1

Basic table:

Date		Units	Cost	Unit Cost
October 1	Beginning inventory	3,500	$70,000	$20.00
October 3	First purchase	4,200	$88,200	$21.00
October 7	First sale	2,600		
October 15	Second sale	1,900		
October 23	Second purchase	2,050	$45,100	$22.00
October 29	Third sale	3,300		
October 31	Third purchase	1,750	$35,875	$20.50

Total units available for sale: 3,500 + 4,200 + 2,050 + 1,750 = 11,500
Total units sold: 2,600 + 1,900 + 3,300 = 7,800
Total units in ending inventory: 11,500 − 7,800 = 3,700
Total cost of goods available for sale: $70,000 + $88,200 + $45,100 + $35,875 = $239,175

a. FIFO
   First Sale, October 7:
   Cost of goods sold (2,600 units)
   2,600 units @ $20.00 (Beginning inventory) $52,000

   Remaining inventory (5,100 units)
     900 units @ $20.00 (Beginning inventory) $18,000
   4,200 units @ $21.00 (First purchase)   88,200
   5,100 units $106,200

HIGH LINER FOODS INCORPORATED 2009 ANNUAL REPORT

Notes to consolidated financial statements

2B) INVENTORIES, COST OF SALES AND DEPRECIATION

The entire amount of the inventory is pledged as security for the Company's short-term bank loans.

INVENTORIES

(in $000s)	January 2, 2010	January 3, 2009
Finished goods – procured	$ 51,156	$ 63,260
Finished goods – manufactured	33,094	24,151
Raw and semi-finished material	22,719	39,557
Supplies, repair parts and other	6,309	8,845
Inventory in transit, paid in advance	6,308	11,050
	$ 119,586	$ 146,863

COST OF SALES AND DEPRECIATION

(in $000s)	Fiscal 2009	Fiscal 2008
Cost of inventories recognized as an expense		
At Cost	$ 492,044	$ 483,911
Reserved inventory disposed	(582)	(2,039)
New inventory reserves created	1,102	582
Cost of sales	$ 492,564	$ 482,454

The value of inventory subject to a reserve was $3.6 million ($3.7 million in 2008).

Depreciation included in:		
Cost of sales	$ 4,785	$ 4,612
Distribution expense	348	353
Selling, general and administrative expense	1,477	1,504
	$ 6,610	$ 6,469

Second Sale, October 15:

Cost of goods sold (1,900 units)

900 units @ $20.00 (Beginning inventory)	$18,000	
1,000 units @ $21.00 (First purchase)	21,000	
1,900 units		$ 39,000

Remaining inventory (3,200 units)

3,200 units @ $21.00 (First purchase)	$67,200	

Third Sale, October 29:

Cost of goods sold (3,300 units)

3,200 units @ $21.00 (First purchase)	$67,200	
100 units @ $22.00 (Second purchase)	2,200	
3,300 units		$ 69,400

Ending inventory (3,700 units)

1,950 units @ $22.00	$42,900	
1,750 units @ $20.50 (Third purchase)	35,875	
3,700 units		$ 78,775

Cost of goods sold: $52,000 + $39,000 + $69,400 = $160,400

Ending inventory: $78,775

COGS + Ending inventory = $160,400 + 78,775 = $239,175 = Goods available for sale

b. Moving average

Calculation of first average cost after the first purchase:

October 1	3,500 units @ $20.00 (Beginning inventory)	$ 70,000
October 3	4,200 units @ $21.00 (First purchase)	88,200
	7,700 units	$ 158,200

First average cost = $158,200 ÷ 7,700 = $20.546

First sale, October 7 (2,600 units)

Cost of goods sold = 2,600 × $20.546 = $53,419.60

Remaining inventory = $158,200 − $53,419.60 = $104,780.40

Second sale, October 15 (1,900 units)

Cost of goods sold = 1,900 × $20.546 = $39,037.40

Remaining inventory = $104,780.40 − $39,037.40 = $65,743.00

Calculation of second average cost after the second purchase:

October 15	3,200 units (Remaining inventory)	$ 65,743.00
	2,050 units @ $22.00 (Second purchase)	45,100.00
	5,250 units	$110,843.00

Second average cost = $110,843 ÷ 5,250 = $21.113

Third sale, October 29 (3,300 units)

Cost of goods sold = 3,300 × $21.113 = $69,672.90

Remaining inventory = $110,843.00 − $69,672.90 = $41,170.10

Calculation of third average cost after the third purchase:

October 29	1,950 units (Remaining inventory)	$ 41,170.10
	1,750 units @ $20.50 (Third purchase)	35,875.00
	3,700 units	$ 77,045.10

Third average cost = $77,045.10 ÷ 3,700 = $20.823

Cost of goods sold: $53,419.60 + $39,037.40 + $69,672.90 = $162,129.90

Ending inventory: $77,045.10

COGS + Ending inventory = $162,129.10 + 77,045.90 = $239,175 = Goods available for sale

SUGGESTED SOLUTION TO PRACTICE PROBLEM 2

All figures in the solution are in thousands.

a. In 2008, the gross margin on sales of $615,993 was $96,542, or 15.7%. In 2009, the gross margin on $627,186 of sales was $102,270, or 16.3%. Note that the sales increased and the gross margin percentage also increased. The increase in the margin from 15.7% to 16.3% makes it easier for High Liner Foods to cover all of its other costs. The company also increased its net income from the previous year by almost 40% (($19,747 − 14,192) ÷ $14,192). High Liner Foods processes and sells seafood products. Because of the decline in the seafood industry, the company faces increasing challenges in getting enough products to process. The fact that it has increased its profits over the previous year indicates that it is effectively controlling its costs.

b. $$\frac{\$492,564}{\frac{(\$119,586 + \$146,863)}{2}} = 3.70$$

365 ÷ 3.7 = 98.6 days

High Liner Foods' inventory turnover is 3.7. It takes about 98.6 days (just over 3 months) for it to process and sell its inventory. Since High Liner Foods freezes most of the seafood that it processes, it can hold the inventory for several months without selling it. Without additional information about High Liner Foods' activities in previous years or about its competitors, it is not possible to comment further on this ratio.

c. Current ratio (2009) = $\dfrac{\$188,250}{\$83,137}$ = 2.27

   Current ratio (2008) = $\dfrac{\$221,128}{\$116,443}$ = 1.90

The current ratio has improved from 2008 to 2009 and is above 2.0, which indicates that the company has sufficient current assets to pay for the current liabilities when they come due. Inventory represents approximately 64% of the current assets in 2009 and approximately 66% in 2008. This means that it has a significant impact on this ratio, and more so in 2008. Without the inventory, the ratio in 2009 would be close to 1.0. The company could experience some difficulty meeting its current liabilities without selling inventory.

APPENDIX

Cost Flow Assumptions Under the Periodic Inventory System

Under the periodic inventory system, all three methods of costing inventory (specific identification, FIFO, and average cost) can be used. Specific identification is determined in the same way under both the periodic and the perpetual system. Because, under the periodic system, the cost of goods sold amount is not determined each time inventory is sold, nor is the inventory account adjusted for the inventory sold, the calculation of cost of goods sold and ending inventory is determined only at the end of the accounting period.

To illustrate FIFO and average cost (called weighted average under the periodic system), we are going to use the same example of Rhoda's Appliances that we used to illustrate the costing assumptions for the perpetual system earlier in the chapter. It is repeated here so that we can refer to it easily.

First-in, First-out (FIFO)

Under the periodic system, the cost of goods sold and ending inventory are not determined during an accounting period. Instead, at the end of each accounting period, the number of units left in inventory is determined either by a physical count or by an estimation method. Using this information, costs are then assigned to both the units sold and those remaining in ending inventory.

Using the Rhoda's Appliances data (Exhibit 7-12) and the FIFO assumption, at the end of the accounting period, we can assign a cost to the cost of goods sold and ending inventory as follows:

Cost of goods sold (26 units)		
6	units @ $450 (beginning inventory)	$ 2,700
+15	units @ $475 (first purchase)	7,125
+ 5	units @ $480 (second purchase)	2,400
26	units	$12,225
Ending inventory (7 units)		
7	units @ $480 (second purchase)	$ 3,360

EXHIBIT 7-12

RHODA'S APPLIANCES, INC.
Inventory of Refrigerators

Date		Units	Unit cost	Total
January 1	Beginning inventory	6	$450	$ 2,700
January 10	Purchase #1	15	475	7,125
January 20	Purchase #2	12	480	5,760
Goods available for sale		33		$15,585
Sale record				
		Units	Unit price	Total
January 15	Sale #1	16	$725	$11,600
January 25	Sale #2	10	750	7,500
		26		$19,100

Note how the sum of units in cost of goods sold and ending inventory (26 + 7) equals the 33 units in goods available for sale. The sum of the dollar amounts ($12,225 + $3,360) equals the dollar amount of the goods available for sale ($15,585). If the dollar amount of the ending inventory were to increase, the dollar amount of the cost of goods sold would have to decrease because the sum of the two must add up to the dollar amount of the goods available for sale. Any errors in counting ending inventory or assigning costs will have an immediate impact on the cost of goods sold and, therefore, net income. You will notice that the cost of goods sold amount, $12,225, and the ending inventory amount, $3,360, are the same as they were under the perpetual system. This will always be the case when using the FIFO cost flow assumption. This should make sense to you because we are assigning costs using the oldest costs and flowing forward through the inventory amounts. Remember the items flowing through the pipe in Exhibit 7-7? Although the end value for cost of goods sold and ending inventory are the same under both methods, the ways we determined those amounts were different.

Weighted Average

The name of this cost assumption has changed to the **weighted average** method because we are going to calculate one average cost by combining the number of units at each unit price. Recall in Exhibit 7-8 how new inventory was added to original inventory and mixed together. Inventory that is sold is therefore a mixture of beginning inventory and the purchases during the period.

In Rhoda's Appliances, the average cost is calculated by taking the total cost of the goods available for sale and dividing it by the total number of refrigerators to produce an average cost per unit.

Calculation of average cost:
$15,585 ÷ 33 = $472.273

Calculation of cost of goods sold:
Number of units sold × average cost per unit = 26 × $472.273 = $12,279.10

Calculation of ending inventory:
Goods available for sale − cost of goods sold = $15,585.00 − $12,279.10 = $3,305.90

If you use the average cost to assign a cost to both the cost of goods sold and ending inventory, because of the rounding of the average cost amount, the sum of the two amounts may not add up to the value of the goods available for sale. It is therefore important to calculate either the cost of goods sold or the ending inventory amount and then subtract that amount from the goods available for sale to find the other amount.

Note that because weighted average has a higher cost of goods sold, it produces a lower pre-tax income than FIFO when prices are rising. Therefore, many companies in Canada choose it for tax purposes. They like the higher net income produced by FIFO for reporting purposes and so will maintain two sets of inventory records. This is acceptable practice. The recent increase in the use of the weighted average method for reporting purposes is an indication that many companies are choosing to maintain only one set of inventory records.

Financial Statement Results

Both of the cost flow assumptions we have discussed are in accordance with IFRS. How different are the results under the periodic and perpetual cost assumptions? Examine Exhibit 7-13 to see the different financial statement effects of each of the two assumptions under each method.

The FIFO costing assumption produces the same results under the periodic and perpetual systems. The weighted (moving) average produces slightly different amounts but maintains the same relationship relative to FIFO. Weighted average continues to produce the lower gross profit, higher cost of goods sold, and lower ending inventory number when prices are rising. Using the costing systems through the periodic system provides less precise amounts (calculated at the end of the accounting period rather than after each sale) and less current information for management to use for decision-making. Management also has less inventory control.

FINANCIAL STATEMENT RESULTS

EXHIBIT 7-13

Periodic System

	Cost flow assumption	
Statement of earnings	FIFO	Weighted average
Sales revenue	$19,100	$19,100
Cost of goods sold	12,225	12,279
Gross profit	$ 6,875	$ 6,821
Statement of financial position		
Inventory	$ 3,360	$ 3,306

Perpetual System

	Cost flow assumption	
Statement of earnings	FIFO	Moving average
Sales revenue	$19,100	$19,100
Cost of goods sold	12,225	12,250
Gross profit	$ 6,875	$ 6,850
Statement of financial position		
Inventory	$ 3,360	$ 3,335

ABBREVIATIONS USED

EDI	Electronic data interchange	LIFO	Last-in, first-out
FIFO	First-in, first-out	LISH	Last-in, still-here
JIT	Just in time	NRV	Net realizable value
LCM	Lower of cost and market	RFID	Radio Frequency ID

SYNONYMS

Entry market ▌ Input market ▌ Wholesale market

Exit market ▌ Output market ▌ Retail market

Entry price ▌ Input price ▌ Replacement cost

Exit price ▌ Output price ▌ Net realizable value

Freight in ▌ Transportation in

GLOSSARY

Cost flow assumption   An assumption made as to how the costs of inventory should be assigned to individual units when it is impossible or impractical to assign costs specifically to units.

Current gross margin   The difference between the current selling price of a unit of inventory and its current replacement cost.

Electronic data interchange (EDI)   A link between two companies with computers allowing inventory to be ordered directly over the computer connection.

Entry market   The market from which goods or materials enter the company; sometimes also referred to as the input or wholesale market.

Exit market   The market in which goods exit the company; sometimes also referred to as the output or retail market.

First-in, first-out (FIFO)   The cost flow assumption that assigns the cost of the first unit into the inventory to the first unit sold.

Freight in   The transportation cost paid when inventory is acquired.

Going-concern assumption   An assumption that the company for which the financial statements are being prepared will continue to exist into the foreseeable future.

Goods available for sale   The units of inventory available to be sold during the period. These units include those available from the beginning inventory plus those produced or purchased during the current period.

Gross margin estimation method   A method for estimating the cost of ending inventory by converting the sales amount to cost of goods sold using the gross margin ratio. The calculated cost of goods sold amount is subtracted from the goods available for sale to determine the ending inventory cost.

Input market   Another name for entry market.

Inventory shrinkage   The losses of inventory due to spoilage, damage, theft, waste, etc.

Inventory turnover   A ratio that measures how fast inventory is sold and how long it is held before it is sold.

Laid-down cost   The inventory costs including invoice cost plus customs, tariff and excise duties, and transportation. Although transportation in, or freight in, should be included in the laid-down cost, it is often treated as a period cost because it is impractical to allocate it to inventory items. In a manufacturing company, the laid-down cost comprises direct materials, direct labour, and overhead.

Last-in, first-out (LIFO)   The cost flow assumption that assigns the cost of the last unit purchased by the company to the first unit sold.

Last-in, still-here (LISH)   The ending inventory units using the FIFO cost flow assumption.

Market   Net realizable value, net realizable value less a profit margin, or replacement cost.

Moving average   A method of assigning costs to units of inventory in which a new average cost is calculated each time new inventory is purchased. This average cost is assigned to sales that occur after the purchase but before the next purchase. It is used under the perpetual inventory system.

Net realizable value (NRV)   A selling price of a unit of inventory less any costs necessary to complete and sell the unit.

Output market   Another name for exit market.

Periodic inventory system   An inventory system in which cost of goods sold is determined by counting ending inventory, assigning costs to these units, and then subtracting the ending inventory value from the sum of the beginning inventory plus purchases for the period.

Perpetual inventory system   An inventory system in which the cost of goods sold is determined at the time a unit is sold.

Replacement cost   The current price at which a unit of inventory can be replaced by the company.

Retail market   Another term for exit market.

Specific identification method   A method of assigning costs to units of inventory in which the cost of a unit can be specifically identified from company records.

Stockout   A situation arising when a company sells all of a specific item of inventory and has no more available (in stock).

Transportation in   A synonym for freight in.

Weighted average   A method of assigning costs to units of inventory in which each unit is assigned the average cost of the units available for sale during the period. This method is used under the periodic inventory system.

Wholesale market   Another term for entry market.

ASSIGNMENT MATERIAL

Assessing Your Recall

7-1   Describe the inventory valuation methods allowed under IFRS.

7-2   Describe how the lower of cost and net realizable standard is applied to inventory under IFRS.

7-3   Define replacement cost and net realizable value, and explain the difference between them.

7-4   Describe the basic differences between the periodic and perpetual inventory systems.

7-5   Discuss the advantages and disadvantages of the periodic inventory system compared with the perpetual inventory system.

7-6   Describe the two cost flow assumptions that are used for determining the value of ending inventory and cost of goods sold.

7-7   Discuss a company's incentives for choosing one cost flow assumption over another. Be sure to include a discussion of the choice from both a reporting and a tax perspective.

7-8   How important is the choice of a cost flow assumption for a company that turns over its inventory rapidly? Explain.

7-9   Under what circumstances would a company want or need to estimate the cost of goods sold or ending inventory?

7-10   Describe the effects the choice of moving average or FIFO may have on the inventory turnover ratio and the current ratio in times of rising prices.

Applying Your Knowledge

7-11 (Inventory valuation decision)

From the opening story, describe the inventory system that Veseys uses. Why is this system appropriate for Veseys? What decisions can Veseys' management make that would not be possible if they had chosen a different inventory system?

7-12 (Calculation of ending inventory, cost of goods sold, and gross margin—perpetual system)

The Soft Touch Company sells leather furniture. The following schedule relates to the company's inventory for the month of April:

				Cost	Sales
April 1	Beginning inventory	75 units		$45,000	
3	Purchase	50 units		31,250	
5	Sale	30 units			$33,000
11	Purchase	25 units		16,250	
15	Sale	55 units			68,750
22	Sale	40 units			48,000
28	Purchase	50 units		33,750	

Soft Touch uses the perpetual inventory system.

Required:

a. Calculate the cost of goods sold and ending inventory under each of the following costing assumptions:
   1. FIFO
   2. Moving average

b. Determine the gross margin under each of the costing assumptions calculated in part "a." Which of the costing assumptions produced the higher gross margin?

7-13 (Calculation of ending inventory, cost of goods sold, and gross margin—periodic system)

If your instructor has assigned the Appendix to this chapter, redo Problem 7-12 assuming that the company uses the periodic inventory system.

7-14 (Calculation of ending inventory and cost of goods sold—perpetual system)

At the beginning of its operations in October 2011, Mastiff Supplies Ltd. began with 8,500 units of inventory that it purchased at a cost of $8.00 each. The company's purchases during October were as follows:

October 5	4,500 units @ $8.00
13	1,500 units @ $7.80
22	7,200 units @ $8.10
29	3,600 units @ $8.30
	17,300 units

Sales during October:

October 3	3,500 units
16	7,800 units
26	8,200 units

Mastiff Supplies uses a perpetual inventory system.

Required:

a. Calculate the cost of goods sold for October using the moving average cost flow assumption.

b. Calculate the cost of goods sold for October using the first-in, first-out cost flow assumption.

c. Which inventory cost flow assumption results in the greater net income for October? Which results in the smaller?

d. Which inventory cost flow assumption results in the larger inventory balance at the end of October? Which results in the smaller?

e. Compare your answers in parts "c" and "d" above and comment on the relationship between these items.

7-15 (Calculation of ending inventory and cost of goods sold—periodic system)

If your instructor has assigned the Appendix to this chapter, redo Problem 7-14 assuming that the company uses a periodic inventory system.

7-16 (Calculation of ending inventory and cost of goods sold—perpetual system)

During the month of March, Glassworks Ltd. had the following information about its inventory available:

		Units	Amount
March 1	Beginning inventory	5,000	$60,000
4	Purchase	3,000	36,300
8	Sale	4,000	
14	Sale	3,000	
22	Purchase	4,000	49,000
28	Sale	3,500	

Required:

a. Assuming Glassworks uses the perpetual inventory system, calculate the cost of goods sold and ending inventory for March under each of the following cost flow assumptions:

i. FIFO

ii. Moving average

b. Which of the cost flow assumptions would produce the higher net income?

7-17 (Calculation of ending inventory and cost of goods sold—periodic system)

If your instructor has assigned the Appendix to this chapter, redo Problem 7-16 assuming that the company uses a periodic inventory system.

7-18 (Calculation of ending inventory and cost of goods sold)

Exquisite Jewellers purchases chiming clocks from around the world for sale in Canada. According to its records, Exquisite Jewellers had the following purchases and sales of clocks in the current year:

Clock No.	Date Purchased	Amount Paid	Date Sold	Sale Price
423	January 5	$2,150	March 8	$3,800
424	March 15	4,500		
425	May 27	4,400	June 16	6,200
426	July 14	2,400	August 9	3,350
427	October 24	3,720		
428	December 5	1,930	December 24	2,640

Exquisite Jewellers has used the average cost method to calculate its cost of goods sold and inventory balances, but is thinking of changing to specific identification. The company calculates an average cost by adding all of the purchases together and dividing by the number of clocks purchased.

Required:

a. Compare the dollar amounts that would be reported as the cost of goods sold and ending inventory under the average cost and specific identification methods.

b. Is average cost an appropriate method to use in this situation? Explain.

c. What conditions generally must exist for specific identification to be used? Explain.

d. Which of the two methods best represents the operating results for Exquisite Jewellers? Explain.

7-19 (Calculation of cost of goods sold and gross profit—perpetual system)

Red Cap Ltd. uses a perpetual inventory system. It recorded the following inventory transactions during 2011:

	Number of Units	Unit Purchase Price	Sale Price
January 1, 2011	40	$7	
January 25	150	$8	
March 6	60	$9	
Sale #1	140		$18
August 7	60	$11	
Sale #2	120		$21

Required:

a. Calculate the cost of goods sold and gross profit for Red Cap Ltd. for 2011 if it uses each of the following cost flow assumptions:
   i. First-in, first-out
   ii. Moving average

b. On the balance sheet, which of the two assumptions provides the more conservative estimate of the carrying value of inventory? Which provides the better estimate of the current cost of replacing the inventory? Explain your answers.

c. Which method provides the more conservative estimate of reported income? Under what circumstances would the opposite be true?

7-20 (Calculation of ending inventory and cost of goods sold—periodic system)

If your instructor has assigned the Appendix to this chapter, redo Problem 7-19 assuming that the company uses a periodic inventory system.

7-21 (Gross margin and the lower of cost and net realizable value)

The Corral Saddle Company's information about merchandise inventories is as follows:

			Ending Inventory	
Year	Purchases	Sales	Cost	Net Realizable Value
2011	$140,000	$115,000	$75,000	$70,000
2012	100,000	175,000	80,000	67,000
2013	155,000	253,000	72,000	80,000
2014	104,000	225,000	31,000	31,000

There was no beginning balance in inventories prior to 2011.

Required:

a. Calculate the gross margin for each year, valuing the ending inventory at acquisition cost. (Hint: Use the following relationship: Beginning inventory + Purchases − Ending inventory = Cost of goods sold.)

b. Calculate the gross margin for each year, valuing the ending inventory at the lower of cost and market value.

c. Compare the gross margin for each year using the two methods, and explain the reason(s) for any differences you observe.

d. Compare the total results (gross margins) over the entire four-year period using the two valuation methods, and explain what you see.

7-22 (Gross margin and the lower of cost and net realizable value)

Lands End Ltd. has been in operation for several years. At the beginning of 2011, there was $412,400 in beginning inventory. The following information about its inventory is available:

			Ending Inventory	
Year	Purchases	Sales	Cost	Net Realizable Value
2011	$2,480,000	$3,470,000	$250,000	$330,000
2012	2,950,000	4,240,000	290,000	280,000
2013	2,110,000	2,940,000	190,000	250,000
2014	2,640,000	3,730,000	250,000	290,000

Required:
a. Calculate the gross margin for each year, valuing the ending inventory at acquisition cost. (Hint: Use the following relationship: Beginning inventory + Purchases − Ending inventory = Cost of goods sold.)
b. Calculate the gross margin for each year, valuing the ending inventory at the lower of cost and market value.
c. Compare the gross margin for each year using the two methods, and explain the reason(s) for any differences you observe.
d. Compare the total results (gross margins) over the entire four-year period using the two valuation methods, and explain what you see.

7-23 (Lower of cost and net realizable value)

Canadian Paper Company (CPC) produces newsprint in its paper mills. At the end of 2011, CPC's chief financial officer noted that the international market price of newsprint had been dropping appreciably. Tonnes of newsprint produced in 2011 at an average cost of $520 per tonne could be sold at the end of December 2012 for only $505 per tonne. CPC has also been working to reduce its production costs, hoping that they can be reduced to $495 per tonne in 2012.

Required:
a. Why is the decline in the market price for newsprint relevant in this type of situation?
b. If CPC has 1,250 tonnes of newsprint on hand on December 31, 2011, at what dollar amount should inventory be reported?
c. What other information would be relevant in determining the year-end reporting amount?
d. Which accounting concepts are relevant in deciding the dollar amount of inventory to be reported? Explain why these concepts are important.

7-24 (Moving average, FIFO, and the lower of cost and market)

Gold Leaf Ltd. began operations in 2011. The following presentation relates to the inventory valuations of the company at the end of the year using different inventory methods.

Date	Moving Average	FIFO	Lower of FIFO Cost and NRV
December 31, 2011	$120,000	$110,000	$105,000
December 31, 2012	235,000	225,000	220,000
December 31, 2013	260,000	245,000	235,000
December 31, 2014	210,000	235,000	235,000

There was no beginning balance of inventory in 2011. The value referred to in the third column is the net realizable value.

Required:
a. For 2010, state whether the prices for purchasing inventory went up or down.
b. For 2014, state whether the prices went up or down.
c. State which of the two inventory methods would show the highest income in each year. (Hint: You will need to calculate the cost of goods sold expense in each year. You can do this by assuming a constant number of purchases in each of the four years under each method. Use the following relationship: Beginning inventory + Purchases − Ending inventory = Cost of goods sold expense.)

d. Which method would show the lowest income for the four years combined? (Hint: You can answer this question much more quickly than part "c." You start on January 1, 2011, with no beginning inventory: what do you end with?)

7-25 (Inventory estimation)

Headstrong Hardware lost most of its inventory in an electrical fire that destroyed the company's warehouse and retail store. Fortunately, the accounting records were backed up on the owner's computer in her home office and could, therefore, be recovered. However, Headstrong uses the periodic inventory system, so without being able to perform a physical count, the company could not determine the amount of inventory that was lost in the fire. In order to process the insurance claim, the insurance company requires Headstrong to prepare a reasonable estimate of the lost inventory.

As Headstrong's accountant, you have been able to gather the following information:
- According to last year's income statement, sales last year were $963,000.
- According to the accounting records, the company's sales during the current year, up to the time of the fire, totalled $678,000.
- According to last year's income statement, the cost of goods sold last year was $597,060.
- According to the accounting records, the company's purchases during the current year, up to the time of the fire, totalled $486,000.
- According to last year's balance sheet, the ending inventory at the end of last year was $88,000.

Required:
Prepare an estimate of the amount of inventory lost in the fire.

7-26 (Inventory estimation)

On April 25, 2011, a flash flood destroyed one of Kane Company's warehouses, destroying all of the inventory inside. The company had inventory at other locations which were not affected by the flood. Fortunately for the company, all of the accounting records were kept in the main office inside a building at a different location. A search through the records revealed the following information:

Purchases up to April 25	$742,500
Cost of inventory on hand January 1	$137,200
Sales up to April 25	$1,028,000
Cost-to-sales ratio for 2011	65%

A count of inventory on hand at the other locations revealed that inventory costed at $121,300 was on hand.

Required:
Determine the cost of the inventory that was destroyed in the flash flood.

7-27 (Inventory estimation)

In the early morning on July 1, 2011, Kiwi Express Company had a major fire. All of the inventory was destroyed. In order to complete the insurance claim, the accountant needed an estimate of the inventory that had been on the premises at the time of the fire. A search through the accounting records (which, luckily, had been kept in another building that was not destroyed by the fire) produced the following information:

2011 cost-to-sales ratio of 58%	
Purchases for the year up to June 30	$1,524,000
Sales for the year up to June 30	$2,333,148
Inventory on hand on January 1, 2011	$416,160

Required:

a. Assuming the 2010 cost-to-sales ratio is appropriate for 2011, calculate how much inventory should have been on hand on June 30, 2011.

b. Assuming the 2011 cost-to-sales ratio was closer to 65%, calculate how much inventory should have been on hand on June 30, 2011.

c. What factors could make the estimate of ending inventory inaccurate?

d. If the company had another site where it had additional inventory that was not destroyed, how would you factor the value of this inventory into your calculation?

7-28 (Ratio analysis and foreign currencies)

Stream Ltd. reported total inventory on January 1 and December 31, 2011, of $180,000 and $150,000, respectively. The cost of goods sold for 2011 was $1,240,000. Stream's nearest competitor reported inventories of $410,000 and $460,000 on January 1 and December 31, 2011, respectively, and reported a cost of goods sold of $2,270,000 for 2008. Total 2011 sales revenues for Stream Ltd. and its competitor were $1,610,000 and $3,365,000, respectively.

Required:

a. Calculate the inventory turnover ratios for the two companies for 2011.

b. Calculate the gross margin percentage (gross margin divided by sales) for the two companies for 2011.

c. On the basis of inventory turnover, which company is moving its inventory faster? Does that mean the inventory is better managed? Explain.

d. On the basis of gross margin percentage, which company is earning a higher profit margin?

e. Which company would you recommend as being better managed? Indicate why.

7-29 (Evaluation of the inventory turnover ratio)

The inventory turnover ratios of Green Grocer, Peaches and Cream (a clothing boutique), and Exotic Cars Ltd. are 18.4, 5.5, and 2.4, respectively.

Required:

a. How is the inventory turnover ratio calculated? What information is provided by this ratio?

b. Is the company with the highest turnover ratio being run the most efficiently? Explain.

c. Evaluate the turnover ratios for the three companies. Are the differences in ratios consistent with what you would expect? Explain.

d. What other ratios would you examine in assessing the companies' operating efficiency?

User Perspective Problems

7-30 (Measurement issues related to ending inventory)

As an auditor, what concerns might you have about the measurement of inventories at year end? If inventory is misstated, what other amounts on the financial statements will be incorrect?

7-31 (Use of ratio analysis during audit procedures)

Auditors typically conduct a preliminary review of a company's financial statements using analytical procedures that include ratio analysis. As an auditor, what ratio(s) would you find useful in auditing amounts related to inventory? Would you be equally concerned if the ratios(s) were unexpectedly high or unexpectedly low? Explain.

7-32 (Ratio analysis and foreign currencies)

Suppose that you are analyzing two competitors, one a Canadian company and the other a company in Europe whose statements are expressed in euros. Discuss whether it is necessary to convert the statements of the European company into Canadian dollars before calculating inventory ratios. Other than the currency used, would you have any concerns with the ratio analysis of inventories for these two competitors?

7-33   (Importance of inventory in loan considerations)

Suppose that you are a loan officer in a financial institution. Describe why you would be interested in the cost of inventory on the balance sheet of a company. Would the selling price of the inventory be of interest to the financial institution? Why? Can you determine the selling price of the inventory from the financial statements? Explain.

7-34   (Decision-making with respect to inventory estimation)

Slick Surf Boards Company reported sales of $595,000 in the first quarter of 2011. Because the company does not keep a running tally of the cost of inventory sold, the controller does not know how much inventory is actually on hand at the end of the quarter. The company, for the first time, is going to prepare quarterly financial reports to issue to its shareholders, but counting the inventory at the end of each quarter is too costly. Therefore, the controller decides to estimate how much inventory is on hand. By looking at the last annual balance sheet, the controller is able to determine that inventory on hand on January 1, 2011, was $88,200, and he knows that an additional $420,000 of inventory was purchased during the first quarter. The company normally earns a 36% gross profit on sales. Based on this information, and using the cost-to-sales method, the controller arrives at what he thinks is a reasonable estimate of the cost of inventory on hand at the end of the first quarter of 2011.

Required:

a. What would you estimate as the cost of Slick Surf Board's inventory on hand at the end of the first quarter of 2011? Explain how you arrived at your estimate.

b. If the controller believes that the gross profit on sales is likely to be closer to 34% in 2011, estimate the cost of Slick Surf Board's inventory on hand at the end of the first quarter of 2011. Comment on the sensitivity of your estimate of the inventory on hand to changes in the gross profit on sales percentage.

c. What other factors might reduce the reliability of using this method to estimate inventory?

d. If the gross margin estimation method works reasonably well for interim estimates of inventory on hand, why not use it at year end as well and avoid altogether the cost of an annual inventory count?

e. Based on your original estimate of Slick Surf Board's inventory at the end of the first quarter, what is your assessment of the company's inventory position? Does the amount seem reasonable? Why might inventory levels change from one quarter to the next?

7-35   (Just-in-time inventory; minimal inventory levels)

Suppose that your company has always used FIFO and that prices have been rising over the years. In order to increase efficiency, you have recommended that the company change its manufacturing process and adopt a just-in-time process, in which the raw materials are purchased just in time for production and goods are produced just in time for sale. The new system will either eliminate or significantly reduce inventory levels.

Required:

a. As you reduce inventory levels during the change to the new policy, what effect will this have on your financial statements?

b. What might be the financial tradeoffs that you should consider in changing your manufacturing process to a just-in-time basis?

c. For a company with just-in-time inventory, what is the impact of the choice of a FIFO or moving average cost flow assumption?

Reading and Interpreting Published Financial Statements

7-36   (The nature of inventory and inventory valuation)

Finning International Inc. is a Canadian company that sells, rents, finances, and provides customer support services (supplies parts and performs maintenance services) for Caterpillar equipment and engines. Caterpillar equipment is used in industries such as mining and forestry, and in large infrastructure projects. The inventory values from the 2009 and 2008 consolidated balance sheets are:

$993,523 thousand (2009) and $1,473,504 thousand (2008).

The cost of sales amounts from the 2009 and 2008 statements of income are:

$3,407,972 thousand (2009) and $4,318,542 thousand (2008).

Refer back to Exhibit 7-4 in this chapter for Note 1(e) on inventory from the summary of significant accounting policies.

**Financial Analysis
Assignments**

Required:
Using the above information, answer the following questions:

a. Calculate the inventory turnover ratios for Finning International Inc. for 2009 and 2008, and comment on any changes. Use the inventory in 2009 and 2008 rather than the average inventory to calculate the ratios.

b. Note 10 to the 2009 financial statements breaks down inventories into three categories: on-hand equipment, parts and supplies, and internal service work in progress. While the revenue on the income statement is broken down into many categories, cost of sales on the income statement is shown as one amount. Explain how this impacts the analysis done in part "a." What other information would you like to be able to obtain from the income statement? How would this help your analysis of the company's inventory management?

c. Note 1(e) in Exhibit 7-4 indicates that Finning uses the specific item basis for on-hand equipment. Explain why this is possible and appropriate.

d. Note 1(e) indicates that Finning uses the average cost basis for the parts and supplies inventory. Why would the specific item basis not be appropriate for this category of inventory?

7-37 (Inventory turnover and valuation)

The 2009 consolidated statement of operations, the asset side of the balance sheet, and the inventory description that is part of Note 1 accompanying the financial statements of **Molson Coors Canada Inc.** are presented in Exhibit 7-14. Molson Coors Canada is a major beer brewing company in Canada. It sells its products mainly in Canada, the United States, and the United Kingdom, but about 9% of its products are sold in other parts of the world. All statement amounts are in millions of U.S. dollars.

Required:
Using the information in these statements, answer the following questions.

a. The asset side of the balance sheet breaks down Molson Coors' inventory into four categories: finished products, those in process, raw materials, and packaging materials. Only the finished products are currently in a state ready for sale. Which categories of inventory do you believe should be used in determining the inventory turnover ratio? Why?

b. In your own words, describe Molson Coors' inventory valuation policies.

c. The excerpt from Note 1 refers to assessing the shelf-life of its products and the creation of a reserve. Describe why the monitoring of the shelf-life is important to Molson Coors. What do you think the purpose of the reserve is?

d. Calculate the inventory turnover ratios for 2009 and 2008 and then convert them into days. Use the inventory values in 2009 and 2008 rather than the average inventory to calculate the ratios. Explain the amounts you selected from the financial statements to use in your calculation, and why.

EXHIBIT 7-14A   **MOLSON COORS CANADA INC. 2009 ANNUAL REPORT**

CONSOLIDATED STATEMENTS OF OPERATIONS
(IN MILLIONS, EXCEPT PER SHARE DATA)

	For the Years Ended		
	December 26, 2009	December 28, 2008	December 30, 2007
Sales	$ 4,426.5	$ 6,651.8	$ 8,319.7
Excise taxes	(1,394.1)	(1,877.5)	(2,129.1)
Net sales	3,032.4	4,774.3	6,190.6
Cost of goods sold	(1,726.9)	(2,840.8)	(3,702.9)
Gross profit	1,305.5	1,933.5	2,487.7
Marketing, general and administrative expenses	(900.8)	(1,333.2)	(1,734.4)
Special items, net	(32.7)	(133.9)	(112.2)
Equity income in MillerCoors	382.0	155.6	—
Operating income	754.0	622.0	641.1
Other (expense) income, net			
Interest expense	(96.6)	(119.1)	(134.9)
Interest income	10.7	17.3	26.6
Debt extinguishment costs	—	(12.4)	(24.5)
Other income (expense), net, includes $46.0 gain in 2009 on related party transaction, see Note 4.	49.4	(8.4)	17.7
Total other expense, net	(36.5)	(122.6)	(115.1)
Income from continuing operations before income taxes	717.5	499.4	526.0
Income tax benefit (expense)	14.7	(96.4)	(1.0)
Income from continuing operations	732.2	403.0	525.0
Loss from discontinued operations, net of tax	(9.0)	(12.1)	(17.7)
Net income	723.2	390.9	507.3
Less: Net income attributable to noncontrolling interests	(2.8)	(12.2)	(15.3)
Net income attributable to Molson Coors Brewing Company	$ 720.4	$ 378.7	$ 492.0
Basic income (loss) per share:			
From continuing operations	$ 3.96	$ 2.14	$ 2.85
From discontinued operations	(0.05)	(0.07)	(0.10)
Basic net income per share	$ 3.91	$ 2.07	$ 2.75
Diluted income (loss) per share:			
From continuing operations	$ 3.92	$ 2.11	$ 2.81
From discontinued operations	(0.05)	(0.07)	(0.10)
Diluted net income per share	$ 3.87	$ 2.04	$ 2.71
Weighted average shares—basic	184.4	182.6	178.7
Weighted average shares—diluted	185.9	185.5	181.4
Amounts attributable to MCBC			
Income from continuing operations, net of tax	$ 729.4	$ 390.8	$ 509.7
Loss from discontinued operations, net of tax	(9.0)	(12.1)	(17.7)
Net income	$ 720.4	$ 378.7	$ 492.0

See notes to consolidated financial statements.

MOLSON COORS CANADA INC. 2009 ANNUAL REPORT

EXHIBIT 7-14B

annual report

CONSOLIDATED BALANCE SHEETS
(IN MILLIONS)

	As of	
	December 26, 2009	December 28, 2008
Assets		
Current assets:		
Cash and cash equivalents	$ 734.2	$ 216.2
Accounts and notes receivable:		
Trade, less allowance for doubtful accounts of $10.1 and $7.9, respectively	513.8	432.9
Affiliates.	52.9	39.6
Current notes receivable and other receivables, less allowance for doubtful accounts of $2.8 and $3.3, respectively	150.5	162.9
Inventories:		
Finished	111.1	89.1
In process	18.3	13.4
Raw materials.	43.6	43.3
Packaging materials	63.2	46.3
Total inventories	236.2	192.1
Maintenance and operating supplies, less allowance for obsolete supplies of $4.1 and $4.6, respectively	17.7	14.8
Other current assets, less allowance for advertising supplies.	47.6	47.1
Discontinued operations	9.9	1.5
Total current assets.	1,762.8	1,107.1
Properties, less accumulated depreciation of $843.4 and $673.5, respectively	1,292.5	1,301.9
Goodwill	1,475.0	1,298.0
Other intangibles, less accumulated amortization of $356.8 and $274.9, respectively	4,534.7	3,923.4
Investment in MillerCoors.	2,613.6	2,418.7
Deferred tax assets.	177.9	75.3
Notes receivable, less allowance for doubtful accounts of $7.3 and $8.1, respectively	48.7	51.8
Other assets	115.9	203.4
Discontinued operations	—	7.0
Total assets.	$12,021.1	$10,386.6

EXHIBIT 7-14C

MOLSON COORS CANADA INC. 2009 ANNUAL REPORT

Excerpt from the Notes to the Statements

Inventories

Inventories are stated at the lower of cost or market. Cost is determined by the first-in, first-out ("FIFO") method. Prior to the formation of MillerCoors, substantially all of the inventories in the United States were determined on the last-in, first-out ("LIFO") method.

We regularly assess the shelf-life of our inventories and reserve for those inventories when it becomes apparent the product will not be sold within our freshness specifications. There are no allowances for obsolete finished goods or packaging materials at December 26, 2009 or at December 28, 2008.

7-38 (Inventory turnover)

The Forzani Group Ltd. is Canada's largest sporting goods retailer. It operates more than 200 stores across Canada under the names Sport Chek, Sport Mart, and Coast Mountain Sports. The company also franchises stores. Note 2(b) to Forzani's 2009 financial statements is included in Exhibit 7-15. The company reported the following amounts for inventory and cost of sales in its January 31, 2010, and February 1, 2009, financial statements.

Inventory:
2010 $316,319 thousand
2009 $291,497 thousand

Cost of sales:
2010 $864,004 thousand
2006 $863,239 thousand

Required:

a. Calculate the inventory turnover (by ratio and by days) for The Forzani Group Ltd. for 2010 and 2009, using the inventory value at each year end instead of the average inventory amount. Comment on the results.

b. What do you think is meant by freight and distribution costs in Note 2(b)? Is it appropriate that these costs be included in inventory cost? Explain.

c. If the company purchases a large shipment of sports shoes from a manufacturer and is given a 10% volume discount on the manufacturer's usual selling price, how and when does Forzani record the discount? Explain whether you think this is appropriate.

EXHIBIT 7-15

THE FORZANI GROUP LTD. 2010 ANNUAL REPORT

Excerpt from the Notes to the Statements

2(b) *Inventory valuation*

Inventory is valued at the lower of laid-down cost and net realizable value. Laid-down cost is determined using the weighted average cost method and includes invoice cost, duties, freight, and distribution costs. Net realizable value is defined as the expected selling price.

Volume rebates and other supplier discounts are included in income when earned. Volume rebates are accounted for as a reduction of the cost of the related inventory and are "earned" when the inventory is sold. All other rebates and discounts are "earned" when the related expense is incurred.

7-39   (Inventory turnover)

Magna International Inc. is a Canadian company operating internationally, supplying techno-logically advanced automotive components, assemblies, systems, and modules, and engineering and assembling complete vehicles mostly for sale to original equipment manufacturers. Because it is a manufacturing company, its inventory is composed of raw materials, work in process, and finished goods. Note 7, Inventories, from its 2009 financial statements is included in Exhibit 7-16. Magna's financial statements are in millions of U.S. dollars.

Magna's cost of goods sold was $15,697 million and $20,982 million for 2009 and 2008, respectively.

> **Required:**
> a. The tooling and engineering inventory is created when Magna does work for a customer, but the customer has not yet been invoiced by Magna for all of the work completed to date. Why is it appropriate to include these costs as inventory? Explain.
> b. Calculate the inventory turnover for Magna in 2009 and 2008 using the inventory value for the given year rather than the average inventory.
>   i.   Cost of goods sold divided by total inventory
>   ii. Cost of goods sold divided by finished goods inventory
>   iii. Cost of goods sold divided by finished goods plus tooling and engineering inventory
> c. Which of the ratios calculated in part "b" do you think is more useful? Why?

MAGNA INTERNATIONAL INC. 2009 ANNUAL REPORT

EXHIBIT 7-16

annual report

Excerpt from the Notes to the Statements

7. INVENTORIES

Inventories consist of:

	2009	2008
Raw materials and supplies	$ 586	$ 605
Work-in-process	176	166
Finished goods	219	228
Tooling and engineering	740	648
	$ 1,721	$ 1,647

Tooling and engineering inventory represents costs incurred on separately priced tooling and engineering services contracts in excess of billed and unbilled amounts included in accounts receivable.

7-40   (Impact of inventory on current ratio; impact of changing sales levels on gross profit)

Cameco Corporation is the world's largest producer of uranium. It also converts the uranium into fuel for light water reactors, as well as Candu reactors. It is a part owner in Bruce Power, which operates a nuclear generating station in Ontario. Total current assets for 2009 and 2008 are $2,527,741 thousand and $2,353,748 thousand respectively. The current liabilities for the same period are $763,057 thousand and $1,566,047 thousand respectively. Its statements of earnings and Note 6, Inventories, for 2009 and 2008 are presented in Exhibit 7-17. Note 2(d) describes Cameco's accounting policy for inventory as follows:

EXHIBIT 7-17A   **CAMECO CORPORATION 2009 ANNUAL REPORT**

annual report

Consolidated Statements of Earnings

For the years ended December 31 ($Cdn thousands, except per share amounts)	2009	(Recast note 25) 2008
Revenue from		
Products and services	$2,314,985	$2,182,553
Expenses		
Products and services sold[i]	1,324,278	1,146,462
Depreciation, depletion and reclamation	240,643	207,453
Administration	135,558	86,392
Exploration	49,061	53,224
Research and development	630	4,998
Interest and other [note 15]	(12,470)	93,281
(Gains) losses on derivatives [note 27]	(243,804)	202,651
Cigar Lake remediation	17,884	11,369
Gain on sale of assets [note 16]	(566)	(4,097)
	1,511,214	1,801,733
Earnings from continuing operations	803,771	380,820
Other expense [note 17]	(36,912)	(39,273)
Earnings before income taxes and minority interest	766,859	341,547
Income tax expense (recovery) [note 18]	52,897	(24,357)
Minority interest	(3,035)	(245)
Earnings from continuing operations	$ 716,997	$ 366,149
Earnings from discontinued operations [note 25]	382,425	83,968
Net earnings	$1,099,422	$450,117
Net earnings per share [note 28]		
Basic		
Continuing operations	$1.84	$1.05
Discontinued operations	0.99	0.24
Total basic earnings per share	$2.83	$1.29
Diluted		
Continuing operations	$1.84	$1.04
Discontinued operations	0.98	0.24
Total diluted earnings per share	$2.82	$1.28
(i) Excludes depreciation, depletion and reclamation expenses of:	$228,317	$198,594

See accompanying notes to consolidated financial statements.

Inventories of broken ore, uranium concentrates, and refined and converted products are valued at the lower of average cost and net realizable value. Average cost includes direct materials, direct labour, operational overhead expenses and depreciation, depletion and reclamation. Net realizable value for finished products is considered to be the estimated selling price in the ordinary course of business, less the estimated costs of completion and selling expenses.

Required:

a. Calculate the current ratio (CA/CL) for both 2009 and 2008. Comment on the impact that inventory has on this ratio in each year.

b. Calculate the gross profit percentage for 2009 and 2008. Revenues increased over this time period. Have the changes in the cost of products and services sold mirrored the changes in revenue? What effect has this had on the gross profit?

c. The description of the accounting policy for inventory states that the average cost includes an expense called "reclamation." When a company closes a mine, it is required by law to perform an environmental cleanup, which may include revegetation of the area and re-sculpting of rock stockpiles to improve water runoff. Why would these costs be accrued and included in the cost of inventory production while the mine is still in operation?

CAMECO CORPORATION 2009 ANNUAL REPORT

EXHIBIT 7-17B

annual report

Excerpt from the Notes to the Statements

6. Inventories

	2009	2008
Uranium		
Concentrate	$310,893	$287,079
Broken ore	18,125	21,396
	329,018	308,475
Fuel Services	124,206	89,635
Total	$453,224	$398,110

Beyond the Book

7-41 (Examination of a company's financial statements)

Choose a Canadian company as directed by your instructor and answer the following questions:

a. What kind of inventory does your company carry?

b. Calculate the inventory turnover for each of the last two years, using the inventory of the year instead of the average inventory. Report any difficulties that you had in finding the appropriate numbers to make this calculation.

c. Describe any significant change that occurred in the inventory balance and try to determine what caused it.

d. Calculate a current ratio for each of the last two years. Describe the significance that inventory has on this ratio in each year.

Cases

7-42 Kinross Gold Corporation

Kinross Gold Corporation is a Canadian company headquartered in Toronto. It explores and develops gold properties in the United States, Canada, Brazil, Chile, and Russia. Rani, a Business Administration student, has recently inherited some money from a grandparent. She intends to create a diversified portfolio of share investments. She has heard that, although they can be risky, investments in gold properties can also be quite profitable. Rani is contemplating investing in Kinross Gold Corporation. She has the annual report, which includes the financial statements (see Exhibit 7-18). She is concerned because the company showed a profit in 2009 but had a significant loss in 2008. More shares were issued in 2009 and if other investors are willing to buy new shares, they obviously have confidence in this company.

Required:

a. Knowing that Kinross explores and develops gold properties, explain the significance of gold inventory on its balance sheet by calculating a current ratio for each year and explaining the impact that inventory has on this ratio.

b. Review the financial statements and draw up a list of questions you think Rani should ask an investment advisor about this company.

c. Look through recent newspaper articles about the price of gold. Should the recent articles give Rani more confidence in investing in Kinross? Explain.

7-43 Flick's Electronics

Jeff Stevenson was recently hired as a new manager for Flick's Electronics. His compensation is composed of a base salary and a bonus based on gross profit. The bonuses are to be paid monthly, as determined by the gross profit for the preceding month.

Flick's Electronics currently uses a periodic inventory system, but Jeff would like to see the company move to a perpetual system. The company's owners are willing to consider the change, provided that Jeff prepares a written analysis outlining the two methods and detailing the benefits and costs of switching to the perpetual system.

Required:

Prepare a report that Jeff could present to the owners of Flick's Electronics to support his request to change to a perpetual inventory system.

7-44 Park Avenue Tire Company

Park Avenue Tire Company has been operating in Winnipeg for more than 30 years and has a very loyal customer base. The company sells and installs tires and the owners pride themselves on the excellent business relationships they have developed with both their customers and suppliers. The company often sells tires on credit, allowing customers to pay their balances within 30 days. Collection of accounts receivable has never been a problem, with most people paying their balances within 60 days.

Park Avenue purchases tires from most of the large national brands and, due to the nature of the business, generally maintains a fairly large inventory. It is essential that the company have the necessary tires on hand to meet customer needs due to increased competition from large retailers such as Canadian Tire and Wal-Mart.

The company has always had sufficient cash to pay its suppliers immediately and take advantage of cash discounts. However, this month, for the first time ever, Park Avenue does not have sufficient cash in the bank to meet its supplier payments. Chris Park, son of the original owner, Ernest Park, is currently operating the business and is very concerned about the company's inability to maintain what he feels are adequate levels of cash.

Your firm has been the accountants for Park Avenue Tire Company for the past 20 years. Chris has approached the firm expressing his concerns and asking for advice on how to solve the

KINROSS GOLD CORPORATION 2009 ANNUAL REPORT

CONSOLIDATED BALANCE SHEETS

As at December 31,

EXHIBIT 7-18A

annual report

(expressed in millions of United States dollars, except share amounts)		2009	2008
Assets			
Current assets			
Cash, cash equivalents and short-term investments	Note 5	$ 632.4	$ 525.1
Restricted cash		24.3	12.4
Accounts receivable and other assets	Note 5	135.5	126.5
Inventories	Note 5	554.4	437.1
Unrealized fair value of derivative assets	Note 8	44.3	23.8
		1,390.9	1,124.9
Property, plant and equipment	Note 5	4,989.9	4,748.0
Goodwill	Note 5	1,179.9	1,181.9
Long-term investments	Note 5	292.2	185.9
Future income and mining taxes	Note 15	–	33.9
Unrealized fair value of derivative assets	Note 8	1.9	8.7
Deferred charges and other long-term assets	Note 5	158.4	104.2
		$ 8,013.2	$ 7,387.5
Liabilities			
Current liabilities			
Accounts payable and accrued liabilities	Note 5	$ 312.9	$ 246.3
Current portion of long-term debt	Note 9	177.0	167.1
Current portion of reclamation and remediation obligations	Note 10	17.1	10.0
Current portion of unrealized fair value of derivative liabilities	Note 8	131.0	128.1
		638.0	551.5
Long-term debt	Note 9	515.2	783.8
Other long-term liabilities	Note 5	543.0	586.6
Future income and mining taxes	Note 15	624.6	622.3
		2,320.8	2,544.2
Non-controlling interest		132.9	56.3
Convertible preferred shares of subsidiary company		–	10.1
Common shareholders' equity			
Common share capital and common share purchase warrants	Note 12	6,448.1	5,873.0
Contributed surplus		169.6	168.5
Accumulated deficit		(838.1)	(1,100.2)
Accumulated other comprehensive loss	Note 6	(220.1)	(164.4)
		5,559.5	4,776.9
Contingencies	Note 19		
Subsequent events	Notes 8, 12, 20		
		$ 8,013.2	$ 7,387.5
Common shares			
Authorized		Unlimited	Unlimited
Issued and outstanding		696,027,270	659,438,293

Signed on behalf of the Board:

John A. Brough
Director

John M.H. Huxley
Director

The accompanying notes are an integral part of these consolidated financial statements

CONSOLIDATED STATEMENTS OF OPERATIONS

For the years ended December 31,

(expressed in millions of United States dollars, except per share and share amounts)

		2009	2008	2007
Revenue				
Metal sales		$ 2,412.1	$ 1,617.0	$ 1,093.0
Operating costs and expenses				
Cost of sales (excludes accretion, depreciation, depletion and amortization)		1,047.1	768.8	580.3
Accretion and reclamation expense		19.3	24.7	10.9
Depreciation, depletion and amortization		447.3	273.8	129.3
		898.4	549.7	372.5
Other operating costs		62.3	7.4	28.7
Exploration and business development		72.5	59.0	47.3
General and administrative		117.7	100.8	69.6
Impairment charges: goodwill	Note 5	–	994.1	–
Operating earnings (loss)		645.9	(611.6)	226.9
Other income (expense) – net	Note 5	(74.3)	(42.7)	189.6
Earnings (loss) before taxes and other items		571.6	(654.3)	416.5
Income and mining taxes expense – net	Note 15	(150.8)	(101.1)	(73.8)
Equity in losses of associated companies		(8.6)	(8.7)	(11.1)
Non-controlling interest		(102.3)	(42.3)	3.2
Dividends on convertible preferred shares of subsidiary		–	(0.8)	(0.8)
Net earnings (loss)		$ 309.9	$ (807.2)	$ 334.0
Earnings (loss) per share				
Basic		$ 0.45	$ (1.28)	$ 0.60
Diluted		$ 0.44	$ (1.28)	$ 0.59
Weighted average number of common shares outstanding (millions)	Note 14			
Basic		691.5	628.6	557.4
Diluted		696.5	628.6	566.1

The accompanying notes are an integral part of these consolidated financial statements

cash flow problems. As part of your analysis, you review the company's financial statements for the past three years. Excerpts from the financial statements are presented below.

	Dec. 31 2012	Dec. 31 2011	Dec. 31 2010
Current assets			
Cash	$ 10,000	$ 35,000	$ 31,500
Accounts receivable	15,000	12,000	9,000
Inventory	169,000	122,000	116,000
Prepaid expenses	6,000	8,000	6,500
Total current assets	$200,000	$177,000	$163,000
Current liabilities			
Accounts payable	$ 62,000	$ 47,000	33,000
Salaries payable	4,200	5,850	3,775
Income tax payable	1,200	1,150	1,950
Total current liabilities	$ 67,400	$ 54,000	$ 38,725

During 2012, credit sales and cost of goods sold were $160,000 and $97,000, respectively. The 2011 and 2010 credit sales were $175,000 and $177,000, and the cost of goods sold for the same periods were $93,000 and $95,000. The accounts receivable and inventory balances at the end of 2009 were $8,000 and $99,000, respectively.

Required:

Prepare a report for Chris Park detailing options that he can take to alleviate the company's cash problems. Remember that you are to present options, not recommendations. As a basis for the report, you should calculate and comment on the following ratios:

a. Current ratio
b. Quick ratio
c. Receivables turnover ratio and average collection period
d. Inventory turnover ratio and days in inventory

7-45 North End Television Services

North End Television Services sells and services a variety of high-end home entertainment products. An inventory count is prepared at each year end to verify the information contained in the company's perpetual inventory system. Once counted, the inventory is valued for the purposes of preparing the financial statements. The following inventory items represent a cross-section of North End's inventory for the year ended June 30, 2011. Because computerized records are maintained and a specific identification method of inventory is applied, the historical cost of each inventory item can easily be determined.

In addition to the historical cost, the store management has also included information detailing net realizable value for each item.

Item	Quantity on hand June 30, 2011	Historical cost (per unit)	Net realizable value (per unit)
Sony DVD Player	4	$125	$225
RCA High Definition 52-Inch Television	2	$1,400	$1,999
Sony High 8 Camcorder	3	$300	$200
JVC Surround Sound System	6	$600	$900
Nikon Digital Camera	4	$190	$395

Tim Cappelino, the manager of North End, is confused about why there is a difference between historical cost and net realizable value. Tim is not an accountant and is unfamiliar with these terms. He is also wondering which number should be used to value the company's inventory on June 30, 2011.

Required:

For the purposes of this case, assume that the above items represent the total inventory of North End Television Services on June 30, 2011.

a. Define for Tim the meaning of historical cost and net realizable value in the context of inventory valuation.
b. Based on Canadian practice, determine for Tim the value of North End's ending inventory on June 30, 2011.

7-46 (Cost flow assumptions)

Jim Wong has been a public accountant for the past 20 years and is now a partner in a prominent accounting firm based in Truro, Nova Scotia. Recently, he was approached by the local chamber of commerce to be a guest speaker at its monthly meeting. Since many members of the chamber are small to mid-sized retailers, Jim decided to prepare a talk on determining inventory values and cost flow assumptions.

It is now Friday afternoon and Jim has just returned to his office following the presentation to the chamber. He is surprised to see messages from two clients who were at the meeting. The first message is from Bryan Cartel, who owns and operates the local Ford dealership. In addition to selling cars, the dealership also has a large service department and maintains an extensive inventory of parts and accessories.

The second caller is Jenny Mead, who manages her family's grocery store. Jim returns the calls and discovers that both businesspeople want further advice on the best cost flow assumption to use in their respective inventory systems.

In particular, Jenny would like to know why her family is using the FIFO approach instead of moving average. From Jim's chamber presentation, she learned that moving average results in lower net income in times of rising prices, and since lower net income means less taxes, she is wondering why Jim has not previously recommended switching to moving average.

Required:

a. Determine which inventory cost flow assumption would best suit the needs of each client. Be prepared to support your recommendation.
b. Writing as Jim, draft a response to Jenny regarding her concerns about the use of moving average in her business. Do you think that the business should change to this method? Why or why not?

7-47 Castle Sight & Sound

You are the sales manager at Castle Sight & Sound, a store that sells high-end televisions, sound systems, and video and computer equipment. Among the various television models are two Pioneer 50-inch digital TVs, one in a black case, purchased through regular channels for $2,600, and the other in a silver case, purchased in a wholesaler's liquidation sale for $1,400. Because the two TVs are identical except for the colour of the case, they have been priced to sell at $3,999.99. This price is competitive with other outlets that are selling similar TVs.

One of your sales reps calls you from the display floor. She has a customer interested in the digital TV with the black case who is willing to pay the asking price of $3,999.99. As you are talking to her, you remember that the digital TV with the silver case was acquired at a much lower cost. Castle Sound uses the specific identification cost method for the high-end equipment that it sells. The following idea occurs to you: if the company sells the digital TV with the black case, it will make a gross profit of $1,399.99. However, if the sales rep were to offer the customer a $200 discount if he bought the digital TV with the silver case, the company will make a gross profit of $2,399.99. You may even be able to get part of the additional $1,000 as a bonus.

Required:

Should you ask the sales rep to offer the $200 discount to the customer if he is willing to buy the digital TV with the silver case? Why or why not? Are there any ethical issues involved in this decision?

7-48   Armstrong Hardware

Armstrong Hardware lost most of its inventory in an electrical fire that destroyed the company's warehouse and retail store. Fortunately, the accounting records were backed up on the owner's computer in her home office and could therefore be recovered.

However, Armstrong uses a periodic inventory system, so without being able to perform a physical count, the company could not determine the amount of inventory lost in the fire. In order to process the insurance claim, the insurance company requires Armstrong to prepare a reasonable estimate of the lost inventory.

As Armstrong's accountant, you have been able to gather the following information:

1. Ending inventory, from the accounting records of last year, was $85,800.

2. In the current year, purchases up to the time of the fire totalled $486,500.

3. According to last year's financial statements, sales and the cost of goods sold were $964,000 and $578,400, respectively.

4. According to this year's accounting records, sales in the current year were $678,000.

Required:

a. Prepare an estimate of the amount of inventory lost in the fire. To ensure the reasonableness of the amount claimed, write a brief memo to the insurance company outlining your approach for determining the amount of inventory destroyed. You should also specify any assumptions used in preparing your estimate.

b. How would this process have differed if Armstrong had used a perpetual instead of a periodic inventory system?

Critical Thinking Questions

7-49   (Inventory decision-making with respect to buying and selling)

You and two of your friends have decided to apply some of the knowledge that you are learning in your business classes. You plan to start a wholesale business, buying goods in the Czech Republic and selling them to small specialty stores. One of your friends has an uncle in the Czech Republic who has some contacts that will enable you to buy the merchandise you want. Another friend has an aunt who owns a trucking company that transports merchandise all over Europe. You hope to use the trucking company to transport your merchandise from the Czech Republic to Rotterdam, in the Netherlands, for shipment to Canada.

You are going to have a meeting to discuss the necessary details surrounding the buying and selling of the inventory. In preparation for the meeting, write a short report outlining the items that you think should be discussed. To make this more realistic and to make your task easier, decide on what types of inventory you are going to buy. The type of inventory you import will affect some of the decisions you need to make.

chapter 8

CAPITAL ASSETS— TANGIBLE AND INTANGIBLE

LEARNING OBJECTIVES

After studying this chapter, you should be able to:

1. Describe the valuation methods for capital assets.

2. Identify the types of asset acquisition costs that are usually capitalized.

3. Explain the purpose of depreciation and implement the most common methods of depreciation, including capital cost allowance.

4. Identify the factors that influence the choice of depreciation method.

5. Describe and implement changes in depreciation estimates and methods.

6. Account for the disposal and writedown (impairment) of capital assets.

7. Describe and implement the depreciation method used most frequently for natural resources.

8. Explain the accounting difficulties associated with intangible assets.

9. Depreciate intangible assets, where appropriate.

10. Calculate the return on assets ratio and discuss the potential implications of the results.

A Canadian Staple's Capital Costs

Nine out of 10 adult Canadians shop at Canadian Tire every year, and 40 percent of Canadians shop there every week, the company website boasts. In fact, the location of Canadian Tire's 475 retail stores allows it to serve more than 90 percent of the Canadian population. It is no surprise, then, that this market reach translates into a significant amount of capital assets, both tangible and intangible. Indeed, the company logo, the instantly recognizable red triangle with the green maple leaf, is a significant intangible asset for the company. However, that specific asset does not have any capitalized asset value on Canadian Tire's balance sheet.

According to Huw Thomas, Canadian Tire's Executive Vice-President, Financial Strategy and Performance, the logo would be on the balance sheet "if we had done a lot of work to create that triangle as a brand." Instead, the creation of the brand's value happened over a long period, and Canadian Tire did not capitalize any costs associated with that process. "If we had," Mr. Thomas continues, "we would have the potential for the creation of further intangibles, because the brand obviously has significant value. But current accounting (and IFRS) doesn't have you carry the value of assets like that on your balance sheet." Intangible assets that have been purchased, however, are carried on the balance sheet. For example, Canadian Tire's acquisition of the Mark's Work Wearhouse chain includes the capitalization of intangibles, such as the company's well-established brand name. All of the goodwill that appears on the balance sheet has been gained through acquisitions, Mr. Thomas says.

On a large acquisition such as Mark's Work Wearhouse, the company calculates the fair value of the various assets it has acquired, including any trademarks. "You create models as to what that trademark might be worth, looking into the future, and then the difference between the total amount that you've paid, less the fair value of the net assets you've acquired, represents goodwill," explains Mr. Thomas. "That becomes an asset that sits on the balance sheet, and every year you have to assess whether the goodwill amount has become impaired." The company would do an impairment assessment for any asset on the balance sheet, whether intangible or tangible, he adds.

Canadian Tire owns 70 percent of the land and buildings for the main stores in its network. The costs to develop a new store location include acquiring the land and the legal costs associated with that purchase, as well as the physical construction of the store itself. As portions of the building are completed, progress payments for the construction are capitalized, Mr. Thomas explains. During the construction period, the company also capitalizes interest costs associated with funding the land purchase, and project costs for the building. "We have a set of specific internal guidelines around what can be capitalized and what can't be," says Mr. Thomas, "and that is consistent with GAAP."

"There are various differences between current accounting under Canadian GAAP and IFRS," Mr. Thomas continues. These differences include the choice to record property and equipment at fair values (under a revaluation model) or at cost, and the IFRS requirement to separately account for and depreciate significant parts of a property and equipment asset. "As IFRS requires borrowing costs that are directly attributable to the construction of a qualifying asset to be capitalized as part of the cost of that asset," concludes Mr. Thomas, "the move to IFRS will not have any significant impact on our accounting for real estate development projects."

Our opening story describes some difficulties associated with recording and reporting capital assets at **Canadian Tire Corporation**, which has significant sums invested in the capital assets that form its extensive retail network and the distribution system (warehouses, trucks, etc.) that supports it. The main accounting issues for these assets include determining the amounts to be recorded as the costs of the assets, how long the company expects to benefit from the assets' use, and how the costs should be transferred to expense during these periods. Each of these issues has significant implications for the amounts that will be reported on both the company's balance sheet and its statement of earnings.

This chapter will discuss the measurement, recording, and reporting issues related to capital assets. In the previous two chapters, we studied current assets whose value would be realized within one year (or the operating cycle). In this chapter, we discuss **capital assets**—assets with lives longer than a year (or the operating cycle) that are used in the company's operations to generate revenue. Long-term investments that also have lives longer than a year are discussed briefly in Appendix B at the end of the text.

Of the capital assets that we are going to study, property, plant, and equipment are the most recognizable. These are a type of non-current asset called **tangible assets**, which are usually defined as those assets with some physical form. ("Tangible" comes from the Latin word meaning "to touch.") In other words, you can usually see these assets and touch them. **Intangible assets**, on the other hand, are non-current assets that are associated with certain legal rights or privileges the company has, such as patents, trademarks, leases, and goodwill.

In the sections that follow, the recognition and valuation issues for capital assets are discussed, much as they were for current assets. Because of the long-term nature of these assets, it is important to address the issue of how to show their effect on the statement of earnings as their cost is expensed over time. The expensing of an asset's cost over time is referred to as **depreciation** (for tangible assets) and **amortization** (for intangible assets).

USER RELEVANCE

Capital assets provide the underlying infrastructure of many companies. They include the real estate, buildings, equipment, vehicles, computers, patents, and so on that companies need to carry out their day-to-day operations. They often require a substantial outlay of funds to acquire, which means that companies will often secure long-term mortgages or other forms of debt to finance them. Another common way to acquire long-lived assets is to lease them. You may find some assets on a statement of financial position labelled as "assets under capital leases."

Because of their importance to business operations, their high costs, and their long lives, the role that capital assets play in a company's success needs to be understood by financial statement users. Users need to monitor the assets' lives so that they can anticipate the future outflows of cash to replace them. They need to know what methods a company has chosen to depreciate its assets, and what impact those methods have on the statement of earnings. They also need to understand that the value carried on the balance sheet for capital assets represents a future benefit that the company expects to earn from using the assets. If the company did not expect to earn the carrying values through its use of the assets, it would be required to write them down (i.e., reduce the carrying values). In most instances, companies expect to earn amounts that are significantly higher than the carrying values of their capital assets.

This chapter will provide you, as a user, with the necessary background information on capital assets so that you can better understand the impact that these assets have on the financial statements.

CAPITAL ASSET RECOGNITION

Assets must have probable future value for the company. The company must also have the right to use them and must have acquired that right through a past transaction. When a company buys a capital asset, both of these conditions exist: it has the right to use the asset and a transaction has occurred. Therefore, the only asset criterion that merits further discussion is the probable future value, which takes at least two forms. Capital assets are used, first and foremost, to generate revenues, usually by producing products, facilitating sales, or providing services. Therefore, the future value is represented by the cash that will eventually be received from the sales of products and services. This type of value is sometimes referred to as **value in use**. Because of the long-term nature of capital assets, these cash flows will be received over several future periods.

The second source of value for capital assets is their ultimate disposal value. Many capital assets are used until the company decides to replace them with a new asset. For example, a business may use a truck for four or five years and then trade it in for a new one. This type of value is called **residual value** (or **resale value**) and can be very important, depending on the type of asset.

Value in use is normally the most appropriate concept for capital assets because companies usually invest in them to use them, not to sell them. Residual value cannot, however, be totally ignored, because it represents the asset's expected value at the end of its use. In Chapter 2, you were introduced to how we use residual value to determine the amount of depreciation that should be recorded.

The difficulty with the value in use concept for capital assets is that the future revenue (and ultimately income) that will be generated by using the asset is inherently uncertain. The company does not know to what extent the demand for its products or services will continue into the future. It also does not know what prices it will be able to command for its products or services. Other uncertainties relate to technology. Equipment can become obsolete as a result of technological change. New technology can give competitors a significant advantage in producing and pricing products. Technological change can also reduce or eliminate the need for the company's product. Consider a manufacturer of cassette tapes when CDs came on the market, or a videotape or VCR manufacturer with the advent of DVDs.

Uncertainty about the asset's value in use also gives rise to uncertainty about its eventual residual value, since the ultimate residual value will depend on whether the asset will have any value in use to the ultimate buyer. There may also be a question of whether a buyer can even be found. Equipment that is made to the original buyer's specifications may not have much residual market value because it may not meet the needs of other potential users.

HOW ARE CAPITAL ASSETS VALUED?

LEARNING OBJECTIVE 1

Describe the valuation methods for capital assets.

In the sections that follow, the discussion is limited to valuation issues regarding property, plant, and equipment, which are similar to those relating to other non-current capital assets. At the end of the chapter, specific concerns and issues regarding natural resources and intangible assets are discussed.

In Canada, property, plant, and equipment are usually valued at historical cost, with no recognition of any other value unless the asset's value becomes "impaired" (i.e., the value of the estimated future cash flows is less than the current carrying value). IFRS allows the recognition of changes in the market values of property, plant, and equipment and you may come across companies that are using market value for their capital assets. Before Canadian practice is discussed in detail, several possible valuation methods will be considered.

Historical Cost

In a historical cost valuation system, the asset's original cost is recorded at the time of acquisition. Changes in the asset's market value are ignored in this system. During the period in which the asset is used, its cost is expensed (depreciated) using an appropriate depreciation method (discussed later in this chapter). Market values are recognized only when the asset is sold. The company then recognizes a gain or loss on the sale, which is determined by the difference between the proceeds from the sale and the **net book value** (or **carrying value**) of the asset at the time of sale. The net book value or carrying value is the original cost less the portion that has been charged to expense in the form of depreciation. This net book value is sometimes called the **depreciated cost** of the asset.

Market Value

Another possible valuation method records capital assets at their market values. There are at least two types of market values: replacement cost and net realizable value.

Replacement Cost

In this version of a market valuation system, the asset is carried at its **replacement cost**—the amount that would be needed to acquire an equivalent asset. At acquisition, the historical cost is recorded because this is the replacement cost at the time of purchase. As the asset is used, its carrying value is adjusted upward or downward to reflect changes in the replacement cost. Unrealized gains and losses are recognized for these changes. The periodic expensing of the asset, in the form of depreciation, has to be adjusted to reflect the changes in the replacement cost. For example, if the asset's replacement cost goes up, the depreciation expense will also have to go up, to reflect the higher replacement cost. A realized gain or loss is recognized upon disposal of the asset. The amount of the gain or loss is determined by the difference between the proceeds from the sale and the depreciated replacement cost at the time of sale.

Net Realizable Value

With a **net realizable value** system, assets are recorded at the amount that could be received by converting them to cash; in other words, from selling them. During the periods when the assets are being used, gains and losses are recognized as their net realizable values change over time. Depreciation in this type of system is based on the net realizable value and is adjusted each time the asset is revalued. The recognition of a gain or loss at the time of sale should be for a small amount, since the asset should be carried at a value close to its resale value at that date. This system is not consistent with the notion of value in use, which assumes that the company has no intention of selling the asset. IFRS allows this valuation system. As Canadian companies adapt to IFRS, companies may opt to use net realizable value.

The word "market" must be used with some care. The preceding discussions assume that both the replacement market and the selling market are the markets in which the company normally trades. There are, however, special markets if a company has to liquidate its assets quickly. The values in these markets can be significantly different from those in normal markets. As long as the company is a going concern, these specialty markets are not appropriate for establishing values for the company's assets. On the other hand, if the company is bankrupt or going out of business, these specialty markets may be the most appropriate places to obtain estimates of the assets' realizable market values. It might be difficult to determine a market value under either method if the assets are very specialized.

INTERNATIONAL PERSPECTIVES

Reports from Other Countries

While most countries value property, plant, and equipment at historical cost, a few (such as France, Switzerland, and the United Kingdom) have allowed revaluations of these assets based on current replacement costs.

These revaluations are seldom made in France, because they would be taxable. In the UK, on the other hand, such revaluations are quite common. The increase in the value of the assets that occurs under the replacement cost valuation is not usually considered part of net income, but (like "other comprehensive income") is recorded directly in the shareholders' equity section of the statement of financial position, in an account called a *revaluation reserve*.

What Is Canadian Practice?

In Canada, most capital assets are valued at their depreciated historical cost (the remaining portion of their original acquisition cost). During the periods of use, the asset's cost is expensed using a depreciation method that is rational, systematic, and appropriate to the asset.

With the adoption of IFRS, some companies may decide to change to the market values for their capital assets. Under this valuation method, the assets are revalued every three or four years. During the intervening years, the assets are depreciated using the same depreciation methods that are used under the cost method. A detailed description of this method is covered in intermediate financial accounting courses.

Under both historical cost and net realizable value, an asset cannot be valued at more than the amount that can be recovered from it. The **net recoverable amount** is the total of all the future cash flows related to the asset, without discounting them to present values. If it is ever determined that an asset's carrying value exceeds its net recoverable amount, the carrying value must be written down and the difference recognized as an **impairment loss**.

ethics in accounting

www.wileyplus.com

Ethics in Accounting

The ability to control the timing of a writedown of property, plant, and equipment provides management with an opportunity to "manage" or manipulate earnings. The issue of earnings management, as described earlier in this text, has been studied by many researchers in an attempt to demonstrate its existence and to estimate its effects. In one study, Belski, Beams, and Brozovsky had business students respond to six situations that involved ethical issues. As the following excerpt from the study shows, the intent of the described actions influenced the students' perception of the potential level of ethical actions:

> The study found that the intent of the earnings management matters. That is, subjects find that managers engaging in earnings management that was deemed opportunistic or selfish were considered more unethical (less ethical) than earnings management behaviour aimed at increasing firm contracting efficiency. Additionally the study found that the method of the manipulation was also important. Accounting estimate manipulations were considered the least ethical followed by economic operating decisions. Changes in accounting method were considered the least unethical.[1]

The writedown (or write-off) of property, plant, and equipment or the change in the useful life or estimated residual value of depreciable assets are ways in which management might attempt to manipulate earnings. The reader of financial statements must be aware of this possibility.

1. W.H. Belski, J.D. Beams, and J.A. Brozovsky, "Ethical Judgments in Accounting: An Examination on the Ethics of Managed Earnings," *Journal of Global Business 2*, no. 2 (2008), pp. 59–68.

Capitalizable Costs

At the date of acquisition, the company must decide which costs associated with the purchase of the asset should be included as a part of the asset's cost, or **capitalized**. The general guideline is that any cost that is necessary to acquire the asset and get it ready for use is a **capitalizable cost**. Any cost incurred that is not capitalized as part of the asset cost would be expensed in the period of the purchase. The following is a partial list of costs that would normally be capitalized (i.e., included in the cost of a capital asset).

EXAMPLES OF CAPITALIZABLE COSTS

Purchase price (less any discounts)
Direct taxes on the purchase price
Interest cost (on self-constructed assets)
Legal costs associated with the purchase
Shipping or transportation costs
Preparation, installation, and set-up costs

The reason for capitalizing ancillary costs (such as taxes on the purchase price, legal costs associated with the purchase, shipping or transportation costs, and preparation, installation, and set-up costs) is the matching principle. If these related costs are recorded as part of the asset's cost, they will be charged to expense in future periods, as depreciation, in order to match them to the revenues that are generated while the asset is being used.

The determination of which costs appropriately belong in an asset account is not always easy. For example, consider a company purchasing new equipment. The salaries of the employees who develop the specifications for the new equipment, negotiate with potential suppliers, and order the equipment are normally not included in the acquisition cost. This is true even though the time spent by these employees is necessary to acquire the asset. On the other hand, if a significant amount of employee time is required to install the new equipment, these employees' wages are usually recorded as part of the cost of the equipment. The costs associated with clearing land in preparation for constructing a new building are usually added to the land account. The cost of digging the hole for the building's foundation, on the other hand, is usually added to the building account.

Land is a unique capital asset. Even after it has been used by a company for several years, land will still be there to be used indefinitely in the future. Therefore, unlike other capital assets, its cost is not depreciated. Consequently, assigning costs to land means that those costs will remain on the statement of financial position forever; they will not appear on the statement of earnings in the future, as depreciation expense.

Related to land is another category of capital assets that are commonly referred to as land improvements. The term **land improvements** refers to things done to the land to improve its usefulness, but which will not last forever. Examples include the installation of fencing, parking lots, lighting, and walkways. It is important to distinguish these types of items from the land itself, because the cost of these land improvements must be depreciated over their expected useful lives.

Deciding which costs to capitalize is also often influenced by income tax regulations. For tax purposes, companies would like to expense as many costs as possible, in order to reduce their taxable income and save on taxes. Capitalizing costs, on the other hand, means that companies have to wait until the assets are depreciated before the costs can be deducted for tax purposes. There is, therefore, an incentive to expense rather than to capitalize costs that are only indirectly related to the acquisition of assets, and companies may decide to expense costs for financial reporting purposes to bolster their arguments that the costs are expenses for tax purposes.

The materiality criterion also plays a part in which costs are capitalized. Small expenditures related to the purchase of an asset may be expensed rather than capitalized, because expensing them is simpler and adding small amounts to the cost of the asset would not change it significantly.

Basket Purchases

Sometimes a company acquires several assets in one transaction. This is called a **basket purchase**. For example, when a forest products company buys timberland, it acquires two distinct assets—land and timber. Therefore, the price paid for the timberland must be divided between the land and the timber, on the basis of their relative fair values at the time of acquisition. This is necessary for three reasons: first, full disclosure requires that each important type of asset be reported separately on the statement of financial position; second, assets that have different rates of depreciation have to be recorded separately in the accounts; and third, some assets, such as land, are not depreciated at all. Suppose that the timberland's purchase price was $880,000 and the fair values of the land and timber were assessed at $250,000 and $750,000, respectively. (Sometimes when assets are acquired in a group it is possible to negotiate a price that is less than the sum of the selling price of the individual assets.)

	Fair value	Percentage	Purchase price	Allocated cost
Land	$ 250,000	25%	$880,000	$220,000
Timber	$ 750,000	75%	$880,000	$660,000
	$1,000,000			$880,000

In this case, the fair value of the land is 25% ($250,000 ÷ $1,000,000) of the total fair value. Therefore, 25% of the total purchase price should be assigned to the land, and the remaining 75% of the cost should be assigned to the timber. Accordingly, a cost of $220,000 (0.25 × $880,000) would be recorded in the land account, and the remaining $660,000 (0.75 × $880,000) of the purchase price would be recorded in the timber account. In the case of timberland, splitting the cost has significant implications for the company because the cost of the land will not be depreciated but the cost of timber will be expensed through depreciation as the timber is harvested.

Another example of a basket purchase is the purchase of a building. Part of the real estate cost must be allocated to the land on which the building is sitting and the remainder to the building. If the building includes various pieces of equipment or furniture, part of the purchase cost will have to be allocated to these items as well. Management's bias in favour of higher income would motivate them to allocate more of the overall cost to the land, and less to the building and other depreciable assets. However, their conflicting desire to pay less income tax would motivate them to allocate a smaller portion of the total cost to the land, and a larger portion to the building and other amortizable assets.

IFRS also requires companies to look within assets such as buildings to see if there are any component parts of the asset that have useful lives that are different from the asset as a whole. For example, assume a company determines that the cost of a building is $750,000 and its useful life is expected to be 35 years. The roof of the building, however, may only last for 15 years. The company should allocate a portion of the original cost of $750,000 to the roof, list the roof as a separate asset and depreciate it over the 15 years.

Interest Capitalization

The issue of **interest capitalization** deserves special consideration. Companies often borrow money to finance the acquisition of a large capital asset. The interest paid on the borrowed money is sometimes capitalized, by including it in the capital asset account rather than recording it as an expense. This is often a major issue for companies that construct some of their own capital assets. For example, some utility and natural resource companies construct their own plant assets. In addition to the costs incurred in the actual construction of these assets (including materials, labour, and overhead), these companies may also incur interest costs if they borrow money to pay for the construction.

Under IFRS, companies can capitalize interest costs for capital assets that are constructed or acquired over time, if the costs are directly attributable to the acquisition. The interest costs can only be capitalized until the capital asset is complete and ready for use, however. Once the asset is ready to use, all subsequent interest costs must be expensed through the statement of earnings.

For assets that are purchased rather than constructed, interest costs are usually not capitalized. The time between acquisition and when it is ready to use is usually too short to make interest capitalization meaningful.

DEPRECIATION CONCEPTS

Depreciation is a systematic and rational method of allocating the cost of capital assets to the periods in which the benefits from the assets are received. This matches the asset's expense in a systematic way to the revenues that are earned in using it, and therefore satisfies the matching principle, described in Chapter 2. The company does not show the capital asset's entire cost as an expense in the period of acquisition, because the asset is expected to help generate revenues over multiple future periods. Matching some portion of a capital asset's cost to the company's revenues, along with its other expenses, results in a measurement of net profit or loss during those periods.

To allocate the expense systematically to the appropriate number of periods, the company must estimate the asset's **useful life**—that is, the periods over which the company will use the asset to generate revenues. The company must also estimate what the asset's ultimate residual value will be at the end of its useful life. It does this by looking at the current selling price of similar assets that are as old as the asset will be at the end of its useful life. Once the asset's useful life and residual value have been estimated, its **depreciable cost** (acquisition cost minus the residual value)—the portion of the asset's cost that is to be depreciated—must then be allocated in a systematic and rational way to the years of useful life. (The term "acquisition cost" refers here to the total capitalized cost of the asset.)

It is important to note that depreciation, as used in accounting, does not refer to valuation. Rather, it is a process of cost allocation. While it is true that a company's capital assets generally decrease in value over time, depreciation normally does not attempt to measure this change in value each period.

The choice of which method to use to allocate a cost across multiple periods will always be somewhat arbitrary. Accounting standards require that the depreciation method reflect the pattern of the economic benefits that are expected to be realized from using the asset. Simply stated, the chosen depreciation method must be a rational and systematic method that is appropriate to the nature of the capital asset and the way it is used by the enterprise. In addition, the method of depreciation and estimates of the useful life and residual value should be reviewed on a regular basis.

Even though accounting standards do not specify which depreciation methods may be used, most companies use one of the methods discussed in the next section.

DEPRECIATION METHODS

As accounting standards developed, rational and systematic methods of depreciation capital assets were created. The simplest and most commonly used method (used by more than 50 percent of Canadian companies) is the **straight-line method** (illustrated in Chapter 2), which allocates the asset's depreciable cost evenly over its useful life. Many accountants have argued in favour of this method for two reasons. First, it is a very simple method to apply. Second, for assets that generate revenues evenly throughout their lives, it properly matches expenses to revenues. It might also be argued that, if an asset physically deteriorates evenly throughout its life, then straight-line depreciation would reflect this physical decline.

A second type of depreciation method recognizes that the usefulness or benefits derived from some capital assets can be measured fairly specifically. This method is usually called the **units-of-activity** or **production method**. Its use requires that the output or usefulness that will be derived from the asset be measurable as a specific quantity. For example, a new truck might be expected to be used for a specific number of kilometres. If so, the depreciation cost per kilometre can be calculated and used to determine each period's depreciation expense, based on the number of kilometres driven during that accounting period.

For certain assets, the decline in their revenue-generating capabilities (and physical deterioration) does not occur evenly over time. In fact, many assets are of most benefit during the early years of their useful lives. In later years, when these assets are wearing out, require more maintenance, and perhaps produce inferior products, the benefits they produce are much lower. This scenario argues for more rapid depreciation in the early years of the asset's life, when larger depreciation expenses will be matched to the larger revenues produced. Methods that match this pattern are known as **accelerated** or **declining-balance methods** of depreciation.

A fourth, but rarely used, depreciation method argues that for some assets the greatest change in usefulness and/or physical deterioration takes place during the last years of the asset's life, rather than in the first years. Capturing this pattern requires the use of a **decelerated** or **compound interest method** of depreciation. Although this type of depreciation method is not used much in practice, it is conceptually consistent with a present-value method of asset valuation.

Exhibit 8-1 illustrates the pattern of depreciation expense under the three methods with predictable methods of depreciation: straight-line, accelerated, and decelerated (these methods are discussed in detail later). Exhibit 8-2 illustrates the pattern of decline in an asset's carrying value under the same methods. The graphs are based on a $10,000 original cost, a 40-year useful life, and zero residual value.

EXHIBIT 8-1

ANNUAL DEPRECIATION EXPENSE

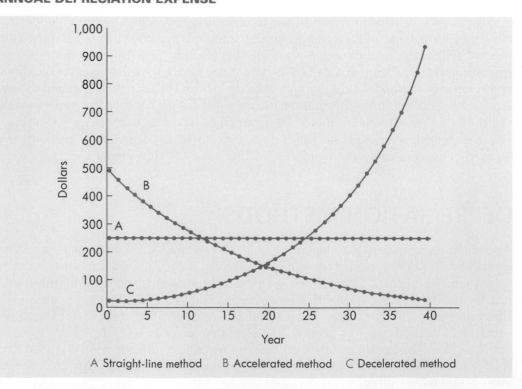

A Straight-line method B Accelerated method C Decelerated method

ASSET CARRYING VALUE

EXHIBIT 8-2

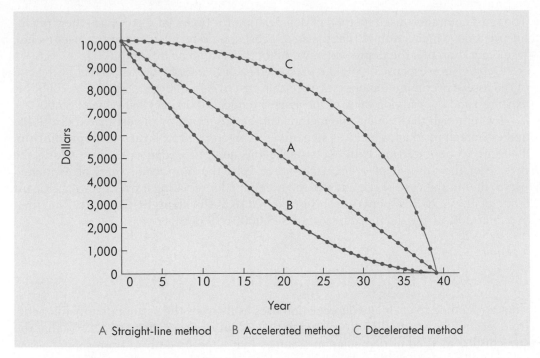

A Straight-line method   B Accelerated method   C Decelerated method

In Exhibit 8-1, you can see that with the straight-line method, the depreciation expense for each period is the same; this produces the even (or straight-line) decline in the asset's carrying value shown in Exhibit 8-2. With the accelerated method, Exhibit 8-1 shows that the annual depreciation expense is higher in the earlier years; this causes a faster decline in the net carrying value during the earlier years of the asset's life, as seen in Exhibit 8-2. For the decelerated method, on the other hand, Exhibit 8-1 shows that the depreciation expense is much lower in the earlier years; this results in a much slower decline in the asset's carrying value during the earlier years of the asset's life, as shown in Exhibit 8-2. However, although the pattern of recognition is different, the total amount of expense taken over the asset's life is the same for all methods. This is evidenced by the fact that, as shown in Exhibit 8-2, all the methods start with a carrying value of $10,000 and end with a carrying value of zero (indicating that each method transfers the entire depreciable cost to expense during the asset's life).

Note that Exhibits 8-1 and 8-2 do not show the units-of-activity or production method because there is usually no consistent or predictable pattern with this method, since the annual amount of depreciation expense depends on the actual usage each year.

To now illustrate each of the depreciation methods, we will use the following example:

EXAMPLE USED FOR DEPRECIATION CALCULATIONS

A company buys equipment for $50,000; the equipment has an estimated useful life of five years and an estimated residual value of $5,000. The total amount to be depreciated over the equipment's life—its depreciable cost—is therefore $45,000 (i.e., $50,000 − $5,000).

Straight-Line Method

The most commonly used method of depreciation for financial reporting is the straight-line method, which assumes that the asset's cost should be allocated evenly over its life. Using our example, the depreciation would be calculated as in Exhibit 8-3.

Depreciation expense of $9,000 is recorded each year for five years, so that by the end of the asset's useful life the entire depreciable cost of $45,000 (i.e., $50,000 − 5,000) is expensed and the carrying value of the asset is reduced to its residual value of $5,000.

Even though the straight-line method can be described by the estimated useful life and estimated residual value, it is sometimes characterized by a **rate of depreciation**. The rate of depreciation with the straight-line method is determined by taking the inverse of the number of years, 1/N, where N is the number of years of estimated useful life. In the case of the asset in the example, depreciating it over five years means a rate of 1 ÷ 5, or 20% per year. This is referred to as the **straight-line rate**. Note that 1 ÷ 5 or 20% of the depreciable cost of $45,000 is $9,000 per year.

Units-of-Activity or Production Method

Another method to calculate depreciation uses as its basis the assumption that benefits from a capital asset are directly related to the output or use of that asset. Note that the straight-line method of depreciation assumes that benefits derived from capital assets are related to time, disregarding how much the assets are actually used during each period. In contrast, the units-of-activity or production method relates benefits to actual usage, which means that it best satisfies the matching principle.

| EXHIBIT 8-3 | **STRAIGHT-LINE METHOD OF DEPRECIATION** |

Acquisition cost	$50,000
Estimated residual value	$ 5,000
Estimated useful life	5 years

Calculation of Depreciation by the Straight-Line Method:

$$\text{Depreciation expense} = \frac{\text{Acquisition cost} - \text{Estimated residual value}}{\text{Estimated useful life}}$$

$$= \frac{\$50,000 - \$5,000}{5 \text{ years}}$$

$$= \$9,000 \text{ per year}$$

Depreciation schedule:

Year	Beginning Net Book Value		Depreciation Expense		Ending Net Book Value
2011	$50,000	=	$ 9,000	=	$41,000
2012	41,000	=	9,000	=	32,000
2013	32,000	=	9,000	=	23,000
2014	23,000	=	9,000	=	14,000
2015	14,000	=	9,000	=	**5,000**
			$45,000		

Under the units-of-activity method, the asset's useful life is estimated and expressed as units of output or activity, rather than years of service. For example, trucks can be depreciated using this method if their expected useful lives can be expressed in kilometres driven or hours used. Machinery used in manufacturing products may have an expected useful life based on the total number of units of output. Depreciation expense is then determined by calculating the depreciation cost per unit, and multiplying this cost per unit by the actual number of units produced or used for the period. The formula for calculating depreciation expense per unit for the units-of-activity or production method is as follows:

$$\text{Depreciation expense per unit} = \frac{(\text{Acquisition cost} - \text{Residual value})}{\text{Estimated total units of output}}$$

To calculate the depreciation expense for the period, simply multiply this per-unit cost by the total number of units produced or used during the period. Exhibit 8-4 illustrates this method using our previous example.

UNITS-OF-ACTIVITY OR PRODUCTION METHOD OF DEPRECIATION

EXHIBIT 8-4

Acquisition cost	$50,000	
Estimated residual value	$ 5,000	
Estimated usage	2011	4,000 units
	2012	5,000 units
	2013	6,000 units
	2014	4,500 units
	2015	3,000 units
		22,500 units

Calculation of Depreciation by the Units-of-Activity or Production Method:

$$\text{Depreciation expense per unit} = \frac{(\text{Acquisition cost} - \text{Residual value})}{\text{Estimated total units of output}}$$

$$= \frac{(\$50,000 - \$5,000)}{22,500 \text{ units}}$$

$$= \$2 \text{ per unit}$$

Depreciation schedule:

Year	Cost per Unit		Units Produced		Depreciation Expense	Ending Net Book Value
2011	$2	×	4,000	=	$ 8,000	$42,000
2012	2	×	5,000	=	10,000	32,000
2013	2	×	6,000	=	12,000	20,000
2014	2	×	4,500	=	9,000	11,000
2015	2	×	3,000	=	6,000	**5,000**
			22,500		**$45,000**	

Accelerated or Declining-Balance Method

The accelerated method of depreciation assumes that most of the benefits from the asset's use are realized in the early years. Most accelerated methods are calculated by multiplying the asset's carrying value by a fixed percentage. Because the carrying value (cost less accumulated depreciation) decreases each year (since the accumulated depreciation increases each year by the amount of the depreciation expense recorded), the resulting amount of depreciation expense decreases each year.

The formula for calculating accelerated or declining-balance depreciation follows:

(Acquisition cost − Accumulated depreciation at beginning of period) ×
Depreciation % = Depreciation expense

The percentage that is used in these calculations is selected by management based on their judgement of how quickly the asset's usefulness will decline. The faster the expected decline, the higher the percentage selected. Different types of capital assets will be assigned different percentages. A capital asset with a relatively long expected useful life (such as a building) would have a fairly small percentage (such as 5% or 10%), while a capital asset with a relatively short expected useful life (such as equipment) would have a larger percentage (such as 20% or 30%).

One method of establishing the percentages to be used is the **double-declining-balance method**. With this method, the percentage selected is double the straight-line rate. Thus, using the example shown in Exhibit 8-3, the acquisition cost of an asset with a five-year expected useful life would be depreciated over five years on a straight-line basis (that is, 1/5 or 20% per year), but would be depreciated at 40% using the double-declining-balance method. However, even though this method appears to be based on fairly concrete numbers, it must be remembered that the 40% rate is very questionable (since the 20% is based on an estimate and doubling it is arbitrary).

Exhibit 8-5 shows the calculation under double-declining-balance depreciation using our ongoing example. Note that, *under this method, the asset's residual value does not directly enter into the calculation of the depreciation expense. Instead, the estimated residual value serves as a constraint; the final net book value should equal the residual value.* In the example in Exhibit 8-5, this means that in 2015 the company has to record $1,480 of depreciation expense, to reduce the asset from its net book value of $6,480 at the end of 2014 to its residual value of $5,000 at the end of 2015.

In this case, only a small amount of depreciation had to be taken in the final year. In other cases, however, a large amount of depreciation expense might have to be recorded in the last year of the asset's life in order to make the final carrying value equal to its residual value. For example, suppose that the residual value of the equipment was expected to be only $2,000 (rather than $5,000). If this were the case, the depreciation schedule would be the same as shown in Exhibit 8-5 except that in 2015 the company would have to record $4,480 of depreciation expense in order to reduce the asset's carrying value from $6,480 at the end of 2014 to its assumed residual value of $2,000 at the end of 2015.

HELPFUL HINT

When using declining-balance depreciation, remember that the residual value is ignored until the final year of the asset's life. At that point, you depreciate whatever amount will reduce the asset's net book value to its residual value.

Recording Depreciation Expense

Regardless of the depreciation method, the recording of the expense is the same. The account Depreciation Expense is debited and Accumulated Depreciation is credited. The credit side of the entry is made to an accumulated depreciation account, not to the

DOUBLE-DECLINING-BALANCE METHOD OF DEPRECIATION

EXHIBIT 8-5

Acquisition cost	$50,000
Estimated residual value	$ 5,000
Estimated useful life	5 years

Calculation of Depreciation by the Double-Declining-Balance Method:

Double-declining-balance rate $= 2 \times$ Straight-line rate

$\qquad\qquad\qquad\qquad\qquad = 2 \times 1/\text{years of life}$

$\qquad\qquad\qquad\qquad\qquad = 2 \times 1/5$

$\qquad\qquad\qquad\qquad\qquad = 2/5 \text{ or } 40\%$

Depreciation schedule:

Year	Cost of Equipment	Beginning Accumulated Depreciation	Beginning Net Book Value	Calculation of Expenses	Depreciation Expense	Ending Net Book Value
2011	$50,000	$ 0	$50,000	40% × 50,000 =	$20,000	$30,000
2012	50,000	20,000	30,000	40% × 30,000 =	12,000	18,000
2013	50,000	32,000	18,000	40% × 18,000 =	7,200	10,800
2014	50,000	39,200	10,800	40% × 10,800 =	4,320	6,480
2015	50,000	43,520	6,480	6,480 − 5,000 =	1,480[a]	**5,000**
					$45,000	

[a] In the final year, the depreciation expense should be whatever amount is needed to make the final net book value equal to the asset's residual value.

asset account. The accumulated depreciation account is a contra asset account that is used to accumulate the total amount of depreciation expense that has been recorded for the capital asset over its lifetime. The asset account shows the asset's acquisition cost, and the accumulated depreciation account shows how much of the cost has already been expensed. To give statement users more information, the accumulated depreciation account is used as an offset to the asset account, instead of reducing the asset directly. If users can see what the original cost was, they may be able to estimate how much the company will have to pay to replace the asset. Also, when the accumulated depreciation is offset against the asset, users can determine how much of the asset has been depreciated and can make a judgement about how soon the asset will need to be replaced.

Capital assets are rarely acquired on the first day of a fiscal year. Most assets are acquired partway through the year, and companies have to then choose among the following accounting conventions for calculating depreciation. One convention is "the nearest whole month" rule. This convention calculates depreciation for the whole month if the asset was purchased in the first half of the month, because the asset was used for most of the month. If the asset was purchased in the last half of the month (the 15th of the month to the end), no depreciation is taken in that month, because the asset was used for less than half a month. A second convention is the "half year" rule. In this convention, half a year's depreciation is taken in the year the asset is acquired and in the year of disposal no matter when the asset was acquired or sold in the year. There are other conventions that can be used but knowing these two is sufficient for now.

In financial statements, companies normally show the total original costs of all tangible capital assets separately by category (such as land, buildings, and equipment) with accumulated depreciation for each category. Some companies show only one total for accumulated depreciation for all the various asset categories. Many companies show only the total net book value (cost less accumulated depreciation) in the statement of financial position, with the details provided in a note to the financial statements.

An example of detailed disclosures regarding property, plant, and equipment (sometimes called *fixed assets*) and related accumulated depreciation is shown in Exhibit 8-6. The information provided by **Finning International Inc.** related to its land, buildings, and equipment in its 2009 annual report is fairly typical of the type of supporting detail that is usually provided in notes accompanying the financial statements. Finning International is the largest Caterpillar dealer, selling, leasing, and servicing Carterpillar's heavy equipment in Canada.

In addition to recording regular depreciation expense, companies must periodically compare their assets' carrying values with the future benefits they expect to derive from their use. If the net book value, or carrying value, of an asset is higher than the future amount recoverable from the asset, it must be written down and a loss recorded to reflect the **impairment** in the asset's value. (Note that this is conceptually similar to the lower of cost and market valuation that is applied to inventories: the value recorded for an asset should not exceed its net realizable value, through use and/or sale.)

CORPORATE INCOME TAXES

The Canada Revenue Agency (CRA) does not allow companies to deduct depreciation expense when calculating their taxable income. However, it does allow a similar type of deduction, called **capital cost allowance** (CCA). In other words, although accountants deduct depreciation expense when they calculate net earnings on the statement of earnings, they have to use capital cost allowance instead of depreciation expense when they calculate the company's taxable income on its income tax return. CCA is calculated in a manner similar to accelerated depreciation, with several exceptions (described below).

EXHIBIT 8-6

annual report

FINNING INTERNATIONAL INC. 2009 ANNUAL REPORT

NOTES TO THE CONSOLIDATED FINANCIAL STATEMENTS

14. CAPITAL ASSETS

LAND, BUILDINGS, AND EQUIPMENT

December 31 ($ THOUSANDS)	2009			2008		
	Cost	Accumulated depreciation	Net book value	Cost	Accumulated depreciation	Net book value
Land	$ 62,761	$ –	$ 62,761	$ 71,224	$ –	$ 71,224
Buildings and equipment	636,546	(216,530)	420,016	610,253	(210,618)	399,635
	$ 699,307	$ (216,530)	$ 482,777	$ 681,477	$ (210,618)	$ 470,859

Land, buildings, and equipment under capital leases of $11.8 million (2008: $12.1 million), net of accumulated depreciation of $3.0 million (2008: $2.9 million), are included above, of which $1.2 million was acquired during the year. Depreciation of buildings and equipment for the year ended December 31, 2009 was $42.3 million (2008: $44.4 million).

Since the depreciation expense for accounting purposes and CCA for tax purposes are usually different amounts, the net carrying value of the capital assets in the company's accounting records will be different from the value in its tax records. For tax purposes, the net carrying value of capital assets is referred to as their **undepreciated capital cost** (UCC). So, while a company's accounting records will show the net book value (NBV) of its capital assets, its tax records will show a different value (the UCC) for these assets. To account for this difference, a **deferred tax asset or liability** results.

While it is not the purpose of this text to teach you about income taxes, which are subject to very complex rules, you should understand the basics of how capital cost allowance works. For tax purposes, capital assets are grouped into *classes* as defined by the *Income Tax Act*. For example, most vehicles are grouped into Class 10 and most equipment into Class 8. Each class has a prescribed rate that is used to calculate the maximum amount that may be deducted. For example, Class 10 has a rate of 30% and Class 8 has a 20% rate. In the year of acquisition, however, the maximum CCA that may be deducted for new assets is half of the normal amount.

Continuing with our previous example of a company that purchases equipment with a cost of $50,000 (and an estimated useful life of five years with a residual value of $5,000), and assuming that the equipment falls into Class 8 with a CCA rate of 20%, for tax purposes the company can deduct the following during the first four years.

Year	First-year reduction	CCA rate for this class	UCC (Original cost–Accumulated CCA)	CCA for the year[2]
2011	1/2 ×	20% ×	($50,000 − 0)	= $5,000
2012		20% ×	($50,000 − $5,000)	= $9,000
2013		20% ×	($50,000 − $14,000)	= $7,200
2014		20% ×	($50,000 − $21,200)	= $5,760

Since the UCC is the equivalent of net book value for tax purposes, it declines each year by the amount of CCA claimed.[3] You should also note that neither the estimated useful life of the asset nor its residual value are relevant for CCA calculations.

We have deliberately not shown 2015 in the table above, because what will be done for tax purposes in the final year of an asset's life depends on several factors that are beyond the scope of an introductory accounting text.

Assuming the company uses straight-line depreciation for accounting purposes, the annual depreciation expense is $9,000 per year (as shown in Exhibit 8-3). Exhibit 8-7 presents some additional data for the company and the calculation of income taxes for the first year of the asset's life, using an income tax rate of 40%.

It seems logical that the tax expense reported on the statement of earnings should be calculated based on the *accounting earnings before tax* that is reported on the statement of earnings, multiplied by the tax rate.[4] In this example, the *tax expense* for the year will be $10,000 (as shown above). However, the amount owed to the CRA will be based on the *taxable income* reported on the company's income tax return. In this

---

2. Companies can claim lower amounts of CCA if they wish. The tax regulations only specify the maximum amounts that can be deducted in any particular year.
3. When capital assets are purchased, their cost is added to the class to increase the UCC. When capital assets are sold, the lesser of the original cost or the proceeds from the sale is deducted from the UCC.
4. More precisely, the tax expense reported in the statement of earnings should be based on the difference between the income taxes payable and the deferred income tax asset.

EXHIBIT 8-7

DEFERRED INCOME TAX CALCULATIONS

Earnings calculations:

	For Accounting Purposes	For Income Tax Purposes
Revenues	$100,000	$100,000
Expenses except depreciation or CCA	(66,000)	(66,000)
Depreciation and CCA	(9,000)	(5,000)
Earnings before tax	$ 25,000	$ 29,000
Income tax expense (40% of $25,000)	$ 10,000	
Income tax payable (40% of $29,000)		$ 11,600
Carrying value of the capital assets:		
NBV ($50,000 − $9,000)	$ 41,000	
UCC ($50,000 − $5,000)		$ 45,000

Deferred income tax asset = 40% × ($41,000 − $45,000) = $1,600

example, the *tax payable* for the year will be $11,600 (as shown above). The difference between these two amounts is recorded as a deferred income tax asset of $1,600.

The journal entry to record the company's taxes is as follows:

Income tax expense (SE)	10,000	
Deferred income tax asset (A)	1,600	
Income tax payable (L)		11,600

As you can see in the preceding entry, the debit to tax expense is less than the credit to the tax payable account. To make the entry balance, we therefore have to debit the difference to a deferred income tax account.

As shown in the lower portion of Exhibit 8-7, the $1,600 difference between the amount of income tax expense for the period and the amount of income tax that has to be paid currently reflects the difference between the carrying values of the capital assets for accounting purposes (NBV of $41,000) and tax purposes (UCC of $45,000), multiplied by the tax rate. Whenever the carrying value of the capital assets for tax purposes is larger than their carrying value for accounting purposes, less tax will be paid in the future because the larger amount remaining for tax purposes will result in larger tax deductions in the future. The deferred income tax amount is therefore recorded as an asset, because it represents a benefit in the form of future income tax reductions.

The deferred income tax account will have a credit balance and be called a deferred income tax liability whenever the carrying value of the capital assets for tax purposes (their UCC) is smaller than their carrying value for accounting purposes (their NBV). When this occurs, more tax will have to be paid in the future, because the smaller UCC will result in smaller future CCA deductions. Thus, a deferred income tax liability represents tax that will have to be paid by the company later in the life of the capital assets, when the CCA deductions for tax purposes will be lower.

In summary, these deferred income tax balances arise from differences between the carrying value of capital assets for tax purposes (i.e., their undepreciated capital cost) compared with their carrying value for accounting purposes (i.e., their net book value). The discussion of income taxes is continued in Chapter 9.

CHOICE OF DEPRECIATION METHOD

Companies are free to use any of the depreciation methods that have been discussed, or other systematic and rational methods that suit their circumstances. The majority of companies use the straight-line method, probably because of its simplicity.

For practical reasons, because CCA is required for income tax purposes, many smaller companies choose to use it for their accounting depreciation as well. By doing so, they only have to do one set of calculations, and their record keeping and tax reporting are simplified.

LEARNING OBJECTIVE 4

Identify the factors that influence the choice of depreciation method.

CHANGES IN DEPRECIATION ESTIMATES AND METHODS

Because the expected useful life and residual value are estimates, the assumptions used in their estimation may change over time. Companies must periodically revisit these estimates to ensure that they are still valid. For example, after an asset has been in service for several years, the company may change its estimate about the asset's remaining useful life. The asset may last longer or deteriorate faster than originally anticipated. Like all accounting estimate changes, a change in an estimate that is used to calculate depreciation is handled prospectively (in current and future periods). Note that there is no restatement of prior periods when an estimate is changed.

LEARNING OBJECTIVE 5

Describe and implement changes in depreciation estimates and methods.

To illustrate how a change in depreciation assumptions is handled, the depreciation example in Exhibit 8-3 will be used. Assume that after the asset has been depreciated for three years the company decides that it has three more years of useful life left (i.e., it is now expected to have a useful life of six rather than five years), and its residual value at the end of the 2016 is expected to be $2,000. Based on these new assumptions, the company will recalculate its depreciation for years 2014, 2015, and 2016. The new calculation is based on the remaining net book value of $23,000 at the end of 2013, as shown in Exhibit 8-3. The revised depreciation schedule will be as shown in Exhibit 8-8.

The disclosure of changes in estimates in financial statements usually describes the nature of the change and the effects on the current year, if they are material. Companies are not required to make this type of disclosure, but voluntary disclosure improves the usefulness of the financial information.

Depreciation amounts can also change when new costs are added to the asset account as a result of major repairs or improvements to the asset. These generally will require new estimates of the asset's useful life and/or residual value, and are handled in the same way as changes in accounting estimates are.

During an asset's life, a company may also decide that a different depreciation method would more appropriately match the depreciation expense with the benefits received from the asset. If the decision to change to a different depreciation method is made as a result of changed circumstances, experience, or new information, the change is treated in the same way as changes in estimates are. The new depreciation method is applied to the asset's carrying value at the time that the change is made, and the company uses the new method over the asset's remaining useful life. If, however, the company determines that the change in depreciation method will provide more reliable and relevant information, the change must be recognized retrospectively by restating prior years' financial statements to incorporate the new depreciation method.

EXHIBIT 8-8

EXAMPLE OF CHANGES IN ESTIMATES OF USEFUL LIFE AND RESIDUAL VALUE

Acquisition cost	$50,000
Original estimate of residual value	$ 5,000
Original estimate of useful life	5 years
Straight-line depreciation per year	$ 9,000
Remaining net book value at end of 2013 [$50,000 − (3 × $9,000)]	$23,000
Changes in estimates in 2014:	
Estimated remaining useful life	3 years
Estimated residual value	$ 2,000

Calculation of Depreciation for Years 2014, 2015, and 2016:

$$\text{Depreciation expense} = \frac{\text{Remaining book value} - \text{Estimated residual value}}{\text{Estimated useful life}}$$

$$= \frac{\$23,000 - \$2,000}{3 \text{ years}}$$

$$= \$7,000 \text{ per year for years 2014, 2015, and 2016}$$

Depreciation schedule:

Year	Beginning Net Book Value	Depreciation Expense	Ending Net Book Value
2011	$50,000	$ 9,000	$41,000
2012	41,000	9,000	32,000
2013	32,000	9,000	23,000
	New calculation for depreciation:	(23,000 − 2,000) ÷ 3 = $7,000	
2014	23,000	7,000	16,000
2015	16,000	7,000	9,000
2016	9,000	7,000	**2,000**
		$48,000	

EARNINGS MANAGEMENT

The decisions about the estimates of useful life and residual value provide opportunities for management to make decisions that affect the net earnings amount on the statement of earnings. The choice of the depreciation method (straight line, declining balance) also provides an opportunity for management to impact the net earnings amount. The IFRS requirement for the choice of depreciation method provides a fair amount of latitude for management.

ADDITIONAL EXPENDITURES ON CAPITAL ASSETS DURING THEIR LIVES

It was mentioned above that new costs may be added to an asset account during the asset's life for major repairs and improvements. Typically, there will also be expenditures for maintenance and minor repairs throughout an asset's life. We must therefore consider how we should account for these types of costs. Should they be capitalized, as part of the asset's cost, or charged directly to expense? If these costs are capitalized, they will be charged to expense over several periods, in the form of depreciation. On the other hand, if they are expensed, they will go directly onto the current period's statement of earnings.

The general guideline to be followed here is that non-routine costs (such as those for major repairs and improvements) are usually capitalized, while the costs of routine items (such as maintenance and minor repairs) are expensed. The former types of costs are likely to increase the future benefits to be received from the asset (by extending its useful life, lowering its operating costs, or increasing its productivity). Therefore, in terms of the matching principle, it makes sense to capitalize these expenditures and then depreciate them over the periods that benefit from them.

> **LEARNING OBJECTIVE 6**
>
> *Account for the disposal and writedown (impairment) of capital assets.*

WRITEDOWNS AND DISPOSALS OF PROPERTY, PLANT, AND EQUIPMENT

Sometimes the future recoverable value of a capital asset (which reflects its ability to generate revenue and contribute to earnings in the future) declines below its carrying value. Some possible reasons for this decline are technological change, damage to the asset, or a change in the company's market. If the recoverable value of an asset is less than its net book value, the company must reduce (or write down) the asset's carrying value. This is accomplished by recognizing a loss on the statement of earnings and increasing the accumulated depreciation account by the amount of the loss. Increasing the accumulated depreciation decreases the net book value of the asset.

For example, suppose that at the end of the 2013, when the book value of the asset in Exhibit 8-3 is $23,000, the company determines that as a result of damage to the equipment the recoverable amount from its future use will be only $20,000. The following entry would be made to record the required writedown:

Loss due to damage to equipment (SE)	3,000	
Accumulated depreciation (XA)		3,000

In all likelihood, subsequent to this decline in value the company would review the asset's estimated useful life and residual value so that changes could be made to the depreciation in future periods, if necessary.

At the end of an asset's useful life, the company usually disposes of it and replaces it with another asset, especially if the line of business is growing and prospering. In lines of business that are declining or being discontinued, old assets are not replaced and may even be sold or written off before they reach the end of their useful lives.

Normally, at the end of an asset's life, it is sold. If the company has accurately projected the residual value, there will be no gain or loss on the sale of the asset. However, if the residual value was not estimated accurately, either a gain or loss will result from this transaction. For example, suppose that the asset in Exhibit 8-3 is sold at the end of its useful life for $6,000. (Recall that its original cost was $50,000 and that its residual value was expected to be $5,000.) The following entry would be made to record its sale:

Cash (A)	6,000	
Accumulated depreciation (XA)	45,000	
Equipment (A)		50,000
Gain on sale of equipment (SE)		1,000

In this entry, the total depreciation recorded during the asset's life is removed from the accumulated depreciation account, at the same time as the original cost is removed from the equipment account. Note that the net of these two amounts is the asset's carrying or net book value at the time of sale, $5,000 ($50,000 − 45,000). Note also that you cannot simply credit the equipment account for the net amount of $5,000, as that would leave $45,000 in the asset account and $45,000 in the accumulated depreciation account when the asset is no longer owned by the company.

If the asset had been worthless at the end of its useful life, the asset's disposal would be recorded as above, except that no cash would be received. If we assume that no cash is received, then the write-off of the asset in our example would result in the following entry:

Accumulated depreciation (XA)	45,000	
Loss on disposal of equipment (SE)	5,000	
Equipment (A)		50,000

Note that, since the asset is worthless, the remaining net book value of $5,000 is written off and recorded as a loss on disposal.

NATURAL RESOURCES

LEARNING OBJECTIVE 7

Describe and implement the depreciation method used most frequently for natural resources.

Companies that deal with natural resources face some unique problems not associated with investments in property, plant, and equipment. For example, consider the situation of oil exploration companies, which incur large costs in their attempts to find oil. Some explorations are successful in finding oil and others are not. Should the costs of unsuccessful exploration be capitalized on the statement of financial position as assets, or should they be written off directly as expenses? If these costs are capitalized as assets, this implies that they have future value. But do they? And if the costs are capitalized, how should they be expensed? That is, what is the useful life of the asset being created, and what is a reasonable pattern of depreciation expense allocation over the useful life?

At the time of writing of this textbook, under IFRS there did not yet exist a standard for the oil and gas industry. Instead, companies were encouraged to continue to use accounting methods that had been used in the past as long as they continued to provide relevant information. In Canada, such companies have a choice of two methods to account for exploration costs: the full cost method and the successful efforts method. The **full cost method** capitalizes the costs of all explorations, both successful and unsuccessful, as long as the expected revenues from all the explorations are estimated to exceed the total costs. (The logic behind capitalizing the costs of unsuccessful exploration efforts is that, even though these attempts were not successful, they are necessary costs of finding oil and will produce future benefits because they will lead to successful attempts.) The **successful efforts method**, on the other hand, capitalizes only the cost of successful explorations and expenses any unsuccessful exploration costs. Sufficient time is allowed to determine whether an effort is or is not successful.

Generally, smaller oil companies use the full cost method, because using the successful efforts method would make their earnings appear to be very uneven from one accounting period to another, depending on the results of the wells they drilled during that particular period. Larger oil companies drill more wells every period, so they tend to use the successful efforts method because it is simpler to apply and its use over a large base does not produce uneven results from period to period.

Exhibit 8-9 includes examples from two companies.

ACCOUNTING FOR EXPLORATION AND DEVELOPMENT COSTS—
FULL COST AND SUCCESSFUL EFFORTS METHODS

EXHIBIT 8-9

ALBERTA OILSANDS INC. 2009 ANNUAL REPORT
Excerpt from Note 2: Significant Accounting Policies
c) Property and equipment
   i) Capitalized costs
      The Company follows the full cost method of accounting for its petroleum and natural gas operations. Under this method all costs relating to the exploration for and development of petroleum and natural gas reserves are capitalized on a country-by-country basis. Costs include lease acquisition costs, geological and geophysical expenses, costs of drilling both productive and nonproductive wells, asset retirement costs and directly related overhead. Proceeds from the sale of properties are applied against capitalized costs, without any gain or loss being realized, unless such sale would alter the rate of depletion and depreciation by more than 20%.

SUNCOR ENERGY INC. 2009 ANNUAL REPORT
Excerpt from Summary of Significant Accounting Policies

(j) *Property, Plant and Equipment*
   The company follows the successful efforts method of accounting for the exploration and development expenditures of oil and gas producing activities. Under the successful efforts method, acquisition costs of proved and unproved properties are capitalized. Costs of unproved properties are transferred to proved properties when proved reserves are confirmed. Exploration costs, including geological and geophysical costs, are expensed as incurred. Exploratory drilling costs are initially capitalized. If it is determined that a specific well does not contain proved reserves, the related capitalized exploratory drilling costs are charged to expense, as dry hole costs, at that time.

Note that **Alberta Oilsands Inc.**, an exploration and development company involved in the petroleum and natural gas industry in the Athabasca region of Alberta, uses the full cost method. It capitalizes the costs of drilling both productive and unproductive wells. In contrast, **Suncor Energy Inc.**, a company involved in oil development in the tar sands of northern Alberta, uses the successful efforts method for its acquisition costs and exploratory drilling costs. Exploratory drilling costs of wells without proven reserves are expensed. Under the full cost method, all exploration costs are first capitalized and then expensed, through depreciation, over the life of the producing wells. Consequently, initial expenses are lower and subsequent depreciation charges are higher. Under the successful efforts method, only the costs associated with successful sites are capitalized and later depreciated over the period of production. Consequently, initial expenses are higher as the costs of the unsuccessful wells are expensed and subsequent depreciation charges are lower.

The depreciation of natural resources is often referred to as **depletion**. The depreciation method most commonly used is the units-of-activity or production method. For example, in the case of an oil field, the total number of barrels of oil expected to be produced from the field would be estimated. The depreciation expense would then be calculated by dividing the capitalized costs by the estimated total number of barrels to be produced from the field, to get a depreciation rate per barrel. This would then be multiplied by the number of barrels extracted each period.

For example, assume that a company estimates a field to contain 2 million barrels of oil. During an accounting period, 500,000 barrels of oil are extracted from the field. If the capitalized costs related to the oil field are $6 million, then the depletion expense recorded for the period would be $1.5 million.

$6,000,000 ÷ 2,000,000 barrels = $3 per barrel
$3 per barrel × 500,000 barrels = $1,500,000

INTANGIBLE ASSETS

As discussed earlier in the chapter, some assets can have probable future value to the company but not have any physical form. The knowledge gained from research and development or the customer awareness and loyalty produced by a well-run promotional campaign are examples of possible intangible assets. The companies that engage in these activities certainly hope that they will benefit from having spent money on them. However, the difficulty of determining the costs of producing intangible assets such as research and development knowledge or customer awareness and loyalty, and of quantifying the benefits that will be derived from them, make intangible assets a troublesome area for accountants. Although accountants would generally agree that these might constitute assets, the inability to provide reliable data concerning their costs and future benefits makes it hard to record these items objectively in the company's accounting system.

The capitalization guideline for intangible assets is that, if they are developed internally, the costs of developing them are expensed as incurred and no asset values are recorded. If intangible assets are purchased from independent entities, however, they can be capitalized at their acquisition costs.

An exception to this general guideline occurs with the **development costs** for a product or process. If certain conditions are met, these development costs may be capitalized and depreciated over the product's useful life. However, the basic **research costs** that occurred prior to any decision to develop the product or process are still expensed. The conditions for capitalization stipulate that the product or process must be clearly definable, technical feasibility must be established, management must intend to market the product in a defined market, and the company must have the resources needed to complete the project. These requirements are intended to ensure that development costs will be capitalized only if the product or process is actually marketable and will therefore produce future benefits in the form of revenues.

INTERNATIONAL PERSPECTIVES

In the United States, both research and development costs are expensed, and the related cash flows are classified as operating activities. This can result in large income differences, as well as differences in cash flows from operations, between a Canadian company and an American one.

The depreciation of an intangible asset is often referred to as amortization. Depreciating the cost of an intangible asset is similar to depreciating other capital assets. The company must estimate the asset's useful life and residual value (if any). Because of the estimation problems associated with intangible assets, this is sometimes very difficult to do. Typically, the method to depreciate intangibles is the straight-line method, with a residual value of zero. The useful life depends on the type of intangible asset. The one aspect of depreciation that is different for intangibles is that the accumulated depreciation account is rarely used. Most companies reduce their intangible assets directly, when they depreciate them. Because of the uncertain valuation of intangibles and the fact that these assets normally cannot be replaced, it is not as important for users to know what the original costs were. For example, the journal entry to record the depreciation of a patent would probably be as follows:

> LEARNING OBJECTIVE 9
>
> *Depreciate intangible assets, where appropriate.*

Depreciation expense (SE)	XXX	
Patents (A)		XXX

When estimating the useful life of an intangible asset, both the economic life and the legal life should be considered. Many intangible assets (such as patents and copyrights) have very well-defined legal lives, but may have less well-defined and shorter economic lives. Any intangible asset that has a definite life should be depreciated over its economic life or its legal life, whichever is shorter.

Note, however, that some intangible assets (such as trademarks and goodwill) have indefinite lives. Intangible assets with indefinite lives should not be depreciated in the usual manner. Instead, each of these assets must be evaluated each year to determine whether there has been any impairment in its value. If there has, the asset should be written down. If there has not, the asset will remain at its current carrying amount until the following year, when it will be evaluated again.

Several types of intangible assets pose special problems. These are discussed in the following sections.

accounting in the news

Biotechnology Intangibles

Small biotech companies are often founded on the strength of intangible assets in the form of scientific patents that hold potential for drug discoveries. The costs associated with developing new drugs, however, are extremely high, and pharmaceutical companies can spend a lot of money with no guarantee of their drugs ever reaching the marketplace. In fact, an Ernst & Young LLP report indicated that, during 2009, the gap between the financing for emerging companies and the larger, more established companies continued to widen. This is despite the fact that 2009 was an exceptional year for biotechnology companies in that the established biotech centres reached profitability for the first time in history. Although revenues fell, cost cutting, efficiency, and new creative models for funding and partnering enabled aggregate profits. Established Canadian biotechs increased the amount of capital raised.

The report, *Beyond Borders: Global Biotechnology Report 2010*, also stated that some research and development funding was directed to projects with potentially faster returns.

Source: Ernst & Young LLP, *Beyond Borders: Global Biotechnology Report 2010*, April 28, 2010.

Advertising

Companies spend enormous amounts of money advertising their products to increase current and future sales. Do expenditures on advertising create an asset for the company? If the advertising is successful, then the answer is probably yes. But how can the company know whether the advertising will be successful and what time periods will receive the benefits? If customers buy the company's products, it may be due to the advertising; but it may also be because they just happened to be in the store and saw them on the shelf, or because their neighbours have one, or because of many other factors. The intent of advertising is clearly to generate future benefits, which would usually lead to recording an asset; but determining the existence of the future benefits and measuring their value can be extremely difficult. These measurement uncertainties are so severe that accountants generally expense all advertising costs in the period in which the advertising occurs. If a company does capitalize this type of cost, it has to provide very strong evidence to support the creation of an asset.

Many companies spend a lot on advertising related to sporting events such as the Olympic Games and the World Cup. In many of these cases, the money is spent not just on advertisements during the games but also on pre-game financial support to the athletes, who then wear clothing and use equipment with the sponsors' logos on it. As you can probably imagine, it is very difficult to know how much future benefit will be received from these expenditures, and over what period of time.

Patents, Trademarks, and Copyrights

Patents, trademarks, and copyrights are legal entitlements that give their owner rights to use protected information. If the protected information has economic value, then the agreements are considered assets. Of course, determining whether they have value or not, and estimating the period over which the rights will continue to have value, can be a difficult task. Each entitlement may have a legal life associated with it, which may

accounting in the news

Advertising for the World Cup

Corporate sponsorship helped make the World Cup a reality in South Africa in 2010 by helping to fund the event's organization. Sponsorships for the 2010 World Cup enabled companies to have exclusive advertising opportunities not open to non-sponsors. Hyundai Kai Motors spent the most money, closely followed by Adidas, Emirates Airline, Sony, Coca-Cola, and Visa International. Spectators to the games (in person and through broadcasts) saw these names flash around the football field during the games, giving the company names maximum exposure. Omnicom Media Group MENA, a global advertising company, saw the advertising spending of companies increase by $60 million during the four weeks of the games. As well, various television companies that purchased the broadcast rights for the games saw their advertising revenues increase dramatically.

Source: Anil Bhoyrul, "World Cup to Net 120% TV Ads Boost—Media Guru," *Arabian Business.Com*, June 6, 2010, http://www.arabianbusiness.com/589832

differ from its economic life. For example, in Canada a patent has a legal life of 20 years, but this does not mean that it will have an economic life of 20 years. The patent on a computer chip, for example, may have a useful economic life of only a few years, as a result of technological innovation. On the other hand, trademarks like *Coca-Cola*® may have an indefinite life. Copyrights have a legal term of the life of the creator plus 50 years. As with any intangible asset, the legal life serves as a maximum in the determination of the asset's useful life for accounting purposes.

A company usually records these types of intangible assets only if it buys them from another entity. The costs of internally developed patents, trademarks, and copyrights are generally expensed, although some easily identifiable costs (such as registration and legal costs associated with obtaining a patent, trademark, or copyright) may be capitalized. These costs are then usually depreciated on a straight-line basis over the asset's estimated useful life.

In some cases, significant costs are subsequently incurred to defend and enforce patents, trademarks, and copyrights. Any costs related to successfully defending or enforcing these rights can be capitalized.

Goodwill

The intangible asset called **goodwill** represents the above-average profits that a company can earn as a result of a number of factors. For example, exceptional management expertise, a desirable location, and excellent employee or customer relations could give one company an economic advantage over other companies in the same industry and enable it to earn above-average profits.

accounting in the news

Patent Protection

In Canada, companies reap the benefits of patent protection laws that give them exclusivity for 20 years before others can use the product or process that has been developed. Many companies seek to expand their patent protection rights by registering their patents in other countries. Monsanto, a large U.S. agrichemical corporation, has developed and patented many genetically modified products and has sought global patent protection for its products.

Monsanto owns a patent for a DNA sequence that provides herbicide resistance in soya beans. It has been unable to obtain patent protection in Argentina for the sequence, although it believes that 95 percent of the soya beans grown in Argentina contain the DNA sequence developed by Monsanto. A Dutch company, Cefetra, was sued by Monsanto for importing soy meal from Argentina that it uses for the production of animal feed. Unable to demand royalties from the farmers in Argentina, Monsanto hoped to be able to get some of the royalties from the purchaser of the soya products. In a landmark decision, the Dutch court ruled that Monsanto's patent rights apply only to live plants and not to the DNA material in the soy meal.

This decision could have a major impact on patent protected products.

Source: Andrew Turley, "DNA Must Do Its Job for Patent Protection," *RCS: Advancing the Chemical Sciences*, July 8, 2010, http://www.rsc.org/chemistryworld/News/2010/July/08071001.asp

Companies incur costs to create these types of goodwill. Advertising campaigns, public service programs, charitable gifts, and employee training programs all require outlays that, to some extent, contribute to the development of goodwill. This type of goodwill is sometimes referred to as internally developed goodwill.

As with other intangible assets, the costs of internally developed goodwill are expensed as they are incurred. In practice, goodwill is recorded as an asset only when it is part of the purchase price paid to acquire another company. Goodwill is not an easily identifiable asset, but is represented by the amount paid by the acquiring company for various valuable but intangible characteristics of the acquired company (such as good location, good management, etc.). These characteristics, in effect, give the acquired company a value that exceeds its identifiable assets (its buildings, inventory, etc.).

The measurement and recognition of goodwill are discussed in more detail in Appendix B at the end of the book. At this point, the most important thing to note about goodwill is that it can be acquired only through the purchase of another company at a price that is greater than the value of its identifiable assets.

As mentioned in an earlier section, an intangible asset with an indefinite life—such as goodwill—is not depreciated. Instead, management is required to periodically review the goodwill's carrying value to determine whether there is evidence that it has been impaired. If it has, the goodwill should be written down (i.e., reduced in value) and an impairment loss recognized.

Examples of the disclosure of goodwill and other intangible assets are shown in Exhibit 8-10 for **Ballard Power Systems Inc.**, which designs, manufactures, sells, and services fuel cell products. As at December 31, 2009, Ballard Power Systems' reported goodwill and other intangible assets accounted for 25 percent of the company's total asset value. By contrast, its property, plant, and equipment constituted only 20 percent of its total assets. This is not uncommon in some industries, especially with high-technology ventures.

Note as well that the value reported for Ballard Power Systems' goodwill ($48.106 million) did not change during the year, which seems to indicate that there was no impairment or writedown, nor any more acquisitions.

HELPFUL HINT

Recorded goodwill arises only when it is externally purchased, and this happens only in situations in which one company buys another company. When the purchase price exceeds the fair value of the identifiable net assets acquired, then the company has purchased goodwill.

EXHIBIT 8-10

EXAMPLE OF A COMPANY WITH LARGE AMOUNTS OF GOODWILL AND OTHER INTANGIBLE ASSETS, BALLARD POWER SYSTEMS INC.

Consolidated Balance Sheets
December 31,
(Expressed in thousands of U.S. dollars)

	2009	2008 (revised— note 1(c)(ii))
Assets		
Current assets:		
Cash and cash equivalents	$ 43,299	$ 54,086
Short-term investments	38,932	31,313
Accounts receivable (notes 4 & 17)	12,903	18,856
Inventories (note 5)	9,168	10,402
Prepaid expenses and other current assets	2,114	1,434
	106,416	116,091

EXAMPLE OF A COMPANY WITH LARGE AMOUNTS OF GOODWILL AND OTHER INTANGIBLE ASSETS (cont'd)

EXHIBIT 8-10

Property, plant and equipment (note 6)	39,320	38,755
Intangible assets (note 7)	824	3,726
Goodwill	48,106	48,106
Investments (note 8)	632	1,765
Other long-term assets	50	–
	$195,348	$208,443
Liabilities and Shareholders' Equity		
Current liabilities:		
Accounts payable and accrued liabilities (notes 9 & 17)	$ 20,321	$ 21,819
Deferred revenue	1,607	947
Accrued warranty liabilities	7,813	3,841
Current portion of obligation under capital lease (note 10)	316	–
	30,057	26,607
Long-term liabilities (notes 11 & 12)	4,632	23,349
Obligation under capital lease (note 10)	1,739	–
	36,428	49,956
Shareholders' equity:		
Share capital (note 13)	835,358	832,711
Contributed surplus (notes 2 & 13)	284,510	283,466
Accumulated deficit	(960,712)	(957,454)
Accumulated other comprehensive loss	(236)	(236)
	158,920	158,487
	$195,348	$208,443

1. (k) Intangible assets:

Intangible assets consist of fuel cell technology acquired from third parties and are recorded at cost. Intangible assets are amortized over their estimated useful lives of 5 to 15 years using the straight-line method.

Costs incurred in establishing and maintaining patents and license agreements are expensed in the period incurred.

(l) Impairment of long-lived assets:

Long-lived assets, including property, plant and equipment, investments, and intangible assets, are reviewed for impairment when events or changes in circumstances indicate that the carrying amount of the asset may not be recoverable. An impairment loss, if any, is recognized when the carrying amount of a long-lived asset exceeds its fair value based on its estimated discounted future cash flows.

(m) Goodwill:

Goodwill represents the excess of the purchase price of an acquired enterprise over the fair value assigned to assets acquired and liabilities assumed.

Goodwill is assessed for impairment at least annually, or more frequently if events or changes in circumstances indicate that the goodwill might be impaired. The assessment of impairment is based on estimated fair market values derived from certain valuation models, which may consider various factors such as normalized and estimated future earnings, price earnings multiples, terminal values and discount rates. An impairment loss, if any, is recognized to the extent that the carrying amount of goodwill exceeds its estimated fair market value.

The Corporation has designated December 31 as the date for the annual impairment test. As at December 31, 2009, date of the last impairment test, goodwill was not considered to be impaired.

accounting in the news

Declining Share Prices and Goodwill

NightHawk Radiology Holdings Inc. provides hospitals and medical centres with radiology-related services. It purchased two companies in 2007 for amounts larger than the fair value of the net assets acquired, resulting in goodwill. A subsequent downturn in the economy resulted in a decline in the market prices of the acquired companies. When NightHawk checked for impairment in 2009, the discounted cash flow analysis was determined to be lower than the carrying value of the goodwill. It therefore wrote off all of the goodwill, $68.7 million, resulting in a net loss for the quarter of $52.6 million.

Source: "NightHawk Gets Goodwill Off Its Books," *Journal of Business*, May 21, 2009, allbusiness.com

Comprehensive Example of Capital Asset Disclosures

Due to the large number of policy issues associated with accounting for capital assets, companies usually have extensive disclosures about them in their notes. Exhibit 8-11 shows excerpts from the summary of significant accounting policies related to property, plant, and equipment, goodwill, and other intangible assets in the 2009 annual report of **Imperial Oil Limited**. The company operates Esso retail gas stations throughout Canada, and is a major Canadian producer of crude oil and natural gas. Notice that the note includes references to the following:

- the successful efforts method of accounting for its exploration and development activities

- its treatment of the costs of maintenance, repairs, and improvements (indicating that only those that prolong the service life or increase the capacity of an asset are capitalized)

- its policy regarding the capitalization of interest charges on capital projects under construction

- extensive discussion of its depreciation and depletion policies, for both tangible and intangible assets (including the methods and estimates of useful lives being used for different types of assets)

- its policy of periodically reviewing its properties and goodwill to check for impairment of their values

EXHIBIT 8-11

annual report

EXAMPLE OF DISCLOSURE OF SIGNIFICANT ACCOUNTING POLICIES RELATED TO CAPITAL ASSETS, IMPERIAL OIL LIMITED, 2009

Property, plant and equipment

Property, plant and equipment are recorded at cost. Investment tax credits and other similar grants are treated as a reduction of the capitalized cost of the asset to which they apply.

The company uses the successful-efforts method to account for its exploration and development activities. Under this method, costs are accumulated on a field-by-field

**EXAMPLE OF DISCLOSURE OF SIGNIFICANT ACCOUNTING POLICIES
RELATED TO CAPITAL ASSETS, IMPERIAL OIL LIMITED, 2009 (cont'd)**

EXHIBIT 8-11

annual report

basis with certain exploratory expenditures and exploratory dry holes being expensed as incurred. Costs of productive wells and development dry holes are capitalized and amortized on the unit-of-production method. The company carries as an asset exploratory well costs if (a) the well found a sufficient quantity of reserves to justify its completion as a producing well and (b) the company is making sufficient progress assessing the reserves and the economic and operating viability of the project. Exploratory well costs not meeting these criteria were charged to expense.

Acquisition costs of proved properties are amortized using the unit-of-production method, computed on the basis of total proved oil and gas reserves. Unproved properties are assessed for impairment individually and valuation allowances against the capitalized costs are recorded based on the estimated economic chance of success and the length of time the company expects to hold the properties. The valuation allowances are reviewed at least annually. Other exploratory expenditures, including geophysical costs and other dry hole costs, are expensed as incurred.

Maintenance and repair costs, including planned major maintenance, are expensed as incurred. Improvements that increase or prolong the service life or capacity of an asset are capitalized.

Production costs are expensed as incurred. Production involves lifting the oil and gas to the surface and gathering, treating, field processing and field storage of the oil and gas. The production function normally terminates at the outlet valve on the lease or field production storage tank. Production costs are those incurred to operate and maintain the company's wells and related equipment and facilities. They become part of the cost of oil and gas produced. These costs, sometimes referred to as lifting costs, include such items as labour cost to operate the wells and related equipment; repair and maintenance costs on the wells and equipment; materials, supplies and energy costs required to operate the wells and related equipment; and administrative expenses related to the production activity.

Depreciation and depletion for assets associated with producing properties begin at the time when production commences on a regular basis. Depreciation for other assets begins when the asset is in place and ready for its intended use. Assets under construction are not depreciated or depleted. Unit-of-production depreciation is applied to those wells, plant and equipment assets associated with productive depletable properties and the unit-of-production rates are based on the amount of proved developed reserves of oil and gas. Depreciation of other plant and equipment is calculated using the straight-line method, based on the estimated service life of the asset. In general, refineries are depreciated over 25 years; other major assets, including chemical plants and service stations, are depreciated over 20 years.

Proved oil and gas properties held and used by the company are reviewed for impairment whenever events or changes in circumstances indicate that the carrying amounts may not be recoverable. Assets are grouped at the lowest level for which there are identifiable cash flows that are largely independent of the cash flows of other groups of assets.

The company estimates the future undiscounted cash flows of the affected properties to judge the recoverability of carrying amounts. Cash flows used in impairment evaluations are developed using annually updated corporate plan investment evaluation assumptions for crude oil commodity prices and foreign-currency exchange

EXHIBIT 8-11

annual report

EXAMPLE OF DISCLOSURE OF SIGNIFICANT ACCOUNTING POLICIES RELATED TO CAPITAL ASSETS, IMPERIAL OIL LIMITED, 2009 (cont'd)

rates. Annual volumes are based on individual field production profiles, which are also updated annually.

In general, impairment analyses are based on proved reserves. Where probable reserves exist, an appropriately risk-adjusted amount of these reserves may be included in the impairment evaluation. An asset would be impaired if the undiscounted cash flows were less than its carrying value. Impairments are measured by the amount by which the carrying value exceeds its fair value.

Acquisition costs for the company's oil sands mining properties are capitalized as incurred. Oil sands mining exploration costs are expensed as incurred. The capitalization of project development costs begins when there are no major uncertainties that exist which would preclude management from making a significant funding commitment within a reasonable time period. Stripping costs of the company's oil sands mining operation during the production phase are expensed when incurred. With the consistently low level of inventory, recognizing stripping costs during the production phase as inventory would not have a significant impact on earnings or inventory value.

Depreciation of oil sands mining and extraction assets begins when bitumen ore is produced on a sustained basis, and depreciation of bitumen upgrading assets begins when feed is introduced to the upgrading unit and maintained on a continuous basis. Assets under construction are not depreciated. Investments in extraction facilities, which separate the crude from sand, as well as the upgrading facilities, are depreciated on a unit-of-production method based on proven developed reserves. Investments in mining and transportation systems are generally depreciated on a straight-line basis over a 15-year life. Other mining related infrastructure costs that are of a long-term nature intended for continued use in or to provide long-term benefit to the operation, such as pre-production stripping, certain roads, etc., are depreciated on a unit-of-production basis based on proven reserves.

Oil sands mining assets held and used by the company are reviewed for impairment whenever events or changes in circumstances indicate that the carrying amounts are not recoverable. The impairment evaluation for oil sands mining assets is based on a comparison of undiscounted cash flows to book carrying value.

Gains or losses on assets sold are included in "investment and other income" in the consolidated statement of income.

Interest capitalization

Interest costs relating to major capital projects under construction are capitalized as part of property, plant and equipment. The project construction phase commences with the development of the detailed engineering design and ends when the constructed assets are ready for their intended use.

Goodwill and other intangible assets

Goodwill is not subject to amortization. Goodwill is tested for impairment annually or more frequently if events or circumstances indicate it might be impaired. Impairment losses are recognized in current period earnings. The evaluation for impairment of goodwill is based on a comparison of the carrying values of goodwill and associated operating assets with the estimated present value of net cash flows from those operating assets.

**EXAMPLE OF DISCLOSURE OF SIGNIFICANT ACCOUNTING POLICIES
RELATED TO CAPITAL ASSETS, IMPERIAL OIL LIMITED, 2009 (cont'd)**

EXHIBIT 8-11

annual report

> Intangible assets with determinable useful lives are amortized over the estimated service lives of the assets. Computer software development costs are amortized over a maximum of 15 years and customer lists are amortized over a maximum of 10 years. The amortization is included in "depreciation and depletion" in the consolidated statement of income.

STATEMENT ANALYSIS CONSIDERATIONS

The choice of depreciation method affects both the value of the assets reported on the statement of financial position and the amount of expense reported on the statement of earnings. The use of different depreciation methods for capital assets can therefore produce significantly different results in the financial statements of two otherwise similar companies. For example, during the first few years of its assets' lives, a company using the straight-line method will show higher carrying values for its capital assets on its statement of financial position, as well as lower expenses on its statement of earnings, than a similar company using an accelerated depreciation method. For many companies, depreciation is one of their largest expenses; consequently, the choice of a depreciation method can have a significant impact on a company's net earnings.

Probably the biggest concerns in the analysis of capital assets are understanding which assets are not reported on the statement of financial position (i.e., those that were developed internally and therefore not recorded as assets), and what market values can be assigned to the capital assets that are reported on the statement of financial position. The historical cost figures for property, plant, and equipment may be very old. Even though the company is not holding these assets for resale, it will have to replace them at some point and, therefore, the replacement cost may be relevant. In Canada, companies are not required to disclose replacement cost information. Under IFRS, however, companies can choose to value their property, plant, and equipment at fair value. Most companies have decided to stay with historical cost because it is easier and less expensive to implement.

Another issue is that the user is not able to determine how much is invested in each component of property, plant, and equipment if these assets are reported as a single amount. This information could be important to users as they attempt to anticipate future outflows of cash for the replacement of these assets. Although some additional information is usually provided in the notes that accompany the financial statements, in most cases it is still not detailed enough to be very useful. Even if a company assigns three separate amounts for property, plant, and equipment, the user is still missing some important pieces of information that could be useful in evaluating the company. For example, if a single amount for buildings is disclosed, the user still does not know how many buildings are included, where they are located, when the buildings were acquired, or when they will have to be replaced. Without this information, the user has no way of determining fair values or replacement costs.

A potentially big problem is that many intangible assets that have been developed internally do not appear on the company's financial statements, because their costs have been expensed as they were developed. For example, it is possible for a company to have developed a patent that will generate revenues for several years. This potentially valuable economic resource is typically not listed as an asset at all. A similar problem arises with respect to goodwill. If it has been developed internally, goodwill will not appear on the company's statement of financial position as an asset, even though it may exist and be very valuable. The large dollar amounts that companies are willing to pay for goodwill when they purchase other companies testify to the substantial value that these assets can have. A failure to consider these assets can lead different analysts to draw significantly different conclusions about a company's value.

A final general concern with regard to financial statement analysis is whether the capital assets listed on the company's statement of financial position are really worth the amounts that are reported. For example, the conditions that gave rise to goodwill at the date of acquisition may have changed since that time. Suppose the goodwill was due to the technical expertise of some key employees of the business that was acquired. If these employees retire, or otherwise leave the company after acquisition, then the goodwill could be worth much less. Although this decline in value may result in an impairment loss being recorded, but due to the way the annual impairment test is conducted, it also might not. For this reason, analysts generally have a considerable amount of skepticism about the value of goodwill and other intangible assets.

Using the Return on Assets (ROA) Ratio

LEARNING OBJECTIVE 10

Calculate the return on assets ratio and discuss the potential implications of the results.

Despite the unknowns associated with capital asset values, a ratio called the **return on assets ratio**, or ROA, is widely used to assess how well management has used the company's assets to generate earnings. This ratio expresses the total return (or earnings) that was earned as a percentage of the total assets that were used to generate the earnings.

The ROA is calculated using the company's net earnings for the period, which does not factor in payments to debtholders or dividend payments to shareholders. Interest expense, however, is deducted in the calculation of net earnings and needs to be added back into the ROA calculation. Interest expense is added back into the net earnings amount so that interest expense and debt payments are treated in a similar way—i.e., the earnings amount should not factor in either of these amounts.

A further complication arises because interest is a deductible expense in the calculation of income tax expense. Therefore, when the net earnings figure is adjusted for the interest expense, we must also adjust the amount of income tax expense. In other words, the tax saving associated with the interest expense deduction must be removed from the earnings. The return on assets is therefore calculated by taking what the net earnings would have been without any interest charges and dividing it by the total assets (expressed as the average for the period, if possible: Assets at beginning of period + Assets at end of period ÷ 2). The following shows how the formula is derived:

$$\text{ROA} = \frac{\text{Earnings without interest}}{\text{Average total assets}}$$

$$= \frac{\text{Net earnings} + [\text{Interest expense} - \text{the Tax saving from the Interest expense}]}{\text{Average total assets}}$$

$$= \frac{\text{Net earnings} + [\text{Interest expense} - (\text{Tax rate} \times \text{Interest expense})]}{\text{Average total assets}}$$

$$= \frac{\text{Net earnings} + [\text{Interest expense} \times (1 - \text{Tax rate})]}{\text{Average total assets}}$$

For **H&M**, the calculation of ROA for the year ended November 30, 2009, is as follows (with the krona amounts shown in thousands):

$$ROA = \frac{\text{Net earnings} + [\text{Interest expense} \times (1 - \text{Tax rate})]}{\text{Average total assets}}$$

$$= \frac{\text{SEK } 16{,}384 + [\text{SEK } 8 \times (1 - 0.28)]}{(\text{SEK } 54{,}363 + \text{SEK } 51{,}243) \div 2}$$

$$= \frac{\text{SEK } 16{,}282 + \text{SEK } 5.76}{\text{SEK } 52{,}803}$$

$$= 0.31 \text{ or } 31\%$$

As is the case with many ratios, a single ROA figure is not as meaningful as a comparison of rates of return over time, or across companies. However, before using ROA to compare different companies, you should check the notes to the financial statements to determine whether the companies' depreciation policies are comparable, as different depreciation policies will affect both the earnings and the total assets. You should also determine whether the companies have recently invested in new assets. This information will be available on the statement of cash flows. The acquisition of new assets will immediately increase the total asset amount but may not immediately increase the company's earnings proportionately; thus, they may temporarily decrease the ROA.

SUMMARY

In this chapter, we described the initial acquisition of capital assets—both tangible and intangible—noting the types of costs that are capitalized and recorded in the asset account. Capital assets include land, buildings, vehicles, equipment, natural resources, intangibles, and many other assets that have a useful life of more than one year. We explored several systematic, rational methods including the straight-line, declining balance, and units-of-output methods that are commonly used to depreciate the cost of capital assets. Depreciation expense is an estimate of the cost arising from the use of the assets each period. It is up to management to determine the appropriate depreciation rates, and to estimate the assets' useful lives and residual values.

We also took a brief look at the Canada Revenue Agency (CRA) in regard to depreciation. Because the CRA requires companies to use capital cost allowance for income tax purposes, there is usually a difference between the tax expense reported on the statement of earnings and the amount of income tax that is actually owed to the CRA. This difference is recorded as a deferred income tax asset or liability.

Because depreciation methods are based on estimates, it is important for management to periodically review the useful life and residual value assumptions to determine if they are still appropriate. If new values are established, the asset's remaining net book value is depreciated over its remaining useful life using the new values. Also, if a company decides to change depreciation method because a new method now seems more appropriate, it will depreciate the remaining depreciable cost of the asset over its remaining useful life using the new method.

We completed the chapter with a discussion of the return on assets ratio, including both its calculation and its limitations.

PRACTICE PROBLEM

Additional Practice Problems

Pete's Trucking Company has a fleet of large trucks that cost a total of $1.5 million. The trucks have an estimated useful life of five years and an estimated residual value of $150,000. For tax purposes, their capital cost allowance (CCA) rate is 30%. The trucks are expected to be driven a total of 5 million kilometres during their lives.

Required:

a. Calculate the annual straight-line depreciation that would be recorded over the lives of these trucks.

b. Prepare a schedule showing depreciation on a units-of-activity basis, if the following usage was expected.

Year 1	950,000 km
Year 2	1,050,000 km
Year 3	1,100,000 km
Year 4	1,000,000 km
Year 5	900,000 km

c. Prepare a schedule showing the depreciation that will result if Pete's Trucking uses the double-declining-balance method.

d. Assume that the trucks were sold at the end of the fourth year for a total of $250,000. Prepare journal entries to record the disposal of the trucks under each of the following assumptions about the depreciation method used by Pete's Trucking:

   i.   straight-line depreciation

   ii.   the units-of-activity method of depreciation

   iii.   double-declining-balance depreciation

e. Briefly explain why there is a gain or loss on the disposal of the trucks in each of these circumstances.

f. Prepare a schedule showing the capital cost allowance that could be deducted for income tax purposes during each of the first four years.

STRATEGIES FOR SUCCESS:

▶ For the units-of-activity method, the "activity" in this case is measured in terms of kilometres driven. Therefore, you need to calculate how much depreciation should be charged for each kilometre, and then multiply this rate by the number of kilometres driven each year.

▶ For the double-declining-balance method, remember that (a) the rate to be used is simply twice the straight-line rate, which is one divided by the years of life, and (b) the rate is applied to the net book value each year (i.e., cost − accumulated depreciation). The residual value is used only in the calculation for the final year, when you have to record whatever amount of depreciation is needed to reduce the net book value of the asset to its residual value.

▶ When you record the disposal of a capital asset, you have to eliminate the cost of the asset (by crediting the asset account); eliminate the depreciation recorded on the asset (by debiting the accumulated depreciation account); record the cash received, if any (by debiting the cash account); and record the gain or loss. A gain—like a revenue—is recorded with a credit; a loss—like an expense—is recorded with a debit.

▶ The calculation of capital cost allowance is similar to the double-declining-balance method, except (a) you use the rate specified by the tax regulations, and (b) in the first year you can deduct only half the usual amount.

SUGGESTED SOLUTION TO PRACTICE PROBLEM

1. The straight-line depreciation would be

$$\text{Depreciation expense} = \frac{\text{Acquisition cost} - \text{Estimated residual value}}{\text{Estimated useful life}}$$

$$= (\$1,500,000 - \$150,000) \div 5 \text{ years}$$

$$= \$270,000 \text{ per year}$$

2. Cost per km = ($1,500,000 − $150,000) ÷ 5,000,000 km

   = $0.27 per km

Depreciation Expense per Year

Year 1: $0.27 per km ×   950,000 km = $256,500
Year 2: $0.27 per km × 1,050,000 km = $283,500
Year 3: $0.27 per km × 1,100,000 km = $297,000
Year 4: $0.27 per km × 1,000,000 km = $270,000
Year 5: $0.27 per km ×   900,000 km = $243,000

3. Double-declining-balance method:

Double-declining-balance rate = twice the straight-line rate

$$= 2 \times 1/5 = 40\%$$

Depreciation schedule for double-declining-balance method (in thousands):

Year	Net Book Value (beginning of year)	Calculation	Depreciation Expense	Accumulated Depreciation
1	$1,500,000	40% × $1,500,000	$600,000	$ 600,000
2	$ 900,000	40% × $ 900,000	$360,000	$ 960,000
3	$ 540,000	40% × $ 540,000	$216,000	$1,176,000
4	$ 324,000	40% × $ 324,000	$129,600	$1,305,600
5	$ 194,400	$194,400 − $ 150,000	$ 44,400	$1,350,000

Notice that, in the final year, the depreciation expense is the difference between the net book value at the beginning of the year and the residual value that should be left in the asset account at the end of the year.

practice problems

d. i. Straight-line method:

Cash (A)	250,000	
Accumulated depreciation (XA)	1,080,00[a]	
Loss on disposal of trucks (SE)	170,000	
Trucks (A)		1,500,000

[a] 4 years at $270,000 per year (from part "a")

ii. Units-of-activity method:

Cash (A)	250,000	
Accumulated depreciation (XA)	1,107,000[b]	
Loss on disposal of trucks (SE)	143,000	
Trucks (A)		1,500,000

[b] $256,500 + $283,500 + $297,000 + $270,000 (from part "b")

iii. Double-declining-balance method:

Cash (A)	250,000	
Accumulated depreciation (XA)	1,305,600[c]	
Gain on disposal of trucks (SE)		55,600
Trucks (A)		1,500,000

[c] from the table in part "c"

e. The actual life of the trucks was only four years, rather than the five years that had been expected; therefore, less of their cost was written off through depreciation, leaving them with higher net book values. In addition, the trucks were sold for $250,000 rather than the $150,000 residual value that had been expected. The combination of these factors creates a gain or loss on disposal.

As can be seen in the journal entry in part "d"(i), under straight-line depreciation, the net book value (acquisition cost − accumulated depreciation) of the trucks had been reduced to $420,000 at the end of year 4 ($1,500,000 − $1,080,000 = $420,000). The trucks were sold for $250,000, which is $170,000 less than their net book value ($420,000 − $250,000 = $170,000). This shortfall is recorded as a loss on the disposal of the trucks.

Similarly, as shown in the journal entry in part "d"(ii), under the units-of-activity method, the net book value (cost − accumulated depreciation) of the trucks had been reduced to $393,000 at the end of year 4 ($1,500,000 − $1,107,000 = $393,000). The trucks were sold for $250,000, which is $143,000 less than their net book value ($393,000 − $250,000 = $143,000), which again results in a loss on the disposal.

As can be seen in the journal entry in part "d"(iii), under double-declining-balance depreciation the net book value (cost − accumulated depreciation) of the trucks had been reduced to $194,400 at the end of year 4 ($1,500,000 − $1,305,600 = $194,400). The trucks were sold for $250,000, which is $55,600 more than their net book value ($250,000 − $194,400 = $55,600). This excess is recorded as a gain on disposal of the trucks.

f. Capital cost allowance schedule (in thousands, rounded to one decimal place):

Year	Undepreciated Capital Cost at Beginning of Year	Calculation		Capital Cost Allowance
1	$1,500,000 − 0 = $1,500,000	1/2 × 30% × $1,500,000	=	$225,000
2	$1,500,000 − 225,000 = $1,275,000	30% × $1,275,000	=	$382,500
3	$1,275,000 − 382,500 = $892,500	30% × $892,500	−	$267,750
4	$892,500 − 267,750 = $624,750	30% × $624,750	=	$187,425

ABBREVIATIONS USED

CCA   Capital cost allowance   ROA   Return on assets
CRA   Canada Revenue Agency   UCC   Undepreciated capital cost
NBV   Net book value

SYNONYMS

Acquisition cost **|** Cost **|** Original cost **|** Capitalized cost
Depreciated cost **|** Net book value **|** Carrying value
Depreciation **|** Amortization
Units-of-activity method **|** Production method

GLOSSARY

Accelerated method   A method of depreciation that allocates a higher portion of an asset's cost to the earlier years of its life than to the later years.

Amortization   A term sometimes used for the depreciation associated with intangible assets that are not natural resources.

Basket purchase   A purchase of assets in which more than one asset is acquired for a single purchase price.

Capital assets   Long-lived assets that are normally used by the company in generating revenues and providing services (e.g., buildings, equipment, etc.).

Capital cost allowance   The deduction permitted by the Canada Revenue Agency for tax purposes, instead of depreciation.

Capitalizable cost   A cost that can be recorded as an asset, rather than being expensed immediately.

Capitalized   A term used to describe a cost that has been recorded as an asset, rather than an expense.

Carrying value   The acquisition cost of a capital asset minus its accumulated depreciation. Synonym for net book value.

Compound interest method   A depreciation method that calculates the expense for a period based on the change in the asset's present value.

Decelerated method   A method of depreciation that allocates a lower portion of an asset's cost to the earlier years of its life than to the later years.

Declining-balance method   A depreciation method that calculates the expense each period by multiplying the rate of depreciation by the asset's carrying value (which declines each period).

Deferred asset or liability   An asset or liability account that arises when there is a difference between the carrying value of assets or liabilities for tax purposes versus those for accounting purposes. With respect to capital assets, it represents the tax effect of the difference between their carrying value for accounting purposes and their carrying value for tax purposes.

Depletion   A term sometimes used to describe the depreciation of the cost of natural resources to expense, over the lives of the resources.

Depreciated cost   The portion of the cost of a capital asset that is to be depreciated over its useful life; the original cost of the asset less its estimated residual value.

Depreciation   The allocation of the cost of capital assets to expense over their useful lives.

Depreciation cost   The calculated depreciation amount for an asset using an acceptable depreciation method.

Development costs   Costs incurred to get a product or service ready for commercial production, after the initial stages of exploration or research (to discover the product or service) have been completed.

Double-declining-balance method   A particular type of declining-balance depreciation method that is calculated by using a percentage rate that is double the rate that would be used for straight-line depreciation.

Earnings management   The practice of choosing revenue and expense methods so that earnings are increased or decreased in particular accounting periods, or smoothed over time.

Full cost method   A method of accounting for the exploration costs of oil and gas exploration companies in which all costs of exploration are capitalized and depreciated, without regard to the success or failure of individual wells. Commonly used in smaller oil and gas companies.

Goodwill   An intangible asset that represents a company's above-average earning capacity as a result of reputation, advantageous location, superior sales staff, expertise of employees, etc. It is only recorded when a company acquires another company and pays more for it than the fair market value of its identifiable net assets.

Impairment loss   The decline in the recoverable value of an asset below its current carrying value. It is recognized as a loss on the statement of earnings.

Intangible asset   A non-physical capital asset that usually involves a legal right, which will provide future economic benefits to the organization.

Interest capitalization   The recording of interest as part of the cost of constructing a capital asset.

Land improvements   Improvements made to land that increase its usefulness, but which have limited lives and therefore have to be depreciated.

Net book value   An asset's carrying value on the company books, found by subtracting its accumulated depreciation from the original cost.

Net realizable value   An asset's selling price minus any costs to complete and sell it, or the net amount of cash that is expected to be obtained from an asset.

Net recoverable amount   The estimated future net cash flow from the use of a capital asset, together with its residual value.

Production method   A method of depreciation that allocates an asset's depreciable cost to the years of its useful life based on the volume of production or usage during each period. Synonym for the units-of-output or units-of-activity method.

Rate of depreciation   A percentage that describes the amount of depreciation to be recorded during a given period. For straight-line depreciation, the rate is the reciprocal of the number of years of useful life.

Replacement cost   An asset's market value, as determined from the market in which the company can purchase the asset, or the cost to reproduce the asset based on current prices of the inputs.

Resale value   An asset's market value, as determined from the market in which it can be sold.

Research costs   Costs incurred to discover new products or service. Subsequent costs to get the products or services ready for commercial production are classified separately, as development costs.

Residual value   A capital asset's estimated net realizable value at the end of its useful life; measured using the current selling price of similar assets that are as old as the asset will be at the end of its useful life.

Return on assets ratio   A measure of the amount of earnings (before deducting interest expense) earned in relation to the value of the assets of the business. Indicates how effectively the assets are being used to generate earnings.

Straight-line method   A method of determining depreciation by dividing the original cost less the estimated residual value by the useful life of the asset. Allocates the same amount as depreciation expense each year.

Straight-line rate   The rate of depreciation for the straight-line method, calculated as the reciprocal of the number of years of useful life (i.e., 1 ÷ years of life).

Successful efforts method   A method of accounting for the exploration and drilling costs of oil and gas exploration companies in which only the costs of exploration for successful wells are capitalized and depreciated. The costs of unsuccessful efforts are charged to expense. Commonly used in larger oil and gas companies.

Tangible asset   An asset that has physical substance.

Undepreciated capital cost   An asset's carrying value for tax purposes. The portion of the asset's original cost that has not yet been deducted as capital cost allowance.

Units-of-activity method   A method of depreciation that allocates an asset's depreciable cost to the years of its useful life as a function of the amount of its usage or production each period. Synonym for units-of-output or production method.

Useful life   An estimate of the period of time over which an asset will have economic value to the company.

Value in use   The value of an asset that is expected to result from using it in the business. Only relevant if the intent is to use the asset rather than sell it.

ASSIGNMENT MATERIAL

Self-Assessment Quiz

Assessing Your Recall

8-1   Describe what is meant by "value in use" versus "resale value," as applied to capital assets.

8-2   Outline the types of costs that should be capitalized for a piece of equipment.

8-3 Describe the procedure that is used to allocate the cost of a basket purchase of assets to each asset that is acquired.

8-4 Explain why interest can be capitalized as part of an asset's construction costs.

8-5 Discuss the purpose of depreciation expense and the possible patterns of depreciation for a company.

8-6 Discuss the factors that should be taken into consideration when choosing a depreciation method.

8-7 Describe how to measure the residual value that is used in depreciation methods.

8-8 Describe how residual value and useful life are used in the calculation of depreciation under the following methods: straight-line, units-of-activity or production, and declining-balance.

8-9 Explain what is done when a company changes its estimate of an asset's useful life and/or residual value partway through the asset's life.

8-10 Explain what capital cost allowance (CCA) is and how it relates to depreciation expense.

8-11 Outline the differences between CCA and declining-balance depreciation.

8-12 Discuss the nature of deferred income taxes in the context of differences between depreciation and CCA.

8-13 Explain what a deferred income tax asset represents.

8-14 Describe the conditions under which intangible assets can be recorded in a company's accounting system, and use research and development costs, patents, and goodwill as examples.

8-15 Describe the guidelines under which the costs of intangible assets can be expensed over the assets' lives, and use research and development costs, patents, and goodwill as examples.

8-16 Discuss the conditions under which a company is required to record an impairment in the value of its capital assets.

Applying Your Knowledge

8-17 (Capitalizing costs related to capital assets)

C & M Securities made several expenditures during the current fiscal year, including the following:

	Amount	Description of Expenditure
1.	$ 50,000	Acquisition of a piece of land to be used as a building site
2.	3,000	Demolition of a small building on the land, to make way for the new building
3.	7,500	Levelling of the land to prepare it for construction of the new building
4.	10,000	Security at the building site during the construction period
5.	24,000	Insurance on the new building, including $10,000 for the time that it was under construction and $14,000 for the remainder of the year
6.	290,000	Construction of the new building
7.	12,000	Paving of a parking lot beside the building
8.	6,000	Decorative landscaping around the building (planting flowers, ornamental shrubs, etc.)
9.	80,000	Purchase of a new piece of equipment
10.	6,000	Sales taxes on the new equipment
11.	3,000	Installation of the new equipment
12.	2,000	Repairs to the new equipment, which was damaged during installation
13.	1,500	Testing and adjustment of the new equipment prior to its use
14.	1,000	Minor repairs to some old equipment
15.	7,000	Major overhaul of an old piece of equipment, extending its useful life by three years
16.	1,200	Routine maintenance of equipment
17.	2,000	Replacement of windows broken by disgruntled employees during a labour dispute

Required:

a. For each of the items listed above, indicate whether the cost should be debited to land, land improvements, buildings, equipment, or an expense account.

b. For each item that was expensed, explain why it was not appropriate to add the amount to an asset.

8-18 (**Acquisition costs and interest capitalization**)

House Builders of Canada decided to expand its facilities and upgrade some of its log preparation equipment. The following events occurred during the year:

Date	Amount	Description of Expenditure
Jan. 2	$ 75,000	Purchased land adjacent to the company's existing property, to be used for the expansion.
6	1,200	Paid legal fees and deed registration fees.
11	4,000	Paid its workers to clear the land on their days off.
15	120,000	Purchased equipment, which was delivered but not yet paid for.
17	900	Purchased building permit for construction of the addition.
20	2,500	Constructed temporary fencing as required by the building permit to enclose the construction site. Upon completion of the addition to the building, the fencing was to be removed.
22	400,000	Construction of a new addition to the main building was started.
25	3,500	Received bill for delivery of the equipment that was received on January 15.
Feb. 1		Paid the amounts owing on the equipment and its delivery.
28	11,000	Paid architect's fees for designing the building addition and supervising its construction.
May 9	380,000	Paid full amount to the construction company upon completion of the building.
11	800	Paid cost to remove temporary fencing.
	500	Sold fence materials to the construction company, reducing the net cost to Home Builders of Canada.
14	2,500	Paid work crews to install the equipment.
24	1,200	Paid for party to celebrate the successful completion of the expansion.
June 7	700	Paid for set-up and adjustment of the new equipment so it would be ready to use.
10	700	Paid for an ad in the local paper to advertise that the company was hiring.

Required:

a. Determine the costs that should be capitalized as assets by Home Builders of Canada in its land, buildings, and equipment accounts.

b. State what should be done with any of the costs that are not capitalized.

c. If Home Builders of Canada borrowed money to finance the expansion, what two options would it have regarding the interest cost?

8-19 (**Acquisition costs; basket purchase**)

Morton Company purchased two machines at an industrial auction. It paid $120,000 for the two machines together, even though machine #1 was appraised at $62,000 and machine #2 was appraised at $70,000.

The company spent $5,000 transporting the two machines to its plant. It spent $6,000 installing machine #1, whereas machine #2 just had to be plugged in. Repairs to get the machines in working order totalled $3,000 for machine #1 and $16,000 for machine #2. Some repairs had been anticipated when the company purchased the machines, but the repair costs for machine #2 were $12,000 higher than expected. The repairs were deemed essential and both machines now work well.

Required:
Calculate the total cost that should be capitalized for each machine.

8-20 (Basket purchase and depreciation)
On March 20, 2011, FineTouch Corporation purchased two machines at auction for a combined total cost of $236,000. The machines were listed in the auction catalogue at $110,000 for machine X and $155,000 for machine Y. Immediately after the auction, FineTouch had the machines professionally appraised so it could increase its insurance coverage. The appraisal put a fair value of $105,000 on machine X and $160,000 on machine Y.

On March 24, FineTouch paid a total of $4,500 in transportation and installation charges for the two machines. No further expenditures were made for machine X, but $6,500 was paid on March 29 for improvements to machine Y. On March 31, 2011, both machines were ready to be used.

The company expects machine X to last five years and to have a residual value of $3,800 when it is removed from service, and it expects machine Y to be useful for eight more years and have a residual value of $14,600 at that time. Due to the different characteristics of the two machines, different depreciation methods will be used for them: machine X will be depreciated using the double-declining-balance method and machine Y using the straight-line method.

Required:
Prepare the journal entries to record the following:
a. The purchase of each machine
b. The transportation, installation, and improvement costs for each machine
c. The depreciation expense to December 31, 2011, for each machine

8-21 (Depreciation calculations and journal entries; two methods)
Polar Company purchased a building with an expected useful life of 40 years for $600,000 on January 1, 2011. The building is expected to have a residual value of $40,000.

Required:
a. Give the journal entries that would be made by Polar to record the building purchase in 2011 and the depreciation expense for 2011 and 2012, assuming straight-line depreciation is used.
b. Repeat part "a," but now assume that double-declining-balance is used.

8-22 (Calculation of depreciation; three methods)
On April 29, 2011, SugarBear Company acquired equipment costing $150,000, which will be depreciated on the assumption that the equipment will be useful for five years and have a residual value of $12,000. The estimated output from this equipment is as follows: 2011—15,000 units; 2012—24,000 units; 2012—30,000 units; 2014—28,000 units; 2015—18,000 units. The company is now considering possible methods of depreciation for this asset.

Required:
a. Calculate what the depreciation expense would be for each year of the asset's life, if the company chooses:
    i. The straight-line method
    ii. The units-of-production method
    iii. The double-declining-balance method
b. Briefly discuss the criteria that a company should consider when selecting a depreciation method.

8-23 (Calculation of depreciation by three methods, plus CCA)

A machine that produces cell phone components is purchased on January 1, 2011, for $100,000. It is expected to have a useful life of four years and a residual value of $10,000. The machine is expected to produce a total of 200,000 components during its life, distributed as follows: 40,000 in 2011; 50,000 in 2012; 60,000 in 2013; and 50,000 in 2014. The company closes its books on December 31 each year.

Required:

a. Calculate the amount of depreciation to be charged each year, using each of the following methods:
   i. Straight-line method
   ii. Production method
   iii. Double-declining-balance method
b. Which method results in the highest depreciation expense:
   i. during the first two years?
   ii. over all four years?
c. Calculate the amount of capital cost allowance that could be claimed in each of the first two years, assuming the machine is subject to a CCA rate of 40%.

8-24 (Depreciation, including CCA; income calculation; deferred tax liability)

On July 1, 2011, Silver Stone Company purchased equipment for a cost of $450,000 with an expected useful life of 15 years and an anticipated residual value of $30,000. This is the company's only capital asset and, for tax purposes, it is a Class 8 asset with a CCA rate of 20%. Silver Stone's income tax rate is 25%.

For the year 2012 (the second year of the equipment's life), Silver Stone reported sales of $1,500,000 and operating expenses other than depreciation of $1,050,000. In addition to the equipment, the company held other assets with a total carrying value of $930,000 on December 31, 2012.

Required:

a. Assuming Silver Stone uses straight-line depreciation, what amount of net earnings will it report for 2012? What will its return on assets be, using the year-end value of the total assets and assuming there is no interest expense?
b. What is the maximum amount of CCA that Silver Stone could claim for tax purposes in 2012? Based on this, how much taxable income will the company have and how much income tax will it have to pay for 2012?
c. Give the journal entry to record the company's income taxes for 2012.
d. If Silver Stone had used double-declining-balance depreciation (in both 2011 and 2012), what amount of net earnings would it have reported for 2012? What would the return on assets have been (again using the year-end value of the total assets and assuming there is no interest expense)?
e. For what type of assets is it appropriate to use double-declining-balance depreciation?

8-25 (Production method depreciation with change in estimate)

A company paid $66,000 for a machine and was depreciating it by the units-of-production method. The machine was expected to produce a total of 150,000 units of product, and to have a residual value of $6,000. During the first two years of use, the machine produced 45,000 units.

At the beginning of the machine's third year of life, its estimated lifetime production was revised from 150,000 to 120,000 units; its estimated residual value was unchanged.

Required:

Calculate the amount of depreciation that should be charged during the third year of the machine's life if 25,000 units are produced that year.

8-26 **(Asset acquisition, subsequent expenditures, change in estimate, and depreciation)**
South Seas Distributors completed the following transactions involving the purchase and operation of a delivery truck:

2011	Transaction Description
May 27	Paid $35,600 for a new truck, plus $4,272 in HST, which can be reclaimed from the federal government. It was estimated that the truck would be sold for $15,000 after four years.
June 9	Paid $3,500 to have special racks installed in the truck. The racks did not increase the truck's estimated resale value. The truck was put into service after the racks were installed.
Dec. 31	Recorded straight-line depreciation on the truck.

2012	
Apr. 5	Paid $650 for repairs to the truck's fender, which was damaged when the driver scraped a loading dock.
July 23	Paid $8,000 to have a refrigerating unit installed in the truck. This increased the truck's estimated resale value by $1,000.
Dec. 31	Recorded straight-line depreciation on the truck.

> *Required:*
> Prepare journal entries to record the above transactions.

8-27 **(Asset expenditures)**
Comfort Zone Housing paid $80,000 for a new air-conditioning system in an existing building.

> *Required:*
> Identify the account that should be debited and briefly explain your reasoning, in each of the following cases:
> a. The expected useful life of the air-conditioning system is the same as the remaining useful life of the building it was installed in.
> b. The air-conditioning system is expected to have a useful life of 15 years, while the building it was installed in is expected to have a remaining useful life of 30 years.

8-28 **(Asset expenditures, changes in estimates, and depreciation)**
Canada Canning Company owns processing equipment that had an initial cost of $106,000, expected useful life of eight years, and expected residual value of $10,000. Depreciation calculations are done to the nearest month using the straight-line method, and depreciation is recorded each December 31.

During the equipment's fifth year of service, the following expenditures were made:

Jan. 7	Lubricated and adjusted the equipment to maintain optimum performance, at a cost of $500.
Mar. 13	Replaced belts, hoses, and other parts that were showing signs of wear on the equipment, at a cost of $350.
June 28	Completed a $14,000 overhaul of the equipment. The work included the installation of new computer controls to replace the original controls, which had become technologically obsolete. As a result of this work, the estimated useful life of the equipment was increased to 10 years and the estimated residual value was increased to $11,000.

> *Required:*
> a. Prepare journal entries to record each of the above transactions.
> b. Calculate the depreciation expense that should be recorded for this equipment in the fourth year of its life, in the fifth year of its life (the year in which the above transactions took place), and in the sixth year of its life.

8-29   (Asset refurbishment, changes in estimates, and depreciation)

At the end of 2011, Spindle Works Inc. owned a piece of equipment that had originally cost $21,000. It was being depreciated by the straight-line method, and had $8,500 of accumulated depreciation recorded as of the end of 2011 after the yearly depreciation was recorded.

At the beginning of 2012, the equipment was extensively refurbished at a cost of $9,500. As a result of this work, the productivity of the equipment was significantly improved, its total estimated useful life was increased from 10 to 14 years, and its residual value was increased from $4,000 to $7,000.

> ***Required:***
> a. Calculate the age of the equipment at the end of 2011.
> b. Give the journal entry to record the refurbishment of the equipment at the beginning of 2012.
> c. Give the adjusting entry to record the depreciation of the equipment at the end of 2012.

8-30   (Acquisition, change in estimates, depreciation, and disposal)

On July 1, 2008, Steelman Company acquired a new machine for $140,000 and estimated it would have a useful life of 10 years and residual value of $7,000. At the beginning of 2011, the company decided that the machine would be used for nine more years (including all of 2011), and at the end of this time its residual value would be only $1,000. On November 1, 2012, the machine was sold for $83,000. The company uses the straight-line method of depreciation and closes its books on December 31.

> ***Required:***
> Give the necessary journal entries for the acquisition, depreciation, and disposal of this asset for the years 2008, 2011, and 2012.

8-31   (Straight-line depreciation with disposal)

On October 4, 2011, C and C Sandblasters Company purchased a new machine for $45,000. It estimated the machine's useful life at 12 years and the residual value at $4,000. On March 25, 2012, another machine was acquired for $70,000. Its useful life was estimated to be 15 years and its residual value $6,000. On May 24, 2013, the first machine was sold for $28,000. The company closes its books on December 31 each year, uses the straight-line method of depreciation, and calculates depreciation to the nearest month.

> ***Required:***
> Give the necessary journal entries for the years 2011 through 2013 for both machines. Include the depreciation of the second machine on December 31, 2013.

8-32   (Straight-line and declining-balance depreciation with disposal)

On March 1, 2011, Zephur Winds Ltd. purchased a machine for $80,000 by paying $20,000 down and issuing a note for the balance. The machine had an estimated useful life of nine years, and an estimated residual value of $8,000. Carson uses the straight-line-method of depreciation and has a December 31 year end. On October 30, 2013, the machine was sold for $62,000.

> ***Required:***
> a. Prepare the journal entry to record the acquisition of the machine.
> b. Assuming that the depreciation was correctly calculated and recorded in 2011 and 2012, prepare the journal entries to update the depreciation and record the sale of the machine on October 30, 2013.
> c. Assume instead that the company used the double-declining-balance method to depreciate the cost of the machine:
>   i. What amount of depreciation would be recorded in 2011 and 2012?
>   ii. What journal entries would be required to update the depreciation and record the sale of the machine on October 30, 2013?

8-33 (Exchange and disposal of capital assets)

On March 31, 2011, Hammer Inc. acquired new machinery by trading in old machinery, paying $15,000 cash, and issuing a 10% note payable for $10,000. The new machinery's estimated life is six years, with a residual value of $3,000.

The old machinery had been acquired on September 30, 2008, for $25,000. At that time, its estimated useful life was 10 years, with a residual value of $1,000. Depreciation was correctly recorded for 2008, 2009, and 2010. On the date of the trade-in, the old machinery's fair market value was approximately the same as its net carrying value.

The company uses the straight-line method of depreciation and closes its books on December 31.

Required:

a. Give the journal entry to record the 2011 depreciation of the old asset, up to the date of the trade-in on March 31.

b. Give the journal entry to record the trade-in of the old asset and the acquisition of the new one. (Hint: The cost of the new asset includes the value of the old asset plus the cash and note given in payment for the new asset.)

c. On March 31, 2017, the machinery acquired in 2011 was retired from service. Give the journal entries that should be made in 2017 related to this machinery, under each of the following assumptions:

   i. The machinery could not be sold, so the company wrote it off.

   ii. The machinery was sold for $5,000.

8-34 (Exchange and disposal of capital assets)

On November 23, 2013, Radon Mines Company acquired new machinery by trading in old machinery and paying $23,000 cash plus another $15,000 borrowed from the bank at 8%. The new machinery's estimated life is six years, with a residual value of $8,000. The company uses the straight-line method of depreciation and has a December 31 year end.

The old machinery was acquired on March 31, 2009, for $25,000. At that time, its estimated useful life was 10 years, with a residual value of $4,000. Depreciation was correctly recorded for 2009, 2010, 2011, and 2012. On the trade-in date, the old machinery's fair market value was approximately the same as its net book value.

Required:

a. Give the journal entries that should be made in 2013 to record the depreciation and trade-in of the old asset, and the acquisition and depreciation of the new asset.

b. On June 30, 2019, the machinery acquired in 2013 was retired from service and sold for $4,000. Give the journal entries that should be made in 2019 related to this machinery.

c. Briefly explain how the answer to part "b" would differ if the residual value of the new machinery was estimated at $10,000 rather than $8,000.

8-35 (Oil and gas exploration, with full cost and successful efforts methods)

Consider the oil and gas exploration companies Wild Cat and Crazy Dog, which have identical histories. Both have been in operation for two years, during which they have each explored five sites a year at a cost of $3 million per site. Only one of the sites each year has proven to be economically viable; the remaining sites were dry holes. The oil reserves in each successful well are estimated at 600,000 barrels, which will be extracted evenly over a six-year period commencing in the year of discovery.

Required:

a. Assuming that Wild Cat Company uses the full cost method of accounting for its exploration expenditures, calculate what it would report for the following:

   i. The value of the oil wells asset on its statement of financial position at the end of each of the two years

   ii. Depreciation expense on its statement of earnings for each of the two years

    b. Assuming that Crazy Dog Company uses the successful efforts method of accounting for its exploration expenditures, calculate what it would report for the following:

        i. The value of the oil wells asset on its statement of financial position at the end of each of the two years

        ii. Depreciation expense on its statement of earnings for each of the two years

    c. At the end of the two-year period, which company has the more valuable oil wells asset? Over the two-year period, which company has been more profitable?

8-36 (Intangibles and depreciation)

Pinetree Manufacturing Company reports both equipment and patents in its statement of financial position.

    Required:

    a. Explain how the cost of each of these types of asset is determined.

    b. If both the equipment and patents were purchased three years ago for $40,000 each and had estimated useful lives of 10 years, what amount would be reported for each of them in the statement of financial position at the end of the current period? Explain.

    c. Financial analysts sometimes ignore intangible assets when analyzing financial statements. Do you think this is appropriate? Explain.

8-37 (Intangibles and depreciation)

Red Bear Ltd. purchased several intangible assets, as follows:

Asset	Purchase Cost
Licence	$ 80,000
Customer list	60,000
Patent	160,000
Copyright	250,000

The following information is also available:

- In addition to the costs listed above, there were legal fees of $12,000 associated with the licence acquisition. The licence is valid in perpetuity, and sales of the products produced under the licence have been strong and are expected to continue at the same level for many decades.

- The customer lists are expected to be useful for the next six years.

- The patent has a legal life of 20 years, but technological changes are expected to render it worthless after about eight years.

- The copyright is good for another 40 years, but nearly all the related sales are expected to occur during the next 10 years.

    Required:

    a. Calculate the annual depreciation expense, if any, that should be recorded for each of these intangible assets.

    b. Show how the intangible assets section of the statement of financial position would be presented four years after acquisition of these assets, assuming that there has been no evidence that their values have been impaired. Assume that a full year of depreciation was taken in the year of acquisition.

8-38 (Cash flow statement—review question)

Comparative statements of financial position and a statement of earnings for Ponderosa Pines Ltd. follow:

Ponderosa Pines Ltd.
Statements of Financial Position
As at December 31, 2011 and 2010

	2011	2010
Current assets		
Cash	$ 70,000	$ 30,000
Accounts receivable, net	250,000	211,000
Inventories	269,000	245,000
Prepaid insurance	18,000	31,000
Total current assets	607,000	517,000
Non-current assets		
Plant and equipment	970,000	958,000
Less: Accumulated depreciation	(180,000)	(102,000)
	790,000	856,000
Patents (net)	65,000	74,000
Investment in Cone Company's common shares	50,000	0
Total non-current assets	905,000	930,000
Total assets	$1,512,000	$1,447,000
Current liabilities		
Accounts payable	$ 205,000	$ 165,000
Accrued liabilities	83,000	155,000
Income taxes payable	24,000	20,000
Dividends payable (see Note 1)	0	21,000
Total current liabilities	312,000	361,000
Non-current liabilities		
Bonds payable	200,000	200,000
Total liabilities	512,000	561,000
Shareholders' equity		
Common shares	450,000	400,000
Retained earnings	550,000	486,000
Total shareholders' equity	1,000,000	886,000
Total liabilities and shareholders' equity	$1,512,000	$1,447,000

Ponderosa Pines Ltd.
Statements of Earnings
For the Year Ended December 31, 2011

Revenues and gain:			
Sales		$878,000	
Dividend revenue		3,000	
Gain on sale of equipment (see Note 2)		2,000	$883,000
Expenses:			
Cost of goods sold		357,000	
Depreciation:			
Plant and equipment	$87,000		
Patents	9,000	96,000	
Other operating expenses		247,000	
Interest expense		13,000	
Income taxes		76,000	789,000
Net income			$ 94,000

Note 1: The company declared cash dividends of $30,000 during 2011.
Note 2: This gain is due to the sale of equipment that had an original cost of $17,000 and a net book value of $8,000 at the time it was sold.

Required:
Prepare a statement of cash flows for Ponderosa Pines Ltd. for the year ended December 31, 2011.

User Perspective Problems

8-39 (Expensing versus capitalizing the cost of tools)

During the current year, a large chain of auto mechanic shops adopted the policy of charging purchases of small tools costing less than $100 to expense as soon as they are acquired. In previous years, the company had carried an asset account, Small Tools, which it had depreciated over the average expected useful lives of the tools. The balance in the Small Tools account represented about 1% of the company's total capital assets, and the depreciation expense on them was 0.3% of its sales revenues. It is expected that the average annual purchases of small tools will be approximately the same amount as the depreciation that would have been charged on them.

Is this in accordance with IFRS? If so, briefly explain why. If not, identify the accounting principle or concept that has been violated and give a brief explanation of the nature of the violation.

8-40 (Nature of depreciation charges)

While discussing the values reported on the statement of financial position for land and buildings, an owner of a company said the following: "Land and buildings should not be recorded separately. They should be treated as a group of related assets. If you view them as a group, no depreciation should be charged on our buildings, because the increase in the value of our land each year more than makes up for any decline in the value of the buildings. Our company is located in a booming commercial area, and land values are rising all the time. In fact, even the value of our buildings has probably been increasing, rather than decreasing."

Comment on the issues raised by the owner.

8-41 (Nature of depreciation charges)

The Piccolo Mondo Company purchased a computer system for $150,000. The company expects to use the system for five years, at which time it will acquire a larger and faster one. The new system is expected to cost $100,000. During the current year, the company debited $20,000 to its depreciation expense account "to provide for one-fifth of the estimated cost of the new computer system."

Is this in accordance with IFRS? If so, briefly explain why. If not, identify the accounting principle or concept that has been violated and give a brief explanation of the nature of the violation.

8-42 (Valuation of capital assets)

Many users of financial statements argue that, for most of the decisions that creditors, investors, analysts, and other users have to make, reporting the market values of companies' assets would be more relevant than other "values." Give two reasons why, despite the opportunity to report capital assets at fair value, companies continue to use historical costs as the basis for reporting these assets.

8-43 (Valuation of assets in discontinued operations)

Suppose that a company decides to discontinue one of its lines of business and sell the related assets. Describe what you think would be the most appropriate valuation basis for the capital assets of the discontinued operations during the interval between when the decision to discontinue the line of business is made and when the assets are sold. As an investor in the company, discuss what disclosures might be most useful to you in these circumstances.

8-44 (Capital assets as collateral for loan)

As a lender, discuss whether you would be more comfortable with a company having long-term assets in the form of (a) property, plant, and equipment, or (b) goodwill, when you consider making a long-term loan to the company.

8-45 (Capital assets as collateral for loan)

As a lender, discuss whether you would prefer to see long-term assets reported at historical cost or fair value. What advantages and disadvantages would you see under each valuation?

8-46 (Auditing and valuation of capital assets)

As an auditor, discuss how you might evaluate a company's property, plant, and equipment to decide whether the value of these assets were impaired and should be written down.

8-47 (Goodwill's effect on financial statements)

In some countries, companies can write off goodwill at the date of acquisition by directly reducing their shareholders' equity; that is, the write-off does not pass through net earnings. Suppose that a Canadian company and a company from a country that allows an immediate write-off of goodwill agreed to purchase the same company for the same amount of money. As a stock analyst, describe how the statements of financial position and statements of earnings would differ for the two companies after the acquisition. Discuss whether this would provide any advantage for either company.

8-48 (Impact of writedowns on remuneration)

Suppose that you are the accounting manager of a division in a large company and your remuneration is partly based on meeting an earnings target. In the current year, it seems certain that your division will not meet its target. You have some property, plant, and equipment that have been idle for a while but have not yet been written off. What incentives do you have to write off this asset during the current year? If you do write it off, how will this affect your future ability to meet the earnings targets for your division?

8-49 (Basket purchase price allocation)

Companies often face a basket purchase situation when they buy real estate, because the acquisition usually involves both the land that is purchased and the building that is located on the land. If you are the accounting manager, how would you go about allocating the real estate's purchase price between the land and the building? Why must you allocate the cost between these two assets? What incentives might you have to allocate a disproportionate amount to either the land or the building?

8-50 (Analysis of an R&D company)

As a stock analyst, discuss any difficulties or inadequacies that you might find with the financial statements of a company that is predominantly a research and development firm.

8-51 (Capital assets and company valuation)

Answer the following questions, assuming that you have been asked to analyze a potential acquisition by your company: (a) Which long-term assets on its financial statements are the most likely to be misstated by their carrying values? Explain your reasoning. (b) Is it possible that the company being considered for acquisition has some long-term assets that do not appear on its financial statements at all? Explain why or how this might occur.

Reading and Interpreting Published Financial Statements

8-52 (Reconstruction of capital asset transactions)

The consolidated statements of income, balance sheets, and cash flows of **Finning International Inc.** are presented in Exhibit 8-12. In addition, Finning International's note regarding its land, buildings, and equipment was presented earlier in this chapter, in Exhibit 8-6. As you may recall, Finning International is the largest Caterpillar dealer, selling, leasing, and servicing the large equipment in Canada.

Financial Analysis Assignments

> *Required:*
> Prepare summary journal entries to reconstruct the transactions that affected Finning International's land, buildings, and equipment in 2009 (i.e., acquisitions, disposals, and depreciation expense). Deal with the total land, buildings, and equipment, rather than the individual components. (Hint: You may find the use of T accounts helpful in reconstructing the events that affected the land, buildings, and equipment, and the accumulated depreciation account during the year.)

EXHIBIT 8-12A

annual report

FINNING INTERNATIONAL INC. 2009 ANNUAL REPORT

CONSOLIDATED STATEMENTS OF INCOME

For years ended December 31

($ THOUSANDS, EXCEPT SHARE AND PER SHARE AMOUNTS)	2009	2008
Revenue		
New equipment	$ 1,984,727	$ 2,928,643
Used equipment	337,806	431,804
Equipment rental	510,439	712,791
Product support	1,892,571	1,899,483
Other	11,998	18,704
Total revenue	4,737,541	5,991,425
Cost of sales	3,407,972	4,318,542
Gross profit	1,329,569	1,672,883
Selling, general, and administrative expenses	1,085,035	1,267,963
Other expenses (income) (Note 2)	37,514	16,801
Goodwill impairment (Note 16)	–	151,373
Earnings before interest and income taxes	207,020	236,746
Finance costs (Notes 3 and 4)	67,608	83,636
Income before provision for income taxes	139,412	153,110
Provision for income taxes (Note 6)	8,589	57,114
Net income	$ 130,823	$ 95,996
Earnings per share (Note 9)		
Basic	$ 0.77	$ 0.56
Diluted	$ 0.77	$ 0.55
Weighted average number of shares outstanding		
Basic	170,607,892	172,361,881
Diluted	170,993,485	173,318,957

The accompanying Notes to the Consolidated Financial Statements are an integral part of these statements.

FINNING INTERNATIONAL INC. 2009 ANNUAL REPORT

CONSOLIDATED BALANCE SHEETS

EXHIBIT 8-12B

annual report

December 31
($ THOUSANDS)

	2009	2008
ASSETS		
Current assets		
Cash and cash equivalents (Note 19)	$ 197,904	$ 109,772
Accounts receivable	622,641	840,810
Service work in progress	62,563	102,607
Inventories (Note 10)	993,523	1,473,504
Other assets (Note 11)	207,030	288,102
Total current assets	2,083,661	2,814,795
Finance assets (Note 12)	32,604	11,671
Rental equipment (Note 13)	691,120	987,835
Land, buildings, and equipment (Note 14)	482,777	470,859
Intangible assets (Note 14)	41,469	38,344
Goodwill (Note 16)	94,254	99,278
Other assets (Note 11)	245,550	297,593
	$ 3,671,435	$ 4,720,375
LIABILITIES		
Current liabilities		
Short-term debt (Note 3)	$ 162,238	$ 193,635
Accounts payable and accruals	749,941	1,316,818
Income tax payable	8,624	3,187
Current portion of long-term debt (Note 3)	24,179	2,643
Total current liabilities	944,982	1,516,283
Long-term debt (Note 3)	991,732	1,410,727
Long-term obligations (Note 17)	110,147	96,296
Future income taxes (Note 6)	108,888	129,965
Total liabilities	$ 2,155,749	$ 3,153,271
Commitments and contingencies (Notes 23 and 24)		
SHAREHOLDERS' EQUITY		
Share capital (Note 7)	557,052	554,966
Contributed surplus	33,509	25,441
Accumulated other comprehensive loss	(293,869)	(176,444)
Retained earnings	1,218,994	1,163,141
Total shareholders' equity	1,515,686	1,567,104
	$ 3,671,435	$ 4,720,375

Signed

FINNING INTERNATIONAL INC. 2009 ANNUAL REPORT

CONSOLIDATED STATEMENTS OF CASH FLOW

For years ended December 31
($ THOUSANDS)

	2009	2008
OPERATING ACTIVITIES		
Net income	$ 130,823	$ 95,996
Add items not affecting cash		
Depreciation and amortization	271,107	326,095
Future income taxes	(7,685)	9,822
Stock-based compensation	11,520	16,924
Gain on disposal of capital assets (Note 2)	(18,313)	(19,892)
Goodwill impairment	–	151,373
Other	1,632	(816)
	389,084	579,502
Changes in working capital items (Note 19)	157,310	(301,369)
Cash provided after changes in working capital items	546,394	278,133
Rental equipment, net of disposals	43,166	(204,800)
Equipment leased to customers, net of disposals	(27,203)	(652)
Cash flow provided by operating activities	562,357	72,681
INVESTING ACTIVITIES		
Additions to capital assets	(107,808)	(100,417)
Proceeds on disposal of capital assets	39,342	50,954
Proceeds on settlement of derivatives	20,020	–
Acquisition of businesses (Notes 11, 15 and 16)	–	(148,639)
Cash used in investing activities	(48,446)	(198,102)
FINANCING ACTIVITIES		
Increase (decrease) in short-term debt	7,663	(198,147)
Increase (decrease) in long-term debt	(344,477)	589,861
Payment on settlement of derivative	–	(8,914)
Issue of common shares on exercise of stock options	1,965	1,919
Repurchase of common shares (Note 7)	–	(147,496)
Dividends paid	(74,970)	(73,997)
Cash provided by (used in) financing activities	(409,819)	163,226
Effect of currency translation on cash balances	(15,960)	10,107
Increase in cash and cash equivalents	88,132	47,912
Cash and cash equivalents, beginning of year	109,772	61,860
Cash and cash equivalents, end of year	$ 197,904	$ 109,772

See supplemental cash flow information, Note 19

8-53 (Accounting policies related to capital assets)

Metro Inc. owns and operates several supermarkets and pharmacies in Quebec and Ontario. Exhibit 8-13 shows Metro's notes on significant accounting policies for intangible assets and goodwill accompanying its 2009 financial statements.

> **Required:**
> a. What major intangible assets does Metro own? Why does the company distinguish between the ones with definite lives and those with indefinite lives?
> b. What method does Metro use to depreciate its intangible assets? Are they depreciated over their legal lives or useful lives? Explain why the treatment is appropriate.
> c. Explain what the prescription files are. How are these related to Metro's major operations?
> d. What is the source of the goodwill that Metro recognizes? Is the goodwill depreciated? Explain how Metro determines and recognizes any impairment loss on the goodwill.

8-54 (Research and development costs)

From its headquarters in Calgary and its development, operations, and marketing facilities in Arizona, Kansas, and Texas, Hemisphere GPS Inc. designs, develops, and manufactures commercial and industrial global positioning systems. The 2009 and 2008 consolidated statements of operations and deficit for Hemisphere GPS are shown in Exhibit 8-14.

As one would expect for a company in a high-technology industry, Hemisphere GPS incurs substantial research and development (R&D) costs. However, the notes accompanying its financial statements reveal that the company's policy is to expense all these costs in the period in which they are incurred.

METRO INC. 2009 ANNUAL REPORT

EXHIBIT 8-13

annual report

notes to consolidated financial statements

INTANGIBLE ASSETS Intangible assets with definite useful lives are recorded at cost and are amortized on a straight-line basis over their useful lives. The amortization method and estimate of the useful lives are reviewed annually.

Leasehold rights	20 to 40 years
Software	3 to 10 years
Improvements and development of retail network loyalty	5 to 20 years
Prescription files	10 years

Intangible assets with indefinite lives, such as banners and private labels and some agreements, are recorded at cost and are not subject to amortization. These assets are tested for impairment annually or more often if events or changes in circumstances indicate that the asset might be impaired. When the impairment test indicates that the carrying amount of the intangible asset exceeds its fair value, an impairment loss is recognized in an amount equal to the excess. The Company uses the royalty-free licensing method and the capitalization of excess earnings before financial costs and income taxes method.

GOODWILL Goodwill represents the excess of the purchase price over the fair value of net assets acquired. Goodwill is tested for impairment annually or more often if events or changes in circumstances indicate that it might be impaired. The impairment test first consists of a comparison of the fair value of the reporting unit to which goodwill is assigned with its carrying amount. When the carrying amount of a reporting unit exceeds its fair value, the fair value of the reporting unit's goodwill is compared with its carrying amount to measure the amount of the impairment loss, if any. Any impairment loss is charged to earnings in the period in which the loss is incurred. The Company uses the indicated earnings method to determine the fair value of its reporting unit.

EXHIBIT 8-14

HEMISPHERE GPS INC. 2009 ANNUAL REPORT

Consolidated Statements of Operations and Deficit

Years ended December 31, 2009 and 2008
(expressed in U.S. dollars)

	2009	2008
Sales	$ 53,638,296	$ 72,663,712
Cost of sales	27,781,060	35,860,059
	25,857,236	36,803,653
Expenses:		
Research and development	8,851,616	8,097,446
Sales and marketing	11,044,783	12,009,367
General and administrative	6,630,584	7,189,844
Stock-based compensation (note 5(d))	719,781	699,875
Amortization	3,145,974	3,427,272
	30,392,738	31,423,804
Income (loss) before undernoted items	(4,535,502)	5,379,849
Foreign exchange loss (gain)	244,332	(625,840)
Interest and other income	(20,697)	(668,673)
Restructuring costs (note 12)	876,094	250,742
Legal fees on settlement of lawsuit	–	151,700
Income (loss) before income taxes	(5,635,231)	6,271,920
Income taxes (note 7)	253,913	175,911
Net income (loss)	(5,889,144)	6,096,009
Deficit, beginning of year	(34,232,193)	(40,469,714)
Adjustment due to adoption of new accounting policy (note 1(d))	–	150,135
Adjustment due to Normal Course Issuer Bid (note 5(e))	–	(8,623)
Deficit, end of year	$(40,121,337)	$(34,232,193)
Net income (loss) per common share:		
Basic and diluted	$ (0.11)	$ 0.11
Weighted average shares outstanding:		
Basic	55,561,676	54,798,890
Diluted	55,561,676	55,132,241

See accompanying notes to consolidated financial statements.

Required:

a. Calculate how much the losses from continuing operations would have been for 2009 and 2008 if Hemisphere GPS had been able to capitalize its R&D costs and then depreciate them on a straight-line basis over a six-year period, commencing in the year in which they were incurred. (Note: In order to do this with the data available, you will have to assume that 2008 was the company's first year of operations.)

b. Compare your results in part "a" to the losses from continuing operations shown in Exhibit 8-14. Are the differences significant?

c. Assume the company continues for many years with approximately the same level of R&D expenditures each year. Will there be a significant difference between its income or loss if the company capitalizes its R&D costs and then depreciates them, rather than expensing these costs in the period in which they are incurred?

8-55 (Accounting for oil and gas properties)

The portion of **Imperial Oil Limited's** summary of significant accounting policies dealing with property, plant, and equipment was presented earlier in this chapter, in Exhibit 8-11. As indicated earlier, Imperial Oil operates Esso retail gas stations throughout Canada and is a major Canadian producer of crude oil and natural gas.

Required:

a. What method does Imperial Oil use to account for its costs related to exploration and development activities? Explain in your own words how these costs are handled under this method.

b. What reason does Imperial Oil give for choosing this method of accounting for costs related to its exploration and development activities? Explain in your own words what you think this means.

c. Is the method that Imperial Oil uses to account for exploration and development costs the method that you would expect a large oil and gas company to use? Explain why or why not.

8-56 (Accounting for mineral properties)

Claude Resources Inc. is a Saskatchewan-based "junior" natural resource company involved in gold mining. Note 2 accompanying its 2009 financial statements outlines its significant accounting policies. The portion of this note related to mineral properties is reproduced in Exhibit 8-15.

Required:

a. Describe how Claude Resources determines the carrying value of its mining properties. What kinds of items are capitalized?

b. Is the method that Claude Resources uses to account for exploration and development costs the method that you would expect a mining company to use? Explain.

c. Describe how Claude Resources records interest on debt that is used for the acquisition and development of mining properties. At what point are the interest costs expensed?

d. Describe in your own words how Claude Resources determines whether its mining properties are impaired.

CLAUDE RESOURCES INC. 2009 ANNUAL REPORT

Notes to Consolidated Financial Statements

Years ended December 31 (Canadian Dollars in Thousands, except as otherwise noted)

MINERAL PROPERTIES

The Company holds various positions in mining interests, including exploration rights, mineral claims, mining leases, unpatented mining leases and options to acquire mining claims or leases. All of these positions are classified as mineral properties for financial statement purposes.

All costs related to the acquisition, exploration and development of mineral properties and the development of milling assets are capitalized on a property by property basis. Development costs on producing properties include only expenditures incurred to develop reserves or for delineation of existing reserves. Interest on debt directly related to the acquisition and development of mineral properties is capitalized until commencement of commercial production. Expenditures for maintenance and repairs are charged to operating expenses as incurred.

Upon commencement of commercial production, the cost of each property is amortized against future income using the unit of production method over estimated recoverable ore reserves. Estimated recoverable ore reserves include proven and probable mineral reserves. Costs which are not considered economically recoverable through mining operations or through sale of reserves, or are related to properties which are allowed to lapse, are expensed. Mining equipment is depreciated over its estimated useful life of three years on a straight-line basis.

The carrying value of mineral properties is reviewed regularly utilizing a two part test and, where necessary, is written down to the estimated fair value. Estimated future cash flow, on an undiscounted basis, is calculated for the property using: estimated recoverable reserves and resources; estimated future metal price realization (considering historical and current prices, price trends and related factors); and, estimated operating and capital cash flows. An impairment loss is recognized when the carrying value of an asset exceeds the sum of undiscounted future net cash flows. An impairment loss is measured at the amount by which the asset's carrying value exceeds its fair value. Where estimates of future cash flows are not available and where other conditions suggest impairment, management assesses if carrying values can be recovered. If the carrying values exceed estimated recoverable values, then the costs are written-down to these values. It is possible that changes can occur that may affect the recoverability of the carrying value of mineral properties. Also, a change in assumptions may significantly impact the potential impairment of these assets.

BEYOND THE BOOK

8-57 (Financial statement disclosures)

Choose a company, as directed by your instructor, and respond to the following:

a. Use the statement of financial position and the notes to the financial statements to prepare an analysis of the capital assets. First list the beginning and ending amounts in the various capital asset and accumulated depreciation accounts and then calculate the net change, in both dollar and percentage terms, for the most recent year.

b. If any of the amounts in part "a" have changed by more than 10 percent, provide an explanation for this change.

c. What percentage of the company's total assets is invested in property, plant, and equipment? Has this percentage changed significantly during the most recent year?

d. What depreciation method(s) does the company use?

e. Use the following formulae to examine the property, plant, and equipment (PPE) for the company:

Average useful life of PPE = Total gross PPE ÷ Annual depreciation expense

Average age of PPE = Total accumulated depreciation ÷ Annual depreciation expense

Note: Remember that depreciation expense may not be separately disclosed in the statement of earnings but will usually appear in the cash flow statement.
Compare your results with any information disclosed in the notes. Do these results make sense?

f. Does the company have any significant intangible assets? If so, describe each of them.

Cases

8-58 Manuel Manufacturing Company

Ramon Manuel, the president of Manuel Manufacturing Company, has e-mailed you to discuss the cost of a new machine that his company has just acquired.

Case Primer

The machine was purchased in Montreal for $150,000. Transporting it from Montreal to the company's Hamilton factory and installing the machine were Manuel's responsibilities. Unfortunately, the machine was seriously damaged during this process and repairs costing $40,000 were required to restore it to its original condition.

Mr. Manuel wants to ensure that he can capitalize these repair costs as part of the cost of the machine, and has therefore consulted you on the following points as he understands them:

1. The cost of a capital asset should include all the costs that are necessary to get it in place and ready for use. The damaged machine was inoperative, so the repairs were definitely necessary.

2. All the other costs related to the transportation and installation of the machine are being capitalized.

3. An asset is a cost that will produce economic benefits in the future. Since the machine will be very productive for the next few years, future periods will definitely benefit from the repairs. Therefore, the repair costs should be capitalized.

4. The matching principle says that expenses should be matched with the revenues they produce. The repairs did not generate any revenue, and therefore this cost should not be considered an expense. As a matter of fact, the machine itself did not generate any revenue in the current fiscal year, since it arrived in early December and was not repaired until late in the month.

Required:

Discuss how Manuel Manufacturing Company should account for the $40,000 cost of the repairs. Ensure that you explain your reasoning and address each of Mr. Manuel's arguments in your reply.

8-59 Eastern and Western Companies

Summary statements of financial position and statement of earnings information for Eastern Company and Western Company, covering the first year of operations for both, follows.

The operations of the two businesses are similar, and both companies have effective corporate income tax rates of 25%. Upon investigation, however, you find the following differences:

- Eastern is financed mainly by shareholders' equity, while Western is financed mainly by long-term debt.

- Eastern depreciates its equipment and buildings using the straight-line method with estimated useful lives of 10 years and 20 years, respectively, while Western depreciates its equipment and buildings using the declining-balance method with rates of 20% and 10%, respectively.

	Eastern	Western
Statement of Financial Position Information		
Total current assets	$ 80,000	$ 75,000
Capital assets		
Land	135,000	130,000
Equipment	200,000	200,000
Accumulated depreciation	(20,000)	(40,000)
Buildings	500,000	500,000
Accumulated depreciation	(25,000)	(50,000)
Total assets	$ 870,000	$ 815,000
Total liabilities	$ 170,000	$ 650,000
Total shareholders' equity	700,000	165,000
Total liabilities and shareholders' equity	$ 870,000	$ 815,000
Statement of Earnings Information		
Revenues	$1,000,000	$1,000,000
Expenses:		
Depreciation	(45,000)	(90,000)
Interest	(17,000)	(65,000)
Other	(783,000)	(775,000)
Income taxes	(38,750)	(17,500)
Net earnings	$ 116,250	$ 52,500

Required:

a. Without adjusting for differences in depreciation policy, which company has the higher rate of return on assets (ROA)?

b. Which company has the higher ROA after adjusting for differences in depreciation policy? (Hint: You can determine this either by using Eastern's depreciation method for Western, or by using Western's depreciation method for Eastern.)

c. Using numbers from this example, explain why you should adjust for differences in depreciation policies when comparing companies.

d. Using numbers from this example, explain why the ROA formula includes an adjustment for interest (after taxes) in the numerator.

e. If you were a shareholder or a potential shareholder in these companies, what other rate-of-return ratio would you want to calculate? Why would this ratio provide different insights than the return on assets ratio?

8-60 Rolling Fields Nursing Home

Rolling Fields Nursing Home purchased land to use for a planned assisted-living community. As a condition of the sale, a title search had to be performed and a survey completed. Rolling Fields incurred both these costs. In order to prepare the land for new construction, a barn that was on the land when it was purchased had to be torn down, and a rocky hill in the middle of the property had to be levelled. A series of streets, sidewalks, water mains, storm drains, and sewers through the planned community also had to be constructed. Finally, street lighting had to be installed and green spaces for recreation and rest had to be landscaped.

The year after the land was purchased, construction of new homes began. The homes are to be owned by Rolling Fields and will be rented on a long-term basis to elderly residents who no longer feel they can live completely on their own but do not yet need nursing home care. Rolling Fields will be responsible for all the maintenance and repair costs associated with the properties. By the end of the year, Phase 1 was complete and 30 homes had been constructed and were occupied. The average cost of each home was $180,000.

In the first year, repair and maintenance costs averaged $1,200 per property. The company also borrowed $4 million to finance the construction of the homes. Interest on the loan for the year was $308,000.

Required:

a. Determine which of the above expenditures should be capitalized.
b. For the expenditures that should be capitalized, identify the appropriate account to which the costs should be charged.
c. For the expenditures that should be capitalized, discuss how each asset class should be depreciated.

8-61 Hugh White

Hugh White is a real estate developer with several properties located throughout St. John's, Newfoundland. Although Mr. White sells most properties upon completion, in some instances he arranges to purchase the property either by himself or in a consortium with other investors.

During the current year, Mr. White was involved in two residential rental properties. The first property was purchased solely by Mr. White. Because it is operated as a proprietorship, he pays personal income taxes on any profits earned by this property. Consequently, he has a strong incentive to maximize expenses on this property in order to minimize its net earnings and his income tax liability.

The second property is very similar in nature to the property owned by Mr. White, but is owned by a group of professionals living in St. John's. They have purchased the property as an investment and hired Mr. White to be the property manager. The group is very concerned with earning a good return on the investment, and consequently Mr. White's compensation is based upon the property's profitability.

During the year, both properties required that new parking lots be constructed. Both new parking lots are significant improvements to the properties, since they are now paved and lighted and have security systems.

Required:

a. In discussions with Mr. White, you discover that he would like to capitalize the costs of the parking lot for which he is the property manager and expense the costs of the parking lot for his own building. What is his rationale for wanting these accounting treatments?
b. What is the appropriate accounting treatment for the costs of both parking lots?

8-62   Maple Manufacturing Company

Maple Manufacturing Company recently purchased a property for use as a manufacturing facility. The company paid $850,000 for a building and four hectares of land. When recording the purchase, the company's accountant allocated $750,000 of the total cost to the building and the remaining $100,000 to the land.

After some investigation and an independent appraisal, you determine that the building is deemed to have a value of only $435,000. You also discover that the property is located near a major highway providing excellent access for shipping, and is therefore quite valuable. Similar properties in the area have been selling for $125,000 per hectare.

Maple Manufacturing is a very successful company and has traditionally reported very high net earnings. Last year, the company paid more than $200,000 in income taxes.

Required:

a. Determine the appropriate allocation between the buildings and land accounts for this basket purchase. (Remember that four hectares of land were purchased.)

b. Why would the company's accountant have wanted to allocate most of the purchase cost to the building rather than to the land?

8-63   Preakness Consulting and Bellevue Services

Preakness Consulting and Bellevue Services are two petroleum engineering firms located in Calgary, Alberta. Both companies are very successful and are looking to attract additional investors to provide them with an infusion of capital to expand. In the past year, both companies had consulting revenue of $1.5 million.

On January 1, 2011, both companies purchased new computer systems. Currently, the only other asset owned by the companies is office equipment, which is fully depreciated. The computer systems, related hardware, and installation cost each company $660,000, and the systems have an expected life of five years. The residual value at the end of the five-year period is expected to be $30,000 in each case.

Preakness has chosen to depreciate the computer equipment using the straight-line method, while Bellevue has taken a more aggressive approach and is depreciating the system using the double-declining-balance method. Both companies have December 31 year ends and a tax rate of 25%. Information on their other expenses is as follows:

	Preakness	Bellevue
Salaries and wages	$ 750,250	$ 747,500
Rent	44,800	46,400
Other operating expenses	110,670	109,790

Required:

a. For each company, prepare a depreciation schedule showing the amount of depreciation expense to be charged each year for the computer system.

b. Prepare statements of earnings for the current year for both companies.

c. How might an unsophisticated investor interpret the financial results from part "b"? Is one company really more profitable than the other?

Critical Thinking Questions

8-64 (Valuation of capital assets)

Four years ago, Litho Printers Ltd. purchased a large, four-colour printing press for $450,000 with the intent of using it for 10 years. Recently, the production manager learned that replacing the press with a comparable new one now would cost $560,000. The manager also estimates that if the company were to sell the existing printing press now it would receive $280,000. On the other hand, the production manager estimates that the company could earn $930,000 from selling materials produced on the press over the next six years.

Required:

a. Under what conditions (if any) should the press be valued at $560,000?
b. Under what conditions (if any) should the press be valued at $280,000?
c. Under what conditions (if any) should the press be valued at $930,000?
d. What value should be assigned to the press in Litho Printers' financial statements?

8-65 (Accounting for idle assets)

Conservative Company purchased a warehouse on January 1, 2006, for $400,000. At the time of purchase, Conservative anticipated that the warehouse would be used to facilitate the expansion of its product lines. The warehouse is being depreciated over 20 years and is expected to have a residual value of $50,000. At the beginning of 2011, the company decided that the warehouse would no longer be used and should be sold for its book value. At the end of 2011, the warehouse still had not been sold and its net realizable value was estimated to be only $260,000.

Required:

a. Calculate the book value of the warehouse on January 1, 2011.
b. Prepare all the journal entries that Conservative should make during 2011 related to the warehouse.
c. If Conservative sells the warehouse in 2012 for $220,000, what entry would be made for the sale?
d. During 2011, the financial vice-president expressed concern that if Conservative put the building up for sale the company might have to report a loss, and he did not want to reduce 2011 earnings. He wanted to continue treating the warehouse as an operating asset. How would the 2011 and 2012 financial statements be different if the warehouse were still treated as an operating asset during 2011? From a shareholder's perspective, do you think the treatment makes any difference? Explain.

chapter 9

CURRENT LIABILITIES, CONTINGENCIES, AND COMMITMENTS

LEARNING OBJECTIVES

After studying this chapter, you should be able to:

1. Describe the recognition criteria and valuation methods for liabilities.

2. Explain why accounts payable are sometimes thought of as "free debt."

3. Understand the issues in accounting for a company's payroll.

4. Explain warranty obligations and how they are accounted for.

5. Explain unearned revenues and describe situations where they must be recorded.

6. Describe the nature of non-financial liabilities and provisions.

7. Understand the concept of constructive obligations.

8. Explain why companies use working capital loans and lines of credit.

9. Calculate the amount of interest owed on various types of short-term notes payable.

10. Explain why any portion of long-term debt that is due within a year is classified as a current liability.

11. Calculate the accounts payable turnover rate and average payment period.

12. Explain contingencies and how they are accounted for.

13. Explain what commitments are and how they are handled.

Good Payroll Systems Help Keep Employees Happy

Mountain Equipment Co-op sells outdoor clothing and gear in stores across Canada, and worldwide through its catalogue and website. Founded in 1971, MEC has a reputation among its members for its helpful, knowledgeable staff, with some 1,670 employees working at its stores in Victoria, Vancouver, North Vancouver, Edmonton, Calgary, Winnipeg, Burlington, Toronto, Ottawa, Montreal, Longueuil, Quebec City, and Halifax, as well as its Vancouver call centre.

As a consumer co-operative—customers pay $5 for a lifetime membership—MEC depends on the dedication of its personnel, including sales staff, who are all active outdoor enthusiasts themselves and do not receive commissions. This is why Controller Doug Wong considers payroll to be the most important aspect of MEC's accounting for liabilities. "Payroll is a huge area," he explains. "In fact, it is our biggest operating expense. It's also an area where there is little margin for error—pay reflects how valued employees feel, and they are understandably sensitive about it. So we endeavour to have accurate payroll, and we do."

Four full-time staff members at MEC's Vancouver head office handle all payroll functions for the stores across Canada, which have salaried and hourly, full- and part-time employees. While inventory, general accounting, and warehouse operations are managed by one program, MEC uses a separate system for payroll. The routine calculations for pay, deductions (for income taxes, the Canada Pension Plan, and Employment Insurance), and benefits (both statutory benefits and supplemental disability and premium health-care plans) is straightforward with today's computerized accounting systems. However, exceptions, such as provincial variations in rules for holiday pay, enhancements to company-sponsored employee benefits like bike and computer loans, or employees leaving, require human intervention or additional calculations.

In the past, hourly employees would fill in time sheets manually, and payroll clerks would then manually enter that data. But MEC implemented an automated time-capture system in 2004. Hourly workers, who are the majority of MEC staff, swipe a card as they arrive and leave, and the number of hours they work is automatically entered into the system, Mr. Wong explains. "This has eliminated much of the data entry work of the payroll group. Now, most of their time is spent dealing with employment changes—new hires, pay changes, leaves of absence, end of employment issues, etc. They also do a fair bit of labour analysis reporting for store and other managers."

MEC can configure the system to track time in many ways, to not only produce accurate results but also provide information that is useful to management. For example, employees can swipe their cards every time they work in a different area of the store—the floor area, the cash area, the stock room, and so forth—keeping store managers informed about how their resources are being allocated. In addition, when employees are scheduled to work in different areas, the time and attendance system can calculate their pay according to their schedules. "This is an example of where MEC leverages technology to effectively and efficiently manage a business process," says Mr. Wong.

People like Doug Wong of Mountain Equipment Co-op understand that good employee relations are important to a successful business. Knowing that errors in payroll can affect employee morale, one way that MEC fosters good relations is through strict attention to detail in its payroll. Smaller businesses, and even some medium-sized and large companies, often find it more cost-effective to use an outside group with expertise in a particular accounting area (such as payroll) rather than to hire employees for this function. MEC once used an outside contractor for its payroll function. However, having grown to the point where it wants more information from its payroll data, MEC has chosen to customize its information flow by making the payroll function an internal one.

Successful businesses also pay attention to obligations owed to people outside the company. A good reputation for paying debts on time enables a company to use credit to operate effectively and to take on new initiatives. A poor credit rating, on the other hand, limits a company's options for outside financing.

In this and the next two chapters, our attention turns to the credit side of the statement of financial position and the accounting for liabilities and shareholders' equity. The common factor is that both liabilities and shareholders' equity can be viewed as sources of assets. Liability holders contribute assets in return for a promise of repayment at some future date, usually with interest. Shareholders contribute assets to the company in return for an ownership interest and the right to share in company profits.

In this chapter, the general nature of liabilities is discussed first, followed by various types of current liabilities. Chapter 10 deals with major non-current liabilities, and shareholders' equity issues are covered in Chapter 11.

USER RELEVANCE

Current liabilities represent obligations that the company must settle within the next year (or operating cycle of the business, if that is longer). Most of these obligations—accounts payable, income taxes payable, wages payable, notes payable, and so on—will require outflows of cash. Users can examine the current liabilities to determine how much cash will be required and to estimate when that cash will need to be paid. Examining the current assets, especially cash, accounts receivable, and short-term investments, provides users with information about the availability of cash. We have already talked about determining how quickly inventory is sold and accounts receivable are collected, using turnover ratios. These help users estimate whether enough cash will be available when the various liabilities come due. If there will not be sufficient cash available, the company will have to go to outside sources—taking on additional short- or long-term debt, or issuing more shares—in order to raise additional cash. Understanding a company's short-term cash needs is essential to determining its current financial health and what may need to be done to ensure its long-term viability.

RECOGNITION CRITERIA FOR LIABILITIES

Liabilities represent the company's obligations arising from past transactions or events. Specifically, to be classified as a liability an item must have the following three characteristics:

- It represents a duty, responsibility, or obligation that imposes an economic burden (i.e., it requires the transfer of assets, the performance of services, or the conferring of some other benefit).

- It is enforceable; the entity has little or no discretion to avoid the obligation. If the entity does not settle it, the creditor usually has the right to pursue legal action.

- The obligation exists at the present time. The exact *amount* may not be determined until a later event has occurred, but the underlying transaction or event creating the obligation has already occurred.

LEARNING OBJECTIVE 1

Describe the recognition criteria and valuation methods for liabilities.

What is uncertain about liabilities is usually the dollar value of the assets, services, or other benefits to be given up, and when they will be given up. To avoid uncertainty about the amount and timing of the settlement, some liabilities, such as accounts payable and most loans, have fixed payment schedules and due dates. For example, in loan agreements the interest and principal payments are specified, as are the dates on which those payments are to be made. Other liabilities, such as warranty obligations, have neither fixed amounts nor fixed dates. For example, the settlement of a warranty obligation will depend on when the customer detects a warranty problem and how much cost the company incurs to fix it. Liabilities, therefore, differ in their degree of uncertainty.

If the obligation is conditional upon some future event, a liability might not be recognized in the financial statements. Suppose, for example, that a company is under investigation by the government for alleged chemical contamination of a river. If the company is found negligent, there could be a significant liability if it is required to clean up the contamination and/or a fine is imposed. However, the company may insist that it is not responsible for the contamination and that the probability that it will be found negligent is low. In such a case, no liability will be recorded in the accounts. However, because a significant amount of assets may have to be transferred in the future, the company would generally disclose information about the investigation and the potential obligation in the notes to its financial statements. Under IFRS, such an item is referred to as a **contingent liability**, meaning that the liability has not been recorded in the accounts, because the obligation is conditional, dependent, or contingent on the occurrence of a low-probability future event.

The ownership criterion that is used for assets does not strictly apply to liabilities, but a similar notion does. Companies should record only those obligations that they will be required to satisfy. For example, if a customer falls on the company's property, sues the company for medical costs, and wins, the company may not be obliged to make the payment. If the company is insured against such claims, the insurance company will make the payment. The company, therefore, would not record the obligation to settle the customer's claim as a liability on its books, because it is the insurance company's obligation. (However, if the insurance does not cover the full amount, the company would record a liability for its portion of the payment.)

It is sometimes hard to determine whether the event giving rise to the obligation has already occurred. For example, in the case of the lawsuit mentioned above, what is the event that gives rise to the obligation? Is it the customer falling, the filing of a lawsuit, or the court's decision? In this case, the probability that an obligation exists increases as each subsequent event occurs. However, the event that gives rise to the ultimate obligation is debatable. More will be said about this later.

Another potentially difficult situation to evaluate can arise when a company signs a binding contract. Suppose, for example, a company signs a contract to purchase 1,000 units of inventory at $30 per unit, to be delivered 60 days from now. Is the signing of the contract the event that gives rise to the obligation to pay for the inventory, or is it the delivery of the inventory? The company's obligation is conditional upon the seller performing its part of the contract, by delivering the goods on time. If the goods are not delivered, then the company will not be obliged to pay. The contract signing creates what is known as a **mutually unexecuted contract** because, at the time of signing, neither the buyer nor the seller have performed their part of the contract. The seller has not delivered any inventory, and the buyer has not paid any cash. Such contracts are normally not recorded in the accounting system, although the company may include information about them in the notes to its financial statements.

A **partially executed contract** is one in which one party has performed part or all of its obligation. In the example just given, the contract would be viewed as partially executed if the buyer paid a $3,000 deposit. The buyer would show an outflow of cash of $3,000, and create an asset account for the right to receive inventory valued at $3,000, called "deposits on purchase contracts" (or something similar). The seller would show an inflow of cash of $3,000 and create a liability account to represent its obligation to deliver inventory valued at $3,000. The liability account would probably be called "unearned revenue." Once inventory valued at $3,000 is delivered to the customer, the obligation will be satisfied and the revenue will be earned. Note that only the amount of the deposit ($3,000) would be recorded at this time, not the full amount of the contract (1,000 units × $30 per unit = $30,000).

VALUATION METHODS FOR LIABILITIES

Just as there are different methods for valuing assets, there are different methods for valuing liabilities. Theoretically, a liability should be valued at its **present value** on the date it is incurred. In practice, however, there are several other possible valuation methods to be considered.

One way to value a liability is to record it at the gross amount of the obligation—i.e., the total of the payments to be made. For example, if an obligation requires a company to pay $1,000 each month for the next three years, the gross obligation would be $36,000. However, while this amount accurately measures the total payments to be made, it may not accurately measure the company's obligation at the time it is reported on the statement of financial position. For example, suppose the obligation is a rental agreement for a piece of machinery. If the rental agreement can be cancelled at any time, the company is only obligated to pay $1,000 each month. The remaining payments will be an obligation only if it keeps using the machinery. If the contract cannot be cancelled, valuing the liability at the full $36,000 would make more sense.

Another reason why the gross obligation may not adequately measure the liability's value is that it ignores the **time value of money**. Suppose that, rather than being a rental payment, the $1,000 each month is to repay a loan (including both interest and principal). In this case, the total payments of $36,000 include both the repayment of principal and the payment of interest. However, since interest only accrues as an obligation as time passes, the only liability that exists initially is for the principal of the loan. For example, if the principal amount of the loan is $30,000 the company could settle the obligation at the outset with a payment of $30,000. The difference ($6,000) between this amount and the $36,000 gross amount is the interest that accrues over time. If the initial liability was recorded at the full $36,000, the company's obligation at the present time would be overstated.

To recognize the time value of money, whenever the interest component is significant companies should record their liabilities at their present values. To do so, both the future principal payments and the interest payments are discounted back to the present time, using the appropriate interest rate. (Present value concepts and calculations are discussed in detail in Chapter 10.) Under this valuation system, the company initially records the obligation at its net present value, rather than the gross amount of the future payments to be made. As time passes, interest expense is recorded, which recognizes the cost of the loan and increases the liability, and payments are made, which decrease the liability.

What Is Canadian Practice?

As stated above, liabilities should, theoretically, be recorded at the present value of the future payments. The interest rate that is used should reflect the type of liability, the duration of the obligation, and the company's creditworthiness. Accordingly, short-term notes payable should be recorded at their present values, and the interest on them should be accrued over time.

However, present-value calculations are generally not used for most short-term liabilities, because either no interest is charged on them or the amounts involved are small and the time to maturity is so short that the difference between the present value of the obligations and the gross amount of the payments would not be material. Therefore, they are simply recorded at the gross amounts that are to be paid.

CURRENT LIABILITIES

Current liabilities are those obligations that require the transfer of assets or services within one year or one operating cycle of the company. As just discussed, most of them are carried on the books at their gross amounts. In order for a company to stay solvent (able to pay its debts when they become due), it must have sufficient current assets on hand and/or generated by its operations to pay the current liabilities. Creditors, such as bankers, will often compare a company's total current assets to its total current liabilities to assess its ability to remain viable. Frequently encountered current liabilities are discussed in the following subsections.

Current Liabilities Related to Operating Activities

Accounts Payable

As you know from earlier chapters, accounts payable occur when a company buys goods or services on credit. They are often referred to as *trade* accounts payable. Payment is generally deferred for a relatively short period of time, such as 30 to 60 days, although longer credit periods are allowed in some industries.

Accounts payable generally do not carry explicit interest charges and are commonly thought of as "free debt." However, there is sometimes a provision for either a

LEARNING OBJECTIVE 2

Explain why accounts payable are sometimes thought of as "free debt."

discount for early payment or a penalty for late payment. In such cases, not taking advantage of the discount, or paying a penalty for being late, can be viewed as equivalent to interest charges.

Wages and Other Payroll Liabilities

LEARNING OBJECTIVE 3

Understand the issues in accounting for a company's payroll.

Wages owed to employees can be another significant current liability. The magnitude depends, in part, on how often the company pays its employees, because the balance in the account reflects the wages that have accrued since the last pay period.

In addition to the wages themselves, most companies provide *fringe benefits* for employees. These costs—for medical insurance, pensions, vacation pay, and other benefits provided by the employer—must also be recognized in the periods in which they occur. Because these may be paid in periods other than when they are earned by the employees, any unpaid costs have to be accrued and liabilities recorded for them.

Canadian companies are also required to act as government agents in collecting certain taxes. For example, companies must withhold income taxes from employees' wages and remit them to the government. The amounts paid to the employees are reduced by the amounts withheld. While these taxes are not an expense to the company (because they come out of the employees' earnings), the company must nevertheless keep track of the amounts deducted from employees' earnings and report a liability to pay these amounts to the government.

The amount of income tax to be deducted from employees' earnings depends on many factors, including their expected annual earnings and their personal exemptions for income tax purposes. Therefore, in the examples and problems in this text we will simply state the amount of personal income tax that is to be withheld from the employees' pay.

Other items, such as Canada Pension Plan (CPP) or Quebec Pension Plan (QPP) and Employment Insurance (EI) contributions, are also deducted from employees' wages and remitted to the government. This further reduces the net amounts that are received by the employees.

In addition to the amounts that are deducted from employees' wages, companies must make their own payments to the government for CPP or QPP, EI, workers' compensation plan premiums, and in some provinces, public health-care premiums. These amounts are recorded as an expense to the employer and are shown as liabilities until they are remitted to the government.

As of mid-2010, CPP was deducted from employees' earnings at the rate of 4.95%, while the rate for EI deductions was 1.73%. (However, there are exemptions and maximums that can complicate the calculations, and these rates can change from year to year.) In addition to collecting the amounts deducted from employees, employers were also required (at the time of writing) to contribute an amount equal to the employees' deductions for CPP, and 1.4 times the amount deducted from their employees for EI.

For example, assume that the employees of Angelique's Autobody Shop have earned wages of $10,000, and that income tax totalling $2,500 is deducted from the employees' cheques. In addition, $495 (4.95% of $10,000) is deducted for CPP and $173 (1.73% of $10,000) is deducted for EI. Beyond these amounts, the employer has to pay an additional $495 (the same amount as deducted from the employees) for CPP, and $242.20 (1.4 times the $173 deducted from the employees) for EI, as the company's contributions. The journal entries to record the payroll would be as follows:

RECORDING DEDUCTIONS FROM THE EMPLOYEES' EARNINGS

Wages expense (SE)	10,000.00	
Employee income taxes payable (L)		2,500.00
CPP contributions payable (L) [4.95% of 10,000]		495.00
EI premiums payable (L) [1.73% of 10,000]		173.00
Cash (A) [10,000 − 2,500 − 495 − 173]		6,832.00

RECORDING CONTRIBUTIONS TO BE MADE BY THE EMPLOYER

Wages expense (SE)	737.20	
CPP contributions payable (L)		
[same amount as from the employees]		495.00
EI premiums payable (L)		
[1.4 times the amount from the employees]		242.20

Note that, although the employees earned $10,000, the amount actually paid to them in this example, after deductions, is only $6,832.00. This is referred to as their *net pay*.

The amounts in the three liability accounts are remitted periodically to the government, according to its regulations. The following journal entry illustrates the remittance of both the employees' deductions and the employer's contributions:

RECORDING THE REMITTANCE (PAYMENT) OF PAYROLL TAXES

Employee income taxes payable (L)	2,500.00	
CPP contributions payable (L) [$495.00 + $495.00]	990.00	
EI premiums payable (L) [$173.00 + $242.20]	415.20	
Cash (A)		3,905.20

Note that the total amount recorded by the employer as an expense ($10,000.00 + $737.20 = $10,737.20) exceeds the amount it agreed to pay the employees ($10,000.00). Because of these extra amounts that the government requires businesses to pay, companies are concerned each time the government makes changes to the Canada/Quebec Pension Plan, Employment Insurance scheme, or other compulsory programs—unless of course, the government reduces the rates. Employers must always take these additional amounts (which are commonly referred to as *payroll taxes*) into account in managing their businesses, because they increase the costs of hiring employees. Workers' Compensation Plan premiums and, in some provinces, public health-care premiums also fall into this category.

Corporate Income Taxes

Canadian companies that are incorporated pay both federal and provincial corporate income taxes, and may also be subject to taxation in other countries in which they operate. As mentioned earlier, the regulations governing the calculation of income for tax purposes differ in many respects from the accounting standards for the calculation of income. (The discussion in Chapter 8 concerning deferred income taxes highlighted this difference; deferred income taxes are discussed in greater detail in Chapter 10.) Nevertheless, the taxes that are payable according to the regulations of the taxing authorities must be recorded as a liability.

accounting in the news

Proposed Pension Plan Increases Called Costly Job Killers

In June 2010, the Canadian Federation of Independent Business (CFIB) spoke out against proposed changes to the Canada Pension Plan (CPP), saying increased premiums would kill jobs in small businesses. Before a meeting of the federal and provincial finance ministers, trade unions proposed doubling CCP premiums and benefits, but the CFIB said that more than 70 percent of small business owners oppose these changes.

The CFIB pointed out the huge up-front cost for any business setting up a pension plan. One of the major challenges for small businesses is whether employees and employers have enough income to dedicate to a pension plan. Nearly half of all small-business owners surveyed by the CFIB said they are unable to provide retirement savings benefits for employees.

The CFIB described the mandatory nature of payroll taxes as "the worst form of taxation for small businesses." It said that if the ministers enacted the proposed increases, the decision would be a "major job killer."

Source: Andrew Binet, "CFIB Opposes Proposed Pension Hikes: Survey," *The Globe and Mail*, June 10, 2010.

The payment of income taxes does not always coincide with the incurrence of the taxes. In Canada, companies are generally required to make monthly income tax payments, usually based on the taxes paid the previous year, so that the government has a steady flow of cash coming in during the year. The deadline for filing a corporate income tax return is six months after the company's fiscal year end, but the balance of taxes owed for the year must generally be paid within two months of the year end and therefore often has to be estimated. Penalties are imposed if the company significantly underestimates the amount of tax payable.

Exhibit 9-1 contains the current liability section of the balance sheet for **Lululemon Athletica Inc.** and illustrates many of the current liabilities related to operating activities discussed so far. Lululemon produces and sells athletic apparel for yoga, running, and dance. Note the size of the liabilities for *accounts payable* (which would be primarily for inventory acquisition costs), *accrued liabilities* (which would include a variety of expenses that have been incurred but not yet paid), *accrued compensation and related expenses* (which would include unpaid salaries and wages, fringe benefits, and payroll taxes), and *income taxes payable* (which would be based on the company's earnings). The liability for unredeemed gift cards will be explained in a later section of this chapter.

Warranty Obligations[1]

When companies sell goods or services, there are often either stated or implied guarantees, or warranties, to the buyers. If a product proves to be defective, the company that manufactured or sold it may have to provide warranty services to repair or replace it. Companies sometimes charge extra for warranties; in other cases they provide warranty coverage at no explicit additional charge. Warranties that are sold separately to

---

1. This section deals with warranties that are provided at no explicit additional charge. Warranties that are sold to customers are dealt with in a later section of this chapter, titled "Warranty Sales."

LULULEMON ATHLETICA INC. 2009 ANNUAL REPORT

CONSOLIDATED BALANCE SHEETS—CURRENT LIABILITIES

	January 31, 2010	February 1, 2009
	(Amounts in thousands, except per share amounts)	
Current liabilities		
Accounts payable	$ 11,028	$ 5,269
Accrued liabilities	17,207	22,103
Accrued compensation and related expenses	10,626	5,862
Income taxes payable	7,742	2,133
Unredeemed gift card liability	11,699	9,278
Other current liabilities	376	690
	58,678	45,335

customers (i.e., those that have an explicit extra charge) are discussed in the following section on unearned revenues; here we deal only with warranties that are provided at no additional charge.

Although, at the time of the product's sale, the company cannot know how much the cost of the warranty services will ultimately be, it should still estimate and accrue the warranty cost in order to match the expense from the warranty to the revenue from the sale. In other words, to satisfy the matching principle, in each accounting period a warranty expense and a warranty liability must be recognized, based on an estimate of the future warranty costs that will be incurred on sales made that period. If the company has been in business for a long time, this estimate can probably be made fairly easily, based on the history of past warranty claims. For new products and new companies, estimating what the future costs will be may be much more difficult.

As an example of a warranty situation, suppose a home appliance company sells 200 refrigerators in 2010, and that each refrigerator has a two-year warranty against mechanical defects. Although the company buys quality merchandise from its suppliers, it is very likely that within two years of sale some of these refrigerators will require warranty services. After reviewing its record of past warranty services, the company estimates that approximately 6% of the refrigerators it sells require warranty services during the first year following their sale, and another 4% require warranty services during the second year after their sale. It also determines that the average cost to repair a refrigerator under the warranty is $150. Over the two-year period of the warranty, the company therefore expects that it will have to spend about $3,000 (10% of 200 units = 20 units; 20 units @ $150 per unit = $3,000) on warranty services for the refrigerators sold in 2010. Of course, this is just an estimate based on averages; the actual costs may be more, or less, than $3,000. However, experience and knowledge of their merchandise usually enable companies to make reasonably accurate estimates of their future warranty costs.

To record the estimated warranty obligation in the period of the sale, the company would make the following journal entry:

RECORDING THE ESTIMATED WARRANTY EXPENSE AND OBLIGATION, AT THE TIME OF SALE

2010			
	Warranty expense (SE)	3,000	
	Estimated warranty obligation (L)		3,000

Note that the entire estimated warranty cost is recorded as an expense in the year of sale, regardless of the length of time covered by the warranty. Whether the warranty costs will be incurred over two years (as in this example) or some other time period is irrelevant for determining the expense to be reported on the statement of earnings. On the statement of financial position, the portion of the obligation that is expected to be settled within a year would be reported as a current liability, and any portion that extends beyond one year would be reported as a non-current liability.

If, during 2011 and 2012 our company spent $1,700 and $1,100, respectively, for warranty work on these refrigerators, it would record these expenditures by reducing the warranty liability account, as follows:

RECORDING THE ACTUAL COSTS INCURRED, AS THE WARRANTY CLAIMS ARE SETTLED

2011			
	Estimated warranty obligation (L)	1,700	
	Cash* (A)		1,700
2012	Estimated warranty obligation (L)	1,100	
	Cash* (A)		1,100

*There could also be credits to various other accounts, such as Inventory (if replacement refrigerators are given to customers), Repair Supplies (for parts used in warranty repairs), and Wages Payable (for labour costs incurred in doing warranty repairs).

In this case, it appears that the company overestimated its warranty costs slightly. It estimated that the costs would total $3,000, but the costs were actually $2,800 ($1,700 + $1,100). As a result, the liability account will have a balance of $200 remaining in it. If this pattern continues for several periods, the company may want to reduce its estimates. However, there will probably be some years when the actual warranty costs are higher than estimated, and in the long run things may average out.

As you can see in the foregoing journal entries, no expense is recorded when actual warranty costs are incurred. Rather, the warranty liability account is debited, to reflect the fact that a portion of the company's obligation has been satisfied.

By estimating its expected future obligation at the same time that it records the sale, the company records the warranty expense in the same accounting period as when the sales revenue is recorded. In this way, the statement of earnings provides a better indication of the profitability of that period's operations. If the company delayed recognizing any expense until it actually incurred the warranty costs, in our example the revenue would be in the 2010 statement of earnings and the expenses would be in the 2011 and 2012 statements of earnings. As a result, the profit reported in 2010 would be overstated. For this reason, if warranty costs are material, companies are required to estimate their expected future warranty obligation, and to record this liability and the related warranty expense at the time of sale.

Warranties thus provide another illustration of the importance of ensuring that the statement of earnings shows a complete picture of the operating results each period, and that the statement of financial position shows the company's true financial position at the end of each period. By recording warranty liabilities, accountants recognize that when goods are sold with warranties companies incur obligations to honour the future claims that will be made.

IFRS INSIGHTS

Recent standards under IFRS have moved towards measuring warranty liabilities as the *sales value* of the goods or services that will be required to satisfy the warranty claims, rather than the company's *acquisition cost* for these goods and services. To illustrate this, recall our example in which the home appliance company estimated that the cost of repairing defective refrigerators would be $3,000 and therefore recorded a warranty obligation of $3,000. Under the new approach, if the repair services that are expected to be required under the warranty could have been *sold* for, say, $4,000, the company would record a liability (in the form of unearned revenue) of $4,000. As a result, the current period's earnings would be $1,000 lower, compared to the method we used. However, if the warranty repairs were eventually done at a cost of $3,000, the company would report a profit of $1,000 on the warranty work in the later period's earnings.

Effectively, the new approach assumes that—even when warranties are provided without any explicit additional charge—part of the sales price of the goods or services is related to the warranties that are provided with them. Put another way, it treats the original sale as a "bundle" consisting of the initial goods or services that have been provided at that point plus the additional goods or services that may be provided in the future under the warranty. This makes the treatment of these warranties consistent with the treatment of warranties that are, in fact, sold separately (discussed in the following section on Unearned Revenues).

Unearned Revenues

In many businesses, customers are required to pay deposits or make down payments prior to receiving goods or services. This creates partially executed contracts between buyers and sellers. Because the sellers have not fulfilled their part of the contract, it would be inappropriate for them to recognize revenue at this point. Therefore, sellers must defer the recognition of revenue from deposits and down payments. These deferrals create liabilities that are known as **unearned revenues** or **deferred revenues**.

Businesses that require prepayments show unearned revenues in the liability section of the balance sheet because, by accepting the money in advance, they incur an obligation to provide the related goods or services (or, failing that, to return the money). Magazine and newspaper publishers that sell subscriptions are among these types of businesses. They receive money for subscriptions in advance, and must initially record this as an asset (cash) offset by a liability (unearned revenue). They earn the revenue later, when they deliver the magazines and newspapers. At that time, they reduce the liability account and record the revenue.

LEARNING OBJECTIVE 5

Explain unearned revenues and describe situations where they must be recorded.

HELPFUL HINT

Remember that revenues cannot be recorded until they have been earned. Consequently, unearned (or deferred) revenues are reported as *liabilities,* on the statement of financial position, rather than as revenues on the statement of earnings. Once the related goods have been delivered or services performed, these amounts are considered earned and an adjusting entry is made to transfer them out of liabilities and into revenues.

Airlines are another example of businesses that receive payments in advance. When a customer pays for a ticket for a future flight, the amount received by the airline must be treated as unearned revenue (a liability) until the flight has been provided; when the flight occurs, the revenue is earned and the liability is eliminated. For example, the current liability section of the balance sheet for WestJet Airlines as at December 31, 2009, included $286,361,000 for Advance Ticket Sales. The accompanying notes stated that "Guest revenues, including the air component of vacation packages, are recognized when air transportation is provided. Tickets sold but not yet used are reported in the consolidated balance sheet as advance ticket sales."

Gift Certificates and Prepaid Cards

The sale of gift certificates and prepaid cards is a major source of unearned revenue for many businesses. According to accounting standards, gift card revenue is recognized only when the cards are redeemed for goods or services. When a gift certificate or prepaid card is sold, the business records the cash received and an offsetting liability, representing its obligation to provide goods or services equal to the value of the card. Later, when the gift card is used, the liability is eliminated and revenue is recognized.

The popularity of gift cards is having a major effect on the sales patterns of many retail businesses. The November-December holiday shopping season is very important to most retailers. However, much of the money spent on gift cards late in the current year shows up in sales revenues early in the next year, when the gift cards are redeemed. Thus, in terms of revenue recognition, selling gift cards during the holiday shopping period shifts revenues to January and February. In particular, gift card activations (when cards are purchased) drop off sharply after December. In contrast, January redemptions (when gift cards are used to purchase something) are very significant. As a result, the usual drop-off in sales from December to January has moderated. The recognition of December gift card sales as revenues in January has given the start of the new year a significant financial boost, in a time that has traditionally been a slow one for retail businesses.

The following example illustrates the journal entries required to record gift certificates or prepaid cards, and their impact on the financial statements.

In December 2011, a company sells gift cards worth $10,000. Twenty percent of these are redeemed in December, for merchandise with a cost of $1,500. Sixty percent of the cards are redeemed in January 2012, for merchandise with a cost of $5,000. The remaining 20 percent of the cards are still outstanding at the end of January.

The journal entries for December 2011 would be as follows:

Cash (A)	10,000	
Unearned revenue/Gift cards (L)		10,000
Unearned revenue/Gift cards (L)	2,000	
Sales (SE)		2,000
20% × $10,000 = $2,000		
Cost of goods sold (SE)	1,500	
Inventory (A)		1,500

The December 31, 2011, statement of financial position would report a liability of $8,000 ($10,000 − $2,000) of unearned revenue related to the outstanding gift cards. The statement of earnings for the month of December would include sales revenue of

$2,000 and cost of goods sold of $1,500, for a gross profit of $500 from the gift cards that were redeemed in December.

The journal entries for January 2012 would be as follows:

Unearned revenue/Gift cards (L)	6,000	
Sales (SE)		6,000
60% × $10,000 = $6,000		
Cost of goods sold (SE)	5,000	
Inventory (A)		5,000

The January 31, 2012, statement of financial position would report a liability of $2,000 ($10,000 − $2,000 − $6,000) of unearned revenue related to the gift cards that are still outstanding. The statement of earnings for January would include sales revenue of $6,000 and cost of goods sold of $5,000, for a gross profit of $1,000 from the gift cards that were redeemed in January.

The current liabilities section of Lululemon Athletica Inc.'s balance sheet (which was presented in Exhibit 9-1) shows that, even though the company has a January 31 year end and many of its gift cards were probably redeemed in January, Lululemon still has a large liability related to unredeemed gift cards included in its current liabilities.

accounting in the news

No End to the Value of Gift Cards

In February 2010, Nova Scotia joined other provinces in banning expiry dates and fees on gift cards. There are two types of gift cards: those for a specific good or service, and those with an associated dollar value. In Nova Scotia, gift cards with a dollar value can no longer have an expiry date. Cards for goods and services purchased before February 1, 2010, will expire as scheduled because the value of the goods or services increase over time; however, cards purchased after this date will not have expiry dates. The regulations also indicate that no fees, such as inactivity fees, can be charged, except customizing or replacement fees, and that the refund policy and contact information must now be included with the cards.

While card buyers benefit from the convenience of gift cards, businesses benefit through both "floatage" and "slippage" (sometimes referred to as "breakage"). Floatage refers to the fact that a gift card–issuing company receives the customer's money without having to deliver the goods or services right away. Slippage refers to the estimated 10 to 15 percent of gift cards that are never redeemed.

Although a little slippage is good, having a large number of unredeemed cards outstanding can create accounting difficulties for companies. This is why many businesses opted to impose expiry dates–that is, until the restrictions introduced by governments. In many provinces, expiry dates are now either not allowed or permitted only in certain circumstances. For example, Nova Scotia's regulations do not apply to charity and promotional cards, prepaid telecom cards, or prepaid cards from credit card companies like Visa or Mastercard.

Sources: Rob Carrick, "Not All Gift Cards Are Created Equal," *The Globe and Mail*, December 1, 2009. Access Nova Scotia, "Nova Scotia Gift Cards," June 6, 2010, http://www.gov.ns.ca/snsmr/access/individuals/nova-scotia-gift-cards

Customer Rewards or Loyalty Programs

Many businesses have customer loyalty programs to encourage their customers to buy from them. Under these programs, points (or other forms of credits) are awarded to customers when they make purchases, and these points can later be redeemed for free goods or services. Some companies participate in general rewards programs, such as *Air Miles*, that are operated by independent entities. In other cases, the loyalty programs are specific to particular companies, such as the *Optimum* rewards program operated by **Shoppers Drug Mart**.

The accounting issues related to these customer loyalty programs are similar to those for warranties. Traditionally, the usual approach was to estimate the cost of the free goods and services that were expected to be provided in the future, and accrue this as an expense in the period when the sales revenue was recorded. The offsetting credit was to a liability account with a title such as Loyalty Program Obligations. Later, when customers redeemed their points for free goods or services, their cost was debited to this liability account, because the obligation had been satisfied. This process ensured that the cost of providing the rewards was matched against the revenues that were generated when the sales were made. Note that this treatment parallels the way in which warranty obligations (discussed earlier) have traditionally been accounted for.

However, as with warranty obligations, recent standards under IFRS have moved towards measuring loyalty program liabilities as the *sales value* of the goods or services that will be required to satisfy the reward redemptions, rather than the company's *acquisition cost* for these goods and services. Thus, if a company estimated that the points awarded in a particular accounting period will be redeemed for goods or services that could have been *sold* for $4,000, it would record a liability (in the form of unearned revenue) of this amount. If the rewards were later provided at a *cost* of $3,000, the company would report a profit of $1,000 from the rewards program in the later period's earnings.

Essentially, the new approach to accounting for customer loyalty programs is to treat the original sale as a "bundle" consisting of two parts: the initial goods or services that are provided at that point, plus the additional goods or services that may be provided in the future under the rewards program. In other words, part of the amount that customers pay when they make purchases is deemed to be for the rewards that will be provided later. Accordingly, the selling company should allocate a portion of the sales revenue to the rewards program and treat it as unearned revenue, until the rewards are delivered.

Warranty Sales[2]

LEARNING OBJECTIVE 6

Describe the nature of non-financial liabilities and provisions.

As a final illustration of a situation involving unearned revenues, consider the case of retailers such as **Future Shop** who sell warranty coverage (either basic or extended) on the products they sell. When customers purchase these warranties, the company has to record the amount received as unearned revenue and carry this as a liability on its statement of financial position, until either the warranty services are provided or the warranty period ends.

---

2. This section deals only with warranties that are sold to customers. Warranties provided at no explicit additional charge are dealt with in an earlier section of this chapter, titled "Warranty Obligations."

Constructive Obligations

In addition to the traditional types of liabilities arising from laws or contracts, IFRS also recognizes a type called a "constructive" liability. **Constructive obligations** can arise when a company has, through its past or present practices, indicated to other parties that it will accept specific responsibilities, and the other parties reasonably expect it to do so. For example, a company might have a long-standing practice of paying a bonus of 5 percent of employees' annual salaries at the end of each year. Therefore, even though it may not be required by law or contract to pay the 5 percent bonus, the company has created the expectation that it will continue to provide it. As a result of its consistent past actions, the company has a constructive obligation. Consequently, if the bonus has not been paid it would be accrued as a liability.

Current Liabilities Related to Financing Activities

Working Capital Loans and Lines of Credit

Companies need to have sufficient current assets or inflows of cash from operations to pay their debts as they become due. At times the current assets may not be converted into cash quickly enough to meet current debt obligation deadlines. To manage these shortfalls, companies have a few options. For example, they can arrange a **working capital loan** with a bank. (As discussed earlier in this book, working capital refers to the amount by which a company's current assets exceed its current liabilities.) This type of short-term loan is often guaranteed (secured) by the company's accounts receivable, inventory, or both. As the inventory is sold and money is collected from the accounts receivable, the amounts received are used to pay off the loan.

Loans or other debts are said to be **secured** whenever specific assets have been pledged to guarantee repayment of the debt. Assets that have been pledged as security for debts are referred to as **collateral**. If the borrower defaults on a secured debt, the lender has the legal right to have the collateral seized and sold, and the proceeds used to repay the debt. If debts are **unsecured**, this means that no specific assets have been pledged as collateral to guarantee their repayment; in such cases, the creditors simply rely on the general creditworthiness of the company.

Another way that companies can deal with temporary cash shortages is to arrange a **line of credit** with a bank. In this case, the bank assesses the company's ability to repay short-term debts and establishes a short-term loan limit that it feels is reasonable. If cheques written by the company exceed its cash balance in the bank, the bank covers the excess by immediately activating the line of credit and establishing a short-term loan. The bank uses subsequent cash deposits by the company to repay the loan. A bank line of credit provides the company with greater flexibility and freedom to take advantage of business opportunities and/or to settle debts.

A company that is using a working capital loan or a line of credit might have a negative cash balance. If so, it must be shown with the current liabilities. For example, at the end of its 2010 fiscal year, **Magnotta Winery Corporation** had an operating line of credit with a limit of $11,500,000. Of this amount, the company had borrowed $5,249,398 on January 31, 2010, which was down from $5,881,325 a year earlier. These amounts were due on demand, and were reported as bank indebtedness in the current liabilities section of Magnotta's balance sheet. The interest rate applicable to this line of credit was the **prime rate**—the loan rate that is offered by banks to their best customers—plus 0.875%. (As you may recall from earlier examples, Magnotta Winery has vineyards in Ontario and Chile and produces, imports, exports, and retails beer and spirits, as well as wine and ingredients for making wine).

Short-Term Notes and Interest Payable

Short-term notes payable represent company borrowings that require repayment in the next year or operating cycle. They either carry explicit interest or are structured so that the difference between the original amount received and the amount repaid represents implicit interest. In either case, interest expense should be recognized over the life of these loan agreements.

Of course, every *note payable* that is recorded by one party (the borrower or debtor) is recorded as a *note receivable* by the other party to the transaction (the lender or creditor). Accordingly, the treatment of notes payable and interest expense in the following discussion parallels the treatment of notes receivable and interest revenue that was discussed in Chapter 6.

LEARNING OBJECTIVE 9

Calculate the amount of interest owed on various types of short-term notes payable.

Illustration of a loan with equal monthly payments that include both interest and principal: Assume that a company borrows $10,000 from a bank at 9% on June 30, to be repaid in equal monthly instalments over six months. (This type of loan is called an **instalment loan**, to indicate that payments are made periodically rather than only at the end of the loan.) The bank determines that the required amount of each monthly payment is $1,710.69. The monthly instalments include reductions of the principal (which is initially $10,000) as well as interest (at the rate of 9% per annum, calculated on the decreasing amount of principal outstanding each month). The following table illustrates how the interest and the reductions of the principal are calculated:

Date	Payment	Interest (Principal Balance × 9% × 1/12)	Principal Reduction (Payment − Interest)	Principal Balance
June 30				$10,000.00
July 31	$ 1,710.69	$ 75.00[a]	$ 1,635.69	$ 8,364.31
Aug. 31	$ 1,710.69	$ 62.73[b]	$ 1,647.96	$ 6,716.35
Sept. 30	$ 1,710.69	$ 50.37	$ 1,660.32	$ 5,056.03
Oct. 31	$ 1,710.69	$ 37.92	$ 1,672.77	$ 3,383.26
Nov. 30	$ 1,710.69	$ 25.37	$ 1,685.32	$ 1,697.94
Dec. 31	$ 1,710.69	$ 12.75[c]	$ 1,697.94	-0-
Total	$10,264.14	$264.14	$10,000.00	

[a] $10,000.00 × 0.09 × 1/12 = $75.00

[b] $8,364.31 × 0.09 × 1/12 = $62.73

[c] with rounding of $0.02 to bring the final principal balance to zero

This type of table is called a **loan amortization table** because it shows how the original amount of the loan is reduced as time passes. The periodic payments on this type of loan are referred to as **blended payments**, because they contain both interest and principal components. Although the total payment is the same amount each period, the portion of each payment that is consumed by interest is reduced as the principal balance is reduced.

Notice that the total interest on the loan ($264.14) is much less than it would have been if the entire $10,000 debt had been outstanding for six months ($10,000 × 9% × 6/12 = $450). This is because monthly payments were made and large portions of these payments were applied to the principal, which reduced the principal amount owing and made the average loan balance outstanding during the six-month period much less than $10,000.

The journal entries to record this loan and the payments on it are as follows:

June 30	Cash (A)	10,000.00	
	Short-term note payable (L)		10,000.00
July 31	Interest expense (SE)	75.00	
	Short-term note payable (L)	1,635.69	
	Cash (A)		1,710.69
Aug. 31	Interest expense (SE)	62.73	
	Short-term note payable (L)	1,647.96	
	Cash (A)		1,710.69
Sept. 30	Interest expense (SE)	50.37	
	Short-term note payable (L)	1,660.32	
	Cash (A)		1,710.69
Oct. 31	Interest expense (SE)	37.92	
	Short-term note payable (L)	1,672.77	
	Cash (A)		1,710.69

Nov. 30	Interest expense (SE)	25.37	
	Short-term note payable (L)	1,685.32	
	Cash (A)		1,710.69
Dec. 31	Interest expense (SE)	12.75	
	Short-term note payable (L)	1,697.94	
	Cash (A)		1,710.69

As shown in the loan amortization table, the principal balance in the short-term note payable account will gradually be reduced as each monthly payment is made, and should be zero when the final payment is made on December 31.

Illustration of a loan with monthly payments of interest only: To illustrate a different type of loan arrangement, we will now consider the case of a company that takes out a six-month loan for $10,000 at 9% on June 30, but with terms that specify that only the interest on the loan is to be paid each month; the principal is to be repaid as a lump sum on December 31.

Note the key difference between this situation and the previous one: in this case, there are no reductions in the principal of the loan during its life. In this type of situation, a loan amortization table is not necessary, because the principal balance remains the same from the start of the loan on June 30 until it is repaid in full on December 31. Consequently, the amount of interest is the same each month, calculated as $10,000 \times 9\% \times 1/12 = \$75$.

The journal entries to record this loan and the payments on it are as follows:

June 30	Cash (A)	10,000.00	
	Short-term note payable (L)		10,000.00
July 31	Interest expense (SE)	75.00	
	Cash (A)		75.00
Aug. 31	Interest expense (SE)	75.00	
	Cash (A)		75.00
Sept. 30	Interest expense (SE)	75.00	
	Cash (A)		75.00
Oct. 31	Interest expense (SE)	75.00	
	Cash (A)		75.00
Nov. 30	Interest expense (SE)	75.00	
	Cash (A)		75.00
Dec. 31	Interest expense (SE)	75.00	
	Short-term note payable (L)	10,000.00	
	Cash (A)		10,075.00

We chose to use the account title Short-Term Note Payable for this liability. However, alternatives such as Short-Term Bank Loan are also commonly used.

Illustration of a loan with no explicit interest charge: Another type of loan arrangement would be for a company to borrow $10,000 on June 30 and sign a note promising to repay $10,450 on December 31. In this case, even though there is no mention of interest, the extra $450 that has to be paid is clearly an interest charge. Over the six-month period of the loan, this interest should be recognized at the rate of $75 per month ($450 ÷ 6 months). In essence, this situation is almost the same as the previous one. The only real difference is that none of the interest is paid until the note becomes due.

The journal entries to record this loan and its repayment are as follows:

June 30	Cash (A)	10,000.00	
	Short-term note payable* (L)		10,000.00
July 31	Interest expense (SE)	75.00	
	Short-term note payable* (L)		75.00
Aug. 31	Interest expense (SE)	75.00	
	Short-term note payable* (L)		75.00
Sept. 30	Interest expense (SE)	75.00	
	Short-term note payable* (L)		75.00
Oct. 31	Interest expense (SE)	75.00	
	Short-term note payable* (L)		75.00
Nov. 30	Interest expense (SE)	75.00	
	Short-term note payable* (L)		75.00
Dec. 31	Interest expense (SE)	75.00	
	Short-term note payable* (L)		75.00
	Short-term note payable** (L)	10,450.00	
	Cash (A)		10,450.00

*Alternatively, Interest Payable could have been credited.

**If Interest Payable had been credited in each of the monthly entries, this entry would have had a debit of $450 to Interest Payable and a debit of $10,000 to Short-Term Note Payable.

Notice that although the note payable states an amount of $10,450, it is initially recorded at its principal amount (or *present value*) of $10,000. The $450 of interest only arises as time passes. Over the term of the loan, the carrying value of the liability increases by $75 per month and reaches its maturity value of $10,450 on December 31, when it is repaid.

Current Portion of Long-Term Debt

When long-term debts (which will be discussed in Chapter 10) come within a year of being due, they must be reclassified as current liabilities. This reclassification enables users to estimate the expected outflow of cash during the following year. Therefore, this liability category, generally known as the **current portion of long-term debt**, is used for all the debt that was originally long-term but is now within one year, or one operating cycle, of being paid off or retired.

LEARNING OBJECTIVE 10

Explain why any portion of long-term debt that is due within a year is classified as a current liability.

In the case of long-term loans, mortgages, or other debt obligations that require monthly or annual payments, the portion that should be reported as a current liability is the amount of principal and any accrued interest from past periods that will be paid within the next year. Remember that interest for future periods is not recorded until it accrues or is paid.

Exhibit 9-2 shows the current liabilities section of the balance sheet for **Shaw Communications Inc.** as of August 31, 2009. Shaw is a diversified Canadian communications company that provides cable television, high-speed Internet, digital phone, mobile telecommunications, and satellite direct-to-home services to subscribers. Notice that the exhibit includes some of the current liabilities related to financing activities discussed in this section of the chapter—working capital loans and lines of credit, and current portions of long-term debts—as well as accounts payable and accrued liabilities, income taxes payable, and unearned revenue. More details of Shaw's current liabilities are provided in the notes that accompany the statements, and users should refer to these for a complete picture of the company's current obligations.

EXHIBIT 9-2

annual report

SHAW COMMUNICATIONS INC. 2009 ANNUAL REPORT

CONSOLIDATED BALANCE SHEETS—CURRENT LIABILITIES

As at August 31 [thousands of Canadian dollars]	2009 $	2008 $
Current		
Bank indebtedness *[note 9]*	–	44,201
Accounts payable and accrued liabilities *[notes 13 and 17]*	563,110	655,756
Income taxes payable	25,320	2,446
Unearned revenue	133,798	124,384
Current portion of long-term debt *[note 9]*	481,739	509
Current portion of derivative instruments *[note 19]*	173,050	1,349
	1,377,017	828,645

STATEMENT ANALYSIS CONSIDERATIONS

LEARNING OBJECTIVE 11

Calculate the accounts payable turnover rate and average payment period.

Current liabilities are, of course, a key component of both the current ratio (i.e., current assets ÷ current liabilities) and the quick ratio (i.e., [current assets − inventories − prepaid expenses] ÷ current liabilities), which were introduced in Chapter 6.

In addition to the current and quick ratios, we can also calculate various turnover ratios related to current liabilities. The most common of these is the **accounts payable turnover** rate, which is calculated as follows:

$$\text{Accounts payable turnover rate} = \frac{\text{Credit purchases}}{\text{Average accounts payable}}$$

The amount of purchases is not usually reported directly in the financial statements. However, the cost of goods sold can be used as a starting point. Making an adjustment for the change in inventories during the period will convert the *cost of goods sold* to the *cost of goods purchased*. As you should recall from Chapter 7, Beginning inventory + Purchases − Ending inventory = Cost of goods sold. Rearranging these terms, the formula to calculate the purchases is as follows:

$$\text{Purchases} = \text{Cost of goods sold} - \text{Beginning inventory} + \text{Ending inventory}$$

For example, using the financial statements in Appendix A we can calculate **H&M**'s purchases as SEK 40,659 (SEK 38,919 − SEK 8,500 + SEK 10,240). Its accounts payable turnover rate for 2009 can then be calculated as follows:

$$\frac{\text{SEK } 40,659^a}{(\text{SEK } 3,667 + \text{SEK } 3,658) \div 2} = 11.1 \text{ times}$$

[a]Assuming that all of H&M's purchases are credit purchases (i.e., made on account). For any large company, this is certainly a reasonable assumption.

H&M's accounts payable turnover ratio indicates that its payables were paid off and replaced by new accounts payable 11.1 times during the year. To make this result easier for users to relate to, many analysts convert the accounts payable turnover rate to an **average payment period** or **days to pay ratio**. This is done by simply dividing the previous result into 365 days per year. Using H&M's data, this produces the following:

$$365 \text{ days} \div 11.1 = 32.9 \text{ days}$$

This indicates that, on average, H&M took 32.9 days to pay its accounts payable in 2009. To assess whether this is a good or bad result, we should compare this to the payment period allowed by the company's creditors, to the results from previous years, and/or to the results for other companies in the same industry.

CONTINGENCIES

The term **contingent liability** (also sometimes referred to as **contingent loss**) refers to a situation in which a liability is conditional; that is, whether there will be a liability depends on some future event. Under IFRS, contingent liabilities are not recorded in the accounts, but they must be disclosed in the notes to the financial statements if they could have a material impact on the company's financial position.

For example, a contingent liability exists when a company has guaranteed another company's debt.[3] This often happens when a subsidiary company takes out a loan and the parent company (the company that owns all or most of the subsidiary's shares) guarantees repayment of the loan. For the parent company, the obligation to repay the loan is a

LEARNING OBJECTIVE 12

Explain contingencies and how they are accounted for.

---

3. Technically, under IFRS such guarantees are governed by a separate set of requirements established for *financial guarantees*. However, at the introductory level the authors do not consider this distinction to be significant.

contingent liability because it will only arise if the subsidiary company defaults on the loan; if the subsidiary repays the loan according to its terms, the parent will have no liability. Another kind of contingent liability exists when a company is the defendant in a lawsuit; it may or may not incur a liability, depending on the outcome of the case.

Because of the uncertainty in such situations, guidelines have been developed to distinguish contingent liabilities (which are disclosed in the notes but not recorded in the accounts) from estimated liabilities or provisions (which *are* recorded in the accounts).

Under IFRS, when there is a contingency a liability should be recorded and reported on the statement of financial position (and a loss recognized and reported on the statement of earnings) if the following criteria are met:

1. *It is probable that some future event will result in the company incurring an obligation* that will require the use of assets or the performance of a service.

2. *The amount of the resulting liability (and loss) can be reasonably estimated.*

HELPFUL HINT

If a possible loss/liability is considered probable and can be reasonably estimated, it should be reported as a loss on the statement of earnings and a liability on the statement of financial position. If the contingency does not satisfy these two criteria but could have a material impact on the financial statements, it should be disclosed in a note.

With respect to point 1, notice that the recognition criterion for assessing the uncertainty of a confirming future event is whether the event's occurrence is considered "probable." This is generally interpreted to mean simply "more likely than not." Clearly, this will often be a very subjective assessment and considerable judgement will have to be exercised.

With respect to point 2, notice that if the amount cannot be measured reliably, no liability is recognized. In the past, companies often avoided having to record probable future liabilities on the basis that they could not be reliably estimated. For example, they sometimes argued that the amount of the liability could range anywhere from a few thousand dollars to hundreds of millions of dollars, and that such a wide range of possible outcomes meant that the amount could not be reasonably estimated. However, under IFRS this should be the case only in very rare circumstances, because, when necessary, an "expected value" method is to be used to measure the liability. If a range of possible outcomes is available, this approach assigns weights to each of the possible outcomes according to their associated probabilities.

To illustrate the calculation of the probability-weighted expected value of a liability, consider the following set of estimated possible outcomes and estimated probabilities:

Possible Amount of Loss and Liability	Estimated Probability of Occurrence	Weighted Value (Amount × Probability)
$50,000	5%	$2,500
$250,000	20%	$50,000
$500,000	30%	$150,000
$750,000	30%	$225,000
$1,000,000	15%	$150,000
	100%	
Probability-weighted expected value		$577,500

Therefore, in this example, if it is considered probable (more likely than not) that there will be a liability, it would be recorded at its expected value of $577,500.

If either of the two criteria is not met (i.e., if the future event that would confirm the obligation is not considered probable, or if it is not possible to estimate the amount reliably), then the liability is not recorded in the accounts. Rather, it is classified as a contingent liability, which means that the company should provide users with information about it in a note disclosure (unless the potential loss is not significant).

IFRS VERSUS ASPE

Under Canada's accounting standards for private enterprises (ASPE), the term *contingent liabilities* is used for the entire spectrum of possible obligations that depend on the occurrence of future events to confirm their existence and/or amount. Some of these are recorded in the accounts, others are only disclosed in the notes, and some are not referred to in the financial statements at all. Under IFRS, the term *contingent liabilities* is only used for those that are not recorded in the accounts.

In addition to this difference in terminology, there are some differences in the criteria for recognizing and measuring these liabilities under Canadian accounting standards for private enterprises, in comparison to IFRS.

With its headquarters in Montreal and operations in eight Canadian provinces and 16 American states, **Canadian National Railway Company** has the largest rail network in Canada and the only transcontinental network in North America. The excerpts from Note 17 to CN's 2009 financial statements presented in Exhibit 9-3 provide details of the company's contingencies related to environmental matters, in part D, and guarantees and indemnifications, in part E. Although the exhibit is a long one, it includes a discussion of some of the difficulties associated with determining the existence and amount of potential obligations, and provides a good example of how contingent liabilities can be disclosed.

EXHIBIT 9-3

annual report

CANADIAN NATIONAL RAILWAY COMPANY 2009 ANNUAL REPORT
Excerpts from Note 17 to Consolidated Financial Statements

D. Environmental matters

The Company's operations are subject to numerous federal, provincial, state, municipal and local environmental laws and regulations in Canada and the United States concerning, among other things, emissions into the air; discharges into waters; the generation, handling, storage, transportation, treatment and disposal of waste, hazardous substances, and other materials; decommissioning of underground and aboveground storage tanks; and soil and groundwater contamination. A risk of environmental liability is inherent in railroad and related transportation operations; real estate ownership, operation or control; and other commercial activities of the Company with respect to both current and past operations.

Known existing environmental concerns
The Company has identified approximately 310 sites at which it is or may be liable for remediation costs, in some cases along with other potentially responsible parties, associated with alleged contamination and is subject to environmental clean-up and enforcement actions... Canadian and U.S. laws generally impose joint and several liability for clean-up and enforcement costs on current and former owners and operators of a site, as well as those whose waste is disposed of at the site, without regard to fault or the legality of the original conduct. The Company has been notified that it is a potentially responsible party for study and clean-up costs at approximately 10 sites ... for which investigation and remediation payments are or will be made or are yet to be determined and, in many instances, is one of several potentially responsible parties.

EXHIBIT 9-3

CANADIAN NATIONAL RAILWAY COMPANY 2009 ANNUAL REPORT (cont'd)
Excerpts from Note 17 to Consolidated Financial Statements

The ultimate cost of addressing these known contaminated sites cannot be definitely established given that the estimated environmental liability for any given site may vary depending on the nature and extent of the contamination, the available cleanup techniques, the Company's share of the costs and evolving regulatory standards governing environmental liability. As a result, a liability is initially recorded when environmental assessments occur and/or remedial efforts are probable, and when the costs, based on a specific plan of action in terms of the technology to be used and the extent of the corrective action required, can be reasonably estimated. Adjustments to initial estimates are recorded as additional information becomes available...

As at December 31, 2009, 2008 and 2007, the Company's provision for specific environmental sites was as follows:

In millions	2009	2008	2007
Balance January 1	$125	$111	$131
Accruals and other	(7)	29	(1)
Payments	(15)	(15)	(19)
Balance December 31	$103	$125	$111

The Company anticipates that the majority of the liability at December 31, 2009 will be paid out over the next five years. However, some costs may be paid out over a longer period. No individual site is considered to be material. Based on the information currently available, the Company considers its provisions to be adequate.

Unknown existing environmental concerns
While the Company believes that it has identified the costs likely to be incurred for environmental matters in the next several years, based on known information, newly discovered facts, changes in laws, the possibility of spills and releases of hazardous materials into the environment and the Company's ongoing efforts to identify potential environmental liabilities that may be associated with its properties may result in the identification of additional environmental liabilities and related costs. The magnitude of such additional liabilities and the costs of complying with future environmental laws and containing or remediating contamination cannot be reasonably estimated due to many factors, including:

(i) the lack of specific technical information available with respect to many sites;

(ii) the absence of any government authority, third-party orders, or claims with respect to particular sites;

(iii) the potential for new or changed laws and regulations and for development of new remediation technologies and uncertainty regarding the timing of the work with respect to particular sites;

(iv) the ability to recover costs from any third parties with respect to particular sites; and

therefore, the likelihood of any such costs being incurred or whether such costs would be material to the Company cannot be determined at this time. There can thus be no assurance that liabilities or costs related to environmental matters will not be incurred in the future, or will not have a material adverse effect on the

CANADIAN NATIONAL RAILWAY COMPANY 2009 ANNUAL REPORT (cont'd)
Excerpts from Note 17 to Consolidated Financial Statements

EXHIBIT 9-3

annual report

Company's financial position or results of operations in a particular quarter or fiscal year, or that the Company's liquidity will not be adversely impacted by such liabilities or costs, although management believes, based on current information, that the costs to address environmental matters will not have a material adverse effect on the Company's financial position or liquidity. Costs related to any unknown existing or future contamination will be accrued in the period in which they become probable and reasonably estimable.

E. Guarantees and indemnifications
... The Company, including certain of its subsidiaries, has granted irrevocable standby letters of credit and surety and other bonds, issued by highly rated financial institutions, to third parties to indemnify them in the event the Company does not perform its contractual obligations. As at December 31, 2009, the maximum potential liability under these guarantees was $463 million, of which $404 million was for workers' compensation and other employee benefits... Of the $463 million of letters of credit and surety and other bonds, $421 million have been drawn on the Company's US$1 billion revolving credit facility.

During 2009, the Company granted guarantees for which no liability has been recorded, as they relate to the Company's future performance. As at December 31, 2009, the Company had not recorded any additional liability with respect to these guarantees, as the Company does not expect to make any additional payments associated with these guarantees...

As another example of a contingency, the selling of accounts receivable with recourse creates a contingent liability for the selling company[4] because it may be required to buy back the receivables under the recourse provision if the customers default on their payments. (Refer to Chapter 6 for further discussion of the sale of accounts receivable.) Exhibit 9-4 illustrates how a company disclosed that it had sold accounts receivable to financial institutions and, as a result, had contingent liabilities in the form of limited recourse obligations for delinquent receivables.

CANADA BREAD COMPANY, LIMITED 2009 ANNUAL REPORT
Note 3 to the Consolidated Financial Statements

EXHIBIT 9-4

annual report

Under a revolving securitization program, the Company has sold certain of its trade accounts receivable to financial institutions. The Company retains servicing responsibilities and retains a limited recourse obligation for delinquent receivables. At December 31, 2009, trade accounts receivable being serviced under this program amounted to $70.0 million (2008: $70.0 million).

---

4. Technically, under IFRS such guarantees are governed by a separate set of requirements established for *financial guarantees*. However, at the introductory level the authors do not consider this distinction to be significant.

INTERNATIONAL PERSPECTIVES

Although, as discussed above, it is considered appropriate in certain circumstances to recognize contingent losses and related contingent liabilities, contingent gains and related contingent assets are not recognized under U.S. GAAP (nor under Canada's Accounting Standards for Private Enterprises). This reflects the principle of conservatism, which suggests that while it may be prudent to anticipate certain losses and liabilities before they are confirmed, gains and assets should not be recognized until they are confirmed. However, International Financial Reporting Standards allow some contingent gains and related contingent assets to be recognized, if it is considered probable that they will be realized.

COMMITMENTS

LEARNING OBJECTIVE 13

Explain what commitments are and how they are handled.

In the course of business, many companies sign agreements committing them to certain future transactions. These are generally described in the notes to the financial statements as **commitments**.

A common example in many types of businesses is **purchase commitments**, which are agreements to purchase items in the future for pre-arranged prices. Some purchase commitments are referred to as **take-or-pay contracts**, which means that the company must pay for a specified quantity at the specified price, whether it actually takes that much from the supplier or not.

As discussed earlier, a purchase commitment is an example of a mutually unexecuted contract and is therefore not recorded as a liability. The company would, however, discuss it in a note to the financial statements if it thought that the commitment could have a material effect on its future operations. Exhibit 9-5 shows an example of this type of disclosure.

EXHIBIT 9-5

annual report

BIG ROCK BREWERY INCOME TRUST 2009 ANNUAL REPORT
Excerpts from Note 13 to the Consolidated Financial Statements

> On June 19, 2009 the Trust entered into an agreement with ENMAX Energy Corporation to provide electricity for a period of three years ... ending July 31, 2012 at a fixed rate of $0.074 / kWh.
>
> In May, 2009 the Trust locked in the ... agreement with Direct Energy to provide natural gas at a fixed price of $6.45 per gigajoule for a period of two years, ending June 30, 2010.
>
> Big Rock has a contract with Rahr Malting Canada Ltd. to supply malt barley for the 2010 fiscal year, at a fixed price of $515 per metric tonne. The barley will be used in the brewery's normal course of business, and delivered, as needed over a reasonable period of time, in quantities to ensure production targets are met.

Disclosures regarding purchase commitments such as these are important because they let users know that the company is planning ahead and arranging future contracts at fixed prices for items that it is going to need in its operations. These types of contracts and commitments are often an important part of a company's **risk management** activities, through which it tries to control the probability and impact of negative events. If prices rise and/or supply shortages occur, the company will benefit from having entered into these commitments in advance. On the other hand, the prices of these items may fall in the marketplace, leaving the company committed to paying prices higher than what would have been paid if no contracts were in place. If this happens, the company will incur losses as a result of having made the purchase commitments. For this reason, any commitments that could have material effects on future operations must be disclosed in the notes to the financial statements.

Also, to enable the users of financial statements to assess risks and estimate future cash flows, companies must disclose any commitments that will require major cash outflows during the next five years. For example, if a company has a long-term loan and a lease contract that commit it to paying significant amounts during the next five years, it must provide schedules of the payments that will be required under these commitments.

Research in Motion, the Canadian company that manufactures the BlackBerry, has such commitments. Exhibit 9-6 presents Note 12 on commitments and contingencies from RIM's 2010 annual report. Notice that part (b) of this note discloses the amounts that the company is committed to pay in each of the next five years under its lease contracts, while part (c) deals with contingencies and describes how RIM handles the uncertainties surrounding intellectual property disputes and legal actions.

EARNINGS MANAGEMENT

Several of the issues discussed in this chapter—such as estimating the value of future warranty services and customer loyalty rewards, and deciding whether contingencies are probable and the related liabilities should be recorded—require management to make estimates and exercise judgement.

You should by now be realizing the extent to which many issues in accounting are quite subjective or involve "grey areas," rather than being totally objective or "black and white." Estimating future bad debts or the expected useful lives of capital assets, deciding whether the value of an asset has been impaired, estimating future costs that will be incurred or the value of future services that will be provided, and deciding whether contingent losses and liabilities are probable and can be reasonably estimated—these all rely on judgement. Management may tend to be biased in exercising such judgement, and the potential impact on the company's earnings and financial position may be significant. Therefore, one of the tasks of auditors is to review the estimates and decisions made by management, to satisfy themselves that the estimates and decisions are fair and reasonable, and that there is no evidence that the financial results are being manipulated.

EXHIBIT 9-6 **RESEARCH IN MOTION INC. 2010 ANNUAL REPORT**

annual report

Excerpt from Notes to the Consolidated Financial Statements

12. COMMITMENTS AND CONTINGENCIES

(a) Credit Facility

The Company has $150.0 million in unsecured demand credit facilities (the "Facilities") to support and secure operating and financing requirements. As at February 27, 2010, the Company has utilized $6.9 million of the Facilities for outstanding letters of credit, and $143.1 million of the Facilities are unused.

(b) Lease commitments

The Company is committed to future minimum annual lease payments under operating leases as follows:

	Real Estate		Equipment and other		Total
For the years ending					
2011	$	35,088	$	1,917	$	37,005
2012		30,611		1,202		31,813
2013		27,841		163		28,004
2014		26,178		—		26,178
2015		21,755		—		21,755
Thereafter		63,631		—		63,631
	$	205,104	$	3,282	$	208,386

For the year ended February 27, 2010, the Company incurred rental expense of $39.6 million (February 28, 2009 — $22.7 million; March 1, 2008 — $15.5 million).

(c) Litigation

On July 23, 2009, the Company settled the Visto Litigation. The key terms of the settlement involved the Company receiving a perpetual and fully-paid license on all Visto patents, a transfer of certain Visto intellectual property, a one-time payment by the Company of $267.5 million and the parties executing full and final releases in respect of the Visto Litigation. Of the total payment by the Company, $163.8 million was expensed as a litigation charge in the second quarter of fiscal 2010. The remainder of the payment was recorded as intangible assets.

The Company is involved in litigation in the normal course of its business, both as a defendant and as a plaintiff. The Company may be subject to claims (including claims related to patent infringement, purported class actions and derivative actions) either directly or through indemnities against these claims that it provides to certain of its partners. In particular, the industry in which the Company competes has many participants that own, or claim to own, intellectual property, including participants that have been issued patents and may have filed patent applications or may obtain additional patents and proprietary rights for technologies similar to those used by the Company in its products. The Company has received, and may receive in the future, assertions and claims from third parties that the Company's products infringe on their patents or other intellectual property rights. Litigation has been and will likely continue to be necessary to determine the scope, enforceability and validity of third-party proprietary rights or to establish the Company's proprietary rights. Regardless of whether claims that the Company is infringing patents or other intellectual property rights have any merit, those claims could be time-consuming to evaluate and defend, result in costly litigation,

EXHIBIT 9-6

annual report

RESEARCH IN MOTION INC. 2010 ANNUAL REPORT (cont'd)

Excerpt from Notes to the Consolidated Financial Statements

divert management's attention and resources, subject the Company to significant liabilities and could have other effects. Additional lawsuits and claims, including purported class actions and derivative actions, may also be filed or made based upon the Company's historical stock option granting practices.

Management reviews all of the relevant facts for each claim and applies judgment in evaluating the likelihood and, if applicable, the amount of any potential loss. Where it is considered likely for a material exposure to result and where the amount of the claim is quantifiable, provisions for loss are made based on management's assessment of the likely outcome. The Company does not provide for claims that are considered unlikely to result in a significant loss, claims for which the outcome is not determinable or claims where the amount of loss cannot be reasonably estimated. Any settlements or awards under such claims are provided for when reasonably determinable.

SUMMARY

This chapter opened with a description of commonly reported current liabilities. It traced the financial statement impact of accounts payable, wages and related payroll liabilities, income taxes, warranty obligations, unearned revenues (including gift certificates and prepaid cards, customer rewards or loyalty programs, and warranty sales), lines of credit, short-term notes, and the current portions of long-term debts. Items significantly affected by *International Financial Reporting Standards* were highlighted, including the concept of constructive obligations. It also described some items that can affect the decisions made by users, but that may or may not be reflected on the financial statements, such as loss contingencies and commitments.

In Chapter 10, our attention turns to non-current liabilities, particularly long-term notes and bonds payable, mortgages, pension obligations, lease liabilities, and deferred income taxes.

PRACTICE PROBLEM

Answer each of the following questions related to various short-term liabilities.

a. Valdez Company borrows $25,000 on September 1, 2011, on a nine-month, 6% note. The interest and principal are due at maturity. The company's fiscal year end is December 31. Give the journal entries to record the transaction on September 1, 2011, the adjustment on December 31, 2011, and the payment on June 1, 2012.

b. Lilly Limited borrows $5,200 on July 1, 2011, and signs a one-year note payable. No interest was specified, but the note requires that Lilly repay $6,000 on June 30, 2012. What amount should Lilly report as interest expense for the year ended December 31, 2011?

c. A clothing store sells $5,000 worth of gift cards in December. In January, cards worth $4,000 are redeemed for merchandise that was purchased by the store in November and carried in its inventory at a cost of $2,500. Make summary journal entries for December and January.

d. Minor Manufacturing has a payroll of $7,200 for its employees. Income tax of $1,080 is deducted from the employees, as well as 5% for CPP and 2% for EI. The company's contributions for CPP and EI total $562. Calculate the total payroll expense for the company, the net amount that is payable to the employees, and the total amount that is payable to the government for this payroll.

e. Welchor Inc. offers a two-year warranty against failure of its products. The estimated cost of repairs and replacements under the warranty (as a percentage of the initial sales revenue) is 2% in the year of the sale and 4% in the following year. Sales and actual warranty costs for 2010 and 2011 (its first two years of operation) were:

	Sales	Actual Warranty Costs Incurred during Year
2010	$2,300,000	$ 45,000
2011	$2,500,000	$140,000

i. What amount of warranty expense should be reported on the statement of earnings for the year ended December 31, 2010?

ii. What amount of warranty obligation should be reported on the December 31, 2010, statement of financial position?

iii. What amount of warranty obligation should be reported on the December 31, 2011, statement of financial position?

f. For each of the following five situations involving a contingency, indicate whether

i. the company should recognize it in the accounts, and hence report it as a loss on the statement of earnings and a liability on the statement of financial position;

ii. the company should not recognize it in the accounts, but should disclose it in a note to the financial statements; or

iii. the company does not need to do anything with respect to this item at this time:

1. The contingency is considered probable; it can be reasonably estimated; it involves a significant amount.

2. The contingency is considered probable; it cannot be reasonably estimated; it involves a significant amount.

3. The contingency is not considered probable; it can be reasonably estimated; it involves a significant amount.

4. The contingency is not considered probable; it can be reasonably estimated; it does not involve a significant amount.

5. The contingency is not considered probable; it cannot be reasonably estimated; it does not involve a significant amount.

STRATEGIES FOR SUCCESS:

▶ If you need guidance with parts "a" or "b," refer to the examples in the section titled "Short-Term Notes and Interest Payable" (pages 596–599).

▶ In part "c," remember that sales revenue is not recorded when gift cards are sold. The amount received for the gift cards is treated as unearned revenue until they are redeemed for merchandise; that is when the real sale occurs.

▶ If you need help with part "d," refer to the examples in the section titled "Wages and Other Payroll Liabilities" (pages 586–587).

▶ In part "e," you may find that using T accounts is helpful for answering parts "ii" and "iii".

▶ If you need guidance with part "f," refer to the criteria in the section titled "Contingencies" (page 602).

SUGGESTED SOLUTION TO PRACTICE PROBLEM

a. September 1, 2011

Cash	25,000	
Note payable		25,000

December 31, 2011

Interest expense ($25,000 × 0.06 × 4/12[a])	500	
Interest payable		500

June 1, 2012

Note payable	25,000	
Interest payable	500	
Interest expense ($25,000 × 0.06 × 5/12[a])	625	
Cash		26,125

[a]Even though this is a nine-month note, the interest is expressed as an annual rate. Therefore, the time factor has to be expressed as a fraction of the year.

b. The difference between the amount that was received ($5,200) and the amount that is to be repaid ($6,000) represents interest of $800. This covers a one-year period, and half of this occurs during the year ended December 31, 2011. Therefore, half of this amount, $400, should be reported as interest expense in 2011.

practice problems

c. December

Cash	5,000	
Unearned gift card revenue		5,000

January

Unearned gift card revenue	4,000	
Sales		4,000
Cost of goods sold	2,500	
Inventory		2,500

d. • The total payroll expense for the company is the gross payroll plus the company's contributions for CPP and EI: $7,200 + $562 = $7,762.

   • The employees' net pay is the gross payroll less the payroll deductions withheld from the employees: $7,200 − $1,080 − (0.05 × $7,200) − (0.02 × $7,200) = $7,200 − $1,080 − $360 − $144 = $5,616.

   • The total amount to be remitted to the government is the sum of the amounts withheld from the employees and the company's contributions: $1,080 + $360 + $144 + $562 = $2,146.

e. i. The expense that should be recognized in 2010 is calculated as follows: (0.02 + 0.04) × $2,300,000 = $138,000. Note that, in accordance with the matching principle, the total expected warranty cost (6% of the sales revenue) should be reported as an expense in the year of the sale.

   ii. The liability that should be reported at the end of 2010 is calculated as follows: $0 beginning balance + $138,000 accrued − $45,000 paid = $93,000 ending balance.

   iii. The liability that should be reported at the end of 2011 is calculated as follows: $93,000 beginning balance + [(0.02 + 0.04) × $2,500,000] accrued − $140,000 paid = $103,000 ending balance.

f. Applying the criteria for contingencies that are discussed on page 602 should lead you to the following conclusions:

   1. The appropriate treatment in these circumstances is alternative (i). Because it satisfies all the criteria, the company should recognize this in the accounts, and report it as a loss on the statement of earnings and a liability on the statement of financial position.

   2. The company should do everything it reasonably can to estimate the amount (including using the probability-weighted expected value method), so that this can be recognized in the accounts. However, if the amount cannot be reasonably estimated the appropriate treatment is alternative (ii). The company should not recognize it in the accounts, but should disclose it in a note to the financial statements.

   3. The appropriate treatment in these circumstances is alternative (ii). Because the event is not considered probable, the company should not recognize it in the accounts, but should disclose it in a note to the financial statements.

   4. The appropriate treatment in these circumstances is alternative (iii). Because the event does not involve a significant amount, the company does not need to do anything at this time.

   5. The appropriate treatment in these circumstances is alternative (iii). Because the event does not involve a significant amount, the company does not need to do anything at this time.

ABBREVIATIONS USED

CPP   Canada Pension Plan   QPP   Quebec Pension Plan
EI   Employment Insurance

SYNONYMS

Average payment period **❙** Days to pay ratio
Contingent liability **❙** Contingent loss
Current portion of long-term debt **❙** Long-term debt due within one year
Deferred revenue **❙** Unearned revenue

GLOSSARY

Accounts payable turnover A ratio that measures how many times per period a company's accounts payable are paid off and replaced by new accounts payable.

Average payment period The average number of days that a company takes to pay for its credit purchases. Synonym for the *days to pay* ratio.

Blended payments Loan payments that consist of both interest and principal, with the total amount remaining constant but the portion for interest becoming smaller as each payment is made.

Collateral An asset that has been pledged as security for a debt. If the borrower defaults on the debt, the lender can have the collateral seized and sold, with the proceeds used to repay the debt.

Commitments Obligations that a company has undertaken which do not yet meet the recognition criteria for liabilities. Significant commitments are disclosed in the notes to the financial statements.

Constructive obligations Liabilities that do not arise from legal or contractual obligations but from a company's past or present practices, which have indicated to other parties that it will accept specific responsibilities and the other parties reasonably expect it to do so.

Contingencies Events or transactions whose effects on the financial statements are conditional on future events.

Contingent liability A liability that is not recorded in the accounts, because it depends on a future event that is not considered probable and/or it cannot be estimated reliably. Significant contingent liabilities are disclosed in the notes.

Contingent loss Synonym for contingent liability.

Current portion of long-term debt The portion of long-term debt that is due within one year (or one operating cycle).

Days to pay ratio The average number of days that a company takes to pay its accounts payable. Synonym for the *average payment period* ratio.

Deferred revenues Cash receipts, from customers, that have not yet met the criteria for revenue recognition. Synonym for *unearned revenues.*

Instalment loan A type of loan in which payments (including both interest and a portion of the principal) are made periodically, rather than only at the end of the loan.

Liability A duty, responsibility, or obligation that imposes an enforceable economic burden on an entity.

Line of credit A borrowing arrangement with a bank, based on a pre-authorized credit limit that allows a company to write cheques for amounts that exceed the balance of cash in its bank account.

Loan amortization table A table that shows how the original amount of a loan is reduced over time, as a result of interest being added and payments being deducted.

Mutually unexecuted contract A contract between two entities in which neither entity has performed its part of the agreement.

Non-financial liabilities Liabilities that are expected to be settled through the delivery of goods or the performance of services, rather than the payment of cash.

Partially executed contract A contract between two entities in which one or both of the parties has performed a portion of its part of the agreement.

Present value The value today of an amount or series of amounts to be received or paid in the future. See also *time value of money*.

Prime rate The interest rate that banks charge their best customers.

Provisions A term used in IFRS to refer to liabilities where there is uncertainty about the timing or the amount of the future expenditures.

Purchase commitment A contract between two entities in which one entity agrees to buy goods or services from another entity, usually at predetermined prices.

Risk management The processes through which organizations identify, assess, and prioritize risks and coordinate the application of resources to monitor and control the probability and impact of negative events.

Secured Loans or other debts are said to be secured when specific assets have been pledged to guarantee repayment of the debt.

Take-or-pay contract A contract in which the buyer must pay for a minimum quantity, whether delivery of the goods is taken or not.

Time value of money The concept that a specified sum of money is worth more if it is paid or received now rather that later (because money received now can be invested to grow to a larger amount later). More generally stated, the value of a specified amount of money decreases as the time until it is paid or received increases.

Unearned revenues Cash receipts from customers that have been received in advance and not yet met the criteria for revenue recognition. Synonym for deferred revenues.

Unsecured Loans or other debts are said to be unsecured when no specific assets have been pledged to guarantee repayment of the debt.

Working capital loan A short-term loan, often on a demand basis, that is arranged with a bank to cover a company's short-term cash shortages.

ASSIGNMENT MATERIAL

Assessing Your Recall

9-1   List three essential characteristics of a liability.

9-2   Explain what a mutually unexecuted contract is and how it is accounted for.

9-3   Describe, in general terms, the appropriate valuation methods for current and non-current liabilities.

9-4   Explain the meaning of the terms "gross pay" and "net pay" in regard to employees' earnings.

9-5   Why do employers often object when the government changes the rates for CPP, QPP, or EI?

9-6   Explain the meaning of the term "payroll taxes."

9-7   Explain why warranty expenses and the actual costs incurred with respect to warranties often do not occur in the same period.

9-8   If a product is sold at the beginning of year 1 with a three-year warranty, should the expected cost of honouring the warranty be spread over years 1, 2, and 3, or recognized entirely in year 1? Explain, with reference to the accounting principle(s) involved.

9-9   Describe the nature of unearned revenues and provide an example.

9-10   Explain why companies record a liability when they sell gift cards.

9-11   Explain the meaning of the term "non-financial liabilities" as it is used in IFRS.

9-12   Explain what a constructive liability is and how it differs from other liabilities.

9-13   Outline what a line of credit is and how it operates.

9-14   Explain what an instalment loan is and how interest expense is calculated for such a loan.

9-15   If a company borrowed $10,000 on September 1 of the current year and signed a note promising to repay $10,600 on August 31 of next year, explain how the interest expense would be determined for this year and next year.

9-16   What is meant by the "current portion of long-term debt"? Why is it recorded with the current liabilities?

9-17   Outline the conditions under which loss/liability contingencies would be recorded in the accounts or disclosed in the notes to the financial statements.

9-18   Explain the meaning of the term "provisions" as it is used in IFRS.

9-19   Describe the circumstances that would require commitments to be recognized in the financial statements.

Applying Your Knowledge

9-20   (Various current liabilities)

Joan's Golf Shop had the following transactions involving current liabilities in its first year of operations:

1. The company ordered golf equipment from suppliers for $546,000, on credit. It paid $505,000 to suppliers during the year.

2. The shop has seven employees, who earned gross wages of $230,000 for the year. From this amount, Joan deducted 22% for income taxes, 5% for Canada Pension Plan deductions, and 2% for Employment Insurance contributions before giving the cheques to her staff. As an employer, she was also required to make additional contributions of 5% for Canada Pension Plan and 2.8% for Employment Insurance. Eleven-twelfths of the amounts due to the government (i.e., all except for the last month) were paid before the end of the year.

3. Joan gives her customers a one-year warranty on golf clubs. She estimated that warranty costs would total 2% of sales. Sales of golf clubs for the year were $1,100,000. During the year, she spent $13,000 to replace faulty golf clubs under the warranty.

4. Some customers order very expensive, custom-made golf clubs. In these cases, Joan requires them to pay a deposit of 50% of the selling price when the order is placed. During the year, deposits totalling $20,000 were received for custom orders. None of these orders have been delivered yet.

   Required:
   a. Prepare journal entries to record the transactions.
   b. Prepare the current liabilities section of the balance sheet as it would appear at the end of the year.

9-21   (Various current liabilities)

Shamsud Ltd. operates on a calendar-year basis. At the beginning of December 2011, the company had the following current liabilities on its books:

Accounts payable	$85,000
Rent payable	10,000
Obligations under warranties	12,000
Unearned revenue	14,000

In December, the following events occurred:

1. Shamsud purchased a new computer system on account at a cost of $28,000, payable on January 15, 2012. In addition to this, $4,000 was paid in cash to have the new system installed and customized to the company's requirements.

2. The company purchased inventory for $93,000 on account and made payments of $86,000 to its suppliers.

3. The rent that was payable at the beginning of December represented the payment that should have been made in November. In December, Shamsud paid the past rent owed, as well as the rent for December and January.

4. By December 31, the company had earned $5,000 of the revenue that was received in advance from customers.

5. Shamsud's employees are paid a total of $2,000 per day. Three work days elapsed between the last payday and the end of the fiscal year. (Ignore deductions for income tax, CPP, and EI.)

6. The company's products are sold with a two-year warranty. Shamsud estimates its warranty expense for the year (not previously recorded) as $16,000. During December, it paid $1,200 in warranty claims.

7. The company borrowed $60,000 from the bank on December 15 at an interest rate of 8%. The principal and interest are due six months from the date of the loan.

8. Since the beginning of 2011, Shamsud has had a five-year note payable of $125,000 outstanding. The note requires that annual interest payments at 7% be made, and that $25,000 of the principal be repaid each January 1.

> **Required:**
> a. Prepare the journal entries to record the December transactions and adjustments. (Ignore the amounts that the company pays for its share of CPP and EI.)
> b. Prepare the current liability section of Shamsud's balance sheet on December 31, 2011.
> c. Explain your treatment of the five-year note payable.

9-22 (Various current liabilities)

Answer each of the following questions related to various short-term liabilities:

a. On September 1, 2011, a company borrowed $100,000 from its bank and signed a nine-month note with 8% interest. The principal and interest on the loan are to be paid when the note matures. What is the total amount related to this loan that should be reported under current liabilities on the company's December 31, 2011, balance sheet?

b. The balance in a company's long-term mortgage payable account on December 31, 2011, is $150,000. This is to be repaid at the rate of $25,000 per year for the next six years. How should this liability be reported on the company's balance sheet on December 31, 2011?

c. During the spring and summer of 2011, the Prairie Predators hockey team sold 2,000 season tickets for the fall 2011–winter 2012 hockey season. Each of the season tickets was sold for $500 and covered 20 games, with 8 to be played in the fall and 12 in the winter. What is the effect on the team's financial statements when the season tickets are sold? What amount of liability (if any) related to the season tickets should be reported on the team's December 31, 2011, balance sheet?

d. Bathurst Beverages collects cash deposits on its returnable bottles and other containers. Past experience indicates that virtually all the bottles and containers will be returned and the deposits refunded. During the current year, the company received $150,000 in such deposits and it disbursed $140,000 for bottles and other containers that were returned. How would this information be reflected in the year-end balance sheet for Bathurst Beverages?

e. During the current year, a company sold 10,000 units of a product that was covered by a two-year warranty. Past experience indicates that approximately 3% of the units sold will require warranty repairs, at an average cost of $50 per unit. The actual costs incurred during the year for repairs under the warranty totalled $7,000. What amount of liability (if any) should be reported on the company's balance sheet at the end of the current year?

f. Shortly before its fiscal year end, a company lost a lawsuit and had damages of $200,000 awarded against it. However, it said that it will appeal the decision in the new year. Its lawyers are confident that the lower court's decision will be reversed. How should this situation be reported in the year-end financial statements? Explain your reasoning.

9-23 (Warranty obligations)

The Athletic Accountant Company produces exercise equipment designed for accountants. Its main product, the Pencil-Pusher Push-Up Platform, is sold with a three-year warranty against defects. The company expects that 1% of the units sold will prove to be defective in the first year after they are sold, 2% will prove to be defective in the second year, and 3% will prove to be defective in the third year. The average cost to repair or replace a defective unit under the warranty is expected to be $60.

The company's sales and warranty costs incurred in its first three years were as follows:

	Units Sold	Actual Costs of Repairs and Replacements under the Warranty Plan
2009	9,000	$ 5,000
2010	12,000	$16,000
2011	17,000	$37,000

Required:
a. Calculate the amount that should have appeared in the warranty obligation (liability) account at the end of 2009.
b. Calculate the amount of warranty expense that should have been recognized in 2010.
c. Considering the costs incurred to the end of 2011, do you think the company's estimates regarding the warranty costs were too high, too low, or just about right? Explain your reasoning.

9-24 (Two types of warranties)

Computers Galore Ltd. sells computers, computer accessories, and software. On its computer sales, the company provides a one-month warranty that is included in the cost of the computer. Claims under the warranties vary from replacing defective parts to providing customers with new computers if repairs cannot be made. During 2011, the estimated cost related to the one-month warranties was $40,000, of which $36,000 had been incurred before year end.

For an additional charge of $100, Computers Galore also offers extended warranty coverage for two years on its computers. This amount is expected to cover the costs associated with the extended warranties. During 2011, Computers Galore sold 800 two-year warranties. The costs incurred during the year for repairs and replacements under these warranties amounted to $31,000.

Required:
a. Prepare journal entries to record the warranty transactions for 2011.
b. Should Computers Galore classify its warranty obligations as current or non-current? Explain.
c. If the actual costs incurred by the company under the extended warranties are less than the amount charged for them, how should the company account for the difference?

9-25 (Revenues and current liabilities)

University Survival Magazine is a small company run by two enterprising university students. They publish an issue of the magazine once a month from September through April. The magazine reports on various university activities and provides information such as how to get the best concert tickets, where the best pizza is sold for the best price, where the good study spots are located, and how to get library personnel to help you with your research assignments.

The magazine is sold either on a prepaid subscription basis for $12.00 for all eight issues, or for $2.00 per issue. During September, 2,000 subscriptions were sold. Up to the end of December, a total of 12,000 single copies were sold.

The owners also pre-sell advertising space in the magazine to local businesses that focus on the student market. During July and August, they signed up several businesses and collected $20,000 in advertising revenues. The advertisements are to be included in all eight issues of the magazine.

The cost of printing and distributing the first four issues of the magazine was $57,000, of which $46,000 was paid by the end of December. Miscellaneous other expenses totalling $2,000 were incurred and paid in cash.

Required:

a. Journalize all the transactions to the end of December.
b. Prepare any necessary adjusting entries on December 31.
c. Prepare a simple statement of earnings for the magazine, for the period from July to December.
d. Calculate the balance in the magazine's cash account on December 31.
e. Write a brief memo to the owners that explains why their net earnings are less than the net cash generated by their operations.

9-26 (Gift card sales and redemptions)

During the month of December, Emile's Electronics sells $7,000 of gift cards. In January, $5,000 of these cards are redeemed for merchandise with a cost of $3,000. In February, a further $1,500 of these cards are redeemed for merchandise with a cost of $1,000. The company uses a perpetual inventory system.

Required:

a. Prepare journal entries to record the transactions for December, January, and February.
b. How much income (if any) was earned in each of these months?
c. What liability (if any) would appear on the company's statement of financial position at the end of each of these months?

9-27 (Short-term note with explicit interest added)

On April 30, 2011, a company borrows $50,000 from its bank and signs a promissory note to repay it in 18 months plus interest of 8% per year. Although no principal payments are to be made until the note matures in 18 months, the interest on the note is to be paid every 6 months. The company's fiscal year end is December 31.

Required:

a. Give the journal entries that would be made in 2011 to record the issuance of the note on April 30 and the first interest payment on October 31.
b. Would an adjusting entry be required on December 31, 2011, related to this note? If so, give the entry.
c. How much interest expense would be reported on the company's statement of earnings for the year ended December 31, 2011?
d. What liabilities related to this loan would be reported on the company's December 31, 2011, statement of financial position? Specify the accounts, amounts, and how they would be classified.

e. Give the journal entries that would be made in 2012 to record the second interest payment on April 30, and the third interest payment and repayment of the principal when the note matures on October 31.

f. How much interest expense would be reported on the company's statement of earnings for the year ended December 31, 2012?

9-28 (Short-term note with no explicit interest)

On August 31, 2011, a company borrows $50,000 from its bank and signs a note promising to repay $53,600 in one year. There is no mention of interest in the loan agreement. The company's fiscal year end is December 31.

Required:

a. Give the journal entry to record the issuance of the note on August 31, 2011.

b. Would an adjusting entry be required on December 31, 2011, related to this note? If so, give the entry.

c. How much interest expense (if any) would be reported on the company's statement of earnings for the year ended December 31, 2012?

d. Give the journal entries to record the repayment of the loan when the note matures on August 31, 2012.

9-29 (Short-term note with equal blended payments)

On October 31, 2011, a company borrows $50,000 from its bank for five months at an annual interest rate of 8%. The loan agreement specifies that it is to be repaid in five equal monthly instalments, and the bank calculates the required payments to be $10,200.89 per month. The company's fiscal year end is December 31.

Required:

a. Prepare an amortization table for this loan, similar to the one shown on page 597.

b. Give the journal entries that would be made in 2011 to record the issuance of the note on October 31 and the first two payments on November 30 and December 31.

c. What is the amount of the liability related to this loan that would be reported on the company's December 31, 2011, statement of financial position?

9-30 (Assessing a contingency)

On April 1, 2010, while shopping for new furniture for her home, a world-renowned pianist, Mia Thorne, tripped on an electrical cable on the showroom floor and broke her wrist. On June 10, 2010, Ms. Thorne sued the furniture store for $5 million. The case came to trial on September 13, 2010, and the court reached a decision on December 23, 2010, finding the store liable and awarding Ms. Thorne the sum of $1.5 million.

Dissatisfied with the first judgement, the furniture store appealed to a higher court on February 3, 2011. The appeal court heard the case beginning on July 18, 2011. On November 25, 2011, the store was again found liable. In this judgement, Ms. Thorne was awarded $2.5 million in damages; however, the furniture store was given three years to pay.

On January 15, 2012, the store negotiated a reduced amount with Ms. Thorne in return for immediate payment, and paid her $2 million in full settlement of the case.

Required:

Review the events in the case and identify the various dates on which a loss and a liability might be recognized. For each of these dates, refer to the criteria for contingent liability and full liability recognition and recommend whether disclosure through a note to the financial statements or a journal entry would be most appropriate, as well as the amount (if any) that should be reported. The company's year end is December 31.

User Perspective Problems

9-31 (Effects of changes in CPP and EI rates)

Suppose you are the general manager of a company with approximately 100 employees and the government has just announced its new rates for contributions to the Canada Pension Plan and Employment Insurance. With respect to employee contributions, assume that the CPP rate is increasing from 5% to 5.5% and the EI rate is increasing from 1.5% to 2%. Also assume that the company's required contribution for CPP is rising from being equal to the employees' contributions to being 1.1 times the employees' contributions, and the company's contribution for EI is increasing from being 1.4 times the employees' contributions to being 1.5 times the employees' contributions.

Required:

a. Assuming that gross wages amount to $6 million per year, calculate the financial impact that these changes will have on (1) the employees' net pay, and (2) the company's payroll costs.

b. Suggest some actions that the company could take to reduce the impact of these rate changes.

9-32 (Accounting for customer loyalty program)

Suppose that you are the manager of a chain of coffee shops and you are planning to launch a loyalty program that will give one free coffee to customers who buy 10 cups of coffee. Customers will be given an electronic "Coffee Club" card, which will be swiped each time they make a purchase. Your computer system will keep track of how many cups each customer has purchased and will automatically award them a free cup when they have purchased 10.

Discuss the income measurement and liability recognition issues that are presented by this type of customer loyalty program. Your answer should explain how and when the revenues associated with the free cups of coffee should be reported. It should also outline some of the issues that will make it difficult to estimate the amount of the liability for future free coffees arising from current sales.

9-33 (Contingencies and investment decisions)

Suppose that you have been asked by your employer to evaluate the potential purchase of another company. The company has been in the chemical business for more than 60 years and has production and distribution facilities in Alberta, Ontario, Texas, and Mexico. Because of the nature of the chemical industry, the company must recognize the possibility of environmental problems related to the manufacture and transportation of its products.

Required:

a. Explain how this issue might affect your evaluation of the potential purchase.

b. Describe the disclosures that you might find in the company's financial statements related to environmental liabilities, and what additional information you would like to have in assessing its liabilities.

9-34 (Commitments and disclosure issues)

Suppose that you are the sales manager for a construction company and you are responsible for securing contracts. As part of the negotiations to construct a new production facility for a customer, you attached a "sweetener" to the contract in the form of an agreement to supply raw materials to the customer at a fixed price over an extended period of time. The price specified in the agreement is the materials' fair market value at the time the construction contract was signed.

Required:

a. What does the accounting department need to know about the "sweetener" to appropriately account for this agreement?

b. Should the financial statements report this transaction? If so, how?

c. Under what circumstances might your answer to part "b" change?

d. What should be disclosed to the shareholders about this agreement?

Reading and Interpreting Published Financial Statements

9-35 (Presentation of liabilities for a financial services company)

Credit Union Central of British Columbia is the primary financial facility and trade association for the independent credit unions that serve the province. Comparative consolidated balance sheets from its 2009 annual report are presented in Exhibit 9-7.

Financial Analysis Assignments

> **Required:**
> a. Notice that Credit Union Central of British Columbia has an item called "loans" listed among its assets. Usually, accounts called "loans" are liabilities. Explain the nature of this item and why it is in the assets section of the balance sheet.
> b. Notice that there is an item called "deposits" listed among the liabilities. Explain how a liability arises related to deposits.
> c. Like many companies in the financial services industry, Credit Union Central of British Columbia does not distinguish between current and non-current liabilities on its balance sheets. Why do you think this is?

CREDIT UNION CENTRAL OF BRITISH COLUMBIA 2009 ANNUAL REPORT

EXHIBIT 9-7

annual report

CONSOLIDATED BALANCE SHEETS | December 31

(Thousands of dollars)	Note	2009	2008	2007
Assets				
Cash	(8)	$ 202,591	$ 228,378	$ 28,529
Securities	(9)	8,254,183	5,299,595	3,745,349
Amounts on deposit with regulated financial institutions	(10)	54,753	126,471	211,058
Loans	(11)	2,165,958	2,425,947	1,482,978
Capital assets	(12)	17,871	15,128	13,834
Other	(13)	360,320	462,265	180,434
		$ 11,055,676	$ 8,557,784	$ 5,662,182
Liabilities				
Notes	(15)	$ 465,289	$ 526,225	$ 968,774
Deposits	(16)	8,879,977	6,938,186	4,223,377
Obligations related to securities sold under repurchase agreements		748,654	193,333	-
Other	(17)	209,826	414,763	150,447
		10,303,746	8,072,507	5,342,598
Subordinated debt	(18)	200,577	50,678	49,671
Members' equity				
Share capital	(19)	162,580	162,580	113,354
Shares to be issued as result of merger	(2)	-	2	-
Contributed surplus	(2)	87,901	87,901	-
Retained earnings		262,056	188,060	167,148
Accumulated other comprehensive income	(20)	38,816	(3,944)	(10,589)
		551,353	434,599	269,913
		$ 11,055,676	$ 8,557,784	$ 5,662,182

9-36   (Interest rates and security)

As mentioned in this chapter, **Magnotta Winery Corporation** has an operating line of credit. Note 4 to the financial statements in Magnotta's 2010 annual report discusses the line of credit:

> **4. Bank Indebtedness:**
>
> Under its credit agreement, the Company has an operating line of credit of $11,500,000. The operating line of credit is due on demand, bears interest at bank prime plus 0.875% (2009 – 0.25%) and is secured by a general security agreement registered against all of the Company's assets. The Company is in compliance with all financial and operating covenants as at January 31, 2010.

Required:

a. What does it mean to have an operating line of credit of $11,500,000 available? What kind of institution is the line of credit likely with?

b. The information regarding the interest rate on Magnotta's line of credit refers to "bank prime." What does this term mean?

c. Magnotta's line of credit bears interest at bank prime plus 0.875% in 2010, compared to bank prime plus 0.250% in 2009. What can you infer from this about the lender's assessment of the company's creditworthiness in 2010 compared to 2009?

d. Is Magnotta's line of credit secured or unsecured? Explain what this means and why a company might prefer to have its debt secured.

9-37   (Line of credit and contingent liability)

As mentioned in the chapter, **Research in Motion Inc.** (RIM) is the Canadian company that developed the famous BlackBerry communications device. To answer the questions that follow, refer to Note 12 from RIM's 2010 financial statements, which appears in Exhibit 9-6 on pages 604–605.

Required:

a. Part (a) of the note describes a demand credit facility. What does RIM use the credit facility for? As at the end of its 2010 fiscal year, what portion of this line of credit had the company used?

b. The demand credit facility is described as unsecured. What does this mean? Would the company be able to get a lower interest rate if its line of credit was secured? Explain.

c. Part (c) of the note describes RIM's involvement in various legal events. For the settlement of the litigation with Vista, RIM expensed $163.8 million. Had this amount been accrued as a liability in the company's previous financial statements? Explain your answer.

d. As a result of the Vista settlement, what amount did RIM record as an intangible asset? Does it seem reasonable that RIM would record some of the costs of a patent lawsuit as an intangible asset? (If you need to review intangible assets, refer back to Chapter 8).

9-38   (Warranties)

As you are probably aware, **Research in Motion Inc.** (RIM) is the Canadian company that developed the BlackBerry communications device. Note 13 to RIM's 2010 financial statements, which appears in Exhibit 9-8, along with the revenue figures from the income statement:

RESEARCH IN MOTION INC. 2010 ANNUAL REPORT

EXHIBIT 9-8

annual report

Excerpt from the Notes to the Consolidated Financial Statements

In thousands of United States dollars

13. PRODUCT WARRANTY

The Company estimates its warranty costs at the time of revenue recognition based on historical warranty claims experience and records the expense in cost of sales. The warranty accrual balance is reviewed quarterly to establish that it materially reflects the remaining obligation based on the anticipated future expenditures over the balance of the obligation period. Adjustments are made when the actual warranty claim experience differs from estimates.

The change in the Company's warranty expense and actual warranty experience from March 3, 2007 to February 27, 2010 as well as the accrued warranty obligations as at February 27, 2010 are set forth in the following table:

Accrued warranty obligations as at March 3, 2007	$ 36,669
Actual warranty experience during fiscal 2008.	(68,166)
Fiscal 2008 warranty provision	116,045
Accrued warranty obligations as at March 1, 2008	84,548
Actual warranty experience during fiscal 2009.	(146,434)
Fiscal 2009 warranty provision	258,757
Adjustments for changes in estimate	(12,536)
Accrued warranty obligations as at February 28, 2009.	184,335
Actual warranty experience during fiscal 2010.	(416,393)
Fiscal 2010 warranty provision	462,834
Adjustments for changes in estimate	21,541
Accrued warranty obligations as at February 27, 2010.	$ 252,317

Excerpt from the Consolidated Statements of Operations

	For the Year Ended		
	February 27, 2010	February 28, 2009	March 1, 2008
Revenue			
Devices and other.	$ 12,535,998	$ 9,410,755	$ 4,914,366
Service and software.	2,417,226	1,654,431	1,095,029
	$ 14,953,224	$ 11,065,186	$ 6,009,395

Required:

a. Based on the note, how much was the warranty expense that was originally recorded in fiscal 2010? How much was the liability on the balance sheet at the end of the same fiscal year?

b. Warranty obligations are based on estimates, and when management revises the estimate they adjust the current year's expense. What was the effect on RIM's warranty expense and the warranty liability as a result of the changes in estimates made in fiscal 2010 and in 2009?

c. Calculate the ratio of the warranty expense to the revenue for each of the three years presented. Assume that the warranties are only related to revenues generated from devices and not from services provided, and ignore the change in estimates in determining the expense. Comment on your findings.

d. Explain how it would be possible for RIM's management to manage its earnings using warranty estimates.

9-39 (Contingent liabilities)

Rogers Communications Inc. provides cell phone and cable access to consumers, operates radio and television stations, publishes consumer magazines and professional publications, and owns the Toronto Blue Jays baseball club. Details of Rogers' contingent liabilities are shown in Exhibit 9-9, which presents two portions of Note 24 to its 2009 financial statements.

EXHIBIT 9-9

annual report

ROGERS COMMUNICATIONS INC. 2009 ANNUAL REPORT

Excerpt from Note 24 to the Consolidated Financial Statements

(A) The CRTC collects two different types of fees from broadcast licensees which are known as Part I and Part II fees. In 2003 and 2004, lawsuits were commenced in the Federal Court alleging that the Part II licence fees are taxes rather than fees and that the regulations authorizing them are unlawful. On December 14, 2006, the Federal Court ruled that the CRTC did not have the jurisdiction to charge Part II fees. On October 15, 2007, the CRTC sent a letter to all broadcast licensees stating that the CRTC would not collect Part II fees due in November 2007. As a result, in the third quarter of 2007, the Company reversed its accrual of $18 million related to Part II fees from September 1, 2006 to June 30, 2007. Both the Crown and the applicants appealed this case to the Federal Court of Appeal. On April 28, 2008, the Federal Court of Appeal overturned the Federal Court and ruled that Part II fees are valid regulatory charges. As a result, during the second quarter of 2008, Cable and Media recorded charges of approximately $30 million and $7 million, respectively, for CRTC Part II fees covering the period from September 1, 2006 to March 31, 2008. In addition to recording $5 million the $2 million in the second quarter of 2008 for Cable and Media, respectively, the Company continued to record these fees on a prospective basis in operating, general and administrative expenses. Leave to appeal the April 28, 2008 Federal Court of Appeal decision was granted by the Supreme Court on December 18, 2008. On October 7, 2009, the Government of Canada announced that a settlement had been reached between the Government of Canada and members of the broadcasting industry with respect to Part II fees. Under the terms of the settlement, the Government agreed to forgive the amounts otherwise owing to it up to August 31, 2009 and the fees going forward will be approximately one-third less than historical rates. As a result, during the fourth quarter of 2009, Cable and Media recorded recoveries in operating, general and administrative expenses of approximately $60 million and $19 million, respectively, for CRTC Part II fees covering periods from September 1, 2006 to August 31, 2009.

(E) In April 2004, a proceeding was brought against Fido and other Canadian wireless carriers claiming damages totalling $160 million, breach of contract, breach of confidence, breach of fiduciary duty and, as an alternative to the damages claims, an order for specific performance of a conditional agreement relating to the use of 38 MHz of MCS Spectrum. In May 2009, the Company settled this litigation for $4 million, which is included in operating, general and administrative expenses for the year ended December 31, 2009.

Required:

a. Summarize the series of events related to the Part II fees described in part (A) to the note. When were amounts expensed or recorded as liabilities, and when were amounts reversed? What caused Rogers to record the Part II fees as expenses in some periods and not record them in other periods? Was there good matching of the expenses with the revenues that gave rise to them throughout the period from 2003 to 2009? Explain.

b. For the lawsuit related to FIDO described in part (E), do you think Rogers accrued an estimated liability for the lawsuit between 2004 and 2009? Support your answer.

9-40 (Loss contingency and liability disclosures)

In May 2010, a powerful blowout and deadly explosion occurred on an oil platform in the Gulf of Mexico owned by **British Petroleum plc** (BP), resulting in a massive oil spill. With the likelihood that rich fishing grounds, hundreds of kilometres of shoreline, and vital wildlife breeding areas would be severely contaminated, the potential cost of the containment and cleanup work was enormous. In addition to the physical restoration costs, there was the possibility that the livelihoods of thousands of people—from shrimp-boat operators to beach-resort workers—would be disrupted for years to come. At the time of writing, lawsuits against BP totalling billions of dollars were being threatened.

Required:

Review BP's group/consolidated financial reports issued from June 30, 2010, onward and prepare a summary of the company's handling of the liability issues related to this incident. (Hint: Your review should include management's comments on these issues, as well as the financial statements and accompanying notes for the BP group.)

9-41 (Commitments)

Headquartered in Quebec, **RONA Inc.** operates approximately 700 stores of various sizes and formats across Canada and is the largest Canadian distributor and retailer of hardware, home renovation, and gardening products. Note 19 accompanying RONA's 2009 financial statements provides details of its major guarantees, commitments, and contingencies. Portions of the note are presented below (amounts in thousands of dollars).

> ### 19. Commitments
>
> In 2005, the Company entered into an eight-year partnership agreement for Olympic and Paralympic sponsorship valued at $60,000. Moreover, in 2006 the Company committed an additional amount of $7,000 to financial support programs for athletes. At December 27, 2009, the balance due on these agreements is $13,725, i.e. $9,925 in 2010, $1,900 in 2011 and $1,900 in 2012.

Required:

a. As at the date of the financial statements (December 31, 2009), did RONA have a liability related to its Olympic and Paralympic commitment? Explain why or why not.

b. Did the information provided in this note have to be disclosed to the readers of the financial statements? Explain your reasoning.

9-42 (Financial statement analysis)

Marks and Spencer is one of the United Kingdom's largest retailers, with over 600 stores in the U.K. and another 300 located internationally, selling clothing, home products, and food. The data in Exhibit 9-10 are excerpts from the 2009 consolidated income statement, balance sheet, and notes of Marks and Spencer Group plc.

EXHIBIT 9-10A   **MARKS AND SPENCER GROUP PLC 2009 ANNUAL REPORT**

annual report

EXCERPT FROM THE CONSOLIDATED INCOME STATEMENT

	Notes	52 weeks ended 28 March 2009 £m	52 weeks ended 29 March 2008 £m
Revenue	2, 3	**9,062.1**	9,022.0
Operating profit	2, 3	870.7	1,211.3
Finance income	6	50.0	64.4
Finance costs	6	(214.5)	(146.6)
Profit on ordinary activities before taxation	4	706.2	1,129.1

EXCERPT FROM THE NOTES TO THE FINANCIAL STATEMENTS

Expense analysis	2009 Total £m	2008 Total £m
Revenue	**9,062.1**	9,022.0
Cost of sales	(5,690.2)	(5,535.2)
Gross profit	3,371.9	3,486.8

EXCERPT FROM THE CONSOLIDATED BALANCE SHEET

	Notes	As at 28 March 2009 £m	As at 29 March 2008 £m
Current assets			
Inventories		536.0	488.9
Other financial assets	17	53.1	48.8
Trade and other receivables	18	285.2	307.6
Derivative financial instruments	22	92.6	18.4
Cash and cash equivalents	19	422.9	318.0
		1,389.8	1,181.7
Current Liabilities			
Trade and other payables	20	1,073.5	976.6
Borrowings and other financial liabilities	21	942.8	878.6
Partnership liability to the Marks & Spencer UK Pension Scheme	21	71.9	50.0
Derivative financial instruments	22	76.2	35.1
Provisions	23	63.6	11.1
Current tax liabilities		78.9	37.5
		2,306.9	1,988.9

MARKS AND SPENCER GROUP PLC 2009 ANNUAL REPORT

EXHIBIT 9-10B

annual report

EXCERPT FROM THE NOTES TO THE FINANCIAL STATEMENTS

Trade and other payables

	2009 £m	2009 £m
Trade payables	**357.0**	226.9
Other payables	**426.6**	425.5
Social security and other taxes	**40.4**	56.1
Accruals and deferred income	**249.5**	268.1
	1,073.5	976.6

Required:
a. Calculate the accounts payable turnover rate for Marks and Spencer for 2008 and 2009. Use the year-end trade payables in your calculations.
b. If you had only used the information available on the financial statements and not the information in the notes, how would your answer to the preceding part have differed?
c. Calculate the current ratio and quick ratio for Marks and Spencer for 2008 and 2009. (Refer to Chapter 6 if you need to review these ratios.)
d. Comment on Marks and Spencer's ability to meet its short-term obligations in 2008 and 2009.
e. Finance costs include interest expense on both current and long-term borrowings. What percentage of revenues did Marks and Spencer spend on finance costs in 2008 and 2009? Explain why you would, or would not, expect interest expense to be a relatively constant proportion of revenues.

Beyond the Book

9-43 (Examine financial statement disclosures)
Choose a company as directed by your instructor and do the following:

a. Prepare an analysis of the current liability accounts by listing the beginning and ending amounts in each of these accounts and calculating the net change, in both dollar and percentage terms, for the most recent year. If the company you have selected does not prepare a classified balance sheet, you will need to determine which liabilities are current.

b. If any account balance changed by more than 10 percent during the year, try to give an explanation for this change. (Hint: Check the notes accompanying the financial statements and the Management Discussion and Analysis section of the annual report.)

c. What percentage of the company's total assets was financed by current liabilities? Did this percentage change significantly during the year?

d. Does the company have any significant estimated liabilities, such as warranties? If so, read any notes discussing these items and summarize the nature of these liabilities.

e. Does the company have unearned revenues? If so, read any notes discussing them and explain the nature of these liabilities.

f. Does the company have any significant contingencies or commitments? Read any related notes and then write a short summary of each significant item. For the contingencies, are you aware of anything that has happened related to these contingencies since the financial statements were issued? If so, give a brief description.

9-44   (Determine current payroll taxes)

Check with employers, an accounting firm, or the Chamber of Commerce and determine the main components of payroll taxes for the province or territory where you are currently located. Also, check the Canada Revenue Agency website and find the current rates for the Canada/Quebec Pension Plan and Employment Insurance, for both deductions from employees and contributions from employers.

Cases

9-45   Greenway Medical Equipment Corporation

At a recent meeting of the board of directors of Greenway Medical Equipment Corporation, the company's chief financial officer, Robert Ables, presented a draft set of financial statements for the year. It is Greenway's corporate policy that the directors be given an opportunity to review the financial statements before they are finalized.

Following the meeting, Mr. Ables received a memo from Dr. Clarise Locklier that included questions about the draft financial statements. Dr. Locklier is a relatively new member of the board of directors and is not familiar with some of the accounting terms and concepts used in the statements. Before voting on approval of the financial statements at the next board meeting, she has several questions she would like to have answered.

MEMORANDUM

To: Robert Ables, CFO
From: Dr. Clarise Locklier, Director
Re: Draft financial statements

I have carefully reviewed the financial statements that you presented to the board last week. Being a physician, I do not have a lot of experience reading accounting information and I am confused about several items presented in the financial statements. I hope that you will clarify the following points for me.

1. I always thought that revenues are reported on the statement of earnings, so I was confused to see unearned revenues listed as a liability on the balance sheet. How can revenues be reported on the balance sheet? As well, if these revenues haven't been earned, shouldn't they be reported in a later period—when they have been earned—rather than in the current period?

2. In one of the notes to the financial statements, you state that the liability for warranty costs is based on an estimate, rather than on the actual warranty repair costs. If we know what our actual costs were for the year, why do we need to use an estimate?

3. I notice that in the current liabilities section of the balance sheet you have listed an item called "current portion of long-term debt." How can debt be current and long-term at the same time? Also, since the long-term debt is also included as a liability on the balance sheet, aren't we overstating our liabilities if we report the debt in this manner?

I would appreciate a response to these questions prior to our next board meeting, so that I can feel more comfortable approving the financial statements.

Thank you for your time in addressing these matters.

Required:
As Robert Ables, prepare a memo to Dr. Locklier addressing her concerns.

9-46 Hanson Consulting

Jenny Shea is renegotiating her contract with her employer, Hanson Consulting. Jenny knows it is important that she negotiate a good contract, because the amount of her raise will become a benchmark for the raises to be received by Hanson's 14 other consultants. Currently, Jenny and the other consultants are receiving payroll transfers into their personal bank accounts averaging $4,000 per month.

Under her existing contract, Jenny is allowed to review Hanson's annual financial statements. She is puzzled when she sees that Hanson is reporting over $900,000 in consulting salaries on its annual statement of earnings, because she knows that she and the other consultants are paid a total of $720,000 per year (i.e., 15 consultants × $4,000 per month × 12 months). Jenny approaches you, the company controller, to see why the consulting salaries on the statement of earnings are higher than the amounts paid to the employees. She suspects that the company may have posted other expenses to the consulting salaries account, in order to improve its bargaining position for the contract negotiations.

Required:
Explain to Jenny why the company's payroll costs are significantly higher than the net amounts being received by the employees.

9-47 Slip-n-Slide Water Park

It is July 31 and the Slip-n-Slide Water Park has just completed its first three months of operations. The company's owners, Kelly and Derek Neil, are very pleased with the results of operations and are trying to prepare the company's first set of financial statements. You have been controller for a local firm for several years and are good friends with Kelly and Derek, so the couple approaches you with some questions about how certain items should be recorded in their financial statements.

Kelly: To promote the park and encourage people to bring their kids to it, we gave away 1,000 coupons for free ice cream cones at our canteen, to be redeemed any time during the summer. We usually charge $1.50 for an ice cream, but the cost is only $0.50 per cone. Two hundred of these coupons have been redeemed already. What should we report about the coupons that have been redeemed, and do we need to report anything about the 800 coupons that haven't been used?

Derek: I can figure out how to record most revenues and expenses, but I don't know how to treat the revenues associated with the 300 season passes that we sold in May and June. They were sold for $60 each and are good for June, July, and August. Holders of season passes have unlimited access to the park for these three months.

Kelly: The other problem we have is that we just took out a $60,000 bank loan. The 10-year loan agreement requires us to repay $500 of the principal of the loan each month, plus interest at the rate of 8%. Since we'll be making payments on this loan in the next year, I think we should record the $60,000 as a current liability; but Derek thinks it should be recorded as a long-term liability, since it will be 10 years before it is fully repaid.

Required:

Provide the owners with advice on how each of these items should be recorded in the July 31 financial statements. Be sure to explain why they should report the items as you recommend.

9-48 Altabet Company

Altabet Company is completing its financial statements for the year ended April 30, 2011. Janet Kramer, Altabet's controller, is reviewing the company's legal correspondence and trying to decide which, if any, of the contingencies facing the company need to be accrued and reported in the financial statements. During her review, Ms. Kramer identified three contingencies:

1. In July 2009, Jeff Altabet, a son of the company's owner, needed to borrow $400,000. He negotiated with a bank for a five-year loan requiring monthly payments of principal and interest. Because he had just graduated and had no credit history, the company guaranteed the note, stating that if Jeff failed to make three consecutive payments Altabet would repay the loan in full. Jeff has invested the money in a business venture that is turning out to be very profitable. He has made every required payment on the note thus far, and expects to be able to repay the remaining balance of $200,000 within the next year. As at April 30, 2011, Ms. Kramer still considers the balance of the loan to be significant.

2. In October 2010, the company was sued for breach of contract concerning the sale of some equipment to a local manufacturer. The manufacturer claims that because Altabet did not deliver the equipment in the period specified by the contract, the manufacturer lost profits of $50,000. Correspondence with Altabet's lawyer indicates that there was no breach of contract, because the manufacturer was late in making the required advance payment and therefore Altabet was justified in delaying the delivery of the equipment. The lawyer feels that this is a nuisance suit and believes there is little possibility of the manufacturer being successful. Ms. Kramer does not consider the potential loss to be significant.

3. In January 2011, Terry Chambers fell on some ice in Altabet's parking lot. As a result of the fall, Ms. Chambers suffered a concussion and a broken arm that required a two-day hospital stay. She is suing Altabet for $600,000 to cover her medical bills, loss of income, and personal suffering. Altabet's lawyer feels that the company will probably lose the suit and has strongly advised it to settle out of court. On April 25, 2011, Altabet instructed its lawyer to offer Ms. Chambers a settlement of $300,000. Although she has not yet responded to the company's offer, the lawyer believes it is a reasonable offer and is hopeful that Ms. Chambers will accept it.

Required:

With reference to the criteria for reporting contingent liabilities, discuss the appropriate treatment for each of the above contingencies with respect to the April 30, 2011, financial statements of Altabet Company.

Critical Thinking Questions

9-49 (Revenue recognition/expense accrual and income measurement)

Software Solutions produces inventory-tracking and supply-chain management software that it sells to large commercial clients. Its main software packages sell for an average of $130,000 each and require the company to customize the programs to suit each buyer's organization and operations. There is no additional charge for this customization service, as it is included in the initial selling price.

The customization work is done by a special team of employees, usually takes several months to complete, and involves significant costs for Software Solutions, averaging $25,000 per sale. If the buyers had to pay for this customization work, the normal charge would average $40,000 per sale.

Aside from the customization work, the company's cost for each software package sold averages $50,000.

Required:
    a. Discuss appropriate accounting treatments for handling the income measurement issues that arise in this type of situation. Describe at least two alternative approaches that could be taken.
    b. Indicate what approach would be appropriate in each of the following situations:
        i. The company wants to treat the software customization unit as a "cost centre." In other words, the customization team is expected to control its costs, but not to generate a profit. (Hint: Under this approach, no revenues are attributed to the customization work.)
        ii. The company wants to treat the software customization unit as a "profit centre." In other words, the customization work is viewed as a profit-generating line of business, separate from the software sales unit. (Hint: Under this approach, a portion of the revenues are attributed to the customization work.)

9-50 (Recognition and disclosure of contingent liabilities)

One of the issues discussed in this chapter is the financial statement recognition and disclosure of contingent liabilities, such as the potential claims associated with litigation and environmental obligations. Loss and liability recognition is dependent on whether it is likely that an asset has been impaired or a liability has been incurred, and the degree to which the loss can be reasonably estimated. Evaluating whether these conditions exist is often a matter of judgement by management and auditors, perhaps more so than with any other issue of recognition or disclosure. Research has shown that reliance on judgement can lead to significant differences among companies, regarding whether and how contingencies are disclosed.

In today's environmentally conscious world, regulatory bodies are making more demands on resource companies to be environmentally responsible. For example, companies involved in mineral or petroleum exploration and development are often required to provide for the cleanup and restoration of resource sites. A review of the annual reports of resource companies reveals that some of these companies report liabilities on their balance sheets in anticipation of these future events, some of these companies disclose contingent liabilities in the notes to their financial statements, and some do or say nothing about these future costs.

Required:
In a brief essay, discuss the criteria that companies should use when deciding on the type of disclosure that is appropriate in accounting for future cleanup and restoration costs, and the practical difficulties they may encounter when they try to implement these criteria.

chapter 10

LONG-TERM DEBT AND OTHER NON-CURRENT LIABILITIES

LEARNING OBJECTIVES

After studying this chapter, you should be able to:

1. Calculate interest and record transactions related to long-term notes and mortgages.

2. Describe the basic characteristics of bonds.

3. Explain how bonds are issued and how the pricing of bonds is affected by market factors.

4. Calculate a bond's selling price and prepare journal entries to record the issuance and subsequent interest payments for bonds sold at par, below par, and above par.

5. Discuss the advantages and disadvantages of leasing.

6. Distinguish between operating leases and capital/finance leases, and prepare journal entries for a lessee under both types of leases.

7. Explain the distinguishing features of defined-contribution pension plans and defined-benefit pension plans.

8. Outline the accounting issues in the reporting of pension plan liabilities.

9. Describe other post-employment benefits and explain how they are treated in Canada.

10. Explain why deferred/future income taxes exist, and describe how they are reported.

11. Record deferred/future income taxes in simple situations.

12. Calculate the debt to total assets ratio and the times interest earned ratio, and comment on a company's financial health using the information from these ratios.

Canada Post Borrows for the Future

In early 2010, Canada Post Corporation announced plans to raise at least $1 billion in the Canadian capital markets, starting in late 2010 or early 2011. Although it has about $55 million in long-term debt, this would be the first time that the Crown corporation has taken on a significant long-term liability.

There are basically three forms of financing, explains Wayne Cheeseman, Canada Post's chief financial officer. "There's internally generated funds, the equity market, or the debt capital markets. Being a Crown corporation, the equity markets aren't open to us. We do generate funds internally, but they won't be sufficient when we look at our long-term plans. So we're looking to the debt capital markets and raising money there, obviously with a plan to pay that off over time."

Canada Post will likely issue the debt in several tranches of $500 million per tranche over five years, says Mr. Cheeseman. At the time of writing, the corporation was in the process of selecting its financial advisors. Details like the number of units, the unit price, and coupon rate would be determined later. "Right now, we're looking at when would be an optimum time for us to go to the markets," says Mr. Cheeseman.

The decision to raise money through debt followed Parliament's assent to a legal amendment that would increase Canada Post's borrowing limit from $300 million to $2.5 billion. "We do have to go back to the Department of Finance to get approval on the terms and conditions, but the legislative approval is in place," says Mr. Cheeseman.

The money raised will be used primarily for Canada Post's Postal Transformation Initiative currently underway. "The Postal Transformation Initiative involves redoing and upgrading our physical and technological platform," says Mr. Cheeseman. The corporation is working to

modernize its operations with several capital projects planned over several years, including new and renovated buildings and updated equipment and systems. The initiative includes building a new processing plant in Winnipeg; replacing part of its current fleet with fuel-efficient, low-emission vehicles; and implementing new sorting equipment in its plants. Once the initiative is completed, the company will have a much greater ability to track and trace parcels, and more accurate address management systems.

"We basically have two goals—to provide an acceptable level of service to all Canadians while remaining financially self-sufficient," says Mr. Cheeseman. These improvements are expected to save Canada Post approximately $250 million a year. "With the cost savings, we're going to take advantage of the coming attrition in the business. It won't be a situation where people lose their jobs. It's simply as they retire, we won't replace a number of people."

With these long-term plans, Canada Post hopes to remain viable and relevant in Canada's rapidly changing and technologically advancing society.

Businesses often use long-term debt or the issuance of new shares as a means of raising outside capital that they can then use to finance growth. By using the new cash to buy long-term assets or invest in other companies, they can improve or expand their existing operations or enter new markets. In the opening story, Canada Post decided to use long-term debt to acquire the funds it needs in order to buy capital assets that will improve its operating efficiency.[1] The story mentions that Canada Post is staggering the debt by issuing it in tranches. French for "slices," the term "tranches" refers to portions of the total amount. This allows the corporation to borrow the funds only as it needs them, thus minimizing its interest charges.

Long-term debt is usually preferable to short-term debt for financing the acquisition of long-term assets, because both the benefits from the expansion efforts and the payments on the debt will be spread over a long period of time. The cash generated from the growth can then be used to repay the debt.

As you will see later in this chapter, companies are usually able to borrow at an interest rate that is lower than the rate of return they will earn from the income-generating activities that the borrowed money will be used for. This phenomenon is called financial leverage, and can be used to increase the rate of return earned by the shareholders.

Sometimes new debt is simply used to pay off old debt, which is referred to as refinancing or rollover of debt. When short-term debt is repaid with the proceeds from long-term debt, a company is able to spread out its debt payments over a longer time period, which means that there is less pressure on short-term cash needs.

USER RELEVANCE

Users of financial statement information need to pay particular attention to the type and extent of debt in a company. All debt must be repaid at some time. In addition to the principal amount, there is usually a requirement to make periodic interest payments. In terms of a company's "cost of capital" (a topic that is studied in finance courses), issuing debt is cheaper than issuing shares. It also does not dilute the current shareholders' ownership interests, as would an issuance of more shares. However, a company cannot rely too extensively on debt for financing: debt involves risks, and stakeholders become concerned if the proportion of debt to equity financing gets too high. When the level of debt is high, lenders demand higher interest rates to compensate for the increased risks.

As a user of financial statements, you should find answers to the following questions when evaluating a company's debt:

- What are the maturity dates and interest rates on the debt? Knowing this will enable you to determine the amount and timing of the future cash flows that will be necessary to meet the debt obligations.

- Are there any special conditions attached to the debt? For example, is the company required to maintain a certain debt/equity ratio or level of retained earnings? Failure to meet debt conditions (called covenants) could make the debt become due immediately, which could have very serious consequences for the business.

1. As a Crown Corporation, Canada Post is owned by the federal government and does not have outside shareholders. It therefore does not have the option of raising equity capital by issuing shares.

- What is the proportion of debt to equity financing? The higher the amount of debt to equity, the greater the risk that the company may have difficulty meeting the debt requirements. Not only could a high proportion of debt to equity result in higher interest rates being charged to the company, it could also make lenders reluctant to extend further credit to the company, which may affect its future financial viability.

- Is the organization using leverage to the advantage of its shareholders? In other words, is it earning a rate of return on its investment that is higher than the cost of the debt? As a user, you will want to examine the company's financial statements to see if leverage is being used effectively.

In this chapter, we are going to illustrate some of the most common non-current liabilities, including long-term loans, bonds payable, lease liabilities, pension and other post-employment benefit liabilities, and deferred income taxes. The general nature of liabilities was discussed in Chapter 9, along with the recognition and valuation criteria for liabilities. You might want to refresh your memory before moving on.

LONG-TERM NOTES AND MORTGAGES

When a company chooses to use long-term debt financing, it can go to various sources to obtain the funds, including the commercial paper market. "Commercial paper" is a promissory note that is sold to another business. In effect, one company (the issuer of the note) borrows funds directly from another (the buyer of the note). However, the commercial paper market is generally used only by large companies that have high credit ratings. More commonly, companies borrow from commercial banks or other financial institutions, much as individuals borrow money to buy a new home or car. These borrowings are often listed on a company's financial statements as long-term notes payable, loans payable, or mortgages.

All types of long-term debt are usually accompanied by a formal agreement between the borrower and the lender that specifies the terms of the loan (such as the interest rate, payment dates, and duration of the loan). In addition, the loan agreement often specifies certain conditions that the borrower must meet during the loan period. These conditions or restrictions on the company are known as **covenants**. The covenants may limit the company's freedom to borrow additional amounts, to sell or acquire assets, or to pay dividends. The restrictions specified in the covenants are intended to protect the lender against the borrower defaulting on the loan.

The accounting for long-term notes payable is much the same as for short-term notes, which was discussed and illustrated in Chapter 9. Long-term borrowings almost always have explicit interest charges, and in most cases these are paid periodically during the life of the loan. However, even if the interest is not explicitly stated or is paid only at maturity, interest expense should be recognized over the life of the loan.

LEARNING OBJECTIVE 1

Calculate interest and record transactions related to long-term notes and mortgages.

Long-Term Loans with Equal Blended Monthly Payments

A **mortgage** loan is simply a long-term debt with a capital asset—such as a building or piece of equipment—pledged as collateral or security for the loan. If the borrower fails to repay the loan according to the specified terms, the lender has the legal right to have the asset seized and sold, and the proceeds from the sale applied to the repayment of the debt.

Mortgages are usually instalment loans. As discussed in Chapter 9, this means that payments are made periodically rather than only at the end of the loan. Also, the periodic payments are usually blended payments, consisting of both interest and principal components. The total amount of the payment is the same each period, but the portion of each payment that is consumed by interest is reduced as the principal balance is reduced.

To illustrate this, we will consider the case of a company that takes out a three-year, $100,000 mortgage on September 30. The interest rate on the loan is 6% per year, and equal blended payments of $3,042.19 are to be made at the end of each month. (This amount can be calculated using the interest tables provided on the inside covers of the book. Simply divide the $100,000 principal, or present value, by the present value factor for an annuity of 36 periods [3 years × 12 months per year = 36 months] at an interest rate of 0.5% per period [6% per year ÷ 12 months per year = 0.5% per month]: $100,000 ÷ 32.87102 = $3,042.19. Alternatively, the monthly payments required to repay the loan can be calculated using the payment function in a financial calculator or computer spreadsheet, such as Excel. Simply enter 0.005 for the interest rate per period, 36 for the number of periods, and 100,000 for the principal or present value. This will return a result of 3,042.19 for the payment.)

Exhibit 10-1 presents a loan amortization table for this mortgage, showing how the first portion of each of the payments is allocated to the monthly interest charge, with the remaining portion being applied to reduce the principal balance of the loan.

Notice that $500 of the first payment is consumed by interest and only $2,542 is left to be applied to the reduction of the principal. By contrast, only $15 of the last payment is consumed by interest, leaving $3,027 to be applied to the reduction of the principal.

The journal entries to record the initial borrowing and the first three payments on the mortgage are as follows:

Sept. 30	Cash (A)	100,000.00	
	Mortgage payable (L)		100,000.00
Oct. 31	Interest expense (SE)	500.00	
	Mortgage payable (L)	2,542.19	
	Cash (A)		3,042.19
Nov. 30	Interest expense (SE)	487.29	
	Mortgage payable (L)	2,554.90	
	Cash (A)		3,042.19
Dec. 31	Interest expense (SE)	474.51	
	Mortgage payable (L)	2,567.68	
	Cash (A)		3,042.19

Long-Term Loans with Monthly Payments of Interest Only

To illustrate a different type of loan arrangement, we will now consider the case of a company that takes out a three-year loan for $100,000 at 6% on September 30, with terms that specify that only the interest on the loan is to be paid each month; the principal is to be repaid as a lump sum when the note matures at the end of the three-year period.

LOAN AMORTIZATION TABLE

EXHIBIT 10-1

For a three-year, 6% mortgage of $100,000 with payments made at the end of each month

Month	Monthly payment	Interest expense (= previous principal balance × 6% × 1/12)	Remaining portion of payment, applied to principal balance	Principal balance outstanding (Initial amount $100,000)
1	3,042.19	500.00[a]	2,542.19	97,457.81
2	3,042.19	487.29[b]	2,554.90	94,902.91
3	3,042.19	474.51	2,567.68	92,335.23
4	3,042.19	461.68	2,580.51	89,754.72
5	3,042.19	448.77	2,593.42	87,161.30
6	3,042.19	435.81	2,606.38	84,554.92
7	3,042.19	422.77	2,619.42	81,935.50
8	3,042.19	409.68	2,632.51	79,302.99
9	3,042.19	396.51	2,645.68	76,657.32
10	3,042.19	383.29	2,658.90	73,998.41
11	3,042.19	369.99	2,672.20	71,326.22
12	3,042.19	356.63	2,685.56	68,640.66
13	3,042.19	343.20	2,698.99	65,941.67
14	3,042.19	329.71	2,712.48	63,229.19
15	3,042.19	316.15	2,726.04	60,503.14
16	3,042.19	302.52	2,739.67	57,763.47
17	3,042.19	288.82	2,753.37	55,010.10
18	3,042.19	275.05	2,767.14	52,242.96
19	3,042.19	261.21	2,780.98	49,461.98
20	3,042.19	247.31	2,794.88	46,667.10
21	3,042.19	233.34	2,808.85	43,858.25
22	3,042.19	219.29	2,822.90	41,035.35
23	3,042.19	205.18	2,837.01	38,198.34
24	3,042.19	190.99	2,851.20	35,347.14
25	3,042.19	176.74	2,865.45	32,481.68
26	3,042.19	162.41	2,879.78	29,601.90
27	3,042.19	148.01	2,894.18	26,707.72
28	3,042.19	133.54	2,908.65	23,799.07
29	3,042.19	119.00	2,923.19	20,875.88
30	3,042.19	104.38	2,937.81	17,938.06
31	3,042.19	89.69	2,952.50	14,985.56
32	3,042.19	74.93	2,967.26	12,018.30
33	3,042.19	60.09	2,982.10	9,036.20
34	3,042.19	45.18	2,997.01	6,039.20
35	3,042.19	30.20	3,011.99	3,027.20
36	3,042.19	14.99[c]	3,027.20	- 0 -
Totals	$109,518.84	$9,518.84	$100,000.00	

[a] $100,000.00 × 0.06 × 1/12 = $500.00
[b] $97,457.81 × 0.06 × 1/12 = $487.29
[c] Adjusted by $0.15 to compensate for rounding and bring the final principal balance to zero

Note the key difference between this situation and the previous one: in this case, there are no reductions in the principal of the loan during its life. In this type of situation a loan amortization table is not necessary, since the principal balance remains the same from the inception of the loan until it is repaid in full at maturity. Consequently, the amount of interest remains the same each month: $100,000 \times 6\% \times 1/12 = \$500$.

The journal entries to record the initial borrowing and the first three interest payments on the note are as follows:

Sept. 30	Cash (A)	100,000.00	
	Long-term note payable (L)		100,000.00
Oct. 31	Interest expense (SE)	500.00	
	Cash (A)		500.00
Nov. 30	Interest expense (SE)	500.00	
	Cash (A)		500.00
Dec. 31	Interest expense (SE)	500.00	
	Cash (A)		500.00

We chose to use the account title "Long-term note payable" for this liability. However, alternatives such as "Long-term bank loan" are also commonly used.

EARNINGS MANAGEMENT

Debt covenants usually include financial measures or tests, such as ratios, that the borrowers must satisfy; otherwise, the debt will become due and payable on demand. As a result, restrictive covenants can create environments that encourage bias in accounting and financial reporting. That is, debt covenants may put so much pressure on companies to achieve the required minimums and pass the tests that managers engage in aggressive accounting and business practices to satisfy the covenants.

Users of financial statements should therefore be aware of the existence and nature of key debt covenants, and alert to the potential for manipulation of the financial statements to satisfy them.

Exhibit 10-2 is an excerpt from the notes to the 2009 financial statements of **WestJet Airlines Inc.**, describing the various components of long-term debt outstanding. Notice that the term loans consist of blended payments of interest and principal, payable monthly or quarterly, and each loan is secured by a specific piece or type of equipment. For 2009, the total amount of property and equipment pledged as security is $1,925,672 thousand. The interest rates vary by loan, depending on when the loans were taken out, and some loans have fixed interest rates while others have floating rates. The last part of the note indicates the loan repayments required over the next five years and the total amount due after that.

BONDS AND DEBENTURES

When a large company wants to borrow long-term funds to support its operations, it does not always have to take a loan from a specific lender such as a bank or other financial institution. Instead, it can get the funds from "the market" by issuing bonds.

WESTJET AIRLINES INC. 2009 ANNUAL REPORT

Excerpt from Note 7 to the Financial Statements

For the years ended December 31, 2009 and 2008
(Stated in thousands of Canadian dollars, except share and per share data)

7. Long-term debt

		2009	2008
Term loans – purchased aircraft	(i)	$ 1,168,381	$ 1,331,083
Term loan – purchased aircraft	(ii)	33,631	—
Term loan – flight simulator	(iii)	6,392	7,265
Term loans – live satellite television equipment	(iv)	493	1,740
Term loan – Calgary Hangar facility	(v)	9,202	9,648
Term loan – Calgary Hangar facility	(vi)	1,678	2,167
		1,219,777	1,351,903
Current portion		171,223	165,721
		$ 1,048,554	$ 1,186,182

(i) 52 individual term loans, amortized on a straight-line basis over a 12-year term, each repayable in quarterly principal instalments ranging from $668 to $955, including fixed interest at a weighted average rate of 5.32%, maturing between 2014 and 2020. These facilities are guaranteed by Ex-Im Bank and secured by one 800-series aircraft, 38 700-series aircraft and 13 600-series aircraft.

(ii) Term loan of US $32,000 repayable in quarterly instalments of US $1,788, including fixed interest at a rate of 4.315%, maturing in 2014. This facility is secured by one 800-series aircraft.

(iii) Term loan repayable in monthly instalments of $91, including floating interest at the bank's prime rate plus 0.88%, with an effective interest rate of 3.13% as at December 31, 2009, maturing in 2011, secured by one flight simulator.

(iv) Three individual term loans, amortized on a straight-line basis over a five-year term, repayable in quarterly principal instalments of $41, including floating interest at the Canadian LIBOR rate plus 0.08%, with a weighted average effective interest rate of 1.80% as at December 31, 2009, maturing in 2010 and 2011. These facilities are for the purchase of live satellite television equipment, are guaranteed by the Ex-Im Bank and are secured by certain 700-series and 600-series aircraft.

(v) Term loan repayable in monthly instalments of $108, including fixed interest at 9.03%, maturing April 2011, secured by the Calgary Hangar facility.

(vi) Term loan repayable in monthly instalments of $50, including floating interest at the bank's prime rate plus 0.50%, with an effective interest rate of 2.75% as at December 31, 2009, maturing April 2013, secured by the Calgary Hangar facility.

The net book value of the property and equipment pledged as collateral for the Corporation's secured borrowings was $1,925,672 as at December 31, 2009 (2008 – $2,012,915).

Future scheduled repayments of long-term debt are as follows:

2010	$ 171,223
2011	183,924
2012	169,992
2013	169,750
2014	170,019
2015 and thereafter	354,869
	$ 1,219,777

Held within the special-purpose entities, as identified in note 1, significant accounting policies, are liabilities of $1,168,907 (2008 – $1,332,859) related to the acquisition of the 52 purchased aircraft and live satellite television equipment, which are included above in the long-term debt balances.

Basic Bond Characteristics

LEARNING OBJECTIVE 2

Describe the basic characteristics of bonds.

A **bond** is a formal agreement between a borrower (the company that issues the bonds) and the lenders (the investors who buy the bonds) that specifies how the borrower is to pay back the lenders, as well as any conditions that the borrower must meet while the bonds are outstanding. The bond's terms, conditions, restrictions, and covenants are usually stated in a document called an **indenture agreement**.

Bonds that are traded in public markets are fairly standardized. The indenture agreement will state a **face value** or principal amount for the bonds, which is usually $1,000 per bond. The face value specifies the cash payment that the borrower will make to the lenders at the bond's **maturity date**. In addition to the cash payment at maturity, most bonds also include semi-annual interest payments to the lenders. The amount of these payments is determined by multiplying the **bond interest rate** by the face value and dividing by two (because the interest payments are semi-annual). The bond interest rate is stated as an annual percentage and is usually not the effective or true interest rate, but simply a rate that determines the periodic amount of the interest payments.

Another important item in the indenture agreement is the collateral (if any) that the company pledges as security to the lenders. If collateral is pledged, it means that, if the company defaults on either the interest payments or the maturity payment, the bondholders can force the pledged assets to be sold in order to settle the debt. A "mortgage bond" has real property (fixed assets) pledged as collateral. A **collateral trust bond** usually has shares and bonds of other companies pledged as collateral.

A bond that carries no specific collateral but is backed by the company's general creditworthiness is known as a **debenture bond**, or simply a debenture. Debenture bonds can be either **senior** or **subordinated** debentures. The distinction between senior and subordinated is the order in which the investors (creditors) are paid in the event of bankruptcy: senior creditors are paid before subordinate claims.

Some indenture agreements specify special provisions that are designed to make the bonds more attractive to investors. **Convertible bonds**, for example, can be exchanged for or converted to a specified number of common shares in the company issuing them.

Sometimes bonds are sold directly to investors through what is referred to as a "private placement". These types of bonds do not trade in public markets. Private placements are usually made to institutional investors, such as the trustees in charge of large pension funds.

Generally, bonds are sold initially to institutional and individual investors through an **investment banker**. The investment banker sells the bonds to its clients before the bonds are traded in the open market, and gets a commission for handling the transaction. The investment banker first consults with the company about its objectives, and helps design an issue that will both meet the company's objectives and attract investors. All the bond features that have been discussed in the previous sections will be considered when structuring the offering.

The investment banker is responsible for the initial sale of the issue to its clients. Because most issues involve larger amounts than one investment banker can easily sell, the investment banker usually forms a syndicate with other investment bankers, who will be jointly responsible for selling the issue. The syndicate members are sometimes known as the **underwriters** of the issue.

Once the bonds have been sold by the investment bankers, they can be freely traded between investors in the bond market—much as shares are traded on the stock market. At this point, any investors can buy or sell the bonds. The prices of the bonds will then fluctuate according to the forces of supply and demand, and with changes in economic conditions.

accounting in the news

Bonds Yield Sweet Returns

UK chocolatier Hotel Chocolat is raising funds in a unique way, by issuing bonds that will pay out in chocolate rather than money. Members of Hotel Chocolat's Tasting Club have been offered two investment options: a three-year £2,000 ($3,030 CAD) bond, for which they will receive a box of chocolates valued at £18 ($27 CAD) every two weeks (equivalent to a 6.7% yield); or a three-year £4,000 ($6,058 CAD) bond that will pay out the equivalent of a 7.3% yield in chocolate. Although the company will be paying yields that are higher than standard bond rates, the cost of making the boxes of chocolates is much less than their market value. With 100,000 Tasting Club members, who already pay for discounts, special offers, and regular home deliveries of chocolate samples, Hotel Chocolat hopes to raise £5 million ($7.5 million CAD) through the bond issue. The transaction is an alternative to bank loan financing, since its size is too small for a typical bond issue. The company has appointed BDO as its advisor and has received approval from the UK Financial Services Authority. It plans to use the funds raised to expand its chain of retail outlets, develop a new plantation in St. Lucia, and expand its business overseas.

Sources: Natalie Harrison, "Candy Bond Investors Get Paid in Chocolate," Reuters, May 24, 2010; Jason Hesse, "Hotel Chocolat Offers a Sweet Deal to Chocoholics," *Real Business—The Champion of UK Enterprise*, http://realbusiness.co.uk/sales_and_marketing/hotel_chocolat_offers_a_sweet_deal_to_chocoholics

Bond Pricing in the Marketplace

Bond prices are established in the marketplace by the economic forces of supply (from companies wanting to sell bonds) and demand (from investors wanting to buy them). The buyers determine what the cash flows are going to be for the bonds—both in the periodic interest payments and the eventual repayment of the principal amount—and the rate of return they want to earn, based on the risk of potential default by the company. They then use these amounts to calculate the present value of the cash flows they will receive from the bonds, to determine the amount they are willing to pay for them.

> **LEARNING OBJECTIVE 3**
>
> *Explain how bonds are issued and how the pricing of bonds is affected by market factors.*

The process of calculating the present value of bonds involves discounting (at the desired earnings rate) the future cash flows from the bonds (periodic interest payments and repayment of principal). Potential buyers determine the yield (or desired rate of return) by looking at the interest rates that could be earned from alternative investments and the relative risk of the particular bond issue. The higher the level of risk, the higher the yield rate has to be. In other words, for buyers to accept a higher risk of default, they have to be compensated for that risk with a higher rate of return. Buyers also have to factor in any special features of the bonds, such as if they are convertible into shares. However, to keep things as simple as possible in the rest of this section, these special features will be ignored as we discuss bond pricing.

The starting point in determining a bond's value is to calculate the cash flows that will be received by the buyer (and paid by the seller). To illustrate the calculation of interest payments and bond values, we will use the following example.

LEARNING OBJECTIVE 4

Calculate a bond's selling price and prepare journal entries to record the issuance and subsequent interest payments for bonds sold at par, below par, and above par.

Baum Company issues bonds on December 31, 2011, with a total face value of $100,000, a bond interest rate of 8%, and a maturity date of December 31, 2014. The company must make a $100,000 payment to the lenders on December 31, 2014, and must make interest payments every six months of $4,000 each. The $4,000 amount is calculated as follows:

Semi-annual interest payment = Face value × Bond interest rate × ½
= $100,000 × 8% × ½
= $4,000

The bond interest rate is sometimes referred to as the **coupon rate**, **stated rate**, or **nominal rate**. All of these terms refer to the rate of interest that is specified in the bond contract and is used to calculate the interest payments.

There will be a total of six interest payments, because there are three years to maturity and two interest payments per year. The interest payments on a bond are typically structured to come at the end of each six-month period. The stream of interest payments is called an **annuity in arrears**, meaning that it is a series of equal payments that are made at the end of each period.

Although these bonds have a face value of $100,000, they may sell for more or less than this amount. Bond selling prices are determined by competitive forces in the bond market, because there are always many other bonds that investors could purchase. If a particular bond issue looks attractive, in comparison to bonds of similar duration and risk, investors will be willing to pay a premium price (i.e., more than the face value) to purchase them. On the other hand, if the terms are unattractive in comparison to bonds of similar duration and risk, investors will only be willing to purchase the bonds if they can do so at a discounted price (i.e., less than their face value).

Case 1: The bond interest rate is lower than the required yield

HELPFUL HINT

There are many terms for interest rates in the context of bonds:

- The interest rate to determine the interest *payments* is referred to as the bond rate, the coupon rate, the stated rate, the nominal rate, or the contract rate.

- The interest rate to determine the selling price of the bonds and the interest *expense* is referred to as the market rate, the effective rate, or the yield.

To illustrate this, suppose that when Baum issues its bonds the competitive interest rate in the market for bonds of similar duration and risk is 10%, compounded semi-annually. This competitive market rate of interest is often called the **yield** or **effective interest rate**. Since investors could buy other, similar bonds and earn a rate of return of 10%, they will not buy Baum's bonds unless they can earn the same rate of return or yield.

To determine exactly how much they are willing to pay for Baum's bonds, investors look at the cash flows that Baum will pay them, and then discount these cash flows using the yield rate of 10%. Exhibit 10-3 shows the timeline and the cash flows for this bond.

Note that the interest payments (the six payments of $4,000 each) are an annuity in arrears and that the maturity payment ($100,000) is a lump-sum cash flow at the end of the sixth period. There are six periods because interest payments are made twice each year. The bonds' issuance price will be determined by calculating the **present value** of these cash flows, based on the 5% semi-annual yield or effective rate of interest.

To calculate the present value of the bonds' future cash flows, we will use the Time Value of Money tables located on the inside covers. Alternatively, the appendix on pages 680–682 shows how the PV (present value) function in Microsoft® Excel can be used to calculate these amounts. These calculations can also be done using a financial

BAUM COMPANY BONDS

EXHIBIT 10-3

Market yield rate	10%
Bond interest rate	8%
Face value (principal)	$100,000
Time to maturity	3 years
Semi-annual yield rate	= Annual yield rate ÷ 2
	= 10% ÷ 2 = 5%
Semi-annual interest payments	= Face value × Annual bond interest rate ÷ 2
	= $100,000 × 8% ÷ 2 = $4,000
Number of semi-annual periods	= Time to maturity × 2
	= 3 years × 2 = 6

Cash flows — interest payments	$4,000	$4,000	$4,000	$4,000	$4,000	$4,000
— principal repayment						$100,000
Number of semi-annual periods from the present time	1	2	3	4	5	6

calculator that has present value functions. To find out how to calculate these amounts on a financial calculator, go to the Study Tools section on the student website at http://www.wiley.com/hoskin.

Study Tools

The two Time Value of Money tables printed on the inside covers contain precalculated factors for various combinations of interest rates and time periods. The present value of the cash flows is determined by multiplying the cash flow amounts by the appropriate factors from the tables. The factors in these tables are sometimes referred to as discount factors, and the results are referred to as **discounted cash flows**.

Notice that the heading on Table 1 is "Present Value Factors for an Annuity in Arrears." Since an annuity is a series of equal payments, Table 1 will be used for the interest payments. By contrast, the heading on Table 2 is "Present Value Factors for a Lump-Sum Payment." Since the principal is repaid only once, as a lump sum when the bonds mature, Table 2 will be used for the principal payment.

To calculate the present value of Baum's bonds, we first need to multiply the amount of the interest payments by the factor from Table 1 for an annuity of 6 periods (since there are 6 interest payments) discounted at an interest rate of 5% (the market rate of interest for each six-month period). Looking in Table 1, where the row for 6 periods intersects with the column for 5%, you will see that the appropriate present value factor is 5.07569. Multiplying the amount of the interest payments ($4,000) by this factor gives $20,302.76. This is the present value of a series of 6 semi-annual future payments of $4,000 each, when the competitive rate of return is 5% per period. This is the amount that investors will be willing to pay now, to receive these interest payments in the future.

Next, we need to multiply the amount of the principal payment by the factor from Table 2 for a lump-sum payment to be made after 6 periods, discounted at the same interest rate of 5% (the yield or market rate). Looking in Table 2, where the row for

6 periods intersects with the column for 5%, you should find the present value factor 0.74622. Multiplying the amount of the principal payment ($100,000) by this factor gives $74,622.00. This is the present value of a future payment of $100,000 after 6 semi-annual periods, when the competitive rate of return is 5% per period. This is the amount that investors will be willing to pay now, to receive this principal payment in the future.

The total present value of the bonds is the sum of these two amounts: $20,302.76 (for the interest) + $74,622.00 (for the principal) = $94,924.76. This is the amount that investors will pay for Baum's bonds. Notice that it is less than the $100,000 face value of the bonds. This is because these bonds pay interest of only 8% (4% semi-annually), while the market rate of interest is 10% (5% semi-annually). Since Baum's bonds pay less interest than comparable bonds from other companies, investors will not be willing to pay full price for them.

Case 2: The bond interest rate is higher than the required yield

How does a different required rate of return or yield affect the value of the bonds? Suppose that instead of 10% the competitive rate of interest in the market for this type of bond is 6%. The only thing that will change in the calculation is the present value factors that are used, as the following shows:

> **Present value of the Baum Company bonds if the market rate of interest is 6% (3% per semi-annual period):**
>
> PV of the bonds = PV of the interest payments + PV of the principal amount
> = amount of each interest payment × PV factor for an annuity
>   for 6 periods at 3% (from Table 1)
> + amount of principal payment × PV factor for a lump sum
>   after 6 periods at 3% (from Table 2)
> = ($4,000 × 5.41719) + ($100,000 × 0.83748)
> = $21,668.76 + $83,748.00
> = $105,416.76

Notice that this is more than the $100,000 face value of the bonds. This is because these bonds pay interest of 8% (4% semi-annually), while the market rate of interest is only 6% (3% semi-annually). Since, under this scenario, Baum's bonds pay more interest than comparable bonds from other companies, investors will be willing to pay extra for them.

In bond pricing terminology, when bonds are sold for more than their face value they are said to be sold at a **premium**. When bonds are sold for less than their face value, they are said to be sold at a **discount**. If they are sold for exactly their face value, they are said to be sold at **par**. You should avoid placing any connotations on the words "premium" and "discount." They do not mean either that the buyers paid too much or that they got a good deal. In competitive financial markets, the amount that investors pay—whether it is premium, discount, or par value—is always the appropriate price for the bond, given the yield or market rate for similar bonds.

Case 3: The bond interest rate is the same as the required yield

What yield rate would have to be used in the example for the bonds to be issued at par? The answer is 8%, because in this case the required yield or market interest rate is the same as the bond interest rate. Whenever the interest rate paid by bonds is exactly equal to the required yield or market rate, the bonds will sell at par. When the bond interest rate is *lower* than the market rate, the bonds will not be very attractive compared to alternative investments and will therefore sell at a *discount*. On the other hand, when the bond interest rate is *higher* than the market rate, the bonds will be relatively attractive and will therefore sell at a *premium*. This should seem logical to you, if you think of it from a buyer's point of view.

You may be wondering why a company would issue (sell) its bonds at other than their par value. Companies generally try to set the interest rate on their bonds to be close to the interest rate that the market will demand (i.e., at what they expect the competitive rate of interest to be). However, when a company decides to issue bonds as a way of raising capital, it is usually a long process. It must first get financial advice and legal advice on aspects of the indenture agreement, and then get the necessary approvals and have the bond certificates printed and ready for issue. By the time the bonds are actually issued to investors, the market's assessment of the company's risk may have changed, and/or general economic conditions may have changed. In such cases, the bond interest rate will differ from the market rate and, as a result, the bonds will sell at a discount or a premium rather than at their par value.

A final point to note about bond pricing terminology is that bond prices are typically expressed out of 100. For example, a $1,000 bond selling for $949 is said to be selling at 94.9, meaning 94.9% of its face value. Similarly, a $1,000 bond selling for $1,054 is said to be selling at 105.4, representing 105.4% of its face value, and a bond selling for its par value is said to be selling at 100.

Calculating Bond Interest Expense and Liability Balances

Exhibit 10-4 presents amortization tables for the Baum Company bonds, under the three scenarios discussed above. These have been prepared in the same way as the amortization tables for various loans, notes, and mortgages presented in Chapter 9 and earlier in this chapter.

In each case, the *interest payment* is calculated using the *face value* and the *bond interest rate*, while the *interest expense* is calculated using the *liability balance* and the *yield* or *market rate*.

Notice that when the bonds are issued at a discount, the liability balance starts at *less* than the face value and *increases* over the life of the bonds, until it equals the face value when the bonds are due for repayment. Conversely, when the bonds are issued at a premium, the bond liability starts at *more* than the face value and *decreases* as each interest payment is made, until it equals the face value when the bonds mature. When the bonds are issued at their par value, the liability balance is the same as the face value over the entire life of the bonds. In each case, the final bond liability equals the principal amount to be repaid when the bonds are due for repayment.

EXHIBIT 10-4

BOND AMORTIZATION TABLES FOR THE BAUM COMPANY EXAMPLE

Case 1: BONDS ISSUED AT A DISCOUNT (bond interest rate is 8%; market rate is 10%)

Interest payment number	Interest payment (= face value × 8% × 1/2)	Interest expense (= previous liability balance × 10% × 1/2)	Difference between interest expense and payment = change in liability balance	Liability balance (initial amount = $94,924.76 issue price)
1	$4,000.00	$4,746.24[a]	$746.24	$ 95,671.00
2	4,000.00	4,783.55[b]	783.55	96,454.55
3	4,000.00	4,822.73	822.73	97,277.28
4	4,000.00	4,863.86	863.86	98,141.14
5	4,000.00	4,907.06	907.06	99,048.20
6	4,000.00	4,951.80[c]	951.80	100,000.00

[a] $94,924.76 × 10% × ½ = $4,746.24
[b] $95,671.00 × 10% × ½ = $4,783.55
[c] adjusted by $0.61 to compensate for rounding and bring the final principal balance to the $100,000 face value

Case 2: BONDS ISSUED AT A PREMIUM (bond interest rate is 8%; market rate is 6%)

Interest payment number	Interest payment (= face value × 8% × 1/2)	Interest expense (= previous liability balance × 6% × 1/2)	Difference between interest expense and payment = change in liability balance	Liability balance (initial amount = $105,416.76 issue price)
1	$4,000.00	$3,162.50[d]	$−837.50	$104,579.26
2	4,000.00	3,137.38[e]	−862.62	103,716.64
3	4,000.00	3,111.50	−888.50	102,828.14
4	4,000.00	3,084.84	−915.16	101,912.98
5	4,000.00	3,057.39	−942.61	100,970.37
6	4,000.00	3,029.63[f]	−970.37	100,000.00

[d] $105,416.76 × 6% × ½ = $3,162.50
[e] $104,579.26 × 6% × ½ = $3,137.38
[f] adjusted by $0.52 to compensate for rounding and bring the final principal balance to the $100,000 face value

Case 3: BONDS ISSUED AT PAR VALUE (bond interest rate and market rate are both 8%)

Interest payment number	Interest payment (= face value × 8% × 1/2)	Interest expense (= liability balance × 8% × 1/2)	Difference between interest expense and payment = change in liability balance	Liability balance (initial amount = $100,000.00 issue price)
1	$4,000.00	$4,000.00	$0.00	$100,000.00
2	4,000.00	4,000.00	0.00	100,000.00
3	4,000.00	4,000.00	0.00	100,000.00
4	4,000.00	4,000.00	0.00	100,000.00
5	4,000.00	4,000.00	0.00	100,000.00
6	4,000.00	4,000.00	0.00	100,000.00

Accounting for Bonds

Continuing with the Baum Company example, we now illustrate the journal entries for bond accounting. The entries to record the issuance of the bonds and the first two interest payments are shown below, for each of the three scenarios developed earlier (issued at a discount, at a premium, and at par). For the interest entries, the amounts are taken from the amortization tables in Exhibit 10-4.

Case 1: Bonds issued at a discount

Journal entry to record the issuance of the bonds:		
Cash (A)	94,924.76	
Bond liability (L)		94,924.76[a]
Journal entry for the first interest payment:		
Interest expense (SE)	4,746.24	
Bond liability (L)		746.24
Cash (A)		4,000.00
Journal entry for the second interest payment:		
Interest expense (SE)	4,783.55	
Bond liability (L)		783.55
Cash (A)		4,000.00

Notice that when bonds are issued at a discount there is a difference between the amount of interest expense and the amount of interest paid in cash, and this difference *increases* the liability balance over the life of the bonds. This is done each interest period, and results in the bond liability at the maturity date equalling the face value of the bonds. Increasing the bond liability is necessary because, when the bonds mature, the company has to repay the full face value of the bonds ($100,000), not just the amount ($94,924.76) that was received when the bonds were issued.

Case 2: Bonds issued at a premium

Journal entry to record the issuance of the bonds:		
Cash (A)	105,416.76	
Bond liability (L)		105,416.76[b]

[a] Traditionally, accountants would have recorded this in two parts: a $100,000.00 credit to Bonds Payable, partially offset by a $5,075.24 debit to a contra-liability account called Discount on Bonds Payable. For the statement of financial position, the contra-liability for the discount on the bonds would be deducted from the bonds payable account, to show the net liability of $94,924.76. As each interest payment was recorded, a portion of the discount would be amortized as interest expense.

Since using a Discount on Bonds Payable account makes the accounting procedures significantly more complex, does not affect the final outcome, and is not encouraged under International Financial Reporting Standards, we use the much simpler approach illustrated above.

[b] Traditionally, accountants would have recorded this in two parts: a $100,000.00 credit to Bonds Payable and a $5,416.76 credit to an adjunct liability account called Premium on Bonds Payable. For the statement of financial position, the adjunct liability for the premium on the bonds would be added to the bonds payable account, to show the total liability of $105,416.76. As each interest payment was recorded, a portion of the premium would be amortized against interest expense.

Since using a Premium on Bonds Payable account makes the accounting procedures significantly more complex, does not affect the final outcome, and is not encouraged under International Financial Reporting Standards, we use the simpler approach illustrated above.

HELPFUL HINT

When calculating bond interest, remember the following:

- The *interest payment* is calculated using the values specified in the bond contract: the *bond interest rate* and the *face value of the bonds*. Since these are both constants, the interest payment is a constant amount—the same for each semi-annual interest period throughout the life of the bonds.

- The *interest expense* is calculated using the *yield* or *market rate* of interest at the time the bonds were issued (the same rate used in the present value calculations that determine the selling price) and the previous *liability balance*. For bonds issued at a discount or a premium, the liability balance changes each period and the interest expense is therefore a different amount each period.

Journal entry for the first interest payment:		
Interest expense (SE)	3,162.50	
Bond liability (L)	837.50	
Cash (A)		4,000.00
Journal entry for the second interest payment:		
Interest expense (SE)	3,137.38	
Bond liability (L)	862.62	
Cash (A)		4,000.00

Notice that when the bonds are issued at a premium the difference between the amount of interest expense and the amount of interest paid in cash *decreases* the liability balance over the life of the bonds. This will result in the bond liability at the maturity date equalling the face value of the bonds. This is logical, because the company will have to repay only the $100,000 face value of the bonds at maturity, not the $105,416.76 that was received when they were issued.

Case 3: Bonds issued at par value

Journal entry to record the issuance of the bonds:		
Cash (A)	100,000.00	
Bond liability (L)		100,000.00
Journal entry for the first interest payment:		
Interest expense (SE)	4,000.00	
Cash (A)		4,000.00
Journal entry for the second interest payment:		
Interest expense (SE)	4,000.00	
Cash (A)		4,000.00

Repayment of Bonds at Maturity

As shown in Exhibit 10-4, whether bonds are issued at a discount, at a premium, or at par, when they reach their maturity date the liability balance equals the face value. Consequently, the journal entry to record the retirement or repayment of the bonds is the same in all three cases. For the Baum Company bonds, the entry is as follows:

Bond liability (L)	100,000.00	
Cash (A)		100,000.00

Early Retirement of Debt

Although a company does not have to pay off its debts until they mature, there are times when it makes sense to pay a debt earlier. This transaction is known as **early retirement**, or **early extinguishment**, of debt.

Some bonds may have a "call feature" that allows the issuing company to buy them back at a predetermined price before they mature. These are referred to as **callable**

bonds. Otherwise, bonds can be retired before maturity by simply buying them in the bond market. Whether they are called or purchased in the open market, it is likely that the bond liability or carrying value of the bonds will be different from the amount paid to retire them. Consequently, a gain or loss will usually arise when debt is retired early.

To demonstrate the accounting for an early retirement of debt, suppose the Baum Company bonds were called or bought back after two years for a price of $101,000.

For case 1, where the bonds were issued at a discount, Exhibit 10-4 shows that the bond liability after two years (i.e., after four interest payments) is $98,141.14. Since the company pays $101,000 to retire a debt that is on the books at only $98,141.14, it records a loss for the difference. The journal entry to record the early retirement of the bonds in this case is as follows:

Bond liability (L)	98,141.14	
Loss on early retirement of bonds (SE)	2,858.86	
Cash (A)		101,000.00

For case 2, where the bonds were issued at a premium, Exhibit 10-4 shows that the bond liability after two years is $101,912.98. Since the company pays only $101,000 to retire a debt that is on the books at $101,912.98, it records a gain equal to the difference. The journal entry to record the early retirement of the bonds in this case is as follows:

Bond liability (L)	101,912.98	
Gain on early retirement of bonds (SE)		912.98
Cash (A)		101,000.00

This case illustrates one reason why a company may decide to retire its debt early: if the cost to retire the debt is lower than the amount of the bond liability on the books, a gain will be recorded. The downside of this, however, is that if the company needs to raise more capital through the use of debt, it may have to pay a higher interest rate for the new debt. If so, the one-time gain on the retirement of the debt in the current period could be offset by ongoing higher interest costs in future periods. Under these circumstances, the company may not really be better off (as suggested by the gain) for having retired its old debt.

For case 3, where the bonds were issued at par value, Exhibit 10-4 shows that the bond liability after two years (or at any point during the life of the bonds) is $100,000. Since $101,000 is paid to retire a debt that is on the books at only $100,000, a loss is recognized for the difference. The journal entry to record the early retirement of the bonds in this case is as follows:

Bond liability (L)	100,000.00	
Loss on early retirement of bonds (SE)	1,000.00	
Cash (A)		101,000.00

EARNINGS MANAGEMENT

The early retirement of debt is a discretionary action by management, and one which can often result in significant gains or losses being reported on the statement of earnings. Users of financial statements should therefore be aware that managers may be tempted to manipulate the financial statements through early debt retirements, and should critically evaluate management's reasoning and the economic justification for any early retirement of debt.

Long-Term Notes or Bonds with No Explicit Interest

Sometimes bonds or long-term notes are issued with no provision for interest on them. This is most commonly done in financing arrangements for the purchase of long-term assets. For example, suppose a company negotiates the purchase of some equipment for $100,000, which is to be paid at the end of three years with no interest added. In this situation, accounting principles would say that the appropriate value for recording this equipment and the related note payable is whatever it would have cost the company to purchase the equipment in cash paid immediately. The true value of the asset is not the $100,000 that will be paid in three years, because surely the equipment could have been acquired for less if the company had purchased it for cash. Similarly, the initial amount of the liability should not be recorded as $100,000, because logically—given the time value of money—the company could settle the debt now for less than the $100,000 that it has agreed to pay after three years.

We can determine the appropriate value for recording the equipment and the related note payable by calculating the *present value* of the $100,000 that is to be paid at the end of three years, using an appropriate interest rate. For example, if the company would normally have been charged an interest rate of 6% annually for a three-year loan, the discounting factor that should be used is 0.83962 (the PV factor for 3 periods at 6%, from Table 2). The present value of this transaction is $100,000 × 0.83962 = $83,962, and the journal entries to record it are as follows.

To record the acquisition of the asset and the issuance of the note:

Equipment (A)	83,962	
Long-term note payable (L)		83,962

To accrue interest for the first year:

Interest expense (SE)	5,038	
Long-term note payable (L)		5,038
6% × 83,962 = $5,038		

To accrue interest for the second year:

Interest expense (SE)	5,340	
Long-term note payable (L)		5,340
6% × (83,962 + 5,038) = $5,340		

To accrue interest for the third year:

Interest expense (SE)	5,660	
Long-term note payable (L)		5,660
6% × (83,962 + 5,038 + 5,340) = $5,660		

To record the payment of the note:

Long-term note payable (L)	100,000	
Cash (A)		100,000

Note that interest expense is recognized—even though none is explicitly charged—and over the life of the note the liability balance is increased to the amount that is due on its maturity date (i.e., $83,962 + $5,038 + $5,340 + $5,660 = $100,000).

LEASES

When a company needs to use an asset such as a piece of machinery, there are two ways it can obtain the use of the asset. One is to purchase it outright. A second is to enter into a **lease agreement** in which another company (the **lessor**) provides the asset and the company that wants to use it (the **lessee**) makes periodic payments to the lessor in exchange for use of the asset over the length of the lease agreement (the **lease term**). There are benefits and costs to both alternatives.

One benefit of purchasing the asset and thereby owning it is that the company can depreciate the asset for tax purposes and, in some cases, obtain an investment tax credit for the purchase. Investment tax credits are incentives provided by the Canada Revenue Agency to encourage investment in certain types of assets. These credits usually take the form of a direct reduction in the company's tax bill, based on a percentage of the asset's cost.

A disadvantage of purchasing the asset is that it ties up capital that could have been used for other purposes. Also, if the company has to borrow to buy the asset, the company's debt ratios and interest coverage ratios will change, which could affect its future borrowing capabilities. (These ratios are discussed later in this chapter, and in Chapter 12.)

Realizing a gain from appreciation in the asset's value is another potential benefit of ownership. Of course, the downside is incurring a loss from the asset's decline in value, which could be dramatic if the asset becomes technologically obsolete or loses its market popularity.

On the other hand, leasing often offers several benefits. The main advantage is that it often provides a low-cost form of financing. This is largely due to the fact that the lessor typically has higher taxable income than the lessee and therefore gets larger tax savings from the capital cost allowance deduction, enabling it to offer attractive terms to the lessee.

Another advantage of leasing is that the lessee does not have to put up its own capital to acquire the asset. It also does not have to borrow to buy the asset, which may mean that its debt and interest coverage ratios will not be affected.

A final advantage of leasing is that, because the lessee does not own the asset, the risk of loss from obsolescence usually falls on the lessor. A related advantage is that the lessee may not want to use the asset for its full useful life. If the company wants to use the asset for only a limited period, there is significantly less risk associated with the residual value if the company leases the asset rather than buying it.

LEARNING OBJECTIVE 5

Discuss the advantages and disadvantages of leasing.

Classification of Leases

The accounting issues for a lessee are best illustrated using two extreme examples. At one extreme, suppose that the lease contract is signed for a relatively short period of time, say two years, whereas the leased asset's useful life is eight years. In this case, it is clear that the lessee is not buying the asset, but is instead renting it for only a short period. The lease contract is a mutually unexecuted rental contract, and the cash payments required by the lease are recorded by the lessee as simply rent expense and an outflow of cash. This type of lease is known as an **operating lease**.

Suppose at the other extreme that the lease contract is signed for the asset's entire useful life and that the title to the asset passes to the lessee at the end of the lease term (which is fairly common, in long lease contracts). In this case, the substance of the

LEARNING OBJECTIVE 6

Distinguish between operating leases and capital/finance leases, and prepare journal entries for a lessee under both types of leases.

transaction is that the lessee has, in effect, bought the asset and agreed to pay for it in instalments, in the form of lease payments. There is essentially no difference between this arrangement and one in which the lessee takes out a long-term loan, uses the funds to buy the asset for cash, and then repays the loan in instalments. The lender, in this case, is the lessor. It seems appropriate for the lessee to account for this as a long-term borrowing and a purchase of a long-term asset. The asset is therefore recorded at its cost (measured as the present value of the lease payments), and is depreciated in the same way that a purchased capital asset would be. The account name for the asset often includes reference to the lease aspect (for example, leased equipment or equipment under lease). The obligation to the lessor is recorded as a non-current liability, and interest expense is recognized over the term of the lease. This type of lease has traditionally been known as a **capital lease**, but under International Financial Reporting Standards is called a **finance lease**.

Although the appropriate accounting procedures for these extreme situations seem fairly clear, the following question arises: What does the company do when the lease is somewhere in between these extremes? To address this issue, criteria have been developed to distinguish capital/finance leases from operating leases. From the lessee's point of view, the lease qualifies as a capital/finance lease if any of the following criteria are met:

CRITERIA FOR A CAPITAL/FINANCE LEASE

1. **The lease transfers ownership of the asset to the lessee by the end of the lease term.**

   Rationale: If the lessee will own the asset at the end of the lease, it is buying the asset; the lease is merely a financing arrangement.

2. **The lessee has an option to purchase the asset at a price that is much lower than its fair value, and it is reasonably certain that this "bargain purchase option" will be exercised.**

   Rationale: If the lessee is likely to buy the asset at the end of the lease, because it can do so at a bargain price, it is ultimately buying the asset.

3. **The lease term is for the major part of the asset's economic life.**

   Rationale: If the lessee will have the use of the asset during most of its useful life, it should treat the transaction as if, in substance, it is buying the asset.

4. **The present value of the minimum lease payments is equal to substantially all of the fair value of the asset.**

   Rationale: If the value being paid to lease the asset is close to the cost of buying it, the lessee should treat the transaction as if, in substance, it is buying the asset.

5. **The leased asset is of such a specialized nature that, without major modifications, only the lessee can use it.**

   Rationale: If the asset would not be of use to anyone else, then it is reasonable to treat it as an asset that is being sold by the lessor and bought by the lessee.

The underlying spirit of these criteria is that, if the lease arrangement substantially transfers the risks and rewards of ownership of the asset to the lessee, it should be classified as a capital/finance lease and treated as an acquisition of a capital asset and a long-term liability.

In terms of the financial statement effects, companies generally have a strong preference for treating leases as operating leases. This keeps the lease obligations off the statement of financial position (creating a situation often referred to as "off-balance-sheet" financing), and there is therefore no effect on the debt to total assets ratio, the debt to equity ratio, or the interest coverage ratios. However, a lease can be treated as an operating lease only if the transaction does not meet any of the above criteria.[3]

IFRS INSIGHTS

The criteria for classifying leases under International Financial Reporting Standards are less specific than under former Canadian GAAP. They are therefore more open to interpretation, and will require accountants and auditors to exercise more judgement.

For example, Canadian GAAP previously specified that if the lease term was *75% or more* of the economic life of the asset, the lease was classified as a capital (finance) lease. By contrast, the comparable IFRS criterion states that if the lease term covers *the major part* of the economic life of the asset, the lease must be classified as a finance lease. It does not state whether the major part means 60%, 75%, or maybe 90%.

Similarly, Canadian GAAP previously specified that if the present value of the lease payments was *90% or more* of the fair value of the asset, the lease was classified as a capital (finance) lease. The comparable IFRS criterion does not specify a percentage. Instead, it states that if the present value of the minimum lease payments is equal to *substantially all* of the fair value of the asset, the lease must be classified as a finance lease.

Accounting for Leases

To illustrate the differences in accounting under a capital/finance lease and an operating lease, we will consider the following simple situation. Suppose that equipment is leased for three years and requires monthly lease payments of $1,000, payable at the end of each month.[4] The implicit interest rate in the lease contract is 12%.

---

3. For situations where a lease is on the borderline of being classified as either an operating lease or a finance lease using the five primary criteria, the following three secondary indicators should also be considered:
   - Any cancellation losses are borne by the lessee.
   - Any gains or losses from fluctuations in the residual value accrue to the lessee.
   - There is a bargain lease renewal option.

   If any of these criteria are met, they indicate that the true substance of the lease is such that it should be classified as a finance lease.

4. Normally, lease payments are made at the *beginning* of each period, rather than at the end. However, this makes the calculations of present value and interest expense somewhat complicated for an introductory text. Therefore, we are making the simplifying assumption that the lease payments are made at the *end* of each period.

If the lease qualifies as an operating lease, the only entry would be to record the payments as rent or lease expense each period. The following entry would be made at the beginning of each month.

MONTHLY JOURNAL ENTRY FOR AN OPERATING LEASE

Equipment rental/lease expense (SE)	1,000	
Cash (A)		1,000

Note that when a lease is treated as an operating lease, the lessee records neither an asset nor a liability—even though it has exclusive use of the asset for the three-year term of the lease, and it is contractually committed to make payments for the duration of the lease.

If the lease qualifies as a capital/finance lease, the transaction must be recorded as the purchase of an asset and a related long-term financing obligation. Both the asset and the obligation would initially be recorded at the present value of the lease payments. In our example, the interest rate per period for use in discounting the future cash flows would be 1% (i.e., the 12% annual rate ÷ 12 months per year). Because the payments are made monthly and the lease term is three years, there would be a total of 36 payments.

Using Table 1 for the present value of an annuity (on the inside covers), the present value of the lease is calculated as follows:

PV of lease payments = $1,000 × PV factor for an annuity of 36 payments
 discounted at 1%
 = $1,000 × 30.10751
 = $30,107.51

The entry to record the acquisition of the asset and the related lease liability at the outset of the lease is as follows:

INITIAL JOURNAL ENTRY FOR A CAPITAL/FINANCE LEASE

Leased equipment (A)	30,107.51	
Lease obligation (L)		30,107.51

The lease obligation will result in the recognition of interest expense, similar to that generated by a long-term note payable. To highlight the similarities, an amortization table for the lease liability is presented in Exhibit 10-5.

The journal entries to record the first two monthly payments are as follows:

CAPITAL/FINANCE LEASE PAYMENT ENTRIES

At the end of the first month:

Interest expense (SE)	301.08	
Lease obligation (L)	698.92	
Cash (A)		1,000.00

CAPITAL/FINANCE LEASE PAYMENT ENTRIES (cont'd)

At the end of the second month:

Interest expense (SE)	294.09	
Lease obligation (L)	705.91	
Cash (A)		1,000.00

AMORTIZATION TABLE FOR LEASE LIABILITY

EXHIBIT 10-5

Payment number	Payment amount	Interest expense (= previous liability balance × 12% × 1/12)	Difference between interest expense and payment = change in liability balance	Liability balance (initial amount = $30,107.51 present value)
1	$ 1,000.00	$ 301.08[a]	$ −698.92	$29,408.59
2	1,000.00	294.09[b]	−705.91	28,702.67
3	1,000.00	287.03	−712.97	27,989.70
4	1,000.00	279.90	−720.10	27,269.59
5	1,000.00	272.70	−727.30	26,542.29
6	1,000.00	265.42	−734.58	25,807.71
7	1,000.00	258.08	−741.92	25,065.79
8	1,000.00	250.66	−749.34	24,316.45
9	1,000.00	243.16	−756.84	23,559.61
10	1,000.00	235.60	−764.40	22,795.21
11	1,000.00	227.95	−772.05	22,023.16
12	1,000.00	220.23	−779.77	21,243.39
13	1,000.00	212.43	−787.57	20,455.83
14	1,000.00	204.56	−795.44	19,660.39
15	1,000.00	196.60	−803.40	18,856.99
16	1,000.00	188.57	−811.43	18,045.56
17	1,000.00	180.46	−819.54	17,226.01
18	1,000.00	172.26	−827.74	16,398.27
19	1,000.00	163.98	−836.02	15,562.26
20	1,000.00	155.62	−844.38	14,717.88
21	1,000.00	147.18	−852.82	13,865.06
22	1,000.00	138.65	−861.35	13,003.71
23	1,000.00	130.04	−869.96	12,133.75
24	1,000.00	121.34	−878.66	11,255.08
25	1,000.00	112.55	−887.45	10,367.63
26	1,000.00	103.68	−896.32	9,471.31
27	1,000.00	94.71	−905.29	8,566.02
28	1,000.00	85.66	−914.34	7,651.68
29	1,000.00	76.52	−923.48	6,728.20
30	1,000.00	67.28	−932.72	5,795.48
31	1,000.00	57.95	−942.05	4,853.44
32	1,000.00	48.53	−951.47	3,901.97
33	1,000.00	39.02	−960.98	2,940.99
34	1,000.00	29.41	−970.59	1,970.40
35	1,000.00	19.70	−980.30	990.11
36	1,000.00	9.89[c]	−990.11	0.00
Totals	$36,000.00	$5,892.49	$30,107.51	

[a] $30,107.51 × 12% × 1/12 = $301.08
[b] $29,408.59 × 12% × 1/12 = $294.09
[c] adjusted by $0.01 to compensate for rounding and bring the final principal balance to zero

In addition, because the leased asset is being treated as if it had been purchased, the equipment must be depreciated. If title to the asset passes to the lessee at the end of the lease, the depreciation will be calculated in the usual way: the asset's useful life will be its physical life, and the residual value (if any) will be deducted. Otherwise, if title does not pass to the lessee at the end of the lease, the useful life of the asset will be limited to the term of the lease—since the company will not be able to use the asset after the lease ends—and any residual value will be irrelevant, because the lessee company will not get the residual value.

In this case, since there is no indication that title to the equipment passes to the lessee at the end of the lease, its useful life (for the lessee) will be equal to the lease term. Also, because the equipment will be returned to the lessor at the end of the lease, there will be no residual value (for the lessee); it must depreciate the entire value of the leased equipment.

If the company uses straight-line depreciation, the monthly depreciation will be $30,107.51 ÷ 36 months = $836.32, and the entry to record it will be as follows:

CAPITAL/FINANCE LEASE DEPRECIATION ENTRY

At the end of each month:

Depreciation expense (SE)	836.32	
Accumulated depreciation—leased equipment (XA)		836.32

The impact of a lease transaction on the financial statements depends on its classification. On the statement of financial position, if the lease arrangement qualifies as a finance lease, both the company's assets and its liabilities will be higher than under an operating lease. On the statement of earnings, the company will report both depreciation expense and interest expense under a finance lease, compared to only equipment rental or lease expense under an operating lease.

In our example, if the lease is classified as a finance lease, the depreciation plus interest expense for the first month will be $836.32 + $301.08 = $1,137.40. By contrast, if the lease is classified as an operating lease, the expense will be $1,000. In the first month, therefore, classification as a finance lease results in higher expenses (and these would be even higher if the company used an accelerated method of depreciation).

The total expenses reported over the entire life of the lease will be the same, however, regardless of which method is used to record the lease transaction. If it is treated as an operating lease, the total expense will be $36,000 (36 payments of $1,000 each). If it is treated as a finance lease, the total expenses will also be $36,000 (consisting of $30,107.51 in depreciation and $5,892.49 in interest expense). The difference, then, is in the pattern of expense recognition over the life of the lease. Operating leases show the same amount of expense each period, while finance leases show more expense in the early periods (when interest charges, and perhaps depreciation, are high) and less expense in later periods.

Although no asset or liability is recorded under operating leases, companies with significant operating leases have to disclose their commitments to pay for these leases—as discussed in Chapter 9. Companies are required to disclose the future lease payments to be made in total and for each of the next five years. Finance lease obligations also require similar disclosures. The future payment obligations associated with leases would typically be shown in a note that relates either to long-term debt or to commitments.

accounting in the news

Lease Fights Prevent Hamilton Hockey Score

Although lease arrangements have several benefits for the lessee, the binding terms of the contract can be problematic—even in the hard-hitting world of the National Hockey League.

One of the main reasons cited for the failure of the 2007 bid by Research In Motion founder, Jim Balsillie, to bring the Nashville Predators to Hamilton, Ontario, was disputes regarding the Predators' arena lease. The NHL said the lease precluded approval of relocation and the league would only consider relocation as part of a sale in cases where a lease was expiring or could be broken unilaterally.

Even when the team filed for bankruptcy in May 2009, the City of Glendale, Arizona—which was then the home to the Predators franchise—objected to any relocation. Balsillie tendered an offer to buy the team after it filed for bankruptcy, still with the goal of moving it to Hamilton, where his experience with leases has been more positive. Indeed, the City of Hamilton voted unanimously to approve a 20-year arena lease agreement with Balsillie for the renovation and use of Copps Coliseum—but only if he eventually succeeds in bringing the hockey team there.

Sources: David Naylor, "Never in Hamilton," *Globe and Mail*, July 14, 2007; Sean Fitz-Gerald, "Balsillie Gets Copps Coliseum Lease as Battle Looms, *National Post*, May 13, 2009.

Like many airlines, **WestJet Airlines Ltd.** leases some of its aircraft, as well as other assets such as land, buildings, and equipment. In WestJet's financial statements, the required disclosures are found in Note 12 for the operating leases and Note 8 for the finance (capital) leases. Excerpts from these notes are presented in Exhibit 10-6.

Notice that the overwhelming majority of WestJet's leases are operating leases rather than finance or capital leases. In fact, the total amount of payments due under its operating leases ($1,613,350 thousand CAD) is over 200 times the total due under its capital leases ($6,822 thousand).

> ### IFRS INSIGHTS
>
> The International Accounting Standards Board has been considering changes to lease accounting that, if adopted as IFRS, could have a significant impact on how leases are accounted for. It seems quite likely that a different accounting model will be adopted, and that the present requirements and practices in accounting for leasing arrangements will no longer apply.

PENSIONS

Pensions are agreements between employers and employees that provide the latter with benefits (income) upon retirement. To the extent that the company is obliged to make payments under these agreements, their costs should be recorded in the years when the company receives the benefits from the work of its employees. In other words,

EXHIBIT 10-6   **WESTJET AIRLINES INC. 2009 ANNUAL REPORT**

annual report

Excerpts from the Notes to the Financial Statements

8. Obligations under capital leases

The Corporation has entered into capital leases relating to a fuel storage facility and ground handling equipment. The obligations are as follows:

2010	$ 943
2011	282
2012	245
2013	245
2014	245
2015 and thereafter	4,862
Total minimum lease payments	$ 6,822
Less weighted average imputed interest at 5.28%	(2,720)
Net minimum lease payments	4,102
Less current portion of obligations under capital leases	(744)
Obligations under capital leases	$ 3,358

12. Commitments and contingencies (continued)

(b) Operating leases and commitments

The Corporation has entered into operating leases and commitments for aircraft, land, buildings, equipment, computer hardware, software licences and satellite programming. As at December 31, 2009, the future payments in Canadian dollars, and when applicable the US-dollar equivalents, under operating leases and commitments are as follows:

	USD	CAD
2010	$ 159,106	$ 189,892
2011	182,562	205,904
2012	187,896	209,340
2013	191,963	210,489
2014	187,498	202,875
2015 and thereafter	520,002	594,850
	$ 1,429,027	$ 1,613,350

As at December 31, 2009, the Corporation is committed to lease an additional six 737-700 aircraft and five 737-800 aircraft for terms ranging between eight and 10 years in US dollars. These aircraft have been included in the above totals.

The Corporation signed a six-year agreement with Bell ExpressVu to provide satellite programming. The agreement commenced in 2004 and can be renewed for an additional four years. During 2009, the Corporation amended its agreement with LiveTV to install, maintain and operate live satellite television on all of the Corporation's aircraft for a term of 10 years. The minimum commitment amounts associated with these agreements have been included in the table totals above.

In 2008, the Corporation signed an agreement with Sabre Airline Solutions (Sabre) to provide the Corporation with a licence to access and use Sabre's reservation system, SabreSonic for a term of eight years. The minimum contract amounts associated with the reservation system have been included in the table totals above.

to be in accordance with the matching principle, pension costs should be recognized when the employees *earn* their pensions, not when they *receive* them. Two kinds of pension plans are commonly used by employers: defined contribution plans and defined benefit plans.

Defined Contribution Pension Plans

In a **defined contribution pension plan**, the employer agrees to make a specified (or defined) contribution to a retirement fund for the employees. The amount is usually set as a percentage of the employees' salaries. Employees sometimes make their own contributions to the same fund, to add to the amounts invested. The amount of the pension benefits that will be paid to the employees in their retirement depends on how well the investments in the retirement fund perform. The employer satisfies its obligation to the employees when it makes the specified payments into the fund. The fund is usually managed by a **trustee** (someone outside the company's employ and control), and the assets are legally separated from the company's other assets, which means they are not reported on the company's statement of financial position.

The accounting for defined contribution funds is straightforward. The company accrues the amount of its obligation to the pension fund, and then records a payment. Because the liability is settled, no other recognition is necessary in the financial statements. The entries to recognize the pension expense and the related payment are as follows:

LEARNING OBJECTIVE 7

Explain the distinguishing features of defined-contribution pension plans and defined-benefit pension plans.

Pension expense (SE)	XXX	
Pension obligation (L)		XXX
Pension obligation (L)	XXX	
Cash (A)		XXX

Companies generally make cash payments that coincide with the accruals, because they cannot deduct the cost for tax purposes if the cash payment is not made. Therefore, with a defined contribution pension plan there is usually no liability balance to report.

Defined Benefit Pension Plans

A **defined benefit pension plan** is more complex. It guarantees to pay the employees a certain amount of money during each year of their retirement. The formula used to calculate how much will be paid usually takes into consideration how long an employee has worked for the company as well as the highest salary (or an average of the highest salaries) that the employee earned while working for the company. For example, a plan might specify that the employee will receive 2% of the average of the highest three years of salaries, multiplied by the number of years that the employee worked for the company. If the employee worked for the company for 30 years and had an average salary of $60,000 for the highest three years, the annual pension benefit would be $36,000 per year (2% × $60,000 × 30 years).

Of course, employees may leave the company at some point prior to their retirement. If the pension benefits belong to employees only as long as they work there, then there may be no obligation on the company's part to pay out pension benefits. In most plans, however, there is a provision for **vesting** the benefits. Benefits that are vested belong to the employees, even if they leave the company.

Because the payments to retired employees will occur many years in the future, pensions represent an estimated future obligation. In estimating the cost of the future obligation today (i.e., the liability's present value), several estimations and projections must be made. These include the length of time the employee will work for the company, the age at which the employee will retire, the employee's average salary during the highest salary years, and the number of years the employee will live after retiring. All these factors will affect the amount and timing of the future cash flows (pension payments). For companies with many employees, the total obligation of the pension plan usually has to be estimated based on the characteristics of the average employee rather than of particular employees. In addition, the company must choose an appropriate interest rate to use for calculating the present value of the future pension payments.

Each year, as employees work for the company, they earn pension benefits that oblige the company to make cash payments at some point in the future. Calculating the present value of the future pension obligation generally requires the services of an **actuary**. The actuary is trained in the use of statistical procedures to make the types of estimates required for pension calculations.

The accounting entries for defined benefit pension plans are essentially the same as the preceding entry for defined contribution plans. The company must accrue the expense and the related obligation to provide pension benefits. The amounts are difficult to estimate in the case of defined benefit plans, but the concept is the same as for defined contribution plans. The entry made to recognize the pension expense is called the **accrual entry**. Setting aside cash to pay for these future benefits is done by making a cash entry, which is sometimes called the **funding entry**. Many employee pension plan agreements have clauses that require the company to fund the pension obligation (i.e., to set aside funds to cover the liability). However, because of the uncertainties associated with the liability amounts, some companies have been reluctant to fully fund their pension obligations.

There is no accounting requirement that the amount expensed be the same as the amount funded. Therefore, the amount of pension expense that is recognized often differs from the amount of cash that is transferred to the trustee in a particular period. A net pension obligation will result if more is expensed than funded, or a net pension asset will exist if the funding is larger than the amount expensed. The calculation of the pension expense to be recorded each period involves many complex factors, and is beyond the scope of this book.

Pension funds are described as **overfunded** if the value of the pension fund assets held by the trustee exceeds the present value of the future pension obligations. In **underfunded** pension plans, the value of the pension fund assets is less than the present value of the future pension obligations. Pension plans in which the fund assets equal the present value of the future obligations are called **fully funded**. The pension fund itself is usually handled by a trustee, and contributions to the fund cannot be returned to the employer except under extraordinary circumstances. To provide sufficient funds to pay the pension benefits, the trustee invests the cash that is transferred to the fund. The trustee then pays benefits to the retired employees out of the pension fund assets.

Pension Plan Disclosures

In Canada, for a defined contribution pension plan, the contribution amounts for the period must be disclosed. For a defined benefit plan, the required disclosures are very extensive. Rather than list all the requirements, we will look at the disclosures provided

accounting in the news

Miners Go on Strike over Changes to Pension Plan

Defined benefit versus defined contribution pension plans were at the heart of the longest nickel strike in Canadian history, in Sudbury and Port Colborne, Ontario. The conflict between the mining company Vale and the United Steelworkers union lasted just under a year, and ended only after both sides made concessions. Among the employees' concessions was acceptance of a change to their pension plan. Under the new labour agreement, new employees will join a defined contribution plan, which is funded by a percentage of the employees' salaries, instead of a defined benefit pension plan, which is funded by the company rather than workers' contributions.

The company's pension plan deficit of about $730 million at the end of 2008 was one of the reasons the giant Brazilian mining company needed to make this change. Many defined benefit plans faced shortfalls when the recession hit, then took an additional beating as financial markets collapsed. These shortfalls can seriously affect a company's finances, since the company is required to put more cash into the plan to keep it solvent.

Sources: "Vale Pension Plan Short $729 million," Thestar.com, February 1, 2010; Peter Koven, "Vale Workers Ratify New Contract," *Financial Post*, July 9, 2010.

by West Fraser Timber Co. Ltd. in Exhibit 10-7. West Fraser Timber has both defined benefit and defined contribution pension plans, as well as some health care and life insurance benefits that it provides to its retired employees.

The note discloses that, for its defined benefit pension plans, West Fraser Timber's pension expense for 2009 was $33.4 million and its funding contributions were $92.6 million. For its defined contribution pension plans, both its pension expense and its funding contributions for 2009 were $1.8 million. Also, the latter part of the note discloses some of the key estimates that have been made regarding the pension plans. For example, West Fraser Timber assumed that its pension plan investments would earn an average annual rate of return of 7%, and that employees' compensation would increase at an average annual rate of 3.5%.

Perhaps the most important thing to note about pensions is that, for defined benefit plans, the amount of any pension plan asset or liability that appears on the company's

WEST FRASER TIMBER CO. LTD. 2009 ANNUAL REPORT

 EXHIBIT 10-7

Excerpts from the Notes to the Financial Statements

annual report

11. Employee future benefits

The Company maintains defined benefit and defined contribution pension plans covering a majority of its employees. The defined benefit plans provide pension benefits based either on length of service or on earnings and length of service. The total pension expense for the defined benefit plans is $33.4 million (2008 — $24.1 million) with total funding contributions of $92.6 million (2008 — $40.6 million). The Company's total funding contributions required for 2010 are expected to be approximately $22.0 million. The Company also provides group life insurance, medical and extended health benefits to certain employee groups for which it contributed $2.1 million (2008 — $1.7 million).

EXHIBIT 10-7

annual report

WEST FRASER TIMBER CO. LTD. 2009 ANNUAL REPORT (cont'd)

Excerpts from the Notes to the Financial Statements

(Figures are in millions of Canadian dollars, except where indicated)

The total pension expense and funding contributions for the defined contribution pension plans is $1.8 million (2008 — $1.7 million).

The status of the defined benefit pension plans and other benefit plans, in aggregate, is as follows:

	Pension plans		Other benefit plans	
	2009	2008	2009	2008
Expense				
Current service cost	$ 22.5	$ 32.6	$ 0.6	$ 1.1
Interest cost on earned benefit obligations	49.6	46.8	3.3	3.1
Actual (gain) loss on plan assets	(87.3)	206.5	—	—
Actual actuarial loss (gain) on benefit obligations	53.6	(133.3)	17.3	(11.8)
Other	(0.3)	1.1	—	—
Expense before adjustments	38.1	153.7	21.2	(7.6)
Difference between expected return and actual return on plan assets	44.2	(263.0)	—	—
Difference between net actuarial gain or loss recognized and actual gain or loss on benefit obligations	(49.2)	133.1	(17.9)	11.8
Difference in other	0.3	0.3	0.5	0.5
Net expense	$ 33.4	$ 24.1	$ 3.8	$ 4.7
Accrued benefit obligations				
Projected benefit obligations — opening	$ 701.2	$ 792.4	$ 44.2	$ 53.5
Current service cost	22.5	32.6	0.6	1.1
Interest cost	49.6	46.8	3.3	3.1
Benefits paid	(43.0)	(41.7)	(2.1)	(1.7)
Actuarial loss (gain)	53.6	(133.3)	17.3	(11.8)
Plan transfers, improvements and other	(1.0)	4.4	(21.1)	—
Projected benefit obligations — ending	$ 782.9	$ 701.2	$ 42.2	$ 44.2
Plan assets				
Fair value — opening	$ 643.1	$ 844.5	$ —	$ —
Actual gain (loss) on plan assets	87.3	(206.5)	—	—
Contributions	59.6	45.1	2.1	1.7
Benefits paid	(43.0)	(41.7)	(2.1)	(1.7)
Plan transfers, improvements and other	(0.4)	1.7	—	—
Fair value — ending	$ 746.6	$ 643.1	$ —	$ —
Funded status of the plans				
Surplus (deficit) — registered plans	$ (45.6)	$ (63.9)	$ (42.2)	$ (44.2)
— supplemental plans	9.3	5.8	—	—
	(36.3)	(58.1)	(42.2)	(44.2)
Contributions after measurement date	39.5	6.4	—	—
	3.2	(51.7)	(42.2)	(44.2)
Unamortized net actuarial loss (gain)	115.5	110.6	6.5	(11.4)
Unamortized past service costs	5.7	6.4	(21.1)	—
Unamortized net transitional amount	(2.0)	(2.1)	1.4	1.9
Net accrued benefit asset (liability)	$ 122.4	$ 63.2	$ (55.4)	$ (53.7)
Represented by				
Deferred pension costs	$ 132.7	$ 78.1	$ —	$ —
Post-retirement obligations (note 7)	(10.3)	(14.9)	(55.4)	(53.7)
	$ 122.4	$ 63.2	$ (55.4)	$ (53.7)

WEST FRASER TIMBER CO. LTD. 2009 ANNUAL REPORT (cont'd)

EXHIBIT 10-7

annual report

Excerpts from the Notes to the Financial Statements

The significant actuarial assumptions used are as follows:

	Pension plans		Other benefit plans	
	2009	2008	2009	2008
To determine benefit obligations at end of year				
Discount rate	6.50%	7.25%	6.50%	7.25%
Expected rate of return on plan assets	7.00%	7.00%	n/a	n/a
Rate of increase in future compensation	3.50%	3.50%	n/a	n/a
To determine benefit expense for the year				
Discount rate	7.25%	5.75%	7.25%	5.75%
Expected rate of return on plan assets	7.00%	7.00%	n/a	n/a
Rate of increase in future compensation	3.50%	3.50%	n/a	n/a

statement of financial position does not represent the plan's funding status. Because of the complex procedures involved in accounting for pension plans (which are beyond the scope of an introductory text), a company might report a net pension plan asset on its statement of financial position, even though its pension plan is *underfunded*. Conversely, a company might report a net pension plan *liability* on its statement of financial position, even though its pension plan is *overfunded*. To determine whether a company's pension plan is underfunded, overfunded, or fully funded, users must read the notes to the financial statements.

For example, Exhibit 10-7 shows the following for West Fraser Timber's defined benefit pension plans at the end of 2009 (in millions):

Projected benefit obligation (the estimated amount of the pension liability)	$782.9
Fair value of the plan assets (held by the trustee, to pay pension benefits)	$746.6
Funded status—plan deficit (the amount by which the plan is underfunded)	($ 36.3)

Despite the fact that its pension plans were underfunded by $36.3 million—which implies that the company has a *liability* for this amount—Exhibit 10-7 shows that a net pension plan asset of $122.4 million was recorded in West Fraser Timber's accounts. On its balance sheet (presented in Exhibit 10-8), this is split between the non-current asset *deferred pension costs* of $132.7 million, and a non-current liability *post-retirement obligations* of $10.3 million (which is included in "Other liabilities"). This illustrates the importance of reading the notes to financial statements.

LEARNING OBJECTIVE 8

Outline the accounting issues in the reporting of pension plan liabilities.

IFRS INSIGHTS

The International Accounting Standards Board has proposed changes to pension accounting that, if adopted as IFRS, could have a significant impact on how pensions are accounted for. In particular, they could greatly reduce or eliminate the smoothing that has commonly occurred in the past because companies were allowed to recognize the effects of changes in the values of their pension plan assets and/or pension benefit obligations gradually, over extended periods of time.

Consolidated Balance Sheets

As at December 31, 2009 and 2008

(in millions of Canadian dollars)	2009	2008
Assets		
Current assets		
Cash and short-term investments	$ 12.0	$ 20.2
Accounts receivable (note 17)	200.6	253.0
Income taxes receivable	67.6	26.8
Inventories (note 3)	407.7	511.6
Prepaid expenses	15.8	29.0
	703.7	840.6
Property, plant, equipment and timber (note 4)	1,624.1	2,040.8
Deferred pension costs (note 11)	132.7	78.1
Goodwill	263.7	263.7
Other assets (note 5)	88.9	101.2
Future income taxes (note 14)	—	87.2
	$ 2,813.1	$ 3,411.6
Liabilities		
Current liabilities		
Cheques issued in excess of funds on deposit	$ 21.8	$ 16.5
Operating loans (note 6)	78.7	29.7
Accounts payable and accrued liabilities	252.6	241.4
Current portion of asset retirement obligations (note 7)	41.5	44.1
Current portion of long-term debt (note 6)	100.3	150.3
	494.9	482.0
Long-term debt (note 6)	315.9	465.3
Other liabilities (note 7)	166.9	167.5
Future income taxes (note 14)	217.2	266.8
	1,194.9	1,381.6
Shareholders' Equity		
Share capital (note 8)	599.7	599.4
Accumulated other comprehensive earnings	(59.8)	1.7
Retained earnings	1,078.3	1,428.9
	1,618.2	2,030.0
	$ 2,813.1	$ 3,411.6

OTHER POST-EMPLOYMENT BENEFITS

As you just saw with West Fraser Timber, employers sometimes offer other types of **post-employment benefits** to their retirees, in addition to pensions. Health care benefits and life insurance are two of the most commonly offered benefits. Until recently, the obligation to provide these benefits was, for the most part, ignored in the financial statements of Canadian companies. Because of publicly funded health care in Canada, corporate obligations and exposure (risk) were limited. Therefore, the costs of providing these benefits were recorded on a pay-as-you-go basis; that is, the costs were expensed as the cash was paid out to the insurance companies that provide the benefits. However, companies are now required to account for these post-employment items in much the same way as they account for pensions.

LEARNING OBJECTIVE 9

Describe other post-employment benefits and explain how they are treated in Canada.

DEFERRED INCOME TAXES

Deferred income taxes (also known as future income taxes) arise because companies use two different systems for calculating their taxes. They use accounting standards for revenues and expenses to determine income tax *expense* on their statement of earnings, and they use Canada Revenue Agency (CRA) calculations of revenues and expenses to determine their income tax *payable* (that is, the amount of tax that must actually be paid to the government). In other words, companies prepare their financial statements according to the requirements of generally accepted accounting principles, but they prepare their income tax returns (which determine the amount of tax they have to pay each year) according to the requirements of the *Income Tax Act* and regulations. Differences between these two sets of calculations result in **deferred income tax assets and liabilities**.

For example, in Chapter 8 we discussed deferred income taxes because companies can use any one of several depreciation methods for accounting purposes but must use capital cost allowances (CCA) for tax purposes. The use of different methods for preparing financial statements and tax returns results in balances in companies' accounting records that are different from the balances in their tax records. These different balances result in deferred income tax effects.

Another area that creates differences between what is reported in the accounting system and what is reported on a company's tax return is warranty costs, which we discussed in Chapter 9. For accounting purposes, the warranty expense deducted from income includes an estimate of future warranty costs, based on the revenue that was recognized in the current period. For tax purposes, however, only the actual amount that the company paid to repair items under warranty during the current period is allowed as a tax deduction.

There are also many other differences between accounting standards and tax regulations that give rise to deferred income taxes.

In Canada, the **liability method** is used to measure deferred income taxes. This method tries to measure the liability that will be incurred to pay more tax in the future, or the benefit that will be derived from paying less tax in the future, that is created by the differences between accounting calculations and tax calculations. Once the tax that is currently owed to the CRA and the deferred income tax have been calculated, the tax expense equals these two items combined (i.e., the income tax expense equals the income tax currently payable plus or minus the deferred income tax amount).

LEARNING OBJECTIVE 10

Explain why deferred/future income taxes exist, and describe how they are reported.

LEARNING OBJECTIVE 11

Record deferred/future income taxes in simple situations.

To illustrate the calculation of deferred income taxes, we will use the data in Exhibit 10-9 for a company that sells products with a three-year warranty. For simplicity, we will assume that the warranty is the only source of difference between the company's accounting records and its tax records.

For accounting purposes, the company estimates the probable costs associated with the warranty and records the total amount as warranty expense in the year of the sale, as well as a liability (warranty obligation). For tax purposes, however, the CRA does not permit a company to deduct the *estimated* warranty expense in calculating its taxable income; the company can only claim a tax deduction for the actual costs that it incurs each year to settle claims under the warranty.

EXHIBIT 10-9

INCOME TAX DATA

Income before tax and warranty expense (same in years 1, 2, and 3)		$10,000
Estimated warranty expense (for accounting purposes)	Year 1 $500	
Actual warranty costs incurred (income tax deductions):	Year 1 $125	
	Year 2 $175	
	Year 3 $200	
Tax rate (same in years 1, 2, and 3)		40%

The liability method requires a calculation of the income tax that will be payable in the future, based on the **temporary differences** (the differences between the accounting records and the tax records) that exist in the current period. In the case of warranties, the company's accounting balances include a warranty liability which represents amounts that will be tax deductions in future periods, when the warranty claims will be paid and deducted on the company's tax returns. This creates a deferred (or future) income tax asset, because fewer taxes will be paid in the future when these amounts are deducted on its tax returns. Exhibit 10-10 illustrates how this occurs.

In part "b" of Exhibit 10-10, for year 1 there is an initial $500 warranty obligation in the accounting records less the actual warranty costs of $125 in the tax records, resulting in a $375 temporary difference (the warranty obligation balance) that is carried forward to year 2. Next, still in year 1, the amount of the reduction in future taxes is calculated. This is done by taking the ending warranty obligation balance (the temporary difference) and multiplying it by the company's tax rate. The $375 balance from year 1 is multiplied by the company's tax rate of 40%, and the result indicates that in future years the company's taxes payable will be reduced by $150 as actual warranty costs are claimed as tax deductions. This amount is then recorded as a deferred income tax asset, to keep a record of the future tax benefits (savings).

In year 2 when this calculation is repeated (using the warranty liability balance carried over from year 1 and the actual warranty costs of year 2), the balance in the deferred income tax asset account is reduced to the amount of tax deductions that remain to be claimed in year 3. The process is then repeated in year 3, until, in our example, the warranty obligation balance has been reduced to zero. At this point, the balance in the deferred income tax account is also zero.

Part "c" of Exhibit 10-10 shows the last step in the income tax calculations, which is to calculate the company's income tax expense. This is done by subtracting the change in the balance of the deferred income tax account (in part "b") from the amount of actual taxes payable to the CRA (in part "a"). Thus, for year 1, we subtract $150 from the $3,950 of income tax payable to arrive at an income tax expense of $3,800 for the year. (An important distinction must be noted here: income tax expense is not the same as

EXHIBIT 10-10

INCOME TAX CALCULATIONS

	Year 1	Year 2	Year 3
a. Calculation of income tax currently payable:			
Income before warranty costs and income tax	$ 10,000	$ 10,000	$ 10,000
Deduct: Actual warranty costs incurred	125	175	200
Taxable income	9,875	9,825	9,800
Tax rate	40%	40%	40%
Tax payable (taxable income × tax rate)	$ 3,950	$ 3,930	$ 3,920
b. Calculation of deferred (or future) income tax:			
Beginning balance in warranty obligation	$ 500	$ 375	$ 200
Deduct: Actual warranty costs incurred	125	175	200
Ending balance in warranty obligation	375	200	0
Tax rate	40%	40%	40%
Deferred tax asset (ending warranty obligation × tax rate)	$ 150	$ 80	$ 0
Increase (decrease) in deferred income tax asset	$ 150	$ (70)	$ (80)
c. Calculation of income tax expense:			
Credit to income tax payable, from part a.	$ (3,950)	$ (3,930)	$ (3,920)
Debit (credit) to deferred tax asset, from part b.	150	(70)	(80)
Debit to income tax expense	$ 3,800	$ 4,000	$ 4,000

income tax payable. Income tax payable is the amount of money that the company currently has to pay to the CRA. Income tax expense includes both the amount of tax that is currently payable and the change in the amount of tax that is deferred to the future.)

The journal entries to record the income taxes calculated in Exhibit 10-10 are as follows:

Year 1	Income tax expense	3,800	
	Deferred income tax	150	
	Income tax payable		3,950
Year 2	Income tax expense	4,000	
	Deferred income tax		70
	Income tax payable		3,930
Year 3	Income tax expense	4,000	
	Deferred income tax		80
	Income tax payable		3,920

HELPFUL HINT

Note that the income tax currently payable and the change in the deferred income tax are calculated first; then the tax expense is simply the amount that will make the journal entry balance.

It should be noted that, to keep the example simple, we created a single warranty obligation in year 1 and then traced it through years 2 and 3. In reality, there would be more sales of products with warranty provisions in years 2 and 3. These new sales would create new warranty obligations, and additional deferred taxes. Dealing with multiple years makes the calculations significantly more complex, but the concept remains the same. Warranty obligations are recognized for accounting purposes in the year of the sale and actual costs are deducted for tax purposes as the obligations are settled. As a result, a deferred tax asset is created in the year of the sale and eliminated over the next two years (because the warranty in our example is for three years).

In Chapter 8, there is an example of deferred income taxes arising from the use of depreciation for accounting purposes versus CCA for tax purposes. You should review the illustration in Exhibit 8-7 and the related discussion on pages 529–530.

Some users misunderstand deferred income taxes, especially if there is a credit balance and it is included with the long-term liabilities. They mistakenly assume that these deferred income taxes represent amounts that are currently owed by the company and should be paid. This assumption is incorrect, because the amount that is currently owed is shown elsewhere—as taxes payable, under current liabilities. Deferred income tax credits on the statement of financial position represent amounts that *will be owed in the future* as a result of current operations. If, as illustrated in Chapter 8, we take the example of deferred income taxes arising because CCA is used for tax purposes while straight-line depreciation is used for accounting purposes, in the early part of an asset's life the tax deduction (CCA) will be larger than the accounting expense (depreciation). This means that the company will pay less tax in the early part of the asset's life. However, in the latter part of the asset's life the CCA deductions will be smaller, which means that the company will have to pay more tax at that time. This is what a credit balance in deferred income taxes represents.

Previously, deferred or future income taxes could appear in various parts of the statement of financial position: as current assets, current liabilities, non-current assets, or non-current liabilities. However, under IFRS they must be classified as non-current. When they have a debit balance, they are reported as non-current assets; more commonly they have a credit balance and are reported as non-current liabilities.

Referring back to Exhibit 10-8 on page 660, you will see that **West Fraser Timber** has future (deferred) income taxes as an account title in two places on its balance sheet. It reports a future tax liability for both 2008 and 2009 ($266.8 and $217.2 million, respectively) grouped with long-term liabilities, and in 2008 it also reports future income taxes of $87.2 million as a non-current asset.

As Exhibit 10-8 illustrates, deferred or future income taxes can be very significant amounts on the statement of financial position. In West Fraser Timber's case, its liability for future income taxes was almost 20 percent of its total liabilities. It is therefore important that users understand what these deferred or future income taxes are. Deferred income tax liabilities represent amounts related to past operations that are expected to become payable in the future. Deferred income tax assets, on the other hand, represent expected future benefits in the form of lower income taxes to be paid in the future, as a result of higher taxes having been paid in the past.

INTERNATIONAL PERSPECTIVES

There are many differences in accounting for income taxes in various parts of the world. In some countries, accounting practices follow the income tax requirements. In these cases, since there are no differences between accounting balances and tax amounts, no deferred income taxes arise. In many other countries, income tax expense is recorded based on a company's taxable income rather than its accounting income. Therefore, no deferred income taxes arise in these cases, either.

OTHER INCOME TAX DISCLOSURES

A number of additional disclosures related to income taxes are usually included either on the financial statements or in the accompanying notes. Although most of these are beyond the scope of an introductory text, we will examine two of the main types.

One of the key tax disclosures is a breakdown of the tax expense (or provision for income taxes) into the amount that is currently payable and the amount that is deferred to the future. To illustrate this, a portion of the consolidated statement of earnings for West Fraser Timber is reproduced in Exhibit 10-11.

WEST FRASER TIMBER CO. LTD. 2009 ANNUAL REPORT

EXHIBIT 10-11

annual report

Excerpts from the Consolidated Statement of Earnings and Comprehensive Earnings

For the years ended December 31, 2009 and 2008

(in millions of Canadian dollars, except earnings per share)	2009	2008
Earnings before income taxes	$ (372.5)	$ (220.4)
Recovery of (provision for) income taxes (note 14)		
Current	57.7	18.8
Future	(26.0)	64.5
	31.7	83.3
Earnings	$ (340.8)	$ (137.1)

Notice that, of West Fraser Timber's total tax expense of $83.3 million for 2008, $18.8 million was to be paid currently and the remaining $64.5 million was expected to become payable in future periods. For 2009, its total tax expense of $31.7 million consisted of $57.7 million that was to be paid currently and an offsetting $26.0 million that was expected to be recovered in future periods. In other words, although West Fraser Timber calculated that its income tax expense for 2009 was $31.7 million, under the tax regulations it was required to make a tax payment of $57.7 million. However, its income taxes that will be payable in future periods are expected to be reduced by $26.0 million.

Another key tax disclosure in the notes is the summary of the temporary differences that have created the deferred income tax amounts. This is illustrated in Exhibit 10-12, which presents Note 14 to West Fraser Timber's financial statements.

Notice that the biggest single source of temporary differences (and hence future taxes) for West Fraser Timber is, as one would expect, differences between the depreciation on its property, plant, equipment and timber, for accounting purposes, and its capital cost allowance claims on these assets, for income tax purposes. Due to the resulting differences between the net book values of these assets in the company's accounts and their undepreciated capital costs in its tax records, West Fraser Timber expects that it will have to pay additional income taxes of $234.7 million in the future. However, there are various other temporary differences listed in the note that partially offset this; consequently, the company reports a net future income tax liability of $217.2 million on its balance sheet.

IFRS VERSUS ASPE

Under current Canadian accounting standards for private enterprises (ASPE), businesses that are privately held are not required to record deferred income taxes; they have the option of simply recording income tax expense equal to the amount of income tax payable each period.

EXHIBIT 10-12

annual report

WEST FRASER TIMBER CO. LTD. 2009 ANNUAL REPORT

Excerpt from Note 14 to the Financial Statements

14. Income taxes

The effective tax rate is different from the statutory tax rates as follows:

	Amount	2009 %	Amount	2008 %
Income tax recovery at statutory rates	$ 111.7	30.0	$ 68.3	31.0
Non-taxable amounts	8.1	2.2	(8.7)	(3.9)
Rate differentials between jurisdictions and on specified activities	11.7	3.2	12.9	5.9
Rate differential on loss carry-backs	8.2	2.2	3.7	1.7
Reduction in statutory income tax rates	4.7	1.2	6.4	2.9
Valuation allowance	(113.8)	(30.6)	—	—
Other	1.1	0.3	0.7	0.2
	$ 31.7	8.5	$ 83.3	37.8

The components of future income taxes are as follows:

	2009	2008
Property, plant, equipment and timber	$ (234.7)	$ (331.2)
Asset retirement obligations	27.6	28.7
Post-retirement obligations	19.4	19.9
Loss carry-forwards	1.6	116.4
Other	(31.1)	(13.4)
	$ (217.2)	$ (179.6)

Presented as follows:

	2009	2008
Future income tax asset	$ —	$ 87.2
Future income tax liability	(217.2)	(266.8)
	$ (217.2)	$ (179.6)

The Company has loss carryforwards not recognized for accounting purposes which expire in various amounts in the years 2021 to 2029.

STATEMENT ANALYSIS CONSIDERATIONS

Two ratios that are commonly used to evaluate a company's ability to repay its obligations are the *debt to total assets* ratio and the *times interest earned* ratio. Exhibit 10-13 presents the statement of earnings and balance sheet of WestJet Airlines Inc., which we will use to demonstrate how these two ratios can provide insights into the financial structure and risk of a company.

The formula for the **debt to total assets ratio** is simply:

$$\frac{\text{Total liabilities}}{\text{Total assets}}$$

EXHIBIT 10-13A

annual report

WESTJET AIRLINES LTD. 2009 ANNUAL REPORT

CONSOLIDATED STATEMENT
OF EARNINGS

For the years ended December 31
(Stated in thousands of Canadian dollars, except per share amounts)

	2009	2008
		Restated – see note 2
Revenues:		
Guest revenues	$ 2,067,860	$ 2,301,301
Charter and other revenues	213,260	248,205
	2,281,120	2,549,506
Expenses:		
Aircraft fuel	570,569	803,293
Airport operations	352,333	342,922
Flight operations and navigational charges	298,762	280,920
Marketing, general and administration	208,316	211,979
Sales and distribution	172,326	170,693
Depreciation and amortization	141,303	136,485
Inflight	112,054	105,849
Aircraft leasing	103,954	86,050
Maintenance	96,272	85,093
Employee profit share	14,675	33,435
	2,070,564	2,256,719
Earnings from operations	210,556	292,787
Non-operating income (expense):		
Interest income	5,601	25,485
Interest expense	(67,706)	(76,078)
Gain (loss) on foreign exchange	(12,306)	30,587
Loss on disposal of property and equipment	(1,177)	(701)
Gain (loss) on derivatives (note 13(b))	1,828	(17,331)
	(73,760)	(38,038)
Earnings before income taxes	136,796	254,749
Income tax expense: (note 9)		
Current	2,690	2,549
Future	35,928	73,694
	38,618	76,243
Net earnings	$ 98,178	$ 178,506
Earnings per share: (note 10(c))		
Basic	$ 0.74	$ 1.39
Diluted	$ 0.74	$ 1.37

The accompanying notes are an integral part of the consolidated financial statements.

EXHIBIT 10-13B

annual report

WESTJET AIRLINES LTD. 2009 ANNUAL REPORT

CONSOLIDATED
BALANCE SHEET

As at December 31
(Stated in thousands of Canadian dollars)

	2009	2008
		Restated – see note 2
Assets		
Current assets:		
Cash and cash equivalents (note 4)	$ 1,005,181	$ 820,214
Accounts receivable	27,654	16,837
Future income tax (note 9)	2,560	8,459
Prepaid expenses, deposits and other (note 14(a))	56,239	53,283
Inventory	26,048	17,054
	1,117,682	915,847
Property and equipment (note 5)	2,307,566	2,269,790
Intangible assets (note 6)	14,087	12,060
Other assets (note 14(a))	54,367	71,005
	$ 3,493,702	$ 3,268,702
Liabilities and shareholders' equity		
Current liabilities:		
Accounts payable and accrued liabilities	$ 231,401	$ 249,354
Advance ticket sales	286,361	251,354
Non-refundable guest credits	64,506	73,020
Current portion of long-term debt (note 7)	171,223	165,721
Current portion of obligations under capital leases (note 8)	744	395
	754,235	739,844
Long-term debt (note 7)	1,048,554	1,186,182
Obligations under capital leases (note 8)	3,358	713
Other liabilities (note 14(a))	19,628	24,233
Future income taxes (note 9)	278,999	241,740
	2,104,774	2,192,712
Shareholders' equity:		
Share capital (note 10(b))	633,075	452,885
Contributed surplus	71,503	60,193
Accumulated other comprehensive loss (note 14(c))	(14,852)	(38,112)
Retained earnings	699,202	601,024
	1,388,928	1,075,990
Commitments and contingencies (note 12)		
	$ 3,493,702	$ 3,268,702

The accompanying notes are an integral part of the consolidated financial statements.
On behalf of the Board:

Sean Durfy, Director

Hugh Bolton, Director

The 2009 and 2008 debt to total assets ratios for WestJet are as follows:

2009	2008
$\dfrac{\$2,104,774}{\$3,493,702} = 60.2\%$	$\dfrac{\$2,192,712}{\$3,268,702} = 67.1\%$

These calculations reveal that in 2008, 67.1% of WestJet's assets were financed through debt. The ratio dropped a little in 2009, to 60.2%. From the company's balance sheet, we can see that there was a slight increase in WestJet's current liabilities but a greater decrease in its non-current liabilities, resulting in a reduction of approximately $88 million in its overall debt; at the same time, its assets increased by $225 million. In short, WestJet was able to increase its assets without increasing its debt, which reduces the financial risk of the company. It would be important to continue to follow this ratio before drawing conclusions about any major shifts in the company's financing strategy.

The **times interest earned ratio** provides a measure of the company's ability to cover its interest expense out of its earnings, by calculating how many times the earnings that are available to cover the interest exceed the interest itself. It is normally calculated as follows:

$$\frac{\text{Earnings before interest and tax}}{\text{Interest}} = \frac{\text{Net earnings} + \text{Interest} + \text{Tax}}{\text{Interest}}$$

The specific calculation required to determine the earnings available to cover the interest charges for a particular company will depend on the format of its statement of earnings. WestJet discloses earnings from operations, an amount that is before interest and taxes (as well as before any other non-operating revenues, expenses, gains, and losses), so in this case it is not necessary to perform a calculation to get the earnings available to cover the interest. The 2009 and 2008 times interest earned ratios for WestJet are as follows:

2009	2008
$\dfrac{\$210,556}{\$67,706} = 3.11 \text{ times}$	$\dfrac{\$292,787}{\$76,078} = 3.85 \text{ times}$

In 2008, WestJet's earnings available to cover interest were almost four times the amount of its interest expense. This indicates that its earnings from operations could fall by about three-quarters before it would be unable to cover its interest charges. Whether this is an adequate cushion depends on the company's line of business and the variability of its earnings. In 2009, the ratio decreased to about three times, indicating that WestJet's earnings from operations could fall by about two-thirds before it would be unable to cover its interest expense.

Thus, the ratio results indicate that WestJet's ability to cover its interest charges deteriorated somewhat. Even though its interest expense decreased in 2009—likely due

LEARNING OBJECTIVE 12

Calculate the debt to total assets ratio and the times interest earned ratio, and comment on a company's financial health using the information from these ratios.

to the decrease in long-term liabilities noted in the debt to total assets ratio—its earnings from operations decreased even more, leaving the company less able to cover its interest charges in 2009 than in 2008. Creditors would watch this ratio for indications that WestJet might become unable to make its scheduled interest payments. They would also read the note describing long-term debt to see if interest costs will continue to decrease, or if any additional debt is taken on that will increase the interest expense and further decrease the ratio.

The biggest concern for most analysts regarding debt is the possibility of unrecorded liabilities. As we saw in the last chapter, commitments and contingent liabilities can have significant effects on a company's health. In this chapter, a company's obligations under operating leases are an example of liabilities that are not reported on the financial statements. Unrecorded liabilities will cause debt ratios to be understated and times interest earned ratios to be overstated. Fortunately, certain disclosures give analysts some help in understanding the effects of these unrecorded liabilities. For example, the disclosure of the next five years of lease payments for operating leases allows analysts to approximate the present value of these lease payments for inclusion in ratio analysis.

In Exhibit 10-6, we saw that WestJet had total commitments of $1,429,027 million related to operating leases. This amount is greater than the total long-term liabilities reported on WestJet's balance sheet. Although the amount disclosed in the notes for the operating leases is not discounted (i.e., not reported at its present value, as other long-term liabilities are) and therefore any direct comparison to the liabilities on the balance sheet is only an approximation, it is clear that if the present value of those obligations were recorded on the balance sheet the ratio of debt to total assets would increase substantially. The times interest earned ratio would also be affected by the portion of the lease payments determined to be interest expense. The effects of other commitments and off-balance-sheet liabilities may be more difficult to estimate, so analysts need to have a good understanding of the company, including its operating, investing, and financing activities, and the types of contracts it enters into, so that these obligations do not come as surprises.

Another concern is whether the carrying values of liabilities reflect their current market values. Because liabilities are recorded at the interest rates that were in effect when the debt originated, changes in market interest rates can cause changes in the value of these liabilities that may not be reflected on the company's books. This does not mean that the company will be paying more or less interest as a result of the changes in market interest rates, but it does mean that the company may be paying more or less than it would if it took out new debt at current rates. Debt carrying values can be adjusted to their fair values either by looking at the debt's market value (for publicly traded debt) or by recalculating the debt's present value using current market interest rates. This, of course, requires detailed information about the terms of the outstanding debt. Another reason why it is important for users to know about changes in interest rates is that companies often refinance their debt, and users need to know what the potential costs are to the company the next time it uses debt financing.

Another risk that analysts should consider is the one posed by debt that is denominated in a foreign currency. As you can imagine, if the company is required to make debt payments in a foreign currency, fluctuations in the exchange rate for that currency can cause increases or decreases in the amount of the liability as expressed in Canadian dollars.

A further risk is that the company may enter into debt agreements in which the interest is not a fixed rate, but floats with interest rates in the economy (sometimes called variable-rate debt). If interest rates go up, the company can find itself having to make significantly higher interest payments. Both these risks can be managed through the use of sophisticated hedging techniques involving financial instruments, such as interest rate and foreign currency options, and swaps. To help readers of financial statements understand these complex transactions and the risks posed to the company, companies in Canada are required to disclose these types of transactions and to provide details concerning the risks that the company faces because of them.

SUMMARY

This chapter completes the discussion of liabilities that started in Chapter 9. Because of the larger amounts being borrowed, the longer time frame involved, and the uncertainty of the future, the risks associated with long-term liabilities are more extensive than those associated with the short-term liabilities discussed in the previous chapter.

The first portion of this chapter outlined different sources of long-term financing available to a company, including borrowing through long-term notes and mortgages. The accounting for these forms of long-term debt is relatively simple, and parallels the accounting for short-term notes that was discussed in Chapter 9.

Large companies often use bonds as a way of raising additional funds for financing growth. Depending on the gap (if any) between the interest rate being offered by the company and the rate being offered in the market for comparable bonds issued by other companies, a company's bonds may be issued at par (face value), above par (at a premium), or below par (at a discount). The chapter described how the issuance price for bonds is established through the use of present value calculations, and how bonds are accounted for, from issuance to retirement.

Another topic discussed in the chapter was leasing—a financing alternative that is used extensively in Canada. When a company needs to acquire or replace a capital asset, it will consider whether it is more advantageous to buy the asset or to lease it. The details of the leasing contracts determine whether they can be accounted for as operating leases or must be accounted for as finance leases. The accounting treatment for each of these types of leases is very different, and was illustrated in the chapter.

Pensions and other post-employment benefits were also discussed, as most large organizations in Canada have pension plans for their employees. The two basic types of pension plans—defined contribution plans and defined benefit plans—were described. We did not go into extensive detail about the accounting for pensions, but rather tried to give you an understanding of what the main issues are and how pension plan information is reported in the financial statements.

Because both leases and pensions are often large items that can have significant effects on the financial statements but may not appear directly in them, knowledge of an organization's lease contracts and pension plans is essential to any evaluation of its current financial position and future prospects.

The final major item in the chapter was a discussion of deferred income taxes, building on the introduction to this topic in Chapter 8. Deferred income taxes are significant amounts in many companies' financial statements, and are often a confusing item for users because they can be either an asset or a liability.

The chapter concluded with a discussion of two ratios that are important in relation to debt: the debt to total assets ratio and the times interest earned ratio. These ratios provide users with a basis for analyzing some of the risks associated with debt financing.

The discussion of specific components of the statement of financial position concludes in the next chapter, with a discussion of shareholders' equity. Following that, we will provide a complete review of the ratios introduced throughout this book and introduce some additional analytical techniques.

PRACTICE PROBLEM 1

Ling Limited issues bonds with a face value of $100,000 and a bond interest rate of 8% on January 1, 2011. The bonds mature in 10 years and pay interest semi-annually on June 30 and December 31.

Required:

a. If the competitive interest rate (or yield) for similar bonds in the market is 6%, how much will investors be willing to pay for these bonds?

b. If the bonds are issued at the price calculated in part "a," what journal entries will Ling Limited make in 2011 to account for these bonds?

c. If the market interest rate (or yield) for similar bonds is 10% (instead of 6%), how much will investors be willing to pay for these bonds?

d. If the bonds are issued at the price calculated in part "c," what entries will the company make in 2011 to account for these bonds?

STRATEGIES FOR SUCCESS:

▶ Begin by calculating the amount of interest that will be paid out each six months. Remember that this is based on the face value of the bonds using the bond interest rate.

▶ Calculate the issuance price using the present value tables printed on the inside covers, a financial calculator, or the Excel function described in the Appendix following these practice problems. If necessary, refer to the section on bond pricing (pages 637–640) for a refresher on how to do this.

▶ Calculate the interest expense for June 30 by multiplying the bond issuance price (the one you calculated using the present value tables) by the yield rate. The difference between the amount of interest *paid* in cash and the amount of interest *expense* is recorded as a debit or a credit to the bond liability account, to make the journal entry balance.

▶ Calculate the interest expense for December 31 by multiplying the new amount of the bond liability by the yield rate. As before, the difference between the amount of interest *paid* and the amount of interest *expense* is recorded as a debit or a credit to the bond liability account, to make the journal entry balance.

PRACTICE PROBLEM 2

On January 1, 2011, Acme Company Ltd. enters into a five-year lease for a computer system. The fair value of the computer system is $35,000. At the end of the lease term, the system will be returned to the lessor, who estimates that it will have no residual value. The lease contract calls for payments of $778.56 at the end of each month. These payments will provide the lessor with a 12% return on the lease contract.

Required:

a. Based on the above facts, how should Acme account for this lease?

b. Construct the entries that Acme should make during the first two months of the lease.

c. Give some reasons why Acme would choose to lease the computer system rather than buy it.

STRATEGIES FOR SUCCESS:

▶ Refer back to the section on leases (pages 647–652), where there were criteria listed for determining whether a lease is an operating lease or finance lease. Read the information about the lease carefully, to see whether any of the finance lease criteria fit for Acme Company. If so, it is a finance lease.

▶ Calculate the present value of the lease using the lease payments ($778.56), the interest rate for one month (12% per year ÷ 12 months), and the duration of the lease in months (12 months per year × 5 years). If you use the tables printed on the inside covers, you will need to use Table 1.

▶ The amount of interest expense incurred for the first month is calculated using the present value of the lease that you determined above.

▶ The interest expense for the second month is calculated using the balance of the lease obligation at the end of the first month (i.e., the original present value of the lease less the changes that you made to the lease obligation account in the first month).

PRACTICE PROBLEM 3

Exhibit 10-14 shows part of the pension footnote for **Teck Cominco Ltd.**, an integrated Canadian natural resource corporation involved in mineral exploration, mining, smelting, and refining.

Required:

a. What kinds of pension plans does Teck Cominco have?

b. How is Teck Cominco accounting for its non-pension retirement benefits? Does its funding match the recognition of the expense for these benefits? Explain.

c. On its income statement, Teck Cominco does not disclose the total expense for retirement benefits. On the balance sheet, it lists "Other liabilities" of $1,029 million. In the notes, it states that this amount includes an accrued pension liability of $54 million for the defined benefit pension plan and $266 million for other post-retirement benefits. What information does this give users about Teck Cominco's retirement benefit plans?

EXHIBIT 10-14

annual report

TECK COMINCO LTD. 2009 ANNUAL REPORT

Excerpts from the Notes to the Financial Statements

2. Significant Accounting Policies

Pension and Other Employee Future Benefits

Defined Benefit Pension Plans

Defined benefit pension plan obligations are based on actuarial determinations. The projected benefit method prorated on services is used to determine the accrued benefit obligation. Actuarial assumptions used in the determination of defined benefit pension plan liabilities and non-pension post-retirement benefits are based upon our best estimates, including discount rate, expected plan performance, salary escalation, expected health care costs and retirement dates of employees. The expected return on plan assets is estimated based on the fair value of plan assets, asset allocation and expected long-term rates of return.

EXHIBIT 10-14

TECK COMINCO LTD. 2009 ANNUAL REPORT (cont'd)
Excerpts from the Notes to the Financial Statements

Past service costs and transitional assets or liabilities are amortized on a straight-line basis over the expected average remaining service period of active employees expected to receive benefits under the plan up to the full eligibility date.

Differences between the actuarial liabilities and the amounts recorded in the financial statements will arise from changes in plan assumptions, changes in benefits, or through experience as results differ from actuarial assumptions. Cumulative differences which are greater than 10% of either the fair value of the plan assets or the accrued benefit obligation, whichever is greater, are amortized over the average remaining service life of the related employees.

Defined Contribution Pension Plans
The cost of providing benefits through defined contribution plans is charged to earnings as the obligation to contribute is incurred.

Non-Pension Post-Retirement Plans
We provide certain health care benefits for certain employees when they retire. The cost of these benefits is expensed over the period in which the employees render services. These non-pension post-retirement benefits are funded by us as they become due.

STRATEGIES FOR SUCCESS:

▶ Read each of the questions and then carefully read the note to the financial statements. You should be able to find the answers in the note.

▶ If necessary, reread the sections on pensions and other post-employment benefits (pages 655–661).

PRACTICE PROBLEM 4

Lund Company purchased a piece of equipment on January 1, 2011, for $41,000. For accounting purposes, the company will depreciate this asset by the straight-line method over its useful life, which is estimated to be eight years. The residual value is estimated to be $1,000. The asset qualifies as a class 10 asset for tax purposes, with a 30% CCA rate. During 2011, Lund generated $18,500 in income before depreciation and taxes. The tax rate in 2011 is 40%. The depreciation of this asset is the only difference between Lund's accounting methods and the tax methods.

Required:

a. Calculate the income taxes payable for 2011 and the deferred income tax liability at the end of 2011. Then construct the journal entry that Lund will make in 2011 to record its taxes.

b. What income tax amounts should be reported on the company's 2011 statement of financial position, and how should they be classified?

c. Prepare a note related to income taxes to accompany the 2011 financial statements.

STRATEGIES FOR SUCCESS:

▶ Begin by calculating the depreciation expense and the capital cost allowance (CCA) for the year. Remember that the CCA claim for the first year of an asset's life is only half the usual amount.

▶ Using the CCA, determine the taxable income for the year. Then multiply this by the tax rate, to calculate the income taxes that are currently payable.

▶ Determine the difference between the undepreciated capital cost of the equipment (Cost − CCA) and its net book value (Cost − Depreciation). Then multiply this by the tax rate to calculate the deferred income taxes.

▶ If the equipment's undepreciated capital cost is higher than its net book value, the deferred income tax will be an asset. If the undepreciated capital cost is lower than the net book value, the deferred income tax will be a liability.

▶ If necessary, reread the section on deferred income taxes (pages 661–664).

SUGGESTED SOLUTION TO PRACTICE PROBLEM 1

Interest to be paid every six months = Face value × Bond interest rate × Time
= $100,000 × 8% × 6/12
= $4,000.00

a. Present value of the Ling Limited bonds at a yield rate of 6%:

PV of bonds = PV of interest payments + PV of maturity payment
= ($4,000 × 14.87747, from Table 1) + ($100,000 × 0.55368, from Table 2)
= $114,877.88

This is the amount that will be received when the bonds are issued.

b.

January 1, 2011—to record issuance of bonds

Cash (A)	114,877.88	
Bond liability (L)		114,877.88

June 30, 2011—to record interest for the first six months

Interest expense[1] (SE)	3,446.34	
Bond liability (L)	553.66	
Cash (A)		4,000.00

[1]Interest expense = Carrying value × Yield rate × Time
= \$114,877.88 × 6% × 6/12
= \$3,446.34

Ending carrying value = Beginning carrying value − Change this period
= \$114,877.88 − 553.66
= \$114,324.22

This is the amount that is used to calculate the interest expense for the next period. Since the bonds were issued for more than face value, their carrying value is reduced each interest period (by debiting the bond liability account).

December 31, 2011—to record interest for the second six months

Interest expense[2] (SE)	3,429.73	
Bond liability (L)	570.27	
Cash (A)		4,000.00

[2]Interest expense = Carrying value × Yield rate × Time
= \$114,324.22 × 6% × 6/12
= \$3,429.73

c. Present value of the bonds at a yield rate of 10%:

PV of bonds = PV of interest payments + PV of maturity payment
= (\$4,000 × 12.46221, from Table 1) + (\$100,000 × 0.37689, from Table 2)
= \$87,537.84

This is the amount that will be received when the bonds are issued.

d.

January 1, 2011—to record issuance of bonds

Cash (A)	87,537.84	
Bond liability (L)		87,537.84

June 30, 2011—to record interest for the first six months

Interest expense[3] (SE)	4,376.89	
Bond liability (L)		376.89
Cash (A)		4,000.00

[3]Interest expense = Carrying value × Yield rate × Time
= \$87,537.84 × 10% × 6/12
= \$4,376.89

Ending carrying value = Beginning carrying value + change this period

$$= \$87,537.84 + 376.89$$
$$= \$87,914.73$$

This is the amount that is used to calculate the interest expense for the next period. Since the bonds were issued for less than face value, their carrying value is increased each interest period (by crediting the bond liability account).

December 31, 2011—to record interest for the second six months

Interest expense[4] (SE)	4,395.74	
Bond liability (L)		395.74
Cash (A)		4,000.00

[4]Interest expense = Carrying value × Yield rate × Time

$$= \$87,914.73 \times 10\% \times 6/12$$
$$= \$4,395.74$$

SUGGESTED SOLUTION TO PRACTICE PROBLEM 2

a. Since the computer system will have no value at the end of the five-year lease term, the lease covers all of the asset's useful life. Therefore, Acme should account for it as a capital asset acquired under a finance lease.

b. The following entries should be made in the first two months.
The present value of the lease payments at 12% per year over 60 months is equal to $778.56 × 44.95504 (Table 1, PV factor for 60 periods at 1%) = $35,000.

JOURNAL ENTRY FOR INCEPTION OF LEASE ON JANUARY 1, 2011

Leased computer system (A)	35,000.00	
Lease obligation (L)		35,000.00

Each month, the interest expense on the outstanding lease obligation and the monthly lease payment must be recorded, with the difference between these two amounts reducing the principal amount. Because this is an annuity in arrears, the payment reduces the principal of the obligation at the end of the month. The following entries would be made:

JOURNAL ENTRY FOR INTEREST AND LEASE PAYMENT ON JANUARY 31, 2011

Interest expense (SE)	350.00	
Lease obligation (L)	428.56	
Cash (A)		778.56

Interest expense = Carrying value × Interest rate × Time

$$= \$35,000 \times 12\% \times 1/12$$
$$= \$350.00$$

Assuming that the corporation depreciates its leased assets on a straight-line basis over the lease term, the following entry would also be made at the end of each month:

JOURNAL ENTRY FOR DEPRECIATION ON JANUARY 31, 2011

Depreciation expense (SE)	583.33	
Accumulated depreciation—leased computer system (XA)		583.33

Straight-line depreciation = ($35,000 + $0) ÷ 60 months
= $583.33 per month

JOURNAL ENTRY FOR INTEREST AND LEASE PAYMENT ON FEBRUARY 28, 2011

Interest expense (SE)	345.71	
Lease obligation (L)	432.85	
Cash (A)		778.56

Interest expense = Carrying value × Interest rate × Time
= ($35,000.00 − $428.56) × 12% × 1/12
= $34,571.44 × 12% × 1/12
= $345.71

JOURNAL ENTRY FOR DEPRECIATION ON FEBRUARY 28, 2011

Depreciation expense (SE)	583.33	
Accumulated depreciation—leased computer system (XA)		583.33

c. There are several reasons why Acme might choose to lease the computer system.

   i. Acme may not have $35,000 available to buy the system. Rather than borrow the $35,000 from the bank, it may choose to lease the asset and make monthly payments.
   ii. The interest rate charged on the lease may be less than what the bank would charge, and/or the duration of the lease financing may be longer than what the bank would provide.
   iii. Because Acme does not own the computer system, if something goes wrong with the system the lessor is responsible for fixing it. It is likely that the lease agreement includes clauses that outline the types of problems that the lessor agrees to fix and the types (if any) that are Acme's responsibility.
   iv. At the end of the five years, Acme is required to return the system to the lessor. This means that it will have to replace it. Thus, the end of the lease term forces Acme to stay technologically current (if you assume that five years is not too long to keep a computer system without replacing it).
   v. There may be clauses in the lease agreement about upgrades to the system and who is responsible for making the upgrades. If the lessor is responsible, it may be to Acme's advantage to lease the system.

SUGGESTED SOLUTION TO PRACTICE PROBLEM 3

a. Teck Cominco Ltd. appears to have both defined benefit and defined contribution pension plans. For its defined benefit pension plans, it mentions actuarial assumptions and the basis of those assumptions. For its defined contribution pension plans, it states that the costs of providing the benefits are charged to earnings as the obligation to contribute is incurred. For these plans, there is no need for information about assumptions, because the amount of the obligation is easily determined.

b. Teck Cominco Ltd. is accounting for its post-employment benefits by accruing them as the employees are working (using methods similar to those for defined benefit pension plans) but not funding them until they become due. The funding is not matching the expense, as the company is not putting any funds aside to cover these costs when the employees retire.

c. Teck Cominco Ltd. is telling users that its pension plans and other post-retirement benefits are not fully funded. The amount Teck Cominco has expensed for these items is greater than the amount that it has deposited in funds to pay for those future benefits.

SUGGESTED SOLUTION TO PRACTICE PROBLEM 4

a. The taxes payable for 2011 and the deferred income tax liability are calculated as shown below.

Depreciation calculation:

($41,000 − $1,000) ÷ 8 = $5,000 per year
The net book value of the asset at the end of 2011 is $41,000 − $5,000 = $36,000. This is the asset's carrying value for accounting purposes.

CCA calculation:

$41,000 × 30% × 50% (for the first year of the asset's life) = $6,150
The undepreciated capital cost at the end of 2011 is $41,000 − $6,150 = $34,850. This is the asset's carrying value for tax purposes.

Since the asset's carrying value for tax purposes is lower, there will be lower tax deductions (in the form of CCA) available in the future. Consequently, the company will have to pay more tax in the future; in other words, a deferred income tax liability exists.

Calculation of taxes currently payable:

Income before CCA	$18,500
Less: CCA	6,150
Taxable income	12,350
Tax rate	40%
Taxes payable	$ 4,940

Calculation of deferred income taxes:

$36,000 − $34,850 = $1,150 difference between the asset's carrying value for accounting purposes and its carrying value for tax purposes.
The deferred income tax liability is $1,150 × 40% tax rate = $460.

Journal entry for income taxes in 2011:

Income tax expense (SE)	5,400	
Income taxes payable (L)	4,940	
Deferred income taxes (L)		460

b. Income taxes payable of $4,940 should be reported as a current liability. Deferred income taxes of $460 should be reported as a long-term liability.

c. The following note regarding income taxes could be included with Lund Company's financial statements:

Income taxes for 2011 consist of:	
Currently payable	$4,940
Deferred income tax	460
Total income tax expense	$5,400

Deferred income taxes have arisen as a result of temporary differences from claiming capital cost allowance for income tax purposes in excess of depreciation expense for accounting purposes. At the end of 2011, these capital assets had a net book value of $36,000 and an undepreciated capital cost of $34,850, resulting in a deferred income tax liability of 40% × ($36,000 − $34,850) = $460.

APPENDIX

Using Excel to Calculate Present Value

The Present Value function within Microsoft® Excel provides an easy way to find the present value of a series of numbers (an annuity, like the interest payments on a bond) and/or a single number (like the principal repayment on a bond). Excel has several formula functions embedded within it, one of which is present value.

The present value function can be accessed in two ways. First, you can access it through the following steps: open Excel and click on any cell. From the tool bar, select *Insert* and then *Function*. Once you are within Function, you will see a list of all of the functions within Excel. Select the *PV* function. The following box will pop up.

PV

Rate   [ ]

Nper   [ ]

Pmt   [ ]

FV   [ ]

Type   [ ]

You can type the information in the boxes to determine the present value of a series of interest payments and the principal amount that is paid at maturity. The following guide will ensure that you put the appropriate values within each box.

Rate = the yield rate per period. (Not the nominal rate of interest stated on the bond, but the effective rate of interest that investors will earn on the bonds.) For a bond that pays interest semi-annually, this is half of the annual yield rate. The rate must be stated as a decimal. For example, if the investors want to earn 8% on the bond, compounded semi-annually, you would type .08/2 or .04 into this box.

Nper = the number of periods to maturity. For example, for a five-year bond with semi-annual interest payments, the number of periods entered in this box would be 5*2 or 10.

Pmt = the interest payment per period, in dollars. For a bond that pays interest semi-annually, this is half of the annual amount, found by using the formula Principal × Rate (the annual rate stated on the bond) × Time.

FV = the single amount that will be paid back at the end of the interest periods; that is, the principal or face value of the bond.

Type = whether the interest payments are made at the end of the period or at the beginning of the period. The examples in the text have the payments made at the end of the period. Since this is a default assumption built into Excel, in these cases you do not have to enter anything here. Otherwise, you can type 0 to specify the end of the period and type 1 for cases in which the payments are made at the beginning of each period.

Let's try an example. Refer back to Exhibit 10-4 and the calculation of the present value of the bonds for Baum Company when the assumptions were as follows for Case 1:

Yield rate	10% compounded semi-annually
Time to maturity	3 years
Face value	$100,000
Bond interest rate	8% paid semi-annually

Based on this, the semi-annual interest payments were $4,000 ($100,000 × 8% × ½). If we put these amounts into the PV function in Excel, it will look like this:

PV

Rate	.05
Nper	6
Pmt	4000
FV	100000
Type	0

= −94924.30739

When you press the Enter key or click on the OK button, ($94,924.31) will appear in the spreadsheet cell. (The PV is presented as a negative amount because Excel treats the present value amount as the amount of cash outflow that would be required today to provide for the future inflows of interest and principal.) This value is slightly more precise than the amount of $94,924.76 that we calculated in the chapter, using the tables printed on the inside covers.

A faster way of finding the present value is to click on a cell in Excel and then type the following into the cell:

= PV(.05,6,4000,100000,0)

This accesses the same present value function that we just did above in the longer way. The amounts within the parentheses are the same ones that are in the table shown above. Excel will remind you what values need to be entered by showing (rate, nper, pmt, [fv], [type]) as soon as you have typed = PV.

As another example, refer back to Exhibit 10-4 and calculate of the present value of the Baum Company bonds using the assumptions for Case 2:

Yield rate	6% compounded semi-annually
Time to maturity	3 years
Face value	$100,000
Bond interest rate	8% paid semi-annually

The semi-annual interest payments will still be $4,000. Only the yield rate has changed. Putting these amounts into the PV function in Excel, it will look like this:

PV	
Rate	.03
Nper	6
Pmt	4000
FV	100000
Type	0
	= −105417.1914

When you press the Enter key or click on the OK button, ($105,417.19) will appear in the spreadsheet cell. (The PV is presented as a negative amount for the same reason as stated above.) This value is more precise than the amount of $105,416.76 that we calculated in the chapter, using the present value tables.

Alternatively, you could simply click on a cell in Excel and type the following:

= PV(.03,6,4000,100000,0)

You now have an alternative way to calculate the present value of bonds or other situations involving future payments.

The main advantage of using a computer spreadsheet such as Excel, rather than interest tables, to calculate present values is that you can do so for any yield rate. For example, if the yield or effective rate of interest for a particular type of bond is 8.75%, compounded semi-annually, you are unlikely to find a set of interest tables with a column for 4.375% (i.e., half of 8.75%). Using Excel, however, you would simply enter the rate as .0875/2 or .04375 and have the result in an instant.

SYNONYMS

Bond interest rate ▍ Coupon rate ▍ Stated rate ▍ Nominal rate ▍ Contract rate
Capital lease ▍ Finance lease
Deferred income taxes ▍ Future income taxes
Early retirement of debt ▍ Early extinguishment of debt
Market rate of interest ▍ Effective rate ▍ Yield

GLOSSARY

Accrual entry   In the context of pension accounting, this is the journal entry to record the pension expense and create the pension obligation.

Actuary   A professional trained in statistical methods who can make detailed estimates of pension costs.

Annuity in arrears   A series of payments of equal amounts made at regular intervals, at the end of each specified period.

Bond   A corporation's long-term borrowing that is evidenced by a bond certificate. The borrowing is characterized by a face value, interest rate, and maturity date.

Bond interest payment The periodic interest payments made on a bond. The payments are typically made semi-annually, and the amount is calculated by multiplying the bond's face value by its interest rate.

Bond interest rate An interest rate that is specified in a bond contract and used to determine the interest payments that are made on the bond. Synonym for coupon rate, stated rate, nominal rate, and contract rate.

Callable bond A bond that specifies that the issuer can choose to buy the bond back, prior to its maturity, at a predetermined price.

Capital lease Synonym for finance lease.

Collateral trust bond A bond that provides marketable securities as collateral in the event of default by the company.

Convertible bond A bond that is convertible under certain conditions into common shares.

Coupon rate The interest rate stated in a bond contract, specifying the interest that will be paid. Synonym for bond rate, stated rate, nominal rate, and contract rate.

Covenants Conditions or restrictions placed on a company that borrows money. The covenants usually require the company to maintain certain minimum ratios and may restrict its ability to pay dividends.

Debenture bond A bond that is issued with no specific collateral.

Debt to total assets ratio A ratio that compares a company's total liabilities to its total assets, to indicate the extent to which the company has used borrowed funds to finance its assets.

Deferred income tax assets Accounts used to represent tax savings related to the current period that are expected to be realized in future periods.

Deferred income tax liabilities Accounts used to represent additional taxes related to the current period that are expected to arise in future periods.

Defined benefit pension plan A pension plan that specifies the benefits that employees will receive in their retirement. The benefits are usually determined based on the number of years of service and the highest salary earned by the employee.

Defined contribution pension plan A pension plan that specifies how much the company will contribute to its employees' pension fund. No guarantee is made of the amount that will be available to the employees upon retirement.

Discount In the context of bond prices, a term used to indicate that a bond is sold or issued at an amount below its face value.

Discounted cash flows Future cash flows that have been converted to their present-value equivalents, by taking the time value of money into consideration.

Effective interest rate The interest rate that reflects the rate of return earned by investors when they purchase a bond, and the real interest cost to the issuer of the bond. It reflects the competitive market rate for similar bonds, and is used in determining the selling price of the bond. Synonym for market rate or yield.

Face value A value in a bond contract that specifies the cash payment that will be made on the bond's maturity date. The face value is also used to determine the periodic interest payments made on the bond.

Finance lease A lease arrangement that the lessee must treat as the acquisition of an asset and a related long-term liability, as if the transaction represented a purchase of the asset with financing. Synonym for capital lease.

Fully funded plan A pension plan in which the value of the plan assets equals the amount of the projected benefit obligation.

Funding entry The journal entry made to show the cash payment made to the trustee of a pension plan, to fund the obligation.

Indenture agreement An agreement that accompanies the issuance of a bond and specifies all the borrowing terms and restrictions, or covenants.

Investment banker The intermediary who arranges the issuance of bonds in the public debt market on behalf of others. The investment banker sells the bonds to its clients before the bonds are traded in the open market.

Lease agreement An agreement between a lessee and a lessor for the rental or effective purchase of an asset.

Lessee The party or entity that is renting or effectively purchasing the asset in a lease arrangement.

Lessor The owner of an asset that is rented or effectively sold to a lessee under a lease arrangement.

Liability method The method of calculating income taxes that is based on the liability that will be incurred to pay more tax in the future (or the benefit that will be derived from paying less tax in the future) arising from temporary differences between accounting calculations and tax calculations.

Maturity date The date in a bond contract that specifies when the final payment is due.

Mortgage A debt for which some type of real (physical) asset is pledged as collateral in the event of default by the company.

Nominal rate The interest rate stated in a bond contract, specifying the interest that will be paid. Synonym for bond rate, coupon rate, stated rate, and contract rate.

Operating lease   A lease in which the lessee does not record an asset and related obligation but treats the lease as a mutually unexecuted contract. Lease expense is then simply recognized as payments are made.

Overfunded   A pension plan in which the value of the plan assets exceeds the amount of the projected benefit obligation.

Par   In the context of bond prices, a term used to indicate that a bond is sold or issued at its face value.

Post-employment benefits   Benefits other than pensions provided to retirees. These benefits are typically health care or life insurance benefits.

Premium   In the context of bond prices, a term used to indicate that a bond is sold or issued at an amount above its face value.

Present value   The value today of an amount or series of amounts to be received or paid in the future.

Senior debenture   A general borrowing of the company that has priority over other types of long-term borrowing in the event of bankruptcy.

Stated rate   The interest rate stated in a bond contract, specifying the interest that will be paid. Synonym for bond rate, coupon rate, nominal rate and contract rate.

Subordinated debenture   A general borrowing of the company that has a lower priority than senior debentures in the event of bankruptcy.

Temporary differences   Differences between accounting and tax reporting that will later reverse themselves and be eliminated. They arise because of the different carrying values of assets and liabilities recorded in a company's accounting records versus its tax records.

Times interest earned ratio   A ratio that calculates how many times a company's earnings available to covered interest charges exceed the interest itself, providing a measure of its ability to cover the interest expense out of its earnings.

Time value of money   The concept that money received now is worth more than money received later (because money received now can be invested to grow to a larger amount later). Conversely, money is worth less, in economic terms, if it is paid later rather than now. More generally stated, the value of money decreases as the time elapsed until it is received or paid increases.

Trustee   In the context of pension plans, an independent party that holds and invests the pension plan assets on behalf of the company and its employees.

Underfunded   A pension plan in which the value of the plan assets is less than the amount of the projected benefit obligation.

Underwriter   An investment bank that arranges and agrees to sell the initial issuance of bonds or other securities.

Vesting   An event by which employees are granted pension benefits even if they leave the company's employ.

Yield   The interest rate that reflects the rate of return earned by investors when they purchase a bond, and the effective interest cost to the issuer of the bond. It reflects the competitive rate available in the market for similar bonds, and is used in determining the selling price of the bond. Synonym for effective rate or market rate.

ASSIGNMENT MATERIAL

Self-Assessment Quiz

Assessing Your Recall

10-1   Explain what a loan amortization table is.

10-2   Explain what a "mortgage" is.

10-3   Explain what "blended payments" are.

10-4   Describe the following terms relating to a bond: indenture agreement, bond covenants, collateral, face value, bond interest rate, interest payments, and maturity date.

10-5   Explain what is meant by the yield rate of interest for a bond issue.

10-6   Distinguish between the stated or nominal rate of interest on a bond and the real or effective rate.

10-7   Discuss how bond prices are determined and how these prices are affected by changes in market interest rates.

10-8   Describe the following terms as they relate to bond prices: par, premium, and discount.

10-9   Explain why some bonds are issued at a discount, and what happens to the carrying value of these bonds between their issuance date and maturity date.

10-10   Describe the accounting procedures or journal entries required when bonds are retired before maturity. Why would a company choose to retire debt early?

10-11   Discuss the benefits of leasing, from the point of view of both the lessee and the lessor.

10-12   List and discuss the criteria that are used to distinguish finance leases from operating leases.

10-13   Outline how finance leases are recorded and accounted for.

10-14   Differentiate between defined contribution pension plans and defined benefit pension plans.

10-15   Explain why vesting of the pension benefits and full funding of the pension plan would be important to employees.

10-16   Explain the difficulties in accounting for a defined benefit pension plan.

10-17   Where is information about a company's pension plan assets and projected benefit obligation presented when its financial statements are prepared?

10-18   Explain the nature of deferred income taxes, including how they arise and what they represent.

10-19   Deferred income taxes are usually a liability, but they can also be an asset. Explain what a deferred income tax asset represents.

10-20   Outline how deferred income taxes are calculated.

10-21   Explain the meaning of the terms "temporary differences" and "permanent differences."

10-22   Explain what the following ratios tell you about a company's financial health: debt to equity ratio and times interest earned ratio.

Applying Your Knowledge

10-23   (Amortization table and journal entries for a mortgage loan)

A company takes out a five-year, $100,000 mortgage on October 1. The interest rate on the loan is 8% per year, and blended payments of $2,027.64 (including both interest and principal) are to be made at the end of each month.

> **Required:**
> a.   The monthly payments will be the same amount each month, throughout the entire term of the loan. Will the interest expense be the same amount each month? Explain briefly.
> b.   Prepare a loan amortization table for this mortgage, similar to the one in Exhibit 10-1. If you do this using a computer spreadsheet such as Excel, you can easily prepare the table for the entire term of the mortgage; if you do it manually, prepare the table for just the first three months.
> c.   Give the journal entries to record the inception of the loan and the first three interest payments.

10-24   (Bond journal entries and financial statement effects)

Spring Water Company Ltd. needed to raise $5 million of additional capital to finance the expansion of its bottled water facility. After consulting an investment banker, it decided to issue bonds. The bonds had a face value of $5 million and an annual interest rate of 7%, paid semi-annually on June 30 and December 31, and will reach maturity on December 31, 2020. The bonds were issued on January 1, 2011, for $4,660,242, which represented a yield of 8%.

> **Required:**
> a.   Spring Water Company issued bonds with a face value of $5 million because it wanted to raise $5 million. However, it succeeded in raising only $4,660,242. Explain why investors were not willing to pay $5 million for the bonds.
> b.   Show the journal entry to record the issuance of the bonds.
> c.   Show the journal entries to record the first two interest payments.
> d.   What amounts will be reported on the financial statements at the end of the first year regarding these bonds?

10-25 (Bonds issued at par—journal entries, including early retirement)

Jason Equipment Ltd. issued 10%, five-year bonds with a face value of $2,800,000 on October 1, 2011. The bonds were issued at par and pay interest on April 1 and October 1 each year. The company's fiscal year end is December 31.

Required:

a. Prepare the journal entry for the issuance of the bonds.
b. Prepare the journal entry for the bonds for December 31, 2011, and explain why it is necessary to prepare a journal entry on December 31 although it does not coincide with an interest payment date.
c. Prepare the journal entries for the interest payments on April 1 and October 1, 2012.
d. On October 1, 2012, after paying the semi annual interest, the company purchased the bonds on the open market and cancelled them. The bonds were purchased at 98 (i.e., at 98% of their face value). Prepare the journal entry to record the purchase and cancellation of the bonds.

10-26 (Bond issuance price, carrying value, and journal entries)

The Standard Mills Corporation issues 1,000 bonds, each with a face value of $1,000, that mature in 12 years. The bonds carry a 6% interest rate and are sold to yield 4%. They pay interest semi-annually.

Required:

a. Calculate the issuance price of the bonds, and show the journal entry to record the issuance.
b. Explain why the issuance price of the bonds is not the same as their face value.
c. Will the carrying value of the liability for these bonds increase over time, or decrease? Explain briefly.
d. Show the journal entries to record the first two interest payments on these bonds.

10-27 (Bond issuance price, journal entries, and carrying value)

KD's Cowboy Bar and Grill Ltd. is a country and western–style restaurant and club chain based in Red Deer, Alberta, that specializes in barbecue food and country music. On January 1, it issued five-year, semi-annual bonds with a face value of $200,000, to provide capital to expand the chain. The bond rate was 8% and on the date of sale the yield rate was 10%. Interest payments are to be made each June 30 and December 31.

Required:

a. Determine the selling price of these bonds and provide the journal entry to record their sale on January 1.
b. Provide the journal entries to record the first two interest payments.
c. What amount will be reported for the bond liability on the year-end statement of financial position?

10-28 (Bond issuance price, journal entries, and early retirement)

On April 1, 2011, Tran Corporation issued $20 million of 8% bonds, with interest payable on March 31 and September 30 each year. The market yield rate for these bonds on the date of issuance was 6%. The bonds were dated April 1, 2011, and had a maturity date of April 1, 2021. The company's fiscal year end is December 31.

Required:

a. Calculate the cash proceeds from the issuance of these bonds.
b. Prepare the journal entries made by the company on April 1, September 30, and December 31, 2011, and on March 31, 2012.
c. On April 1, 2012, the company retired the bonds by purchasing them on the open market at 101 (i.e., at 101% of their face value). Prepare the journal entry (or entries) required to record the early retirement of the bonds.

    d. Explain how a company could record a gain on the early retirement of its bonds even though the amount it paid to repurchase them was more than their face value.

10-29 (Bond issuance prices and journal entries at various yield rates)

Alphabet Toy Company has plans for a plant expansion and needs to raise additional capital to pay for the construction. The company is considering issuing seven-year, 6% mortgage bonds with a par value of $1 million. The bonds will pay interest semi-annually.

Required:

    a. What are mortgage bonds? Explain how the fact that these are mortgage bonds would affect the interest rate dictated by the market (the yield rate).

    b. Calculate the amount of cash the company will receive if the bonds are sold at a yield rate of:

        i. 6%

        ii. 8%

        iii. 4%

    c. Prepare the journal entry Alphabet Toy would record at the time of the issuance of the bonds under each of the alternative yields. Also prepare the journal entries to record the interest expense for the first two periods under each alternative.

10-30 (Bond selling price, journal entries, carrying value, and early retirement)

Eraser Equipment Company Inc. issued $400,000 of 9% bonds maturing in six years. The bonds pay interest semi-annually and are issued to yield 8%.

Required:

    a. Calculate the issuance price of the bonds and give the journal entry to record the issuance.

    b. Give the journal entries to record the first two interest payments.

    c. Calculate the carrying value of the bonds one year after issuance (that is, at the beginning of the second year).

    d. Calculate the market value of the bonds one year after issuance, if the market yield has increased to 10%.

    e. Compare the carrying value (calculated in part "c") and the market value of the bonds (calculated in part "d") one year after issuance, and explain why a difference exists.

    f. Assuming the company retires the bonds at the beginning of the second year by purchasing them in the open market, give the journal entry to record this. (Hint: The amount that you calculated in part "d" should be used in this entry.)

10-31 (Bond calculations and early retirement—partial information)

Black Company issued 10-year, 6% bonds on January 1, 2011. These bonds pay interest every June 30 and December 31. A partial amortization table follows:

Date	Interest Payment	Interest Expense	Liability Balance
Jan. 1, 2011			$43,205.00
June 30, 2011	$1,500.00	$1,728.20	$43,433.20
Dec. 31, 2011	_____	_____	_____

Required:

    a. Calculate the face value of the bonds that were issued on January 1, 2011.

    b. Calculate the yield rate of interest on these bonds.

    c. Complete the amortization table for 2011.

    d. On January 1, 2012, Black retired the bonds at 98 (i.e., at 98% of their face value). Prepare the journal entry to record the retirement of the bonds.

10-32 (Bond calculations and early retirement—partial information)

Crystal Gems Company issued 10-year, 6% bonds on January 1, 2011. These bonds pay interest every June 30 and December 31. A partial amortization table follows:

Date	Interest Payment	Interest Expense	Liability Balance
Jan. 1, 2011			$232,700.00
June 30, 2011	$ 6,000.00	$ 4,654.00	$231,354.00
Dec. 31, 2011	_____	_____	_____
June 30, 2012	_____	_____	_____
Dec. 31, 2012	_____	_____	_____

Required:

a. Calculate the face value of the bonds that were issued on January 1, 2011.
b. Calculate the yield rate of interest applicable to these bonds.
c. Complete the amortization table for 2011 and 2012.
d. On January 1, 2013, Crystal Gems retired the bonds by repurchasing them at a price of $208,000. Prepare the journal entry to record the repurchase and retirement of the bonds.

10-33 (Finance lease—journal entries and financial statement balances)

On January 1, 2011, ABC Manufacturing Corporation leased a machine to Start Corporation. The machine had cost ABC $480,000 to manufacture, and would normally have sold for about $600,000. The 10-year lease was classified as a finance lease for accounting purposes.

The machine is expected to have a total useful life of 12 years. However, it will be returned to ABC at the end of the 10-year lease. The lease agreement requires equal semi-annual payments of $44,936 to be made each June 30 and December 31, which reflects an annual interest rate of 10%. Start Corporation closes its books annually on December 31.

Required:

a. Calculate the present value of the payments that will be made under this lease agreement.
b. Provide the journal entry that should be made by Start Corporation on January 1, 2011, to record the inception of the lease.
c. Over what period of time—10 years or 12 years—should Start Corporation depreciate this machine? Explain briefly.
d. Assuming that Start Corporation uses straight-line depreciation, provide the journal entry that should be made each December 31 to record the depreciation of this asset.
e. Provide the journal entries that should be made by Start Corporation to record the lease payments on:
   i. June 30, 2011
   ii. December 31, 2011
   iii. June 30, 2012
   iv. December 31, 2012
f. What values will be reported on Start Corporation's December 31, 2012, statement of financial position for the leased machine and the lease obligation?
g. What values related to the lease will be reported on Start Corporation's statement of earnings for the year ended December 31, 2012?

10-34 (Finance lease—journal entries and financial statement balances)

On July 1, 2011, XYZ Manufacturing Corporation leased equipment to Good Company. The equipment had cost XYZ $500,000 to manufacture, and would normally have sold for about $700,000. The eight-year lease was classified as a finance lease for accounting purposes.

The equipment is expected to have a total useful life of 10 years. However, it will be returned to XYZ at the end of the lease. The lease agreement requires equal quarterly payments of $25,566 to be made each September 30, December 31, March 31, and June 30. These payments reflect an annual interest rate of 8%. Good Company closes its books semi-annually, on June 30 and December 31.

Required:

a. Calculate the present value of the payments that will be made under this lease agreement, and show the journal entry that should be made by Good Company on July 1, 2011, to record the inception of the lease.

b. Over what period of time should Good Company depreciate this equipment? Explain your reasoning.

c. Assuming that Good Company uses straight-line depreciation, provide the journal entry that should be made on December 31, 2011, and June 30, 2012, to record the depreciation of the equipment.

d. Provide the journal entries that should be made by Good Company to record the lease payments on:
   i. September 30, 2011
   ii. December 31, 2011
   iii. March 31, 2012
   iv. June 30, 2012

e. What values related to the lease will be reported on Good Company's statement of earnings for the six months ended June 30, 2012?

f. What values related to this lease will be reported on the company's June 30, 2012, statement of financial position?

10-35 (Lease classification, journal entries, and financial statement effects)

Transprovincial Buslines experienced a major increase in the volume of its business in the last three months of 2011. Consequently, on January 1, 2012, the company leased a new bus from BigBus Leasing Ltd. Transprovincial could have purchased the bus for $400,000 but decided to lease it instead.

The 10-year lease agreement on the bus requires Transprovincial to pay $5,000 per month at the end of each month starting January 31, 2012. At the end of the lease term, title to the bus transfers to Transprovincial. The lease is structured with a 9% interest rate. The bus is expected to have a useful life of 15 years and will be depreciated on a straight-line basis with no anticipated residual value.

Required:

a. Is the above lease a finance lease or an operating lease? Explain why, referring to the criteria for classifying leases.

b. Assuming that Transprovincial records the lease on the bus as a finance lease, calculate the present value of the lease payments and give the journal entry that should be made to record the inception of the lease on January 1, 2012.

c. Should Transprovincial depreciate the bus over 10 years or over 15 years? Explain.

d. Assuming that Transprovincial records depreciation at the end of each month, give the journal entry that should be made to record depreciation for the months of January and February, 2012.

e. Give the journal entry that should be made to record the lease payments for January and February, 2012.

f. What amounts related to the lease would appear on Transprovincial's statement of earnings for the month of February, and on its statement of financial position as of the end of February?

10-36 **(Lease classification, journal entries, and financial statement effects)**
Titan Ltd. entered into an agreement to lease manufacturing equipment. The following terms are
included in the lease:

- Payments required semi-annually on June 30 and December 31: $9,327 each
- Estimated useful life of equipment: 15 years
- Lease term: 10 years

At the end of the lease term, Titan has the option to acquire the equipment for $10,000.
The terms of the lease reflect an annual interest rate of 10%. The lease started January 1, 2011.
At that time, the equipment could have been purchased for $120,000.

Required:

a. Is the above lease a finance lease or an operating lease? Explain why, referring to the
criteria for classifying leases.

b. Assuming that Titan records the lease as a finance lease, calculate the present value
of the lease payments. (Hint: Include the present value of the $10,000 purchase
option to be paid at the end of 10 years.)

c. Give the journal entry that should be made to record the inception of the lease on
January 1, 2011.

d. Should Titan depreciate the equipment over 10 years or over 15 years? Explain.

e. Assuming that Titan uses straight-line depreciation, give the journal entry that should
be made to record depreciation on December 31, 2011.

f. Give the journal entries that should be made to record the lease payments made on
June 30 and December 31, 2011.

g. What amounts related to the lease would appear on Titan's December 31, 2011, statement of financial position?

10-37 **(Lease classification, journal entries, and financial statement effects)**
The *Provincial Star* newspaper signed an agreement on January 1, 2011, to lease a truck for $800
per month for the next four years to deliver its newspapers. These payments are to be made on
the last day of each month, and reflect an interest rate of 6% on the lease. The truck will be
returned to the lessor at the end of the lease term. The *Provincial Star* depreciates its assets using
the straight-line method and closes its books monthly.

Required:

a. Assuming that the truck's fair market value is $70,000 and its expected useful life is
10 years, how should the *Provincial Star* account for this lease? Explain, referring to
the criteria for classifying leases.

b. Assuming that the truck's fair market value is $40,000 and its expected useful life is
six years, how should the *Provincial Star* account for this lease? Explain, referring to
the criteria for classifying leases.

c. Assuming that this lease should be classified as an operating lease:
   i. Provide the appropriate accounting entries for the first two months of 2011.
   ii. State what (if anything) the *Provincial Star* would indicate about this lease on its
   statement of financial position at the end of the first two months.

d. Assuming that this lease should be classified as a finance lease:
   i. Provide the appropriate accounting entries for the first two months of 2011.
   ii. Show what (if anything) the *Provincial Star* would indicate about this lease on its
   statement of financial position at the end of the first two months.

10-38 **(Income taxes and warranty provisions)**
At the end of its first year of operations, Margaret's Manufacturing had earnings of $180,000,
before income taxes. One of the expenses that was deducted in determining this amount was

product warranty expense of $50,000. However, the amount that was spent to settle product warranty claims during the year (the amount that is deductible for income tax purposes) was only $30,000. The income tax rate was 35%.

Required:
a. What amount of product warranty obligation will be reported as a liability on the company's balance sheet at the end of the year?
b. Calculate the company's taxable income for the year and the amount of tax that is currently payable.
c. Calculate the amount of deferred income tax related to the product warranty. State whether it is a deferred tax asset or a deferred tax liability, and explain your reasoning.
d. What amount of income tax expense will be reported on the company's statement of earnings for the year?

10-39   (Income taxes and warranty provisions)
The Hudson Motor Company manufactures engines for small airplanes. The company offers its customers a warranty for five years or 5,000 flying hours. In 2010, the company sold engines valued at $3,000,000 and estimated that the future warranty costs on these engines would be 5% of sales. It incurred costs of $25,000 associated with warranty work on engines during 2010 and $35,000 during 2011.

Required:
a. Calculate the deferred income tax asset or liability amount associated with the warranty in 2010. The tax rate is 35%.
b. Calculate the deferred income tax asset or liability balance that would appear on the statement of financial position at the end of 2011.
c. Where on the statement of financial position would the deferred income tax balance be reported?

10-40   (Income taxes and capital assets)
On January 1, 2010, Precision Machining Company purchased a new machine costing $46,000. The company uses straight-line depreciation for book purposes and capital cost allowance (CCA) for tax purposes. The machine has an estimated useful life of eight years and a $2,000 residual value. For tax purposes, the machine is in an asset class with a CCA rate of 20%. The company's tax rate is 30% and it closes its books on December 31. In both 2010 and 2011, its earnings before depreciation and taxes are $100,000.

Required:
a. Calculate the income tax amounts for 2010 and 2011, and give the journal entries for recording the taxes for each year. (Hint: The solution to Practice Problem 4 at the end of this chapter illustrates the steps to be followed in doing this.)
b. What amounts would appear on the balance sheet for the deferred income tax asset or liability for 2010 and 2011? Where on the balance sheet would these amounts be reported?
c. If you were a banker reviewing this company's financial statements in anticipation of granting it a loan, what importance would you place on the deferred income tax asset or liability balances? Explain.

10-41   (Income taxes and capital assets)
On January 1, 2010, Canadian Corporation purchased a new capital asset costing $51,000. The company estimated the asset would have a useful life of five years and a $3,000 residual value. The company uses straight-line amortization for book purposes, and the asset qualifies for a 30% capital cost allowance (CCA) rate for tax purposes. The company closes its books on December 31, its earnings before depreciation and taxes are $90,000 in both 2010 and 2011, and the income tax rate is 40%.

Required:

a. Calculate the depreciation expense and the CCA for 2010 and 2011, and determine what the net book value of the asset and its undepreciated capital cost will be at the end of each of these years.

b. Calculate the income taxes payable in 2010 and 2011, and determine what the deferred income tax asset or liability balance will be at the end of each of these years. (Hint: You should find that the deferred income tax account will be an asset at the end of 2010 and a liability at the end of 2011.)

c. Explain why the deferred income tax account changes as it does, over this two-year period.

d. Give the journal entry to record the company's income taxes for 2010 and 2011.

10-42   (Income taxes and capital assets)

At the beginning of 2010, Maritime Manufacturing Company acquired a capital asset costing $500,000 that was expected to have a residual value of approximately $50,000 at the end of its productive life. The company decided to depreciate it using the production method, which resulted in depreciation expense of $70,000 in 2010 and $60,000 in 2011. For tax purposes, a capital cost allowance rate of 20% was applicable to this asset. In 2010, the company had earnings before depreciation and tax of $400,000. The income tax rate was 45%.

Required:

a. Calculate the amount of income tax payable for 2010.

b. What is the balance in the deferred income taxes account at the end of 2010? Be sure to specify whether it is an asset or a liability.

c. Explain briefly what this balance (in the deferred income taxes account) represents.

d. Calculate the amount of income tax expense for the company in 2010.

e. What amount of capital cost allowance can be deducted in 2011?

f. By what amount will the deferred income taxes account change during 2011?

g. What will be the balance in the deferred income taxes account at the end of 2011? Again, be sure to specify whether it will be an asset or a liability.

h. Explain briefly how the balance in the deferred income taxes account is related to the asset's carrying values (i.e., the net book value for accounting purposes and the undepreciated capital cost for tax purposes).

User Perspective Problems

10-43   (Blended payments)

From a management perspective, what is the advantage of having long-term loans such as mortgages structured to be repaid through equal, blended monthly payments?

10-44   (Collateral for long-term debt)

As a potential lender considering making a long-term loan to a company, discuss how much comfort you might get from knowing what long-term assets the company has, specifically in the form of (1) property, plant, and equipment and (2) goodwill. As well as the existence of these assets, what else would you like to know?

10-45   (Seniority of liabilities)

In assessing the riskiness of investing in a particular bond, discuss the importance of being aware of the seniority of various company liabilities.

10-46   (Bond covenants)

Why do bond investors like to see restrictive covenants included in bond indenture agreements? Give two examples of common bond covenants, and explain why each would be beneficial to bond investors.

10-47 (Operating leases)

Suppose that you are a stock analyst and you are evaluating a company that has a significant number of operating leases.

Required:

a. Discuss the potential misstatement of the financial statements that may occur because of this treatment. Specifically, address the impact of this type of accounting on the debt to total assets ratio and return on total assets ratio.
b. Using disclosures provided in the notes to the financial statements, explain how you could adjust the statements to address the issues discussed in part "a."

10-48 (Finance leases)

A shareholder recently charged that the financial statements of a company in which he owned shares were false and misleading because a large amount of computer equipment, which the company leased from a financial institution and did not actually own, was included among the company's capital assets. Is the company's treatment appropriate? Explain.

10-49 (Lease classification criteria)

"If two separate companies were each to lease identical capital assets under identical lease terms, the finance lease criteria used under International Financial Reporting Standards will ensure that each company reports the transaction in the same way."

As a financial statement analyst, would you agree or disagree with this statement? Explain.

10-50 (Impact of lease classification on earnings)

Suppose that your company leases a valuable asset and you are a manager whose remuneration is partially tied to the company meeting a particular earnings target. How is your ability to meet the earnings target affected by the decision to record the lease transaction as either an operating lease or finance lease? Which accounting treatment would you prefer? Does your answer depend on whether you are in the early years of the lease rather than the later years?

10-51 (Lease or buy decision)

Starburst Brewery Ltd. must replace some of its old copper equipment with new stainless steel equipment. The controller is unsure whether to lease the equipment or purchase it with borrowed money.

If purchased, the equipment will cost $800,000 and have an estimated useful life of 16 years and no residual value. The company's bank is willing to provide the $800,000 to Starburst, through a 10 year note bearing 8% annual interest payable at the end of each year. The principal amount would be due at the end of the 10 years.

A local rental company is willing to lease the equipment to Starburst for 12 years at an interest rate of 7%. At the end of each year, Starburst would be required to pay the leasing company $100,000. At the end of the lease period, title to the equipment would remain with the lessor.

Required:

a. Calculate the present value of the future cash flows under both arrangements.
b. State what amounts would appear in Starburst's statement of earnings and statement of financial position for the first year, under both alternatives. (Assume the new equipment is acquired on January 1.)
c. What factors, other than cash payments directly related to financing, might be important to the decision?
d. Which of the two financing alternatives would you recommend to the controller? Why?

10-52 (Pension plan alternatives)

Describe the two main types of pension plans. As a manager, which type of plan would you recommend to the company's senior executives? Explain. As an employee, which plan would you prefer? Explain.

10-53 (Post-employment benefits)

Accountants now have to accrue the cost and record the future obligation for post-employment benefits. In the past, the cost of these benefits was simply recorded as it was incurred (the pay-as-you-go approach). As a manager, explain why you would prefer to continue to use the pay-as-you-go method. What accounting concepts support the change in accounting method from the pay-as-you-go approach to recognizing the future obligation before the employees retire?

10-54 (Unrecorded liabilities)

In assessing the risk of investing in a company, stock analysts are often very concerned that there may be liabilities that do not appear on the company's financial statements. Discuss the major types of these "off-balance-sheet" liabilities, and describe the information about them that may be included in the notes to the financial statements.

10-55 (Risks associated with liabilities)

Notes to the financial statements regarding liabilities typically include the interest rates and payment terms on major debts, as well as details of any foreign currency repayment requirements. Why are such disclosures important to a financial statement analyst?

10-56 (Valuation of liabilities)

Does the concept of fair market value apply to liabilities? Is the market value the same as the book or carrying value reported on the statement of financial position? Explain. Which value would be more relevant to financial statement users?

10-57 (Deferred income taxes as liabilities)

Some users of financial statements do not believe that deferred income tax liabilities meet the criteria for recognition as liabilities. Discuss deferred income tax liabilities in terms of the criteria for recognizing liabilities, and provide your own arguments about whether they satisfy the criteria.

10-58 (Deferred income taxes and lending decisions)

As a potential lender, discuss how you might view the nature of a deferred income tax liability on a company's statement of financial position, and whether you would treat it in the same way as you would a long-term bank loan.

Reading and Interpreting Published Financial Statements

10-59 (Revolving debt facility)

Headquartered in Toronto, **Maple Leaf Foods Inc.** is a food processing company with operations across Canada, the United States, Europe, and Asia. It produces meats and meal products, as well as fresh and frozen pork, chicken, and turkey products, and also produces livestock nutrition products and pet foods in its agribusiness group. Note 8 to the company's 2009 financial statements provides details of Maple Leaf's long-term debt. An excerpt follows:

> **8. e. Long-term debt**
>
> The Company has an unsecured revolving debt facility with a principal amount of $870.0 million. The maturity date is May 31, 2011. This facility can be drawn in Canadian dollars, U.S. dollars, or British pounds, and bears interest based on bankers' acceptance rates for Canadian dollar loans and LIBOR for U.S. dollar and British pound loans. As at December 31, 2009, $476.6 million of the revolving facility was utilized (2008: $559.8 million)...

Required:
a. What is a revolving debt facility?
b. The revolving debt facility is described as unsecured. What does this mean?

c. Why would a company want to be able to borrow in Canadian dollars, U.S. dollars or British pounds? How does this capability affect the company's financial risk?

d. How much is outstanding on the revolving debt facility as at December 31, 2009? Do you know what currency the company borrowed that sum in? Explain.

10-60 (Long-term debt)

Suncor Energy Inc. is a major developer in the oil sands of Northern Alberta. Note 17 to Suncor's financial statements (Exhibit 10-15) describes the company's long-term debt as at December 31, 2009.

Required:

a. Suncor has revolving-term debt. Explain in your own words what the major features of this type of debt are.

b. The revolving-term debt bears interest at variable interest rates. What advantages are there for a company to borrow at variable interest rates? How does this affect the risk of investing in Suncor?

c. Suggest possible reasons why the company has borrowed in U.S. dollars. How does this affect the risk of investing in Suncor?

d. The company has not disclosed the minimum cash payments that it must make on its debt over the next five years and a cumulative amount for the years after the fifth year. Why would this type of disclosure be important to users?

e. You would expect that a company in the oil industry would lease some of its facilities and equipment. Does Suncor have any leases? How do you know? What kind of leases are they?

SUNCOR ENERGY INC. 2009 ANNUAL REPORT

EXHIBIT 10-15

annual report

Excerpts from the Notes to the Financial Statements

17. LONG-TERM DEBT AND CREDIT FACILITIES

($ millions)	2009	2008
Fixed-term debt, redeemable at the option of the company		
6.85% Notes, denominated in U.S. dollars, due in 2039 (US$750)[i]	785	918
6.80% Notes, denominated in U.S. dollars, due in 2038 (US$900)	972	—
6.50% Notes, denominated in U.S. dollars, due in 2038 (US$1150)	1 204	1 408
5.95% Notes, denominated in U.S. dollars, due in 2035 (US$600)	578	—
5.95% Notes, denominated in U.S. dollars, due in 2034 (US$500)	523	612
5.35% Notes, denominated in U.S. dollars, due in 2033 (US$300)	266	—
7.15% Notes, denominated in U.S. dollars, due in 2032 (US$500)	523	612
6.10% Notes, denominated in U.S. dollars, due in 2018 (US$1250)[i]	1 308	1 531
6.05% Notes, denominated in U.S. dollars, due in 2018 (US$600)	643	—
5.00% Notes, denominated in U.S. dollars, due in 2014 (US$400)[ii]	429	—
4.00% Notes, denominated in U.S. dollars, due in 2013 (US$300)	313	—
7.00% Debentures, denominated in U.S. dollars, due in 2028 (US$250)	271	—
7.875% Debentures, denominated in U.S. dollars, due in 2026 (US$275)	325	—
9.25% Debentures, denominated in U.S. dollars, due in 2021 (US$300)	402	—
5.39% Series 4 Medium Term Notes, due in 2037	600	600
5.80% Series 4 Medium Term Notes, due in 2018[iii]	700	700
6.70% Series 2 Medium Term Notes, due in 2011[iv]	500	500
	10 342	6 881
Revolving-term debt, with interest at variable rates		
Commercial paper[v], bankers' acceptances and LIBOR loans		
(interest rate at December 31, 2009 – 0.7%, 2008 – 2.2%)	3 244	934

EXHIBIT 10-15

SUNCOR ENERGY INC. 2009 ANNUAL REPORT (cont'd)

annual report   Excerpts from the Notes to the Financial Statements

17. LONG-TERM DEBT AND CREDIT FACILITIES (cont'd)

($ millions)	2009	2008
Total unsecured long-term debt	**13 586**	7 815
Secured long-term debt	**13**	13
Capital leases(vi)	**326**	103
Fair value of interest swaps	**18**	25
Deferred financing costs	**(63)**	(72)
	13 880	7 884
Current portion of long-term debt		
Capital leases(vii)	**(14)**	(9)
Fair value of interest swaps	**(11)**	(9)
Total current portion of long-term debt	**(25)**	(18)
Total long-term debt	**13 855**	7 866

(i) In June 2008, the company issued 6.10% Notes with a principal amount of US$1.25 billion and 6.85% Notes with a principal amount of US$750 million under an amended US$3.65 billion debt shelf prospectus. These notes bear interest, which is paid semi-annually, and mature on June 1, 2018, and June 1, 2039, respectively. The net proceeds received were added to our general funds, which were used for our working capital needs, sustaining capital expenditures, growth capital expenditures and to repay outstanding commercial paper borrowings.

(ii) These notes, acquired on August 1, 2009 under the merger with Petro-Canada, were originally issued by PC Financial Partnership, a wholly-owned finance subsidiary of Petro-Canada. Suncor has fully and unconditionally guaranteed the notes.

(iii) In May 2008, the company issued 5.80% Medium Term Notes with a principal amount of $700 million under an outstanding $2,000 million debt shelf prospectus. These notes bear interest, which is paid semi-annually, and mature on May 22, 2018. The net proceeds received were added to our general funds to repay outstanding commercial paper, which originally funded our working capital needs, sustaining capital expenditures and growth capital expenditures.

(iv) The company has entered into interest rate swap transactions. The swap transactions result in an average effective interest rate that is different from the stated interest rate of the related underlying long-term debt instruments.

	Principal Swapped	Swap	Effective Interest Rate	
Description of Swap Transaction	($ millions)	Maturity	2009	2008
Swap of 6.70% Medium Term Notes to floating rates	200	2011	2.0%	4.8%

(v) The company is authorized to issue commercial paper to a maximum of $2.5 billion having a term not to exceed 365 days. Commercial paper is supported by available committed credit facilities, (see Credit facilities below).

(vi) Interest rates on capital leases range from 4.7% to 13.4%, and maturity dates range from 2012 to 2037.

Credit facilities

During 2009, the company acquired $4,524 million of available credit facilities in the merger with Petro-Canada. At December 31, 2009, the company had available credit facilities of $8,188 million, of which $4,208 million was unutilized, as follows:

($ millions)	2009
Facility that is fully revolving for 364 days, has a term period of one year and expires in 2010	61
Facility that is fully revolving for a period of four years and expires in 2013	209
Facilities that are fully revolving for a period of five years and expire in 2013	7 320
Facilities that can be terminated at any time at the option of the lenders	598
Total available credit facilities	8 188
Credit facilities supporting outstanding revolving-term debt	(3 244)
Credit facilities supporting standby letters of credit	(736)
Total unutilized credit facilities	4 208

Certain of the notes and debentures of the company were acquired in the merger described in note 2 and were accounted for at their fair value at the date of acquisition, which was higher than the principal amount. The difference between the fair value and the principal amount of these debts of $121 million is being amortized over the remaining life of the debt acquired.

10-61 (Long-term debt)

Loblaw Companies Limited distribute food, general merchandise, and financial products and services across Canada, through Superstore, Extra Foods, Dominion, Fortinos, No Frills, Independent, Zehrs, Dominion and Provigo, as well as Loblaws stores. Their brands include President's Choice, no name, and Joe Fresh Style. Exhibit 10-16 contains excerpts from three notes related to long-term liabilities accompanying Loblaw Companies Limited's 2009 financial statements. All dollar amounts in the notes are in millions.

LOBLAW COMPANIES LIMITED 2009 ANNUAL REPORT

 **EXHIBIT 10-16A**

annual report

Excerpts from Note 16 to the Financial Statements

Note 16. Long Term Debt

	2009	2008
Loblaw Companies Limited Notes		
5.75%, due 2009	$ –	$ 125
7.10%, due 2010	300	300
6.50%, due 2011	350	350
5.40%, due 2013	200	200
6.00%, due 2014	100	100
4.85%, due 2014	350	–
7.10%, due 2016	300	300
6.65%, due 2027	100	100
6.45%, due 2028	200	200
6.50%, due 2029	175	175
11.40%, due 2031		
– principal	151	151
– effect of coupon repurchase	(67)	(55)
6.85%, due 2032	200	200
6.54%, due 2033	200	200
8.75%, due 2033	200	200
6.05%, due 2034	200	200
6.15%, due 2035	200	200
5.90%, due 2036	300	300
6.45%, due 2039	200	200
7.00%, due 2040	150	150
5.86%, due 2043	55	55
Private Placement Notes		
6.48%, due 2013 (US $150 million)	158	180
6.86%, due 2015 (US $150 million)	158	181
Long Term Debt Secured by Mortgage		
5.49%, due 2018 (see note 11)	96	–
VIE loans payable[1] (see note 27)	163	152
Capital lease obligations[1] (see note 18)	64	62
Other	2	9
Total long term debt	4,505	4,235
Less amount due within one year	343	165
	$ 4,162	$ 4,070

During 2008, the Company issued United States Dollar ("USD") $300 of fixed rate notes in a private placement debt financing which contains certain financial covenants (see note 21). The notes were issued in two equal tranches of USD $150 with 5 and 7 year maturities at interest rates of 6.48% and 6.86%, respectively.

EXHIBIT 10-16B

annual report

LOBLAW COMPANIES LIMITED 2009 ANNUAL REPORT

Excerpts from Notes 18 and 21 to the Financial Statements

Note 18. Leases

As Lessee

Future minimum lease payments relating to the Company's operating leases are as follows:

	Payments due by year						2009 Total	2008 Total
	2010	2011	2012	2013	2014	Thereafter		
Operating lease payments	$ 211	$ 192	$ 166	$ 146	$ 126	$ 664	$ 1,505	$1,623
Sub-lease income	(38)	(34)	(30)	(27)	(20)	(55)	(204)	(183)
Net operating lease payments	$ 173	$ 158	$ 136	$ 119	$ 106	$ 609	$ 1,301	$1,440

As Lessor

Fixed assets on the consolidated balance sheets include cost of properties held for leasing purposes of $755 (2008 – $603) and related accumulated depreciation of $211 (2008 – $173). Rental income for the year ended January 2, 2010 from these operating leases totaled $47 (2008 – $45).

Capital Leases

Capital lease obligations of $64 (2008 – $62) are included in the consolidated balance sheet as at year end (see note 16). The capital lease obligations are related to leased properties and equipment of the VIEs that provides distribution and warehousing services. The amount due within one year is $8 (2008 – $8).

Note 21. Capital Management

Covenants and Regulatory Requirements

The committed credit facility which the Company entered into during the first quarter of 2008 (see note 15) and the USD $300 fixed-rate private placement notes which the Company issued during the second quarter of 2008 (see note 16) both contain certain financial covenants. The covenants under both agreements include maintaining an interest coverage ratio as well as a leverage ratio, which the Company measures on a quarterly basis. These ratios are defined in the respective agreements. As at January 2, 2010, the Company was in compliance with both of these covenants.

---

a. Looking at Loblaw's series of notes outstanding and the recent private placement, what do you think the relationship is between interest rates and the length of time to maturity of a loan? As an investor, explain why this relationship would be important to you.

b. Compare the rate of interest on the long-term debt secured by a mortgage that is due in 2018 to the note due in 2016. Why do you think the debt due in 2018 has a lower interest rate than the note due in 2016?

c. Explain why Loblaw would spread out the maturities of their debt over such a long period of time. When they issued the private placement notes, why did they not arrange to have both tranches mature at the same time?

d. What is meant by a private placement?

e. Are capital (finance) leases a major form of long-term financing for Loblaw? Support your answer.

f. Does Loblaw use many operating leases? Why might an analyst be concerned with Loblaw's operating leases?

g. What type of covenants are attached to Loblaw's long-term debt? Explain why these covenants would be useful to lenders or investors. (Hint: The times interest earned ratio is sometimes referred to as an interest coverage ratio. A leverage ratio is one that measures the amount of debt in a company's capital structure, relative to either the assets or the shareholders' equity.)

10-62 (Long-term debt)

Bombardier Inc. is an international provider of aerospace and transportation equipment and solutions. Exhibit 10-17 presents excerpts from Note 13 to Bombardier's 2010 financial statements, which describes the company's long-term debt. All amounts are in millions of U.S. dollars.

EXHIBIT 10-17

annual report

BOMBARDIER INC. 2010 ANNUAL REPORT

Excerpts from Note 13 to the Financial Statements

13 LONG-TERM DEBT

Long-term debt was as follows as at January 31:

				Interest rate			**2010**	2009
	Amount in currency of origin 2010/2009	Currency	Fixed/ Variable[1]	Contractual 2010/2009[1]	After effect of fair value hedges 2010/2009	Maturity	**Amount**	Amount
Senior notes	679	EUR	Variable	4.53%/ 7.74%	n/a	Nov. 2013	**$ 933**	$ 858
	385	USD	Fixed	8.00%	3-month Libor +2.91	Nov. 2014	**419**	430
	785	EUR	Fixed	7.25%	3-month Libor +4.83/ 6-month Euribor +3.36	Nov. 2016	**1,139**	1,028
Notes	550	USD	Fixed	6.75%	3-month Libor +2.28	May 2012	**597**	587
	500	USD	Fixed	6.30%	3-month Libor +1.60	May 2014	**550**	551
	250	USD	Fixed	7.45%	n/a	May 2034	**247**	247
Debentures	150	CAD	Fixed	7.35%	n/a	Dec. 2026	**139**	120
Other[2]	138/131[3]	Various	Fix./var.	7.42%/ 7.21%	n/a	2011-2027	**138**	131
							$4,162	$3,952

1 For variable-rate debt, the interest rate represents the average rate for the fiscal year. All interests on long-term debt are payable semi-annually, except for the Senior note due in November 2013, for which they are payable quarterly, and for the other debts for which the timing of interest payments is variable.

2 Includes $76 million relating to obligations under capital leases as at January 31, 2010 ($66 million as at January 31, 2009).

3 Amounts are expressed in U.S. dollars.

n/a: Not applicable

EXHIBIT 10-17

annual report

BOMBARDIER INC. 2010 ANNUAL REPORT (cont'd)

Excerpts from Note 13 to the Financial Statements

All long-term debt items rank pari-passu and are unsecured.

The carrying value of long-term debt includes principal repayments, transaction costs and the basis adjustments related to derivatives designated in a fair value hedge relationships. The following table presents the principal repayment of the long-term debt:

	Debt	Capital leases	Total
2011	$ 3	$ 8	$ 11
2012	3	10	13
2013	554	10	564
2014	943	3	946
2015	888	3	891
Thereafter	1,528	42	1,570
	$3,919	$ 76	$3,995

In addition, refer to Note 30 – Subsequent event for the issuance and repurchase of Notes subsequent to year-end.

Required:

a. Bombardier has three senior notes outstanding, with two in euros (one at a fixed rate and one at a floating rate) and one in U.S. dollars. They are due at different times. Why would the company choose to issue three different kinds of debt rather than consolidate all of its financing needs into one note?

b. In the list of all of its long-term debt, Bombardier has senior notes, notes, and debentures. Briefly highlight the differences between these three types of debt instruments.

c. The company has debt instruments denominated in several different currencies. What advantages would there be for Bombardier in this strategy? (Hint: Think about where Bombardier does business.)

10-63 (Leases)

Ballard Power Systems Inc. designs, manufactures, and sells fuel cells and has its head office, research and development, and manufacturing facilities in Burnaby, British Columbia. Exhibit 10-18 presents Note 10 from Ballard's 2009 financial statements, which describes the company's capital (finance) lease obligations.

Required:

Based on the information in the note, explain why Ballard's lease for the production and test equipment is classified as a finance (capital) lease rather than an operating lease.

BALLARD POWER SYSTEMS INC. 2009 ANNUAL REPORT

EXHIBIT 10-18

annual report

Excerpt from Note 10 to the Financial Statements

(Tabular amounts expressed in thousands of U.S. dollars)

10. Obligations under capital lease:

The Corporation leases certain production and test equipment under a capital lease expiring in December 2014. Under the terms of the lease, the Corporation must either (i) purchase the equipment in December 2014 for its residual value equal to 20% of the initial cost, or (ii) enter into a new lease agreement for the residual value. Minimum future lease payments are as follows:

Year ending December 31		
2010	$	359
2011		359
2012		359
2013		359
2014		759
Total minimum lease payments		2,195
Less imputed interest at 2.25%		(140)
Total obligation under capital lease		2,055
Current portion of obligation under capital lease		316
Long-term portion of obligation under capital lease	$	1,739

10-64 (Pensions and other long-term benefits)

An excerpt from Note 18 to the 2009 financial statements of The **Lindt & Sprüngli Group**, dealing with employee benefits, is presented in Exhibit 10-19. As you probably know, Lindt & Sprungli is a Swiss-based manufacturer of fine chocolates.

Required:
a. What types of pension plans and other long-term benefit plans does Lindt & Sprüngli have?
b. In Lindt & Sprüngli's 2009 statement of earnings, what are the total expenses related to the pension and long-term benefit plans?
c. What is the total pension plan obligation for Lindt & Sprüngli as at December 31, 2009?
d. What is the total fair value of pension plan assets for Lindt & Sprüngli as at December 31, 2009?
e. Are Lindt & Sprüngli's pension plans underfunded or overfunded, and by what amount?
f. What is the net asset or liability related to pension plans that is reported on Lindt & Sprüngli's balance sheet as at December 31, 2009?

EXHIBIT 10-19

annual report

LINDT & SPRÜNGLI 2009 ANNUAL REPORT

Excerpt from Note 18 to the Financial Statements

18. PENSION PLANS AND OTHER LONG-TERM EMPLOYEE BENEFITS

In accordance with local laws and practices, the Group operates various benefit plans. Among these plans are defined benefits and defined contribution plans. These plans cover the majority of employees for death, disability and retirement. There are also plans for anniversary benefits or other benefits related to years of service, which qualify as plans for other long-term employee benefits.

Benefits are usually dependent on one or more factors such as the number of years the employee was covered in the plan, age, insurable salary and to some extent on the accumulated old age capital. The assets of the funded pension plans are held within separate foundations or insurances and may not revert to the employer.

The economic benefit available, as reduction in future employer contributions, is determined annually according to the applicable plan rules and the statutory requirement in the jurisdiction of the plan based on IFRIC 14. During the financial year 2009, the Group recognized an increase in the economic benefit net of deferred taxes of CHF 4.1 million (CHF 20.7 million in 2008) in the income statement.

Defined benefits pension plans and other long-term employee benefits — The following amounts have been recorded in the income statement as personnel expense:

Employee benefits expense

	Pension plans		Other long-term employee benefits	
CHF million	2009	2008	2009	2008
Current service cost	10.2	9.8	2.7	1.3
Interest on obligation	14.3	14.3	0.4	0.4
Expected return on plan assets	−42.4	−69.8	−	−
Changes in unrecognized assets (IAS 19.58)	87.3	−557.8	−	−
Gains (−) / losses (+) on curtailments or settlements	−1.6	−	−	−
Net actuarial gains (−) / losses (+) recognized	−63.4	583.5	0.1	0.1
Past service costs	−	−1.0	−	0.2
Total included in employee benefits expense	**4.4**	**−21.0**	**3.2**	**2.0**
Actual return on plan assets	111.2	−542.4		

Changes in the present value of the defined benefit obligation

	Pension plans		Other long-term employee benefits	
CHF million	2009	2008	2009	2008
Defined benefit obligation as at January 1	**392.7**	**399.8**	**8.0**	**7.7**
Current service cost	10.2	9.8	2.7	1.3
Plan participants' contributions	3.2	3.6	−	−
Interest on obligation	14.3	14.3	0.4	0.4
Benefits and net transferal paid through pension assets	−19.2	−13.4	−	−
Benefits paid by employer	−3.9	−6.0	−1.2	−0.9
Curtailments and settlements	−1.5	−	−	−
Actuarial gains (−) / losses (+)	−3.6	−4.8	0.1	0.1
Past service costs and others	−	−1.0	−	0.2
Currency translation	−	−9.6	−	−0.8
Defined benefit obligation as at December 31	**392.2**	**392.7**	**10.0**	**8.0**

LINDT & SPRÜNGLI 2009 ANNUAL REPORT (cont'd)

EXHIBIT 10-19

annual report

Changes in the fair value of plan assets

CHF million	Pension plans 2009	Pension plans 2008
Fair value of plan assets as at January 1	**877.5**	**1,424.5**
Plan participants' contributions	3.2	3.6
Contributions by employer	1.9	6.0
Benefits and net transferal paid through pension assets	−19.2	−13.4
Expected return on plan assets	42.4	69.8
Actuarial gains (+) / losses (−)	68.8	−612.1
Currency translations	−	−0.9
Fair value of plan assets as at December 31	**974.6**	**877.5**

The pension assets are composed of the following essential asset classes:

Asset classes

Valuation date December 31	Pension plans 2009 in %	Pension plans 2008 in %
Equities	80	78
Bonds	8	9
Real estate	9	9
Others including cash	3	4
Total	**100**	**100**

The pension assets as at December 31, 2009, include shares of the Lindt & Sprüngli Group with a market value of CHF 786.0 million (CHF 702.2 million in 2008). The market value of real estate rented by the Group is CHF 13.8 million (CHF 12.2 million in 2008).

Expected employer contributions for 2010 amount to CHF 2.1 million.

The net position of pension obligations in the balance sheet can be summarized as follows:

Amount recognized in the balance sheet

CHF million Valuation date December 31	Pension plans 2009	Pension plans 2008	Other long-term employee benefits 2009	Other long-term employee benefits 2008
Present value of funded obligation	372.6	372.0	−	−
Fair value of plan assets	−974.6	−877.5	−	−
Underfunding (+) / Overfunding (−)	−602.0	−505.5	−	−
Present value of unfunded obligations	19.7	20.7	10.0	8.0
Unrecognized actuarial gains (+) / losses (−)	24.5	15.6	−	−
Unrecognized past service costs	−	0.1	−	−
Unrecognized prepaid pension cost	602.6	515.3	−	−
Net liability	**44.8**	**46.2**	**10.0**	**8.0**

Amounts in the balance sheet

	Pension plans 2009	Pension plans 2008	Other 2009	Other 2008
Pension liabilities	125.6	124.0	10.0	8.0
Assets (prepaid pension funds)[1]	−80.8	−77.8	−	−
Net liability	**44.8**	**46.2**	**10.0**	**8.0**

1) See note 9.

10-65   (Income tax disclosures)

Research In Motion Limited—or RIM—is a leading designer, manufacturer, and marketer of wireless solutions for the worldwide mobile communications market, including the BlackBerry communications device. Exhibit 10-20 presents a portion of Note 10 to RIM's 2010 financial statements, with details about its income taxes.

Required:
a. For the fiscal years ending in 2010 and 2009, calculate the percentage of RIM's provision for income taxes that had to be paid in the current period and the percentage that was deferred to the future.
b. For the fiscal years ending in 2010 and 2009, calculate the percentage of RIM's total provision for income taxes that was Canadian and the percentage that was foreign.

10-66   (Debt to total assets and times interest earned ratios)

The 2009 consolidated balance sheet and statement of earnings for **Maple Leaf Foods Inc.**, a global food processing company based in Toronto, are included in Exhibit 10-21.

Required:
a. Calculate the debt to total assets ratios and the times interest earned ratios for the years ending December 31, 2009 and 2008. (Hint: The "non-controlling interest" amount on the balance sheet should not be included in total liabilities.)
b. Identify the major factors that caused the changes in these ratios.
c. Write a short report commenting on the results of the ratio calculations in part "a."

10-67   (Debt to total assets and times interest earned ratios)

Carnival Corporation & Group plc is a global company that operates several cruise lines— including Carnival Cruises, Princess Cruises, and Holland America—offering cruises in Europe, North America, and Australia. The statement of operations and consolidated balance sheet from Carnival's 2009 annual report are presented in Exhibit 1-10 A and B on pages 66–67.

Required:
a. Calculate the debt to total assets ratios and the times interest earned ratios for 2009 and 2008.
b. Identify the major factors that contributed to the changes in these ratios.
c. Write a short report commenting on the results of the ratio calculations that you did in part "a."

EXHIBIT 10-20

annual report

RESEARCH IN MOTION LIMITED 2009 ANNUAL REPORT
Excerpt from Note 10 to the Financial Statements

In thousands of United States dollars, except share and per share data, and except as otherwise indicated.

The provision for (recovery of) income taxes consists of the following:

	For the year ended		
	February 27, 2010	February 28, 2009	March 1, 2008
Provision for (recovery of) income taxes:			
Current			
Canadian	$ 695,790	$ 880,035	$ 555,895
Foreign	62,642	68,501	31,950
Deferred			
Canadian	20,965	(36,013)	(73,294)
Foreign	29,969	(4,776)	2,102
	$ 809,366	$ 907,747	$ 516,653

EXHIBIT 10-21A

annual report

MAPLE LEAF FOODS INC. 2009 ANNUAL REPORT

consolidated balance sheets

As at December 31

(In thousands of Canadian dollars)	2009	2008
ASSETS		
Current assets		
Cash and cash equivalents	$ 29,316	$ 365,518
Accounts receivable (Note 3)	200,317	139,144
Inventories (Note 4)	349,909	377,414
Income and other taxes recoverable	18,067	20,971
Future tax asset (Note 18)	4,301	19,787
Prepaid expenses and other assets	15,328	32,289
	$ 617,238	$ 955,123
Property and equipment (Note 5)	1,135,056	1,169,435
Other long-term assets (Note 6)	328,063	329,070
Future tax asset (Note 18)	22,116	24,854
Goodwill	857,278	876,261
Other intangible assets (Note 7)	97,913	97,358
	$ 3,057,464	$ 3,452,101
LIABILITIES AND SHAREHOLDERS' EQUITY		
Current liabilities		
Bank indebtedness	$ 4,274	$ 8,894
Accounts payable and accrued charges	489,182	600,924
Current portion of long-term debt (Note 8)	206,147	179,244
Other current liabilities	37,837	28,456
	$ 737,413	$ 817,518
Long-term debt (Note 8)	834,557	1,200,224
Future tax liability (Note 18)	27,851	37,903
Other long-term liabilities (Note 9)	187,523	179,039
Non-controlling interest	81,070	74,447
Shareholders' equity (Note 12)	1,189,050	1,142,970
	$ 3,057,464	$ 3,452,101

Contingencies and commitments (Note 21)

See accompanying Notes to the Consolidated Financial Statements

EXHIBIT 10-21B

annual report

MAPLE LEAF FOODS INC. 2009 ANNUAL REPORT

consolidated statements of earnings

Years ended December 31

(In thousands of Canadian dollars except share amounts)	2009	2008
Sales	$ 5,221,602	$ 5,242,602
Cost of goods sold	4,487,378	4,622,409
Gross margin	$ 734,224	$ 620,193
Selling, general and administrative expenses	538,113	491,778
Earnings from operations before the following:	$ 196,111	$ 128,415
Product recall, restructuring and other related costs (Note 11)	(31,145)	(102,812)
Other income (Note 16)	3,613	24,864
Earnings from operations before interest and income taxes	$ 168,579	$ 50,467
Interest expense (Note 17)	81,234	88,651
Earnings (loss) from operations before income taxes	$ 87,345	$ (38,184)
Income taxes (Note 18)	27,296	(8,538)
Earnings (loss) from operations before non-controlling interest	$ 60,049	$ (28,646)
Non-controlling interest	7,902	7,211
Net earnings (loss)	$ 52,147	$ (36,857)
Basic earnings (loss) per share (Note 15)	$ 0.40	$ (0.29)
Diluted earnings (loss) per share (Note 15)	$ 0.39	$ (0.29)
Weighted average number of shares (millions)	129.8	126.7

See accompanying Notes to the Consolidated Financial Statements.

BEYOND THE BOOK

10-68 (Analysis of a company's liabilities)

Choose a company as directed by your instructor and do the following:

a. Prepare a quick analysis of the non-current liability accounts by listing the beginning and ending amounts in these accounts and calculating the net change, in both dollar and percentage terms, for the most recent year.

b. If any of the accounts changed by more than 10%, try to give an explanation for the change.

c. What percentage of the company's total liabilities is in the form of long-term bank loans? Long-term bonds? Have these percentages changed significantly over the last year?

d. What interest rates is the company paying on its long-term debt? (Hint: You will probably need to look in the notes to the financial statements to find the answer to this question.)

e. Calculate the company's debt to total assets ratio and its times interest earned ratio. To the extent that you can, based on this limited analysis, comment on the company's financial health in terms of its level of debt and interest expense.

f. Read the company's note on income taxes and answer the following questions:

   i. What are the major items that caused the company's effective tax rate to be different from the statutory tax rate?

   ii. What are the major items that created deferred (or future) income tax assets and/or liabilities for the company?

Cases

10-69 Regal Cars

Regal Cars has been manufacturing exotic automobiles for more than 50 years. It has always prided itself on its top-quality products and high levels of customer satisfaction. All Regal Cars are hand-built to the purchasers' individual specifications. In the past year, the popularity of Regal Cars has increased dramatically following a promotional campaign in which Regal provided complimentary cars to star members of the local NHL team. To meet the increasing demand, Mark Quaid, the president and largest shareholder of Regal Cars, is considering partially automating the production line.

To finance the conversion of the manual production line to a robotic system, Quaid will have to raise more than $1 million in capital. The company has been in the Quaid family for more than 50 years and Mark is unwilling to sell shares and risk diluting his family's equity in the business. As an alternative to equity financing, he has identified three potential sources of debt financing and has asked you to explain how each option would affect the company's financial statements.

Option 1—Bank loan

A national bank has offered to lend Regal the necessary funds in the form of a 10-year, 12% bank loan. Annual payments of $100,000 plus interest will be required. Because of the loan's size, the bank would require Mark Quaid to personally guarantee the loan with a mortgage on the family estate.

Option 2—Bond issue

Regal can issue 10-year, 10% bonds for the amount required. Currently, similar bonds in the market are providing a return of 10%.

Option 3—Lease

Regal can lease the equipment. The lease would require annual payments of $104,000 over a 10-year lease period. The present value of these payments, at an annual interest rate of 8%, would be $697,850. The equipment is expected to have a useful life of 12 years and to be worth about $100,000 at the end of the 10 years.

> **Required:**
> Prepare a memo to Mark Quaid discussing how each of these options would affect the company's financial statements. You should also include in your memo any other pertinent observations that could influence the financing decision he has to make.

10-70 Jonah Fitzpatrick

Jonah Fitzpatrick would like to start investing and is considering purchasing some of the bonds being issued by Jennings Financial. Details of the bond issue were outlined in a recent article in *Financial Times Magazine*. The following is an excerpt from the article:

> Jennings Financial is planning to issue a series of bonds to help finance the acquisition of a large manufacturing facility. In consultation with its investment bankers, the company has decided to issue $100 million of 8%, five-year bonds. Each bond will be denominated at $1,000. The bonds will be classified as senior debenture bonds and will be sold to yield a return of 10%. Because this is such a large issue, the investment banker is required to underwrite the issue. However, given the company's historical performance and financial strength, a syndicate is willing to guarantee the entire issue.

Jonah is unfamiliar with bond issues and approaches Mike Jacobs, his stockbroker, with some basic questions.

Jonah: I've always invested in equity securities, Mike, but I want to consider investing in the bonds being issued by Jennings Financial. I know very little about bonds, though, so I have a few questions.

Mike: Sure thing, Jonah. Just e-mail your questions and I'll get back to you later today.

Required:

Jonah has just sent Mike the following e-mail. Draft an appropriate response.

Mike, here are my questions on the Jennings bonds. I look forward to hearing from you.

1. The advertisement for the bond issue states that the bonds will be 8% bonds but will yield 10%. Why are there two interest rates? Which interest rate should I use to determine how much I'll earn on the bonds?

2. What are debenture bonds? Will I have any security if the company defaults on these bonds?

3. What is the role of the investment banker? What does it mean to use a syndicate?

4. What if I need my money back before the end of the five-year period? Does the five-year term mean that I would be locked into this investment for five years?

10-71 Wasselec's Moving and Storage

Wasselec's Moving and Storage is a small company based in Hamilton, Ontario. It operates in both the residential and commercial markets. To serve its various clients, Wasselec's owns two large moving trucks (tractor-trailer units), six medium-sized cartage trucks, two large vans, and two cars. Because its business relies on its vehicles, it has always been the company's policy to purchase new vehicles on a regular rotation basis. Its accountant and vehicle service manager have established guidelines that trigger the purchase of a new vehicle. For example, the large vans are replaced every 200,000 kilometres, the tractors every 10 years, and the trailers every 15 years.

The president of the company recently read an article about the increasing trend toward leasing. She wonders if Wasselec's should start leasing its vehicles instead of buying them, and has asked the chief financial officer (CFO) for guidance in this matter. In turn, the CFO has asked you, a recent addition to the company's staff, to prepare a summary of the advantages and disadvantages of ownership versus leasing.

Required:

Draft a memo to the CFO summarizing the advantages and disadvantages of ownership and leasing, with reference to the types of assets currently owned by Wasselec's Moving and Storage. The CFO is very busy, so your memo should be concise.

10-72 Grant's Ice Cream Shop

Jack and Gillian Grant, owners of Grant's Ice Cream Shop, have recently expanded their business by moving into a second location in a nearby town. To open the second location, the company had to obtain three large ice cream machines. To buy the machines would have cost over $15,000, so Jack and Gillian decided to lease them instead.

The lease term is for five years and the machines are expected to have a useful life of eight to 10 years. According to the lease contract, the present value of the lease payments over the lease term is $12,000 and the Grants will have the option to purchase the leased machines for $1,000 at the end of the five-year lease term. Their fair market value is expected to be approximately $4,000 at the end of the lease.

Jack Grant is thrilled with the arrangement. "Not only do we get the machines that we need without a large initial cash outlay, but we don't have to record any liability on the statement of financial position; we can just report the annual lease payments as equipment rental expense on the statement of earnings."

Required:

Is Jack correct in assuming that the lease payments will be recorded as an expense and that no debt will have to be reported on the statement of financial position as a result of this transaction? Explain your answer fully, by referring to the criteria for lease classification and the appropriate accounting treatment for this type of lease.

10-73 Peterson Corporation

As part of recent contract negotiations, Peterson Corporation has presented two pension plan options to its employees. The employees are to vote on which plan they would like the company to implement. Peterson Corporation owns and operates a chain of grocery stores throughout western Canada and employs more than 3,000 people. Most employees have little education and very limited accounting knowledge. Your cousin, Karen Cooper, is a cashier at a Peterson store located in Kamloops, British Columbia, and she has asked you for help in determining which pension option to vote for. She is confused over the terminology used in the proposal and would like you to explain the two alternatives in simpler terms, so that she can make an informed decision.

Option 1

The company will establish a defined contribution pension plan. The company will contribute 10% of the employee's gross wages to the pension plan each pay period. Vesting will occur immediately and the funds will be placed with an independent trustee to be invested. Employees will have the option of contributing additional funds to the plan.

Option 2

The company will establish a defined benefit plan. The plan will guarantee that each employee will receive 2% of the average of their highest five years of salary multiplied by the number of years the employee works for the company. The plan will be fully employer-funded and the pension entitlement will vest after five years of continuous service.

> **Required:**
> Briefly explain to Karen the difference between the two pension plan options. You should remember that Karen is unfamiliar with pension terminology and you therefore have to explain some of the terms used in the plan descriptions.

Critical Thinking Question

10-74 (Pension plan disclosures)

For defined benefit pension plans, a formula has been devised for calculating the pension expense to be recognized each accounting period. The amount of funding (i.e., cash transferred from the company to the pension plan trustee) is usually a different amount than the expense. When the amount of cash that is transferred is less than the pension expense that is recognized, a liability for the difference results. When the opposite occurs (i.e., the amount of cash transferred to the trustee is greater than the pension expense), an asset results.

The difference between the two amounts in any particular period is a reflection of the pension plan being either overfunded or underfunded that individual period. However, these amounts are usually insignificant compared with the corporation's total liability for the pension plan and its cumulative status in terms of being overfunded or underfunded.

> **Required:**
> Describe the current disclosure requirements for pensions. Should a company be required to include a liability on the statement of financial position that reflects its total future obligation with respect to its pension plan? What impact would such a requirement have on the debt to total assets ratio? Are users of financial statements being given enough information about pension plans to allow them to make informed decisions?

SHAREHOLDERS' EQUITY

LEARNING OBJECTIVES

After studying this chapter, you should be able to:

1. Distinguish among the different types of business organizations and explain the advantages and disadvantages of each.

2. Describe the different types of shares and explain why corporations choose to issue a variety of share types.

3. Prepare journal entries for share transactions, including the issuance and payment of dividends.

4. Describe the different types of dividends and explain why companies might opt to issue one type of dividend rather than another.

5. Describe what a stock split is and explain how it is accounted for.

6. Describe what an employee stock option is and explain how it is accounted for.

7. Explain the structure and purpose of the statement of retained earnings and the statement of changes in equity.

8. Calculate the book value and market value of a corporation.

9. Calculate and interpret the price/earnings ratio and the return on shareholders' equity ratio.

The Market's Ups and Downs Are More Than Entertainment

Perhaps you're a devoted fan of the Canadian comedy *This Hour Has 22 Minutes*; or a parent, aunt, or uncle of a preschooler who can't miss episodes of *Franny's Feet* or *Animal Mechanicals*; or maybe you took in a screening of the Academy Award winning documentary *Bowling for Columbine*—in all cases, you've seen the work of the people behind DHX Media Ltd.

Shares in DHX Media began trading on the Toronto Stock Exchange and the AIM exchange in London in May 2006. At the time, the company issued 8.7 million common shares at a price of $2.35 per share, raising $20.45 million. It used the proceeds to acquire DECODE Entertainment Inc., repay debt, and finance international growth.

Before the initial public offering, DHX Media had been known as Halifax Film, which is now a subsidiary of the larger company. Halifax Film develops and produces original film and television programming, including *22 Minutes*, *Animal Mechanicals*, and the feature film *Shake Hands with the Devil*. Founders Michael Donovan and Charles Bishop also produced *Bowling for Columbine* when they were principals with Salter Street Films, which was purchased by Alliance Atlantis. They formed Halifax Film in 2004.

DHX Media's subsidiary DECODE Entertainment internationally distributes television and interactive programming for children and youth. Meanwhile, its Vancouver-based subsidiary, Studio B Productions, creates proprietary production and interactive content, and does service work for outside producers, including the hit series *Martha Speaks* for PBS.

The production and worldwide distribution of children's programming, as well as the subsequent merchandizing licensing, is DHX's main focus. However, a portion of its efforts are also devoted to the quality comedy and theatrical productions that the company's older audience enjoys, such as the prime-time drama *The Guard*.

As successful as the company is, DHX shares have nonetheless followed the ups and downs of the market and by August 2010 were trading at about $0.94 per share. The company had issued an aggregate 44.5 million common shares at an average price of $1.40 per share. In addition, through a normal course issuer bid initiated in 2009, the company repurchased a total of 260,925 of its own shares at market price, averaging $0.76 per share.

"The reality is, with a $40-million market capitalization company, unfortunately a different set of rules apply," explains David Regan, executive vice president, corporate development and investor relations. "DHX is a microcap without much of a free float of shares because many of the shares are locked up with the principals." The company's founders and some directors own 38 percent of DHX's shares. "You don't necessarily get the rational response you might expect with a bigger company that's got a wider following and more volume associated with its shares," Mr. Regan adds.

DHX shares, along with those of fellow microcap companies, were hit hard in late 2008 as the credit crises caused market panic and a flight to liquidity. However, consistent operating results have buoyed the share price since then. Ongoing projects like *This Hour Has 22 Minutes* and *The Guard* provide a stable source of production revenue, while increasing international distribution helps drive profit margins.

The opening story describes how a company, Halifax Film, created a new company, **DHX Media**, and moved in 2006 from being a private corporation to a public corporation. A private corporation has shareholders, but those shareholders are usually a relatively small group (compared with a publicly traded company) and most likely know each other and have similar objectives for the company. Shares of a private company are not available for purchase on a public stock exchange, like the Toronto Stock Exchange (TSE), and because of the limited number of shareholders it is more difficult to buy and/or sell an ownership interest. A private company can become a public company by issuing additional shares to the public in an initial public offering (IPO). Once DHX Media went public with its IPO in May 2006, it increased its access to funds, increased its number of shareholders, and lost some control over who its shareholders are. DHX Media's financial statements are public information now and the company must produce quarterly and annual reports for the stock exchange and its shareholders. When it was a private corporation, it produced financial information for its shareholders but not for the stock exchange or the general public. DHX Media saw the issuance of the IPO as an opportunity to expand not only its capital base, but also its ownership base. It used the new funds to purchase another company, DECODE Entertainment Inc., pay down some of its debt, and finance some of its international initiatives. In 2009 the company bought back some of the shares held by the public, which reduced the number of shares outstanding, but the company remained a public company. Later in this chapter, we will look at why a company might buy back its shares.

As the following shows, however, a company can also go from being a public company to a private one.

accounting in the news

Going Private

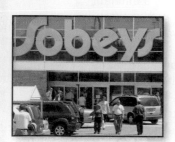

For many companies, the ultimate goal is to go public, giving them access to a lot of money through the stock market. But others choose to go private. In June 2007, Stellarton, N.S.–based **Empire Co. Ltd.** acquired all the outstanding common shares of **Sobeys Inc.** that it did not previously own, thus taking Canada's second-largest grocery chain private. Empire, whose key businesses include food retailing, real estate, and corporate investment activities, made its bid on April 26, 2007, offering 53 percent more than Sobeys' closing price the previous day, or $58 per share. Sobeys shareholders and the Supreme Court of Nova Scotia approved the plan in early June, and common shares in Sobeys were delisted from the Toronto Stock Exchange on June 18. The transaction cost Empire approximately $1,062 million.

Sources: "Empire Bid for Sobeys Gets Court Approval," Bloomberg, June 14, 2007; Empire Company Limited news release, June 15, 2007.

A company often gets taken private when one of its shareholders already owns a significant amount of the company. In the case of Empire Co. Ltd., it owned 71.2 percent of Sobeys prior to making a bid to buy the remainder of the shares. A major shareholder will often seek to own 100 percent of the shares so that it can exert total control over the operations and strategy of the purchased company. Owning all of the company enables Empire Co. to keep information about Sobeys' operations from its competitors in the grocery industry.

In this chapter, we are going to delve more deeply into the components of shareholders' equity, which represents a residual amount (assets minus liabilities) and measures the investment that owners have made in the company. However, before getting into a detailed discussion of the components of shareholders' equity in a corporation, we will take a short detour to discuss why knowing more about shareholders' equity is important to users and we will look at alternative forms of business organization.

USER RELEVANCE

The chances are relatively high that in the future you will invest in companies, either directly by buying shares or indirectly by buying mutual funds. As a future shareholder, you need to understand how your ownership interest is measured and disclosed in the financial statements. So far in this book, we have talked only about common shares. In reality, there are several different kinds of shares (ownership interests). With the help of financial experts, companies design and create financial instruments that have a variety of features to provide investors with different levels of risk and return. These instruments also have varying rights and privileges. You should know what some of those features are so that you can more accurately assess the value of your ownership interest through the particular types of shares that you own. In addition, when a company raises more capital by issuing new shares, you will need to be aware of how that new issuance affects your current holdings.

Sometimes investors buy shares to receive a periodic dividend payment. More frequently, however, shares are purchased in anticipation of the share value increasing so that the shares can be sold in the future for a profit. Let's now take a brief look at some of the different forms of business organization.

FORMS OF ORGANIZATION

As discussed briefly in Chapter 1, there are different forms of business organization. While almost all companies in Canada are established as corporations, the other forms of business include sole proprietorships, partnerships, limited partnerships, and Crown corporations. The form of organization has implications for the liability of the owners, and the taxation of the business income. We will first briefly describe the three main forms of business and their accounting implications. Then we will discuss the liability, taxation, and other important advantages and disadvantages of each form.

Sole Proprietorship

The simplest form of business is the **sole proprietorship**. The sole proprietorship is a single-owner business. All profits and losses belong to the owner, and all decisions are made either by the owner or under the owner's direction. It is probably this aspect of control that keeps the proprietorship form of business alive. Most owners like to be the ones making decisions and to be active in the day-to-day operations. Proprietorships can be small, single-unit operations, or they can be larger operations with units in several places.

LEARNING OBJECTIVE 1

Distinguish among the different types of business organizations and explain the advantages and disadvantages of each.

Because the sole proprietor does not have to report to shareholders, there is also less concern about preparing reports according to accounting standards. The owner might deviate from established standards if using a different method will produce information that was more useful in making the decisions necessary to run the business. For example, for tax purposes, sole proprietors are required to combine the profits or losses from their businesses with their personal income; there is no separate taxation as there is for corporations. To simplify bookkeeping, many sole proprietorships therefore only follow taxation rules in determining their income. On the other hand, if the hope is to secure a bank loan for the business, the sole proprietor might want to follow Canadian standards, since loan officers could insist on seeing financial statements prepared according to GAAP. GAAP statements might also be required if the sole proprietorship operates in an industry that is regulated. In Canada, a proprietorship has two forms of acceptable GAAP from which to choose—either IFRS or APSE.

Regarding owners' equity accounts, there is little reason for the owner to distinguish the initial investment from the earnings retained in the business. For this reason, the owner's equity section of a sole proprietorship typically has only one account, which is sometimes called **owner's capital**. This account is used when the owner puts new capital into the business, when the business earns income (revenues and expenses are closed to this account), and when the owner withdraws cash from the business. Cash withdrawn from the business for personal use is usually referred to as a withdrawal by the owner. These withdrawals are similar to dividends in a corporation.

Partnership

A second form of business organization is the **partnership**, which is very similar to a sole proprietorship. In a partnership, two or more individuals agree to conduct business together. The partners' involvement in the partnership can vary greatly and the partners' rights and responsibilities are generally specified in a document called a **partnership agreement**. This document is very important because it specifies how the partners will make decisions about the business, including how they will share in profits and losses, as well as how the assets will be distributed if the partnership is dissolved. When there is no partnership agreement, the distribution of assets and profits is assumed to be equal for all partners. If the partners intend to share profits in some other proportion, this must be stated in a partnership agreement.

The accounting for the owners' equity section of a partnership requires that the partnership keep a separate account for each partner, usually called the partner's **capital account**. Each period, the partnership's profits or losses must be distributed among the partners' capital accounts. This is usually a relatively complex process that takes into consideration issues such as the form of contributions and withdrawals by partners during the year. Were contributions loans or capital? Were withdrawals expenses of the partnership or the partner's share of profits? Sometimes there is also an account for each partner called a **drawings account**. This is an account that keeps track of the amounts withdrawn by the partner during the period. It is similar to a dividends declared account in a corporation in that it records payments made to owners. In the case of the drawings account, at the end of each accounting period it is closed into the capital account of the specific partner. As with sole proprietorships, such withdrawals are not taxable.

Detailed accounting procedures for partnerships are sometimes covered in advanced accounting texts and will not be discussed here. Other than owners' equity, the accounting for partnership transactions is essentially the same as for corporations.

Corporation

The third major form of business organization is the **corporation**, which has been the focus of most of this book. The basics of accounting for shareholders' equity in a company have been covered in preceding chapters. Later in this chapter, details will be provided concerning more complex transactions that involve shareholders' equity.

A corporation differs from a sole proprietorship and a partnership in at least three significant ways: limited liability, taxation, and its status as a separate legal entity.

The fact that the corporation is legally separate from its shareholders normally provides its shareholders with limited liability, discussed later, and usually results in a distinct separation between the owners and the corporation's operations. The corporation has a board of directors, who are the ultimate decision-makers in the business. They are elected by the shareholders and select (hire and fire) the management team that runs the day-to-day business operations.

Limited Liability Differences in the Different Forms of Organization

The owners of sole proprietorships and partnerships have **unlimited liability**, which means they assume all the risk if the business runs into trouble. They are personally 100 percent liable for all debts of the business. If a stakeholder makes a claim against the company, both the business assets and the owner's personal property (if necessary) may be used to fulfill the obligation and satisfy the claim. This aspect of unlimited liability makes many single owners and partners consider establishing the business as a corporation rather than a sole proprietorship.

The status of a corporation as a separate legal entity allows the corporate shareholders to have **limited liability** for the debts of the companies they own. They cannot be made to pay for the company's debts out of their personal assets (unless they give personal guarantees). The most a shareholder can lose is the amount of the investment in the shares. Creditors cannot seek satisfaction of their claims from the personal assets of corporate shareholders. Limited liability is obviously an advantage of the corporate form of organization.

Some types of partnerships, called **limited partnerships**, also have limited liability for some of the partners. These partnerships allow partners to assume different responsibilities and risks in a partnership. In limited partnerships, there are general partners and limited partners. **General partners** normally make day-to-day decisions about the business, share in profits and losses, and have unlimited liability. If the partnership defaults on its debts, creditors can sue one, more than one, or all of the general partners, taking both business and personal assets. **Limited partners** have limited liability, but also have limited involvement in the partnership. They normally invest in the partnership and share in its profits and losses, but they do not make day-to-day decisions about operations. Creditors typically cannot sue them if the partnership runs into financial difficulty.

In recent years, most provinces have changed the accounting legislation that governs the terms and structure of professional accountants and their activities. Historically, accounting firms were partnerships, with all partners having unlimited liability. Under the new legislation, professional accountants have a form of limited liability in that they are no longer unconditionally liable for all of the actions of all of the other partners. They now have personal liability only with respect to their own acts and the acts of those employees working under them. This is a new form of limited partnership. Accounting firms with this form of limited partnership have LLP at the end of their name, which stands for Limited Liability Partnership.

Taxation Differences in the Different Forms of Organization

For tax purposes, because it flows through to the individual owners, the income of partnerships and sole proprietorships is not taxed at the business level. Instead it is included in the owner's personal tax return in the year it is earned, regardless of whether it was paid out to the owner or not. Personal tax is then assessed according to the individual owner's tax bracket. If amounts are withdrawn by the owner in a subsequent year, he is not taxed on that withdrawal, because the income tax was already paid on this amount in the year it was earned.

Because corporations are viewed as separate legal entities, the Canada Revenue Agency (CRA) and provincial governments impose corporate taxes on the income they earn. This corporate tax is in addition to the personal income tax that shareholders pay on their personal income when they receive dividends or when they sell their shares and experience a gain or loss. An incorporated small business can obtain a tax advantage through tax deferral when profits are retained in the business. The corporation pays the corporate taxes in the year the income is earned. Corporate tax rates vary by the type of income earned and the size of the business, but in general are lower than personal taxes on the same level of earnings. The tax to be paid by the individual shareholders on dividends or capital gains (if they sell their shares for a gain) is deferred until dividends are received or the shares are sold, which could be in subsequent years. It is then taxed at the individual level. Corporate income is, therefore, subject to double taxation: once when the corporation pays taxes on corporate income when it is earned, and again when the shareholders pay taxes on dividends distributed by the corporation. This does not necessarily mean that the corporate form results in more tax being paid. The sum of the corporate tax and individual tax for a small business is approximately equal to the individual tax on business income, but only the corporate tax is paid in the year the income is earned. The individual portion can be deferred to a later period, if the profits are not paid out in the same year they are earned. For larger corporations that cannot take advantage of the small business tax rate, the tax effect could be a disadvantage of the corporate form. However, the income tax rules include methods intended to reduce the impact of this double taxation.

Other Advantages and Disadvantages in the Different Forms of Organization

There are other advantages and disadvantages to each form of business. For example, incorporation, the process of becoming a corporation, requires a significant amount of paperwork and regulation, which makes a corporation more difficult to form than a sole proprietorship or partnership. (Although partnerships can be formed without any written agreement, a written partnership agreement prepared with legal assistance is advisable in order to avoid possible disagreements among the partners.) Once established, corporations can raise additional capital much more easily than proprietorships or partnerships, since they can issue more shares, or bonds, as discussed in Chapter 10. Partnerships and sole proprietorships are limited to the assets contributed by the owners and to profits that are earned by the business and not withdrawn; they cannot usually raise additional capital by issuing more shares or bonds.

It is much easier to change your ownership interest if you are a shareholder than if you are a partner or a sole proprietor. If the company is public, you simply sell your shares on the stock market. If the company is private, you can sell your shares to other existing owners or a new owner. In contrast, if you no longer want to own a proprietorship, you must sell the whole business or close it down. If you are a partner and want to withdraw from a partnership, you must convince the other partners to buy you out or find another partner to buy your ownership interest.

Lastly, there are additional costs to operating as a corporation in the form of filing corporate tax returns or, if required, preparing audited financial statements or meeting other ongoing regulatory costs. When establishing a new business, it is important to weigh all the issues before deciding on the organizational form that will work best.

In Canada, corporations own the vast majority of business assets and almost all large businesses are organized as corporations. That is why we focus on accounting for corporations in this text.

CORPORATIONS

Let's look at corporations in more detail. Shareholders of corporations require certain types of legal protection, especially because the owners of most corporations are absentee shareholders; that is, they are not intimately involved in the day-to-day business operations. This protection is provided by the laws of the jurisdiction under which the company is incorporated. In Canada, companies may be incorporated under the federal *Canada Business Corporations Act*, or under similar acts that have been established in the provinces and territories. When investors decide to establish a business in the form of a corporation, they must first decide under which act they want to be incorporated. Normally, most companies in Canada are incorporated under the laws of the province or territory in which the business, or at least the head office, is located. Companies that intend to carry out business interprovincially or internationally may decide that being incorporated under federal legislation will give them more options. After deciding on where to be incorporated, the founding investors prepare a document called the **articles of incorporation**. The articles of incorporation include information about what type of business the company will conduct, how the board of directors will be organized, who the management will be, and what kinds of shares will be issued, as well as other information. The exact content of the articles will depend on the decisions of the incorporating shareholders. Once the company has been incorporated, the articles of incorporation can generally be amended only by a shareholder vote.

SHARES

For accounting purposes, the most important section of the articles of incorporation is the description of the shares that will be issued. The maximum number of shares that the company can issue is specified in the articles. These are referred to as the **authorized shares**. Shares that have been sold by the company are known as **issued shares**. In the past, companies would establish a fixed number of authorized shares that they assumed would carry them for many years. However, when a company is first starting up, it may be difficult to anticipate that it will ever issue the full number of shares that it sets as its authorized limit. (Remember our opening story? **DHX Media** issued 8.7 million common shares in its first public offering.) To give you some perspective on share numbers, consider that **Le Château Inc.**, a medium-sized company, had 24.5 million shares issued by the end of January 2010. The **Royal Bank of Canada**, one of the largest companies in Canada, had 1,423.4 million common shares issued at the end of April 2010. In the United States, **Microsoft** had issued 8,763.8 million shares by the middle of April 2010. The magnitude of these numbers is difficult to conceive when starting a company. Indeed some companies have subsequently found that issuing all the authorized shares was not really that hard to do. Increasing the number of authorized shares in such cases requires a change in the articles of incorporation, which in turn requires a vote by the shareholders. To overcome the problem of reaching the authorized limit set in the articles of incorporation, many companies today instead establish an unlimited number of authorized shares in their articles of incorporation. This allows them the greatest freedom to issue shares as a means for raising capital.

In the past, the articles of incorporation could also specify a dollar amount to attach to each share. This dollar amount was known as the **par value**. When the shares were issued, the par value of each share was credited to the shares account and the excess was credited to an account called additional paid-in capital, or contributed surplus in excess of par. The amount credited to the shares account (in this case, the par value of the shares) is referred to as the **legal capital** and must be kept intact. Except under specific circumstances, it cannot be paid out as dividends. This provides protection for creditors.

Under most jurisdictions in Canada, par value shares are no longer permitted. Instead, most companies issue **no par value shares**. When no par value shares are issued, the total amount received for the shares is credited to the shares account. This results in a larger amount of legal capital that must be maintained in the company, and thus provides greater protection for creditors.

The articles of incorporation also specify the classes or types of shares that can be issued by the company, if more than one class of shares is to be issued. Financial statement users can usually find information about the authorized, issued, and different types of shares in the notes to the financial statements. An example of this disclosure, Note 8 for Le Château Inc., is shown in Exhibit 11-1. You may recall from earlier chapters that Montreal-based Le Château is a major Canadian retailer of men's and women's clothing, footwear, and accessories. As a medium-sized Canadian company, it is a good company to use throughout the chapter to illustrate the concepts of shareholders' equity in a Canadian context. Note that the excerpts used in this chapter are from the 2009 annual report but they include figures up to January 30, 2010, the company's fiscal year end. It is called the 2009 annual report because most of the months it covers (11 out of 12) are from 2009. When reading the report, we will be focusing on numbers in the 2010 column, which covers the 12 months from February 1, 2009, to January 30, 2010.

Le Château has two classes of common shares and three classes of preferred shares (which can be issued in series). As at January 30, 2010, there were no preferred shares issued. There were 19,973,464 Class A subordinate voting shares and 4,560,000 Class B multiple voting shares issued. In many companies, more than one class is authorized so that the company has more flexibility in attracting different kinds of investors. For example, some investors want the assurance of regular dividends to provide a steady income; others prefer no regular dividends but hope for increasing share values so that they can earn capital gains when they eventually sell their shares.

LE CHÂTEAU INC. 2009 ANNUAL REPORT

EXHIBIT 11-1

annual report

EXCERPT FROM NOTE 8 ON CAPITAL STOCK

8. CAPITAL STOCK
Authorized
An unlimited number of non-voting First, Second and Third Preferred Shares issuable in series.
An unlimited number of Class A subordinate voting shares.
An unlimited number of Class B voting shares.

Principal features

[a] With respect to the payment of dividends and the return of capital, the shares rank as follows:

First Preferred
Second Preferred
Third Preferred
Class A and Class B

[b] Subject to the rights of the Preferred shareholders, the Class A subordinate voting shareholders are entitled to a non-cumulative preferential dividend of $0.0125 per share, after which the Class B shareholders are entitled to a non-cumulative dividend of $0.0125 per share; any further dividends declared in a fiscal year must be declared and paid in equal amounts per share on all the Class A and Class B Shares then outstanding without preference or distinction.

[c] Subject to the foregoing, the Class A and Class B Shares rank equally, share for share, in earnings.

[d] The Class A subordinate voting shares carry one vote per share and the Class B Shares carry 10 votes per share.

[e] The Articles of the Corporation provide in effect that if there is an accepted or completed offer for more than 20% of the Class B Shares or an accepted or completed offer to more than 14 holders thereof at a price in excess of 115% of their market value [as defined in the Articles of the Corporation], each Class A subordinate voting share will be, at the option of the holder, converted into one Class B Share for the purposes of accepting such offer, unless at the same time an offer is made to all holders of the Class A subordinate voting shares for a percentage of such shares at least equal to the percentage of Class B Shares which are the subject of the offer and otherwise on terms and conditions not less favourable. In addition, each Class A subordinate voting share shall be converted into one Class B Share if at any time the principal shareholder of the Company or any corporation controlled directly or indirectly by him ceases to be the beneficial owner, directly or indirectly, and with full power to exercise in all circumstances the voting rights attached to such shares, of shares of the Corporation having attached thereto more than 50% of the votes attached to all outstanding shares of the Corporation.

Issued and outstanding

	January 30, 2010		January 31, 2009	
	Number of shares	$	Number of shares	$
Class A subordinate voting shares				
Balance – beginning of year	19,663,464	30,595	18,502,964	31,216
Conversion of multiple voting shares	—	—	2,000,000	176
Issuance of subordinate voting shares upon exercise of options	310,000	2,696	81,200	614
Cancellation of shares pursuant to stock repurchase program	—	—	(920,700)	(1,548)
Reclassification from contributed surplus due to exercise of share options	—	642	—	137
Balance, end of year	19,973,464	33,933	19,663,464	30,595
Class B multiple voting shares				
Balance, beginning of year	4,560,000	402	6,560,000	578
Conversion to subordinate voting shares	—	—	(2,000,000)	(176)
	4,560,000	402	4,560,000	402
Balance, end of year	24,533,464	34,335	24,223,464	30,997

EXHIBIT 11-1 **LE CHÂTEAU INC. 2009 ANNUAL REPORT (cont'd)**

8. CAPITAL STOCK [Cont'd]

In September 2008, the principal shareholder of the Company converted 2,000,000 Class B voting shares with a paid-up capital of $176,153 into Class A subordinate voting shares.

Dividends

During the year, the Company declared dividends in the amount of $17,064,000 [2009 – $21,602,000, which included a one-time dividend of $0.25 per Class A subordinate voting share and Class B voting share amounting to $6,220,000 that was paid on August 19, 2008].

The different classes of shares differ in the rights that accrue to their holders. Two major classes of shares, common shares and preferred shares, are discussed in the following subsections. Different classes of shares can be authorized within each of these two major types. As noted for Le Château, some companies have multiple classes of common shares and multiple classes (sometimes these are called series) of preferred shares. Le Château's Class A shares carry one vote per share, whereas the Class B shares carry 10 votes per share.

Corporations generally issue shares through a firm of investment bankers, known as underwriters, in much the same way that bonds are issued (see Chapter 10 for a discussion of this process). When common or preferred shares are issued, the details and features of the shares being issued are discussed in a legal document called a **prospectus**, which is distributed to potential investors when shares (or bonds) are initially sold.

LEARNING OBJECTIVE 2

Describe the different types of shares and explain why corporations choose to issue a variety of share types.

Common Shares

Every corporation must have one class of shares that represents the company's basic voting ownership rights. These shares are normally referred to as **common shares** (or, in most of the world outside North America, **ordinary shares**). Common shares carry a basic set of rights that allow the owner to share proportionately (based on the number of shares held) in all of the following:

1. Profits and losses

2. The selection of corporate management

3. Net assets upon liquidation

4. Subsequent issues of shares (although not all jurisdictions in Canada provide for this basic right)

PROFITS AND LOSSES Rather than establishing complex income-sharing rules similar to a partnership, a corporation retains control over the distribution of its profits. Different classes of shares are entitled to different portions of the earnings. Normally, preferred shares are restricted to the amounts of their dividends and no more. Common shares normally have no restrictions on their rights to share in earnings, once the claims of the creditors and the preferred shareholders have been satisfied.

It is sometimes useful to think of a corporation's profits or losses as being allocated to its shares. The resulting per-share figure is useful in determining whether the corporation's profits are increasing or decreasing on an individual share basis. The earnings per share figure (EPS) that corporations calculate provides a measure of performance that all shareholders can use. Recall from Chapter 4 that this calculation consists of dividing the corporation's net earnings by the average number of common shares outstanding during the year. A weighted average is used if the number of common shares outstanding changed during the year.

If a corporation opts to pay dividends (it is not obliged to do so), owners of the same class of shares receive a proportionate share of earnings in the form of dividends. Corporations, in addition to reporting earnings per share, often report dividends per share. As will be seen shortly, the right to share in dividend distributions may be amended for different classes of shares, especially for preferred shares.

SELECTION OF CORPORATE MANAGEMENT   Common shareholders also have the right to vote on the selection of the corporation's board of directors. The standard rule for voting is one share equals one vote; so the more shares an individual owns, the greater the influence that individual has. The board of directors then represents the shareholders, and most decisions are made by a vote of the board of directors rather than a vote of all shareholders. The board of directors hires (and fires) the company's top-level management and also declares the dividends that are paid to shareholders. The board is ultimately responsible for the financial information that is prepared by management and examined by auditors. Since the bankruptcy of **Enron Corporation** and a few other major companies in the United States, regulators have been developing stronger rules to govern who can be a board member and what their responsibilities should be. The *Sarbanes-Oxley Act*, which was passed by the United States Congress in 2002, stipulates that a board must have five financially literate members who are appointed for five years. Most Canadian corporations are now implementing the requirements of the *Sarbanes-Oxley Act* in Canada, either because they are required to as subsidiaries of U.S. companies or as owners of U.S. subsidiaries, or because they simply recognize the value of having a responsible board.

NET ASSETS UPON LIQUIDATION   The third right of common shareholders is the right to share in the net assets upon liquidation. If a company goes bankrupt or otherwise liquidates, there is an established order in which creditors and shareholders are paid. Common shareholders come last on that list; whatever is left after creditors and preferred shareholders are paid is then divided proportionately among them, based on their relative number of shares. This means that common shareholders bear the highest risk, since there may be nothing left for them. On the other hand, they could reap the largest benefit if there is a substantial sum left over.

SUBSEQUENT ISSUES OF SHARES   The fourth right of common shares is the right to share proportionately in any new issuance of shares. This is called the **pre-emptive right**. Pre-emptive rights are not automatic. They must be explicitly stated in the articles of incorporation. This right allows current shareholders to retain their proportionate interest in the company when new shares are issued. For example, a shareholder owning 20 percent of a company's shares has the pre-emptive right to purchase 20 percent of any new shares of that class that may be issued. Without this right, an investor that had a **controlling interest** in a company (i.e., more than 50 percent of the outstanding shares) could lose that controlling interest if the new shares were issued to another investor. Of course, this scenario is unlikely because controlling interest includes the right to vote for the company's directors; so directors who support the majority owner will likely be elected. The greatest protection is for shareholders who have a **minority** or **non-controlling interest** in a company. Pre-emptive rights prevent their ownership interests from being diluted.

Multiple Classes of Shares

When more than one class of common shares is issued, each class is distinguished by some amendment to the fundamental rights just described. For example, a second class of non-voting common shares might be issued that may be entitled to conversion to voting common shares under certain conditions. This obviously affects the control that holders of the voting common shares have over the company's operations. There might also be differences in the rights to share in the assets' liquidation values. As mentioned earlier, Le Château Inc. has two classes of common shares that differ primarily in the voting rights assigned to each class. The various features of those two classes are as shown in Exhibit 11-1. This format of classes with different voting features is common in companies where the business was initially a family or private company and the original family or group of shareholders wishes to retain the majority of the voting power when additional shares are issued. The following Accounting in the News story about **Magna International Inc.** indicates that it can be expensive to get the founding shareholders to give up their control.

In addition to the rights just mentioned, different classes of common shares may also pay dividends on a different basis, although each outstanding share within any class of shares will be paid the same amount.

accounting in the news

Mega Deal for Magna Founder

In the summer of 2010, an Ontario court approved Magna International's controversial plan to buy out founder Frank Stronach's controlling shares for $863 million in cash and stock—a ruling that Canada's major pension funds planned to appeal.

The deal with Stronach would eliminate the automotive supplier's dual-class share structure, which was believed to affect the value of the company's common shares. The Canada Pension Plan Investment Board, the Ontario Teachers' Pension Plan, and the British Columbia Management Corp. condemned the deal, saying the price is unfair, sets a bad precedent for other companies who might eliminate similar share structures, and favours the Stronach Trust at the expense of Magna's other shareholders.

Those against the deal agree that eliminating the dual-class share structure would be good for the company; however, they balk at the cost, which works out to a 1,800 percent premium for Stronach's multiple-voting shares. Under the deal, Magna would give Stronach $300 million in cash and 9 million new common shares in return for his multiple voting shares. He would also get an estimated $120 million in consulting fees over four years and remain chairman of the company.

The Ontario court judge who ruled in favour of the plan described the deal as fair and balanced, indicating that a shareholder vote backed the deal and Magna's stock price rose the day it was announced. As well, shareholders who disapprove were free to sell their holdings.

Source: Jeff Gray, "Pension Plans to Appeal Magna Ruling," *Globe and Mail*, August 18, 2010.

Preferred Shares

Preferred shares (or, as they are called in most of the world outside North America, **preference shares**) are shares that have preference over common shares with regard to dividends. This does not mean that preferred shareholders are guaranteed to receive dividends, but if dividends are declared, they will receive them before common shareholders do. In addition to the preference for dividends, normally there is also some preference over net assets if the company is liquidated. Another difference between common and preferred shares is that preferred shares are usually non-voting.

The preferred dividend amount may be stated as a dollar amount per share, such as a $2 preferred share issue, which would pay a dividend of $2 per share per year or as a percentage of the issue price of the preferred share. For example, in 2009, **BMO Financial Group** (the Bank of Montreal) had nine different types of preferred shares issued, including the two series described in Exhibit 11-2.

EXHIBIT 11-2

annual report

BMO FINANCIAL GROUP 2009 ANNUAL REPORT

EXCERPT FROM NOTE 21 SHARE CAPITAL

Note 21: Share Capital

- 14,000,000 4.5% Non-Cumulative Perpetual Class B Preferred shares, Series 13, at a price of $25.00 per share, representing an aggregate issue price of $350 million.

- Class B – Series 15 shares are redeemable at our option starting May 25, 2013 for $25.00 cash per share, plus a premium if we redeem the shares before May 25, 2017. The shares carry a non-cumulative quarterly dividend of $0.3625 per share.

The note indicates that BMO's Class B Series 15 preferred shares pay dividends of $0.3625 quarterly, or $1.45 annually. The Series 13 shares pay a dividend of 4.5% of $25.00 ($1.125 annually), also on a quarterly basis. For both the company issuing the preferred shares and an investor purchasing a share, one of the risks of a fixed dividend rate that is established when the shares are issued is that, if economic circumstances change, the rates may not provide investors with an adequate rate of return on their investment if competitive rates rise, or, they may prove to be very expensive for the company if rates subsequently fall. The BMO Series 13 preferred shares were issued in October 2007, when a 4.5% dividend seemed reasonable relative to the level of interest rates and other investment opportunities. However, if interest rates rise significantly, investors may decide they would prefer other investments that pay higher rates of return and BMO's preferred shares would become less attractive as an investment. To protect against this risk, some companies now issue preferred shares that reset the dividend rate periodically. As at October 2009, the **Royal Bank of Canada** had 17 different series of preferred shares outstanding, of which eight have the reset feature. The dividends are based on a prescribed rate, varying on the eight series from 1.93% to 4.13% above the Government of Canada five-year bond rate, and are reset on average every five years.

There are other features of preferred shares with which you need to be familiar. Preferred shares may be **cumulative**. Cumulative means that if a dividend is not declared on the preferred shares in one year, it carries over into the next year. In the second year, both the prior year's preferred dividend and the current year's preferred dividend must be declared before any common dividends can be declared. Dividends from prior years that have not been declared are called **dividends in arrears**. Although most preferred shares issued by companies are cumulative, in the case of both BMO and the Royal Bank, none of the series of preferred shares is cumulative.

Convertible preferred shares can be converted, at the shareholder's option, into common shares (or sometimes other types of preferred shares) based on a ratio stated in the articles of incorporation. **CCL Industries Ltd.** has an interesting share capital arrangement. CCL Industries is a Toronto-based world leader in specialty packaging and labelling solutions for the consumer products and health care industries. It has Class A shares that are voting and convertible into Class B shares on a one-for-one basis. The Class B shares are non-voting but, in all other major respects, rank equal to the Class A shares. Currently, the dividend on Class A shares has been set at 5 cents less than that for the Class B shares. As a result, each year some Class A shareholders convert to Class B shares; that is, they give up the right to vote in order to receive the higher dividend.

Redeemable preferred shares can be bought back by the company (retired) at a price and time specified in the articles of incorporation, and at the issuing company's option. All of BMO's preferred share issues are redeemable. The Series 13 shares in Exhibit 11-2 are redeemable starting February 25, 2012, for $25.00 cash per share, plus a premium if they are redeemed before February 25, 2016. The Series 15 have similar terms but different dates. Other series have different terms, including the option to convert the preferred shares into a different series of preferred shares if they are not redeemed. As a potential investor in BMO's preferred shares, you would need to read the articles very carefully to understand all of the features of your preferred shares, including dividend rates and redemption terms. **Retractable preferred shares** are similar to redeemable shares in that they can be sold back to the company (retired) at the shareholder's option. The price that must be paid for them and the periods of time when they can be sold are also specified in the articles of incorporation.

The last feature we are going to discuss is participation. **Participating preferred shares** are preferred shares that not only have a preference with regard to dividends, but, if dividends are declared to common shareholders beyond the level declared to the preferred shareholders, the preferred shareholders also share in the excess dividends. Most preferred shares are non-participating, but Le Château has the participating feature on its Class A and Class B common shares.

As noted earlier, the variety of features and different types of shares provide investors with different levels of risk and return. This allows companies to raise financing from different types of investors—those who might prefer the steady dividends of preferred shares, or others who are willing to forego dividends and assume more risk in the hope of higher returns. Targeting different types of investors increases the pool of capital available to the company.

While the features of various classes of shares differ, the accounting issues related to all of them are basically the same. Therefore, in the sections that follow, we limit the discussion to common shares.

Accounting for the Issuance of Common Shares

When common shares are issued for cash, the company accounts for these proceeds by debiting the cash account and crediting a share capital account. This share capital account is sometimes referred to as **paid-in capital** or legal capital.

To illustrate the issuance entry, suppose that Rosman Company issues 1,000 no par value common shares for $15 a share. The following entry would be made:

LEARNING OBJECTIVE 3

Prepare journal entries for share transactions, including the issuance and payment of dividends.

SHARE ISSUANCE ENTRY WITH NO PAR VALUE

Cash (A)	15,000	
Share capital (SE)		15,000
To record issuance of 1,000 shares with no par value for $15 per share.		

As explained earlier in the chapter, in the past Canadian companies were permitted to issue shares that had a stated value (also known as par value). With stated or par value shares, only the total of the par value was credited to the share capital account, and any remaining amount was credited to another equity account. Although they are seldom seen in Canada now, the use of par values for shares is still very common internationally.

To illustrate the issuance entry for par value shares, suppose that Rosman Company issued 1,000 common shares for $15 a share that had a par value of $10 per share. The following entry would be made:

HELPFUL HINT

Remember that, to provide protection for creditors, the amount credited to the share capital account cannot be paid out as dividends.

SHARE ISSUANCE ENTRY WITH A PAR VALUE

Cash (A)	15,000	
Share capital (SE)		10,000
Contributed capital (SE)		5,000
To record issuance of 1,000 shares with a $10 par value for $15 per share.		

Note that the additional $5 per share (the amount in excess of par) is recorded in an account called Contributed Capital. This account is sometimes called Contributed Surplus in Excess of Par, or Additional Paid-In Capital.

Repurchased Shares

Companies can decide to buy back some of their own shares after their issuance. In 2009, for instance, DHX Media in the opening story repurchased 260,925 of its shares. A company might do this because it wants to reduce the number of shares outstanding. When there are fewer shares outstanding, the company's income is divided among fewer shares and the earnings per share therefore rises, which might increase the share price. Or it may repurchase some of its shares because it wants to use those shares to satisfy its stock option plans (discussed later) rather than issue new shares. Shares that have been repurchased by the issuing company are sometimes referred to as **treasury shares**. In most jurisdictions in Canada, repurchased shares are cancelled immediately upon purchase. In a few jurisdictions, they are not cancelled and are held in the accounting system as treasury shares. They are considered issued but not outstanding.

Three terms are used to refer to the number of company shares: authorized shares, issued shares, and **outstanding shares**. The maximum number of shares that can be issued by the company according to the articles of incorporation is the authorized shares. As mentioned earlier, many companies avoid the possible limitations that might result from an authorized limit by stating that they have the right to issue an unlimited number of shares. Those that have been sold (issued) by the company are considered issued shares. As long as the shares remain in the possession of shareholders outside the company, they are considered outstanding. If, however, the company repurchases some of its own shares and holds them, the shares remain issued but are no longer outstanding. If the company cancels the shares, they will cease to be issued and will revert to the status of only being authorized.

The repurchase of shares reduces the share capital account by the amount that the shares were originally issued for. In addition, if the company buys them back at a higher or lower price than it issued them for, there is a form of gain or loss on the repurchase. The gain or loss is not considered part of the company's earnings, however; it is recorded in either the retained earnings account or the contributed surplus account. The appendix to this chapter provides more detail about accounting for share repurchases and treasury shares.

DIVIDENDS, STOCK SPLITS, AND EMPLOYEE STOCK OPTIONS

Cash Dividends

LEARNING OBJECTIVE 4

Describe the different types of dividends and explain why companies might opt to issue one type of dividend rather than another.

Dividends are payments to shareholders from the total net earnings retained by a company in the retained earnings account. Dividends are a payment in return for the company's use of the shareholders' money. They are paid to shareholders only if the board of directors has voted to declare a dividend. The declaration of a cash dividend makes the dividend a legal liability of the company. Dividends are not paid on treasury shares as these are held internally by the company, and companies cannot pay dividends to themselves. They are paid only on outstanding shares.

Here is an example of a dividend notice. On June 9, 2010, Le Château issued a press release to announce that it was paying a quarterly dividend of $0.175 a share on its Class A subordinate voting shares and Class B voting shares. The dividend was payable on August 17, 2010, to shareholders of record on July 30, 2010. This announcement was reported in several financial newspapers in Canada so that investors would know that a dividend was forthcoming.

Three dates are important in the **dividend declaration** process. The first is the **date of declaration**. This is the date on which the board of directors votes to declare a dividend. For Le Château, that date is June 9, 2010. On the date of declaration, the company records its obligation to pay the dividend. Suppose that Le Château had 25,000,000 common shares outstanding at that time. The journal entry to record the declaration would be the following:

CASH DIVIDEND DECLARATION ENTRY		
Dividends declared (SE)	4,375,000	
Dividends payable (L)		4,375,000
2,500,000 × $0.175 = $4,375,000		

You might recall from Chapter 3 that the debit is usually to a dividends declared account, which is a temporary account that is closed to the retained earnings account at the end of the accounting period. Companies typically declare dividends quarterly, and the dividends declared account accumulates all four quarterly dividends by the end of the fiscal year. Not all companies use a dividends declared account, however, as some prefer to debit dividends directly to retained earnings.

In declaring the dividend, the board of directors specifies that the dividend is payable to shareholders of record on the **date of record**. This second important date is the date on which a shareholder must own the shares in order to receive the dividend. For Le Château, that date is the close of business on July 30, 2010. The date of record is typically at least two weeks after the declaration date. This delay allows investors to make informed decisions about buying and selling the stock relative to whether or not they will receive the dividend. If a shareholder sells shares before the date of record, the new owner of the shares will then be entitled to receive the dividend.

In the stock market, traders talk about the **ex-dividend day**. The ex-dividend day is the day on which shares are sold without the right to receive the dividend. Purchasing the shares on or after the ex-dividend day means that the buyer will not receive the dividend; it belongs to the seller, because the seller is recorded as having owned the shares on the date of record. As you might expect, the share price decreases on the ex-dividend day, to reflect the loss of this dividend. The ex-dividend date is usually two days before the date of record. For Le Château it is July 28, 2010.

A few weeks after the date of record, the company pays the dividend. This third important date is called the **date of payment**. Le Château's date of payment was August 17, 2010. Again, a delay is needed so that the company can update its list of shareholders and calculate the total amount of dividends owed to each. This total amount is calculated as the dividend per share times the number of shares outstanding.

At the date of record, no journal entry is made. The company is simply trying to find out who owns the shares on this date to determine who is entitled to receive a dividend cheque. On the payment date, the company sends out the cheques to the shareholders and must make an entry to record the reduction in cash and the payment of the liability. Le Château would make the following journal entry for the payment of the dividend:

CASH DIVIDEND PAYMENT ENTRY		
Dividends payable (L)	4,375,000	
Cash (A)		4,375,000

The following diagram summarizes the dividend paying process:

DATE TIME LINE			
June 9	July 28	July 30	August 17
Date of declaration	*Ex-dividend date*	*Date of record*	*Date of payment*
Dividend recorded; liability established.	No journal entry required.	No journal entry required.	Cash paid; liability eliminated.

Property Dividends

It is also possible for a company to declare a dividend that will be settled with some resource other than cash. Dividends of this type are called **property dividends** or **dividends in kind.** These dividends are relatively rare because the assets other than cash that can be paid out are necessarily limited to assets that can be divided into small, equal parts. There is a story of a liquor company that was short on cash but long on excess inventory and declared a dividend of one bottle per share. Whether this actually happened or not is not as important as the concept it illustrates. If a company issues a property dividend, it must be able to give the same amount per share to each share-holder. In May 2000, **BCE Inc.** owned approximately 37% of **Nortel Networks**. It decided to distribute 35% of its 37% investment to its shareholders in the form of a dividend. BCE shareholders received 1.57 Nortel shares for every BCE common share held. This was a property dividend. The major accounting question for property dividends is how to value the dividend. Should the property be valued at its fair market value, or at its cost? In Canada, property dividends are valued at their fair market value because this represents the value that the company is giving up to pay the dividend.

Stock Dividends

Stock dividends are dividends that are satisfied by issuing additional company shares to shareholders, instead of cash or property. Stock dividends can be used to issue dividends when the company does not want to use, or is not in a position to use, any of its assets for dividends. Shareholders who receive stock dividends have the option of keeping the new shares or selling them for cash.

Whereas issuing a cash or property dividend reduces a company's overall value (because cash or other assets have been removed), issuing a stock dividend does not. For example, assume that a company has 100,000 shares outstanding. These shares are held by 10 different people, each with 10,000 shares. In other words, each owns 10% of the company. If the company issues a 20% stock dividend, it will issue 20,000 additional shares (100,000 shares × 20%), or 2,000 for every 10,000 shares held. Each shareholder will now have 12,000 shares and the company will have 120,000 shares outstanding. While the company's value was divided among 100,000 shares before, now the same value is divided among 120,000 shares. The company's overall value has not changed, nor has the percentage ownership of each of the shareholders—they still own 10% each—but the value attached to each share is a little less.

If shareholders are no better off after a stock dividend than they were before, why would a company issue such a dividend? There are a couple of good reasons. First, it is possible that the shareholders are better off. Going back to our example, if the shares' market value prior to the stock dividend was $10 a share, the market would have valued the company at $1,000,000 ($10 × 100,000 shares). After the stock dividend, there are 120,000 shares so their market value should drop to $8.33 ($1,000,000 ÷ 120,000 shares). If the market price drops to $8.33, each shareholder is no better off. However, often the market price does not fully compensate for the increase in the number of shares. If the market price only drops to $8.50, for example, the shareholders are better off. The market value of a 10% interest would now be $102,000 ($8.50 × 12,000 shares), where before it was $100,000 ($10 × 10,000 shares).

The second reason for issuing a stock dividend is that it provides an opportunity for the company to capitalize its retained earnings. When cash or property dividends are declared and subsequently issued, a temporary account called dividends declared is used. At the end of the accounting period, this account is closed into retained earnings, causing it to decrease. When stock dividends are issued, the same procedure is followed, and retained earnings decrease. However, at the same time that retained earnings decreases, the share capital account increases because more shares were issued. Because the amount in the share capital account represents stated or legal capital (meaning that it cannot be used to issue dividends), the company has taken an amount out of an account from which dividends can be issued and put it in an account from which they cannot, thus capitalizing it. This effectively indicates that the amount is now permanently invested in the company, which increases protection for the creditors. Companies that have a substantial accumulation of retained earnings but do not have cash available for a dividend will sometimes issue stock dividends to reduce the retained earnings amount.

As with property dividends, the question that underlies stock dividends is the following: What value should be attached to the shares that are issued? Should the shares' fair market value be used, or should some other value be selected?

To answer this question, consider the following extreme situations. When a stock dividend is declared, it is stated as a percentage of the outstanding shares. Suppose a company declares a 100% stock dividend. This means that each shareholder will receive one additional share for each one that is currently held. No cash changes hands in this transaction. What would you expect to happen to the shares' market value? It is likely that a share's value would be cut in half. There is no change in the value of the company's assets or liabilities, only a doubling of the number of shares that represent ownership. If there is no change in the company's value, then the price per share should adjust for the number of new shares that have been issued. This suggests that the value of the new shares issued is zero.

At the other extreme, suppose the company issues one additional share as a stock dividend. The recipient of the share can probably sell it for the fair market value of the existing shares on that date. Assuming that there are large numbers of shares already on the market, it is unlikely that the price per share would adjust for the issuance of this one additional share. In this case, then, the fair market value of the share issued would seem to measure the dividend's value. In theory, the market price should adjust for the issuance of new shares in any stock dividend, regardless of the number of shares issued. As a practical matter, however, it is unlikely that the market will fully adjust for very small stock dividends, which makes the shares' fair market value a reasonable measure of the value given up by the company.

How, then, does the company value the shares that are issued in a stock dividend? Since most stock dividends represent relatively small percentages of the shares issued (similar to the second extreme example), most companies account for them by using the shares' fair market value on the date of declaration.

The market price that is used to record the issuance of a small stock dividend should be the market price on the date the dividend is declared. Unlike for a cash or property dividend, the board of directors has the power to revoke the stock dividend at any time prior to its actual issuance. This means that the dividend does not represent a legal liability to the company on the date of declaration. For this reason, some companies do not record a journal entry on the date of declaration. If an entry is recorded, the credit part of the entry is made to a shareholders' equity account called stock dividends *issuable* and not to a dividends *payable* account. Upon issuance, the credit is made to the shares account and the stock dividends issuable account is removed.

To illustrate, suppose that a company decides to issue a 5% stock dividend when 100,000 shares are outstanding and the market price for a single share is $30. That is, the company will issue 5,000 additional shares, with a value of $30 each. The following journal entries would be made for the declaration and issuance:

SMALL STOCK DIVIDEND ENTRIES

Declaration of stock dividend		
Dividends declared (SE)	150,000	
Stock dividend issuable (SE)		150,000
Issuance of stock dividend		
Stock dividend issuable (SE)	150,000	
Share capital (SE)		150,000

Stock Splits

LEARNING OBJECTIVE 5

Describe what a stock split is and explain how it is accounted for.

Very similar to a stock dividend, a **stock split** increases the number of shares outstanding and is usually stated as a ratio. In a two-for-one stock split, each share currently held by shareholders is exchanged for two new shares. When this is done, the numbers of shares authorized and outstanding are adjusted to compensate for the increase. For example, in a two-for-one split, the number of shares outstanding is doubled. Splits typically involve large numbers of shares, and the arguments for large stock dividends that were discussed earlier apply here as well. As the additional shares do not increase or decrease the company's value, the shares' market price simply adjusts to compensate for the split.

Exhibit 11-3 presents information about a stock split in the management discussion and analysis section of Le Château Inc.'s 2008 Annual Report.

EXHIBIT 11-3

LE CHÂTEAU INC. 2008 ANNUAL REPORT

annual report

EXCERPT FROM THE FINANCIAL STATEMENTS

At the annual meeting of shareholders held on June 27, 2007, the shareholders approved the split of the Class A subordinate voting shares and Class B voting shares on a four-for-one basis. The record date for the split was July 18, 2007 and shares began trading on an "as split" basis at the opening of business on July 16, 2007. All share and per share information presented in the MD&A and the audited consolidated financial statements reflect the effects of the stock split retroactively.

The share price for Le Château fell from \$65.07 the day before the split to \$16.27 the day of the split, reflecting the fact that every share had been converted into four shares.

In accounting for a stock split, there is no change in the dollar amounts of any of the shareholders' equity accounts, and no journal entry is made in the accounting system. The only change is in the number of shares issued and outstanding. This change can be accomplished with an informal or **memorandum entry** in the accounting system. That is, a notation is made about the details of the stock split and the new numbers of shares, but no accounts are debited or credited.

Why would a company want to quadruple the number of shares outstanding? The main reason is that a stock split improves the marketability of a company's shares. As a company grows, the market value of its shares generally rises. The share price can get quite high. As the price rises, fewer investors have the necessary funds to buy the shares.

To lower the price so that it is within reach of more investors, the company may split its shares, which will cut the market price per share. For example, as its share price has escalated, Microsoft has split its shares nine times since the shares were first issued to the public in 1986. A single share from 1986 is equivalent to 288 shares as of July 2010.

Exhibit 11-4 summarizes the effects on the financial statements of the different types of dividends we have discussed.

COMPARISON OF DIFFERENT TYPES OF DIVIDENDS AND STOCK SPLITS

EXHIBIT 11-4

Effect on:	Cash Dividend	Property Dividend	Stock Dividend	Stock Split
Total assets	Cash decreases	The asset distributed decreases	No effect	No effect
Share capital	No effect	No effect	Increases	No effect
Retained earnings	Decreases	Decreases	Decreases	No effect
Total shareholders' equity	Decreases	Decreases	No effect	No effect
Number of shares outstanding	No effect	No effect	Increases	Increases

Employee Stock Options

A **stock option** on common shares is an agreement between two parties to either buy or sell shares at a fixed price, called the **exercise price** or **strike price**, at some future date. One type of option is the one granted by a company to its employees and senior executives that allows them to purchase the company's shares at a fixed price. Called an **employee stock option**, it is generally used as a form of compensation and as an incentive to employees. If employees are also shareholders, they may work harder for the company so that it grows and they can then benefit as their shares increase in value. For senior executives, a stock option plan aligns their goals with those of the shareholders, to increase company value and share price. The agreement usually contains a **service period** that the employees must work before they can exercise the options. When the time comes for employees to exercise their options, they pay the exercise price, obtain the shares, and can either sell them for the current market price and realize a profit, or continue to hold the shares in hopes that the price will go up even further. Employee stock option plans provide an incentive for the employees to work hard to improve the company's performance, so that the shares' market price will exceed the exercise price. Obviously, if the share price never exceeds the exercise price, the employees will not exercise their options or benefit from the plan.

It is not uncommon for large corporations to compensate their senior executives with stock option plans. It is also not uncommon for the exercise price on those plans to be significantly below the current market value. If, through effective management, the executives can increase the company's value, which will translate into an increase in the market value of the company's shares, both the executives and the company benefit.

The Accounting in the News story below gives an idea of the potential size of the benefit to a senior executive of having stock options and owning shares. **Potash Corporation of Saskatchewan Inc.** is the world's largest fertilizer producer, with approximately 20 percent of the world's productive capacity for potash, phosphate, and

LEARNING OBJECTIVE 6

Describe what an employee stock option is and explain how it is accounted for.

nitrogen. PotashCorp made news in the summer of 2010 when it was the target of a takeover offer. A takeover is when another company (BHP in this case) wants to buy enough of the target company's (PotashCorp's) shares to have a controlling interest in it. The company making the offer usually bids more than the current share price of the target company to encourage existing shareholders to sell their shares. Reading the story, you might wonder why the strike prices of the stock options were so low. There are two reasons: first, the stock option plans were probably created several years before, at a time when those exercise prices may not have been so different from the shares' market price and, second, BHP was offering a premium over the current share price.

accounting in the news

Executive Stock Worth Millions in Takeover

The chief executive officer of PotashCorp, Bill Doyle, could have made at least $370 million if BHP Billiton had succeeded in its $130-per-share takeover bid of the Saskatchewan-based company. The CEO could have made even more if a higher bid from another company had come. Doyle owns 2.9 million stock options exercisable at strike prices from about $10 to about $60 a share. He also owns almost 470,000 ordinary shares, according to the company's February 2010 regulatory filling. According to company policy, if there is a change of control, "all outstanding non-exercisable options granted to the executive become exercisable," implying that he would receive a lump sum immediately. In addition, Doyle would receive three years' salary and the average of the last three years' bonuses. PotashCorp said the vast majority of executive compensation was "tied directly to their ability to generate long-term value for the company's shareholders," adding, "Anyone who has been a long-term shareholder of PotashCorp has benefited from tremendous value creation." In November 2010 the federal government rejected the initial bid. BHP Billiton subsequently withdrew their efforts to acquire PotashCorp.

Source: Javier Blas and William MacNamara, "PotashCorp Chief in Line for $370m," *Financial Times*, August 19, 2010.

Companies are required to disclose details regarding their employee stock option plans. Exhibit 11-5 shows the stock option plan outstanding for Le Château on January 30, 2010. Note that the plan is for key company employees, directors, and consultants. The exercise price varies from a low of $7.56 to a high of $15.14, and the stock options have a maximum term of five years after the grant date. The market price on January 29, 2010, was close to $13.80 so the probability of the options with the lower exercise prices being exercised is high. During 2009, 215,500 new options were granted, 310,000 were exercised, and 4,000 were cancelled, expired, or forfeited.

With respect to employee stock option plans, the major question for accounting purposes is how to record compensation expense for this type of incentive-based plan. If an option's exercise price is at or above the current market price, does that mean it is worthless? The answer is no. There is generally an extended period of time over which the employee can exercise the option. There may, however, be an **expiration date** specified, after which the option can no longer be exercised. The option will be of some value (in present-value terms) if there is some probability that the share price will exceed the exercise price before the option expires. The more likely this is, the higher the value of the option.

LE CHÂTEAU INC. 2009 ANNUAL REPORT

EXHIBIT 11-5

annual report

EXCERPT FROM NOTE 8 ON CAPITAL STOCK

Stock option plan

Under the provisions of the stock option plan, the Company may grant options to key employees, directors and consultants to purchase Class A subordinate voting shares. The maximum number of Class A subordinate voting shares issuable from time to time under the Plan is 12% of the aggregate number of Class A subordinate voting shares and Class B Shares issued and outstanding from time to time. The option price may not be less than the closing price for the Class A subordinate voting shares on the Toronto Stock Exchange on the last business day before the date on which the option is granted. The stock options may be exercised by the holder, progressively, over a period of 5 years from the date of granting. Under certain circumstances, the vesting period can be accelerated.

A summary of the status of the Company's stock option plan as of January 30, 2010, and changes during the years then ended is presented below:

	January 30, 2010		January 31, 2009	
	Shares	Weighted average exercise price $	Shares	Weighted average exercise price $
Outstanding at beginning of year	1,172,800	12.64	1,267,600	12.26
Granted	215,500	9.40	—	—
Exercised	(310,000)	8.70	(81,200)	7.56
Cancelled / expired	(4,000)	10.75	(13,600)	7.56
Outstanding at end of year	1,074,300	13.14	1,172,800	12.64
Options exercisable at end of the year	415,600	13.41	352,640	11.99

The 215,500 stock options granted during the year will expire on April 22, 2014.

The following table summarizes information about the stock options outstanding at January 30, 2010:

Range of exercise prices $	Number outstanding at January 30, 2010 #	Weighted average remaining life	Weighted average exercise price $	Number of options exercisable at January 30, 2010 #	Weighted average exercise price $
7.56	42,800	0.3 years	7.56	42,800	7.56
9.40	213,500	4.2 years	9.40	—	—
11.75 – 13.37	178,000	0.9 years	11.77	116,800	11.76
15.14	640,000	2.2 years	15.14	256,000	15.14
	1,074,300	2.3 years	13.14	415,600	13.41

	2010 $	2009 $
Contributed surplus, beginning of year	2,460	1,761
Stock-based compensation expense	341	836
Exercise of share options	(642)	(137)
Contributed surplus, end of year	2,159	2,460

EXHIBIT 11-5

annual report

LE CHÂTEAU INC. 2009 ANNUAL REPORT (cont'd)

EXCERPT FROM NOTE 8 ON CAPITAL STOCK

Compensation expense recorded in the consolidated financial statements during the year for stock options amounted to $341,000 [2009 – $836,000]. During the second quarter ended August 1, 2009, modifications were made to 160,000 options granted to a former director. Of these options, 80,000 were not vested at the time of the modification, which resulted in a reversal of previously recognized stock-based compensation expense amounting to $212,000. The modification to vested options was expensed in the second quarter and the modifications to the unvested options will be expensed over their revised vesting period. In the fourth quarter ended January 30, 2010, there was a reversal of stock-based compensation expense in the amount of $125,000 related to the cancellation of 80,000 non-vested options to a former employee. These modifications are reflected in the tables above.

During the year ended January 30, 2010, the Company granted 215,500 stock options [2009 – nil] to purchase Class A subordinate voting shares. The weighted-average grant date fair value of stock options granted during 2009 was $1.47 per option. The fair value of each option granted was determined using the Black-Scholes option pricing model and the following weighted-average assumptions:

	Assumptions
Risk-free interest rate	1.36%
Expected life	2.9 years
Expected volatility in the market price of the shares	41.2%
Expected dividend yield	7.4%

Employee stock options generally cannot be traded, because they are restricted to the employees to whom they are issued. As they do not trade in a market, their value can only be estimated, and methods have therefore been developed that enable accountants to determine a value for stock options. In the Le Château example in Exhibit 11-5, the company used the Black-Scholes option pricing model to determine a fair value of the option grants issued in 2009. The fair value of the options granted determines the total compensation expense, which is recorded by the company on a straight-line basis over the service period specified in the agreement. As disclosed in Exhibit 11-5, Le Château recorded compensation expense of $341,000 related to stock options in its 2010 statement of earnings.

To illustrate the calculation of the expense related to employee stock options, assume Maple Company issued 5,000 options to its CEO on January 1, 2010. The share price at that date was $25.00, the exercise price of the options is $30.00 and they can only be exercised after three years of service (January 1, 2013). Using the Black-Scholes option pricing model, the options are determined to have a total fair value of $6,000. The total compensation expense is the $6,000 fair value of the options, and the expense, recorded straight-line over the three year service period, would be $2,000 per year ($6,000 ÷ 3). Because the shares have not yet been issued, the credit entry would be to contributed surplus, the same equity account used earlier for the excess portion of par value shares.

When the employee exercises the option (buys the shares from the company at the stated price), the company records the receipt of the cash proceeds from the employee and the issuance of the shares. The shares are valued at the amount of cash received by the company plus an amount equal to the total amount that was recorded as compensation expense over the service period.

For Maple Company, if the CEO exercises the options on July 31, 2013, when the share price was $38.00, the CEO would pay to the company the agreed-upon exercise price of $30.00 per share and receive the 5,000 shares. The shares would be valued at $156,000, the total of the cash received ($30.00 × 5,000) plus the $6,000 ($2,000 per year for three years) that was recorded in contributed surplus over the life of the options.

Note that the CEO effectively bought shares worth $38.00 for $30.00, and the lower price is his reward for successfully managing the company over the three years while the share price rose. For the company and its other shareholders, only $150,000 was received for these shares when they could have been sold for $190,000 ($38.00 × 5,000). The issuance of shares for less than their market price is sometimes a controversial point for other shareholders, because it dilutes the value of their shares.

EARNINGS MANAGEMENT

If a portion of a senior executive's compensation is based on stock options or increases in share price, there can be a concern that management might use earnings management to increase their compensation. Share prices are affected by earnings per share (EPS) and generally increase when EPS increases. If the share price increases, it is likely that the stock options will then become more valuable to the executive. Although share prices also reflect the underlying fundamentals and cash flow of the company, which cannot be altered by accounting choices, management could try to select accounting policies or accounting estimates that increase net earnings in the short term. For example, management might overestimate the useful lives of depreciable assets or underestimate the bad debt expense, and hope that the share price will rise even though nothing in the fundamentals or cash flow of the company has changed. This risk is a particular concern in the short term and is one of the reasons stock options often require a service period of several years before they can be exercised. Although ratios, trend analysis, and careful examination of the notes to the financial statements can be helpful, such manipulation may be difficult to detect in the short term. In the long term, however, these techniques and other information about the company can enable users to determine whether management is manipulating net earnings or EPS.

When employee stock options are exercised, additional shares are issued. This causes a dilution of earnings per share because the earnings for the company are now divided among a larger number of shares. To prevent continuous dilution as a result of the exercise of stock options, many companies repurchase their own shares to offset those that are issued when stock options are exercised.

STATEMENT OF RETAINED EARNINGS AND STATEMENT OF CHANGES IN EQUITY

In this chapter we saw transactions that affect the retained earnings account, and others that affect the share capital accounts. Financial statement users are interested in changes during the year in these accounts. Companies following IFRS summarize changes in the shareholders' equity accounts in a separate statement, the statement of changes in equity. Before the adoption of IFRS, most Canadian public companies used the simpler statement of retained earnings, which only details changes in the retained earnings account. Private companies following APSE are still allowed to use it. For companies preparing only a statement of retained earnings, changes in the share capital accounts are summarized in the notes to the financial statements, as we saw in Exhibit 11-1 for Le Château. Because you may be using company statements that date from before IFRS, as well as statements of companies that follow ASPE, we will show both the retained earnings statement and the statement of changes in equity.

Statement of Retained Earnings

LEARNING OBJECTIVE 7

Explain the structure and purpose of the statement of retained earnings and the statement of changes in equity.

In Chapter 3 when we needed to complete the statement of financial position, we calculated the ending balance in retained earnings using the format shown below. The statement of retained earnings follows that same simple format. It starts with the opening balance of retained earnings at the beginning of the year. Then it shows the net earnings or loss for the year, which comes directly from the statement of earnings. Dividends declared in the year are then deducted. Next appear any other items that affect retained earnings. Finally, the balance of retained earnings at the end of the year appears. This ending balance is what appears on the statement of financial position.

> Retained earnings at the end of the preceding period
> \+ Net earnings (or − Net loss) for the current period
> − Dividends declared in the current period
> ───
> = Retained earnings at the end of the current period

An example is shown in Exhibit 11-6A for Le Château. Note that the balance of retained earnings at the beginning of the 2010 fiscal year was $107,914 thousand, net earnings for the year were $29,837 thousand, and dividends of $17,064 thousand were declared. As discussed earlier, Le Château paid dividends on the two classes of common shares: Class A subordinate voting and Class B multiple voting. There are no preferred shares issued and outstanding, so no dividends were paid on preferred shares. The ending balance of $120,687 thousand is the amount that appears for retained earnings on the January 30, 2010, balance sheet.

If you examine the 2009 column of Le Château's statement of retained earnings, you will see a deduction of $8,989 thousand for the excess of cost over stated value of the Class A subordinate voting shares that were purchased and cancelled. Le Château repurchased some of its own outstanding shares and paid more for them than it had received when the shares were issued. The excess paid reduces retained earnings, similar to if the company had incurred a loss. The accounting for share repurchases is discussed further in the appendix to this chapter.

You may see other adjustments reported on the statement of retained earnings. If financial statements are restated for changes in accounting policies or corrections of errors, the effects of those changes are often included on the statement of retained earnings. If the change arises from a prior period, however, it should not be reported on the statement of earnings, which measures current period performance. Instead, the adjustment is made directly to retained earnings. (An example of a change in accounting policy that results in a direct adjustment to retained earnings is shown in Exhibit 11-7.)

The shareholders' equity section of Le Château's balance sheet is shown in Exhibit 11-6B and includes the capital stock and retained earnings information we have discussed so far.

LE CHÂTEAU INC. 2009 ANNUAL REPORT

EXHIBIT 11-6A

annual report

CONSOLIDATED STATEMENTS OF RETAINED EARNINGS Years ended January 30, 2010 and January 31, 2009
[In thousands of Canadian dollars]

	2010 $	2009 $
	[52 weeks]	[53 weeks]
Balance, beginning of year	107,914	99,884
Excess of cost over stated value of Class A subordinate voting shares purchased and cancelled	—	(8,989)
Net earnings	29,837	38,621
	137,751	129,516
Dividends declared [note 8]	17,064	21,602
Balance, end of year	120,687	107,914

LE CHÂTEAU INC. 2009 ANNUAL REPORT

EXHIBIT 11-6B

annual report

EXCERPT FROM CONSOLIDATED BALANCE SHEETS As at January 30, 2010 and January 31, 2009
[In thousands of Canadian dollars]

	2010 $	2009 $
Shareholders' equity		
Capital stock [note 8]	34,335	30,997
Contributed surplus [note 8]	2,159	2,460
Retained earnings	120,687	107,914
Accumulated other comprehensive income [note 17]	40	1,043
Total shareholders' equity	157,221	142,414

Statement of Changes in Equity

The statement of changes in equity, sometimes called the statement of shareholders' equity, summarizes the changes in all of the equity accounts and is usually presented in a columnar format. Exhibit 11-7 shows an example of this statement for Toronto-based **Rogers Communications Inc.**, which provides cable and cell phone access to subscribers and operates various media and entertainment outlets. When the statement is presented in columnar format it is essentially a table. The columns represent the different shareholders' equity accounts we have discussed in the chapter, while the rows summarize the transactions that occurred during the period. Instead of reporting the comparative figures of the previous year beside the current year's figures, the previous year is presented in the top rows, while the current year is in the rows at the bottom of the statement. Rogers' statement starts with the opening balances from December 31,

2007, then restates the opening retained earnings for a change in an accounting policy. The middle section of the table indicates the transactions that occurred during the 2008 year, and the bottom of the statement reflects the transactions for 2009, ending with the December 31, 2009, balances. Companies might report the ending balance of each account in the shareholders' equity section of the statement of financial position (as in the Le Château example in Exhibit 11-6B), or alternatively just as a single total figure for shareholders 'equity (as Rogers does, in the amount of $4,273 million, in Exhibit 11-7 B).

EXHIBIT 11-7A

ROGERS COMMUNICATIONS INC. 2009 ANNUAL REPORT

annual report

CONSOLIDATED STATEMENTS OF SHAREHOLDERS' EQUITY
(IN MILLIONS OF CANADIAN DOLLARS)

Years ended December 31, 2009 and 2008	Class A Voting shares Amount	Number of shares (000s)	Class B Non-Voting shares Amount	Number of shares (000s)	Contributed surplus	Retained earnings (Restated – note 2(p)(i))	Accumulated other comprehensive income (loss)	Total shareholders' equity (Restated – note 2(p)(i))
Balances, December 31, 2007	$ 72	112,462	$ 471	527,005	$ 3,689	$ 342	$ 50	$ 4,624
Change in accounting policy related to goodwill and intangible assets (note 2(p)(i))	–	–	–	–	–	(11)	–	(11)
As restated, January 1, 2008	72	112,462	471	527,005	3,689	331	50	4,613
Net income for the year	-	–	–	–	–	1,002	–	1,002
Shares issued on exercise of stock options	–	–	21	502	–	–	–	21
Dividends declared	–	–	–	–	–	(638)	–	(638)
Repurchase of Class B Non-Voting shares (note 18(c))	–	–	(4)	(4,077)	(129)	(4)	–	(137)
Other comprehensive loss	–	–	–	–	–	–	(145)	(145)
Balances, December 31, 2008	72	112,462	488	523,430	3,560	691	(95)	4,716
Net income for the year	–	–	–	–	–	1,478	–	1,478
Shares issued on exercise of stock options	–	–	9	294	–	–	–	9
Dividends declared	–	–	–	–	–	(721)	–	(721)
Repurchase of Class B Non-Voting shares (note 18(c))	–	–	(41)	(43,776)	(1.256)	(50)	–	(1,347)
Other comprehensive income	–	–	–	–	–	–	138	138
Balances, December 31, 2009	$ 72	112,462	$ 456	479,948	$ 2,304	$ 1,398	$ 43	$ 4,273

See accompanying notes to consolidated financial statements.

EXHIBIT 11-7B

ROGERS COMMUNICATIONS INC. 2009 ANNUAL REPORT
Excerpt from Consolidated Balance Sheet

annual report

Shareholders' equity section of the consolidated balance sheet

(IN MILLIONS OF CANADIAN DOLLARS)	December 31, 2009	December 31, 2008
Shareholders' equity (note 18)	$ 4,273	$ 4,716

In Rogers' statement of changes in equity, the first four columns show the changes in the two classes of common shares. Like Le Château, Rogers has two classes of common shares: one is the voting class and the other a non-voting class of common shares. For each class, the dollar amount in millions and the number of shares in thousands is shown. Looking at the first two columns for the Class A voting shares, there were 112,462 thousand shares outstanding at December 31, 2007, for which the company had received $72 million when the shares were issued, and no changes occurred over the two years shown; in other words, Rogers did not issue or repurchase any Class A shares. Companies do not have to disclose the number of shares issued in the statement, and could choose to disclose this non-financial information in the notes instead, as Le Château does. The two columns for the Class B non-voting shares indicate that shares were both issued and repurchased over the two years. The opening balance as at December 31, 2007, consisted of 527,005 thousand shares issued for $471 million. In both 2008 and 2009, Rogers issued more shares when stock options were exercised (502 thousand for $21 million in 2008; 294 thousand for $9 million in 2009), and repurchased some shares (4,077 thousand in 2008; 43,776 thousand in 2009). Only the average carrying value of the shares repurchased is deducted from the share capital account. The excess paid to repurchase the shares—above their average carrying value—reduces contributed surplus and retained earnings. The accounting for this is discussed further in the appendix. As mentioned earlier, companies frequently repurchase shares to prevent the dilution of existing shareholders when stock options are issued, or for other reasons.

The next three columns, Contributed surplus, Retained earnings, and Accumulated other comprehensive income, indicate the changes in those equity accounts over the period. Rogers' contributed surplus is affected by the repurchase of shares, decreasing in both 2008 and 2009. The changes in retained earnings are the same as the ones described earlier in the statement of retained earnings: it increases by the net income earned ($1,002 million in 2008; $1,478 million in 2009), decreases by dividends declared ($638 million in 2008; $721 million in 2009), and, for Rogers, is also affected by the repurchase of the Class B shares and the change in accounting policy at the start of 2008. The ending balance as at December 31, 2009, is $1,398 million.

Other comprehensive income was introduced in Chapter 4. Certain gains and losses incurred by a company are reported in other comprehensive income rather than net earnings. These gains and losses arise from transactions that are beyond the scope of an introductory text, and include gains and losses on some types of investments, some foreign currency translation adjustments, or when a company might be using more complex financial instruments to hedge events. As explained in Chapter 4, other comprehensive income is reported either in a separate statement or at the bottom of the statement of earnings directly below net earnings. Other comprehensive income is added to net earnings to determine the total comprehensive income for the year. These other comprehensive gains and losses affect shareholders' wealth but are not included in retained earnings. Instead, they are included in **accumulated other comprehensive income** on the statement of financial position. Accumulated other comprehensive income is like a separate type of retained earnings. It is the "retained earnings" account for other comprehensive income. It has an opening balance equal to the ending balance of the prior period, increases with gains in other comprehensive income (or decreases with losses), and has an ending balance that is reported as part of shareholders' equity. Some of the gains or losses reported in accumulated other comprehensive income eventually are transferred to net earnings, but that is best left for more advanced accounting courses. Rogers' opening accumulated other comprehensive income at the beginning of January 2008 was $50 million. Rogers reported a loss of

$145 million in 2008 and income of $138 million in 2009 from the activities reported as other comprehensive income, resulting in an ending balance of $43 million on December 31, 2009.

You might wonder why it is necessary to keep the other comprehensive gains and losses in a separate account in the shareholders' equity section and not include them directly in retained earnings. The reason is that the transactions that give rise to these gains and losses are not yet realized by the company. For example, let's say Rogers' other comprehensive gains and losses arose from changes in the market value of certain securities. The securities owned might have increased in value, leading to the gain recognized in other comprehensive income; but the company has not sold the securities yet, so the final gain could be higher or lower, or even a loss. Remember that dividends are paid from retained earnings, which are earnings that the company has realized through completed events. If Rogers included the $138 million of other comprehensive income reported in 2009 in its retained earnings, shareholders might expect a larger dividend. But Rogers is not certain that it will actually sell the securities for a gain of that amount. Remember that in 2008 the securities fell in value, because the company reported an other comprehensive loss during that year. Shareholders need to be aware of the effect of the changes in the value of the assets, because that gives them a more complete understanding of the value of their shareholdings; but it would be premature to treat these unrealized gains and losses as part of retained earnings and available for distribution as dividends.

IFRS VERSUS ASPE

Companies using ASPE prepare the statement of retained earnings instead of the more detailed statement of changes in shareholders' equity. These companies do not report other comprehensive income or the corresponding equity account, accumulated other comprehensive income. The gains and losses that give rise to other comprehensive income either do not exist under ASPE or are booked directly to equity and shown as a separate account in equity (for example, currency translation gains or losses on certain types of foreign subsidiaries).

IFRS INSIGHTS

The biggest difference between Canada and some other countries is the establishment of reserves. Reserves in other countries can be used to set aside retained earnings in separate accounts so that they are not available to pay dividends and are an extra cushion for the protection of creditors. The part set aside is termed "appropriated retained earnings" and the amount remaining is called "unappropriated retained earnings."

Another way reserves can be used is to record changes in the value of assets or liabilities that do not pass through the statement of earnings. Chapter 8 discussed the possible changes in values arising from revaluing capital assets to market value. In Canada, the resulting gains or losses would become part of *accumulated other comprehensive income*. In many other countries, they would be reported as reserves within shareholders' equity.

H&M, in Appendix A, uses the term "reserves" on its group changes in equity statement (see page A12) to account for changes arising from its hedging activities. Again, this reserve account is similar to accummulated other comprehensive income.

In Canada, use of the word "reserve" is generally discouraged because users of financial statements may believe it refers to cash that has been set aside, which is incorrect. In Canada, its use is limited to references to appropriations of retained earnings.

FINANCIAL STATEMENT ANALYSIS

The analysis of the shareholders' equity section of the financial statements normally involves assuming the perspective of an investor. Investors monitor their investment's value to assess company performance and their rate of return. We will look at three different measures that investors and analysts use when assessing investment performance. The investors' return is affected by the value of the shares they own, and share value for a public company is reflected in the stock market. Investors will therefore want to use market information, in addition to the company's financial statements, for a better understanding of their position. Not surprisingly then, some of these measures use market data and look at the relationship between the market and the company's reported performance.

Book Value and Market Value

Investors and analysts will refer to the book value or the market value of a company to monitor the value of their investment. The shareholders' equity represents the net assets (assets minus liabilities) of a company and is also referred to as the **book value** of the company. It is the value of the shareholders' investment in the company, based on the values recorded in the accounting books. It values the investment at the original amount contributed by shareholders plus the retained earnings (undistributed earnings) and accumulated other comprehensive income that accrues to them. Whether the book value fairly reflects the fair value of the company depends on whether the assets and liabilities fairly reflect their market values.

By this point in your study of accounting, you understand that some assets and liabilities are recorded at their market values, and some are not. The book value represents the value of the shareholders' investment based on the conventions of the accounting models. For some industries, like financial institutions, where many of the assets and liabilities are at market value, the book value will be a close approximation of market value. For industries whose assets are primarily recorded at historical cost—for example, an industrial manufacturing company—the book value understates the true value of the investment.

Using the partial balance sheet in Exhibit 11-6B, the book values for Le Château on December 31, 2010 and 2009, are $157,221 thousand and $142,414 thousand, respectively. However, as will be seen below, its market values on those dates were quite different.

LEARNING OBJECTIVE 8

Calculate the book value and market value of a corporation.

The **market value** of a company is measured by multiplying the market price per share by the number of shares outstanding. This total amount may be different from the sum of the company's assets less liabilities at market value. The combination of assets in a company may produce synergies or goodwill (discussed in Chapter 8), both of which increase a company's value above the value of its identifiable assets on the company's statement of financial position. In addition, there may be intangible assets that are not recorded on the company's statement of financial position. The share price of a company tries to reflect all of the components of value in the company, including intangibles and growth opportunities. Share prices are also affected by economic factors such as interest rates or market attitudes to risk, and fluctuate daily in the stock markets.

Investors often use a range of values or recent prices to estimate market value. Recall that Le Château has two classes of shares. Class A with one vote per share, and Class B with 10 votes per share. The Class B shares do not trade on the stock market, so we can only obtain a market price for the Class A shares. However, the two classes share equally in earnings and dividends, so we will assume that the Class B shares would be worth at least the same value as the Class A shares. (As they have extra voting rights, they would likely be worth more, so our assumption of equality is conservative.) Based on this assumption, the market value of Le Château as at January 30, 2010, and January 31, 2009, is as follows:

Le Château Inc. Market Value

	2010	2009
Number of Class A shares outstanding	19,973,464	19,663,464
Number of Class B shares outstanding	4,560,000	4,560,000
Market price per share	$13.82	$8.30
Total market value of all shares	$339,052,000	$201,055,000

Note that for 2010 the market value is more than twice the book value of $157,221,000, illustrating the potentially large difference that can exist between the two measures.

Price/Earnings Ratio

LEARNING OBJECTIVE 9

Calculate and interpret the price/earnings ratio and the return on shareholders' equity ratio.

A key ratio that involves shareholders' equity is earnings per share (EPS). We introduced this ratio in Chapter 4 and are returning to it now. Earnings per share provides a measure of the earnings relative to the number of common shares outstanding. It is useful for tracking the return per share earned by the company over time. This ratio can also be related to the current market price per share, by calculating the **price/earnings ratio** or multiple. This is calculated as follows:

$$\frac{\text{Market price per share}}{\text{Earnings per share}}$$

The price/earnings ratio relates the accounting earnings to the market price at which the shares trade. If two companies in the same industry had the same earnings per share of $5, and Company A's shares were selling for $25 and Company B's shares were selling for $50, the price/earnings ratios would be different. Company A's price/earnings ratio would be 5 ($25 ÷ $5) and Company B's would be 10 ($50 ÷ $5). This indicates that the market is placing a higher value on Company B's shares. There are probably many reasons for the higher valuation, such as an assessment of higher earning potential in the future, a lower risk with respect to debt repayment, or an assessment of its future competitive position. The price/earnings ratios for Le Château for its Class A non-voting shares for the basic earnings per share were as follows in 2010 and 2009:

$$\text{January 29, 2010} \qquad \$13.82 \div \$1.23 = 11.24$$
$$\text{January 30, 2009} \qquad \$8.30 \div \$1.56 = 5.32$$

The price/earnings ratio rose in the year ending January 31, 2010 primarily because the share price rose significantly in that year.

When evaluating a company's price/earnings ratio, it is important to compare it with those of other companies in the same industry. This comparison gives the user information about how the market is valuing the company in relation to others.

Return on Shareholders' Equity Ratio

Another useful indicator of profitability is the return on shareholders' equity, or simply the **return on equity ratio** (ROE). This is a more general measure than earnings per share because it relates the earnings available to common shares to the total of the common shareholders' equity. It is calculated as follows:

$$\text{ROE} = \frac{\text{Net earnings} - \text{Preferred dividends}}{\text{Average common shareholders' equity}}$$

Preferred dividends need to be subtracted from the net earnings because preferred shareholders have a prior claim on the earnings through preferred dividends, which must be declared and paid before any dividends are paid on common shares. We want this ratio to determine a measure of return to the common shares only. Common shareholders' equity is the shareholders' equity less any amounts that represent owners other than common shareholders. This means that the amount in the preferred shares account would need to be subtracted from the total shareholders' equity to arrive at common shareholders' equity.

This ratio tells you the rate of return that the common shareholders are earning on the amount that they have invested in the company. The following are the rates of return for Le Château in 2010 and 2009:

Le Château Inc. ROE

	2010	2009
Net earnings	$29,837	$38,621
Average shareholders' equity	1/2 ($157,221 + $142,414)	1/2 ($142,414 + $133,605)
ROE	19.6%	28.0%

Le Château has no preferred shares issued, so all the net earnings accrue to the common shareholders. The return to common shareholders decreased in 2010 because 2010 earnings decreased significantly. Further analysis would be necessary to determine the reasons for the decrease in earnings, but a portion of it can likely be explained by the economic crisis and slowdown that occurred in the latter half of 2008. Despite the decline, the common shareholders earned a hefty 19.6% return on their investment in Le Château in 2010.

Chapter 12 includes a more detailed discussion of other types of analysis that involve shareholders' equity.

SUMMARY

This chapter discussed the most common forms of business organization: sole proprietorships, partnerships, and corporations. Advantages and disadvantages for each form were discussed. Because the predominant business structure is the corporation, this form was explored in more detail. Particular attention was paid to shares. Corporations authorize different types or classes of shares with the intention of attracting capital investment. These shares come with different rights and privileges, which were also outlined in the chapter.

Shareholders can be given a return from the company in the form of dividends. Dividends can come in various forms: cash, property, or stock. This section of the chapter concluded with a brief discussion about stock splits and employee stock option plans.

Because the chapter concerns shareholders' equity, we discussed the fourth financial statement which, depending on the company, is either the statement of retained earnings or the statement of changes in shareholders' equity. Examples from Le Château and Rogers Communications were included as illustrations.

The chapter concluded with three measures used to help investors evaluate shareholders' equity: book and market values, the price/earnings ratio, and the return on shareholders' equity ratio. This concludes the discussion of the primary accounts on the statement of financial position.

In the final chapter of the book, financial statement analysis is summarized. You have already been introduced to most of the ratios discussed in Chapter 12, but some new ratios and other analytical techniques are introduced, and there is extensive discussion of how the results of the quantitative analysis can be interpreted. The book ends with a further discussion of complex companies in Appendix B, to help you understand some of the issues related to intercompany strategic investments.

PRACTICE PROBLEM

WILEY PLUS
www.wileyplus.com

Additional Practice Problems

Balukas Company had the following shareholders' equity section balances at December 31, 2010:

Share capital	$4,700,000
(Unlimited number of common shares authorized; 240,000 issued)	
Retained earnings	4,000,000
Total shareholders' equity	$8,700,000

During 2011, the following transactions occurred:

1. On January 2, 2011, Balukas declared a cash dividend of $1.50 per share to shareholders of record on January 27, 2011, payable February 15, 2011.

2. On March 15, 2011, Balukas issued 10,000 new shares and received proceeds of $40 per share.

3. On June 29, 2011, Balukas declared and paid a 10% stock dividend. The market price of Balukas' shares on June 29, 2011, was $45 per share.

4. On June 30, 2011, Balukas declared a cash dividend of $1.50 per share to shareholders of record on July 15, 2011, payable on July 31, 2011.

5. On September 1, 2011, Balukas issued 100,000 new shares at $50 per share.

6. On December 31, 2011, Balukas declared a four-for-one stock split.

Additional information:

7. Net income for 2011 was $1,500,000.

8. The market price of the shares on December 31, 2011, was $13.00

Required:

a. Construct journal entries for each of the transactions as they occurred during 2011.

b. If a transaction does not require a journal entry, explain why.

c. What will be the balance in the retained earnings account as at December 31, 2011?

d. What is the average carrying value of the common shares at the end of 2011? (Hint: The average carrying value is the total amount in the common shares account divided by the number of shares outstanding.)

e. Explain why the average carrying value calculated in part "d" differs from the market value of the shares.

STRATEGIES FOR SUCCESS:

▶ You should start by reading the information given about the shareholders' equity section of the statement of financial position at the end of 2010. It tells you the kind of shares the company has, how many have been issued, and how much has been paid for the shares. You can use the information about the number of shares and the amount that has been paid for them to calculate an average price per share.

▶ As you work through the various transactions that occurred in 2011, it would be helpful to create a spreadsheet so that you can keep track of changes to the amounts in the common shares and retained earnings accounts, as well as the number of shares that are being issued. Remember that dividends are paid on the number of shares outstanding at a given date, so you need to be able to determine how many there are.

▶ It is important to show your work so that your instructor can see how you are thinking through the problem. In the solution to this practice problem, we have included all of the calculations for each transaction. If you do not have the right amount in your journal entry, it may only be a calculation error but it may also be a fundamental error in understanding. Seeing your work will help your instructor provide you with the appropriate assistance.

SUGGESTED SOLUTION TO PRACTICE PROBLEM 1

a. 1. January 2, 2011—Declaration of a Cash Dividend

Dividend declared (SE)	360,000[a]	
Dividend payable (L)		360,000

February 15, 2011—Payment of Dividend to Shareholders

Dividend Payable (L)	360,000	
Cash (A)		360,000

a. (240,000 × $1.50) = $360,000

practice problems

2. March 15, 2011—Common Share Issuance Entry (10,000 shares)

Cash (A)	400,000	
Share capital (SE)		400,000

3. June 29, 2011—Small Stock Dividend Entries

Declaration

Dividend declared (SE)	1,125,000[b]	
Stock dividend issuable (SE)		1,125,000

Issuance

Stock dividend issuable (SE)	1,125,000	
Share capital (SE)		1,125,000

b. Number of shares = 240,000 + 10,000 = 250,000 shares
   250,000 shares × 10% × $45 per share = $1,125,000
   25,000 new shares issued

4. June 30, 2011—Declaration of Dividend

Dividends declared (SE)	412,500[c]	
Dividends payable (L)		412,500

July 31, 2011—Payment of Dividend to Shareholders

Dividends payable (L)	412,500	
Cash (A)		412,500

c. (250,000 shares + 25,000 shares) = 275,000 shares
   275,000 shares × $1.50 per share = $412,500

5. September 1, 2011—Issuance of New Shares (100,000 shares)

Cash (A)	5,000,000	
Share capital (SE)		5,000,000

100,000 shares × $50.00 per share

6. No entry is needed. However, a memorandum entry could be made to indicate that the number of shares outstanding has changed from 375,000 (275,000 + 100,000) to 1,500,000 (375,000 × 4 = 1,500,000).

b. No journal entry was required for transaction f. During a stock split or a large stock dividend, the number of shares increases but the company's value does not change. The purpose of the stock split is to lower the current market price of the company's shares. In the four-for-one split that was used in the practice problem, the market price would immediately drop to one-quarter of the price before the split. The lower price would make the shares accessible to more investors.

c. The balance in the retained earnings account will be:
   $4,000,000 + 1,500,000 − $360,000 − $1,125,000 − $412,500 = $3,602,500.
   Opening balance + Net income − Dividends = Ending balance

d. The average carrying value of the common shares will be:
   $11,225,000[d] ÷ 1,500,000 = $7.48
   d. See the calculation of carrying value in the table below.

e. The average carrying value considers the average price that the shares were issued at throughout the company's existence, whereas the market price values all shares at the current market price. The opening balance implied an average cost of 4,700,000 ÷ 240,000 = $19.58 before taking into account the 4:1 split, or $19.58 ÷ 4 = $4.895 after the split. The market price of the shares has been increasing throughout the company's life, reflecting increased expectations for future earnings. The shares issued during this year were closer to the market value (when adjusted for the split, the range for the year is from $40 ÷ 4 = $10 to $50 ÷ 4 = $12.50). However, the market value is greater than the average value. The stock market values the company at more than the sum of the cost of its equity and retained earnings.

Working spreadsheet to accompany the practice problem

Date	Number of Common Shares	Common Share Account	Retained Earnings Account
January 1, 2011	240,000	$ 4,700,000	$ 4,000,000
January 2, 2011			(360,000)
March 15, 2011	10,000	$ 400,000	
Balance	250,000	$ 5,100,000	
June 29, 2011	25,000	$ 1,125,000	(1,125,000)
Balance	275,000	$ 6,225,000	
June 30, 2011			($412,500)
September 1, 2011	100,000	$ 5,000,000	
Balance	375,000		
December 31, 2011			
Stock Split	1,500,000		
Net earnings			$ 1,500,000
Ending balance	1,500,000	$11,225,000	$ 3,602,500

APPENDIX

REPURCHASE OF SHARES AND TREASURY SHARES

There are several reasons for a company to repurchase its shares. Depending on the jurisdiction that the company is incorporated in, the shares are either cancelled or held as treasury shares. Accounting for the repurchase is similar for either situation, but the presentation differs.

Repurchased and Cancelled

When a company repurchases its own shares, the amount in the share capital account must be reduced since the shares are no longer outstanding. When a company buys back shares, the price per share that it pays is usually different from what it received per share when they were originally issued, creating a type of either gain or loss on the repurchase. Gains and losses incurred by a company on buying back their own shares are not recorded on the statement of earnings. Transactions on the statement of earnings represent transactions with parties outside the company. As the shareholders are considered part of the company, transactions with them are not reported on the statement of earnings. In addition, repurchasing shares is not an activity that is part of normal company operations, as the company was not incorporated to earn money by trading in its own shares. As a general rule, companies never earn revenues/gains or incur expenses/losses from transactions involving their own equities. Gains and losses from share repurchases are still reported as part of shareholders equity, however. Gains are recorded as increases in contributed surplus, and losses as a reduction in either contributed surplus or retained earnings.

When a company repurchases its own shares, a credit is made to cash for the total cost of the shares. The debit to reduce share capital is determined by using the average carrying value, dividing the total amount in the share capital account by the total number of shares outstanding before the repurchase. The difference in these two entries is the gain or loss.

As an example, suppose that Lee Industries Ltd. had the following shareholders' equity:

Share capital (150,000 shares outstanding)	$1,500,000
Retained earnings	500,000
Total shareholders' equity	$2,000,000

The average carrying value of its shares was $10 ($1,500,000 ÷ 150,000). If Lee repurchases 1,000 shares for $9 each, it is paying $1 less than the average carrying value. Share capital will be reduced by $10,000 ($10 × 1,000 shares). The $1 per share difference is credited to a separate account called contributed surplus. The entry to record this repurchase would be as follows:

Share capital (SE)	10,000	
Cash (A)		9,000
Contributed surplus (SE)		1,000

Subsequent to this transaction, the shareholders' equity would include the following:

Share capital	$1,490,000
Contributed surplus	1,000
Retained earnings	500,000
Total shareholders' equity	$1,991,000

Note that the total shareholders' equity has decreased from $2,000,000 to $1,991,000, or $9,000—the amount paid to repurchase the shares.

If Lee had paid $12 per share, it would have paid $2 more than the average issue price per share of $10. In this case, the $2 extra per share would reduce shareholders' equity. Normally, the $2 is debited to retained earnings as follows:

Share capital (SE)	10,000	
Retained earnings (SE)	2,000	
Cash (A)		12,000

Subsequent to this transaction, the shareholders' equity would include the following:

Share capital	$1,490,000
Retained earnings	498,000
Total shareholders' equity	$1,988,000

In this case the total shareholders' equity decreased from $2,000,000 to $1,988,000, or by $12,000. Again, this is the amount paid by the company to repurchase the shares.

If there had been a previous repurchase of shares that created a contributed surplus account (similar to the first part of this example), the contributed surplus account could have been debited instead of retained earnings, but the contributed surplus account never has a debit (negative) balance.

In the statement of shareholders' equity for Rogers in Exhibit 11-7A, Rogers repurchased Class B shares in both 2008 and 2009. In both years the amount reported in share capital decreased ($4 million in 2008; $9 million in 2009), reflecting the average cost of the shares, and the excess price Rogers paid on the repurchase reduced contributed surplus and retained earnings in both years. How the amount is split between those accounts is covered in more advanced accounting courses.

Treasury Shares

The calculations and logic are the same for treasury shares, but the presentation is different. Instead of debiting share capital directly, the treasury shares are shown in a contra account as a reduction from the share capital account. The shares are still issued, so the original share capital is still valid, but they are not outstanding. The issued shares minus those held as treasury shares are the outstanding shares. The net effect is the same as the earlier examples.

Exhibit 11-8 shows an example in Note 16 of the financial statements of **Metro Inc.**, which owns a large number of grocery stores in Eastern Canada. Metro has an unlimited number of First Preferred Shares, Class A Subordinate Shares, and Class B Shares. No preferred shares have been issued. The Class A shares have one voting right per share, are participating, and are convertible into Class B shares in case of a takeover bid. The Class B shares have 16 votes per share, are participating, and are convertible into Class A shares.

When the treasury shares are later reissued, the treasury shares account will be credited and any excess amount above the average carrying value of the shares—$10 per share in our earlier example—that is received for the shares is credited to contributed surplus. If they are issued at an amount below $10 per share, retained earnings or contributed surplus is debited, as was done when the treasury shares were first acquired. Further details on the accounting for treasury share transactions can be found in more advanced accounting texts.

METRO INC. 2009 ANNUAL REPORT

EXHIBIT 11-8

annual report

16 CAPITAL STOCK

AUTHORIZED Unlimited number of First Preferred Shares, non-voting, without par value, issuable in series.

Unlimited number of Class A Subordinate Shares, bearing one voting right per share, participating, convertible into Class B Shares in the event of a takeover bid involving Class B Shares, without par value.

Unlimited number of Class B Shares, bearing 16 voting rights per share, participating, convertible in the event of disqualification into an equal number of Class A Subordinate Shares on the basis of one Class A Subordinate Share for each Class B Share held, without par value.

OUTSTANDING

	Class A Subordinate Shares		Class B Shares		Total	
	Number (Thousands)		Number (Thousands)			
Balance as at September 29, 2007	113,683	$ 713.2	804	$ 1.6	$	714.8
Shares issued for cash	661	11.4	–	–		11.4
Shares redeemed for cash, excluding premium of $92.1	(4,552)	(28.6)	–	–		(28.6)
Acquisition of treasury shares, excluding premium of $0.7	(40)	(0.2)	–	–		(0.2)
Stock options exercised	–	0.2	–	–		0.2
Conversion of Class B Shares into Class A Subordinate Shares	54	0.1	(54)	(0.1)		–
Balance as at September 27, 2008	109,806	$ 696.1	750	$ 1.5	$	697.6
Shares issued for cash	2,044	44.0	–	–		44.0
Shares redeemed for cash, excluding premium of $116.2	(3,989)	(26.3)	–	–		(26.3)
Acquisition of treasury shares, excluding premium of $3.6	(115)	(0.7)	–	–		(0.7)
Released treasury shares	52	0.3	–	–		0.3
Stock options exercised	–	1.8	–	–		1.8
Conversion of Class H Shares into Class A Subordinate Shares	32	0.1	(32)	(0.1)		–
Balance as at September 26, 2009	107,830	$ 715.3	718	$ 1.4	$	716.7

SYNONYMS

Exercise price ❙ Strike price
Minority interest ❙ Non-controlling interest
Property dividends ❙ Dividends in kind

GLOSSARY

Accumulated other comprehensive income   A component of shareholders' equity representing the cumulative amount of unrealized increases and decreases in the values of the net assets of the entity. Once realized, these gains/losses are transferred to retained earnings.

Articles of incorporation   A document filed with federal or provincial regulatory authorities when a business incorporates under that jurisdiction. The articles include, among other items, the authorized number of shares and dividend preferences for each class of shares that is to be issued.

Authorized shares   The maximum number of shares that a company is authorized to issue under its articles of incorporation.

Capital account   An account used in a partnership or proprietorship to record the investment and accumulated earnings of each owner.

Common shares   Certificates that represent portions of ownership in a corporation. These shares usually carry a right to vote.

Controlling interest   The holding of enough common shares (usually greater than 50%) to give the investor the ability to set the strategic, operating, investing, and financing policies for the company.

Convertible preferred shares   Preferred shares that are exchangeable or convertible into a specified number of common shares.

Corporation   A form of business in which the shareholders have limited liability and the business entity is taxed directly. Shareholders receive distributions from the entity in the form of dividends.

Cumulative preferred shares   Preferred shares that accumulate dividends from periods even if there is no dividend declaration. These accumulated dividends, called dividends in arrears, must be paid before a dividend can be declared for common shareholders.

Date of declaration   The date on which the board of directors votes to declare a dividend. On this date, the dividend becomes legally payable to shareholders.

Date of payment   The date on which a dividend is paid to shareholders.

Date of record   The date on which a shareholder must own the shares in order to receive the dividend from a share.

Dividend declaration   An action by a corporation's board of directors that legally obliges the corporation to pay a dividend.

Dividends   Payments made to shareholders that represent a return on their investment in a company. Dividends are paid only after they are declared by the board of directors.

Dividends in arrears   Dividends on cumulative preferred shares that have not yet been declared from a prior year.

Dividends in kind   A dividend that is satisfied with the transfer of some type of property other than cash. Synonym for property dividend.

Drawings account   An account used in a partnership or proprietorship to record the cash withdrawals by owners.

Employee Stock Options   An option granted to an employee to buy shares at a fixed price, usually as part of an incentive compensation plan.

Ex-dividend day   The date on which shares are sold in the market without the most recently declared dividend.

Exercise price   The price per share that the holder of a stock option is required to pay if the holder exercises the option.

Expiration date   The date by which a stock option holder must either exercise the option or lose it.

General partners   The partners who have unlimited liability in a limited partnership.

Issued shares   The shares of a corporation that have been issued.

Legal capital   The amount that is recorded in the common share account when the shares are first issued.

Limited liability   A feature of share ownership that restricts the liability of shareholders to the amount they have invested in the corporation. Also available to limited partners in a limited partnership.

Limited partners   The partners in a limited partnership that have limited liability.

Limited partnership   A partnership that allows some partners to have limited liability (limited partners) and others to have unlimited liability (general partners).

Market value   The amount that an item would generate if it were sold.

Memorandum entry   An entry made to record a stock split. No amounts are affected; only the record of the number of shares issued is affected.

Minority interest   A block of shares owed by an investor that represents less that 50% of the outstanding shares. Synonym for non-controlling interest.

Non-controlling interest   A block of shares owed by an investor that represents less than 50% of the outstanding shares. Synonym for minority interest.

No par value shares   Shares that have no par value associated with them.

Ordinary shares   A synonym for common shares used primarily outside North America.

Outstanding shares   The number of shares that are held by individuals or entities outside the corporation (not including treasury shares).

Owner's capital   An account used in a sole proprietorship to record the owner's investments in the company, plus income earned less withdrawals.

Paid-in capital   The amount paid by an investor to purchase shares in a corporation when they are first issued.

Participating preferred shares   Preferred shares that can also participate in dividends declared beyond the level specified by the preferred shares, that is, beyond the fixed dividend payout specified in the preferred shares contract.

Partnership   A form of business in which the owners have unlimited legal liability and the business entity is not taxed directly; the income from the entity passes through to the partners' individual tax returns.

Partnership agreement   An agreement between the partners in a partnership that specifies how they will share in the risks and rewards of ownership.

Par value   A value per share of common shares set in the articles of incorporation.

Pre-emptive right   The right of shareholders to share proportionately in new issuances of shares.

Preference shares   A synonym for preferred shares used primarily outside North America.

Preferred shares   An ownership right in which the shareholder has some preference as to dividends; that is,

if dividends are declared, the preferred shareholders receive them first. Other rights that are normally held by common shareholders may also be changed in preferred shares; for example, many issues of preferred shares are non-voting.

Price/earnings (P/E) ratio   A performance ratio that compares the market price per share with the earnings per share.

Property dividend   A dividend that is satisfied with the transfer of some type of property other than cash. Synonym for dividend in kind.

Prospectus   A document filed with a securities commission by a corporation when it wants to issue public debt or shares.

Redeemable preferred shares   Preferred shares that can be bought back (redeemed) by the corporation under certain conditions and at a price stated in the articles of incorporation.

Retractable preferred shares   Shares that can be sold back to the company (retired) at the shareholder's option. The price that must be paid for them and the periods of time within which they can be sold are specified in the articles of incorporation.

Return on equity ratio   A ratio that compares the net earnings (or income or profit) for the period to the shareholders' equity in the company.

Service period   The period the employees need to work before they can exercise their employee stock option.

Sole proprietorship   A form of business in which there is a single owner (sole proprietor). This form is characterized by unlimited liability to the owner and exemption from corporate taxation.

Stock dividend   A distribution of additional common shares to shareholders. Existing shareholders receive shares in proportion to the number of shares they already own.

Stock option   An agreement between two parties to either buy or sell shares at a fixed price, called the exercise price, at some future date.

Stock split   A distribution of new shares to shareholders. The new shares take the place of existing shares, and existing shareholders receive new shares in proportion to the number of old shares they already own.

Treasury shares   Shares that are repurchased by a corporation and held internally. Repurchased shares are normally cancelled immediately upon purchase.

Unlimited liability   A characteristic of sole proprietorships and partnerships where the owners are personally responsible for the liabilities incurred by the business entity.

ASSIGNMENT MATERIAL

Assessing Your Recall

11-1   Describe the owners' legal liability and tax status in the following forms of business: corporations, sole proprietorships, partnerships, and limited partnerships.

11-2   Discuss the purpose and importance of a partnership agreement.

11-3   Many companies start as small companies, often as sole proprietorships. What factors could cause the owner to consider changing the ownership structure of a corporation?

11-4   Explain the different roles and responsibilities of a general partner and a limited partner.

11-5   Describe what is contained in a company's articles of incorporation and what significance they have for the accounting system.

11-6   List and briefly describe the four rights that common shareholders typically have in a corporation.

11-7   Discuss how preferred shares differ from common shares.

11-8   Briefly describe what each of the following features means in a preferred share issue: participating, cumulative, convertible, and redeemable.

11-9   Briefly describe each of the following terms: authorized shares, issued shares, and outstanding shares.

11-10   Describe the process of declaring and paying a cash dividend, including information about the declaration date, date of record, and payment date.

11-11   Discuss the nature of a stock dividend and why a distinction is made between small and large stock dividends.

11-12   Explain why companies might declare a stock dividend rather than a cash dividend.

11-13   Discuss why companies issue employee stock options and what immediate and potential effects these options have on a company's financial results.

11-14   Explain why a company might repurchase its own shares in the open market.

11-15   Differentiate between the book value and the market value of a company's equity.

11-16   Describe what the price/earnings ratio is intended to tell users about a company.

11-17   Explain why the return on shareholders' equity provides information on the rate of return to common shareholders only.

Applying Your Knowledge

11-18   **(Taking a company public)**
In our opening story, **DHX Media** decided to "go public." What reasons could it have for making this decision?

11-19   **(Taking a company private)**
In 2006, **Empire Co. Ltd.**, the majority shareholder of Sobeys Inc., bought all of the outstanding shares of Sobeys that it did not already own, thus making it a privately held corporation. What reasons could it have for deciding to take Sobeys private?

11-20 (Selecting a business entity)

Indicate whether each of the following business entities is more likely to be established as a sole proprietorship (SP), partnership (P), or corporation (C). Provide reasons for your choice.

    a. A small legal practice set up by two recent law school graduates
    b. A restaurant with six locations in southern Alberta
    c. A second-hand outdoor equipment store owned by Rose Johnston
    d. A mining company operating in Quebec
    e. A hairdressing salon operated by three stylists
    f. An independent house-painting business owned and operated by one person

11-21 (Selecting a business entity)

Indicate whether each of the following business entities is more likely to be established as a sole proprietorship (SP), partnership (P), or corporation (C). Provide reasons for your choice.

    a. A bottled water company that operates out of Quebec and delivers bottled water to offices, businesses, and homes in Quebec
    b. A dental practice with four dentists
    c. A company that employs tree cutters and contracts out their services to logging companies
    d. A dog kennel operation that raises and trains guard dogs
    e. A national chain of building supply stores
    f. A picture-framing business operating out of a mall location in Hamilton, Ontario

11-22 (Business formation)

Albert Wong just graduated from university and is planning to start his own software development company. He is debating whether to set up practice as a sole proprietor or establish a corporate entity and serve as its president.

Required:
    a. What advantages are there to operating as a sole proprietorship?
    b. What advantages are there to operating as a corporation?
    c. Which form of business organization would his customers likely prefer? Why?
    d. Which form of business organization would his creditors likely prefer? Why?
    e. Which form of business will be most advantageous to Albert Wong if he expects the business to grow rapidly? Why?

11-23 (Business formation)

Jasmine Sparks has just finished a clothing design program at one of the local colleges, where her instructors praised her creativity. Each year, clothing designed by the students is sold to the public. As her designs sold very quickly, Jasmine is considering starting her own company to design clothing for teens. She realizes that she will need some financial backing to get started.

Required:
    a. What advantages and disadvantages are there to setting up her business as a sole proprietorship?
    b. What advantages are there to beginning operations as a sole proprietorship and then switching to a partnership when she expands?
    c. What advantages and disadvantages are there to operating as a corporation?
    d. Which form of business organization would her customers likely prefer? Why?
    e. Which form of business will be most advantageous to her if she wants to maintain control as the business expands? Why?

11-24   (Business formation)

Three friends, Abe, Ben, and Candice, all recently qualified as CAs (Chartered Accountants) and have decided to leave the large national firm they work for to start their own small firm (ABC CA). They are going to share office space and hire one administrative staff person. Each person will be responsible for providing the services to the clients they introduce to the firm.

- a. What form of organization would you recommend for ABC?
- b. What are the advantages and disadvantages of the form you recommended in part "a"?
- c. Which form of business organization would the clients of ABC likely prefer? Why?
- d. The three principals have agreed that if the practice grows they will consider adding additional CAs to the firm. What implications would this have for the organization of ABC?

11-25   (Equity transactions)

Southern Exposure Ltd. begins operations on January 2, 2010. During the year, the following transactions affect shareholders' equity:

1. Southern Exposure authorizes the issuance of 1 million common shares and 100,000 preferred shares, which pay a dividend of $2 per share.

2. A total of 240,000 common shares are issued for $5 a share.

3. A total of 15,000 preferred shares are issued for $14 per share.

4. The full annual dividend on the preferred shares is declared and paid.

5. A dividend of $0.10 per share is declared on the common shares but is not yet paid.

6. The company has earnings of $150,000 for the year. (Assume revenues of $750,000 and total expenses of $600,000.)

7. The dividends on the common shares are paid.

8. A 5% stock dividend is declared on the common shares and distributed. On the date of declaration, the shares' market price was $5.50.

Required:

- a. Prepare journal entries to record the above transactions, including the closing entries for the net earnings.
- b. Prepare the shareholders' equity section of the statement of financial position as at December 31, 2010.
- c. Why would an investor choose to purchase the common shares rather than the preferred shares? Or vice versa?

11-26   (Share issuance, dividends, financial statement preparation)

The Equitee Corporation was incorporated on January 2, 2010, with two classes of share capital: an unlimited number of common shares and $3 cumulative non-voting preferred shares with an authorized limit of 50,000. Equitee is not a public company (the shares do not trade on a stock exchange). During the first year of operations, the following transactions occurred:

1. The company issued 3,000 preferred shares for a total of $75,000 cash, and 10,000 common shares for $20 per share.

2. It issued 4,000 common shares in exchange for a parcel of land. The land had an estimated fair market value of $120,000. The current market value of the company's common shares was not known. (Hint: When shares are issued in exchange for another asset, you value the transaction at the more reliable of the two values, the asset received or the shares given up.)

3. The company earned revenues of $1,050,000 and its expenses were $925,000 during the year.

4. No dividends were declared during the first year of operations.

During the second year of operations, the following transactions occurred:

5. In November, the company's board of directors declared cash dividends sufficient to be able to pay a dividend of $4 on each common share. The dividends were payable on December 14. (Hint: Remember that no dividends can be paid on the common shares until the dividends in arrears on the preferred shares are paid.)

6. In December, the cash dividends from November were paid.

7. In September, the board of directors declared and distributed a 10% stock dividend on the common shares. The estimated market value of the common shares at the time was $24 per share.

8. The company earned $1,200,000 in revenue and incurred $1,025,000 in expenses during the second year.

Required:

a. Use a spreadsheet or table format like the one in the practice problem to track the changes in all of the shareholders' equity accounts over the two-year period. Prepare the shareholders' equity section of the statement of financial position at the end of the second year.

b. Why would the owners have designated the preferred shares as non-voting?

11-27 (Equity transactions, financial statement preparation)

Pharma Shop Ltd. was a mid-sized public company that had been in operation for many years. On December 31, 2010, it had an unlimited number of common shares authorized and 5,200,000 shares issued at an average value of $25 per share. As well, there were 5,000,000 preferred shares authorized, with 250,000 of them issued at $20 per share. The balance in retained earnings was $26,610,000. The balance in accumulated other comprehensive income was $525,000. The preferred shares paid an annual dividend of $2 per share. During 2011, the following transactions affected shareholders' equity:

1. In total, 200,000 common shares were issued at $30 per share.

2. The preferred dividend for the year was declared and paid.

3. A 10% common stock dividend was declared when the market price was $33 per share. The shares were distributed one month after the declaration.

4. In early December 2011, a dividend of $1.50 per share was declared on the common shares. The date of record was December 15, 2011. The dividend will be paid the following year.

5. The company earned income of $14,820,000 and had an other comprehensive loss of $145,000.

6. On December 31, 2011, the company declared a two-for-one stock split on common shares.

Required:

a. Use a spreadsheet or table format like the one in the practice problem to track all of the changes in the shareholders' equity accounts in 2011.

b. Prepare the statement of changes in shareholders' equity for 2011 and the shareholders' equity section of the statement of financial position as at the end of 2011. (Hint: The statement of changes in shareholders' equity will be similar to the table from part "a" but similar transactions, like dividends, will be grouped into one line.)

11-28 (Share issuance, repurchase, and cancellation)

On December 31, 2010, the shareholders' equity section of Eastwood Inc.'s statement of financial position appeared as follows:

Share capital, preferred shares, no par, $8 dividend, non-voting, redeemable at $103, 100,000 shares authorized, 30,000 shares issued	$ 3,000,000
Share capital, common shares, 500,000 shares issued, unlimited number of shares authorized	4,400,000
Retained earnings	5,120,000
Accumulated other comprehensive income	345,000
Total shareholders' equity	$12,856,000

During 2011, the following events occurred:

1. Eastwood issued 120,000 additional common shares for $15 per share.

2. The company declared and paid the dividend on the preferred shares for the first half of the year.

3. Immediately after paying the preferred dividend for the first half of the year, the company repurchased and cancelled all the preferred shares at the redemption price of $103 per share.

4. The company declared and distributed a 5% stock dividend when the market price of the share was $46 per share.

5. In November, the share price had risen to $100 per share, so the board of directors voted to split the shares five-for-one.

6. Late in December, the board declared a cash dividend on the common shares of $0.50 per share payable in early January 2010. In past years, the dividend had generally been about $2.00 per share.

7. The company earned income of $720,000 for 2011 and other comprehensive income of $85,000.

Required:

a. Use a spreadsheet or table format like the one in the practice problem to track all of the changes in the shareholders' equity accounts in 2011. Use the table to prepare the statement of changes in shareholders' equity for 2011.

b. Prepare the shareholders' equity section of the statement of financial position as at the end of 2011.

c. If you owned 50,000 common shares on January 1, 2011, and did not buy or sell any shares during the year, how has your ability to influence the management of the company changed over the year? Did you need to consider the existence of preferred shares on January 1, 2011? Explain.

d. What effect did each dividend (stock dividend and cash dividend) have on the financial statements?

e. What reasons might the company have for declaring a stock dividend?

f. What reasons might the company have for splitting the shares?

g. If you were a common shareholder, would you be happy or unhappy with the stock dividend and stock split? Explain.

h. What do you think about the reduction in the cash dividend from $2.00 to $0.50? Explain.

i. Why would an investor purchase common shares rather than preferred shares? Or vice versa?

j. Give possible reasons for a company to change its equity financing by eliminating its preferred shares and issuing more common shares.

11-29 (Statement of changes in shareholders' equity)

The following information was available for The Gibson Group Inc. (TGGI) for 2011:

1. Class A common shares, 10 votes per share, unlimited authorized, 7,530,000 issued and outstanding on January 1, 2011, for $18,825,000. Class B common shares, 1 vote per share, unlimited authorized, 25,432,000 issued and outstanding for $216,172,000.

2. January 1, 2011, balance of $252,475,000 in retained earnings and $674,000 in accumulated other comprehensive income.

3. During September, TGGI bought back and cancelled 750,000 Class B shares. The total cost of the buyback was $7,875,000 and the average value of the shares repurchased was $8.50. Any difference between the average carrying value and the repurchase price should be recorded in retained earnings.

4. In December, TGGI paid dividends of $1.25 on all shares outstanding.

5. Net earnings for 2011 were $85,993,000 and other comprehensive income was $43,000.

Required:
a. Prepare TGGI's statement of changes in shareholders' equity for 2011.
b. What portion of net earnings did TGGI pay out in dividends?

11-30 (Stock dividends)

Sealand Company has 80,000 common shares outstanding. Because it wants to use its cash flow for other purposes, the company has decided to issue stock dividends to its shareholders. The market price of each Sealand Company share is $26.

Required:
a. Give the journal entry, if any, if the company decides to issue a 10% stock dividend.
b. Give the journal entry, if any, if the company decides to issue a 100% stock dividend.
c. What should happen to the market price of the company's shares in part "a"? In part "b"?

11-31 (Change in shareholders' equity)

The shareholders' equity of Deer Ltd. at the end of 2010 and 2009 appeared as follows:

	2010	2009
Share capital, preferred shares, no par, $2 cumulative, 2,000,000 shares authorized, 25,000 shares issued	$ 200,000	$ 200,000
Share capital, no par, 5,000,000 common shares authorized, 1,200,000 common shares issued (2009—1,000,000 shares)	5,000,000	4,000,000
Retained earnings	3,920,000	3,160,000
Total shareholders' equity	$9,120,000	$7,360,000

During 2010, Deer paid a total of $125,000 in cash dividends.

Required:
a. Assuming the preferred shares were not in arrears, how was the $125,000 in cash dividends distributed between the two classes of shares?
b. Assuming the preferred share dividends were in arrears for one year, how was the $125,000 in cash dividends distributed between the two classes of shares?
c. Both common shares and retained earnings changed during the year. Provide journal entries that would account for the changes.

11-32 (Dividend distributions)

Flatfish Limited reported the following items in shareholders' equity on December 31, 2010:

Share capital: Preferred shares, $5 cumulative dividend, 150,000 shares issued and outstanding	$15,000,000
Share capital: Common shares, 750,000 issued and outstanding	30,000,000
Retained earnings	25,000,000

Required:

a. No dividends were declared in 2008 or 2009; however, in 2010 cash dividends of $5,000,000 were declared. Calculate how much would be paid to each class of shares.

b. Assuming that the number of common shares remained constant throughout 2010, what was the cash dividend per share distributed to the common shareholders?

c. Early in 2011 when its common shares were selling at $59 per share, the company declared a 10% stock dividend. Describe the impact that this declaration will have on the shareholders' equity accounts.

d. Explain why a company would choose to issue a stock dividend rather than a cash dividend.

11-33 (Dividend distributions)

Holt Company paid out cash dividends at the end of each year as follows:

Year	Dividends
2009	$150,000
2010	$175,000
2011	$250,000

Required:

a. Assuming that Holt had 250,000 no par value common shares and 10,000 no par value, $7, non-cumulative preferred shares, how much cash would be paid out in 2009, 2010, and 2011 to each class of shares?

b. Assuming that Holt had 100,000 no par value common shares, and 5,000 no par value, $4, cumulative preferred shares that were three years in arrears as at January 1, 2009, how much cash would be paid out in 2009, 2010, and 2011 to each class of shares?

11-34 (Equity transactions)

The following information relates to the shareholders' equity section of McLaren Ltd. (in thousands):

	Dec. 31, 2010	Dec. 31, 2009
Share capital, preferred shares (15,000 shares issued and outstanding)	$ 4,500	$ 4,500
Share capital, common shares (250,000 shares issued and outstanding at end of 2009)	?	6,250
Contributed surplus—stock options	0	25
Retained earnings	6,400	3,750
Total shareholders' equity	?	$14,525

1. Early in 2010, 30,000 common shares were issued at $28 per share.

2. Midway through the year, cash dividends of $210,000 and $300,000 were paid to common shareholders and preferred shareholders, respectively.

3. Just before year end, the company acquired 15,000 of its own shares at $30 per share and cancelled them. Any difference between the price paid and the average value of the shares was recorded in retained earnings.

4. Immediately thereafter, the company issued 5,000 common shares when employees exercised options under employee stock option plans. The options had an exercise price of $20 and $25,000 of compensation expense that had been recognized during the service period for these options and recorded in contributed surplus.

Required:

a. Calculate the ending balance in common shares at the end of 2010.

b. Determine the number of common shares issued and outstanding at the end of 2010.

c. Calculate the amount of net income reported in 2010.

11-35   (Book value, market value, EPS)

Woods Inc. is a provincially incorporated company working in software development. The company was initially owned by a group of 40 investors that included the four original founders, their friends and families, and employees. The company is authorized to issue 50 million common shares; at the beginning of 2011 there were 1 million outstanding, with all of them owned by the initial group. The recorded value of these shares was $2.5 million. Due to the company's rapid success, management decided to raise funds for further growth by issuing more shares. In 2011, the company went public with an initial public offering (IPO) that sold 5 million shares and raised $50 million. Other information is as follows:

1. After losses in the early years, the company recently had positive earnings. The opening balance of retained earnings on January 1, 2011, was $1,200,000.

2. In 2011, net earnings were $2,500,000.

3. On December 31, 2011, the shares were trading at $10.50.

Required:

a. What percentage of the company does the original group of investors own after the IPO? How could the group have maintained their control of the company? How would that have likely influenced the price of the shares sold?

b. Calculate and compare the book value and market value of Woods Inc. on December 31, 2011. Explain why they might be different.

c. What was the EPS amount for 2011 based on the end of year number of shares outstanding?

d. If you were an investor who bought shares in the IPO, would you be surprised that dividends were not paid in 2011?

11-36   (Statement of earnings and statement of retained earnings)

The following are selected account balances from Eastern Shore Ltd.'s trial balance on December 31, 2010.

	Debits	Credits
Assets	$21,390,000	
Liabilities		$6,712,500
Amortization expense	105,000	
Common dividends declared	225,000	
Share capital		6,885,000
Cost of goods sold	1,020,000	
Interest expense	90,000	
Miscellaneous expense	300,000	
Preferred dividends declared	69,000	
Preferred shares		3,750,000
Retained earnings		3,915,000
Revenues		2,326,500
Wage expense	390,000	
	$23,589,000	$23,589,000

Required:

a. Prepare Eastern Shore's statement of earings and retained earnings statement in good form for the year ended December 31, 2010. (Hint: At what date is the retained earnings balance of $3,915,000 measured? How can you tell?)

b. Prepare the shareholders' equity section of the statement of financial position as at December 31, 2010.

c. Based on this information, does it appear likely that Eastern Shore will be able to continue paying common and preferred dividends at similar levels in the future? Explain.

d. Why might viewing Eastern Shore's statements or earnings for the previous few years help you in answering part "c"? What other information would you find helpful in reaching a conclusion?

User Perspective Problems

11-37 (New share issuance)

As a loan officer at a bank, six months ago you helped Cedar Ltd. arrange a $1.5-million, 20-year mortgage. Cedar Ltd. has just announced an issuance of new shares from which it intends to raise $5 million. How do you think this new issuance will affect the bank's outstanding loan? Identify some positive and negative outcomes.

11-38 (Accounting in a sole proprietorship)

A friend of yours has decided to start her own home decorating business. She has decided to establish the business as a sole proprietorship and to operate out of her home for now. Because she already owns a computer and all the required design software, she thinks she will be able to run the business initially without any outside financing. She is trying to decide how to prepare her financial statements and has come to you for advice. She asks you to explain what type of accounting system to use. Specifically, she is not sure if she needs to follow IFRS ("Whatever that is!" she says) or GAAP, or if she can just track the cash flow in her bank account. To help her out, first outline the differences in the accounting approaches that she has identified and any other approaches that you think might be appropriate. Then briefly explain the advantages and disadvantages of each system for her particular business and recommend one.

11-39 (Share repurchase and EPS)

A company has just announced a major repurchase of its own shares. Explain the likely effect on the company's EPS and share price.

11-40 (Stock dividends)

The shareholders' equity section of Golden Corporation's comparative balance sheet at the end of 2010 and 2009 was presented as follows at a recent shareholders' meeting:

	Dec. 31, 2010	Dec. 31, 2009
Share capital, common shares, no par value, 500,000 shares authorized, 290,000 shares issued and outstanding	$4,720,000	$4,000,000
Retained earnings	2,066,000	2,555,000
Total shareholders' equity	$6,786,000	$6,555,000

The following items were also disclosed at the shareholders' meeting: net income for 2010 was $666,000; a 16% stock dividend was issued on December 14, 2010, when the market value was $18 per share; the market value per share on December 31, 2010, was $16; management has put aside $900,000 and plans to borrow $200,000 to help finance a new plant addition, which is expected to cost a total of $1,000,000; and the customary $1.74 per share cash dividend was revised to $1.50 for the cash dividend declared and issued in the last week of December 2010.

As part of their shareholders' goodwill program, management asked shareholders to write down any questions they might have concerning the company's operations or finances. As assistant controller, you are given the shareholders' questions.

> *Required:*
> Prepare brief but reasonably complete answers to the following questions:
>
> a. What did Golden do with the cash proceeds from the stock dividend issued in December?
> b. What was the book value per share at the end of 2009 and 2010?
> c. I owned 5,000 shares of Golden in 2009 and have not sold any shares. How much more or less of the corporation do I own on December 31, 2010, and what happened to the market value of my interest in the company?
> d. I heard someone say that stock dividends don't give me anything I didn't already have. Why did you issue one? Are you trying to fool us?
> e. Instead of a stock dividend, why didn't you declare a cash dividend and let us buy the new shares that were issued?

f. Why are you cutting back on the dividends I receive?

g. If you have $900,000 put aside for the new plant addition that will cost $1,000,000, why are you borrowing $200,000 instead of just the missing $100,000?

11-41 (Cash dividends)

You have been considering buying some common shares of Sherlock Ltd., which has 1.5 million common shares outstanding. While the company has been through difficult times, it is now doing better and your main concern is whether you will receive cash dividends. In addition to the common shares, the company has 50,000 no par, $8, Class A preferred shares outstanding that are non-cumulative and non-participating. The company also has 10,000, no par, $7.50, Class B preferred shares outstanding. These shares are non-participating but are cumulative. The normal dividend was paid on both classes of preferred shares until last year, when no dividends were paid. This year, however, Sherlock is doing well and is expecting net income of $2.1 million. The company has not yet declared its annual dividends but has indicated that it plans to pay total dividends equal to 35% of net income.

a. If you were to immediately buy 100 shares of Sherlock Ltd., what amount of common dividend would you expect to receive?

b. If you were to immediately buy 100 shares of Sherlock Ltd., what amount of common dividend would you expect to receive if the Class B preferred shares were non-cumulative?

11-42 (Stock dividends and splits)

Peninsula Minerals Ltd.'s share capital consists of an unlimited number of common shares, with 9.3 million outstanding. After some early successes, the company has failed to locate new mineral deposits and has also decreased its estimates of the amount of minerals in existing mines. As a result, earnings per share and the share price have been declining and are currently $0.17 and $0.68 per share, respectively. Peninsula Minerals is considering a reverse stock split (one that decreases the number of shares outstanding instead of increasing them) of 1:3.

a. What is the current price/earnings ratio?

b. What is the current market value of the company?

c. Why would any company want to reverse split its shares? What would be the likely effect of the reverse split on the EPS and share price?

d. Would repurchasing shares achieve the same result as a reverse split? What is the likely reason that management prefers a reverse split over repurchasing shares?

e. If the board of directors approves the reverse split, how many shares will be outstanding?

f. Assuming the price/earnings ratio is the same after the reverse split as it was before the split, what will Peninsula Minerals' share price be after the reverse split?

11-43 (Retained earnings and dividends)

You are considering purchasing some Stanley Ltd. common shares. Although Stanley recently had to make heavy expenditures for new capital assets, the company has been relatively profitable over the years and prospects for the future look good. The summarized statement of financial position at the end of 2010 is as follows:

Cash	$ 37,500
Other current assets	740,500
Capital assets (net)	4,702,000
Total	$5,480,000
Current liabilities	$ 414,000
Long-term debt	2,000,000
Share capital, common shares	1,000,000
Retained earnings	2,066,000
Total	$5,480,000

The company has 150,000 common shares outstanding, and its earnings per share have increased by at least 10% in each of the last 10 years. In several recent years, earnings per share increased by more than 14%. Given the company's earnings and the amount of retained earnings, you judge that it could easily pay cash dividends of $3 or $4 per share, resulting in hardly a dent in retained earnings.

Required:

a. Discuss whether it is likely that you would receive a cash dividend from Stanley during the next year if you were to purchase its shares.

b. Discuss whether it is likely that you would receive a cash dividend from Stanley during the next five years if you were to purchase its shares.

c. In making an investment decision, would it help you to know whether Stanley has paid dividends in the past? Explain.

d. Suppose Stanley borrowed $2 million cash on a five-year bank loan to provide working capital and additional operating flexibility. While no collateral would be required, the loan would stipulate that no dividends be paid in any year in which the ratio of long-term debt to equity was greater than 60%.

   i. If Stanley were to enter into the loan agreement, would you be likely to receive a dividend next year?

   ii. Would you be likely to receive a dividend at some point in the next five years? (Hint: What would you expect to happen to the statement of financial position values for long-term debt and for equity?)

11-44   (Return on investment)

Windmere Corporation's statement of financial position at December 31, 2010, appears as follows:

Cash	$ 63,000
Other current assets	1,106,000
Capital assets (net)	7,140,000
Total	$8,309,000
Current liabilities	$ 546,000
Long-term debt	1,400,000
Preferred shares	700,000
Share capital—common shares	2,100,000
Retained earnings	3,563,000
Total	$8,309,000

For the year just ended, Windmere reported net earnings of $540,000. During the year, the company declared preferred dividends of $50,000 and common dividends of $300,000.

Required:

a. Calculate the following ratios for Windmere:

   i. Return on assets, using net income in the calculation

   ii. Return on common shareholders' equity

b. Assume that the company issued $1.4 million of common shares at the beginning of last year and paid off the long-term debt, and that the company's interest expense related to its long-term debt for last year was $70,000, after taxes.

   i. What would the return on common shareholders' equity be? (Hint: Remember that shareholders' equity is affected by net earnings.)

   ii. Would shareholders be better or worse off?

   iii. Does switching from debt to equity financing always have this effect on the return on common shareholders' equity? Explain.

c. Assume that the long-term debt remains as shown on the balance sheet and that the company issued an additional $700,000 of common shares last year and used the proceeds to redeem and cancel the preferred shares.

i. What would the return on common shareholders' equity be?

ii. Would shareholders be better or worse off?

iii. Does switching from preferred equity financing to common equity financing always have this effect on the return on common shareholders' equity? Explain.

Reading and Interpreting Published Financial Statements

11-45 (Capital stock)

Note 8 to the January 30, 2010, financial statements of **Le Château Inc.** is shown in Exhibit 11-1. All dollar amounts are in thousands.

Financial Analysis
Assignments

Required:

i. Describe the differences between the Class A subordinate voting shares and Class B voting shares with respect to the following:

   i. Their ability to influence the selection of management and to influence company decision-making

   ii. The amount and priority of expected dividends

b. If you own 100,000 Class A subordinate voting shares, what proportion of total votes do you control? If you own 100,000 Class B voting shares, what proportion of total votes do you control?

c. Why would investors choose to purchase the Class A rather than the Class B shares? Or vice versa?

d. Why might Class B shareholders choose to convert their shareholdings into Class A shares, as described in Principal Feature part [e]?

11-46 (Capital stock, equity analysis, international company)

Use the 2009 financial statements for **H&M** in Appendix A to answer the following questions:

a. What types of share capital does H&M have?

b. How does the presentation of the shareholders' equity section for H&M on the group balance sheet differ from the shareholders' equity sections presented in this chapter?

c. What portion of earnings did H&M pay out as dividends in 2008 and 2009?

d. Calculate H&M's ROE for 2009 and 2008 and comment on your findings. (For the 2008 ratio, you will need to use year-end equity instead of average).

e. On November 30, 2009, H&M's share price was SEK 206.50. Calculate the price/earnings ratio as at that date.

f. What was the book value and market value of H&M as at November 30, 2009? Comment on the difference, if any.

11-47 (Types of shares, equity transactions, stock options)

With corporate offices in Quebec, **RONA Inc.** operates approximately 700 stores of various sizes and formats across Canada and is the largest Canadian distributor and retailer of hardware, renovation, and gardening products. Exhibit 11-9 presents the shareholders' equity section of the balance sheet, the statement of retained earnings, and excerpts from Notes 20 and 21 from RONA's consolidated financial statements for 2009. All amounts are in thousands.

Required:

a. i. How many types of shares does RONA have authorized?

   ii. What are the main differences in the types?

   iii. Why would a company have different types of shares authorized?

b. Are there any preferred shares outstanding?

c. Explain all of the changes in retained earnings in 2009.

d. i. Why do companies have share option plans for their employees?

   ii. Explain why compensation cost appears to be recorded in contributed surplus.

   iii. What method does RONA use to estimate the fair value of its stock option plans?

   iv. What is the likely reason that there is no compensation expense related to the May 1, 2002, plan that was expensed in 2008 and 2009?

EXHIBIT 11-9A   **RONA INC. 2009 ANNUAL REPORT**

annual report

CONSOLIDATED FINANCIAL STATEMENTS
December 27, 2009 and December 28, 2008
(In thousands of dollars)

	2009	2008 (Restated – Note 2)
Shareholders' equity		
Capital stock (Note 20)	$ 603,756	$ 426,786
Retained earnings	1,161,808	1,028,876
Contributed surplus	13,475	12,563
	1,779,039	1,468,225
	$ 2,749,883	$ 2,478,918

EXHIBIT 11-9B   **RONA INC. 2009 ANNUAL REPORT**

annual report

CONSOLIDATED RETAINED EARNINGS
CONSOLIDATED CONTRIBUTED SURPLUS
Years ended December 27, 2009 and December 28, 2008
(In thousands of dollars)

	2009	2008 (Restated – Note 2)
Consolidated Retained Earnings		
Balance, beginning of year, as previously reported	$ 1,053,166	$ 892,967
Change in accounting policy – Goodwill and intangible assets (Note 2)	(24,290)	(20,542)
Restated balance, beginning of year	1,028,876	872,425
Net earnings	138,252	156,451
	1,167,128	1,028,876
Expenses relating to the issue of common shares, net of income tax recovery of $2,042	5,320	–
Balance, end of year	$ 1,161,808	$ 1,028,876
Consolidated Contributed Surplus		
Balance, beginning of year	$ 12,563	$ 11,045
Compensation cost relating to stock option plans	946	1,518
Exercise of stock options	(34)	–
Balance, end of year	$ 13,475	$ 12,563

RONA INC. 2009 ANNUAL REPORT

EXHIBIT 11-9C

annual report

CONSOLIDATED FINANCIAL STATEMENTS

20. Capital stock

Authorized

Unlimited number of shares

  Common shares

  Class A preferred shares, issuable in series

    Series 5, non-cumulative dividend equal to 70% of prime rate, redeemable at their issuance price

  Class B preferred shares, 6% non-cumulative dividend, redeemable at their par value of $1 each

  Class C preferred shares, issuable in series

    Series 1, non-cumulative dividend equal to 70% of prime rate, redeemable at their par value of $1,000 each

  Class D preferred shares, 4% cumulative dividend, redeemable at their issue price. Beginning in 2003, these shares are redeemable at their issue price over a maximum period of ten years on the basis of 10% per year (Note 17)

Issued and fully paid:

The following table presents changes in the number of outstanding common shares and their aggregate stated value:

	2009		2008	
	Number of shares	Amount	Number of shares	Amount
Balance, beginning of year	115,819,699	$ 423,477	115,412,766	$ 418,246
Issuance in exchange for common share subscription deposits	328,692	3,744	197,854	3,349
Issuance under stock option plans	113,775	502	89,000	309
Issuance in exchange for cash[a]	13,391,217	172,736	120,079	1,573
Balance before elimination of reciprocal shareholdings	129,653,383	600,459	115,819,699	423,477
Elimination of reciprocal shareholdings	(80,251)	(524)	(72,396)	(435)
Balance, end of year	129,573,132	599,935	115,747,303	423,042
Deposits on common share subscriptions, net of eliminations of joint ventures[b]		3,821		3,744
		$ 603,756		$ 426,786

(a) In June 2009, the Company issued 13,374,500 common shares at a price of $12.90 per share for total gross proceeds of $172,531.

(b) Deposits on common share subscriptions represent amounts received during the year from affiliated and franchised merchants in accordance with commercial agreements. These deposits are exchanged for common shares on an annual basis. If the subscription deposits had been exchanged for common shares as at December 27, 2009, the number of outstanding common shares would have increased by 251,114.

RONA INC. 2009 ANNUAL REPORT

EXHIBIT 11-9D

annual report

CONSOLIDATED FINANCIAL STATEMENTS

21. Stock-based compensation

Stock option plans

Stock option plan of May 1, 2002

The Company adopted a stock option plan for designated senior executives which was approved by the shareholders on May 1, 2002. A total of 2,920,000 options were granted at that date. Options granted under the plan may be exercised since the Company made a public share offering on November 5, 2002. The Company could grant options for a maximum of 3,740,000 common shares. As at December 27, 2009, the 2,920,000 options granted have an exercise price of $3.47 and of this number, 1,645,500 options (1,538,500 options as at December 28, 2008) were exercised.

The fair value of each option granted was estimated at the grant date using the Black-Scholes option-pricing model. Calculations were based upon a market price of $3.47, an expected volatility of 30%, a risk-free interest rate of 4.92%, an expected life of four years and 0% expected dividend. The fair value of options granted was $1.10 per option according to this method.

No compensation cost was expensed with respect to this plan for the years ended December 27, 2009 and December 28, 2008.

Stock option plan of October 24, 2002

On October 24, 2002, the Board of Directors approved another stock option plan for designated senior executives of the Company and for certain designated directors. The total number of common shares which may be issued pursuant to the plan will not exceed 10% of the common shares issued and outstanding less the number of shares subject to options granted under the stock option plan of May 1, 2002. These options become vested at 25% per year, if the market price of the common share has traded, for at least 20 consecutive trading days during the twelve-month period preceding the grant anniversary date, at a price equal to or higher than the grant price plus a premium of 8% compounded annually.

On March 8, 2007, the Board of Directors approved certain modifications to the plan. These modifications, approved by the shareholders at the annual shareholders' meeting on May 8, 2007, establish that this plan is no longer applicable to the designated directors of the Company and provide for the replacement of the terms and conditions for granting options under the plan by a more flexible mechanism for setting the terms and conditions for granting options. The Board of Directors will adopt the most appropriate terms and conditions relative to each type of grant. For the options granted on March 8, 2007, February 29, 2008, December 9, 2008 and March 11, 2009, the Board approved the option grants with vesting over a four-year period following the anniversary date of the grants at 25% per year.

11-48 (Ratios)

Using the consolidated statement of earnings for RONA Inc. in Exhibit 11-10 and the partial balance sheet in Exhibit 11-9A, calculate the ratios below. The market price of RONA's shares on December 27, 2009, was $15.38.

a. Calculate RONA's book and market values. Explain why they are different.
b. Calculate the price/earnings ratio.
c. Calculate the return on common shareholders' equity for 2008 and 2009 and comment on your findings. (For the 2008 ratio, you will need to use year-end equity instead of average.)

EXHIBIT 11-10 **RONA INC. 2009 ANNUAL REPORT**

annual report

CONSOLIDATED EARNINGS
Years ended December 27, 2009 and December 28, 2008
(In thousands of dollars, except earnings per share)

2009

	2009	2008 (Restated – Note 2)
Sales	$ 4,677,359	$ 4,891,122
Earnings before the following items (Note 6)	332,994	364,729
Interest on long-term debt	20,951	28,106
Interest on bank loans	2,586	2,134
Depreciation and amortization (Notes 12, 14, 15)	103,160	100,958
	126,697	131,198
Earnings before income taxes and non-controlling interest	206,297	233,531
Income taxes (Note 7)	62,714	71,928
Earnings before non-controlling interest	143,583	161,603
Non-controlling interest	5,331	5,152
Net earnings and comprehensive income	$ 138,252	$ 156,451
Net earnings per share (Note 27)		
Basic	$ 1.12	$ 1.35
Diluted	$ 1.11	$ 1.34

The accompanying notes are an integral part of the consolidated financial statements.

11-49 (Shares, share options, dividend policy)

West Fraser Timber Co. Ltd. is a forest products company operating in British Columbia, Alberta, and the southeastern United States, producing lumber and related wood products. In Exhibit 10-8 on p. 660, you will find the consolidated balance sheets, and in Exhibit 11-11, you will find the statement of changes in equity and an excerpt from Note 8 to West Fraser's 2009 financial statements. All amounts are in millions.

Required:

a. West Fraser has a limited number of authorized shares on each class of shares. Why do many companies today prefer to have an unlimited authorized number of shares?

b. What was the average value of the shares issued and outstanding as at December 31, 2008? What was the average price of the shares issued in 2009? Explain why those two values are not the same.

c. West Fraser has a share option plan for its directors, officers, and employees. What is a share option plan and why would the company issue options to these groups? What compensation expense did West Fraser record in 2009 related to stock options?

d. In 2008 and 2009, West Fraser had negative earnings. How much did it lose in each year? How much did the company pay in dividends in each of those years? How is it possible to pay dividends when earnings are negative? Why is West Fraser continuing to pay dividends when earnings are negative?

WEST FRASER TIMBER CO. LTD. 2009 ANNUAL REPORT

EXHIBIT 11-11A

annual report

Consolidated Statement of Changes in Equity

For the years ended December 31, 2009 and 2008

(in millions of Canadian dollars)	Number of shares	Amount	Translation of foreign operations	Retained earninngs	Total equity
	Issued capital				
Balance — January 1, 2008	42,805,086	$ 599.3	$ (93.2)	$ 1,590.0	$ 2,096.1
Changes in equity for 2008					
Foreign exchange translation gain on investment in self-sustaining foreign operations	—	—	94.9	—	94.9
Share purchase loans received	—	0.1	—	—	0.1
Earnings for the year	—	—	—	(137.1)	(137.1)
Dividends	—	—	—	(24.0)	(24.0)
Balance — December 31, 2008	42,805,086	599.4	1.7	1,428.9	2,030.0
Changes in equity for 2009					
Foreign exchange translation loss on investment in self-sustaining foreign operations	—	—	(61.5)	—	(61.5)
Issuance of Common shares	10,723	0.3	—	—	0.3
Earnings for the year	—	—	—	(340.8)	(340.8)
Dividends	—	—	—	(9.8)	(9.8)
Balance — December 31, 2009	42,815,809	$ 599.7	$ (59.8)	$ 1,078.3	$ 1,618.2

8. Share capital

Authorized

200,000,000 Common shares, without par value

20,000,000 Class B Common shares, without par value

10,000,000 Preferred shares, issuable in series, without par value

Issued

	2009		2008	
	Number	Amount	Number	Amount
Common	40,009,331	$ 599.4	39,998,608	$ 599.1
Class B Common	2,806,478	0.3	2,806,478	0.3
Total Common	42,815,809	$ 599.7	42,805,086	$ 599.4

Share capital transactions during 2009

The Company issued 10,723 Common shares for $0.3 million.

Share capital transactions during 2008

78,728 Class B Common shares were exchanged for Common shares.

Rights and restrictions of Common shares

Common shares and Class B Common shares are equal in all respects except that each Class B Common share may at any time be exchanged for one Common share.

Dividends payable

Dividends declared and unpaid at December 31, 2009 amounted to $1.3 million (2008 — $6.0 million) and are included in accounts payable and accrued liabilities.

Share option plan

The Company has a share option plan for its directors, officers and employees under which it may grant options to purchase up to 5,005,506 Common shares. The exercise price of a share option is the closing price of a Common share on the trading day immediately preceding the grant date. Options vest at the earlier of the date of retirement or death and 20% per year from the grant date, and expire after 10 years. The Company has recorded an expense of $3.4 million (2008 — recovery of $2.3 million) in selling, general and administration expense related to the share option plan.

11-50 (Share structures, initial stock offerings, ratios)

Montreal-based **Dollarama Inc.** sells consumer products and general merchandise for $2 or less throughout Canada. The statement of shareholders' equity and company's balance sheet, and a portion of Note 11 from its 2009 financial statements are presented in Exhibit 11–12. Exhibit 11-12 also describes some of the changes that the company made to its share structure before and after it went public in October 2009.

Required:

a. Describe the changes that the company made to its capital structure when it went public. Why were these changes necessary before going public?

b. Prior to the company going public, a group of shareholders controlled Dollarama through various types of shares that were all converted into common shares at the time of the IPO. After the initial public offering (IPO), what percentage of the votes (including the shares issued in the stock split) does that controlling group still own? What percentage of the common stock share capital did the group contribute?

c. Calculate the total debt to equity ratio for 2009 and 2010 (total liabilities divided by total shareholders' equity). Comment on the change in the ratio. If you were a creditor of Dollarama, how would you feel about the change?

d. How much money did Dollarama raise in its IPO? By how much did its share capital increase compared to 2009? Explain the difference, if any.

e. Is it possible to compare the ROE for Dollarama for 2009 and 2010? Why or why not?

DOLLARAMA INC. 2009 ANNUAL REPORT

EXHIBIT 11-12A

annual report

Consolidated Statements of Shareholders' Equity

(expressed in thousands of Canadian dollars)	Capital stock $	Contributed surplus $	Retained earnings $	Accumulated other comprehensive income (loss) $	Shareholders' equity $
Balance – February 3, 2008	35,304	10,071	31,526	(4,993)	71,908
Net loss for the year	–	–	(15,504)	–	(15,504)
Other comprehensive income					
Unrealized gain on derivative financial instruments, net of reclassification adjustments and income taxes of $21,435	–	–	–	45,550	45,550
Total comprehensive income					30,046
Stock-based compensation (note 12)	–	283	–	–	283
Balance – February 1, 2009	35,304	10,354	16,022	40,557	102,237
Net earnings for the year	–	–	72,863	–	72,863
Other comprehensive income					
Unrealized loss on derivative financial instruments, net of reclassification adjustments and income taxes of $22,465	–	–	–	(50,648)	(50,648)
Total comprehensive income					22,215
Stock-based compensation (note 12)	–	7,118	–	–	7,118
Issuance of common shares, net of issuance expenses of $27,775 and related income taxes of $6,455 (note 1)	278,680	–	–	–	278,680
Conversion of amounts due to shareholders into common shares (note 11)	204,446	–	–	–	204,446
Balance – January 31, 2010	518,430	17,472	88,885	(10,091)	614,696

The sum of retained earnings and accumulated other comprehensive income (loss) amounted to $78,794 as of January 31, 2010 (February 1, 2009 – $56,579).

EXHIBIT 11-12B   **DOLLARAMA INC. 2009 ANNUAL REPORT**

annual report

Consolidated Balance Sheets

(expressed in thousands of Canadian dollars)	As of January 31, 2010 $	As of February 1, 2009 $
Assets		
Current Assets		
Cash and cash equivalents	93,057	66,218
Accounts receivable	1,453	2,998
Deposits and prepaid expenses	4,924	4,710
Merchandise inventories	234,684	249,644
Derivative financial instruments (note 10)	3,479	33,175
	337,597	356,745
Property and Equipment (note 3)	138,214	129,878
Goodwill	727,782	727,782
Other Intangible Assets (note 4)	113,302	115,210
Derivative financial instruments (note 10)	5,342	33,423
	1,322,237	1,363,038
Liabilities		
Current Liabilities		
Accounts payable	31,694	39,729
Accrued expenses and other (note 5)	46,825	37,760
Income taxes payable	23,445	5,692
Derivative financial instruments (note 10)	55,194	–
Current portion of long-term debt (note 6)	1,925	15,302
	159,083	98,483
Long-Term Debt (note 6)	468,591	806,384
Due To Shareholders (note 7)	–	256,077
Future Income Taxes (note 17)	49,879	71,759
Other Liabilities (note 8)	29,988	28,098
	707,541	1,260,801
Commitments (note 9)		
Shareholders' Equity		
Capital Stock (note 11)	518,430	35,304
Contributed Surplus	17,472	10,354
Retained Earnings	88,885	16,022
Accumulated Other Comprehensive Income (Loss)	(10,091)	40,557
	614,696	102,237
	1,322,237	1,363,038

DOLLARAMA INC. 2009 ANNUAL REPORT

EXHIBIT 11-12C

annual report

EXCERPT FROM NOTE 11

As described in note 1, as of the date of the closing of the initial public offering, the Corporation reorganized its capital structure. As a result of the reorganization, the Corporation has the following capital structure:

a) Authorized
   Unlimited number of common shares, voting and participating, without par value
   Unlimited number of preferred shares, without par value, non-voting and non-participating
   Prior to the reorganization, the authorized capital stock of the Corporation was composed of Class A and B common shares, and Class A, B and C preferred shares.

b) The table below summarizes the number of common and preferred shares issued before and after the reorganization and the effect of the reorganization on the capital structure of the Corporation.

	Number of units			Amount		
	Before reorganization		After reorganization	Before reorganization		After reorganization
	Class A	Class B	Common shares	Class A $	Class B $	Common shares $
Balance – February 3, 2008	33,929,931	8,645,886	–	33,930	1,374	–
Balance – February 1, 2009	33,929,931	8,645,886	–	33,930	1,374	–
Conversion of Class A and B common shares into common shares of Dollarama Inc.	(33,929,931)	(8,645,886)	42,575,817	(33,930)	(1,374)	35,304
Stock split (1:03 for 1:00)	–	–	1,290,689	–	–	–
Conversion of junior subordinated notes	–	–	7,105,503	–	–	124,346
Conversion of Class A preferred shares	–	–	2,204,995	–	–	38,587
Conversion of Class B preferred shares	–	–	2,372,074	–	–	41,513
Issuance of common shares, net of issuance cost and taxes	–	–	17,142,857	–	–	278,680
Balance – January 31, 2010	–	–	72,691,935	–	–	518,430

BEYOND THE BOOK

11-51 (Examination of shareholders' equity for real company)
Choose a company as directed by your instructor and answer the following questions:

a. Prepare a quick analysis of the shareholders' equity accounts by listing their beginning and ending amounts and calculating the net change for the most recent year in both dollar and percentage terms.

b. If any of the accounts changed by more than 10%, explain why.

c. For each type of share authorized by the company, list the nature of the issue, the number of shares (authorized, issued, and outstanding), whether it is par value or no par value, the market price at the end of the year, and any special features of the issue.

d. What was the company's market value at the end of the most recent year? Compare this with the company's book value and discuss why these amounts are different. Be as specific as possible.

e. Did the company pay dividends in the most recent year? If so, what was the dividend per share and has this amount changed over the past three years?

f. Did the company declare any stock dividends or have a stock split during the most recent year? If so, describe the nature of the event and the effects on the shareholders' equity section.

Cases

Case Primer

11-52 Manonta Sales Company
Manonta Sales Company's summary balance sheet and income statement as at December 31, 2010, follow:

Statement of Financial Position (in thousands)

Current assets	$150,000
Net property, plant, and equipment	75,000
Total assets	$225,000
Current liabilities	$95,000
Long-term debt	90,000
Shareholders' equity	40,000
Total liabilities and shareholders' equity	$225,000

Statement of Earnings (in thousands)

Sales	$460,000
Cost of goods sold, operating, and other expenses	420,000
Earnings before income taxes	40,000
Income taxes	14,000
Net earnings	$ 26,000
Earnings per share	$1.30

The long-term debt has an interest rate of 6% and is convertible into 9.0 million common shares. After carefully analyzing all available information about Manonta, you decide the following events are likely to happen. First, Manonta will increase its earnings before income taxes by 10% next year because of increased sales. Second, the effective tax rate will stay the same. Third, the holders of long-term debt will convert it into shares on January 1, 2011. Fourth, the current multiple of earnings per share to market price of 20 will increase to 24 if the debt is converted, because of the reduced risk.

You own 100 common shares of Manonta and are trying to decide whether you should keep or sell them. You decide you will sell the shares if you think their market price is not likely to increase by at least 10% next year.

Required:
Based on the information available, should you keep the shares or sell them? Support your answer with a detailed analysis.

11-53 Tribec Wireless Inc.

Tribec Wireless Inc. had the following shareholders' equity section as at December 31, 2010:

Common shares, no par value, unlimited number authorized, 2 million issued and outstanding	$4,000,000
Retained earnings	1,958,476
Total shareholders' equity	$5,958,476

In 2007 and 2008, Tribec paid a cash dividend of $0.75 per share. In 2009, the company expanded operations significantly and the board of directors decided to retain earnings in the business rather than pay them out as a cash dividend. In lieu of the cash dividend, the board voted to distribute a 10% stock dividend. In December 2010, the company returned to its previous dividend policy and again paid a $0.75 cash dividend.

In 2007, you inherited 5,000 shares of Tribec Wireless. At that time, the shares were trading at $5 per share. Given the tremendous growth in the wireless market, by 2009 when the stock dividend was distributed the company's shares were trading at $80 per share. After the stock dividend, the share price dropped slightly but has since risen again, and as at December 31, 2010, they were trading at $82 per share.

Required:
a. From Tribec's perspective, how would the accounting for the stock dividend distributed in 2009 differ from the accounting for the cash dividends paid in the other years?
b. Immediately after the stock dividend, the price of the Tribec shares dropped slightly. Does this mean the value of the company (and your investment) decreased due to the payment of the stock dividend?
c. Prepare a schedule illustrating the total amount of cash dividends you have received since inheriting the Tribec shares. What is the value of your investment on December 31, 2010?

11-54 Blooming Valley Custom Landscaping

Blooming Valley Custom Landscaping provides landscaping services to a variety of clients in southern Ontario. The company's services include planting lawns and shrubs and installing outdoor lighting and irrigation systems, as well as constructing decks and gazebos. The company also remains very busy in the winter by using its trucks for snow removal. Blooming Valley would like to extend its operations into the northern United States, but Jack Langer, the owner, feels that the company would require at least $2 million in new capital before such a venture could be successful. Langer is excited about the prospects of expanding because his projections indicate that the company could earn an additional $750,000 in income before interest and taxes.

Currently, Blooming Valley has no long-term debt and is entirely owned by the Langer family, with 300,000 common shares outstanding. The company's current net income before tax is $900,000, with a tax rate of 25% that is not expected to change if the expansion goes ahead. As the family does not have sufficient financial resources to undertake the expansion, it would be essential to obtain outside financing. Mr. Langer is considering three financing options:

Option 1
The first option is to borrow, using a conventional bank loan. Interest on the loan would be 9% annually with monthly payments of principal and interest required.

Option 2

The second possibility is to issue 100,000 common shares to a local venture capitalist. As part of the plan, the venture capitalist would be given a seat on the board of directors and would also have a say in the day-to-day running of the company.

Option 3

The final option is to sell 100,000 non-voting cumulative preferred shares. The preferred shares would have an annual dividend of $2.85. A number of investors have expressed interest in purchasing these shares.

Required:

a. Calculate the effect of each financing option on the company's earnings per share. Which option will result in the highest earnings per share?
b. Recommend an option to Mr. Langer and explain your reasoning. Be sure to consider both quantitative and qualitative factors as part of your analysis.

11-55 Thai restaurant

Sam Able, Abby Moss, and Kendra McDonald have just graduated from the Toronto Culinary Institute and are excited about opening their own restaurant. The three want to open a trendy Thai restaurant in Toronto and have been busy looking for the perfect location. Sam, who completed several business management courses as part of his degree, has estimated that the three will require $600,000 at a minimum to start the business. This would provide cash for rent, equipment, supplies, and advertising, as well as small salaries for the three graduates until the restaurant is up and running.

Having recently graduated, none of the three has significant assets to invest in the venture. Sam's parents are willing to loan them $75,000, but they want to see a solid business plan before committing to the loan. Sam and Abby are willing to work full-time in the business, but Kendra has a small child and feels that initially she may not be able to work full-time. Instead, she would be willing to work nights and weekends when her husband is home to take care of the baby.

The three friends recently had a meeting to discuss matters and try to decide on how to form the business. Sam has proposed that they incorporate, but the others are concerned about the additional cost of incorporation and wonder if it would not be better to operate as a partnership. They feel that they need additional information before making this decision and decide to ask you, an independent business consultant, for advice.

Required:

a. Prepare a report for the three friends outlining how operating as a partnership differs from incorporating. Be sure to include the advantages and disadvantages of each form of organization.
b. Based on the information available, make a preliminary recommendation to your clients about the form of organization that will best suit their needs.

11-56 Teed's Manufacturing Corporation

Teed's Manufacturing Corporation has the following shareholders' equity at December 1, 2010:

Shareholders' Equity	
Share capital	
$2 preferred shares, no par value, cumulative, 20,000 shares authorized, 16,000 shares issued	360,000
Common shares, no par value, unlimited number of shares authorized, 60,000 shares issued	600,000
Total share capital	960,000
Retained earnings	687,500
Total shareholders' equity	$1,647,500

The company was formed in January 2008 and there has been no change in share capital since that time. It is now December 1, 2010, and after a very strong year, the company has just declared a $160,000 cash dividend to shareholders of record as at February 10, 2011. The dividend payment date is February 28, 2011. Teed's has always used business earnings for further expansion and has never paid a dividend before.

Jan Kielly owns 500 shares of Teed's Manufacturing common stock and is curious to know how much of a dividend she will receive. She is confused about the difference between preferred and common stock and wonders why the preferred shareholders would purchase shares in a company without having the right to vote. Finally, she is confused about the differences between the declaration date, date of record, and payment date. She wants to know when she will actually receive her dividend.

> *Required:*
> a. Determine how much of the dividend will be paid to the preferred shareholders and how much to the common shareholders.
> b. Prepare a memo addressing Jan's questions.

Critical Thinking Question

11-57 (Stock options)

Corporate executives are normally remunerated with a package that consists of a combination of one or more of the following:

a. Salary
b. Perks such as company cars, expense accounts, nice offices, and club memberships
c. Bonuses based on net income
d. Bonuses based on gross sales
e. Stock option plans

Required:

Discuss the impact of each of the above items on the actions of executives. What would each item encourage the executive to achieve? Which of these actions might be beneficial to the company? Which might be harmful? If you were designing a remuneration package for executives running a company you owned, what would you include? Explain your choices.

APPLYING YOUR KNOWLEDGE AND A USER PERSPECTIVE

The Impact of Accounting Policy Choices on Financial Statements—An Integrative Project

At the end of its first year of operations, Commerce Corporation had the following account balances before making any adjustments:

Commerce Corporation
Unadjusted Trial Balance December 31, 2010

	Debits	Credits
Cash	$ 10,590	
Accounts Receivable	26,570	
Allowance for Doubtful Accounts	890	
Inventory	17,010	
Prepaid Insurance	3,500	
Vehicle	25,370	—
Accumulated Depreciation: Vehicle		
Equipment	66,120	—
Accumulated Depreciation: Equipment		
Building	164,430	—
Accumulated Depreciation: Building		
Land	31,340	
Patent	20,450	
Trademark	18,020	
Accounts Payable		$ 28,440
Accrued Liabilities		14,740
Estimated Warranty Liability		—
Estimated Lawsuit Damages Payable		—
Unearned Service Revenue		—
Bonds Payable (90,000 face value)		102,230
Share Capital: Common Shares		166,300
Retained Earnings		—
Sales (all on credit)		185,680
Service Revenue		19,630
Cost of Goods Sold	71,980	
Bad Debts Expense	—	
Depreciation Expense: Vehicle	—	
Depreciation Expense: Equipment	—	
Depreciation Expense: Building	—	
Depreciation Expense: Patent	—	
Loss on Writedown of Trademark	—	
Product Warranty Expense	—	
Other Operating Expenses	60,750	
Interest Expense	—	
Loss from Lawsuit Damages	—	
Totals	**$517,020**	**$517,020**

To assist you in making year-end adjustments, the following additional information is available.

Information for adjustments involving accounting policy choices and estimates:

1. The company wrote off an account receivable during the year, in the amount of $890. Because it was the company's first year of operations, there was no balance in the allowance for doubtful accounts prior to this write-off. This is why there is a debit balance in the allowance for doubtful accounts in the unadjusted trial balance.

   At the end of the year, the company is considering whether to use the percentage of sales or the aging of receivables method for estimating the amount that will prove to be uncollectible. The sales manager estimates that the bad debts expense will total 2% of sales revenue, while the office administrator (who has done an aging analysis of the receivables) estimates that the company should provide an allowance equal to 6% of the year-end balance in accounts receivable.

2. The company made the following purchases and sales during the year (listed in chronological order):

Purchased	1,500 units at a cost of $42,000
Sold	300 units
Purchased	1,000 units at a cost of $29,980
Sold	700 units
Purchased	500 units at a cost of $17,010
Sold	1,500 units

   During the year, the company used the FIFO method for determining the cost of goods sold. However, it has not yet prepared its financial statements and is now considering using the moving average costing method instead.

3. The vehicle was purchased on May 1, and the company estimates that it will have a useful life of six years or 150,000 kilometres, with a residual value of $3,000. The company will depreciate it using either the straight-line method or the units-of-activity method. During 2010, the vehicle was driven 15,000 kilometres.

4. The equipment was purchased in late January and put into service at the end of March. It will be depreciated on the double-declining-balance basis. Estimates of its service life range from seven years with a residual value of $5,000 to 10 years with a residual value of $1,000.

5. The building was purchased in early March and will be depreciated on the straight-line basis. It is expected to have a useful life of 30 years, with a residual value between zero and $30,000.

6. The company acquired a patent midway through the year. It has a legal life of 20 years; however, it is almost certain that a competitor will develop a superior product that will make this patent obsolete within five to 10 years.

7. At the beginning of the year, the company registered its trademark, which management believes is increasing in value as it becomes more widely known to the public. However, some members of the board of directors think that actions taken by competitors during the year have impaired the value of the company's trademark by 50%.

8. The company sells its products with a two-year warranty. Estimates of the costs that will be incurred under the warranty vary from 2% to 6% of the sales revenue. There have not yet been any claims under the warranty.

9. The company is being sued by one of its suppliers for breach of contract. The company's lawyers have warned that it will probably lose the lawsuit and be held liable for damages of $25,000. However, some of the company's officers have argued that this is "just a guess," and that there is no way of knowing what the outcome of the case will be. At year end, the company is considering whether to recognize this contingency in the accounts or simply disclose it in the notes that accompany the financial statements. (Unless your instructor tells you otherwise, use the effective interest method for calculating the interest expense and amortizing the premium on the bonds.)

Information for other adjustments:

10. The balance in the prepaid insurance account represents the cost of a one-year policy that began on February 1.

11. One-third of the balance in the service revenue account represents advance payments from customers for work that is to be done in 2011.

12. The balance in the bonds payable account represent 10-year 10% bonds that were issued on September 1, when the competitive yield rate for similar bonds in the market was 8%. The first interest payment is scheduled to be made on March 1, 2011.

Required:

a. Determine what adjustments, if any, to make for items 1 through 12 above, *assuming that your objective is to report the highest possible net earnings (or the lowest possible net loss)* for the year, while still complying with International Financial Reporting Standards (IFRS). Make the appropriate adjustments and then prepare a single-step statement of earnings for the year ended December 31, 2010, and a statement of financial position as of December 31, 2010.

b. Repeat part "a," *assuming that your objective is to report the lowest possible net earnings (or the highest possible net loss)* for the year, while still complying with IFRS.

c. Calculate the difference between the net earnings or loss in part "a" and the net earnings or loss in part "b," and comment briefly on whether you think the difference is significant.

d. Calculate the following ratios at the end of the year, under your results for both part "a" and part "b," and comment briefly on whether you think the differences between the two sets of ratio values are significant:

    i. Current ratio
    ii. Quick Ratio
    iii. Debt to equity ratio (defined as total liabilities divided by total shareholders' equity)
    iv. Return on shareholders' equity*

*Since this was the company's first year of operations and there were no opening balances, use the year-end balances, rather than averages, when calculating this.

Notes:

- Your adjustments (if any) for items 1 to 9 above should be different in part "a" and part "b"; however, your adjustments for items 10 to 12 will be the same for both parts.

- All the accounts that are needed to complete this project are listed in the trial balance; you should not have to open any additional accounts.

- You should not do any rounding during your calculations; only your final results are to be rounded. All monetary amounts should be rounded to the nearest dollar. Ratios should be calculated to two decimal places.

- If you are in doubt about whether a liability is current or long-term, you should be conservative and categorize it as a current liability.

chapter 12

FINANCIAL STATEMENT ANALYSIS

LEARNING OBJECTIVES

After studying this chapter, you should be able to:

1. Explain why knowledge of the business is important when drawing conclusions about a company's future financial health.

2. Describe the various ways of analyzing a company's financial statements.

3. Identify the types of ratios that are best at providing insights for specific decisions.

4. Calculate specific ratios that are used to assess a company's profitability, short-term liquidity, activity, and solvency, and explain how the ratios can be interpreted.

5. Calculate and explain the uses of the earnings per share ratio and the price/earnings ratio.

6. Understand the differences that might affect the ratio analysis of non-manufacturing or non-retail companies.

7. Understand the need to exercise caution when interpreting ratios.

8. Use ratios to assess a company's financial health through an analysis of its performance and financial position.

A Real-Life Exercise in Financial Management

Proper analysis of financial statements requires a good understanding of the statements' various components. No one knows this better than a group of finance students at Simon Fraser University in Vancouver, B.C., who are putting their knowledge into action with the Student Investment Advisory Service (SIAS).

The SIAS was established in 2003 when a group of about 15 students in the university's Master's in Financial Risk Management program were given the opportunity to manage a fund, which then was worth approximately $6.5 million, representing about 5 percent of the total SFU endowment funds, says adjunct professor Derek Yee. In the following years, two other student groups joined the SIAS: master's students from the Financial Risk Management Program are calculating risk measures and offering advice on ways to reduce risks, and some undergraduates studying finance are acting as junior analysts.

The SIAS gives students the opportunity to apply what they have learned in the classroom. "As part of the normal portfolio management process, an Investment Policy Statement describes the parameters that the students must operate within," explains Professor Yee. The students invest in three asset classes—cash, fixed income (Canadian), and equity (Canadian and global).

"We use a top-down approach," says Enrico Chua, a student in the Master's in Financial Risk Management program, whose role was Canadian equity sector head for health care. "We first look at global macroeconomic factors like GDP, inflation, and interest rates. Then we look for industries that have wide economic moat and other competitive factors before drilling down to the individual companies." The students then identify undervalued companies in good industries by looking into their financial statements. "We obtain at least five years of historical financial data from the company's balance sheet and statement of cash flow. Based on the accounting information and our understanding of the future

business plans of the company, we forecast cash flows. We then use the discounted cash-flow method to come up with the fair value price of the stock." The students also compare this target company with its peers to assess its competitive advantages. They write a report outlining the major financial information, valuation, and performance ratios, which they present to the SIAS group and Professor Yee for discussion, and then vote on whether to take action.

To review past performance, the students meet quarterly with their client, SFU's vice president of finance, who is responsible for the endowment funds' management. A business council composed of investment professionals from major financial institutions also critiques the students' performance. "Tough questions and constructive comments from the business council help shape and improve how we manage the fund," says Mr. Chua. Following this quarterly review, the students meet with Professor Yee to discuss how they can improve SIAS.

And results have been good. The original $6.5 million had increased to about $9.2 million by the end of 2009. Some months, the SIAS outperforms the market, while other months are less successful. As Professor Yee points out, performance is only one measure; another is risk. "The students have a mandate to preserve wealth and they give that a higher priority than attempting to maximize return."

The SIAS group at Simon Fraser University provides investment advice for some of the university's endowed funds. Not many students get the opportunity to work with real investments. The Master's in Financial Risk Management was a new program when the SIAS group was formed, but with the assistance of students from other SFU programs, the SIAS team is able to do a thorough analysis of potential investment options. One of the avenues of analysis that the SIAS group uses at the start of each investigation is financial statement analysis. The information that is gathered from the evaluation of the financial statements and their notes then forms the basis for their decision to go forward with further investigation. However, financial statement analysis is not the only basis on which they make their recommendations. They go on to look at discounted cash flow, perform a risk analysis, and complete their thorough analysis of the industry in which the company operates. Although financial statement analysis does not answer all questions, it does provide signals about financial health, cash flow, and operating efficiency.

Having worked your way through the previous chapters of this book, you now know the main issues in accounting, you can read and understand most of the items on financial statements, you are aware of the various methods that can be used to measure and report transactions, and you understand some of the limitations that affect the numbers on the statements. As we move through the various methods and ratios of financial analysis in this chapter, we are going to refer to some of the ratios that you have already seen in this text. In the first 11 chapters of this book, we described the basic components of the financial reporting system and how accounting numbers are accumulated and recorded. In most of these chapters, we also identified ratios that use the material that was being discussed. In this chapter, we pull all of these ratios together and summarize how financial information can be analyzed.

USER RELEVANCE

As a user, you need to analyze financial information effectively so that you can make knowledgeable decisions. This involves more than a basic understanding of what each individual statement means. You need to understand the relationships among the three major financial statements and the methods that produce the numbers. You also need to compare and contrast these relationships over time and among different companies. Our current discussion was left until this chapter because proper analysis requires a good understanding of all financial statement components.

As we worked through the material in the book, we introduced the ratios that pertained to the topics under discussion. While this has given you some tools, they are not organized cohesively, and you now need to think about analysis as a structured activity. You need to know what information will help you make informed decisions and then identify the tools that will give you that information. With this in mind, the ratios in this chapter have been organized according to decision-making needs.

This chapter provides an overview of financial statement analysis and a discussion of the basic ratios used. However, because financial statement analysis is very complex, it can serve only as an introduction. Remember two things as you work through this chapter. First, there is no definitive set of rules or procedures that dictate how to analyze financial statements. Second, every analysis should be tailored to suit the underlying reason for making the analysis. These two features make comprehensive analysis quite complex. A more detailed discussion of financial statement analysis is left to more advanced texts.

OVERVIEW OF FINANCIAL STATEMENT ANALYSIS

Financial statements are typically analyzed for a specific purpose. An investment analyst or a stockbroker, for example, may undertake an analysis in order to recommend that a client buy or sell shares. A bank's commercial loans officer may perform an analysis of a client's financial statements to decide whether the client will be capable of paying back a loan the bank is considering. A student looking for a job may analyze a company to decide whether it is a suitable company to work for.

Each analyst will tailor the analysis to the demands of the decision to be made. For example, a banker trying to decide whether to make a short-term loan may restrict the analysis to the company's short-term cash-producing capabilities. The investment analyst, on the other hand, may focus on its long-term financial health.

In this chapter, we take a very general approach to financial statement analysis. While no particular decision is considered as the various ratios are discussed, we do discuss decision contexts where one particular ratio may be more helpful than others. Before turning to specific ratios, however, and whatever the decision to be made, one of the first things you have to do is understand the business.

Understanding the Business

Understanding the business means more than understanding a company's financial statements. It means having a grasp of the operating activities of the business, the underlying economics, the risks involved, and the external economic factors that are crucial to the company's long- and short-term health. It means that you must understand the various types of businesses that the company is engaged in. For example, a large company such as **Rogers Communications Inc.** is involved in more than just providing cell phone and cable access to consumers. In its wireless division, it provides wireless voice and data communications services. The cable division provides cable television services and high speed Internet. The media group not only operates radio and television stations, including Citytv in Toronto and The Shopping Channel, but also publishes consumer magazines and professional publications, and owns the Toronto Blue Jays Baseball Club. An analyst who thinks that Rogers is only in the telephone and cable business has a very inaccurate view of the risks involved in lending Rogers money or in buying its shares.

Companies follow different strategies to achieve success. Although a detailed discussion of corporate strategy is beyond the scope of this book, you should be familiar with a few basic strategies that companies follow. The two most common strategies are being a low-cost producer and following a product differentiation. A low-cost producer focuses on providing goods or services at the lowest possible cost and selling at low prices. To be successful, these companies need to sell a high volume of goods at the lower prices. This strategy works best when competing products are similar and price is the most important decision factor for customers. Discount grocery chains or discount retailers usually follow this strategy. The other strategy is to sell products that are specialized or to provide superior service that customers are willing to pay a premium for. If the company can make a higher profit margin on the goods or services provided, it does not need to sell as many goods to make the same level of total profit as a company that sells more for less—they can succeed with a lower volume. Gourmet grocery or specialty stores and high-end retailers usually follow this strategy. Understanding the company's strategy will help you interpret the financial results and explain differences if, for example, you are trying to compare a discounter to a specialty store and are wondering why the results are so different.

LEARNING OBJECTIVE 1

Explain why knowledge of the business is important when drawing conclusions about a company's future financial health.

A basic understanding of the company's range of business activities, including their recent achievements and management's future expectations for them, can usually be had by reading the first sections of the company's annual report. The first half of the annual report in North America is divided into two parts. The first part contains the description of the company, some general highlights of the year, and letters to the shareholders from the CEO and the chief financial officer. Following that is the Management Discussion and Analysis (MD&A). This is a very important section for an analyst to read, because in it management must discuss many aspects of the company's financial performance in greater detail. It should include a discussion not only of past results, but also of management's expectations for the future and the risks the company is facing. The intention of the MD&A is to allow the user to see the company through the eyes of management. Although this descriptive section of most annual reports does not explain everything you need to know about the company, it does provide some insight into what the company does and the types of risks it faces. You should also listen to the financial news and read financial newspapers and magazines to find additional information about the company and the industry in which it operates. Once you have an overall view of the types of businesses operated by the company, you should next read the financial statements, including the auditor's report and the notes to the financial statements. The financial statements are usually found in the second half of an annual report.

For purposes of illustration in this chapter, we are going to use the financial statements of **SOCIÉTÉ BIC (BIC)**. Headquartered in a suburb of Paris, France, BIC is familiar to most students as a world leader in the stationery (pens and other office supplies), lighter, and shaver markets. In 2010, as a result of acquisitions in 2009, BIC added advertising and promotional products (custom printed calendars, bags, pens, and so on) as a fourth product area. BIC's strategy, as indentified in its annual report, is to focus on generating sales growth with new products and extension of its product line, both focused on innovation. The company's goal is to produce consistent quality products at a lower cost, either in-house or, to a lesser extent, by outsourcing, to increase flexibility or to take advantage of new technologies. BIC sells its products to office product stores and other retailers, and to distributors and wholesalers. The company prepares its financial statements in French in accordance with regulations governing the stock market in Paris, and refers to the English translation used in this chapter (and available on the companion website) as a reference document. In the remainder of the chapter, we will refer to the document as an annual report, as it is similar in format and content to the other annual reports we have used throughout the book.

Reading the Financial Statements

The first thing to read in the financial statements is the auditor's report, as it states whether appropriate accounting policies were followed and whether the statements present the company's operating results and financial position fairly. This report is important because the auditor is an independent third party who is stating a professional opinion on the fairness of the numbers and disclosures reported in the financial statements. The role of the auditor and the audit report were introduced in Chapter 1.

Remember that the auditor's report does not guarantee the accuracy of the information contained in the financial statements. Financial statements are prepared by management, and management has primary responsibility for them. Auditors express their opinion on whether the financial statements present the information fairly according to generally accepted accounting principles. The auditor's report does not indicate whether the information contained in the financial statements is good or bad. It is the reader's responsibility to interpret the information provided.

An example of a typical *unqualified* auditor's opinion, provided by Grant Thornton and Deloitte & Associates Chartered Accountants for the 2009 financial statements of BIC, is shown in Exhibit 12-1. As you may recall from Chapter 1, an unqualified (or "clean") audit opinion is one in which the auditors do not express any concerns, reservations, or qualifications regarding the financial statements. Without any exceptions, they state that, in their professional opinion, the financial statements give a true and fair view of the company's financial position and the results of its operations in accordance with generally accepted accounting principles. This is what the users of the financial statements want to see; any other type of audit opinion warrants very careful consideration.

One of the differences in the presentation of the financial statements under French GAAP is that the auditor's report is found *after* the financial statements and notes, as opposed to the traditional North American presentation, where it is presented before the financial statements. Similar to Canadian audit reports, BIC's audit report contains three components: the auditors express their opinion on the financial statements, state their justifications, and outline the specific procedures they used.

After reading the auditor's report, the second step is to read each of the major financial statements to ensure that the results make sense for the types of activities that the company is engaged in. Use your knowledge from this course to look for unusual account titles and unusually large dollar items. For example, if there is a large loss item on the statement of earnings, the nature of the loss is important. Is it an item that could be expected to continue into the future, or is it a non-continuing item?

Unusual account titles may indicate that the company is involved in a line of business that is new, which could have serious implications for future operations. For example, if a manufacturer suddenly shows lease receivables on its statement of financial position, this probably indicates that it has started to lease assets, as well as sell them. The leasing business is very different from the manufacturing business and exposes the company to different types of risk. You must take this new information into consideration when evaluating the company.

A reading of the financial statements is not complete unless the notes to the financial statements are read carefully. Because the major financial statements provide summary information only, there is not much room on them to provide all the details that are necessary for a full understanding of the company's transactions. The notes provide a place for more detail and discussion about many items on the financial statements. Also pay attention in the notes to the summary of the company's significant accounting policies. Remember that IFRS allows considerable flexibility in choosing accounting methods, and different choices result in different amounts on the financial statements, so you should be aware of the choices that management made. These will generally be listed in the first note to the financial statements.

Once you have an overall understanding of the business and the financial statements, you can begin a detailed analysis of the financial results.

EXHIBIT 12-1   **SOCIÉTÉ BIC 2009 ANNUAL REPORT**

annual report

Statutory Auditors' report on the financial statements

➤ FOR THE YEAR ENDED DECEMBER 31, 2009

This is a free translation into English of the statutory auditors' report issued in French and is provided solely for the convenience of English speaking users. The statutory auditors' report includes information specifically required by French law in such reports, whether modified or not. This information is presented below the opinion on the Company financial statements and includes an explanatory paragraph discussing the auditors' assessments of certain significant accounting and auditing matters. These assessments were considered for the purpose of issuing an audit opinion on the Company financial statements taken as a whole and not to provide separate assurance on individual account captions or on information taken outside of the Company financial statements. This report should be read in conjunction with, and construed in accordance with, French law and professional auditing standards applicable in France.

To the Shareholders,

In accordance with our appointment as statutory auditors at your Annual General Meeting, we hereby report to you for the year ended December 31, 2009 on:

- the audit of the accompanying financial statements of SOCIÉTÉ BIC;
- the justification of our assessments;
- the specific procedures and disclosures required by law.

These financial statements have been approved by the Board of Directors. Our role is to express an opinion on these financial statements, based on our audit.

I.   Opinion on the financial statements

We conducted our audit in accordance with professional standards applicable in France. Those standards require that we plan and perform the audit to obtain reasonable assurance about whether the financial statements are free of material misstatement. An audit includes examining, using sample testing techniques or other selection methods, evidence supporting the amounts and disclosures in the financial statements. An audit also includes assessing the accounting principles used and significant estimates made by management, as well as evaluating the overall financial statement presentation. We believe that the audit evidence we have obtained is sufficient and appropriate to provide a basis for our opinion.

In our opinion, the financial statements give a true and fair view of the financial position and the assets and liabilities of the Company as of December 31, 2009 and the results of its operations for the year ended in accordance with accounting principles generally accepted in France.

II.   Justification of our assessments

Pursuant to Article L. 823-9 of the French Commercial Code (*Code de commerce*) governing the justification of our assessments, we bring to your attention the following matters:

Note 2 d) to the financial statements presents the accounting rules and methods adopted with respect to the valuation of long-term investments. We verified the appropriateness of these accounting methods and, where necessary, the consistency of values in use attributed to equity investments with the values adopted for the preparation of the consolidated financial statements.

These assessments were performed as part of our audit approach for the financial statements taken as a whole and contributed to the expression of the opinion in the first part of this report.

III.   Specific procedures and disclosures

We have also performed the other procedures required by law, in accordance with professional standards applicable in France.

We have no matters to report as to the fair presentation and consistency with the financial statements of the information given in the Board of Directors' report and in the documents addressed to shareholders with respect to the financial position and the financial statements.

Concerning the information given in accordance with the requirements of Article L. 225-102-1 of the French Commercial Code (*Code de commerce*) relating to remunerations and benefits received by the corporate officers and any other commitments made in their favor, we have verified its consistency with the financial statements, or with the underlying information used to prepare these financial statements and, where applicable, with the information obtained by your company from companies controlling your company or controlled by it. Based on this work, we attest that this information is accurate and fair.

Pursuant to the law, we have verified that the Board of Directors' report contains the appropriate disclosures as to the identity of and percentage interests and votes held by shareholders.

Paris and Neuilly-sur-Seine, February 26, 2010

The Statutory Auditors

Grant Thornton	**Deloitte & Associés**
French Member of Grant Thornton International	
Gilles HENGOAT	Jean-François VIAT
	Dominique JUMAUCOURT

Retrospective versus Prospective Analysis

As discussed earlier, most analysis is done with a particular objective in mind, and as most objectives involve making decisions that have future consequences, it follows, therefore, that almost every analysis of a set of financial statements is, in one way or another, concerned with the future. Because of this, you should make a **prospective** (forward-looking) **analysis** of the company to try to determine what the future will bring. For example, commercial loans officers in banks try to forecast companies' future cash flows to ensure that loans will be repaid.

LEARNING OBJECTIVE 2

Describe the various ways of analyzing a company's financial statements.

The problem with prospective analysis is that the world is an uncertain place; no one can predict the future with complete accuracy. Analysts, however, are expected to make recommendations based on their predictions of what the future outcomes will be for specified companies. In trying to predict the future, some of the most reliable sources of data you have are the results of a company's past operations, as summarized in the financial statements. To the extent that the future follows past trends, you can do a **retrospective analysis** to assist in predicting the future. You must also understand the economics of a company well enough to know when something fundamental has changed in the economic environment to make it unlikely that the company's past results will predict the future. In such a situation, you cannot rely on the retrospective data.

If you believe that retrospective data may be useful in predicting the future, a complete analysis of those data is in order. Two major types of analysis of retrospective data are time-series and cross-sectional analyses.

Time-Series versus Cross-Sectional Analysis

In a **time-series analysis**, the analyst examines information from different time periods for the same company, to look for any patterns in the data over time. For example, you may look at the sales data over a five-year period to determine whether sales are increasing, decreasing, or remaining stable. This would have important implications for the company's future sales. The assumption underlying a time-series analysis is that there is some predictability in the time series; that is, past data can be used to predict the future. Without this assumption, there is no reason to do a time-series analysis.

Many companies recognize the importance of time-series information and provide five- or 10-year summaries to assist in making this analysis. In the first part of its annual report, BIC prepares a review covering a three-year period. Because this is not adequate for the purpose of a trend analysis, Exhibit 12-2 extracts some of the key accounts from BIC's analysis and has extended the summary to five years using data from earlier annual reports. In BIC's information, it is interesting to note that both net sales and group net income increased from 2005 to 2007, and then fell in 2008. Sales growth rebounded to a new, higher level of sales in 2009, and although net income increased over 2008, it was still below the amounts earned from 2005 to 2007. The income from operations (income after all operating expenses but before tax and interest expense) exhibited the same pattern as the net income.

A review of the balance sheet items presented shows that assets grew substantially between 2008 and 2009, as a result of the acquisitions BIC made to establish itself in the promotional products market and an acquisition of a stationery company in India, undertaken to increase the company's presence in that geographic market. It appears that the acquisitions were financed by increases in both non-current borrowings and equity. A review of the cash flow statement information indicates that BIC spent a large sum on investing activities in 2009, but the cash generated from operations increased

EXHIBIT 12-2   **SOCIÉTÉ BIC**

Comparison of Key Figures

(in millions of euros (except share data)	2005	2006	2007	2008	2009
Selected Income Statement Items					
Net sales	1,380.1	1,448.1	1,456.1	1,420.9	1,562.7
Gross profit	674.1	709.6	715.0	669.9	719.7
Group net income	156.4	170.2	172.9	144.9	151.7
Earnings per share (in euros)	3.11	3.43	3.51	3.00	3.15
Number of shares	50,330,582	49,661,931	49,244,579	48,357,724	48,151,691
Selected Balance Sheet Items					
Shareholders' equity	1,052.5	1,111.9	1,174.5	1,172.1	1,304.3
Current borrowings and bank overdraft	24.0	30.5	29.1	21.8	53.7
Non-current borrowings	0.8	26.5	23.3	11.1	161.5
Total assets	1,567.7	1,623.3	1,631.1	1,632.4	2,029.1
Selected Cash Flow Statement Items					
Net cash from operating activities	170.6	245.3	197.8	225.1	343.1
Net cash from investing activities	(71.7)	(98.0)	(81.9)	(81.6)	(216.9)
Net cash from financing activities	(153.6)	(80.1)	(89.2)	(101.6)	100.0
Closing cash and cash equivalents	103.5	166.5	198.5	225.5	478.9

and it had a very large cash and cash equivalents balance (€478.9 million) at the end of the year. Some companies include non-financial data, such as the number of employees or number of retail outlets, in their financial summaries. BIC included the number of shares outstanding.

After this brief review, an analyst would now have identified that although the company's stated strategy may be growth and producing quality products at low costs, the company has not achieved that consistently over the period. The analyst will be interested in further analyzing the performance of the company to try to determine the reasons for the lower level of net income and to assess whether BIC will be able to repay the additional debt it has taken on.

A **cross-sectional analysis** compares the data from one company with the data from another company for the same time period. Usually, the comparison is with another company in the same industry (a competitor perhaps), or with an average of the other companies in the industry. For example, you might look at the growth in sales for **General Motors of Canada** compared with the growth in sales for **Ford of Canada**. Other cross-sectional analyses might compare companies across different industries (General Motors of Canada compared with Rogers), different countries (General Motors of Canada compared with Nissan of Japan), and so forth. However, any cross-sectional comparisons must consider that different industries may have different accounting principles (for example, accounting principles for banks and insurance companies are slightly different from those for most other industries). Comparing across countries is more difficult if different accounting standards are used in different countries. However, investment analysts want to recommend the best investment strategy to their clients

HELPFUL HINT

A word of caution: Some companies, like BIC, present their financial information with the earliest year closest to the account titles. Most companies present their information the other way, with the most recent year closest to the account titles. When you are reading financial statements, be careful to observe the format used or you may end up thinking sales are falling when they are growing!

using as wide a range of investments as possible. To make the best recommendation, they must consider the return versus risk trade-off across many companies. They must, therefore, directly compare companies in different industries and different countries. One of the advantages of the growing use of IFRS in Canada and around the world is that there will be fewer accounting differences and, therefore, easier comparisons.

The choice of which type of analysis to conduct is driven, in part, by the type of decision that motivated the analysis. In a lending situation, for example, the commercial loans officer will use a time-series analysis of the company in conjunction with a cross-company comparison. The time-series analysis is important because it will help the lender determine the company's ability to repay any money loaned. As part of the decision-making process, the lender must also be aware of industry trends in order to get an overall assessment of how well a particular company performs relative to its competitors. This information will help ascertain the company's future viability.

Data to Be Used

The type of data that is used in a time-series or cross-sectional analysis will vary depending on the purpose of the analysis. Three general types of frequently used data are raw financial data, common size data, and ratio data.

Raw Financial Data

Raw financial data are the data that appear directly in the financial statements. An example of a time-series analysis of this type of data would be time-series data available in the annual report from the income statements, cash flow statements, and balance sheets, similar to that shown for BIC in Exhibit 12-2. Cross-sectional analysis can also be used with this type of data. For example, you might compare total revenues across companies in the same industry for the past three years. Annual reports may also contain data other than strictly financial data, such as numbers of employees or sales volumes expressed in physical units rather than dollars.

In the remainder of the chapter, data from BIC's financial statements will be used to illustrate various types of analyses. These raw financial statement data appear in Exhibit 12-3, which includes the balance sheets, income statements, and cash flow statements.

Common Size Data

Although a company's raw data can reveal much about its performance, certain relationships are more easily understood when some elements of the raw data are compared with other elements. For example, in the income statement for BIC in Exhibit 12-3B, you can see that sales increased from €1,456,088 thousand in 2007 to €1,562,696 thousand in 2009. Cost of goods has also increased over this period from €741,063 thousand to €842,952 thousand. What happened to gross profit margins, on a relative basis? This is a question of the relationship between the costs and the revenues. One way to address this question is to compare the cost of goods sold expressed as a proportion of the sales revenue. Often, this is done by preparing a set of financial statements called **common size** statements.

EXHIBIT 12-3A   **SOCIÉTÉ BIC 2009 ANNUAL REPORT**

annual report

Consolidated balance sheet for the year ended December 31, 2009

➡ **ASSETS**

(in thousand euros)	Notes	DEC. 31, 2007	DEC. 31, 2008	DEC. 31, 2009
Property, plant and equipment	10-1, 10-2	344,716	348,029	372,511
Investment properties	10-3	14,984	7,693	2,547
Goodwill	11	193,673	195,264	215,047
Intangible assets	12	39,312	36,763	40,155
Interests in associates	13	78	27	67,101
Other non-current assets	14	19,518	20,057	12,567
Deferred tax assets	22	91,558	108,762	110,664
Derivative financial instruments	16-f, 23	120	2,064	1
Non-current assets		**703,959**	**718,659**	**820,593**
Inventories	15-1	333,341	304,322	300,973
Income tax advance payments		11,283	21,712	8,373
Trade and other receivables	15-2, 16-e	345,984	315,108	361,172
Other current assets		11,556	11,343	8,863
Current derivative financial instruments	16-f, 23	473	16,472	5,906
Other derivative instruments	16-f, 23	–	–	1,896
Other current financial assets		22,789	18,476	40,113
Cash and cash equivalents		200,547	224,992	480,343
Assets held for sale	10-4	1,125	1,322	890
Current assets		**927,098**	**913,747**	**1,208,529**
TOTAL ASSETS		**1,631,057**	**1,632,406**	**2,029,122**

SOCIÉTÉ BIC 2009 ANNUAL REPORT (cont'd)

EXHIBIT 12-3A

▶ EQUITY AND LIABILITIES

(in thousand euros)	Notes	DEC. 31, 2007	DEC. 31, 2008	DEC. 31, 2009
Share capital	17	186,439	183,858	184,231
Accumulated profits		1,001,990	1,021,385	1,113,245
Translation reserve		(12,407)	(43,236)	(5,080)
Cash flow hedge derivatives		(1,758)	9,887	11,669
Group Shareholders' equity		**1,174,264**	**1,171,894**	**1,304,065**
Minority interest		219	219	219
Shareholders' equity		**1,174,483**	**1,172,113**	**1,304,284**
Non-current borrowings	19	23,321	11,078	161,466
Other non-current liabilities		–	125	118
Retirement benefit obligation	21-2	104,099	150,562	153,649
Provisions	20	27,969	28,741	36,676
Deferred tax liabilities	22	18,311	23,957	19,390
Non-current hedging contracts	16-f, 23	315	147	672
Non-current liabilities		**174,015**	**214,610**	**371,971**
Trade and other payables	15-2	92,352	92,134	120,430
Current borrowings	19	29,097	21,806	53,695
Current tax due		29,352	7,528	20,735
Other current liabilities		129,955	119,273	149,777
Other derivative intruments	16-f, 23	11	2,134	–
Current hedging contracts	16-f, 23	1,792	2,808	8,230
Current liabilities		**282,559**	**245,683**	**352,867**
TOTAL EQUITY AND LIABILITIES		**1,631,057**	**1,632,406**	**2,029,122**

EXHIBIT 12-3B   SOCIÉTÉ BIC 2009 ANNUAL REPORT

annual report

Consolidated income statement for the year ended December 31, 2009

(in thousand euros)	Notes	DEC. 31, 2007	DEC. 31, 2008	DEC. 31, 2009
Net sales	3	1,456,088	1,420,909	1,562,696
Cost of goods	4	(741,063)	(750,973)	(842,952)
Gross profit		**715,025**	**669,936**	**719,744**
Distribution costs	4	(234,574)	(237,679)	(258,436)
Administrative expenses	4	(142,100)	(143,102)	(159,457)
Other operating expenses	4	(94,749)	(84,992)	(76,857)
Other operating income and expense	5	12,204	5,396	(8,987)
Income from operations		**255,806**	**209,559**	**216,007**
Income from cash and cash equivalents	6	11,249	10,011	11,271
Finance costs	6	(5,859)	(3,248)	(8,531)
Income before tax		**261,196**	**216,322**	**218,747**
Income tax expense	7	(87,762)	(71,386)	(70,843)
Net income from consolidated entities		**173,434**	**144,936**	**147,904**
Income from associates	13	–	–	3,820
Net income from continued operations		173,434	144,936	151,724
Net income from discontinued operations		–	–	–
Income before minority interest		**173,434**	**144,936**	**151,724**
Minority interest		(557)	–	–
Group net income		**172,877**	**144,936**	**151,724**
Earnings per share (in euros)	8	3.51	3.00	3.15
Diluted earnings per share (in euros)(*)	8	3.50	3.00	3.14
Weighted average number of shares outstanding net of treasury shares	8	49,244,579	48,357,724	48,151,691

(*) Diluted items are options for subscribing for new shares and free shares.

SOCIÉTÉ BIC 2009 ANNUAL REPORT

EXHIBIT 12-3C

annual report

Consolidated cash flow statement for the year ended December 31, 2009

(in thousand euros)	Notes	DEC. 31, 2007	DEC. 31, 2008	DEC. 31, 2009
Operating activities				
Net income	PL	172,877	144,936	151,724
Adjustments to reconcile net income to net cash:				
Minority interest	PL	557	–	–
Amortization of intangible, tangible assets and investment properties	4, 10, 11, 12	79,191	74,522	75,024
Impairment loss	4, 5, 10-2	1,454	397	5,095
Antalis Promotional Products negative goodwill	5, 11-2	–	–	(10,250)
Retirement benefits	21-3	12,739	13,166	26,832
Other provisions (excluding provisions on current assets)		(3,965)	2,363	3,964
Hedging and derivative instruments	23	(3,574)	2,845	250
Option premium expense		2,301	517	305
Recognition of share-based payments	18, SHEQ	5,731	5,365	5,705
Deferred tax variation	7, 22	(3,033)	8,737	(6,611)
Income from associates	13	–	–	(3,820)
(Gain)/ Loss from disposal of fixed assets	5, 10, 12	(2,865)	(1,603)	(555)
Cash flow		**261,413**	**251,245**	**247,663**
(Increase)/ Decrease in net working capital	15-2	(54,160)	41,756	92,005
Payments related to employee benefits	21	(16,939)	(34,073)	(25,264)
Financial expense/(income)	6	(2,625)	(3,276)	(2,227)
Interests (paid)/ received		2,599	1,931	4,298
Income tax expense	7	90,913	59,497	77,464
Income tax paid		(83,425)	(91,976)	(50,799)
NET CASH FROM OPERATING ACTIVITIES		**197,776**	**225,104**	**343,140**
Investing activities				
Proceeds on disposal of property, plant and equipment	5, (a)	8,272	4,045	7,115
Purchases of property, plant and equipment	10	(69,321)	(75,528)	(47,639)
Purchases of patents and trademarks	12	(7,294)	(7,876)	(5,429)
Acquisition of equity investment	13, (b)	–	–	(63,271)
(Increase)/ Decrease in other investments	(h)	(528)	(746)	11,161
Acquisition of subsidiaries	11, (c)	(13,051)	(1,487)	(118,848)
NET CASH FROM INVESTING ACTIVITIES		**(81,922)**	**(81,592)**	**216,911)**

EXHIBIT 12-3C SOCIÉTÉ BIC 2009 ANNUAL REPORT (cont'd)

annual report

Consolidated cash flow statement for the year ended December 31, 2009

(in thousand euros)	Notes	DEC. 31, 2007	DEC. 31, 2008	DEC. 31, 2009
Financing activities				
Dividends paid	SHEQ, (d)	(64,190)	(65,428)	(65,001)
Minority interest buy back		(3,657)	–	–
Borrowings/(Repayments)	19, (i)	2,822	(14,180)	190,347
Repayments of obligations under finance leases	26	(512)	(172)	1,033
Purchase of financial instruments	(e)	(423)	(587)	(127)
(Purchase)/ Sale of other current financial assets	(f)	4,207	3,971	(19,416)
Increase in treasury shares and exercise of stock options	17, (g)	(27,422)	(25,245)	3,175
NET CASH FROM FINANCING ACTIVITIES		**(89,175)**	**(101,641)**	**110,011**
Net increase/(decrease) in cash and cash equivalents		26,679	41,871	236,240
Opening cash and cash equivalents	BS	166,507	198,513	222,471
Exchange difference		5,327	(17,913)	20,174
CLOSING CASH AND CASH EQUIVALENTS	BS	**198,513**	**222,471**	**478,885**

PL: See consolidated income statement.

SHEQ: See consolidated statement of changes in equity.

BS: See consolidated balance sheet.

In a common size statement of earnings, all line items are expressed as percentages of sales. Exhibit 12-4 presents a common size income statement for BIC, with every item calculated as a percentage of net sales.

We observed from the key figures in Exhibit 12-2 that sales have been increasing for BIC, except in 2008, but net income had fallen in 2007 and did not fully recover when sales did in 2009. This common size statement of earnings gives us a better understanding of those changes. It shows that BIC's cost of goods as a proportion of sales has been increasing over the three-year period, and that proportionate net income has been decreasing. Cost of goods has gone from 50.9% of sales to 53.9%, a full 3% increase. It is costing BIC more to produce the goods it sells. This has caused the gross profit to fall from 49.1% to 46.1% and signals to the user that BIC has been ineffective in controlling its major costs. It is not clear if the increase reflects a shift to selling more products that are more expensive to produce, if increases in sales prices have not kept pace with increases in cost, if price cuts were required due to competitive or economic conditions, or if cost control has just been ineffective. An analyst would want to try to find out more information, either from management or from performing additional analysis, about the cause of the change. An analyst will examine a company's financial statements carefully when sales are rising or falling. If sales are rising and the cost of those sales rises proportionately more than the sales themselves, the new sales are costing the company more and management should be looking for ways to control the costs.

EXHIBIT 12-4 SOCIÉTÉ BIC
Common Size Statements of Income

EXHIBIT 12-4

	2007	2008	2009
Net sales	100.0%	100.0%	100.0%
Cost of goods	50.9%	52.9%	53.9%
Gross profit	49.1%	47.1%	46.1%
Distribution costs	16.1%	16.7%	16.5%
Administrative expenses	9.8%	10.1%	10.2%
Other operating expenses	6.5%	6.0%	4.9%
Other operating income and expenses[1]	(0.8%)	(0.4%)	0.6%
Income (loss) from operations	17.6%	14.7%	13.8%
Income from cash and cash equivalents	0.8%	0.7%	0.7%
Finance costs	0.4%	0.2%	0.5%
Income before tax	17.9%	15.2%	14.0%
Income tax expense	6.0%	5.0%	4.5%
Net income from consolidated entities	11.9%	10.2%	9.5%
Income from associates			0.2%
Net income from continuing operations	11.9%	10.2%	9.7%
Income before minority interest	11.9%	10.2%	9.7%
Minority interests	0.0%		
Group net income	11.9%	10.2%	9.7%

1 The negative values for 2007 and 2008 indicate that these amounts are income; they are shown as negative because they are grouped with the expenses.

As a percentage of sales, when all other costs remain the same, an increase in the cost of sales results in an identical decrease in net income. Imagine if you sell an item for $1.00 and it now costs you $0.03 more to make or acquire the item than it did last year. This means there will be $0.03 less to spend on other items or left over as net income. For BIC, net income as a percentage of sales actually decreased by 2.2% over the period, from 11.9% of sales to 9.7%. As BIC experienced a 3% increase in its cost of goods sold, it must have been able to control other operating costs well enough to prevent net income from declining by the full 3% of the rise in its cost of goods sold. Many other items on the income statement are proportionately similar to 2007, although the operating expenses seem to be declining relative to sales. This could indicate that management is doing a better job at controlling those operating expenses. As well, income tax as a proportion of sales decreased, but income tax expense is generally not under management's control. The signals on this common size statement are mixed—cost of goods is increasing but other expenses decreased slightly. Overall, however, the net effect is a decrease in net income.

Common size statements could also be prepared for the balance sheet and the cash flow statement. The common size data could then be used in a time-series analysis, as they were earlier, or they could be used in a cross-sectional analysis of different companies. In fact, common size statements are particularly useful in cross-sectional analysis because they allow you to compare companies of different sizes.

Ratio Data

Common size data are useful for making comparisons of data items within a given financial statement, but they are not useful for making comparisons across the various financial statements. Ratios, on the other hand, compare a data element from one statement with an element from another statement, or with an element in the same statement. These ratios can then be used in a time-series or cross-sectional analysis. Ratio data are potentially the most useful analytical tool because they reveal information about relationships between the financial statements.

Although ratios tell you about the relationship between two figures and changes in that relationship from year to year, or compared to another company, they do not tell you the reason for the changes. You will usually need to do further research and analysis, or talk to management, to understand the reasons for the changes. Sometimes changes in ratios are referred to as red flags—they identify areas that the user needs to investigate further.

To illustrate the relationships that can be analyzed using ratio analysis, the remainder of the chapter is devoted to discussing various ratios and their calculation and interpretation. Most of them have already been introduced in previous chapters, but a discussion of the ratios as they relate to one another should help you to better understand and appreciate the usefulness of ratio analysis.

Before you begin ratio analysis, it is important to remember that financial statements are based on IFRS. This means that they involve certain accounting policy choices, assumptions, and estimates. As well, many of the assets and liabilities are reported at historical cost values rather than market values. Consequently, the limitations inherent in the financial statements are carried over into the ratios that are used to evaluate them.

RATIOS

LEARNING OBJECTIVE 3

Identify the types of ratios that are best at providing insights for specific decisions.

Ratios explain relationships among data in the financial statements. The relationships differ across companies, if for no other reason than that the companies' underlying transactions are different. For example, a manufacturing company is very concerned about the management of inventory and focuses on various ratios related to inventory. A bank, on the other hand, has no inventory and would not be able to calculate such ratios. It might, however, be very concerned about the loans that it makes, whereas a manufacturer would probably not have any items comparable to loans receivable.

Because of the differences across companies, it is impossible for us to address all the ratio issues related to all types of industries. The main focus of our discussion will, therefore, be restricted to BIC, but most of our discussion also applies to companies in other manufacturing and retailing industries. At the end of the chapter, we include a brief discussion of ratio analysis for non-retailing/manufacturing companies in areas where there may be differences in interpretation.

The ratios that will be discussed are divided into four general categories, but you will see that they are all related. The categories are performance, short-term liquidity, activity, and long-term solvency. Most of these ratios apply to any company regardless of the nature of its business, but some (such as inventory ratios) apply only to certain types of businesses. A fifth group of ratios applicable to equity analysis will also be discussed.

Before the calculations of the various ratios are presented, one general caveat is given. There are often several ways to calculate a given ratio. Therefore, it makes sense to understand the basis of a calculation before you attempt to interpret it. The use of ratios in this book will be consistent with the definitions given. However, if you use similar ratios from other sources, you should check the definition used in that source to make sure that it is consistent with your understanding of the ratio.

Profitability Ratios

LEARNING OBJECTIVE 4

Calculate specific ratios that are used to assess a company's profitability, short-term liquidity, activity, and solvency, and explain how the ratios can be interpreted.

Net earnings and cash flow as measures of performance have already been discussed in Chapters 2 and 4. Although much can be learned from studying the statement of earnings and statement of cash flows, in both their raw data and common size forms, the ratios discussed in this section complement that understanding and also draw out some of the relationships between these statements and the balance sheet.

Net Profit

In Chapter 2 we used the profit margin ratio, or more correctly the **net profit margin**, to measure a company's profitability relative to its revenues. This ratio provides information about the company's ability to control all costs and is calculated by dividing the company's net earnings by the revenues that produce those earnings:

$$\text{Net profit margin} = \frac{\text{Net earnings}}{\text{Revenues}}$$

The net profit margin is a good starting point to determine if a company is profitable, but it does not provide any information about how that profit was achieved or what resources were required to earn it. Were the earnings mostly from the company's primary operations, or did the company have significant earnings from investment income or one-time gains from selling other assets? When trying to predict a company's future earnings, the current sources and types of earnings are an important consideration. A company cannot sell off assets continuously and expect to stay in operation for long.

Earlier in the chapter, we identified different strategies a company could be using. Is the company's strategy to produce at the lowest cost and sell a high volume? Or does it sell a differentiated or premium product at a higher margin and lower volume? Answers to these questions can be obtained by looking at other margin ratios calculated from the statement of earnings.

Gross Profit

The **gross profit margin** measures the proportion of sales revenue available to pay all other operating costs after the costs of goods sold. It is calculated as gross profit divided by revenues. It is a key ratio in assessing a company's profitability. The cost of goods sold is, for most businesses, the largest single cost incurred and companies need to pay close attention to this margin to ensure that there is enough money available after those costs to pay all other expenses. Changes in this ratio would indicate a change in the product's profitability and may indicate changes in the cost structure or pricing policy.

$$\text{Gross profit margin} = \frac{\text{Gross profit}}{\text{Revenues}}$$

Some companies choose not to disclose the cost of goods sold separately on the statement of earnings because they do not want competitors to know that information. In those situations, the cost of goods sold is usually grouped with other operating costs and an *operating profit margin* is shown. Calculating a ratio for that margin would also be useful, but would not provide the same level of information as a gross margin and a separate analysis of operating costs.

BIC does disclose the cost of goods sold separately on its income statement, and both the net profit margin and gross profit margin were calculated as part of the common size income statement in Exhibit 12-4 and are repeated here. In 2009, for every €1 BIC made in sales, it had €0.461 left over after covering the cost of the item that contributed to the €1 in sales. And after paying all other costs, it had €0.097 left in profit on the €1 of sales.

It should be apparent to you that gross profit margin and cost of goods sold are reciprocal figures. If BIC had €0.461 of gross profit left over from the euro in sales after paying for the related cost of goods sold, it must have cost BIC €0.639 (€1 − €0.461) to earn that euro in sales. Some analyses focus on the cost to make the good—a cost of goods sold percentage—whereas the gross profit margin ratio views it from the gross profit margin perspective. The conclusions drawn from either approach would be the same.

In the discussion of both the financial highlights and the common size income statement, we raised concerns that BIC's profitability was declining. We now see that net profit margin decreased by 0.5% from 2008 to 2009, but gross profit margin decreased by more, 1.0%. BIC has less money available after producing its goods to pay other costs. It appears that costs have been rising faster than selling prices. This could be due to several factors. It may be due to poor cost controls. It may be that the company has chosen (or been forced) to lower prices relative to costs. Or perhaps there has been a change in BIC's product mix and it is selling more low margin items than previously. Further analysis or discussions with management would be necessary to know the exact cause, but the concern has been identified. The fact that the net profit margin did not decrease by the same amount as the gross profit margin indicates that BIC is doing a better job of controlling (is spending less per euro of sales) its other costs. This is a positive sign.

PROFIT MARGINS—SOCIÉTÉ BIC

Net profit margin

2008	2009
$\dfrac{€144,936}{€1,420,909} = 10.2\%$	$\dfrac{€151,724}{€1,562,696} = 9.7\%$

Gross profit margin

$\dfrac{€669,936}{€1,420,909} = 47.1\%$	$\dfrac{€719,744}{€1,562,696} = 46.1\%$

In addition to the profitability of earnings relative to revenues, it is important to examine the earnings relative to the amount invested to earn those earnings. If two companies generate the same amount of net earnings, but one company requires twice as many assets to do so, that company would clearly be a less desirable investment.

In Chapter 4, a performance ratio called the return on investment (ROI) was briefly discussed in generic terms as a measure of an investment's performance.

The generic form of the ROI calculation can be used to formulate several different ratios, depending on the perspective taken in measuring performance. For example, one perspective is that of the shareholders, who make an investment in the company and want to measure the performance of their investment. **Return on equity (ROE)**, which we also saw in Chapters 4 and 11, is a form of the ROI measure that captures the return to shareholders.

A second perspective is that of management. Management obtains resources from both shareholders and debt holders. Those resources are then invested in assets. The return generated by the investment in assets is then used to repay the debt holders and the shareholders. The profitability of the investment in assets is, therefore, very important. First seen in Chapter 8, **return on assets (ROA)** captures this type of ROI.

In this chapter, both ROA and ROE are considered.

Return on Assets (ROA)

Company management must make two fundamental business decisions. The first is the type of assets in which the company should invest (sometimes referred to as the investment decision), and the second is whether to seek more financing to increase the amount that the company can invest in assets (referred to as the financing decision). The ROA ratio, in this book, separates the investment decision from the financing decision. Regardless of the mix of debt and shareholder financing, this ratio asks the following question: What type of return is earned on the investment in assets? From this perspective, the return on the investment in assets should be calculated prior to any payments or returns to the debt holders or shareholders. Net earnings is a measure that is calculated before any returns to shareholders, but after the deduction of interest to the debt holders. Therefore, the net earnings, if it is to be used as a measure of return on assets, must be adjusted for the effects of interest expense so that the financing effects are removed from the earnings amount, resulting in a measure of the earnings generated by the assets that is available to pay both debt holders and shareholders.

A complicating factor in calculating this ratio is that interest is deductible in the calculation of income tax expense. Therefore, if interest expense is to be removed from the net earnings figure, we must also adjust the amount of income tax expense that would result. In other words, the tax savings (i.e., the reduction in income tax expense) associated with this interest deduction must also be removed. The ROA ratio is then calculated as the ratio of the return (income before interest) divided by the investment in total assets, as follows:

$$\text{ROA} = \frac{\text{Earnings before interest}}{\text{Average total assets}}$$

$$= \frac{\text{Net earnings} + \text{Interest expense} - \text{Tax saving of interest expense}}{\text{Average total assets}}$$

$$= \frac{\text{Net earnings} + \text{Interest expense} - (\text{Tax rate} \times \text{Interest expense})}{\text{Average total assets}}$$

$$= \frac{\text{Net earnings} + [\text{Interest expense} \times (1 - \text{Tax rate})]}{\text{Average total assets}}$$

Many companies show interest expense as a separate item on the statement of earnings. The interest expense for BIC is included in the finance costs on the income statement, and can be determined from reading Note 6, which is shown in Exhibit 12-5. Also included in the finance costs are gains or losses on some types of foreign currency exchanges and derivatives used for hedging, both of which are beyond the scope of this book.

EXHIBIT 12-5

annual report

SOCIÉTÉ BIC 2009 ANNUAL REPORT
Excerpt from Note 6: Finance Costs/Revenue

NOTE 6.   FINANCE COSTS/REVENUE

(in thousand euros)	DEC. 31, 2007	DEC. 31, 2008	DEC. 31, 2009
Interest income from cash and cash equivalents	8,219	4,428	6,189
Interest on bank deposits	3,030	5,583	5,082
Income from cash and cash equivalents	**11,249**	**10,011**	**11,271**
Interest expense	(8,691)	(6,735)	(9,043)
Hedging instruments revaluation	3,574	(712)	493
Net financial FOREX difference	(742)	4,199	19
Finance costs	**(5,859)**	**(3,248)**	**(8,531)**
FINANCE (COSTS)/REVENUE	**5,390**	**6,763**	**2,740**

The effective income tax rate can be calculated by dividing the income tax expense on the income statement by the income before tax (in 2009, €70,843 ÷ €218,747 = 32.4%). Based on the data for BIC, the calculation of the ROA for 2009 and 2008 has the following results:

RETURN ON ASSETS (ROA)—SOCIÉTÉ BIC

2008

$$\frac{€144{,}936 + [€6{,}735 \times (1 - 33\%)]}{\dfrac{€1{,}631{,}057 + €1{,}632{,}046}{2}} = 9.2\%$$

2009

$$\frac{€151{,}724 + [€9{,}043 \times (1 - 32.4\%)]}{\dfrac{€1{,}632{,}046 + €2{,}029{,}122}{2}} = 8.6\%$$

The 8.6% ROA in 2009 indicates that BIC earned 8.6% on the average total assets before making any payments to the suppliers of capital. This 8.6% should be compared with the 9.2% ROA earned in 2008. The decrease in the ROA is consistent with the decrease in profitability that we observed with the net profit margin and the increase in total assets in the common size financial statements. It should be compared with the ROA of other companies of similar risk.

The ROA is useful in measuring the overall profitability of the funds invested in the company assets. However, comparisons of ROAs across industries must be made with care. The level of ROA reflects, to some extent, the risk that is inherent in the type of assets that the company invests in. Investors trade off the risk for the return. The more risk investors take, the higher the return they demand. If the company invested its assets in a bank account (a very low-risk investment), it would expect a lower return than if it invested in oil exploration equipment (a high-risk business). Although this factor cannot explain all the variations in ROA between companies, it must be kept in mind. It may be more appropriate either to do a time-series analysis of this ratio, or to compare it cross-sectionally with a direct competitor in the same business. Data obtained from a source of industry ratios, such as Dun and Bradstreet, can provide you with median measures of ROA that can be used for comparison purposes to determine whether the calculated ROA of a specific company is reasonable or not.

There exists a useful breakdown of the ROA ratio that can provide insight into what caused a change in the ROA. The most common breakdown of this ratio is as follows:

$$\text{ROA} = \frac{\text{Net earnings} + [\text{Interest expense} \times (1 - \text{Tax rate})]}{\text{Average total assets}}$$

$$= \frac{\text{Net earnings} + [\text{Interest expense} \times (1 - \text{Tax rate})]}{\text{Sales revenue}} \times \frac{\text{Sales revenue}}{\text{Average total assets}}$$

$$= \text{Profit margin ratio} \times \text{Total asset turnover}$$

This breakdown of the ROA ratio into a profit margin ratio and a total asset turnover allows the analyst to assess some of the reasons for a company's ROA having gone up or down. Note that this is not the same **profit margin ratio** as the net profit margin ratio calculated earlier, because it is calculated using the profit or earnings before the after-tax interest expense. Changes in this ratio would indicate a change in the product's profitability and may indicate changes in the company's cost structure or pricing policy. The **total asset turnover** is the ratio of sales to total assets, or the dollars of sales generated per dollar of investment in assets. Changes in this ratio could reflect an increase or decrease in sales volume or major changes in the level of investment in company assets.

The breakdown for BIC in 2009 would be as follows:

ROA BREAKDOWN—SOCIÉTÉ BIC

2008

$$\frac{€144,936 + [€6,735 \times (1 - 33\%)]}{€1,420,909} \times \frac{€1,420,909}{\dfrac{€1,631,057 + €1,632,046}{2}} = 10.5\% \times 0.87 = 9.2\%$$

2009

$$\frac{€151,724 + [€9,043 \times (1 - 32.4\%)]}{€1,562,696} \times \frac{€1,562,696}{\dfrac{€1,632,046 + €2,029,122}{2}} = 10.1\% \times 0.85 = 8.6\%$$

These calculations indicate that in 2009 BIC earned the 8.6% ROA by achieving a profit margin of 10.1% and a total asset turnover of 0.85 times. Note that the decrease in the ROA from 2008 was a result of both a decrease in the profit margin (from 10.5% to 10.1%) and a small decrease in the total asset turnover ratio (0.87 to 0.85). So declining profitability is not the only difficulty BIC faced; there was also a decrease in sales generated per euro of assets. That could reflect declining efficiency of assets, or investment in new assets that have yet to reach their full potential to generate sales. The decrease in total asset turnover is small, and would need to be compared to other years or other companies before a conclusion could be reached about whether it should be of concern to an analyst. We saw earlier that BIC's assets grew as a result of an acquisition in 2009, and it appears that those assets have been able to generate close to BIC's traditional level of sales. The decrease in profitability, however, is consistent with earlier concerns we identified about BIC's performance in recent years.

Earlier in the chapter, we identified two strategies a company could be pursuing. The same ROA could be achieved by companies in the same industry with different strategies. For example, a discount retailer operates on smaller profit margins and hopes to make that up by generating a larger volume of sales relative to its investment in assets (giving it a higher asset turnover). Discounters generally have less invested in their retail stores. Other full-price retailers have a much larger investment in assets relative to their sales volume (giving them a lower asset turnover), and they must therefore charge higher prices (giving them a higher profit margin) to achieve a comparable ROA. Both businesses face the same general sets of risks and should earn comparable ROAs.

Return on Equity (ROE)

Return on equity (ROE), mentioned earlier in this section, is the return that shareholders earn on their investment in the company. There is an additional issue that must be understood in calculating this ratio. If there is more than one class of shares (generally the second class would be preferred shares), the ROE calculation should be done from the point of view of the common shareholders. This means that any payments to the other classes of shares (preferred dividends, for example) should be deducted from net earnings in the numerator of this ratio, because these amounts are not available to the common shareholders. Similarly, the denominator in such cases should include only the shareholders' equity accounts that belong to common shareholders. This usually means that the preferred shares equity account is subtracted from the total shareholders' equity to arrive at the common shareholders' equity.

The calculation of a company's ROE is as follows:

$$\text{ROE} = \frac{\text{Net earnings} - \text{Perferred dividends}}{\text{Average common shareholders' equity}}$$

As BIC only has common shares, we do not have to consider preferred shares and their related dividends. However, the minority interest that is shown in BIC's shareholders' equity section is not an investment by common shareholders; it reflects the fact that BIC does not own 100 percent of some of the subsidiaries that it controls. Minority interests are discussed further in Appendix B, but for now it is enough for you to understand that they are not included in common shareholders' equity and hence the denominator for BIC is the Group Shareholders' equity amount from the balance sheet.

HELPFUL HINT

When removing the preferred dividends for this calculation, you need to remove the dividends that were owed in the current year for preferred shares that are cumulative. If the current year's owed dividends are removed each year, it is not necessary to remove the dividends in arrears that were paid in a given year since prior years already included them in an ROE calculation.

For BIC, the calculation of ROE is as follows:

RETURN ON EQUITY (ROA)—SOCIÉTÉ BIC

2008

$$\frac{€144{,}936 - 0}{\dfrac{€1{,}174{,}264 + €1{,}171{,}894}{2}} = 12.4\%$$

2009

$$\frac{€151{,}724 - 0}{\dfrac{€1{,}171{,}894 + €1{,}304{,}065}{2}} = 12.3\%$$

This calculation shows that BIC earned a 12.3% ROE in 2009, indicating that it earned an average of 12.3% on the average shareholders' equity balances. This is down slightly from the previous year's ROE of 12.4%, but not as much as the ROA decreased. Just as with the ROA, this ROE of 12.3% should be compared with the ROE of other similar companies, or with the results of BIC over time. Cross-sectional comparisons of ROE (among different companies) are difficult for the same reason that similar comparisons of ROA are difficult. Differences in the risks involved should result in differences in returns. Differences in the risks cannot, however, always explain large differences in returns, as there are many factors that affect ROE.

Leverage

Comparing the ROE calculated for BIC with the associated ROA shows that the company, while earning only an 8.6 % return on assets, showed a return of 12.3% on the shareholders' equity. This higher return on equity results from the company's successful use of financial leverage. Financial **leverage** simply means that some of the funds obtained to invest in assets came from debt holders rather than shareholders. A company that has a larger proportion of debt to shareholders' equity is said to be highly leveraged.

In the case of a totally shareholder-financed company—that is, a company with no debt—the ROE (assuming there is only one class of shares) would equal the ROA. There would be no interest expense and, therefore, the numerators of both ratios would be the same. The denominators would also be the same because the accounting equation (assets = liabilities + shareholders' equity) would be adjusted for the absence of any liabilities (assets = shareholders' equity).

To understand the effects of leverage, consider first the data in Exhibit 12-6 for the fictitious Baker Company, which we assume to be 100% equity-financed. Note that in this example, Baker generates a 15% return on its assets before taxes (earnings before interest and taxes ÷ assets = $150 ÷ $1,000). After the 40% corporate income taxes, this translates into a 9% after-tax return (ROA). Note also that the ROE is the same as the after-tax ROA, because there is no debt and therefore no leverage effect.

The key to financial leverage is the relationship between the after-tax cost of borrowing and the return on assets. When a company borrows money, it invests that money in assets and earns the company's return on assets on that amount. The cost of using those funds is the after-tax cost of borrowing. If the cost to borrow is less than the return that the company can earn on the funds, then the wealth of the company will increase. If it costs the company more to borrow than it can earn on the funds, the wealth of the company will decrease.

It is necessary to use the after-tax cost of the debt in the comparison, as opposed to just the interest rate, because interest expense, as we saw earlier, is tax deductible and therefore generates tax savings for a company. The taxes saved are the tax rate times the

EXHIBIT 12-6

BAKER COMPANY
Case A: 100% Equity-Financed

Statement of Financial Position

Assets		$ 1,000	Liabilities	$ 0
			Shareholders' equity	1,000
Total		$ 1,000	Total	$ 1,000

Statement of Earnings

Earnings before interest and taxes	$150.00
Interest	0
Earnings before taxes	150.00
Income taxes (40%)	60.00
Net earnings	$ 90.00

ROA $90 ÷ $1,000	9.0%
ROE $90 ÷ $1,000	9.0%

interest expense. The net cost to the company is therefore the interest paid minus the taxes saved. For example, if a company borrows $400 at a rate of 10% and the tax rate is 40%, the net after-tax cost would be as follows:

$$\text{Net cost of borrowing} = \text{Interest expense} - (\text{Tax rate} \times \text{Interest expense})$$
$$= \$40.00 - (0.40 \times \$40.00) = \$24.00$$
$$\text{OR Interest expense} \times (1 - \text{Tax rate})$$
$$= \$40 \times (1 - 0.40) = \$24.00$$

Now consider the data in Exhibit 12-7 for Baker Company, which assumes that the company is only 60% equity-financed. To keep the illustration simple, all liabilities are considered interest-bearing at the rate of 10%. There are two statements of earnings presented, Case B where the earnings before interest and taxes (EBIT) is the same as in Case A, $150, and Case C where EBIT has fallen to $75.

In Exhibit 12-7, several things should be noted. The first is that in Case B the ROA (9%) is the same as in the all-equity case in Exhibit 12-6 because the amount of assets has not changed; only the amount of debt has changed. Before interest and tax, the assets should be earning exactly what they would have earned in a 100%-shareholder-financed company. In Case C, when EBIT has fallen by half (from $150 to $75), the ROA has fallen by the same amount (from 9% to 4.5%).

Note that in Case B the ROE (11%) is greater than the ROA (9%). This occurs because the company was able to borrow at an after-tax interest rate that was less than the rate it could earn by investing in assets. The before-tax borrowing rate in Case B is 10%. To adjust this to an after-tax rate, we multiply it by 1 minus the tax rate: 10% × (1 − 0.40) = 6%. Thus, the after-tax cost of debt is 6%, whereas the after-tax return on assets (ROA) is 9%. This increases the ROE for the shareholders.

BAKER COMPANY
Case B and Case C: 60% Equity-Financed, Interest Rate 10%

EXHIBIT 12-7

Statement of Financial Position

Assets	$ 1,000	Liabilities	$ 400
		Shareholders' equity	600
Total	$ 1,000	Total	$ 1,000

Statement of Earnings	Case B	Case C
Earnings before interest and taxes	$150.00	$ 75.00
Interest (0.10 × $400)	40.00	40.00
Earnings before taxes	110.00	35.00
Income taxes (40%)	44.00	14.00
Net earnings	$ 66.00	$ 21.00

ROA	[$66 + {$40 × (1 − 0.4)}] ÷ $1,000 = $90 ÷ $1,000 =	9.0%	
	[$21 + {$40 × (1 − 0.4)}] ÷ $1,000 = $45 ÷ $1,000 =		4.5%
ROE	$66 ÷ $600 =	11.0%	
	$21 ÷ $600 =		3.5%

The increase in the ROE in Case B occurs because, when the company borrowed $400 its net cost of borrowing was $24, but it was able to generate $36 (9% × $400) in income from the borrowed funds. The difference is $12, which goes to the shareholders as an incremental return. Therefore, the shareholders earn a $54 (9% of $600) return on the money that they invested, plus the excess return of $12 that is earned on the money that was borrowed, for total earnings of $66. Thus, without any further investment on their part, their percentage return (ROE) over what they could have earned as a 100%-equity-financed company is improved from 9% to 11% ($66 ÷ $600).

In Case C, the ROE (3.5%) is less than the ROA (4.5%). This occurs because the after-tax cost of borrowing at 6% is now greater than the 4.5% return on assets. As a result, the company is incurring the same net borrowing cost of $24 to earn a return of $18 (4.5% × $400). If you are paying more to obtain funds than you can earn by investing them, overall wealth is going to suffer. Note that although the ROA fell by half, the ROE plunged by more than this, from 11% to 3.5%. This is much less than the ROE of 9% in the 100%-equity-financed case; the shareholders would have been better off if the company had not borrowed at all.

This, then, is the advantage and risk of leverage. The shareholders can improve their return (ROE) if the company can borrow funds at an after-tax borrowing rate that is less than the ROA. However, this is a big *if*. A company that leverages itself is committed to making fixed interest payments to debt holders prior to earning a return for its shareholders. It is betting that the return on assets will be higher than the after-tax cost of its borrowing. If it is wrong and the after-tax cost of borrowing is greater than the ROA, the return to the shareholders (ROE) will fall below what the company could have earned with no debt at all.

If leveraging the company a little is potentially a good thing, as Case B in Exhibit 12-7 illustrated, why not leverage it a lot? In other words, why not borrow funds to finance most of the company's assets? For example, why not have 80% debt and 20% equity in the company?

Case D in Exhibit 12-8 illustrates the kind of return that the company could expect if it had 80% debt financing and the same 10% interest rate and EBIT as Case B in Exhibit 12-7.

A return of 21% is certainly very attractive, compared with the ROE of 11% that could be achieved with a 60% equity-financed company. The problem with this financing strategy is that the riskiness of an investment in Baker Company will be much higher in Case D (with 80% debt and only 20% equity) than in Case B. With high interest charges to be covered, if the company's ROA drops, the ROE will plunge—and may become negative—very rapidly.

The amount of leverage that a company can use is affected by several factors, including the stability of operating cash flows and the types of assets employed by the company. The cost of borrowing for a company increases as the amount of leverage increases. As the company adds more and more debt to its capital structure, it is committing itself to higher and higher fixed interest payments and increasing the risk of not being able to repay the borrowed funds. The increased obligations could perhaps force the company into bankruptcy. Because of the increased risk, as the company increases its level of debt it has to pay higher interest rates. When its borrowing cost starts to equal or exceed its ROA, it will become unattractive to lenders if it seeks further funds.

As we saw in our simple examples, return on equity improves relative to a 100%-equity-financed company when a company begins to use leverage and the ROA is greater than the after-tax cost of borrowing. But as the company continues to increase the amount of debt there is a point where the increasing risk, and hence increasing cost

EXHIBIT 12-8	

BAKER COMPANY

Case D: 20% Equity-Financed, Interest Rate 10%

Statement of Financial Position				
Assets	$ 1,000	Liabilities		$ 800
		Shareholders' equity		200
Total	$ 1,000	Total		$ 1,000

Statement of Earnings	
Earnings before interest and taxes	$150.00
Interest (0.10 × $800)	80.00
Earnings before taxes	70.00
Income taxes (40%)	28.00
Net earnings	$ 42.00

ROA [$42 + {$80 × (1 − 0.4)}] ÷ $1,000 = $90 ÷ $1,000 =   9.0%

ROE $42 ÷ $200 =   21.0%

of borrowing, starts to exceed the benefits, and the return on equity starts to decrease. The level of leverage that would maximize the return on equity is sometimes called the company's optimal capital structure. This **optimal capital structure** exists in theory but is more difficult to determine in the real world. It is true, however, that as you look across industries, different types of businesses have different average levels of debt financing (i.e., leverage). This indicates that, based on the risk characteristics of those industries, the companies in those industries borrow up to the point that they think is beneficial to their shareholders, and no further.

In the notes to its financial statements, BIC discloses that interest rates on its borrowings varied from 2.80% to 11.50%, before taxes. Rates on different borrowings vary depending on the terms and conditions of the debt, as well as the length of time until its maturity and what the market interest rates were at the time the debt was issued. BIC's tax rate was approximately 32.4%, which means its after-tax interest rate ranged from 1.9% to 7.8%. If its ROA was 8.6%, BIC was earning a higher return on its assets than it paid to borrow money. Its ROE of 12.3% illustrates how BIC's use of leverage boosted its ROA into a higher return to its shareholders.

A company's use of leverage can be judged, to some extent, by the difference between its ROE and its ROA, as the hypothetical Baker Company example and BIC's results show. In addition, several other ratios are used to measure the amount of leverage the company employs, as well as how well it uses that leverage. These ratios include the debt to equity ratio and the times interest earned ratio, which are discussed in a later section on solvency.

The following story indicates that if a company gets an appropriate level of leverage and controls costs, the results can be an increase in its share price.

accounting in the news

Cott Has Caught Analysts' Attention

Prospects were not looking good for Cott Corp. in 2009, but the private-label beverage maker's recent transformation has changed some analysts' minds. Cott Corp. shares rose by as much as 7 percent in September 2010 after the company was rated "Buy" in new coverage from Deutsche Bank. Other analysts were also now recommending Cott as a buying opportunity. Their reason is management's return to basics—lean infrastructure, disciplined cost management, a quality low-cost product, healthy customer relations, and a sound balance sheet. In addition, Cott's acquisition of the private-label juice maker Cliffstar Corp. was seen as a significant strategic step forward, providing the company with a better product balance and making it more consistently profitable. Efforts to deleverage the company's balance sheet were also creating value in the short to intermediate term. So, although Cott is not likely to be a fast revenue grower, its improved cost discipline and synergies from Cliffstar should allow the company to generate a steady margin and free cash flow in the future.

Source: David Pett, "Cott Shares Soar," *Financial Post*, September 21, 2010. http://business.financial-post.com/2010/09/21/cott-shares-soar/

Short-Term Liquidity Ratios

As discussed in Chapter 1, liquidity refers to a company's ability to convert assets into cash to pay liabilities. A basic understanding of the company's short-term liquidity position should result from a consideration of the financial statements, particularly the statement of cash flows, as well as the turnover rates discussed in the next section on activity ratios. Understanding the liquidity position requires knowledge of the leads and lags in the company's cash-to-cash cycle, discussed in Chapters 4 and 5. Managing a company's cash cycle is sometimes also referred to as working capital management. You will recall from earlier chapters that **working capital** = current assets − current liabilities. In addition, at least three ratios provide quantitative measures of short-term liquidity: the current and quick ratios, and the operating cash flow to short-term debt ratio.

Current Ratio

The **current ratio** is calculated by comparing the total current assets with the total current liabilities, as follows:

$$\text{Current ratio} = \frac{\text{Current assets}}{\text{Current liabilities}}$$

Remember that current assets are those that are going to be converted into cash in the next year (or the company's operating cycle, if it is longer than one year), and current liabilities are going to require the use of cash or other assets in the next year. As such, this ratio should be greater than 1; otherwise, it is difficult to see how the company will remain solvent in the coming year. The rule of thumb for this ratio for most industries is that it should be 1 or more, and, to be conservative, approximately 2. However, the size of this ratio depends on the type of business and the types of assets and liabilities that are considered current. For example, a company that sells primarily on a cash basis and does not have any accounts receivable, like a grocery store, normally has a low current ratio.

One caveat: the current ratio is subject to manipulation by a company at year end. This ratio may not, therefore, be a very reliable measure of liquidity. As a simple example, consider a company that has $100 in current assets and $50 in current liabilities at the end of a given year. Its current ratio would be 2 ($100 ÷ $50). Suppose that $25 of the $100 is in cash and the rest is in inventory. Suppose further that the company uses up all of its $25 in cash to pay $25 of current liabilities at year end. The current ratio becomes 3 ($75 ÷ $25) and the company looks more liquid. However, it is actually less liquid; in fact, it is virtually illiquid in the short term, because it has no cash and must sell its inventory and wait until it collects on the sale of that inventory before it will have any cash to pay its bills. In this case, the current ratio is deceptive.

The current ratios for BIC are as follows:

CURRENT RATIO—SOCIÉTÉ BIC	
2008	**2009**
$\dfrac{€913{,}747}{€245{,}683} = 3.72$	$\dfrac{€1{,}208{,}529}{€352{,}867} = 3.42$

The current ratio of 3.42 in 2009 is a slight decline from the 3.72 of the previous year. With the ratio above 2 in both years, however, BIC appears able to comfortably handle its short-term obligations. Upon reviewing the components of current assets, we can see that cash and cash equivalents more than doubled over 2008 and is the largest current asset in 2009. There was also an increase in accounts receivable. Despite both these changes, which should increase liquidity, the current ratio decreased. This is because almost all of the current liabilities increased—accounts payable, current borrowings, and other current liabilities. The increase in the current obligations of the company offset the increase in assets and BIC is less liquid than in 2008. Despite this drop, the company appears to be healthy with respect to liquidity.

It is important to note that it is possible for a company to be *too liquid*—to have too much money invested in assets such as cash and accounts receivable that do not generate any returns for the company. Then again, an increase in cash and cash equivalents might be part of the company's strategy. Maybe the company needs liquid assets for a planned purchase or acquisition early in the next year. Finding answers to questions like these is why it is important for an analyst to understand the business and to talk to management or do additional research before drawing conclusions.

Quick Ratio

One problem with the current ratio is that some assets in the current section are less liquid than others. For example, inventory is usually less liquid than accounts receivable, which are less liquid than cash. In some industries, inventory is very illiquid, because of the long period of time that it may have to be held before sale. Consider, for example, the holding period in the manufacture of 12-year-old Scotch whisky. The current ratio in such cases will not adequately measure the company's short-term liquidity, because the inventory will not be converted into cash for a very long time. In this case, the **quick ratio** is a better measure of short-term liquidity. It differs from the current ratio in that only the most liquid current assets (cash, accounts receivable, and short-term investments) are included in the numerator. Other current assets, such as inventories and prepaid expenses, are excluded from this ratio. Prepaid expenses do not convert into cash. Instead they used cash in the past and the company will be saving cash in the future because amounts have been paid in advance. The ratio is calculated as follows:

$$\text{Quick ratio} = \frac{\text{Cash + Accounts receivable + Short-term investments}}{\text{Current liabilities}}$$

The rule of thumb for this ratio is that it should be approximately 1 or more. A quick ratio of 1 means that the very short-term current assets are equal to the total current liabilities. Again, the desirable level for this ratio depends on the type of industry.

Some judgement is necessary when reviewing BIC's balance sheet to determine which current assets should be included in this ratio. Some of the account titles are not completely clear with respect to understanding how easily the asset could be converted into cash, and do not have accompanying notes to guide the user. The "other current financial assets" are most likely short-term investments, and hence should be included in the quick ratio. Recall from Chapter 6 that financial assets include marketable securities or short-term investments. The "income tax advanced payments" and "other current assets" are more likely similar to prepaids and would not be included in the ratio. The derivative instruments—"Current financial" and "Other"—are more difficult to discern. The quick ratio is intended to be a more stringent test of a company's liquidity than the current ratio; therefore, conservatism would dictate that if we are not certain about an item it is better to exclude it. The "Assets held for sale" will generate cash, but the timing and amount of the cash flow is uncertain, and the amounts are small. It is best to exclude this account as well. Based on those classifications, the calculation is as follows:

QUICK RATIO—SOCIÉTÉ BIC

2008	2009
$\dfrac{€224,992 + €18,476 + €315,108}{€245,683} = 2.27$	$\dfrac{€480,343 + €40,113 + €361,172}{€352,867} = 2.50$

The quick ratio of 2.50 in 2009 is slightly higher than the quick ratio of 2.27 in 2008, which should not be surprising. Remember that when we discussed the current ratio we noted major increases in BIC's most liquid assets—cash and receivables. The increase in these most liquid of assets is reflected in the increased quick ratio. In both years, the quick ratio is well above the 1.0 rule of thumb amount and brings us back to the concern that perhaps the company has too much invested in assets that do not produce much (if any) return.

Taken together, the current ratio and quick ratio indicate that BIC's liquidity position seems to be healthy but that more information would be useful. Just reviewing these two years illustrates the importance of time-series analyses in understanding a ratio. Going back further than the two years would enable you to see whether a current ratio above 3 and a quick ratio above 2 are normal. Cross-sectional analyses should also be undertaken with other companies that manufacture plastic consumer products.

Operating Cash Flow to Short-Term Debt Ratio

In Chapter 5, we discussed the importance of the information on the cash flow statement, how it is prepared, and how it should be interpreted. (You may want to refer to Chapter 5 to refresh your understanding of how to interpret the information on the cash flow statement.) The cash flow statement details the inflows and outflows of cash from operating, financing, and investing activities. The **operating cash flow to short-term debt ratio** is another measure of the company's ability to meet its short-term debt. It is calculated as follows:

$$\text{Operating cash flow to short-term debt} = \frac{\text{Operating cash flow}}{\text{Short-term debt and current maturities of long-term debt}}$$

Like the current ratio and the quick ratio, the higher this ratio is, the better the company can meet its short-term debt obligations. For BIC, the results for 2009 and 2008 are as follows:

OPERATING CASH FLOW TO SHORT-TERM DEBT RATIO— SOCIÉTÉ BIC

2008	2009
$\dfrac{€225{,}104}{€245{,}683} = 0.92$	$\dfrac{€343{,}140}{€352{,}867} = 0.97$

The operating cash flow to short-term debt ratio of 0.97 in 2009 has increased from the 0.92 of the previous year. The increase indicates that BIC can more comfortably handle its short-term debt obligations; in fact, BIC could almost completely pay off all of its short-term obligations with the operating cash flow generated in the year. Both long-term and short-term debt have increased in 2009 as a result of the acquisitions undertaken, but the cash from operations has also increased, so BIC's ability to meet its short-term obligations continues to look strong.

Activity Ratios

The activity ratios provide additional insight into the major decisions management makes regarding asset use and liquidity. The total asset turnover ratio, discussed earlier as a component of the ROA, is a measure of a company's total asset utilization. There are three other turnover ratios we will discuss to better understand liquidity and assess management's policies concerning accounts receivable, inventory, and accounts payable. They relate to the three policy decisions that were discussed in Chapter 5 regarding the company's cash flow performance. They are the accounts receivable, inventory, and accounts payable turnovers. These ratios provide some quantitative measures of the lead/lag relationships that exist between the revenue and expense recognition and the cash flows related to these three items.

Total Asset Turnover

The total asset turnover ratio measures the dollar amount of sales generated for each dollar invested in assets. Companies acquire assets to generate net earnings, and the first step in generating net earnings is to generate sales. Consider a business that has a single asset that will be used to produce the goods for sale. If management decides to expand by purchasing a second asset, would the sales level double? Perhaps the sales might not double immediately if the second machine were not yet operating at full capacity, but if the company wants to maintain the same level of efficiency its objective would be to have the sales level double. By examining the ratio of sales to assets, the asset turnover ratio, we can assess how efficiently the company is using its assets. This is a different measure than merely comparing net income to see if it has doubled, because other factors such as cost control influence net income. By differentiating between the effect on sales versus net income, managers and analysts can determine if the company's difficulties lie in generating sales, or in controlling costs. The solutions to those two problems are different, so determining which one is the source of the problem is important for effective management.

As calculated for ROA (on page 801), the total asset turnover for BIC in 2009 was 0.85, down slightly from 0.87 in 2008. It appears that with BIC's recent acquisitions, its efficiency has fallen slightly. Trend analysis would be useful to determine if the decrease is due solely to the acquisitions or is a longer term concern.

Accounts Receivable Turnover

The **accounts receivable turnover ratio** attempts to provide information about the company's accounts receivable policy. This ratio was introduced in Chapter 6, when the management of accounts receivables and other short-term liquid assets was discussed. This ratio measures how many times during a year the accounts receivable balance turns over—that is, how many times old receivables are collected and replaced by new receivables. It is calculated as follows:

$$\text{Accounts receivable turnover} = \frac{\text{Credit sales}}{\text{Average accounts receivable}}$$

When data from financial statements are used, the assumption is usually made that all sales were on account, because there is usually no information in the financial statements about the percentage of credit sales (or sales on account) versus cash sales. If the turnover ratio were being prepared for internal use by management, this type of information would be available and only credit sales would be used when calculating this ratio. It is probable that most of BIC's sales are credit sales, since it sells its products to retailers and wholesale distributors. Companies that sell directly to the public, like grocery stores, tend to sell primarily on a cash basis and hence have few (if any) credit sales. Additionally, the ratio should only include receivables related to credit sales, often referred to as *trade receivables*, and not other miscellaneous receivables (for example, receivables related to expected tax refunds or advances to employees). The description in BIC's balance sheet is "trade and other receivables," and although the breakdown is available in the notes, for simplicity we will assume they are all related to sales.

Using BIC's data, the ratio is as follows:

ACCOUNTS RECEIVABLE TURNOVER—SOCIÉTÉ BIC

2008	2009
$\dfrac{€1,420,9009}{\dfrac{€345,984 + €315,108}{2}} = 4.30 \text{ times}$	$\dfrac{€1,562,696}{\dfrac{€315,108 + €361,172}{2}} = 4.62 \text{ times}$

The level of the accounts receivable turnover depends on several factors, especially the normal credit terms granted by the company. If the company normally allows 30 days for customers to pay, and if customers actually pay in 30 days, the resulting accounts receivable turnover would be 12 times, because there would be one month of sales always outstanding in accounts receivable. If the normal credit term is 60 days, the resulting accounts receivable turnover would be 6 times (because 365 days ÷ 60 days is approximately 6 times). To determine how effectively a company is collecting its receivables, it is necessary to compare the turnover rate to the company's credit terms.

With an accounts receivable turnover of 4.62 times, it appears that BIC is collecting its receivables in 79 days (since 365 days ÷ 4.62 = 79). We do not know how this compares to BIC's actual credit terms, because we do not know the company's credit policies. If its credit terms are 60 days, the company is not collecting its receivables on a timely basis; that is, customers on average are taking longer to pay than the terms given. If the credit terms are 90 days, then it appears customers are paying more quickly and BIC is benefitting from the earlier cash inflows. BIC's 2009 turnover is higher than in 2008 (4.30 times), indicating that it is turning the receivables over more quickly— that is, the company is collecting the receivables a little faster than in 2008, improving the cash inflow. The increase would be a good signal of improving cash collections and maybe improved liquidity.

An accounts receivable turnover ratio that indicates the company is collecting its accounts receivable more slowly than the credit terms imply, or more slowly than others in the industry, could indicate that the company is having trouble collecting its accounts receivable. Is the company selling to customers that do not pay? Does the company still have old accounts receivable that should be written off on its books? Has it been making an adequate allowance for bad debts? Depending on the answers to these and other similar questions, a high level of accounts receivable may not always be associated with high levels of liquidity or good cash management.

The turnover number can also be converted into a measure of the days necessary to collect the average receivable, by dividing the numbers of days in one year by the turnover ratio. Although they measure the same thing, users may find that the average days to collect is easier to interpret than accounts receivable turnover numbers. Although companies probably do not sell goods or collect receivables every day of the year, the convention is to use 365 days. The average days to collect for BIC follows:

DAYS TO COLLECT ACCOUNTS RECEIVABLE—SOCIÉTÉ BIC

2008	2009
$\dfrac{365 \text{ days}}{4.30} = 84.9 \text{ days}$	$\dfrac{365 \text{ days}}{4.62} = 79.0 \text{ days}$

As noted earlier, you cannot simply look at the 79.0 days and decide whether it is bad or good. You need to know what the credit terms are, and if the average monthly sales are fairly equal, since large sales in the last month of the fiscal year would result in an apparently lower turnover (due to higher accounts receivable balances at year end) and a higher number of days to collect. You also need to know the proportion of total sales that are made on credit. To analyze both of these ratios more fully, we should also consider a time-series analysis and a cross-sectional analysis with competitors.

Inventory Turnover

The **inventory turnover** ratio gives the analyst some idea of how fast inventory is sold or, alternatively, how long the inventory is held prior to sale. This ratio was introduced in Chapter 7. The calculation of the turnover is similar to that of the accounts receivable turnover, with a measure of the flow of inventory in the numerator, and a measure of the balance in inventory in the denominator. It is calculated as follows:

$$\text{Inventory turnover} = \frac{\text{Cost of goods sold}}{\text{Average inventory}}$$

Note that the numerator contains the cost of goods sold, not the sales value of the goods sold (revenues). Total sales revenue, while it does measure the flow of goods sold to customers, would be inappropriate in the numerator because it is based on the inventory's *selling price*, while the denominator is measured at *cost*. Cost of goods sold is measured at cost and is therefore more appropriate.

The number of days that inventory is held can be calculated from the turnover ratio in the same way as was the accounts receivable turnover ratio. BIC's results for both of these ratios follow:

INVENTORY TURNOVER AND DAYS IN INVENTORY—SOCIÉTÉ BIC

2008

$$\frac{€750,973}{\dfrac{€333,341 + €304,322}{2}} = 2.36 \text{ times}$$

2009

$$\frac{€842,952}{\dfrac{€304,322 + €300,973}{2}} = 2.79 \text{ times}$$

$$\textbf{DAYS INVENTORY HELD} = \frac{\textbf{365 days}}{\textbf{Inventory turnover}}$$

$$\frac{365 \text{ days}}{2.36} = 155.0 \text{ days}$$

$$\frac{365 \text{ days}}{2.79} = 131.0 \text{ days}$$

The average number of days that inventory is held depends on the type of inventory produced, used, or sold. In BIC's case, remember that its major operations are the sale of stationery, lighter, and shaver products to both retailers and wholesalers. The 131 days, therefore, refers to the average length of time that costs remain in inventory, from original processing to sale of the products to customers. Because the product is not perishable, this length of time could be reasonable. Before making this assumption, however, you would want to review this turnover over time and against the inventory turnover ratios of other companies producing and selling plastic consumer goods. BIC's 2009 inventory turnover is higher than in 2008, indicating that BIC is holding the goods for fewer days in 2009. The shorter the holding time, the less money tied up in inventory, which is generally a good sign.

One limitation that must be considered when interpreting the inventory turnover ratio is that many companies do not disclose the cost of goods sold amount on the statement of earnings. They will sometimes skip from the revenue amount directly to earnings before other operating expenses. In such cases, you will need to find the cost of goods sold by subtracting earnings before other operating expenses from gross revenue. Another problem with determining this ratio is that some companies combine the cost of goods sold with other operating expenses. The resulting figure is, therefore, larger than the cost of goods sold figure and the resulting inventory turnover is larger as well (making it look as if the company is turning it over more quickly). Under these circumstances, it is important to treat this ratio with some skepticism.

BIC is a manufacturing company, and the inventory turnover ratio that we calculated used all types of its inventory: finished goods, work in process, and raw materials. A more appropriate inventory turnover measure could be to use only the finished goods amounts, which could be done as BIC discloses the components of its inventory in Note 15-1. It would be interesting to see the impact of using just finished goods in this ratio, but for simplicity we will not recalculate the inventory turnover ratio here.

An inventory turnover ratio that is significantly different from that of others in the industry, or the company's in previous years, may be a warning sign. If the ratio is lower, it could indicate that the company is having trouble selling its inventory, or perhaps has obsolete inventory on hand that (similar to a low accounts receivable turnover) overstates the company's current ratio and levels of liquidity. If the inventory turnover ratio is too high, there is a risk the company's inventory level might be too low—it might be losing sales if it does not have enough items on hand to meet orders. Seasonal or unusual inventory transactions at the end of the year could also affect the inventory ratios. As with other ratios, we should consider both time-series and cross-sectional analysis of the inventory ratios.

Accounts Payable Turnover

The **accounts payable turnover** ratio is similar to the accounts receivable ratio, but provides information about the company's accounts payable policy. In its ideal form, it would be calculated as follows:

$$\text{Accounts payable turnover} = \frac{\text{Credit purchases}}{\text{Average accounts payable}}$$

The problem with this calculation is that a company's credit purchases do not appear directly in the financial statements. An alternative formula sometimes used for this ratio is to use the cost of goods sold in place of credit purchases, because the cost of goods sold appears in the statement of earnings. If the level of inventories did not change dramatically during the period, this would be a good approximation.

However, the purchases can also be estimated by adjusting the cost of goods sold for the changes in inventory during the period. Recall from Chapter 7 that beginning inventory + cost of goods purchased − ending inventory = cost of goods sold. Rearranging this equation to solve for purchases gives the following:

$$\text{Purchases} = \text{Cost of goods sold} - \text{Beginning inventory} + \text{Ending inventory}$$

For BIC, the calculations are as follows:

ACCOUNTS PAYABLE TURNOVER AND DAYS TO PAY—SOCIÉTÉ BIC

2008	2009
PURCHASES	
€750,973 − €333,341 + €304,322 = €721,954	€842,952 − €304,322 + €300,973 = €839,603

ACCOUNTS PAYABLE TURNOVER

$$\frac{€721,954}{\dfrac{€92,352 + €92,134}{2}} = 7.83 \text{ times} \qquad \frac{€839,603}{\dfrac{€92,134 + €120,430}{2}} = 7.90 \text{ times}$$

$$\text{DAYS TO PAY} = \frac{365 \text{ days}}{\text{Accounts payable turnover}}$$

$$\frac{365 \text{ days}}{7.83} = 46.6 \text{ days} \qquad \frac{365 \text{ days}}{7.90} = 46.2 \text{ days}$$

As with the accounts receivable, the accounts payable turnover ratio can be converted into a days to pay figure indicating, on average, how long it takes BIC to pay its payables. Also similar to the accounts receivable, the interpretation of the "days to pay" ratio depends on the credit terms. If the terms are 30 days, BIC appears to be taking significantly longer than this to pay; if the terms are 60 days, BIC appears to be paying too quickly. If a company is paying too quickly, it is not taking advantage of the fact that accounts payable normally do not charge interest and hence are "free" credit. However, if the company is paying too slowly, there may be interest charges for late payments. Again, cross-sectional and time-series analyses should be undertaken.

Another thing to consider is that for a manufacturing company many items other than purchases affect the cost of goods sold. For example, a manufacturing company such as BIC will probably include the amortization of its production equipment (which does not affect accounts payable) in the cost assigned to the inventory it produces. Therefore, the estimate of purchases will likely be overstated, and consequently the turnover ratio will be overstated. Also, as noted with the accounts receivable turnover ratio, we should only use accounts payable that arise from purchases and trade payables, and not other payable amounts that a company might have outstanding, such as interest payable. In BIC's case, the account title "trade and other payables" implies that other amounts are included. In BIC's case, we cannot really understand the payables ratios without knowing more details of the amounts that are included in the cost of goods sold and other payables.

Solvency Ratios

Solvency, or long-term liquidity, refers to the company's ability to pay its obligations in the long term (meaning more than one year into the future). A time-series analysis of the statement of cash flows and the patterns of cash flow over time should provide much of the insight you need to assess a company's abilities to pay its long-term debt. Two dimensions are used to assess solvency: (1) risk, based on the level of leverage in the company, and (2) coverage, based on the company's ability to meet its interest and debt payments. There are at least four ratios that are generally used in the assessment of long-term liquidity: the debt to equity ratio, the debt to total assets ratios, the times interest earned ratio, and the operating cash flow to total debt ratio. The first two of these are often referred to as leverage ratios, and the latter two as coverage ratios.

Leverage Ratios: Debt to Equity Ratio and Debt to Total Assets Ratio

From our earlier discussion about leverage, you know that leverage means a company uses debt to finance some of its assets and that the more leverage a company has, the riskier its situation is and the higher its fixed commitments to pay interest are. Comparing the amount of debt with the amount of equity in a company is important in assessing its ability to pay off these debts in the long term. There are different ratios that can be used to assess the extent to which a company is leveraged. We will use the two that have been introduced earlier in the book: debt to equity and debt to total assets.

The **debt to equity ratio** expresses the company's total debt as a percentage of its total shareholders' equity, and is calculated as follows:

$$\text{Debt to equity} = \frac{\text{Total liabilities}}{\text{Shareholders' equity}}$$

BIC's debt to equity ratio follows:

DEBT TO EQUITY RATIO—SOCIÉTÉ BIC

2008	2009
$= \dfrac{€245{,}683 + €214{,}610}{€1{,}172{,}113} = 0.39$	$= \dfrac{€352{,}867 + €371{,}971}{€1{,}304{,}065} = 0.56$

The debt to equity ratio tells you that the amount of debt BIC uses in its financing has increased from 39% of the amount of its equity in 2008 to 56% in 2009. In other words, BIC's debt has increased to slightly more than half of its equity. Despite the increase in the use of debt, BIC still uses equity more than debt to finance its assets. If the ratio were equal to 1, it would indicate that equal amounts of debt and equity are used to finance assets.

The second ratio, **debt to total assets**, focuses on what portion of a company's assets is financed by debt. It is calculated as the ratio of the total liabilities to total assets (or total liabilities plus the shareholders' equity), as follows:

$$\text{Debit to total assets} = \frac{\text{Total liabilities}}{\text{Total assets}}$$

For BIC, this ratio is the following:

DEBT TO TOTAL ASSETS RATIO—SOCIÉTÉ BIC

2008	2009
$= \dfrac{€245{,}683 + €214{,}610}{€1{,}632{,}046} = 0.28$	$= \dfrac{€352{,}867 + €371{,}971}{€2{,}029{,}122} = 0.36$

This ratio shows that for BIC the portion of its total assets financed by debt increased from 28% in 2008 to 36% in 2009—the same trend as the debt to equity ratio. A review of BIC's balance sheet indicates a large increase in non-current borrowings from 2008 to 2009 (from €11,078 to €161,466) and an increase in current borrowings (from €21,806 to €53,695). These increases, totalling €182,277, would explain the increase in both of the leverage ratios. Why has there been such a dramatic increase in the debt? Recall that BIC made acquisitions in 2009: a review of the notes to the financial statements indicates that the acquisitions were financed primarily by five-year loans. The increase in borrowings is a bit surprising, given the large amounts of cash and cash equivalents on hand that we identified in the analysis of short-term liquidity. BIC has more than enough cash on hand to pay off the long-term debt in full. Perhaps the company intends to use the funds in the near future for other projects or to pay dividends to shareholders. Having calculated these ratios, analysts would now try to find answers to the questions they raise. Ratio calculations are just the starting point for analysts when evaluating a company.

The two leverage ratios have portrayed similar messages to the user in different ways. Because of the variety of ways in which this information can be determined, you need to know exactly what formula was used so that you can appropriately interpret the results. Is the level of debt represented in these ratios appropriate for BIC? Again, a cross-sectional analysis could reveal whether the company has excessive debt compared with other companies. A time-series analysis could reveal the trend over time. As a general guide, however, the average corporate debt on the books of non-financial companies is somewhere between 45 percent and 50 percent of total assets. With a ratio of 36 percent in 2009, BIC is below that average—despite the increase from 2008.

Coverage Ratios: Times Interest Earned Ratio and Operating Cash Flow to Total Debt Ratio

In addition to determining the level of risk that a company is exposed to through its use of debt to finance its assets, users want to assess the company's ability to meet the interest and principal payments that arise from the debt obligations. Again we will use two ratios in our analysis, the times interest earned ratio and the operating cash flow to total debt ratio.

The **times interest earned (TIE) ratio** compares the amount of earnings available to pay interest to the level of interest expense. Because interest is tax-deductible, the earnings available to pay interest would be the earnings prior to the payment of interest and taxes. The easiest way to find the earnings before interest and taxes is to start with the net earnings amount and add the income taxes and interest expense to it. One complication in the calculation of this ratio is that companies capitalize interest when they construct long-term assets to use in operations. This means that instead of expensing interest, a company can record the interest in an asset account. This generally happens only when a company is constructing an asset and incurs interest on money borrowed to finance the construction. In such cases, the adjustment to the ratio is that the amount of interest capitalized should be added to the denominator. The ratio is therefore calculated as follows:

$$\text{Times interest earned} = \frac{\text{Earnings before interest and taxes}}{\text{Interest (including capitalized interest)}}$$

In the notes to the financial statements, BIC does not say anything about capitalizing interest on assets constructed over time. We therefore do not need to adjust the denominator. Earlier in the chapter, when calculating the ROA for BIC, we used Note 6 to determine what portion of the finance costs on the income statement is interest expense. The ratio for BIC is therefore calculated as follows:

TIMES INTEREST EARNED—SOCIÉTÉ BIC

2008	2009
$= \dfrac{€144,936 + €71,386 + €6,735}{€6,735} = 33.1$	$= \dfrac{€147,904 + €70,843 + €9,043}{€9,043} = 25.2$

Included in BIC's group net income is income from associates: investments that BIC has in other companies that allow it to influence the companies' operations but not control the companies (discussed in Appendix B). Our objective, however, is to determine the available earnings to pay interest expense, which are found higher up in the income statement. We could have started with group net income and then added back the income from associates, but it is easier to start with BIC's net income from consolidated entities. In fact, because BIC discloses income before tax separately on its income statement, we could also have just started there and not had to add back the income tax expense. Different companies choose to disclose different amounts of detail at the bottom of the statement of earnings. To be consistent with the definition given, we used a net income figure as a starting point, but as your experience and confidence in reading and interpreting financial statements grow you may find different ways to get to the same amount.

BIC's times interest earned ratios are very comfortable, despite the decrease from 33.1 in 2008 to 25.2 in 2009. The 25.2 indicates that BIC could pay its interest costs 25 times from its available earnings. This ratio helps potential lenders assess the margin of safety as it answers the question of whether the company will likely be able to meet its interest obligations. As a lender, a low times interest earned ratio would be a concern. While BIC's ratio did decline, it would only become a concern to lenders if it continued to decline by the same amount over several years. As it is, the results are consistent with the leverage ratios we examined earlier. BIC has taken on more long-term debt, so a user would expect that increase to cause an increase in interest payments and a decrease in the times interest earned ratio. Since earnings would have to drop to 1/25 of their current level for the company to have trouble paying its interest expense, lenders would see the current TIE ratio as a very positive indicator of BIC's solvency.

The second coverage ratio and final one in this solvency section is the **operating cash flow to total debt ratio**. This ratio measures the company's ability to cover its total debt with the annual operating cash flow. Like the operating cash flow to short-term debt, the higher this ratio, the stronger the indication of the company's ability to generate cash and pay its debt. The ratio is calculated as follows:

$$\text{Operating cash flow to total debt} = \frac{\text{Operating cash flow}}{\text{Total debt}}$$

This ratio is broader than the previous operating cash flow ratio, which included only short-term debt. Because not all of the debt will need to be paid at once, this ratio can safely be less than 1.

For BIC, the ratio is as follows:

OPERATING CASH FLOW TO TOTAL DEBT—SOCIÉTÉ BIC

2008	2009
$= \dfrac{€225,104}{€245,683 + €214,610} = 0.49$	$= \dfrac{€343,100}{€352,867 + €371,971} = 0.47$

In the calculation of this ratio, we have assumed that BIC's total debt is the same as its total liabilities. Some analysts might prefer to focus strictly on the borrowing liabilities, such as long-term debt, and not include such items as warranty provisions, which may be satisfied by providing products or services as opposed to cash. The use of total liabilities is a more conservative approach, and results in a more stringent assessment of a company's solvency.

Operating cash flow increased from 2008 to 2009, but as we have noted, total liabilities also increased over the same period. The decrease in the ratio therefore is very small, from 0.49 to 0.47. What this ratio tells us is that almost half of BIC's total liabilities could be paid off with the current levels of operating cash flow.

Another way of looking at this ratio is to determine how many years of operating cash flow at the current level would be required to pay off the total debt. In 2009, the ratio of 0.47 could be converted into 2.11 years, by inverting the ratio (€724,838/€343,140). In other words, with the current level of operating cash flow, it would take the company just over two years to generate enough cash to pay off all the debt existing in 2009. Remember that some of the debt must be paid off in the following year and the rest over several years, depending on the maturity dates associated with the debt. You would need to read the notes associated with the long-term debt to determine if the current level of operating cash flow will be sufficient for the company's future cash needs. All of BIC's long-term debt is repayable in instalments over the next five years, which means that with an operating cash flow to total debt ratio of 0.47 the company is relatively comfortable in its ability to repay its debt from operating cash flows.

Investors use different ratios to screen investments for different factors they are interested in. The Accounting in the News story above explains how Warren Buffet uses ratios, including some we have talked about, to screen potential investments. Warren Buffett is an American investor, and the primary shareholder and CEO of Berkshire Hathaway, based in Omaha, Nebraska. He is sometimes referred to as the "Oracle of Omaha." Through Berkshire Hathaway, a company with a market capitalization of more than US$200 billion, he follows a philosophy of value investing and holds investments in a large number of diverse companies, including The Coca-Cola Company, GEICO Insurance, *The Washington Post*, and Wells Fargo.

Equity Analysis Ratios

LEARNING OBJECTIVE 5

Calculate and explain the uses of the earnings per share ratio and the price/earnings ratio.

Equity analysts are interested in the long-term risk and return of the company, as measured by many of the ratios discussed so far. But equity analysts and investors are uniquely interested in the relative value of the company's shares. They use valuation techniques that you will learn about in finance courses to value a share, or an entire company, and compare those values to current market prices to determine if the company is an attractive investment. There are two ratios related to the financial statements that are used in their analysis, the earnings per share ratio and the price-earnings multiple.

Basic Earnings Per Share

The **basic earnings per share ratio** is quoted quite often in the financial press and is of great interest to shareholders. Introduced in Chapter 4 in its simplest form, it is the company's net earnings divided by the weighted average number of common shares outstanding. Although this ratio may be of some help in analyzing a company's results, its usefulness is limited. The major problem with using it as a measure of performance is that it ignores the level of investment. Companies with the same earnings per share might have very different rates of return, depending on their investment in net assets. The other limitation is that the shares of different companies are not equivalent, and companies with the same overall level of profit may have different earnings per share figures because they have a different number of shares outstanding. For these reasons,

accounting in the news

Buying Like Buffett

Everyone would like to know what Warren Buffett's next acquisition might be. The Oracle of Omaha makes no secret about what Berkshire Hathaway Inc. is looking for. Companies interested in having Mr. Buffett as a partner have to be large, with at least US$75 million in pre-tax earnings, demonstrated consistent earning power, good returns on equity, little or no debt, and a simple business. Considering the essential ingredients that catch Berkshire Hathaway's attention, the *Financial Post* sifted through the 3,261 companies included in the Google Finance stock screener to find those that might be attractive to Mr. Buffett and Berkshire. The criteria included financial health, steady growth, and consistent profitability.

The first criterion—a market capitalization of at least US$5 billion—weeded out the bulk, leaving 620 names. The criteria then applied included a return on equity of at least 8% over the past five years, a net profit margin of at least 10%, a five-year earnings per share growth of at least 10%, total debt of no more than 20% of equity, and a current ratio of at least 2.5. After the final two criteria regarding price—shares trading at no more than 1.5 times book value and twice sales per share—were applied, the screener provided one name, that of J.M. Smucker & Co. Based in Orrville, Ohio, and operating in Canada as Smucker Foods. The company began as an apple cider mill in 1897 and now makes jam, peanut butter, coffee, shortening and oils, canned milk, and baking mixes. Through a combination of expansion and acquisition, it holds the leading U.S. market share in seven food categories. The company's current ratio is a strong 3.74, debt is a modest 16% of assets, while the company's operating margin is a healthy 18.3%. Finally, the shares themselves trade at just 13.3 times trailing earnings, 1.34 times book value, and 1.57 times sales per share.

Smucker's relatively simple business, combined with its long history of steady growth and profitability, makes it attractive, but as Mr. Buffett has said, past performance is no indication of future profitability. As Mr. Buffett has also said, "If past history was all there was to the game, the richest people would be librarians."

Source: Richard Morrison, "What Would Warren Buffett Buy?" *Financial Post*, September 11, 2010, http://www.financialpost.com/What+would+Warren+Buffett/3510564/story.html

the best use of the earnings per share figure is in a time-series analysis rather than in a cross-sectional analysis.

Basic earnings per share is usually a very simple number that considers only the net earnings, preferred dividends, and weighted average number of common shares outstanding. Every published financial statement shows this figure.

The earnings per share calculation represents the earnings per *common* share. Therefore, if the company also issues preferred shares, the effects of the preferred shares must be removed in calculating the ratio. Similar to ROE, any dividends that are paid to preferred shareholders should be deducted from net earnings because that amount of earnings is not available to common shareholders. The number of preferred shares outstanding should also be left out of the denominator. The calculation of basic earnings per share then becomes the following:

$$\text{Basic earnings per share} = \frac{\text{Net earnings} - \text{Preferred dividends}}{\text{Weighted average number of common shares outstanding}}$$

The preferred dividends that should be deducted are the cumulative preferred dividends for the year, whether they are declared in the year or not, and any non-cumulative preferred dividends that have been declared in the year. As Chapter 11 stated, cumulative means that if a dividend is not declared on the preferred shares in one year, the dividends then carry over into the next year. In the second year, both the prior year's preferred dividends and the current year's preferred dividends must be declared before any common dividends can be declared.

Note in Exhibit 12-3B on the income statement for BIC that there is a basic earnings per share of €3.15 in 2009. If BIC had discontinued some of its operations during the year, there would have been earnings per share amounts on the statement of earnings both before the discontinued operations and after. The reason for multiple amounts is that the company would have removed this amount from the normal continuing operations and shown it separately. When users review the financial statements, it is usually with two objectives in mind: first, to see how the company did during the past year, and second, to assess how it might do in the future. Because of this focus on the future, it is important for companies to isolate discontinued operations from continuing operations as only the latter are a good indicator of future operations.

Diluted Earnings Per Share

In addition to preferred shares, another complicating factor in the calculation of earnings per share arises when the company issues securities that are convertible into common shares. Examples of these types of securities are convertible debt, convertible preferred shares, and stock options. The key feature of these securities is that they are all convertible into common shares under certain conditions. If additional common shares are issued upon their conversion, the earnings per share number could decrease because of the larger number of shares that would be outstanding. This is called the potential dilution of earnings per share.

At the end of a given accounting period, the presence of convertible securities creates some uncertainty about how to report the earnings per share number. Should the company report the earnings per share without considering the potentially dilutive effects of the convertible securities, or should it disclose some information that would allow readers of the financial statements to understand these effects? To provide the best information for users of financial statements, we should disclose information about the dilutive effects of convertible securities.

Diluted earnings per share is calculated assuming the worst-case scenario. This means that the company identifies all the dilutive securities that will have a negative effect on the earnings per share amount if they are converted. For example, if convertible preferred shares are converted to common shares, the number of common shares outstanding will increase, increasing the size of the denominator in the calculation. At the same time, the numerator (net earnings − preferred dividends) will also increase: if the preferred shares are now common shares, there will no longer be any preferred dividends, so all the net earnings will be available to the common shareholders. Because both the numerator and the denominator increase, the effect of a conversion on earnings per share is not always negative. Under the worst-case scenario for determining diluted earnings per share, the calculation includes only those conversions that would have a negative effect on earnings per share. The calculation of diluted earnings per share is a heads-up calculation for users. It attempts to tell them how much the earnings per share could decline in the future, if all the dilutive convertible securities were converted to common shares.

The calculation of diluted earnings per share is complex, and beyond the scope of an introductory text. At this stage, the important thing is that you understand what the amount of diluted earnings per share represents.

BIC has stock options and performance shares that are dilutive. Performance shares are shares that will be granted if certain performance objectives are met by executives. As a result of these items, in 2009, the company reported a diluted earnings per share amount of €3.14 (compared with the basic earnings per share of €3.15). If the company had discontinued operations, it would have disclosed a diluted earnings per share from continuing operations and from net earnings, for the reasons mentioned earlier. For BIC, stock options and performance shares have caused the diluted earnings per share amounts to be lower than the basic earnings per share amounts. However, the decline from €3.15 to €3.14 is not a very significant drop. Shareholders should not be very concerned about the potential future conversion of the stock options and performance shares to common shares, because they will have only a small negative effect on the earnings per common share.

In sum, financial statements may include several earnings per share figures, the main ones being the basic earnings per share and the diluted earnings per share. You will often find the earnings per share figures at the bottom of the statement of earnings.

Price/Earnings Ratio

The **price/earnings ratio**, or **multiple**, was introduced in Chapter 11 and compares the price per share on the stock market with the company's earnings per share. Calculated as the market price of a share divided by the current earnings per share, this ratio is thought of by many analysts as the amount that investors are willing to pay for a dollar's worth of earnings. The interpretation of this ratio is somewhat difficult because stock market price levels are affected by many factors and are not well understood. It might help to think of the multiple in terms of its inverse. If a company is earning $1 per common share and its shares are selling for $20 on the stock market, this indicates that the current multiple is 20 (i.e., the current price of the stock is 20 times the current earnings per share). The inverse of this multiple is 1/20, or 5%. This indicates that the shares are returning 5% in the form of earnings per share when compared with the market price.

On December 31, 2009, the company's year end, BIC's common shares were trading on the Euronext Paris Exchange at approximately €48.30 per share. Its price/earnings ratio at that date would therefore have been 15.3 (€48.30/€3.15). The other way of considering its earnings in relation to its share price is to consider the inverse. The company earned €3.15 on shares that were trading at €48.30, which is a return of 6.5%.

Remember that the earnings per share is the portion of the earnings that is attributable to an individual share: it is not the amount that the company normally pays out as a dividend to each shareholder. A shareholder earns a return from both receiving dividends and from the change in the price of the share. Therefore, the return calculated from the price multiple may differ from the return actually earned. Many factors affect the level of stock market prices, including the prevailing interest rates and the company's future prospects. It is sometimes useful to think that the market price reflects the present value of all of the company's future expected earnings. Companies with a low growth potential or higher levels of risk tend to have lower price/earnings ratios, because investors are not willing to pay as much per dollar of earnings if the earnings are not expected to grow much or are more risky. Conversely, companies with high growth potential or lower levels of risk tend to have higher price/earnings ratios.

Many factors ultimately affect the price/earnings ratio, but the earnings per share figure serves as an important link between the accounting numbers produced in the financial statements and the stock market price of the company's shares.

NON-MANUFACTURING OR NON-RETAIL COMPANY ANALYSIS

LEARNING OBJECTIVE 6

Understand the differences that might affect the ratio analysis of non-manufacturing or non-retail companies.

Although the discussion in this chapter applies to most companies in most industries, some differences for non-manufacturing or non-retail companies should be noted. As an example of a non-manufacturing or non-retail company, consider the analysis of a financial services company such as a bank, an insurance company, or a finance company. These companies invest in very different kinds of assets than manufacturers or retailers, and they obtain their financing from different sources. The assets of financial services companies consist of almost no inventories and relatively little property, plant, and equipment. The majority of their assets are loans that they have made to their customers, or other investments. The assets of most non-financial companies consist mainly of property, plant, and equipment, inventories, and receivables.

The liability sections of financial services companies' statements of financial position are also very different from those of manufacturers or retailers. The first major difference is the debt to equity ratio. Financial services companies tend to have considerably higher debt to equity ratios than manufacturers or retailers because of the large amounts of cash received from depositors. The cash you put on deposit in a bank, an asset to you, is a liability to the bank. In the insurance industry, the high ratio results from amounts owed to policy holders. Second, the liabilities of financial services companies such as banks tend to be predominantly short-term in nature because of the deposits received from customers, which are normally payable on demand. Many customers, however, leave amounts with these companies for long periods of time. This means that, although they are technically short-term because the customer can withdraw the funds at any time, in reality they are often long-term in nature.

The higher leverage employed by financial services companies reflects, in part, the lower risk of the types of assets that they invest in. In addition to employing financial leverage, manufacturers also use something called operating leverage. **Operating leverage** involves investing in large amounts of property, plant, and equipment (capital assets with fixed depreciation costs). The property, plant, and equipment allow manufacturers to make their own inventory rather than buying finished goods from outside suppliers. When goods are purchased from suppliers the costs are essentially variable costs and if the sales fall costs can be easily reduced. However, when companies produce their own goods and use large amounts of capital assets, the production costs consist more of fixed costs, costs that do not change when the volume of production changes. The risk is that the manufacturers must operate at a sufficient volume for their profit from the sale of goods to cover their fixed costs. At large volumes, this makes manufacturing companies very profitable, but at low volumes, they generate large losses because the fixed costs cannot be covered at lower sales volumes. Partially because of the amount of operating leverage, lenders generally do not lend as much to manufacturers as they lend to financial services companies.

A complete analysis of financial services companies is beyond the scope of this book. However, it is hoped that this brief discussion of some of the differences between these companies and manufacturers and retailers will provide some insight into how an analysis of these companies may differ.

INTERPRETING THE RATIOS

A final word of caution is necessary when interpreting the ratios you have calculated. The real value of a good analysis is in the interpretation, not merely the calculation, of the ratios. When interpreting ratios, you should be careful to say more than whether the ratio increased or decreased. It is necessary to *interpret* the change. As we have seen, some ratios are better when they increase, like the return ratios, while for other ratios an increase might indicate a worsening of a position. It may also be possible for a small increase in a ratio to indicate improvement, but too large an increase to indicate a concern. For example, a small increase in the debt to equity ratio may indicate an improved use of leverage; but if the ratio gets too big it might indicate that the firm is over-leveraged and becoming too risky. Similarly, an increase in the current ratio may indicate improved liquidity; but if it is too high there might be problems with too much inventory on hand, or collecting accounts receivable.

You should also be careful not to draw conclusions too easily from limited amounts of data. In this chapter—due to time and space constraints—we were limited to only two years of ratios for BIC and no cross-sectional comparisons with other companies or the industry. Looking at longer time-series and cross-sectional comparisons with other companies or industry data would greatly improve the analysis.

Bear in mind that ratios are sometimes referred to as red flags, meaning that they can indicate areas that require further investigation or analysis, but they do not explain the change. For example, a decrease in inventory turnover does not explain *why* inventory turnover slowed down. In a complete analysis of our sample company, SOCIÉTÉ BIC, an analyst would seek more information and discussion with management before making any decisions.

> **LEARNING OBJECTIVE 7**
>
> *Understand the need to exercise caution when interpreting ratios.*

> **HELPFUL HINT**
>
> When commenting on ratios and trends, be sure to use evaluative or interpretative terms. Do not simply make superficial, mathematical observations; show that you understand what the figures *mean*. For example, do not simply say that a ratio or percentage is higher/lower or increasing/decreasing. Instead, try to use terms such as stronger/weaker, better/worse, improving/ deteriorating, when you describe the numeric results.

SUMMARY

At this point in the book, we have discussed all the major financial statements and specific accounting methods and principles that apply to each category within the asset, liability, and shareholders' equity sections of the statement of financial position. We have devoted this final chapter to methods you can use to gain some insight into how to interpret the information that you find reported on the financial statements. By comparing amounts on one financial statement with related amounts on another financial statement, we are able to assess the impact of various items on a company's health and future prospects. We restricted the discussion to fairly simple companies to make it easier for you to learn the basics.

In Appendix B at the back of the book, you will find additional information about more complex organizations. These are companies (usually called parent companies) that buy an interest in other companies (called subsidiaries) to obtain control of the subsidiaries' resources. The majority of the real companies reported in this book are parent companies that have subsidiaries. A company is a parent company if it prepares consolidated (or group) financial statements. If you look back through the examples of financial statements that we showed you in the book, you will see that most of them are consolidated (or group) statements. Complex issues arise in accounting for parent companies, such as how to represent the resources controlled by their shareholders.

Ratio Summary
Exhibit 12-9 summarizes the ratios that were developed in the chapter.

EXHIBIT 12-9

RATIO SUMMARY

Profitability Ratios

$$\text{Net profit margin} = \frac{\text{Net earnings}}{\text{Revenues}}$$

$$\text{Gross profit margin} = \frac{\text{Gross profit}}{\text{Revenues}}$$

$$\text{ROA} = \text{Profit margin ratio} \times \text{total asset turnover}$$

$$= \frac{\text{Net earnings} + [\text{Interest expense} \times (1 - \text{Tax rate})]}{\text{Sales revenue}} \times \frac{\text{Sales revenue}}{\text{Average total assets}}$$

$$\text{ROE} = \frac{\text{Net earnings} - \text{Preferred dividends}}{\text{Average common shareholders' equity}}$$

Short-Term Liquidity Ratios

$$\text{Current ratio} = \frac{\text{Current assets}}{\text{Current liabilities}}$$

$$\text{Quick ratio} = \frac{\text{Cash} + \text{Accounts receivable} + \text{Marketable securities}}{\text{Current liabilities}}$$

$$\frac{\text{Operating cash flow}}{\text{to short-term debt}} = \frac{\text{Operating cash flow}}{\text{Short-term debt and current maturities of long-term debt}}$$

Activity Ratios

$$\text{Accounts receivable turnover} = \frac{\text{Credit sales}}{\text{Average accounts receivable}}$$

$$\text{Inventory turnover} = \frac{\text{Cost of goods sold}}{\text{Average inventory}}$$

$$\text{Accounts payable turnover} = \frac{\text{Credit purchases}}{\text{Average accounts payable}}$$

Solvency Ratios

$$\text{Debt to equity} = \frac{\text{Total liabilities}}{\text{Shareholders' equity}}$$

$$\text{Debt to total assets} = \frac{\text{Total liabilities}}{\text{Total assets}}$$

$$\text{Times interest earned} = \frac{\text{Net earnings} + \text{Taxes} + \text{Interest}}{\text{Interest}}$$

$$\text{Operating cash flow to total debt} = \frac{\text{Operating cash flow}}{\text{Total debt}}$$

Equity Analysis Ratios

$$\text{Basic earnings per share} = \frac{\text{Net earnings} - \text{Preferred dividends}}{\text{Weighted average number of common shares outstanding}}$$

$$\text{Price/earnings ratio} = \frac{\text{Stock market share price}}{\text{Earnings per share}}$$

PRACTICE PROBLEM

The statements of earnings and retained earnings, cash flow statements, and balance sheets of **Le Château Inc.** are shown in Exhibit 12-10. As you will recall from earlier chapters, Le Château is a major, Montreal-based Canadian retailer of men's and women's clothing, footwear, and accessories. Calculate the following ratios for the year ending January 30, 2010, based on the data in the financial statements. Comment on what the ratios tell us about the financial position of Le Château and what further analyses you should undertake. Note that the financial statements are from the 2009 annual report but the fiscal year end for the company is January 30, 2010. Therefore, when reading the 2009 annual report, you will be calculating the ratios based on the 2010 column. With a January year end, the figures include 11 months of 2009—hence the title as the 2009 annual report.

Additional Practice Problems

EXHIBIT 12-10A

annual report

LE CHÂTEAU INC. 2009 ANNUAL REPORT

CONSOLIDATED BALANCE SHEETS As at January 30, 2010 and January 31, 2009
[In thousands of Canadian dollars]

	2010 $	2009 $
ASSETS [note 2]		
Current		
Cash and cash equivalents	23,411	10,034
Short-term investments [note 3]	45,000	56,643
Accounts receivable	2,454	4,791
Income taxes receivable	1,602	—
Derivative financial instruments	59	1,530
Inventories [note 4]	61,234	54,012
Prepaid expenses	1,308	778
Total current assets	135,068	127,788
Long-term investments [note 3]	10,000	—
Fixed assets [notes 5 and 7]	88,437	86,156
Intangible assets [note 6]	2,527	2,487
	236,032	216,431
LIABILITIES AND SHAREHOLDERS' EQUITY		
Current		
Accounts payable and accrued liabilities	27,151	25,403
Dividend payable	4,293	4,239
Income taxes payable	—	2,285
Current portion of capital lease obligations	—	1,008
Current portion of long-term debt [note 7]	11,752	8,746
Future income taxes [note 9]	19	487
Total current liabilities	43,215	42,168
Long-term debt [note 7]	21,464	18,982
Future income taxes [note 9]	3,910	3,176
Deferred lease inducements	10,222	9,691
Total liabilities	78,811	74,017
Shareholders' equity		
Capital stock [note 8]	34,335	30,997
Contributed surplus [note 8]	2,159	2,460
Retained earnings	120,687	107,914
Accumulated other comprehensive income [note 17]	40	1,043
Total shareholders' equity	157,221	142,414
	236,032	216,431

Commitments, contingencies and guarantees [notes 11 and 16]
See accompanying notes

EXHIBIT 12-10B

annual report

LE CHÂTEAU INC. 2009 ANNUAL REPORT

CONSOLIDATED STATEMENT OF CASH FLOWS Years ended January 30, 2010 and January 31, 2009
[In thousands of Canadian dollars]

	2010 $ [52 weeks]	2009 $ [53 weeks]
OPERATING ACTIVITIES		
Net earnings	29,837	38,621
Adjustments to determine net cash from operating activities		
Depreciation and amortization	17,216	16,705
Write-off of fixed assets	538	585
Amortization of deferred lease inducements	(1,540)	(1,414)
Future income taxes	734	(642)
Stock-based compensation [note 8]	341	836
	47,126	54,691
Net change in non-cash working capital items related to operations [note 13]	(7,554)	(15,402)
Deferred lease inducements	2,071	2,532
Cash flows related to operating activities	41,643	41,821
FINANCING ACTIVITIES		
Repayment of capital lease obligations	(1,008)	(1,384)
Proceeds of long-term debt	15,000	18,000
Repayment of long-term debt	(9,512)	(10,074)
Issue of capital stock upon exercise of options	2,696	614
Purchase of Class A subordinate voting shares for cancellation	—	(10,537)
Dividends paid	(17,010)	(20,496)
Cash flows related to financing activities	(9,834)	(23,877)
INVESTING ACTIVITIES		
Decrease in short-term investments	11,643	9,711
Increase in long-term investments	(10,000)	—
Additions to fixed assets and intangible assets	(20,075)	(21,467)
Cash flows related to investing activities	(18,432)	(11,756)
Increase in cash and cash equivalents	13,377	6,188
Cash and cash equivalents, beginning of year	10,034	3,846
Cash and cash equivalents, end of year	23,411	10,034
Supplementary information:		
Interest paid during the year	1,503	1,798
Income taxes paid during the year	15,929	22,009

See accompanying notes

LE CHÂTEAU INC. 2009 ANNUAL REPORT

EXHIBIT 12-10C

annual report

CONSOLIDATED STATEMENTS OF EARNINGS Years ended January 30, 2010 and January 31, 2009
[In thousands of Canadian dollars]

	2010 $	2009 $
	[52 weeks]	[53 weeks]
Sales	321,733	345,614
Cost of sales and expenses		
Cost of sales and selling, general and administrative	260,010	271,119
Depreciation and amortization	17,216	16,705
Write-off of fixed assets [note 5]	538	585
Interest on long-term debt and capital lease obligations	1,503	1,798
Interest income	(780)	(2,299)
	278,487	287,908
Earnings before income taxes	43,246	57,706
Provision for income taxes [note 9]	13,409	19,085
Net earnings	29,837	38,621
Net earnings per share [note 10]		
Basic	1.23	1.56
Diluted	1.22	1.55
Weighted average number of shares outstanding	24,339,461	24,795,576

See accompanying notes

Profitability Ratios:

a. Net profit margin

b. Gross profit margin

c. ROA (broken down into the profit margin ratio and total asset turnover, using 31% for the tax rate)

d. ROE

Short-Term Liquidity Ratios:

e. Current ratio

f. Quick ratio

g. Operating cash flow to short-term debt ratio

Activity Ratios:

h. Accounts receivable turnover

i. Inventory turnover

j. Accounts payable turnover

Solvency Ratios:

k. Debt to equity ratio

l. Debt to total assets ratio

m. Times interest earned ratio

n. Operating cash flow to total debt ratio

www.wileyplus.com

LEARNING OBJECTIVE 8

Use ratios to assess a company's financial health through an analysis of its performance and financial position.

practice problems

STRATEGIES FOR SUCCESS:

▶ Make a copy of the financial statements from Le Château and lay them out so that you can move easily between them without having to flip through the pages of the book. Next, open your textbook to the Ratio Summary (Exhibit 12-9) so that you have the formulae for the ratios close to you.

▶ Calculate each ratio by following the formula and finding the amounts on the financial statements.

▶ The comments on the ratios are the hardest part, because one ratio by itself tells you very little. Refer back to the discussion in your notes, or in the text, regarding what each ratio indicates, and then try to put in words what your calculated ratio amounts mean. The comments about BIC in the body of the chapter can also be used as guides on how to interpret the amounts you have calculated.

SUGGESTED SOLUTION TO PRACTICE PROBLEM

Ratios for Le Château Inc., for the year ending January 30, 2010:

(Amounts used in the ratios are in thousands of dollars.)

a. Net profit margin

$$\text{Net profit margin} = \frac{\text{Net income}}{\text{Sales}} = \frac{\$29,837}{\$321,733} = 9.3\%$$

b. Gross profit margin

$$\text{Gross profit margin} = \frac{\text{Gross profit}^1}{\text{Sales}} = \frac{(\$321,733 - \$260,010)}{\$321,733} = 19.2\%$$

1 Gross profit = Sales − Cost of sales

Note that in the case of Le Château the cost of sales included selling, general, and administrative expenses, so this ratio understates the true gross profit.

c. Return on assets

$$\text{ROA} = \text{Profit margin ratio} \times \text{Total asset turnover}$$

$$= \frac{\text{Net earnings} + [\text{Interest expense} \times (1 - \text{Tax rate})]}{\text{Sales revenue}} \times \frac{\text{Sales revenue}}{\text{Average total assets}}$$

$$= \frac{\$29,837 + [\$1,503 \times (1 - 0.31)]}{\$321,733} \times \frac{\$321,733}{\dfrac{\$236,062 + \$216,431}{2}}$$

$$= 9.6\% \times 1.42 = 13.6\%$$

d. Return on equity

$$\text{ROE} = \frac{\text{Net earnings} - \text{Preferred dividends}}{\text{Average shareholders' equity}}$$

$$= \frac{\$29,837 - 0^a}{\dfrac{\$157,221 + \$142,414}{2}}$$

$$= 19.9\%$$

[a] Although the company had Class A subordinated shares, it has always treated them as equivalent to the Class B multi-voting common shares because they are fully participating. The earnings per share amount is calculated using both the Class A Non-voting shares and the Class B shares. The company has preferred shares authorized, but none outstanding. See Chapter 11 for further discussion of Le Château's share capital.

e. Current ratio

$$\text{Current ratio} = \frac{\text{Current assets}}{\text{Currenty liabilities}}$$

$$= \frac{\$135,098}{\$43,215}$$

$$= 3.13$$

f. Quick ratio

$$\text{Quick ratio} = \frac{\begin{array}{c}\text{Cash and cash equivalents} + \text{Accounts receivable} +\\ \text{Short-term investments} + \text{Income taxes receivable}^a\end{array}}{\text{Current liabilities}}$$

$$= \frac{\$23,441 + \$45,000 + \$2,454 + \$1,602}{\$43,215}$$

$$= 1.68$$

[a] Income taxes receivable would arise from an income tax refund due to the company and would be an expected inflow in the near term; therefore they are included in the ratio. The nature of the derivative financial instruments is unknown, so it is more conservative to exclude them. As the amounts are very small, there would be little effect on the ratio either way.

g. Operating cash flow to short-term debt ratio

$$\frac{\text{Operating cash flow}}{\text{to short-term debt}} = \frac{\text{Operating cash flow}}{\text{Short-term debt and current maturities of long-term debt}}$$

$$= \frac{\$41,643}{\$11,752^a}$$

$$= 3.5$$

[a] The company does not have any short-term debt (no bank loans or lines of credit); therefore only the current portion of long-term debt is used.

h. Accounts receivable turnover

$$\text{Accounts receivable turnover} = \frac{\text{Credit sales}}{\text{Average accounts receivable}}$$

$$= \frac{\$321,733^a}{\dfrac{\$2,454 + \$4,791}{2}}$$

$$= 88.8 \text{ times}$$

$$\text{Days to collect} = \frac{365 \text{ days}}{\text{Receivable turnover}}$$

$$= \frac{365 \text{ days}}{88.8}$$

$$= 4 \text{ days}$$

[a] Total sales were used because no amount for credit sales was given. Because the total amount does include some cash sales, the accounts receivable turnover will be inflated. For Le Château, a retail business, most of its sales would be cash. Even if a customer pays with a credit card, Le Château collects that amount from the credit card company within a few days. It is the credit card company that has the receivable outstanding from the customer. Therefore this ratio has little meaning for this business.

i. Inventory turnover

$$\text{Inventory turnover} = \frac{\text{Cost of goods sold}}{\text{Average inventory}}$$

$$= \frac{\$260,010^a}{\dfrac{\$61,234 + \$54,012}{2}}$$

$$= 4.5 \text{ times}$$

$$\text{Days inventory held} = \frac{365 \text{ days}}{\text{Inventory turnover}}$$

$$= \frac{365 \text{ days}}{4.5}$$

$$= 81 \text{ days}$$

[a] Cost of sales and selling, general, and administrative expenses were used because the company did not disclose cost of goods sold separately. Because other operating expenses were included in the numerator, the inventory turnover will be inflated. It will actually take longer to sell the inventory than is indicated by this ratio.

j. Accounts payable turnover

$$\text{Accounts payable turnover} = \frac{\text{Credit purchases}^a}{\text{Average accounts payable}}$$

$$= \frac{\$260,010 - \$54,012 + \$61,234}{\dfrac{\$27,151 + \$25,403}{2}}$$

$$= 10.2$$

$$\text{Days to pay} = \frac{365 \text{ days}}{\text{Payable turnover}}$$

$$= \frac{365 \text{ days}}{10.2}$$

$$= 36 \text{ days}$$

^{a}Credit purchases = cost of goods sold − beginning inventory + ending inventory. As noted in the inventory turnover ratio, the cost of sales includes selling, general, and administrative expenses, which might overstate this ratio. However, the accounts payable number also includes accrued liabilities, some of which could arise from the operating expenses. The combination of these two factors makes this ratio difficult to interpret or to compare to other companies.

k. Debt to equity

$$\text{Debt to equity} = \frac{\text{Total liabilities}}{\text{Shareholders' equity}}$$

$$= \frac{\$78,811}{\$157,221}$$

$$= 50.1\%$$

l. Debt to total assets

$$\text{Debt to total assets} = \frac{\text{Total liabilities}}{\text{Total assets}}$$

$$= \frac{\$78,811}{\$236,032}$$

$$= 33.4\%$$

m. Times interest earned

$$\text{TIE} = \frac{\text{Net earnings} + \text{Taxes} + \text{Interest}}{\text{Interest}}$$

$$= \frac{\$29,837 + \$13,409 + \$1,503}{\$1,503}$$

$$= 29.8 \text{ times}$$

n. Operating cash flow to total debt

$$\text{Operating cash flow to total} = \frac{\text{Operating cash flow}}{\text{Total debt}^{a}}$$

$$= \frac{\$41,643}{\$78,811}$$

$$= 0.53$$

[a] Total liabilities is used for total debt as it is the most conservative measure.

Profitability Ratios

In analyzing the performance of any company, first consider the net earnings and its trend. For Le Château, the net earnings amount is positive but lower than in 2009. On reviewing the statement of earnings, both sales and net earnings decreased from 2009 to 2010, a result of the difficult retail environment during the economic slowdown of the period. Net earnings decreased by more than sales (22% vs. 7%). The net profit margin of 9.3% is therefore likely lower than in 2009.

Next, consider the ROA and ROE ratios. Despite the drop in earnings, ROA and ROE appear to be good. ROA is 13.6% and the ROE is 19.9%. The ROE of 19.9% is significantly larger than the ROA and indicates that the company is using leverage effectively. From the breakdown in the ROA calculation, the strong performance by Le Château can be attributed to its profit margin (9.6%), and not its asset turnover (1.42 times). With a gross profit margin (after selling, general, and administrative expenses) of 19.2%, Le Château appears to have a reasonable markup on its merchandise, but comparing the results of previous years and competitors would be useful.

Further analyses would include common size financial statements to determine the trends in the cost of goods sold and other expenses (shown in Exhibit 12-11), and trend analyses of the ROA and ROE.

EXHIBIT 12-11

LE CHÂTEAU INC.
Common Size Income Statement

	2010	2009
Sales	100.0%	100.0%
Cost of sales and selling, general, and administrative	80.8%	78.4%
Depreciation and amortization	5.4%	4.8%
Write-off of fixed assets	0.2%	0.2%
Interest on long-term debt and capital lease obligations	0.5%	0.5%
Interest income	−0.2%	−0.7%
Total expenses	86.6%	83.3%
Earnings before income taxes	13.4%	16.7%
Provision for income taxes	4.2%	5.5%
Net earnings	9.3%	11.2%

These common size statements show that, as expected, the net profit margin declined in 2010. Cost of sales and general expenses increased by 2.4% and total expenses by 3.4%, but lower income taxes resulted in the net profit margin decreasing by less than 2.0%. These common size earnings statements indicate some concern about the company's profitability compared to the previous year. If many of the costs are fixed, and if sales recover in 2011, profitability should improve as well; if sales do not recover, or 2010 reflects new rising costs, then profitability may continue at this lower level in the future.

Short-Term Liquidity Ratios

The current ratio is high at 3.13. The difference between the current ratio and the quick ratio of 1.68 indicates that the company has about half of its current assets tied up in inventory, which would be reasonable for a retailer. The high level of both the current ratio and the quick ratio shows that Le Château has a good liquidity position and will be able it to pay its liabilities as they come due. The cash flow from operations on the cash flow statement is positive and significantly larger than the net earnings amount. This, combined with the fact that the company's sales are primarily cash, provides evidence that the company does not have a cash flow problem. The operating cash flow to short-term debt ratio at 3.5 shows that the company generates enough cash from operations to settle short-term debt. Overall liquidity appears strong for Le Château, despite the decrease in sales and net earnings.

Activity Ratios

The turnover figures are interesting and some may be distorted. As a retailer, Le Château sells primarily for cash, which is confirmed in the accounts receivable turnover of 88.8 times, indicating there are only 4 days of sales in accounts receivable. In calculating the ratio, we were not able to use credit sales, because that amount was not disclosed. Most likely only a very small portion of sales are on credit. Using the total sales amount to calculate this ratio has obviously affected the turnover rate; by how much, we cannot determine. The inventory turnover of 4.5 times indicates that there is enough inventory on hand to cover 81 days of sales. In the retail fashion business, there are normally four selling seasons, and Le Château's turnover appears to indicate that inventory is sold once per season. This is likely similar to other fashion retailers.

The accounts payable turnover of 10.2 times indicates that the company pays its suppliers an average of 36 days after incurring the obligation. However, this ratio is obviously distorted by the inclusion of accrued liabilities in the denominator and the cost of sales and selling, general, and administrative expenses in the numerator. As there are more items included than just the amounts owed to suppliers of inventory, this ratio is impossible to interpret.

Solvency Ratios

Le Chateau Inc.'s debt to equity ratio is 50%, indicating that total debt is half of equity or, as the debt to total assets ratio indicates, the company is approximately one-third financed by debt, and two-thirds by equity. Looking at the balance sheet, you can see that approximately one-third of total liabilities are accounts payable. Large payables would be expected in a company with large amounts of inventory, such as Le Château. As noted in the discussion of the profitability ratios, Le Château has been able to make good use of leverage to increase its ROE above its ROA. Should Le Château increase its leverage more? High debt/equity ratios require a stable market for the products sold. With the fall in sales and earnings that the company has experienced in the past year, it is unlikely that an increase in leverage would be viewed favourably by the lending or equity markets. The company needs to maintain flexibility in case sales are slow to recover to previous levels. Le Château is probably not looking to increase its leverage, and with the strong short-term liquidity position noted earlier could even reduce its leverage if necessary.

practice problems

The times interest earned ratio of 29.8 indicates that Le Château can pay its interest expense almost 30 times from its earnings before interest; this is a very strong position. The operating cash flow to total debt ratio of 0.53 indicates that the company could repay its entire debt in two years from operating cash flows. The high times interest earned ratio plus the strong operating cash flow to total debt ratio indicate that the current level of debt in the company is not a problem for Le Château; it is in a good position to pay its interest and meet its total debt obligations.

Interesting information can be found in the cash flow statement. In 2010, the cash inflow from operating activities was positive and did not decrease from 2009, even though net earnings decreased. Cash is being used to invest in property and equipment, and long-term investments, which is also a good sign. The company has both repaid long-term debt and been able to raise money from new debt. Le Château consistently pays large dividends. As an investor, if you were looking for an investment that would pay you periodically in the form of dividends, Le Château may be a good choice.

In conclusion, Le Chateau's sales and net earnings fell in 2010 compared to 2009, likely as a result of the economic slowdown. But the company has strong short-term liquidity and good solvency; it continues to pay dividends and appears to be well situated to weather the slowdown. Le Chateau's profitability in 2011 will be a key indicator of the company's future potential. Will sales recover and costs return to historical lower levels?

ABBREVIATIONS USED

EPS	Earnings per share	ROE	Return on equity
P/E ratio	Price/earnings ratio	TIE	Times interest earned
ROA	Return on assets		

GLOSSARY

Accounts payable turnover   The number of times that accounts payable are replaced during the accounting period. It is usually calculated as the credit purchases divided by the average accounts payable.

Accounts receivable turnover   The number of times that accounts receivable are replaced during the accounting period. It is calculated as the credit sales divided by the average accounts receivable.

Basic earnings per share   A measure of a company's performance, calculated by dividing the earnings for the period that are available to common shareholders by the weighted average number of common shares that were outstanding during the period.

Common size data   Data that are prepared from the financial statements and which express each element of the statement as a percentage of a denominator value. On the statement of earnings, the denominator value is usually the net sales revenues. On the statement of financial position, the denominator is total assets.

Cross-sectional analysis   A type of financial statement analysis in which one company is compared with other companies, either within the same industry or across industries, for the same time period.

Current ratio   A measure of a company's short-term liquidity. It is measured as the ratio of the company's current assets divided by the current liabilities.

Debt to equity ratio   A measure of a company's leverage. There are numerous definitions of this ratio, but the one used in this chapter is total liabilities divided by total equity.

Debt to total assets   A measure of a company's leverage calculated as total liabilities divided by total assets.

Diluted earnings per share   A type of earnings per share calculation whose purpose is to provide the lowest possible earnings per share figure under the assumption that all the company's convertible securities and options have been converted into common shares. It measures the maximum potential dilution in earnings per share that would occur under these assumed conversions.

Gross profit margin   A profitability ratio that compares the gross profit to a company's sales. It measures what portion of each sales dollar is available to cover other expenses after covering the cost of goods sold.

Inventory turnover   The number of times that inventory is replaced during the accounting period. It is calculated as the cost of goods sold divided by the average inventory.

Leverage   A company's use of debt to improve the return to shareholders.

Net profit margin   A profitability measure that compares a company's net earnings to its total revenues. It measures what portion of each sales dollar is left after covering all the expenses.

Operating cash flow to short-term debt ratio   A short-term liquidity ratio that measures a company's ability to cover its short-term debt with the cash flow generated from operations.

Operating cash flow to total debt ratio   A long-term liquidity ratio that measures a company's ability to cover all its debt with the cash flow generated from operations.

Operating leverage   The replacement of variable costs with fixed costs in the operation of the company. If a sufficient volume of sales is achieved, the investment in fixed costs can be very profitable.

Optimal capital structure   A theoretical point at which the company's leverage maximizes the return to the shareholders.

Price/earnings (P/E) ratio   A performance ratio that compares the market price per share with the earnings per share.

Profit margin ratio   A profitability measure that compares a company's after-tax but before-interest income with its revenues, used when calculating ROA.

Prospective analysis   A financial statement analysis of a company that attempts to look forward in time to predict future results.

Quick ratio   A measure of a company's short-term liquidity, calculated by dividing the current assets less inventories and, in most cases, prepaid items by the current liabilities.

Raw financial data   The data that appear directly in the financial statements.

Retrospective analysis   A financial statement analysis of a company that looks only at historical data.

Return on assets (ROA)   A measure of profitability that measures the return on the investment in assets. It is calculated by dividing the earnings after tax but before interest by the average total assets during the accounting period. The ROA ratio can be split into the profit margin ratio and the total asset turnover ratio.

Return on equity (ROE)   A measure of profitability that measures the return on the investment made by common shareholders. It is calculated by dividing the net earnings less dividends for preferred shares by the average common shareholders' equity during the accounting period.

Time-series analysis   A type of financial statement analysis in which data are analyzed over time.

Times interest earned (TIE) ratio   A measure of a company's long-term liquidity. It measures the company's ability to make its interest payments. It is calculated by dividing the earnings before interest and taxes by the interest expense.

Total asset turnover ratio   A measure of company performance that shows the number of dollars of sales that is generated per dollar of investment in total assets. It is calculated by dividing the sales revenue by the average total assets for the accounting period.

Working capital   The difference between current assets and current liabilities. It is a function of the company's management of the cash cycle and a component of short-term liquidity.

ASSIGNMENT MATERIAL

Assessing Your Recall

12-1   Explain why knowledge of a business is important when using ratio analysis. What aspects of the business should you learn more about?

12-2   Describe the information that a user can get from reading the auditors' report.

12-3   Would an investor find retrospective analysis or prospective analysis more useful in making investment decisions? Why is the other technique used?

12-4   Compare and contrast time-series analysis and cross-sectional analysis.

12-5   Identify the four main types of ratios used in this chapter to analyze a company. What does each group of ratios attempt to measure?

12-6   Write the formula for calculating each of the following ratios:

    a. Net profit margin
    b. Gross profit margin
    c. ROA (broken down into the profit margin percentage and total asset turnover rate)
    d. ROE
    e. Accounts receivable turnover
    f. Inventory turnover
    g. Accounts payable turnover
    h. Current ratio
    i. Quick ratio
    j. Operating cash flow to short-term debt ratio
    k. Debt to equity ratio
    l. Debt to total assets
    m. Times interest earned ratio
    n. Operating cash flow to total debt ratio

12-7   Explain how the accounts receivable and inventory turnover ratios can be useful in assessing a company's liquidity.

12-8   Why are ratios that use cash flows useful under accrual-based accounting?

12-9   Describe leverage, and explain how it is shown in the ROA and ROE ratios.

12-10   Explain, using the profit margin and total asset turnover ratios, how two companies in the same business (use retail clothing stores as an example) can earn the same ROA, yet have very different operating strategies.

12-11   Explain what an analyst might determine from preparing a common size statement of earnings.

12-12   Explain how the current ratio can be manipulated as a measure of liquidity.

12-13   Describe how earnings per share is calculated, and discuss the purpose of producing basic and diluted earnings per share ratios for a company.

12-14   What kinds of analysts are interested in the P/E ratio? Explain why the P/E ratios for two companies in the same industry might be different.

Applying Your Knowledge

12-15   (Common size analysis and differences in profitability)
Comparative financial statement data for First Company and Foremost Company, two competitors, follow:

	First Company		Foremost Company	
	2010	2009	2010	2009
Net sales	$337,500		$1,950,000	
Cost of goods sold	202,500		1,092,000	
Operating expenses	68,250		468,000	
Interest expense	3,375		37,800	
Income tax expense	17,400		70,500	
Current assets	165,000	$142,500	1,020,000	$ 780,000
Capital assets (net)	420,000	367,500	1,530,000	1,425,000
Current liabilities	52,500	42,750	225,000	2,400,000
Long-term liabilities	67,500	95.250	630,000	540,000
Share capital	345,000	270,000	1,200,000	1,125,000
Retained earnings	120,000	102,000	495,000	300,000

Required:

a. Prepare a common size analysis of the 2010 statement of earnings data for First Company and Foremost Company.

b. Calculate the return on assets and the return on shareholders' equity for both companies. For the ROA, break it down into its two component ratios.

c. Comment on the relative profitability of these companies.

d. Identify two main reasons for the difference in their profitability.

12-16 (Common size analysis and differences in profitability and leverage)

Comparative financial statement data for Cool Brewery Company and Northern Beer Company, two competitors, follow (amounts in thousands):

	Cool Brewery Company		Northern Beer Company	
	2010	2009	2010	2009
Net sales	$206,700		$40,500	
Cost of goods sold	100,500		15,300	
Operating expenses	85,400		17,190	
Interest expense	7,800		370	
Income tax expense	4,700		1,130	
Current assets	98,000	$ 90,500	12,700	$ 9,900
Long-term assets (net)	210,000	209,600	29,100	30,700
Current liabilities	71,900	60,800	3,900	4,000
Long-term liabilities	103,900	117,500	8,000	7,400
Share capital	51,200	48,500	17,800	16,700
Retained earnings	81,000	73,300	12,100	12,500

Required:

a. Prepare a common size analysis for 2008 for Cool Brewery Company and Northern Beer Company.

b. Calculate the return on assets and the return on shareholders' equity for both companies. For the ROA, break it down into its two component ratios.

c. Comment on the relative profitability of these companies.

d. Identify two main reasons for the difference in their profitability.

e. Calculate the debt to equity ratio for both companies.

f. Compare the use of leverage by these companies.

12-17 (General financial statement analysis)

The following is an abbreviated balance sheet for Grizzly Grocers:

Grizzly Grocers Ltd.
Statement of Financial Position
As at December 31, 2010

Assets		Liabilities and Equities	
Cash	$ 8,600	Accounts payable	$ 9,500
Accounts receivable	15,500	Short-term note payable	1,800
Inventory	10,900	Mortgage payable	25,000
Land	15,000	Share capital	12,000
Building and equipment	30,000	Retained earnings	31,700
Total assets	$80,000	Total liabilities and equity	$80,000

The company had net earnings of $20,000 on sales of $180,000.

Required:

a. Calculate Grizzly Grocers' current ratio.
b. Calculate the company's debt to equity ratio.
c. Calculate the company's working capital.
d. Calculate the company's net profit margin.
e. Assuming that you have just learned that a credit sale of $10,000 that was included in the sales amount actually occurred three days after the end of the fiscal year, revise the statement of financial position and sales amount to correct this error. Recalculate the ratios in parts "a" to "d."

12-18 (Liquidity ratios)

The financial data for Alouette Resources are as follows (amounts in thousands):

	2009	2010	2011	2012
Current assets				
Cash	$ 120	$ 80	$ 140	$ 160
Accounts receivable	400	520	480	430
Inventories	650	920	1,240	1,810
Other current assets	100	100	150	100
	$1,270	$1,620	$2,010	$2,500
Current liabilities				
Accounts payable	$ 600	$ 660	$ 780	$ 820
Accrued salaries	70	100	120	150
Other current liabilities	100	150	160	300
	$ 770	$ 910	$1,060	$1,270

Required:

a. Calculate the current and quick ratios for 2009 through 2012.
b. Comment on the short-term liquidity position of Alouette Resources.
c. Which ratio do you think is the better measure of short-term liquidity for Alouette Resources? Can you tell? Explain. What would your answer depend on?

12-19 (Accounts receivable turnover)

The Super Gym Company Limited sells fitness equipment to retail outlets and fitness centres. The majority of these sales are on credit. The financial data related to accounts receivable over the last three years are as follows:

	2009	2010	2011
Accounts receivable	$ 181,200	$ 192,400	$ 186,000
Sales	1,634,200	1,788,600	1,947,500

Required:

a. Calculate the accounts receivable turnover for each year. For 2009, use the accounts receivable in 2009. For the other two years, use the average accounts receivable.
b. Calculate the average number of days required to collect the receivables in each year.
c. As a user of this information, describe what trends you see. What additional information would you like to have to help you understand the trends?

12-20 (Accounts receivable turnover)

The financial data for Michaels' Foods Inc. and Sunshine Enterprises Ltd. for the current year are as follows (amounts in thousands):

	Annual Sales	Accounts Receivable Jan. 1	Accounts Receivable Dec. 31
Michaels' Foods	$60,600	$6,200	$8,100
Sunshine Enterprises	30,100	1,800	2,050

Required:

a. Calculate the accounts receivable turnover for each company.
b. Calculate the average number of days required by each company to collect its receivables.
c. Which company appears to be more efficient at handling its accounts receivable?
d. What additional information would be helpful in evaluating management's handling of the collection of accounts receivable?

12-21 (Inventory turnover)

Information on the activities of Novel-T Toy Company is as follows:

	2008	2009	2010	2011	2012
Cost of goods sold	$893,100	$1,002,700	$1,174,500	$1,326,300	$1,391,780
Average inventory	128,450	157,100	206,310	323,420	442,990

Required:

a. Do a time-series analysis of the inventory turnover for each year. Also calculate the average number of days that inventories are held for the respective years.
b. Is Novel-T Toy Company managing its inventories efficiently? Do you have enough information to answer this question? If not, what else do you need to know?
c. Provide an example of a situation where management may deliberately reduce inventory turnover, but still be operating in the company's best long-term interests.

12-22 (Inventory turnover)

The financial data for Ken's Fresh Fruits Incorporated and Al's Supermarket Corporation for the current year are as follows:

	Annual Cost of Goods Sold	Inventory Jan. 1	Inventory Dec. 31
Ken's Fresh Fruits	$ 9,875,600	$ 695,000	$ 695,600
Al's Supermarket	53,885,000	4,776,500	1,040,500

Required:

a. Calculate the inventory turnover for each company.
b. Calculate the average number of days the inventory is held by each company.
c. Knowing the type of inventory these companies sell, comment on the reasonableness of the inventory turnover. Which company manages its inventory more efficiently?
d. Which company would be a more profitable investment? Can we tell? Explain.
e. What are the potential problems with fast inventory turnovers? Would these be a concern for Ken's Fresh Fruits?

12-23 (Inventory turnover)

Clearwater Company and Sparkling Springs are competitors in the bottled water industry. Their financial data (in thousands of dollars) for the current year are as follows:

	Annual Cost of Goods Sold	Inventory Jan. 1	Inventory Dec. 31
Clearwater Company	$100,600	$39,100	$44,800
Sparkling Springs	15,300	4,700	3,050

Required:

a. Calculate the inventory turnover for each company.
b. Calculate the average number of days the inventory is held by each company.
c. Knowing the type of inventory these companies sell, comment on the reasonableness of the inventory turnover. Which company manages its inventory more efficiently?
d. Which company would be a more profitable investment? Can we tell? Explain.

12-24   (Analysis using selected ratios)

The following ratios and other information are based on a company's comparative financial statements for a two-year period:

	2010	2011
Current ratio	1.84	2.20
Quick ratio	1.07	.89
Debt to total assets ratio	.43	.58
Debt to equity ratio	.75	1.38
Earnings per share	.24	.15
Gross profit margin	42.3%	45.6%
Total assets	$2,143,702	$3,574,825
Current assets	$ 965,118	$1,462,763

Required:

a. What is the amount of current liabilities at the end of 2011?
b. What is the amount of total debt at the end of 2011?
c. What is the total shareholders' equity at the end of 2011?
d. Do you think this company is a retail company, a financial institution, or a service organization? Explain.
e. If the company has 1,650,200 common shares outstanding for most of 2011 and has issued no other shares, what are its net earnings for 2011?
f. Based on the information available, what is your assessment of the company's liquidity? Explain.
g. Given the limited information, what is your assessment of the company's overall financial position? Explain.
h. What changes do you see between 2010 and 2011 that appear particularly significant? What explanations might there be for these changes?

12-25   (Analysis using selected ratios)

HomeStar Corp. is a national chain of retail hardware stores with total assets of $2.5 billion. Selected financial ratios for HomeStar are as follows:

	2010	2009	2008
Current ratio	2.35	2.38	2.39
Quick ratio	.56	.51	.58
Inventory turnover	5.57	5.33	5.27
Debt to equity ratio	.68	.87	.86
Return on assets	7.3%	9.0%	9.8%
Total asset turnover	1.96	2.08	2.16
Gross profit margin	7.71%	8.36%	8.73%
Net profit margin	3.28%	3.87%	4.19%
Return on equity	11.4%	15.1%	16.8%

Required:

The economic slowdown that started in 2008 was difficult for HomeStar. Briefly discuss what these financial ratios indicate about how HomeStar was affected by the slowdown. Which measures deteriorated over the period? Which ratios indicate positive action taken by HomeStar during the period?

12-26 (Activity ratios)

The following financial information is for Ambroise Industries Inc.:

	2010	2009
Sales	$5,000,000	$4,500,000
Cost of goods sold	2,250,000	2,025,000
Accounts receivable	585,500	558,800
Inventory	770,800	707,400
Accounts payable	200,750	195,250
Total assets	1,875,200	1,690,500

Ambroise is a distributor of auto parts operating in eastern Ontario that offers 30-day terms and has all sales on credit. The company has a large inventory due to the number of parts it stocks for different makes and models of cars. Most of its suppliers offer terms of 30 days, and Ambroise tries to stay on good terms with its supplies by paying on time.

Required:
a. What is the average time it takes Ambroise to collect its accounts receivable? How does that compare with the credit terms that the company offers?
b. What is the average length of time that inventory is on hand?
c. What is the average length of time that it takes Ambroise to pay its payables? How does that compare to the credit terms it is offered?
d. The operating cycle is the length of time from when a company purchases an item of inventory to when it collects cash from its sale. How long is Ambroise's operating cycle?
e. Assume that Ambroise finances its inventory with a working capital loan from the bank. If Ambroise could improve its inventory management system and reduce the inventory holding period to an average of 50 days, how much lower would the company's bank loan be?

12-27 (ROE and ROA)

The following financial information relates to Smooth Suds Brewery Ltd. (amounts in thousands):

	2007	2008	2009
Sales	$18,360	$25,840	$36,120
Average total assets	23,715	31,965	47,340
Average shareholders' equity	24,664	32,415	51,515
Net income	715	1,845	3,580
Interest expense	120	150	210
Tax rate	25%	30%	30%

Required:
For each year, calculate the following:
a. Return on shareholders' equity (ROE)
b. Return on assets (ROA), broken down into (i) the profit margin percentage and (ii) the total asset turnover rate
c. Comment on the profitability of Smooth Suds Brewery Ltd.

12-28 (ROE and ROA)

Cathay Glass Company's summarized statement of financial position is as follows:

Total assets	$500,000	Liabilities	$200,000
		Shareholders' equity	300,000
	$500,000		$500,000

The interest rate on the liabilities is 7% and the income tax rate is 35%. There are no preferred shares, and net earnings for the year are $13,650.

Required:

a. What is the company's after-tax cost of debt?
b. Calculate the ROE and ROA for Cathay Glass.
c. Explain what causes the ROE to be equal to the ROA.
d. How could Cathay Glass increase its ROE?
e. Calculate the earnings before interest and taxes.
f. Assume that the interest rate is now 9% and that the income tax rate remains at 35%. Calculate the net earnings, ROA, and ROE for Cathay Glass.
g. Compare the ROE in parts "b" and "f" and explain why there is a difference.

12-29   (Debt to equity, debt to total assets, and times interest earned)

Artscan Enterprises' financial data are as follows:

	2009	2010	2011
Income before interest and taxes	$1,650	$ 2,625	$3,300
Interest	150	340	435
Current liabilities	600	800	1,200
Non-current liabilities	2,000	4,000	4,500
Shareholders' equity	4,250	5,500	7,250

Required:

a. Calculate the debt to equity, debt to total assets, and times interest earned ratios.
b. Comment on the long-term solvency position of Artscan Enterprises.

12-30   (Debt to equity, debt to total assets, and times interest earned)

Silver City Ltd.'s financial data are as follows:

	2009	2010	2011
Income before interest and taxes	$6,900	$7,200	$5,700
Interest	380	340	280
Current liabilities	1,010	1,900	2,700
Non-current liabilities	5,500	6,100	5,200
Shareholders' equity	6,500	6,900	7,600

Required:

a. Calculate the debt to equity, debt to total assets, and times interest earned ratios.
b. Comment on the long-term solvency position of Silver City Ltd.

12-31   (Transaction effects on ratios)

Two lists follow: one for ratios and another for transactions.

Ratios:

a. Current ratio
b. Quick ratio
c. Accounts receivable turnover
d. Inventory turnover
e. Debt to total assets
f. ROA
g. ROE

Transactions:

1. Goods costing $200,000 are sold to customers on credit for $380,000.
2. Accounts receivable of $140,000 are collected.
3. Inventory costing $110,000 is purchased from suppliers.
4. A long-term bank loan for $500,000 is arranged with the bank, and the company receives the cash at the beginning of the year.
5. The bank loan carries an interest rate of 18% and the interest payment is made at the end of the year.
6. The company uses $40,000 to buy short-term investments.
7. New common shares are issued for $250,000.

Required:

State the immediate effect (increase, decrease, or no effect) of each transaction on each ratio. You may want to format your answer in a table with the ratios down the left, and the transactions across the top.

12-32 (Earnings per share)

In 2010, Signal Communications Ltd. reported earnings per share of $0.34. Signal had 28.1 million common shares outstanding during 2010 and 2011, and no preferred shares. In 2011, Signal reported net income of $10,926,000.

Required:

a. What were the net earnings for 2010?
b. Calculate the earnings per share for 2011.
c. Will Signal also disclose a diluted earnings per share amount? Explain.
d. Assume that in December 2010 Signal decided to split its common shares three for one. What effect will this have on the earnings per share amount calculated in "b"? Will the earnings per share amount for 2010 be affected as well? Explain.

12-33 (Equity analysis ratios)

Caltron Electronics has 3,000,000 common shares and 400,000 preferred shares outstanding. The preferred shares pay a dividend of $4.00 per share and are convertible into 800,000 common shares. During the year, Caltron earned net earnings of $9,800,000. The price/earnings ratio for the electronics industry is 12.5 times.

Required:

a. Calculate the basic earnings per share that should be reported in the financial statements.
b. Why is it important that the notes to the financial statements describe the preferred shares as convertible?
c. If Caltron purchased its own preferred shares on the market and cancelled them, what impact would this have on earnings per share in future years?
d. Estimate the market price of the common shares for Caltron at the end of the year.
e. What return are Caltron's shares earning, based on the earnings per share?
f. Lightning Electronics, a competitor of Caltron, reported earnings per share of $3.50 for the same period. Do you think Lightning is a better investment than Caltron? Explain your reasoning.

12-34 (Analysis of assets)

You have inherited money from your grandparents and a friend suggests that you consider buying shares in Galena Ski Products. Because you may need to sell the shares within the next two years to finance your university education, you start your analysis of the company data by calculating (1) working capital, (2) the current ratio, and (3) the quick ratio. Galena's statement of financial position is as follows:

Current assets	
Cash	$154,000
Inventory	185,000
Other current assets	21,000
Non-current assets	
Land	50,000
Building and equipment	145,000
Other	15,000
Total	$570,000
Current liabilities	$165,000
Long-term debt	190,000
Share capital	80,000
Retained earnings	135,000
Total	$570,000

Required:

a. What amount of working capital is currently maintained? Comment on the adequacy of this amount.

b. Your preference is to have a quick ratio of at least 0.80 and a current ratio of at least 2.00. How do the existing ratios compare with your criteria? Based on these two ratios, how would you evaluate the company's current asset position?

c. The company currently sells only on a cash basis and had sales of $900,000 this past year. How would you expect a change from cash to credit sales to affect the current and quick ratios?

d. Galena's statement of financial position is presented just before the start of shipments for its fall and winter season. How would your evaluation change if these balances existed in late February, following completion of its primary business for the skiing season?

e. How would Galena's situation as either a public company or private company affect your decision to invest?

12-35   (Ratio analysis over time)

The following information comes from the accounting records of Hercep Ltd. for the first three years of its existence:

	2009	2010	2011
Statement of Financial Position			
Assets			
Cash	$ 22,500	$ 20,000	$ 25,000
Accounts receivable	67,500	50,000	145,000
Inventory	110,000	130,000	220,000
Capital assets (net)	430,000	450,000	500,000
Other assets	232,000	210,000	266,400
	$ 862,000	$ 860,000	$1,156,400
Liabilities and equity			
Current liabilities	100,000	$ 50,000	$ 100,000
Long-term debt	200,000	250,000	500,000
Share capital—common shares	525,000	525,000	525,000
Retained earnings	37,000	35,000	31,400
	$ 862,000	$ 860,000	$1,156,400
Statement of Earnings			
Sales	$ 700,000	$ 800,000	$ 900,000
Cost of goods sold	(420,000)	(540,000)	(630,000)
Other expenses	(170,000)	(220,000)	(218,000)
	110,000	40,000	52,000
Income tax	(33,000)	(12,000)	(15,600)
Net earnings	$ 77,000	$ 28,000	$ 36,400

In each of the three years, Hercep paid 10% interest on its long-term debt, and the current liabilities were non-interest bearing. In addition, the company made half of its first year's sales on credit, and made one-third of the second and third years' sales on credit. Hercep's shares sold for $12.75, $10.00, and $12.75 at the end of the years 2009, 2010, and 2011, respectively. The company also declared and paid dividends of $40,000, $30,000, and $40,000 in 2009, 2010, and 2011, respectively.

Required:

Based on this information, analyze and comment on the changes in the company's performance and its management of accounts receivable and inventory from 2009 to 2011.

12-36 (Ratio analysis of two companies)

You have obtained the financial statements of A-Tec and Bi-Sci, two new companies in the high-tech industry. Both companies have just completed their second full year of operations. You have acquired the following information for an analysis of the companies (amounts in thousands):

	A-Tec		Bi-Sci	
	2010	2009	2010	2009
Cash	$ 10	$ 0	$ 25	$ 25
Accounts receivable	195	140	120	100
Inventory	130	100	110	100
Other current assets	5	5	5	5
Capital assets (net)	350	300	230	180
Current liabilities	110	125	50	50
Long-term debt	200	220	0	0
Share capital—common shares	100	100	220	220
Retained earnings	280	100	220	120
Sales (all credit sales)	1,900	1,300	1,250	1,200
Cost of goods sold	1,250	900	910	900
Interest expense	20	22	–	–
Taxes (30%)	77	56	64	56
Net earnings	180	130	150	130

Required:

a. Calculate the following ratios for the two companies for the two years:
   i. Current ratio
   ii. Accounts receivable turnover
   iii. Inventory turnover
   iv. Total asset turnover
   v. Debt to equity
   vi. Times interest earned
   vii. Gross margin ratio
   viii. Net profit margin
   ix. ROA
   x. ROE

b. Write a brief analysis of the two companies based on the information given and the ratios calculated. Be sure to discuss issues of short-term liquidity, activity, solvency, and profitability. Which company appears to be the better investment for the shareholder? Explain. Which company appears to be the better credit risk for the lender? Explain. Is there any other information you would like to have to complete your analysis?

12-37 (Compare ratios and comment on results)

Selected financial data for two intense competitors in a recent year follow (amounts in millions):

	Zeus Corporation	Mars Company
Statement of earnings data:		
Net sales	$ 3,350	$ 6,810
Cost of goods sold	2,980	5,740
Selling and administrative expenses	95	410
Interest expense	130	175
Other expenses	8	0
Income taxes	62	110
Net earnings	$ 75	$ 375

Cash flow statement data:

Net cash inflow from operating activities	$ 125	$ 260
Net increase in cash during the year	10	37

Statement of financial position data:
End-of-year balances:

Current assets	$ 1,020	$ 1,620
Property, plant, and equipment (net)	1,865	2,940
Other assets	720	1,020
Total assets	$ 3,605	$ 5,580
Current liabilities	575	830
Long-term debt	2,220	3,130
Total shareholders' equity	810	1,620
Total liabilities and shareholders' equity	$ 3,605	$ 5,580

Beginning-of-year balances:

Total assets	$ 3,250	$ 5,160
Total shareholders' equity	750	1,245

Other data:

Average net receivables	$ 350	$ 790
Average inventory	290	575

Required:

a. For each company, calculate the following ratios:
   i. Average collection period (in days) for receivables
   ii. Average holding period (in days) for inventory
   iii. Current ratio
   iv. Debt to total assets
   v. Times interest earned
   vi. Return on assets
   vii. Return on equity
b. Compare the financial position and performance of the two companies, and comment on their relative strengths and weaknesses.

User Perspective Problems

12-38 (Use of ratios in debt restrictions)

Contracts with lenders typically place restrictions on a company's activities in an attempt to ensure that the company will be able to repay both the interest and the principal on the debt owed to the lenders. These restrictions are frequently stated in terms of ratios. For instance, a restriction could be that the debt to equity ratio cannot exceed 1.0. If it does exceed 1.0, the debt covered by the restrictions becomes due immediately. Two commonly used ratios are the current ratio and the debt to equity ratio. Explain why these might be used as restrictions. How do they protect the lender?

12-39 (Cross-sectional analysis)

In using cross-sectional analysis to evaluate performance, what factors should an investor match in choosing companies for comparison? Why are these factors important?

12-40 (Use of ratios for performance measurement)

A company's business strategy often leads to better performance on some financial statement ratios rather than others. For example, management of a high-volume retailer may deliberately keep prices low, reducing the gross margin percentage, in order to achieve a high inventory turnover. Give an example of another conflict between financial statement ratios, where management's attempt to improve one ratio may result in decreased performance on the other ratio.

12-41 (Use of ROA in performance measurement)

Management compensation plans typically specify performance criteria in terms of financial statement ratios. For instance, a plan might specify that management must achieve a certain level of return on investment—for example, ROA. If managers were trying to maximize their compensation, how could they manipulate the ROA ratio to achieve this goal?

12-42 (Use of ratios for investing decisions)

The Accounting in the News story on page 821 describes how Warren Buffet screens potential investments for his company, Berkshire Hathaway. Explain what each of the ratios mentioned in the article would tell Berkshire Hathaway about the companies being considered as potential investments. Are there any other ratios that Berkshire Hathaway could use to determine the same information about these companies? Explain your choices.

12-43 (Use of cash flow ratios)

There is judgement involved in preparing financial statements. For example, management must often estimate warranty expense and bad debts expense. Management may also need to select an accounting policy if generally accepted accounting principles allow a choice. Ultimately, these estimates and decisions affect the determination of net earnings. Do you believe that financial statement ratios using cash flows are more reliable than measures of performance that use net income? Discuss.

12-44 (Ratio analysis and auditors)

Auditors review the financial statements to determine whether the information reported has been collected, summarized, and reported according to generally accepted accounting principles. Although auditors are not expected to identify fraud, they do perform tests to see if there are any apparent abnormalities. If an auditor wanted to ensure that a company's sales revenues were not overstated, how might the auditor use ratio analysis to detect a possible overstatement?

12-45 (Using ratios to evaluate creditworthiness)

You are the lending officer in a bank and a new customer has approached you for a working capital loan. A working capital loan is intended to help a business finance the fluctuations in daily cash flows that arise from the lead-lag relationships of operating a business. Explain how you would use the accounts receivable turnover ratio, inventory turnover ratio, and accounts payable turnover ratio to assist you in your analysis.

12-46 (Use of ratios in decision-making)

Managers, investors, and creditors usually have a specific focus when making decisions about a business.

> *Required:*
>
> Each of the following independent cases asks one or more questions. Identify the ratio or ratios that would help the user answer the question and/or identify areas for further analysis:
> a. A company's net earnings have declined. Is the decrease in net earnings due to
>   i. a decrease in sales or an increase in cost of goods sold?
>   ii. an increase in total operating expenses?
>   iii. an increase in a specific expense, such as tax expense?
> b. Is the company collecting its accounts receivables on a timely basis?
> c. Does the company rely more heavily on long-term debt financing than other companies in the same industry?
> d. In a comparison of two companies, which company is using its assets more effectively?
> e. In a comparison of two companies, which company has used the capital invested in it more profitably?
> f. Has the decline in the economy affected the company's ability to pay its accounts payable?
> g. Has the company been successful in reducing its investment in inventories as a result of installing a new ordering system?

Reading and Interpreting Published Financial Statements

12-47 (Ratio analysis for H&M)

The financial statements for **H&M** are in Appendix A. Alternatively, you can refer to Exhibits 1-3 and 1-4 on pages 23 and 26 to get the data needed for these questions.

Required:

Use the financial statements to answer the following questions:
a. Calculate the following ratios for 2009 and 2010. For the 2009 ratios, use the year-end balance sheet amounts, rather than an average for the year.
  i. Gross profit margin
  ii. Net profit margin
  iii. Inventory turnover
  iv. Debt to equity
  v. ROA and ROE. For the ROA, use the two components of the ratio.
b. Comment on H&M's profitability and use of leverage over the period.

12-48 (Comparison of two companies in same industry)

The Practice Problem at the end of the chapter contains the financial statements and ratios for Le Château Inc. In Canada, Le Château and H&M are direct competitors in the fashion retail market for young adults.

Required:

Use the information from the Practice Problem, the financial statements of H&M in Appendix A, and the ratios calculated in problem 12-47 to answer the following questions:
a. Compare the inventory turnover and gross margin for the two companies. Are there any factors that make this comparison less reliable?
b. Compare the profitability and ROA for the two companies. What do you think explains the differences?
c. Compare the ROE and use of leverage for the two companies. Which company provides a higher return to its shareholders? Which company has more financial risk from the point of view of the shareholders?
d. Discuss the reasons doing a direct cross-sectional comparison of these two companies. Discuss the reasons for not doing one.

12-49 (Ratio analysis for Shoppers Drug Mart)

Financial Analysis Assignments

Shoppers Drug Mart Corporation is a licensor of over 1,170 full-service retail drug stores across Canada. The 2009 consolidated statement of earnings, balance sheet, and excerpts from the statement of cash flows for Shoppers Drug Mart are shown in Exhibit 12-12 (amounts in thousands).

Required:

Based on these financial statements, answer each of the following questions:
a. Calculate the following ratios for both 2009 and 2008, and comment on the changes. For the 2008 ratios, use the year-end balance sheet amounts, rather than an average for the year.
  i. ROA (split into profit margin percentage and total asset turnover rate)
  ii. ROE (no preferred shares outstanding)
  iii. Times interest earned
  iv. Operating cash flow to short-term debt
b. Comment on the use of leverage by Shoppers Drug Mart, using appropriate ratios to support your analysis.
c. The balance sheet of Shoppers Drug Mart includes intangible assets, which includes prescription files, developed technology, customer relations, and goodwill. How significant is the impact of these assets on the ROA calculated above? As a potential investor, would you have any particular concerns about the extent of intangible assets? Explain.

SHOPPERS DRUG MART CORPORATION, LIMITED 2009 ANNUAL REPORT

EXHIBIT 12-12A

annual report

Consolidated Balance Sheets

As at January 2, 2010 and January 3, 2009
[In thousands of dollars]

	2009	2008
Assets		
Current		
Cash	$ 44,391	$ 36,567
Accounts receivable	471,029	448,476
Inventory (Note 3)	1,852,441	1,743,253
Income taxes recoverable	–	8,835
Future income taxes (Notes 2 and 6)	86,161	84,770
Prepaid expenses and deposits (Notes 2 and 4)	75,573	59,327
	2,529,595	2,381,228
Property and equipment (Notes 2 and 7)	1,566,024	1,331,363
Goodwill (Notes 2 and 8)	2,481,353	2,427,239
Intangible assets (Notes 2 and 9)	258,766	212,279
Other assets (Note 2)	16,716	12,114
Total assets	$ 6,852,454	$ 6,364,223
Liabilities		
Current		
Bank indebtedness (Note 10)	$ 270,332	$ 240,844
Commercial paper (Note 10)	260,386	339,943
Short-term debt (Note 10)	–	197,845
Accounts payable and accrued liabilities	964,736	1,018,505
Income taxes payable	17,046	–
Dividends payable	46,748	46,709
	1,559,248	1,843,846
Long-term debt (Note 11)	946,098	647,250
Other long-term liabilities (Note 12)	347,951	303,117
Future income taxes (Note 6)	42,858	30,803
	2,896,155	2,825,016
Associate interest	130,189	118,678
Shareholders' equity		
Share capital (Note 13)	1,519,870	1,514,207
Contributed surplus (Note 14)	10,274	10,625
Accumulated other comprehensive loss (Note 18)	(1,125)	(3,442)
Retained earnings (Note 2)	2,297,091	1,899,139
	2,295,966	1,895,697
	3,826,110	3,420,529
Total liabilities and shareholders' equity	$ 6,852,454	$ 6,364,223

The accompanying notes are an integral part of these consolidated financial statements.

EXHIBIT 12-12B SHOPPERS DRUG MART CORPORATION, LIMITED 2009 ANNUAL REPORT

annual report

Consolidated Statements of Earnings

52 weeks ended January 2, 2010 and 53 weeks ended January 3, 2009
(In thousands of dollars, except per share amounts)

	2009	2008
Sales	$ 9,985,600	$ 9,422,911
Operating expenses		
Cost of goods sold and other operating expenses (Notes 2 and 3)	8,841,170	8,350,367
Amortization	248,794	205,371
Operating income	895,636	867,173
Interest expense (Note 5)	58,215	63,952
Earnings before income taxes	837,421	803,221
Income taxes (Notes 2 and 6)		
Current	249,776	254,159
Future	2,737	(5,083)
	252,513	249,076
Net earnings (Note 2)	$ 584,908	$ 554,145
Net earnings per common share (Notes 2 and 13)		
Basic	$ 2.69	$ 2.55
Diluted	$ 2.69	$ 2.55

The accompanying notes are an integral part of these consolidated financial statements.

EXHIBIT 12-12C SHOPPERS DRUG MART CORPORATION, LIMITED 2009 ANNUAL REPORT

annual report

Excerpts from the Consolidated Statements of Cash Flows

52 weeks ended January 2, 2010 and 53 weeks ended January 3, 2009
(In thousands of dollars)

	2009	2008
Operating activities		
Net earnings (Note 2)	$ 584,908	$ 554,145
Items not affecting cash		
Amortization (Note 2)	250,202	204,533
Future income taxes (Note 2)	2,737	(5,083)
(Gain) loss on disposal of property and equipment	(3,456)	3,436
Stock-based compensation (Note 14)	694	1,498
	835,085	758,529
Net change in non-cash working capital balances (Notes 2 and 15)	(177,724)	(328,806)
Increase in other long-term liabilities	35,757	45,609
Cash flows from operating activities	693,118	475,332

12-50   (Ratio analysis for Maple Leaf Foods Inc.)

Maple Leaf Foods Inc. is a major Canadian food processor with three major lines of business: meat products, agricultural feed, and bakery products. The company's 2009 consolidated statement of cash flows is presented in Exhibit 5-20 on page 374, and its consolidated balance sheet and statement of earnings are presented in Exhibits 10-21A and B on pages 705 and 706.

> ### Required:
> Based on these financial statements, answer each of the following questions:
> a. Calculate the following ratios for both 2009 and 2008, and comment on the company's profitability and use of leverage. For the 2008 ratios, use the year-end balance sheet amounts, rather than an average for the year.
>   i.   ROA (broken down into profit margin percentage and total asset turnover rate)
>   ii. ROE (no preferred shares)
> b. Calculate the following operating ratios for both 2009 and 2008 and comment on the results:
>   i.   Current ratio
>   ii.   Quick ratio
>   iii. Accounts receivable turnover
>   iv.   Inventory turnover
>   v.   Operating cash flow to short-term debt
> c. Examine Maple Leaf Foods' consolidated statements of cash flows and comment on any significant differences in the company's cash-related activities during 2006 and 2005.
> d. Based on your analysis in parts "a" and "b," comment on the company's liquidity.
> e. The statement of earnings includes an expense related to "product recall and restructuring cost." Note 11 describes this as the cost related to severance and lease termination in the processed protein operations, and from the consolidation of the pasta and sandwich operations in 2009. In 2008, $102.8 million was related to product recalls and ongoing restructuring costs. By showing the cost as a separate item on the statement of earnings, how is management hoping that investors will interpret this cost? How significant is the cost to the operating results in 2008 and 2009?

12-51   (Ratio analysis for Magnotta Winery Corporation)

Magnotta Winery Corporation has vineyards in Ontario and Chile, and produces, imports, exports, and retails beer and spirits, as well as wine and ingredients for making wine. The company's 2010 financial statements are shown in Exhibits 2-13A, B and C on pages 136 to 138.

> ### Required:
> a. Prepare a common size income statement for both 2010 and 2009 and comment on any significant changes.
> b. Analyze the company's liquidity by calculating the following ratios for 2010 and 2009:
>   i.   Current ratio
>   ii.   Quick ratio
>   iii. Accounts receivable turnover
>   iv.   Inventory turnover
>   v.   Accounts payable turnover
> c. How does the nature of the business that Magnotta Winery is in help you to explain the ratios calculated in part "b"? Based on the accounts receivable turnover, what credit terms do you think Magnotta Winery offers its customers?
> d. The market prices of Magnotta Winery's shares on January 31, 2010 and 2009, were $1.70 and $1.40, respectively. What were the price/earnings multiples for those dates? If the P/E multiple had stayed at the 2009 level, what would the share price have been on January 31, 2010?

Beyond the Book

12-52 (Ratio analysis of company)

Choose a company as directed by your instructor and answer the following questions:

    a. Using the ratios given in the text, prepare an analysis of the company for the past two years with respect to profitability, liquidity, activity, solvency, and earnings per share ratios.

    b. Even though the ratios calculated in part "a" do not span a long period of time, discuss the company's financial health. Would you invest in it? Why or why not?

Cases

12-53 Cedar Appliance Sales and Service Ltd.

Cedar Appliance Sales and Service Ltd. owns several retail and service centres in northern British Columbia. Financial ratios for the company for the years ended December 31, 2010 and 2009, are provided below. For comparative purposes, industry averages have also been provided.

Ratio	2010	2009	Industry Average
Current ratio	1.6:1	1.7:1	2:1
Quick ratio	0.75:1	0.80:1	1:1
Accounts receivable turnover	8 times	7.75 times	12 times
Inventory turnover	4 times	3.8 times	7 times

The company is in the process of opening two new retail outlets and will need to obtain a line of credit to finance receivables and inventory. To receive a competitive interest rate on its line of credit, it needs to ensure that its liquidity ratios are close to the average for the industry. In particular, the company would like to see the current ratio at 2:1. The company has hired you, an independent consultant, to suggest how it might improve its liquidity ratios.

In preparing your report, you have gathered the following additional information:

    1. The company's credit terms to its customers are net 45 days; no discounts are provided for early payment.

    2. The company policy is to pay accounts payable every 45 days regardless of the credit terms. Many supplier invoices offer discounts for payments within 30 days.

    3. Cedar's policy is to keep high amounts of inventory on hand to ensure that customers will have maximum selection.

Required:

Propose several steps that Cedar Appliance Sales and Service Ltd. might take to improve its liquidity. All suggestions must be ethical.

12-54 Albert Long

Albert Long has just been awarded a large academic scholarship. As he had already saved enough money from his summer job to pay for his current year's expenses, he has decided to invest the scholarship to maximize the funds he will have available for the next school year. Because he will need the money in about a year, Albert wants to invest in a fairly stable company and has decided that RBC Financial seems to be a very profitable investment.

Albert has obtained the company's annual report and has completed a very thorough ratio analysis. However, he has relied heavily on financial statements to perform the ratio analysis and only skimmed the other components of the annual report. You are a good friend of Albert's and explain to him that, although ratio analysis provides a good indication as to a company's financial strength, there is much more information available that an informed investor should consider before making any investment decisions.

Required:

Albert has asked you to help him investigate RBC Financial further. Other than ratio analysis, give him four examples of information that an investor might want to examine in order to fully understand a business. Where might this information be available?

12-55   Hencky Corporation

The management of Hencky Corporation is developing a loan proposal to present to a local investor. The company is looking for a $1-million loan to finance the research and development costs of producing a revolutionary new hand-held computer. Most of the loan proceeds will be spent on intangible costs, such as salaries, and this will therefore be a very risky investment. Because of the risk associated with the project, the investor is requiring some assurance that the company is currently solvent and operating as a going concern.

As the accountant for Hencky Corporation, you have used the most recent financial statements to calculate the following ratios:

	2010	2009
Current ratio	1.8:1	1.7:1
Quick ratio	1.10:1	1.08:1
Receivables turnover	10 times	11 times
Inventory turnover	6 times	5 times
Debt to equity ratio	25.2%	35.8%

Required:

Provide an explanation of how each of the above ratios should be interpreted and what they specifically tell you about Hencky's solvency and ability to continue as a going concern.

Critical Thinking Questions

12-56   (Discuss value of comparability)

One qualitative characteristic that underlies financial accounting is comparability. As you will recall, comparability refers to similarities of financial information between different companies, and consistency of the financial information produced by a company over time. Two of the many ways of achieving comparability are by limiting the number of different ways transactions may be recorded, and by specifying how assets, liabilities, equities, revenues, and expenses will be disclosed in the financial statements.

One argument against comparability is that it limits companies' ability to choose among accounting methods, and thus may result in disclosures that may not be agreeable to management or best suited to the particular circumstances.

Required:

Discuss the pros and cons of comparability, with reference to the analysis of financial statements.

12-57   (Use of subsidiaries to manage debt financing)

A major reason why companies such as General Motors form finance subsidiaries (separate companies that they control) is the potential to increase leverage as they seek ways to finance the manufacture and sale of their products. Such subsidiaries are referred to as "captive" finance subsidiaries.

Required:

Explain why a company that finances its operations through a subsidiary has greater debt capacity than a similar company that finances its operations internally.

H&M

ANNUAL REPORT PART 2

H&M in figures 2009

Dress €19.95

PART 2 H&M IN FIGURES 2009
including the Annual Accounts and Consolidated Accounts

THE ANNUAL ACCOUNTS AND CONSOLIDATED ACCOUNTS

The annual report on H&M's operations in 2009 is in two parts: Part 1 is H&M in words and pictures 2009 and Part 2 is H&M in figures 2009 including the Annual Accounts and Consolidated Accounts.

ADMINISTRATION REPORT

The Board of Directors and the Managing Director of H & M Hennes & Mauritz AB (publ), 556042-7220, domiciled in Stockholm, Sweden, herewith submit their annual report and consolidated accounts for the financial year 1 December 2008–30 November 2009.

BUSINESS

The Group's business consists mainly of the sale of clothing and cosmetics to consumers.

H&M's business concept is to offer fashion and quality at the best price. According to H&M's expansion principle, every store is to have the best commercial location. The business is operated from leased store premises, through internet and catalogue sales and on a franchise basis. At the end of the financial year, H&M was present in 35 markets and the operations in eight of these are on a franchise basis. The total number of stores at the end of the financial year was 1,988, of which 36 are franchise stores, 23 are COS stores, 35 are Monki stores, ten are Weekday stores and one is a Cheap Monday store. Internet and catalogue sales are offered in Sweden, Norway, Denmark, Finland, the Netherlands, Germany and Austria. The new home textile range, H&M Home, is sold via internet and catalogue and at a showroom in Stockholm.

Focusing on the customer, H&M's own designers work with pattern designers and buyers to create a broad and varied range for the fashion conscious. H&M's own design and buying department creates the collections centrally. To ease the flow of goods, H&M is increasingly using the concept of regional grouping. This means that products are purchased and distributed to a group (region) of sales countries. The products are then allocated to the sales countries in the region according to demand in each market.

To facilitate this regional grouping and support the considerable ongoing expansion, the Group structure went through a review and restructuring process in 2007. Among other things, this process involved transferring the central design, buying, logistics and stock-keeping functions to a separate company, H & M Hennes & Mauritz GBC AB, as of 1 June 2007. This company owns the products until they are delivered to the stores. At the same time, the production unit in Hong Kong was reinforced and made into a central procurement department for the Group. This resulted in a new internal pricing model within the Group, the full effect of which was realised in 2008.

H&M does not own any factories but instead outsources product manufacturing to around 700 independent suppliers through H&M's 16 local production offices in Asia and Europe. To guarantee the quality of the products and that manufacturing takes place under good working conditions, H&M works in close cooperation with the suppliers. The production offices are responsible for ensuring that orders are placed with the correct supplier, that the products are manufactured at the right price and are of good quality, and that they are delivered at the right time. The production offices also check that manufacturing takes place under good working conditions. H&M's own auditors check that the suppliers live up to H&M's environmental requirements and high standards with respect to the employment terms of the suppliers' employees. H&M applies the company's Code of Conduct for long-term improvements for employees of the suppliers who manufacture the company's products.

Tests, such as chemical and laundry tests, are carried out on a continuous basis at the production offices and at external laboratories. The goods are subsequently transported by sea, rail, road or air to various distribution centres. From there the goods are distributed directly to the stores and/or to central regional replenishment centres.

The best price is achieved by having few middlemen, buying in large volumes, buying the right product from the right market, being cost-conscious in every part of the organisation and having efficient distribution processes.

ENVIRONMENT AND CORPORATE SOCIAL RESPONSIBILITY

H&M acts in many markets as both a buyer and a seller. This requires H&M to act responsibly and in a sustainable way with respect to the environment and social responsibility. The head of environment and corporate social responsibility issues has been a member of the executive management team for around ten years.

One area of focus is to develop sustainable materials and production methods, such as using organic cotton. H&M's sustainability strategy involves incorporating sustainability work into day-to-day routines in all areas of the company's operations.

The company publishes a sustainability report every year. The report is available at www.hm.com/csr.

EMPLOYEES

H&M's business is characterised by a fundamental respect for the individual. This applies to everything from fair pay, reasonable work hours and freedom of association, to the opportunity to grow and develop within the company. The company's values – the spirit of H&M – which have been in place since the days of H&M's founder, Erling Persson, are based, among other things, on the ability of the employees to use their common sense to take responsibility and use their own initiative.

H&M has grown significantly since its beginnings in 1947 and at the end of the financial year had around 76,000 employees. The average number of employees in the Group, converted to full-time positions, was 53,476 (53,430), of which 4,874 (4,924) are employed in Sweden.

Around 79 percent of the employees were women and 21 percent were men. Women held 77 percent of the positions of responsibility within the company, such as store managers and country managers.

SIGNIFICANT EVENTS

The Group opened 275 (234*) stores and closed 25 (18) stores during the financial year. Of the new stores, 18 (8) were opened on a franchise basis. The rate of expansion has been high; there was a net addition of 250 (216) stores during the financial year,

* including 13 Monki stores and 7 Weekday stores which were added through H&M's acquisition of FaBric Scandinavien AB.

ADMINISTRATION REPORT

which is 25 more than originally planned. The increase in the number of stores added compared to what was originally planned is largely due to the economic downturn which provided opportunities for new store projects, and to the fact that a number of store contracts scheduled for the first quarter of 2010 were completed earlier than planned, allowing these stores to be opened in the fourth quarter of 2009.

Russia and Lebanon became new H&M markets during the year. The first stores in Moscow opened in the spring, while the first franchise stores in Beirut opened during the autumn and were very well received. The opening of H&M's first stores in Beijing was another example of successful establishments during the year.

The proportion of refurbished stores remained at the same high level as the previous year. The investments and costs associated with new and refurbished stores calculated per unit were lower than the previous year.

H&M works continually on developing its offering to the customer. In 2009 H&M continued to develop internet and catalogue sales and concepts such as COS, Monki, Weekday and H&M Home.

Internet and catalogue sales developed well during the year. H&M Home – fashion for the home – which was launched in February 2009 via internet and catalogue sales channels was well received. In 2009 H&M Home's offering was complemented by a showroom on Drottninggatan in Stockholm where customers can purchase products directly.

During the year, the store chains Weekday and Monki opened their first stores outside Scandinavia, in Germany. During the year 19 Monki stores were opened and one was closed. Two Weekday stores were opened and the first Cheap Monday store was opened in Copenhagen in the autumn.

The COS – Collection of Style – brand offers a collection for women, men and children in a higher price segment. Ten stores were opened in 2009 and at the end of the financial year, there were 23 COS stores in total in the UK, Germany, the Netherlands, Belgium, Denmark, France and Spain.

SALES AND PROFITS

Sales excluding VAT increased during the financial year by 15 percent compared to the previous year and amounted to SEK 101,393 m (88,532). The H&M Group's sales including VAT amounted to SEK 118,697 m (104,041), an increase of 14 percent. In local currencies the increase was 4 percent and in comparable units sales decreased by 5 percent.

The gross profit for the financial year amounted to SEK 62,474 m (54,468), equivalent to 61.6 percent (61.5) of sales.

After deducting selling and administrative expenses, the operating profit amounted to SEK 21,644 m (20,138). This represents an operating margin of 21.3 percent (22.7).

The operating profit for the financial year has been charged with depreciation of SEK 2,830 m (2,202). The Group's net financial income amounted to SEK 459 m (1,052).

Profit after financial items was SEK 22,103 m (21,190), an increase of 4 percent compared to the previous year.

The Group's profit for the financial year after applying a tax rate of 25.9 percent (27.8) was SEK 16,384 m (15,294), which represents earnings per share of SEK 19.80 (18.48) and an increase of 7 percent.

The profit for the year represents a return on shareholders' equity of 42.2 percent (44.3) and a return on capital employed of 56.7 percent (61.1).

COMMENTS ON PROFITS

The sales increase during the year was weak, which is deemed to be due to several factors; mainly the recession and restrained consumption and the fact that the market has been discount-driven.

In a time of significant exchange rate fluctuation, H&M's policy* of hedging the mark-up on internal sales of goods to the subsidiaries had a major impact – both negative and positive – on the gross margin in the year's different quarters. There was a total negative effect of approximately SEK 370 m on gross profit during the financial year, which is equivalent to a negative effect of 0.4 percentage units on the gross margin. Despite this, the company achieved a gross margin of 61.6 percent (61.5) mainly due to greater surplus capacity among suppliers and more efficient buying processes.

Cost control within the Group was successful throughout the financial year. Selling and administrative expenses increased by 18.9 percent. In local currencies the increase was 9 percent, which is entirely related to the company's expansion. Selling and administrative expenses in relation to sales excluding VAT increased to 40.3 percent (38.8), which is mainly explained by weak sales during the year. Costs in comparable stores, which were adjusted effectively for the recession, were lower than the previous year.

The 20 percent increase in stock-in-trade compared to the same period the previous year is largely explained by the company's expansion and the fact that sales in the fourth quarter were lower than planned. As sales were weak during the fourth quarter, the stock-in-trade as of 30 November 2009, contains a larger proportion of mainly weather-dependent garments compared to the same period the previous year. This will lead to larger markdowns during the first quarter of 2009/2010 and thereby affect the gross margin negatively compared to the same quarter the previous year.

* For information about the amended currency hedging policy, see page 6.

TAXES

The tax rate for the 2008/2009 financial year was 25.9 percent (27.8). On 1 January 2009 the Swedish corporate tax rate was reduced to 26.3 percent from its previous level of 28 percent. In autumn 2009 it was made clear that the new, lower Swedish corporate tax rate would begin to affect the Group already in the 2008/2009 financial year. The tax expense for the year was thus SEK 225 m lower than originally estimated.

For the full year 2009/2010 the tax rate is expected to be 26 percent.

PARENT COMPANY

The parent company had no external sales (136) during the financial year. Profit after financial items amounted to SEK15,267 m (15,395). Investments in fixed assets amounted to SEK -94 m (-185).

FINANCIAL POSITION AND CASH FLOW

The Group's total assets had increased as of 30 November 2009 by 6 percent, amounting to SEK 54,363 m (51,243).

The Group's cash flow for the financial year amounted to SEK -3,607 m (5,292). Current operations generated a positive cash flow of SEK 17,973 m (17,966). The cash flow was affected by, among other things, dividends of SEK -12,825 m (-11,584), investments in fixed assets of SEK -5,686 m (-5,193), and short-term financial investments with a term of four to twelve months amounting to SEK -3,001 m (4,900). Liquid funds and short-term investments amounted to SEK 22,025 m (22,726).

Stock-in-trade increased by 20 percent compared to the same date the previous year and amounted to SEK 10,240 m (8,500). This represents 10.1 percent (9.6) of sales excluding VAT. Stock-in-trade accounted for 18.8 percent (16.6) of the total assets.

The Group's equity/assets ratio was 74.7 percent (72.1) and the percentage of risk-bearing capital was 78.5 percent (75.7).

Shareholders' equity shared between the outstanding 827,536,000 shares as of 30 November 2009 equalled SEK 49.08 (44.65).

LIQUIDITY MANAGEMENT

In 2009 the longest investment period was 12 months. The Group does not use any derivative instruments in the interest-bearing securities market, nor does the Group trade in shares or similar instruments. See also Note 2, Financial risks.

EVENTS AFTER THE CLOSING DAY

EXPANSION AND FUTURE DEVELOPMENT

H&M's growth target is to increase the number of stores by 10–15 percent per year while maintaining high profitability and at the same time increase the sales within comparable units. H&M remains positive towards the future expansion and the company's business opportunities. For the 2009/2010 financial year a net addition of around 240 stores is planned, 25 of which will be Monki and Weekday stores and 12 will be COS stores. Most of the new stores will be in the US, the UK, China, France, Germany and Italy. The refurbishment of existing stores is expected to remain at the same high level as in 2008/2009.

As previously communicated, the following store openings are planned for 2010:

The first store in Seoul, South Korea will be launched in the spring and the second in the autumn of 2010.

Israel will be a new franchise market in 2010 and the first three stores are planned to open in the spring in Tel Aviv, Jerusalem and Haifa.

H&M is planning to start internet sales in the UK in autumn 2010.

CHANGED CURRENCY HEDGING POLICY

H & M Hennes & Mauritz AB changed its internal transfer pricing model within the Group in the second half of 2007. This involved, among other things, the introduction of currency hedging for the mark-up on the internal sales of goods to the subsidiaries in order to secure part of the Group's gross earnings in Swedish kronor.

During a time of significant exchange rate fluctuation in the autumn of 2008 and spring of 2009, the currency hedging for the mark-up of internal sales of goods to the subsidiaries had a major impact, both negative and positive, on the gross margin in different quarters of the year. To avoid such effects in the future, the company has decided to end the hedging of the internal mark-up with effect from 1 December 2009 and thereby return to the previous practice of applying currency hedging for the Group's flow of goods only. Although the currency hedging for the internal mark-up to the subsidiaries ended as of 1 December 2009, there are outstanding forward contracts that were entered into before 1 December 2009 and that will mature in the first half-year 2009/2010. This means that the majority of the internal mark-up for the first quarter is currency-hedged, which is expected to have a positive impact on the gross margin based on current exchange rates. For the second quarter, a somewhat smaller proportion of the internal mark-up is currency-hedged and is therefore estimated, at current currency rates, to have a more limited effect on the gross margin than in the first quarter of 2009/2010.

During the year the part of the Group's flow of goods (around 10 percent) that was not currency-hedged had an impact on the gross margin that varied substantially in the various quarters due to rapid and significant exchange rate fluctuation. In order to decrease such effects in the future the company has therefore also, with effect from 1 December 2009, decided to apply currency hedging for 100 percent of the Group's flow of goods instead of 90 percent as previously.

GUIDELINES FOR REMUNERATION OF SENIOR EXECUTIVES

At the Annual General Meeting on 4 May 2009 a resolution for guidelines for remuneration of senior executives within H&M in accordance with the Swedish Companies Act was approved. The guidelines below are effective until the 2010 Annual General Meeting.

The term "senior executives" covers the Managing Director, other members of the executive management team, country managers and certain key individuals. The number of individuals covered by the term senior executives is currently around 40.

Compensation to senior executives is based on factors such as work tasks, expertise, position, experience and performance. Senior executives are compensated at competitive market rates. H&M has a presence in more than 30 countries and therefore levels of compensation may vary between countries. Senior executives receive a fixed salary, pension benefits and other benefits such as car benefits. The largest portion of the remuneration consists of a fixed salary. For information on the variable portion, see the section below.

ADMINISTRATION REPORT

In addition to the ITP plan, the executive management team and certain key individuals are covered either by a defined benefit or a defined premium pension plan. The retirement age for these individuals is between 60 and 65 years of age. Members of executive management and country managers employed by a subsidiary abroad are covered by local pension arrangements as well as a defined benefit pension plan. The retirement age for these is in accordance with local retirement age rules. The cost of these commitments is partly covered by separate insurance policies.

The period of notice for senior executives varies between three and twelve months. No severance pay agreements exist within H&M other than for the Managing Director.

PENSION TERMS ETC. FOR MANAGING DIRECTOR ROLF ERIKSEN

The retirement age for Managing Director Rolf Eriksen is 65, which he reaches in autumn 2009. During the first three years of his retirement, Rolf Eriksen will receive a pension equivalent to 65 percent of his fixed salary followed by a lifetime pension equivalent to 50 percent of the same salary.

VARIABLE REMUNERATION

Managing Director Rolf Eriksen, country managers, certain senior executives and certain key individuals are included in a bonus scheme. The size of the bonus per person is based on 0.1 percent of the increase in the dividend approved by the Annual General Meeting and the fulfilment of targets in their respective areas of responsibility. The maximum bonus per person and year has been set at SEK 0.3 m net after tax. Net after tax means that income tax and social fees are not included in the calculation. In the case of the Head of Sales, the bonus is based on 0.2 percent of the dividend increase, with a maximum of SEK 0.6 m net after tax. For Managing Director Rolf Eriksen, the bonus is 0.3 percent of the dividend increase up to a maximum of SEK 0.9 m net after tax. The bonuses that are paid out must be invested entirely in shares in the company which must be held for at least five years. Since H&M is present in markets with varying personal income tax rates, the net model has been chosen because it is considered fair that the recipients in the different countries should be able to purchase the same number of H&M shares for the amounts that are paid out. The future Managing Director may be covered by the bonus scheme according to the principles and within the parameters outlined above.

In individual cases other members of executive management, key individuals and country managers may, at the discretion of the Managing Director and the Chairman of the Board, receive one-off payments up to a maximum of 30 percent of their fixed yearly salary.

MISCELLANEOUS

The Board of Directors may deviate from these guidelines in individual cases where there is a particular reason for doing so.

THE BOARD's PROPOSED GUIDELINES FOR REMUNERATION OF SENIOR EXECUTIVES FOR ADOPTION AT THE 2010 AGM

See below for the Board's proposals to the 2010 AGM.

The term "senior executives" covers the Managing Director, other members of executive management, country managers and other key individuals. The number of individuals covered by the term senior executives is currently around 40.

Compensation for senior executives is based on factors such as work tasks, expertise, position, experience and performance. Senior executives are compensated at what are considered by the company to be competitive market rates.

H&M is present in more than 30 countries and the levels of compensation may therefore vary from country to country. Senior executives receive a fixed salary, pension benefits and other benefits such as car benefits. The largest portion of the remuneration consists of the fixed salary. For information on variable components, see the section below.

In addition to the ITP plan, executive management and certain key individuals are covered by either a defined benefit or defined contribution pension plan. The retirement age for these individuals varies between 60 and 65 years. Members of executive management and country managers who are employed by a subsidiary abroad are covered by local pension arrangements and a defined contribution plan. The retirement age for these is in accordance with local retirement age rules. The cost of these commitments is partly covered by separate insurance policies.

The period of notice for senior executives varies from three to twelve months. No severance pay is payable within H&M, except in the case of the Managing Director.

PENSION TERMS ETC. FOR THE MANAGING DIRECTOR

The retirement age for the Managing Director is 65. The Managing Director is covered by the ITP plan and a defined contribution plan. The total pension cost shall not exceed a total of 30 percent of the Managing Director's fixed salary. The Managing Director is entitled to 12 months' notice. In the event the company cancels the employment contract, the Managing Director will receive severance pay of an additional year's salary.

VARIABLE REMUNERATION

The Managing Director, country managers, certain senior executives and certain key individuals are included in a bonus scheme. The size of the bonus per person is based on 0.1 percent of the increase in the dividend approved by the Annual General Meeting and the fulfilment of targets in their respective areas of responsibility. The maximum bonus per person and year has been set at SEK 0.3 m net after tax. Net after tax means that income tax and social fees are not included in the calculation. In the case of the Head of Sales, the bonus is based on 0.2 percent of the dividend increase, with a maximum of SEK 0.6 m net after tax. For the Managing Director, the bonus is 0.3 percent of the dividend increase up to a maximum of SEK 0.9 m net after tax. The bonuses that are paid out must be invested entirely in shares in the company, which must be held for at least five years. Since H&M is present in markets with varying personal income tax rates, the net model has been chosen because it is considered fair that the recipients in the different countries should be able to purchase the same number of H&M shares for the amounts that are paid out.

In individual cases other members of executive management, key individuals and country managers may, at the discretion of the Managing Director and the Chairman of the Board, receive one-off payments up to a maximum of 30 percent of their fixed yearly salary.

MISCELLANEOUS

The Board of Directors may deviate from these guidelines in individual cases where there is a particular reason for doing so.

NUMBER OF SHARES ETC.

The total number of shares in H&M is 827,536,000, of which 97,200,000 are class A shares (ten votes per share) and 730,336,000 class B shares (one vote per share). Class A shares are not listed. Ramsbury Invest AB, of which the principal owner is Stefan Persson, holds all 97,200,000 class A shares which represent 57.1 percent of the votes, and 3,200,000 class B shares which represent 0.2 percent of the votes. In addition, Stefan Persson holds 186,274,400 class B shares which represent 10.9 percent of the votes. This means that, in total, Stefan Persson personally or through companies holds 68.2 percent of the votes and 34.6 percent of the total number of shares.

RISKS AND UNCERTAINTIES

A number of factors may affect H&M's results and business. Most of these can be dealt with through internal routines, while some are influenced more by external factors. There are risks and uncertainties related to fashion, weather conditions, climate change, trade interventions and foreign currencies, but also in connection with expansion into new markets, launching new concepts, changes in consumer behaviour or how the brand is managed.

FASHION

Operating in the fashion industry is a risk in itself. Fashion is a perishable item and there is always a risk that a part of one of the collections will not be well received by the customers.

Within each concept H&M must have the right volumes and achieve the right balance in the mix between fashion basics and trend items. To optimise fashion precision, H&M buys items on an ongoing basis throughout the season.

The purchasing patterns are relatively similar in the various markets, although differences do exist. The start of a season and the duration of a season may, for example, vary from country to country. Delivery dates and product volumes for the various countries are therefore adjusted accordingly.

THE WEATHER

H&M's products are purchased and launched in stores on the basis of normal weather patterns. Major deviations from normal conditions may affect sales. The effect is the greatest if there is a major deviation at the beginning of a season.

CHANGES IN PURCHASING BEHAVIOUR

There is also a risk that changes in the global economy may change consumer purchasing behaviour. It is therefore important to be aware of such changes and to have a flexible buying model that can be adjusted to different market conditions.

CLIMATE CHANGE

There is a risk that H&M's business may be affected by future regulation and increased costs, e.g. in the form of emissions trading and carbon taxes in H&M's various sales markets. These can essentially be regarded as competition-neutral. The risks that may arise as a result of climate change and natural disasters primarily in production countries can be considered as very limited bearing in mind H&M's flexible business model which can be adapted quickly to changed circumstances.

TRADE INTERVENTION

Buying costs may be affected by decisions at the national level on export/import subsidies, customs duties, textile quotas, embargos etc. The effects primarily impact customers and companies in individual markets. Global companies with operations in many countries are affected to a lesser extent and among global corporations trade interventions may be regarded as largely competition-neutral.

FOREIGN CURRENCIES

The most significant currencies in which the Group's purchasing takes place are the US dollar and the euro. Fluctuation in the US dollar/euro exchange rate is the single largest transaction exposure for the Group. To hedge flow of goods in foreign currencies and thereby reduce the effects of future exchange rate fluctuation, 90 percent of the Group's flow of goods are hedged under forward contracts on an ongoing basis throughout the year.

ADMINISTRATION REPORT

Starting on 1 December 2009, 100 percent of the Group's flow of goods (compared to 90 percent in the past) are being hedged and at the same time hedging of the mark-up of internal goods flows to the subsidiaries is being discontinued. For more information see the text under the heading "Changed currency hedging policy."

In addition to the effects of transaction exposure, translation effects also impact the Group's results due to changes in exchange rates between the local currencies of the various foreign subsidiaries against the Swedish krona compared to the same period the previous year. The underlying profit/loss in a market may be unchanged in the local currency, but may increase or decrease when converted into the Swedish currency depending on whether the Swedish krona has weakened or strengthened.

Translation effects also arise in respect of the Group's net assets on consolidation of the foreign subsidiaries' balance sheets. No exchange rate hedging, so-called equity hedging, is carried out for this risk. See also Note 2, Financial risks.

For more information on currency hedging and financial risks, see Note 2, Financial risks.

DIVIDEND POLICY

H&M's financial goal is to enable the company to continue enjoying good growth and to be prepared to exploit future business opportunities. It is essential that the company's expansion is able to proceed as in the past with continued high degree of financial strength and continued freedom of action.

Based on this policy, the Board of Directors has determined that the dividend should equal around half of the profit after taxes. In addition, the Board may propose the distribution of surplus liquidity.

The Board of Directors has decided to propose to the 2010 Annual General Meeting a dividend of SEK 16.00 per share (15.50), which is equivalent to 81 percent (84) of the Group's profit after tax.

PROPOSED DISTRIBUTION OF EARNINGS

At the disposal of the Annual General Meeting	SEK	15,298,171,245
The Board of Directors and the Managing Director propose a dividend of SEK 16.00 per share	SEK	13,240,576,000
To be carried forward as retained earnings	SEK	2,057,595,245
	SEK	15,298,171,245

The Board of Directors is of the opinion that the proposed distribution of earnings is justifiable taking into consideration the financial position and future freedom of action of the Group and the parent company, and observing the requirements that the nature and extent of the business, its risks and future expansion plans impose on the Group's and the parent company's equity and liquidity.

GROUP INCOME STATEMENT
SEK M

1 DECEMBER – 30 NOVEMBER	2009	2008
Sales including VAT	118,697	104,041
Sales excluding VAT, Note 3, 4	101,393	88,532
Cost of goods sold, Note 6, 8	-38,919	-34,064
GROSS PROFIT	**62,474**	**54,468**
Selling expenses, Note 6, 8	-38,224	-32,185
Administrative expenses, Note 6, 8, 9	-2,606	-2,145
OPERATING PROFIT	**21,644**	**20,138**
Interest income	467	1,060
Interest expense	-8	-8
PROFIT AFTER FINANCIAL ITEMS	**22,103**	**21,190**
Tax, Note 10	-5,719	-5,896
PROFIT FOR THE YEAR	**16,384**	**15,294**

All profit is assignable to the parent company H & M Hennes & Mauritz AB's shareholders.

	2009	2008
Earnings per share, SEK*	19.80	18.48
Number of shares	827,536,000	827,536,000

* Before and after dilution.

GROUP BALANCE SHEET
SEK M

30 NOVEMBER	2009	2008
ASSETS		
FIXED ASSETS		
Intangible fixed assets		
Brands, Note 11	396	443
Customer relations, Note 11	110	123
Leasehold rights, Note 11	744	659
Goodwill, Note 11	424	431
	1,674	1,656
Tangible fixed assets		
Buildings and land, Note 12	492	480
Equipment, tools, fixtures and fittings, Note 12	14,319	11,961
	14,811	12,441
Long-term receivables	551	476
Deferred tax receivables, Note 10	1,246	1,299
TOTAL FIXED ASSETS	18,282	15,872
CURRENT ASSETS		
Stock-in-trade	10,240	8,500
Current receivables		
Accounts receivable	1,990	1,991
Other receivables	889	1,206
Prepaid expenses, Note 13	937	948
	3,816	4,145
Short-term investments, Note 14	3,001	–
Liquid funds, Note 15	19,024	22,726
TOTAL CURRENT ASSETS	36,081	35,371
TOTAL ASSETS	54,363	51,243

30 NOVEMBER	2009	2008
EQUITY AND LIABILITIES		
EQUITY		
Share capital, Note 17	207	207
Reserves	1,514	1,410
Retained earnings	22,508	20,039
Profit for the year	16,384	15,294
TOTAL EQUITY	40,613	36,950
Long-term liabilities*		
Provisions for pensions, Note 18	254	228
Deferred tax liabilities, Note 10	2,038	1,818
Other provisions, Note 19	368	368
	2,660	2,414
Current liabilities**		
Accounts payable	3,667	3,658
Tax liabilities	439	1,279
Other liabilities	2,531	3,255
Accrued expenses and prepaid income, Note 21	4,453	3,687
	11,090	11,879
TOTAL LIABILITIES	13,750	14,293
TOTAL EQUITY AND LIABILITIES	54,363	51,243
Pledged assets and contingent liabilities	–	–

* Only provisions for pensions are interest-bearing.
** No current liabilities are interest-bearing.

GROUP CHANGES IN EQUITY
SEK M

All shareholders' equity is attributable to the shareholders of the parent company H & M Hennes & Mauritz AB since there are no minority interests. See also Note 19.

	SHARE CAPITAL	TRANSLATION EFFECTS	HEDGING RESERVES	RETAINED EARNINGS	TOTAL SHAREHOLDERS' EQUITY
Shareholders' equity, 1 December 2008	207	1,942	-532	35,333	36,950
Translation effects, hedging reserves	–	-386	680	–	294
Deferred tax	–	–	-190	–	-190
Income and expenses posted directly to equity	–	-386	490	–	104
Profit for the year	–	–	–	16,384	16,384
Total income and expenses	–	-386	490	16,384	16,488
Dividend	–	–	–	-12,825	-12,825
Shareholders' equity, 30 November 2009	**207**	**1,556**	**-42**	**38,892**	**40,613**

	SHARE CAPITAL	TRANSLATION EFFECTS	HEDGING RESERVES	RETAINED EARNINGS	TOTAL SHAREHOLDERS' EQUITY
Shareholders' equity, 1 December 2007	207	263	–	31,623	32,093
Translation effects, hedging reserves	–	1,679	-739	–	940
Deferred tax	–	–	207	–	207
Income and expenses posted directly to equity	–	1,679	-532	–	1,147
Profit for the year	–	–	–	15,294	15,294
Total income and expenses	–	1,679	-532	15,294	16,441
Dividend	–	–	–	-11,584	-11,584
Shareholders' equity, 30 November 2008	**207**	**1,942**	**-532**	**35,333**	**36,950**

The Group's managed capital consists of shareholders' equity. The Group's goal with respect to managing capital is to enable good growth to continue and to be prepared to exploit business opportunities. It is essential that the expansion, as in the past, proceeds with continued high degree of financial strength and continued freedom of action. Based on this policy, the Board of Directors has established a dividend policy whereby the dividend should equal around half of the profit for the year after tax. In addition, the Board may propose that surplus liquidity may also be distributed. H&M meets the capital requirements set out in the Swedish Companies Act. No other external capital requirements exist.

GROUP CASH FLOW STATEMENT
SEK M

1 DECEMBER – 30 NOVEMBER	2009	2008
Profit after financial items*	22,103	21,190
Provision for pensions	26	72
Depreciation	2,830	2,202
Tax paid	-6,468	-5,940
Cash flow from current operations before changes in working capital	18,491	17,524
Cash flow from changes in working capital		
Current receivables	-71	-1,343
Stock-in-trade	-1,740	-183
Current liabilities	1,293	1,968
CASH FLOW FROM CURRENT OPERATIONS	17,973	17,966
Investment activities		
Investments in leasehold rights	-180	-446
Investments in/sale of buildings and land	-25	-23
Investments in fixed assets	-5,481	-4,724
Adjustment of consideration/acquisition of subsidiaries	7	-555
Change in short-term investments, 4–12 months	-3,001	4,900
Other investments	-75	-242
CASH FLOW FROM INVESTMENT ACTIVITIES	-8,755	-1,090
Financing activities		
Dividend	-12,825	-11,584
CASH FLOW FROM FINANCING ACTIVITIES	-12,825	-11,584
CASH FLOW FOR THE YEAR	-3,607	5,292
Liquid funds at beginning of financial year	22,726	16,064
Cash flow for the year	-3,607	5,292
Exchange rate effect	-95	1,370
Liquid funds at end of financial year**	19,024	22,726

* Interest paid for the Group amounts to SEK 8 m (8). Received interest for the Group amounts to SEK 466 m (1,070).
** Liquid funds and short-term investments at the end of the financial year amounted to SEK 22,025 m (22,726).

PARENT COMPANY INCOME STATEMENT
SEK M

1 DECEMBER – 30 NOVEMBER	2009	2008
Sales including VAT	–	136
Sales excluding VAT	–	136
Internal sales excluding VAT, Note 5	5,521	5,175
Cost of goods sold, Note 8	–	-32
GROSS PROFIT	**5,521**	**5,279**
Selling expenses, Note 6, 8	-1,898	-1,773
Administrative expenses, Note 6, 8, 9	-1,561	-1,388
OPERATING PROFIT	**2,062**	**2,118**
Dividend from subsidiaries	13,092	12,839
Interest income	113	438
Interest expense	0	0
PROFIT AFTER FINANCIAL ITEMS	**15,267**	**15,395**
Year-end appropriations, Note 23	-41	-663
Tax, Note 10	-608	-534
PROFIT FOR THE YEAR	**14,618**	**14,198**

PARENT COMPANY BALANCE SHEET
SEK M

30 NOVEMBER	2009	2008
ASSETS		
FIXED ASSETS		
Tangible fixed assets		
Buildings and land, Note 12	51	58
Equipment, tools, fixtures and fittings, Note 12	363	356
	414	414
Financial fixed assets		
Shares and participation rights, Note 24	572	583
Receivables from subsidiaries	705	345
Long-term receivables	30	13
Deferred tax receivables, Note 10	56	51
	1,363	992
TOTAL FIXED ASSETS	1,777	1,406
CURRENT ASSETS		
Current receivables		
Receivables from subsidiaries	8,072	8,579
Tax receivables	627	143
Other receivables	13	46
Prepaid expenses, Note 13	14	12
	8,726	8,780
Short-term investments, Note 14	3,001	–
Liquid funds, Note 15	3,644	6,525
TOTAL CURRENT ASSETS	15,371	15,305
TOTAL ASSETS	17,148	16,711

30 NOVEMBER	2009	2008
EQUITY AND LIABILITIES		
EQUITY		
Restricted equity		
Share capital, Note 17	207	207
Restricted reserves	88	88
	295	295
Non-restricted equity		
Retained earnings	681	783
Profit for the year	14,618	14,198
	15,299	14,981
TOTAL EQUITY	15,594	15,276
UNTAXED RESERVES, NOTE 25	825	782
Long-term liabilities		
Provisions for pensions, Note 18	211	193
Current liabilities*		
Accounts payable	133	98
Other liabilities	245	219
Accrued expenses and prepaid income, Note 21	140	143
	518	460
TOTAL LIABILITIES	729	653
TOTAL EQUITY AND LIABILITIES	17,148	16,711
Pledged assets	–	–
Contingent liabilities, Note 26	11,292	11,751

* No current liabilities are interest-bearing.

PARENT COMPANY CHANGES IN EQUITY
SEK M

	SHARE CAPITAL	RESTRICTED RESERVES	RETAINED EARNINGS	TOTAL SHAREHOLDERS' EQUITY
Shareholders' equity, 1 December 2008	207	88	14,981	15,276
Group contributions provided	–	–	-2,044	-2,044
Tax effect of group contributions provided	–	–	572	572
Result of merger	–	–	-3	-3
Dividend	–	–	-12,825	-12,825
Profit for the year	–	–	14,618	14,618
Shareholders' equity, 30 November 2009	**207**	**88**	**15,299**	**15,594**

	SHARE CAPITAL	RESTRICTED RESERVES	RETAINED EARNINGS	TOTAL SHAREHOLDERS' EQUITY
Shareholders' equity, 1 December 2007	207	88	12,367	12,662
Dividend	–	–	-11,584	-11,584
Profit for the year	–	–	14,198	14,198
Shareholders' equity 30 November 2008	**207**	**88**	**14,981**	**15,276**

PARENT COMPANY CASH FLOW STATEMENT
SEK M

1 DECEMBER–30 NOVEMBER	2009	2008
Profit after financial items*	15,267	15,395
Provision for pensions	18	80
Depreciation	94	88
Tax paid	-525	-701
Cash flow from current operations before changes in working capital	**14,854**	**14,862**
Cash flow from changes in working capital		
Current receivables	-1,503	-2,261
Stock-in-trade	–	407
Current liabilities	58	-117
CASH FLOW FROM CURRENT OPERATIONS	**13,409**	**12,891**
Investment activities		
Investments in/sale of buildings and land	4	-2
Investments in equipment	-98	-183
Adjustment of consideration/Acquisition of subsidiaries	7	-566
Change in short-term investments, 4–12 months	-3,001	4,900
Other investments	-377	-348
CASH FLOW FROM INVESTMENT ACTIVITIES	**-3,465**	**3,801**
Financing activities		
Dividend	-12,825	-11,584
CASH FLOW FROM FINANCING ACTIVITIES	**-12,825**	**-11,584**
CASH FLOW FOR THE YEAR	**-2,881**	**5,108**
Liquid funds at beginning of financial year	6,525	1,417
Cash flow for the year	-2,881	5,108
Liquid funds at end of financial year	3,644	6,525

* Interest paid for the parent company amounts to SEK 0 m (0).
  Received interest for the parent company amounts to SEK 113 m (436).

NOTES TO THE FINANCIAL STATEMENTS

CORPORATE INFORMATION

The parent company H & M Hennes & Mauritz AB (publ) is a limited company domiciled in Stockholm, Sweden. The parent company's corporate identity number is 556042-7220. The company's share is listed on the Stockholm stock exchange, NASDAQ OMX Stockholm AB. The Group's business consists mainly of the sale of clothing and cosmetics to consumers. The company's financial year is 1 December–30 November. The Annual Report was approved for publication by the Board of Directors on 27 January 2010 and will be submitted to the Annual General Meeting for approval on 29 April 2010.

The holding of Ramsbury Invest AB (formerly Stefan Persson Placering AB) of shares in H & M Hennes & Mauritz AB represents 12.1 percent of all shares and around 57.3 percent of the total voting power. Ramsbury Invest AB (556423-5769) is thus formally the parent company of H & M Hennes & Mauritz AB.

1 ACCOUNTING PRINCIPLES

BASIS FOR PREPARATION OF THE ACCOUNTS

The consolidated accounts have been prepared in accordance with the International Financial Reporting Standards (IFRS) issued by the International Accounting Standard Board (IASB) and the interpretations provided by the International Financial Reporting Interpretations Committee (IFRIC). Since the Parent Company is a company within the EU, only IFRS approved by the EU are applied. The consolidated accounts also contain disclosures in accordance with the Swedish Financial Reporting Board's recommendation RFR 1.2, Supplementary Accounting Rules for Groups.

The financial statements are based on historical acquisition costs, apart from certain financial instruments which are reported at fair value.

The parent company's functional currency is Swedish kronor which is also the reporting currency for the parent company and for the Group. Unless otherwise indicated, all amounts are reported in millions of Swedish kronor (SEK m).

The parent company

In the preparation of its financial statements, the parent company has applied the Swedish Financial Reporting Board's recommendation RFR 2.2, Accounting for Legal Entities. The Swedish Accounts Act has also been applied. The main deviation from the Group's accounting principles is that the parent company does not apply IAS 39.

CHANGES IN ACCOUNTING PRINCIPLES AND DISCLOSURE REQUIREMENTS

The accounting principles and disclosure requirements applied for 2008/2009 are the same as those applied in the previous year with the exception of the following:

– IFRIC 13 Customer Loyalty Programmes (effective from 2008/2009) – requires that rewards from customer loyalty programmes be accounted for as a separate component in the sale transaction in which they are awarded, and that the amount of proceeds allocated to the award credits, measured at fair value be reported as deferred income and distributed over the periods when the obligation is fulfilled. The application of this requirement has not involved any change in the reported profit or financial position.

FUTURE ACCOUNTING PRINCIPLES AND DISCLOSURE REQUIREMENTS

A number of new standards, changes and interpretations of existing standards have been published but have not yet entered into force. The standards, amendments and interpretations below, which are deemed applicable to the Group, are not expected to have any effect on the consolidated accounts on their introduction beyond the provision of supplementary information in certain cases:

– IFRS 3 Business Combinations (revisions) and related revisions to IAS 27 Consolidated and Separate Financial Statements (effective from 2009/2010) – affect the accounting of possible future acquisitions and disposals and transactions with minority shareholders.

– IFRS 7, Financial Instruments: Disclosures, revision (effective from 2009/2010) – involves greater disclosure with respect to financial instruments.

– IFRS 8 Operating Segments (effective from 2009/2010) – contains disclosure requirements with respect to the Group's operating segments and requires that financial statements be based on the internal segments determined by the executive management and the accounting principles applied. H&M does not believe that the new standard will require any change to segment reporting.

– Revised IAS 1 Presentation of Financial Statements (effective from 2009/2010) – the revision requires, among other things, that items previously reported in the shareholders' equity calculation but that are not shareholder transactions be presented in an expanded income statement or in a separate report attached to the income statement. The Group will present a separate report.

ESTIMATES AND ASSESSMENTS

The preparation of the Annual Report and consolidated accounts requires estimates and assumptions to be made as well as judgements in the application of the accounting principles. These affect recorded amounts for assets, liabilities, income, expenses and supplementary information. The estimates and assumptions are reviewed regularly and are based on historical experience, other relevant factors and expectations for the future. The actual outcome may therefore deviate from the estimates and assumptions made. It is the company's assessment that the estimates and assumptions made in the financial statements up to 30 November 2009 will not significantly affect the results and position for the forthcoming financial year.

CONSOLIDATED ACCOUNTS

General

The consolidated accounts cover the parent company and its subsidiaries. Subsidiaries are included in the consolidated accounts from the date of acquisition, which is the date on which the parent company gains a determining influence, and are included in the consolidated accounts until such date as the determining influence ends. The acquisition method is used in the preparation of the consolidated accounts. The net assets of acquired subsidiaries are determined based on a valuation of the fair value of the assets, liabilities and contingent liabilities at the time of acquisition. If the acquisition cost of the subsidiary's shares exceeds the calculated value at the time of acquisition of the Group's share of the net identifiable assets of the acquired company, the difference is reported as goodwill upon consolidation. If the acquisition cost is less than the finally established value of the net identifiable assets, the difference is reported directly in the income statement. The financial reports for the parent company and the subsidiaries included in the consolidated accounts cover the same period and have been prepared in accordance with the accounting principles that apply to the Group. Intra-group transactions such as income, expenses, receivables and liabilities, as well as unrealised gains and losses are eliminated entirely in the preparation of the consolidated accounts.

Minority interests
In 2008 H&M acquired 60 percent of the shares in FaBric Scandinavien AB. The parties have reached an agreement whereby H&M has the opportunity/obligation to acquire the remaining shares within three to seven years. The calculated value of the put options allocated to minority shareholders in connection with the acquisition is reported as a provision for an additional contingent consideration. Therefore no minority interest is reported. Any change in fair value of the put options/consideration will be reported as an adjustment of goodwill.

Translation of foreign subsidiaries
Assets and liabilities in foreign subsidiaries are translated at the exchange rate on the closing date, while the income statement is translated at the average exchange rate for the financial year. The translation difference arising from this, and also as a result of the fact that the net investment is translated at a different exchange rate at the end of the year than at the beginning of the year, is posted directly to equity as a translation reserve. On disposal of a foreign business the accumulated exchange rate differences in the income statement are posted together with the profit or loss on disposal. Where foreign businesses are concerned, the accumulated translation differences attributable to the period before 1 December 2004 – the date of adoption of IFRS – have been set at zero in accordance with the transitional rules in IFRS 1.

FOREIGN CURRENCY
Receivables and liabilities in foreign currencies are converted at the exchange rate on the closing date. Exchange rate differences arising on translation are reported in the income statement with the exception of exchange rate differences in respect of loans, which are to be regarded as net investment in a foreign business. Such exchange rate differences are posted directly to equity as translation effects.

INCOME
The Group's income is generated mainly by sales of clothing and cosmetics to consumers. Sales revenue is reported less value-added tax, returns and discounts as sales excluding VAT in the income statement. Income is reported in connection with sale/delivery to the customer. Franchise sales have two components: sales of goods to franchisees, which are reported on delivery of the goods, and franchise fees, which are reported when the franchisee sells goods to the consumer. The Group's income exhibits seasonal variations. The first quarter of the financial year is normally the weakest and the last quarter the strongest. Interest income is reported as it is earned.

MARKETING
Advertising costs and other marketing activities are expensed on a continuous basis.

INTANGIBLE FIXED ASSETS
Intangible fixed assets with a finite useful life are reported at cost less accumulated amortisation and any accumulated write-downs. Amortisation is distributed linearly over the assets' expected useful life. See also Note 8 and Note 11.

Goodwill is the amount by which the acquisition cost exceeds the fair value of the Group's share in the acquired subsidiary's identifiable net assets upon acquisition. Goodwill on acquisition of subsidiaries is reported as intangible assets. Intangible assets with an indefinite useful life including goodwill are tested annually for impairment. If the book value of the asset exceeds the recoverable amount (the highest of the net realisable value and the value in use) the necessary amount is written down. Any write-down is recognised in profit/loss.

TANGIBLE FIXED ASSETS
Costs relating to intangible fixed assets are reported in the balance sheet if it is likely that the company will gain from the future financial benefits associated with the asset and if the asset's acquisition cost can be reliably calculated. Costs relating to on-going maintenance and repair are reported as an expense in the period in which they arise. Tangible fixed assets are reported at cost less accumulated depreciation and any accumulated write-downs. Depreciation is distributed linearly over the asset's expected useful life. No depreciation is applied to land. See also Note 8 and Note 12. The book value of tangible fixed assets is tested for impairment. If the asset's book value exceeds the recoverable amount (the highest of the net realisable value and the value in use) the required amount is written down. Any write-down is recognised in profit/loss.

LEASING
Leasing agreements in which a substantial portion of the risks and benefits of ownership are retained by the lessor are classified as operational leases. Financial leases exist when the financial risks and benefits associated with the ownership of an object are essentially transferred from the lessor to the lessee, regardless

of whether the legal ownership belongs to the lessor or the lessee. Assets held under financial leasing agreements are reported as fixed assets and future payment commitments are reported as liabilities in the balance sheet. As of the closing day the Group had no leasing agreement reported according to the rules for financial leases. Minimal leasing agreements relating to operational leases are recognised in the income statement as an expense and distributed linearly over the term of the agreement. The Group's main leasing agreements are rental agreements for premises. Variable (sales-based) rents are recognised in the same period as the corresponding sales.

FINANCIAL INSTRUMENTS

Financial instruments are assessed and recognised in accordance with the rules in IAS 39. Financial instruments recognised in the balance sheet include on the assets side, liquid funds, accounts receivable, short-term investments, long-term receivables and derivatives. On the liabilities and equity side are accounts payables and derivatives. Financial instruments are recognised in the balance sheet when the Group becomes a party to the contractual terms of the instrument. Financial assets are removed from the balance sheet when the contractual rights to the cash flows from the asset cease. Financial liabilities are removed from the balance sheet when the obligation is met, cancelled or ends.

The Group classifies its financial instruments in the following categories:

Financial assets and liabilities at fair value through profit or loss
This category consists of two sub-groups: financial assets and liabilities held for trading, and other financial assets and liabilities that the company initially chose to place in this category when they were first recognised. Assets and liabilities in this category are assessed continually at fair value, with changes in value recognised in profit/loss.

Loans receivable and accounts receivable
This category primarily covers cash and bank balances as well as accounts receivable. Cash and bank balances are valued at the accrued acquisition cost. Accounts receivable have a short expected term and are recognised at the original invoiced amount without discount, with deductions for doubtful receivables.

Financial assets held to maturity
Financial assets held to maturity are assets with payment flows that are fixed or that can be established in advance and with a fixed term which the Group has the express intention and capacity to hold until maturity. Assets in this category are valued at accrued acquisition cost, with the effective interest rate being used to calculate the value. As of the closing date, all of the Group's short-term investments fell into this category.

Financial assets that may be sold
This category contains financial assets that were either placed in this category at the time of acquisition or have not been classified in any other category. These are valued continually at fair value, with changes in value recognised in equity. No financial assets have been classified in this category.

Other financial liabilities
Financial liabilities that are not held for trading are assessed at their accrued acquisition value. Accounts payable fall into this category. These have a short expected term and are recognised at the nominal amount with no discounting.

Reporting of derivatives used for hedging purposes
All derivatives are reported initially and continually at fair value in the balance sheet. The result of revaluation of derivatives used for hedging is reported as described in the section Derivatives and Hedge Accounting.

LIQUID FUNDS

Liquid funds consist of cash and bank balances as well as short-term investments with a maximum term of three months from the date of acquisition. These investments carry no significant risk of changes in value.

DERIVATIVES AND HEDGE ACCOUNTING

The Group's policy is for derivatives to be held for hedging purposes only. Derivative instruments comprise forward currency contracts used to hedge the risk of exchange rate fluctuation for internal and external flow of goods.

H&M applies hedge accounting in accordance with IAS 39. To meet the requirements of hedge accounting there must be a clear link to the hedged item. In addition, the hedge must effectively protect the hedged item, hedge documentation must have been prepared and the effectiveness must be measurable.

In hedge accounting, derivatives are classified as cash flow hedging or as fair value hedging. As of 30 November 2008 and 2009 all of the Group's derivatives were in the cash flow hedging category. How these hedging transactions are reported is described below.

Hedging of forecast currency flows – cash flow hedging
Derivatives that hedge the forecast flow are reported in the balance sheet at fair value. Changes in value are reported directly in equity in the hedge reserve until such time as the hedged flow is recognised in the income statement, at which time the hedging instrument's accumulated changes in value are transferred to the income statement where they then correspond to the profit/loss effects of the hedged transaction.

Hedging of contracted currency flows
When a hedging instrument is used to hedge fair value, the hedges are reported at fair value in the balance sheet and, correspondingly, the contracted flow is also reported at fair value with regard to the currency risk being hedged. Changes in the value of a derivative are reported in the income statement together with changes in the value of the hedged item. Cash flow hedging may also be used for contracted flow of goods.

NOTES TO THE FINANCIAL STATEMENTS

STOCK-IN-TRADE

Stock-in-trade is valued at the lower of the acquisition cost and the net realisable value. From the moment the goods are transferred from the supplier to the transport service provider appointed by H&M, the goods are owned according to civil law by H&M and become part of H&M's reported stock-in-trade. Goods that have not yet arrived at a store are valued at their actual acquisition cost including the cost of customs duties and freight.

For stock-in-trade in the stores the acquisition cost is determined by reducing the selling price by the calculated gross margin (retail method). The net realisable value is the estimated market value less the calculated selling expenses.

PENSIONS

H&M has several different plans for benefits after employment has ended. The plans are either defined benefit or defined contribution plans. Defined contribution plans are reported as an expense in the period in which the employee performs the service to which the benefit relates. Defined benefit plans are assessed separately for the respective plan based on the benefits earned during the previous and current periods. The defined benefit obligations less the fair value of managed assets are reported under the heading "Provisions for Pensions." Defined benefit plans are primarily found in Sweden. Pension obligations are assessed annually with the help of independent actuaries according to the so-called Projected Unit Credit Method. The assessment is made using actuarial assumptions. These assumptions include such things as the discount rate, anticipated salary and pension increases as well as the expected return on managed assets. Changes in the actuarial assumptions and outcomes that deviate from the assumptions give rise to actuarial gains or losses. Such gains or losses are recognised in profits in the year they arise.

For salaried employees in Sweden, H&M applies the ITP plan through an insurance policy with Alecta. According to the statements issued by the Swedish Financial Reporting Board (UFR 3), this is a defined benefit plan that covers a number of employers. The plan will be reported as a defined contribution plan until the company gains access to the information allowing this plan to be reported according to the rules for defined benefit plans.

Alecta's surplus may be allocated to the insured employer and/or the insured employees. As of 30 September 2009, Alecta's consolidation ratio was 136 percent (126). The consolidation ratio is calculated as fair value of managed assets as a percentage of the obligations, calculated in accordance with Alecta's actuarial assumptions. This calculation is not in line with IAS 19. See Note 18 for further information.

OTHER PROVISIONS

Provisions are reported in the balance sheet when there is an undertaking as a result of an event occurring and it is likely that an outflow of resources will be required for the undertaking and when the amount can be reliably estimated. Other provisions include additional contingent consideration relating to put options allocated to minority shareholders.

INCOME TAX

Income taxes in the income statement represent current and deferred corporation tax payable by Swedish and foreign subsidiaries. Current tax is tax that will be paid or received in respect of the current year as well as adjustments to current tax attributable to previous periods. The income tax rate in force in each country is applied. For more information see Note 10.

Deferred tax is calculated according to the balance sheet method based on temporary differences arising between reported and fiscal values of assets and liabilities. Deferred tax is calculated using the tax rates that are expected to apply in the period when the receivables are deducted or the liabilities are settled, based on the tax rates (and the tax legislation) in force on the closing date. Deferred tax receivables are recognised for all temporary differences unless they relate to goodwill or an asset or a liability in a transaction that is not a company acquisition and that, at the time of acquisition, affects neither the reported nor taxable profit or loss for the period. Also, temporary differences relating to investments in subsidiaries and associated companies are taken into account only to the extent it is likely that the temporary difference will be reversed in the foreseeable future. Deferred tax receivables for temporary differences and loss carry-forwards are recognised only to the extent it is likely that these will be able to be utilised. As of the closing date, the Group had no loss carry-forwards that were not matched by reported deferred tax receivables.

The recorded values of deferred tax receivables are tested as of each closing date and reduced where it is no longer deemed likely that they will be able to be utilised.

CASH FLOW STATEMENT

The cash flow statement is prepared according to the indirect method. The reported cash flow covers only transactions involving payments in or out.

SEGMENT REPORTING

The Group's business consists mainly of sales of clothing and cosmetics to consumers. Internal follow-up is carried out by country. In order to clearly present the information for different segments, the operations are divided into three geographical areas: the Nordic region, Euro Zone countries excluding Finland, and the Rest of the World. The risks and opportunities are similar in each segment. The parent company and subsidiaries with no external sales are reported in a separate Group-wide segment. There is no internal division into different business segments and thus reporting in secondary segments is not relevant. Transactions between segments take place on normal commercial terms.

2 FINANCIAL RISKS

The Group's financing and management of financial risk is done centrally within the Group's finance department and is done according to a financial policy established by the Board of Directors. The financial policy is the most important financial control tool for the company's financial activities and establishes the framework within which the company works. The Group's accounting principles for financial instruments, including derivatives, are described in Note 1.

In the course of doing business the Group is exposed to risk associated with financial instruments, such as liquid funds, short-term investments, accounts receivable and accounts payable. The Group also executes transactions involving currency derivatives for the purpose of managing currency risk that arises in the course of the Group's business.

The risks relating to these instruments are primarily the following:
- Interest risk associated with liquid funds and short-term investments.
- Currency risk associated with foreign currency flows.
- Credit risk associated with financial assets and derivative positions.

INTEREST RISK

Interest risk is the risk that the value of a financial instrument will vary due to changes in market interest rates. Interest risk relates to the risk that the Group's exposure to changes in market interest rates may affect net profit. The Group's exposure to risk from changes in interest rates relates to liquid funds and short-term investments. The original term of the investments as of the closing date is a maximum of twelve months by the closing date. The financial policy permits investments of up to two years. The Group's liquid funds and short-term investments as of the closing date amounted to SEK 22,025 m. An interest rate increase of 0.5 percentage units on this amount would increase interest income by SEK 110 m. A corresponding decrease in the interest rate would reduce the interest income by the same amount.

CURRENCY RISK

Currency risk is, among other things, the risk that the value of financial instruments or future cash flows will vary due to changes in exchange rates.

Currency exposure associated with financial instruments
H&M's currency risk associated with financial instruments is mainly related to financial investments, accounts payable and derivatives. To reduce currency risk associated with financial investments, any surplus liquidity is invested in local currencies in the respective country. Most of the surplus liquidity is in Sweden and is invested in SEK. The Group's accounts payable in foreign currencies are mainly handled in Sweden and are to a large extent hedged through forward contracts. Based on this, a change in the value of the Swedish krona of 2 percent in relation to other currencies would result in an insignificant momentary effect on profit related to the financial instrument holdings as of the closing date. A strengthening of the Swedish krona would have a positive effect on the hedge reserve in equity in the amount of around SEK 250 m before taking into account the tax effect.

The Group's exposure to outstanding derivative instruments is reported in Note 16.

The Group's operating profit for the year was affected by exchange rate differences relating to flow of goods in the amount of SEK -170 m (31).

Transaction exposure associated with commercial flows
The payment flows in the form of payments in foreign currencies for accounts receivable and payable expose the Group to currency risk. To manage the currency risk relating to changes in exchange rates, the Group hedges its currency risk within the framework of the financial policy. The currency risk exposure is dealt with at the central level. Most of the Group's sales are made in euro and the Group's most significant purchase currencies are the US dollar and the euro. Fluctuation in the US dollar/euro exchange rates is the single largest transaction exposure within the Group. To hedge the flow of goods in foreign currencies and thereby reduce the effects of future exchange rate fluctuation, the majority of the Group's flow of goods (90 percent) were hedged under forward contracts on an ongoing basis throughout the 2008/2009 financial year. Since the sole purpose of this currency management is to reduce risk, only exposure to the flow of goods is hedged.

In 2009 a review was conducted of the Group's currency flows and as a result, two changes were made:
- Starting on 1 December 2009, 100 percent of the Group's product buying will be currency-hedged, compared to 90 percent previously, for the purpose of reducing the volatility caused by exchange rate fluctuation.
- Starting on 1 December 2009 the company will discontinue the hedging of the internal mark-up for the internal flow of goods to the subsidiaries.

For more information see under the heading "Changed currency hedging policy" in the Administration Report.

Translation exposure on consolidation of units outside Sweden
In addition to the effects of transaction exposure, the profits are also affected by translation effects as a result of changes in exchange rates for the local currencies of the various foreign subsidiaries against the Swedish krona, compared to the same period the previous year. The underlying profit/loss in a market may be unchanged in the local currency, but when converted into SEK may increase in SEK if the Swedish krona has weakened or decrease if the Swedish krona has strengthened. Translation effects affect the Group's net assets on consolidation of the foreign companies' balance sheets (translation exposure in the balance sheet). No exchange rate hedging (equity hedging) is carried out for this risk.

CREDIT RISK

Credit risk is the risk that a party in a transaction involving financial instruments may not be able to fulfil its commitment and thereby cause a loss to the other party. Credit exposure arises when liquid funds including short-term investments are invested, but also arises in the form of counterparty risk associated with trading in derivatives. To limit credit risk, forward contract transactions are only executed with counterparties with a good credit rating, and funds are only invested in banks with a minimum rating of A-1/A- (Standard & Poor) and P2/A3 (Moody's). Maximum credit exposure as of 30 November 2009 is equivalent to the book value of liquid assets of SEK 19,024 m, short-term investments SEK 3,001 m, accounts receivables SEK 1,990 m and other SEK 811 m, totalling SEK 24,826 m. The accounts

---

NOTES TO THE FINANCIAL STATEMENTS

---

receivables are shared between a large number of customers with low amounts per customer. The average debt was around SEK 2,000 (2,000). The loss on accounts receivables was insignificant.

3 SEGMENT REPORTING

	2009	2008
Nordic region		
External net sales	16,302	15,323
Operating profit	692	1,154
Operating margin, %	4.2	7.5
Assets, excluding tax receivables	5,037	4,059
Liabilities, excluding tax liabilities	1,639	1,168
Investments	375	268
Depreciation	259	198
Euro Zone excluding Finland		
External net sales	57,229	49,961
Operating profit	2,545	2,938
Operating margin, %	4.4	5.9
Assets, excluding tax receivables	16,601	14,190
Liabilities, excluding tax liabilities	3,307	2,911
Investments	2,789	2,439
Depreciation	1,374	1,051
Rest of the world		
External net sales	27,862	23,248
Operating profit	1,298	1,196
Operating margin, %	4.7	5.1
Assets, excluding tax receivables	10,711	9,234
Liabilities, excluding tax liabilities	1,875	1,601
Investments	2,135	1,827
Depreciation	1,015	823
Group functions		
Net sales to other segments	57,510	51,558
Operating profit	17,109	14,850
Operating margin, %	29.7	28.8
Assets, excluding tax receivables	20,768	22,461
Liabilities, excluding tax liabilities	4,452	5,516
Investments	387	659
Depreciation	182	130
Eliminations		
Net sales to other segments	-57,510	-51,558
Total		
External net sales	101,393	88,532
Operating profit	21,644	20,138
Operating margin, %	21.3	22.7
Assets, excluding tax receivables	53,117	49,944
Liabilities, excluding tax liabilities	11,273	11,196
Investments	5,686	5,193
Depreciation	2,830	2,202

4 NET SALES BY COUNTRY

	2009	2008
Sweden	6,323	5,973
Norway	4,482	4,235
Denmark	3,411	3,102
UK	6,723	6,401
Switzerland	5,615	4,534
Germany	25,289	21,434
Netherlands	6,220	5,710
Belgium	2,894	2,581
Austria	4,598	4,195
Luxembourg	371	316
Finland	2,086	2,013
France	7,070	6,686
USA	7,173	6,264
Spain	5,448	5,006
Poland	2,033	2,081
Czech Republic	561	564
Portugal	773	634
Italy	3,013	2,229
Canada	1,972	1,629
Slovenia	517	500
Ireland	476	418
Hungary	251	254
Slovakia	157	115
Greece	403	253
China	1,513	827
Japan	1,111	188
Russia	319	
Franchise	591	390
Total	**101,393**	**88,532**

5 ROYALTIES FROM GROUP COMPANIES

The parent company's internal sales include royalties from Group companies of SEK 5,521 m (5,145).

6 SALARIES, OTHER REMUNERATION AND PAYROLL OVERHEADS

2009	Board, MD, executive management salary	Salary other employees	Payroll overheads total	*of which* pens. total	*of which* pens. Board, MD exec. mgmt
Sweden, parent company	54	408	240	81	28
Subsidiaries	61	13,015	2,862	140	6
Group total	**115**	**13,423**	**3,102**	**221**	**34**

2008	Board, MD, executive management salary	Salary other employees	Payroll overheads total	*of which* pens. total	*of which* pens. Board, MD exec. mgmt
Sweden, parent company	49	372	263	128	85
Subsidiaries	52	11,324	2,434	90	4
Group total	**101**	**11,696**	**2,697**	**218**	**89**

NOTES TO THE FINANCIAL STATEMENTS

BOARD FEES

Board fees for the year as approved by the 2008 AGM amounted to SEK 4.25 m (4.25). Board fees were paid as follows:

	SEK
Stefan Persson, Chairman	1,350,000
Fred Andersson	375,000
Mia Brunell Livfors	375,000
Lottie Knutson	375,000
Sussi Kvart	450,000
Bo Lundquist	450,000
Stig Nordfelt	500,000
Karl-Johan Persson*	—
Melker Schörling	375,000

* Karl-Johan Persson received no Board fees as he is employed by the company.

As of the AGM on 4 May 2009 the Board consists of seven ordinary members elected by the AGM. There are also two employee representatives with two deputies for these positions. Seven members of the Board are women, four are men and four of the eleven are employed by the company.

REMUNERATION TO SENIOR EXECUTIVES

Based on a resolution regarding guidelines passed by the 2009 AGM. See the Administration Report page 6.

REMUNERATION TO THE MANAGING DIRECTOR

Rolf Eriksen was the Managing Director until 30 June 2009. On 1 July 2009 Karl-Johan Persson took over as Managing Director.

Remuneration to the former Managing Director
Remuneration to the former Managing Director for the 2009 financial year in the form of salary, fees and benefits amounted to SEK 15.8 m (16.8) which included a bonus of SEK 2.1 m (2.1). The pension expenses for the former Managing Director during the year amounted to SEK 16.0 m (60.2). The change in the year's pension commitments entered as liabilities for the former Managing Director include actuarial gains of SEK 3.8 m (actuarial losses of 38). The total pension commitments entered as liabilities, which are based on the fact that the former Managing Director will receive a pension for the first three years of his retirement equivalent to 65 percent of his fixed salary followed by a lifelong pension equivalent to 50 percent of the same salary, amount to SEK 152.2 m (136.7). The former Managing Director retired on 1 September 2009.

Remuneration to the current Managing Director
Remuneration to the current Managing Director for the period from 1 July 2009 to 30 November 2009 in the form of salary and benefits amounted to SEK 4.6 m. No bonus was paid out in 2009. Pension benefits for the current Managing Director is covered by a defined contribution plan and by the ITP plan. The total pension cost shall not exceed a total of 30 percent of

the Managing Director's fixed salary. The pension expenses for the current Managing Director amounted to SEK 1.4 m.

The Managing Director is entitled to a 12-month period of notice. In the event the company cancels his employment contract, the Managing Director will also receive severance pay of an extra year's salary. The Managing Director's terms of employment are determined by the Board of Directors.

REMUNERATION TO OTHER MEMBERS OF EXECUTIVE MANAGEMENT

Remuneration to other members of the executive management team in the form of salary and benefits were paid in the amount of SEK 42.9 m (38.5) which included bonuses of SEK 2.7 m (2.6). Pension expenses relating to other members of executive management during the year amounted to SEK 11.8 m (24.9). The other members of executive management are 12 (12) individuals, five of whom are women.

In addition to the Managing Director, the executive management team consists of the heads of the following functions: Finance, Buying, Production, Sales, Expansion, IR, Accounts, Marketing, HR, Communications, Corporate Social Responsibility and Security. There are rules in place for these individuals with respect to supplements to retirement pension beyond the ITP plan. The retirement age varies between 60 and 65. The cost of this commitment is partially covered by separate insurance policies.

In addition, bonuses amounting to SEK 5.6 m (8.0) were paid out to country managers. No severance pay agreements exist within the Group other than for the Managing Director as described above. The terms of employment for other members of executive management are determined by the Managing Director and the Chairman of the Board.

7 AVERAGE NUMBER OF EMPLOYEES

	2009 Total	Male %	2008 Total	Male %
Sweden	4,874	21	4,924	21
Norway	1,546	10	1,575	7
Denmark	1,419	6	1,335	6
UK	4,562	23	4,275	24
Switzerland	1,813	13	1,599	12
Germany	11,114	19	10,746	19
Netherlands	2,196	17	2,395	19
Belgium	1,480	21	1,332	15
Austria	1,881	10	1,986	10
Luxembourg	134	12	134	11
Finland	782	8	840	10
France	3,498	27	3,396	25
USA	4,253	31	6,820	31
Spain	4,009	18	4,528	20
Poland	2,452	19	1,956	21
Czech Republic	263	11	281	6
Portugal	646	20	606	25
Italy	1,632	29	1,052	30
Canada	1,096	23	1,011	22
Slovenia	139	14	129	15
Ireland	236	20	220	15
Hungary	135	15	135	12
Slovakia	69	19	65	38

NOTES TO THE FINANCIAL STATEMENTS

	2009 Total	Male %	2008 Total	Male %
Greece	262	19	247	20
China	1,521	30	1,109	26
Japan	442	42	203	33
Russia	374	31	26	23
South Korea	44	32		
Other countries	604	51	505	48
Group total	53,476	21	53,430	21

SICKNESS ABSENCE WITHIN THE PARENT COMPANY

	Sickness absence as % of reg. working hours		% of sickness absence lasting over 60 days	
	2009	2008	2009	2008
Female employees	2.8	2.6	24.8	35.4
Male employees	2.1	1.7	17.5	5.9
Employees in age group < 30 years	2.6	1.9	15.9	
Employees in age group 30–49 years	2.5	2.3	21.3	29.2
Employees in age group > 50 years	1.9	1.3	38.7	
Total	2.5	2.2	21.9	24.7

8 DEPRECIATION

Depreciation has been calculated at 12 percent of the acquisition cost of equipment and leasehold rights, and 20 percent for computer equipment and vehicles, based on their estimated useful life. Depreciation on brands and customer relations relating to FaBric Scandinavien AB is assessed at 10 percent of the acquisition cost. Buildings are depreciated at 3 percent of their acquisition cost. No depreciation is applied to land values. Depreciation for the year is reported in the income statement as follows:

	GROUP		PARENT COMPANY	
	2009	2008	2009	2008
Cost of goods sold	310	245		11
Selling expenses	2,350	1,825		73
Administrative expenses	170	132	94	4
Total	2,830	2,202	94	88

9 AUDIT FEES

	GROUP		PARENT COMPANY	
	2009	2008	2009	2008
Ernst & Young				
Audit assignments	16.7	14.5	2.2	2.2
Other assignments	15.2	14.0	0.1	0.6
Other auditors				
Audit assignments	3.2	2.9	–	–
Other assignments	1.8	1.1	–	–
Total	36.9	32.5	2.3	2.8

10 TAX

	GROUP		PARENT COMPANY	
	2009	2008	2009	2008
Tax expense (-) *tax receivable (+):*				
Current tax				
Tax expense for the period	-5,630	-5,034	-40	-556
Tax effect of group contributions provided	–	–	-572	–
Adjusted tax expense for previous years	–	-1	-1	3
Total	-5,630	-5,035	-613	-553
Deferred tax receivable (+) / tax expense (-) in respect of temporary differences in				
stock-in-trade	130	32	–	–
loss carry-forward	–	1		
pension provisions	7	20	5	19
tax allocation reserve	-79	-1,017		
intangible fixed assets	18	10		
other temporary differences	-165	93		
Total	-89	-861	5	19
Total	-5,719	-5,896	-608	-534
Reconciliation between current tax rate and effective tax rate:				
Expected tax expense according to the Swedish tax rate of 28%	-6,189	-5,933	-4,263	-4,126
Effect of changed tax rate in Sweden	225			
Difference in foreign tax rates	261	279		
Non-deductible/non-taxable	-128	-153	-15	-8
Other	112	-88		
Tax for previous years	–	-1	-2	3
Tax-free dividend subsidiaries			3,666	3,597
Total	-5,719	-5,896	-614	-534
Reported deferred tax receivable relates to:				
Pensions	84	56	56	51
Loss carry-forward in subsidiaries	0	3		
Temporary differences in stock-in-trade	978	819		
Hedge reserve	21	207		
Other temporary differences	163	214	–	–
Total	1,246	1,299	56	51

	GROUP	
	2009	2008
Reported deferred tax expense relates to		
Intangible fixed assets	142	159
Tangible fixed assets	456	432
Stock-in-trade	291	210
Tax allocation reserve	1,073	1,017
Other temporary differences	76	
Total	**2,038**	**1,818**

11 INTANGIBLE FIXED ASSETS

	GROUP	
	2009	2008
Brand*		
Opening acquisition cost	470	
Acquisitions during the year	–	470
Closing acquisition cost	470	470
Opening amortisation	-27	
Amortisation for the year	-47	-27
Closing accumulated amortisation	-74	-27
Closing book value	**396**	**443**
Customer relations*		
Opening acquisition cost	131	
Acquisitions during the year	–	131
Closing acquisition cost	131	131
Opening amortisation	-8	
Amortisation for the year	-13	-8
Closing accumulated amortisation	-21	-8
Closing book value	**110**	**123**
Leasehold rights		
Opening acquisition cost	890	476
Acquisitions during the year	180	446
Sales/disposals	7	-77
Translation effects	9	45
Closing acquisition cost	1,086	890
Opening amortisation	-231	-210
Sales/disposals	12	77
Amortisation for the year	-122	-74
Translation effects	-1	-24
Closing accumulated amortisation	-342	-231
Closing book value	**744**	**659**
Goodwill*		
Opening acquisition cost	431	
Acquisitions during the year	–	431
Adjusted consideration FaBric Scandinavien AB	-7	
Closing acquisition	424	431

* Brand, customer relations and goodwill assets have been added through the acquisition in 2008 of the company FaBric Scandinavien AB, which was a cash-generating unit. A goodwill impairment test was carried out at the end of 2009. The impairment test is based on a calculation of value in use. The value in use has been assessed based on discounted cash flows according to the forecasts for the next ten years and with an annual growth rate of 2 percent in subsequent years. A discount rate of 12 percent before tax was used. The cash flows are based on H&M's business plan. The growth rate of 2 percent is based on H&M's assessment of the opportunities and risks associated with the business. The discount rate is based on an average weighted capital cost that is estimated to be on a par with the external requirements that the market imposes for similar companies. No impairment was identified and H&M is of the opinion that reasonable possible changes in the variables above would not have such a significant impact that the recovery value would be reduced to a lower amount than the booked value. An adjustment of the consideration for FaBric Scandinavien AB of SEK 7 m was made and this reduced the reported goodwill value.

12 BUILDINGS, LAND & EQUIPMENT

	GROUP		PARENT COMPANY	
	2009	2008	2009	2008
Buildings				
Opening acquisition cost	596	564	109	107
Acquisitions during the year	29	23	–	2
Sales/disposals	-4	-35	-4	–
Translation effects	8	44	–	–
Closing acquisition cost	629	596	105	109
Opening depreciation	-184	-158	-54	-51
Sales/disposals	–	4	–	–
Depreciation for the year	-18	-16	-3	-3
Translation effects	-5	-14	–	–
Closing accumulated depreciation	-207	-184	-57	-54
Closing book value	**422**	**412**	**48**	**55**
Land				
Opening acquisition cost	68	60	3	3
Acquisitions during the year	–	0	–	–
Sales/disposals	–	–	–	–
Translation effects	2	8	–	–
Closing book value	**70**	**68**	**3**	**3**

The tax assessment values for the Swedish properties amount to SEK 73 m (71). The book value of these amounts to SEK 51 m (58).

	2009	2008	2009	2008
Equipment				
Opening acquisition cost	21,020	16,173	769	736
Acquisitions during the year	5,481	4,724	98	183
Sales/disposals	-2,266	-1,346	-131	-150
Translation effects	-659	1,469	–	–
Closing acquisition cost	23,576	21,020	736	769
Opening depreciation	-9,059	-7,352	-413	-478
Sales/disposals	2,115	1,203	131	150
Depreciation for the year	-2,630	-2,077	-91	-85
Translation effects	317	-833	–	–
Closing accumulated depreciation	-9,257	-9,059	-373	-413
Closing book value	**14,319**	**11,961**	**363**	**356**

NOTES TO THE FINANCIAL STATEMENTS

The Group has no significant leasing agreements other than the rental agreements for rented premises entered into at normal market rates. Rental costs for the 2009 financial year amounted to SEK 12,249 m (9,776), of which sales-based rent amounted to SEK 888 m (740).

Rent according to the Group's rental agreements (basic rent including any sales-based rent) amounts to SEK m:

Rental commitment 2010	9,383
Rental commitment 2011–2014	26,416
Rental commitment 2015 and thereafter	18,546

13 PREPAID COSTS

	GROUP		PARENT COMPANY	
	2009	2008	2009	2008
Prepaid rent	697	642	5	4
Other items	240	306	9	8
Total	937	948	14	12

14 SHORT-TERM INVESTMENTS

	GROUP		PARENT COMPANY	
	2009	2008	2009	2008
Short-term investments 4–12 months	3,001		3,001	
Total	3,001		3,001	

The balance sheet item includes interest-bearing investments, i.e. investments in securities issued by banks or in short-term bank deposits.

15 LIQUID FUNDS

	GROUP		PARENT COMPANY	
	2009	2008	2009	2008
Cash and bank balances	6,629	3,028	143	8
Short-term investments 0–3 months	12,395	19,698	3,501	6,517
Total	19,024	22,726	3,644	6,525

Investment are made on market terms and interest rates are between 0.16 and 5.5 percent. The difference in interest rates depends on the currency in which the funds are invested.

16 FORWARD CONTRACTS

The table below shows the outstanding forward contracts as of the closing date:

Currency pair SELL/BUY	Book value and fair value		Nominal amount		Average remaining term in months	
	2009	2008	2009	2008	2009	2008
NOK/SEK	-24	-1	762	830	4	4
GBP/SEK	31	-27	1,308	1,210	4	4
DKK/SEK	-7	-46	667	637	4	4
CHF/SEK	-16	-90	1,432	1,209	4	4
EUR/SEK	-82	-820	11,862	11,950	4	4
PLN/SEK	-18	9	472	633	4	4
USD/SEK	38	-216	1,053	1,380	4	4
CAD/SEK	2	–	449	–	4	–
JPY/SEK	-20	–	509	–	4	–
SEK/USD	2	550	5,082	5,338	3	3
SEK/EUR	19	66	1,040	1,423	2	2
Total	-75	-575	24,636	24,610		

Forward contracts with a positive market value amount to SEK 260 m (660), which is reported under Other current receivables. Forward contracts with a negative market value amount to SEK 335 m (1,234), which is reported under Other current liabilities.

Of the outstanding forward contracts, losses of SEK 16 m were recorded in the income statement with changes in value of the underlying hedged item. Residual fair value of SEK 60 m was recorded in the hedge reserve in equity.

The fair value was established based on listed prices.

17 SHARE CAPITAL

The share capital is divided between 97,200,000 class A shares (ten votes per share) and 730,336,000 class B shares (one vote per share). There are no other differences between the rights associated with the shares. The total number of shares is 827,536,000.

18 PROVISIONS FOR PENSIONS

	GROUP		PARENT COMPANY	
	2009	2008	2009	2008
Capitalised value of defined benefit obligations	335	299	238	219
Fair value of managed assets	-81	-71	-27	-26
Provisions for pension obligations recorded in the balance sheet	254	228	211	193
Opening balance, 1 December	228	156	193	113
Reported pension expenses, net	38	82	23	84
Premiums paid	-5	-4	-2	-2
Pensions paid out	-7	-6	-3	-2
Recorded amount of defined benefit obligations, 30 November	254	228	211	193

The amounts recorded as pension expenses include the following items:

	GROUP		PARENT COMPANY	
	2009	2008	2009	2008
Expenses for service during the current year	34	23	23	18
Interest expense	11	10	7	7
Expected return on managed assets	-3	-3	-1	-1
Actuarial gains (-) and losses (+)	-4	51	-6	59
Changes in foreign exchange rates for plans valued in a currency other than the reporting currency	0	1	–	1
Reported pension expenses, net	**38**	**82**	**23**	**84**

The cost of defined contribution pension plans amounts to SEK 193 m (135).

Significant actuarial assumptions on the balance sheet date (weighted average amounts)

Discount rate	3.61%	3.30%	3.50%	3.00%
Expected return on managed assets	3.57%	3.76%	3.25%	3.25%
Future salary increases	4.63%	4.67%	5.00%	5.00%
Future pension increases (inflation)	3.00%	2.06%	2.00%	2.00%

19 OTHER PROVISIONS

	GROUP	
	2009	2008
Provision for additional consideration for FaBric Scandinavien AB	368	368
Total	**368**	**368**

H&M acquired 60 percent of the shares in the fashion company FaBric Scandinavien AB in 2008. At the time of the acquisition the parties signed an agreement giving H&M the opportunity/obligation to acquire the remaining shares within three to seven years. The assessed value of the put options allocated to minority shareholders in connection with the acquisition is reported as a provision for an additional contingent consideration. Therefore no minority interest is reported. At the time of the acquisition the provision was SEK 368 m. Any change in fair value of the put options/additional consideration will be recorded as an adjustment of goodwill.

20 FINANCIAL ASSETS AND LIABILITIES BY CATEGORY

2009	Loan receivables and accounts receivable	Financial assets held to maturity	Deriv. for hedging recog. at fair value in equity	Other financial liabilities	Total booked value
Other long-term receivables		551	–	–	551
Accounts receivable	1,990	–	–	–	1,990
Other receivables	–	–	260	–	260
Short-term investments	–	3,001	–	–	3,001
Liquid funds	12,395	6,629	–	–	19,024
Total financial assets	**14,385**	**10,181**	**260**	**–**	**24,826**
Accounts payable	–			3,667	3,667
Other liabilities	–		335	–	335
Total financial liabilities	**–**	**–**	**335**	**3,667**	**4,002**

NOTES TO THE FINANCIAL STATEMENTS

2008	Loan receivables and accounts receivable	Financial assets held to maturity	Deriv. for hedging recog. at fair value in equity	Other financial liabilities	Total booked value
Other long-term receivables	–	476	–	–	476
Accounts receivable	1,991	–	–	–	1,991
Other receivables	–	–	660	–	660
Short-term investments	–	–	–	–	0
Liquid funds	3,028	19,698	–	–	22,726
Total financial assets	5,019	20,174	660		25,853
Accounts payable	–	–	–	3,658	3,658
Other liabilities	–	–	1,234	–	1,234
Total financial liabilities	–	–	1,234	3,658	4,892

The fair value of all assets and liabilities corresponds to the book value since the assets and liabilities that are recognised at the accrued acquisition cost have short remaining terms.

21 ACCRUED EXPENSES AND DEFERRED INCOME

	GROUP		PARENT COMPANY	
	2009	2008	2009	2008
Holiday pay liability	569	524	42	35
Payroll overheads	383	425	48	52
Payroll liability	489	512	10	3
Costs relating to premises	1,476	1,032	4	1
Other accrued overheads	1,536	1,194	36	52
Total	4,453	3,687	140	143

22 RELATED PARTY DISCLOSURES

Ramsbury Invest AB is the parent company of H & M Hennes & Mauritz AB. The H&M Group leases the following store premises in properties directly or indirectly owned by Stefan Persson and family: Drottninggatan 50–52 in Stockholm, Drottninggatan 56 in Stockholm, Kungsgatan 55 in Gothenburg, Stadt Hamburgsgatan 9 in Malmö, Amagertorv 23 in Copenhagen and Oxford Circus in London, and since January 2008 premises for H&M's head office in Stockholm. Rent is paid at market rates and totalled SEK 193 m (156) for the financial year.

Karl-Johan Persson has received remuneration in the form of a salary and benefits amounting to SEK 5.1 m (0.7) for work carried out during the financial year as Head of H&M's expansion until 30 June 2009 and from 1 July 2009 as Managing Director for H & M Hennes & Mauritz AB. More information regarding salaries and other remuneration to related parties is provided in Note 6.

23 APPROPRIATIONS

	PARENT COMPANY	
	2009	2008
Provision for tax allocation reserve	-43	-662
Depreciation in excess of plan	2	-1
Total	-41	-663

24 PARTICIPATIONS IN GROUP COMPANIES

All Group companies are wholly-owned except FaBric Scandinavien AB which is owned to 60 percent. The parties have also signed an agreement under which H&M has the opportunity/obligation to acquire the remaining shares within three to seven years.

2009	Corporate ID number	No. of shares	Book value	Domicile
Parent company shareholding				
Bekå AB	556024-2488	450	1.3	Stockholm
H & M Hennes & Mauritz Sverige AB	556151-2376	1,250	0.1	Stockholm
H & M Rowells AB	556023-1663	1,150	0.6	Stockholm
H & M Hennes & Mauritz GBC AB	556070-1715	1,000	2.6	Stockholm
H & M Hennes & Mauritz International B.V.		40	0.1	Netherlands
H & M India Private Ltd		1,633,500	2.9	India
H & M Hennes & Mauritz Japan KK		99	11.7	Japan
FaBric Scandinavien AB	556663-8522	828	552.9	Tranås
H & M Hennes & Mauritz International AB	556782-4890	1,000	0.1	Stockholm
Total			572.3	

2009	Corporate ID number	Domicile
Subsidiaries' holdings		
H & M Hennes & Mauritz AS		Norway
H & M Hennes & Mauritz A/S		Denmark
H & M Hennes & Mauritz UK Ltd		UK
H & M Hennes & Mauritz SA		Switzerland
H & M Hennes & Mauritz B.V. & Co. KG		Germany
Impuls GmbH		Germany
H & M Hennes & Mauritz Logistics GBC GmbH		Germany
H & M Hennes & Mauritz Logistics GmbH & Co. KG		Germany
H & M Hennes & Mauritz Holding BV		Netherlands
H & M Hennes & Mauritz Netherlands BV		Netherlands
H & M Hennes & Mauritz USA BV		Netherlands
H & M Hennes & Mauritz Belgium NV		Belgium
H & M Hennes & Mauritz GesmbH		Austria
H & M Hennes & Mauritz OY		Finland
H & M Hennes & Mauritz SARL		France
H & M Hennes & Mauritz LP		USA
Hennes & Mauritz SL		Spain
H & M Hennes & Mauritz sp. z o.o.		Poland
H & M Hennes & Mauritz logistics sp. z o.o.		Poland
H & M Hennes & Mauritz CZ, s.r.o.		Czech Republic
Hennes & Mauritz Lda		Portugal
H & M Hennes & Mauritz S.r.l.		Italy
H & M Hennes & Mauritz Inc.		Canada
H & M Hennes & Mauritz d.o.o.		Slovenia
H & M Hennes & Mauritz (Ireland) Ltd		Ireland
H & M Hennes & Mauritz Kft		Hungary
H & M Hennes & Mauritz Far East Ltd		Hong Kong
Puls Trading Far East Ltd		Hong Kong
H & M Hennes & Mauritz Holding Asia Ltd		Hong Kong
H & M Hennes & Mauritz Ltd		Hong Kong
Hennes & Mauritz (Shanghai) Commercial Ltd Co		China
H & M Hennes & Mauritz SK s.r.c.		Slovakia
H & M Hennes & Mauritz A.E.		Greece
Monki AB	556686-8609	Tranås
Weekday AB	556427-8926	Stockholm
Weekday Brands AB	556675-8438	Tranås
Weekday A/S		Denmark
H & M Hennes & Mauritz LLP Russia		Russia
H & M Hennes & Mauritz TR Tekstil ltd sirketi		Turkey
H & M Hennes & Mauritz Ltd		South Korea
FaBric Sales Norway AS		Norway
FaBric Sales AB & Co. KG		Germany

During the year the following subsidiaries merged into H & M Hennes & Mauritz AB. The merger of wholly-owned limited companies took place through absorption. The effective date for all of the mergers was 28 October 2009. The companies being absorbed were not active during the 2009 financial year. According to the Swedish Accounting Standards Board's recommendation BFNAR 1999:1 item 24, the amounts of the merged assets and liabilities are not stated in the published version of the annual accounts as the amounts are insignificant.

556005-5047	Big is Beautiful, BiB AB
556027-7351	Carl Axel Petterssons AB
556030-1052	K.E. Persson AB
556056-0889	AB Hennes
556099-0706	Carl-Axel Herrmode AB
556125-1421	Mauritz AB

25 UNTAXED RESERVES

	PARENT COMPANY	
	2009	2008
Tax allocation reserve tax 09	662	662
Tax allocation reserve tax 10	43	
Depreciation in excess of plan	120	120
Total	**825**	**782**

26 CONTINGENT LIABILITIES

	PARENT COMPANY	
	2009	2008
Parent company's lease guarantees	11,292	11,751
Total	**11,292**	**11,751**

27 KEY RATIO DEFINITIONS

Return on equity:
Profit for the year in relation to average shareholders' equity.

Return on capital employed:
Profit after financial items plus interest expense in relation to average shareholders' equity plus average interest-bearing liabilities.

Share of risk-bearing capital:
Shareholders' equity plus deferred tax liability in relation to the balance sheet total.

Equity/assets ratio:
Shareholders' equity in relation to the balance sheet total.

Equity per share:
Shareholders' equity divided by number of shares.

P/E ratio:
Price per share divided by earnings per share.

Comparable units:
Comparable units refers to the stores and the internet and catalogue sales countries that have been in operation for at least one financial year. H&M's financial year is from 1 December to 30 November.

AUDITORS' REPORT

To the Annual General Meeting of H & M Hennes & Mauritz AB (publ) Corporate identity number 556042-7220

We have audited the annual accounts, consolidated accounts, accounting records and the administration of the Board of Directors and the Managing Director of H & M Hennes & Mauritz AB for the financial year 1 December 2008 to 30 November 2009. The company's annual accounts and consolidated accounts are included in this document on pages 4–31. These accounts, the administration of the company and compliance with the Annual Accounts Act in the preparation of the annual report and the application of IFRS international accounting standards, as adopted by the EU, and of the Annual Accounts Act to the consolidated accounts are the responsibility of the Board of Directors and the Managing Director. Our responsibility is to express an opinion on the annual accounts, the consolidated accounts and the administration based on our audit.

Our audit was conducted in accordance with generally accepted auditing standards in Sweden. This means that we planned and performed the audit in order to obtain a high, but not absolute, degree of assurance that the annual accounts and consolidated accounts are free from material misstatement. An audit includes examining, on a test basis, evidence supporting the amounts and disclosures in the accounts. An audit also includes assessing the accounting principles used and their application by the Board and the Managing Director and evaluating the significant assessments made by the Board and the Managing Director in preparing the annual accounts and consolidated accounts, as well as assessing the overall presentation of information in the annual accounts and the consolidated accounts. As a basis for our opinion concerning discharge from liability, we examined significant decisions, actions taken and circumstances in the company to be able to determine the liability, if any, to the company of any Board member or the Managing Director. We also examined whether any Board member or the Managing Director has, in any other way, acted in contravention of the Companies Act, the Annual Accounts Act or the Articles of Association. We believe that our audit provides a reasonable basis for our opinion set out below.

The annual report has been prepared in accordance with the Annual Accounts Act and gives a true and fair view of the company's and the Group's earnings and financial position in accordance with generally accepted accounting principles in Sweden.

The consolidated accounts have been compiled in accordance with IFRS international accounting standards, as adopted by the EU, and the Annual Accounts Act and give a true and fair view of the Group's earnings and financial position. The administration report is consistent with the other section of the annual accounts and the consolidated accounts.

We recommend to the Annual General Meeting that the income statement and balance sheet of the parent company and the Group be adopted, that the profit for the parent company be dealt with in accordance with the proposal in the administration report and that the members of the Board of Directors and the Managing Director be discharged from liability for the financial year.

Stockholm, 28 January 2010

Ernst & Young AB

Erik Åström
Authorised Public Accountant

FIVE YEAR SUMMARY

1 DECEMBER – 30 NOVEMBER

FINANCIAL YEAR	2009	2008	2007	2006	2005
Sales including VAT, SEK m	118,697	104,041	92,123	80,081	71,886
Sales excluding VAT, SEK m	101,393	88,532	78,346	68,400	61,262
Change from previous year, %	+15	+13	+15	+12	+14
Operating profit, SEK m	21,644	20,138	18,382	15,298	13,173
Operating margin, %	21.3	22.7	23.5	22.4	21.5
Depreciation for the year, SEK m	2,830	2,202	1,814	1,624	1,452
Profit after financial items, SEK m	22,103	21,190	19,170	15,808	13,553
Profit after tax, SEK m	16,384	15,294	13,588	10,797	9,247
Liquid funds and short-term investments, SEK m	22,025	22,726	20,964	18,625	16,846
Stock-in-trade, SEK m	10,240	8,500	7,969	7,220	6,841
Equity, SEK m	40,613	36,950	32,093	27,779	25,924
Number of shares, thousands*	827,536	827,536	827,536	827,536	827,536
Earnings per share, SEK*	19.80	18.48	16.42	13.05	11.17
Equity per share, SEK*	49.08	44.65	38.78	33.57	31.33
Cash flow from current operations per share, SEK*	20.92	21.71	18.59	14.57	12.25
Dividend per share, SEK	16.00**	15.50	14.00	11.50	9.50
Return on shareholders' equity, %	42.2	44.3	45.4	40.2	38.4
Return on capital employed, %	56.7	61.1	63.7	58.7	56.3
Share of risk-bearing capital, %	78.5	75.7	78.5	80.0	80.2
Equity/assets ratio, %	74.7	72.1	76.9	78.1	78.1
Total number of stores	1,988	1,738	1,522	1,345	1,193
Average number of employees	53,476	53,430	47,029	40,855	34,614

* Before and after dilution.
** Proposed by the Board of Directors.

Definitions of key figures, see Note 27.
The International Financial Reporting Standards (IFRS) are applied from 2005/2006. The restatement of the 2004/2005 figures according to IFRS has not involved any adjustment.

CORPORATE GOVERNANCE REPORT 2009
H & M HENNES & MAURITZ AB

> Corporate governance is basically about how companies are to be run in order to safeguard the interests of the shareholders.

H&M applies the Swedish Code of Corporate Governance and has therefore prepared this corporate governance report in accordance with the Code. This corporate governance report for 2009 describes H&M's corporate governance, management and administration as well as internal control of financial reporting. The report is not part of the formal Annual Report and has not been reviewed by the company's auditors.

The Code is based on the principle "comply or explain," which means that companies applying the Code may deviate from individual rules provided they give an explanation of the deviation, describe the chosen alternative and provide the reasons for the deviation.

Deviation from the Code:
– The Chairman of the Board is the chairman of the Election Committee. The reason for this is described in the section on the Election Committee.

H&M's CORPORATE GOVERNANCE STRUCTURE 2009

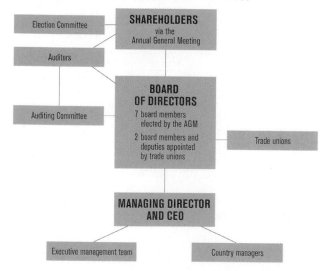

H&M's corporate governance is regulated by both external regulations and internal control documents.

Examples of external regulations:
– the Swedish Companies Act
– accounting legislation including the Swedish Bookkeeping Act and Annual Accounts Act
– NASDAQ OMX Stockholm AB Rules for issuers
– Swedish Code of Corporate Governance

Examples of internal control documents:
– Articles of Association
– instructions and work plan for the Board of Directors and the Managing Director
– Code of Ethics
– policies and guidelines

SHAREHOLDERS AND ANNUAL GENERAL MEETING

The general meeting is the company's highest decision-making body and is the forum in which shareholders exercise their right to decide on the company's affairs. The shareholders registered directly in the register of shareholders and who have given notice of their attendance on time are entitled to participate in the meeting and vote for the total number of shares they hold. The shareholders who cannot be present in person may be represented by proxy.

The general meeting is convened once a year in order to carry out tasks such as adopting the annual accounts and consolidated accounts, discharging the members of the Board of Directors and the Managing Director from liability and deciding how the profit for the past financial year is to be allocated. The meeting is called the Annual General Meeting (AGM) and elects the Board of Directors and, when necessary, auditors for the forthcoming period of office. Extraordinary general meetings may be convened where there is a particular need to do so. At the end of the financial year H&M had 172,057 shareholders. H&M's share is listed on NASDAQ OMX Stockholm AB. Information materials from H&M's most recent Annual General Meetings are published under Investor Relations/Corporate Governance/Annual General Meeting at www.hm.com. Here there is also information about the right of shareholders to raise matters at the meeting and when such requests must be received by H&M so that the matter is certain to be included in the agenda in the notice to attend. The e-mail address is indicated for those shareholders who wish to submit their questions in advance to H&M.

ANNUAL GENERAL MEETING 2009

H&M's Annual General Meeting was held on 4 May 2009 in Victoriahallen at the Stockholm International Fairs. 1,404 shareholders participated in the meeting, representing 81.3 percent of the votes and 61.5 percent of the capital. H&M's Board of Directors, executive management and Election Committee as well as the company's two auditors attended the meeting.

The main resolutions passed were the following:
– Lawyer Sven Unger was elected as chairman of the meeting.
– The balance sheets and income statements for the parent company and the Group were adopted.
– A dividend to shareholders of SEK 15.50 per share was approved.
– The Board members and the Managing Director were discharged from liability for the 2007/2008 financial year.
– The number of Board members elected by the meeting to serve until the next AGM was set at seven with no deputies elected by the meeting.

– Mia Brunell Livfors, Lottie Knutson, Sussi Kvart, Bo Lundquist, Stig Nordfelt, Stefan Persson and Melker Schörling were re-elected as ordinary members by the AGM. Fred Andersson had declined re-election and Karl-Johan Persson, who took over as the new Managing Director and CEO of H&M on 1 July 2009, resigned his position on the Board at the AGM. Stefan Persson was re-elected as Chairman of the Board.

– The fees paid to the Board members until the next AGM were set at SEK 3,875,000 in total, to be distributed as follows: Chairman of the Board, SEK 1,350,000; Board members, SEK 375,000; members of the Auditing Committee an extra SEK 75,000; and the chairman of the Auditing Committee, an extra SEK 125,000.

– The accounting firm Ernst & Young AB was elected as auditor for the company for a four-year period, i.e. until the end of the 2013 AGM.

– The proposed principles for the Election Committee were approved.

– The proposed guidelines for remuneration for senior executives were approved.

The minutes from the Annual General Meeting were posted on the website within two weeks of the meeting. Materials from the meeting, such as the notice to attend the meeting, the Board's statement concerning allocation of profits and the Managing Director's address and presentation and the minutes etc. were translated into English and published on the website.

Votes and capital represented at H&M's Annual General Meetings

YEAR	% OF VOTES	% OF CAPITAL
2007	80.9	60.7
2008	80.9	60.7
2009	81.3	61.5

ANNUAL GENERAL MEETING 2010

H&M's Annual General Meeting 2010 will be held on Thursday, 29 April in Victoriahallen at the Stockholm International Fairs. To register to attend the 2010 AGM, see H&M in Figures 2009 page 47 or www.hm.com under Investor Relations/Corporate Governance/Annual General Meeting 2010.

ELECTION COMMITTEE

The Election Committee is the general meeting's body that prepares the necessary information as a basis for decisions at the general meeting as regards election of the Board of Directors, Chairman of the Board, auditors and the chairman of the Annual General Meeting, as well as fees to the Board and auditors, and principles for the Election Committee. An account of the work of the Election Committee ahead of each AGM is available in a separate document on the website. Starting from the 2008 Annual General Meeting, the members of H&M's Election Committee are elected by the general meeting.

COMPOSITION OF THE ELECTION COMMITTEE AND WORK

The members of the Election Committee were elected by the 2009 AGM. The Election Committee was elected on the basis of its principles, which, in brief, state that the Election Committee shall be made up of the Chairman of the Board and four other members, each representing one of the four biggest shareholders as of 28 February 2009, apart from the shareholder that the Chairman of the Board represents. The principles include a procedure for replacing any member who leaves the Election Committee before the Committee's work is complete. To read the principles in full, see the document "Account of the work of H&M's Election Committee 2009" under Investor Relations/Corporate Governance/Election Committee at www.hm.com.

The composition of the Election Committee following election at the 2009 AGM was:

– Stefan Persson, Chairman of the Board
– Lottie Tham, representing Lottie Tham
– Staffan Grefbäck, representing Alecta
– Jan Andersson, representing Swedbank Robur Fonder
– Peter Lindell, representing AMF Pension

The composition of the Election Committee meets the Code's requirement with respect to independent members.

H&M deviated from Code rule 2.4 which states, among other things, that the Chairman of the Board shall not be the chairman of the Election Committee. The Election Committee appointed Chairman of the Board Stefan Persson as chairman of the Election Committee during the year on the grounds that this is deemed an obvious choice in view of the ownership structure of H&M.

Since the 2009 AGM the Election Committee has held two meetings at which minutes were taken and the Committee was also in contact between these meetings. At the Election Committee's first meeting Stefan Persson gave a verbal account of the work of the Board during the year. The conclusion was that the Board had worked effectively over the course of the year.

The Board's work is presented so that the Election Committee can make the best possible assessment of the Board's competence and experience. The Election Committee also discussed the size of the Board, its composition and fees for Board members.

No special fees were paid to the Election Committee's chairman or to any of the other members of the Election Committee.

The Election Committee's work in preparation for the next AGM is not yet complete and more information will be presented before the 2010 AGM.

Shareholders wishing to submit proposals to the Election Committee can do so either to individual members of the Election Committee or by letter to:

H & M Hennes & Mauritz AB
Election Committee
106 38 Stockholm
Sweden

valberedningen@hm.com

THE BOARD OF DIRECTORS

The task of the Board of Directors is to manage the company's affairs on behalf of the shareholders. The Board members are elected by the shareholders at the Annual General Meeting for the period until the next AGM. Under Swedish law, trade unions have the right to appoint employee representatives with deputies to the company's Board.

In addition to laws and recommendations, H&M's Board work is regulated by the Board's work plan which contains rules on the distribution of work between the Board and the Managing Director, financial reporting, investments and financing. The work plan, which also contains a work plan for the Auditing Committee, is established once a year.

According to the Articles of Association, H&M's Board is to consist of at least three but no more than twelve members elected by the AGM and no more than the same number of deputies.

The Annual General Meeting determines the exact number of Board members. Since the 2009 AGM the Board has consisted of seven ordinary members and no deputies. There are also two employee representatives and two deputies for these positions. The Board is comprised of seven women and four men and four out of eleven are employed by the company. For facts on H&M's Board members, see page 42. The Board members are to devote the time and attention that their assignment for H&M requires. New Board members receive introductory instruction which, among other things, includes meetings with the heads of various functions.

During the financial year, H&M normally holds five regular board meetings and one statutory board meeting. Extraordinary board meetings are held when the need arises. The Managing Director attends all board meetings, except when the Managing Director's work is being evaluated. The Managing Director reports to the Board on the operational work within the Group and ensures that the Board is given relevant and objective information on which to base its decisions. Other members of the management team, such as the CFO and Chief Accountant, also attend in order to provide the Board with financial information. The Board is assisted by a secretary who is not a member of the Board.

WORK OF THE BOARD IN 2009

H&M's Board held six Board meetings and one statutory meeting during the financial year. One of the meetings is usually an extended meeting and in 2009 it took place in Copenhagen in Denmark and included a visit to a number of stores.

The attendance of the Board members is reported in the table entitled "Composition of the Board of Directors and Attendance in 2009." The former Managing Director Rolf Eriksen attended all of the Board meetings until 30 June 2009. Karl-Johan Persson, in his role as Managing Director, has attended all Board meetings from 1 July 2009.

The Board meetings begin with a discussion of the company's financial situation, with sales, costs and results as the main focus. The Board takes decisions on the interim reports and the Annual Report. Accounting and auditing matters are dealt with within the Auditing Committee and reported back to the Board.

Matters dealt with at the Board meetings in 2009 included the company's main aims for the year, sales development, the focus on costs, currency hedging, the rate of expansion and the results of expansion into for example Russia, Beijing and Lebanon. The Board also reviewed the executive management team's updated risk assessment. In addition, the Managing Director reported on the status of concepts such as COS and H&M Home, the integration of FaBric Scandinavien AB as well as developments in the buying process and internet and catalogue sales, future marketing campaigns, the refurbishment of stores, development of IT support, preparations for expansion into South Korea and the franchise countries, Israel and Jordan etc. The Board has kept itself informed of the company's CSR and environmental work. Decisions taken by the Board in 2009 included among other things the following: the launch of internet sales in the UK in 2010, investments for the total number of stores and the level of the investments.

A committee within the Board consisting of Stefan Persson, Melker Schörling and Bo Lundquist handled the managing director issue as Rolf Eriksen had announced that he would retire in 2009. The Board appointed Karl-Johan Persson, formerly Head of H&M's expansion, Business development, Brand and new business as the new Managing Director and CEO for H&M Hennes & Mauritz AB, taking up the position on 1 July 2009. The Board believes that Karl-Johan Persson has the background, competence and experience needed to lead H&M into the future. Karl-Johan Persson knows the company well and understands its culture. He also has excellent leadership skills.

During the year the Board discussed strategic matters such as competition and development opportunities, and also revised its financial policy. In connection with the Board's review of the proposed Annual Report for 2009, auditor Erik Åström gave an account of the year's audit work.

COMPOSITION OF THE BOARD AND ATTENDANCE IN 2009

NAME	YEAR	INDEPENDENT[1]	INDEPENDENT[2]	FEES[3](SEK)	BOARD MEETINGS	AUDITING COMMITTEE	SHARE-HOLDING	SHARES HELD BY RELATED PARTIES
Stefan Persson, Chairman	1979	No	No	1,350,000	7/7		186,274,400	97,200,000[4] 3,200,000[5]
Fred Andersson[6]	1990	Yes	Yes	375,000	3/4		800	
Mia Brunell Livfors	2008	Yes	Yes	375,000	7/7			300[7]
Lottie Knutson	2006	Yes	Yes	375,000	7/7		600	
Sussi Kvart	1998	Yes	Yes	450,000	7/7	4/4	2,200	850
Bo Lundquist	1995	Yes	Yes	450,000	7/7	4/4		20,000[8]
Stig Nordfelt	1987	Yes	Yes	500,000	7/7	4/4	4,000	
Karl-Johan Persson[6]	2006	No	No	–	3/4		6,066,000	
Melker Schörling	1998	Yes	No	375,000	6/7		114,000[9]	
Marianne Broman, employee rep.	1995	No	No		7/7		70	145
Margareta Welinder, employee rep.	2007	No	No		5/7			
Tina Jäderberg, deputy employee rep.	2007	No	No		7/7			
Agneta Ramberg, deputy employee rep.	1997	No	No		6/7			

1) Independent of the company and company management in accordance with the Swedish Code of Corporate Governance.
2) Independent of major shareholders in the company in accordance with the Swedish Code of Corporate Governance.
3) Fees as resolved at the 2008 Annual General Meeting. The fees relate to the period until the next AGM is held and have been paid out during 2009.
4) Class A shares owned through Ramsbury Invest AB.
5) Class B shares owned through Ramsbury Invest AB.
6) Fred Andersson and Karl-Johan Persson resigned from the Board at the 2009 AGM.
7) Shares held together with related parties
8) Shares owned through Bo Lundquist's company Smideseken AB.
9) Shares owned through Melker Schörling AB.

There are no outstanding share or share price related incentive programmes for the Board of Directors.

INDEPENDENCE OF BOARD MEMBERS

The composition of H&M's Board meets the independence requirements set by NASDAQ OMX Stockholm AB and the Code. This means that the majority of the Board members elected by the general meeting are independent of the company and company management. At least two of these are also independent of the company's major shareholders.

FINANCIAL REPORTING

H&M's financial reporting is carried out in compliance with the laws, statutes, agreements and recommendations that apply to companies listed on NASDAQ OMX Stockholm AB. It falls to the Board of Directors to ensure the quality of financial reporting with the help, for example, of the Auditing Committee (see text below). More information is available in the section on internal control of financial reporting.

H&M's AUDITING COMMITTEE

The Board's Auditing Committee is responsible for making preparations for the Board's work on quality assurance of the company's financial reporting and internal control. The Committee is also the main channel of communication between the Board and the company's auditors. This work involves handling auditing issues and financial reports published by the company.

H&M's Auditing Committee is made up of three Board members. The Committee is appointed annually by the Board of Directors at the statutory Board meeting held in conjunction with the AGM. The Auditing Committee, which consists of chairman Stig Nordfelt and members Sussi Kvart and Bo Lundquist, has held four meetings at which minutes were taken in 2009. The Auditing Committee's composition meets the Code's requirements with respect to independent members.

Authorised Public Accountant Erik Åström attended the Auditing Committee meetings and reported on the auditing assignments. The meetings were also attended by Jyrki Tervonen, CFO and Anders Jonasson, Chief Accountant, among others. The Committee's meetings are minuted and the minutes are then distributed to the Board members.

During the year the Committee addressed issues concerning the company's financial reporting including interim reports and the Annual Report. The Auditing Committee checks that the company effectively carries out its internal control and risk management processes. During the year the Auditing Committee discussed the company's currency hedging policy and the monitoring of the internal pricing model, and gathered information on the scope and focus of auditing assignments, as well as on integration of FaBric Scandinavien and IT development within the Group.

CORPORATE GOVERNANCE REPORT

AUDITORS

The auditors are appointed by the shareholders at the Annual General Meeting every four years. The Auditors scrutinise the company's annual financial statements, consolidated statements and accounts, and the management of the company by the Board and Managing Director.

At the 2009 AGM the registered accounting firm Ernst & Young AB was elected as auditor for H&M for a four-year period, i.e. until the end of the 2013 Annual General Meeting. Authorised Public Accountant Erik Åström from Ernst & Young holds the main responsibility for auditing assignments.

As previously, the 2009 AGM resolved that the auditors' fees should be paid based on the invoices submitted.

Ernst & Young AB is a member of a global network used for auditing assignments for most of the Group companies and meets H&M's requirements with respect to competence and geographical coverage. The auditors' independent status is guaranteed partly by legislation and professional ethics rules, partly by the accounting firm's internal guidelines and partly by the Auditing Committee's guidelines regulating which assignments the accounting firm is permitted to conduct in addition to the audit.

Authorised Public Accountant Erik Åström conducts auditing assignments for a number of listed companies, such as Hakon Invest, Modern Times Group, Saab, Svenska Handelsbanken and Apoteket.

The fees invoiced by the auditors over the past three financial years are as follows:

AUDIT FEES (SEK M)

	GROUP			PARENT COMPANY		
	2009	2008	2007	2009	2008	2007
Ernst & Young						
Audit assignments	16.7	14.5	12.8	2.2	2.2	2.4
Other assignments	15.2	14.0	18.4	0.1	0.6	11.5
Other auditors						
Audit assignments	3.2	2.9	2.5	–	–	–
Other assignments	1.8	1.1	1.3	–	–	–
Total	36.9	32.5	35.0	2.3	2.8	13.9

MANAGING DIRECTOR

The Managing Director is appointed by the Board of Directors and is responsible for the daily management of the company as directed by the Board. This means that the Managing Director must place particular importance on recruiting senior executives, buying and logistics matters, pricing strategy and sales, marketing, expansion, development of the stores, internet and catalogue sales and IT development. The Managing Director reports to the Board on H&M's development and makes the necessary preparations for taking decisions on investments, expansion, etc. The role of Managing Director includes contact with the financial markets, the media and the authorities.

Rolf Eriksen, who retired in 2009, was Managing Director of H&M until 30 June 2009. Karl-Johan Persson took over as Managing Director on 1 July 2009.

INFORMATION ABOUT THE MANAGING DIRECTOR

Karl-Johan Persson, born in 1975, has been the Managing Director and Chief Executive Officer of H & M Hennes & Mauritz AB since 1 July 2009.

Before taking over as Managing Director, Karl-Johan Persson held an operational role within H&M from 2005, including working as Head of expansion, Business development and Brand and new business. Karl-Johan Persson has since 2000 been a member of the boards of H&M's subsidiaries in Denmark, Germany, the US and the UK. Between the years 2006 and 2009 he was also a member of the Board of H&M's parent company.

Between 2001 and 2004 Karl-Johan Persson was CEO of European Network. Karl-Johan holds a BA in Business Administration from the European Business School in London.

His current external board assignments are the Swedish Chamber of Commerce in the UK and the GoodCause foundation. Karl-Johan Persson's H&M shareholding amounts to 6,066,000 shares.

EXECUTIVE MANAGEMENT TEAM AND COUNTRY MANAGERS

H&M has a matrix organisation in which country managers and the members of the executive management team report directly to the Managing Director (see section on control environment). The matrix organisation consists of the sales countries, headed by the country managers, and the central functions/departments for which the executive management team is responsible.

In addition to the Managing Director, the executive managements team comprises twelve people, five of whom are women. These are responsible for the following functions: Finance, Buying, Production, Sales, Expansion, Accounting, Human Resources, Marketing, Communications, IR, Security and Corporate Social Responsibility.

GUIDELINES FOR REMUNERATION PAID TO SENIOR EXECUTIVES

In accordance with the Swedish Companies Act the 2009 Annual General Meeting adopted guidelines for remuneration of senior executives within H&M. To view the full guidelines, please refer to the Administration Report on page 6 of H&M in figures 2009.

H&M has no remuneration committee since the Board of Directors deems it more appropriate for the entire Board to carry out the tasks of a remuneration committee. The Board prepares proposals for guidelines for remuneration to senior executives and these proposals are presented at the Annual General Meetings. The Board decides on the Managing Director's salary according to the guidelines adopted at the 2009 AGM. The terms of employment for other senior executives are decided by the Managing Director and the Chairman of the Board. No severance pay agreements exist within H&M other than for the Managing Director.

INTERNAL CONTROL

This description of H&M's internal control and risk management has been prepared in accordance with sections 10.5 and 10.6 of the Swedish Code of Corporate Governance. The description is not part of the formal Annual Report.

The Board of Directors is responsible for the company's internal control, the overall aim of which is to safeguard the company's assets and thereby its shareholders' investment. Internal control and risk management are part of the Board's and the management's control and follow-up responsibilities the purpose of which is to ensure that the business is managed in the most appropriate and effective manner possible.

H&M uses the COSO framework as a basis for internal control with respect to financial reporting. The COSO framework, which is issued by the Committee of Sponsoring Organizations of the Treadway Commission, is made up of five components: control environment, risk assessment, control activities, information and communication as well as monitoring.

CONTROL ENVIRONMENT

The control environment forms the basis of internal control, because it includes the culture that the Board and management communicate and by which they work. The control environment is made up primarily of ethical values and integrity, expertise, management philosophy, organisational structure, responsibility and authority, policies and guidelines, as well as routines.

Of particular importance is that management documents such as internal policies, guidelines and manuals exist in significant areas and that these provide the employees with solid guidance. Within H&M there exists above all a Code of Ethics; a policy that permeates the entire company since it describes the way in which the employees should act within the company and in business transactions with suppliers.

H&M's internal control structure is based on:
– The division of work between the Board of Directors, the Auditing Committee and the Managing Director, which is clearly described in the Board's formal work plan. The executive management team and the Auditing Committee report regularly to the Board based on established routines.
– The company's organisation and way of carrying on business, in which roles and the division of responsibility are clearly defined.
– Policies, guidelines and manuals; of these, the Code of Ethics, the financial policy, the information policy, the communications policy and the store instructions are examples of important overall policies.
– Awareness among the employees of the maintenance of effective control over financial reporting.
– Control activities, checks and balances, analysis, reporting.

H&M has a matrix organisation, which means that those on the executive management team are responsible for performance within their function in each country (the vertical arrows). The country managers are responsible for profitability in their country and thereby have overall responsibility for all the functions within their operations (the horizontal arrows). The country organisation is in turn divided into regions, with a number of stores in each region.

All the companies within the H&M Group have the same structure and accounting system with the same chart of accounts. This simplifies the creation of appropriate routines and control systems, which facilitates internal control and comparisons between the various companies.

There are detailed instructions for the store staff that control daily work in the stores. Many other guidelines and manuals are also available within the Group. In most cases these are drawn up in the central departments at the head office in Stockholm

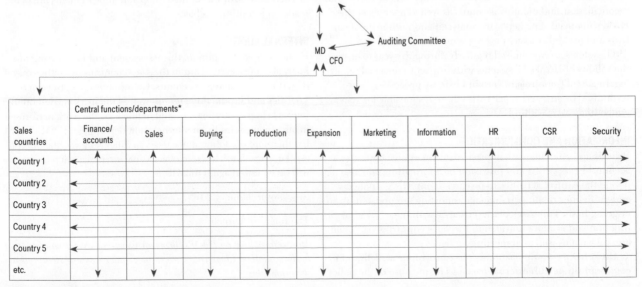

Sales countries	Central functions/departments*									
	Finance/accounts	Sales	Buying	Production	Expansion	Marketing	Information	HR	CSR	Security
Country 1										
Country 2										
Country 3										
Country 4										
Country 5										
etc.										

* Executive management team

CORPORATE GOVERNANCE REPORT

and then communicated to the respective department in the country offices. Each central department regularly reviews its guidelines and manuals to see which ones need updating and whether new guidelines need to be developed.

RISK ASSESSMENT

H&M carries out regular risk analysis to review the risks of errors within its financial reporting. At the end of each financial year the main risks within financial reporting are updated in a group-wide document. The same is done for operational risk. These documents are reviewed by the Auditing Committee and then sent on to the Board of Directors.

Operational risks are also documented on an ongoing basis. During the year the overall risk analysis was updated in order to obtain a general idea of the main risks within each function as well as the systems and methods that are in place to mini-mise any impact of a risk.

Where financial reporting is concerned, H&M has identified certain areas with a higher intrinsic risk of errors, including stock-in-trade shrinkage, cash-desk manipulation, misappropriation of merchandise and the impact of exchange rate fluctuation and taxes.

For a more detailed description of H&M's risks, see the Admin-istration Report, page 8 and Note 2 Financial risks, page 21 in H&M in Figures 2009.

To limit the risks there are appropriate policies and guidelines as well as processes and controls within the business.

CONTROL ACTIVITIES

There are a number of control activities built into every process to ensure that the business is run effectively and that financial reporting on every reporting occasion provides a fair and true picture. The control activities, which aim to prevent, find and correct inaccuracies and non-compliance, are at all levels and in all parts of the organisation. Within H&M the control activities include effective control and analysis of sales statistics, account reconciliation, and monthly accounts as well as analysis of these. H&M's financial statements are analysed and both manual con-trols and feasibility assessments are made.

IT systems are scrutinised regularly during the year to ensure the validity of H&M's IT systems with respect to financial report-ing. In 2009 IT controls in certain business processes were scrutinised by an external party with those responsible for systems and system areas within H&M.

INFORMATION AND COMMUNICATION

Policies and guidelines are of particular importance for accurate accounting, reporting and provision of information, and also define the control activities to be carried out. H&M's policies and guidelines relating to financial reporting are updated on an ongoing basis. This takes place primarily within each central function and is communicated to the sales countries via e-mail and intranet as well as at meetings.

H&M has a communications policy providing guidelines for communication with external parties. The purpose of the policy is to ensure that all information obligations are met and that the information provided is accurate and complete.

Financial information is provided via:
– H&M's Annual Report
– Interim reports, the full year report and monthly sales reports
– Press releases on events that may significantly impact the share price
– H&M's website www.hm.com

MONITORING

As part of the company's 2009 internal control work, the central departments carried out assessments of the respective functions in the sales countries using the COSO model based partly on general issues and partly on department-specific issues. This work resulted in a plan of action for each central department containing the areas that should be improved to further strengthen internal control.

At the stores, annual controls are performed by internal shop controllers with the aim of determining the strengths and weak-nesses of the stores and how any shortcomings can be corrected. Follow-up and feedback with respect to any deviations found during the assessment of internal control constitute a central part of internal control work.

The Board of Directors and the Auditing Committee continuously evaluate the information provided by the executive management team, including information on internal control. The Auditing Committee's task of monitoring the efficiency of internal control by the management team is of particular interest to the Board. This work includes checking that steps are taken with respect to any problems detected and suggestions made during the assessment by the central departments and internal shop controllers as well as by external auditors. The work on internal control during the year has further increased awareness of internal control within the Group and improvements are being made on a continuous basis.

INTERNAL AUDIT

In the company's opinion, the assessment and monitoring of internal control carried out in the sales countries by all the central departments – such as Accounts, Communications, Security, Logistics and Production etc. – as well as the work carried out by internal shop controllers are well in line with the work performed in other companies by an internal audit department. H&M's Board has therefore not found it necessary to establish a specific internal audit department. The issue of a specific internal audit department will be reviewed again in 2010.

Stockholm, January 2010

The Board of Directors

More information on H&M's corporate governance work can be found in the section on Corporate Governance under Investor Relations at www.hm.com.

THE H&M SHARE

KEY RATIOS PER SHARE	2009	2008	2007	2006	2005
Shareholders' equity per share, SEK	49.08	44.65	38.78	33.57	31.33
Earnings per share, SEK	19.80	18.48	16.42	13.05	11.17
Change from previous year, %	+7	+13	+26	+17	+27
Dividend per share, SEK	16.00*	15.50	14.00	11.50	9.50
Market price on 30 November, SEK	412.30	298.00	399.00	319.00	253.00
P/E ratio	21	16	24	24	23

* Board's proposal.

DISTRIBUTION OF SHARES, 30 NOVEMBER 2009

SHAREHOLDINGS	NO. OF SHAREHOLDERS	%	NO. OF SHARES	%	AVERAGE SHARES PER SHAREHOLDER
1–1,000	160,702	93.4	29,132,149	3.5	181
1,001–5,000	8,558	5.0	18,965,696	2.3	2,216
5,001–10,000	1,185	0.7	8,746,473	1.1	7,381
10,001–50,000	1,057	0.6	22,398,802	2.7	21,191
50,001–100,000	177	0.1	12,699,713	1.5	71,750
100,001–	378	0.2	735,593,167	88.9	1,946,014
Total	**172,057**	**100**	**827,536,000**	**100**	**4,810**

MAJOR SHAREHOLDERS, 30 NOVEMBER 2009	NO. OF SHARES	% OF VOTING RIGHTS	% OF TOTAL SHARES
Stefan Persson and family	304,872,400	69.3	36.8
Lottie Tham and family	44,040,200	2.6	5.3
Alecta Pensionsförsäkring	28,685,000	1.7	3.5
JP Morgan Chase Bank	27,483,130	1.6	3.3
Swedbank Robur Fonder	20,036,338	1.2	2.4
AMF Pensionsförsäkring	15,421,912	0.9	1.9
Clearstream Banking	14,604,117	0.9	1.8
Handelsbanken Fonder	13,572,452	0.8	1.6
SSB CL Omnibus AC	12,436,921	0.7	1.5
Folksam KPA Förenade Liv	8,979,005	0.5	1.1

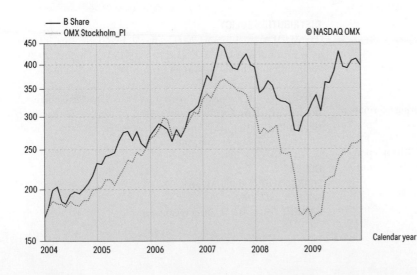

ANNUAL GENERAL MEETING

The Annual General Meeting 2010 will be held at Victoriahallen, Stockholm International Fairs, Stockholm, on Thursday, 29 April at 3 p.m.

Shareholders who are registered in the share register print-out as of Friday 23 April 2010 and who give notice of their intention to attend the AGM no later than Friday, 23 April 2010, will be entitled to participate in the AGM.

NOMINEE SHARES

Shareholders whose shares are registered in the name of a nominee must re-register their shares in their own name in order to be entitled to participate in the AGM. In order to re-register shares in time, shareholders should request temporary owner registration, which is referred to as voting right registration, well in advance of 23 April.

NOTICE

Shareholders must provide notice of their intention to participate in the Annual General Meeting by post, fax, telephone or via H&M's website to:

H & M Hennes & Mauritz AB
Head Office/Carola Echarti-Ardéhn
106 38 Stockholm
Sweden
Telephone: +46 (0)8 796 55 00
Fax: +46 (0)8 796 55 44
www.hm.com/arsstamma

Shareholders must provide their name, civil identity number and telephone number (daytime) when providing notice of their intention to participate.

DIVIDEND

The Board of Directors and the Managing Director have decided to propose to the Annual General Meeting a dividend for 2009 of SEK 16.00 per share. The Board of Directors has proposed 4 May 2010 as the record day. With this record day, Euroclear Sweden AB (formerly VPC AB) is expected to pay the dividend on 7 May 2010. To be guaranteed dividend payment, the H&M shares must have been purchased no later than 29 April 2010.

FINANCIAL INFORMATION

H & M Hennes & Mauritz AB will provide the following information:

8 April 2010	Three month report
29 April 2010	Annual General Meeting 2010 at 3 p.m. at Victoriahallen, Stockholm International Fairs, Stockholm
24 June 2010	Half-year report
29 September 2010	Nine month report
27 January 2011	Full-year report

As previously, we plan to publish sales figures for each month on the 15th of the subsequent month. If the 15th falls on a weekend, the sales figures will be published on the following weekday. However, H&M plans to publish the sales figures for February, May, August and December in each of the subsequent Interim reports.

This information is available at www.hm.com

CONTACT DETAILS

HEAD OFFICE

H & M Hennes & Mauritz AB
Mäster Samuelsgatan 46A
106 38 Stockholm
Sweden
Tel: +46 (0)8 796 55 00

For information about H&M and addresses of the country offices, please see www.hm.com

CEO Karl-Johan Persson
FINANCE Jyrki Tervonen
ACCOUNTS Anders Jonasson
SALES Jonas Guldstrand
BUYING Madeleine Persson
DESIGN Ann-Sofie Johansson
PRODUCTION Karl Gunnar Fagerlin
CORPORATE SOCIAL RESPONSIBILITY Ingrid Schullström
EXPANSION Stefan Larsson
BUSINESS DEVELOPMENT Björn Magnusson
BRAND AND NEW BUSINESS Jörgen Andersson
MARKETING Anna Tillberg Pantzar
COMMUNICATIONS Kristina Stenvinkel
INVESTOR RELATIONS Nils Vinge
HUMAN RESOURCES Sanna Lindberg
IT Kjell-Olof Nilsson
LOGISTICS Danny Feltmann
SECURITY Angelika Giese

DISTRIBUTION POLICY

The H&M Annual Report 2009 comes in two parts: Part 1: H&M in words and pictures 2009, and Part 2: H&M in figures 2009 including the Annual Report and Consolidated Accounts.

H&M sends out the printed version of Parts 1 and 2 to shareholders who have specifically expressed an interest in receiving the printed version. The Annual Report is also available to read and download at www.hm.com

COVER

PHOTOGRAPHY Camilla Åkrans
MODEL Natasha Poly
GARMENT Dress, H&M Garden Collection

ACCOUNTING FOR INTERCOMPANY INVESTMENTS

Throughout this text we have shown you excerpts of financial statements from various Canadian and international companies. Without exception, all of those financial statements were consolidated financial statements. Consolidated financial statements become necessary when one company buys a controlling ownership interest in another company, thus creating a more complex organization and the need for more complete financial reporting than for an individual company. Before we end this text, we want to provide you with a broad understanding of how financial statements become consolidated, and the implications of using consolidated statements for decision-making.

Because an investment in a company's common shares carries with it a right to vote, one company can influence and, under the right circumstances, control the activities of another company. As a result of this, some important financial reporting issues arise for organizations that are considered complex due to intercompany investments. We start with a brief discussion of the purpose of such intercompany investments, and then turn to aspects of their accounting and analysis.

PURPOSE OF INTERCOMPANY INVESTMENTS

A company may have many reasons for acquiring an ownership interest in another company. Buying the shares of another company may be viewed as a good short-term or long-term investment, with such investments broadly classified into two types: non-strategic and strategic.

Non-strategic investments are ones where the investing company (the one buying the shares) has little or no influence over the operations of the other company. The equity securities that a company carries in its current asset account, called short-term investments (or marketable securities), which were discussed in Chapter 6, are examples of this type of investment. If the shares are bought for this reason, the number of shares purchased is usually small compared with the number of outstanding shares. Consequently, the acquiring company has little influence or control over the affairs of the company in which it has invested. Such investments are sometimes called **passive investments** or **portfolio investments** because the acquiring company cannot exercise any influence or control over the decisions of the acquired company. Some non-strategic investments can also be long-term, if management's intention is to hold the security for long-term returns.

A second major reason for obtaining ownership of the shares of another company is to influence or control the decisions that the other company makes. These are **strategic investments**, in which the acquiring company (the **investor**) intends to a have long-term strategic relationship with the acquired company (the **investee**). Common targets for this kind of purchase are competitors, suppliers, and customers. Acquiring a block of shares in a supplier or customer allows the acquiring company to exercise some influence over the production, buying, and selling decisions of the acquired company, which may benefit the acquiring company. If the block of shares purchased is large enough, the acquiring company could have a controlling interest in a competitor, which would allow it to increase its market share by increasing its productive capacity, its geographic market, or both. Buying a controlling interest in a supplier or customer allows the company to ensure a market in which it can buy its raw materials (in the case of a supplier), or sell and distribute its product (in the case of a customer).

Buying a supplier or customer is sometimes referred to as **vertical integration**. **George Weston Limited** is an example of a company that is vertically integrated. It owns 100 percent of Weston Foods, a producer of baked goods, and 62.5 percent of Loblaw Companies Limited, a distributor of food, drug, and general merchandise where the Weston baked goods, among other things, are sold. It had previously also owned dairy and bottling operations that supplied Loblaw.

Combining with a competitor is sometimes referred to as **horizontal integration**. Horizontal integration may offer benefits that come from economies of scale. The company may be able to reduce its workforce or use a single distribution system to avoid duplication of effort. It might also allow the company to enter and compete in different segments of the market. **Cara Operations Limited**, a large private Canadian corporation, is an example of a company that is horizontally integrated. Cara owns several different restaurant and food services businesses, including Swiss Chalet, Harvey's, Kelsey's, and Montana's Cookhouse. Through the different chains, it competes in both the fast food segment of the restaurant business and the casual dining segment.

Another reason for buying and controlling another company is **diversification**. If a company is in a seasonal business, it can protect itself from seasonal declines in one business by investing in another business that is counter-seasonal. **Seasonal businesses** are those that have significant peaks and valleys of activity during the year. A greeting card company is an example of a seasonal business. Some cards, such as birthday cards, are purchased relatively evenly throughout the year. Other cards, such as Christmas and Valentine cards, cause peaks in revenue generation. Such a company may wish to diversify by buying into an automobile dealership business. The peak times for the dealership are likely to be the late summer, when the new cars are introduced, and early spring, when people anticipate travelling over the summer. The greeting card business and the automobile dealership would have peak activities at different times, which would help to even out the revenue flows for the whole business.

Algoma Central Corporation is an example of a diversified Canadian business. Its main focus of operation is marine transportation. It operates several ships, organizes the transportation of goods, provides for the repair and maintenance of ships, and provides marine-engineering services. This business depends not only on the type of goods shipped, but also on the economic environment of the countries to and from which it transports goods. Algoma has countered some of the shipping industry's cyclical nature by investing in commercial real estate. It owns and manages various commercial properties in Ontario. This business is also subject to the economic environment, but is much more localized and would be unlikely to experience the same peaks and valleys as marine transportation.

METHODS OF OBTAINING INFLUENCE AND CONTROL

Perhaps the simplest way to obtain control of the assets of another company is to purchase the assets directly from that company. This is called an **asset purchase**. The accounting for asset purchases is discussed in Chapter 8. If several assets are acquired at one time, such as in the acquisition of an entire division or plant, a single price may be negotiated. As discussed in Chapter 8, this type of purchase is called a basket purchase. The total cost of the purchased assets must be allocated to the individual assets based on their relative fair market values.

When a company buys all the assets of another company, this does not give it influence or control over the second company: the buyer only controls the assets it has purchased. The company that sold the assets can continue to operate, but must now make arrangements to use different assets to generate revenue. An asset purchase does not require consolidated financial statements. Once the new assets are recorded in the accounting system of the buying company, there are no further accounting implications.

The only way to obtain influence or control over another company is to buy its common shares in a **share acquisition**. The investor purchases the shares from the shareholders of the investee in exchange for cash, some of its own shares, some of its debt, or with a combination of all three (cash, shares, and debt). In a share acquisition, the investor can obtain a large degree of influence or control over the investee by acquiring more shares. That influence or control is obtained by exercising the voting rights that the investor obtains with the shares. Ultimate control over the investee's assets and liabilities will occur when the percentage ownership of the voting rights is greater than 50 percent. This is called a **controlling interest**.

An investor can sometimes effectively control an investee even though it owns less than 50 percent of the shares. This can occur in situations where the remaining shares are owned by a large number of investors, none of whom has a very large percentage ownership in the investee (the shares are said to be **widely held** in such situations). For example, if an investor owns, say, 40 percent of an investee and the rest of the shares are widely held, the investor may be able to effectively control the investee's assets and liabilities. Because it is possible to control with less than 50 percent, control is defined as occurring when one company has the "power to govern the financial and operating policies of an entity so as to obtain benefits from its activities."[1]

In a share acquisition, the investee remains a separate legal entity from the investor. The investor company is like any other owner in that it has limited liability with regard to the investee's debts. The investor's liability is limited to the amount invested in the shares. The separation of the legal status of the two companies is one reason this form of acquisition is appealing. The tax status of each company is also separate. Each company must file its own return. For accounting purposes, the separate legal status also means that the investor and the investee each keep their own accounting records, even if the investor has acquired 100 percent of the investee's shares. This presents an accounting problem if the investor controls the investee, because they are, in substance, one accounting entity.

1. *CICA Handbook*, Part I IAS 27, para. 4.

VALUATION ISSUES AT DATE OF ACQUISITION

In any type of acquisition, whether the purchase is of a single asset or an entire company, the fundamental accounting valuation method at the time of acquisition is historical cost. Thus, the new asset or the investment in the investee is recorded at its cost. If the asset is acquired with a payment of cash, the amount of cash serves as the proper measure of the cost. If debt is exchanged for the asset or company, the present value of the debt should be used as the measure of cost.

When shares are issued in the acquisition, their fair market value at the date of acquisition should be used as the measure of cost. A problem exists in valuing shares when the share issue is large, because the number of shares outstanding increases significantly and the value of the investment acquired is not exact. How the market will adjust the existing share price to reflect this acquisition is not known at the date of the transaction. In these situations, instead of using the value of the shares to measure the acquisition, accountants sometimes turn to the fair market value of the assets acquired to measure the value of the shares given up.

Share Acquisition

In a share acquisition, the investor records the acquisition cost in an investment account. There is no breakdown of this cost into individual assets and liabilities in the investor's books, because the assets and liabilities do not technically belong to the investor; they remain the investee's legal property or legal obligation. An investor that owns a large enough percentage of the investee's shares may control the assets economically, through its voting rights, but it does not hold the title to the assets. Nor is it legally obliged to settle the liabilities. Under IFRS, we currently use the **acquisition method** to account for an acquisition of a controlling interest.

When a share acquisition results in gaining control of another company, the acquiring company (investor) is called the **parent** and the acquired company (investee) is called the **subsidiary**. As previously explained, both the parent company and the subsidiary company are separate legal entities that keep separate books, prepare separate financial statements, and pay separate taxes. To provide users with information about the whole economic entity or group (parent and subsidiaries), accountants prepare **consolidated financial statements**, which add the components of the various financial statements of the parent and the subsidiaries together. The consolidated statements enable users to see the total cash that the entity controls, the total inventory it owns, the total revenues it earns, and so forth. Complications arise in the consolidation process if there have been transactions between the parent and the subsidiaries. Because such transactions occur within the group or economic entity (parent and subsidiaries), they are deemed not to have occurred and they must be eliminated. More will be said about this later.

The annual report for **H&M** presented in Appendix A shows the financial statements for both the parent company and the group, or consolidated, financial statements. Normally in North America the parent company's financial statements are not presented in the annual report, only the consolidated ones. H&M's report gives us an opportunity to see the difference between the two sets of financial statements.

The Parent Company financial statements for H&M (pages A13–A16) present the legal view of the parent company. The shares it owns in all of the subsidiaries are reported on the Parent Company Balance Sheet in Financial Fixed Assets under the heading "Shares and participation rights." The amount reported is SEK572 million. The names of all of the individual subsidiaries owned by H&M are listed in Note 24, shown in Exhibit B-1. The SEK572 million represents the cost paid by H&M for the shares of the subsidiaries. It is equal to the net asset value of those companies at the time of acquisition (remember, net asset value = assets − liabilities).

H&M 2009 ANNUAL REPORT
Excerpt from Note 24 to the Financial Statements

EXHIBIT B-1

annual report

24 PARTICIPATIONS IN GROUP COMPANIES

All Group companies are wholly-owned except FaBric Scandinavien AB which is owned to 60 percent. The parties have also signed an agreement under which H&M has the opportunity/obligation to acquire the remaining shares within three to seven years.

2009	Corporate ID number	No. of shares	Book value	Domicile
Parent company shareholding				
Bekå AB	556024-2488	450	1.3	Stockholm
H & M Hennes & Mauritz Sverige AB	556151-2376	1,250	0.1	Stockholm
H & M Rowells AB	556023-1663	1,150	0.6	Stockholm
H & M Hennes & Mauritz GBC AB	556070-1715	1,000	2.6	Stockholm
H & M Hennes & Mauritz International B.V.		40	0.1	Netherlands
H & M India Private Ltd		1,633,500	2.9	India
H & M Hennes & Mauritz Japan KK		99	11.7	Japan
FaBric Scandinavien AB	556663-8522	828	552.9	Tranås
H & M Hennes & Mauritz International AB	556782-4890	1,000	0.1	Stockholm
Total			**572.3**	

In contrast, the Group Balance Sheet for H&M (page A10) includes all of the individual assets and liabilities of the subsidiaries added to the parent's assets and liabilities. Note that there is no "Shares and participation rights" asset on the group balance sheet; that single amount for the net assets is replaced by all of the assets and liabilities. When all of the assets of the subsidiaries are included (instead of only the net assets) the total group assets are SEK54,363 million, more than three times greater than the SEK17,148 million that the parent H&M reported! You can easily see how the group or consolidated financial statements paint a more complete picture of the assets that are under the control of H&M than the parent financial statements did.

As well as providing information about the total entity, consolidated financial statements hide information about the individual companies in the group. Because users are usually not given information about these individual companies, they have difficulty determining the risks and rewards contributed by each. To address this problem, if a company, through its activities, is involved in various industries or geographic locations, it is required to disclose segmented information in the notes to its financial statements. The segmented information provides some breakdown of accounts in the different segments (industries or geographic locations) so that users can evaluate the segments' potential future impact on the total entity. Note 3 on Segmented Information (page A22) from the H&M annual report provides information about sales, operating profits, and assets and liabilities in different regions. The information is still very highly aggregated—only a total asset and liability figure net of tax assets or liabilities is reported, not individual ones—but it helps a reader understand some of the risks and opportunities facing the enterprise.

As mentioned earlier, when the parent purchases a controlling number of shares in a subsidiary company, it has an investment on its books that it has recorded at the cost of the purchase. Because another company is being controlled and consolidated financial statements are therefore going to be prepared, the transaction is viewed as a basket purchase. The cost to acquire the subsidiary needs to be allocated to the subsidiary's individual assets and liabilities based on their fair market values at the date of acquisition, just as with any other basket purchase. This allocation is not recorded on the actual books of either the parent or the subsidiary, but instead is determined during the work sheet preparation of the consolidated financial statements. When the subsidiary's assets and liabilities are added to those of the parent so that consolidated financial statements can be prepared, it is the fair values of the subsidiary's assets and liabilities at the date of acquisition that are added to the historical cost assets and liabilities of the parent. The fair value at the date of acquisition is the "cost" to the parent company of these assets and liabilities and is normally different from the cost of the same assets and liabilities when the subsidiary purchased them.

The Acquisition Method

When allocating the purchase price, all the assets and liabilities in the subsidiary are first measured at their fair market values. Some assets that did not exist on the subsidiary's books may be found and included in this measurement process. For example, if the subsidiary developed a patent or a trademark internally, the costs of such an item would have been expensed (see Chapter 8 for a discussion of whether to capitalize or expense the costs of these types of assets). The parent would need to identify all the assets that the subsidiary owned or had the right to use, and establish values for those items using current items similar to them in the market, estimations of future benefits, or appraisals as a guide. By buying the shares, the parent is now also controlling these assets, and part of the acquisition cost should be allocated to them if they have a measurable market value. All of these assets and liabilities—those on the books and those that have value but are not on the books—are known as the subsidiary's **identifiable net assets**. In the year that a parent buys a subsidiary, the components of the assets and liabilities that were purchased will be disclosed in the notes to the consolidated financial statements. In 2008, H&M acquired 60 percent of Swedish fashion company FaBric Scandinavien AB. Exhibit B-2 is an excerpt from Note 21 of the 2008 financial statements and itemizes how the total acquisition cost of SEK927 million was allocated to the assets and liabilities. Note that SEK470 million was allocated to an intangible fixed asset for Brands, which had not previously been recognized on FaBric's financial statements.

H&M 2008 ANNUAL REPORT
Note 21 to the Financial Statements

21 COMPANY ACQUISITION

As announced in a press release on 6 March 2008, H&M has signed an agreement to acquire the privately owned Swedish fashion company FaBric Scandinavien AB, which designs and sells fashion under a number of own brands, such as Cheap Monday, and operates the store chains Weekday and Monki. Following approval by the relevant competition authorities, H&M acquired 60 percent of the shares in the company for SEK 551 m in cash on 30 April 2008. Thus FaBric Scandinavien AB is included in the consolidated accounts from 1 May 2008. The parties also signed an agreement under which H&M has the opportunity/obligation to acquire the remaining shares within three to five years. The assessed value of the put options allocated to minority shareholders in connection with the acquisition is reported as a provision for an additional contingent consideration. Therefore no minority interest is reported. At the time of acquisition the provision was SEK 368 m. Any change in fair value of the put options/additional consideration will be recorded as an adjustment of goodwill. The total consideration including the provision for put options allocated to minority shareholders is calculated at SEK 919 m. To this are added acquisition costs of SEK 8 m, making the total acquisition cost SEK 927 m. The acquisition gives rise to goodwill of SEK 431 m after intangible fixed assets identified relating to the brands of SEK 470 m and customer relations of SEK 131 m and a deferred tax liability of SEK 169 m. Goodwill arising from the acquisition relates to synergy effects etc. achieved due, among other things, to economies of scale in production, logistics, expansion and know-how in the existing organisation.

The assets and liabilities included in the acquisition are as follows:

SEK m	Reported value in FaBric Scandinavien AB	Value according to acquisition analysis
Intangible fixed assets		
– Brands*		470
– Customer relations*		131
– Leasehold rights	8	8
Tangible fixed assets	42	42
Financial fixed assets	1	1
Stock-in-trade	48	48
Other current assets	51	51
Liquid funds	4	4
Deferred tax liabilities	-5	-174
Non current liabilities	-22	-22
Current liabilities	-63	-63
Acquired identifiable net assets		**496**
Goodwill		431
Total	**64**	**927**
Consideration for shares in subsidiary		551
Acquisition expenses		8
Provision for additional consideration/put options		368
Total acquisition cost		**927**

* The utilisation period for these assets has been assessed as ten years.

FaBric Scandinavien AB's result after tax for the shortened financial year, 1 May 2008 to 30 November 2008, amounted to SEK 9 m, sales excluding VAT for the same period amounted to SEK 218 m.

If the purchase price is more than the fair market value of the identifiable net assets (often referred to as **excess fair market value**), another asset called **goodwill** must be reported (see Chapter 8). It represents all the unidentifiable intangible reasons that motivated the investor to pay more for the investee than the sum of the fair market values of the purchased company's individual assets and liabilities. For example, perhaps the investor expects to earn extra future cash flows as a result of economies of scale or synergies, or perhaps the business is located in a high-traffic area and so has a greater chance at higher revenues than businesses located elsewhere. Perhaps the sales personnel in the business have created a loyal customer following that leads to consistent revenues, or previous advertising campaigns may have made this a well-known business. In H&M's acquisition of FaBric, of the SEK927 million total acquisition cost, SEK496 million was allocated to identifiable assets and liabilities (including the intangible asset Brands discussed earlier). The balance of the cost, SEK431 million, was recognized as goodwill. If, on the other hand, the purchase price is less than the fair value of the identifiable net assets, negative goodwill is created. This negative goodwill is recognized as a gain on the purchase in the year it occurs. This is a topic for an advanced accounting course.

INCOME RECOGNITION ISSUES SUBSEQUENT TO ACQUISITION

Income recognition issues subsequent to acquisition are a consequence of the valuation decisions made at the date of acquisition. In the following subsections, these issues are discussed for asset acquisitions and share acquisitions.

Asset Purchases

Subsequent to purchase, these are accounted for in the same way as any other acquisition of assets. If the asset acquired is property, plant, or equipment, it is amortized like any other such asset. If the asset purchased is inventory, it ultimately affects the cost of goods sold when it is sold.

Share Acquisitions

The accounting treatment of income subsequent to a share acquisition depends on the level of control that the investor exerts over the investee. As examples of the conceptual differences, consider two extreme cases. The first case is one in which the investor owns only a few shares in the investee, and the second is one in which the investor buys 100 percent of the investee's shares.

Case 1

If the investor buys only a few shares of the investee, it has virtually no control or influence over the investee. The investor cannot dictate the dividend policy or any other strategic policy to the investee. As indicated earlier, this is a non-strategic investment. The shareholders of the investor company in such a situation are unlikely to be interested in the full details of the investee's operating performance. They are probably more interested in the cash flows that have come in from their investment (dividends) and in the current market value of the investment. Therefore, income recognition should show dividend revenue and the change in the value of the investment. As noted in Chapter 6, held-for-trading investments are valued at their fair market value, and any gains or losses resulting from the change since the last valuation are recognized in income of the period.

Case 2

In this case, where the investor owns 100 percent of the investee's shares, the investor's shareholders will likely want to know the operating details of the investee's performance because they economically control all of its assets and liabilities. For example, if the investee that was purchased was a competitor, the sales results of the purchasing company's product are the combined results of the investor and the investee. To show only the details for the investor would be misleading in terms of the resources controlled by the shareholders. The investor's shareholders would probably find information about the two companies' combined assets and liabilities more useful than simply a listing of the investor's assets and liabilities. A set of statements that conveys this information is a set of consolidated financial statements, as mentioned earlier. Consolidated financial statements are prepared as if the investor and investee were one legal company, because the two companies represent one economic accounting entity.

What Is Canadian Practice?

This section of the appendix will describe the guidelines that have been established under IFRS for the acquisition of various blocks of shares. It is important to understand these guidelines because they tell you how companies will describe their various acquisitions and how they are accounting for them. You will need to know the various methods used so that you can understand each one's effects on the financial statements.

Under IFRS, control is determined by the investor's power to govern the financial and operating policies of the investee so as to obtain benefits from its activities. As mentioned previously, this usually means that the investor owns more than 50 percent of the investee's voting shares; but in some situations, as mentioned previously, control can occur with less than 50 percent ownership.

Because control is evidenced by the ability to determine certain activities in another company, IFRS provides guidelines or recommended cut-offs for the percentages of ownership (in voting shares) that require different accounting treatments. Exhibit B-3 outlines these cut-offs:

- Small investments (less than 20 percent), ones that we will refer to as non-strategic investments, are accounted for as either held-for-trading or available-for-sale. Held-for-trading investments were covered in Chapter 6. For the purpose of the discussion in this appendix, we will assume non-strategic investments are classified as available-for-sale. Non-strategic investments can be subdivided into those that are current, which we usually label "short-term investments," and those that are non-current, which are generally labelled "investments" and are long-term.

- Larger investments where control is present (greater than 50 percent) require consolidation; that is, consolidated financial statements must be prepared.

- For investments that fall between these two extremes, the companies are considered to be associated and the acquiring company is considered to have significant influence over activities in the investee. Significant influence is evidenced by being able to elect a person to the board of directors, having significant transactions between the two companies, or having an exchange of technology or managerial personnel. When significant influence exists, another method, called the equity method, is required. Each of these methods is discussed in detail in the following pages.

The percentage cut-offs identified in Exhibit B-3 are only a guide. If a company can demonstrate that it possesses either more or less control than the percentage ownership indicates, it can apply a different method. For example, a company may only own 15 percent of another company but, due to the volume of intercompany transactions, or the ability to elect someone to the board of directors, the investor may be able to exercise significant influence over the investee. The key issue in determining the appropriate accounting method to be used is not the percentage of ownership, per se, but whether the investor has significant influence or control over the investee. Each method carries its own set of accounting implications for the company, as discussed in the following subsections.

ACCOUNTING METHODS FOR INVESTMENTS

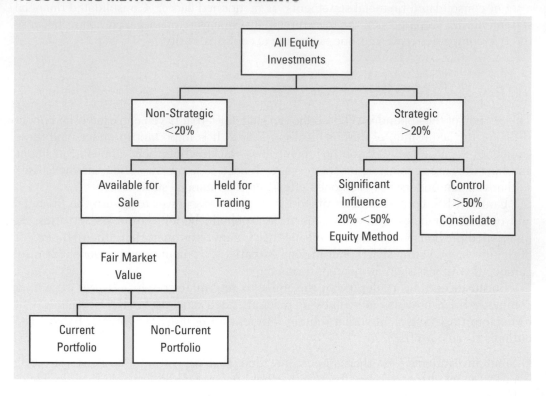

Available for Sale

In Chapter 6, we identified four types of financial instruments: held-for-trading, available-for-sale, held-to-maturity, and loans and receivables. For simplicity, we assumed that all short-term investments were held for-trading, but management classifies the investment based on its intention and the features of the asset. Management can elect to not classify an investment as held for trading and instead classify it as available for sale. These investments are reported at their market value on each statement of financial position date, but the gains and losses arising from the change in market values are reported in other comprehensive income and not directly in net earnings. When an available-for-sale security is sold, the gains and losses are said to be realized and they are reclassified from other comprehensive income to net earnings. The basic difference between the two methods is that under the available-for-sale classification fluctuations in the market value of the security will not affect net earnings until the asset is sold. The reasoning behind this treatment is that, because the fluctuations in value are not a result of management decisions, the unrealized gains and losses should not be considered part of regular operations as depicted on the statement of earnings. Any dividends received while owning the shares are reported as investment income under both methods.

The details of the distinction between the held-for-trading and available-for-sale classifications are best left for intermediate level accounting courses. What you need to understand for the purpose of this appendix is that under both methods the investments are carried at market value on the statement of financial position; however, although the gains and losses on held-for-trading securities are recognized in net earnings as they occur, gains and losses on available-for-sale investments are recognized in net earnings only when the securities are sold.

Available-for-sale investments can be classified as either current or non-current assets, depending on management's intended holding period. For example, if management expects to build a new production facility in two years, it may start setting aside some cash or excess funds in investments. As management intends to hold the securities for longer than a year, the securities would be classified as non-current assets; but if management did need those funds before then, the securities would be available for management to sell.

It is possible for there to be no market value that is readily available for a security that management has designated as available for sale. This would be the case if the securities were part of a private corporation, or for some other reason were not actively trading on the stock market (for example, if the company were in bankruptcy protection). In these cases, it is not possible to value the investment at market value on the statement of financial position date and the cost method is instead used.

Cost Method

In the **cost method**, the investment is carried in the investment account at its cost. During the period in which the investment is held, dividend revenue is recognized as investment income. Because the security is not revalued to market, there are no gains and losses recognized until the security is sold.

IFRS INSIGHTS

The International Accounting Standards Board (IASB) has approved a new standard, IFRS 9, which replaces the existing standard for financial instruments. The new standard is not mandatory until January 1, 2013, and will modify some of the accounting for non-strategic investments and eliminate the option to use the cost method. The material in this appendix reflects the existing standard, although companies may choose to adopt the new standard before 2013.

Consolidation Method

As explained earlier in this appendix, **consolidation** is required when an investor (parent company) controls the activities of an investee (subsidiary). For instructional purposes, we will assume here that the investor owns more than 50 percent of the investee's outstanding shares. Because the subsidiary is still legally a separate company, the parent company records its investment in the subsidiary company in an investment account in the parent company's accounting system. However, because the parent company, through its ownership of the majority of shares, controls the subsidiary's assets and liabilities, it is probably more useful to the parent company's shareholders to report the full details of the subsidiary's assets, liabilities, and earnings, rather than a single amount in the investment account and a single amount of income from the subsidiary on the statement of earnings. The purpose of consolidating, therefore, is to replace the investment account with the subsidiary's individual assets and liabilities. On the consolidated financial statements, it then looks as though the two companies are one; that is, as if they had merged. You must recognize, however, that this is simply an "as if" representation of the combined company. The accounting systems are not merged. In fact, the consolidated statements are prepared on "working papers"; no actual entries are made to either company's accounting system.

Because consolidation reflects an acquisition, the consolidated statements are prepared using the fair market value of the subsidiary's assets and liabilities acquired, as well as any goodwill. These amounts are combined with the book values of the parent's assets and liabilities.

Equity Method

Between the two extremes of no control and complete control lies the situation in which the two companies are associated and the investor can significantly influence the investee but not completely control its decisions. Canadian practice is to refer to these investments as "investments in **significantly influenced companies**," whereas IFRS uses the term "investment in **associated companies**." In practice you may see both terms. The accounting method used, the **equity method**, tries to strike some middle ground between showing all the assets, liabilities, and income items in the financial statements (consolidation) and showing only the dividend revenue from the investment (available-for-sale method). The equity method requires that the investor reflect the effects of its proportionate share of the investee's financial results. Its share of the net assets (assets minus liabilities) is therefore reported as a single line item, "Investment in shares," or "Investment in associated companies," on the investor's statement of financial position. Its share of the net earnings is also reported as a single revenue item, "Equity in earnings of investee," on the statement of operations. Because of the netting of assets and liabilities as well as revenues and expenses, this method is sometimes referred to as **one-line consolidation**.

To illustrate the entries made in a simple case using the available-for-sale method and the equity method, let us assume the following facts and refer to the investee as the associate company. The investor bought 30 percent of the associate's outstanding shares for $10,000. During the first year of the investment, the associate's earnings were $3,000 and dividends of $1,000 were declared. At the end of the year, the market value of the associate's shares was $11,000. In Case A, it is assumed that the 30 percent does not give the investor significant influence (available-for-sale method required), and in Case B, it is assumed that significant influence is present (equity method required). The entries that the investor makes to account for the investment in the first year are as follows:

CASE A (AVAILABLE-FOR-SALE METHOD)			CASE B (EQUITY METHOD)		
Investor's entry to record the acquisition of the shares:					
Investment in Shares (A)	10,000		Investment in Shares (A)	10,000	
Cash (A)		10,000	Cash (A)		10,000
Investor's entry to record the earnings of the associate:					
No entry			Investment in Shares (A)	900[a]	
			Equity in Earnings of Investee (SE)		900
Investor's entry to record dividends received from the associate:					
Cash (A)	300[b]		Cash (A)	300	
Dividend Revenue (SE)		300	Investment in Shares (A)		300
Investor's entry to record the change in the market value of the shares:					
Investment in Shares (A)	1,000		No entry		
Other Comprehensive Income (SE)		1,000			

[a] Investor's percentage ownership × earnings of associate = 30% × $3,000 = $900.
[b] Investor's percentage ownership × dividends of associate = 30% × $1,000 = $300.

Under the equity method, the entry to record the earnings shows that the investment account increases by the investor's share of the associated company's earnings. The investment account represents the investor's investment in the associate (its share of the associate's equity) and, as the associate company earns income and increases its shareholders' equity, the investor's records reflect that increase in value by the increase in the investment account. The credit part of this entry is to the statement of earnings in a line item called "**Equity in earnings of investee**" (abbreviated as EEI).

The entry to record the associate's dividends causes a decrease in the investor's investment account. This should make sense because, on the associate company's books, the declaration of dividends causes a decrease in the shareholders' equity of the company. Because the investor's investment account measures its share of that equity, the investment account should decrease with the declaration of dividends. Another way to think about this is to imagine that the investment represents a deposit in a savings account. The interest on the savings account would be equivalent to the subsidiary's earnings. Withdrawals from the savings account would be the equivalent of the dividends declared. Withdrawals decrease the balance in the savings account in the same way that dividends reduce the investment account.

The effects of those entries on the statement of operations and statement of financial position year-end balance are summarized in the following table:

	AVAILABLE-FOR-SALE	EQUITY METHOD
Investment in Shares (A)	$11,000	$10,600[a]
Investment income (SE)	300	900
Other comprehensive income	1,000	Not applicable

[a] 10,000 + 900 − 300

CONSOLIDATION PROCEDURES AND ISSUES

There are many procedures and issues that are important to understanding consolidated statements, but they are complex enough that an advanced accounting course is usually necessary to thoroughly understand them. To give you a general idea of the procedures that are necessary under consolidation, we will show you the consolidation of a subsidiary that is 100 percent owned. This will be followed by a discussion of the issues surrounding the handling of a subsidiary that is less than 100 percent owned, and of intercompany transactions.

Consolidation Procedures—100 Percent Acquisition

To illustrate the concepts behind the preparation of a consolidated set of financial statements, we will consider a share acquisition in which the parent acquires 100 percent of the subsidiary. To make the example as concrete as possible, let's assume that the statements of financial position of the parent (referred to as Parent Company) and the subsidiary (referred to as Sub Company) just prior to the acquisition are as shown in Exhibit B-4.

EXHIBIT B-4

PARENT AND SUBSIDIARY STATEMENTS OF FINANCIAL POSITION

	Parent Company	Sub Company
Assets other than PP&E	$2,200	$1,500
Property, plant, and equipment	1,800	1,000
Total assets	$4,000	$2,500
Total liabilities	$2,000	$1,500
Shareholders' equity	2,000	1,000
Total liabilities and shareholders' equity	$4,000	$2,500

Assume that, at acquisition, Parent Company pays $1,400 in cash for all the outstanding shares of Sub Company. Because the book value of Sub Company's equity (net assets) is $1,000 at the date of acquisition, Parent Company has paid $400 more than the book value of the acquired company's assets and liabilities. Assume further that $250 of this $400 relates to the additional fair market value of Sub's property, plant, and equipment. It will be assumed that the fair market value of Sub's other assets and liabilities are equal to their book values. This means that the remainder of the $400, or $150, is due to goodwill. Exhibit B-5 illustrates these assumptions.

Parent Company records its investment in an account called Investment in Sub Company. Because Parent Company owns more than 50 percent of the shares of Sub Company, it controls Sub Company and will have to prepare consolidated financial statements. For its part, because Sub Company remains a separate legal entity, it will continue to record its transactions in its own accounting system. Parent Company will also continue to keep track of its own transactions in its own accounting system on what are known as the **parent-only books**. At the end of each accounting period, the two entities' separate financial statements will be combined on a work sheet to produce the consolidated financial statements, as if the two companies were one legal entity. Because the Investment in Sub Company account will be replaced in the consolidation process by the individual assets and liabilities of Sub Company, it does not really matter, from a consolidated point of view, how Parent accounts for its investment on the parent-only statements. However, it will make a difference in the parent-only financial statements. Some companies use the equity method to account for the investment,

EXHIBIT B-5

REPRESENTATION OF THE PURCHASE PRICE COMPOSITION

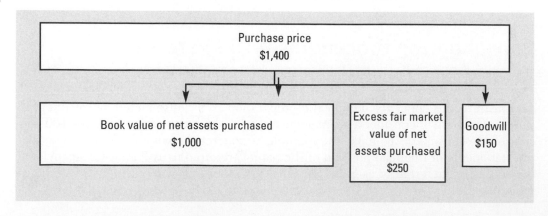

and some use the cost method. Assuming that Parent Company uses the equity method, the investment entry is as follows:

INVESTMENT ENTRY		
Investment in Sub Company (A)	1,400	
Cash (A)		1,400

After recording the investment, the statements of financial position of Parent Company and Sub Company will appear as in Exhibit B-6.

PARENT AND SUBSIDIARY STATEMENTS OF FINANCIAL POSITION
At Date of Acquisition

EXHIBIT B-6

	Parent Company	Sub Company
Assets other than PP&E	$ 800	$1,500
Property, plant, and equipment	1,800	1,000
Investment in Sub Company	1,400	–
Total assets	$4,000	$2,500
Total liabilities	$2,000	$1,500
Shareholders' equity	2,000	1,000
Total liabilities and shareholders' equity	$4,000	$2,500

To prepare a consolidated statement of financial position for Parent Company at the date of acquisition, the Investment in Sub Company account must be replaced by the individual assets and liabilities of Sub Company. This would normally be done on a set of **consolidating working papers**. The consolidating entries that are discussed next are made on the consolidating working papers, and no entries would be made directly in either the parent company's or the subsidiary company's accounting system. The accountant starts the working papers by placing the financial statements as prepared by the parent company and the subsidiary side by side, as shown in Exhibit B-7. The working papers will then have columns for the consolidating entries and for the consolidated totals. Note that the exhibit shows debit and credit columns for all four items.

CONSOLIDATING WORKING PAPERS

EXHIBIT B-7

Account	Parent Company Debit	Parent Company Credit	Sub Company Debit	Sub Company Credit	Consolidating Entries Debit	Consolidating Entries Credit	Consolidated Totals Debit	Consolidated Totals Credit
Assets other than PP&E	800		1,500					
Property, plant, and equipment	1,800		1,000					
Investment in Sub Company	1,400							
Liabilities		2,000		1,500				
Shareholders' equity		2,000		1,000				
Totals	4,000	4,000	2,500	2,500				

On the consolidating working papers, each row will be added across to obtain the consolidated totals. If no adjustments are made to the balances shown in Exhibit B-7, several items will be double-counted. First, the subsidiary's net assets will be counted twice: once in the individual accounts of Sub and again as the net amount in Parent's investment account. One or the other of these two amounts must be eliminated. Because the idea of consolidated statements is to show the subsidiary's individual assets and liabilities in the consolidated totals, the best option is to eliminate the parent's investment account. The second item that will be counted twice is in the shareholders' equity section. The only outside shareholders of the consolidated company are the parent company's shareholders. The shareholders' equity represented by the subsidiary's balances is held by the parent company. The shareholders' equity section of the subsidiary must, therefore, be eliminated. Both of these items are eliminated in a working paper entry called an **elimination entry**. The elimination entry for our example is as follows:

WORKING PAPER ELIMINATION ENTRY		
Shareholders' Equity—Sub Company (SE)	1,000	
???	400	
Investment in Sub Company (A)		1,400

In the preceding entry, you can see that, in order to balance the entry, additional debits totalling $400 are needed. What does this $400 difference represent? It represents the excess amount that Parent Company paid for its interest in Sub Company over the net assets' book value. Remember the assumption that this excess is broken down into $250 for the excess of the fair market value of property, plant, and equipment over its book value, and $150 for goodwill. Therefore, the complete entry would be as follows:

WORKING PAPER ELIMINATION ENTRY (ENTRY 1)		
Shareholders' Equity—Sub Company (SE)	1,000	
Property, plant, and equipment (A)	250	
Goodwill (A)	150	
Investment in Sub Company (A)		1,400

As a result of the elimination entry, the consolidating working papers would appear as in Exhibit B-8. The working paper entries are numbered so that you can follow them from the journal entry form to the working paper form.

Note that shareholders' equity on a consolidated basis is the same as on the parent company's books. This is true because all that consolidation has really done is replace the net assets represented in the investment account with the individual assets and liabilities that make up the subsidiary's net assets. In this sense, the statements of the parent company (which are referred to as the parent-only statements) portray the same net results to the shareholders as the consolidated statements. However, the consolidated statements present somewhat different information to the shareholders in that ratios, such as the debt to equity ratio, can be quite different from those found in parent-only statements. For example, from Exhibit B-8 you can calculate the debt to equity ratio for the parent-only statements as 1.0 ($2,000/$2,000), whereas in the consolidated statements, it is 1.75 ($3,500/$2,000). This occurs because consolidating

CONSOLIDATING WORKING PAPERS
(Statement of Financial Position Only)

Account	Parent Company Debit	Parent Company Credit	Sub Company Debit	Sub Company Credit	Consolidating Entries Debit	Consolidating Entries Credit	Consolidated Totals Debit	Consolidated Totals Credit
Assets other than PP&E	800		1,500				2,300	
Property, plant, and equipment	1,800		1,000		(1) 250		3,050	
Goodwill	–		–		(1) 150		150	
Investment in Sub Company	1,400					1,400 (1)		
Liabilities		2,000		1,500				3,500
Shareholders' equity		2,000		1,000	(1) 1,000			2,000
Totals	4,000	4,000	2,500	2,500	1,400	1,400	5,500	5,500

the two companies produces a leverage ratio that reflects both the parent's and the sub's debt, yet only the parent's equity. However, although the debt to equity ratio appears to be less favourable on the consolidated statements, users must remember that Sub Company is a separate legal entity and is responsible for its own debts. Parent Company has limited liability. For this reason, creditors such as banks prefer to see parent-only financial statements when they assess a company's ability to repay debt.

Now consider what the financial statements of Parent Company and Sub Company might look like one year after acquisition. The two companies' accounts are shown in Exhibit B-9 (remember that EEI stands for equity in earnings of the investee).

PARENT AND SUBSIDIARY STATEMENTS OF FINANCIAL POSITION AND STATEMENTS OF EARNINGS

One Year after Acquisition	Parent Company	Sub Company
Statement of financial position		
Assets other than PP&E	$1,400	$1,950
Property, plant, and equipment	1,850	850
Investment in Sub Company	1,475	–
Total assets	$4,725	$2,800
Total liabilities	$2,330	$1,700
Shareholders' equity	2,395	1,100
Total liabilities and shareholders' equity	$4,725	$2,800
Statement of earnings		
Revenues	$1,500	$1,000
Expenses other than depreciation	(860)	(700)
Depreciation expense	(250)	(150)
Equity in Sub Company's Earnings (EEI)	125	—
Net earnings	$ 515	$ 150
Dividends declared	$ 120	$ 50

Using the equity method, Parent Company would make the following entries in its parent-only books to account for its investment:

ENTRIES USING THE EQUITY METHOD
(ON PARENT COMPANY'S BOOKS)

Parent's share (100%) of Sub's income:

Investment in Sub Company (A)	150	
EEI (SE)		150

Parent's share (100%) of Sub's dividends:

Cash (A)	50	
Investment in Sub Company (A)		50

After these entries, the ending balance in the investment account will be $1,500 ($1,400 + $150 − $50). However, you will note in the statements in Exhibit B-9 that the investment account has a balance of $1,475. The difference in these amounts is due to the fact that Parent Company paid more than the book value for the net assets of Sub Company. As we assumed earlier, Parent Company paid $400 more than the book value ($1,000). The $400 is due to the extra fair market value of property, plant, and equipment ($250) and goodwill ($150). Subsequent to acquisition, the property, plant, and equipment must be depreciated and the depreciation is shown as part of the EEI. Assume that the property, plant, and equipment have a remaining useful life of 10 years, have a residual value of zero, and are depreciated using the straight-line method. Therefore, Parent Company must take an additional $25 ($250 ÷ 10 years) in depreciation expense over what is shown on the books of Sub Company. The depreciation of the property, plant, and equipment means that Parent Company has to report an additional $25 in expenses during each year subsequent to acquisition. Using the equity method, Parent Company shows these additional expenses as a part of the EEI. The following entry is made (in addition to those shown earlier):

DEPRECIATION ENTRY UNDER EQUITY METHOD
(ON PARENT COMPANY'S BOOKS)

EEI (SE)	25	
Investment in Sub Company (A)		25

With this additional entry, the balance in the Investment in Sub Company account is $1,475, exactly the balance shown in Exhibit B-9.

The $150 of goodwill is not amortized. Instead, it is checked each year to determine if its value has been impaired. To keep our example simple, we are going to assume that there is no impairment and the goodwill is still worth $150.

The consolidated working papers at the end of the first year are presented in Exhibit B-10. You should note that they are shown in the **trial balance phase**. In the trial balance phase, the temporary statement of earnings and dividends declared accounts still have balances that have not been closed to retained earnings. (See Chapter 3 if you need to refresh your memory about the meaning of the trial balance phase and the closing process.) Note that shareholders' equity has the same balance as it had at the beginning of the year.

In the year subsequent to acquisition, three basic consolidating working paper entries are made if the parent company is using the equity method to account for the investment on the parent-only financial statements. In addition to eliminating the investment account and the shareholders' equity accounts discussed earlier, the EEI must be eliminated, as must the subsidiary's dividends declared account. Otherwise, the subsidiary's income would be counted twice, once as EEI and a second time as the individual revenue and expense items. Dividends declared by the subsidiary are inter-company transfers of cash, from a consolidated point of view. They are not dividends to outside shareholders and, as such, they should be eliminated in the consolidation process. The entry to eliminate EEI and dividends will be called the reversal of current year entries because the entry is, in effect, removing income and dividends recognized during the period. Once these two entries have been made, the third set of entries recognizes the extra depreciation expense discussed earlier. Exhibit B-10 shows the consolidating working paper entries.

CONSOLIDATING WORKING PAPERS
(One Year After Acquisition)

EXHIBIT B-10

Account	Parent Company Debit	Parent Company Credit	Sub Company Debit	Sub Company Credit	Consolidating Entries Debit	Consolidating Entries Credit	Consolidated Totals Debit	Consolidated Totals Credit
Assets other than PP&E	1,400		1,950					
Property, plant, and equipment	1,850		850					
Goodwill								
Investment in Sub Company	1,475							
Liabilities		2,330		1,700				
Shareholders' equity		2,000[a]		1,000[a]				
Revenues		1,500		1,000				
Expenses other than depreciation	860		700					
Depreciation expense	250		150					
EEI		125						
Dividends declared	120		50					
Totals	5,955	5,955	3,700	3,700				

[a] Beginning of period balances (trial balance phase).

CONSOLIDATING WORKING PAPER ENTRIES

Reversal of current year entries (Entry 1):

EEI (SE)	125	
Dividends Declared (SE)		50
Investment in Sub Company (A)		75

Investment elimination entry (Entry 2):

Shareholders' Equity (SE)	1,000	
Property, Plant, and Equipment (A)	250	
Goodwill (A)	150	
Investment in Sub Company (A)		1,400

Extra Depreciation of PP&E (Entry 3):

Depreciation Expense (SE)	25	
Property, Plant, and Equipment (A)		25
or Accumulated Depreciation (XA)		

The preceding entries are added to the consolidating working papers as shown in Exhibit B-11A and the consolidated financial statements that are prepared. Note that a separate accumulated depreciation account has not been provided and that the amount of extra depreciation for the period has simply been credited to the property, plant, and equipment account. You can think of property, plant, and equipment as a net account—that is, as net of accumulated depreciation.

Note that this is exactly the same as the net earnings that was reported by Parent Company using the equity method, as shown in Exhibit B-9. This will always be the case when the parent company uses the equity method to account for its investment in a subsidiary. As mentioned earlier, the equity method is sometimes referred to as a

EXHIBIT B-11A

CONSOLIDATING WORKING PAPERS
(One Year After Acquisition)

Account	Parent Company Debit	Parent Company Credit	Sub Company Debit	Sub Company Credit	Consolidating Entries Debit	Consolidating Entries Credit	Consolidated Totals Debit	Consolidated Totals Credit
Assets other than PP&E	1,400		1,950				3,350	
Property, plant, and equipment, net	1,850		850		(2) 250	25 (3)	2,925	
Goodwill					(2) 150		150	
Investment in Sub Company	1,475					75 (1)		
						1,400 (2)		
Liabilities		2,330		1,700				4,030
Shareholders' equity		2,000ᵃ		1,000ᵃ	(2) 1,000			2,000
Revenues		1,500		1,000				2,500
Expenses other than depreciation	860		700				1,560	
Depreciation expense	250		150		(3) 25		425	
EEI		125				(1) 125		–
Dividends declared	120		50			50 (1)	120	
Totals	5,955	5,955	3,700	3,700	1,550	1,550	8,530	8,530

ᵃ Beginning of period balances (trial balance phase).

CONSOLIDATED STATEMENTS OF FINANCIAL POSITION AND STATEMENTS OF EARNINGS

One year after acquisition

Statement of financial position

Assets other than PP&E	$ 3,500
Property, plant, and equipment	2,925
Goodwill	150
Total assets	$ 6,425
Total liabilities	$ 4,030
Shareholders' equity	2,395[a]
Total liabilities and shareholders' equity	$ 6,425

Statement of earnings

Revenues	$ 2,500
Expenses other than depreciation	(1,560)
Depreciation expense	(425)
Net earnings	$ 515

[a]Shareholders' equity = opening shareholders' equity + net earnings − dividends
= 2,000 + 515 − 120 = $2,395

one-line consolidation. It is a one-line consolidation because the statement of financial position effects of consolidation are captured in the one-line item called the investment account. The statement of earnings effects of consolidation are captured in the one-line item called EEI. The only difference, then, between the equity method and a full consolidation is that the one-line items are replaced with the full details of the subsidiary's assets and liabilities on the statement of financial position and the full details of the subsidiary's revenues and expenses on the statement of earnings.

Consolidation Procedures—Less Than 100 Percent Acquisition

One complication that arises in many acquisitions is that the parent company does not always acquire 100 percent of the subsidiary's shares. Suppose, for example, that Parent Company buys 80 percent of the shares of Sub Company for $1,120. The balance sheets of Parent Company and Sub Company immediately after acquisition are the same as in Exhibit B-6.

Assume that the same fair market values of the assets and liabilities apply to Sub Company as before. The only asset that had extra fair market value is property, plant, and equipment, with an excess value of $250. Even though Parent Company only purchased 80 percent of Sub Company, when it prepares the consolidated financial statements it will include 100 percent of the fair value of the assets and liabilities of Sub Company. The consolidated financial statements portray the assets and liabilities under Parent's control, and they do *control* 100 percent of the assets and liabilities, even if they only *own* 80 percent. Additionally, although we only know what Parent paid for its

80 percent, we can use that value to determine what the fair value of 100 percent of Sub is, and apply that when determining goodwill. The calculation of goodwill would be made as follows:

ALLOCATION OF THE PURCHASE PRICE	
Purchase price paid for 80% of Sub Company	$ 1,120
Purchase price implied for 100% (1,120 ÷ 0.80)	1,400
Less 100% of book value acquired	(1,000)
Less 100% of extra fair market value	(250)
100% of Goodwill	$ 150

Because Parent Company controls Sub Company, it must prepare consolidated financial statements. When it prepares consolidated financial statements, Parent Company adds 100 percent of Sub Company's assets, liabilities, revenues, and expenses to its own accounts. But Parent Company only owns 80 percent of Sub Company. It must, therefore, show 20 percent as being owned by the other shareholders. It does this by creating an account called **non-controlling interest** (NCI) or sometimes **minority interest**. The NCI account is located in the shareholders' equity section on the consolidated balance sheet. It contains 20 percent of the market value of Sub Company, $280 (20% of $1,400). There is another NCI account that represents 20 percent of Sub Company's net earnings. It appears as a deduction from the consolidated entity's net earnings so that consolidated net earnings include only the 80 percent of Sub's earnings that belongs to Parent Company, plus Parent's own net earnings. These two NCI accounts allow the parent to consolidate 100 percent of its subsidiary and then to "back out" the part that does not belong to it.

To illustrate NCI (minority interest) disclosure, we have included the fiscal 2009 income statement and net assets (shareholders' equity) section of the balance sheet of **Nippon Steel Corporation** in Exhibit B-12. Nippon is involved in steel production, transportation, and related businesses, and has investments in over 250 other companies worldwide, with 190 of its investment subsidiaries accounted for through consolidation. Nippon's ownership interest in these subsidiaries ranges from 51 percent to 100 percent. One hundred percent of the income and losses from all of these subsidiaries is included on Nippon's income statement in the 2009 income before income taxes and minority interest amount of ¥11,242 million. The minority interest (NCI) of ¥6,728 million on the income statement represents the amount of the subsidiaries' income that Nippon does not own. On the balance sheet, 100 percent of the subsidiaries' assets and liabilities are included in the total assets and liabilities. The minority interest (NCI) of ¥491,294 million on the balance sheet represents the portion of those net assets not owned by Nippon.

We can also see the importance of other investments to Nippon. In approximately 60 of the investee companies, Nippon only exercises significant influence and uses the equity method to account for those investments. The income earned from these investees on the income statement is ¥34,756 million, roughly 20 percent of the total income before taxes and minority interest. The balance sheet account representing these investments is in the fixed asset section and is not shown in the exhibit.

NIPPON STEEL CORPORATION 2010 ANNUAL REPORT

(2) Consolidated Statements of Income

Millions of yen

	Fiscal 2008	Fiscal 2009
Operating revenues :		
Net sales	4,769,821	**3,487,714**
Cost of sales	4,105,778	**3,156,497**
Gross margin	664,042	**331,216**
Selling, general and administrative expenses	321,112	**299,211**
Operating profit	342,930	**32,005**
Non-operating profit and loss :		
Non-operating profit :		
Interest and dividend income	25,085	**16,656**
Equity in net income of unconsolidated subsidiaries and affiliates	58,876	**34,756**
Other	24,090	**26,170**
	108,051	**77,583**
Non-operating loss :		
Interest expenses	19,813	**19,803**
Other	95,029	**77,952**
	114,842	**97,755**
Ordinary profit	336,140	**11,833**
Special profit :		
Gain on sales of tangible fixed assets	13,342	**5,809**
	13,342	**5,809**
Special loss :		
Loss on valuation of investments in securities	68,402	**–**
Penalty		**6,400**
	68,402	**6,400**
Income before income taxes and minority interest	281,079	**11,242**
Income taxes - current	145,113	**52,440**
Income taxes - deferred	(31,753)	**(36,396)**
Minority interest in net income of consolidated subsidiaries	12,641	**6,728**
Net income (loss)	155,077	**(11,529)**

EXHIBIT B-12B

annual report

NIPPON STEEL CORPORATION 2010 ANNUAL REPORT

Excerpt from the Consolidated Balance Sheet

Millions of yen

NET ASSETS	March 31, 2009	March 31, 2010
Shareholders' equity :		
Common stock	419,524	419,524
Capital surplus	114,333	114,345
Retained earnings	1,458,622	1,441,248
Less: Treasury stock, at cost	(262,152)	(262,004)
	1,730,328	1,713,114
Valuation and transaction adjustments :		
Unrealized gains on available-for-sale securities	22,665	158,364
Deferred hedge income (loss)	(1,149)	(1,846)
Unrealized gains on revaluation of land	11,187	10,759
Foreign currency translation adjustments	(94,348)	(36,010)
	(61,645)	131,267
Minority interest in consolidated subsidiaries	506,126	491,294
Total net assets	2,174,809	2,335,676
Total liabilities and net assets	4,870,680	5,002,378

When a parent owns less than 100 percent of a subsidiary, the accounting can become quite complex. The discussion of these aspects will be left to more advanced texts. It is enough that you understand what the non-controlling interest accounts represent.

Consolidations—Intercompany Transactions

One final complication that deserves mentioning is the impact that intercompany transactions have on the consolidated financial statements. When a parent company buys a controlling interest in a supplier or a customer, it is likely that there are many transactions between the two companies. Prior to the acquisition, these transactions are viewed as taking place between two independent parties, but after the acquisition, they are viewed as transactions within a single economic entity and are referred to as intercompany transactions.

Sales of goods and services between a parent and a subsidiary cannot be viewed as completed transactions unless there has been a sale of the goods or services outside the consolidated entity. Therefore, any profits (revenues and expenses) from those transactions that are not completed by a sale outside the consolidated entity must be eliminated. If there are remaining balances in accounts receivable and accounts payable that relate to intercompany transactions, these, too, must be removed.

To show you this elimination process briefly, consider the following example. Company A owns 100 percent of Company B. During 2010, Company A sells a parcel of land to Company B for $60,000. This land had originally cost Company A $45,000. Company A records the transaction on its books as follows:

Cash (A)	60,000	
Land (A)		45,000
Gain on sale of land (SE)		15,000

Company B records the acquisition of the land as follows:

Land (A)	60,000	
Cash (A)		60,000

Note that cash went out of one company and into the other company, but the consolidated entity still has the same amount of cash. Land went from $45,000 on one company's statement of financial position to $60,000 on the other company's statement of financial position. To the consolidated entity, this is the same parcel of land that was on last year's consolidated statement of financial position at its historical cost of $45,000. If it is not reduced back to $45,000 on the consolidated statement of financial position, it will be overstated. If we allowed the sale price of items sold in intercompany transactions to appear on the consolidated financial statements, the two entities could sell items back and forth merely to increase asset values and record gains when, in reality, no external transactions with independent third parties took place. The gain on the sale of land must also be removed from the consolidated statement of earnings. No gain can be recognized by the consolidated entity, because the land has not been sold to an outside party. The journal entry to eliminate this unrealized gain and increase in the value of the asset on the consolidating working papers would be as follows:

Gain on sale of land (SE)	15,000	
Land (A)		15,000

An entry similar to this would have to be repeated on the consolidating working papers each year, when the consolidated financial statements are prepared. However, the entry in subsequent years would have a debit to Retained Earnings rather than to Gain on Sale of Land because in future years the statement of earnings will not have the gain reported. The gain caused the retained earnings of Company A to increase in the year that the land was sold to Company B.

Entries similar to these are prepared for all the intercompany transactions that occur between the two entities.

STATEMENT ANALYSIS CONSIDERATIONS

The consolidation of a subsidiary considerably changes the appearance of both the statement of earnings and the statement of financial position compared to the parent-only financial statements. The statement of earnings is different only in its detail; the controlling interest's share of net earnings for the period is the same regardless of whether or not the subsidiary is consolidated. The statement of financial position can be dramatically affected when the investment in the subsidiary account is replaced by all of the assets and liabilities of the subsidiary, and this impacts many ratios.

Earlier in the appendix, the effect that consolidation has on the debt to equity ratio was described using the information provided in Exhibit B-8. The debt to equity ratio for Parent Company was 1.0, whereas the debt to equity ratio for the consolidated entity was 1.75. Users who need information about an entity's ability to repay debt should not rely solely on consolidated financial statements. These statements contain the liabilities of all the companies in the consolidated group of companies, but each of those companies is only responsible for its own debt. However, a parent and its subsidiaries often guarantee each other's debt, because this could result in lending institutions charging lower interest rates or loaning larger amounts. When the debt is guaranteed, the consolidated debt to equity ratio is useful, because all the consolidated assets are available to service the debt.

Other ratios will also be affected. The ROA ratio, for example, divides the net earnings before interest by the average total assets. With consolidation, the numerator changes to the extent that the subsidiary's interest expense is included on the consolidated statement of earnings and is, therefore, added back to the net earnings. The denominator (average total assets) also changes because the investment account is replaced by the subsidiary's individual assets and liabilities. In the example in Exhibit B-9, the parent's total assets prior to consolidation were $4,725. After consolidation, |the total assets were $6,425 (Exhibit B-11). This large increase would certainly affect the ROA. The ROA prior to consolidation (ignoring interest expense which was not shown in the example) would have been 10.9 percent ($515/$4,725). After consolidation, the ROA was 8.0 percent ($515/$6,425).

The current ratio will also be affected. The current assets and liabilities that are embedded in the investment account are shown in full detail when they are consolidated, as the subsidiary's current assets and liabilities are added to the parent's when they are consolidated. Because our example in Exhibit B-8 does not distinguish current liabilities from long-term liabilities, it is not possible to demonstrate the change that would occur. Obviously, the quick ratio will also be affected by consolidation, for the same reason as for the current ratio.

Shareholders, potential investors, and most other outside users may not be able to determine the impact that various subsidiaries have on the consolidated financial statements. If a parent owns 100 percent of a subsidiary, the subsidiary will often not provide financial statements for external users other than the Canada Revenue Agency. A lender would be able to request individual financial statements from any company that wanted to borrow funds, but most other external users would not have this luxury. This means that users should have some understanding of how ratios are affected by the consolidation process.

If the parent owns less than 100 percent of the shares, the subsidiary must publish publicly available financial statements if it is traded on the stock market. Users then have the opportunity to get more information about the components of the consolidated entity. However, a 100 percent-owned subsidiary does not trade on a stock exchange and does not need to make its financial statements public.

SUMMARY

In this appendix, we provided more background information to improve your understanding of consolidated financial statements. You learned about the different levels of investments in other companies, from non-strategic investments to significant influence investments to controlled subsidiaries. Through simple examples, we demonstrated the acquisition of a 100 percent-owned subsidiary. We expanded your knowledge through a discussion of non-wholly owned subsidiaries and of intercompany transactions. We concluded the appendix with a brief discussion of the impact of the consolidation process on ratio analysis.

The environment of corporate financial reporting is one of constant change and growing complexity. This book has introduced you to most of the fundamental concepts and principles that guide bodies such as the International Accounting Standards Board, as they consider new business situations and issues. You should think of the completion of this appendix as the end of your introduction to and initial understanding of corporate financial reporting. As accounting standard-setting bodies and regulators adjust and change the methods and guidelines used to prepare financial statements, you must constantly educate yourself so that you understand the impacts of these changes on the financial statements of your company or of other companies that are of interest to you.

IFRS VERSUS ASPE

Accounting for strategic investments is one of the areas where the accounting may differ for companies that prepare their financial statements using Canada's Accounting Standards for Private Enterprises. For significantly influenced investments, the investor company can choose to use either the equity method or the cost method. For subsidiaries, the investor company may choose to use the cost method or equity method, or to prepare consolidated financial statements. The investor must use the same method for all investments in each category. Consolidated financial statements do provide a more complete picture of the assets, liabilities, revenues, and expenses under the investor company's control, but as you have seen in this appendix, even very simple consolidated financial statements are more time consuming and complex to prepare. Many private enterprises can adequately assess the performance of all of the companies under their control by studying the financial statements of the individual companies, and they are usually familiar with the extent of intercompany transactions between the companies. In those situations, the preparation of consolidated financial statements may not be necessary.

PRACTICE PROBLEM

Peck Company (parent) bought 100 percent of the shares of Spruce Company (subsidiary) on January 1, 2011, for $600,000. On that date, the shareholders' equity section of Spruce Company was as follows:

Common shares	$125,000
Retained earnings	75,000
Total shareholders' equity	$200,000

www.wileyplus.com

Additional Practice Problems

practice problem

Peck paid $400,000 more for Spruce than the book value of the assets acquired. This excess amount was attributed partially to land ($50,000) and equipment ($250,000); the remainder was attributed to goodwill. The equipment had a remaining useful life of 10 years and an expected residual value of zero. Peck depreciates its assets using the straight-line method.

The following represents the trial balances of Peck and Spruce as at December 31, 2011 (the end of the fiscal year):

Trial Balance, December 31, 2011

Account	Peck Company Debit	Peck Company Credit	Spruce Company Debit	Spruce Company Credit
Cash	$ 780,000		$ 240,000	
Accounts receivable	400,000		200,000	
Inventory	525,000		350,000	
Investment in Spruce	695,000		–	
PP&E	800,000		600,000	
Accumulated depreciation		$ 300,000		$ 200,000
Accounts payable		425,000		290,000
Long-term debt		900,000		580,000
Common shares		700,000		125,000
Retained earnings (January 1, 2011)		400,000		75,000
Revenues		5,000,000		2,000,000
Expenses (other than depreciation)	4,200,000		1,700,000	
Depreciation	100,000		100,000	
Equity in Spruce's earnings		175,000		–
Dividends declared	400,000		80,000	
Totals	$7,900,000	$7,900,000	$3,270,000	$3,270,000

Required:

a. Reconstruct the entries that Peck made during 2011 to account for its investment in Spruce using the equity method.

b. Prepare a set of consolidating working papers for Peck and Spruce for 2011, showing the consolidating entries and the amounts that will appear in the consolidated financial statements.

c. Calculate the following ratios for Peck Company, using (i) its parent-only financial statement information and (ii) the consolidated entity information. (Hint: It might be easier to first prepare the statements of earnings and retained earnings for the year in order to determine the closing retained earnings balances that would appear on the statements on financial position.)

   1. Debt to equity ratio

   2. Return on equity

   3. Return on assets

   4. Current ratio

SUGGESTED SOLUTION TO PRACTICE PROBLEM

a. Using the equity method, the following entries would be made:

At acquisition

Investment in Spruce (A)	600,000	
Cash (A)		600,000

At year end

Spruce's net earnings are calculated as follows:

Revenues	$2,000,000
Expenses other than depreciation	1,700,000
Depreciation	100,000
Net earnings	$ 200,000

To recognize dividends: Since Peck's share of Spruce's earnings is 100 percent, the following entry would be made:

Investment in Spruce (A)	200,000	
Equity in Spruce's Earnings (SE)		200,000

To recognize dividends: As Spruce declared $80,000 in dividends and Peck's share is 100 percent, the following entry would be made:

Cash (A)	80,000	
Investment in Spruce (A)		80,000

To recognize depreciation of the fair value increment on the equipment: At the date of acquisition, Peck paid $400,000 more for the Spruce shares than the book value of the net assets. This excess amount would be attributable to the following items:

Land	$ 50,000
Equipment	250,000
Goodwill	100,000
Total	$ 400,000

The land is not depreciated, but the excess amount due to the equipment must be depreciated. Since Peck uses straight-line depreciation, the extra depreciation expense would be $25,000 per year ($250,000 ÷ 10 years). Using the equity method, the extra expenses would be recognized with the following entry:

Equity in Spruce's Earnings (SE)	25,000	
Investment in Spruce (A)		25,000

The goodwill is not amortized, but must be written down if there is evidence that its value has been impaired.

Based on these entries, the investment account balance would be $695,000 (600,000 + 200,000 − 80,000 − 25,000) and the equity in Spruce's earnings would be $175,000 (200,000 − 25,000), both as shown in the trial balance.

b. The consolidating working paper entries are as follows.

To reverse current income and dividends:

Equity in Spruce Earnings (SE)	175,000	
Dividends Declared (SE)		80,000
Investment in Spruce (A)		95,000

To eliminate the investment account and shareholders' equity and to recognize extra fair market value and goodwill:

Common Shares (SE)	125,000	
Retained Earnings (SE)	75,000	
PP&E (A) (Land $50,000 + Equipment $250,000)	300,000	
Goodwill (A)	100,000	
Investment in Spruce (A)		600,000

To depreciate the extra fair market value of the equipment:

Depreciation Expense (SE)	25,000	
Accumulated Depreciation (XA)		25,000

The consolidating working papers are shown in Exhibit B-13.

EXHIBIT B-13	**CONSOLIDATING WORKING PAPERS**

Peck Company and Spruce Company, 2011—100% Acquisition

Account	Peck Company Debit	Peck Company Credit	Spruce Company Debit	Spruce Company Credit	Consolidating Entries Debit	Consolidating Entries Credit	Consolidated Totals Debit	Consolidated Totals Credit
Cash	780,000		240,000				1,020,000	
Accounts receivable	400,000		200,000				600,000	
Inventory	525,000		350,000				875,000	
Property, plant, & equipment	800,000		600,000		(2) 300,000		1,700,000	
Accumulated depreciation		300,000		200,000		25,000 (3)		525,000
Goodwill					(2) 100,000		100,000	
Investment in Spruce	695,000					95,000 (1)	–	
						600,000 (2)		
Accounts payable		425,000		290,000				715,000
Long-term debt		900,000		580,000				1,480,000
Common shares		700,000		125,000	(2) 125,000			700,000
Retained earnings		400,000[a]		75,000[a]	(2) 75,000			400,000
Revenues		5,000,000		2,000,000				7,000,000
Expenses other than depreciation	4,200,000		1,700,000				5,900,000	
Depreciation expense	100,000		100,000		(3) 25,000		225,000	
EEI		175,000			(1) 175,000		–	
Dividends declared	400,000		80,000			80,000 (1)	400,000	
Totals	7,900,000	7,900,000	3,270,000	3,270,000	800,000	800,000	10,820,000	10,820,000

[a]Beginning of period balances (trial balance phase)

c. Statements of Earnings and Retained Earnings for 2011:

	Peck Company — Parent Only	Peck Company — Consolidated
Revenues	$5,000,000	$7,000,000
Expenses	(4,200,000)	(5,900,000)
Depreciation expense	(100,000)	(225,000)
EEI	175,000	–
Net earnings	$ 875,000	$ 875,000
Opening retained earnings	400,000	400,000
Dividends paid	(400,000)	(400,000)
Ending retained earnings	$ 875,000	$ 875,000

i. Parent-Only   ii. Consolidated Entity

1. Debt to equity

$\$1,325,000 \div 1,575,000^a = 0.84$ $\$2,195,000 \div 1,575,000^b = 1.39$

[a]$700,000 + 875,000 = \$1,575,000$
[b]$700,000 + 875,000 = \$1,575,000$

2. Return on equity

$\$875,000 \div 1,575,000 = 0.56$ $\$875,000 \div 1,575,000 = 0.56$

3. Return on assets

$\$875,000 \div 2,900,000^a = 0.30$ $\$875,000 \div 3,770,000^b = 0.23$

[a]$780,000 + 100,000 + 525,000 + 800,000 - 300,000 + 695,000 = \$2,900,000$
[b]$1,020,000 + 600,000 + 875,000 + 1,700,000 - 525,000 + 100,000 = \$3,770,000$

4. Current ratio

$\$1,705,00^a \div 425,000 = 4.0$ $\$2,495,000^b \div 715,000 = 3.5$

[a]$780,000 + 400,000 + 525,000 = \$1,705,000$
[b]$1,020,000 + 600,000 + 875,000 = \$2,495,000$

SYNONYMS

Non-controlling interest **I** Minority interest
Non-strategic investment **I** Passive investment **I** Portfolio investment
Significantly influenced company **I** Associated company

ABBREVIATIONS USED

EEI	Equity in earnings of investee	PP&E	Property, plant, and equipment
NCI	Non-controlling interest		

practice problem

GLOSSARY

Acquisition method An accounting method to record the acquisition of another company. The acquisition is treated as a purchase, and the assets and liabilities acquired are measured at their fair market value. Because this is typically a basket purchase, the cost is allocated to the individual assets and liabilities based on their fair market values.

Asset purchase An acquisition of assets from another company in which the acquiring company purchases the assets directly rather than buying a controlling interest in the shares of the other company. Title to the assets passes to the acquiring company.

Associated company The IFRS term to describe a company that has been invested in by another company and where the investor has the power and ability to participate in financial and operating decisions of the investee but does not have control over it. Synonym for significantly influenced company.

Consolidated financial statements Financial statements that represent the total financial results of a parent company and its various subsidiaries as if they were one company, even though they are separate legal entities.

Consolidating working papers A work sheet that adjusts the financial statements of a parent and its subsidiaries so that the statements can be combined to show the consolidated financial statements.

Consolidation An accounting method that companies are required to use to represent their ownership in other companies when they have control over the activities of these other companies. The method requires the preparation of consolidated financial statements.

Controlling interest The amount of ownership of a subsidiary that a parent company must have in order to control the subsidiary's strategic operating, financing, and investing activities. An ownership interest of greater than 50 percent usually meets this criterion.

Diversification A reason for acquiring ownership in another company. Diversification typically implies that the acquired company is in a business that is very different from the acquiring company's business. The idea is to find a new business that is counter-cyclical to the company's current business.

Elimination entry A working paper consolidating entry that eliminates the balance in the Investment in subsidiary account against the shareholders' equity accounts of the subsidiary. At the same time, if the price paid by the parent company exceeds the book value of the subsidiary's shareholders' equity section, the excess fair market value of the net assets acquired and goodwill are recognized as part of the entry.

Equity in earnings of investee (EEI) An account used in a parent company's books to record its share of the subsidiary's net earnings for the period using the equity method.

Equity method A method that companies use to account for their ownership in companies in which they have significant influence. This is usually true when the percentage of ownership is between 20 percent and 50 percent. In addition, this method is often used in parent-only statements to account for the investment in a subsidiary. In the latter case, the account will be eliminated on the consolidating working papers at the end of the year when consolidated financial statements are prepared.

Excess fair market value The difference between the fair market value and book value of the net assets of a subsidiary company when its shares are acquired by a parent company.

Goodwill An intangible asset that arises when a parent company acquires ownership in a subsidiary company and pays more for the shares than the fair market value of the underlying net identifiable assets at the date of acquisition. The difference between the price paid and these net assets' fair market value is the value of the goodwill. It can represent expected excess earnings that result from, for example, the subsidiary's reputation, its exceptional sales staff, or an advantageous location.

Horizontal integration A type of acquisition in which a parent company buys a competitor company in order to gain a larger market share or to expand its markets geographically.

Identifiable net assets The assets and liabilities that can be specifically identified at the date of a merger or acquisition. Some of the identifiable assets, such as patents and trademarks, may not have been recorded on the subsidiary's books.

Investee A company whose shares are acquired by another company.

Investor A company that acquires shares of another company as an investment.

Minority interest The portion of a less-than 100 percent-owned subsidiary that is owned by other shareholders. Synonym for non-controlling interest.

Non-controlling interest (NCI) The portion of a less-than 100 percent-owned subsidiary that is owned by other shareholders. Synonym for minority interest.

Non-strategic investment An investment by one company in another company in which the acquiring company has little or no influence over the operations of the acquired company. Synonym for passive investment or portfolio investment.

One-line consolidation A term to describe the equity method because it produces the same net results as the full consolidation method, except that the subsidiary's results are shown in a single line on the statement of financial position (the investment account) and a single line on the statement of earnings (the equity in earnings of investee).

Parent company A company that acquires control (usually by purchasing more than 50 percent of another company's voting shares) of another company. The acquired company is referred to as a subsidiary.

Parent-only books The accounting records of a parent company that have not been combined with its subsidiary's records in consolidated financial statements.

Passive investment An investment by one company in another company in which the acquiring company has no ability to control or influence the decisions of the acquired company. Synonym for non-strategic investment or portfolio investment.

Portfolio investment An investment by one company in another company in which the acquiring company has no ability to control or influence the decisions of the acquired company. A synonym for non-strategic investment or passive investment.

Seasonal business A business that is subject to significant swings in the level of its activity according to the time of year, such as the greeting card business.

Share acquisition An acquisition of another company that is accomplished through the purchase of its shares. The acquired company continues as a separate legal entity.

Significantly influenced company A company where the investor company has the power and ability to participate in financial and operating decisions of the investee but does not have control over the investee. Synonym for associated company.

Strategic investment An investment by one company in another company where the investor company intends to a have long-term strategic relationship with the acquired company.

Subsidiary A company controlled by another company (the parent). The parent controls the subsidiary's strategic operating, financing, and investing decisions, usually by owning more than 50 percent of its outstanding shares.

Trial balance phase A phase in the preparation of financial statements in which the temporary accounts still contain revenue, expense, and dividend accounts from the period and have not been closed out to retained earnings.

Vertical integration A type of merger or acquisition in which a parent company buys a supplier or customer company in order to ensure a supply of raw materials or a market for its end product.

Widely held shares Shares of a company that are held by a large number of individuals or institutions, such that no single shareholder has significant influence over the company's decisions.

ASSIGNMENT MATERIAL

Additional Practice Problems

Assessing Your Recall

B-1 Identify and briefly explain the major reasons for a company to buy shares in another company.

B-2 Exhibit B-1 provided information about the subsidiaries of H&M. The largest investment is in FaBric Scandinavien AB. The acquisition of FaBric in 2008 is described in Exhibit B-2. Explain briefly the possible strategic reasons for H&M to have acquired a controlling interest in FaBric. Would this investment be an example of horizontal or vertical integration?

B-3 Compare and contrast a share acquisition and an asset acquisition in terms of their effects on the financial statements.

B-4 What factors other than the percentage of ownership could you use to determine if a company has significant influence over an investee?

B-5 Briefly describe the IRFS guidelines for accounting for long-term acquisitions in the shares of other companies. In your description, identify the criteria used to distinguish the various accounting methods.

B-6 Explain the nature of goodwill and how it arises in the context of an acquisition.

B-7 The equity method is sometimes referred to as a one-line consolidation. Explain.

B-8 Discuss what a consolidation is trying to accomplish.

B-9 Consolidating working paper entries are needed to eliminate double accounting for certain items on the parent's and subsidiary's books. Explain which items would be accounted for twice if the subsidiary company's books were added directly to the parent's books.

B-10 Explain the accounting alternatives that are available to a company that follows Accounting Standards for Private Enterprise GAAP and which has just purchased control of another company. Explain why consolidated financial statements might not be more useful for these companies.

Applying Your Knowledge

B-11 (Accounting alternatives for investments)
On January 1, 2010, Rain Inc. purchased a 20 percent interest in Waterworks Ltd. by buying 50,000 shares for $8.00 per share. During 2010, Waterworks earned income of $160,000 and paid dividends of $20,000. On December 31, 2010, the market value of Waterworks shares was $8.80.

> *Required:*
> a. Compare the investment income reported on Rain's statement of earnings under each of the following methods of accounting for the investment in Waterworks:
>   i. Cost method
>   ii. Available-for-sale method
>   iii. Equity method
> b. Compare the balance in the investment account on Rain's statement of financial position as at January 1, 2010, and December 31, 2010, under each of the following methods of accounting for the investment in Waterworks:
>   i. Cost method
>   ii. Available-for-sale method
>   iii. Equity method
> c. What factors should Rain consider to determine whether or not to use the equity method?

B-12 (Investments ranging from 10 percent to 100 percent)
On April 1, Red Tin Company acquired some common shares of Timber Steel Company. The book value of Timber Steel's net assets on April 1 was $10 million, and the market value of the net assets was $12.5 million. During the year, Timber Steel had net earnings of $1 million and declared dividends of $600,000.

> *Required:*
> For each of the following assumptions, give the amount of income recognized by Red Tin Company from its investment in Timber Steel Company and show the beginning and ending balances for the investment account on Red Tin's books. Both companies close their books annually on December 31. Assume that any excess fair market value is to be depreciated straight-line over five years. Goodwill, if any, is not amortized. In each case, the shares' market value on December 31 is the same as the acquisition price.

a. The acquisition price is $1,500,000 for 15 percent of Timber Steel's common shares.
b. The acquisition price is $3,125,000 for 25 percent of Timber Steel's common shares.
c. The acquisition price is $6,000,000 for 45 percent of Timber Steel's common shares.
d. The acquisition price is $13,000,000 for 100 percent of Timber Steel's common shares.

B-13 (Acquisition of 100 percent-owned subsidiaries)

On January 1, 2011, Down Company purchased 100 percent ownership of Topp Company for $120,000 and 100 percent of Steady Company for $300,000. Immediately after the purchases, the companies reported the following amounts:

	Total Assets	Total Liabilities	Total Shareholders' Equity
Down Company	$950,000	$250,000	$ 700,000
Topp Company	180,000	60,000	120,000
Steady Company	500,000	200,000	300,000

Required:
Assuming that Down Company prepares a consolidated statement of financial position immediately after the purchase of the two companies, answer the following questions:
a. What amount of total assets will be reported?
b. What amount of total liabilities will be reported?
c. What amount of total shareholders' equity will be reported?
d. Why is it necessary to eliminate the balance in Down's investment accounts for each of the two subsidiaries when preparing a consolidated statement of financial position?

B-14 (Acquisition alternatives for 100 percent purchase)

Hartney Limited decided to acquire 100 percent of Southern Company for $450,000. To pay for the acquisition, Hartney's management concluded it could (1) sell temporary investments it holds and pay cash, (2) issue new bonds and use the cash receipts, or (3) issue common shares with a market value of $450,000 in exchange for the Southern shares.

Required:
Answer each of the following questions and explain why your answer is appropriate:
a. Under which of the alternatives will total liabilities in the consolidated statement of financial position be greater than the amount reported by Hartney prior to the purchase of Southern's shares?
b. Under which of the alternatives will total assets in the consolidated statement of financial position be greater than the amount reported by Hartney prior to the purchase of Southern's shares?
c. Under which of the alternatives will total shareholders' equity in the consolidated statement of financial position be greater than the amount reported by Hartney prior to the purchase of Southern's shares?
d. Which of the alternatives would appear to increase the risk of investing in Hartney Company?
e. Which of the alternatives would appear to reduce the risk of investing in Hartney Company?

B-15 (Significant influence investment)

On January 1, 2010, Waxton Company acquired a portion of the common shares of Ball Company. The data relating to the acquisition and the first year of operations are as follows:

	Common Shares Acquired	Book Value of Net Assets as at Jan. 1, 2010	Market Value of Net Assets as at Jan. 1, 2010	Acquisition Price	Net Earnings for Year	Dividends Declared for Year
Ball Company	40%	$6,000,000	$7,500,000	$3,200,000	$2,500,000	$1,000,000

Both companies close their books annually on December 31. Goodwill, if any, is not amortized. Property, plant, and equipment acquired have a remaining useful life of six years, have a residual value of zero, and are amortized using the straight-line method. Any excess fair market value in the transaction relates to property, plant, and equipment. The market value of the Ball Company shares held on December 31 was $4 million.

Required:
Show the journal entries (including for the acquisition) to account for Waxton's investment in Ball during the year.

B-16   (Consolidation of 100 percent-owned subsidiary)
Large Company owns all the common shares of Small Company. The statements of earnings for the companies for 2011 contained the following amounts:

	Large Co.	Small Co.
Sales revenue	$600,000	$300,000
Cost of goods sold	400,000	160,000
Gross profit	200,000	140,000
Dividend income from subsidiary	90,000	
Operating expenses	(130,000)	(50,000)
Net earnings	$160,000	$ 90,000

During 2011, Small purchased inventory for $10,000 and immediately sold it to Large at cost. Large has not yet sold this inventory.

Required:
Answer the following questions about the consolidated statement of earnings for 2011:
a. What amount will be reported as sales revenue?
b. What amount will be reported as cost of goods sold?
c. What amount will be reported as dividend income from subsidiary?
d. What amount will be reported as operating expenses?
e. Why are some of the amounts that are reported in the consolidated statement of earnings not equal to the sum of the amounts from the statements of the parent and subsidiary?

B-17   (Consolidation of 100 percent-owned subsidiary)
On January 1, Lid Company acquired 100 percent of the common shares of Ant Company at a price of $1.5 million. The book value of Ant Company's net assets on January 1 was $1,250,000. The net assets' book value approximates the fair value at the date of acquisition. During the year, Ant earned $340,000 and declared dividends of $290,000. At the end of the year, the dividends receivable of Lid Company included an amount of $290,000 that was due from Ant Company. (Hint: Lid's statement of financial position would have a dividend receivable and Ant's would have a dividend payable. The consolidated entity cannot owe money to itself. Therefore, both of these accounts must be removed on the working papers before consolidated financial statements are prepared.) Goodwill, if any, will not be amortized.

Required:
a. Show the journal entries for the acquisition of the common shares and other entries during the year, assuming that Lid uses the equity method on its own books.
b. Prepare the consolidating working paper entries.

B-18   (Consolidation of 100 percent-owned subsidiary)
Jennie's Plumbing and Heating recently purchased 100 percent of the shares of Ron's Repair Service. The statements of financial position for the two companies immediately after the purchase of Ron's shares were as follows:

	Jennie's Plumbing	Ron's Repair
Cash	$ 30,000	$ 8,000
Accounts receivable	75,000	30,000
Inventory	120,000	72,000
Investment in Ron's Repair	225,000	
Buildings and equipment	450,000	240,000
Less: Accumulated depreciation	(165,000)	(80,000)
Total assets	$735,000	$270,000
Accounts payable	$ 90,000	$ 75,000
Taxes payable	105,000	45,000
Common shares	300,000	100,000
Retained earnings	240,000	50,000
Total liabilities and equity	$735,000	$270,000

On the statement of financial position date, Ron's Repair owes Jennie's Plumbing $15,000 on accounts payable.

Required:

a. Prepare a consolidated statement of financial position for Jennie's Plumbing and its subsidiary.

b. Why are the shareholders' equity balances of Ron's Repair not included in the consolidated statement of financial position?

c. Monona Wholesale Supply has extended credit of $10,000 to Jennie's Plumbing, and Winona Supply Company has extended credit of $10,000 to Ron's Repair. Which supplier has the stronger claim on the consolidated cash balance? Explain.

d. Jennie's Plumbing has applied to Sussex Bank for a $100,000 short-term loan to open a showroom for bathroom and kitchen fixtures. Accounts receivable will be used as collateral and Jennie's Plumbing has provided the bank with its consolidated statement of financial position prepared immediately after the acquisition of Ron's Repair. From the bank's perspective, how would you rate the sufficiency of the collateral? Explain.

e. If Jennie's Plumbing had purchased only 80 percent of the shares of Ron's Repair, an item labelled "Non-controlling interest" would have been reported on the statement of financial position. What does the amount assigned to the non-controlling interest represent?

B-19 (Consolidation of 100 percent-owned subsidiary)

The statements of financial position as at December 31 for Porter and Associates and Rachel Excavation follow:

	Porter	Rachel
Assets		
Cash	$ 196,000	$ 10,000
Accounts receivable	150,000	40,000
Inventory	300,000	40,000
Capital assets	400,000	130,000
Total assets	$1,046,000	$ 220,000
Liabilities and Shareholders' Equity		
Accounts payable	$ 80,000	$ 20,000
Long-term liabilities	300,000	50,000
Common shares	540,000	100,000
Retained earnings	126,000	50,000
Total liabilities and shareholders' equity	$1,046,000	$ 220,000

As at December 31, the market values of Rachel's inventories and capital assets were $70,000 and $120,000, respectively. Liabilities are at fair market value on the statement of financial position.

On December 31, Porter and Associates purchased Rachel Excavation for $180,000 cash. The preceding statements of financial position were prepared immediately before the acquisition.

Required:
a. Prepare the journal entry recorded by Porter to recognize the acquisition.
b. Prepare a consolidating working paper and a consolidated statement of financial position.

B-20 (Consolidation of 100 percent-owned subsidiary)

The following are the statements of financial position and statements of earnings for Jungle Company and Forest Company as at December 31, 2011.

Statements of Financial Position as at December 31, 2011:

	Jungle Company	Forest Company
Assets		
Cash	$ 29,000	$ 15,000
Accounts receivable	35,000	45,500
Investment in Forest Company	130,000	–
Other assets	61,000	74,500
Total assets	$255,000	$135,000
Liabilities and shareholders equity		
Accounts payable	$ 39,500	$ 20,000
Other current liabilities	10,500	10,000
Common shares	150,000	80,000
Retained earnings	55,000	25,000
Total liabilities and shareholders' equity	$255,000	$135,000

Statements of Earnings for the Year Ended December 31, 2011:

	Jungle Company	Forest Company
Sales revenue	$100,000	$ 60,000
Cost of goods sold	(55,000)	(35,000)
Depreciation	(25,000)	(5,000)
EEI	20,000	–
Net earnings	$ 40,000	$ 20,000
Dividends declared	$ 25,000	$ 15,000

On January 1, 2011, Jungle had acquired 100 percent of the common shares of Forest Company for $125,000. The shareholders' equity sections of Jungle Company and Forest Company on January 1 were as follows:

	Jungle Company	Forest Company
Common shares	$150,000	$ 80,000
Retained earnings	40,000	20,000
Total	$190,000	$100,000

The fair market value of Forest's net assets equalled their book values on the date of acquisition. Goodwill, if any, will not be amortized.

Required:
a. Prepare the consolidating working papers supported by the necessary working paper journal entries.
b. Prepare the consolidated statement of financial position and statement of earnings.

B-21 (Accounting for subsidiary)

Varwood Company Ltd. is a subsidiary of Tabor Company Ltd. The statements of financial position for Varwood Company and for the consolidated entity on December 31, 2011, contained the following balances:

	Varwood Company	Consolidated Amounts for Tabor Company and Subsidiary
Cash and receivables	$ 80,000	$120,000
Inventory	150,000	260,000
Land	70,000	200,000
Building and equipment	150,000	450,000
Less: Accumulated depreciation	(70,000)	(210,000)
Total assets	$380,000	$820,000
Accounts payable	$ 40,000	$ 70,000
Notes payable	90,000	290,000
Non-controlling interest		100,000
Common shares	80,000	180,000
Retained earnings	170,000	180,000
Total liabilities and shareholders' equity	$380,000	$820,000

Required:

a. Does Tabor own 100 percent or less than 100 percent of Varwood's common shares? How do you know?

b. What percentage of Varwood's assets and liabilities is included in the consolidated statement of financial position? Explain.

c. What is the amount of cash and accounts receivable reported by Tabor on December 31, 2011, if (i) there are no intercompany receivables and payables, and (ii) Tabor's accounts receivable include a $20,000 receivable from Varwood?

d. Must Tabor share a portion of Varwood's net earnings with others? Explain. What portion of the earnings from Tabor's separate operations must be shared with the other shareholders of Varwood?

e. Which of parts "a" through "d" can only be answered by looking at the consolidated financial statements?

B-22 (Consolidation of 100 percent-owned subsidiary)

On December 31, 2011, Multi Corp. acquired 100 percent of the outstanding shares of Littleton Company Ltd. for $64,000. The market values of Littleton's assets and liabilities on that date were as follows:

Cash	$ 6,000
Accounts receivable	9,000
Inventory	15,000
Capital assets	40,000
Accounts payable	(14,000)
Long-term notes payable	(16,000)

The statements of financial position on December 31, 2011, prior to acquisition, were as follows:

	Multi Corp.		Littleton Co.	
Account	Debit	Credit	Debit	Credit
Cash	$ 65,000		$ 6,000	
Accounts receivable	70,000		9,000	
Notes receivable	35,000			
Inventory	120,000		10,000	
Capital assets	230,000		35,000	

Account	Multi Corp. Debit	Multi Corp. Credit	Littleton Co. Debit	Littleton Co. Credit
Accounts payable		$ 90,000		$14,000
Long-term notes payable		130,000		16,000
Common shares		200,000		22,000
Retained earnings		100,000		8,000
Totals	$520,000	$520,000	$60,000	$60,000

Required:
a. Prepare the consolidating working papers that will be used to prepare the consolidated statement of financial position.
b. Prepare the consolidated statement of financial position.

B-23 (Consolidation of 100 percent-owned subsidiary)

On January 1, 2011, Neptune Company Ltd. acquired 100 percent of the outstanding shares of Baker Company Ltd. The acquisition price was $500,000, which included $40,000 related to the excess fair market value of the capital assets acquired. The shareholders' equity as at January 1, 2011, was as follows:

	Neptune Co.	Baker Co.
Common shares	$1,000,000	$300,000
Retained earnings	20,000	100,000
Total	$1,020,000	$400,000

During the year, Neptune Company lent $100,000 to Baker Company, which was to be repaid by December 31, 2011; however, $40,000 was still due at year end. The trial balances of Neptune and Baker on December 31, 2011, were as follows:

Account	Neptune Co. Debit	Neptune Co. Credit	Baker Co. Debit	Baker Co. Credit
Current assets	$ 300,000		$180,000	
Capital assets	700,000		400,000	
Investment in Baker	502,000		–	
Cost of goods sold	400,000		150,000	
Other expenses	50,000		20,000	
Dividends declared	100,000		60,000	
Current liabilities		$ 170,000		$ 70,000
Non-current liabilities		200,000		100,000
Common shares		1,000,000		300,000
Retained earnings		20,000		100,000
Sales revenue		600,000		240,000
EEI		62,000		
Totals	$2,052,000	$2,052,000	$810,000	$810,000

The capital assets' entire fair market value is to be depreciated using the straight-line method. The remaining useful life is five years, and the residual value is zero. Goodwill, if any, will not be amortized.

Required:
a. Prepare the consolidating working papers supported by the necessary working paper journal entries.
b. Prepare the consolidated statement of financial position.

B-24 (Equity method and consolidation of 100 percent-owned subsidiary)

On January 1, 2011, Casey Incorporated acquired 100 percent of the outstanding common shares of both Smith Company Ltd. and List Company Ltd. The details of the acquisitions and the earnings of both companies are as follows:

	Smith Co.	List Co.
Book value of net assets as at 1/1/11	$140,000	$175,000
Acquisition price	150,000	200,000
Earnings (loss) for 2011	(20,000)	15,000
Dividends declared for 2011	–	10,000

Goodwill, if any, will not be amortized. Assume that the net assets' fair market value on January 1, 2011, is the same as the book values.

Required:
a. Construct the journal entries that Casey will make in 2011 to account for these investments on its own books, assuming it uses the equity method.
b. Prepare the consolidating working paper entries for the consolidation of these investments as of December 31, 2011, assuming the entries in part "a" have been recorded.

B-25 (Acquisition of subsidiary)

The following is a summary of the January 1, 2011, statement of financial position of the private company Alsop Ltd., prior to any acquisition:

Assets	$180,000	Liabilities	$90,000
		Shareholders' equity	90,000
Total	$180,000	Total	$180,000

On January 1, 2011, Alsop acquired 100 percent of the outstanding common shares of Martin Monthly for $62,000 cash. At the time of the acquisition, the fair market values of Martin's assets and liabilities were $86,000 and $64,000, respectively. During 2011, Martin operated as a subsidiary of Alsop, and recognized $15,000 of net earnings and paid a $10,000 dividend.

Required:
a. Provide the journal entry to record the acquisition, and prepare Alsop's consolidated statement of financial position as at January 1, 2011.
b. Account for the acquisition using the equity method. Provide the journal entry to record the acquisition, and prepare Alsop's statement of financial position as at January 1, 2011.
c. Calculate the debt to equity ratios produced by the two methods of accounting for this investment. Explain why Alsop's management might wish to use the equity method instead of preparing consolidated financial statements.
d. Provide the journal entries that would be made by Alsop to record the income earned and the dividends paid by Martin during 2011, assuming that Alsop used the equity method.

B-26 (Acquisition of subsidiary)

The following are the statements of financial position for Trident Inc. and Gum Company Ltd. as at December 31, 2011 (prior to any acquisition):

	Trident Inc.	Gum Co.
Assets		
Current assets	$175,000	$ 65,000
Non-current assets	500,000	130,000
Total assets	$675,000	$195,000
Liabilities and shareholders' equity		
Current liabilities	$ 85,000	$ 28,000
Non-current liabilities	190,000	57,000
Common shares	350,000	100,000
Retained earnings	50,000	10,000
Total liabilities and shareholders' equity	$675,000	$195,000

After those statements were prepared on December 31, 2011, Trident Inc. issued 5,000 shares having a market value of $300,000 in exchange for all 7,500 Gum shares. Included in the $300,000 purchase price was $100,000 for the excess fair market value of the non-current assets. All other Gum assets and liabilities had values equal to their book values.

> **Required:**
> a. Construct the entry that Trident would make on its books to account for its investment in Gum.
> b. Prepare a consolidated statement of financial position as at December 31, 2011.
> c. Describe the groups of shareholders that own Trident after the acquisition. Do you think the original shareholders of Trident still control the company?

B-27 (Calculation of consolidated net earnings)

Refer to the data in Problem B-26. For 2011, the details of the net earnings and dividends reported by the two companies were as follows:

	Trident Inc.	Gum Co.
Net earnings	$250,000	$75,000
Dividends declared	$225,000	$65,000

> **Required:**
> What are the net earnings of Trident Inc. on a consolidated basis?

B-28 (Preparation of consolidated statement of earnings)

Refer to the data in Problem B-26 and assume that the net earnings and dividends declared for 2012 are as follows:

	Trident Inc.	Gum Co.
Revenues	$700,000	$280,000
Cost of goods sold	400,000	160,000
Other expenses	95,000	30,000
Net earnings	$205,000	$ 90,000
Dividends declared	$150,000	$ 75,000

Trident's net earnings exclude the earnings from its investment in Gum. Goodwill is not depreciated, and any excess fair market value of non-current assets is to be depreciated using the straight-line method over a 10-year useful life with a zero residual value.

> **Required:**
> Prepare a consolidated statement of earnings for 2012.

Reading and Interpreting Published Financial Statements

B-29 (Business acquisitions)

In its 2008 annual report, **Rogers Communications Inc.** described several acquisitions it undertook to expand its media empire. Two of the acquisitions are described in the excerpts of Note 4 in Exhibit B-14. (Note that Rogers used the purchase method to account for its acquisitions. This is the method used in Canada prior to the adoption of IFRS, but for the purposes of these questions the accounting is the same as the acquisition method.)

www.wileyplus.com

Financial Analysis Assignments

ROGERS COMMUNICATIONS INC. 2008 ANNUAL REPORT

NOTES TO THE CONSOLIDATED FINANCIAL STATEMENTS

---

4. BUSINESS COMBINATIONS AND DIVESTITURES

(A) 2008 ACQUISITIONS AND DIVESTITURES

(i) Outdoor Life Network:

On July 31, 2008, the Company acquired the remaining two-thirds of the shares of Outdoor Life Network that it did not already own, for cash consideration of $39 million. The acquisition was accounted for using the purchase method with the results of operations consolidated with those of the Company effective July 31, 2008. The purchase price allocation is preliminary pending finalization of valuations of the net indentifiable assets acquired. The preliminary estimated fair values of the assets acquired and liabilities assumed are as follows:

Purchase price	$	39
Current assets	$	11
Current liabilities		(3)
Preliminary fair value of net assets acquired	$	8
Goodwill	$	31

The goodwill has been allocated to the Media reporting segment and is not tax deductible.

(iii) channel m:

On April 30, 2008, the Company acquired the assets of Vancouver multicultural television station channel m, from Multivan Broadcast Corporation, for cash consideration of $61 million. The acquisition was accounted for using the purchase method with the results of operations consolidated with those of the Company effective April 30, 2008. The fair values of the assets acquired and liabilities assumed, which were finalized during 2008 are as follows:

Purchase price	$	61
Current assets	$	5
Broadcast licence	$	9
PP&E		6
Current liabilities		(7)
Fair value of net assets acquired	$	13
Goodwill	$	48

The goodwill has been allocated to the Media reporting segment and is tax deductible.

Required:

a. Prior to the new acquisition in 2008, Rogers already owned part of the Outdoor Life Network (OLN). What type of investment was OLN on Rogers' books prior to the 2008 acquisition? Which accounting method did Rogers most likely use to account for OLN at that time? What type of investment is OLN now? What method does Rogers most likely use to account for OLN now?

b. In the acquisition of channel m, Rogers purchased the net assets. What is the difference from an accounting perspective between purchasing the net assets and purchasing the shares?

c. One of the assets listed in the purchase of channel m is "Broadcast licence." What type of asset is this? Do you think it was listed on channel m's balance sheet at the time of the purchase? Support your answer.

d. Do these acquisitions represent vertical or horizontal investments for Rogers? Explain.

B-30 (Increase in business acquisition)

In its 2009 annual report, **Maple Leaf Foods Ltd.** described its acquisition of additional shares of Canada Bread Company Limited for $32.6 million. The details are included in Note 20 in Exhibit B-15.

EXHIBIT B-15 **MAPLE LEAF FOODS LTD. 2009 ANNUAL REPORT**

annual report

notes to the consolidated financial statements

20. ACQUISITIONS AND DIVESTITURES

(c) On July 17, 2008, the Company purchased 458,000 additional shares in Canada Bread Company, Limited ("Canada Bread") for cash consideration of $32.6 million, increasing the Company's ownership interest in Canada Bread from 88.0% to 89.8%. During the second quarter of 2009, the Company finalized the purchase equation for these purchases, allocating $11.4 million of the purchase price to the net tangible assets of Canada Bread at the acquisition date, $1.1 million to intangible assets and $20.1 million to goodwill.

Required:

a. Prior to the purchase of the additional shares in 2008, Maple Leaf Foods already owned part of Canada Bread. What accounting method was Maple Leaf Foods using to account for its investment in Canada Bread prior to the acquisition? What accounting method is Maple Leaf Foods most likely using after purchasing the additional shares in Canada Bread?

b. How was the purchase price allocated? Explain briefly what goodwill is.

c. The balance sheet and statement of earnings for Maple Leaf Foods are available in Exhibit 10-21 on pages (705–706). Explain briefly what the non-controlling interest accounts on the two statements represent. (Note: Maple Leaf Foods has other subsidiary companies in addition to Canada Bread.)

B-31 (Acquisition of subsidiary)

Use the balance sheet of **Brickworks Limited**, an Australia-based company, in Exhibit B-16 to answer the following questions.

Required:

a. Explain the difference between the consolidated figures and parent entity figures on the balance sheet.

b. Does Brickworks own a controlling interest in all of its investee companies? Explain.

BRICKWORKS LIMITED 2009 ANNUAL REPORT

BALANCE SHEET AS AT 31 JULY 2009

	NOTE	CONSOLIDATED		PARENT ENTITY	
		31 JULY 09 $000	**31 JULY 08** $000	**31 JULY 09** $000	**31 JULY 08** $000
CURRENT ASSETS					
Cash assets	8	17,916	37,808	1,361	15,852
Receivables	9(a)	68,747	83,428	-	-
Held for trading financial assets	10	23	30	-	-
Inventories	12(a)	147,292	137,935	-	-
Land held for resale	13(a)	50,461	95,108	-	-
Prepayments		5,020	4,497	1,138	878
TOTAL CURRENT ASSETS		289,459	358,806	2,499	16,730
NON-CURRENT ASSETS					
Receivables	9(b)	200	200	717,708	630,858
Other financial assets	11	-	-	193,698	248,437
Inventories	12(b)	8,699	7,230	-	-
Land held for resale	13(b)	30,722	34,649	-	-
Investments accounted for using the equity method	14	1,133,580	740,255	-	-
Property, plant and equipment	15	399,809	500,203	-	645
Intangible assets	16	272,099	271,513	-	-
Prepayments		704	1,792	704	1,792
TOTAL NON-CURRENT ASSETS		1,845,813	1,555,842	912,110	881,732
TOTAL ASSETS		2,135,272	1,914,648	914,609	898,462
CURRENT LIABILITIES					
Payables	17(a)	88,255	73,070	688	2,297
Interest-bearing liabilities	18(a)	67,000	262,865	67,000	262,865
Derivative financial instruments	19(a)	511	(347)	519	(486)
Current tax liabilities		8,620	18,782	5,728	19,049
Provisions	20(a)	25,348	22,095	-	300
TOTAL CURRENT LIABILITIES		189,734	376,465	73,935	284,025
NON-CURRENT LIABILITIES					
Payables	17(b)	-	2,047	152,992	511
Interest-bearing liabilities	18(b)	333,000	300,000	333,000	300,000
Derivative financial instruments	19(b)	517	-	517	-
Provisions	20(b)	25,059	13,560	544	544
Deferred taxes	21	215,514	109,107	899	11,858
TOTAL NON-CURRENT LIABILITIES		574,090	424,714	487,952	312,913
TOTAL LIABILITIES		763,824	801,179	561,887	596,938
NET ASSETS		1,371,448	1,113,469	352,722	301,524
EQUITY					
Contributed equity	22	146,521	144,892	146,521	144,892
Reserves	23	353,572	359,550	96,124	96,279
Retained profits	24	871,355	609,027	110,077	60,353
TOTAL EQUITY		1,371,448	1,113,469	352,722	301,524

B-32 (Business acquisitions)

Use the 2010 annual report for **HMV Group plc** on the companion website to answer the following questions.

Required:

a. Note 15 describes HMV's acquisition of MAMA Group plc in 2010. Did HMV pay by issuing shares or paying cash?
b. Why did HMV pay an amount in excess of the fair value of the net assets acquired?
c. In the table in Note 15, why is the value of the intangibles for HMV (Group) greater than their book value (the value on MAMA's books at acquisition)?
d. On the balance sheet, explain what the account "Investments in subsidiaries and joint ventures" represents. Why does it appear on the company balance sheet, but not the group balance sheet?
e. Does HMV, the parent company, have any investments in companies where it exercises significant influence or do only the subsidiaries have that type of investment? Explain.

Critical Thinking Question

B-33 (Strategic planning of future growth)

As explained at the beginning of this appendix, companies buy all or parts of other companies for many reasons. You might assume that this type of activity is undertaken only by large corporations, but many owners of small businesses will also establish or buy subsidiaries as they start to expand. Often these small subsidiaries represent a specific niche in the owner's business that allows the owner to undertake various activities without exposing the whole organization to the risk of failure.

Assume that you are the owner of a small business. Your initial business is installing carpets and you have a crew of three people doing the installations for you. Your ultimate goal is to do finishing contract work on residential and commercial construction and to be controlling a multimillion-dollar operation. Think about the path that could be taken so that you can expand your business from carpet installation to your eventual goal. Draft an expansion plan that would take you gradually from one to the other. Include in your plan the purchase or establishment of subsidiaries.

subject index

company index

photo credits

TIME VALUE OF MONEY TABLES

TABLE 1   PRESENT VALUE OF AN ANNUITY IN ARREARS

Periods	0.50%	0.75%	1.00%	1.50%	2.00%	3.00%	4.00%	5.00%	6.00%	7.00%	8.00%	9.00%	10.00%	11.00%	12.00%	13.00%
1	0.99502	0.99256	0.99010	0.98522	0.98039	0.97087	0.96154	0.95238	0.94340	0.93458	0.92593	0.91743	0.90909	0.90090	0.89286	0.88496
2	1.98510	1.97772	1.97040	1.95588	1.94156	1.91347	1.88609	1.85941	1.83339	1.80802	1.78326	1.75911	1.73554	1.71252	1.69005	1.66810
3	2.97025	2.95556	2.94099	2.91220	2.88388	2.82861	2.77509	2.72325	2.67301	2.62432	2.57710	2.53129	2.48685	2.44371	2.40183	2.36115
4	3.95050	3.92611	3.90197	3.85438	3.80773	3.71710	3.62990	3.54595	3.46511	3.38721	3.31213	3.23972	3.16987	3.10245	3.03735	2.97447
5	4.92587	4.88944	4.85343	4.78264	4.71346	4.57971	4.45182	4.32948	4.21236	4.10020	3.99271	3.88965	3.79079	3.69590	3.60478	3.51723
6	5.89638	5.84560	5.79548	5.69719	5.60143	5.41719	5.24214	5.07569	4.91732	4.76654	4.62288	4.48592	4.35526	4.23054	4.11141	3.99755
7	6.86207	6.79464	6.72819	6.59821	6.47199	6.23028	6.00205	5.78637	5.58238	5.38929	5.20637	5.03295	4.86842	4.71220	4.56376	4.42261
8	7.82296	7.73661	7.65168	7.48593	7.32548	7.01969	6.73274	6.46321	6.20979	5.97130	5.74664	5.53482	5.33493	5.14612	4.96764	4.79877
9	8.77906	8.67158	8.56602	8.36052	8.16224	7.78611	7.43533	7.10782	6.80169	6.51523	6.24689	5.99525	5.75902	5.53705	5.32825	5.13166
10	9.73041	9.59958	9.47130	9.22218	8.98259	8.53020	8.11090	7.72173	7.36009	7.02358	6.71008	6.41766	6.14457	5.88923	5.65022	5.42624
11	10.67703	10.52067	10.36763	10.07112	9.78685	9.25262	8.76048	8.30641	7.88687	7.49867	7.13896	6.80519	6.49506	6.20652	5.93770	5.68694
12	11.61893	11.43491	11.25508	10.90751	10.57534	9.95400	9.38507	8.86325	8.38384	7.94269	7.53608	7.16073	6.81369	6.49236	6.19437	5.91765
13	12.55615	12.34235	12.13374	11.73153	11.34837	10.63496	9.98565	9.39357	8.85268	8.35765	7.90378	7.48690	7.10336	6.74987	6.42355	6.12181
14	13.48871	13.24302	13.00370	12.54338	12.10625	11.29607	10.56312	9.89864	9.29498	8.74547	8.24424	7.78615	7.36669	6.98187	6.62817	6.30249
15	14.41662	14.13699	13.86505	13.34323	12.84926	11.93794	11.11839	10.37966	9.71225	9.10791	8.55948	8.06069	7.60608	7.19087	6.81086	6.46238
16	15.33993	15.02431	14.71787	14.13126	13.57771	12.56110	11.65230	10.83777	10.10590	9.44665	8.85137	8.31256	7.82371	7.37916	6.97399	6.60388
17	16.25863	15.90502	15.56225	14.90765	14.29187	13.16612	12.16567	11.27407	10.47726	9.76322	9.12164	8.54363	8.02155	7.54879	7.11963	6.72909
18	17.17277	16.77918	16.39827	15.67256	14.99203	13.75351	12.65930	11.68959	10.82760	10.05909	9.37189	8.75563	8.20141	7.70162	7.24967	6.83991
19	18.08236	17.64683	17.22601	16.42617	15.67846	14.32380	13.13394	12.08532	11.15812	10.33560	9.60360	8.95011	8.36492	7.83929	7.36578	6.93797
20	18.98742	18.50802	18.04555	17.16864	16.35143	14.87747	13.59033	12.46221	11.46992	10.59401	9.81815	9.12855	8.51356	7.96333	7.46944	7.02475
24	22.56287	21.88915	21.24339	20.03041	18.91393	16.93554	15.24696	13.79864	12.55036	11.46933	10.52876	9.70661	8.98474	8.34814	7.78432	7.28288
36	32.87102	31.44681	30.10751	27.66068	25.48884	21.83225	18.90828	16.54685	14.62099	13.03521	11.71719	10.61176	9.67651	8.87859	8.19241	7.59785
48	42.58032	40.18478	37.97396	34.04255	30.67312	25.26671	21.19513	18.07716	15.65003	13.73047	12.18914	10.93358	9.89693	9.03022	8.29716	7.67052
60	51.72556	48.17337	44.95504	39.38027	34.76089	27.67556	22.62349	18.92929	16.16143	14.03918	12.37655	11.04799	9.96716	9.07356	8.32405	7.68728
120	90.07345	78.94169	69.70052	55.49845	45.35539	32.37302	24.77409	19.94268	16.65135	14.28146	12.49878	11.11075	9.99989	9.09088	8.33332	7.69230
240	139.58077	111.14495	90.81942	64.79573	49.56855	33.30567	24.99796	19.99984	16.66665	14.28571	12.50000	11.11111	10.00000	9.09091	8.33333	7.69231
360	166.79161	124.28187	97.21833	66.35324	49.95992	33.33254	24.99998	20.00000	16.66667	14.28571	12.50000	11.11111	10.00000	909091	8.33333	7.69231